P9-BYH-409

∎ For Students

MyAccountingLab provides students with a personalized interactive learning environment, where they can learn at their own pace and measure their progress.

Interactive Tutorial Exercises ▼

MyAccountingLab's homework and practice questions are correlated to the textbook, and they regenerate algorithmically to give students unlimited opportunity for practice and mastery. Questions include guided solutions, DemoDoc examples, and learning aids for extra help at point-of-use, and they offer helpful feedback when students enter incorrect answers.

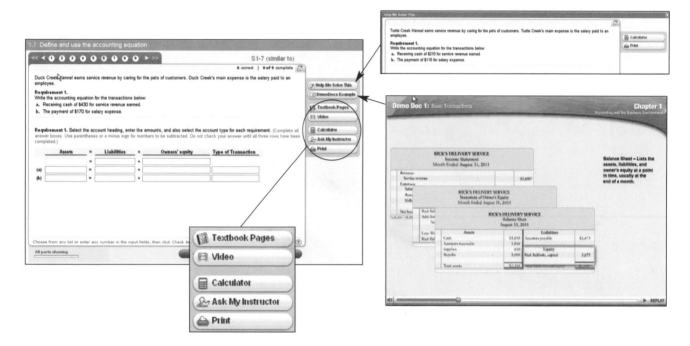

Study Plan for Self-Paced Learning ▶

MyAccountingLab's study plan helps students monitor their own progress, letting them see at a glance exactly which topics they need to practice. MyAccountingLab generates a personalized study plan for each student based on his or her test results, and the study plan links directly to interactive, tutorial exercises for topics the student hasn't yet mastered. Students can regenerate these exercises with new values for unlimited practice, and the exercises include guided solutions and multimedia learning aids to give students the extra help they need.

View a guided tour of MyAccountingLab at http://www.myaccountinglab.com/support/tours.

MANAGERIAL ACCOUNTING

SECOND EDITION

Karen Wilken Braun
Case Western Reserve University

Wendy M. Tietz
Kent State University

Walter T. Harrison, Jr.
Baylor University

Prentice Hall

Boston   Columbus   Indianapolis   New York   San Francisco   Upper Saddle River
Amsterdam   Cape Town   Dubai   London   Madrid   Milan   Munich   Paris   Montreal   Toronto
Delhi   Mexico City   Sao Paulo   Sydney   Hong Kong   Seoul   Singapore   Taipei   Tokyo

VP/Publisher: Natalie Anderson
AVP/Executive Editor: Jodi McPherson
Acquisitions Editor: Jodi Bolognese
Director of Marketing, Intro Markets: Kate Valentine
AVP/Executive Editor, Media: Richard Keaveny
AVP/Executive Producer, Media: Lisa Strite
Director, Product Development: Pamela Hersperger
Editorial Project Manager: Rebecca Knauer
Editorial Media Project Manager: Allison Longley
Development Editor: Mignon Tucker, J.D. Brava
   360° Publishing Solutions
Supplements Development Editor: Claire Hunter
Editorial Assistant: Terenia McHenry
Marketing Manager: Maggie Moylan

Marketing Assistant: Justin Jacob
Senior Managing Editor, Production: Cynthia Zonneveld
Production Media Project Manager: John Cassar
Production Project Manager: Carol O'Rourke
Permissions Coordinator: Charles Morris
Senior Operations Supervision: Natacha Moore
AV Project Manager: Rhonda Aversa
Art Director: Anthony Gemmellaro
Cover Design: Anthony Gemmellaro
Composition: GEX Publishing Services
Full-Service Project Management:
   GEX Publishing Services
Printer/Binder: Courier
Typeface: 8/10 Sabon

Credits and acknowledgments borrowed from other sources and reproduced, with permission, in this textbook appear on appropriate page within text and on page 826.

Copyright © 2010, 2008 Pearson Education, Inc., publishing as Prentice Hall, Upper Saddle River, New Jersey, 07446. All rights reserved. Manufactured in the United States of America. This publication is protected by Copyright, and permission should be obtained from the publisher prior to any prohibited reproduction, storage in a retrieval system, or transmission in any form or by any means, electronic, mechanical, photocopying, recording, or likewise. To obtain permission(s) to use material from this work, please submit a written request to Pearson Education, Inc., Permissions Department, One Lake Street, Upper Saddle River, New Jersey, 07446.

Many of the designations by manufacturers and seller to distinguish their products are claimed as trademarks. Where those designations appear in this book, and the publisher was aware of a trademark claim, the designations have been printed in initial caps or all caps.

Library of Congress Cataloging-in-Publication Data
Braun, Karen Wilken
  Managerial accounting / Karen Wilken Braun, Wendy M. Tietz, Walter T. Harrison, Jr. -- 2nd ed.
    p. cm.
  Includes bibliographical references and index.
  ISBN-10: 0-13-609116-4
  ISBN-13: 978-0-13-609116-5
  1. Managerial accounting. I. Tietz, Wendy M. II. Harrison, Walter T. III. Title.
  HF5657.4.B36 2008
  658.15'11--dc22   2009032886

10 9 8 7 6 5 4 3 2 1

Prentice Hall
is an imprint of

PEARSON

ISBN-13: 978-0-13-609116-5
ISBN-10: 0-13-609116-4

BRIEF CONTENTS

CONTENTS

Cost-Volume-Profit Analysis 362
CHAPTER 7

Short-Term Business Decisions 420
CHAPTER 8

The Master Budget and Responsibility Accounting 474
CHAPTER 9

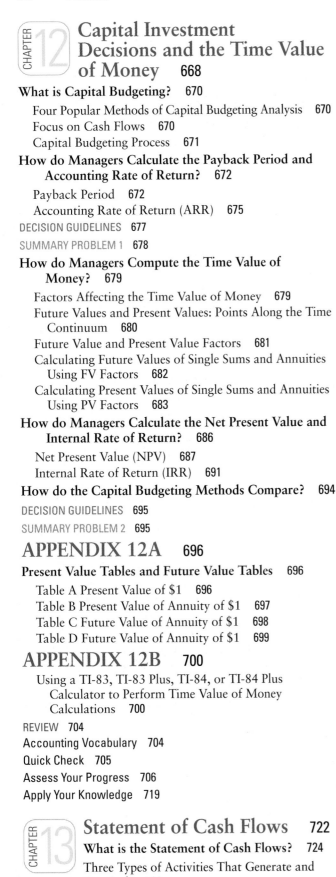

With
Managerial Accounting
Student Text, Study Resources,
and MyAccountingLab
students will have more
"I get it!"
moments.

Students will "get it" anytime, anywhere

Students understand (or "get it") right after the instructor does a problem in class. Once they leave the classroom, however, students often struggle to complete the homework on their own. This frustration can cause them to give up on the material altogether and fall behind in the course, resulting in an entire class falling behind as the instructor attempts to keep everyone on the same page.

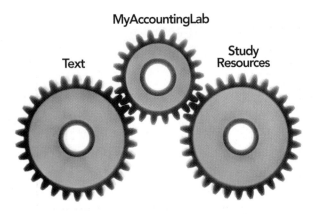

MyAccountingLab

Text

Study Resources

With the *Managerial Accounting, Second Edition* **Student Learning System,** all the features of the student textbook, study resources, and online homework system are designed to work together to provide students with the consistency, repetition, and high level of detail that will keep both the instructor and students on track, providing more "I get it!" moments inside and outside the classroom.

Replicating the Classroom Experience with Demo Doc Examples

The Demo Doc Examples consist of entire problems, worked through step-by-step, from start to finish, narrated with the kind of comments that instructors would say in class. The Demo Docs are available in specific chapters of the text and for every chapter in the study guide. In addition to the printed Demo Docs, Flash® animated versions are available so that students can watch the problems as they are worked through while listening to the explanations and details. Demo Docs will aid students when they are trying to solve exercises and problems on their own, duplicating the classroom experience outside of class.

DEMO DOC CHAPTER 2

Preparing a Schedule of Cost of Goods Manufactured and Income Statement

Learning Objective 5

US Granite manufactures granite kitchen and bathroom countertops. US Granite's accounting records show the following information for the year ended December 31, 2010:

Sales revenue	$1,105,000
Raw materials inventory, Jan. 1, 2010*	11,000
Raw materials inventory, Dec. 31, 2010	15,000
Work in process inventory, Jan. 1, 2010	33,000
Work in process inventory, Dec. 31, 2010	54,000
Finished goods inventory, Jan. 1, 2010	36,000
Finished goods inventory, Dec. 31, 2010	50,000
Purchases of direct materials	275,000
Direct labor	144,000
Manufacturing overhead	240,000
Operating expenses (selling, general, and administrative)	325,000

*US Granite's Raw Materials Inventory account only contains direct materials (any indirect materials are used immediately, rather than stored for later use).

Requirements

1. Prepare US Granite's schedule of cost of goods manufactured for the year ended December 31, 2010.
2. Prepare US Granite's income statement for the year ended December 31, 2010.

DEMO DOC Solution

Requirement 1

Prepare US Granite's schedule of cost of goods manufactured for the year ended December 31, 2010.

The cost of goods manufactured is just what it sounds like: It's all of the cost incurred by a company to make a finished product during the year. Notice that the term is past tense: *manufactured*. In other words, this is just the cost associated with all units that were actually *finished* during the year, so it does *not* include any costs associated with units that were worked on but *not finished* during the year. Those costs need to remain in Work in Process Inventory at the end of the year.

Before we get started on the schedule, recall from Chapter 2 that manufacturers use three production inputs to make their product:

- Direct materials (physical components required to manufacture the product)
- Direct labor (such as assembly line workers, machine operators, and so forth)
- Manufacturing overhead (such as depreciation on the factory and machinery factory utilities, and so forth)

Gear art © Pep I Dreamstime.com

with the Student Learning System!

Consistency, Repetition, and a High Level of Detail Throughout the Learning Process

The concepts, materials, and practice problems are presented with clarity and consistency across all mediums—textbook, study resources, and online homework system. No matter which platform students use they will continually experience the same look, feel, and language, minimizing confusion and ensuring clarity.

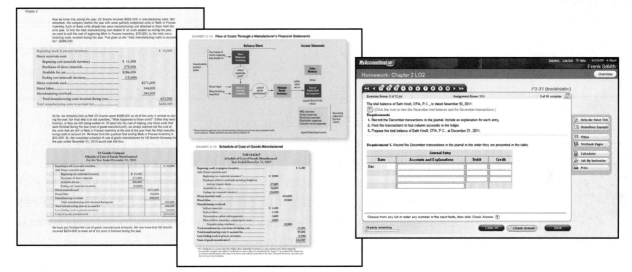

Experiencing the Power of Practice with MyAccountingLab: www.myaccountinglab.com

MyAccountingLab is an online homework system that gives students more "I get it!" moments through the power of practice. With **MyAccountingLab** students can do the following:

- Work on the exact end-of-chapter material and/or similar problems assigned by the instructor.
- Use the Study Plan for self-assessment and customized study outlines.
- Use the Help Me Solve This tool for a step-by-step tutorial.
- View the Demo Docs Example to see an animated demonstration of where the numbers came from.
- Watch a Video to see additional information pertaining to the lecture.
- Open Textbook Pages to find the material they need to get help on specific problems.

Managerial Accounting, 2e presents students with the fundamentals they need to know followed by extensive opportunities for practice. By building their accounting skills with strong coverage and effective practice, students will be able to see the business implications of what they're learning so that they can apply it in their future careers.

Focused Coverage

Managerial Accounting, 2e is concise and straightforward without sacrificing the explanations that clarify concepts! The key to capturing students' attention isn't just about being concise—which is why this text presents concepts in a way that gets students to the point without omitting vital information for the sake of brevity. The result is an accessible and understandable text that helps students make connections about the business significance of accounting information.

NEW! Adjusted Chapter Order
Based on extensive market feedback, the layout of the second edition reflects the order in which instructors teach the topics as well as the order that makes the most sense to students. This allows for increased comprehension of the material.

Coverage Specifics

Revised Costing Chapters
The Activity-Based Costing chapter now follows the Job Costing chapter since it is a natural extension to a traditional job costing environment. For both chapters the authors use Life Fitness, a manufacturer of fitness equipment, as the focus company so that students can easily compare and contrast the different costing methods within the same business context. To give instructors more flexibility of coverage, all journal entries associated with job costing and process costing are isolated in the final section of the chapter.

Revised Budgeting Chapters

The focus of this chapter switched from a merchandising to a manufacturing context to provide the most comprehensive coverage of master budgets. The appendix compares and contrasts the budgets of service, manufacturing, and merchandising budgets.

Revised Financial Statement Analysis Chapter

The authors use a large retailer to present the concept, then feature Target in both Summary Problems, and then use leading competitors such as JC Penney, Kohl's, and Wal-Mart to illustrate, compare, and analyze the financial statements from both a company and industry point of view.

NEW! Statement of Cash Flows Chapter

This edition now offers a separate chapter on the statement of cash flows (Ch 13) which shows students how to interpret the statement and deepens their understanding of the importance of cash to a business' survival and expansion.

IFRS ⊕ NEW! International Financial Reporting Standards (IFRS), Sustainability, and Other Emerging Issues Integrated throughout the Text

IFRS, international accounting issues, XBRL, sustainability, and corporate responsibility are added to ensure that students learn the current trends in the business environment. These emerging IFRS and international issues are denoted throughout the text with a global icon.

Merchandising Companies' Inventoriable Product Costs

Merchandising companies' inventoriable product costs include *only* the cost of purchasing the inventory from suppliers plus any costs incurred to get the merchandise to the merchandiser's place of business and ready for sale. Typically, these additional costs include freight-in costs and import duties or tariffs, if the products were purchased from overseas. Why does the cost of the inventory include freight-in charges? Think of the last time you purchased a shirt from a catalog such as L.L.Bean. The catalog may have shown the shirt's price as $30, but by the time you paid the shipping and handling charges, the shirt really cost you around $35. Likewise, merchandising companies pay freight-in charges to get the goods to their place of business (plus import duties if the goods were manufactured overseas). These charges become part of the cost of their inventory.

For instance, Home Depot's inventoriable product costs include what the company paid for its store merchandise plus freight-in and import duties. Home Depot records these costs in an asset account—Inventory—until it *sells* the merchandise. Once the merchandise sells, it belongs to the customer, not Home Depot. Therefore, Home Depot takes the cost out of its inventory account and records it as an expense—the *cost of goods sold*. Home Depot expenses costs incurred in other elements of the value chain as period costs. For example, Home Depot's period costs include store operating expenses (such as salaries, utilities, and depreciation) and advertising expenses.

Focused Coverage

NEW! Headers in a Question & Answer Format
Most headers in the chapters are written as thought-provoking questions followed by clear, direct answers. The Q & A format allows students to read with purpose, focusing on the concept and its relevance. This format reinforces how the accounting information is used to answer questions and make decisions in business.

Which Business Activities Make Up the Value Chain?

Many people describe Toyota, General Mills, and Dell as manufacturing companies. But it would be more accurate to say that these are companies that *do* manufacturing. Why? Because companies that do manufacturing also do many other things. Toyota also conducts research to determine what type of new technology to integrate into next year's models. Toyota designs the new models based on its research and then produces, markets, distributes, and services the cars. These activities form Toyota's **value chain**— the activities that add value to the company's products and services. The value chain is pictured in Exhibit 2-3.

Decision Guidelines

Summarizing the chapter's key terms, concepts, and formulas in the context of business decisions, Decision Guidelines can be found at the midpoint and end of each chapter. They reinforce how the accounting information students are learning is used to make decisions in business.

Decision Guidelines

BUILDING BLOCKS OF MANAGERIAL ACCOUNTING

As a manufacturer, Dell needs to know how to calculate its inventoriable product costs for external reporting. Dell also needs to know many characteristics about its costs (that is, which are controllable, which are relevant to different decisions, which are fixed, and so forth) in order to plan and make decisions.

Decision	Guidelines
How do you compute cost of goods sold?	*Service companies:*
	No cost of goods sold because they don't sell tangible goods
	• *Merchandising companies:*

Beginning inventory
+ Purchases plus freight-in and import duties, if any
= Cost of goods available for sale
− Ending inventory
= Cost of goods sold

NEW! "Why is this important?" Feature

To help students focus on the business significance of managerial accounting, the authors added marginal notations called "Why is this important?" There are several of these notes in each chapter to help students make connections between accounting and the business environment.

Why is this important?

"All activities in the value chain are important, yet each costs money to perform. Managers must understand how decisions made in one area of the value chain will affect the costs incurred in other areas of the value chain."

Coordinating Activities Across the Value Chain

Many of the value chain activities occur in the order discussed here. However, managers cannot simply work on R&D and not think about customer service until after selling the car. Rather, cross-functional teams work on R&D, design, production, marketing, distribution, and customer service simultaneously. As the teams develop new model features, they also plan how to produce, market, and distribute the redesigned vehicles. They also consider how the new design will affect warranty costs. Recall from the last chapter that management accountants typically participate in these cross-functional teams. Even at the highest level of global operations, Toyota uses cross-functional teams to implement its business goals and strategy.

The value chain in Exhibit 2-3 also reminds managers to control costs over the value chain as a whole. For example, Toyota spends more in R&D and product design to increase the quality of its vehicles, which, in turn, reduces customer service costs. Even though R&D and design costs are higher, the total cost of the vehicle—as measured throughout the entire value chain—is lower as a result of this trade off. Enhancing its reputation for high-quality products has also enabled Toyota to increase its market share and charge a slightly higher selling price than some of its competitors.

Accounting in Business

The second edition continues to focus on the business significance of accounting information. The authors cover a variety of business settings (manufacturing, retail, and service sectors) and present full coverage of job costing and budgeting in service firms (Chs 3 and 9). They also cover all costs throughout the value chain rather than only the inventoriable product costs. Combined with careful consideration of the depth of coverage on the more "cost-oriented" topics, *Managerial Accounting, 2e* offers instructors and students an easy-to-read, balanced text.

www.pearsonhighered.com/braun

Extensive Practice

The concepts learned throughout the text are reinforced with a thorough, extensive, and clear set of practice opportunities. Once students read through the chapters, it's imperative for them to immediately apply the concepts learned to make connections. The end-of-chapter material, along with **MyAccountingLab**, provides students with ample opportunities to practice.

NEW! Rewritten End-of-Chapter Material

Important concepts such as ethics, Sarbanes-Oxley, and globalization need to be reinforced in the end-of-chapter material in order to cement student understanding. New coauthor Wendy Tietz, an experienced accounting and technology educator, has rewritten all the end-of-chapter material in this text to thoroughly support key chapter topics and to remain consistent with the rest of the text.

An Extensive Set of End-of-Chapter Material and Tools

The EOC Philosophy: The end-of-chapter material has been structured so that students progress from simple, computational exercises to a mixture of computational and conceptual exercises, building their confidence as they build their skills. In addition, there is a solid offering of end-of-chapter exercises and problems, which mix cost-oriented and conceptual requirements. This structure helps students think about what the numbers mean in addition to how to calculate them.

Application and Analysis

2-1 Costs in the Value Chain at a Real Company and Cost Objects

Choose a company with which you are familiar that manufactures a product. In this activity, you will be making reasonable assumptions about the activities involved in the value chain for this product; companies do not typically publish information about their value chain.

Basic Discussion Questions

1. Describe the product that is being produced and the company that produces it.
2. Describe the six value chain business activities that this product would pass through from its inception to its ultimate delivery to the customer.

NEW! Multi-Media and Analytical Emphasis: Every chapter now features "Discussion & Analysis" and "Application & Analysis" features suitable for use in class, online, and/or outside of class. These opportunities for analysis help students grasp the underlying concepts. Popular multi-media are used to engage the student in this level of thinking.

NEW! "B" Exercises Added to the Text: In addition to an "A" set of exercises students will receive additional practice with a new set of "B" exercises that have been added to this text. For even more practice, these exercises come with alternative versions in **MyAccountingLab**.

Exercises —Group B

E2-32B Identify types of companies and their inventories (*Learning Objective 1*)

Complete the following statements with one of the terms listed here. You may use a term more than once, and some terms may not be used at all.

Wholesalers	Work in process inventory	Service companies
Manufacturing companies	Raw materials inventory	Retailers
Finished goods inventory	Inventory (merchandise)	Merchandising companies

NEW! CMA Sample Problems: In order to give students ample exposure to the Certified Management Accountant exam, CMA sample problems appear at the end of selected chapters for students to practice.

Updated Demo Docs: Demo Docs are fully worked-through problems that weave computation and concepts together in a step-by-step format for guided reinforcement of chapter concepts and skills. These strategically placed, worked-through problems reflect the chapter content, occurring only where students need them the most. Additional Demo Docs, including animated versions, are available for every chapter in the study guide and in MyAccountingLab.

DEMO DOC 2

Preparing a Schedule of Cost of Goods Manufactured and Income Statement

Learning Objective 5

US Granite manufactures granite kitchen and bathroom countertops. US Granite's accounting records show the following information for the year ended December 31, 2010:

Sales revenue	$1,105,000
Raw materials inventory, Jan. 1, 2010*	11,000
Raw materials inventory, Dec. 31, 2010	15,000
Work in process inventory, Jan. 1, 2010	33,000
Work in process inventory, Dec. 31, 2010	54,000
Finished goods inventory, Jan. 1, 2010	36,000
Finished goods inventory, Dec. 31, 2010	50,000
Purchases of direct materials	275,000
Direct labor	144,000
Manufacturing overhead	240,000
Operating expenses (selling, general, and administrative)	325,000

*US Granite's Raw Materials Inventory account only contains direct materials (any indirect materials are used immediately, rather than stored for later use).

Requirements

1. Prepare US Granite's schedule of cost of goods manufactured for the year ended December 31, 2010.
2. Prepare US Granite's income statement for the year ended December 31, 2010.

New and Revised Summary Problems and Solutions: Found at the mid- and end-of-chapter points, these problems and solutions provide students with guided learning of the chapter material. By presenting these problems and solutions at the mid and end of the chapter, the summary problems reinforce the concepts, enabling students to absorb and master the material in more manageable pieces.

Summary Problem 2

Requirements

1. Show how to compute cost of goods manufactured. Use the following amounts: direct materials used ($24,000), direct labor ($9,000), manufacturing overhead ($17,000), beginning work in process inventory ($5,000), and ending work in process inventory ($4,000).

2. Auto-USA spent $300 million in total to produce 50,000 cars this year. The $300 million breaks down as follows: The company spent $50 million on fixed costs to run its manufacturing plants and $5,000 of variable costs to produce each car. Next year, it plans to produce 60,000 cars using the existing production facilities.

   a. What is the current *average cost* per car this year?

   b. Assuming there is no change in fixed costs or variable costs per unit, what is the *total forecasted cost* to produce 60,000 cars next year?

   c. What is the *forecasted average cost* per car next year?

   d. Why does the average cost per car vary between years?

MyAccountingLab®

NEW! End-of-Chapter Material Integrated with MyAccountingLab: www.myaccountinglab.com
Students need practice and repetition in order to successfully learn the fundamentals of accounting. *Managerial Accounting, 2e* now contains an additional set of exercises in the text for instructors to choose from. In **MyAccountingLab** alternative exercises and problems and algorithmic versions are all auto-graded for unlimited practice.

www.pearsonhighered.com/braun

Rock-Solid Understanding: Study Aids

MyAccountingLab

www.myaccountinglab.com

MyAccountingLab is web-based tutorial and assessment software for accounting that gives students more "I get it!" moments. **MyAccountingLab** provides students with a personalized interactive learning environment where they can complete their course assignments with immediate tutorial assistance, learn at their own pace, and measure their progress.

In addition to completing assignments and reviewing tutorial help, students have access to the following resources in **MyAccountingLab:**

- Pearson eText
- Study Guide
- Animated Demo Docs
- Excel in Practice
- Videos
- Audio and Student PowerPoints
- Working Papers in both Excel and PDF
- MP3 Files with Chapter Objectives and Summaries
- Flashcards

Study Guide and Study Guide CD with Demo Docs

This chapter-by-chapter learning aid, reviewed by the authors, helps students learn managerial accounting while getting the maximum benefit from study time. For each chapter there is an explanation of each Learning Objective; additional Demo Docs; Quick Practice, True/False and Multiple Choice questions; Quick Exercises; and Do It Yourself questions—all available with solutions. Animated Demo Docs are available on the accompanying Study Guide CD in Flash so students can easily refer to them when they need them.

Student Resource Website: www.pearsonhighered.com/braun

- Excel in Practice
- Working Papers in both Excel and PDF

Student Reference Cards

IFRS Student Reference Card

International Financial Reporting Standards Student Reference Card

This four-page laminated reference card includes an overview of IFRS, why it matters and how it compares to U.S. standards, and highlights key differences between IFRS and U.S. GAAP.

Math for Accounting Student Reference Card

Math for Accounting Student Reference Card

This six-page laminated reference card provides students with a study tool for the basic math they will need to be successful in accounting, such as rounding, fractions, converting decimals, calculating interest, break-even analysis, and more!

Rock-Solid Supplements: Author-Driven Instructor Resources

The primary goal of the Instructor Resources is to help instructors deliver their course with ease, using any delivery method—traditional, self-paced, or online. *Every resource has been written or reviewed by the author team.*

MyAccountingLab®

www.myaccountinglab.com

MyAccountingLab is web-based tutorial and assessment software for accounting that not only gives students more "I get it!" moments, but also provides instructors the flexibility to make technology an integral part of their course or a supplementary resource for students. And, because practice makes perfect, MyAccountingLab offers exactly the same end-of-chapter material found in the text along with algorithmic options that can be assigned for homework. MyAccountingLab also features the same look and feel for exercises and problems so that students are familiar and comfortable working with the material.

Instructor's Manual

The author-reviewed Instructor's Manual, available electronically or in print, offers course-specific content including a guide to available resources, a roadmap for using MyAccountingLab, a first day handout for students, sample syllabi, guidelines for teaching an online course, and content-specific material including chapter overviews, teaching outlines, student summary handouts, lecture outline tips, assignment grids, ten-minute quizzes, and more!

Instructor Resource Center: www.pearsonhighered.com/braun

For the instructor's convenience, many of the instructor resources are available for download from the textbook's catalog page or from MyAccountingLab. Available resources include the following:

- **Solutions Manual,** written by coauthor Wendy Tietz, contains the fully worked-through and accuracy-checked solutions for every question, exercise, and problem in the text.
- **Author-Written Test Item File with TestGen Software** offers over 1,600 multiple choice, true/false, and problem solving questions that are correlated by Learning Objective and difficulty level as well as AACSB and AICPA standards.
- **Four Sets of Author-Reviewed Instructor PowerPoints** give instructors flexibility and choices for their courses. There are 508 Compliant Instructor PowerPoints with extensive notes for on-campus or online classes, Student PowerPoints, Clicker Response System (CRS) PowerPoints, and Audio Narrated PowerPoints.
- **Excel in Practice**
- **Image Library**
- **Working Papers and Solutions in Excel and PDF formats**
- **Instructor's Manual**

Course Cartridges

Course Cartridges for Blackboard, WebCT, CourseCompass, and other learning management systems are available upon request.

www.pearsonhighered.com/braun

Changes to the Second Edition

Students and Instructors will both benefit from a variety of new content and features in the second edition:

New Coauthor. For this edition, Wendy Tietz, of Kent State University, contributed as coauthor. Dr. Tietz is an award-winning and experienced accounting and technology educator, and a past contributor to the end-of-chapter materials for several of the market-leading managerial accounting texts. Together, the authors refined their philosophy for the end-of-chapter and supplementary material for the second edition. Feedback from editorial surveys indicated that the end-of-chapter material in managerial accounting texts either, a) assumed too much knowledge on the part of the students, and/or, b) focused too much on calculation rather than the conceptual uses of the information. Throughout all the chapters, readers will notice not only new, multi-media features (Application & Analysis) for instructors and students, but also incorporation of this market feedback. Specifically:

- The homework progresses from simple to complex and builds logically at each step as students work through quick checks, short exercises, exercises and problems, as well as the cases, analytical portion, and CMA (Certified Management Accounting) adapted test problems. Students will gain confidence as they work through the end-of-chapter material assigned.
- A solid offering of end-of-chapter exercises and problems that mix cost-oriented and conceptual requirements are found throughout the text. This structure helps students think about what the numbers mean in addition to how to calculate them.

Chapter Order Revised. Based on extensive market feedback, the authors revised the table of contents to reflect how instructors teach the course, and to follow the order that best enables students' understanding and comprehension of the material:

- **Revised Costing Chapters.** The Activity-Based Costing chapter (formerly Ch 5, now Ch 4) has been moved to follow Job Costing (Ch 3) since it is a natural extension of a traditional job costing environment. Life Fitness, a fitness equipment manufacturer, is used as the focus company in both chapters so that students can easily compare and contrast the different costing methods within the same business context. The Job Costing chapter now focuses on teaching students how companies find the cost of a job using source documents, and then uses job cost information to make business decisions. To give instructors more flexibility of coverage, all journal entries associated with job costing have been isolated in the final section of the chapter. A full example of job costing at a service firm, including the calculation of a professional billing rate, is illustrated in the appendix.
- **Financial Statement Analysis Chapter.** This chapter has been fully revised, including the end-of-chapter materials. The authors use a large retailer similar to Target to present the concept and then use Target in both Summary Problems. The standard ratios of leading competitors such as JC Penney, Kohl's, and Wal-Mart are now compared and discussed to illustrate financial statement analysis. Unlike other texts on the market, the use of a competitor like Target allows students to analyze the financial statements from both a company and industry point of view.
- **Revised Budgeting Chapter.** The focus of this chapter (formerly Ch 10, now Ch 9) switched from a merchandising to a manufacturing context to provide the most comprehensive coverage of master budgets. The authors have also increased the coverage of budget practices and processes at the beginning of the chapter. The appendix compares and contrasts the budgets of service, manufacturing, and merchandising budgets.

- **New Chapter on Statement of Cash Flows (Chapter 13).** The authors increased coverage of the statement of cash flows in this edition to support the frequency of coverage of this topic in the managerial course. The new chapter shows students how to interpret the statement and deepens their understanding of the importance of cash to a business' survival and expansion.

International Financial Reporting Standards (IFRS) and Global Issues Integration. The changes on the global accounting landscape are fast approaching. In order to fully inform students of these upcoming changes, applicable topics are denoted by icons and footnotes where relevant and practical.

"Why is this important?" To help students focus on the business significance of managerial accounting and make the connections between accounting and the business environment, the authors added marginal notations called "Why is this important?" (several in each chapter).

Business Decision-Making Focus. Most major headings in the chapter have been re-written in a question and answer format so that students can appreciate the impact of managerial accounting information on business decision-making as they are learning how to calculate and understand that information.

Extensive Revision of the End-of-Chapter Materials. In every chapter of the text, the material was restructured so that students progress from simple computational questions (short exercises) to a mixture of computational/conceptual exercises, and on to the more complex conceptual analysis (problems). This progression allows students to attain confidence and achieve mastery of the material. Highlights of additional material added to this edition include the following:

- **A & B exercises and problems in the book PLUS three alternate versions of each exercise and problem in MyAccountingLab.**
- **Additional Set of Exercises in the Text.** In addition to an "A" set of exercises, students will receive additional practice with a new set of "B" exercises that have been added to this text. These questions can be assigned, completed, and graded in **MyAccountingLab.**
- **Application & Analysis Cases.** These new cases require students to analyze real-life scenarios and to apply management accounting concepts or use skills acquired from their study of accounting. Some of these cases require Internet research or use of other media sources familiar to them (YouTube, etc). These cases are also designed specifically to be extremely flexible: they can be used as in-class group work, individual at-home assignments, or online course work.
- **Discussion & Analysis.** New questions are available to provide meaningful opportunities for classroom discussions that can help students make connections between accounting and the business environment.
- **Certified Management Accountant (CMA) Adapted Problems.** In order to assess accounting majors understanding of material in a simulated certified testing format, CMA Adopted problems were added to selected chapters throughout the text.
- **Accreditation Compliant End-of-Chapter materials.** As in the last edition, the authors reviewed and revised course materials in order to comply with higher education accreditation requirements.

Accuracy Process. Three accuracy checkers verified not only the end-of-chapter materials but also the in-chapter figures and illustrations to ensure the level of accuracy instructors expect and need.

www.pearsonhighered.com/braun

ACKNOWLEDGMENTS

We'd like to extend a special thank you to our reviewers, who took the time to help us develop teaching and learning tools for Managerial Accounting courses to come. We value and appreciate your commitment, dedication, and passion for your students and the classroom:

Managerial Accounting, 2e

Revision Plan Reviewers

Felix E. Amenkhienan, Radford University

Molly Brown, James Madison University

David Centers, Grand Valley State University

Sandra Cereola, James Madison University

Mike Chatham, Radford University

Julie Chenier, Louisiana State University

Thomas Clevenger, Washburn University

Robert Cornell, Oklahoma State University

David L. Davis, Tallahassee Community College

Patricia A. Doherty, Boston University School of Management

Jimmy Dong, Sacramento City College

Gene B. Elrod, The University of North Texas

Robert Everett, Lewis & Clark Community College

Dr. Kurt Fanning, Grand Valley State University

Amanda Farmer, University of Georgia

Janice Fergusson, University of South Carolina

Ben Foster, University of Louisville

Mary Anne Gaffney, Temple University

Lisa Gillespie, Loyola University - Chicago

Christopher Harper, Grand Valley State University

Audrey S. Hunter, Broward College

Mark Judd, University of San Diego

Harold T. Little, Western Kentucky University

D. Jordan Lowe, Arizona State University, West Campus

Diane Marker, University of Toledo

Linda Marquis, Northern Kentucky University

David Mautz, University of North Carolina, Wilmington

Mallory McWilliams, San Jose State University

Robert Meyer, Parkland College

Mehmet Ozbilgin, Baruch College, City University of New York

Glenn Pate, Palm Beach Community College

Sheldon Peng, Washburn University

Tamara Phelan, Northern Illinois University

Cindy Powell, Southern Nazarene University

Paulette A. Ratliff-Miller, Grand Valley State University

Anwar Salimi, California State Polytechnic University

Kathryn Savage, Northern Arizona University

Dennis Stovall, Grand Valley State University

Gloria Stuart, Georgia Southern University

Gracelyn V. Stuart-Tuggle, Palm Beach Community College, South

Lloyd Tanlu, University of Washington

Linda Tarrago, Hillsborough Community College

John Virchick, Chapman University

Chapter Reviewers

Lisa Dutchik, Kirkwood Community College

Diane Eure, Texas State University

Amanda Farmer, University of Georgia

Janice H. Fergusson, University of South Carolina

Lisa Gillespie, Loyola University - Chicago

Nancy Jones, California State University - Chico

David Juriga, St. Louis Community College

Diane Marker, University of Toledo

Olin Scott Stovall, Abilene Christian University

Don Trippeer, SUNY Oneonta

Judith Zander, Grossmont College

Supplements Authors

Excel in Practice Templates: Diane Marker, University of Toledo

Instructor's Manual: Judith Zander, Grossmont College

PowerPoints: Robin Turner, Rowan-Cabarrus Community College

Study Guide: Diane Marker, University of Toledo; Amanda Farmer, University of Georgia

Solutions Manual: Wendy Tietz, Kent State University

Test Item File: Wendy Tietz, Kent State University

Supplements Reviewers

Diane Marker, University of Toledo

Diane Tanner, University of North Florida

Previous Edition

Nasrollah Ahadiat *California State Polytechnic University*

Markus Ahrens *St. Louis Community College*

Vern Allen *Central Florida Community College*

Michael T. Blackwell *West Liberty State College*

Charles Blumer *St. Charles Community College*

Kevin Bosner *SUNY Genesco*

Anna Boulware *St. Charles Community College*

Nina E. Brown *Tarrant County College*

Helen Brubeck *San Jose State University*

Cheryl Copeland *California State University Fresno*

Patrick Cunningham *Dawson Community College*

Alan B. Czyzewski *Indiana State University*

Darlene K. Edwards *Bellingham Technical College*

Anita Ellzey *Harford Community College*

Jean Fornasieri *Bergen Community College*

Shirley Glass *Macomb Community College*

Sueann Hely *West Kentucky Community & Technical College*

Ken Koerber *Bucks County Community College*

Pamela Legner *College of DuPage*

Elliott Levy *Bentley College*

Lizbeth Matz *University of Pittsburgh at Bradford*

Florence McGovern *Bergen Community College*

Kitty O'Donnell *Onondaga Community College*

Deborah Pavelka *Roosevelt University*

Donald Reynolds *Calvin College*

Doug Roberts *Appalachian State University*

Christine Schalow *California State University, San Bernadino*

Tony Scott *Norwalk Community College*

David Skougstad *Metropolitan State College of Denver*

Gracelyn V. Stuart *Palm Beach Community College*

Iris Stuart *California State University, Fullerton*

Diane Tanner *University of North Florida*

Andy Williams *Edmonds Community College*

Your authors keep a blog called *Teaching Managerial Accounting* where they share teaching ideas and resources. We would like to hear your ideas too! Please visit us at the link found under the Instructor Resources section in MyAccountingLab.

Karen Wilken Braun is currently a faculty member of the Weatherhead School of Management at Case Western Reserve University. From 1996 to 2004, Professor Braun was on the faculty of the J.M. Tull School of Accounting at the University of Georgia, where she received the Outstanding Accounting Teacher of the Year award from the UGA chapter of Alpha Kappa Psi.

Professor Braun is a Certified Public Accountant, a member of the American Accounting Association (AAA), She is also a member of the AAA's Management Accounting Section as well as the Teaching, Learning and Curriculum Section.

Dr. Braun received her Ph.D. from the University of Connecticut, where she was an AICPA Doctoral Fellow, a Deloitte & Touche Doctoral Fellow, and an AAA Doctoral Consortium Fellow. She received her B.A., summa cum laude, from Luther College, where she was a member of Phi Beta Kappa and received the Outstanding Accounting Student award from the Iowa Society of Certified Public Accountants.

She gained public accounting experience while working at Arthur Andersen & Co. and accumulated additional business and management accounting experience as Corporate Controller for Gemini Aviation, Inc.

Professor Braun and her husband, Cory, have two daughters, Rachel and Hannah. In her free time she enjoys playing tennis, gardening, skiing, hiking, and music.

Wendy M. Tietz is currently a faculty member in the Department of Accounting in the College of Business Administration at Kent State University, where she has taught since 2000. Prior to Kent State University, she was on the faculty at The University of Akron. She teaches in a variety of formats, including large sections, small sections, and web-based sections. She has received numerous college and university teaching awards while at Kent State University.

Professor Tietz is a Certified Public Accountant, a Certified Management Accountant, and a Certified Information Systems Auditor. She is a member of the American Accounting Association, the Institute of Management Accountants, the American Institute of Certified Public Accountants, and ISACA®. She is also a member of the AAA's Management Accounting Section as well as the Teaching, Learning and Curriculum Section. She has published in Issues in Accounting Education and in Accounting Education: An International Journal and regularly presents at AAA regional and national meetings.

Professor Tietz received her Ph.D. from Kent State University. She received both her M.B.A. and B.S.A from The University of Akron. She worked in industry for several years, both as a controller for a financial institution and as the operations manager and controller for a recycled plastics manufacturer.

Professor Tietz and her husband, Russ, have two sons who are both in college. In her spare time, she enjoys playing tennis, bike riding, reading, and learning about new technology.

Walter T. Harrison, Jr. is Professor Emeritus of Accounting at the Hankamer School of Business, Baylor University. He received his B.B.A. degree from Baylor University, his M.S. from Oklahoma State University, and his Ph.D. from Michigan State University.

Professor Harrison, recipient of numerous teaching awards from student groups as well as from university administrators, has also taught at Cleveland State Community College, Michigan State University, the University of Texas, and Stanford University.

A member of the American Accounting Association and the American Institute of Certified Public Accountants, Professor Harrison has served as Chairman of the Financial Accounting Standards Committee of the American Accounting Association, on the Teaching/Curriculum Development Award Committee, on the Program Advisory Committee for Accounting Education and Teaching, and on the Notable Contributions to Accounting Literature Committee.

Professor Harrison has lectured in several foreign countries and published articles in numerous journals, including *The Accounting Review, Journal of Accounting Research, Journal of Accountancy, Journal of Accounting and Public Policy, Economic Consequences of Financial Accounting Standards, Accounting Horizons, Issues in Accounting Education*, and *Journal of Law and Commerce*.

He is co-author of *Financial Accounting*, Eighth Edition, 2009 (with Charles T. Horngren and C. William (Bill) Thomas), published by Prentice Hall. Professor Harrison has received scholarships, fellowships, and research grants or awards from PriceWaterhouse Coopers, Deloitte & Touche, the Ernst & Young Foundation, and the KPMG Foundation.

To Cory, Rachel, and Hannah who fill my life with joy
Karen Braun

To Russ, Jonathan, and Nicholas who enrich my life
through laughter and love
Wendy Tietz

To Billie Harrison who taught me to pursue excellence in all things
Tom Harrison

In 1988, Outback Steakhouse's cofounders decided to

create a chain of four or five restaurants that would generate enough income to let them have a nice lifestyle, stay in the Tampa Bay area, and play golf. That was then; this is now. Outback Steakhouse, Inc., currently owns over 1,400 restaurants that operate in all 50 states and in 21 different countries. In addition to steakhouses, Outback also owns six other award-winning restaurant brands, including Carrabba's Italian Grill and Bonefish Grill. Annual sales have topped $3.9 billion, and operating income is over $152 million. How did Outback become so successful? Part of the answer is managerial accounting. Outback won't invest in a new restaurant location unless the projected annual sales are at least double the initial cost of the location's property, improvements, and equipment. Outback motivates restaurant managers by requiring them to buy into the property for $25,000 and sign a five-year contract. In exchange, the manager receives an annual base salary of plus 10% of the location's cash flow, resulting in an average pay of over $118,000. Outback's founders also decided that the cost of replacing overworked managers and employees would exceed profits from lunchtime business. So, they bucked the industry trend and open only for dinner. As a result, managers have incentives to ensure their restaurant is profitable and employee turnover is far lower than industry standards.

Sources: www.osirestaurantpartners.com; www.outbacksteakhouse.com; "Bounce of the Kangaroo," Maddux Business Report, September 2004, pp. 18–23; "Inside Outback," Nation's Restaurant News, March 27, 1995, pp. 51–69.

CHAPTER 1

Introduction to Managerial Accounting

Learning Objectives

1 Identify managers' four primary responsibilities

2 Distinguish financial accounting from managerial accounting

3 Describe organizational structure and the roles and skills required of management accountants within the organization

4 Describe the role of the Institute of Management Accountants (IMA) and use its ethical standards to make reasonable ethical judgments

5 Discuss and analyze the implications of regulatory and business trends

As the Outback story shows, managers use accounting information for much more than preparing annual financial statements. They use managerial accounting (or management accounting) information to guide their actions and decisions. These decisions might include opening new restaurants, adding new items to the menu, or outsourcing the desserts to a local bakery or caterer. Management accounting information helps management decide whether any or all of these actions will be profitable. In this chapter, we'll introduce managerial accounting and discuss how managers use it to fulfill their duties. We will also explore how managerial accounting differs from financial accounting, and discuss the role of management accountants within the organization. Finally, we will discuss the regulatory and business environment in which today's managers and management accountants operate.

What is Managerial Accounting?

As you will see throughout the book, managerial accounting is very different from financial accounting. Financial accounting focuses on providing stockholders and creditors with the information they need to make investment and lending decisions. This information takes the form of financial statements: the balance sheet, income statement, statement of shareholders' equity, and statement of cash flows. Managerial accounting focuses on providing internal management with the information it needs to run the company efficiently and effectively. This information takes many forms depending on management's needs.

To understand the kind of information managers need, let's first look at their primary responsibilities.

Managers' Four Primary Responsibilities

1 Identify managers' four primary responsibilities

Managerial accounting helps managers fulfill their four primary responsibilities, as shown in Exhibit 1-1: planning, directing, controlling, and decision making.

EXHIBIT 1-1 **Managers' Four Primary Responsibilities**

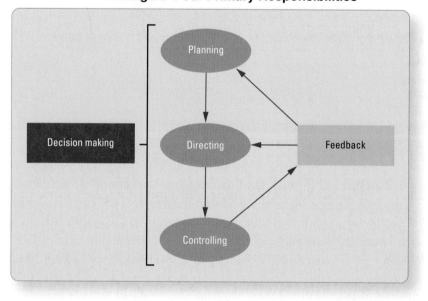

- **Planning** involves setting goals and objectives for the company and determining how to achieve them. For example, one of Outback's goals is to generate more sales. One strategy to achieve this goal is to open more restaurants, so management may plan to build and begin operating 25 new steakhouses next year. Managerial accounting translates these plans into **budgets**—the quantitative expression of a plan. Management analyzes the budgets before proceeding to determine whether its expansion plans make financial sense.

- **Directing** means overseeing the company's day-to-day operations. Management uses product cost reports, product sales information, and other managerial accounting reports to run daily business operations. Outback uses product sales data to determine which menu items are generating the most sales and then uses that information to adjust menus and marketing strategies.

- **Controlling** means evaluating the results of business operations against the plan and making adjustments to keep the company pressing toward its goals. Outback uses performance reports to compare each restaurant's actual performance against the budget and then uses that *feedback* to take corrective actions if needed. If actual costs are higher than planned, or actual sales are lower than planned, then management may revise its plans or adjust operations. Perhaps the newly opened steakhouses are not generating as much income as budgeted. As a result, management may decide to increase local advertising to increase sales.

■ Management is continually **making decisions** while it plans, directs, and controls operations. Outback must decide where to open new restaurants, which restaurants to refurnish, what prices to set for meals, what entrees to offer, and so forth. Because Outback is in business to generate profits for its stockholders, management must consider the financial impact of each of these decisions. Managerial accounting gathers, summarizes, and reports cost and revenue data relevant to each of these decisions.

A Road Map: How Managerial Accounting Fits In

This book will show you how managerial accounting information helps managers fulfill their responsibilities. The rest of the text is organized around the following themes:

1. **Managerial Accounting Building Blocks** Chapter 1 helps you understand more about the management accounting profession and today's business environment. Chapter 2 teaches you some of the language that is commonly used in managerial accounting. Just as musicians must know the notes to the musical scale, management accountants *and* managers must understand managerial accounting terms to effectively use managerial accounting information to run the business.

2. **Determining Unit Cost (Product Costing)** How does a company decide how high to set its prices? It must first figure out how much it costs to make its product or deliver its service. Outback must calculate the cost of each item on the menu to set prices high enough to cover costs and generate a profit. This is tougher than it sounds. Outback's cost to prepare and serve each meal includes more than just the cost of the ingredients. Outback's cost also includes the chefs' and servers' wages and benefits, restaurant lease payments, property taxes, utilities, business and alcohol licenses, and so forth. Chapters 3, 4, and 5 discuss how businesses determine their product costs. Once management knows its product costs, it uses that information for decision making, planning, directing, and controlling.

3. **Making Decisions** Before Outback opened any restaurants, management determined how many meals it would have to serve just to break even—that is, just to cover costs. Management had to understand how costs behave before it could calculate a *breakeven* point. Chapters 6 and 7 discuss how costs behave, how to determine a breakeven point, and how managers use cost behavior knowledge to make good decisions and accurate forecasts. Then, Chapter 8 walks you through some very common business decisions, such as *outsourcing* and pricing. For example, should Outback outsource its desserts—that is, have another company make them? Many restaurants do. Chapter 12 shows you how managers decide whether to invest in new equipment, new locations, and new projects.

4. **Planning** Budgets are management's primary tool for expressing its plans. Chapter 9 discusses all of the components of the *master budget* and the way a large company like Outback uses the budgeting process to implement its business goals and strategies.

5. **Controlling and Evaluating** Management uses *budget variances*—the difference between actual costs and the budget—to control operations. Chapters 9 and 10 show how management uses variance analysis to determine how and where to adjust operations. Chapter 11 discusses other tools that management can use to determine whether individual segments of the company are reaching the company's goals. Finally, Chapters 13 and 14 describe how the statement of cash flows and financial statement analysis can be used to evaluate the company as a whole.

Differences Between Managerial Accounting and Financial Accounting

Managerial accounting information differs from financial accounting information in many respects. Exhibit 1-2 summarizes these differences. Take a few minutes to study the exhibit (on the next page), and then we'll apply it to Outback.

Distinguish financial accounting from managerial accounting **2**

Outback's *financial accounting* system is geared toward producing annual and quarterly consolidated financial statements that will be used by investors and creditors to make investment and lending decisions. The financial statements, which must be prepared

EXHIBIT 1-2   Managerial Accounting Versus Financial Accounting

MANAGERIAL ACCOUNTING	ISSUE	FINANCIAL ACCOUNTING
Internal users such as managers.	Who are the primary users of the information?	External users, such as creditors, stockholders, and government regulators.
To help managers plan, direct, and control business operations and make business decisions.	What is the purpose of the information?	To help external users make investing and lending decisions.
Any internal accounting report deemed worthwhile by management.	What is the primary accounting product?	Financial statements.
Management determines what it wants in a report, and how it wants it formatted. Reports are prepared only when management believes the benefit of using the report exceeds the cost of preparing the report.	What must be included in the report, and how must it be formatted?	Generally accepted accounting principles (GAAP) determine the content and format of financial statements.
While some information is based on past transactions, managerial accounting focuses on the future. It provides information on both external and internal transactions.	What is the underlying basis of the information?	The information is based on historical transactions with external parties.
The data must be relevant.	What information characteristic is emphasized?	The data must be reliable and objective.
Segments of the business, such as products, customers, geographical regions, departments, and divisions.	What business "unit" is the report about?	The company as a whole (consolidated financial statements). Limited segment data is provided in the footnotes.
It depends on management's needs. Some reports are prepared daily, while others may be prepared only one time.	How often are the reports prepared?	Annually and quarterly.
There are no independent audits. However, the company's internal audit function may examine the procedures used in preparing the reports.	Does anyone verify the information?	Independent certified public accountants (CPAs) audit the annual financial statements of publicly traded companies and express an opinion on the fairness of the financial information they contain.
No authoritative body requires managerial accounting reports.	Is the information required by an outside group/government agency?	Yes, the Securities and Exchange Commission (SEC) requires publicly traded companies to issue annual audited financial statements.
Management carefully considers behavioral implications when designing the managerial accounting system.	Is there any concern over how the reports will affect employee behavior?	The concern is about adequacy of disclosure; behavioral implications are secondary.

in accordance with Generally Accepted Accounting Principles (GAAP), objectively summarize the transactions that occurred between Outback and external parties during the previous year. The SEC requires that the annual financial statements of publicly traded companies be audited by independent certified public accountants (CPAs). Outback's financial statements are useful to its investors and creditors, but they do not provide management with enough information to run the company effectively.

Outback's *managerial accounting* system is designed to provide its managers with the accounting information they need to plan, direct, control, and make decisions. There are no GAAP-type standards or audits required for managerial accounting. Outback's managers tailor the company's managerial accounting system to provide the information they need to help them make better decisions. Outback must weigh the benefits of the system (information that helps managers make decisions that increase profits) against the costs to develop and run the system. The costs and benefits of any particular managerial accounting system differ from one company to another. Different companies create different systems, so Outback's system will differ from Toyota's system.

In contrast to financial statements, most managerial accounting reports focus on the *future*, providing *relevant* information that helps managers make profitable business decisions. For example, before putting their plans into action, Outback's managers determine if their plans make sense by quantitatively expressing them in the form of budgets. Outback's managerial accounting reports may also plan for and reflect *internal* transactions, such as the daily movement of beverages and dry ingredients from central warehouses to individual restaurant locations.

To make good decisions, Outback's managers need information about smaller units of the company, not just the company as a whole. For example, management uses revenue and cost data on individual restaurants, geographical regions, and individual menu items to increase the company's profitability. Regional data helps Outback's management decide where to open more restaurants. Sales and profit reports on individual menu items help management choose menu items and decide what items to offer on a seasonal basis. Rather than preparing these reports just once a year, companies prepare and revise managerial accounting reports as often as needed.

When designing the managerial accounting system, management must carefully consider how the system will affect employees' behavior. Employees try to perform well on the parts of their jobs that the accounting system measures. If Outback restaurant managers were evaluated only on their ability to control costs, they may use cheaper ingredients or hire less experienced servers. Although these actions cut costs, they can hurt profits if the quality of the meals or service declines as a result. As another example, Outback wants to focus each restaurant manager's attention on cash flow. As a result, Outback pays its restaurant managers a percentage of the restaurant's cash flows in addition to a base salary.

What Role do Management Accountants Play?

Let's look at how management accountants fit into the company's organizational structure, how their roles are changing, and the skills they need to successfully fill their roles. We'll also look at their professional association, their average salaries, and their ethical standards.

Describe organizational structure and the roles and skills required of management accountants within the organization   **3**

Organizational Structure

Most corporations are too large to be governed directly by their stockholders. Therefore, stockholders elect a **board of directors** to oversee the company. Exhibit 1-3 (on the next page) shows a typical organizational structure with the green boxes representing employees of the firm and the orange and blue boxes representing nonemployees.

The board meets only periodically, so they hire a **chief executive officer (CEO)** to manage the company on a daily basis. The CEO hires other executives to run various aspects of the organization, including the **chief operating officer (COO)** and the **chief financial officer (CFO)**. The COO is responsible for the company's operations, such as research and development (R&D), production, and distribution. The CFO is responsible for all of the company's financial concerns. The **treasurer** and the **controller** report directly to the CFO. The treasurer is primarily responsible for raising capital (through issuing stocks and bonds) and investing funds. The controller is usually responsible for general financial accounting, managerial accounting, and tax reporting.

The New York Stock Exchange requires that listed companies have an **internal audit function**. The role of the internal audit function is to ensure that the company's internal controls and risk management policies are functioning properly. The internal audit department reports directly to a subcommittee of the board of directors called the **audit committee**. The

EXHIBIT 1-3 **Typical Organizational Structure**

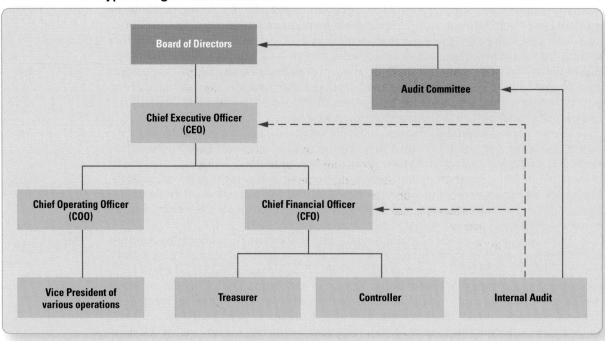

audit committee oversees the internal audit function as well as the annual audit of the financial statements by independent CPAs. Both the internal audit department and the independent CPAs report directly to the audit committee for one very important reason: to ensure that management will not intimidate them or bias their work. However, since the audit committee meets only periodically, it is not practical for the audit committee to manage the internal audit function on a day-to-day basis. Therefore, the internal audit function also reports to a senior executive, such as the CFO or CEO, for administrative matters.

When you look at the organizational chart pictured in Exhibit 1-3, where do you think management accountants work? It depends on the company. Management accountants used to work in accounting departments and reported directly to the controller. Now, over half of management accountants are located throughout the company and work on cross-functional teams. **Cross-functional teams** consist of employees representing various functions of the company, such as R&D, design, production, marketing, distribution, and customer service. Cross-functional teams are effective because each member can address business decisions from a different viewpoint. These teams often report to various vice presidents of operations. Management accountants often take the leadership role in the teams. Here is what two managers had to say in a study about management accountants:[1]

> Finance (the management accountant) has a unique ability and responsibility to see across all the functions and try and make sense of them. They have the neat ability to be a member of all of the different groups (functions) and yet not be a member of any of them at the same time. (U.S. West)

> Basically the role of the financial person on the team is analyzing the financial impact of the business decision and providing advice. Does this make sense financially or not? (Abbott Laboratories)

The Changing Roles of Management Accountants

Technology has changed the roles of management accountants. Management accountants no longer perform routine mechanical accounting tasks. Computer programs perform those tasks. Yet, management accountants are in more demand than ever before. Company managers used to view management accountants as "scorekeepers" or "bean counters" because they spent most of their time recording historical transactions. Now, they view management accountants as internal consultants or business advisors.

---

[1]*Counting More, Counting Less: The 1999 Practice Analysis of Management Accounting*, Institute of Management Accountants, Montvale, NJ, 1999.

Does this mean that management accountants are no longer involved with the traditional task of recording transactions? No. Management accountants must still ensure that the company's financial records adequately capture economic events. They help design the information systems that capture and record transactions and make sure that the information system generates accurate data. They use professional judgment to record nonroutine transactions and make adjustments to the financial records as needed. Management accountants still need to know what transactions to record and how to record them, but they let technology do most of the routine work.

Freed from the routine mechanical work, management accountants spend more of their time planning, analyzing, and interpreting accounting data and providing decision support. Because their role is changing, management accountants rarely bear the job title "management accountant" anymore; managers often refer to them as business management support, financial advisors, business partners, or analysts. Here is what two management accountants have said about their jobs:[2]

> We are looked upon as more business advisors than just accountants, which has a lot to do with the additional analysis and forward-looking goals that we are setting. We spend more of our time analyzing and understanding our margins, our prices, and the markets in which we do business. People have a sense of purpose; they have a real sense of "I'm adding value to the company." (Caterpillar, Inc.)

> Accounting is changing. You're no longer sitting behind a desk just working on a computer, just crunching the numbers. You're actually getting to be a part of the day-to-day functions of the business. (Abbott Laboratories)

Why is this important?

"Management accountants act as internal business advisors. They provide the financial information and in-depth analysis that managers need to make good business decisions."

The Skills Required of Management Accountants

Because computers now do the routine "number crunching," do management accountants need to know as much as they did 20 years ago? The fact is, management accountants now need to know *more*! They have to understand what information management needs and how to generate that information accurately. Therefore, management accountants must be able to communicate with the computer/IT system programmers to create an effective information system. Once the information system generates the data, management accountants interpret and analyze the raw data and turn it into *useful* information management can use.[3]

> Twenty years ago we would say, "Here are the costs and you guys need to figure out what you want to do with them." Now we are expected to say, "Here are the costs and this is why the costs are what they are, and this is how they compare to other things, and here are some suggestions where we could possibly improve." (Caterpillar, Inc.)

Today's management accountants need the following skills:[4]

- Solid knowledge of both financial and managerial accounting
- Analytical skills
- Knowledge of how a business functions
- Ability to work on a team
- Oral *and* written communication skills

The skills shown in Exhibit 1-4 (on the next page) are critical to these management accountants:

> We're making more presentations that are seen across the division. So you have to summarize the numbers . . . you have to have people in sales understand what those numbers mean. If you can't communicate information to the individuals, then the

[2]*Counting More, Counting Less: The 1999 Practice Analysis of Management Accounting*, Institute of Management Accountants, Montvale, NJ, 1999.
[3]*Counting More, Counting Less: The 1999 Practice Analysis of Management Accounting*, Institute of Management Accountants, Montvale, NJ, 1999.
[4]Gary Siegel and James Sorenson, *What Corporate America Wants in Entry-Level Accountants*, Institute of Management Accountants, Montvale, NJ, 1994.

information is never out there; it's lost. So, your communication skills are very important. (Abbott Laboratories)

Usually when a nonfinancial person comes to you with financial questions, they don't really ask the right things so that you can give them the correct answer. If they ask you for cost, well, you have to work with them and say, "Well, do you want total plant cost, a variable cost, or an accountable cost?" Then, "What is the reason for those costs?" Whatever they're using this cost for determines what type of cost you will provide them with. (Caterpillar, Inc.)

Chapter 2 explains these cost terms. The point here is that management accountants need to have a solid understanding of managerial accounting, including how different types of costs are relevant to different situations. Additionally, they must be able to communicate that information to employees from different business functions.

EXHIBIT 1-4 **The Skills Required of Management Accountants**

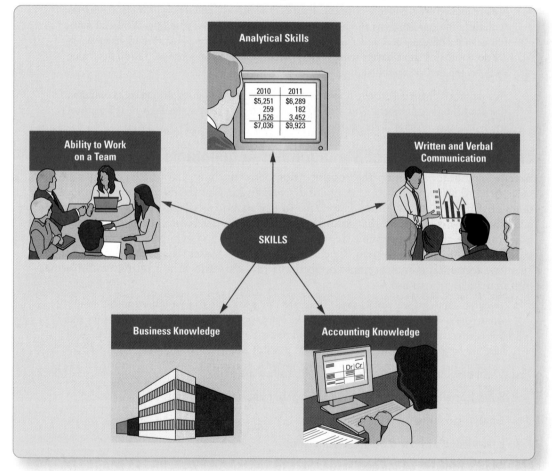

Professional Association

4 Describe the role of the Institute of Management Accountants (IMA) and use its ethical standards to make reasonable ethical judgments

The **Institute of Management Accountants (IMA)** is the professional association for management accountants. The mission of the IMA is to provide a dynamic forum for management accounting and finance professionals to develop and advance their careers through certification, practice development, education, networking, and advocacy of the highest ethical and professional practice. The IMA also wants to educate society about the role management accountants play in organizations. According to the IMA, about 85% of accountants work in organizations, performing the roles discussed earlier. The IMA publishes a monthly journal called *Strategic Finance*. (Prior to 1999, the journal was called *Management Accounting*; but as the role of management accountants changed, so did the journal's title.) The journal addresses current topics of interest to management accountants and helps them keep abreast of recent techniques and trends.

The IMA also issues the **Certified Management Accountant (CMA)** certification. To become a CMA you must pass a rigorous examination and maintain continuing professional education. The CMA exam focuses on managerial accounting topics similar to those discussed in this book, as well as economics and business finance. While most employers do not require the CMA certification, management accountants bearing the CMA designation tend to command higher salaries and obtain higher-level positions within the company. You can find out more about the IMA and the CMA certification it offers at its Web site: www.imanet.org.

Average Salaries of Management Accountants

The average salaries of management accountants reflect their large skill set. Naturally, salaries will vary with the accountant's level of experience, his or her specific job responsibilities, and the size and geographical location of the company. However, to give you a general idea, in 2008, the average salary of IMA members with 1–5 years of experience was $82,504. The average salary of all IMA members was $104,092. In general, those professionals with the CMA certification earned salaries that were about 30% higher than members with no certification. You can obtain more specific salary information in the IMA's 2008 Salary Survey.[5]

Robert Half International, Inc., also publishes a free yearly guide to average salaries for all types of finance professionals. The guide also provides information on current hiring trends. To obtain a free copy of the *Salary Guide*, go to www.roberthalf.com.

Ethics

Management accountants continually face ethical challenges. The IMA has developed principles and standards to help management accountants deal with these challenges. The principles and standards remind us that society expects professional accountants to exhibit the highest level of ethical behavior. The IMA's *Statement on Ethical Professional Practice* requires management accountants to do the following:

- Maintain their professional competence
- Preserve the confidentiality of the information they handle
- Uphold their integrity
- Perform their duties with credibility

These ethical standards are summarized in Exhibit 1-5, while the full *Statement of Ethical Professional Practice* appears in Exhibit 1-6.

Why is this important?

"At the root of all business relationships is trust. Would you put your money in a bank that you didn't trust, invest in a company you knew was 'cooking the books,' or loan money to someone you thought would never pay you back? As a manager, your trust in the other party's ethical behavior, and vice versa, will be a vital component to the business decisions you make."

EXHIBIT 1-5 Summary of Ethical Standards

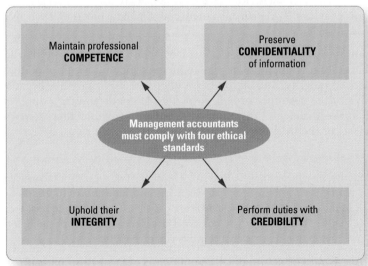

To resolve ethical dilemmas, the IMA suggests that management accountants first follow their company's established policies for reporting unethical behavior. If the conflict is not resolved through the company's procedures, the management accountant should consider the following steps:

- Discuss the unethical situation with the immediate supervisor unless the supervisor is involved in the unethical situation. If so, notify the supervisor at the next higher managerial level. If the immediate supervisor involved is the CEO, notify the audit committee or board of directors.

- Discuss the unethical situation with an objective advisor, such as an IMA ethics counselor. The IMA offers a confidential "Ethics Hotline" to its members. Members may call the hotline and discuss their ethical dilemma. The ethics counselor will not provide a specific resolution but will clarify how the dilemma relates to the IMA's *Statement of Ethical Professional Practice* shown in Exhibit 1-6.

- Consult an attorney regarding legal obligations and rights.

Examples of Ethical Dilemmas

Unfortunately, the ethical path is not always clear. You may want to act ethically and do the right thing, but the consequences can make it difficult to decide what to do. Let's consider several ethical dilemmas in light of the *Statement of Ethical Professional Practice*:

Dilemma #1

Sarah Baker is examining the expense reports of her staff, who counted inventory at Top-Flight's warehouses in Arizona. She discovers that Mike Flinders has claimed but not included hotel receipts for over $1,000 of accommodation expenses. Other staff, who also claimed $1,000, did attach hotel receipts. When asked about the receipts, Mike admits that he stayed with an old friend, not in the hotel, but he believes that he deserves the money he saved. After all, the company would have paid his hotel bill.

By asking to be reimbursed for hotel expenses he did not incur, Flinders violated the IMA's integrity standards (conflict of interest in which he tried to enrich himself at the company's expense). Because Baker discovered the inflated expense report, she would not be fulfilling her ethical responsibilities of integrity and credibility if she allowed the reimbursement.

Dilemma #2

As the accountant of Entreé Computer, you are aware of your company's weak financial condition. Entreé is close to signing a lucrative contract that should ensure its future. To do so, the controller states that the company must report a profit this year (ending December 31). He suggests, "Two customers have placed orders that are really not supposed to be shipped until early January. Ask production to fill and ship those orders on December 31 so we can record them in this year's sales."

The resolution of this dilemma is less clear-cut. Many people believe that following the controller's suggestion to manipulate the company's income would violate the standards of competence, integrity, and credibility. Others would argue that because Entreé Computer already has the customer orders, shipping the goods and recording the sale in December is still ethical behavior. You might discuss the available alternatives with the next managerial level or the IMA ethics hotline counselor.

Dilemma #3

As a new accounting staff member at Central City Hospital, your supervisor has asked you to prepare the yearly *Medicare Cost Report*, which the government uses to determine its reimbursement to the hospital for serving Medicare patients. The report requires specialized knowledge that you don't believe you possess. The supervisor is busy planning for the coming year and cannot offer much guidance while you prepare the report.

This situation is not as rare as you might think. You may be asked to perform tasks that you don't feel qualified to perform. The competence standard requires you to perform

EXHIBIT 1-6   IMA Statement of Ethical Professional Practice

Members of IMA shall behave ethically. A commitment to ethical professional practice includes: overarching principles that express our values, and standards that guide our conduct.

Principles
IMA's overarching ethical principles include: Honesty, Fairness, Objectivity, and Responsibility. Members shall act in accordance with these principles and shall encourage others within their organizations to adhere to them.

Standards
A member's failure to comply with the following standards may result in disciplinary action.

I. Competence
Each member has a responsibility to:
1. Maintain an appropriate level of professional expertise by continually developing knowledge and skills.
2. Perform professional duties in accordance with relevant laws, regulations, and technical standards.
3. Provide decision support information and recommendations that are accurate, clear, concise, and timely.
4. Recognize and communicate professional limitations or other constraints that would preclude responsible judgment or successful performance of an activity.

II. Confidentiality
Each member has a responsibility to:
1. Keep information confidential except when disclosure is authorized or legally required.
2. Inform all relevant parties regarding appropriate use of confidential information. Monitor subordinates' activities to ensure compliance.
3. Refrain from using confidential information for unethical or illegal advantage.

III. Integrity
Each member has a responsibility to:
1. Mitigate actual conflicts of interest. Regularly communicate with business associates to avoid apparent conflicts of interest. Advise all parties of any potential conflicts.
2. Refrain from engaging in any conduct that would prejudice carrying out duties ethically.
3. Abstain from engaging in or supporting any activity that might discredit the profession.

IV. Credibility
Each member has a responsibility to:
1. Communicate information fairly and objectively.
2. Disclose all relevant information that could reasonably be expected to influence an intended user's understanding of the reports, analyses, or recommendations.
3. Disclose delays or deficiencies in information, timeliness, processing, or internal controls in conformance with organization policy and/or applicable law.

Institute of Management Accountants. Adapted with permission (2006).

professional duties in accordance with laws, regulations, and technical standards; but laws and regulations are always changing. For this reason, the competence standard also requires you to continually develop knowledge and skills. CPAs and CMAs are required to complete annual continuing professional education (about 40 hours per year) to fulfill this responsibility. However, even continuing professional education courses will not cover every situation you may encounter.

In the Medicare cost report situation, advise your supervisor that you currently lack the knowledge required to complete the Medicare cost report. By doing so, you are complying with the competence standard that requires you to recognize and communicate any limitations that would preclude you from fulfilling an activity. You should ask for training on the report preparation and supervision by someone experienced in preparing the report. If the supervisor denies your requests, you should ask him or her to reassign the Medicare report to a qualified staff member.

Dilemma #4

> Your company is negotiating a large multiyear sales contract that, if won, would substantially increase the company's future earnings. At a dinner party over the weekend, your friends ask you how you like your job and the company you work for. In your enthusiasm, you tell them not only about your responsibilities at work but also about the contract negotiations. As soon as the words pop out of your mouth, you worry that you've said too much.

This situation is difficult to avoid. You may be so excited about your job and the company you work for that information unintentionally "slips out" during casual conversation with friends and family. The confidentiality standard requires you to refrain from disclosing information or using confidential information for unethical or illegal advantage. Was the contract negotiation confidential? If so, would your friends invest in company stock in hopes that the negotiations increase stock prices? Or were the negotiations public knowledge in the financial community? If so, your friends would gain no illegal advantage from the information. Recent cases, such as those involving Martha Stewart, remind us that insider trading (use of inside knowledge for illegal gain) has serious consequences. Even seemingly mundane information about company operations could give competitors an advantage. Therefore, it's best to disclose only information that is meant for public consumption.

Unethical Versus Illegal Behavior

Finally, is there a difference between unethical and illegal behavior? Not all unethical behavior is illegal, but all illegal behavior is unethical. For example, consider the competence standard. The competence standard states that management accountants have a responsibility to provide decision support information that is accurate, clear, concise, and timely. Failure to follow this standard is unethical but in most cases not illegal. Now, consider the integrity standard. It states that management accountants must abstain from any activity that might discredit the profession. A management accountant who commits an illegal act is violating this ethical standard. In other words, ethical behavior encompasses more than simply following the law. The IMA's ethical principles include honesty, fairness, objectivity, and responsibility—principles that are much broader than what is codified in the law.

Decision Guidelines

Managerial Accounting and Management Accountants

Outback made the following considerations in designing its managerial accounting system to provide managers with the information they need to run operations efficiently and effectively.

Decision	Guidelines
What is the primary purpose and focus of managerial accounting?	Managerial accounting provides information that helps managers plan, direct, and control operations and make better decisions; it has a • *future* orientation. • *focus on relevance* to business decisions.
How do managers design a company's managerial accounting system that is not regulated by GAAP?	Managers design the managerial accounting system so that the benefits (from helping managers make wiser decisions) outweigh the costs of the system.
Where should management accountants be placed within the organizational structure?	In the past, most management accountants worked in isolated departments. Now, over 50% of management accountants are deployed throughout the company and work on cross-functional teams. Management must decide which structure best suits its needs.

Decision	Guidelines
What skills should management accountants possess?	Because of their expanding role within the organization, most management accountants need financial and managerial accounting knowledge, analytical skills, knowledge of how a business functions, ability to work on teams, and written and oral communication skills.
By what ethical principles and standards should management accountants abide?	The IMA's overarching ethical *principles* include the following: • Honesty • Objectivity • Fairness • Responsibility The IMA's ethical *standards* include the following: • Competence • Integrity • Confidentiality • Credibility

Summary Problem 1

Requirements

1. Each of the following statements describes a responsibility of management. Match each statement to the management responsibility being fulfilled.

Statement	Management Responsibility
1. Identifying alternative courses of action and choosing among them	a. Planning
2. Running the company on a day-to-day basis	b. Decision making
3. Determining whether the company's units are operating according to plan	c. Directing
4. Setting goals and objectives for the company and determining strategies to achieve them	d. Controlling

2. Are the following statements more descriptive of managerial accounting or financial accounting information?

   a.   Describes historical transactions with external parties

   b.   Is not required by any authoritative body, such as the SEC

   c.   Reports on the company's subunits, such as products, geographical areas, and departments

   d.   Is intended to be used by creditors and investors

   e.   Is formatted in accordance with GAAP

3. Each of the following statements paraphrases an ethical responsibility. Match each statement to the standard of ethical professional practice being fulfilled. Each standard may be used more than once or not at all.

Responsibility	Standard of Ethical Professional Practice
1. Do not disclose company information unless authorized to do so.	a. Competence
2. Continue to develop skills and knowledge.	b. Confidentiality
3. Don't bias the information and reports presented to management.	c. Integrity
4. If you do not have the skills to complete a task correctly, do not pretend you do.	d. Credibility
5. Avoid actual *and* apparent conflicts of interest.	

Solutions

Requirement 1

1. (b) Decision making
2. (c) Directing
3. (d) Controlling
4. (a) Planning

Requirement 2

a. Financial accounting
b. Managerial accounting
c. Managerial accounting
d. Financial accounting
e. Financial accounting

Requirement 3

1. (b) Confidentiality
2. (a) Competence
3. (d) Credibility
4. (a) Competence
5. (c) Integrity

What Regulatory and Business Issues Affect Today's Management Accountants?

5 Discuss and analyze the implications of regulatory and business trends

The business world is continually changing. Let's look at some of the current regulatory and business issues that affect managers and the managerial accounting systems that support them. These issues include the Sarbanes-Oxley Act (SOX), International Financial Reporting Standards (IFRS), Extensible Business Reporting Language (XBRL), and the shifting economy. After considering these issues, we'll look at some of the tools companies use to compete in the global marketplace.

Sarbanes-Oxley Act of 2002

As a result of corporate accounting scandals, such as those at Enron and WorldCom, the U.S. Congress enacted the **Sarbanes-Oxley Act of 2002 (SOX)**. The purpose of SOX is to restore trust in publicly traded corporations, their management, their financial statements, and their auditors. SOX enhances internal control and financial reporting requirements and establishes new regulatory requirements for publicly traded companies and their independent auditors. Publicly traded companies have spent millions of dollars upgrading their internal controls and accounting systems to comply with SOX regulations.

As shown in Exhibit 1-7, SOX requires the company's CEO and CFO to assume responsibility for the financial statements and disclosures. The CEO and CFO must certify that the financial statements and disclosures fairly present, in all material respects, the operations and financial condition of the company. Additionally, they must accept responsibility for establishing and maintaining an adequate internal control structure and procedures for financial reporting. The company must have its internal controls and financial reporting procedures assessed annually.

EXHIBIT 1-7 Some Important Results of SOX

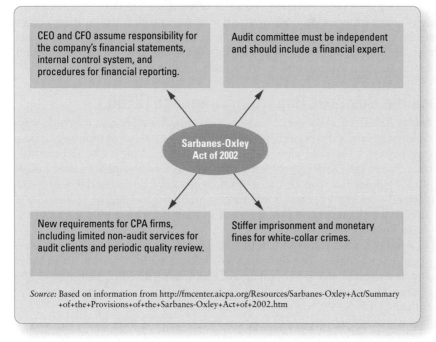

CEO and CFO assume responsibility for the company's financial statements, internal control system, and procedures for financial reporting.

Audit committee must be independent and should include a financial expert.

Sarbanes-Oxley Act of 2002

New requirements for CPA firms, including limited non-audit services for audit clients and periodic quality review.

Stiffer imprisonment and monetary fines for white-collar crimes.

Source: Based on information from http://fmcenter.aicpa.org/Resources/Sarbanes-Oxley+Act/Summary +of+the+Provisions+of+the+Sarbanes-Oxley+Act+of+2002.htm

SOX also requires audit committee members to be independent, meaning that they may not receive any consulting or advisory fees from the company other than for their service on the board of directors. In addition, at least one of the members should be a financial expert. The audit committee oversees not only the internal audit function but also the company's audit by independent CPAs.

To ensure that CPA firms maintain independence from their client company, SOX does not allow CPA firms to provide certain non-audit services (such as bookkeeping and financial information systems design) to companies during the same period of time in which they are providing audit services. If a company wants to obtain such services from a CPA firm, it must hire a different firm to do the non-audit work. Tax services may be provided by the same CPA firm if preapproved by the audit committee. The audit partner must rotate off the audit engagement every five years, and the audit firm must undergo quality reviews every one to three years.

SOX also increases the penalties for white-collar crimes such as corporate fraud. These penalties include both monetary fines and substantial imprisonment. For example, knowingly destroying or creating documents to "impede, obstruct, or influence" any federal investigation can result in up to 20 years of imprisonment.[6] Since its enactment in 2002, SOX has significantly affected the internal operations of publicly traded corporations and their auditors. SOX will continue to play a major role in corporate management and the audit profession.

> ## Why is this important?
>
> "SOX puts more pressure on companies, their managers, and their auditors to ensure that investors get financial information that fairly reflects the company's operations."

International Financial Reporting Standards (IFRS)

As a result of globalization, the need for consistent reporting standards for all companies in the world has grown. As a result, the SEC is currently considering whether to require all publicly traded companies to adopt **International Financial Reporting Standards (IFRS)** within the next few years. In many instances, IFRS vary from GAAP. While the transition to IFRS may be time consuming and expensive, in the long run it should

---

[6]Go to www.AICPA.org to learn more about SOX.

actually save companies money and make the markets more efficient. Currently, a company operating in several different countries often must prepare several sets of financial statements using different accounting standards. As a result of IFRS, these companies will only need to prepare one set of financial statements that will be acceptable to all countries that have adopted IFRS. You can keep abreast of current IFRS developments and implications for accounting information at www.IFRS.com or www.IASB.org.

Extensible Business Reporting Language (XBRL)

Wouldn't it be nice if managers, analysts, investors, and regulators could easily access public company information over the Internet without having to *manually* read pdf documents and extract the data they need for decision making? The **Extensible Business Reporting Language (XBRL)** enables companies to release financial and business information in a format that can be quickly, efficiently, and cost-effectively accessed, sorted, and analyzed over the Internet. XBRL uses a standardized coding system to "tag" each piece of reported financial and business data so that it can be read by computer programs, rather than human eyes.

For example, *Sales Revenue* would be tagged with the same code by all companies so that a computer program could extract *Sales Revenue* information from an individual company or a selected group of companies. This standardized tagging system allows computers, rather than humans, to sift through financial reports and extract only the information that is needed. XBRL has several advantages:

- It decreases the need for laborious, manual searches though corporate reports for specific pieces of information.

- It decreases the time companies will spend converting their financial information into various government-prescribed formats.

- It will allow managers to easily compare their results to other companies and to industry averages.

- Investors and managers can "slice and dice" financial information however they want, to suit their decision making needs.

- It should promote the more consistent use of financial terminology since all data must be tagged using a preset, yet extensible, classification system.

Because of these benefits, the SEC is requiring that all publicly traded companies begin using XBRL for filing their financial reports. This mandatory requirement is being phased in over the next few years, with the 500 largest U.S. companies being required to use XBRL in 2009. The U.S. joins Australia, Canada, China, Japan, the United Kingdom, and other countries in mandating the use of XBRL for publicly-traded companies. You can keep abreast of XBRL developments at www.XBRL.org and www.sec.gov.

Shifting Economy

In the last century, North American economies have shifted away from manufacturing toward service. Service companies provide health care, communication, transportation, banking, and other important benefits to society. Service companies now make up the largest sector of the U.S. economy. The U.S. Census Bureau expects services, especially technology and health-care services, to be among the fastest-growing industries over the next decade. Even companies that traditionally carried out manufacturing, such as General Electric (GE), are shifting toward selling more services.

Managerial accounting has its roots in the industrial age of manufacturing. Most traditional managerial accounting practices were developed to fill the needs of manufacturing firms. However, since the U.S. economy has shifted away from manufacturing, managerial accounting has shifted, too. The field of managerial accounting has *expanded* to meet the needs of service and merchandising firms as well as manufacturers. For example, consider the following:

1. Manufacturers still need to know how much each unit of their product costs to manufacture. In addition to using this information for inventory valuation and pricing

decisions, manufacturers now use cost information to determine whether they should outsource production to another company or to an overseas location.

2. Service companies also need cost information to make decisions. They need to know the cost of providing a service rather than manufacturing a product. For example, banks must include the cost of servicing checking and savings accounts in the fees they charge customers. And hospitals need to know the cost of performing appendectomies to justify reimbursement from insurance companies and from Medicare.

3. Retailers need to consider importing costs when determining the cost of their merchandise. Because many goods are now produced overseas rather than domestically, determining the cost of a product is often more difficult than it was in the past. Management accountants need to consider foreign currency translation, shipping costs, and import tariffs when determining the cost of imported products.

Management accounting has expanded to meet decision-making needs for all types of businesses, including those that wish to compete globally.

How do Companies Compete in Today's Global Marketplace?

The barriers to international trade have fallen over the past decades, allowing foreign companies to compete with domestic firms. Firms that are not highly efficient, innovative, and responsive to business trends will vanish from the global market. However, global markets also provide highly competitive domestic companies with great opportunities for growth.

Globalization has several implications for managerial accounting:

- Stiffer competition means managers need more accurate and timely information to make wise business decisions. Companies can no longer afford to make decisions by the "seat of their pants." Detailed, accurate, and real-time cost information has become a necessity for survival.

- Companies must decide whether to expand sales and/or production into foreign countries. To do so, managers need comprehensive estimates of the costs of running international operations and the benefits that can be reaped.

- Companies can learn new management techniques by observing their international competitors. For example, the management philosophy of lean production, first developed in Japan by Toyota, is now being used by many U.S. companies to cut costs, improve quality, and speed production.

In the following sections we'll briefly describe several tools that companies use to compete in the global marketplace. How do managers decide which of these initiatives to undertake? They use **cost benefit analysis**, which weighs the expected costs of taking an action against the expected benefits of the action.

Sustainability and Social Responsibility

In recent years there has been a growing movement toward sustainability and social responsibility by both consumers and the corporate world. **Sustainability** is the ability to meet the needs of the present without compromising the ability of future generations to meet their own needs.[7] To move towards environmental sustainability, companies are introducing "green initiative"—ways of doing business that do not have negative consequences on the earth's resources. They've also recognized the need to be socially responsible—carefully considering how their business affects employees, consumers, and local citizens. Many companies have introduced means of "giving back" to their local communities, by monetarily supporting local schools and charities. Businesses are now viewing sustainability and social responsibility as opportunities for innovation and business development. These initiatives not only "do the right thing," but they also can lead to economic profits by increasing demand for a company's products and services.

---

[7]1987 World Commission on Environment and Development, www.un.org/documents/ga/res/42/ares42-187.htm.

Tools for Time-Based Competition

The Internet, electronic commerce (e-commerce), and other new technologies speed the pace of business. Think about your last trip to the grocery store or Wal-Mart. Did you use the self-scanning checkout? Retailers install expensive self-scanning technology to cut labor costs and give shoppers an alternative to standing in longer checkout lines. Some studies have shown that, on average, the self-scanning checkout process is really not faster. However, shoppers *perceive* the checkout time to be faster because they are actively engaged rather than passively standing in line. Businesses are doing whatever they can to shorten the time customers have to wait for their orders. Why? Because *time* is the latest competitive weapon in business.

Advanced Information Systems

Many small businesses use QuickBooks or Peachtree software to track their costs and to develop the information that owners and managers need to run the business. But large companies are turning to **enterprise resource planning** (**ERP**) systems that can integrate all of a company's worldwide functions, departments, and data. ERP systems such as SAP, Oracle, and PeopleSoft gather company data into a centralized data warehouse. The system feeds the data into software for all of the company's business activities, from budgeting and purchasing to production and customer service.

Advantages of ERP systems include the following:

- Companies streamline their operations before mapping them into ERP software. Streamlining operations saves money.

- ERP helps companies respond quickly to changes. A change in sales instantly ripples through the ERP's purchases, production, shipping, and accounting systems.

- An ERP system can replace hundreds of separate software systems, such as different software in different regions, or different payroll, shipping, and production software.

ERP is expensive and requires a large commitment of time and people. Major installations cost Fujitsu and Allstate over $40 million, but the expected benefits from the system are greater.

E-commerce

To survive in a competitive, globally wired economy, companies use the Internet in everyday operations such as budgeting, planning, selling, and customer service. Just as you and I may use the Web to place orders for merchandise, companies use business-to-business e-commerce to complete transactions with each other. Electronic purchases between businesses are often untouched by human hands, generate little if any paper, and avoid the time and cost of processing paperwork.

STOP & THINK

Electronically billing (e-billing) customers has become popular. Analysts estimate the following:
1. Companies save $7 per invoice by billing customers electronically.
2. The average large company issues 800,000 invoices a year.
3. The average cost of installing an e-billing system is $500,000. Should companies that issue 800,000 invoices a year consider e-billing?

Answer: Yes, these companies should consider e-billing. Comparing expected benefits to costs reveals significant expected net benefits from e-billing:

Expected benefits:	
800,000 invoices × $7 savings per invoice	$5,600,000
Expected costs:	
Installation of e-billing system	(500,000)
Net expected benefits	$5,100,000

E-commerce is also an important means of **supply-chain management**, where companies exchange information with suppliers to reduce costs, improve quality, and speed delivery of goods and services from suppliers to the company itself. For example, companies that supply component parts to Dell use the Internet to access Dell's daily inventory levels and current demand for parts. Access to real-time information lets suppliers automate the size of the next day's shipment, which in turn helps Dell cut order-to-delivery times and control costs.

Lean production

Lean production is both a philosophy and a business strategy of manufacturing without waste. The more waste that is eliminated, the lower the company's costs will be. Why is this important? With lower costs, companies are better able to compete. One primary goal of a lean production system is to eliminate the waste of *time and money* that accompanies large inventories. Inventory takes time to store and unstore. The costs of holding inventory can add up to 25% or more of the inventory's value. Also, inventory that is held too long quickly becomes obsolete because of changing technology and consumer tastes.

Companies that advocate lean production usually adopt the **just-in-time (JIT)** inventory philosophy that was first pioneered by Toyota. By manufacturing product *just in time* to fill customer orders, and no sooner, companies are able to substantially reduce the quantity of raw materials and finished product kept on hand. This, in turn, reduces storage costs (warehousing and associated security, utilities, and shrinkage costs) and handling costs (labor costs associated with storing and unstoring inventory). Since companies are making inventory *just in time* to fill customer orders, they must be able to produce a quality product very quickly. Therefore, lean companies focus on reducing **throughput time**, the time between buying raw materials and selling finished products, while still maintaining high quality. In Chapter 4, we'll look at some of the unique features of a lean production system.

> ### Why is this important?
> "To survive in the global marketplace, businesses must quickly respond to customer demand, providing high-quality products and services at a reasonable price."

Total Quality Management

All companies, not just lean producers, must deliver high-quality goods and services to remain competitive. **Total quality management (TQM)** is one key to succeeding in the global economy. The goal of TQM is to delight customers by providing them with superior products and services. As part of TQM, each business function examines its own activities and works to improve performance by *continually* setting higher goals. In Chapter 4, we'll discuss how companies analyze the costs associated with their current level of quality as well as the costs of quality improvement initiatives.

ISO 9001:2008

Many firms want to demonstrate their commitment to continuous quality improvement. The International Organization for Standardization (ISO), made up of 157 member countries, has developed international quality management standards and guidelines. Firms may become **ISO 9001:2008** certified by complying with the quality management standards set forth by the ISO and undergoing extensive audits of their quality management processes. The prestigious certification gives firms a competitive advantage in the global marketplace. Many companies will purchase supplies only from firms bearing the ISO 9001 certification. To better understand the ISO's global impact, consider the following: by 2006, over 897,000 certificates had been issued to firms in 170 countries! The certification does not only apply to manufacturing firms. Service firms account for over 32% of all certificates issued. The American Institute of Certified Public Accountants was the first professional membership organization in the United States to earn the ISO 9001 certification.

Decision Guidelines

The Changing Regulatory and Business Environment

Successful companies have to respond to changes in the regulatory and business environment. Here are some of the decisions managers need to consider.

Decision	Guidelines
What companies need to comply with SOX?	Publicly traded companies must comply with SOX. Many of the law's specific requirements focus on implementing adequate internal controls and financial reporting procedures and maintaining independence from the company's auditors.
How will IFRS benefit international companies?	Companies that operate in more than one country will no longer be required to prepare multiple financial statements using different standards for each country in which they operate. Rather, they will prepare one set of financial statements in accordance with International Financial Reporting Standards (IFRS).
How will XBRL help managers?	XBRL will allow managers to more easily obtain and analyze publicly available financial data from their competitors, from companies they may wish to purchase, or from companies in which they may want to invest.
How do companies compete in a global economy?	They use advanced information systems, e-commerce, supply-chain management, lean production, and TQM to compete more effectively. They consider becoming ISO 9001:2008 certified.
How do companies decide whether to undertake new initiatives such as international expansion, ERP, lean production, and TQM?	They use cost-benefit analysis: comparing the estimated benefits of the initiative with the estimated costs. They undertake the project if benefits exceed costs.

Summary Problem 2

EZ-Rider Motorcycles is considering whether to expand into Germany. If gas prices increase, the company expects more interest in fuel-efficient transportation such as motorcycles. As a result, the company is considering setting up a motorcycle assembly plant on the outskirts of Berlin.

EZ-Rider Motorcycles estimates it will cost $850,000 to convert an existing building to motorcycle production. Workers will need training, at a total cost of $65,000. The additional costs to organize the business and to establish relationships is estimated to be $150,000.

The CEO believes the company can earn sales profits from this expansion (before considering the costs in the preceding paragraph) of $1,624,000.

Requirement

Use cost-benefit analysis to determine whether EZ-Rider should expand into Germany.

Solution

The following cost-benefit analysis indicates that the company should expand into Germany:

Expected Benefits:		
Expected profits from expansion sales..		$ 1,624,000
Expected Costs:		
Conversion of building to manufacturing plant..	$850,000	
Workforce training...	65,000	
Organizing business and establishing relationships.................................	150,000	
Total expected costs...		(1,065,000)
Net expected benefits		$ 559,000

Accounting Vocabulary

Audit Committee. (p. 7)   A subcommittee of the board of directors that is responsible for overseeing both the internal audit function and the annual financial statement audit by independent CPAs.

Board of Directors. (p. 7)   The body elected by shareholders to oversee the company.

Budget. (p. 4)   Quantitative expression of a plan that helps managers coordinate and implement the plan.

Certified Management Accountant (CMA). (p. 11)   A professional certification issued by the IMA to designate expertise in the areas of managerial accounting, economics, and business finance.

Chief Executive Officer (CEO). (p. 7)   The position hired by the board of directors to oversee the company on a daily basis.

Chief Financial Officer (CFO). (p. 7)   The position responsible for all of the company's financial concerns.

Chief Operating Officer (COO). (p. 7)   The position responsible for overseeing the company's operations.

Controller. (p. 7)   The position responsible for general financial accounting, managerial accounting, and tax reporting.

Controlling. (p. 4)   One of management's primary responsibilities; evaluating the results of business operations against the plan and making adjustments to keep the company pressing toward its goals.

Cost-Benefit Analysis. (p. 22)   Weighing costs against benefits to help make decisions.

Cross-Functional Teams. (p. 8)   Corporate teams whose members represent various functions of the organization, such as R&D, design, production, marketing, distribution, and customer service.

Decision Making. (p. 5)   One of management's primary responsibilities; identifying possible courses of action and choosing among them.

Directing. (p. 4)   One of management's primary responsibilities; running the company on a day-to-day basis.

Enterprise Resource Planning (ERP). (p. 20)   Software systems that can integrate all of a company's worldwide functions, departments, and data into a single system.

Extensible Business Reporting Language (XBRL). (p. 18)   A data tagging system that enables companies to release financial and business information in a format that can be quickly, efficiently, and cost-effectively accessed, sorted, and analyzed over the Internet.

International Financial Reporting Standards (IFRS). (p. 17)   The SEC has recently moved to adopt IFRS for all publicly traded companies within the next few years. In many instances, IFRS vary from GAAP.

Institute of Management Accountants (IMA). (p. 10)   The professional organization that promotes the advancement of the management accounting profession.

Internal Audit Function. (p. 7)   The corporate function charged with assessing the effectiveness of the company's internal controls and risk management policies.

ISO 9001:2008. (p. 21)   A quality-related certification issued by the International Organization for Standardization (ISO). Firms may become ISO 9001:2008 certified by complying with the quality management standards set forth by the ISO and undergoing extensive audits of their quality management processes.

Just-in-time (JIT). (p. 21)   An inventory philosophy first pioneered by Toyota in which a product is manufactured *just in time* to fill customer orders. Companies adopting JIT are able to substantially reduce the quantity of raw materials and finished product kept on hand.

Lean Production. (p. 21)   A philosophy and business strategy of manufacturing without waste.

Planning. (p. 4)   One of management's primary responsibilities; setting goals and objectives for the company and deciding how to achieve them.

Sarbanes-Oxley Act of 2002 (SOX). (p. 16)   A congressional act that enhances internal control and financial reporting requirements and establishes new regulatory requirements for publicly traded companies and their independent auditors.

Supply-Chain Management. (p. 21)   Exchange of information with suppliers to reduce costs, improve quality, and speed delivery of goods and services from suppliers to the company itself and on to customers.

Sustainability. (p. 19)   The ability to meet the needs of the present without compromising the ability of future generations to meet their own needs.

Throughput Time. (p. 21)   The time between buying raw materials and selling finished products.

Treasurer. (p. 7)   The position responsible for raising the firm's capital and investing funds.

Total Quality Management (TQM). (p. 21)   A management philosophy of delighting customers with superior products and services by continually setting higher goals and improving the performance of every business function.

Quick Check

1. *(Learning Objective 1)* Which of the following is *not* one of the four primary responsibilities of management?
   a. Controlling
   b. Costing
   c. Directing
   d. Planning

2. *(Learning Objective 2)* Which of the following about managerial accounting is *true*?
   a. GAAP requires managerial accounting.
   b. Internal decision makers use managerial accounting.
   c. CPAs audit managerial accounting reports.
   d. Managerial accounting reports are usually prepared on an annual basis.

3. *(Learning Objective 2)* Which of the following is *not* a characteristic of managerial accounting information?

   a. Emphasizes relevance
   b. Focuses on the future more than the past
   c. Provides detailed information about parts of the company, not just the company as a whole
   d. Emphasizes reliability

4. *(Learning Objective 3)* What company position is in charge of raising the firm's capital?

   a. Director of internal audit
   b. Controller
   c. COO
   d. Treasurer

5. *(Learning Objective 3)* Which of the following statements is *true*?

   a. The COO reports to the CFO.
   b. The treasurer reports to the CEO.
   c. The Internal Audit Department reports to the audit committee.
   d. The controller reports to the internal auditor.

6. *(Learning Objective 3)* To get a job as a management accountant in most companies, you must

   a. join the IMA.
   b. be certified as a CMA.
   c. be certified as a CPA.
   d. None of the above

7. *(Learning Objective 3)* In addition to accounting knowledge, management accountants must possess all of the following skills *except*

   a. written communication skills.
   b. knowledge of how a business functions.
   c. computer programming skills.
   d. analytical skills.

8. *(Learning Objective 4)* A management accountant who refuses an expensive gift from a software salesperson meets the ethical standard of

   a. credibility.
   b. confidentiality.
   c. integrity.
   d. competence.

9. *(Learning Objective 5)* Which of the following is *not* one of the provisions of the Sarbanes-Oxley Act of 2002?

   a. The company's auditors assume responsibility for the financial statements.
   b. The penalties (i.e., prison time and fines) for corporate fraud were increased.
   c. At least one audit committee member should be a financial expert.
   d. The CEO and CFO must certify that the financial statements fairly present the company's operations and financial condition.

10. *(Learning Objective 5)* All of the following tools help companies compete in today's market *except*

   a. JIT.
   b. KJD.
   c. ERP.
   d. TQM.

ASSESS YOUR PROGRESS

Learning Objectives

 1 Identify managers' four primary responsibilities

 2 Distinguish financial accounting from managerial accounting

3 Describe organizational structure and the roles and skills required of management accountants within the organization

 4 Describe the role of the Institute of Management Accountants (IMA) and use its ethical standards to make reasonable ethical judgments

 5 Discuss and analyze the implications of regulatory and business trends

Short Exercises

S1-1 Roles of managers *(Learning Objective 1)*

Describe the four primary roles of managers and the way they relate to one another.

S1-2 Contrast managerial and financial accounting *(Learning Objective 2)*

Managerial accounting differs from financial accounting in several areas. Specify whether each of the following characteristics relates to managerial accounting or financial accounting.

   a. Reports tend to be prepared for the parts of the organization rather than the whole organization
   b. Primary users are internal (for example, company managers)

   c. Governed by Generally Accepted Accounting Principles (GAAP)
   d. Main characteristic of data is that it must be reliable and objective
   e. Reports are prepared as needed
   f. Not governed by legal requirements
   g. Primary users are external (i.e., creditors, investors)
   h. Focused on the future
   i. Reporting is based mainly on the company as a whole
   j. Reports are prepared usually quarterly and annually
   k. Information is verified by external auditors
   l. Focused on the past
   m. Main characteristic of data is that it must be relevant

S1-3 Accounting roles in the organization *(Learning Objective 3)*

The following is a list of job duties or descriptions. For each item, specify whether it would be most likely to describe the duties or responsibilities of someone working for the treasurer, the controller, or in the Internal Auditing Department.
   a. Performing cash counts at branch offices
   b. Preparing journal entries for month-end closing
   c. Issuing company stock
   d. Ensuring that the company's internal controls are functioning properly
   e. Creating an analysis about whether to lease or buy a delivery truck
   f. Calculate the cost of a product
   g. Issuing company bonds
   h. Check to make sure that company risk management procedures are being followed
   i. Work with various departments in preparing operating budgets for the upcoming year
   j. Oversee accounts payable activities
   k. Invests company funds
   l. Report to the audit committee of the board of directors *and* to a senior executive, such as the CFO or CEO
   m. Prepares company tax returns

S1-4 Role of internal audit function *(Learning Objective 3)*

The following table lists several characteristics. Place a check mark next to those items which pertain directly to the internal audit function and its role within the organization.

Characteristic	Check (✓) if related to internal auditing
a. Helps to ensure that company's internal controls are functioning properly	
b. Reports to treasurer or controller	
c. Required by the New York Stock Exchange if company stock is publicly traded on the NYSE	
d. Reports directly to the audit committee	
e. Ensures that the company achieves its profit goals	
f. Is part of the accounting department	
g. Usually reports to a senior executive (CFO or CEO) for administrative matters	
h. Performs the same function as independent certified public accountants	
i. External audits can be performed by the internal auditing department	

S1-5 Importance of ethical standards *(Learning Objective 4)*

Explain why each of the four broad ethical standards in the IMA's *Statement of Ethical Professional Practice* is necessary.

S1-6 Violations of ethical standards *(Learning Objective 4)*

The IMA's *Statement of Ethical Professional Practice* (Exhibit 1-6) requires management accountants to meet standards regarding the following:

- Competence
- Confidentiality
- Integrity
- Credibility

Consider the following situations. Which guidelines are violated in each situation?

a. You tell your brother that your company will report earnings significantly above financial analysts' estimates.

b. You see that other employees take home office supplies for personal use. As an intern, you do the same thing, assuming that this is a "perk."

c. At a conference on e-commerce, you skip the afternoon session and go sightseeing.

d. You failed to read the detailed specifications of a new general ledger package that you asked your company to purchase. After it is installed, you are surprised that it is incompatible with some of your company's older accounting software.

e. You do not provide top management with the detailed job descriptions they requested because you fear they may use this information to cut a position from your department.

S1-7 Identify current competitive tools *(Learning Objective 5)*

Companies are facing a great amount of change in every facet of their operations today. To remain competitive, companies must keep abreast of current developments in several areas. You recently got together with a group of friends who work for different companies. Your friends share information about their current challenges in adopting new tools or complying with new regulations. Excerpts from the conversation are presented in the following section. Tell whether each excerpt describes XBRL, ISO 9001:2008, e-commerce, the Sarbanes-Oxley Act (SOX), or enterprise resource planning (ERP) systems.

a. Suzanne: My company is working to demonstrate its commitment to continuous quality improvement. We are currently undergoing an extensive audit of our quality management processes. We hope to gain a competitive advantage through this process.

b. Ying: We have just installed a system at our company that integrates all of our company's data across all systems. We have one central data warehouse that contains information about our suppliers, our customers, our employees, and our financial information. The software retrieves information from this single data warehouse and all systems are integrated. The process of implementing this system has been very expensive and time-consuming, but we are reaping the benefits of being more streamlined, of being able to respond more quickly to changes in the market, and of not having several different software systems operating independently.

c. Steve: I just started a new job in the Auditing Department. My new duties include assisting in the development of testing procedures and methods for determining internal controls effectiveness. I also oversee the testing for assurance of compliance with corporate policies. I am coordinating the review of SEC filings with our external auditors. I also am responsible for preparing periodic compliance status reports for management, the audit committee, and the external auditors.

d. Keisha: We have been working on a system to tag all of the financial information in our quarterly and annual reports so that our financial information can be shared easily. We will be able to attach a tag to each piece of financial information. For example, we can tag our "net profits" wherever it appears in the financial reports. Any user accessing the financial reports would then be able to download the numbers for "net profits." Our stockholders and the analysts will be able to retrieve the information they need quickly, efficiently, and cost-effectively.

e. Roland: My company has been shifting much of our purchasing system to the Internet. We are now able to complete many of our business-to-business transactions via the Web, which generates little to no paperwork, lessens the chance of error, and decreases the costs of each transaction.

Exercises–Group A

E1-8A Managers' responsibilities *(Learning Objective 1)*

Categorize each of the following activities as to which management responsibility it fulfills: planning, directing, controlling, or decision making. Some activities may fulfill more than one responsibility.

a. Management conducts variance analysis by comparing budget to actual.

b. Management reviews hourly sales reports to determine the level of staffing needed to service customers.

c. Management decides to increase sales growth by 10% next year.

d. Management uses information on product costs to determine sales prices.

e. To lower product costs, management moves production to Mexico.

E1-9A Define key terms *(Learning Objectives 1 & 2)*

Complete the following statements with one of the terms listed here. You may use a term more than once, and some terms may not be used at all.

Budget	Creditors	Managerial accounting	Planning
Controlling	Financial accounting	Managers	Shareholders

a. Companies must follow GAAP in their _____ systems.

b. Financial accounting develops reports for external parties such as _____ and _____.

c. When managers evaluate the company's performance compared to the plan, they are performing the _____ role of management.

d. _____ are decision makers inside a company.

e. _____ provides information on a company's past performance to external parties.

f. _____ systems are not restricted by GAAP but are chosen by comparing the costs versus the benefits of the system.

g. Choosing goals and the means to achieve them is the _____ function of management.

h. _____ systems report on various segments or business units of the company.

i. _____ statements of public companies are audited annually by CPAs.

E1-10A Identify users of accounting information *(Learning Objective 3)*

For each of the following users of financial accounting information and managerial accounting information, specify whether the user would primarily use financial accounting information or managerial accounting information or both.

1. Potential shareholders

2. Loan officer at the company's bank

3. Manager of the Sales Department

4. Bookkeeping Department

5. Managers at regional offices

6. IRS agent

7. Current shareholders

8. Wall Street analyst

9. News reporter

10. Company controller

11. Board of directors

12. SEC employee

13. External auditor (public accounting firm)

14. Internal auditor

E1-11A Classify roles within the organization *(Learning Objective 3)*

Complete the following statements with one of the terms listed here. You may use a term more than once, and some terms may not be used at all.

Audit committee	Board of directors	CEO	CFO
Treasurer	Controller	Cross-functional teams	COO

a. The _____ and the _____ report to the CEO.
b. The internal audit function reports to the CFO or _____ and the _____.
c. The _____ is directly responsible for financial accounting, managerial accounting, and tax reporting.
d. The CEO is hired by the _____.
e. The _____ is directly responsible for raising capital and investing funds.
f. The _____ is directly responsible for the company's operations.
g. Management accountants often work with _____.
h. A subcommittee of the board of directors is called the _____.

E1-12A Professional organization and certification *(Learning Objective 4)*

Complete the following sentences:
a. The _____ is the professional association for management accountants.
b. The Institute offers a professional certification called the _____, which focuses on managerial accounting topics, economics, and business finance.
c. The Institute finds that people holding the _____ certification earn, on average, _____% more than those without the certification.
d. The Institute's monthly publication, called _____, addresses current topics of interest to management accountants.
e. The Institute says that approximately _____% of accountants work in organizations rather than at CPA firms.

E1-13A Ethical dilemma *(Learning Objective 4)*

Mary Gonzales is the controller at Automax, a car dealership. She recently hired Cory Loftus as a bookkeeper. Loftus wanted to attend a class on Excel spreadsheets, so Gonzales temporarily took over Loftus's duties, including overseeing a fund for topping off a car's gas tank before a test drive. Gonzales found a shortage in this fund and confronted Loftus when he returned to work. Loftus admitted that he occasionally uses this fund to pay for his own gas. Gonzales estimated that the amount involved is close to $300.

Requirements

1. What should Gonzales do?

2. Would you change your answer to the previous question if Gonzales was the one recently hired as controller and Loftus was a well-liked, longtime employee who indicated that he always eventually repaid the fund?

E1-14A Classify ethical responsibilities *(Learning Objective 4)*

According to the IMA's *Statement of Ethical Professional Practice* (Exhibit 1-6), management accountants should follow four standards: competence, confidentiality, integrity, and credibility. Each of these standards contains specific responsibilities. Classify each of the following responsibilities according to the standard it addresses.
Responsibility:

1. Refrain from using confidential information for unethical or illegal advantage.

2. Maintain an appropriate level of professional expertise by continually developing knowledge and skills.

3. Communicate information fairly and objectively.

4. Recognize and communicate professional limitations that would preclude responsible judgment or successful performance of an activity.

5. Mitigate actual conflicts of interest. Regularly communicate with business associates to avoid apparent conflicts of interest. Advise all parties of any potential conflicts.

6. Provide decision support information and recommendations that are accurate, clear, concise, and timely.

7. Abstain from engaging in or supporting any activity that might discredit the profession.

8. Disclose all relevant information that could reasonably be expected to influence an intended user's understanding of the reports, analyses, or recommendations.

9. Inform all relevant parties regarding the appropriate use of confidential information. Monitor subordinates' activities to ensure compliance.

10. Perform professional duties in accordance with relevant laws, regulations, and technical standards.

11. Refrain from engaging in any conduct that would prejudice carrying out duties ethically.

12. Keep information confidential except when disclosure is authorized or legally required.

13. Disclose delays or deficiencies in information, timeliness, processing, or internal controls in conformance with organization policy and/or applicable law.

E1-15A Define key terms (Learning Objective 5)

Complete the following statements with one of the terms listed here. You may use a term more than once, and some terms may not be used at all.

E-commerce	Shift to service economy	XBRL
Sarbanes-Oxley Act of 2002	Just in time	Future
Present	Throughput time	ISO 9001: 2008
IFRS	Lean production	Supply-chain management
Total quality management	ERP	Cross-functional teams

a. _____ is a language that utilizes a standardized coding system companies use to tag each piece of financial and business information in a format that can be quickly and efficiently accessed over the Internet.

b. _____ involves the exchange of information with suppliers to reduce costs, improve quality, and speed delivery of goods and services from suppliers to the company and its customers.

c. The _____ was enacted to restore trust in publicly traded corporations, their management, their financial statements, and their auditors.

d. The goal of _____ is to meet customers' expectations by providing them with superior products and services by eliminating defects and waste throughout the value chain.

e. Most of the costs of adopting ERP, expanding into a foreign market, or improving quality are incurred in the _____; but most of the benefits occur in the _____.

f. _____ is the time between buying raw materials and selling the finished products.

g. _____ serves the information needs of people in accounting as well as people in marketing and in the warehouse.

h. Firms adopt _____ to conduct business on the Internet.

i. Firms acquire the _____ certification to demonstrate their commitment to quality.

j. _____ is a philosophy that embraces the concept that the lower the company's waste, the lower the company's costs.

k. _____ is a data tagging system that enables companies to release financial and business information in a format that can be quickly, efficiently, and cost-effectively accessed, sorted, and analyzed over the Internet.

l. The SEC is expected to require the adoption of _____ for all publicly traded companies within the next few years, which differs from the GAAP that companies are currently required to use.

m. Toyota first pioneered an inventory philosophy in which a product is manufactured _____ to fill customer orders; companies are able to substantially reduce the quantity of raw materials and finished goods inventories.

n. _____ is a management philosophy of delighting customers with superior products and services by continually setting higher goals and improving the performance of every business function.

E1-16A Summarize the Sarbanes-Oxley Act *(Learning Objective 5)*

You just obtained an entry-level job as a management accountant. Other newly hired accountants have heard of the Sarbanes-Oxley Act of 2002 (SOX), but don't know much about it (they attended a different university). Write a short memo to your colleagues discussing the reason for SOX, the goal of SOX, and some of the specific requirements of SOX that will affect your company.

E1-17A Lean production cost-benefit analysis *(Learning Objective 5)*

Wild Rides manufactures snowboards. Shawn Mobbs, the CEO, is trying to decide whether to adopt a lean production model. He expects that adopting lean production would save $97,000 in warehousing expenses and $46,000 in spoilage costs. Adopting lean production will require several one-time up-front expenditures: (1) $13,500 for an employee training program, (2) $37,000 to streamline the plant's production process, and (3) $8,000 to identify suppliers that will guarantee zero defects and on-time delivery.

Requirements

1. What are the total costs of adopting lean production?

2. What are the total benefits of adopting lean production?

3. Should Wild Rides adopt lean production? Why or why not?

Exercises—Group B

E1-18B Managers' responsibilities *(Learning Objective 1)*

Categorize each of the following activities as to which management responsibility it fulfills: planning, directing, controlling, or decision making. Some activities may fulfill more than one responsibility.

a. The store manager posts the employee time schedule for the next week so that employees know when they are working.

b. The manager of the Service Department investigates why the actual hours spent on a recent repair job exceeded the standard for that type of repair by more than 20%.

c. Management creates a sales budget for the upcoming quarter.

d. Top management selects a location for a new store.

e. Management is designing a new sales incentive program for the upcoming year.

E1-19B Define key terms *(Learning Objectives 1 & 2)*

Complete the following statements with one of the terms listed here. You may use a term more than once, and some terms may not be used at all.

Budget	Creditors	Managerial accounting	Planning
Controlling	Financial accounting	Managers	Shareholders

a. _____ systems are chosen by comparing the costs versus the benefits of the system and are not restricted by GAAP.

b. CPAs audit the _____ statements of public companies.

c. Financial accounting develops reports for external parties such as _____ and _____.

d. Companies must follow GAAP in their _____ systems.

e. Decision makers inside a company are the _____.

f. Choosing goals and the means to achieve them is the _____ function of management.

g. _____ systems report on various segments or business units of the company.

h. When managers evaluate the company's performance compared to the plan, they are performing the _____ role of management.

i. Information on a company's past performance is provided to external parties by _____.

E1-20B   Identify users of accounting information *(Learning Objective 3)*

For each of the following users of financial accounting information and managerial accounting information, specify whether the user would primarily use financial accounting information or managerial accounting information or both.

1. Reporter from the *Wall Street Journal*

2. Regional division managers

3. SEC examiner

4. Bookkeeping Department

5. Division controller

6. External auditor (public accounting firm)

7. Loan officer at the company's bank

8. State tax agency auditor

9. Board of directors

10. Manager of the Service Department

11. Wall Street analyst

12. Internal auditor

13. Potential investors

14. Current stockholders

E1-21B   Classify roles within the organization *(Learning Objective 3)*

Complete the following statements with one of the terms listed here. You may use a term more than once, and some terms may not be used at all.

Audit committee	Board of directors	CEO	CFO
Treasurer	Controller	Cross-functional teams	COO

a. Management accountants often work with _____.

b. The _____ and the _____ report to the CEO.

c. A subcommittee of the board of directors is called the _____.

d. Raising capital and investing funds are the direct responsibilities of the _____.

e. Financial accounting, managerial accounting, and tax reporting are the direct responsibilities of the _____.

f. The internal audit function reports to the CFO or _____ and the _____.

g. The CEO is hired by the _____.

h. The company's operations are the direct responsibility of the _____.

E1-22B   Professional organization and certification *(Learning Objective 4)*

Complete the following sentences:

a. The _____ is the professional association for management accountants.

b. The Institute says that approximately _____ % of accountants work in organizations rather than at CPA firms.

   c. The Institute's monthly publication, called _____, addresses current topics of interest to management accountants.

   d. The Institute offers a professional certification called the _____, which focuses on managerial accounting topics, economics, and business finance.

   e. The Institute finds that people holding the _____ certification earn, on average, _____% more than those without the certification.

E1-23B Ethical dilemma *(Learning Objective 4)*

Richard Welsh is the controller at Sangood Kitchens, a large food and kitchen store. He recently hired Helen Smith as a bookkeeper. Smith wanted to attend a class on information systems, so Welsh temporarily took over Smith's duties, including overseeing a fund for giving in-store cooking and product demonstrations. Welsh discovered a shortage in this fund and confronted Smith on it. Smith admitted that she occasionally uses the fund to pay for her own store purchases. Welsh estimated that the amount involved is close to $500.

Requirements

1. What should Welsh do?

2. Would you change your answer to the previous question if Welsh was the one recently hired as controller and Smith was a well-liked, longtime employee who indicated that she always eventually repaid the fund?

E1-24B Classify ethical responsibilities *(Learning Objective 4)*

According to the IMA's *Statement of Ethical Professional Practice* (Exhibit 1-6), management accountants should follow four standards: competence, confidentiality, integrity, and credibility. Each of these standards contains specific responsibilities. Classify each of the following responsibilities according to the standard it addresses.
Responsibility:

1. Keep information confidential except when disclosure is authorized or legally required.

2. Communicate information fairly and objectively.

3. Refrain from using confidential information for unethical or illegal advantage.

4. Inform all relevant parties regarding the appropriate use of confidential information. Monitor subordinates' activities to ensure compliance.

5. Mitigate actual conflicts of interest. Regularly communicate with business associates to avoid apparent conflicts of interest. Advise all parties of any potential conflicts.

6. Maintain an appropriate level of professional expertise by continually developing knowledge and skills.

7. Recognize and communicate professional limitations that would preclude responsible judgment or successful performance of an activity.

8. Disclose all relevant information that could reasonably be expected to influence an intended user's understanding of the reports, analyses, or recommendations.

9. Disclose delays or deficiencies in information, timeliness, processing, or internal controls in conformance with organization policy and/or applicable law.

10. Perform professional duties in accordance with relevant laws, regulations, and technical standards.

11. Abstain from engaging in or supporting any activity that might discredit the profession.

12. Refrain from engaging in any conduct that would prejudice carrying out duties ethically.

13. Provide decision support information and recommendations that are accurate, clear, concise, and timely.

E-commerce	Shift to service economy	XBRL
IFRS	ERP	Future
Present	Just in time	ISO 9001: 2008
Cross-functional teams	Lean production	Supply-chain management
Sarbanes-Oxley Act of 2002	Total quality management	Throughput time

E1-25B Define key terms (*Learning Objective 5*)

Complete the following statements with one of the terms listed here. You may use a term more than once, and some terms may not be used at all.

a. _____ is a language that utilizes a standardized coding system companies use to tag each piece of financial and business information in a format that can be quickly and efficiently accessed over the Internet.

b. _____ involves the exchange of information with suppliers to reduce costs, improve quality, and speed delivery of goods and services from suppliers to the company and its customers.

c. Toyota first pioneered an inventory philosophy in which a product is manufactured _____ to fill customer orders; companies are able to substantially reduce the quantity of raw materials and finished goods inventories.

d. The _____ was enacted to restore trust in publicly traded corporations, their management, their financial statements, and their auditors.

e. _____ is a management philosophy of delighting customers with superior products and services by continually setting higher goals and improving the performance of every business function.

f. The goal of _____ is to meet customers' expectations by providing them with superior products and services by eliminating defects and waste throughout the value chain.

g. Most of the costs of adopting ERP, expanding into a foreign market, or improving quality are incurred in the _____; but most of the benefits occur in the _____.

h. _____ is the time between buying raw materials and selling the finished products.

i. _____ serves the information needs of people in accounting as well as people in marketing and in the warehouse.

j. Firms adopt _____ to conduct business on the Internet.

k. Firms acquire the _____ certification to demonstrate their commitment to quality.

l. _____ is a philosophy that embraces the concept that the lower the company's waste, the lower the company's costs.

m. _____ is a data tagging system that enables companies to release financial and business information in a format that can be quickly, efficiently, and cost-effectively accessed, sorted, and analyzed over the Internet.

n. The SEC is expected to require the adoption of _____ for all publicly traded companies within the next few years, which differs from the GAAP that companies are currently required to use.

E1-26B Summarize the Sarbanes-Oxley Act (*Learning Objective 5*)

At a family gathering, your grandmother comes to you and asks you, since you have taken many business classes, to explain the Sarbanes-Oxley Act of 2002 (SOX). She has heard about SOX on television and the Internet but does not really understand it. Explain to your grandmother the reason for SOX, the goal of SOX, and some of the specific requirements of SOX.

E1-27B Lean production cost-benefit analysis *(Learning Objective 5)*

Snow Wonderful manufactures snowboards. John Gallagher, the CEO, is trying to decide whether to adopt a lean production model. He expects that adopting lean production would save $95,000 in warehousing expenses and $48,500 in spoilage costs. Adopting lean production will require several one-time up-front expenditures: (1) $12,500 for an employee training program, (2) $36,000 to streamline the plant's production process, and (3) $8,750 to identify suppliers that will guarantee zero defects and on-time delivery.

Requirements

1. What are the total costs of adopting lean production?

2. What are the total benefits of adopting lean production?

3. Should Snow Wonderful adopt lean production? Why or why not?

Problems—Group A

P1-28A Management processes and accounting information *(Learning Objectives 1 & 2)*

Allison Hopkins has her own chain of music stores, Hopkins' Music. Her stores sell musical instruments, sheet music, and other related items. Music lessons and instrument repair are also offered through the stores. Hopkins' Music also has a Web site that sells music merchandise. Hopkins' Music has a staff of 80 people working in six departments: Sales, Repairs, Lessons, Web Development, Accounting, and Human Resources. Each department has its own manager.

Requirements

1. For each of the six departments, describe at least one decision/action for each of the four stages of management (planning, directing, controlling, and decision-making). Prepare a table similar to the following for your answer:

	Planning	Directing	Controlling	Decision Making
Sales				
Repairs				
Lessons				
Web Development				
Accounting				
Human Resources				

2. For each of the decisions/actions you described in Part 1, identify what information is needed for that decision/action. Specify whether that information would be generated by the financial accounting system or the managerial accounting system at Hopkins' Music.

P1-29A Ethical dilemmas *(Learning Objective 4)*

Kate Royer is the new controller for EDU Software, which develops and sells educational software. Shortly before the December 31 fiscal year-end, Matt Adams, the company president, asks Royer how things look for the year-end numbers. He is not happy to learn that earnings growth may be below 15% for the first time in the company's five-year history. Adams explains that financial analysts have again predicted a 15% earnings growth for the company and that he does not intend to disappoint them. He suggests that Royer talk to the assistant controller, who can explain how the previous controller dealt with this situation. The assistant controller suggests the following strategies:

a. Persuade suppliers to postpone billing until January 1.

b. Record as sales certain software awaiting sale that is held in a public warehouse.

c. Delay the year-end closing a few days into January of the next year so that some of next year's sales are included as this year's sales.

   d. Reduce the allowance for bad debts (and bad debts expense).

   e. Postpone routine monthly maintenance expenditures from December to January.

Requirement

1. Which of these suggested strategies are inconsistent with IMA standards? What should Royer do if Adams insists that she follow all of these suggestions?

P1-30A ERP cost-benefit analysis *(Learning Objective 5)*

As CEO of SeaSpray Marine, Ron Greenwood knows it is important to control costs and to respond quickly to changes in the highly competitive boat-building industry. When IDG Consulting proposes that SeaSpray Marine invest in an ERP system, he forms a team to evaluate the proposal: the plant engineer, the plant foreman, the systems specialist, the human resources director, the marketing director, and the management accountant.

A month later, management accountant Mike Cobalt reports that the team and IDG estimate that if SeaSpray Marine implements the ERP system, it will incur the following costs:

   a. $350,000 in software costs

   b. $80,000 to customize the ERP software and load SeaSpray's data into the new ERP system

   c. $125,000 for employee training

The team estimates that the ERP system should provide several benefits:

   a. More efficient order processing should lead to savings of $185,000.

   b. Streamlining the manufacturing process so that it maps into the ERP system will create savings of $275,000.

   c. Integrating purchasing, production, marketing, and distribution into a single system will allow SeaSpray Marine to reduce inventories, saving $220,000.

   d. Higher customer satisfaction should increase sales, which, in turn, should increase profits by $150,000.

Requirements

1. If the ERP installation succeeds, what is the dollar amount of the benefits?

2. Should SeaSpray Marine install the ERP system? Why or why not? Show your calculations.

3. Why did Greenwood create a team to evaluate IDG's proposal? Consider each piece of cost-benefit information that management accountant Cobalt reported. Which person on the team is most likely to have contributed each item? (*Hint:* Which team member is likely to have the most information about each cost or benefit?)

P1-31A E-commerce cost-benefit analysis *(Learning Objective 5)*

Sun Gas wants to move its sales order system to the Web. Under the proposed system, gas stations and other merchants will use a Web browser and, after typing in a password for the Sun Gas Web page, will be able to check the availability and current price of various products and place an order. Currently, customer service representatives take dealers' orders over the phone; they record the information on a paper form, then manually enter it into the firm's computer system.

CFO Carrie Smith believes that dealers will not adopt the new Web system unless Sun Gas provides financial assistance to help them purchase or upgrade their PCs. Smith estimates this one-time cost at $750,000. Sun Gas will also have to invest $150,000 in upgrading its own computer hardware. The cost of the software and the consulting fee for installing the system will be $230,000. The Web system will enable Sun Gas to eliminate 25 clerical positions. Smith estimates that the new system's lower labor costs will have saved the company $1,357,000.

Requirement

1. Use a cost-benefit analysis to recommend to Smith whether Sun Gas should proceed with the Web-based ordering system. Give your reasons, showing supporting calculations.

P1-32A Continuation of P1-31A: revised estimates *(Learning Objective 5)*

Consider the Sun Gas proposed entry into e-commerce in P1-31A. Smith revises her estimates of the benefits from the new system's lower labor costs. She now thinks the savings will be only $933,000.

Requirements

1. Compute the expected benefits of the Web-based ordering system.

2. Would you recommend that Sun Gas accept the proposal?

3. Before Smith makes a final decision, what other factors should she consider?

Problems—Group B

P1-33B Management processes and accounting information *(Learning Objectives 1 & 2)*

David Doors has his own electronics retail chain, Circuit Pro. His stores sell computer parts, audio-visual equipment, consumer electronics, and related items. Custom computer building and electronics repair are also offered. In addition, Circuit Pro has a Web site to sell its merchandise. Circuit Pro has a staff of 90 people working in six departments: Sales, Customization, Repairs, Web Development, Accounting, and Human Resources. Each department has its own manager.

Requirements

1. For each of the six departments, describe at least one decision/action for each of the four stages of management (planning, directing, controlling, and decision-making). Prepare a table similar to the following for your answer:

	Planning	Directing	Controlling	Decision Making
Sales				
Customization				
Repairs				
Web Development				
Accounting				
Human Resources				

2. For each of the decisions/actions you described in Part 1, identify what information is needed for that decision/action. Specify whether that information would be generated by the financial accounting system or the managerial accounting system at Circuit Pro.

P1-34B Ethical dilemmas *(Learning Objective 4)*

Kara Williams is the new controller for Colors, a designer and manufacturer of sportswear. Shortly before the December 31 fiscal year-end, Lashea Lucas (the company president) asks Williams how things look for the year-end numbers. Lucas is not happy to learn that earnings growth may be below 10% for the first time in the company's five-year history. Lucas explains that financial analysts have again predicted a 12% earnings growth for the company and that she does not intend to disappoint them. She suggests that Williams talk to the assistant controller, who can explain how the previous controller dealt with this situation. The assistant controller suggests the following strategies:

a. Postpone planned advertising expenditures from December to January.

b. Do not record sales returns and allowances on the basis that they are individually immaterial.

c. Persuade retail customers to accelerate January orders to December.

d. Reduce the allowance for bad debts (and bad debts expense).

e. Colors ships finished goods to public warehouses across the country for temporary storage until it receives firm orders from customers. As Colors receives orders, it directs the warehouse to ship the goods to nearby customers. The assistant controller suggests recording goods sent to the public warehouses as sales.

Requirement

1. Which of these suggested strategies are inconsistent with IMA standards? What should Williams do if Lucas insists that she follow all of these suggestions?

P1-35B ERP cost-benefit analysis *(Learning Objective 5)*

As CEO of AquaBoat Marine, Rick Wilson knows its important to control costs and to respond quickly to changes in the highly competitive boat-building industry. When IDG Consulting proposes that AquaBoat Marine invest in an ERP system, he forms a team to evaluate the proposal: the plant engineer, the plant foreman, the systems specialist, the human resources director, the marketing director, and the management accountant. A month later, management accountant Matt Cook reports that the team and IDG estimate that if AquaBoat Marine implements the ERP system, it will incur the following costs:

a. $360,000 in software costs
b. $95,000 to customize the ERP software and load SeaSpray's data into the new ERP system
c. $115,000 for employee training

The team estimates that the ERP system should provide several benefits:

a. More efficient order processing should lead to savings of $185,000.
b. Streamlining the manufacturing process so that it maps into the ERP system will create savings of $270,000.
c. Integrating purchasing, production, marketing, and distribution into a single system will allow AquaBoat Marine to reduce inventories, saving $230,000.
d. Higher customer satisfaction should increase sales, which, in turn, should increase the present value of profits by $155,000.

Requirements

1. If the ERP installation succeeds, what is the dollar amount of the benefits?

2. Should AquaBoat Marine install the ERP system? Why or why not? Show your calculations.

3. Why did Greenwood create a team to evaluate IDG's proposal? Consider each piece of cost-benefit information that management accountant Cook reported. Which person on the team is most likely to have contributed each item? (*Hint:* Which team member is likely to have the most information about each cost or benefit?)

P1-36B E-commerce cost-benefit analysis *(Learning Objective 5)*

Mid-West Gas wants to move its sales order system to the Web. Under the proposed system, gas stations and other merchants will use a Web browser and, after typing in a password for the Mid-West Gas Web page, will be able to check the availability and current price of various products and place an order. Currently, customer service representatives take dealers' orders over the phone; they record the information on a paper form, then manually enter it into the firm's computer system.

CFO Carrie Smith believes that dealers will not adopt the new Web system unless Mid-West Gas provides financial assistance to help them purchase or upgrade their PCs. Smith estimates this one-time cost at $760,000. Mid-West Gas will also have to invest $155,000 in upgrading its own computer hardware. The cost of the software and the consulting fee for installing the system will be $225,000.

The Web system will enable Mid-West Gas to eliminate 25 clerical positions. Smith estimates that the benefits of the new system's lower labor costs will have a present value of $1,370,000.

Requirement

1. Use a cost-benefit analysis to recommend to Smith whether Mid-West Gas should proceed with the Web-based ordering system. Give your reasons, showing supporting calculations.

P1-37B Continuation of P1-36B: revised estimates *(Learning Objective 5)*

Smith revises her estimates of the benefits from the new system's lower labor costs. She now thinks the saving will be only $925,000.

Requirements

1. Compute the expected benefits of the Web-based ordering system.

2. Would you recommend that Mid-West Gas accept the proposal?

3. Before Smith makes a final decision, what other factors should she consider?

APPLY YOUR KNOWLEDGE

Decision Case

C1-38   Ethical standards *(Learning Objective 4)*

The IMA's *Statement of Ethical Professional Practice* (Exhibit 1-6) can be applied to more than just managerial accounting. It is also relevant to college students. Explain at least one situation that shows how each IMA standard is relevant to your experiences as a student. For example, the ethical standard of competence would suggest not cutting classes.

Ethical Issue

I1-39   Ethical dilemma *(Learning Objective 4)*

Ricardo Valencia recently resigned his position as controller for Tom White Automotive, a small, struggling foreign car dealer in Austin, Texas. Valencia has just started a new job as controller for Mueller Imports, a much larger dealer for the same car manufacturer. Demand for this particular make of car is exploding, and the manufacturer cannot produce enough cars to satisfy demand. Each manufacturer's regional sales managers is given a certain number of cars. Each regional sales manager then decides how to divide the cars among the independently owned dealerships in the region. Because most dealerships can sell every car they receive, the key is getting a large number of cars from the manufacturer's regional sales manager.

Valencia's former employer, Tom White Automotive, received only about 25 cars a month. Consequently, the dealership was not very profitable.

Valencia is surprised to learn that his new employer, Mueller Imports, receives over 200 cars a month. Valencia soon gets another surprise. Every couple of months, a local jeweler bills the dealer $5,000 for "miscellaneous services." Franz Mueller, the owner of the dealership, personally approves the payment of these invoices, noting that each invoice is a "selling expense." From casual conversations with a salesperson, Valencia learns that Mueller frequently gives Rolex watches to the manufacturer's regional sales manager and other sales executives. Before talking to anyone about this, Valencia decides to work through his ethical dilemma by answering the following questions:

1. What is the ethical issue?
2. What are my options?
3. What are the possible consequences?
4. What should I do?

Team Project

T1-40   Interviewing a local company about e-commerce *(Learning Objective 5)*

Search the Internet for a nearby company that also has a Web page. Arrange an interview with a management accountant, a controller, or another accounting/finance officer of the company. Before you conduct the interview, answer the following questions:

1. What is the company's primary product or service?
2. Is the primary purpose of the company's Web site to provide information about the company and its products, to sell online, or to provide financial information for investors?
3. Are parts of the company's Web site restricted so that you need password authorization to enter? What appears to be the purpose of limiting access?
4. Does the Web site provide an e-mail link for contacting the company?

   At the interview, begin by clarifying your answers to questions 1–4 and ask the following additional questions:

5. If the company sells over the Web, what benefits has the company derived? Did the company perform a cost-benefit analysis before deciding to begin Web sales?

Or

If the company does not sell over the Web, why not? Has the company performed a cost-benefit analysis and decided not to sell over the Web?

6. What is the biggest cost of operating the Web site?

7. Does the company make any purchases over the Internet? What percentage?

8. How has e-commerce affected the company's managerial accounting system? Have the management accountant's responsibilities become more or less complex? more or less interesting?

9. Does the company use Web-based accounting applications such as accounts receivable or accounts payable?

10. Does the company use an ERP system? If so, does it view the system as a success? What have been the benefits? the costs?

Prepare a report describing the results of your interview.

Quick Check Answers
1. *b* 2. *b* 3. *d* 4. *d* 5. *c* 6. *d* 7. *c* 8. *c* 9. *a* 10. *b*

For online homework, exercises, and problems that provide you with immediate feedback, please visit www.myaccountinglab.com.

Discussion & Analysis

1. What are the four main areas of management's responsibility? How are these four areas interrelated? How does managerial accounting support each of the responsibility areas of managers?

2. What is the Sarbanes-Oxley Act of 2002 (SOX)? How does SOX affect financial accounting? How does SOX impact managerial accounting? Is there any overlap between financial and managerial accounting in terms of the SOX impact? If so, what are the areas of overlap?

3. Why is managerial accounting more suitable for internal reporting than financial accounting?

4. A company currently has all of its managerial accountants reporting to the controller. What might be inefficient about this organizational structure? How might the company restructure? What benefits would be offered by the restructuring?

5. What skills are required of a management accountant? In what college courses are these skills taught or developed? What skills would be further developed in the workplace?

6. What is the Institute of Management Accountants (IMA)? How could being in a member of a professional organization help a person's career?

7. How might a Certified Management Accountant (CMA) certification benefit a person in his or her career? How does the CMA certification differ from the Certified Public Accountant (CPA) certification? What skills are assessed on the CMA exam?

8. What are the four ethical standards in the Institute of Management Accountants' *Statement of Ethical Professional Practice*? Describe the meaning of each of the four standards. How does each of these standards impact planning, directing, controlling, and decision making?

9. How has technology changed the work of management accountants? What other business trends are influencing managerial accounting today? How do these other trends impact management accountants' roles in the organization?

10. What significant regulatory trends are impacting accounting in general today? How do these regulatory trends affect the field of managerial accounting?

Application & Analysis

1-1 Accountants and Their Jobs

Basic Discussion Questions

1. When you think of an accountant, whom do you picture? Do you personally know anyone (family member, friend, relative) who's chosen career is accounting? If so, does the person "fit" your description of an accountant or not?

2. Before reading Chapter 1, what did you picture accountants doing, day-in and day-out, at their jobs? From where did this mental picture come (e.g., movies, first accounting class, speaking with accountants, etc.)?

3. What skills are highly valued by employers? What does that tell you about "what accountants do" at their companies?

4. Chapter 1 includes several quotes from accountants at Abbott Laboratories, Caterpillar, and U.S. West. After reading these quotes and from what you know about accountants, how would you describe the role/job responsibilities of accountants?

5. Many accounting majors start their careers in public accounting. Do you think most of them stay in public accounting? Discuss what you consider to be a typical career track for accounting majors.

6. If you are not an accounting major, how do the salaries of accountants compare with your chosen field? How do the opportunities compare (i.e., demand for accountants)?

Classroom Applications

Web: Post the discussion questions on an electronic discussion board. Have small groups of students choose 2–3 of the questions to discuss in their groups.

Classroom: Form groups of 3–4 students. Each group is assigned a question and will have 5–10 minutes to prepare a short presentation of the group's response to the question, which the group will present to the class.

Independent: Research answers to each of the questions. Turn in a 2–3 page typed paper (12 point font, double-spaced with 1" margins). Include references.

1-2 Ethics at Enron

Watch the movie "Enron: The Smartest Guys in the Room" (Magnolia Home Entertainment, 2005, Los Angeles, California).

Basic Discussion Questions

1. Do you think such behavior is common at other companies or do you think this was a fairly isolated event?

2. How important is the "tone at the top" (the tone set by company leadership)?

3. Do you think you could be tempted to follow along if the leadership at your company had the same mentality as the leadership at Enron, or do you think you would have the courage to "just say no" or even be a "whistle-blower"?

4. Why do you think some people can so easily justify (at least to themselves) their unethical behavior?

5. In general, do you think people stop to think about how their actions will affect other people (e.g., the elderly in California who suffered due to electricity blackouts) or do they just "do their job"?

6. What was your reaction to the psychology experiment shown in the DVD? Studies have shown that unlike the traders at Enron (who received large bonuses), most employees really have very little to gain from following a superior's directive to act unethically. Why then do some people do it?

7. Do you think people weigh the potential costs of acting unethically with the potential benefits?

8. You are a business student and will someday work for company or own a business. How will watching this movie impact the way you intend to conduct yourself as an employee or owner?

9. The reporter from *Fortune* magazine asked the question, "How does Enron make its money?" Why should every employee and manager (at every company) know the answer to this question?

10. In light of the "mark-to-market" accounting that enabled Enron to basically record any profit it wished to record, can you understand why some of the cornerstones of financial accounting are "conservatism" and "recording transactions at historical cost"?

11. How did employees of Enron (and employees of the utilities company in Oregon) end up losing billions in retirement funds?

Classroom Applications

Web: Post the discussion questions on an electronic discussion board. Have small groups of students choose 3–5 of the questions to discuss in their groups.

Classroom: Watch the movie before class. Once in class, form groups of 3–4 students. Each group is assigned a question and will have 5–10 minutes to prepare a short presentation of the group's response to the question, which the group will present to the class.

Independent: Watch the movie and take notes. You'll need to turn in a copy of your notes for full credit (without the notes you will only be eligible for ½ credit). Leave your notes handwritten. Also, turn in a 2–4 page typed paper in which you give your gut reaction to the movie. *Your paper should not be a summary of the movie; it should be your reaction to the movie.* In your paper, try to address *most* of the questions.

   For additional Application & Analysis projects and implementation tips, see the Instructor Resources in MyAccountingLab.com.

With the introduction of the Prius, Toyota became the

front-runner in offering fuel-efficient vehicles with cutting edge technology. Ten years after the Prius's debut, Toyota is still committed to developing new environmentally friendly vehicles that "redefine what it means to be environmentally considerate." Not only has Toyota introduced award-winning vehicles, but also award-winning manufacturing plants. Toyota's use of solar energy, waste-water recycling, and improved manufacturing robotics has decreased the harmful consequences of manufacturing on the environment. At the same time, these "green" initiatives have cut plant energy costs and improved productivity.

To understand whether these and other investments were worth it, Toyota's managers needed to understand their costs across all business functions. They also needed to consider which costs should be *increased*, and which costs should be *reduced*. For example, by spending *more* money on green technologies, product quality and safety improvements, Toyota has increased its market share and decreased warranty and liability costs. On the other hand, Toyota's cost reduction efforts in production saved the company over $1.19 billion dollars in 2008. For example, to offset rising raw material costs, Toyota's engineers have figured out ways to decrease the quantity of materials needed without sacrificing performance and quality. They also work with suppliers to help them reduce their own costs, so that the cost savings can be passed on. In this chapter, we talk about many costs: costs that both managers and management accountants must understand to successfully run a business.

Sources: Toyota.com, 2008 Annual Report.

CHAPTER 2

Building Blocks of Managerial Accounting

Learning Objectives

1. Distinguish among service, merchandising, and manufacturing companies

2. Describe the value chain and its elements

3. Distinguish between direct and indirect costs

4. Identify the inventoriable product costs and period costs of merchandising and manufacturing firms

5. Prepare the financial statements for service, merchandising, and manufacturing companies

6. Describe costs that are relevant and irrelevant for decision making

7. Classify costs as fixed or variable and calculate total and average costs at different volumes

So far, we have seen how managerial accounting provides information that managers use to run their businesses more efficiently. Managers must understand basic managerial accounting terms and concepts before they can use the information to make good decisions. This terminology provides the "common ground" through which managers and accountants communicate. Without a common understanding of these concepts, managers may ask for (and accountants may provide) the wrong information for making decisions. As you will see, different types of costs are useful for different purposes. Both managers and accountants must have a clear understanding of the situation and the types of costs that are relevant to the decision at hand.

| 1 | Distinguish among service, merchandising, and manufacturing companies |

What are the Most Common Business Sectors and Their Activities?

Before we talk about specific types of costs, let's consider the three most common types of companies and the business activities in which they incur costs.

Service, Merchandising, and Manufacturing Companies

Organizations other than not-for-profits and governmental agencies are in business to generate profits for their owners. The primary means of generating that profit generally fall into one of three categories:

Service Companies

Service companies are in business to sell intangible services—such as health care, insurance, banking, and consulting—rather than tangible products. Recall from the last chapter that service firms now make up the largest sector of the U.S. economy. Because these types of companies sell services, they generally don't have inventory. Some service providers carry a minimal amount of supplies inventory; however, this inventory is generally used for internal operations—not sold for profit. Service companies incur costs to provide services, develop new services, advertise, and provide customer service. For many service providers, salaries and benefits make up over 70% of their costs.

Merchandising Companies

Merchandising companies such as Wal-Mart and JCPenney resell tangible products they buy from suppliers. For example, Wal-Mart buys clothing, toys, and electronics and resells them to customers at higher prices than what it pays its own suppliers for these goods. Merchandising companies include retailers (such as Wal-Mart) and wholesalers. **Retailers** sell to consumers like you and me. **Wholesalers**, often referred to as "middlemen," buy products in bulk from manufacturers, mark up the prices, and then sell those products to retailers.

Because merchandising companies sell tangible products, they have inventory. The cost of inventory includes the cost merchandisers pay for the goods *plus* all costs necessary to get the merchandise in place and ready to sell, such as freight-in costs and any import duties or tariffs. A merchandiser's balance sheet reports just one inventory account called "Inventory" or "Merchandise Inventory." Besides incurring inventory-related costs, merchandisers also incur costs to operate their retail stores and Web sites, advertise, research new products and new store locations, and to provide customer service.

Manufacturing Companies

Manufacturing companies use labor, plant, and equipment to convert raw materials into new finished products. For example, Toyota's production workers use the company's factories (production plant and equipment) to transform raw materials, such as steel, into high-performance automobiles. Manufacturers sell their products to retailers or wholesalers at a price that is high enough to cover their costs and generate a profit.

Because of their broader range of activities, manufacturers have three types of inventory (pictured in Exhibit 2-1):

1. **Raw materials inventory:** *All raw materials used in manufacturing.* Toyota's raw materials include steel, glass, tires, upholstery fabric, engines, and other automobile components. It also includes other physical materials used in the plant, such as machine lubricants and janitorial supplies.

2. **Work in process inventory:** *Goods that are partway through the manufacturing process but not yet complete.* At Toyota, the work in process inventory consists of partially completed vehicles.

3. **Finished goods inventory:** *Completed goods that have not yet been sold.* Toyota is in business to sell completed cars, not work in process. Once the vehicles are completed, they are no longer considered work in process, but rather they become part of finished goods inventory. Manufacturers sell units from finished goods inventory to merchandisers or directly to consumers.

EXHIBIT 2-1   Manufacturers' Three Types of Inventory

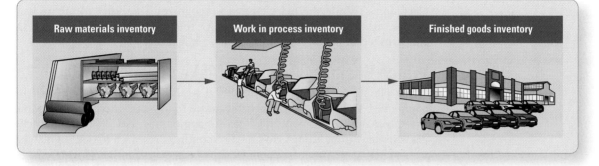

Exhibit 2-2 summarizes the differences among service, merchandising, and manufacturing companies.

EXHIBIT 2-2   Service, Merchandising, and Manufacturing Companies

	Service Companies	Merchandising Companies	Manufacturing Companies
Examples	Advertising agencies Banks Law firms Insurance companies	Amazon.com Kroger Wal-Mart Wholesalers	Procter & Gamble General Mills Dell Computer Toyota
Primary Output	Intangible services	Tangible products purchased from suppliers	New tangible products made as workers and equipment convert raw materials into new finished products
Type(s) of Inventory	None	Inventory (or Merchandise Inventory)	Raw materials inventory Work in process inventory Finished goods inventory

STOP & THINK

What type of company is Outback Steakhouse, Inc.?

Answer: Some companies don't fit nicely into one of the three categories discussed previously. Restaurants are usually considered to be in the service sector. However, Outback has some elements of a service company (it serves hungry patrons), some elements of a manufacturing company (its chefs convert raw ingredients into finished meals), and some elements of a merchandising company (it sells ready-to-serve bottles of wine and beer).

Why is this important?

"All employees should have an understanding of their company's basic business model. The Enron scandal was finally brought to light as a result of someone seriously asking, "How does this company actually make money?" If the business model does not make logical sense, something fishy may be going on."

2 Describe the value chain and its elements

As the "Stop & Think" shows, not all companies are strictly service, merchandising, or manufacturing firms. Recall from Chapter 1 that the U.S. economy is shifting more toward service. Many traditional manufacturers, such as General Electric (GE), have developed profitable service segments that provide much of their company's profits. Even merchandising firms are getting into the "service game" by selling extended warranty contracts on merchandise sold. Retailers offer extended warranties on products ranging from furniture and major appliances to sporting equipment and consumer electronics. While the merchandiser recognizes a liability for these warranties, the price charged to customers for the warranties greatly exceeds the company's cost of fulfilling its warranty obligations.

Which Business Activities Make up the Value Chain?

Many people describe Toyota, General Mills, and Dell as manufacturing companies. But it would be more accurate to say that these are companies that *do* manufacturing. Why? Because companies that do manufacturing also do many other things. Toyota also conducts research to determine what type of new technology to integrate into next year's models. Toyota designs the new models based on its research and then produces, markets, distributes, and services the cars. These activities form Toyota's **value chain**—the activities that add value to the company's products and services. The value chain is pictured in Exhibit 2-3.

EXHIBIT 2-3   The Value Chain

Value Chain

| Research and development | Design | Production or purchases | Marketing | Distribution | Customer service |

The value chain activities also cost money. To set competitive, yet profitable selling prices, Toyota must consider all of the costs incurred along the value chain, not just the costs incurred in manufacturing vehicles. Let's briefly consider some of the costs incurred in each element of the value chain.

Research and development

Design

Research and Development (R&D): *Researching and developing new or improved products or services and the processes for producing them.* Toyota continually engages in researching and developing new technologies to incorporate in its vehicles (such as fuel cells, pre-crash safety systems, and "smart keys,") and in its manufacturing plants (such as environmentally friendly and efficient manufacturing robotics). Toyota currently spends over $9.56 billion a year in R&D.

Design: *Detailed engineering of products and services and the processes for producing them.* Toyota's goal is to design vehicles that create total customer satisfaction, including satisfaction with vehicle style, features, safety, and quality. As a result, Toyota updates the design of older models (such as the Corolla) and designs new prototypes (such as the new ultra-energy efficient "iQ" model) on a regular basis. Part of the design process also includes determining how to mass-produce the vehicles. Because Toyota produces over 8.9 million vehicles per year, engineers must design production plants that are efficient, yet flexible enough to allow for new features and models.

Production or Purchases: *Resources used to produce a product or service or to purchase finished merchandise intended for resale.* For Toyota, the production activity includes all costs incurred to *make* the vehicles. These costs include raw materials (such as steel), plant labor (such as machine operators' wages and benefits), and manufacturing overhead (such as factory utilities and depreciation on the factory). As you can imagine, factories are very expensive to build and operate. Toyota has earmarked over $1.3 billion dollars just to build and equip a new Prius manufacturing plant in Mississippi.

Production or
purchases

For a merchandiser such as Best Buy, this value chain activity includes the cost of purchasing the inventory that the company plans to sell to customers. It also includes all costs associated with getting the inventory to the store, including freight-in costs and any import duties and tariffs that might be incurred if the merchandise was purchased from overseas.

Marketing: *Promotion and advertising of products or services.* The goal of marketing is to create consumer demand for products and services. Toyota uses print advertisements in magazines and newspapers, billboards, television commercials, and the Internet to market its vehicles. Some companies use sponsorship of star athletes and sporting events to market their products. Each method of advertising costs money, but adds value by reaching different target customers.

Marketing

Distribution: *Delivery of products or services to customers.* Toyota sells most of its vehicles through traditional dealerships. However, more customers are ordering "build-your-own" vehicles through Toyota's Web site. Toyota's distribution costs include the costs of shipping the vehicles to retailers and the costs of administering Web-based sales portals. Other industries use different distribution mechanisms. For example, Tupperware primarily sells its products through home-based parties while Amazon.com sells only through the Internet. Until recently, Lands' End sold only through catalogs and the Web.

Distribution

Customer Service: *Support provided for customers after the sale.* Toyota incurs substantial customer service costs, especially in connection with warranties on new car sales. Toyota generally warranties its vehicles for the first three years and/or 36,000 miles, whichever comes first. While Toyota has earned a reputation for excellent quality and has the lowest warranty claim rates in the industry, any malfunction or defect that occurs during the warranty period must be corrected at Toyota's expense. Even with its low warranty claims rate, warranty claims costs the company roughly $4 billion dollars per year.[1]

Customer
service

Coordinating Activities Across the Value Chain

Many of the value chain activities occur in the order discussed here. However, managers cannot simply work on R&D and not think about customer service until after selling the car. Rather, cross-functional teams work on R&D, design, production, marketing, distribution, and customer service simultaneously. As the teams develop new model features, they also plan how to produce, market, and distribute the redesigned vehicles. They also consider how the new design will affect warranty costs. Recall from the last chapter that management accountants typically participate in these cross-functional teams. Even at the highest level of global operations, Toyota uses cross-functional teams to implement its business goals and strategy.

The value chain pictured in Exhibit 2-3 also reminds managers to control costs over the value chain as a whole. For example, Toyota spends more in R&D and product design to increase the quality of its vehicles, which, in turn, reduces customer service costs. Even though R&D and design costs are higher, the total cost of the vehicle—as measured throughout the entire value chain—is lower as a result of this trade off. Enhancing its reputation for high-quality products has also enabled Toyota to increase its market share and charge a slightly higher selling price than some of its competitors.

> ### Why is this important?
>
> "All activities in the value chain are important, yet each costs money to perform. Managers must understand how decisions made in one area of the value chain will affect the costs incurred in other areas of the value chain."

---

[1]http://www.warrantyweek.com/archive/ww20060620.html, Auto Warranty vs. Quality.

The value chain applies to service and merchandising firms as well as manufacturing firms. For example, an advertising agency such as Saatchi & Saatchi incurs the following:

- *Design* costs to develop each client's ad campaign

- *Marketing* costs to obtain new clients

- *Distribution* costs to get the ads to the media

- *Customer service* costs to address each client's concerns

<table>
<tr><td>**3**</td><td>Distinguish between direct and indirect costs</td></tr>
</table>

How do Companies Define Cost?

How do companies such as Bank of America and Toyota determine how much it costs to serve a customer or produce a Prius? Before we can answer this question, let's first consider some of the specialized language that accountants use when referring to costs.

Cost Objects, Direct Costs, and Indirect Costs

A **cost object** is anything for which managers want a separate measurement of cost. Toyota's cost objects may include the following:

- Individual units (a specific, custom-ordered Prius)

- Different models (the Prius, Rav4, and Corolla)

- Alternative marketing strategies (sales through dealers versus built-to-order Web sales)

- Geographic segments of the business (United States, Europe, Japan)

- Departments (Human Resources, R&D, Legal)

Costs are classified as either direct or indirect with respect to the cost object. A **direct cost** is a cost that can be traced to the cost object. For example, say the cost object is one Prius. Toyota can trace the cost of tires to a specific Prius; therefore, the tires are a direct cost of the vehicle. An **indirect cost** is a cost that relates to the cost object but cannot be traced to it. For example, Toyota incurs substantial cost to run a manufacturing plant, including utilities, property taxes, and depreciation. Toyota cannot build a Prius without incurring these costs, so the costs are related to the Prius. However, it's impossible to trace a specific amount of these costs to one Prius. Therefore, these costs are considered indirect costs of a single Prius.

As shown in Exhibit 2-4, the same costs can be indirect with respect to one cost object yet direct with respect to another cost object. For example, plant depreciation, property

EXHIBIT 2-4 **The Same Cost Can Be Direct or Indirect, Depending on the Cost Object**

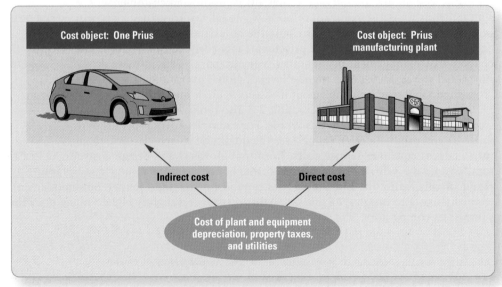

taxes, and utilities are indirect costs of a single Prius. However, if management wants to know how much it costs to run the Prius manufacturing plant, the plant becomes the cost object; so the same depreciation, tax, and utility costs are direct costs of the manufacturing facility. Whether a cost is direct or indirect depends on the specified cost object. In most cases, we'll be talking about a unit of product (such as one Prius) as the cost object.

If a company wants to know the *total* cost attributable to a cost object, it must **assign** all direct *and* indirect costs to the cost object. Assigning a cost simply means that you are "attaching" a cost to the cost object. Why? Because the cost object caused the company to incur that cost. In determining the cost of a Prius, Toyota assigns both the cost of the tires *and* the cost of running the manufacturing plant to the Priuses built at the plant.

Toyota assigns direct costs to each Prius by **tracing** those costs to specific vehicles. This results in a very precise cost figure, giving managers great confidence in the cost's accuracy. However, because Toyota cannot trace indirect costs to specific vehicles, it must **allocate** these costs between all of the vehicles produced at the plant. The allocation process results in a less precise cost figure being assigned to the cost object (one vehicle). We will discuss the allocation process in more detail in the following two chapters; but for now, think of allocation as dividing up the total indirect costs over all of the units produced, just as you might divide a pizza among friends. Exhibit 2-5 illustrates these concepts.

Why is this important?

"As a manager making decisions, you'll need different types of cost information for different types of decisions. To get the information you really want, you'll have to be able to communicate with the accountants using precise definitions of cost."

EXHIBIT 2-5 **Assigning Direct and Indirect Costs to Cost Objects**

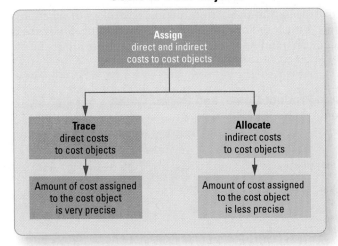

Costs for Internal Decision Making and External Reporting

Let's look more carefully at how companies determine the costs of one of the most common cost objects: products. As a manager, you'll want to focus on the products that are most profitable. But which products are these? To determine a product's profitability, you subtract the cost of the product from its selling price. But how do you calculate the cost of the product? Most companies use two different definitions of costs: (1) total costs for internal decision making and (2) inventoriable product costs for external reporting. Let's see what they are and how managers use each type of cost.

4 Identify the inventoriable product costs and period costs of merchandising and manufacturing firms

Total Costs for Internal Decision Making

Total costs include the costs of *all resources used throughout the value chain*. For Toyota, the total cost of a particular model, such as the Prius, is the total cost to research, design, manufacture, market, distribute, and service that model. Before launching a new model, managers predict the total costs of the model to set a selling price that will cover *all costs* plus return a profit. Toyota also compares each model's sale revenue to its total cost to determine which models are most profitable. Perhaps Rav4s are more profitable than Corollas. Marketing can then focus on advertising and promoting the most profitable models. We'll talk more about total costs in Chapter 8, where we discuss many common business decisions. For the next few chapters, we'll concentrate primarily on inventoriable product costs.

Inventoriable Product Costs for External Reporting

GAAP does not allow companies to use total costs to report inventory balances or Cost of Goods Sold in the financial statements. For external reporting, GAAP allows only a *portion* of the total cost to be treated as an inventoriable product cost. GAAP specifies which costs are inventoriable product costs and which costs are not. **Inventoriable product costs** include *only* the costs incurred during the "production or purchases" stage of the value chain (see Exhibit 2-6). Inventoriable product costs are treated as an asset (inventory) until the product is sold. Hence, the name "inventoriable" product cost. When the product is sold, these costs are removed from inventory and expensed as cost of goods sold. Since inventoriable product costs include only costs incurred during the production or purchases stage of the value chain, all cost incurred in the *other* stages of the value chain must be expensed in the period in which they are incurred. Therefore, we refer to R&D, design, marketing, distribution, and customer service costs as **period costs**.

> Period costs are often called "operating expenses" or "selling, general, and administrative expenses" (SG&A) on the company's income statement. Period costs are *always* expensed in the period in which they are incurred and *never* become part of an inventory account.

Exhibit 2-6 shows that a company's total cost has two components: inventoriable product costs (those costs treated as part of inventory until the product is sold) and period costs (those costs expensed in the current period regardless of when inventory is sold). GAAP requires this distinction for external financial reporting. Study the exhibit carefully to make sure you understand how the two cost components affect the income statement and balance sheet.

EXHIBIT 2-6 **Total Costs, Inventoriable Product Costs, and Period Costs**

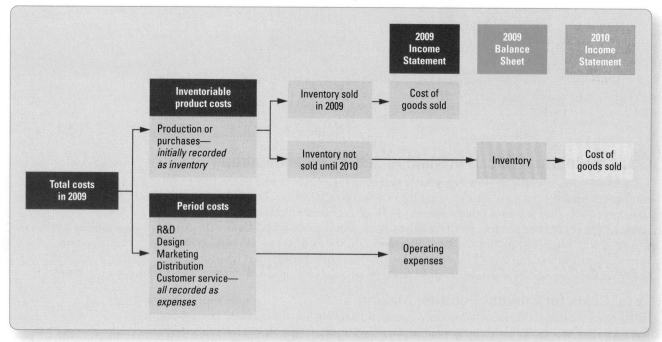

Now that you understand the difference between inventoriable product costs and period costs, let's take a closer look at the specific costs that are inventoriable in merchandising and manufacturing companies.

Merchandising Companies' Inventoriable Product Costs

Merchandising companies' inventoriable product costs include *only* the cost of purchasing the inventory from suppliers plus any costs incurred to get the merchandise to the merchandiser's place of business and ready for sale. Typically, these additional costs include freight-in costs and import duties or tariffs, if the products were purchased from overseas. Why does the cost of the inventory include freight-in charges? Think of the last time you purchased a shirt from a catalog such as L.L.Bean. The catalog may have shown the shirt's price as $30, but by the time you paid the shipping and handling charges, the shirt really cost you around $35. Likewise, merchandising companies pay freight-in charges to get the goods to their place of business (plus import duties if the goods were manufactured overseas). These charges become part of the cost of their inventory.

For instance, Home Depot's inventoriable product costs include what the company paid for its store merchandise plus freight-in and import duties. Home Depot records these costs in an asset account—Inventory—until it *sells* the merchandise. Once the merchandise sells, it belongs to the customer, not Home Depot. Therefore, Home Depot takes the cost out of its inventory account and records it as an expense—the *cost of goods sold*. Home Depot expenses costs incurred in other elements of the value chain as period costs. For example, Home Depot's period costs include store operating expenses (such as salaries, utilities, and depreciation) and advertising expenses.

Some companies, such as Pier 1 Imports, refer to their cost of goods sold as "cost of sales." However, we use the more specific term *cost of goods sold* throughout the text because it more aptly describes the actual cost being expensed in the account—the inventoriable product cost of the goods themselves.

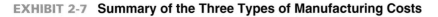

STOP & THINK

What are the inventoriable product costs for a service firm such as H&R Block?

Answer: Service firms such as H&R Block have no inventory of products for sale. Services cannot be produced today and stored up to sell later. Because service firms have no inventory, they have no inventoriable product costs. Instead, they have only period costs that are expensed as incurred.

Manufacturing Companies' Inventoriable Product Costs

Manufacturing companies' inventoriable product costs include *only* those costs incurred during the production element of the value chain. As shown in Exhibit 2-7, manufacturers such as Toyota incur three types of manufacturing costs when making a vehicle: direct materials, direct labor, and manufacturing overhead.

EXHIBIT 2-7   Summary of the Three Types of Manufacturing Costs

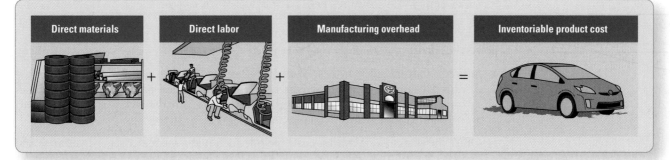

Direct Materials (DM)

Manufacturers convert raw materials into finished products. **Direct materials** are the *primary* raw materials that become a physical part of the finished product. The Prius's direct materials include steel, tires, engines, upholstery, carpet, dashboard instruments, and so forth.

Toyota can trace the cost of these materials (including freight-in and import duties) to specific units or batches of vehicles; thus, they are considered direct costs of the vehicles.

Direct Labor (DL)

Although many manufacturing facilities are highly automated, most still require some direct labor to convert raw materials into a finished product. **Direct labor** is the cost of compensating employees who physically convert raw materials into the company's products. At Toyota, direct labor includes the wages and benefits of machine operators and technicians who assemble the parts and wire the electronics to build the completed vehicles. These costs are *direct* with respect to the cost object (the vehicle) because Toyota can *trace* the time each of these employees spends working on specific units or batches of vehicles.

Manufacturing Overhead (MOH)

The third production cost is manufacturing overhead. **Manufacturing overhead** *includes all manufacturing costs other than direct materials and direct labor.* In other words, manufacturing overhead includes *all indirect manufacturing costs.* Manufacturing overhead is also referred to as factory overhead because all of these costs relate to the factory. As shown in Exhibit 2-8, manufacturing overhead has three components: indirect materials, indirect labor, and other indirect manufacturing costs.

EXHIBIT 2-8 **Components of Manufacturing Overhead**

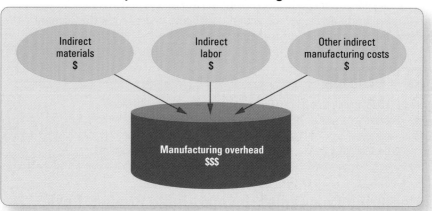

- **Indirect materials** include materials used in the plant that are not easily traced to individual units. For example, indirect materials often include janitorial supplies, oil and lubricants for the machines, and any physical components of the finished product that are very inexpensive. For example, Toyota might treat the invoice sticker placed on each vehicle's window as an indirect material rather than a direct material. Even though the cost of the sticker *could* be traced to the vehicle, it wouldn't make much sense to do so. Why? Because the cost of tracing the sticker to the vehicle outweighs the benefit management receives from the increased accuracy of the information. Therefore, Toyota treats the cost of the stickers as an indirect material, which becomes part of manufacturing overhead.

- **Indirect labor** includes the cost of all employees *in the plant* other than those employees directly converting the raw materials into the finished product. For example, at Toyota, indirect labor includes the salaries, wages, and benefits of plant forklift operators, plant security officers, plant janitors, and plant supervisors.

- **Other indirect manufacturing costs** include such plant-related costs as insurance and depreciation on the plant and plant equipment, plant property taxes, plant repairs and maintenance, and plant utilities. Indirect manufacturing costs have grown in recent years as manufacturers automate their plants with the latest technology.

In summary, *manufacturing overhead includes all manufacturing costs, other than direct materials and direct labor.*

Review: Inventoriable Product Costs or Period Costs?

Exhibit 2-9 summarizes the differences between inventoriable product costs and period costs for service, merchandising, and manufacturing companies. Study this exhibit carefully. When are such costs as depreciation, insurance, utilities, and property taxes inventoriable product costs? *Only* when those costs are related to the manufacturing plant. When those costs are related to nonmanufacturing activities such as R&D or marketing, they are treated as period costs. Service companies and merchandisers do no manufacturing, so they always treat depreciation, insurance, utilities, and property taxes as period costs. When you studied financial accounting, you studied nonmanufacturing firms. Therefore, salaries, depreciation, insurance, and taxes were always expensed.

EXHIBIT 2-9 **Inventoriable Product Costs and Period Costs for Service, Merchandising, and Manufacturing Companies**

	Inventoriable Product Costs	Period Costs
Accounting Treatment	• Initially recorded as inventory • Expensed as *Cost of Goods Sold* only when inventory is sold	• Always recorded as an expense • Never considered part of inventory
Type of Company:		
Service company	• None	• All costs along the value chain • For example, salaries, depreciation expense, utilities, insurance, property taxes, and advertising
Merchandising company	• Purchases of merchandise • Freight-in; customs and duties	• All costs along the value chain *except* for the purchases element • For example, salaries, depreciation expense, utilities, insurance, property taxes, advertising, and freight-out
Manufacturing company	• Direct materials • Direct labor • Manufacturing overhead (including indirect materials, indirect labor, and other indirect manufacturing costs)	• All costs along the value chain *except* for the production element • For example, R&D; freight-out; all expenses for executive headquarters (separate from plant), including depreciation, utilities, insurance, and property taxes; advertising; and CEO's salary

Prime and Conversion Costs

Managers and accountants sometimes talk about certain combinations of manufacturing costs. As shown in Exhibit 2-10 on the next page, **prime costs** refer to the combination of direct materials and direct labor. Prime costs used to be the primary costs of production. However, as companies have automated production with expensive machinery, manufacturing overhead has become a greater cost of production. **Conversion costs** refer to the combination of direct labor and manufacturing overhead. These are the costs of *converting* direct materials into finished goods.

Additional Labor Compensation Costs

The cost of labor, in all areas of the value chain, includes more than the salaries and wages paid to employees. The cost also includes company-paid fringe benefits such as health insurance, retirement plan contributions, payroll taxes, and paid vacations. These costs are very expensive. Health insurance premiums, which have seen double-digit increases for many years, often amount to $500–$1,500 per month for *each* employee electing family coverage. Many companies also contribute an amount equal to 3% to 6% of their

EXHIBIT 2-10 **Prime and Conversion Costs**

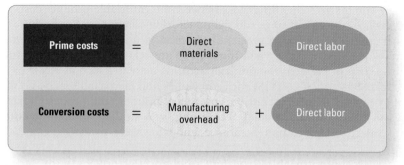

employees' salaries to company-sponsored retirement 401(k) plans. Employers must pay Federal Insurance Contributions Act (FICA) payroll taxes to the federal government for Social Security and Medicare, amounting to 7.65% of each employee's gross pay. In addition, most companies offer paid vacation and other benefits. Together, these fringe benefits usually cost the company an *additional* 35% beyond gross salaries and wages. Thus, an assembly-line worker who makes a $40,000 salary costs Toyota approximately another $14,000 (= $40,000 × 35%) in fringe benefits. Believe it or not, for automobiles manufactured in the United States, the cost of health care assigned to the vehicle is greater than the cost of the steel in the vehicle! Throughout the remainder of this book, any references to wages or salaries also include the cost of fringe benefits.

Decision Guidelines

Building Blocks of Managerial Accounting

Dell engages in *manufacturing* when it assembles its computers, *merchandising* when it sells them on its Web site, and support *services* such as start-up and implementation services. Dell had to make the following types of decisions as it developed its accounting systems.

Decision	Guidelines
How do you distinguish among service, merchandising, and manufacturing companies? How do their balance sheets differ?	*Service companies:* • Provide customers with intangible services • Have no inventories on the balance sheet *Merchandising companies:* • Resell tangible products purchased ready-made from suppliers • Have only one category of inventory *Manufacturing companies:* • Use labor, plant, and equipment to transform raw materials into new finished products • Have three categories of inventory: 1. Raw materials inventory 2. Work in process inventory 3. Finished goods inventory
What business activities add value to companies?	All of the elements of the value chain, including the following: • R&D • Design • Production or Purchases • Marketing • Distribution • Customer Service

Decision	Guidelines
What costs should be assigned to cost objects such as products, departments, and geographic segments?	Both direct and indirect costs are assigned to cost objects. Direct costs are traced to cost objects, whereas indirect costs are allocated to cost objects.
Which product costs are useful for internal decision making, and which product costs are used for external reporting?	Managers use *total costs* for internal decision making. However, GAAP requires companies to use only *inventoriable product costs* for external financial reporting.
What costs are treated as inventoriable product costs under GAAP?	• *Service companies:* No inventoriable product costs • *Merchandising companies:* The cost of merchandise purchased for resale plus all of the costs of getting the merchandise to the company's place of business (for example, freight-in and import duties) • *Manufacturing companies:* Direct materials, direct labor, and manufacturing overhead
How are inventoriable product costs treated on the financial statements?	Inventoriable product costs are initially treated as assets (inventory) on the balance sheet. These costs are expensed (as cost of goods sold) on the income statements when the products are sold.

Summary Problem 1

Requirements

1. Classify each of the following business costs into one of the six value chain elements:

    a. Costs associated with warranties and recalls

    b. Cost of shipping finished goods to overseas customers

    c. Costs a pharmaceutical company incurs to develop new drugs

    d. Cost of a 30-second commercial during the SuperBowl™

    e. Cost of making a new product prototype

    f. Cost of assembly labor used in the plant

2. For a manufacturing company, identify the following as either an inventoriable product cost or a period cost. If it is an inventoriable product cost, classify it as direct materials, direct labor, or manufacturing overhead.

    a. Depreciation on plant equipment

    b. Depreciation on salespeoples' automobiles

    c. Insurance on plant building

    d. Marketing manager's salary

    e. Cost of major components of the finished product

    f. Assembly-line workers' wages

    g. Costs of shipping finished products to customers

    h. Forklift operator's salary

Solutions

Requirement 1

a. Customer service

b. Distribution

c. Research and Development

d. Marketing

e. Design

f. Production

Requirement 2

a. Inventoriable product cost; manufacturing overhead

b. Period cost

c. Inventoriable product cost; manufacturing overhead

d. Period cost

e. Inventoriable product cost; direct materials

f. Inventoriable product cost; direct labor

g. Period cost

h. Inventoriable product cost; manufacturing overhead

How are Inventoriable Product Costs and Period Costs Shown in the Financial Statements?

> **5** Prepare the financial statements for service, merchandising, and manufacturing companies

The difference between inventoriable product costs and period costs is important because these costs are treated differently in the financial statements. All costs incurred in the production or purchases area of the value chain are inventoriable product costs that remain in inventory accounts until the merchandise is sold—then, these costs become the cost of goods sold. However, costs incurred in all other areas of the value chain (R&D, design, marketing, distribution, and customer service) are period costs, which are expensed on the income statement in the period in which they are incurred. Keep these differences in mind as we review the income statements of service firms (which have no inventory), merchandising companies (which purchase their inventory), and manufacturers (which make their inventory). We'll finish the section by comparing the balance sheets of these three different types of companies.

Service Companies

Service companies have the simplest income statement. Exhibit 2-11 shows the income statement of eNow!, a group of e-commerce consultants. The firm has no inventory and thus, no inventoriable product costs, so eNow!'s income statement has no Cost of Goods Sold. Rather, all of the company's costs are period costs, so they are expensed in the current period as "operating expenses."

EXHIBIT 2-11 Service Company Income Statement

eNOW! Income Statement Year Ended December 31, 2009		
Revenues		$ 160,000
Operating expenses:		
Salary expense	$106,000	
Office rent expense	18,000	
Depreciation expense—furniture and equipment	3,500	
Marketing expense	2,500	
Total operating expenses		(130,000)
Operating income		$ 30,000

In this textbook, we always use "operating income" rather than "net income" as the bottom line on the income statement since internal managers are particularly concerned with the income generated through operations. To determine "net income," we would have to deduct interest expense and income taxes from "operating income" and add back interest income. In general, "operating income" is simply the company's income before interest and income taxes.

Merchandising Companies

In contrast with service companies, merchandisers' income statements feature Cost of Goods Sold as the major expense. Consider Apex Showrooms, a merchandiser of lighting fixtures. Apex's *only* inventoriable product costs are the costs of the chandeliers and track lights that it purchases from suppliers, plus freight-in and any import duties. Merchandisers such as Apex compute the Cost of Goods Sold as follows:[2]

	Beginning inventory	$ 9,500	What Apex had at the beginning of the period
+	Purchases, freight-in and import duties	110,000	What Apex bought during the period
=	Cost of goods available for sale	119,500	Total available for sale during the period
−	Ending inventory	(13,000)	What Apex had left at the end of the period
=	Cost of goods sold	$106,500	What Apex sold during the period

Exhibit 2-12 shows Apex's complete income statement, where we have highlighted the Cost of Goods Sold computation. Many companies do not show the computation of Cost of Goods Sold directly on the face of the income statement, preferring to only show the Cost of Goods Sold figure that was obtained through the calculation performed above ($106,500). However, either presentation is acceptable. Cost of Goods Sold is then deducted from Sales Revenue to determine the company's gross profit. Finally, all operating expenses (period costs) are deducted from gross profit to arrive at the company's operating income.

EXHIBIT 2-12 **Merchandiser's Income Statement**

APEX SHOWROOMS
Income Statement
Year Ended December 31, 2009

Sales revenue		$ 150,000
Cost of goods sold:		
Beginning inventory	$ 9,500	
Purchases, freight-in and import duties	110,000	
Cost of goods available for sale	119,500	
Ending inventory	(13,000)	
Cost of goods sold		106,500
Gross profit		43,500
Operating expenses:		
Showroom rent expense	5,000	
Sales salary expense	4,000	9,000
Operating income		$ 34,500

Manufacturing Companies

Exhibit 2-13 shows the income statement of Top-Flight, a manufacturer of golf clubs. Compare its income statement with the merchandiser's income statement in Exhibit 2-12. The only difference is that the merchandiser (Apex) uses *purchases and freight-in* in computing Cost of Goods Sold, whereas the manufacturer (Top-Flight) uses the *cost of goods manufactured* (we've highlighted both in blue). Notice that the term **cost of goods manufactured** is in the past tense. It was the cost of manufacturing the goods that

---

[2]Even companies that use perpetual inventory systems during the year recalculate Cost of Goods Sold in this manner before preparing their annual financial statements.

Top-Flight *finished making during 2009*. This is the manufacturer's cost to obtain new finished goods that are ready to sell. Thus, it is the counterpart to the merchandiser's *purchases*. Next, we'll show you how to calculate the cost of goods manufactured.

EXHIBIT 2-13 Manufacturer's Income Statement

TOP-FLIGHT
Income Statement
Year Ended December 31, 2009

Sales revenue...		$65,000
Cost of goods sold:		
Beginning finished goods inventory...................................	$ 6,000	
Cost of goods manufactured*	42,000	
Cost of goods available for sale.......................................	48,000	
Ending finished goods inventory	(8,000)	
Cost of goods sold...		40,000
Gross profit..		25,000
Operating expenses:		
Sales salary expense	3,000	
Delivery expense	7,000	10,000
Operating income..		$15,000

*From the Schedule of Cost of Goods Manufactured in Exhibit 2-15.

Calculating the Cost of Goods Manufactured

The cost of goods manufactured summarizes the cost of activities that take place in a manufacturing plant over the period. Let's begin by reviewing these activities, which are pictured in Exhibit 2-14. The manufacturer starts by buying direct materials, which are stored in

EXHIBIT 2-14 Flow of Costs Through a Manufacturer's Financial Statements

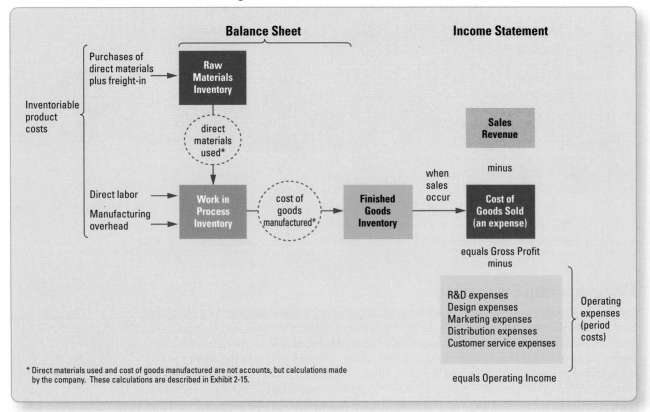

* Direct materials used and cost of goods manufactured are not accounts, but calculations made by the company. These calculations are described in Exhibit 2-15.

Raw Materials Inventory until they are needed for production. Only those *direct materials used* in production are transferred out of Raw Materials Inventory and into Work in Process Inventory. During production, the company uses direct labor and manufacturing overhead to convert these direct materials into a finished product. All units currently being worked on are in Work in Process Inventory. When the units are completed, they are moved out of Work in Process Inventory into Finished Goods Inventory. The amount transferred into finished goods inventory during the year is the *cost of goods manufactured.*

The finished units remain in Finished Goods Inventory until they are sold. When the manufacturer *sells* finished units, the cost of those units becomes the Cost of Goods Sold on the income statement. Costs incurred in nonmanufacturing elements of the value chain are expensed in the period incurred as operating expenses. Exhibit 2-14 shows that these operating expenses are deducted from gross profit to obtain operating income.

With this overview in mind, let's walk through Exhibit 2-15 which shows how Top-Flight computes its cost of goods manufactured—the cost of the goods the plant *finished* during 2009. For simplicity, we'll assume that Top-Flight's raw materials inventory contains only direct materials.[3]

Exhibit 2-15 shows that Top-Flight begins 2009 with $2,000 of partially completed golf clubs that remained on the plant floor at the close of business on December 31, 2008.

During 2009, Top-Flight's production plant *used* $14,000 of direct materials, $19,000 of direct labor, and $12,000 of manufacturing overhead. The sum of these three costs ($45,000) represents the total manufacturing costs incurred during the year. Adding the total manufacturing costs incurred *during* the year ($45,000) to the *beginning* Work in Process Inventory balance ($2,000) gives the total manufacturing costs to account for ($47,000). This figure represents the total manufacturing cost assigned to *all* goods the plant worked on during the year.

EXHIBIT 2-15 **Schedule of Cost of Goods Manufactured**

<table>
<tr><td colspan="3" align="center">**TOP-FLIGHT**
Schedule of Cost of Goods Manufactured
Year Ended December 31, 2009</td></tr>
<tr><td>**Beginning work in progress inventory**</td><td></td><td>$ 2,000</td></tr>
<tr><td>Add: Direct materials used</td><td></td><td></td></tr>
<tr><td>Beginning raw materials inventory*</td><td>$ 9,000</td><td></td></tr>
<tr><td>Purchases of direct materials including freight-in and any import duties</td><td>27,000</td><td></td></tr>
<tr><td>Available for use</td><td>36,000</td><td></td></tr>
<tr><td>Ending raw materials inventory</td><td>(22,000)</td><td></td></tr>
<tr><td>**Direct materials used**</td><td>$14,000</td><td></td></tr>
<tr><td>**Direct labor**</td><td>19,000</td><td></td></tr>
<tr><td>**Manufacturing overhead:**</td><td></td><td></td></tr>
<tr><td>Indirect materials</td><td>$ 1,500</td><td></td></tr>
<tr><td>Indirect labor</td><td>3,500</td><td></td></tr>
<tr><td>Depreciation—plant and equipment</td><td>3,000</td><td></td></tr>
<tr><td>Plant utilities, insurance, and property taxes</td><td>4,000</td><td></td></tr>
<tr><td>Manufacturing overhead</td><td>12,000</td><td></td></tr>
<tr><td>**Total manufacturing costs incurred during year**</td><td></td><td>45,000</td></tr>
<tr><td>**Total manufacturing costs to account for**</td><td></td><td>47,000</td></tr>
<tr><td>**Less: Ending work in process inventory**</td><td></td><td>(5,000)</td></tr>
<tr><td>**Costs of goods manufactured**</td><td></td><td>$42,000</td></tr>
</table>

*For simplicity, we assume that Top-Flight's Raw Materials Inventory account contains only direct materials because the company uses indirect materials as soon as they are purchased. In Chapter 3, we expand the discussion to include manufacturers who store both direct and indirect materials in the Raw Materials Inventory account until they are used in production.

---

[3]We assume that Top-Flight uses its indirect materials as soon as they are purchased rather than storing them in Raw Materials Inventory. In Chapter 3, we expand the discussion to include manufacturers who store indirect materials in the Raw Materials Inventory account until they are used in production.

The plant finished most of these goods and sent them to Finished Goods Inventory, but some were not finished. By the close of business on December 31, 2009, Top-Flight had spent $5,000 on partially completed golf clubs that were still in work in process inventory.

By subtracting the cost of the units still in work in process inventory ($5,000)[4] from the total costs to account for ($47,000), Top-flight is able to calculate the *cost of goods manufactured during 2009*. This figure is then used in Exhibit 2-13 to complete the Cost of Goods Sold calculation.

Flow of Costs Through Inventory Accounts

Exhibit 2-16 diagrams the flow of costs through Top-Flight's three inventory accounts. Notice how the final amount at each stage flows into the next stage. The format is the same for all three inventory accounts:

- Each inventory account starts with a beginning inventory balance.

- Top-Flight adds costs to each inventory account (it adds direct materials *purchased* to Raw Materials Inventory; it adds direct materials *used*, direct labor, and manufacturing overhead to Work in Process Inventory; and it adds the cost of goods manufactured to Finished Goods Inventory).

- Top-Flight subtracts the ending inventory balance to find out how much inventory passed through the account during the period *and on to the next stage*. At all stages, the flow of costs follows the flow of physical goods.

EXHIBIT 2-16 **Flow of Costs Through Top-Flight's Inventory Accounts**

Raw Materials Inventory		
Beginning inventory		$ 9,000
+ Direct materials purchased plus freight-in*		27,000
= Direct materials available for use		36,000
− Ending inventory		(22,000)
= Direct materials used*		$ 14,000

Work in Process Inventory		
Beginning inventory		$ 2,000
+ Direct materials used	$14,000	
+ Direct labor	19,000	
+ Manufacturing overhead	12,000	
Total manufacturing costs incurred during the year		45,000
= Total manufacturing costs to account for		47,000
− Ending inventory		(5,000)
= Cost of goods manufactured		$ 42,000

Finished Goods Inventory		
Beginning inventory		$ 6,000
+ Cost of goods manufactured		42,000
= Cost of goods available for sale		48,000
− Ending inventory		(8,000)
= Cost of goods sold		$ 40,000

*For simplicity, we assume that Top-Flight's Raw Materials Inventory account contains only direct materials because the company uses indirect materials as soon as they are purchased. In Chapter 3, we expand the discussion to include manufacturers who store both direct and indirect materials in the Raw Materials Inventory account until they are used in production.

---

[4]We'll discuss how managers calculate the cost of work in process inventory in Chapters 3–5.

Take time to see how the Schedule of Cost of Goods Manufactured (Exhibit 2-15) captures the flow of costs through the Raw Materials and Work in Process Inventory accounts. The Income Statement (Exhibit 2-13) captures the flow of costs through the Finished Goods Inventory account. Some manufacturers combine the flow of costs through *all three* inventory accounts into one combined Schedule of Cost of Goods Manufactured and Cost of Goods Sold, and then show only the resulting Cost of Goods Sold figure ($40,000) on the income statement.

Comparing Balance Sheets

Now that we've looked at the income statement for each type of company, let's turn our attention to the balance sheet. The only difference in the balance sheets of service, merchandising, and manufacturing companies relates to inventories. Exhibit 2-17 shows how the current asset sections of eNOW! (service company), Apex Showrooms (merchandising company), and Top-Flight (manufacturing company) might differ at the end of 2009. eNOW! has no inventory at all, Apex Showrooms has a single category of inventory, and Top-Flight has three categories of inventory (raw materials, work in process, and finished goods).

EXHIBIT 2-17 **Current Asset Sections of Balance Sheets**

eNOW! (SERVICE COMPANY)

Cash	$ 4,000
Accounts receivable	5,000
Prepaid expenses	1,000
Total current assets	$10,000

APEX SHOWROOMS (MERCHANDISING COMPANY)

Cash	$ 4,000
Accounts receivable	5,000
Inventory (Exhibit 2-12)	13,000
Prepaid expenses	1,000
Total current assets	$23,000

TOP-FLIGHT (MANUFACTURING COMPANY)

Cash		$ 4,000
Accounts receivable		5,000
Inventories:		
Raw materials inventory (Exhibit 2-15)	22,000	
Work in process inventory (Exhibit 2-15)	5,000	
Finished goods inventory (Exhibit 2-13)	8,000	
Total inventories		35,000
Prepaid expenses		1,000
Total current assets		$45,000

6 Describe costs that are relevant and irrelevant for decision making

What Other Cost Terms are Used by Managers?

So far in this chapter, we have discussed direct versus indirect costs and inventoriable product costs versus period costs. Now let's turn our attention to other cost terms that managers and accountants use when planning and making decisions.

Controllable Versus Uncontrollable Costs

When deciding to make business changes, management needs to distinguish controllable costs from uncontrollable costs. In the long run, most costs are **controllable**, meaning management is able to influence or change them. However, in the short run, companies are often "locked in" to certain costs arising from previous decisions. These are called **uncontrollable costs**. For example, Toyota has little or no control over the property tax and insurance costs of their existing plants. These costs were "locked in" when Toyota built its plants. Toyota could replace existing production facilities with different-sized plants in different areas of the world that might cost less to operate, but that would take time. To see *immediate* benefits, management must change those costs that are controllable at the present. For example, management can control costs of research and development, design, and advertising. Sometimes Toyota's management chose to *increase* rather than decrease these costs in order to successfully gain market share. However, Toyota was also able to *decrease* other controllable costs, such as the price paid for raw materials, by working with its suppliers.

Relevant and Irrelevant Costs

Decision making involves identifying various courses of action and then choosing among them. When managers make decisions, they focus on those costs and revenues that are relevant to the decision. For example, Toyota plans to build a new state-of-the-art Prius production facility in the United States. After considering alternative locations, management decided to build the facility in Blue Springs, Mississippi. The decision was based on relevant information such as the **differential cost** of building and operating the facility in Mississippi versus building and operating the facility in other potential locations. Differential cost refers to the difference in cost between two alternatives.

Say you want to buy a new car. You narrow your decision to two choices: the Nissan Sentra or the Toyota Corolla. As shown in Exhibit 2-18, the Sentra you like costs $14,480, whereas the Corolla costs $15,345. Because sales tax is based on the sales price, the Corolla's sales tax is higher. However, your insurance agent quotes you a higher price to insure the Sentra ($365 per month versus $319 per month for the Corolla). All of these costs are relevant to your decision because they differ between the two cars.

EXHIBIT 2-18 Comparison of Relevant Information

	Sentra	Corolla	Differential Cost
Car's price	$14,480	$15,345	$ (865)
Sales tax (8%) (rounded to the nearest dollar)	1,158	1,228	(70)
Insurance*	21,900	19,140	2,760
Total relevant costs	$37,538	$35,713	$1,825

*Over the five years (60 months) you plan to keep the car.

Other costs are not relevant to your decision. For example, both cars run on regular unleaded gasoline and have the same fuel economy ratings, so the cost of operating the vehicles is about the same. Likewise, you don't expect cost differences in servicing the vehicles because they both carry the same warranty and have received excellent quality ratings in *Consumer Reports*. Because you project operating and maintenance costs to be the *same* for both cars, these costs are irrelevant to your decision. In other words, they won't influence your decision either way. Based on your analysis, the differential cost is $1,825 in favor of the

Corolla. Does this mean that you will choose the Corolla? Not necessarily. The Sentra may have some characteristics you like better, such as a particular paint color, more comfortable seating, or more trunk space. When making decisions, management must also consider qualitative factors (such as effect on employee morale) in addition to differential costs.

Another cost that is irrelevant to your decision is the cost you paid for the vehicle you currently own. Say you just bought a Ford F-150 pickup truck two months ago, but you've decided you need a small sedan rather than a pickup truck. The cost of the truck is a **sunk cost**. Sunk costs are costs that have already been incurred. Nothing you do now can change the fact that you already bought the truck. Thus, the cost of the truck is not relevant to your decision of whether to buy the Sentra versus the Corolla. The only thing you can do now is (1) keep your truck or (2) sell it for the best price you can get.

Management often has trouble ignoring sunk costs when making decisions, even though it should. Perhaps it invested in a factory or a computer system that no longer serves the company's needs. Many times, new technology makes management's past investments in older technology look like bad decisions, even though they weren't at the time. Management should ignore sunk costs because its decisions about the future cannot alter decisions made in the past.

Fixed and Variable Costs

Managers cannot make good plans and decisions without first knowing how their costs behave. Costs generally behave as fixed costs or variable costs. We will spend all of Chapter 6 discussing cost behavior. For now, let's look just at the basics. **Fixed costs** stay constant in total over a wide range of activity levels. For example, let's say you decide to buy the Corolla, so your insurance cost for the year is $3,828 ($319 per month × 12 months). As shown in Exhibit 2-19, your total insurance cost stays fixed whether you drive your car 0 miles, 1,000 miles, or 10,000 miles during the year.

Classify costs as fixed or variable and calculate total and average costs at different volumes   **7**

EXHIBIT 2-19 Fixed Cost Behavior

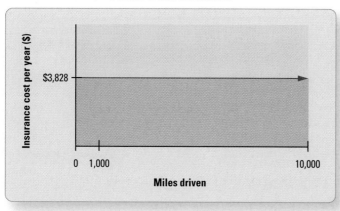

However, the total cost of gasoline to operate your car varies depending on whether you drive 0 miles, 1,000 miles, or 10,000 miles. The more miles you drive, the higher your total gasoline cost for the year. If you don't drive your car at all, you won't incur any costs for gasoline. Your gasoline costs are **variable costs**, as shown in Exhibit 2-20. Variable costs change in total in direct proportion to changes in volume. To accurately forecast the total cost of operating your Corolla during the year, you need to know which operating costs are fixed and which are variable.

How Manufacturing Costs Behave

Most companies have both fixed and variable costs. Manufacturing companies know that their direct materials are variable costs. The more cars Toyota makes, the higher its total cost for tires, steel, and parts. The behavior of direct labor is harder to characterize. Salaried employees are paid a fixed amount per year. Hourly wage earners are paid only when they work. The

Why is this important?

"Most business decisions depend on how costs are expected to change at different volumes of activity. Managers can't make good decisions without first understanding how their costs behave."

EXHIBIT 2-20 **Variable Cost Behavior**

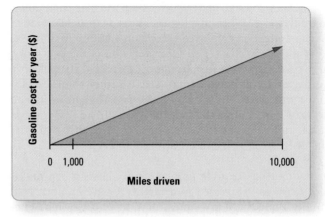

more hours they work, the more they are paid. Nonetheless, direct labor is generally treated as a variable cost because the more cars Toyota produces, the more assembly-line workers and machine operators it must employ. Manufacturing overhead includes both variable and fixed costs. For example, the cost of indirect materials is variable, while the cost of property tax, insurance, and straight-line depreciation on the plant and equipment is fixed. The cost of utilities is partially fixed and partially variable. Factories incur a certain level of utility costs just to keep the lights on. However, when more cars are produced, more electricity is used to run the production equipment. Exhibit 2-21 summarizes the behavior of manufacturing costs.

EXHIBIT 2-21 **The Behavior of Manufacturing Costs**

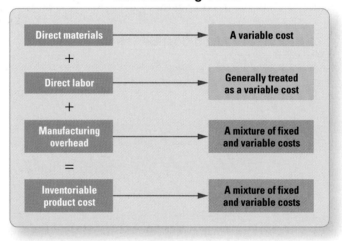

Calculating Total and Average Costs

Why is cost behavior important? Managers need to understand how costs behave to predict total costs and calculate average costs. In our example, we'll look at Toyota's total and average *manufacturing* costs; but the same principles apply to nonmanufacturing costs.

Let's say Toyota wants to estimate the total cost of manufacturing 10,000 Prius cars next year. To do so, Toyota must know 1) its total fixed manufacturing costs, and 2) the variable cost of manufacturing each vehicle. Let's assume total fixed manufacturing costs for the year at the Prius plant are $20,000,000 and the variable cost of manufacturing each Prius is $5,000.[5] How much total manufacturing cost should Toyota budget for the year? Toyota calculates it as follows:

Total fixed cost + (Variable cost per unit × Number of units) = Total cost

$20,000,000 + ($5,000 per vehicle × 10,000 vehicles) = $70,000,000

[5]All references to Toyota in this hypothetical example were created by the author solely for academic purposes and are not intended in any way to represent the actual business practices of, or costs incurred by, Toyota Motor Corporation.

What is the **average cost** of manufacturing each Prius next year? It's the total cost divided by the number of units:

$$\frac{\text{Total cost}}{\text{Number of units}} = \text{Average cost per unit}$$

$$\frac{\$70,000,000}{10,000 \text{ vehicles}} = \$7,000 \text{ per vehicle}$$

If Toyota's managers decide they need to produce 12,000 Prius cars instead, can they simply predict total costs as follows?

$$\text{Average cost per unit} \times \text{Number of units} = \text{Total cost???}$$

$$\$7,000 \quad \times \quad 12,000 \quad = \$84,000,000???$$

No! They cannot! Why? *Because the average cost per unit is NOT appropriate for predicting total costs at different levels of output.* Toyota's managers should forecast total cost based on cost behavior:

$$\text{Total fixed cost} + (\text{Variable cost per unit} \times \text{Number of units}) = \text{Total cost}$$

$$\$20,000,000 + (\ \$5,000 \text{ per vehicle} \times 12,000 \text{ vehicles}\ ) = \$80,000,000$$

Why is the *correct* forecasted cost of $80 million less than the *faulty* prediction of $84 million? The difference stems from fixed costs. Remember, Toyota incurs $20 million of fixed manufacturing costs whether it makes 10,000 vehicles or 12,000 vehicles. As Toyota makes more Prius cars, the fixed manufacturing costs are spread over more vehicles, so the average cost per vehicle declines. If Toyota ends up making 12,000 vehicles, the new average manufacturing cost per Prius decreases as follows:

$$\frac{\text{Total cost}}{\text{Number of units}} = \text{Average cost per unit}$$

$$\frac{\$80,000,000}{12,000 \text{ vehicles}} = \$6,667 \text{ per vehicle (rounded)}$$

The average cost per unit is lower when Toyota produces more vehicles because it is using the fixed manufacturing costs more efficiently—taking the same $20 million of resources and making more vehicles with it.

> *The moral of the story: The average cost per unit is valid only at ONE level of output—the level used to compute the average cost per unit. Thus, NEVER use average costs to forecast costs at different output levels; if you do, you will miss the mark!*

Finally, a **marginal cost** is the cost of making *one more unit*. Fixed costs will not change when Toyota makes one more Prius unless the plant is operating at 100% capacity and simply cannot make one more unit. (If that's the case, Toyota will need to incur additional costs to expand the plant.) So, the marginal cost of a unit is simply its variable cost.

As you have seen, management accountants and managers use specialized terms for discussing costs. They use different costs for different purposes. Without a solid understanding of these terms, managers are likely to make serious judgment errors.

Decision Guidelines

Building Blocks of Managerial Accounting

As a manufacturer, Dell needs to know how to calculate its inventoriable product costs for external reporting. Dell also needs to know many characteristics about its costs (that is, which are controllable, which are relevant to different decisions, which are fixed, and so forth) in order to plan and make decisions.

Decision	Guidelines
How do you compute cost of goods sold?	*Service companies:* No cost of goods sold because they don't sell tangible goods • *Merchandising companies:* Beginning inventory + Purchases plus freight-in and import duties, if any = Cost of goods available for sale − Ending inventory = Cost of goods sold • *Manufacturing companies:* Beginning finished goods inventory + Cost of goods manufactured = Cost of goods available for sale − Ending finished goods inventory = Cost of goods sold
How do you compute the cost of goods manufactured?	Beginning work in process inventory + Total manufacturing costs incurred during year (direct materials used + direct labor + manufacturing overhead) = Total manufacturing costs to account for − Ending work in process inventory = Cost of goods manufactured
How do managers decide which costs are relevant to their decisions?	Costs are relevant to a decision when they differ between alternatives and affect the future. Thus, *differential costs* are relevant, whereas *sunk costs* and costs that don't differ are not relevant.
How should managers forecast total costs for different production volumes?	To forecast total costs, managers should compute the following: Total cost = Total fixed costs + (Variable cost per unit × Number of units) Managers should *not* use a product's *average cost* to forecast total costs because it will change as production volume changes. As production increases, the average cost per unit declines (because fixed costs are spread over more units).

Summary Problem 2

Requirements

1. Show how to compute cost of goods manufactured. Use the following amounts: direct materials used ($24,000), direct labor ($9,000), manufacturing overhead ($17,000), beginning work in process inventory ($5,000), and ending work in process inventory ($4,000).

2. Auto-USA spent $300 million in total to produce 50,000 cars this year. The $300 million breaks down as follows: The company spent $50 million on fixed costs to run its manufacturing plants and $5,000 of variable costs to produce each car. Next year, it plans to produce 60,000 cars using the existing production facilities.

   a. What is the current *average cost* per car this year?

   b. Assuming there is no change in fixed costs or variable costs per unit, what is the *total forecasted cost* to produce 60,000 cars next year?

   c. What is the *forecasted average cost* per car next year?

   d. Why does the average cost per car vary between years?

Solutions

Requirement 1

Cost of goods manufactured:

Beginning work in process inventory		$ 5,000
Add: Direct materials used	24,000	
Direct labor	9,000	
Manufacturing overhead	17,000	
Total manufacturing costs incurred during the period		50,000
Total manufacturing costs to account for		55,000
Less: Ending work in process inventory		(4,000)
Cost of goods manufactured		$51,000

Requirement 2

a.
   Total cost ÷ Number of units = Current average cost
   $300 million ÷ 50,000 cars = $6,000 per car

b.
   Total fixed costs + Total variable costs = Total projected costs
   $50 million + (60,000 cars × $5,000 per car) = $350 million

c.
   Total cost ÷ Number of units = Projected average cost
   $350 million ÷ 60,000 cars = $5,833 per car

d. The average cost per car decreases because Auto-USA will use the same fixed costs ($50 million) to produce more cars next year. Auto-USA will be using its resources more efficiently, so the average cost per unit will decrease.

REVIEW

Accounting Vocabulary

Allocate. (p. 49) To assign an *indirect* cost to a cost object.

Assign. (p. 49) To attach a cost to a cost object.

Average cost. (p. 65) The total cost divided by the number of units.

Controllable Costs. (p. 62) Costs that can be influenced or changed by management.

Conversion Costs. (p. 53) The combination of direct labor and manufacturing overhead costs.

Cost Object. (p. 48) Anything for which managers want a separate measurement of costs.

Cost of Goods Manufactured. (p. 57) The cost of manufacturing the goods that were *finished* during the period.

Customer Service. (p. 47) Support provided for customers after the sale.

Design. (p. 46) Detailed engineering of products and services and the processes for producing them.

Differential Cost. (p. 62) The difference in cost between two alternative courses of action.

Direct Cost. (p. 48) A cost that can be traced to a cost object.

Direct Labor. (p. 52) The cost of compensating employees who physically convert raw materials into the company's products; labor costs that are directly traceable to the finished product.

Direct Materials. (p. 51) Primary raw materials that become a physical part of a finished product and whose costs are traceable to the finished product.

Distribution. (p. 47) Delivery of products or services to customers.

Finished Goods Inventory. (p. 45) Completed goods that have not yet been sold.

Fixed Costs. (p. 63) Costs that stay constant in total despite wide changes in volume.

Indirect Cost. (p. 48) A cost that relates to the cost object but cannot be traced to it.

Indirect Labor. (p. 52) Labor costs that are difficult to trace to specific products.

Indirect Materials. (p. 52) Materials whose costs are difficult to trace to specific products.

Inventoriable Product Costs. (p. 50) All costs of a product that GAAP requires companies to treat as an asset (inventory) for external financial reporting. These costs are not expensed until the product is sold.

Manufacturing Company. (p. 44) A company that uses labor, plant, and equipment to convert raw materials into new finished products.

Manufacturing Overhead. (p. 52) All manufacturing costs other than direct materials and direct labor; also called factory overhead and indirect manufacturing cost.

Marginal Cost. (p. 65) The cost of producing one more unit.

Marketing. (p. 47) Promotion and advertising of products or services.

Merchandising Company. (p. 44) A company that resells tangible products previously bought from suppliers.

Other Indirect Manufacturing Costs. (p. 52) All manufacturing overhead costs aside from indirect materials and indirect labor.

Period Costs. (p. 50) Cost that are expensed in the period in which they are incurred; often called Operating Expenses, or Selling, General, and Administrative Expenses.

Prime Costs. (p. 53) The combination of direct material and direct labor costs.

Production or Purchases. (p. 47) Resources used to produce a product or service, or to purchase finished merchandise intended for resale.

Raw Materials Inventory. (p. 44) All raw materials (direct materials and indirect materials) not yet used in manufacturing.

Research and Development (R&D). (p. 46) Researching and developing new or improved products or services or the processes for producing them.

Retailer. (p. 44) Merchandising company that sells to consumers.

Service Company. (p. 44) A company that sells intangible services rather than tangible products.

Sunk Cost. (p. 63) A cost that has already been incurred.

Total Costs. (p. 49) The cost of all resources used throughout the value chain.

Trace. (p. 49) To assign a *direct* cost to a cost object.

Uncontrollable Costs. (p. 62) Costs that cannot be changed or influenced in the short run by management.

Value Chain. (p. 46) The activities that add value to a firm's products and services; includes R&D, design, production or purchases, marketing, distribution, and customer service.

Variable Costs. (p. 63) Costs that change in total in direct proportion to changes in volume.

Wholesaler. (p. 44) Merchandising companies that buy in bulk from manufacturers, mark up the prices, and then sell those products to retailers.

Work in Process Inventory. (p. 44) Goods that are partway through the manufacturing process but not yet complete.

Quick Check

1. *(Learning Objective 1)* Sears, Roebuck and Co. is a
   a. service company.
   b. retailer.
   c. wholesaler.
   d. manufacturer.

2. *(Learning Objective 2)* The cost of oranges at a fruit juice manufacturer is an example of a cost from which element in the value chain?
   a. Design
   b. Production
   c. Marketing
   d. Distribution

3. *(Learning Objective 2)* Which is *not* an element of Toyota's value chain?
   a. Administrative costs
   b. Cost of shipping cars to dealers
   c. Salaries of engineers who update car design
   d. Cost of print ads and television commercials

4. *(Learning Objective 3)* For Toyota, which is a direct cost with respect to the Prius?
   a. Depreciation on plant and equipment
   b. Cost of vehicle engine
   c. Salary of engineer who rearranges plant layout
   d. Cost of customer hotline

5. *(Learning Objective 3)* Which one of the following costs would be considered a direct cost of serving a particular customer at a McDonald's restaurant?
   a. The salary of the restaurant manager
   b. The depreciation on the restaurant building
   c. The cost of the hamburger patty in the sandwich the customer ordered
   d. The cost of heating the restaurant

6. *(Learning Objective 4)* Which of the following is *not* part of Toyota's manufacturing overhead?
   a. Insurance on plant and equipment
   b. Depreciation on its North American corporate headquarters
   c. Plant property taxes
   d. Plant utilities

7. *(Learning Objective 4)* The three basic components of inventoriable product costs are direct materials, direct labor, and
   a. cost of goods manufactured.
   b. manufacturing overhead.
   c. cost of goods sold.
   d. work in process.

8. *(Learning Objective 5)* In computing cost of goods sold, which of the following is the manufacturer's counterpart to the merchandiser's purchases?
   a. Direct materials used
   b. Total manufacturing costs incurred during the period
   c. Total manufacturing costs to account for
   d. Cost of goods manufactured

9. *(Learning Objective 6)* Which of the following is irrelevant to business decisions?
   a. Differential costs
   b. Sunk costs
   c. Variable costs
   d. Qualitative factors

10. *(Learning Objective 7)* Which of the following is *true*?
    a. Total fixed costs increase as production volume increases.
    b. Total fixed costs decrease as production volume decreases.
    c. Total variable costs increase as production volume increases.
    d. Total variable costs stay constant as production volume increases.

ASSESS YOUR PROGRESS

Learning Objectives

1 Distinguish among service, merchandising, and manufacturing companies

2 Describe the value chain and its elements

3 Distinguish between direct and indirect costs

4 Identify the inventoriable product costs and period costs of merchandising and manufacturing firms

5 Prepare the financial statements for service, merchandising, and manufacturing companies

6 Describe costs that are relevant and irrelevant for decision making

7 Classify costs as fixed or variable and calculate total and average costs at different volumes

Short Exercises

S2-1 Identify type of company from balance sheets *(Learning Objective 1)*

The current asset sections of the balance sheets of three companies follow. Which company is a service company? Which is a merchandiser? Which is a manufacturer? How can you tell?

X-Treme		Y-Not?		Zesto	
Cash.............................	$ 2,500	Cash.............................	$3,000	Cash......................................	$ 2,000
Accounts receivable......	5,500	Accounts receivable......	6,000	Accounts receivable.............	5,000
Inventory......................	8,000	Prepaid expenses	500	Raw materials inventory	1,000
Prepaid expenses	300	Total............................	$9,500	Work in process inventory	800
Total............................	$16,300			Finished goods inventory........	4,000
				Total.....................................	$12,800

S2-2 Identify types of companies and inventories *(Learning Objective 1)*

Fill in the blanks with one of the following terms: *manufacturing, service, merchandising, retailer(s), wholesaler(s), raw materials inventory, merchandise inventory, work in process inventory, finished goods inventory, freight-in, the cost of merchandise.*

a. _____ companies generally have no inventory.
b. Boeing is a _____ company.
c. Merchandisers' inventory consists of _____ and _____.
d. _____ companies carry three types of inventories: _____, _____, and _____.
e. Prudential Insurance Company is a _____ company.
f. Two types of _____ companies include _____ and _____.
g. Direct materials are stored in _____.
h. Sears is a _____ company.
i. Manufacturers sell from their stock of _____.
j. Labor costs usually account for the highest percentage of _____ companies' costs.
k. Partially completed units are kept in the _____.

S2-3 Label value chain functions *(Learning Objective 2)*

List the correct value chain element for each of the six business functions described below.
a. Delivery of products and services
b. Detailed engineering of products and services and the processes for producing them
c. Promotion and advertising of products or services
d. Investigating new or improved products or services and the processes for producing them
e. Support provided to customers after the sale
f. Resources used to make a product or obtain finished merchandise

S2-4 Classify costs by value chain function *(Learning Objective 2)*

Classify each of Hewlett-Packard's (HP's) costs as one of the six business functions in the value chain.
a. Depreciation on Roseville, California, plant
b. Costs of a customer support center Web site
c. Transportation costs to deliver laser printers to retailers such as Best Buy
d. Depreciation on research lab
e. Cost of a prime-time TV ad featuring the new HP logo

f. Salary of scientists at HP laboratories who are developing new printer technologies

g. Purchase of plastic used in printer casings

h. Salary of engineers who are redesigning the printer's on-off switch

i. Depreciation on delivery vehicles

j. Plant manager's salary

S2-5 Classify costs as direct or indirect *(Learning Objective 3)*

Classify the following as direct or indirect costs with respect to a local Blockbuster store (the store is the cost object). In addition, state whether Blockbuster would trace or allocate these costs to the store.

a. Store utilities

b. The CEO's salary

c. The cost of the DVDs

d. The cost of national advertising

e. The wages of store employees

f. The cost of operating the corporate payroll department

g. The cost of Xbox, PlayStation, and Nintendo games

h. The cost of popcorn and candy sold at the store

S2-6 Classify inventoriable product costs and period costs *(Learning Objective 4)*

Classify each of Georgia-Pacific's costs as either inventoriable product costs or period costs. Georgia-Pacific is a manufacturer of paper, lumber, and building material products.

a. Depreciation on the gypsum board plant

b. Purchase of lumber to be cut into boards

c. Life insurance on CEO

d. Salaries of scientists studying ways to speed forest growth

e. Cost of new software to track inventory during production

f. Cost of electricity at one of Georgia-Pacific's paper mills

g. Salaries of Georgia-Pacific's top executives

h. Cost of chemical applied to lumber to inhibit mold from developing

i. Cost of TV ads promoting environmental awareness

S2-7 Classify a manufacturer's costs *(Learning Objective 4)*

Classify each of the following costs as a period cost or an inventoriable product cost. If you classify the cost as an inventoriable product cost, further classify it as direct material (DM), direct labor (DL), or manufacturing overhead (MOH).

a. Depreciation on automated production equipment

b. Telephone bills relating to customer service call center

c. Wages and benefits paid to assembly-line workers in the manufacturing plant

d. Repairs and maintenance on factory equipment

e. Lease payment on administrative headquarters

f. Salaries paid to quality control inspectors in the plant

g. Property insurance—40% of building is used for sales and administration; 60% of building is used for manufacturing

h. Standard packaging materials used to package individual units of product for sale (for example, cereal boxes in which cereal is packaged)

S2-8 Classify costs incurred by a dairy processing company *(Learning Objective 4)*

Each of the following costs pertains to DairyPlains, a dairy processing company. Classify each of the company's costs as a period cost or an inventoriable product cost. Further classify inventoriable product costs as direct material (DM), direct labor (DL), or manufacturing overhead (MOH).

Cost	Period Cost or Inventoriable Product Cost?	DM, DL, or MOH?
1. Cost of milk purchased from local dairy farmers		
2. Lubricants used in running bottling machines		
3. Depreciation on refrigerated trucks used to collect raw milk from local dairy farmers		
4. Property tax on dairy processing plant		
5. Television advertisements for DairyPlains' products		
6. Gasoline used to operate refrigerated trucks delivering finished dairy products to grocery stores		
7. Company president's annual bonus		
8. Plastic gallon containers in which milk is packaged		
9. Depreciation on marketing department's computers		
10. Wages and salaries paid to machine operators at dairy processing plant		
11. Research and development on improving milk pasteurization process		

S2-9 Determine total manufacturing overhead (Learning Objective 4)

Snap's manufactures disposable cameras. Suppose the company's March records include the items described below. What is Snap's total manufacturing overhead cost in March?

Glue for camera frames	$ 250
Depreciation expense on company cars used by sales force	3,000
Plant depreciation expense	10,000
Interest expense	2,000
Company president's salary	25,000
Plant supervisor's salary	4,000
Plant janitor's salary	1,000
Oil for manufacturing equipment	25
Flashbulbs	50,000

S2-10 Compute Cost of Goods Sold for a merchandiser (Learning Objective 5)

Given the following information for Circuits Plus, an electronics e-tailer, compute the cost of goods sold.

Web site maintenance	$ 7,000
Delivery expenses	1,000
Freight-in	3,000
Import duties	1,000
Purchases	40,000
Ending inventory	5,500
Revenues	60,000
Marketing expenses	10,000
Beginning inventory	3,500

S2-11 Prepare a retailer's income statement *(Learning Objective 5)*

Salon Secrets is a retail chain specializing in salon-quality hair care products. During the year, Salon Secrets had sales of $38,230,000. The company began the year with $3,270,000 of merchandise inventory and ended the year with $3,920,000 of inventory. During the year, Salon Secrets purchased $23,450,000 of merchandise inventory. The company's selling, general, and administrative expenses totaled $6,115,000 for the year. Prepare Salon Secrets' income statement for the year.

S2-12 Calculate direct materials used *(Learning Objective 5)*

You are a new accounting intern at Sunny's Bikes. Your boss gives you the following information and asks you to compute the cost of direct materials used (assume that the company's raw materials inventory contains only direct materials).

Purchases of direct materials	$16,000
Import duties	1,000
Freight-in	200
Freight-out	1,000
Ending raw materials inventory	1,500
Beginning raw materials inventory	4,000

S2-13 Compute Cost of Goods Manufactured *(Learning Objective 5)*

Smith Manufacturing found the following information in its accounting records: $524,000 of direct materials used, $223,000 of direct labor, and $742,000 of manufacturing overhead. The Work in Process Inventory account had a beginning balance of $76,000 and an ending balance of $85,000. Compute the company's Cost of Goods Manufactured.

S2-14 Consider relevant information *(Learning Objective 6)*

You have been offered an entry-level marketing position at two highly respectable firms: one in Los Angeles, California, and one in Sioux Falls, South Dakota. What quantitative and qualitative information might be relevant to your decision? What characteristics about this information make it relevant?

S2-15 Classify costs as fixed or variable *(Learning Objective 7)*

Classify each of the following personal expenses as either fixed or variable. In some cases, your answer may depend on specific circumstances. If so, briefly explain your answer.
a. Apartment rental
b. Television cable service
c. Cost of groceries
d. Water and sewer bill
e. Cell phone bill
f. Health club dues
g. Bus fare

Exercises—Group A

E2-16A Identify types of companies and their inventories *(Learning Objective 1)*

Complete the following statements with one of the terms listed here. You may use a term more than once, and some terms may not be used at all.

Finished goods inventory	Inventory (merchandise)	Service companies
Manufacturing companies	Merchandising companies	Work in process inventory
Raw materials inventory	Wholesalers	

a. _____ produce their own inventory.

b. _____ typically have a single category of inventory.

c. _____ do not have tangible products intended for sale.

d. _____ resell products they previously purchased ready-made from suppliers.

e. _____ use their workforce and equipment to transform raw materials into new finished products.

f. _____ sell to consumers.

g. Swaim, a company based in North Carolina, makes furniture. Partially completed sofas are _____. Completed sofas that remain unsold in the warehouse are _____. Fabric and wood are _____.

h. For Kellogg's, corn, cardboard boxes, and waxed paper liners are classified as _____.

i. _____ buy in bulk from manufacturers and sell to retailers.

E2-17A   Classify costs along the value chain for a retailer *(Learning Objective 2)*

Suppose Radio Shack incurred the following costs at its Charleston, South Carolina, store:

Research on whether store should sell satellite radio service	$ 400	Payment to consultant for advice on location of new store	$2,500
Purchases of merchandise	30,000	Freight-in	3,000
Rearranging store layout	750	Salespeople's salaries	4,000
Newspaper advertisements	5,000	Customer complaint department	800
Depreciation expense on delivery trucks	1,000		

Requirements

1. Use the following format to classify each cost according to its place in the value chain.

R&D	Design	Purchases	Marketing	Distribution	Customer Service

2. Compute the total costs for each value chain category.

3. How much are the total inventoriable product costs?

E2-18A   Classify costs along the value chain for a manufacturer *(Learning Objectives 2 & 3)*

Suppose the cell phone manufacturer Samsung Electronics provides the following information for its costs last month (in hundreds of thousands):

Salaries of telephone salespeople	$ 5	Transmitters	$61
Depreciation on plant and equipment	65	Rearrange production process to accommodate new robot	2
Exterior case for phone	6	Assembly-line workers' wages	10
Salaries of scientists who developed new model	12	Technical customer support hotline	3
Delivery expense to customers via UPS	7	1-800 (toll-free) line for customer orders	1

Requirements

1. Use the following format to classify each cost according to its place in the value chain. (*Hint:* You should have at least one cost in each value chain function.)

		Production					
R&D	Design of Products or Processes	Direct Materials	Direct Labor	Manufacturing Overhead	Marketing	Distribution	Customer Service

2. Compute the total costs for each value chain category.

3. How much are the total inventoriable product costs?

4. How much are the total prime costs?

5. How much are the total conversion costs?

E2-19A Classify costs as direct or indirect *(Learning Objective 3)*

Classify each of the following costs as a *direct cost* or an *indirect cost* assuming the cost object is the Produce Department (fruits and vegetables) of a local grocery store.

a. Produce manager's salary

b. Cost of the produce

c. Store utilities

d. Bags and twist ties provided to customers in the Produce Department for packaging fruits and vegetables

e. Depreciation expense on refrigerated produce display shelves

f. Cost of shopping carts and baskets

g. Wages of checkout clerks

h. Cost of grocery store's advertisement flyer placed in the weekly newspaper

i. Store manager's salary

j. Cost of equipment used to peel and core pineapples at the store

k. Free grocery delivery service provided to senior citizens

l. Depreciation on self-checkout machines

E2-20A Define cost terms *(Learning Objectives 3 & 4)*

Complete the following statements with one of the terms listed here. You may use a term more than once, and some terms may not be used at all.

Prime costs	Cost objects	Inventoriable product costs
Assigned	Direct costs	Fringe benefits
Period costs	Assets	Cost of goods sold
Indirect costs	Conversion costs	Total costs

a. _____ can be traced to cost objects.

b. _____ are expensed when incurred.

c. _____ are the combination of direct materials and direct labor.

d. Compensation includes wages, salaries, and _____.

e. _____ are treated as _____ until sold.

f. _____ include costs from only the production or purchases element of the value chain.

g. _____ are allocated to cost objects.

h. Both direct and indirect costs are _____ to _____.

i. _____ include costs from every element of the value chain.

j. _____ are the combination of direct labor and manufacturing overhead.

k. _____ are expensed as _____ when sold.

l. Manufacturing overhead includes all _____ of production.

E2-21A   Classify and calculate a manufacturer's costs (Learning Objectives 3 & 4)

An airline manufacturer incurred the following costs last month (in thousands of dollars):

a. Airplane seats	$ 250
b. Depreciation on administrative offices	60
c. Assembly workers' wages	600
d. Plant utilities	120
e. Production supervisors' salaries	100
f. Jet engines	1,000
g. Machine lubricants	15
h. Depreciation on forklifts	50
i. Property tax on corporate marketing office	25
j. Cost of warranty repairs	225
k. Factory janitors' wages	30
l. Cost of designing new plant layout	175
m. Machine operators' health insurance	40
TOTAL	$2,690

Requirements

1. If the cost object is an airplane, classify each cost as one of the following: direct material (DM), direct labor (DL), indirect labor (IL), indirect materials (IM), other manufacturing overhead (other MOH), or period cost. (*Hint:* Set up a column for each type of cost.) What is the total for each type of cost?

2. Calculate total manufacturing overhead costs.

3. Calculate total inventoriable product costs.

4. Calculate total prime costs.

5. Calculate total conversion costs.

6. Calculate total period costs.

E2-22A   Prepare the current assets section of the balance sheet (Learning Objective 5)

Consider the following selected amounts and account balances of Lords:

Cost of goods sold	$104,000	Prepaid expenses	$ 6,000
Direct labor	47,000	Marketing expense	30,000
Direct materials used	20,000	Work in process inventory	40,000
Accounts receivable	80,000	Manufacturing overhead	26,000
Cash	15,000	Finished goods inventory	63,000
Cost of goods manufactured	94,000	Raw materials inventory	10,000

Requirement

1. Show how this company reports current assets on the balance sheet. Not all data are used. Is this company a service company, a merchandiser, or a manufacturer? How do you know?

E2-23A   Prepare a retailer's income statement (Learning Objective 5)

Robbie Roberts is the sole proprietor of Precious Pets, an e-tail business specializing in the sale of high-end pet gifts and accessories. Precious Pets' sales totaled $987,000 during the most recent year. During the year, the company spent $56,000 on expenses relating to Web site maintenance; $22,000 on marketing; and $25,000 on wrapping, boxing, and shipping the goods to customers. Precious Pets also spent $642,000 on inventory purchases and an additional $21,000 on freight-in charges. The company started the year with $17,000 of inventory on hand and ended the year with $15,000 of inventory. Prepare Precious Pets' income statement for the most recent year.

E2-24A Compute direct materials used and cost of goods manufactured (Learning Objective 5)

Danielle's Die-Cuts is preparing its Cost of Goods Manufactured Schedule at year-end. Danielle's accounting records show the following: The Raw Materials Inventory account had a beginning balance of $13,000 and an ending balance of $17,000. During the year, Danielle purchased $58,000 of direct materials. Direct labor for the year totaled $123,000, while manufacturing overhead amounted to $152,000. The Work in Process Inventory account had a beginning balance of $21,000 and an ending balance of $15,000. Compute the Cost of Goods Manufactured for the year. (*Hint:* The first step is to calculate the direct materials used during the year. Model your answer after Exhibit 2-15.)

E2-25A Compute cost of goods manufactured and cost of goods sold (Learning Objective 5)

Compute the cost of goods manufactured and cost of goods sold for Strike Marine Company for the most recent year using the amounts described below. Assume that raw materials inventory contains only direct materials.

	Beginning of Year	End of Year		End of Year
Raw materials inventory	$25,000	$28,000	Insurance on plant	$ 9,000
Work in process inventory	50,000	35,000	Depreciation—plant building and equipment	13,000
Finished goods inventory	18,000	25,000	Repairs and maintenance—plant	4,000
Purchases of direct materials		78,000	Marketing expenses	77,000
Direct labor		82,000	General and administrative expenses	29,000
Indirect labor		15,000		

E2-26A Continues E2-25A: Prepare income statement (Learning Objective 5)

Prepare the income statement for Strike Marine Company in E2-25A for the most recent year. Assume that the company sold 32,000 units of its product at a price of $12 each during the year.

E2-27A Work backwards to find missing amounts (Learning Objective 5)

Smooth Sounds manufactures and sells a new line of MP3 players. Unfortunately, Smooth Sounds suffered serious fire damage at its home office. As a result, the accounting records for October were partially destroyed—and completely jumbled. Smooth Sounds has hired you to help figure out the missing pieces of the accounting puzzle. Assume that Smooth Sounds' raw materials inventory contains only direct materials.

Work in process inventory, October 31	$ 1,500
Finished goods inventory, October 1	4,300
Direct labor in October	3,000
Purchases of direct materials in October	9,000
Work in process inventory, October 1	0
Revenues in October	27,000
Gross profit in October	12,000
Direct materials used in October	8,000
Raw materials inventory, October 31	3,000
Manufacturing overhead in October	6,300

Requirement

1. Find the following amounts:
   a. Cost of goods sold in October
   b. Beginning raw materials inventory
   c. Ending finished goods inventory
   (*Hint:* You may find Exhibits 2-15 and 2-16 helpful.)

E2-28A Determine whether information is relevant *(Learning Objective 6)*

Classify each of the following costs as relevant or irrelevant to the decision at hand and briefly explain your reason.

a. Cost of operating automated production machinery versus the cost of direct labor when deciding whether to automate production
b. Cost of computers purchased six months ago when deciding whether to upgrade to computers with a faster processing speed
c. Cost of purchasing packaging materials from an outside vendor when deciding whether to continue manufacturing the packaging materials in-house
d. The property tax rates in different locales when deciding where to locate the company's headquarters
e. The type of gas (regular or premium) used by delivery vans when deciding which make and model of van to purchase for the company's delivery van fleet
f. Depreciation expense on old manufacturing equipment when deciding whether to replace it with newer equipment
g. The fair market value of old manufacturing equipment when deciding whether to replace it with new equipment
h. The interest rate paid on invested funds when deciding how much inventory to keep on hand
i. The cost of land purchased three years ago when deciding whether to build on the land now or wait two more years
j. The total amount of the restaurant's fixed costs when deciding whether to add additional items to the menu

E2-29A Describe other cost terms *(Learning Objectives 6 & 7)*

Complete the following statements with one of the terms listed here. You may use a term more than once, and some terms may not be used at all.

Differential costs	Irrelevant costs	Controllable costs
Marginal costs	Fixed costs	Average cost
Uncontrollable costs	Sunk costs	Variable costs

a. Managers cannot influence _____ in the short run.
b. Total _____ decrease when production volume decreases.
c. For decision-making purposes, costs that do not differ between alternatives are _____.
d. Costs that have already been incurred are called _____.
e. Total _____ stay constant over a wide range of production volumes.
f. The _____ is the difference in cost between two alternative courses of action.
g. The product's _____ is the cost of making one more unit.
h. A product's _____ and _____, not the product's _____, should be used to forecast total costs at different production volumes.

E2-30A Classify costs as fixed or variable *(Learning Objective 7)*

Classify each of the following costs as fixed or variable:
a. Thread used by a garment manufacturer
b. Property tax on a manufacturing facility
c. Yearly salaries paid to sales staff
d. Gasoline used to operate delivery vans
e. Annual contract for pest (insect) control
f. Boxes used to package breakfast cereal at Kellogg's

g. Straight-line depreciation on production equipment

h. Cell phone bills for sales staff—contract billed at $.03 cents per minute

i. Wages paid to hourly assembly-line workers in the manufacturing plant

j. Monthly lease payment on administrative headquarters

k. Commissions paid to the sales staff—5% of sales revenue

l. Credit card transaction fee paid by retailer—$0.20 per transaction plus 2% of the sales amount

m. Annual business license fee from city

n. Cost of ice cream sold at Baskin-Robbins

o. Cost of shampoo used at a hair salon

E2-31A Compute total and average costs (*Learning Objective 7*)

Fizzy-Cola spends $1 on direct materials, direct labor, and variable manufacturing overhead for every unit (12-pack of soda) it produces. Fixed manufacturing overhead costs $5 million per year. The plant, which is currently operating at only 75% of capacity, produced 20 million units this year. Management plans to operate closer to full capacity next year, producing 25 million units. Management doesn't anticipate any changes in the prices it pays for materials, labor, and manufacturing overhead.

Requirements

1. What is the current total product cost (for the 20 million units), including fixed and variable costs?

2. What is the current average product cost per unit?

3. What is the current fixed cost per unit?

4. What is the forecasted total product cost next year (for the 25 million units)?

5. What is the forecasted average product cost next year?

6. What is the forecasted fixed cost per unit?

7. Why does the average product cost decrease as production increases?

Exercises—Group B

E2-32B Identify types of companies and their inventories (*Learning Objective 1*)

Complete the following statements with one of the terms listed here. You may use a term more than once, and some terms may not be used at all.

Wholesalers	Work in process inventory	Service companies
Manufacturing companies	Raw materials inventory	Merchandising companies
Finished goods inventory	Inventory (merchandise)	

a. _____ do not sell tangible products.

b. _____ buy in bulk from manufacturers and sell to retailers.

c. _____ produce their own inventory.

d. _____ typically have only one category of inventory.

e. Keller, a company based in Montana, builds bicycles. Partially completed bikes are _____. Completed bikes that remain unsold in the warehouse are _____ . Aluminum and plastic are _____.

f. _____ sell merchandise to consumers.

g. _____ transform raw materials into new finished products using their workforce and equipment.

h. _____ resell products they previously purchased ready-made from suppliers.

i. For Sony, blank compact discs, CD cases, and unprinted case liners are classified as _____ .

E2-33B Classify costs along the value chain for a retailer (*Learning Objective 2*)

Suppose Accessory Shack incurred the following costs at its Buffalo, New York, store.

Research on whether store should sell satellite radio service	$ 500	Payment to consultant for advice on location of new store........................	$2,200
Purchases of merchandise............................	32,000	Freight-in	3,600
Rearranging store layout............................	800	Salespeople's salaries............................	4,500
Newspaper advertisements.........................	5,800	Customer complaint department............	900
Depreciation expense on delivery trucks............	1,900		

Requirements

1. Classify each cost according to its place in the value chain.

R&D	Design	Purchases	Marketing	Distribution	Customer Service

2. Compute the total costs for each value chain category.

3. How much are the total inventoriable product costs?

E2-34B Classify costs along the value chain for a manufacturer (*Learning Objectives 2 & 3*)

Suppose the cell phone manufacturer Plum Electronics provides the following information for its costs last month (in hundreds of thousands):

Salaries of telephone salespeople	$ 4	Transmitters..	$58
Depreciation on plant and equipment	55	Rearrange production process to accommodate new robot..................	1
Exterior case for phone	8	Assembly-line workers' wages....................	9
Salaries of scientists who developed new model.........	11	Technical customer-support hotline	3
Delivery expense to customers via UPS................	5	1-800 (toll-free) line for customer orders....	2

Requirements

1. Classify each of these costs according to its place in the value chain. (*Hint:* You should have at least one cost in each value chain function.)

		Production					
R&D	Design of Products or Processes	Direct Materials	Direct Labor	Manufacturing Overhead	Marketing	Distribution	Customer Service

2. Compute the total costs for each value chain category.

3. How much are the total inventoriable product costs?

4. How much are the total prime costs?

5. How much are the total conversion costs?

E2-35B Classify costs as direct or indirect (*Learning Objective 3*)

Classify each of the following costs as a *direct cost* or an *indirect cost* assuming the cost object is the Garden Department of a local hardware store.
a. Garden manager's salary
b. Cost of shopping carts and baskets
c. Wages of checkout clerks
d. Cost of the merchandise

e. Depreciation expense on demonstration water feature

f. Cost of hardware store's advertisement flyer placed in the weekly newspaper

g. Depreciation on self-checkout machines

h. Bags provided to garden customers for packaging small items

i. Store manager's salary

j. Free garden delivery service provided to senior citizens

k. Cost of equipment used to plant and water plants at the store

l. Store utilities

E2-36B Define cost terms (Learning Objectives 3 & 4)

Complete the following statements with one of the terms listed here. You may use a term more than once, and some terms may not be used at all.

Assigned	Indirect costs	Cost objects
Assets	Fringe benefits	Total costs
Cost of goods sold	Direct costs	Prime costs
Period costs	Inventoriable product costs	Conversion costs

a. _____ include costs from only the production or purchases element of the value chain.

b. _____ are allocated to cost objects.

c. The combination of direct materials and direct labor is _____.

d. The combination of direct labor and manufacturing overhead is _____.

e. Both direct and indirect costs are _____ to _____.

f. All _____ of production are included in manufacturing overhead.

g. _____ are expensed when incurred.

h. Wages, salaries, and _____ are considered compensation.

i. _____ include costs from every element of the value chain.

j. _____ can be traced to cost objects.

k. Until sold, _____ are treated as _____.

l. _____ are expensed as _____ when sold.

E2-37B Classify and calculate a manufacturer's costs (Learning Objectives 3 & 4)

An airline manufacturer incurred the following costs last month (in thousands of dollars).

a.	Airplane seats	$ 270
b.	Depreciation on administrative offices	70
c.	Assembly workers' wages	690
d.	Plant utilities	140
e.	Production supervisors' salaries	150
f.	Jet engines	1,200
g.	Machine lubricants	35
h.	Depreciation on forklifts	90
i.	Property tax on corporate marketing offices	15
j.	Cost of warranty repairs	215
k.	Factory janitors' wages	40
l.	Cost of designing new plant layout	180
m.	Machine operators' health insurance	60
	TOTAL	$3,155

Requirements

1. If the cost object is an airplane, classify each cost as one of the following: direct material (DM), direct labor (DL), indirect labor (IL), indirect materials (IM), other manufacturing overhead (other MOH), or period cost. What is the total for each type of cost?

2. Calculate total manufacturing overhead costs.

3. Calculate total inventoriable product costs.

4. Calculate total prime costs.

5. Calculate total conversion costs.

6. Calculate total period costs.

E2-38B Prepare the current assets section of the balance sheet *(Learning Objective 5)*

Consider the following selected amounts and account balances of Esquires:

Cost of goods sold	$107,000		Prepaid expenses	$ 5,600
Direct labor	45,000		Marketing expense	28,000
Direct materials used	20,100		Work in process inventory	38,000
Accounts receivable	79,000		Manufacturing overhead	22,000
Cash	14,900		Finished goods inventory	63,000
Cost of goods manufactured	92,000		Raw materials inventory	10,400

Requirement

1. Show how Esquires reports current assets on the balance sheet. Not all data are used. Is Esquires a service merchandiser, or a manufacturer? How do you know?

E2-39B Prepare a retailer's income statement *(Learning Objective 5)*

Mike Leaver is the sole proprietor of Prestigious Pets, an e-tail business specializing in the sale of high-end pet gifts and accessories. Prestigious Pets' sales totaled $1,060,000 during the most recent year. During the year, the company spent $53,000 on expenses relating to Web site maintenance, $33,000 on marketing, and $28,500 on wrapping, boxing, and shipping the goods to customers. Prestigious Pets also spent $643,000 on inventory purchases and an additional $20,500 on freight-in charges. The company started the year with $15,500 of inventory on hand, and ended the year with $12,800 of inventory. Prepare Prestigious Pets' income statement for the most recent year.

E2-40B Compute direct materials used and cost of goods manufactured *(Learning Objective 5)*

Lawrence's Die-Cuts is preparing its Cost of Goods Manufactured Schedule at year end. Lawrence's accounting records show the following: The Raw Materials Inventory account had a beginning balance of $18,000 and an ending balance of $14,000. During the year, Lawrence purchased $66,000 of direct materials. Direct labor for the year totaled $135,000 while manufacturing overhead amounted to $155,000. The Work in Process Inventory account had a beginning balance of $27,000 and an ending balance of $21,000. Compute the Cost of Goods Manufactured for the year. (*Hint:* The first step is to calculate the direct materials used during the year.)

E2-41B Compute cost of goods manufactured and cost of goods sold *(Learning Objective 5)*

Compute the cost of goods manufactured and cost of goods sold for South Marine Company for the most recent year using the amounts described next. Assume that raw materials inventory contains only direct materials.

	Beginning of Year	End of Year		End of Year
Raw materials inventory	$28,000	$30,000	Insurance on plant.....................................	$10,500
Work in process inventory	44,000	37,000	Depreciation—plant building	
Finished goods inventory............	13,000	29,000	and equipment..................................	13,400
Purchases of direct materials.........		76,000	Repairs and maintenance—plant.............	4,300
Direct labor...............................		81,000	Marketing expenses..................................	78,000
Indirect labor		41,000	General and administrative expenses..........	26,500

E2-42B   Continues E2-41B: Prepare income statement (Learning Objective 5)

Prepare the income statement for South Marine Company for the most recent year. Assume that the company sold 37,000 units of its product at a price of $14 each during the year.

E2-43B   Work backwards to find missing amounts (Learning Objective 5)

Great Sounds manufactures and sells a new line of radio players. Unfortunately, Great Sounds suffered serious fire damage at its home office. As a result, the accounting records for October were partially destroyed and completely jumbled. Great Sounds has hired you to help figure out the missing pieces of the accounting puzzle. Assume that Great Sounds' raw materials inventory contains only direct materials.

Work in process inventory, October 31..	$ 1,800
Finished goods inventory, October 1..	4,700
Direct labor in October..	3,900
Purchases of direct materials in October	9,100
Work in process inventory, October 1..	0
Revenues in October	27,200
Gross profit in October...	12,100
Direct materials used in October...	8,500
Raw materials inventory, October 31..	3,600
Manufacturing overhead in October	6,000

Requirement

1. Find the following amounts:
   a. Cost of goods sold in October
   b. Beginning raw materials inventory
   c. Ending finished goods inventory

E2-44B   Determine whether information is relevant (Learning Objective 6)

Classify each of the following costs as relevant or irrelevant to the decision at hand and briefly explain your reason.
   a. Cost of barcode scanners purchased six months ago when deciding whether to upgrade to scanners that are faster and easier to use

b. The fair market value of an ice cream truck when deciding whether to replace it with a newer ice cream truck

c. Cost of operating automated production machinery versus the cost of direct labor when deciding whether to automate production

d. Cost of purchasing packaging materials from an outside vendor when deciding whether to continue manufacturing the packaging materials in-house

e. The cost of an expansion site purchased two years ago when deciding whether to sell the site or to expand business to it now

f. The property tax rates in different locales when deciding where to locate the company's headquarters

g. The interest rate paid on invested funds when deciding how much inventory to keep on hand

h. The gas mileage of delivery vans when deciding which make and model of van to purchase for the company's delivery van fleet

i. Depreciation expense on old manufacturing equipment when deciding whether to replace it with newer equipment

j. The total amount of a coffee shop's fixed costs when deciding whether or not to introduce a new drink line

E2-45B **Describe other cost terms** *(Learning Objectives 6 & 7)*

Complete the following statements with one of the terms listed here. You may use a term more than once, and some terms may not be used at all.

Variable costs	Sunk costs	Differential costs
Marginal costs	Uncontrollable costs	Average cost
Fixed costs	Irrelevant costs	Controllable costs

a. In the short run, managers cannot influence _____.

b. Costs that do not differ between alternatives are _____, for decision-making purposes.

c. Total _____ decrease when production volume decreases.

d. A product's _____ and _____, not the product's _____, should be used to forecast total costs at different production volumes.

e. Total _____ stay constant over a wide range of production volumes.

f. _____ are costs that have already been incurred.

g. The cost of making one more unit is the product's _____.

h. The difference in cost between two alternative courses of action is the _____.

E2-46B **Classify costs as fixed or variable** *(Learning Objective 7)*

Classify each of the following costs as fixed or variable:

a. Credit card transaction fee paid by retailer—$0.20 per transaction plus 2% of the sales amount

b. Yearly salaries paid to marketing staff

c. Gasoline used to drive company shuttle

d. Syrup used by an ice cream parlor

e. Property tax on an electronics factory

f. Annual contract for company landscaping

g. Boxes used to package computer components at Dell

h. Wages paid to hourly retail staff at the company store

i. Annual web hosting fee for company Web site

j. Cost of coffee sold at Starbucks

k. Monthly lease payment on branch office

l. Straight-line depreciation on production equipment

m. Rental car fees for company business travelers—contract billed at $0.25 per mile

n. Commissions paid to the sales staff—7% of sales revenue

o. Cost of paint used at an auto body shop

E2-47B   Compute total and average costs (Learning Objective 7)

Grand Cola spends $1 on direct materials, direct labor, and variable manufacturing overhead for every unit (12-pack of soda) it produces. Fixed manufacturing overhead costs $6 million per year. The plant, which is currently operating at only 85% of capacity, produced 15 million units this year. Management plans to operate closer to full capacity next year, producing 20 million units. Management doesn't anticipate any changes in the prices it pays for materials, labor, or manufacturing overhead.

Requirements

1. What is the current total product cost (for the 15 million units), including fixed and variable costs?

2. What is the current average product cost per unit?

3. What is the current fixed cost per unit?

4. What is the forecasted total product cost next year (for the 20 million units)?

5. What is the forecasted average product cost next year?

6. What is the forecasted fixed cost per unit?

7. Why does the average product cost decrease as production increases?

Problems—Group A

P2-48A   Classify costs along the value chain (Learning Objectives 2 & 4)

ShaZam Cola produces a lemon-lime soda. The production process starts with workers mixing the lemon syrup and lime flavors in a secret recipe. The company enhances the combined syrup with caffeine. Finally, ShaZam dilutes the mixture with carbonated water. ShaZam Cola incurs the following costs (in thousands):

Plant utilities	$ 750
Depreciation on plant and equipment	3,000
Payment for new recipe	1,000
Salt	25
Replace products with expired dates upon customer complaint	50
Rearranging plant layout	1,100
Lemon syrup	18,000
Lime flavoring	1,000
Production costs of "cents-off" store coupons for customers	600
Delivery truck drivers' wages	250
Bottles	1,300
Sales commissions	400
Plant janitors' wages	1,000
Wages of workers who mix syrup	8,000
Customer hotline	200
Depreciation on delivery trucks	150
Freight-in on materials	1,500
Total	$38,325

Requirements

1. Use the following format to classify each of these costs according to its place in the value chain. (*Hint:* You should have at least one cost in each value chain function.)

	Design of Products or Processes	Production			Marketing	Distribution	Customer Service
R&D		Direct Materials	Direct Labor	Manufacturing Overhead			

2. Compute the total costs for each value chain category.

3. How much are the total inventoriable product costs?

4. Suppose the managers of the R&D and design functions receive year-end bonuses based on meeting their unit's target cost reductions. What are they likely to do? How might this affect costs incurred in other elements of the value chain?

P2-49A   Prepare income statements *(Learning Objective 5)*

Part One: In 2009, Hannah Summit opened Hannah's Pets, a small retail shop selling pet supplies. On December 31, 2009, her accounting records show the following:

Inventory on December 31, 2009	$10,250
Inventory on January 1, 2009	15,000
Sales revenue	54,000
Utilities for shop	2,450
Rent for shop	4,000
Sales commissions	2,300
Purchases of merchandise	27,000

Requirement

1. Prepare an income statement for Hannah's Pets, a merchandiser, for the year ended December 31, 2009.

Part Two: Hannah's Pets was so successful that Hannah decided to manufacture her own brand of pet toys—Best Friends Manufacturing. At the end of December 2010, her accounting records show the following:

Work in process inventory, December 31, 2010	$ 720
Finished goods inventory, December 31, 2009	0
Finished goods inventory, December 31, 2010	5,700
Sales revenue	105,000
Customer service hotline expense	1,000
Utilities for plant	4,600
Delivery expense	1,500
Sales salaries expense	5,000
Plant janitorial services	1,250
Direct labor	18,300
Direct material purchases	31,000
Rent on manufacturing plant	9,000
Raw materials inventory, December 31, 2009	13,500
Raw materials inventory, December 31, 2010	9,275
Work in process inventory, December 31, 2009	0

Requirements

1. Prepare a schedule of cost of goods manufactured for Best Friends Manufacturing for the year ended December 31, 2010.

2. Prepare an income statement for Best Friends Manufacturing for the year ended December 31, 2010.

3. How does the format of the income statement for Best Friends Manufacturing differ from the income statement of Hannah's Pets?

Part Three: Show the ending inventories that would appear on these balance sheets:

1. Hannah's Pets at December 31, 2009

2. Best Friends Manufacturing at December 31, 2010

P2-50A   Fill in missing amounts *(Learning Objective 5)*

Certain item descriptions and amounts are missing from the monthly schedule of cost of goods manufactured below and the income statement of Tretinik Manufacturing. Fill in the missing items.

TRETINIK MANUFACTURING COMPANY

_____ June 30

Beginning _____			$ 21,000
Add: Direct _____:			
Beginning raw materials inventory	$ X		
Purchases of direct materials	51,000		
_____	78,000		
Ending raw materials inventory	(23,000)		
Direct _____		$ X	
Direct _____		X	
Manufacturing overhead		40,000	
Total _____ costs _____			166,000
Total _____ costs			X
Less: Ending _____			(25,000)
_____			$ X

TRETINIK MANUFACTURING COMPANY

_____ June 30

Sales revenue		$ X
Cost of goods sold:		
Beginning _____	$115,000	
_____	X	
Cost of goods _____	X	
Ending _____	X	
Cost of goods sold		209,000
Gross profit		254,000
_____ expenses:		
Marketing expense	99,000	
Administrative expense	X	154,000
_____ income		$ X

P2-51A   Identify relevant information *(Learning Objective 6)*

You receive two job offers in the same big city. The first job is close to your parents' house, and they have offered to let you live at home for a year so you won't have to incur expenses for housing, food, or cable TV. This job pays $30,000 per year. The second job is far from your parents' house, so you'll have to rent an apartment with parking ($6,000 per year), buy your own food ($2,400 per year), and pay for your own cable TV ($600 per year). This job pays $35,000 per year. You still plan to do laundry at your parents' house once a week if you live in the city, and you plan to go into the city once a week to visit with friends if you live at home. Thus, the cost of operating your car will be about the same either way. In addition, your parents refuse to pay for your cell phone service ($720 per year), and you can't function without it.

Requirements

1. Based on this information alone, what is the net difference between the two alternatives (salary, net of relevant costs)?

2. What information is irrelevant? Why?

3. What qualitative information is relevant to your decision?

4. Assume that you really want to take Job #2, but you also want to live at home to cut costs. What new quantitative and qualitative information will you need to incorporate into your decision?

P2-52A   Calculate the total and average costs (Learning Objective 7)

The owner of Pizza-House Restaurant is disappointed because the restaurant has been averaging 3,000 pizza sales per month, but the restaurant and wait staff can make and serve 5,000 pizzas per month. The variable cost (for example, ingredients) of each pizza is $2.00. Monthly fixed costs (for example, depreciation, property taxes, business license, and manager's salary) are $6,000 per month. The owner wants cost information about different volumes so that he can make some operating decisions.

Requirements

1. Fill in the following chart to provide the owner with the cost information he wants. Then use the completed chart to help you answer the remaining questions.

Monthly pizza volume	2,500	3,000	5,000
Total fixed costs	$	$	$
Total variable costs			
Total costs			
Fixed cost per pizza	$	$	$
Variable cost per pizza			
Average cost per pizza			
Sales price per pizza	$10.00	$10.00	$10.00
Average profit per pizza			

2. From a cost standpoint, why do companies such as Pizza-House Restaurant want to operate near or at full capacity?

3. The owner has been considering ways to increase the sales volume. He believes he could sell 5,000 pizzas a month by cutting the sales price from $10 a pizza to $9.50. How much extra profit (above the current level) would he generate if he decreased the sales price? (Hint: Find the restaurant's current monthly profit and compare it to the restaurant's projected monthly profit at the new sales price and volume.)

Problems—Group B

P2-53B Classify costs along the value chain (*Learning Objectives 2 & 4*)

Best Value Cola produces a lemon-lime soda. The production process starts with workers mixing the lemon syrup and lime flavors in a secret recipe. The company enhances the combined syrup with caffeine. Finally, Best Value dilutes the mixture with carbonated water. Best Value Cola incurs the following costs (in thousands):

Plant utilities	$ 750
Depreciation on plant and equipment	2,800
Payment for new recipe	1,040
Salt	25
Replace products with expired dates upon customer complaint	45
Rearranging plant layout	1,400
Lemon syrup	17,000
Lime flavoring	1,120
Production costs of "cents-off" store coupons for customers	470
Delivery truck drivers' wages	285
Bottles	1,310
Sales commissions	400
Plant janitors' wages	1,050
Wages of workers who mix syrup	8,000
Customer hotline	190
Depreciation on delivery trucks	200
Freight-in on materials	1,300
Total	$37,385

Requirements

1. Classify each of these costs according to its place in the value chain. (*Hint:* You should have at least one cost in each value chain function.)

	Design of Products or	Production					
R&D	Processes	Direct Materials	Direct Labor	Manufacturing Overhead	Marketing	Distribution	Customer Service

2. Compute the total costs for each value chain category.

3. How much are the total inventoriable product costs?

4. Suppose the managers of the R&D and design functions receive year-end bonuses based on meeting their unit's target cost reductions. What are they likely to do? How might this affect costs incurred in other elements of the value chain?

P2-54B Prepare income statements *(Learning Objective 5)*

Part One: In 2009, Lindsey Conway opened Lindsey's Pets, a small retail shop selling pet supplies. On December 31, 2009, her accounting records show the following:

Inventory on December 31, 2009	$ 9,400
Inventory on January 1, 2009	12,200
Sales revenue	55,000
Utilities for shop	1,500
Rent for shop	3,400
Sales commissions	4,100
Purchases of merchandise	34,500

Requirement

1. Prepare an income statement for Lindsey's Pets, a merchandiser, for the year ended December 31, 2009.

Part Two: Lindsey's Pets succeeded so well that Lindsey decided to manufacture her own brand of pet toys—Best Friends Manufacturing. At the end of December 2010, her accounting records show the following:

Work in process inventory, December 31, 2010	$ 4,000
Finished goods inventory, December 31, 2009	0
Finished goods inventory, December 31, 2010	3,000
Sales revenue	103,000
Customer service hotline expense	1,400
Utilities for plant	4,500
Delivery expense	2,500
Sales salaries expense	4,200
Plant janitorial services	1,150
Direct labor	20,000
Direct material purchases	39,000
Rent on manufacturing plant	8,400
Raw materials inventory, December 31, 2009	10,000
Raw materials inventory, December 31, 2010	8,000
Work in process inventory, December 31, 2009	0

Requirements

1. Prepare a schedule of cost of goods manufactured for Best Friends Manufacturing for the year ended December 31, 2010.

2. Prepare an income statement for Best Friends Manufacturing for the year ended December 31, 2010.

3. How does the format of the income statement for Best Friends Manufacturing differ from the income statement of Lindsey's Pets?

Part Three: Show the ending inventories that would appear on these balance sheets:

1. Lindsey's Pets at December 31, 2009.

2. Best Friends Manufacturing at December 31, 2010.

P2-55B   Fill in missing amounts *(Learning Objective 5)*

Certain item descriptions and amounts are missing from the monthly schedule of cost of goods manufactured and income statement of Chili Manufacturing Company. Fill in the missing items.

Chili Manufacturing Company

_____ June 30

Beginning _____			$ 27,000
Add: Direct _____:			
Beginning raw materials inventory	$ X		
Purchases of direct materials	56,000		
_____	80,000		
Ending raw materials inventory	(28,000)		
Direct _____		$ X	
Direct _____		X	
Manufacturing overhead		43,000	
Total _____ costs _____			$174,000
Total _____ costs _____			X
Less: Ending _____			(21,000)
_____			$ X

Chili Manufacturing Company

_____ June 30

Sales revenue		$ X
Cost of goods sold:		
Beginning _____	$114,000	
_____	X	
Cost of goods _____	X	
Ending _____	X	
Cost of goods sold		228,000
Gross profit		242,000
_____ expenses:		
Marketing expense	98,000	
Administrative expense	X	166,000
_____ income		$ X

P2-56B   Identify relevant information *(Learning Objective 6)*

You receive two job offers in the same big city. The first job is close to your parents' house, and they have offered to let you live at home for a year so you won't have to incur expenses for housing, food, or cable TV. This job pays $49,000 per year. The second job is far away from your parents' house, so you'll have to rent an apartment with parking ($9,000 per year), buy your own food ($3,500 per year), and pay for your own cable TV ($550 per year). This job pays $54,000 per year. You still plan to do laundry at your parents' house once a week if you live in the city and plan to go into the city once a week to visit with friends if you live at home. Thus, the cost of operating your car will be about the same either way. Additionally, your parents refuse to pay for your cell phone service ($690 per year), and you can't function without it.

Requirements

1. Based on this information alone, what is the net difference between the two alternatives (salary, net of relevant costs)?

2. What information is irrelevant? Why?

3. What qualitative information is relevant to your decision?

4. Assume you really want to take Job #2, but you also want to live at home to cut costs. What new quantitative and qualitative information will you need to incorporate in your decision?

P2-57B Calculate the total and average costs (Learning Objective 7)

The owner of Brooklyn Restaurant is disappointed because the restaurant has been averaging 5,000 pizza sales per month but the restaurant and wait staff can make and serve 10,000 pizzas per month. The variable cost (for example, ingredients) of each pizza is $1.20. Monthly fixed costs (for example, depreciation, property taxes, business license, manager's salary) are $5,000 per month. The owner wants cost information about different volumes so that he can make some operating decisions.

Requirements

1. Fill in the chart to provide the owner with the cost information he wants. Then use the completed chart to help you answer the remaining questions.

Monthly pizza volume	2,500	5,000	10,000
Total fixed costs			
Total variable costs			
Total costs			
Fixed cost per pizza			
Variable cost per pizza			
Average cost per pizza			
Sales price per pizza	$ 5.50	$ 5.50	$ 5.50
Average profit per pizza			

2. From a cost standpoint, why do companies such as Brooklyn Restaurant want to operate near or at full capacity?

3. The owner has been considering ways to increase the sales volume. He believes he could sell 10,000 pizzas a month by cutting the sales price from $5.50 a pizza to $5.00. How much extra profit (above the current level) would he generate if he decreased the sales price? (*Hint:* Find the restaurant's current monthly profit and compare it to the restaurant's projected monthly profit at the new sales price and volume.)

APPLY YOUR KNOWLEDGE

Decision Case

C2-58 Determine ending inventory balances (Learning Objective 5)

PowerBox designs and manufactures switches used in telecommunications. Serious flooding throughout North Carolina affected PowerBox's facilities. Inventory was completely ruined, and the company's computer system, including all accounting records, was destroyed.

Before the disaster recovery specialists clean the buildings, Annette Plum, the company controller, is anxious to salvage whatever records she can to support an insurance claim for the destroyed inventory. She is standing in what is left of the Accounting Department with Paul Lopez, the cost accountant.

"I didn't know mud could smell so bad," Paul says. "What should I be looking for?"

"Don't worry about beginning inventory numbers," responds Annette. "We'll get them from last year's annual report. We need first-quarter cost data."

"I was working on the first-quarter results just before the storm hit," Paul says. "Look, my report's still in my desk drawer. But all I can make out is that for the first quarter, material purchases were $476,000 and that direct labor, manufacturing overhead (other than indirect materials), and total manufacturing costs to account for were $505,000, $245,000, and $1,425,000, respectively. Wait, and cost of goods available for sale was $1,340,000."

"Great," says Annette. "I remember that sales for the period were approximately $1.7 million. Given our gross profit of 30%, that's all you should need."

Paul is not sure about that, but decides to see what he can do with this information. The beginning inventory numbers are as follows:

- Raw materials, $113,000
- Work in process, $229,000
- Finished goods, $154,000

He remembers a schedule he learned in college that may help him get started.

Requirements

1. Exhibit 2-16 resembles the schedule Paul has in mind. Use it to determine the ending inventories of raw materials, work in process, and finished goods.

2. Draft an insurance claim letter for the controller, seeking reimbursement for the flood damage to inventory. PowerBox's insurance representative is Gary Streer, at Industrial Insurance, 1122 Main Street, Hartford, CT 06268. The policy number is #3454340-23. PowerBox's address is 5 Research Triangle Way, Raleigh, NC 27698.

Discussion & Analysis

1. Briefly describe a service company, a merchandising company, and a manufacturing company. Give an example of each type of company, but do not use the same examples as given in the chapter.

2. How do service, merchandising, and manufacturing companies differ from each other? How are service, merchandising, and manufacturing companies similar to each other? List as many similarities and differences as you can identify.

3. What is the value chain? What are the six types of business activities found in the value chain? Which type(s) of business activities in the value chain generate costs that go directly to the income statement once incurred? What type(s) of business activities in the value chain generate costs that flow into inventory on the balance sheet?

4. Compare direct costs to indirect costs. Give an example of a cost at a company that could be a direct cost at one level of the organization but would be considered an indirect cost at a different level of that organization. Explain why this same cost could be both direct and indirect (at different levels).

5. What is meant by the term "inventoriable product costs"? What is meant by the term "period costs"? Why does it matter whether a cost is an inventoriable product cost or a period cost?

6. Compare inventoriable product costs to period costs. Using a product of your choice, give examples of inventoriable product costs and period costs. Explain why you categorized your costs as you did.

7. Describe how the income statement of a merchandising company differs from the income statement of a manufacturing company. Also comment on how the income statement from a merchandising company is similar to the income statement of a manufacturing company.

8. How are the cost of goods manufactured, the cost of goods sold, the income statement, and the balance sheet related for a manufacturing company? What specific items flow from one statement or schedule to the next? Describe the flow of costs between the cost of goods manufactured, the cost of goods sold, the income statement, and the balance sheet for a manufacturing company.

9. What makes a cost relevant or irrelevant when making a decision? Suppose a company is evaluating whether to use its warehouse for storage of its own inventory or whether to rent it out to a local theater group for housing props. Describe what information might be relevant when making that decision.

10. Explain why "differential cost" and "variable cost" do *not* have the same meaning. Give an example of a situation in which there is a cost that is a differential cost but *not* a variable cost.

Quick Check Answers
1. *b* 2. *b* 3. *a* 4. *b* 5. *c* 6. *b*
7. *b* 8. *d* 9. *b* 10. *c*

For online homework, exercises, and problems that provide you with immediate feedback, please visit www.myaccountinglab.com.

Application & Analysis

2-1 Costs in the Value Chain at a Real Company and Cost Objects

Choose a company with which you are familiar that manufactures a product. In this activity, you will be making reasonable assumptions about the activities involved in the value chain for this product; companies do not typically publish information about their value chain.

Basic Discussion Questions

1. Describe the product that is being produced and the company that produces it.

2. Describe the six value chain business activities that this product would pass through from its inception to its ultimate delivery to the customer.

3. List at least three costs that would be incurred in each of the six business activities in the value chain.

4. Classify each cost you identified in the value chain as either being an inventoriable product cost or a period cost. Explain your justification.

5. A cost object can be anything for which managers want a separate measurement of cost. List three different potential cost objects *other* than the product itself for the company you have selected.

6. List a direct cost and an indirect cost for each of the three different cost objects in #5. Explain why each cost would be direct or indirect.

Classroom Applications

Web: Post the discussion questions on an electronic discussion board. Have small groups of students choose a company that manufactures a product.

Classroom: Form groups of 3–4 students. Your group should choose a company that manufactures a product. Prepare a five minute presentation about your group's company and product which addresses the listed questions.

Independent: Research answers to each of the questions. Turn in a 2–3 page typed paper (12 point font, double-spaced with 1" margins).

For additional Application & Analysis projects and implementation tips, see the Instructor Resources in MyAccountingLab.com.

CMA-1. Roberta Johnson is the manager of Sleep-Well Inn, one of a chain of motels located throughout the U.S. An example of an operating cost at Sleep-Well that is both direct and fixed is

a. Johnson's salary.

b. water.

c. toilet tissue.

d. advertising for the Sleep-Well Inn chain.

CMA-2. The Profit and Loss Statement of Madengrad Mining, Inc., includes the following information for the current fiscal year.

Sales	$160,000
Gross profit	48,000
Year-end finished good inventory	58,300
Opening finished good inventory	60,190

The cost of goods manufactured by Madengrad for the current fiscal year is

a. $46,110.

b. $49,890.

c. $110,110.

d. $113,890.

CMA-3. The schedule of cost of goods manufactured of Gruber Fittings, Inc., shows the following balances for its fiscal year-end.

Direct manufacturing labor	$ 280,000
Manufacturing overhead	375,000
Ending work-in-process inventory	230,000
Raw materials used in production	450,000
Cost of goods manufactured	1,125,000

The value of the work-in-process inventory at the beginning of the fiscal year was

    a. $625,000.

    b. $250,000.

    c. $210,000.

    d. $20,000.

(CMA Adapted)

Life Fitness, a division of the Brunswick Corporation,

is currently the global leader in fitness equipment. The company's roots began in the 1970s with the introduction of the world's first-ever computerized exercise bike, the Lifecycle. Since then, the company has grown to design, manufacture, and market over 300 different cardio and strength-training products, including treadmills, elliptical cross-trainers, stair climbers, and of course, exercise bikes. While the company's growth has been propelled in part by consumers' ever-increasing zeal for personal fitness, the company has also grown through carefully analyzing the profit margins on each of its products, and adjusting its operations and pricing accordingly.

How does the company figure out the profit margins on each of its 300 different models? Life Fitness would first determine how much it costs to manufacture each type of exercise machine. Each batch of identical units produced (for example, 50 units of the X4 Elliptical Cross-Trainer) is called a "job." The company's job costing system traces the direct materials and direct labor used by each job. The company then allocates some manufacturing overhead to each job. By summing the direct materials, direct labor, and manufacturing overhead assigned to each job, the company can figure out how much it costs to make each cross-trainer in the job. The company could then use this cost information to make vital business decisions, such as the following:

- Setting selling prices that will lead to profits on each product
- Identifying opportunities to cut costs
- Determining which products are most profitable and therefore deserve the most marketing emphasis

Managers also need cost information on each exercise machine in order to prepare the company's financial statements. The cost is used to determine the following:

- The cost of goods sold for the income statement
- The cost of the inventory for the balance sheet

Sources:
Brunswick Corporation 2008 Annual Report
http://us.corporate.lifefitness.com

Job Costing

Learning Objectives

1 Distinguish between job costing and process costing

2 Understand the flow of production and how direct materials and direct labor are traced to jobs

3 Compute a predetermined manufacturing overhead rate and use it to allocate MOH to jobs

4 Determine the cost of a job and use it to make business decisions

5 Compute and dispose of overallocated or underallocated manufacturing overhead

6 Prepare journal entries for a manufacturer's job costing system

7 (Appendix) Use job costing at a service firm as a basis for billing clients

Whether you plan a career in marketing, engineering, production, general management, or accounting, you'll need to understand how much it costs to produce the company's products. Life Fitness's marketing team needs to know how much it costs to produce a treadmill to set the selling price high enough to cover costs and provide a profit. Engineers study the materials, labor, and manufacturing overhead that go into each elliptical cross-trainer to pinpoint new cost-cutting opportunities. Production managers need to know whether it's cheaper to produce each bike's video screen or *outsource* (buy) the video screens from a supplier. General managers use cost data to identify the most profitable models and guide marketing to boost sales of those products. And the accounting department uses product costs to determine the cost of goods sold and inventory for the financial statements.

Because it is so important for managers in all areas of the business to know how much it costs to manufacture each product, in this chapter and the next, we show you how to determine these costs. We'll be concentrating our attention on one element of the value chain: production. Keep in mind that Life Fitness also incurs costs in all other areas of the value chain (researching and designing new models, as well as marketing, distributing, and providing customer service on existing models). However, most manufacturers first concentrate on understanding their *production* costs, and then factor in other operating costs to make sound business decisions.

In the next section we'll summarize the two most popular methods of determining how much it costs to manufacture a product.

What Methods are Used to Determine the Cost of Manufacturing a Product?

Most manufacturers use one of two product costing systems in order to find the cost of producing their products:

■ Process costing

■ Job costing

The end goal of both product costing systems is the same: to find the cost of manufacturing one unit of product. However, the manner in which this goal is achieved differs. Management chooses the product costing system that works best for its particular manufacturing environment. Let's go over the basics of each system and identify the types of companies that would be most likely to use them.

Process Costing

Process costing is used by companies that produce extremely large numbers of identical units through a series of uniform production steps or processes. Because each unit is identical, in theory, each unit should cost the same to make. In essence, process costing averages manufacturing costs across all units so that each identical unit bears the same cost.

For example, let's assume Pace Foods uses two processes to make picante sauce: (1) cleaning and chopping vegetables and (2) mixing and bottling the sauce. First, Pace accumulates the costs incurred in the cleaning and chopping process over a period of time. The costs incurred in this process include the cost of the vegetables themselves, as well as cleaning and chopping the vegetables. The company averages the costs of this process over all units passing through the process during the same period of time.

For example, let's say Pace spends $500,000 on purchasing, cleaning, and chopping the vegetables to make one million jars of picante sauce during the month. Then the average cost per jar of the cleaning and chopping process, including the cost of the vegetables themselves is as follows:

$$\text{Cleaning and chopping process} = \frac{\$500,000}{1,000,000 \text{ jars}} = \$0.50 \text{ per jar}$$

That's the unit manufacturing cost for just the first production process. Now the cleaned and chopped vegetables go through the second production process, mixing and bottling, where a similar calculation is performed to find the average cost of that process. Again, this process would include any raw materials used, such as the cost of the glass jars themselves, as well as the cost of mixing the sauce and filling the jars with the sauce. Let's say the average cost to mix and bottle each jar of sauce is $0.25.

Now Pace can figure out the total cost to manufacture each jar of picante sauce:

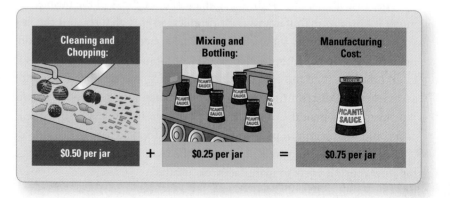

Each jar of picante sauce is identical to every other jar, so each bears the same average cost: $0.75. Once managers know the cost of manufacturing each jar, they can use that information to help set sales prices and make other business decisions. To generate a profit, the sales price will have to be high enough to cover the $0.75 per jar manufacturing cost as well as the company's operating costs incurred along other areas of the value chain (marketing, distributing, and so forth) during the period.

We'll delve more deeply into process costing in Chapter 5. For now, just remember that any company that mass-produces identical units of product will most likely use process costing to determine the cost of making each unit. The following industries and companies are further examples of companies that use process costing:

- Oil refining—Texaco, ExxonMobile, BP (British Petroleum)

- Food and beverages—Kellogg's, Coca-Cola, Campbell's, General Mills, Kraft

- Consumer toiletries and paper products—Kimberly-Clark, Proctor and Gamble

Job Costing

Whereas process costing is used by companies that mass manufacture identical units, **job costing** is used by companies that produce unique, custom-ordered products, or relatively small batches of different products. Each unique product or batch of units is considered a separate "job." Different jobs can vary considerably in direct materials, direct labor, and manufacturing overhead costs, so job costing accumulates these costs separately for each individual job. For example, Dell custom-builds each personal computer based on the exact components the customer orders. Since each PC is unique, Dell treats each order as a unique job. Life Fitness produces each of its 300 different models of exercise machines in relatively small, separate batches. Each batch of exercise machines produced is considered a separate job. Job costing would also be used by Boeing (airplanes), custom-home builders (unique houses), high-end jewelers (unique jewelry), and any other manufacturers that build custom-ordered products.

Why is this important?

"Managers need the most accurate cost information they can get in order to make good business decisions. They will choose a costing system (usually **job costing** or **process costing**) based on which system best fits their operations."

However, job costing is not limited to manufacturers. Professional service providers such as law firms, accounting firms, consulting firms, and marketing firms use job costing to determine the cost of serving each client. People working in trades such as mechanics, plumbers, and electricians also use job costing to determine the cost of performing separate jobs for clients. In both cases, the job cost is used as a basis for billing the client. In the appendix to this chapter we'll go over a complete example of how a law firm would use job costing to bill its clients.

In summary, companies use job costing when their products or services vary in terms of materials needed, time required to complete the job, and/or the complexity of the production process. Because the jobs are so different, it would not be reasonable to assign them equal costs. Therefore, the cost of each job is compiled separately. We'll spend the rest of this chapter looking at how companies compile, record, and use job costs to make important business decisions. Before moving on, take a look at Exhibit 3-1, which summarizes the key differences between job and process costing.

EXHIBIT 3-1 Differences Between Job and Process Costing

	Job Costing	Process Costing
Cost object:	Job	Process
Outputs:	Single units or small batches with large difference between jobs	Large quantities of identical units
Extent of averaging:	Less averaging—costs are averaged over the small number of units in a job (often 1 unit in a job)	More averaging—costs are averaged over the many identical units that pass through the process

STOP & THINK

Do all manufacturers use job costing or process costing systems?

Answer: Some manufacturers use a hybrid of these two costing systems if neither "pure" system mirrors their production environment very well. For example, clothing manufacturers often mass produce the same product over and over (dress shirts) but use different materials on different batches (cotton fabric on one batch and silk fabric on another). A hybrid costing system would have some elements of a process costing system (averaging labor and manufacturing overhead costs equally across all units) and some elements of a job costing system (tracing different fabric costs to different batches).

How do Manufacturers Determine a Job's Cost?

 2 Understand the flow of production and how direct materials and direct labor are traced to jobs

As we've just seen, manufacturers use job costing if they produce unique products or relatively small batches of different products. Life Fitness produces each of its 300 different models in relatively small batches, so it considers each batch a separate job. In this section, we will show you how Life Fitness determines the cost of producing Job 603, a batch of 50 identical X4 Elliptical Cross-Trainers[1]. The company's market for these cross-trainers includes health and fitness clubs, college student fitness centers, professional athletic teams, city recreation departments, and direct sales to customers for home fitness gyms. As we walk through the process, keep in mind that most companies maintain the illustrated documents in electronic, rather than hard copy form. Even so, the basic information stored in the documents and the purpose for the documents remains the same.

Overview: Flow of Inventory Through a Manufacturing System

Before we delve into Life Fitness's job costing system, let's take a quick look at how the physical products, as well as costs, flow through the company. As you learned in Chapter 2, manufacturers such as Life Fitness, maintain three separate types of inventory: Raw Materials, Work in Process, and Finished Goods. The cost of each of these inventories is reflected on the company's balance sheet.

As shown in Exhibit 3-2, Raw Materials (RM) Inventory is maintained in a storeroom, near the factory, until the materials are needed in production. As soon as these materials are transferred to the factory floor, they are no longer considered raw materials because they have become part of the work in process in the factory. Work in Process (WIP) Inventory consists of all products that are part-way through the production process. As soon as the manufacturing process is complete, the products are moved out of the factory and into a Finished Goods (FG) Inventory storage area, or warehouse, where they will await sale and shipment to a customer. Finally, when the products are shipped to customers, the cost of manufacturing those products becomes the Cost of Goods Sold (CGS) shown on the company's income statement.

---

[1]All references to Life Fitness in this hypothetical example were created by the author solely for academic purposes and are not intended, in any way, to represent the actual business practices of, or costs incurred by, Life Fitness, Inc.

EXHIBIT 3-2 **Flow of Inventory Through a Manufacturing System**

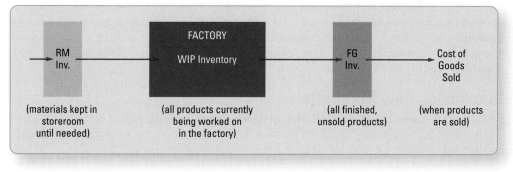

Keep this basic flow of inventory in mind as we delve into Life Fitness's job costing system.

Scheduling Production

Job costing begins with management's decision to produce a batch of units. Sometimes companies produce a batch of units just to meet a particular customer order. For example, the Chicago Bears may custom order treadmills that have characteristics not found on other models. This batch of unique treadmills would become its own job. On the other hand, most companies also produce **stock inventory** for products they sell on a regular basis. They want to have stock available to quickly fill customer orders. By forecasting demand for the product, the manufacturer is able to estimate the number of units that should be produced during a given time period. As shown in Exhibit 3-3, the **production schedule** indicates the quantity and types of inventory that are scheduled to be manufactured during the period. Depending on the company, the types of products it offers, and production time required, production schedules may cover periods of time as short as one day (Dell, producing customized laptops) or as long as one year or more (Boeing, manufacturing 737 airplanes).

EXHIBIT 3-3 **Monthly Production Schedule**

Production Schedule
For the Month of December

Job	Model Number	Stock or Customer	Quantity	Scheduled Start Date	Scheduled End Date
603	X4 Cross-Trainer	For stock	50	12/2	12/6
604	T5-0 Treadmill	For stock	60	12/7	12/17
605	Custom T6-C Treadmill	Chicago Bears	15	12/18	12/21
606	Custom S3-C Stair-Climber	Chicago Bears	12	12/22	12/24
	FACTORY CLOSED FOR HOLIDAYS and ANNUAL MAINTENANCE			12/25	12/31

The production schedule is very important in helping management determine the direct labor and direct materials that will be needed during the period. To complete production on time, management must make sure it will have an appropriate number of available factory workers with the specific skill-sets required for each job. Management also needs to make sure it will have all of the raw materials needed for each job. How does management do this? We'll see in the next section.

Purchasing Raw Materials

Production engineers prepare a **bill of materials** for each job. The bill of materials is like a recipe card: It simply lists of all of the raw materials needed to manufacture the job. Exhibit 3-4 illustrates a partial bill of materials for Job 603:

EXHIBIT 3-4   Bill of Materials (Partial Listing)

Bill of Materials

Job: 603

Model: X4 Elliptical Cross-Trainer   **Quantity:** 50 units

Part Number	Description	Quantity Needed
HRM50812	Heart rate monitor	50
LCD620	LCD entertainment screen	50
B4906	Front and rear rolling base	100
HG2567	Hand grips	100
FP689	Foot platform	100
	Etc.	

After the bill of materials has been prepared, the purchasing department checks the raw materials inventory to determine what raw materials are currently in stock, and what raw materials must be purchased. Each item has its own **raw materials record**. As shown in Exhibit 3-5, a raw materials record details information about each item in stock: the number of units received, the number of units used, and the balance of units currently in stock. Additionally, the raw materials record shows how much each unit costs to purchase, as well as the cost of the units used and cost of the units still in raw materials inventory.

EXHIBIT 3-5   Raw Materials Record

Raw Materials Record

Item No.: HRM50812   **Description:** Heart rate monitor

	Received			Used				Balance		
Date	Units	Cost	Total	Requisition Number	Units	Cost	Total	Units	Cost	Total
11-25	100	$60	$6,000					100	$60	$6,000
11-30				#7235	70	$60	$4,200	30	$60	$1,800

By looking at the materials record pictured in Exhibit 3-5, the purchasing department sees that only 30 heart rate monitors are currently in stock, whereas the bill of materials for Job 603 (Exhibit 3-4) shows that 50 heart rate monitors are needed for the job. Therefore, the purchasing department will need to buy 20 more monitors. The purchasing department also needs to consider other jobs that will be using heart rate monitors in the near future, as well as the time it takes to obtain the monitors from the company's suppliers. According to the production schedule, Job 603 is scheduled to begin production on December 2; therefore, the purchasing department needs to make sure all necessary raw materials are on hand by that date.

Life Fitness's purchasing department will issue a **purchase order** to its suppliers for the needed parts. For control purposes, incoming shipments of raw materials are counted and recorded on a **receiving report**, which is typically just a duplicate of the purchase order but without the quantity pre-listed on the form. Life Fitness's accounting department will not pay the **invoice** (bill from the supplier) unless it agrees with the quantity of parts both ordered *and* received. By matching the purchase order, receiving report and invoice, Life Fitness ensures that it pays for only those parts that were ordered and received, *and nothing more*. This is an important control that helps companies avoid scams in which businesses are sent and billed for inventory that that was not ordered.

Besides serving as a basis for determining what raw materials to buy, the raw materials records also form the basis for valuing the Raw Materials Inventory account. On a given date, by adding together the balances in the individual raw materials records, the company is able to substantiate the total Raw Materials Inventory shown on the balance sheet. For example, as shown in Exhibit 3-6, on November 30, Life Fitness had $1,800 of heart rate monitors in stock, $24,000 of LCD entertainment screens, $1,200 of roller bases, and so forth. When combined, these individual balances sum to the Raw Materials Inventory balance shown on the Life Fitness's November 30 balance sheet.

EXHIBIT 3-6 Individual Raw Materials Records Sum to the Raw Materials Inventory Balance

Heart Rate Monitors

Date	Received	Used	Balance
11-30			$1,800

LCD Entertainment Screen

Date	Received	Used	Balance
11-30			$24,000

Roller Base

Date	Received	Used	Balance
11-30			$1,200

Hand Grips

Date	Received	Used	Balance
11-30			$500

Wheels

Date	Received	Used	Balance
11-30			$3,000

Foot Platform

Date	Received	Used	Balance
11-30			$1,000

Life Fitness
Balance Sheet
November 30

Assets:	Liabilities and Owners' Equity:
Cash	Accounts Payable
Accounts Receivable	Wages and Salaries Payable
Raw Materials Inventory	Other Liabilities
Work in Process Inventory	Total Liabilities
Finished Goods Inventory	Common Stock
Total Current Assets	Retained Earnings
Property and Equipment	Total Owners' Equity
Total Assets	Total Liabilities and Owners' Equity

Using a Job Cost Record to Accumulate Job Costs

Once the necessary raw materials have arrived, and production is ready, Job 603 will be started. A **job cost record**, as pictured in Exhibit 3-7, will be used to accumulate all of the direct materials and direct labor used on the job, as well as the manufacturing overhead allocated to the job.

EXHIBIT 3-7 **Job Cost Record**

Job Cost Record

Job Number: 603

Customer: For stock

Job Description: 50 units of X4 Elliptical Cross-Trainers

Date Started: Dec. 2   Date Completed: _____

Manufacturing Cost Information:	Cost Summary
Direct Materials	
	$
Direct Labor	
	$
Manufacturing Overhead	
	$
Total Job Cost	$
Number of Units	÷ 50 units
Cost per Unit	$

Shipping Information:

Date	Quantity Shipped	Units Remaining	Cost Balance

Each job will have its own job cost record. Note that the job cost record is merely a form (electronic or hard copy) for keeping track of the three manufacturing costs associated with each job: direct materials, direct labor, and manufacturing overhead. As we saw in the last section, the individual raw materials records sum to the total Raw Materials Inventory shown on the balance sheet. Likewise, as shown in Exhibit 3-8, the job cost records on *incomplete* jobs sum to the total Work in Process Inventory shown on the balance sheet.

As shown near the bottom of Exhibit 3-7, job cost records usually also contain details about what happens to the units in the job after it has been completed and sent to the finished goods warehouse. These details include the date and quantity of units shipped to customers, the number of units remaining in finished goods inventory, and the cost of these units. The balance of *unsold* units from *completed* job cost records sum to the total Finished Goods Inventory on the balance sheet.

Why is this important?

"**Job cost records** keep track of all manufacturing costs assigned to individual jobs so that managers know how much it cost to make each product."

Tracing Direct Materials Cost to a Job

As you can see, the job cost records serve a vital role in a job costing system. Now let's take a look at how Life Fitness accumulates manufacturing costs on the job cost record. We'll begin by looking at how direct material costs are traced to individual jobs.

Once production is ready to begin Job 603, it will need many of the parts shown on the bill of materials (Exhibit 3-4). According to the production schedule (Exhibit 3-3) this job is scheduled to take five days to complete, so the production crew may not want all of the raw materials at once. Each time production needs some raw materials, it will fill out a **materials requisition**.

EXHIBIT 3-8 **Job Cost Records on *Incomplete* Jobs Sum to the WIP Inventory Balance**

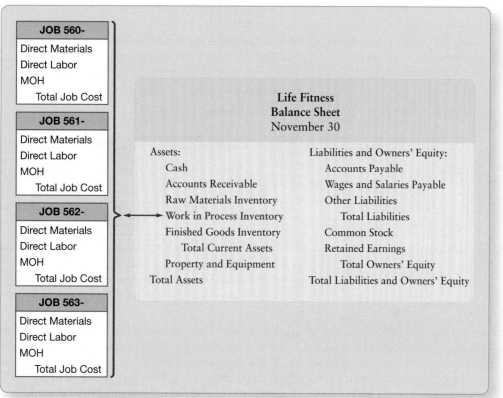

As shown in Exhibit 3-9, the materials requisition is a form itemizing the raw materials currently needed from the storeroom. Again, this is normally an electronic form, but we show the hard copy here.

EXHIBIT 3-9 **Materials Requisition**

Materials Requisition

Date: 12/2   Number: #7568

Job: 603

Part Number	Description	Quantity	Unit Cost	Amount
HRM50812	Heart rate monitor	50	$60	$3,000
LCD620	LCD entertainment screen	50	$100	5,000
B4906	Front and rear rolling base	100	$5	500
	Total			$8,500

As soon as the materials requisition is received by the raw materials storeroom, workers **pick** the appropriate materials and send them to the factory floor. Picking is just what it sounds like: storeroom workers pick the needed materials off of the storeroom shelves. The unit cost and total cost of all materials picked are posted to the materials requisition based on the cost information found in the individual raw materials records. The individual raw materials records are also updated as soon as the materials are picked. For example, in

Exhibit 3-10, we show how the raw material record for heart rate monitors is updated after requisition #7568 (Exhibit 3-9) has been picked. In most companies, this mundane task is now performed automatically by the company's computerized bar coding system.

EXHIBIT 3-10 Raw Materials Record Updated for Materials Received and Used

Raw Materials Record

Item No.: HRM50812   Description: Heart rate monitor

	Received			Used				Balance		
Date	Units	Cost	Total	Requisition Number	Units	Cost	Total	Units	Cost	Total
11-25	100	$60	$6,000					100	$60	$6,000
11-30				#7235	70	$60	$4,200	30	$60	$1,800
12-1	75	$60	$4,500					105	$60	$6,300
12-2				#7568	50	$60	$3,000	55	$60	$3,300

Finally, the raw materials requisitioned for the job are posted to the job cost record. As shown in Exhibit 3-11, each time raw materials are requisitioned for Job 603, they are posted to the direct materials section of the job cost record. They are considered direct materials (rather than indirect materials), since they can be traced specifically to Job 603. By using this system to trace direct materials to specific jobs, managers know *exactly* how much direct material cost is incurred by each job.

EXHIBIT 3-11 Posting Direct Materials Used to the Job Cost Record

Job Cost Record

Job Number: 603

Customer: For stock

Job Description: 50 units of X4 Elliptical Cross-Trainers

Date Started: Dec. 2   Date Completed: _____

Manufacturing Cost Information:	Cost Summary
Direct Materials	
Req. #7568: $ 8,500 (shown in Exhibit 3-9)	
Req. #7580: $14,000	
Req. #7595: $13,500	
Req. #7601: $ 4,000	$ 40,000
Direct Labor	
	$
Manufacturing Overhead	
	$
Total Job Cost	$
Number of Units	÷ 50 units
Cost per Unit	$

Tracing Direct Labor Cost to a Job

Now let's look at how direct labor costs are traced to individual jobs. All direct laborers in the factory fill out **labor time records**. As shown in Exhibit 3-12, a labor time record simply records the time spent by each employee on each job he or she worked on throughout the day. Often times, these records are kept electronically. Rather than using old-fashioned time tickets and punch clocks, factory workers now "swipe" their bar-coded employee identification cards on a computer terminal and enter the appropriate job number. Based on the employee's unique hourly wage rate, the computer calculates the direct labor cost to be charged to the job.

EXHIBIT 3-12 **Labor Time Record**

Labor Time Record

Employee: Hannah Smith   **Week:** 12/2 – 12/9

Hourly Wage Rate: $20   **Record #:** 324

Date	Job Number	Start Time	End Time	Hours	Cost
12/2	602	8:00	11:00	3	$60
12/2	603	12:00	5:00	5	$100
12/3	603	8:00	4:00	8	$160
12/4 etc.					

For example, in Exhibit 3-12, we see that Hannah Smith, who is paid a wage rate of $20 per hour, worked on both Jobs 602 and 603 during the week. Hannah spent five hours working on Job 603 on December 2. Therefore, $100 of direct labor cost ($20 × 5) will be charged to Job 603 for Hannah's work on that date. On December 3, Hannah's eight hours of work on Job 603 resulted in another $160 ($20 × 8) of direct labor being charged to the job. The cost of each direct laborer's time will be computed using each employee's unique wage rate, just as done with Hannah Smith's time. Then, as shown in Exhibit 3-13 (on the next page), the information from the individual labor time records is posted to the direct labor section of the job cost record. Again, this posting is normally done automatically by the company's computer system.

As you can see, by tracing direct labor cost in this fashion, jobs are charged only for the direct labor actually incurred in producing the job.

What about employee benefits, such as employee-sponsored retirement plans, health insurance, payroll taxes, and other benefits? As discussed in Chapter 2, these payroll-related benefits often add another 30% or more to the cost of gross wages and salaries. Some companies factor, or load, these costs into the hourly wage rate charged to the jobs. For example, if a factory worker earns a wage rate of $10 per hour, the job cost records would show a loaded hourly rate of about $13 per hour, which would include all benefits associated with employing the worker. However, since coming up with an *accurate* loaded hourly rate such as this is difficult, many companies treat these extra payroll-related costs as part of manufacturing overhead, rather than loading these costs into the direct labor wage rates. We'll talk about how all manufacturing overhead costs are handled in the next section.

Allocating Manufacturing Overhead to a Job

So far we have traced the direct materials cost and direct labor cost to Job 603. Recall, however, that Life Fitness incurs many other manufacturing costs that cannot be directly traced to specific jobs. These indirect manufacturing costs, otherwise known as manufacturing overhead, include depreciation on the factory plant and equipment, utilities to run the plant, property taxes and insurance on plant, equipment maintenance, the salaries of

Compute a predetermined manufacturing overhead rate and use it to allocate MOH to jobs

EXHIBIT 3-13 Posting Direct Labor Used to the Job Cost Record

Job Cost Record

Job Number: 603

Customer: For stock

Job Description: 50 units of X4 Elliptical Cross-Trainers

Date Started: Dec. 2   **Date Completed:** _____

Manufacturing Cost Information:	Cost Summary
Direct Materials	
Req. #7568: $ 8,500	
Req. #7580: $14,000	
Req. #7595: $13,500	
Req. #7601: $ 4,000	$ 40,000
Direct Labor	
No. #324 (30 hours): $100, $160, etc. (shown in Exhibit 3-12)	
No. #327 (40 hours): $240, $240, etc.	
No. #333 (36 hours): $100, $120, etc.	
Etc.	
(a total of 500 direct labor hours)	$ 10,000
Manufacturing Overhead	
	$
Total Job Cost	$
Number of Units	÷ 50 units
Cost per Unit	$

plant janitors and supervisors, machine lubricants, and so forth. Because of the nature of these costs, we cannot tell exactly how much of these costs are attributable to producing a specific job. Therefore, we cannot trace these costs to jobs, as we did with direct materials and direct labor. Rather, we will have to allocate some reasonable amount of these costs to each job. Why bother? Generally accepted accounting principles (GAAP) mandate that manufacturing overhead *must* be treated as an inventoriable product cost for financial reporting purposes. The rationale is that these costs are a *necessary* part of the production process: Jobs could not be produced without incurring these costs. Let's now look at how companies allocate manufacturing overhead costs to jobs.

What Does Allocating Mean?

Allocating manufacturing overhead[2] to jobs simply means that we will be "splitting up" or "dividing" the total manufacturing overhead costs among the jobs we produced during the year. There are many different ways we could "split up" the total manufacturing overhead costs among jobs. For example, there are a number of different ways you could split up a pizza pie among friends: You could give equal portions to each friend, you could give larger portions to the largest friends, or you could give larger portions to the hungriest friends. All in all, you have a set amount of pizza, but you could come up with several different reasonable bases for splitting it among your friends (based on number of friends, size of friends, or hunger level of friends).

Likewise, a manufacturer has a total amount of manufacturing overhead that must be split among all of the jobs produced during the year. Since each job is unique in size and resource requirements, it wouldn't be fair to

> ## Why is this important?
>
> "Managers use the **Predetermined MOH rate** as a way to 'spread' (allocate) indirect manufacturing costs, like factory utilities, among all products produced in the factory during the year."

[2]The term "applying" manufacturing overhead is often used synonymously with "allocating" manufacturing overhead.

allocate an equal amount of manufacturing overhead to each job. Rather, management needs some other reasonable basis for splitting up the total manufacturing overhead costs among jobs. In this chapter, we'll discuss the most basic method of allocating manufacturing overhead to jobs. This method has traditionally been used by most manufacturers. In the next chapter, we'll discuss some ways companies can improve this basic allocation system.

Steps to Allocating Manufacturing Overhead

Manufacturers follow four steps to implement this basic allocation system. The first three steps are taken *before the year begins*:

Step 1) **The company estimates its total manufacturing overhead costs for the coming year.** This is the total "pie" to be allocated. For Life Fitness, let's assume management estimates total manufacturing overhead costs for the year to be $1 million.

Step 2) **The company selects an allocation base and estimates the total amount that will be used during the year.** This is the *basis* management has chosen for "dividing up the pie." For Life Fitness, let's assume management has selected direct labor hours as the allocation base. Furthermore, management estimates that 62,500 of direct labor hours will be used during the year.

Ideally, the allocation base should be the **cost driver** of the manufacturing overhead costs. As the term implies, a cost driver is the primary factor that causes a cost. For example, in many companies (like Life Fitness), manufacturing overhead costs rise and fall with the amount of work performed in the factory. Because of this, most companies in the past have used either direct labor hours or direct labor cost as their allocation base. This information was also easy to gather from the labor time records or job cost records. However, for manufacturers who have automated much of their production process, machine hours is a more appropriate allocation base because the amount of time spent running the machines drives the utility, maintenance, and equipment depreciation costs in the factory. As you'll learn in Chapter 4, some companies even use multiple allocation bases to more accurately allocate manufacturing overhead costs to individual jobs. The important point is that the allocation base selected should bear a strong relationship to the manufacturing overhead costs.

Step 3) **The company calculates its *predetermined* manufacturing overhead (MOH) rate using the information estimated in Steps 1 and 2:**

$$\text{Predetermined MOH rate} = \frac{\text{Total estimated manufacturing overhead costs}}{\text{Total estimated amount of the allocation base}}$$

For example, Life Fitness calculates its **predetermined manufacturing overhead (MOH) rate** as follows:

$$\text{Predetermined MOH rate} = \frac{\$1,000,000}{62,500 \text{ DL hours}} = \$16 \text{ per direct labor hour}$$

This rate will be used throughout the coming year. It is not revised, unless the company finds that either the manufacturing overhead costs or the total amount of the allocation base being used in the factory (direct labor hours for Life Fitness) have substantially shifted away from the estimated amounts. If this is the case, management might find it necessary to revise the rate part way through the year.

Why does the company use a *predetermined* MOH rate, based on *estimated or budgeted data*, rather than an actual MOH rate based on actual data for the year? In order to get actual data, the company would have to wait until the *end of the year* to set its MOH rate. By then, the information is too late to be useful for making pricing and other decisions related to individual jobs. Managers are willing to sacrifice some accuracy in order to get timely information on how much each job costs to produce.

Once the company has established its predetermined MOH rate, it uses that rate throughout the year as jobs are produced to calculate the amount of manufacturing overhead to allocate to each job, as shown in Step 4.

Step 4) The company allocates some manufacturing overhead to each individual job as follows:

MOH allocated to a job = Predetermined MOH rate × Actual amount of allocation base used by the job

Let's see how this works for Life Fitness's Job 603. Since the predetermined MOH rate is based on direct labor hours ($16 per DL hour), we'll need to know how many direct labor hours were used on Job 603. From Exhibit 3-13, we see that Job 603 required a total of 500 DL hours. This information was collected from the individual labor time records and summarized on the job cost record. Therefore, we calculate the amount of manufacturing overhead to be allocated to Job 603 as follows:

MOH to be allocated to Job 603 = $16 per direct labor hour × 500 direct labor hours
= $8,000

The $8,000 of manufacturing overhead allocated to Job 603 is now posted to the job cost record, as shown in Exhibit 3-14.

EXHIBIT 3-14   Posting Manufacturing Overhead and Completing the Job Cost Record

Job Cost Record

Job Number: 603

Customer: For stock

Job Description: 50 units of X4 Elliptical Cross-Trainers

Date Started: Dec. 2   **Date Completed:** Dec. 6

Manufacturing Cost Information:	Cost Summary
Direct Materials	
Req. #7568: $ 8,500	
Req. #7580: $14,000	
Req. #7595: $13,500	
Req. #7601: $ 4,000	$ 40,000
Direct Labor	
No. #324 (30 DL hours): $100, $160, etc.	
No. #327 (40 DL hours): $240, $210, etc.	
No. #333 (36 DL hours): $80, $120, etc.	
Etc.	
(a total of 500 DL hours)	$ 10,000
Manufacturing Overhead	
$16/ DL hour × 500 DL hours = $8,000	$ 8,000
Total Job Cost	$ 58,000
Number of Units	÷ 50 units
Cost per Unit	$ 1,160

When is Manufacturing Overhead Allocated to Jobs?

The point in time at which manufacturing overhead is allocated to the job depends on the sophistication of the company's computer system. In most sophisticated systems, some manufacturing overhead is allocated to the job each time some of the allocation base is posted to the job cost record. In our Life Fitness example, every time an hour of direct labor is posted to the job, $16 of manufacturing overhead would also be posted to the job. In less sophisticated systems, manufacturing overhead is allocated only once: as soon as the job is complete and the total amount of allocation base used by the job is known (as shown in Exhibit 3-14). However, if the balance sheet date (for example, December 31) arrives before the job is complete, Life Fitness would need to allocate some manufacturing overhead to the job based on the number of direct labor hours used on the job thus far. Only by updating the job cost records will the company have the most accurate Work in Process Inventory on its balance sheet.

STOP & THINK

Assume Life Fitness's managers had chosen direct labor *cost* as its MOH allocation base, rather than direct labor *hours*. Furthermore, assume management estimated direct labor would cost $1,200,000 for the year.

1. Assuming direct labor cost as the allocation base, calculate the company's predetermined MOH rate.
2. How much MOH would have been allocated to Job 603?

Answer:

1. Predetermined MOH rate $= \dfrac{\$1,000,000}{\$1,200,000 \text{ of DL cost}} = \dfrac{.8333 \text{ or } 83.33\%}{\text{of direct labor cost}}$

2. MOH allocated to Job 603 $= 83.33\% \times \begin{array}{c}\$10,000 \text{ direct labor cost} \\ \text{(from Exhibit 3-14)}\end{array}$

$$= \$8,333$$

Note that this allocation differs from that shown in Exhibit 3-14 ($8,000). That's because the amount of MOH allocated to an individual job will depend upon the allocation base chosen by management. While there is no one "correct" allocation, the most *accurate* allocation occurs when the company uses the MOH cost driver as its allocation base.

Completing the Job Cost Record and Using it to Make Business Decisions

As shown in Exhibit 3-14, now that all three manufacturing costs have been posted to the job cost record, Life Fitness can determine the total cost of Job 603 ($58,000) as well as the cost of producing each of the 50 identical units in the job ($1,160 each). Let's look at a few ways this information is used by management.

Determine the cost of a job and use it to make business decisions   **4**

REDUCING FUTURE JOB COSTS   Management will use the job cost information to control costs. By examining the exact costs traced to the job, management might be able to determine ways of reducing the cost of similar jobs produced in the future. For example, are the heart rate monitors costing more than they did on previous jobs? Perhaps management can renegotiate its contract with its primary suppliers, or identify different suppliers that are willing to sell the parts more cheaply, without sacrificing quality.

What about direct labor costs? By examining the time spent by various workers on the job, management may be able to improve the efficiency of the process so that less production time is required. Management will also examine the hourly wage rates paid to the individuals who worked on the job to determine if less skilled, and therefore less costly workers could accomplish the same production tasks, freeing up the more highly skilled employees for more challenging work.

ASSESSING AND COMPARING THE PROFITABILITY OF EACH MODEL

Management will also use job cost information to determine the profitability of the various models. Assume the X4 Elliptical Cross-Trainer is listed on the company's Web site at a sales price of $1,900. That means the company can expect the following gross profit on each unit sold:

Unit sales price...	$1,900
Unit cost (computed on job cost record in Exhibit 3-14).........................	1,160
Gross profit..	$ 740

This profit analysis shows that the company would generate a gross profit of $740 on each unit sold from this job. While this may seem fairly high, keep in mind that companies incur many operating costs, outside of its manufacturing costs, that must be covered by the gross profit earned by product sales. For example, in 2008, Life Fitness spent over $17 million researching and developing new features and models of exercise equipment! Managers will compare the gross profit on this model to the gross profit of other models to determine which products to emphasize selling. Obviously, management will want to concentrate on marketing those models that yield the higher profit margins.

DEALING WITH PRICING PRESSURE FROM COMPETITORS   Management can also use this information to determine how it will deal with pricing pressure. Say a competitor drops the price of its similar elliptical cross-trainer to $1,500. The profit analysis shows that Life Fitness could drop its sales price to $1,500 and still generate $340 of gross profit on the sale ($1,500 – $1,160). In fact, Life Fitness could *undercut* the competitors by charging less than $1,500 to generate additional sales and perhaps increase its market share.

ALLOWING DISCOUNTS ON HIGH-VOLUME SALES   Often times, customers will expect discounts for high-volume sales. For example, say the City of Westlake wants to order 40 of these cross-trainers for the city's recreation center and has asked for a 25% volume discount off of the regular sales price. If Life Fitness won't agree to the discount, the city will take its business to the competitor. Can Life Fitness agree to this discount and still earn a profit on the sale? Let's see:

Discounted sales price (75% of $1,900)...	$1,425
Unit cost (computed on job cost record in Exhibit 3-14).........................	1,160
Gross profit..	$ 265

These calculations show that the discounted sales price will still be profitable. We'll talk more about special orders like this in Chapter 8.

BIDDING FOR CUSTOM ORDERS   Management also uses product cost information to bid for custom orders. You may recall from the production schedule (Exhibit 3-3) that the Chicago Bears placed an order for 15 custom treadmills. Management can use the job cost records from past treadmill jobs to get a good idea of how much it will cost to complete the custom order. For example, the custom treadmills may require additional components not found on the standard models. Life Fitness will factor in these additional costs to get an estimate of the total job cost before it is produced. Life Fitness will most likely use **cost-plus pricing** to determine a sales price for the custom job. When companies use cost-plus pricing, they take the cost of the job (from the estimated or actual job cost record) and add a markup to help cover operating expenses and generate a profit:

Why is this important?

"Once managers know how much it costs to make a job, they use that information to do the following:
- Find cheaper ways of producing similar jobs in the future
- Figure out which products are most profitable
- Establish prices for custom-ordered jobs."

Cost plus price = Cost + Markup on cost

Usually, the markup percentage or final bid price is agreed upon in a written contract before the company goes ahead with production. Let's say the Bears have agreed to pay production cost plus a 40% markup. If the job cost record shows a total job cost of $25,000 for the 15 treadmills, then the sales price is calculated as follows:

$$\text{Cost-plus price} = \$25,000 + (40\% \times \$25,000)$$
$$= \$35,000$$

PREPARING THE FINANCIAL STATEMENTS   Finally, the job cost information is critical to preparing the company's financial statements. Why? Because the information is used to figure out the total Cost of Goods Sold shown on the income statement, as well as the Work in Process and Finished Goods Inventory accounts shown on the balance sheet. Every time a cross-trainer from Job 603 is sold, its cost ($1,160) becomes part of the Cost of Goods Sold during the period. Likewise, every time a cross-trainer from the job is sold, the balance in Finished Goods Inventory is reduced by $1,160. As shown earlier (Exhibit 3-8), the cost-to-date of unfinished jobs remains in the company's Work in Process Inventory.

In the second half of the chapter we'll tackle some other issues involved with job costing. Before you move on, take time to review the Decision Guidelines and try your hand at the Summary Problem.

Decision Guidelines

Job Costing

Life Fitness uses a job costing system that assigns manufacturing costs to each batch of exercise machines that it makes. These guidelines explain some of the decisions Life Fitness made in designing its costing system.

Decision	Guidelines
Should we use job costing or process costing?	Managers use the costing system that best fits their production environment. Job costing is best suited to manufacturers that produce unique, custom-built products or relatively small batches of different products, like Life Fitness. Process costing is best suited to manufacturers that mass produce identical units in a series of uniform production processes.
How do we figure out how much each job costs to manufacture?	The exact amount of direct materials and direct labor can be traced to individual jobs using materials requisitions and labor time records. However, the exact amount of manufacturing overhead attributable to each job is unknown, and therefore *cannot* be traced to individual jobs. To deal with this issue, companies *allocate* some manufacturing overhead to each job.
Should we use a predetermined manufacturing overhead rate or the actual manufacturing overhead rate?	While it would be more accurate to use the actual manufacturing overhead rate, companies would have to wait until the end of the year to have that information. Most companies are willing to sacrifice some accuracy for the sake of having timely information that will help them make decisions throughout the year. Therefore, most companies use a predetermined overhead rate to allocate manufacturing overhead to jobs as they are produced throughout the year.
How do we calculate the predetermined MOH rate?	$$\text{Predetermined MOH rate} = \frac{\text{Total estimated manufacturing overhead cost}}{\text{Total estimated amount of the allocation base}}$$
What allocation base should we use for allocating manufacturing overhead?	If possible, companies should use the cost driver of manufacturing overhead as the allocation base. The most common allocation bases are direct labor hours, direct labor cost, and machine hours. Some companies use multiple bases in order to more accurately allocate MOH. This topic will be covered in Chapter 4.
How should we allocate manufacturing overhead to individual jobs?	The MOH allocated to a job is calculated as follows: $$= \text{Predetermined MOH rate} \times \text{Actual amount of allocation base used by the job}$$

Summary Problem 1

E-Z-Boy Furniture makes sofas, loveseats, and recliners. The company allocates manufacturing overhead based on direct labor hours. E-Z-Boy estimated a total of $2 million of manufacturing overhead and 40,000 direct labor hours for the year.

Job 310 consists of a batch of 10 recliners. The company's records show that the following direct materials were requisitioned for Job 310:

    Lumber: 10 units at $30 per unit

    Padding: 20 yards at $20 per yard

    Upholstery fabric: 60 yards at $25 per yard

Labor time records show the following employees (direct labor) worked on Job 310:

    Jesse Slothower: 10 hours at $12 per hour

    Becky Wilken: 15 hours at $18 per hour

    Chip Lathrop: 12 hours at $15 per hour

Requirements

1. Compute the company's predetermined manufacturing overhead rate.

2. Compute the total amount of direct materials, direct labor, and manufacturing overhead that should be shown on Job 310's job cost record.

3. Compute the total cost of Job 310, as well as the cost of each recliner produced in Job 310.

Solution

1. The predetermined MOH rate is calculated as follows:

$$\text{Predetermined MOH rate} = \frac{\text{Total estimated manufacturing overhead cost}}{\text{Total estimated amount of the allocation base}}$$

For E-Z-Boy:

$$\text{Predetermined MOH rate} = \frac{\$2,000,000}{40,000 \text{ direct labor hours}} = \$50 \text{ per direct labor hour}$$

2. The total amount of direct materials ($2,200) and direct labor ($570) incurred on Job 310 is determined from the materials requisitions and labor time records, as shown on the following job cost record. Since the job required 37 direct labor hours, we determine the amount of manufacturing overhead to allocate to the job is as follows:

$$= \text{Predetermined MOH rate} \times \text{Actual amount of allocation base used by the job}$$
$$= \$50 \text{ per direct labor hour} \times 37 \text{ direct labor hours used on Job 310}$$
$$= \$1,850$$

These costs are summarized on the following job cost record:

Job Cost Record

Job Number: 310

Job Description: 10 recliners

Manufacturing Cost Information:	Cost Summary
Direct Materials	
Lumber: 10 units × $30 = $300	
Padding: 20 yards × $20 = $400	
Fabric: 60 yards × $25 = $1,500	$ 2,200
Direct Labor	
Slothower: 10 hours × $12 = $120	
Wilken: 15 hours × $18 = $270	
Lathrop: 12 hours × $15 = $180	
Total hours: 37 hours	$ 570
Manufacturing Overhead	
37 direct labor hours × $50 = $1,850	$ 1,850
Total Job Cost	$ 4,620
Number of Units	÷ 10 units
Cost per Unit	$ 462

3. The direct materials ($2,200), direct labor ($570), and manufacturing overhead ($1,850) sum to a total job cost of $4,620, as previously shown. When averaged over the 10 recliners in the job, the cost per recliner is $462.

How do Managers Deal with Underallocated or Overallocated Manufacturing Overhead?

In the first half of the chapter, we showed how managers find the cost of producing a job. Direct materials and direct labor were traced to each job using materials requisitions and labor time records, while manufacturing overhead was allocated to each job using a predetermined overhead rate. **At the end of the period, all manufacturers will have a problem to deal with: Invariably, they will have either underallocated manufacturing overhead or overallocated manufacturing overhead** to the jobs worked on during the period.

Recall that manufacturing overhead was allocated to jobs using a *predetermined rate* which was calculated using *estimates* of the company's total annual manufacturing costs and *estimates* of the total annual allocation base (such as direct labor hours). By the end of the period, the *actual* manufacturing overhead costs incurred by the company will be known, and no doubt, will differ from the total amount allocated to jobs during the period.

Compute and dispose of overallocated or underallocated manufacturing overhead

5

For example, suppose Life Fitness incurred the following *actual* manufacturing overhead costs during the month of December:

Manufacturing Overhead Incurred	Actual MOH Costs
Indirect materials used (janitorial supplies, machine lubricants, etc.)	$ 2,000
Indirect labor (janitors' and supervisors' wages, etc.)	13,000
Other indirect manufacturing costs	
(Plant utilities, depreciation, property taxes, and insurance etc.)	10,000
Total actual manufacturing overhead costs incurred	$25,000

Now let's look at the total amount of manufacturing overhead that was *allocated* to individual jobs during the month (using the predetermined manufacturing overhead rate of $16 per direct labor hour). For simplicity, we'll assume only two jobs were worked on during December.

Job	Amount of MOH Allocated to Job
603 (from Exhibit 3-14) ($16 per DL hour × 500 DL hours)	$ 8,000
604 (not shown) ($16 per DL hour × 1,000 DL hours)	16,000
Total MOH allocated to jobs ($16 per DL hour × 1,500 DL hours)	$24,000

Notice that we don't need to have the individual job cost records available to figure out the total amount of MOH allocated to jobs during the period. Rather, we could do the following calculation to arrive at the same $24,000 figure:

Total MOH allocated = Predetermined MOH rate × Actual *total* amount of allocation base used on all jobs

= $16 per DL hour × 1,500 direct labor hours

= $24,000 total MOH allocated to jobs during the period

Now we simply compare the amount of MOH actually incurred during the period with the amount of MOH that was allocated to jobs during the same period. The difference between the *actual manufacturing overhead costs incurred* and the amount of manufacturing overhead *allocated to jobs* shows that Life Fitness *underallocated* manufacturing overhead by $1,000 during December:

Actual manufacturing overhead costs **incurred**	$25,000
Manufacturing overhead **allocated** to jobs	24,000
Underallocated manufacturing overhead	$ 1,000

By underallocating manufacturing overhead, Life Fitness *did not allocate enough* manufacturing overhead cost to the jobs worked on during the period. In other words, the jobs worked on during the period should have had a total of $1,000 more manufacturing overhead cost allocated to them than the job cost records indicated. These jobs have been undercosted, as shown in Exhibit 3-15. If, on the other hand, a manufacturer finds that the amount of manufacturing overhead allocated to jobs is *greater* than the actual amount of manufacturing overhead incurred, we would say that manufacturing overhead had been overallocated, resulting in overcosting these jobs.

What do manufacturers do about this problem? *Assuming that the amount of under- or overallocation is immaterial, or that most of the inventory produced during the period has been sold,* manufacturers typically adjust the Cost of Goods Sold shown on the income statement for the total amount of the under- or overallocation. Why? Because the

EXHIBIT 3-15 **Underallocated Versus Overallocated Manufacturing Overhead**

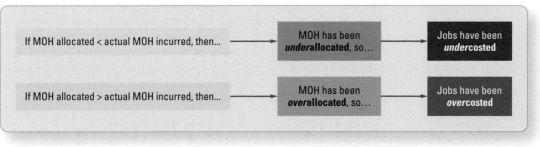

actual cost of producing these goods differed from what was initially reported on the job cost records. Since the job cost records were used as a basis for recording Cost of Sold at the time the units were sold, the Cost of Goods Sold will be wrong unless it is adjusted. As shown in Exhibit 3-16, by increasing Cost of Goods Sold when manufacturing overhead has been underallocated, or by decreasing Cost of Goods Sold when manufacturing overhead has been overallocated, the company actually corrects the error that exists in Cost of Goods Sold.

EXHIBIT 3-16 **Correcting Cost of Goods Sold for Underallocated or Overallocated MOH**

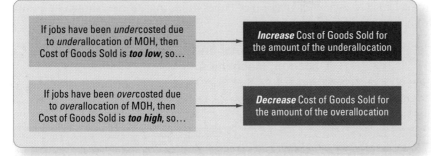

What if the amount of under- or overallocation is large, and the company has *not* sold almost all of the jobs it worked on during the period? Then the company will prorate the total amount of under- or overallocation among Work in Process Inventory, Finished Goods Inventory, and Cost of Goods Sold based on the current status of the jobs worked on during the period. For example, if 30% of the jobs are still in Work in Process, 20% are still in Finished Goods, and 50% were sold, then the total amount of underallocation ($1,000 in the case of Life Fitness) would be roughly allocated as follows: 30% ($300) to Work in Process Inventory, 20% ($200) to Finished Goods Inventory, and 50% ($500) to Cost of Goods Sold. The exact procedure for prorating is covered in more advanced accounting textbooks.

How do Manufacturers Treat Non-Manufacturing Costs?

Job costing in manufacturing companies has *traditionally* focused on assigning only production-related costs to jobs. This is why our Life Fitness example focuses on assigning only manufacturing costs (direct materials, direct labor, and manufacturing overhead) to jobs. The focus on manufacturing costs arises because GAAP requires that the accounting records treat only inventoriable costs as assets. Costs incurred in other elements of the value chain (period costs) are not assigned to products for external financial reporting, but instead, are treated as operating expenses.

However, manufacturers often want to know more than just the cost to manufacture a product; they want to know the *total* cost of researching and developing, designing, producing, marketing, distributing, and providing customer service for new or existing products. *In other words, they want to know the total cost of the product across the entire value chain.* Managers use this information to guide internal decisions, such as setting long-run average sale prices. But how do managers figure this out? The same principles of tracing direct costs and allocating indirect costs apply to all costs incurred in other elements of the value chain. Managers can add these non-manufacturing costs to the inventoriable job costs to build *the total cost of the product across the value chain*. Keep in mind that these non-manufacturing costs are assigned to products *only* for internal decision making, *never* for external financial reporting because GAAP does not allow it. For financial reporting, non-manufacturing costs must *always* be expensed in the period in which they are incurred as operating expenses on the income statement.

What Journal Entries are Needed in a Manufacturer's Job Costing System?

6 Prepare the journal entries for a manufacturer's job costing system

Now that you know how manufacturers determine job costs and how those costs are used to make business decisions, let's look at how these costs are entered into the company's general ledger accounting system. We'll consider the journal entries needed to record the flow of costs through Life Fitness's accounts during the month of December. We'll use the same examples used earlier in the chapter. For the sake of simplicity, we'll continue to assume that Life Fitness only worked on two jobs during the month:

Job 603: 50 units of the X4 Elliptical Cross-Trainers

Job 604: 60 units of the T5 Treadmill

You may wish to review the basic mechanics of journal entries, shown in Exhibit 3-17, before we begin our discussion.

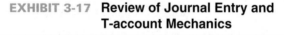

EXHIBIT 3-17 **Review of Journal Entry and T-account Mechanics**

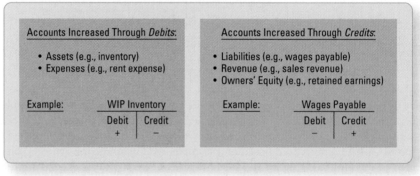

Additionally, keep in mind the flow of inventory that was first described in Exhibit 3-2. You may find this visual reminder helpful as we describe how the journal entries reflect the flow of inventory through the manufacturing system. Each arrow represents a journal entry that must be made to reflect activities that occur along the process: purchasing raw materials, using direct materials, using direct labor, recording actual MOH costs, allocating MOH to jobs, moving the jobs out of the factory after completion, and finally selling the units from a job.

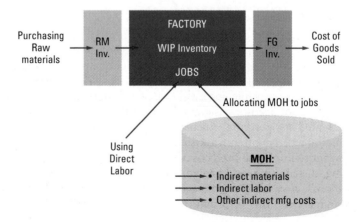

Purchase of Raw Materials

Life Fitness's purchase manager uses the bill of materials and raw materials records to determine what raw materials to purchase. Assume that Life Fitness ordered and received $90,000 of raw materials during December. Once the materials are received and verified against the purchase order and the invoice received from the supplier, the purchase is recorded as follows:

(1)	Raw Materials Inventory	90,000	
	Accounts Payable		90,000
	(to record purchases of raw materials)		

These materials will remain in the raw materials storeroom until they are needed for production. The liability in Accounts Payable will be removed when the supplier is paid.

Use of Direct Materials

Recall that direct materials are the primary physical components of the product. Each time production managers need particular direct materials for Jobs 603 and 604, they fill out a materials requisition informing the storeroom to pick the materials and send them into the manufacturing facility. Once these materials are sent into production, they become part of the work in process on Jobs 603 and 604, so their cost is added to the job cost records, as shown next:

JOB 603: Cross-Trainers	
Direct Materials	$40,000
Direct Labor..	
Manufacturing Overhead......................	
Total Job Cost	

JOB 604: Treadmills	
Direct Materials	$72,000
Direct Labor..	
Manufacturing Overhead......................	
Total Job Cost	

From an accounting perspective, the cost of these materials must also be moved into Work in Process Inventory (through a debit) and out of Raw Materials Inventory (through a credit). The following journal entry is made:

(2)	Work in Process Inventory (40,000 + 72,000)	112,000	
	Raw Materials Inventory		112,000
	(to record the use of direct materials on jobs)		

Recall from the first half of the chapter, that the individual job cost records form the underlying support for the Work in Process Inventory account shown on the Balance Sheet.[3] Therefore, the amount posted to the general ledger account ($112,000) must be identical to the sum of the amounts posted to the individual job cost records ($40,000 + $72,000 = $112,000).

Use of Indirect Materials

Indirect materials are materials used in the manufacturing plant that *cannot* be traced to individual jobs, and therefore are *not* recorded on any job cost record. Examples include janitorial supplies used in the factory and machine lubricants for the factory machines. Once again, materials requisitions inform the raw materials storeroom to release these materials. However, instead of becoming part of the Work in Process for

---

[3]The job cost records of unfinished jobs form the subsidiary ledger for the Work in Process Inventory account. Recall that a **subsidiary ledger** is simply the supporting detail for a general ledger account. Many other general ledger accounts (such as Accounts Receivable, Accounts Payable, Plant & Equipment) also have subsidiary ledgers. The raw material inventory records form the subsidiary ledger for the Raw Materials Inventory account, while the job cost records on completed, unsold jobs form the subsidiary ledger for the Finished Goods Inventory account.

a particular job, the indirect materials used in the factory ($2,000) become part of the Manufacturing Overhead account. Therefore, the Manufacturing Overhead account is debited (to increase the account) and Raw Materials Inventory is credited (to decrease the account) as follows:

(3)	Manufacturing Overhead	2,000	
	Raw Materials Inventory		2,000
	(to record the use of indirect materials in the factory)		

All indirect manufacturing costs, including indirect materials, indirect labor, and other indirect manufacturing costs (such as plant insurance and depreciation) are accumulated in the Manufacturing Overhead account. The Manufacturing Overhead account is a temporary account used to "store" or "pool" indirect manufacturing costs until those costs can be allocated to individual jobs.

We can summarize the flow of materials costs through the T-accounts as follows:

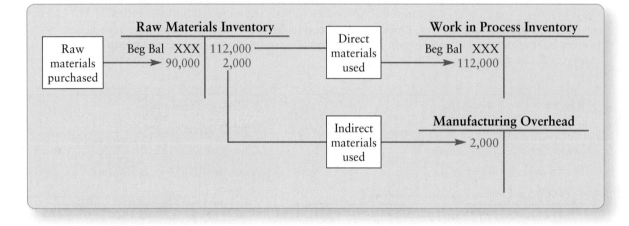

Use of Direct Labor

The labor time records of individual factory workers are used to determine exactly how much time was spent directly working on Jobs 603 and 604. The cost of this direct labor is entered on the job cost records, as shown:

JOB 603: Cross-Trainers	
Direct Materials	$40,000
Direct Labor	$10,000
Manufacturing Overhead	
Total Job Cost	

JOB 604: Treadmills	
Direct Materials	$72,000
Direct Labor	$20,000
Manufacturing Overhead	
Total Job Cost	

Again, since the job cost records form the underlying support for Work in Process Inventory, an identical amount ($10,000 + $20,000 = $30,000) must be debited to the Work in Process Inventory account. Wages Payable is credited to show that the company has a liability to pay its factory workers.

(4)	Work in Process Inventory ($10,000 + $20,000)	30,000	
	Wages Payable		30,000
	(to record the use of direct labor on jobs)		

The Wages Payable liability will be removed on payday when the workers receive their paychecks.

Use of Indirect Labor

Recall that indirect labor consists of the salary, wages, and benefits of all factory workers that are *not* directly working on individual jobs. Examples include factory janitors, supervisors, and forklift operators. Since their time cannot be traced to particular jobs, the cost of employing these factory workers during the month ($13,000) cannot be posted to individual job cost records. Thus, we record the cost of indirect labor as part of Manufacturing Overhead, *not* Work in Process Inventory:

(5)	Manufacturing Overhead	13,000	
	Wages Payable		13,000
	(to record the use of indirect labor in the factory)		

Again, the Wages Payable liability will be removed on payday when the workers receive their paychecks.

We can summarize the flow of manufacturing labor costs through the T-accounts as follows:

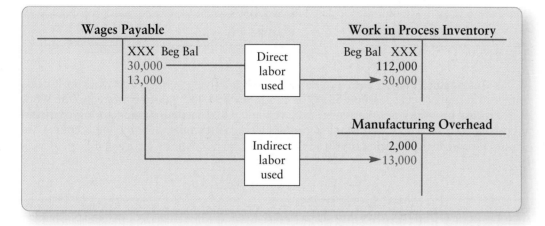

Incurring Other Manufacturing Overhead Costs

We have already recorded the indirect materials and indirect labor used in the factory during December by debiting the Manufacturing Overhead account. However, Life Fitness incurs other indirect manufacturing costs, such as plant utilities ($3,000), plant depreciation ($4,000), plant insurance ($1,000) and plant property taxes ($2,000) during the period. All of these other indirect costs of operating the manufacturing plant during the month are also accumulated in the Manufacturing Overhead account until they can be allocated to specific jobs:

(6)	Manufacturing Overhead	10,000	
	Accounts Payable *(for electric bill)*		3,000
	Accumulated Depreciation—Plant and Equipment		4,000
	Prepaid Plant Insurance *(for expiration of prepaid insurance)*		1,000
	Plant Property Taxes Payable *(for taxes to be paid)*		2,000
	(to record other indirect manufacturing costs incurred during the month)		

After recording all other indirect manufacturing costs, the Manufacturing Overhead account appears as follows:

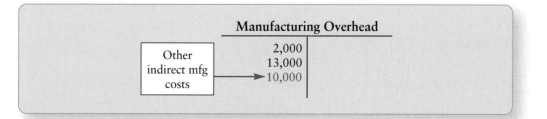

Allocating Manufacturing Overhead to Jobs

Life Fitness allocates some manufacturing overhead to each job worked on during the month using its predetermined manufacturing overhead rate, calculated in the first half of the chapter to be $16 per direct labor hour. The total direct labor hours used on each job is found on the labor time records, and is usually summarized on the job cost records. Assume Job 603 used 500 DL hours and Job 604 used 1,000 DL hours. Then the amount of manufacturing overhead allocated to each job is determined as follows:

Job 603: $16 per DL hour × 500 DL hours = $8,000

Job 604: $16 per DL hour × 1,000 DL hours = $16,000

JOB 603: Cross-Trainers	
Direct Materials	$40,000
Direct Labor (500 DL hrs)	10,000
Manufacturing Overhead.....................	8,000
Total Job Cost	

JOB 604: Treadmills	
Direct Materials	$72,000
Direct Labor (1,000 DL hrs).................	20,000
Manufacturing Overhead.....................	16,000
Total Job Cost	

Again, since the job cost records form the underlying support for Work in Process Inventory, an identical amount ($8,000 + $16,000 = $24,000) must be debited to the Work in Process Inventory account. Since we accumulated all actual manufacturing overhead costs *into* an account called Manufacturing Overhead (through debiting the account), we now allocate manufacturing overhead costs *out* of the account by crediting it.

(7)		Work in Process Inventory ($8,000 + $16,000)	24,000	
		Manufacturing Overhead		24,000
		(to allocate manufacturing overhead to specific jobs)		

By looking at the Manufacturing Overhead T-account, you can see how actual manufacturing overhead costs are accumulated in the account through debits, while the amount of manufacturing overhead allocated to specific jobs is credited to the account:

Completion of Jobs

Once the job has been completed, the three manufacturing costs shown on the job cost record are summed to find the total job cost. If the job consists of more than one unit, the total job cost is divided by the number of units to find cost of each unit:

JOB 603: Cross-Trainers		JOB 604: Treadmills	
Direct Materials	$40,000	Direct Materials	$ 72,000
Direct Labor	10,000	Direct Labor	20,000
Manufacturing Overhead	8,000	Manufacturing Overhead	16,000
Total Job Cost	$58,000	Total Job Cost	$108,000
Number of Units	÷ 50	Number of Units	÷ 60
Cost per Unit	$ 1,160	Cost per Unit	$ 1,800

The jobs are physically moved off of the plant floor and into the finished goods warehouse. Likewise, in the accounting records the jobs are moved out of Work in Process Inventory (through a credit) and into Finished Goods Inventory (through a debit):

(8)	Finished Goods Inventory (58,000 + 108,000)	166,000	
	Work in Process Inventory		166,000
	(to move the completed jobs out of the factory and into		
	Finished Goods)		

The T-accounts show the movement of completed jobs off of the factory floor:

Work in Process Inventory			Finished Goods Inventory	
Beg Bal XXX	166,000	Move completed jobs	Beg Bal XXX	
112,000			► 166,000	
30,000				
24,000				
End Bal XXX				

Sale of Units

For simplicity, let's assume that Life Fitness only had one sale during the month: It sold 40 cross-trainers from Job 603 and all 60 treadmills from Job 604 to the City of Westlake for its recreation centers. The sales price was $1,425 for each cross-trainer and $2,500 for each treadmill. Like most companies, Life Fitness uses a perpetual inventory system so that its inventory records are always up to date. Two journal entries are needed. The first journal entry records the revenue generated from the sale and shows the amount due from the customer:

(9)	Accounts Receivable (40 × $1,425) + (60 × $2,500)	207,000	
	Sales Revenue		207,000
	(to record the sale of 40 cross-trainers and 60 treadmills)		

The second journal entry reduces the company's Finished Goods Inventory, and records the Cost of Goods Sold. From the job cost record, we know that each cross-trainer produced in Job 603 cost $1,160 to make while each treadmill from Job 604 cost $1,800 to make. Therefore, the following entry is recorded:

(10)	Cost of Goods Sold (40 × $1,160) + (60 × $1,800)	154,400	
	Finished Goods Inventory		154,400
	(to reduce finished goods inventory and record cost of goods sold)		

The following T-accounts show the movement of the units out of Finished Goods Inventory and into Cost of Goods Sold:

Operating Expenses

During the month, Life Fitness also incurred $32,700 of operating expenses to run its business. For example, Life Fitness incurred salaries and commissions ($20,000) for its sales people, office administrators, research and design staff, and customer service representatives. It also needs to pay rent ($3,300) for its office headquarters. The company also received a bill from its advertising agency for marketing expenses incurred during the month ($9,400). *All costs incurred outside of manufacturing function of the value chain* would be expensed in the current month as shown in the following journal entry.

(11)	Salaries and Commission Expense	20,000	
	Rent Expense	3,300	
	Marketing Expenses	9,400	
	Salaries and Commissions Payable		20,000
	Rent Payable		3,300
	Accounts Payable		9,400
	(to record all non-manufacturing costs incurred during the month)		

All non-manufacturing expenses will be shown as "operating expenses" on the company's income statement.

Closing Manufacturing Overhead

As a final step, Life Fitness must deal with the balance in the manufacturing overhead account. Since the company uses a *predetermined* manufacturing overhead rate to allocate manufacturing overhead to individual jobs, the total amount allocated to jobs will most likely differ from the amount of manufacturing overhead actually incurred.

Let's see how this plays out in the Manufacturing Overhead T-account:

1. All manufacturing overhead costs *incurred* by Life Fitness were recorded as *debits* to the Manufacturing Overhead account. These debits total $25,000 of actual manufacturing overhead incurred.

2. On the other hand, all manufacturing overhead *allocated* to specific jobs ($8,000 + $16,000) was recorded as *credits* to the Manufacturing Overhead account:

This leaves a debit balance of $1,000 in the Manufacturing Overhead account, which means that manufacturing overhead has been underallocated during the month. More manufacturing overhead costs were incurred than were allocated to jobs. Since Manufacturing Overhead is a temporary account, not shown on any of the company's financial statements, it must be closed out (zeroed out). Since most of the inventory produced during the period has been sold, Life Fitness will close the balance in Manufacturing Overhead to Cost of Goods Sold as follows:

(12)	Cost of Goods Sold	1,000	
	Manufacturing Overhead		1,000
	(to close the manufacturing overhead account)		

As a result of this entry, 1) the Manufacturing Overhead account now has a zero balance, and 2) the balance in Cost of Goods Sold has increased to correct for the fact that the jobs had been undercosted during the period.

If, in some period, Life Fitness overallocates its overhead, the journal entry to close Manufacturing Overhead would be the opposite of that shown: Manufacturing Overhead would need to be debited to zero it out; and Cost of Goods Sold would need to be credited to reduce it as a result of having overcosted jobs during the period.

Now you have seen how all of the costs flow through Life Fitness's accounts during December. Exhibit 3-18 shows the company's income statement that results from these journal entries:

EXHIBIT 3-18   Income Statement After Adjusting for Underallocated Manufacturing Overhead

Life Fitness Income Statement December 31	
Sales Revenue	$207,000
Less: Cost of Goods Sold	155,400
Gross Profit	51,600
Less: Operating Expenses	32,700
Operating Income	$ 18,900

Decision Guidelines

Job Costing

As a result of using a predetermined manufacturing overhead rate to allocate manufacturing overhead to jobs, manufacturers will invariably either underallocate or overallocate manufacturing overhead. The following decision guidelines describe the implications as well as other decisions that need to be made in a job costing environment.

Decision	Guidelines
If we have underallocated (or overallocated) manufacturing overhead, what does it mean about the cost of the jobs produced during the period?	If manufacturing overhead has been *underallocated*, it means that the jobs have been *undercosted* as a result. In other words, not enough manufacturing overhead cost was posted on the job cost records. On the other hand, if manufacturing overhead has been *overallocated*, it means that the jobs have been *overcosted*. Too much manufacturing overhead cost was posted on the job cost records.
What do we do about overallocated or underallocated manufacturing overhead?	Assuming most of the inventory produced during the period has been sold, manufacturers generally adjust the Cost of Goods Sold for the total amount of the under or overallocation. If a significant portion of the inventory is still on hand, then the adjustment will be prorated between WIP, Finished Goods, and Cost of Goods Sold.
How do we know whether to increase or decrease Cost of Goods Sold?	If manufacturing overhead has been overallocated, then Cost of Goods Sold is too high, and must be decreased. If manufacturing overhead has been underallocated, then Cost of Goods Sold is too low, and must be increased.
How does job costing work at a service firm?	Job costing at a service firm is very similar to job costing at a manufacturer. The main difference is that the company is allocating operating expenses, rather than manufacturing costs, to each client job. In addition, since there are no Inventory or Cost of Goods Sold accounts, no journal entries are needed to move costs through the system.
Can manufacturers also allocate operating expenses to jobs?	For *internal decision making only*, operating expenses can also be assigned to jobs. However, operating expenses are *never* assigned to jobs for external financial reporting purposes. Direct operating costs would be traced to jobs (such as the sales commission on a particular job or the design costs related to a particular job) while indirect operating cost (such as the lease of the corporate headquarters) would be allocated to jobs.

Summary Problem 2

Fashion Fabricators makes custom handbags and accessories for high-end clothing boutiques. Record summary journal entries for each of the following transactions that took place during the month of January, the *first* month of the fiscal year.

Requirements

1. $150,000 of raw materials were purchased on account.

2. During the month $140,000 of raw materials were requisitioned. Of this amount, $135,000 were traced to specific jobs, while the remaining materials were for general factory use.

3. Manufacturing labor (both direct and indirect) for the month totaled $80,000. It has not yet been paid. Of this amount, $60,000 was traced to specific jobs.

4. The company recorded $9,000 of depreciation on the plant building and machinery. In addition $3,000 of prepaid property tax expired during the month. The company also received the plant utility bill for $6,000.

5. Manufacturing overhead was allocated to jobs using a predetermined manufacturing overhead rate of 75% of direct labor *cost*. (*Hint:* Total direct labor cost is found in Requirement 3.)

6. Several jobs were completed during the month. According to the job cost records these jobs cost $255,000 to manufacture.

7. Sales (all on credit) for the month totaled $340,000. According to the job cost records, the units sold cost $250,000 to manufacture. Assume the company uses a perpetual inventory system.

8. The company incurred operating expenses of $60,000 during the month. Assume that 80% of these were for marketing and administrative salaries and the other 20% were lease and utility bills related to the corporate headquarters.

9. In order to prepare its January financial statements, the company had to close its manufacturing overhead account.

10. Based on the transactions previously incurred, prepare the January income statement for Fashion Fabrics.

Solution

1. $150,000 of raw materials were purchased on account.

	Raw Materials Inventory	150,000	
	Accounts Payable		150,000
	(*to record purchases of raw materials*)		

2. During the month $140,000 of raw materials were requisitioned. Of this amount, $135,000 were traced to specific jobs, while the remaining materials were for general factory use.

	Work in Process Inventory	135,000	
	Manufacturing Overhead	5,000	
	Raw Materials Inventory		140,000
	(*to record the use of direct materials and indirect materials*)		

3. Manufacturing labor (both direct and indirect) for the month totaled $80,000. It has not yet been paid. Of this amount, $60,000 was traced to specific jobs.

	Work in Process Inventory (*for direct labor*)	60,000	
	Manufacturing Overhead (*for indirect labor*)	20,000	
	Wages Payable		80,000
	(*to record the use of direct labor and indirect labor*)		

4. The company recorded $9,000 of depreciation on the plant building and machinery. In addition $3,000 of prepaid property tax expired during the month. The company also received the plant utility bill for $6,000.

	Manufacturing Overhead	18,000	
	Accumulated Depreciation—Plant and Equipment		9,000
	Prepaid Plant Property Tax (*for expiration of property tax*)		3,000
	Accounts Payable (*for electric bill*)		6,000
	(*to record other indirect manufacturing costs incurred during the month*)		

5. Manufacturing overhead was allocated to jobs using a predetermined manufacturing overhead rate of 75% of direct labor cost. (*Hint:* Total direct labor cost is found in Requirement 3.)

	Work in Process Inventory (75% × $60,000 of direct labor)	45,000	
	Manufacturing Overhead		45,000
	(*to allocate manufacturing overhead to jobs*)		

continued

6. Several jobs were completed during the month. According to the job cost records these jobs cost $255,000 to manufacture.

Finished Goods Inventory		255,000	
Work in Process Inventory			255,000
(to move the completed jobs out of the factory and into Finished Goods)			

7. Sales (all on credit) for the month totaled $340,000. According to the job cost records, the units sold cost $250,000 to manufacture. Assume the company uses a perpetual inventory system.

Accounts Receivable		340,000	
Sales Revenue			340,000
(to record the sales and receivables)			

Cost of Goods Sold		250,000	
Finished Goods Inventory			250,000
(to reduce finished goods inventory and record cost of goods sold)			

8. The company incurred operating expenses of $60,000 during the month. Assume that 80% of these were for marketing and administrative salaries and the other 20% were lease and utility bills related to the corporate headquarters.

Salaries Expense		48,000	
Lease and Utilities Expense		12,000	
Salaries and Wages Payable			48,000
Accounts Payable			12,000
(to record all non-manufacturing costs incurred during the month)			

9. In order to prepare its January financial statements, the company had to close its manufacturing overhead account.

An analysis of the manufacturing overhead account *prior to closing* shows the following:

Manufacturing Overhead	
(ACTUAL)	**(ALLOCATED)**
5,000	45,000
20,000	
18,000	
	2,000

Manufacturing Overhead		2,000	
Cost of Goods Sold			2,000
(to close the manufacturing overhead account to CGS)			

10. Based on the transactions previously incurred, prepare the January income statement for Fashion Fabrics.

Fashion Fabrics Income Statement January 31	
Sales Revenue	$340,000
Less: Cost of Goods Sold**	248,000
Gross Profit	92,000
Less: Operating Expenses	60,000
Operating Income	$ 32,000

(** $250,000 – $2,000 closing adjustment)

APPENDIX 3A

How do Service Firms Use Job Costing to Determine the Amount to Bill Clients?

Use job costing at a service firm as a basis for billing clients

7

So far this chapter we have illustrated job costing in a manufacturing environment. However, job costing is also commonly used by service firms (such as law firms, accounting firms, marketing firms, and consulting firms) and by trades people (such as plumbers, electricians, and auto mechanics). At these firms, the work performed for each individual client is considered a separate job. Service firms need to keep track of job costs so that they have a basis for billing their clients. As shown in Exhibit 3-19, the direct costs of serving the client are traced to the job, whereas the indirect costs of serving the client are allocated to the job.

EXHIBIT 3-19 Assigning Costs to Client Jobs

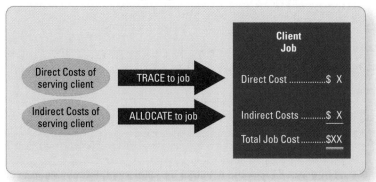

The amount billed to the client is determined by adding a profit markup to the total job cost. The main difference between job costing at a manufacturer and job costing at a service firm is that the indirect costs of serving the client are all *operating expenses*, rather than inventoriable product costs. In the next section, we will illustrate how job costing is used at Barnett & Associates law firm to determine how much to bill Client 367.

What Costs are Considered Direct Costs of Serving the Client?

The most significant direct cost at service firms is direct professional labor. In our example, direct professional labor is the attorney's time spent on clients' cases. Attorneys use labor time records to keep track of the amount of time they spend working on each client. Since most professionals are paid an annual salary rather than an hourly wage rate, firms estimate the hourly cost of employing their professionals based on the number of hours the professionals are expected to work on client jobs during the year. For example, say Attorney Theresa Fox is paid a salary of $100,000 per year. The law firm expects her to spend 2,000 hours a year performing legal work for clients (50 weeks × 40 hours per week). Therefore, for job costing purposes, the law firm converts her annual salary to an hourly cost rate as follows:

$$\frac{\$100,000 \text{ annual salary}}{2,000 \text{ hours per year}} = \$50 \text{ per hour}$$

If the labor time record indicates that Fox has spent 14 hours on Client 367, then the direct professional labor cost traced to the client is calculated as follows:

$$14 \text{ hours} \times \$50 \text{ per hour} = \$700 \text{ of direct professional labor}$$

At a law firm, very few other costs will be directly traceable to the client. Examples of other traceable costs might include travel and entertainment costs, or court filing fees related directly to specific clients. When trades people such as auto mechanics or plumbers use job costing, they trace their time to specific client jobs, just like attorneys do. In addition, they also trace the direct materials costs (such as the cost of new tires, an exhaust pipe, or garbage disposal) to the jobs on which those materials were used.

What Costs are Considered Indirect Costs of Serving the Client?

The law firm also incurs general operating costs, such as office rent, the salaries of office support staff, and office supplies. These are the indirect costs of serving *all* of the law firm's clients. These costs cannot be traced to specific clients, so the law firm will allocate these costs to client jobs using a *predetermined indirect cost allocation rate*. This is done using the same four basic steps as we used earlier in the chapter for a manufacturer. The only real difference is that we are allocating indirect operating expenses, rather than indirect manufacturing costs (manufacturing overhead).

Step 1) Estimate the total indirect costs for the coming year. Before the fiscal year begins, the law firm estimates the total indirect costs that will be incurred in the coming year follow:

Office rent	$190,000
Office supplies, telephone, internet access, and copier lease	10,000
Office support staff	70,000
Maintaining and updating law library for case research	25,000
Advertising	3,000
Sponsorship of the symphony	2,000
Total indirect costs	$300,000

Step 2) Choose an allocation base and estimate the total amount that will be used during the year. Next, the law firm chooses a cost allocation base. Service firms typically use professional labor hours as the cost allocation base because the time spent on client jobs is probably the main driver of indirect costs. For example, Barnett & Associates estimates that attorneys will spend a total of 10,000 professional labor hours working on client jobs throughout the coming year.

Step 3) Compute the predetermined indirect cost allocation rate. The predetermined indirect cost allocation rate is found as follows:

$$\text{Predetermined indirect cost allocation rate} = \frac{\text{Total estimated indirect costs}}{\text{Total estimated amount of the allocation base}}$$

$$= \frac{\$300,000 \text{ total indirect costs}}{10,000 \text{ professional labor hours}}$$

$$= \$30 \text{ per professional labor hour}$$

Step 4) **Allocate indirect costs to client jobs using the predetermined rate.** Throughout the year, indirect costs are allocated to individual client jobs using the predetermined indirect cost allocation rate. For example, assume Theresa Fox was the only attorney who worked on Client 367. Since Fox spent 14 hours working on Client 367, the amount of indirect cost allocated to the job is computed as follows:

= Predetermined indirect cost allocation rate × Actual amount of allocation base used by the job

= $30 per professional labor hour × 14 professional labor hours

= $420

Finding the Total Cost of the Job and Adding a Profit Markup

Barnett & Associates can now determine the total cost of serving Client 367:

Direct costs traced to Client 367 ($50 per hour × 14 hours).....................	$ 700
Indirect costs allocated to Client 367 ($30 per hour × 14 hour)	420
Total cost of serving Client 367	$1,120

Once the total job cost is known, Barnett & Associates can determine the amount to bill the client. Let's assume that Barnett & Associates wants to achieve a 25% profit over its costs. To achieve this profit, Barnett would bill Client 367 as follows:

Job cost + Markup for Profit = Amount to bill the client

$1,120 + (25% × $1,120) = $1,400

Invoicing the Client Using a Professional Billing Rate

When service firms and trades people bill their clients, they rarely show the actual direct costs of providing the service, the allocation of indirect costs, or the profit they earned on the job. Rather, these figures are "hidden" from the client's view. How is this done? By incorporating these costs and profit components in the labor rate, often known as the **billing rate**, charged to the customer. Consider the last time you had your vehicle repaired. A typical mechanic billing rate exceeds $48 per hour, yet the mechanic employed by the auto repair shop does not actually earn a $48 per hour wage rate.

> ### Why is this important?
>
> "Service companies and trades (such as law firms, auto repair shops, and plumbers) use job costing to determine how much to bill their clients."

Let's look at the calculations a service firm performs "behind the scenes" to determine its hourly billing rates. Barnett & Associates determines Theresa Fox's billing rate as follows:

Professional labor cost per hour..	$ 50
Plus: Indirect cost allocation rate per hour	30
Total hourly cost...	$ 80
Multiplied by the 25% profit markup..	× 1.25
Hourly billing rate for Theresa Fox...	$100

Whenever Theresa Fox performs legal work for a client, her time will be billed at $100 per hour. Remember, this is the *price* Barnett & Associates charges its clients for any work performed by Theresa Fox. The actual invoice to Client 367 would look similar to Exhibit 3-20.

EXHIBIT 3-20 Invoice to Client

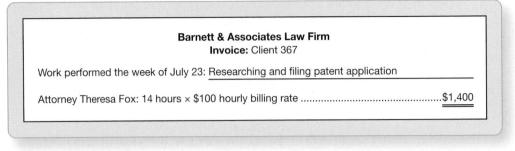

Barnett & Associates Law Firm
Invoice: Client 367

Work performed the week of July 23: Researching and filing patent application

Attorney Theresa Fox: 14 hours × $100 hourly billing rate $1,400

What Journal Entries are Needed in a Service Firm's Job Costing System?

The journal entries required for job costing at a service firm are much simpler than those used at a manufacturing company. That's because service firms typically have no inventory; hence, there is no need to record the movement of inventory through the system. Rather, all costs at a service company are treated as period costs, meaning they are immediately recorded as operating expenses when they are incurred (for example, salaries expense, rent expense, telephone expense, supplies expense, and so forth). The tracing of direct costs and allocation of indirect costs is performed *only* on the client's job cost record; *not* through journal entries to the company's general ledger.

REVIEW

Accounting Vocabulary

Bill of Materials. (p. 102)   A list of all of the raw materials needed to manufacture a job.

Billing Rate. (p. 131)   The labor rate charged to the customer, which includes both cost and profit components.

Cost Driver. (p. 109)   The primary factor that causes a cost.

Cost-Plus Pricing. (p. 112)   A pricing approach in which the company adds a desired level of profit to the product's cost.

Job Cost Record. (p. 103)   A written or electronic document that lists the direct materials, direct labor, and manufacturing overhead costs assigned to each individual job.

Job Costing. (p. 99)   A system for assigning costs to products or services that differ in the amount of materials, labor, and overhead required. Typically used by manufacturers that produce unique, or custom-ordered products in small batches; also used by professional service firms.

Invoice. (p. 103)   Bill from a supplier.

Labor Time Record. (p. 107)   A written or electronic document that identifies the employee, the amount of time spent on a particular job, and the labor cost charged to a job.

Materials Requisition. (p. 104)   A written or electronic document that requests specific materials be transferred from the raw materials inventory storeroom to the production floor.

Overallocated Manufacturing Overhead. (p. 115)   The amount of manufacturing overhead allocated to jobs is more than the amount of manufacturing overhead costs actually incurred; results in jobs being overcosted.

Pick. (p. 105)   Storeroom workers remove items from raw materials inventory that are needed by production.

Predetermined Manufacturing Overhead Rate. (p. 109)   The rate used to allocate manufacturing overhead to individual jobs; calculated before the year begins as follows: total estimated manufacturing overhead costs divided by total estimated amount of allocation base.

Process Costing. (p. 98)   A system for assigning costs to a large numbers of identical units that typically pass through a series of uniform production steps. Costs are averaged over the units produced such that each unit bears the same unit cost.

Production Schedule. (p. 101)   A written or electronic document indicating the quantity and types of inventory that will be manufactured during a specified time frame.

Purchase Order. (p. 103)   A written or electronic document authorizing the purchase of specific raw materials from a specific supplier.

Raw Materials Record. (p. 102)   A written or electronic document listing the number and cost of all units used and received, and the balance currently in stock; a separate record is maintained for each type of raw material kept in stock.

Receiving Report. (p. 103)   A written or electronic document listing the quantity and type of raw materials received in an incoming shipment; the report is typically a duplicate of the purchase order without the quantity prelisted on the form.

Stock Inventory. (p. 101)   Products normally kept on hand in order to quickly fill customer orders.

Subsidiary Ledger. (p. 119)   Supporting detail for a general ledger account.

Underallocated Manufacturing Overhead. (p. 115)   The amount of manufacturing overhead allocated to jobs is less than the amount of manufacturing overhead costs actually incurred; this results in jobs being undercosted.

Quick Check

1. *(Learning Objective 1)* Which of the following companies would be most likely to use a job costing system rather than a process costing system?
   a. Steel manufacturer
   b. Legal firm
   c. Beverage bottler
   d. Paint manufacturer

2. *(Learning Objective 1)* Would the advertising agency Saatchi & Saatchi use job or process costing? What about a Georgia-Pacific paper mill?
   a. Saatchi & Saatchi—job costing
      Georgia-Pacific—job costing
   b. Saatchi & Saatchi—process costing
      Georgia-Pacific—process costing
   c. Saatchi & Saatchi—process costing
      Georgia-Pacific—job costing
   d. Saatchi & Saatchi—job costing
      Georgia-Pacific—process costing

3. *(Learning Objective 2)* In a job costing system, all of the following statements about materials are correct *except* for which of the following?
   a. A materials requisition is used to request materials needed from the storeroom.
   b. The job cost record for a job will contain all direct material used for that particular job.
   c. Materials that cannot be traced to a particular job are treated as manufacturing overhead.
   d. All materials are always classified as direct materials.

4. *(Learning Objective 4)* How does Dell's management use product cost information?
   a. To set prices of its products
   b. To decide which products to emphasize
   c. To identify ways to cut production costs
   d. All of the above

5. *(Learning Objective 3)* The formula to calculate the amount of manufacturing overhead to allocate to jobs is
   a. predetermined overhead rate times the actual amount of the allocation base used by the specific job.
   b. predetermined overhead rate divided by the actual allocation base used by the specific job.
   c. predetermined overhead rate times the actual manufacturing overhead used on the specific job.
   d. predetermined overhead rate times the estimated amount of the allocation base used by the specific job.

6. *(Learning Objective 3)* Averaging is involved in computing unit product costs when
   a. using process costing but not when using job order costing.
   b. using job order costing but not when using process costing.
   c. using both job order costing and process costing.
   d. averaging is not involved when using either job costing or process costing.

7. *(Learning Objective 4)* For which of the following reasons would John Barnett, owner of the Barnett Associates law firm, want to know the total costs of a job (serving a particular client)?
   a. To determine the fees charged to the client
   b. For inventory valuation
   c. For external reporting
   d. All of the above

8. *(Learning Objective 5)* If the company underestimates the amount of allocation base when calculating its predetermined manufacturing overhead rate but estimates the amount of manufacturing overhead costs correctly, the amount of manufacturing overhead allocated for the year will be
   a. underallocated.
   b. overallocated.
   c. exactly equal to the actual manufacturing overhead for the year.
   d. unable to determine from the information given.

9. *(Learning Objective 5)* If manufacturing overhead is overallocated for the period by $200, then
   a. the $200 should be prorated between Work in Process inventory, Finished Goods inventory, and Cost of Goods Sold.
   b. actual manufacturing overhead is greater than allocated manufacturing overhead.
   c. jobs have been overcosted during the period.
   d. Cost of Goods Sold should be adjusted by an increase of $200.

10. *(Learning Objective 6)* When Dell *uses* direct labor, it *traces* the cost to the job by debiting
    a. Direct Labor.
    b. Wages Payable.
    c. Manufacturing Overhead.
    d. Work in Process Inventory.

ASSESS YOUR PROGRESS

Learning Objectives

1 Distinguish between job costing and process costing

2 Understand the flow of production and how direct materials and direct labor are traced to jobs

3 Compute a predetermined manufacturing overhead rate and use it to allocate MOH to jobs

4 Determine the cost of a job and use it to make business decisions

5 Compute and dispose of overallocated or underallocated manufacturing overhead

6 Prepare journal entries for a manufacturer's job costing system

7 (Appendix) Use job costing at a service firm as a basis for billing clients

Short Exercises

S3-1 Decide on product costing system *(Learning Objective 1)*

Would the following companies use job costing or process costing?
a.   A manufacturer of fiberglass insulation
b.   A residential plumbing contractor
c.   A manufacturer of fiber optic cabling
d.   A custom home builder
e.   A hospital

S3-2 Determine the flow of costs between inventory accounts *(Learning Objective 2)*

Parker's Wood Amenities is a manufacturing plant that makes picnic tables, benches, and other outdoor furniture. Indicate which inventory account(s) would be affected by the following actions, which occur at Parker's in the process of manufacturing its standard picnic tables. Also indicate whether the inventory account would increase or decrease as a result of the action.

Action	Raw Materials Inventory	Work in Process Inventory	Finished Goods Inventory
a. Lumber is delivered by the supplier to the plant, where it is stored in a materials storeroom until needed.			
b. Lumber is requisitioned from the storeroom to be used for tops and seats for the tables.			
c. Factory workers cut the lumber for the tables.			
d. Ten tables are completed and moved to the inventory storage area to await sale.			
e. A customer purchases a table and takes it home.			

S3-3 Compute various manufacturing overhead rates *(Learning Objective 3)*

Therrien Pools manufactures swimming pool equipment. Therrien estimates total manufacturing costs next year to be $1,200,000. Therrien also estimates it will use 50,000 direct labor hours and incur $1,000,000 of direct labor cost next year. In addition, the machines are expected to be run for 40,000 hours. Compute the predetermined manufacturing overhead rate for next year under the following independent situations:

1. Assume that Therrien uses direct labor hours as its manufacturing overhead allocation base.

2. Assume that Therrien uses direct labor cost as its manufacturing overhead allocation base.

3. Assume that Therrien uses machine hours as its manufacturing allocation base.

S3-4 Continuation of S3-3: compute total allocated overhead (Learning Objective 3)

Use your answers from S3-3 to determine the total manufacturing overhead allocated to Therrien's manufacturing jobs in the following independent situations:

1. Assume that Therrien actually used 52,300 direct labor hours.

2. Assume that Therrien actually incurred $1,025,000 of direct labor cost.

3. Assume that Therrien actually ran the machines 39,500 hours.

4. Briefly explain what you have learned about the total manufacturing overhead allocated to production.

S3-5 Continuation of S3-4: determine over- or underallocation (Learning Objectives 3 & 5)

Use your answers from S3-4 to determine the total overallocation or underallocation of manufacturing overhead during the year. Actual manufacturing costs for the year totaled $1,225,000.

1. Assume that Therrien used direct labor hours as the allocation base.

2. Assume that Therrien used the direct labor cost as the allocation base.

3. Assume that Therrien used machine hours as the allocation base.

4. Were there any situations in which jobs were costed correctly? If not, when were they overcosted? When were they undercosted?

S3-6 Calculate rate and analyze year-end results (Learning Objectives 3 & 5)

Rainbow manufactures wooden backyard playground equipment. Rainbow estimated $1,785,000 of manufacturing overhead and $2,100,000 of direct labor cost for the year. After the year was over, the accounting records indicated that the company had actually incurred $1,700,000 of manufacturing overhead and $2,200,000 of direct labor cost.

1. Calculate Rainbow's predetermined manufacturing overhead rate assuming that the company uses direct labor cost as an allocation base.

2. How much manufacturing overhead would have been allocated to manufacturing jobs during the year?

3. At year-end, was manufacturing overhead overallocated or underallocated? By how much? (Hint: Use a T-account to aid in your analysis.)

S3-7 Calculate job cost and billing (Learning Objectives 2 & 4)

Troy James is the owner of a business that sells and installs home theater systems. He just completed a job for a builder consisting of the installation of twelve home theater systems in a new condominium complex. The installations required materials totaling $17,400 and 72 hours of direct labor hours at a wage rate of $20 per hour. Overhead is allocated to jobs using a predetermined overhead rate of $5 per direct labor hour.

1. What is the total cost of the job?

2. What is the average unit cost (per theater system installed)?

3. If Troy charges a price to the builder that is 150% of the total job cost, what price will he charge for the job?

S3-8 Calculate job cost and billing at appliance repair service (Learning Objectives 2 & 4)

A-1 Appliance provides repair services for all makes and models of home appliances. A-1 Appliance charges customers for labor on each job at a rate of $50 per hour. The labor rate is high enough to cover actual technician wages of $20 per hour, to cover shop overhead (allocated at a cost of $12 per hour), and to provide a profit. A-1 Appliance charges the customer "at cost" for parts and materials. A recent customer job consisted of $37 in parts and materials and two hours of technician time.

1. What was A-1 Appliance's cost for this job? Include shop overhead in the cost calculation.

2. How much was charged to the customer for this repair job?

S3-9 Ramifications of overallocating and underallocating jobs *(Learning Objectives 2 & 5)*

Answer the following questions:

1. Why do managers use a *predetermined* manufacturing overhead allocation rate rather than the *actual* rate to cost jobs?

2. Jobs will typically be overcosted or undercosted. Is one worse than the other? Explain your thoughts.

S3-10 Record purchase and use of materials *(Learning Objective 6)*

Trekker manufactures backpacks. Its plant records include the following materials-related transactions:

Purchases of canvas (on account)	$70,000
Purchases of thread (on account)	1,100
Material requisitions:	
Canvas	63,000
Thread	280

Make the journal entries to record these transactions. Post these transactions to the Raw Materials Inventory account. If the company had $35,680 of Raw Materials Inventory at the beginning of the period, what is the ending balance of Raw Materials Inventory?

S3-11 Record manufacturing labor costs *(Learning Objective 6)*

Art Glass reports the following labor-related transactions at its plant in Seattle, Washington.

Plant janitor's wages	600
Plant supervisor's wages	900
Glassblowers' wages	76,000

Record the journal entries for the incurrence of these wages.

S3-12 Recompute job cost at a legal firm *(Learning Objectives 3, 4, & 7)*

In the Barnett Associates example in the appendix to this chapter, suppose Fox's annual salary is $110,000 rather than $100,000. Also suppose the Barnett's attorneys are expected to work a total of 12,000 direct labor hours rather than 10,000 direct labor hours.

1. What would be the hourly (cost) rate to Barnett Associates of employing Fox?

2. What direct labor cost would be traced to Client 367?

3. What is the indirect cost allocation rate?

4. What indirect costs will be allocated to Client 367?

5. What is the total job cost for client 367?

Exercises—Group A

E3-13A   Identify type of costing system *(Learning Objective 1)*

For each of the following companies, specify whether each company would be more likely to use job costing or process costing.

a. Jumbo airline manufacturer

b. Oil refinery

c. Custom cabinet manufacturer

d. Cereal manufacturer

e. Dentist office

   f. Auto body repair shop

   g. Mainframe computer manufacturer

   h. CPA firm

   i. Print shop

   j. Paper manufacturer

   k. Movie production company

   l. Hospital

  m. Prescription eyewear retailer with on-site lab

   n. Brewery

E3-14A Describe the flow of costs in a job cost shop *(Learning Objective 2)*

Simple Sign Company is a manufacturer of routered outdoor signs made from recycled plastic lumber (HDPE). The following table contains events that occur in the manufacture and sale of signs by Simple Sign Company. Put the events in the order in which they would occur by designating the step number in the Order column. Also indicate with a "+" or a "−" whether that account would increase or decrease as a result of the event.

Event	Order	Raw Materials Inventory	WIP Inventory	FG Inventory	Cost of Goods Sold	No effect on inventory or COGS
a. The eight basic "Entrance" signs are completed and are stored in the finished goods warehouse.						
b. Six sheets of the HDPE sheets are taken from the stockroom to be cut down into 12 half sheets, which is a common dimension for signs made by Simple Sign Company.						
c. The customer is billed for the five basic "Entrance" signs.						
d. Mark Hawkins, an employee of Simple Sign Company, routers the lettering for eight basic "Entrance" signs on eight of the half sheets.						
e. An order of recycled plastic lumber (HDPE) sheets, the primary component in making the outdoor routered signs, is received by Simple Sign Company. The HDPE sheets are stored in the stockroom until needed in production.						
f. An order is received for five basic "Entrance" signs and the signs are shipped to the customer.						

E3-15A   Understanding key document terms in a job cost shop *(Learning Objective 2)*

Match each of the following statements with the corresponding document term.

Statement	Term
1. Incoming shipments of raw materials are counted and recorded on this document, a(n) _____, which does not include pre-printed quantities or prices.	a. Bill of materials
	b. Job cost record
2. The time spent by each employee on each job he or she worked on throughout the day is detailed on a(n) _____.	c. Production schedule
	d. Purchase order
3. A supplier would issue a(n) _____ to bill the customer for products the customer ordered and received.	e. Raw materials record
	f. Labor time record
4. Information about each item in stock, including number of units received and the balance of units currently in stock, would be found on a(n) _____.	g. Receiving report
	h. Materials requisition
5. A listing of all of the raw materials needed to manufacture the job would be found on a(n) _____.	i. Invoice
6. A(n) _____ itemizes the raw materials currently needed from the storeroom and provides documentation of authorization for the request.	
7. The _____ indicates the quantity and types of inventory that are planned to be manufactured during the given time period.	
8. A(n) _____ is used to accumulate all of the direct materials and direct labor used on a job, as well as the manufacturing overhead allocated to the job.	
9. A(n) _____ is authorization for a supplier to ship products at a given price.	

E3-16A   Understand the flow of costs in a job cost shop *(Learning Objective 2)*

Smythe Feeders manufactures bird feeders for wild bird specialty stores. In September, Smythe Feeders received an order from Wild Birds, Inc., for 20 platform bird feeders. The order from Wild Birds, Inc., became Job Number 1102 at Smythe Feeders.

A materials requisition for Job 1102 is presented in the following section. In addition to the materials requisition, the labor time records (partial) for the week that these feeders were made are presented. Other products were also being produced during that week, so not all of the labor belongs to Job 1102.

Materials Requisition
Number: #1250

Date: 9/14

Job: 1102

Part Number	Description	Quantity	Unit Cost	Amount
WOCD06	Rough-hewn cedar planks	40	$2.50	
SSF0304	Stainless steel fasteners	80	$0.50	
AS222	Reinforced aluminum screens	20	$1.50	
	Total			

Labor Time Record

Employee: Greg Henderson   **Week:** 9/14 – 9/20

Hourly Wage Rate: $12   **Record #:** 912

Date	Job Number	Start Time	End Time	Hours	Cost
9/14	1102	9:00	2:00		
9/14	1103	2:00	5:00		
9/15 etc.					

Labor Time Record

Employee: Andrew Peck   **Week:** 9/14 – 9/20

Hourly Wage Rate: $8   **Record #:** 913

Date	Job Number	Start Time	End Time	Hours	Cost
9/14	1101	8:00	12:00		
9/14	1102	12:00	4:00		
9/15	1103	8:00	10:00		
9/15 etc.					

Job Cost Record

Job Number: 1102

Customer: Wild Birds, Inc.

Job Description: 20 Model 3F (platform bird feeders)

Date Started: Sep. 14   **Date Completed:** _____

Manufacturing Cost Information:	Cost Summary
Direct Materials	
Req. # :	
Direct Labor	
No. #	
No. #	
Manufacturing Overhead	
9 hours × $2 per direct labor hour	$ 18
Total Job Cost	
Number of Units	÷
Cost per Unit	

Requirements

1. Calculate the total for the Materials Requisition form. Post the information (cost and requisition number) from the Materials Requisition form to the Job Cost Record in the appropriate boxes.

2. Complete the labor time records for each of the employees. Once the labor time record is completed, post the information relevant to Job #1102 to the Job Cost Record for Job Cost #1102.

3. Manufacturing overhead has already been added to the Job Cost Record. Complete the Job Cost Record by calculating the total job cost and the cost per unit. Remember that this job consisted of 20 feeders (units).

E3-17A   Compute a predetermined overhead rate and calculate cost of jobs *(Learning Objectives 3 & 4)*

Lakeland Heating & Cooling installs and services commercial heating and cooling systems. Lakeland uses job costing to calculate the cost of its jobs. Overhead is allocated to each job based on the number of direct labor hours spent on that job. At the beginning of the current year, Lakeland estimated that its overhead for the coming year would be $60,000. It also anticipated using 4,000 direct labor hours for the year. In November, Lakeland started and completed the following two jobs:

	Job 101	Job 102
Direct materials used	$17,000	$12,000
Direct labor hours used	120	78

Lakeland paid a $22 per hour wage rate to the employees who worked on these two jobs.

Requirements

1. What is Lakeland's predetermined overhead rate based on direct labor hours?

2. Calculate the overhead to be allocated based on direct labor hours to each of the two jobs.

3. What is the total cost of Job 101? What is the total cost of Job 102?

E3-18A   Compute a predetermined overhead rate and calculate cost of job *(Learning Objectives 3 & 4)*

Dellroy Restaurant Supply manufactures commercial stoves and ovens for restaurants and bakeries. Dellroy uses job costing to calculate the costs of its jobs with direct labor cost as its manufacturing overhead allocation base. At the beginning of the current year, Dellroy estimated that its overhead for the coming year would be $300,000. It also anticipated using 25,000 direct labor hours for the year. Dellroy pays its employees an average of $20 per direct labor hour. Dellroy just finished Job 371, which consisted of two large ovens for a regional bakery. The costs for Job 371 were as follows:

	Job 371
Direct materials used	$13,000
Direct labor hours used	110

Requirements

1. What is Dellroy's predetermined manufacturing overhead rate based on direct labor cost?

2. Calculate the manufacturing overhead to be allocated based on direct labor cost to Job 371.

3. What is the total cost of Job 371?

E3-19A   Determine the cost of a job and use it for pricing *(Learning Objectives 2 & 4)*

Playtime Industries manufactures custom-designed playground equipment for schools and city parks. Playtime expected to incur $664,000 of manufacturing overhead cost, 41,500 of direct labor hours, and $830,000 of direct labor cost during the year (the cost of direct labor is $20 per hour). The company allocates manufacturing overhead on the basis of direct labor hours. During May, Playtime completed Job 301. The job used 155 direct labor hours and required $12,700 of direct materials. The City of Westlake has contracted to purchase the playground equipment at a price of 20% over manufacturing cost.

Requirements

1. Calculate the manufacturing cost of Job 301.

2. How much will the City of Westlake pay for this playground equipment?

E3-20A Calculate job cost, billing, and profit at a car care center *(Learning Objectives 2, 4, & 7)*

Conrad's Car Care Center specializes in providing car tune-ups, brake jobs, and tire replacements for most vehicle makes and models. Conrad's charges customers for materials "at cost" but charges labor at a rate of $84 per hour. The labor rate is high enough to cover actual mechanic wages ($24 per hour), to cover shop overhead (allocated at a cost of $16 per hour), and to provide a profit. Cory recently had a 60,000-mile service performed on his Honda Pilot. Materials used on the job included $9.95 for oil and filter, $60.45 for transmission fluid exchange, $20.86 for the air filter, and $33.02 for the cabin filter. The mechanic spent 1.25 hours on the job.

Requirements

1. How much was charged to the customer for this work?

2. What was Conrad's cost for this job?

3. How much profit did Conrad's earn on this job?

E3-21A Understanding key terms *(Learning Objectives 1, 2, 3, & 4)*

Listed next are several terms. Complete the following statements with one of these terms. You may use a term more than once, and some terms may not be used at all.

Cost allocation	Cost driver	Job costing	Process costing
Cost tracing	Job cost record	Materials requisition	

a. A _____ shows the accumulation of costs of an individual job.

b. _____ is used by companies that produce small quantities of many different products.

c. A _____ is the primary factor that causes costs.

d. Georgia-Pacific pulverizes wood into pulp to manufacture cardboard. The company would use a _____ system.

e. To record costs of maintaining thousands of identical mortgage files, financial institutions such as Money Tree would use a _____ system.

f. _____ is assigning direct costs to cost objects.

g. Companies that produce large numbers of identical products use _____ systems for product costing.

h. The computer repair service that visits your home and repairs your computer would use a _____ system.

i. A _____ is manufacturing personnel's request that materials be moved to the production floor.

j. _____ is assigning indirect costs to cost objects.

E3-22A Determine the cost of a job *(Learning Objectives 2, 3, & 4)*

E-Z-Boy started and finished Job 310 during April. The company's records show that the following direct materials were requisitioned for Job 310:

Lumber: 50 units at $9 per unit

Padding: 15 yards at $20 per yard

Upholstery fabric: 30 yards at $25 per yard

Labor time records show the following employees (direct labor) worked on Job 310:

Vince Owens: 10 hours at $10 per hour

Patrick Erin: 15 hours at $15 per hour

E-Z-Boy allocates manufacturing overhead at a rate of $9 per direct labor hour.

Requirements

1. Compute the total amount of direct materials, direct labor, and manufacturing overhead that should be shown on Job 310's job cost record.

2. Job 310 consists of five recliners. If each recliner sells for $600, what is the gross profit per recliner?

E3-23A   Compare bid prices under two different allocation bases *(Learning Objectives 3 & 4)*

Middleton Recycling recycles newsprint, cardboard, and so forth, into recycled packaging materials. For the coming year, Middleton Recycling estimates total manufacturing overhead to be $360,000. The company's managers are not sure if direct labor hours (estimated to be 10,000) or machine hours (estimated to be 15,000 hours) is the best allocation base to use for allocating manufacturing overhead. Middleton Recycling bids for jobs using a 30% markup over total manufacturing cost.

After the new fiscal year began, Wisconsin Paper Supply asked Middleton Recycling to bid for a job that will take 2,000 machine hours and 1,600 direct labor hours to produce. The direct labor cost for this job will be $12 per hour, and the direct materials will total $25,000.

Requirements

1. Compute the total job cost and bid price if Middleton Recycling decided to use direct labor hours as the manufacturing overhead allocation base for the year.

2. Compute the total job cost and bid price if Middleton Recycling decided to use machine hours as the manufacturing overhead allocation base for the year.

3. In addition to the bid from Middleton Recycling, Wisconsin Paper Supply received a bid of $125,000 for this job from Sun Prairie Recycling. What are the ramifications for Middleton Recycling?

E3-24A   Job cost and bid price at a consulting firm *(Learning Objectives 3 & 4)*

Black Consulting, a real estate consulting firm, specializes in advising companies on potential new plant sites. Black Consulting uses a job cost system with a predetermined indirect cost allocation rate computed as a percentage of expected direct labor costs.

At the beginning of the year, managing partner Tony Black prepared the following plan, or budget, for the year:

Direct labor hours (professionals)	17,000 hours
Direct labor costs (professionals)	$2,669,000
Office rent	350,000
Support staff salaries	1,194,300
Utilities	324,000

Land Resources is inviting several consulting firms to bid for work. Black estimates that this job will require about 220 direct labor hours.

Requirements

1. Compute Black Consulting's (a) hourly direct labor cost rate and (b) indirect cost allocation rate.

2. Compute the predicted cost of the Land Resources job.

3. If Black wants to earn a profit that equals 50% of the job's cost, how much should he bid for the Land Resources job?

E3-25A   Analyze manufacturing overhead *(Learning Objectives 3 & 5)*

Freeman Foundry in Charleston, South Carolina, uses a predetermined manufacturing overhead rate to allocate overhead to individual jobs based on the machine hours required. At the beginning of the year, the company expected to incur the following:

Manufacturing overhead costs	$ 600,000
Direct labor cost	1,500,000
Machine hours	75,000

At the end of the year, the company had actually incurred the following:

Direct labor cost	$1,210,000
Depreciation on manufacturing plant and equipment	480,000
Property taxes on plant	20,000
Sales salaries	25,000
Delivery drivers' wages	15,000
Plant janitors' wages	10,000
Machine hours	55,000 hours

Requirements

1. Compute Freeman's predetermined manufacturing overhead rate.
2. How much manufacturing overhead was allocated to jobs during the year?
3. How much manufacturing overhead was incurred during the year? Is manufacturing overhead underallocated or overallocated at the end of the year? By how much?
4. Were the jobs overcosted or undercosted? By how much?

E3-26A   Record manufacturing overhead (*Learning Objectives 5 & 6*)

Refer to the data in Exercise 3-25A. Freeman's accountant found an error in the expense records from the year reported. Depreciation on manufacturing plant and equipment was actually $400,000, not the $480,000 that had originally reported. The unadjusted Cost of Goods Sold balance at year-end was $600,000.

Requirements

1. Prepare the journal entry(s) to record manufacturing overhead costs incurred.
2. Prepare the journal entry to record the manufacturing overhead allocated to jobs in production.
3. Use a T-account to determine whether manufacturing overhead is underallocated or overallocated and by how much.
4. Record the entry to close out the underallocated or overallocated manufacturing overhead.
5. What is the adjusted ending balance of Cost of Goods Sold?

E3-27A   Determine transactions from T-accounts (*Learning Objectives 2 & 6*)

Use the following T-accounts to determine the cost of direct materials used and indirect materials used.

Raw Materials Inventory				Work in Process Inventory		
Balance	16			Balance	32	
Purchases	230	X				
Balance	24			Direct materials	Y	Cost of goods manufactured 744
				Direct labor	320	
				Manufacturing overhead	200	
				Balance	8	

E3-28A Record journal entries *(Learning Objectives 2, 3, 5, & 6)*

The following transactions were incurred by Dutch Fabricators during January, the first month of its fiscal year.

Requirements

1. Record the proper journal entry for each transaction.
   a. $190,000 of materials were purchased on account.
   b. $174,000 of materials were used in production; of this amount, $152,000 was used on specific jobs.
   c. Manufacturing labor and salaries for the month totaled $225,000. A total of $190,000 of manufacturing labor and salaries was traced to specific jobs, while the remainder was indirect labor used in the factory.
   d. The company recorded $20,000 of depreciation on the plant and plant equipment. The company also received a plant utility bill for $10,000.
   e. $81,000 of manufacturing overhead was allocated to specific jobs.

2. By the end of January, was manufacturing overhead overallocated or underallocated? By how much?

E3-29A Analyze T-accounts *(Learning Objectives 2, 3, 5, & 6)*

Touch Enterprises produces LCD touch screen products. The company reports the following information at December 31. Touch Enterprises began operations on January 31 earlier that same year.

Work in Process Inventory		Wages Payable		Manufacturing Overhead		Finished Goods Inventory		Raw Materials Inventory	
30,000	123,000	70,000	70,000	2,000	48,000	123,000	111,000	52,000	32,000
60,000				10,000					
48,000		Balance 0		37,000					

Requirements

1. What is the cost of direct materials used?
2. What is the cost of indirect materials used?
3. What is the cost of direct labor?
4. What is the cost of indirect labor?
5. What is the cost of goods manufactured?
6. What is the cost of goods sold (before adjusting for any under- or overallocated manufacturing overhead)?
7. What is the actual manufacturing overhead?
8. How much manufacturing overhead was allocated to jobs?
9. What is the predetermined manufacturing overhead rate as a percentage of direct labor cost?
10. Is manufacturing overhead underallocated or overallocated? By how much?

E3-30A Prepare journal entries *(Learning Objectives 2, 3, & 6)*

Record the following transactions in Micro Speakers' general journal.
   a. Received bill for Web site expenses, $3,400.
   b. Incurred manufacturing wages, $15,000, 70% of which was direct labor and 30% of which was indirect labor.

c. Purchased materials on account, $14,750.

d. Used in production: direct materials, $7,000; indirect materials, $3,000.

e. Recorded manufacturing overhead: depreciation on plant, $13,000; prepaid plant insurance expired, $1,700; plant property tax, $4,200 (credit Property Tax Payable).

f. Allocated manufacturing overhead to jobs, 200% of direct labor costs.

g. Cost of jobs completed during the month: $33,000.

h. Sold all jobs (on account) completed during the month for $52,000. Assume a perpetual inventory system.

E3-31A Record completion and sale of jobs *(Learning Objectives 2 & 6)*

September production generated the following activity in Digital Connection's Work in Process Inventory:

Work in Process Inventory		
Sep 1 Bal	16,000	
Direct materials used	29,000	
Direct labor assigned to jobs	32,000	
Manufacturing overhead allocated to jobs	12,000	

Production completed in September but not recorded yet consists of Jobs B-78 and G-65, with total costs of $41,000 and $37,000, respectively.

Requirements

1. Compute the balance of Work in Process Inventory at September 30.

2. Prepare the journal entry for the production completed in September.

3. Prepare the journal entry to record the sale (on credit) of Job G-65 for $45,000. Assume a perpetual inventory system.

4. What is the gross profit of Job G-65? What other costs must this gross profit cover?

Exercises–Group B

E3-32B Identify type of costing system *(Learning Objective 1)*

For each of the following companies, specify whether each company would be more likely to use job costing or process costing.

a. Doctor's office

b. Hospital

c. Oil refinery

d. Textile (fabric) manufacturer

e. Corporate caterer

f. Ice cream manufacturer

g. Advertising agency

h. Computer chip manufacturer

i. Small engine repair shop

j. Soft drink bottler

k. Photography studio

l. Satellite manufacturer

m. Sugar manufacturer

n. Menswear custom tailor

E3-33B Describe the flow of costs in a job cost shop *(Learning Objective 2)*

Outdoor Furniture Company is a manufacturer of outdoor furniture made from recycled plastic lumber (HDPE). The following table contains events that occur in the manufacture and sale of signs by Outdoor Furniture Company. Put the events in the order in which they would occur by designating the step number in the Order column. Also indicate with a "+" or a "–" whether that account would increase or decrease as a result of the event.

Event	Order	Raw Materials Inventory	WIP Inventory	FG Inventory	Cost of Goods Sold	No effect on inventory or COGS
a. John Hosbach, an employee of Outdoor Furniture Company, drills holes into the cut lumber so that these pieces can be used in building the basic model of outdoor table.						
b. An order of recycled plastic lumber, the primary component in making the outdoor tables, is received by Outdoor Furniture Company. The plastic lumber is stored in the stockroom until needed in production.						
c. An order is received for five of the basic model outdoor tables and the tables are shipped to the customer.						
d. Several of the plastic lumber boards are taken from the stockroom to be cut down into the lengths used in the basic model of the outdoor table.						
e. The customer is billed for the five basic model outdoor tables.						
f. Twelve of the basic model outdoor tables are completed and are stored in the finished goods warehouse.						

E3-34B   Understanding key document terms in a job cost shop (*Learning Objective 2*)

Match each of the following statements with the corresponding document term.

Statement	Term
1. A supplier would issue a(n) _____ to bill the customer for products the customer ordered and received.	a. Invoice
2. The quantity and types of inventory that are planned to be manufactured during the given time period are indicated on the _____.	b. Receiving report
3. On a(n) _____ would be a listing of all the raw materials needed to manufacture the job.	c. Labor time record d. Purchase order
4. A(n) _____ itemizes the raw materials currently needed from the storeroom and provides documentation of authorization for the request.	e. Production schedule f. Bill of materials
5. A(n) _____ details the time spent by each employee on the job he or she worked on throughout the day.	g. Raw materials record h. Materials requisition
6. Information about each item in stock, including number of units received and the balance of units currently in stock, would be found on a(n) _____.	i. Job cost record
7. A(n) _____ is used to accumulate all of the direct materials and direct labor used on a job, as well as the manufacturing overhead allocated to the job.	
8. Authorization for a supplier to ship products at a given price is a(n) _____.	
9. A(n) _____ is where incoming shipments of raw materials are counted and recorded, but it does not include pre-printed quantities or prices.	

E3-35B   Understand the flow of costs in a job cost shop (*Learning Objective 2*)

Hamilton Feeders manufactures bird feeders for wild bird specialty stores. In September, Hamilton Feeders received an order from Wild Birds, Inc., for 24 platform bird feeders. The order from Wild Birds, Inc., became Job Number 1102 at Hamilton Feeders.

A materials requisition for Job 1102 is presented in the following section. In addition to the materials requisition, the labor time records (partial) for the week that these feeders were made are presented. Other products were also being produced during that week, so not all of the labor belongs to Job 1102.

Materials Requisition
Number: #1250

Date: 9/14

Job: 1102

Part Number	Description	Quantity	Unit Cost	Amount
WOCD06	Rough-hewn cedar planks	44	$2.50	
SSF0304	Stainless steel fasteners	84	$1.00	
AS222	Reinforced aluminum screens	28	$1.50	
	Total			

Labor Time Record

Employee: Greg Henderson

Week: 9/14 – 9/20

Hourly Wage Rate: $14

Record #: 912

Date	Job Number	Start Time	End Time	Hours	Cost
9/14	1102	8:00	12:00		
9/14	1103	12:00	4:00		
9/15 etc.					

Labor Time Record

Employee: Andrew Peck

Week: 9/14 – 9/20

Hourly Wage Rate: $6

Record #: 913

Date	Job Number	Start Time	End Time	Hours	Cost
9/14	1101	9:00	12:00		
9/14	1102	12:00	5:00		
9/15	1103	9:00	11:00		
9/15 etc.					

Job Cost Record

Job Number: 1102

Customer: Wild Birds, Inc.

Job Description: 20 Model 3F (platform bird feeders)

Date Started: Sep. 14   **Date Completed:** _____

Manufacturing Cost Information:	Cost Summary
Direct Materials	
Req. #:	
Direct Labor	
No. #	
No. #	
Manufacturing Overhead	
9 hours × $2 per direct labor hour	$ 18
Total Job Cost	
Number of Units	
Cost per Unit	

Requirements

1. Calculate the total for the Materials Requisition form. Post the information (cost and requisition number) from the Materials Requisition form to the Job Cost Record in the appropriate boxes.

2. Complete the labor time records for each of the employees. Once the labor time record is completed, post the information relevant to Job #1102 to the Job Cost Record for Job Cost #1102.

3. Manufacturing overhead has already been added to the Job Cost Record. Complete the Job Cost Record by calculating the total job cost and the cost per unit. Remember that this job consisted of 24 feeders (units).

E3-36B   Compute a predetermined overhead rate and calculate cost of jobs *(Learning Objectives 3 & 4)*

Dansville Heating & Cooling installs and services commercial heating and cooling systems. Dansville uses job costing to calculate the cost of its jobs. Overhead is allocated to each job based on the number of direct labor hours spent on that job. At the beginning of the current year, Dansville estimated that its overhead for the coming year would be $64,800. It also anticipated using 4,050 direct labor hours for the year. In May, Dansville started and completed the following two jobs:

	Job 101	Job 102
Direct materials used	$16,000	$13,500
Direct labor hours used	175	82

Dansville paid a $20 per hour wage rate to the employees who worked on these two jobs.

Requirements

1. What is Dansville's predetermined overhead rate based on direct labor hours?

2. Calculate the overhead to be allocated based on direct labor hours to each of the two jobs.

3. What is the total cost of Job 101? What is the total cost of Job 102?

E3-37B   Compute a predetermined overhead rate and calculate cost of job *(Learning Objectives 3 & 4)*

Elkland Restaurant Supply manufactures commercial stove and ovens for restaurants and bakeries. Elkland uses job costing to calculate the costs of its jobs with direct labor cost as its manufacturing overhead allocation base. At the beginning of the current year, Elkland estimated that its overhead for the coming year will be $292,600. It also anticipated using 27,500 direct labor hours for the year. Elkland pays its employees an average of $19 per direct labor hour. Elkland just finished job 371, which consisted of two large ovens for a reginonal bakery. The costs for Job 371 were as follows:

	Job 371
Direct materials used	$17,500
Direct labor hours used	165

Requirements

1. What is Elkland's predetermined manufacturing overhead rate based on direct labor cost?

2. Calculate the manufacturing overhead to be allocated based on direct labor hours to Job 371.

3. What is the total cost of Job 371?

E3-38B   Determine the cost of a job and use it for pricing *(Learning Objectives 2 & 4)*

All Wood Industries manufactures custom-designed playground equipment for schools and city parks. All Wood expected to incur $637,500 of manufacturing overhead cost, 42,500 of direct labor hours, and $860,000 of direct labor cost during the year (the cost of direct labor is $38 per hour). The company allocates manufacturing overhead on the basis of direct labor hours. During May, All Wood completed Job 305. The job used 180 direct labor hours and required $13,000 of direct materials. The City of Ogdenville has contracted to purchase the playground equipment at a price of 23% over manufacturing cost.

Requirements

1. Calculate the manufacturing cost of Job 305.

2. How much will the City of Ogdenville pay for this playground equipment?

E3-39B Calculate job cost, billing, and profit at a car care center *(Learning Objectives 2, 4, & 7)*

Alan's Car Care Center specializes in providing car tune-ups, brake jobs, and tire replacements for most vehicle makes and models. Alan's charges customers for materials "at cost" but charges labor at a rate of $87 per hour. The labor rate is high enough to cover actual mechanic wages ($29 per hour), to cover shop overhead (allocated at a cost of $18 per hour), and to provide a profit. Giles recently had a 45,000-mile service performed on his car. Materials used on the job included $15.50 for oil and filter, $65.45 for transmission fluid exchange, $21.35 for the air filter, and $32.78 for the cabin filter. The mechanic spent 1.75 hours on the job.

Requirements

1. How much was charged to the customer for this work?

2. What was Alan's cost for this job?

3. How much profit did Alan's earn on this job?

(Round all your answers to two decimal places.)

E3-40B Understanding key terms *(Learning Objectives 1, 2, 3, & 4)*

Listed next are several terms. Complete the following statements with one of these terms. You may use a term more than once, and some terms may not be used at all.

Materials requisition	Cost allocation	Job cost record	Process costing
Job cost record	Cost driver	Job costing	

a. The process of assigning direct costs to cost objects is called _____.

b. The local hospital would use a _____ system.

c. A paint manufacturer such as Sherwin-Williams would use a _____ system.

d. A _____ is manufacturing personnel's request that materials be moved to the production floor.

e. Companies that produce small qualities of many different products would use _____.

f. The process of assigning indirect costs to cost objects is called _____.

g. A _____ is the primary factor that causes costs.

h. To record costs of maintaining thousands of identical mortgage files, lending companies such as Quicken Loans would use a _____ system.

i. Companies that produce large numbers of identical products use _____ systems for product costing.

j. The direct materials, direct labor, and manufacturing overhead associated with an individual job are accumulated on a _____.

E3-41B Determine the cost of a job *(Learning Objectives 2, 3, & 4)*

Fontaine Furniture started and finished Job 310 during March. The company's records show that the following direct materials were requisitioned for Job 310:

> Lumber: 47 units at $9 per unit
>
> Padding: 17 yards at $18 per yard
>
> Upholstery fabric: 32 yards at $23 per yard.

Labor time records show the following employees (direct labor) worked on Job 310:

> Jeff Inglis: 8 hours at $12 per hour
>
> Patrick Erin: 12 hours at $14 per hour.

Fontaine Furniture allocates manufacturing overhead at a rate of $8 per direct labor hour.

Requirements

1. Compute the total amount of direct materials, direct labor, and manufacturing overhead that should be shown on Job 310's job cost record.

2. Job 310 consists of seven recliners. If each recliner sells for $700, what is the gross profit per recliner?

E3-42B Compare bid prices under two different allocation bases *(Learning Objectives 3 & 4)*

Wellington Recycling recycles newsprint, cardboard, and so forth, into recycled packaging materials. For the coming year, Wellington Recycling estimates total manufacturing overhead to be $360,360. The company's managers are not sure if direct labor hours (estimated to be 10,010) or machine hours (estimated to be 18,018 hours) is the best allocation base to use for allocating manufacturing overhead. Wellington Recycling bids for jobs using a 29% markup over total manufacturing cost.

After the new fiscal year began, Lundy Paper Supply asked Wellington Recycling to bid for a job that will take 1,995 machine hours and 1,750 direct labor hours to produce. The direct labor cost for this job will be $12 per hour, and the direct materials will total $25,400.

Requirements

1. Compute the total job cost and bid price if Wellington Recycling decided to use direct labor hours as the manufacturing overhead allocation base for the year.

2. Compute the total job cost and bid price if Wellington Recycling decided to use machine hours as the manufacturing overhead allocation base for the year.

3. In addition to the bid from Wellington Recycling, Lundy Paper Supply received a bid of $124,500 for this job from Kearns Recycling. What are the ramifications for Wellington Recycling?

E3-43B Job cost and bid price at a consulting firm *(Learning Objectives 3 & 4)*

Tibbs Consulting, a real estate consulting firm, specializes in advising companies on potential new plant sites. Tibbs Consulting uses a job costing system with a predetermined indirect cost allocation rate computed as a percentage of direct labor costs. At the beginning of the year, managing partner Kenneth Tibbs prepared the following plan, or budget, for the year:

Direct labor hours (professionals)	14,000 hours
Direct labor costs (professionals)	$2,150,000
Office rent	250,000
Support staff salaries	870,000
Utilities	350,000

Chance Resources is inviting several consultants to bid for work. Tibbs estimates that this job will require about 200 direct labor hours.

Requirements

1. Compute Tibbs Consulting's (a) hourly direct labor cost rate and (b) indirect cost allocation rate.

2. Compute the predicted cost of the Chance Resources job.

3. If Tibbs wants to earn a profit that equals 35% of the job's cost, how much should he bid for the Chance Resources job?

E3-44B Analyze manufacturing overhead *(Learning Objectives 3 & 5)*

Smith Foundry in Charleston, South Carolina, uses a predetermined manufacturing overhead rate to allocate overhead to individual jobs based on the machine hours required. At the beginning of the year, the company expected to incur the following:

Manufacturing overhead costs	$ 560,000
Direct labor cost	1,700,000
Machine hours	80,000

At the end of the year, the company had actually incurred the following:

Direct labor cost	$1,230,000
Depreciation on manufacturing plant and equipment	490,000
Property taxes on plant	18,500
Sales salaries	24,000
Delivery drivers' wages	16,000
Plant janitors' wages	11,000
Machine hours	57,000 hours

Requirements

1. Compute Smith's predetermined manufacturing overhead rate.

2. How much manufacturing overhead was allocated to jobs during the year?

3. How much manufacturing overhead was incurred during the year? Is manufacturing overhead underallocated or overallocated at the end of the year? By how much?

4. Were the jobs overcosted or undercosted? By how much?

E3-45B   Record manufacturing overhead *(Learning Objectives 5 & 6)*

Refer to the data in Exercise E3-44B. Smith's accountant found an error in the expense records from the year reported. Depreciation on manufacturing plant and equipment was actually $305,000, not the $490,000 it had originally reported. The unadjusted Cost of Goods Sold balance at year-end was $630,000.

Requirements

1. Prepare the journal entry(s) to record manufacturing overhead costs incurred.

2. Prepare the journal entry to record the manufacturing overhead allocated to jobs in production.

3. Use a T-account to determine whether manufacturing overhead is underallocated or overallocated, and by how much.

4. Record the entry to close out the underallocated or overallocated manufacturing overhead.

5. What is the adjusted ending balance of Cost of Goods Sold?

E3-46B   Determine transactions from T-accounts *(Learning Objectives 2 & 6)*

Use the following T-accounts to determine the cost of direct materials used and indirect materials used.

Raw Materials Inventory		
Balance	20	
Purchases	235	X
Balance	65	

Work in Process Inventory		
Balance	10	
Direct materials	Y	Cost of goods manufactured 550
Direct labor	305	
Manufacturing overhead	130	
Balance	20	

E3-47B   Record journal entries *(Learning Objectives 2, 3, 5, & 6)*

The following transactions were incurred by Whooley Fabricators during January, the first month of its fiscal year.

Requirements

1. Record the proper journal entry for each transaction.

   a. $205,000 of materials were purchased on account.

   b. $174,000 of materials were used in production; of this amount, $146,000 was used on specific jobs.

   c. Manufacturing labor and salaries for the month totaled $210,00. $200,000 of the total manufacturing labor and salaries was traced to specific jobs, while the remainder was indirect labor used in the factory.

   d. The company recorded $16,000 of depreciation on the plant and plant equipment. The company also received a plant utility bill for $14,000.

   e. $56,000 of manufacturing overhead was allocated to specific jobs.

2. By the end of January, was manufacturing overhead overallocated or underallocated? By how much?

E3-48B   Analyze T-accounts *(Learning Objectives 2, 3, 5, & 6)*

LCDs For You produces LCD touch screen products. The company reports the following information at December 31. LCDs For You began operations on January 31 earlier that same year.

Work in Process Inventory		Wages Payable		Manufacturing Overhead		Finished Goods Inventory		Raw Materials Inventory	
28,000	125,500	73,000	73,000	7,500	42,000	125,500	111,500	57,500	35,500
60,000				13,000					
42,000		Balance 0		41,500					

Requirements

1. What is the cost of direct materials used?

2. The cost of indirect materials used?

3. What is the cost of direct labor?

4. The cost of indirect labor?

5. What is the cost of goods manufactured?

6. What is the cost of goods sold (before adjusting for any under- or overallocated manufacturing overhead)?

7. What is the actual manufacturing overhead?

8. How much manufacturing overhead was allocated to jobs?

9. What is the predetermined manufacturing overhead rate as a percentage of direct labor cost?

10. Is manufacturing overhead underallocated or overallocated? By how much?

E3-49B   Prepare journal entries *(Learning Objectives 2, 3, & 6)*

Record the following transactions in Super Speakers' general journal.

   a. Received bill for Web site expenses, $2,200.

   b. Incurred manufacturing wages, $19,000, 55% of which was direct labor and 45% of which was indirect labor.

   c. Purchased materials on account, $18,000.

   d. Used in production: direct materials, $9,500; indirect materials, $4,000.

   e. Recorded manufacturing overhead: depreciation on plant, $14,000; prepaid plant insurance expired, $1,700; plant property tax, $3,500 (credit Property Tax Payable).

f. Allocated manufacturing overhead to jobs, 190% of direct labor costs.

g. Cost of jobs completed during the month, $38,000.

h. Sold all jobs (on account) completed during the month for $62,000. Assume a perpetual inventory system.

E3-50B Record completion and sale of jobs *(Learning Objectives 2 & 6)*

July production generated the following activity in Ciano Piano's Work in Process Inventory:

Work in Process Inventory		
Jul 1 Bal	15,750	
Direct materials used	28,600	
Direct labor assigned to jobs	32,150	
Manufacturing overhead allocated to jobs	12,250	

Completed Production in July not recorded yet consists of Jobs C-55 and G-72, with total costs of $40,600 and $36,900, respectively.

Requirements

1. Compute the balance of Work in Process Inventory at July 31.

2. Prepare the journal entry for the production completed in July.

3. Prepare the journal entry to record the sale (on credit) of Job G-72 for $43,900. Assume a perpetual inventory system.

4. What is the gross profit of Job G-72? What other costs must this gross profit cover?

Problems—Group A

P3-51A Analyze Manufacturing Overhead *(Learning Objectives 3 & 5)*

Suit Up produces uniforms. The company allocates manufacturing overhead based on the machine hours each job uses. Suit Up reports the following cost data for the past year:

	Budget	Actual
Direct labor hours	7,000 hours	6,200 hours
Machine hours	6,920 hours	6,400 hours
Depreciation on salespeople's autos	$22,000	$22,000
Indirect materials	50,000	52,000
Depreciation on trucks used to deliver uniforms to customers	14,000	12,000
Depreciation on plant and equipment	65,000	67,000
Indirect manufacturing labor	40,000	43,000
Customer service hotline	19,000	21,000
Plant utilities	18,000	20,000
Direct labor cost	70,000	85,000

Requirements

1. Compute the predetermined manufacturing overhead rate.

2. Calculate the allocated manufacturing overhead for the past year.

3. Compute the underallocated or overallocated Manufacturing Overhead. How will this under-allocated or overallocated Manufacturing Overhead be disposed of?

4. How can managers use accounting information to help control manufacturing overhead costs?

P3-52A   Use job costing at an advertising agency *(Learning Objectives 3, 4, & 7)*

Adnet.com is an Internet advertising agency. The firm uses a job cost system in which each client is a different "job." Adnet.com traces direct labor, software licensing costs, and travel costs directly to each job (client). The company allocates indirect costs to jobs based on a predetermined indirect cost allocation rate based on direct labor hours.

At the beginning of the current year, managing partner Ricky Buena prepared a budget:

Direct labor hours (professional)	17,500 hours
Direct labor costs (professional)	$1,750,000
Support staff salaries	305,000
Rent and utilities	95,000
Supplies	15,000
Lease payments on computer hardware	285,000

During January of the current year, Adnet.com served several clients. Records for two clients appear here:

	GoVacation.com	Port Armour Golf Resort
Direct labor hours	460 hours	32 hours
Software licensing costs	$1,490	$280
Travel costs	$9,000	$ 0

Requirements

1. Compute Adnet.com's predetermined indirect cost allocation rate for the current year based on direct labor hours.

2. Compute the total cost of each job.

3. If Adnet.com wants to earn profits equal to 20% of sales revenue, how much (what total fee) should it charge each of these two clients?

4. Why does Adnet.com assign costs to jobs?

P3-53A   Use job costing at a consulting firm *(Learning Objectives 3, 4, & 7)*

WB Design is a Web site design and consulting firm. The firm uses a job cost system in which each client is a different "job." WB Design traces direct labor, licensing costs, and travel costs directly to each job (client). It allocates indirect costs to jobs based on a prede-termined indirect cost allocation rate computed as a percentage of direct labor costs.

At the beginning of the current year, managing partner Mary Milici prepared the following budget:

Direct labor hours (professional)	8,000 hours
Direct labor costs (professional)	$1,000,000
Support staff salaries	80,000
Computer lease payments	46,000
Office supplies	25,000
Office rent	49,000

Later that same year in November, WB Design served several clients. Records for two clients appear here:

	Organic Foods	SunNow.com
Direct labor hours...	750 hours	50 hours
Licensing costs	$ 1,850	$160
Travel costs...	$14,150	$ 0

Requirements

1. Compute WB Design's predetermined indirect cost allocation rate for the current year.

2. Compute the total cost of each of the two jobs listed.

3. If Milici wants to earn profits equal to 20% of sales revenue, how much (what total fee) should she charge each of these two clients?

4. Why does WB Design assign costs to jobs?

P3-54A Prepare job cost record *(Learning Objectives 2, 3, & 4)*

Geolander manufactures tires for all-terrain vehicles. Geolander uses job costing and has a perpetual inventory system.

On September 22, Geolander received an order for 100 TX tires from ATV Corporation at a price of $55 each. The job, assigned number 298, was promised for October 10. After purchasing the materials, Geolander began production on September 30 and incurred the following direct labor and direct materials costs in completing the order:

Date	Labor Time Record No.	Description	Amount
9/30	1896	12 hours @ $20	$240
10/3	1904	30 hours @ $19	570

Date	Materials Requisition No.	Description	Amount
9/30	437	60 lb. rubber @ $18	$1,080
10/2	439	40 meters polyester fabric @ $12	480
10/3	501	100 meters steel cord @ $10	1,000

Geolander allocates manufacturing overhead to jobs on the basis of the relation between expected overhead costs ($540,000) and expected direct labor hours (20,000). Job 298 was completed on October 3 and shipped to ATV on October 5.

Requirements

1. Prepare a job cost record for Job 298 similar to Exhibit 3-7.

2. Calculate the total profit and the per-unit profit for Job 298.

P3-55A Determine and record job costs *(Learning Objectives 2, 3, 4, & 6)*

Getaway Homes manufactures prefabricated chalets in Colorado. The company uses a perpetual inventory system and a job cost system in which each chalet is a job. The following events occurred during May:

a. Purchased materials on account, $405,000.

b. Incurred total manufacturing wages of $111,600, which included both direct labor and indirect labor. Used direct labor in manufacturing as follows:

	Direct Labor
Chalet 13	$14,800
Chalet 14	28,500
Chalet 15	19,200
Chalet 16	21,000

c. Requisitioned direct materials in manufacturing as follows:

	Direct Materials
Chalet 13	$41,100
Chalet 14	56,800
Chalet 15	62,100
Chalet 16	66,000

d. Depreciation of manufacturing equipment used on different chalets, $20,000.
e. Other overhead costs incurred on Chalets 13–16:

Equipment rentals paid in cash	$10,400
Prepaid plant insurance expired	6,000

f. Allocated overhead to jobs at the predetermined rate of 60% of direct labor cost.
g. Chalets completed: 13, 15, and 16.
h. Chalets sold on account: 13 for $99,000 and 16 for $141,900.

Requirements

1. Record the preceding events in the general journal.

2. Open T-accounts for Work in Process Inventory and Finished Goods Inventory. Post the appropriate entries to these accounts, identifying each entry by letter. Determine the ending account balances assuming that the beginning balances were zero.

3. Summarize the job costs of the unfinished chalet and show that this equals the ending balance in Work in Process Inventory.

4. Summarize the job cost of the completed chalet that has not yet been sold and show that this equals the ending balance in Finished Goods Inventory.

5. Compute the gross profit on each chalet that was sold. What costs must the gross profit cover for Getaway Homes?

P3-56A Determine flow of costs through accounts *(Learning Objectives 2 & 6)*

CarNut reconditions engines. Its job cost records yield the following information. CarNut uses a perpetual inventory system.

Job No.	Date Started	Date Finished	Sold	Total Cost of Job at March 31	Total Manufacturing Cost Added in April
1	2/26	3/7	3/9	$1,400	
2	2/3	3/12	3/13	1,600	
3	3/29	3/31	4/3	1,300	
4	3/31	4/1	4/1	500	$ 400
5	4/8	4/12	4/14		700
6	4/23	5/6	5/9		1,200

Requirements

1. Compute CarNut's cost of (a) work in process inventory at March 31 and April 30, (b) finished goods inventory at March 31 and April 30, and (c) cost of goods sold for March and April.

2. Make summary journal entries to record the transfer of completed jobs from Work in Process Inventory to Finished Goods Inventory for March and April.

3. Record the sale of Job 5 on account for $1,600.

4. Compute the gross profit for Job 5. What costs must the gross profit cover?

Problems—Group B

P3-57B Analyze Manufacturing Overhead *(Learning Objectives 3 & 5)*

Root Company produces uniforms. The company allocates manufacturing overhead based on the machine hours each job uses. Root Company reports the following cost data for 2008:

	Budget	Actual
Direct labor hours..	7,400 hours	6,600 hours
Machine hours	7,250 hours	6,800 hours
Depreciation on salespeople's autos	$21,500	$21,500
Indirect materials	48,500	54,500
Depreciation on trucks used to deliver uniforms to customers	13,500	11,000
Depreciation on plant and equipment	63,500	65,000
Indirect manufacturing labor.............................	40,500	42,500
Customer service hotline	18,000	20,500
Plant utilities..	18,500	19,500
Direct labor cost...	72,500	84,000

Requirements

1. Compute the predetermined manufacturing overhead rate.

2. Calculate the allocated manufacturing overhead for the past year.

3. Compute the underallocated or overallocated Manufacturing Overhead. How will this underallocated or overallocated Manufacturing Overhead be disposed of?

4. How can managers use accounting information to help control manufacturing overhead costs?

P3-58B Use job costing at an advertising agency *(Learning Objectives 3, 4, & 7)*

PelicanAds.com is an Internet advertising agency. The firm uses a job cost system in which each client is a different "job." PelicanAds.com traces direct labor, software licensing costs, and travel costs directly to each job (client). The company allocates indirect costs to jobs based on a predetermined indirect cost allocation rate computed as a percentage of direct labor costs.

At the beginning of the current year, managing partner Ricky Beuna prepared a budget:

Direct labor hours (professional)	8,000 hours
Direct labor costs (professional)	$1,600,000
Support staff salaries	190,000
Rent and utilities	41,000
Supplies	23,000
Lease payments on computer hardware	66,000

During January of the current year, PelicanAds.com served several clients. Records for two clients appear here:

	AllVacations.com	Port Adak Golf Resort
Direct labor hours	760 hours	50 hours
Software licensing costs	$2,000	$150
Travel costs	$9,000	$ 0

Requirements

1. Compute PelicanAds.com's predetermined indirect cost allocation rate for the current year based on direct labor hours.
2. Compute the total cost of each job.
3. If PelicanAds.com wants to earn profits equal to 20% of sales revenue, how much (what total fee) should it charge each of these two clients?
4. Why does PelicanAds.com assign costs to jobs?

P3-59B Use job costing at a consulting firm *(Learning Objectives 3, 4, & 7)*

Cardinal Design is a Web site design and consulting firm. The firm uses a job cost system, in which each client is a different job. Cardinal Design traces direct labor, licensing costs, and travel costs directly to each job (client). It allocates indirect costs to jobs based on a predetermined indirect cost allocation rate computed as a percentage of direct labor costs.

At the beginning of the current year, managing partner Mary Milici prepared the following budget:

Direct labor hours (professional)	6,250 hours
Direct labor costs (professional)	$1,000,000
Support staff salaries	120,000
Computer leases	45,000
Office supplies	25,000
Office rent	60,000

Later that same year in November, Cardinal Design served several clients. Records for two clients appear here:

	Delicious Treats	GoGreen.com
Direct labor hours	770 hours	55 hours
Software licensing costs	$ 2,500	$400
Travel costs	10,000	$ 0

Requirements

1. Compute Cardinal Design's predetermined indirect cost allocation rate for the current year.

2. Compute the total cost of each of the two jobs listed.

3. If Milici wants to earn profits equal to 20% of sales revenue, how much (what total fee) should she charge each of these two clients?

4. Why does Cardinal Design assign costs to jobs?

P3-60B   Prepare job cost record *(Learning Objectives 2, 3, & 4)*

Great Quality manufactures tires for all-terrain vehicles. Great Quality uses job costing and has a perpetual inventory system. On November 22, Great Quality received an order for 170 TX tires from ATV Corporation at a price of $60 each. The job, assigned number 298, was promised for December 10. After purchasing the materials, Great Qualtiy began production on November 30 and incurred the following direct labor and direct materials costs in completing the order:

Date	Labor Time Record No.	Description	Amount
11/30	1896	12 hours @ $20	$240
12/3	1904	30 hours @ $14	420

Date	Materials Requisition No.	Description	Amount
11/30	437	60 lbs. rubber @ $12	$ 720
12/2	439	40 meters polyester fabric @ $16	640
12/3	501	100 meters steel cord @ $10	1,000

Great Quality allocates manufacturing overhead to jobs on the basis of the relation between expected overhead costs ($529,000) and expected direct labor hours (23,000). Job 298 was completed on December 3 and shipped to ATV on December 5.

Requirements

1. Prepare a job cost record for Job 298 similar to Exhibit 3-7.

2. Calculate the total profit and the per-unit profit for Job 298.

P3-61B   Determine and record job costs *(Learning Objectives 2, 3, 4, & 6)*

Divine Homes manufactures prefabricated chalets in Colorado. The company uses a perpetual inventory system and a job cost system in which each chalet is a job. The following events occurred during May:

a. Purchased materials on account, $480,000.

b. Incurred total manufacturing wages of $116,000, which included both direct labor and indirect labor. Use direct labor in manufacturing as follows:

	Direct Labor
Chalet 13	$14,300
Chalet 14	28,700
Chalet 15	19,100
Chalet 16	21,500

c. Requisitioned direct materials in manufacturing as follows:

	Direct Materials
Chalet 13	$41,900
Chalet 14	56,900
Chalet 15	62,400
Chalet 16	66,800

d. Depreciation of manufacturing equipment used on different chalets, $6,700.
e. Other overhead costs incurred on Chalets 13–16:

Equipment rentals paid in cash	10,800
Prepaid plant insurance expired	3,000

f. Allocated overhead to jobs at the predetermine rate of 60% of direct labor cost.
g. Chalets completed: 13, 15, and 16.
h. Chalets sold on account: 13 for $97,000; 16 for $149,000.

Requirements

1. Record the events in the general journal.

2. Post the appropriate entries to the T-accounts, identifying each entry by letter. Determine the ending account balances, assuming that the beginning balances were zero.

3. Add the costs of the unfinished chalet, and show that this total amount equals the ending balance in the Work in Process Inventory account.

4. Summarize the job cost of the completed chalet that has not yet been sold and show that this equals the ending balance in Finished Goods Inventory.

5. Compute gross profit on each chalet that was sold. What costs must gross profit cover for Divine Homes?

P3-62B Determine flow of costs through accounts *(Learning Objectives 2 & 6)*

EnginePro reconditions engines. Its job costing records yield the following information. EnginePro uses a perpetual inventory system.

Job No.	Date Started	Date Finished	Sold	Total Cost of Job at April 30	Total Manufacturing Cost Added in May
1	3/26	4/7	4/9	$1,400	
2	3/3	4/12	4/13	1,200	
3	4/29	4/30	5/3	1,600	
4	4/30	5/1	5/1	700	$ 700
5	5/8	5/12	5/14		900
6	5/23	6/6	6/9		1,700

Requirements

1. Compute EnginePro's cost of (a) work in process inventory at April 30 and May 31, (b) finished goods inventory at April 30 and May 31, and (c) cost of goods sold for April and May.

2. Make summary journal entries to record the transfer of completed jobs from Work in Process to Finished Goods for April and May.

3. Record the sale of Job 5 for $2,100.

4. Compute the gross profit for Job 5. What costs must the gross profit cover?

APPLY YOUR KNOWLEDGE

Decision Cases

C3-63   Issues with cost of job *(Learning Objectives 2, 3, & 4)*

Hegy Chocolate is located in Cleveland. The company prepares gift boxes of chocolates for private parties and corporate promotions. Each order contains a selection of chocolates determined by the customer, and the box is designed to the customer's specifications. Accordingly, Hegy Chocolate uses a job cost system and allocates manufacturing overhead based on direct labor cost.

One of Hegy Chocolate's largest customers is the Bailey and Choi law firm. This organization sends chocolates to its clients each Christmas and also provides them to employees at the firm's gatherings. The law firm's managing partner, Peter Bailey, placed the client gift order in September for 500 boxes of cream-filled dark chocolates. But Bailey and Choi did not place its December staff-party order until the last week of November. This order was for an additional 100 boxes of chocolates identical to the ones to be distributed to clients.

Hegy Chocolate budgeted the cost per box for the original 500-box order as follows:

Chocolate, filling, wrappers, box	$14.00
Employee time to fill and wrap the box (10 min.)	2.00
Manufacturing overhead	1.00
Total manufacturing cost	$17.00

Ben Hegy, president of Hegy Chocolate, priced the order at $20 per box.

In the past few months, Hegy Chocolate has experienced price increases for both dark chocolate and direct labor. *All other costs have remained the same.* Hegy budgeted the cost per box for the second order as follows:

Chocolate, filling, wrappers, box	$15.00
Employee time to fill and wrap the box (10 min.)	2.20
Manufacturing overhead..	1.10
Total manufacturing cost..	$18.30

Requirements

1. Do you agree with the cost analysis for the second order? Explain your answer.

2. Should the two orders be accounted for as one or two jobs in Hegy Chocolate's system?

3. What sales price per box should Hegy set for the second order? What are the advantages and disadvantages of this price?

C3-64   Issues with the manufacturing overhead rate *(Learning Objectives 2, 3, & 4)*

All Natural manufactures organic fruit preserves sold primarily through health food stores and on the Web. The company closes for two weeks each December to allow employees to spend time with their families over the holiday season. All Natural's manufacturing overhead is mostly straight-line depreciation on its plant and air-conditioning costs for keeping the berries cool during the summer months. The company uses direct labor hours as the allocation base. President Kara Wise has just approved new accounting software and is telling Controller Melissa Powers about her decision.

"I think this new software will be great," Wise says. "It will save you time in preparing all of those reports."

"Yes, and having so much more information just a click away will help us make better decisions and help control costs," replies Powers. "We need to consider how we can use the new system to improve our business practices."

"And I know just where to start," says Wise. "You complain each year about having to predict the weather months in advance for estimating air-conditioning costs and direct labor hours for the denominator of the predetermined manufacturing overhead rate, when professional meteorologists can't even get tomorrow's forecast right! I think we should calculate the predetermined overhead rate on a monthly basis."

Controller Powers is not so sure this is a good idea.

Requirements

1. What are the advantages and disadvantages of Wise's proposal?

2. Should All Natural compute its predetermined manufacturing overhead rate on an annual basis or a monthly basis? Explain.

Team Project

T3-65   Finding the cost of flight routes *(Learning Objectives 2, 3, & 4)*

Major airlines such as American, Delta, and Continental are struggling to meet the challenges of budget carriers such as Southwest and JetBlue. Suppose Delta CFO Edward Bastian has just returned from a meeting on strategies for responding to competition from budget carriers. The vice president of operations suggests doing nothing: "We just need to wait until these new airlines run out of money. They cannot be making money with their low fares." In contrast, the vice president of marketing, not wanting to lose marketing share, suggests cutting Delta's fares to match the competition. "If JetBlue charges only $75 for that flight from New York, so must we!" Others, including CFO Bastian, emphasize the potential for cutting costs. Another possibility is starting a new budget airline within Delta. Imagine that CEO Gerald Grinstein cuts the meeting short and directs Bastian to "get some hard data."

As a start, Bastian decides to collect cost and revenue data for a typical Delta flight and then compare it to the data for a competitor. Assume that he prepares the following schedule:

	Delta	JetBlue
Route: New York to Tampa......................	Flight 1247	Flight 53
Distance..	1,011 miles	1,011 miles
Seats per plane	142	162
One-way ticket price	$80–$621*	$75
Food and beverage	Meal	Snack

*The highest price is first-class airfare.

Excluding food and beverage, Bastian estimates that the cost per available seat mile is $0.084 for Delta, compared to $0.053 for JetBlue. (That is, the cost of flying a seat for one mile—whether or not the seat is occupied—is $0.084 for Delta and $0.053 for JetBlue.) Assume that the average cost of food and beverage is $5 per passenger for snacks and $10 for a meal.

Split your team into two groups. Group 1 should prepare its response to Requirement 1 and Group 2 should prepare its response to Requirement 2 before the entire team meets to consider Requirements 3–6.

Requirements

1. Group 1 uses the data to determine the following for Delta:
   a. The total cost of Flight 1247 assuming a full plane (100% load factor)
   b. The revenue generated by Flight 1247 assuming a 100% load factor and average revenue per one-way ticket of $102
   c. The profit per Flight 1247 given the responses to a and b
2. Group 2 uses the data to determine for JetBlue:
   a. The total cost of Flight 53 assuming a full plane (100% load factor)
   b. The revenue generated by Flight 53 assuming a 100% load factor
   c. The profit per Flight 53 given the responses to a and b
3. The entire team meets, and both groups combine their analyses. Based on the responses to Requirements 1 and 2, carefully evaluate each of the four alternative strategies discussed in Delta's executive meeting.
4. CFO Bastian wants additional data before he meets again with Delta's CEO. Each group should repeat the analyses in *both* Requirements 1 and 2 using another Delta route in Requirement 1 and a budget airline other than JetBlue in Requirement 2 (other budget airlines include America West, with a cost per available seat mile of about $0.065, and Southwest Airlines, with a cost per available seat mile of about $0.063). Information on flights, available seats, airfares, and mileage are available on airline Web sites.
5. The analysis in this project is based on several simplifying assumptions. As a team, brainstorm factors that your quantitative evaluation does not include but that may affect a comparison of Delta's operations against budget carriers.
6. Prepare a memo from CFO Bastian addressed to Delta CEO Grinstein summarizing the results of your analyses. Be sure to include the limitations of your analyses identified in Requirement 5. Use the following format for your memo.

Quick Check Answers

1. *b* 2. *d* 3. *d* 4. *d* 5. *a* 6. *c*
7. *a* 8. *b* 9. *c* 10. *d*

For online homework, exercises, and problems that provide you with immediate feedback, please visit www.myaccountinglab.com.

Date: _____

To: CEO Gerald Grinstein

From: CFO Edward Bastian

Subject: Delta's Response to Competition from Budget Airlines

Discussion & Analysis

1. Why would it be inappropriate for a custom home builder to use process costing?

2. For what types of products is job costing appropriate? Why? For what types of products is process costing appropriate? Why?

3. What product costs must be allocated to jobs? Why must these costs be allocated rather than assigned?

4. When the predetermined manufacturing overhead rate is calculated, why are estimated costs and cost driver levels used instead of actual dollars and amounts?

5. Why should manufacturing overhead be allocated to a job even though the costs cannot be directly traced to a job? Give at least two reasons.

6. Why does management need to know the cost of a job? Discuss at least five reasons.

7. Why is it acceptable to close overallocated or underallocated manufacturing overhead to Cost of goods sold rather than allocating it proportionately to Work in process inventory, Finished goods inventory, and Cost of goods sold? Under what circumstances would it be advisable to allocate the overallocated or underallocated manufacturing overhead to Work in process inventory, Finished goods inventory, and Cost of goods sold?

8. Describe a situation that may cause manufacturing overhead to be overallocated in a given year. Also describe a situation that may cause manufacturing overhead to be underallocated in a given year.

9. Explain why cost of goods sold should be lower if manufacturing overhead is overallocated. Should operating income be higher or lower if manufacturing overhead is overallocated? Why?

10. What account is credited when manufacturing overhead is allocated to jobs during the period? What account is debited when manufacturing overhead costs are incurred during the period? Would you expect these two amounts (allocated and incurred manufacturing overhead) to be the same? Why or why not?

Application & Analysis

3-1 *Unwrapped* or *How It's Made*

Product Costs and Job Costing Versus Process Costing

Go to www.YouTube.com and search for clips from the show *Unwrapped* on Food Network or *How It's Made* on the Discovery Channel. Watch a clip for a product you find interesting.

Basic Discussion Questions

1. Describe the product that is being produced and the company that makes it.

2. Summarize the production process that is used in making this product.

3. What raw materials are used to make this product?

4. What indirect materials are used to make this product?

5. Describe the jobs of the workers who would be considered "direct labor" in the making this product.

6. Describe the jobs of the workers who would be considered "indirect labor" in the making this product.

7. Define manufacturing overhead. In addition to the indirect materials and indirect labor previously described, what other manufacturing overhead costs would be incurred in this production process? Be specific and thorough. Make reasonable "guesses" if you do not know for sure.

8. Would a job-order costing system or a process costing system be used for this production process? Give specific reasons for your choice of which costing system would be most appropriate for this manufacturer.

Classroom Applications

Web: Post the discussion questions on an electronic discussion board. Have small groups of students choose a product for each group. Each student should watch the clip for the product for his or her group.

Classroom: Form groups of 3–4 students. Your group should choose a product and its clip to view. After viewing the clip, prepare a five minute presentation about your group's product that addresses the listed questions.

Independent: Research answers to each of the questions. Turn in a 2–3 page typed paper (12 point font, double-spaced with 1" margins). Include references and the URL for the clip that you viewed.

For additional Application & Analysis projects and implementation tips, see the Instructor Resources in MyAccountingLab.com.

CMA-1. A review of the year-end accounting records of Elk Industries discloses the following information:

Raw materials	$ 80,000
Work in process	128,000
Finished goods	272,000
Cost of goods sold	1,120,000

The company's underapplied overhead equals $133,000. On the basis of this information, Elk's cost of goods sold is most appropriately reported as

a. $987,000.

b. $1,213,100.

c. $1,218,000.

d. $1,253,000.

CMA-2. Wagner Corporation applies factory overhead based upon machine hours. At the beginning of the year, Wagner budgeted factory overhead at $250,000 and estimated that 100,000 machine hours would be used to make 50,000 units of product. During the year, the company produced 48,000 units, using 97,000 machine hours. Actual overhead for the year was $252,000. Under a standard cost system, the amount of factory overhead applied during the year was

a. $240,000.

b. $242,500.

c. $250,000.

d. $252,000.

(CMA Adapted)

DEMO DOC

Job Costing for Manufacturers

(*Learning Objectives 1, 2, & 6*)

Douglas Art manufactures specialized art for customers. Suppose Douglas has the following transactions during the month:

a. Raw materials were purchased on account for $67,000.

b. Materials costing $45,000 were requisitioned for production. Of this total, $40,000 were traced to individual jobs, while $5,000 were requisitioned for general factory use.

c. $32,000 of labor was incurred in the factory. Of the total labor costs, $30,000 was traced to specific jobs worked on during the month. The remainder of the factory labor cost related to indirect labor.

d. Manufacturing overhead is allocated to production using the predetermined overhead rate of 75% of direct labor cost.

e. Jobs costing $67,000 were completed during the month.

f. Douglas sold several jobs during the month for a total price of $106,000. These jobs cost $65,000 to produce. Assume all sales are made on account. Also assume that Douglas uses a perpetual inventory system.

Requirements

1. **What type of product costing system would Douglas use? Justify your answer.**

2. **What document would Douglas use to show the direct materials, direct labor, and manufacturing overhead costs assigned to each individual job?**

3. **Prepare journal entries for each transaction.**

DEMO DOC Solution

Requirement 1

What type of product costing system would Douglas use?

Job Costing System—companies that manufacture batches of unique or specialized products would use a job costing system to accumulate costs for each job or batch.

Requirement 2

What document would Douglas use to show the direct materials, direct labor, and manufacturing overhead costs assigned to each individual job?

Douglas would use a job cost record to show the direct materials, direct labor, and manufacturing overhead costs assigned to each individual job. Managers use the job cost record to see how they can use materials and labor more efficiently. For example, if a job's costs exceed its budget, managers must do a better job controlling costs on future jobs, or raise the sale price on similar jobs, to be sure that the company remains profitable.

Requirement 3

Prepare journal entries for each transaction.

a. **Raw materials were purchased on account for $67,000.**

When materials are purchased you need to record an increase in raw materials inventory, so you would debit Raw Materials Inventory (an asset) for the cost of the materials, $67,000.

continued

Since the materials were purchased on account, you also need to record a liability to your suppliers, so you would credit Accounts Payable (a liability) for $67,000.

Raw Materials Inventory	67,000	
Accounts Payable		67,000

b. Materials costing $45,000 were requisitioned for production. Of this total, $40,000 were traced to individual jobs, while $5,000 were requisitioned for general factory use.

When materials are requisitioned, it means that they moved from raw materials inventory into production.

The direct materials traced to specific jobs is posted to individual job cost records. Since the job cost records form the supporting detail for the Work in Process Inventory account, the cost of these direct materials is debited directly to Work in Process Inventory, increasing the asset by $40,000.

The materials that cannot be traced to a specific job (indirect materials) would be debited to manufacturing overhead (an increase of $5,000).

Because we are taking the materials out of the raw materials inventory, we reduce this asset with a credit for the total amount of the materials requisitioned ($45,000).

Work in Process Inventory	40,000	
Manufacturing Overhead	5,000	
Raw Materials Inventory		45,000

c. $32,000 of labor was incurred in the factory. Of the total labor costs, $30,000 was traced to specific jobs worked on during the month. The remainder of the factory labor cost related to indirect labor.

The amount of direct labor traced to individual jobs is posted to individual job cost records. Once again, since the job cost records form the supporting detail for the Work in Process Inventory account, the cost of direct labor is debited to Work in Process Inventory. The rest of the labor, $2,000, is for indirect labor, such as factory supervisors, forklift operators, and janitors. Indirect labor cannot be traced to specific jobs; therefore, it is debited to Manufacturing Overhead.

We credit Wages Payable to show a liability to our factory employees until they are paid on the company's payday.

Work in Process Inventory	30,000	
Manufacturing Overhead	2,000	
Wages Payable		32,000

d. Manufacturing overhead is allocated to production using the predetermined overhead rate of 75% of direct labor cost.

Manufacturing overhead consists of all of the indirect costs of running the manufacturing plant, such as depreciation on the plant and equipment, salaries of the janitors, utilities, and property taxes and insurance on the plant. It is impossible to trace these costs to each job; therefore, manufacturers allocate some of these costs to each job using a predetermined overhead rate. Since Douglas Art's predetermined manufacturing overhead rate is 75% of direct labor cost, the total amount of manufacturing overhead allocated to production for the month is as follows:

$$75\% \times \$30,000 \text{ of direct labor (from part c)} = \$22,500$$

Keep in mind that each individual job cost record would show the amount of manufacturing overhead allocated to that particular job (75% of the direct labor cost traced to the job).

Here, we just computed the *total* amount of manufacturing overhead allocated to *all jobs* worked on during the month.

All actual manufacturing overhead costs are recorded as debits to the Manufacturing Overhead account. To take cost *out* of the account and assign it to specific jobs in production, we credit the Manufacturing Overhead account:

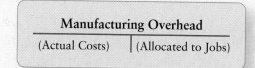

Manufacturing Overhead	
(Actual Costs)	(Allocated to Jobs)

To record the amount of manufacturing overhead allocated to jobs, we debit Work in Process Inventory. We then take this cost out of the Manufacturing Overhead account through a credit, as shown in the previous T-account.

	Work in Process Inventory	22,500	
	Manufacturing Overhead		22,500

e. Jobs costing $67,000 were completed during the month.

When jobs are completed, the direct materials, direct labor, and manufacturing overhead costs shown on the job cost records are added together to determine the total cost of the jobs. Then the jobs are moved off the plant floor and into the finished goods storage area until they are shipped to customers. In the accounting records, we also show the movement of these completed jobs by transferring the cost of the jobs from one inventory account to the next. Since all inventory accounts are assets, we debit the accounts to increase them and credit the accounts to decrease them. Thus, the following entry shows an increase in the Finished Goods Inventory and a decrease in the Work in Process Inventory:

	Finished Goods Inventory	67,000	
	Work in Process Inventory		67,000

f. Douglas sold several jobs during the month for a total price of $106,000. These jobs cost $65,000 to produce. Assume all sales are made on account. Also assume that Douglas uses a perpetual inventory system.

We need to make two journal entries here. The first journal entry records the sale of the art to customers at a sales price of $106,000. Therefore, the following entry records an increase in the accounts receivable and an increase in sales revenue for the year:

	Accounts Receivable	106,000	
	Sales Revenue		106,000

The second entry is made assuming that Douglas has a perpetual inventory system. In a perpetual inventory system, companies show the costs of goods sold at the time they make a sale. They also show that the inventory sold is no longer theirs—it has been sold to the customer. So, they make the following journal entry to increase the Cost of Goods Sold (through a debit) and decrease the amount of inventory they have on hand (through a credit):

	Cost of Goods Sold	65,000	
	Finished Goods Inventory		65,000

When Life Fitness began, it only had one product:

the Lifecycle computerized exercise bike. Since it was the first of its kind, the Lifecycle had no immediate competition. However, as the success of the company increased, other companies began to produce their own brands of fitness equipment. In addition, Life Fitness expanded its product offerings to include computerized treadmills, elliptical cross-trainers, and stair climbers.[1]

Let's suppose that, as a result of the increase in competition and product diversity, managers found they needed better, more accurate product cost information to help guide their business decisions and remain competitive.[2] A traditional job costing system would have ensured that the direct material and direct labor costs traced to each product were correct. However, the traditional method of allocating manufacturing overhead costs may not have been doing a good enough job of matching overhead costs to the products that used those overhead resources.

Life Fitness's managers may have needed a more refined cost allocation system: one that wasn't based on a single, predetermined manufacturing overhead rate. By using either *departmental overhead rates* or *activity-based costing (ABC)* to allocate manufacturing overhead, the company would be able to more accurately determine the cost of individual jobs or products. ABC could also help managers cut costs by highlighting the cost of each activity performed during production. In addition, it could help them identify the costs associated with providing high-quality products to their customers. With more accurate cost information in hand, managers would be able to secure Life Fitness's continued leadership in the market for fitness equipment.

[1]uscorporate.lifefitness.com
[2]All references to Life Fitness in this chapter are hypothetical, unless otherwise noted, and were created by the author solely for academic purposes. The examples are not intended, in any way, to represent the actual business practices of, or costs incurred by, Life Fitness, Inc.

CHAPTER 4

Activity-Based Costing, Lean Production, and the Costs of Quality

As the chapter opening story illustrates, most companies have experienced increased competition over the past few decades. In addition, companies have sought to expand their customer base by offering a more diversified line of products. Both of these factors are good for consumers, who now enjoy more product options at very competitive prices. However, these factors also present unique challenges to business managers and the accounting systems that support them. To thrive in a globally competitive market, companies must provide value to the customer by delivering a high-quality product at an attractive price, while managing costs so the company still earns a profit. This chapter will introduce several tools that today's managers use to make their companies competitive:

■ Refined costing systems: Departmental Overhead Rates and Activity-Based Costing (ABC)

■ Lean production systems

■ Total quality management and the costs of quality

Why and How do Companies Refine Their Cost Allocation Systems?

Organizations from Dell to Carolina Power and Light to the U.S. Marine Corps use refined cost allocation systems. Why? Because simple cost allocation systems don't always do a good job of matching the cost of overhead resources with the products that consume those resources. The following example illustrates why.

Simple Cost Allocation Systems Can Lead to Cost Distortion

David, Matt, and Marc are three college friends who share an apartment. They agree to split the following monthly costs equally:

Rent and utilities	$570
Cable TV	50
High-speed Internet access	40
Groceries	240
Total monthly costs	$900

Each roommate's share is $300 ($900/3).

Things go smoothly for the first few months. But then David calls a meeting: "Since I started having dinner at Amy's each night, I shouldn't have to chip in for the groceries." Matt then pipes in: "I'm so busy studying and using the Internet that I never have time to watch TV. I don't want to pay for the cable TV anymore. And Marc, since your friend Jennifer eats here most evenings, you should pay a double share of the grocery bill." Marc replies, "If that's the way you feel, Matt, then you should pay for the Internet access since you're the only one around here who uses it!"

What happened? The friends originally agreed to share the costs equally. But they are not participating equally in watching cable TV, using the Internet, and using the groceries. Splitting these costs equally is not equitable.

The roommates could use a cost allocation approach that better matches costs with the people who participate in the activities that cause those costs. This means splitting the cable TV costs between David and Marc, assigning the Internet access cost to Matt, and allocating the grocery bill one-third to Matt and two-thirds to Marc. Exhibit 4-1 compares the results of this refined cost allocation system with the original cost allocation system.

EXHIBIT 4-1   More-Refined Versus Less-Refined Cost Allocation System

	David	Matt	Marc	Total
More-refined cost allocation system:				
Rent and utilities	$190	$190	$190	$570
Cable TV	25	0	25	50
High-speed Internet access	0	40	0	40
Groceries	0	80	160	240
Total costs allocated	$215	$310	$375	$900
Less-refined original cost allocation system	$300	$300	$300	$900
Difference	$ (85)	$ 10	$ 75	$ 0

No wonder David called a meeting! The original cost allocation system charged him $300 a month, but the refined system shows that a more equitable share would be only $215. The new system allocates Marc $375 a month instead of $300. David was paying for resources he did not use (Internet and groceries), while Marc was not paying for all of the resources (groceries) he and his guest consumed. The simple cost allocation system the roommates initially devised had ended up distorting the cost that should be charged to each roommate: David was *overcharged* by $85 while Matt and Marc were *undercharged* by an equal, but offsetting amount ($10 + $75 = $85). Notice that the total "pool" of monthly costs ($900) is the same under both allocation systems. The only difference is *how* the pool of costs is *allocated* among the three roommates.

Just as the simple allocation system had resulted in overcharging David, yet undercharging Matt and Marc, many companies find that the simple overhead cost allocation system described in the last chapter results in "overcosting" some of their jobs or products while "undercosting" others. **Cost distortion** occurs when some products are overcosted while other products are undercosted by the cost allocation system. As we'll see in the following sections, companies often refine their cost allocation systems to minimize the amount of cost distortion caused by the simpler cost allocation systems. By refining their costing systems, companies can more equitably assign indirect costs (such as manufacturing overhead) to their individual jobs, products, or services. As a result, less cost distortion occurs and managers have more accurate information for making vital business decisions. For example, now each of the roommates has better information about his actual living costs. This information will be useful if they ever consider moving out on their own.

In the following section, we will be describing how refined cost allocation systems can be used to better allocate manufacturing overhead (indirect manufacturing costs) to specific products to reduce cost distortion. However, keep in mind that the same principles apply to allocating *any* indirect costs to *any* cost objects. Thus, even merchandising and service companies, as well as governmental agencies, can use these refined cost allocation systems to provide their managers with better cost information.

Why is this important?

"With better cost information, managers are able to make more profitable decisions. One company reported triple sales and a five-fold increase in profits after it implemented a refined costing system. By using better cost information for quoting jobs, management was able generate a more profitable mix of job contracts."[3]

[3]Hicks, Douglas. "Yes, ABC is for small business, too," *Journal of Accountancy*, Aug. 1999; p. 41.

Review: Using a Plantwide Overhead Rate to Allocate Indirect Costs

In the last chapter, we assumed that Life Fitness allocated its manufacturing overhead costs using one predetermined MOH rate ($16 per DL hour). This rate was based on management's estimate of the total manufacturing overhead costs for the year ($1 million) and estimate of the total amount of the allocation base (62,500 DL hours) for the year.[4] The rate was calculated as follows:

$$\text{Predetermined MOH rate} = \frac{\$1,000,000}{62,500 \text{ DL hours}} = \$16 \text{ per direct labor hour}$$

This rate is also known as a **plantwide overhead rate**, because any job produced in the plant, whether it be treadmills, elliptical cross-trainers, or stair climbers, would be allocated manufacturing overhead using this single rate. It wouldn't matter whether the job was worked on in one department or many departments during the production process: The same rate would be used throughout the plant.

Let's see how this works for Life Fitness. In Chapter 3, we followed a job in which each elliptical cross-trainer required about 10 direct labor hours to make.[5] We'll continue to assume that each elliptical made by the company requires 10 direct labor hours to make. Let's also assume that each treadmill requires 10 direct labor hours to make. Exhibit 4-2 shows how manufacturing overhead would be allocated to a job in which one elliptical was made, and another job in which one treadmill was made, using the plantwide overhead rate.

[4]All references to Life Fitness in this hypothetical example, were created by the author solely for academic purposes and are not intended, in any way, to represent the actual business practices of, or costs incurred by, Life Fitness, Inc.
[5]Job 603, a batch of 50 elliptical cross-trainers, required 500 DL hours to complete. Thus, the average time spent on each unit was 10 DL hours.

EXHIBIT 4-2 **Allocating Manufacturing Overhead Using a Plantwide Overhead Rate**

	Plantwide Overhead Rate		Actual Use of Allocation Base		MOH Allocated to One Unit
Elliptical	$16 per DL hour	×	10 DL hours	=	$160
Treadmill	$16 per DL hour	×	10 DL hours	=	$160

The plantwide allocation system is illustrated in Exhibit 4-3.

EXHIBIT 4-3 **Plantwide Allocation System**

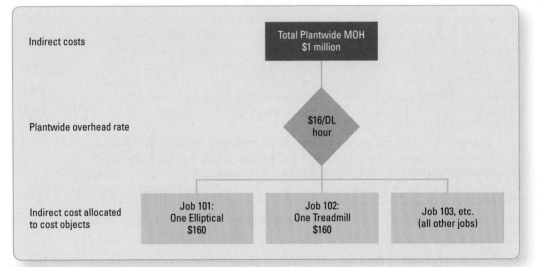

Using Departmental Overhead Rates to Allocate Indirect Costs

> **1** Develop and use departmental overhead rates to allocate indirect costs

The plantwide allocation system described above works well for some companies, but may end up distorting costs if the following conditions exist:

1. Different departments incur different amounts and types of manufacturing overhead.

2. Different jobs or products use the departments to a different extent.

If these circumstances exist, the company should strongly consider refining its cost allocation system. Let's see if these conditions exist at Life Fitness.

CONDITION 1: DO DIFFERENT DEPARTMENTS HAVE DIFFERENT AMOUNTS AND TYPES OF MOH COSTS? As shown in Exhibit 4-4, let's assume Life Fitness has two primary production departments: Machining and Assembly. The Machining Department has a lot of machinery, which drives manufacturing overhead costs such as machine depreciation, utilities, machine lubricants, and repairs and maintenance. Let's say these overhead costs are estimated to be $400,000 for the year. On the other hand, the Assembly Department does not incur as many of these types of overhead costs. Rather, the Assembly Department's manufacturing overhead costs include more indirect labor for supervision, quality inspection, and so forth. These manufacturing overhead costs are expected to total $600,000 for the year.

Exhibit 4-4 shows that the first condition is present: Each department incurs different types and amounts of MOH. Life Fitness expects to incur a total of $1 million of manufacturing overhead: $400,000 relates to the Machining Department while $600,000 relates to the Assembly Department.

**EXHIBIT 4-4 Machining and Assembly Departments'
Manufacturing Overhead**

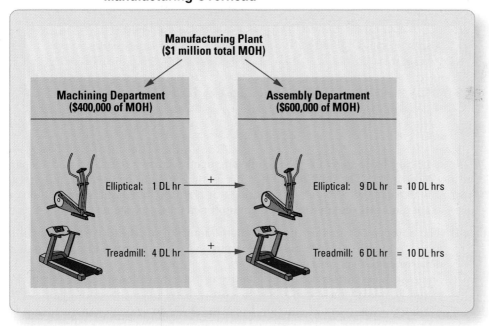

CONDITION 2: DO DIFFERENT PRODUCTS USE THE DEPARTMENTS TO A DIFFERENT EXTENT?

While both ellipticals and treadmills take 10 direct labor hours in total to make, Exhibit 4-4 also shows that ellipticals and treadmills spend *different* amounts of time in each production department. Each elliptical only requires 1 DL hour in the Machining Department, but requires 9 DL hours in the Assembly Department. Contrast that with a treadmill, which spends more time in Machining to fabricate some of its components (4 DL hours) but less time in Assembly (6 DL hours). As a result of these differences, the second condition is also present. The company's cost allocation system would be much more accurate if it took these differences into account when determining how much manufacturing overhead to allocate to each product.

Since both conditions are present, the company should consider "fine-tuning" its cost allocation systems by establishing separate manufacturing overhead rates, known as **departmental overhead rates,** for each department. That means that Life Fitness will establish one manufacturing overhead rate for the Machining Department and another overhead rate for the Assembly Department. These rates are then used to allocate manufacturing overhead to jobs or products based on the extent to which each product uses the different manufacturing departments.

Exhibit 4-5 shows the circumstances favoring the use of departmental overhead rates rather than a single, plantwide overhead rate.

**EXHIBIT 4-5 Circumstances Favoring Departmental
Overhead Rates**

> Departmental overhead rates increase the accuracy of job costs when....
>
> • Each department incurs different types and amounts of manufacturing overhead
> • Each product, or job, uses the departments to a different extent.

Four Basic Steps to Computing and Using Departmental Overhead Rates

In Chapter 3, we used four steps for allocating manufacturing overhead. These steps are summarized in Exhibit 4-6 on the next page.

EXHIBIT 4-6   Four Basic Steps for Allocating Manufacturing Overhead

1. Estimate the total manufacturing overhead costs (MOH) for the coming year.
2. Select an allocation base and estimate the total amount that will be used during the year.
3. Calculate the predetermined overhead rate by dividing the total estimated MOH costs by the total estimated amount of the allocation base.
4. Allocate some MOH cost to each job worked on during the year by multiplying the predetermined MOH rate by the actual amount of the allocation base used by the job.

The same four basic steps are used to allocate manufacturing overhead using departmental overhead rates. The only real difference is that we will be calculating *separate rates* for *each* department. Let's now take a look at how the four basic steps outlined in Exhibit 4-6 are modified slightly to implement a refined costing system.

Step 1) **The company estimates the total manufacturing overhead costs that will be incurred in *each department* in the coming year. These estimates are known as departmental overhead cost pools.**

Some of these costs are easy to identify or trace to different departments. For example, management can trace the cost of lease payments and repairs to the machines used in the Machining Department. Management can also trace the cost of employing supervisors and quality control inspectors to the Assembly Department. However, other overhead costs are more difficult to identify with specific departments. For example, the depreciation, property taxes and insurance on the entire plant would have to be split, or allocated, between the individual departments, most likely based on the square footage occupied by each department in the plant.

As shown in Exhibit 4-4, Life Fitness has determined that $400,000 of its total estimated MOH relates to its Machining Department, while the remaining $600,000 relates to its Assembly Department.

Department	Total Departmental Overhead Cost Pool
Machining	$ 400,000
Assembly	$ 600,000
TOTAL MOH	$1,000,000

Step 2) **The company selects an allocation base for *each department* and estimates the total amount that will be used during the year.**

The allocation base selected for each department should be the cost driver of the costs in the departmental overhead pool. Often, manufacturers will use different allocation bases for the different departments. For example, machine hours might be the best allocation base for a very automated Machining Department that uses machine robotics extensively. However, direct labor hours might be the best allocation base for an Assembly Department.

Let's assume that Life Fitness's Machining Department uses a lot of human-operated machinery, therefore the number of direct labor hours used in the department is identical to the number of hours the machines are run. While machine hours is the real cost driver, direct labor hours will make an adequate surrogate. As a result, management has selected direct labor hours as the allocation base for both departments. Recall that Life Fitness estimates using a total of 62,500 direct labor hours during the year. Of this amount, management expects to use 12,500 in the Machining Department and 50,000 in the Assembly Department.

Department	Total Amount of Departmental Allocation Base
Machining..	12,500 DL hours
Assembly..	50,000 DL hours

Step 3) The company calculates its departmental overhead rates using the information estimated in Steps 1 and 2:

$$\text{Departmental overhead rate} = \frac{\text{Total estimated departmental overhead cost pool}}{\text{Total estimated amount of the departmental allocation base}}$$

Therefore, Life Fitness calculates its departmental overhead rates as follows:

$$\text{Machining Department overhead rate} = \frac{\$400,000}{12,500 \text{ DL hours}} = \$32 \text{ per DL hour}$$

$$\text{Assembly Department overhead rate} = \frac{\$600,000}{50,000 \text{ DL hours}} = \$12 \text{ per DL hour}$$

These first three steps are performed before the year begins, using estimated data for the year. Thus, departmental overhead rates are also "predetermined," just like the "plantwide" predetermined manufacturing overhead rate discussed in Chapter 3. The first three steps, performed before the year begins, are summarized in Exhibit 4-7.

EXHIBIT 4-7 **Steps to Calculating the Departmental Overhead Rates**

Department	Step 1: Total Departmental Overhead Cost Pool		Step 2: Total Amount of Departmental Allocation Base		Step 3: Departmental Overhead Rate
Machining	$400,000	÷	12,500 DL hours	=	$32 per DL hour
Assembly	$600,000	÷	50,000 DL hours	=	$12 per DL hour

Once these rates have been established, the company uses them throughout the year to allocate manufacturing overhead to each job as it is produced, as shown in Step 4.

Step 4) The company allocates some manufacturing overhead from *each* department to the individual jobs that use those departments.

The amount of MOH allocated from each department is calculated as follows:

MOH allocated to job = Departmental overhead rate × Actual amount of departmental allocation base used by job

Exhibit 4-8 shows how these departmental overhead rates would be used to allocate manufacturing to a job in which one elliptical is produced.

EXHIBIT 4-8 **Allocating MOH to One Elliptical Using Departmental Overhead Rates**

Department	Departmental Overhead Rate (from Exhibit 4-7)		Actual Use of Departmental Allocation Base (from Exhibit 4-4)		MOH Allocated to One Elliptical
Machining	$32 per DL hour	×	1 DL hours	=	$ 32
Assembly	$12 per DL hour	×	9 DL hours	=	108
Total					$140

Exhibit 4-9 shows how the same rates would be used to allocate manufacturing overhead to another job in which one treadmill is produced. Because the treadmill spends more time in the Machining Department, but less time in the Assembly Department, the amount of MOH allocated to the treadmill differs from the amount allocated to the elliptical in Exhibit 4-8.

EXHIBIT 4-9 **Allocating MOH to One Treadmill Using Departmental Overhead Rates**

Department	Departmental Overhead Rate (from Exhibit 4-7)		Actual Use of Departmental Allocation Base (from Exhibit 4-4)		MOH Allocated to One Elliptical
Machining	$32 per DL hour	×	4 DL hours	=	$128
Assembly	$12 per DL hour	×	6 DL hours	=	72
Total					$200

Exhibit 4-10 illustrates the company's departmental cost allocation system.

EXHIBIT 4-10 **Departmental Cost Allocation System**

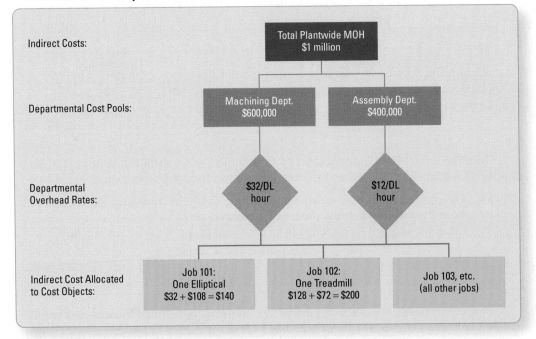

Had the Plantwide Overhead Rate Been Distorting Product Costs?

We have just seen that Life Fitness's refined cost allocation system allocates $140 of MOH to each elliptical, and $200 of MOH to each treadmill (Exhibit 4-10). Does this differ from the amount that would have been allocated to each unit using Life Fitness's original plantwide rate? Yes. Recall from Exhibit 4-2 that if Life Fitness uses a plantwide overhead rate, $160 of manufacturing overhead would be allocated to either type of equipment, simply because both types of equipment require the *same total* number of direct labor hours (10 DL hours) to produce.

The plantwide allocation system does not pick up on the nuances of how many direct labor hours are used by the products in *each* department. Therefore, it was not able to do a very good job of matching manufacturing overhead costs to the products that use those costs. As a result, the plantwide rate would have overcosted each elliptical, but undercosted each treadmill, as shown in Exhibit 4-11.

EXHIBIT 4-11 **Cost Distortion Caused by Plantwide Overhead Rate**

	Plantwide Overhead Rate MOH Allocation (from Exhibit 4-2)	Departmental Overhead Rates MOH Allocation (from Exhibits 4-8 and 4-9)	Amount of Cost Distortion
Elliptical..................	$160	$140	$20 *overcosted*
Treadmill	$160	$200	$40 *undercosted*

On the other hand, the refined cost allocation system recognizes the cost differences between departments and the usage difference between jobs. Therefore, the refined costing system does a *better job of matching* each department's overhead costs to the products that use the department's resources. This is the same thing we saw with the three roommates: The refined costing system did a better job of matching the cost of resources (cable, Internet, groceries) to the roommates who used those resources. Because of this better matching, we can believe that the departmental overhead rates *more accurately allocate* MOH costs.

STOP & THINK

Do companies always have separate production departments, such as Machining and Assembly, for each step of the production process?

Answer: No. Rather than basing production departments on separate processing steps, some companies have separate production departments for each of their products. For example, Life Fitness could have one department for producing treadmills, another department for producing ellipticals, and yet another department for producing stair climbers. Each department would have all of the equipment necessary for producing its unique product. Departmental overhead rates would be formulated using the same four basic steps discussed above to determine a unique departmental overhead rate for each department. The only difference is that each product (for example, a treadmill) would travel through *only one* department (the Treadmill Department) rather than traveling through separate production departments (Machining and Assembly). Always keep in mind that the accounting system should reflect the actual production environment.

Using Activity-Based Costing to Allocate Indirect Costs

We just saw how companies can refine their cost allocation systems by using departmental overhead rates. If a company wants an even more refined system, one that reduces cost distortion to a minimum, it will use activity-based costing (ABC). **Activity-based costing (ABC)** focuses on *activities*, rather than departments, as the fundamental cost objects. ABC recognizes that activities are costly to perform, and each product manufactured may require different types and amounts of activities. Thus, activities become the building blocks for compiling the indirect costs of products, services, and customers. Companies such as Coca-Cola and American Express use ABC to more accurately estimate the cost of resources required to produce different products, to render different services, and to serve different customers.

Think about the three roommates for a moment. The most equitable and accurate cost allocation system for the roommates was one in which the roommates were charged only for the *activities* in which they participated, and the *extent* to which they participated in those activities. Likewise, activity-based costing generally causes the *least* amount of cost distortion among products because indirect costs are allocated to the products based on the (1) *types* of activities used by the product and (2) the *extent* to which the activities are used.

Develop and use activity-based costing (ABC) to allocate indirect costs

2

Four Basic Steps to Computing and Using Activity Cost Allocation Rates

ABC requires the same four basic steps listed in Exhibit 4-6. The main difference between an ABC system and a plantwide or departmental cost allocation system is that ABC systems have *separate* cost allocation rates for *each activity* identified by the company.

Step 1) The company first identifies its primary activities and then estimates the total manufacturing overhead costs associated with *each activity*. These are known as the activity cost pools.

Let's assume Life Fitness has determined that the following activities occur in its plant: First the machines must be set-up to meet the particular specifications of the production run. Next, raw materials must be moved out of the storeroom and into the machining department, where some of the parts for the units are fabricated. Once the fabricated parts have been inspected, they are moved into the assembly department, along with additional raw materials that are needed from the storeroom. The units are then assembled by direct laborers, while production engineers supervise the process. All units are inspected during and after assembly. Upon passing inspection, each unit is packaged so that it is not damaged during shipment. Finally, the units are moved to the finished goods warehouse where they await shipment to customers. These activities are pictured in Exhibit 4-12.

EXHIBIT 4-12   Primary Activities Identified in the Manufacturing Plant

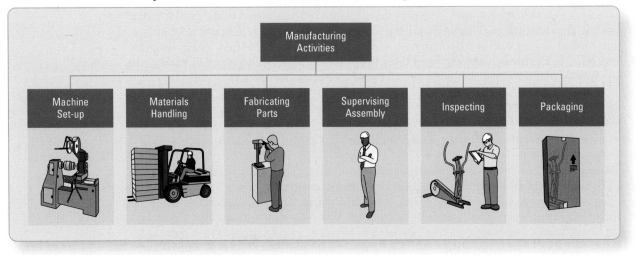

As part of this step, management must determine how much of the total estimated $1 million of MOH relates to each activity. Exhibit 4-13 shows some of the specific MOH costs that management has identified with each activity, along with the total estimated amount of each activity cost pool.

EXHIBIT 4-13   Activity Cost Pools

Activity	MOH Costs Related to the Activity	Total Activity Cost Pool
Machine Set-up	Indirect labor used to set-up machines	$ 80,000
Materials Handling	Forklifts, gas, operators' wages	200,000
Fabricating Parts	Machine lease payments, electricity, repairs	300,000
Supervising Assembly	Production engineers' labor	150,000
Inspecting	Testing equipment, inspection labor	170,000
Packaging	Packaging equipment	100,000
	TOTAL MOH	**$1,000,000**

Keep in mind that all of the costs in the activity costs pools are MOH costs; direct labor costs and direct materials costs are *not included* because they will be directly traced to specific jobs and therefore do not need to be allocated. That is why we only include supervisory labor in the overhead cost pool for the assembly activity. The machine operators and assembly-line workers are considered direct labor, so their cost will be traced to individual jobs, not allocated as part of MOH.

Step 2) The company selects an allocation base for *each activity* and estimates the total amount that will be used during the year.

When selecting an allocation base for each activity, the company should keep the following in mind:

- The allocation base selected for each activity should be the *cost driver* of the costs in that particular activity cost pool.

- The company will need to keep track of how much of the allocation base each job or product uses. Therefore, the company must have the means to collect usage information about each allocation base. Thankfully, bar-coding, and other technological advances have helped make data collection easier and less costly in recent years.

Let's assume that Life Fitness has identified a cost driver for each activity, and has plans for how it will collect usage data. Exhibit 4-14 shows the selected allocation bases along with the total estimated amounts for the year.

EXHIBIT 4-14   Activity Allocation Bases and Total Estimated Amount of Each

Activity	Activity Allocation Base	Total Estimated Amount of Allocation Base
Machine Set-up	Number of set-ups	8,000 set-ups
Materials Handling	Number of parts moved	400,000 parts
Fabricating Parts	Machine hours	12,500 machine hours
Supervising Assembly	Direct labor hours	50,000 DL hours
Inspecting	Number of inspections	34,000 inspections
Packaging	Cubic feet packaged	400,000 cubic feet

Step 3) The company calculates its activity cost allocation rates using the information estimated in Steps 1 and 2.

The formula for calculating the activity cost allocation rates is as follows:

$$\text{Activity cost allocation rate} = \frac{\text{Total estimated activity cost pool}}{\text{Total estimated activity allocation base}}$$

Exhibit 4-15 shows how this formula is used to compute a unique cost allocation rate for each of the company's production activities.

Once again, these rates are calculated based on estimated, or budgeted, costs for the year. Hence, they too are "predetermined" before the year begins. Then, during the year, the company uses them to allocate manufacturing overhead to specific jobs, as shown in Step 4.

EXHIBIT 4-15 **Computing Activity Cost Allocation Rates**

Activity	Step 1: Total Activity Cost Pool (from Exhibit 4-13)		Step 2: Total Amount of Activity Allocation Base (from Exhibit 4-14)		Step 3: Activity Cost Allocation Rate
Machine Set-up	$ 80,000	÷	8,000 set-ups	=	$10.00 per set-up
Materials Handling	200,000	÷	400,000 parts	=	$ 0.50 per part
Fabricating Parts	300,000	÷	12,500 machine hours	=	$24.00 per machine hour
Supervising Assembly	150,000	÷	50,000 DL hours	=	$ 3.00 per DL hour
Inspecting	170,000	÷	34,000 inspections	=	$ 5.00 per inspection
Packaging	100,000	÷	400,000 cubic feet	=	$ 0.25 per cubic foot

Step 4) The company allocates some manufacturing overhead from *each* activity to the individual jobs that use the activities.

The formula is as follows:

MOH allocated to job = Activity cost allocation rate × Actual amount of activity allocation base used by job

Exhibit 4-16 shows how these activity cost allocation rates would be used to allocate manufacturing overhead to a job in which one elliptical was produced.

EXHIBIT 4-16 **Allocating MOH to One Elliptical Using ABC**

Activity	Activity Cost Allocation Rate (from Exhibit 4-15)		Actual Use of Activity Allocation Base (information collected on job)		MOH Allocated to One Elliptical
Machine Set-up	$10.00 per set-up	×	2 set-ups	=	$ 20
Materials Handling	$ 0.50 per part	×	20 parts	=	10
Fabricating	$24.00 per machine hour	×	1 machine hour	=	24
Supervising Assembly	$ 3.00 per DL hour	×	9 DL hours	=	27
Inspecting	$ 5.00 per inspection	×	3 inspections	=	15
Packaging	$ 0.25 per cubic foot	×	52 cubic feet	=	13
Total					$109

Exhibit 4-17 shows how the same activity cost allocation rates are used to allocate MOH to a job in which one treadmill was produced.

EXHIBIT 4-17 **Allocating MOH to One Treadmill Using ABC**

Activity	Activity Cost Allocation Rate (from Exhibit 4-15)		Actual Use of Departmental Allocation Base (information collected on job)		MOH Allocated to One Treadmill
Machine Set-up	$10.00 per set-up	×	4 set-ups	=	$ 40
Materials Handling	$ 0.50 per part	×	26 parts	=	13
Fabricating	$24.00 per machine hour	×	4 machine hour	=	96
Supervising Assembly	$ 3.00 per DL hour	×	6 DL hours	=	18
Inspecting	$ 5.00 per inspection	×	6 inspections	=	30
Packaging	$ 0.25 per cubic foot	×	60 cubic feet	=	15
Total					$212

Exhibit 4-18 illustrates the company's ABC system.

EXHIBIT 4-18 **Illustration of the Company's ABC System**

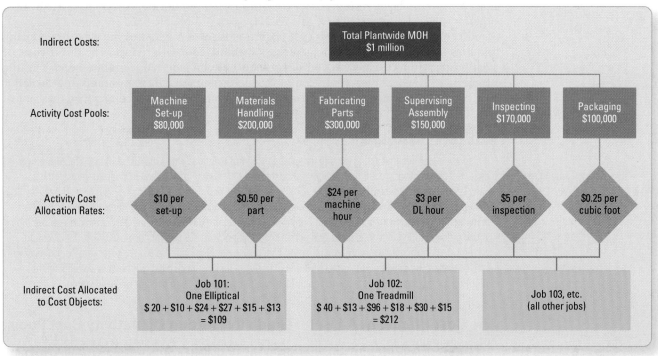

One Last Look at Cost Distortion: Comparing the Three Allocation Systems

Exhibit 4-19 compares the amount of manufacturing overhead that would have been allocated to each elliptical and each treadmill, using the three cost allocation systems that we have discussed: 1) a single plantwide overhead rate, 2) departmental overhead rates, and 3) ABC.

EXHIBIT 4-19 **Comparing the Three Cost Allocation Systems**

	Plantwide Overhead Rate (Exhibit 4-2)	Departmental Overhead Rates (Exhibit 4-8 & 4-9)	Activity Based Costing (Exhibit 4-16 & 4-17)
Elliptical..................	$160	$140	$109
Treadmill	$160	$200	$212

As you can see, each allocation system renders different answers for the amount of MOH that should be allocated to each elliptical and treadmill. Which is correct?

ABC costs are generally thought to be the most accurate because ABC takes into account 1) the *specific resources* each product uses (for example, inspecting resources) and 2) the *extent* to which they use these resources (for example three inspections of the elliptical, but six inspections of the treadmill).

Exhibit 4-19 shows that the plantwide rate had been severely distorting costs: Each elliptical had been overcosted by $51 ($160 − $109) and each treadmill had been under-costed by $52 ($160 − $212). Here, we have only looked at two units produced during the year. However, if we consider all of the products the company produced during the year, we will see that the total amount by which some products have been overcosted will equal the total amount by which other products have been undercosted. Why? Because $1 million of MOH is being allocated: If some products are allocated too much MOH, then other products are allocated too little MOH.

Keep in mind that all of this cost distortion is solely a result of the way the company allocates its indirect costs (manufacturing overhead) to each product. The direct costs of each product (direct materials and direct labor) are known with certainty because of the precise way in which they are traced to the job using materials requisitions and the labor time records of the machinists and assembly personnel who worked directly on these units.

STOP & THINK

If a company refines its costing system using departmental overhead rates or ABC, will manufacturing overhead still be overallocated or underallocated by the end of the year (as we saw in Chapter 3 when the company used a plantwide overhead rate)?

Answer: Yes. The use of *any predetermined* allocation rate will result in the over- or underallocation of manufacturing overhead. That's because *predetermined* rates are developed using *estimated* data before the actual manufacturing overhead costs and actual cost driver activity for the year are known. Refined costing systems decrease cost distortion *between* products, but do not eliminate the issue of over- or underallocating total manufacturing overhead.[6] As described in Chapter 3, Cost of Goods Sold will need to be adjusted at year-end for the *total* amount by which manufacturing overhead has been over- or underallocated.

The Cost Hierarchy: A Useful Guide for Setting Up Activity Cost Pools

Some companies use a classification system, called the cost hierarchy, to establish activity cost pools. Companies often have hundreds of different activities. However, to keep the ABC system manageable, companies need to keep the system as simple as possible, yet refined enough to accurately determine product costs.[7] The cost hierarchy, pictured in Exhibit 4-20, helps managers understand the nature of each activity cost pool, and what drives it.

EXHIBIT 4-20 The Cost Hierarchy

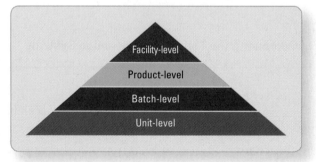

There are four categories of activity costs in this hierarchy, each determined by the underlying factor that drives its costs:

1. **Unit-level activities**—activities and costs incurred for every unit. Examples include inspecting and packaging *each* unit the company produces.

2. **Batch-level activities**—activities and costs incurred for every batch, regardless of the number of units in the batch. One example would be machine set-up. Once the machines are set-up for the specifications of the production run, the company could produce a batch of 1, 10, or 100 units, yet the company only incurs the machine set-up cost once for the entire batch.

---

[6]In some cases, ABC may reduce the total amount of over- or underallocation. How? Some activity cost pools may be overallocated, while others are underallocated, resulting in an offsetting total effect.

[7]When ABC system implementations fail, it is often due to managers' development of an overly complex system with too many cost pools and too many different cost drivers. After several redesigns of their ABC systems, Coca-Cola and Allied Signal both found that the simpler designs resulted in just as much accuracy. G. Cokins, "Learning to Love ABC," *Journal of Accountancy*, August 1999, pp. 37–39.

3. **Product-level activities**—activities and costs incurred for a particular product, regardless of the number of units or batches of the product produced. Examples include the cost to research, develop, design, and market new models.

4. **Facility-level activities**—activities and costs incurred no matter how many units, batches, or products are produced in the plant. An example is facility upkeep: the cost of depreciation, insurance, property tax, and maintenance on the entire production plant.

By considering how the costs of different activities are consumed (at the unit, batch, product, or facility level), managers are often able to maintain a relatively simple, yet accurate ABC system. After initially identifying perhaps 100 different activities, managers may be able to settle on 5–15 cost pools by combining those activities (for example, batch-level activities) that behave the same way into the same cost pools.

STOP & THINK

Do the journal entries used to record job costing differ if a manufacturer uses a refined cost allocation system (departmental overhead rates or ABC) rather than a single, plantwide overhead rate?

Answer: The journal entries used for a refined costing system are essentially the same as those described in Chapter 3 for a traditional job costing system. The only difference is that the company may decide to use *several* MOH accounts (one for each department or activity cost pool) rather than *one* MOH account. By using several MOH accounts, the manufacturer obtains more detailed information on each cost pool. This information may help managers make better estimates when calculating allocation rates the next year.

How do Managers Use the Improved Cost Information?

We've just seen how companies can increase the accuracy of their product costing systems by using departmental overhead rates or ABC. Now let's consider how managers use this improved cost information to run their companies more effectively and efficiently.

> Understand the benefits and limitations of ABC/ABM systems   **3**

Activity-Based Management (ABM)

Activity-based management (ABM) refers to using activity-based cost information to make decisions that increase profits while satisfying customers' needs. Life Fitness can use ABC information for pricing and product mix decisions, for helping to identify ways of cutting costs, and for routine planning and control decisions.

Pricing and Product Mix Decisions

The information provided by ABC showed Life Fitness's managers that ellipticals cost *less* to make and treadmills cost *more* to make than indicated by the original plantwide cost allocation system. As a result, managers may decide to change pricing on these products. For example, the company may be able to reduce its price on ellipticals to become more price-competitive. Or the company may decide to leave the price where it is, yet try to increase demand for this product since it is more profitable than originally assumed. On the other hand, managers will want to reevaluate the price charged for treadmills. The price must be high enough to cover the cost of producing and selling the treadmills, while still being low enough to compete with other companies and earn Life Fitness a reasonable profit.

After implementing ABC, companies often realize they were overcosting their high-volume products and undercosting their low-volume products. Plantwide overhead rates based on volume-sensitive allocation bases (such as direct labor hours), end up allocating more cost to high-volume products, and less cost to low volume products. However, ABC recognizes that not all indirect costs are driven by the number of units produced. That is to say, not all costs are unit-level costs. Rather, many costs are incurred at the batch-level or product-level where they can be spread over the number of units in the batch or in the product-line. As shown in Exhibit 4-21, ABC tends to increase the unit cost of low-volume products (that have fewer units over which to spread batch-level and product-level costs), and decrease the unit cost of high-volume products.

EXHIBIT 4-21   **Typical Result of ABC Costing**

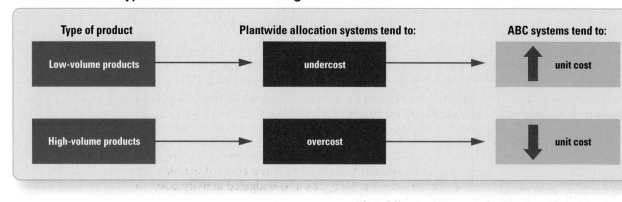

As a result of using ABC, many companies have found that they were actually losing money on some of their products while earning much more profit than they had realized on other products! By shifting the mix of products offered away from the less profitable and towards the more profitable, companies are able to generate a higher operating income.

Cutting Costs

Most companies adopt ABC to get more accurate product costs for pricing and product mix decisions, but they often reap even *greater benefits* by using ABM to pinpoint opportunities to cut costs. For example, using ABC allowed Life Fitness to better understand what drives its manufacturing overhead costs. The plantwide allocation system failed to pinpoint what was driving manufacturing overhead costs. Hence, managers could not effectively determine which costs could be minimized. Once the company switched to ABC, managers realized that it costs $10 each time a machine is set-up, $5 for each inspection, and so forth. Now, production managers have a "starting place" for cutting costs.

Once managers identify the company's activities and their related costs, managers can analyze whether all of the activities are really necessary. As the term suggests, **value-added activities** are activities for which the customer is willing to pay because these activities add value to the final product or service. In other words, these activities help satisfy the customer's expectations of the product or service. For example, fabricating component parts and assembling the units are value-added activities because they are necessary for changing raw materials into high-quality ellipticals and treadmills.

On the other hand, **non-value-added activities** (also referred to as **waste activities**), are activities that neither enhance the customer's image of the product or service nor provide a competitive advantage. These types of activities, such as storage of inventory and movement of parts from one area of the factory to another, could be reduced or removed from the process with no ill effect on the end product or service. The goal of **value-engineering**, as described in Exhibit 4-22, is to eliminate all waste in the system by making the company's processes as effective and efficient as possible. That means eliminating, reducing, or simplifying all non-value-added activities, and examining whether value-added activities could be improved.

EXHIBIT 4-22   **The Goal of Value-Engineering**

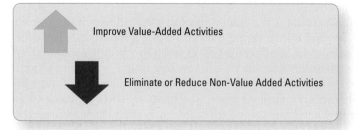

One way of determining whether an activity adds value is to ask if it could be eliminated or reduced by improving another part of the process. For example, could the movement of parts be eliminated or reduced by changing the factory layout? Could inventory storage be eliminated if the company only purchased the raw materials that were needed for each day's production run? Could inspection be reduced if more emphasis was placed on improving the production process, training employees, or using better quality inputs? In the second half of the chapter we'll discuss tools that many companies have adopted to identify and eliminate these costly non-value-added activities. These tools include lean manufacturing techniques and total quality management.

Routine Planning and Control Decisions

In addition to pricing, product mix, and cost-cutting decisions, Life Fitness can use ABC in routine planning and control. Activity-based budgeting uses the costs of activities to create budgets. Managers can compare actual activity costs to budgeted activity costs to determine how well they are achieving their goals.

Using ABC Outside of Manufacturing

Our chapter example revolved around using refined costing systems at a manufacturing company to more accurately allocate manufacturing overhead. However, merchandising and service companies also find ABC useful. These firms use ABC to allocate the cost of *operating activities* (rather than production activities) among product lines or service lines to figure out which are most profitable.

For example, Wal-Mart may use ABC to allocate the cost of store operating activities such as ordering, stocking, and customer service among its housewares, clothing, and electronics departments. An accounting firm may use ABC to allocate secretarial support, software costs, and travel costs between its tax, audit, and consulting clients. Even manufacturers may use ABC to allocate operating activities, such as research and development, marketing, and distribution costs to different product lines. ABC has also been used to determine customer profitability, not just product or service profitability. Firms use the same four basic steps discussed above, but apply them to indirect *operating* costs rather than indirect *manufacturing* costs (MOH). Once again, managers can use the data generated by ABC to determine which products or services to emphasize, to set prices, to cut costs, and to make other routine planning and control decisions.

STOP & THINK

Can governmental agencies use ABC/ABM to run their operations more efficiently?

Answer: ABC/ABM is not just for private-sector companies. Several governmental agencies, including the U.S. Postal Service (USPS) and the City of Indianapolis, have successfully used ABC/ABM to run their operations more cost-effectively. For example, in the past the USPS accepted customer payments only in the form of cash or checks. After using ABC to study the cost of its revenue collection procedures (activities), the USPS found that it would be cheaper to accept debit and credit card sales. Accepting debit and credit card sales also produced higher customer satisfaction, allowing the USPS to better compete with private mail and package carriers.

The City of Indianapolis was able to save its taxpayers millions of dollars after using ABC to study the cost of providing city services (activities) to local citizens. Once the city determined the cost of its activities, it was able to obtain competitive bids for those same services from private businesses. As a result, the city outsourced many activities to private-sector firms for a lower cost.[8]

Passing the Cost Benefit Test

Like all other management tools, ABC/ABM must pass the cost-benefit test. The system should be refined enough to provide accurate product costs but simple enough for managers to understand. In our chapter example, ABC increased the number of allocation rates from the single plantwide allocation rate in the original system to six activity cost allocation rates. ABC systems are even more complex in real-world companies that have many more activities and cost drivers.

---

[8]T. Carter, "How ABC changed the Post Office," *Management Accounting*, February 1998, pp. 28–36.
H. Meyer, "Indianapolis Speeds Away," *The Journal of Business Strategy*, May/June 1998, pp. 41–46.

Circumstances Favoring ABC/ABM Systems

ABC and ABM pass the cost-benefit test when the benefits of adopting ABC/ABM exceed the costs.

The benefits of adopting ABC/ABM are higher for companies in competitive markets because

- accurate product cost information is essential for setting competitive sales prices that still allow the company to earn a profit.

- ABM can pinpoint opportunities for cost savings, which increase the company's profit or are passed on to customers through lower prices.

The benefits of adopting ABC/ABM are higher when the risk of cost distortion is high, for example, when

- the company produces many different products that use different types and amounts of resources. (If all products use similar types and amounts of resources, a simple plantwide allocation system works fine.)

- the company has high indirect costs. (If the company has relatively few indirect costs, it matters less how they are allocated.)

- the company produces high volumes of some products and low volumes of other products. (Plantwide allocation systems based on a volume-related driver, such as direct labor hours, tend to overcost high-volume products and undercost low-volume products.)

We have seen that ABC offers many benefits. However, the cost and time required to implement and maintain an ABC system are often quite high. Some companies report spending up to two to four years to design and implement their ABC systems. The larger the company, the longer it usually takes. Top management support is crucial for the success of such an expensive and time consuming initiative. Without such support, ABC implementations might easily be abandoned for an "easier" allocation system. Since we know ABC systems are costly to implement, how can a company judge the costs involved with setting one up?

The costs of adopting ABC are generally lower when the company has

- accounting and information system expertise to develop the system. However, even "canned" accounting packages offer ABC modules. Small companies often find that Excel spreadsheets can be used to implement ABC, rather than integrating ABC into their general ledger software.

- information technology such as bar coding, optical scanning, Web-based data collection, or data warehouse systems to record and compile cost driver data.

Are real-world companies glad they adopted ABC?

Usually, but not always. A survey shows that 89% of the companies using ABC data say that it was worth the cost.[9] Adoption is on the rise among financial companies such as American Express, utilities such as Indianapolis Power and Light, and nonprofits such as the U.S. Marine Corps. But ABC is not a cure-all. As the controller for one Midwest manufacturer said, "ABC will not reduce cost; it will only help you understand costs better to know what to correct."

Signs That the Old System May Be Distorting Costs

Broken cars or computers simply stop running. But unlike cars and computers, even broken or outdated costing systems continue to report "product costs." How can you tell whether a cost system is broken and needs repair? In other words, how can you tell whether an existing cost system is distorting costs and needs to be refined by way of departmental rates or ABC?

---

[9]K. Krumwiede, "ABC: Why It's Tried and How It Succeeds," *Management Accounting*, April 1998, pp. 32–38.

A company's product cost system may need repair in the following situations:
Managers don't understand costs and profits:

- In bidding for jobs, managers lose bids they expected to win and win bids they expected to lose.
- Competitors with similar high-volume products price their products below the company's costs but still earn good profits.
- Employees do not believe the cost numbers reported by the accounting system.

The cost system is outdated:

- The company has diversified its product offerings since the allocation system was first developed.
- The company has reengineered its production process but has not changed its accounting system to reflect the new production environment

Decision Guidelines

Refined Costing Systems

Several years ago, Dell decided that it needed to refine its costing system. Starting with an Excel spreadsheet, Dell developed a simple ABC system that focused on the ten most critical activities. Here are some of the decisions Dell faced as it began refining its cost system.

Decision	Guidelines
How do we develop an ABC system?	1. Identify the activities and estimate the total MOH associated with each activity. These are known as the activity cost pools. 2. Select a cost allocation base for each activity and estimate the total amount that will be used during the year. 3. Calculate an activity cost allocation rate for each activity. 4. Allocate some MOH from each activity to the individual jobs that use the activities.
How do we compute an activity cost allocation rate?	$$\dfrac{\text{Total estimated activity cost pool}}{\text{Total estimated activity allocation base}}$$
How do we allocate an activity's cost to a job?	$$\begin{array}{c}\text{Activity cost}\\\text{allocation rate}\end{array} \times \begin{array}{c}\textbf{Actual amount of}\\\textbf{activity allocation}\\\textbf{base used by job}\end{array}$$
What types of decisions would benefit from the use of ABC?	Managers use ABC data in ABM to make decisions on the following: • Pricing and product mix • Cost cutting • Routine planning and control
What are the main benefits of ABC?	• More accurate product cost information • More detailed information on costs of activities and associated cost drivers help managers control costs.

continued

Decision	Guidelines
When is ABC most likely to pass the cost-benefit test?	• The company is in a competitive environment and needs accurate product costs. • The company makes different products that use different amounts of resources. • The company has high indirect costs. • The company produces high volumes of some products and lower volumes of other products. • The company has accounting and information technology expertise to implement the system. • The old cost system appears to be "broken."
How do we tell when a cost system needs to be refined?	• Managers lose bids they expected to win and win bids they expected to lose. • Competitors earn profits despite pricing high-volume products below our costs. • Employees do not believe cost numbers. • The company has diversified the products it manufactures. • The company has reengineered the production process but not the accounting system.

Summary Problem 1

Indianapolis Auto Parts (IAP) has a seat manufacturing department that uses ABC. IAP's activity cost allocation rates include the following:

Activity	Allocation Base	Activity Cost Allocation Rate
Machining	Number of machine hours	$30.00 per machine hour
Assembling	Number of parts	0.50 per part
Packaging	Number of finished seats	0.90 per finished seat

Suppose Ford has asked for a bid on 50,000 built-in baby seats that would be installed as an option on some Ford SUVs. Each seat has 20 parts and the direct materials cost per seat is $11. The job would require 10,000 direct labor hours at a labor wage rate of $25 per hour. In addition, IAP will use a total of 400 machine hours to fabricate some of the parts required for the seats.

Requirements

1. Compute the total cost of producing and packaging 50,000 baby seats. Also compute the average cost per seat.

2. For bidding, IAP adds a 30% markup to total cost. What price will the company bid for the Ford order?

3. Suppose that instead of an ABC system, IAP has a traditional product costing system that allocates manufacturing overhead at a plantwide overhead rate of $65 per direct labor hour. The baby-seat order will require 10,000 direct labor hours. Compute the total cost of producing the baby seats and the average cost per seat. What price will IAP bid using this system's total cost?

4. Use your answers to Requirements 2 and 3 to explain how ABC can help IAP make a better decision about the bid price it will offer Ford.

Solution

Requirement 1

Total Cost of Order and Average Cost per Seat:

Direct materials: 50,000 seats × $11.00 per seat	$ 550,000
Direct labor: 10,000 DL hours × $25.00 per DL hour........................	250,000
Manufacturing overhead:	
Machining, 400 machine hours × $30 per machine hour............	12,000
Assembling, (50,000 × 20 parts) × $0.50 per part......................	500,000
Packaging, 50,000 seats × $0.90 per seat....................................	45,000
Total cost of order..	$1,357,000
Divide by number of seats..	÷ 50,000
Average cost per seat..	$ 27.14

Requirement 2

Bid Price (ABC System):

> Bid price ($1,357,000 × 130%) = $1,764,100

Requirement 3

Bid Price (Traditional System):

Direct materials: 50,000 seats × $11.00	$ 550,000
Direct labor: 10,000 DL hours × $25.00 per DL hour............................	250,000
Manufacturing overhead: 10,000 DL hours × $65 per DL hour.............	650,000
Total cost of order...	$1,450,000
Divide by number of seats...	÷ 50,000
Average cost per seat...	$ 29.00
Bid price ($1,450,000 × 130%)...	$1,885,000

Requirement 4

IAP's bid would be $120,900 higher using the plantwide overhead rate than using ABC ($1,885,000 versus $1,764,100). Assuming that the ABC system more accurately captures the costs caused by the order, the traditional plantwide overhead system overcosts the order. This leads to a higher bid price that reduces IAP's chance of winning the bid. The ABC system shows that IAP can increase its chance of winning the bid by bidding a lower price and still make a profit.

How do Traditional and Lean Production Systems Differ?

ABC and ABM often reveal the high costs of activities such as (1) buying, storing, and moving inventories and (2) producing poor-quality products and services. So, it is not surprising that many "best practices" companies have linked their ABC/ABM systems to lean production and quality initiatives. In this section of the chapter, we'll discuss some of the differences between traditional production systems and lean production systems. In the final section, we'll describe the cost of quality framework and show how it can be used to guide managers' decisions.

> Describe a lean production system **4**

Traditional Production Systems

Traditional production systems are often described as "push systems." Once the production schedule for the period has been determined, products are "pushed" through the manufacturing process and then stored in finished goods inventory until sold. Traditional systems often keep large inventories of raw materials, work in process, and finished goods on hand. Why?

1. Companies often buy more raw materials than they need because the materials may be of poor quality. As a result, the materials may not be usable or may break during production and require replacement.

2. Companies often make products in large batches to spread setup costs over many units. As a result, companies often buy large quantities of raw materials and then have large quantities of finished units.

3. Companies often keep extra work in process inventory *between* departments so that each department will have something to continue working on in the event production stops or slows in an earlier department. For example, in Exhibit 4-23, we see the series of production steps required to produce drill bits from bar stock (the raw materials). If the company keeps some work in process inventory *between* the grinding and smoothing operations, the smoothing operation can continue even if the shaping or grinding operations slows or come to a halt as a result of machine break down, absence due to sick workers, or other production problems.

EXHIBIT 4-23   **Sequence of Operations for Drill-Bit Production**

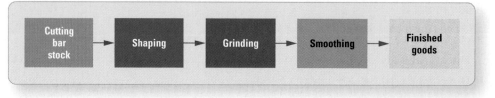

Companies often keep large inventories to protect themselves from uncertainty. Large raw material inventories protect against delayed deliveries from suppliers. Large finished goods inventories protect against lost sales if customer demand is higher than expected.

These are all valid reasons for keeping large inventories. So why are large inventories a problem?

1. Inventories use cash. Companies incur interest expense or forgo interest revenue on that cash. If a company has to borrow money to pay for inventory, it incurs interest expense on the loan. Even if a company uses its own cash to fund the inventory, it misses the opportunity to earn interest on that cash. In other words, if the cash were not used to purchase excessive inventory, the company could invest it and earn a return.

2. Large inventories often hide quality problems, production bottlenecks, and obsolescence. Inventory may spoil, be broken or stolen, or become obsolete as it sits in storage and waits to be used or sold. Companies in the high-tech and fashion industries are particularly susceptible to inventory obsolescence. What would Dell do with computer chips purchased six months earlier? The chips would be obsolete and unusable.

3. The activities of storing and taking items out of storage is very expensive. ABC and ABM have helped uncover the cost of these non-value-added activities.

Because of the problems associated with large inventories, many companies are now striving to use lean production systems that keep inventories to a minimum.

Lean Production Systems

Lean production is both a philosophy and a business strategy of manufacturing without waste. One primary goal of a lean production system is to eliminate the waste of time and money that accompanies large inventories. Therefore, lean companies adopt a "Just-in-Time" (JIT) inventory philosophy. As the name suggests, JIT inventory focuses on purchasing raw materials *just in time* for production and then completing finished goods *just in time* for delivery to customers. By doing so, companies eliminate the waste of storing and unstoring raw materials and finished goods, as pictured in Exhibit 4-24.

EXHIBIT 4-24   **Traditional System Versus JIT System**

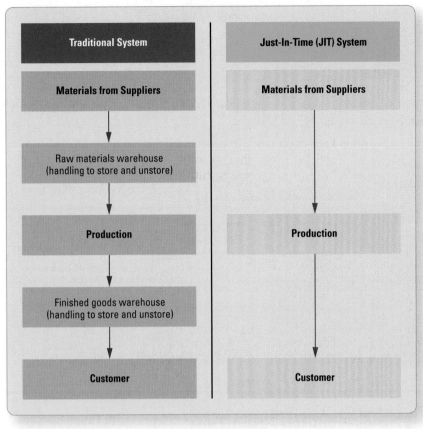

For example Dell workers receive orders via a monitor and assemble a desktop computer every 3–5 minutes. Most days, workers finish more than 25,000 computers, which ship directly to customers. However, the plant rarely holds more than two *hours* of inventory![10] How do they do it?

Most companies that adopt lean production have several common characteristics that help minimize the amount of inventory that is kept on hand, yet enable the company to quickly satisfy customer demand. These characteristics are described next.

Production Occurs in Self-Contained Cells

A traditional drill-bit manufacturer would group all cutting machines in one area, all shaping machines in another area, all grinding machines in a third area, and all smoothing machines in a fourth area, as illustrated in Panel A of Exhibit 4-25 (see next page). After switching to lean production, the company would group the machines in self-contained production cells as in Panel B of Exhibit 4-25. The goal is continuous production without interruptions or work in process inventories. These self-contained production cells minimize the time and cost involved with physically moving parts across the factory to other departments.

Broad Employee Roles

Employees working in production cells do more than operate a single machine. They also conduct maintenance, perform setups, inspect their own work, and operate other machines. For example, look at Panel B of Exhibit 4-25. A worker in the Drill Bit Production Cell 1 would be cross-trained to operate all of the machines (cutting, shaping, grinding, and smoothing) in that cell. This cross-training boosts morale and lowers costs. Employees who perform a number of duties rather than one repetitive duty tend to have higher job satisfaction.

---

[10]Kathryn Jones, "The Dell Way," Business 2.0, February 2003, www.business2.com.

EXHIBIT 4-25 Equipment Arrangement in Traditional and Lean Production Systems

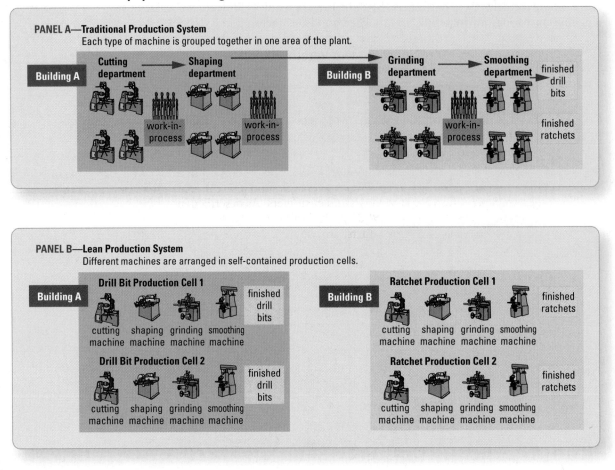

Small Batches Produced Just in Time

Lean companies schedule production in small batches *just in time* to satisfy customer needs. As a result, they don't need to carry extra finished goods inventory. In this "demand-pull system," the customer order—the "demand"—triggers the start of the production process and "pulls" the batch through production. Each order, even if very small, is usually its own batch. Even raw materials are usually not purchased until a customer order is received. The "demand-pull" system extends back to suppliers of materials who end up making frequent, small deliveries of defect-free raw materials just in time for production. The lean "pull" system replaces the traditional "push" system in which large quantities of raw materials are "pushed" through the production process to be stored in finished goods inventory until sold.

Shortened Setup Times

Since the product is not started until a customer order is received, lean companies must focus on reducing the time it takes to setup the machines used for more than one product. Employee training and technology helped Toyota cut setup times from several hours to a few minutes. This increases flexibility in scheduling production to meet customer orders, which, in turn, increases customer satisfaction and company profits.

Shortened Manufacturing Cycle Times

Lean companies must also produce their products very quickly. Dell's manufacturing cycle time is 3–5 minutes. GED Integrated Solutions, a window manufacturer, used to require three weeks to complete an order. GED has cut manufacturing cycle time to three to five days. Within six years after adopting lean production, Harley-Davidson reduced the time to produce a motorcycle by 77%. Shorter manufacturing times also protect companies from foreign competitors whose cheaper products take longer to ship. Delivery speed has become a competitive weapon.

Emphasis on Quality

Lean companies focus on producing their products right the *first* time, *every* time. Why? First, they have no backup stock to give to waiting customers if they run into production problems. Second, defects in materials and workmanship can slow or shut down production. Lean companies cannot afford the time it takes to rework faulty products. Lean companies emphasize "building-in" quality rather than "inspecting-in" quality (that is, hoping to catch defective units through sample inspections).

Supply-Chain Management

Because there are no inventory buffers, lean production requires close coordination with suppliers. These suppliers must guarantee *on-time delivery* of *defect-free* materials. *Supply-chain management* is the exchange of information with suppliers and customers to reduce costs, improve quality, and speed delivery of goods and services from the company's suppliers, through the company itself, and on to the company's end customers. As described in Chapter 1, suppliers that bear the ISO 9001:2008 certification have proven their ability to provide high-quality products, and thus, tend to be suppliers for lean manufacturers.

Are There Any Drawbacks to a Lean Production System?

While companies such as Toyota, Carrier, and Dell credit lean production for saving them millions of dollars, the system is not without problems. With no inventory buffers, lean producers are vulnerable when problems strike suppliers or distributors. For example, Ford cut production of its SUVs in response to the tire shortage resulting from Firestone's tire recall. It also had to shut down five of its U.S. plants when engine deliveries from Canadian suppliers were late due to security-related transportation delays in the wake of the World Trade Center attacks.

> ### Why is this important?
>
> "In order to compete and remain profitable, manufacturers must cut costs by becoming as efficient as possible. Lean production has become an important tool for cutting costs, especially the costs associated with carrying inventory."

How do Managers Improve Quality?

As discussed previously, lean companies strive for high-quality production. Poor-quality materials or defective manufacturing processes can slow or even shut down production. Since a lean production system only produces what is currently needed, it is essential that production consistently generates high-quality products.

> Describe and use the cost of quality framework **5**

To meet this challenge, many companies adopt **total quality management (TQM)**. The goal of TQM is to provide customers with superior products and services. Each business function in the value chain continually examines its own activities to improve quality and eliminate defects and waste. Those companies that have already adopted ABC have a head start. They have already identified their primary activities, so now they can concentrate on making those activities more efficient or finding ways to eliminate any non-value-added activities.

Most companies find that if they invest more in the front end of the value chain (R&D and design), they can generate savings in the back end of the value chain (production, marketing, distribution, and customer service). Why? Because carefully designed products and manufacturing processes reduce manufacturing time, inspections, rework, and warranty claims. World-class companies such as Toyota, who have adopted TQM, *design* and *build* quality into their products rather than having to *inspect* and *repair* later, as many traditional manufacturers do.

Costs of Quality

As part of TQM, many companies prepare cost of quality reports. **Cost of quality reports** categorize and list the costs incurred by the company related to quality. Once managers know the extent of their costs of quality, they can start to identify ways for the company to improve quality, while at the same time controlling costs.

Quality-related costs generally fall into four different categories: prevention costs, appraisal costs, internal failure costs, and external failure costs. These categories form the framework for a cost of quality report. We'll briefly describe each next.

1. **Prevention costs** are costs incurred to *avoid* producing poor-quality goods or services. Often, poor quality is caused by the variability of the production process or the complexity of the product design. To reduce the variability of the production process, companies often automate as much of the process as possible. Employee training can help decrease variability in nonautomated processes. In addition, reducing the complexity of the product design or manufacturing process can prevent the potential for error: The fewer parts or processes, the fewer things that can go wrong. Frequently, companies need to literally "go back to the drawing board" (the R&D and design stages of the value chain) to make a significant difference in preventing production problems. For example, Dell reengineered its assembly process to cut in half the number of times humans touch the hard drive. As a result, the hard-drive failure rate dropped 40%. Likewise, HP was able to reduce its defect rate by significantly reducing the number of parts that went into a desktop printer.

2. **Appraisal costs** are costs incurred to *detect* poor-quality goods or services. Intel incurs appraisal costs when it tests its products. One procedure, called burn-in, heats circuits to a high temperature. A circuit that fails the burn-in test is also likely to fail in customer use. Nissan tests 100% of the vehicles that roll off the assembly lines at its plant in Canton, Mississippi. Each vehicle is put through the paces on Nissan's all-terrain test track. Any problems are identified before the vehicle leaves the plant.

3. **Internal failure costs** are costs incurred on defective units *before* delivery to customers. For example, if Nissan does identify a problem, the vehicle is reworked to eliminate the defect before it is allowed to leave the plant. In the worst-case scenario, a product may be so defective that it cannot be reworked and must be completely scrapped. In this case, the entire cost of manufacturing the defective unit, plus any disposal cost, would be an internal failure cost.

4. **External failure costs** are costs incurred because the defective goods or services are not detected until *after* delivery is made to customers. For example, Maytag recently recalled 250,000 washing machines because water was leaking on the electrical connections, which had the potential to cause an electrical short and ignite the circuit boards. Along with incurring substantial cost for repairing or replacing these recalled washers, the publicity of this defect could cause significant damage to the company's reputation. Damage to a company's reputation from selling defective units to end customers can considerably harm the company's future sales. Unsatisfied customers will avoid buying from the company in the future. Even worse, unsatisfied customers tend to tell their neighbors, family, and friends about any poor experiences with products or services. As a result, a company's reputation for poor quality can increase at an exponential rate. To capture the extent of this problem, external failure costs should include an estimate of how much profit the company is losing due to having a bad reputation for poor quality.

Exhibit 4-26 lists some common examples of the four different costs of quality. Most prevention costs occur in the R&D and design stages of the value chain. In contrast, most appraisal and internal failure costs occur in the production element of the value chain. External failure costs occur in the customer service stage. Managers make trade-offs among these costs. Many prevention costs are incurred only periodically, while internal and external failure costs are ongoing. One expert estimates that $0.08 spent on prevention saves most manufacturers $1.00 in failure costs.

Prevention and appraisal costs are sometimes referred to as "conformance costs" since they are the costs incurred to make sure the product or service conforms to its intended design. In other words, these are the costs incurred to make sure the product is *not* defective. On the other hand, internal and external failure costs are sometimes

EXHIBIT 4-26   Four Types of Quality Costs

Prevention Costs	Appraisal Costs
Training personnel	Inspection of incoming materials
Evaluating potential suppliers	Inspection at various stages of production
Using better materials	Inspection of final products or services
Preventive maintenance	Product testing
Improved equipment	Cost of inspection equipment
Redesigning product or process	

Internal Failure Costs	External Failure Costs
Production loss caused by downtime	Lost profits from lost customers
Rework	Warranty costs
Abnormal quantities of scrap	Service costs at customer sites
Rejected product units	Sales returns and allowances due to
Disposal of rejected units	quality problems
Machine breakdowns	Product liability claims
	Cost of recalls

referred to as "non-conformance costs." These are the costs incurred because the product or service *is* defective.

The costs of quality are not limited to manufacturers. Service firms and merchandising companies also incur costs of quality. For example, CPA firms spend a lot of money providing ongoing professional training to their staff. They also develop standardized audit checklists to minimize the variability of the audit procedures performed for each client. These measures help to *prevent* audit failures. Both audit managers and partners review audit work papers to *appraise* whether the audit procedures performed and evidence gathered are sufficient on each audit engagement. If audit procedures or evidence is deemed to be lacking (*internal failure*), the audit manager or partner will instruct the audit team to perform additional procedures before the firm will issue an audit opinion on the client's financial statements. This parallels the "rework" a manufacturer might perform on a product that isn't up to par. Finally, recent audit failures, such as those at Enron and WorldCom, illustrate just how expensive and devastating *external failure* can be to a CPA firm. The once prestigious international CPA firm Arthur Andersen & Co. actually went out of business because of the reputation damage caused by its audit failure at Enron.

Now that we have examined the four costs of quality, let's see how they can be presented to management in the form of a Costs of Quality report. Let's assume Global Fitness, another manufacturer of fitness equipment, is having difficulty competing with Life Fitness because it doesn't have the reputation for high quality that Life Fitness enjoys. To examine this issue, management has prepared the Costs of Quality report shown in Exhibit 4-27.

Notice how Global Fitness identifies, categorizes, and quantifies all of the costs it incurs relating to quality. Global Fitness also calculated the percentage of total costs of quality that is incurred in each cost category. This helps company managers see just how *little* they are spending on conformance costs (prevention and appraisal). Most of their costs are internal and external failure costs. The best way to reduce these failure costs is to invest more in prevention and appraisal. Global Fitness managers can now begin to focus on how they might be able to prevent these failures from occurring.

Why is this important?

"Businesses compete with each other on the basis of price and quality. Costs of Quality reports help managers determine how they are spending money to ensure that consumers get the best quality product for the price."

EXHIBIT 4-27   Global Fitness's Costs of Quality Report

	Costs Incurred	Total Costs of Quality	Percentage of Total Costs of Quality (rounded)
Prevention Costs:			
Employee training	$ 125,000		
Total prevention costs		$ 125,000	6%*
Appraisal Costs:			
Testing	$ 175,000		
Total appraisal costs		$ 175,000	8%
Internal Failure Costs:			
Rework	$ 300,000		
Cost of rejected units	50,000		
Total internal failure costs		$ 350,000	17%
External Failure Costs:			
Lost profits from lost sales due to impaired reputation	$1,000,000		
Sales return processing	175,000		
Warranty costs	235,000		
Total external failure costs		$1,410,000	69%
Total costs of quality		$2,050,000	100%

*The percentage of total is computed as the total cost of the category divided by the total costs of quality.
 For example: 6% = $125,000 ÷ $2,050,000.

Using the Costs of Quality Framework to Aid Decisions

After analyzing the Cost of Quality report, the CEO is considering spending the following amounts on a new quality program:

Inspect raw materials	$100,000
Reengineer the production process to improve product quality	750,000
Supplier screening and certification	25,000
Preventive maintenance on plant equipment..	75,000
Total costs of implementing quality programs......................................	$950,000

Although these measures won't completely eliminate internal and external failure costs, Global Fitness expects this quality program to *reduce* costs by the following amounts:

Reduction in lost profits from lost sales due to impaired reputation...........	$ 800,000
Fewer sales returns to be processed	150,000
Reduction in rework costs...	250,000
Reduction in warranty costs..	225,000
Total cost savings...	$1,425,000

According to these projections, Global Fitness's quality initiative will cost $950,000 but result in total savings of $1,425,000—for a net benefit of $475,000. In performing a cost-benefit analysis, some companies will simply compare all of the projected costs ($950,000) with all of the projected benefits ($1,425,000) as shown previously. Other companies like to organize their cost-benefit analysis by cost category so that managers have a better idea of how the quality initiative will affect each cost category. Exhibit 4-28 shows that by increasing prevention costs (by $850,000) and appraisal costs (by $100,000), Global Fitness will be able to save $250,000 in internal failure costs and $1,175,000 in external failure costs. In total, Global Fitness expects a net benefit of $475,000 if it undertakes the quality initiative. By spending more on conformance costs (prevention and appraisal costs), Global Fitness saves even more on non-conformance costs (internal and external failure costs).

EXHIBIT 4-28 **Cost-Benefit Analysis of Global Fitness's Proposed Quality Program**

	Additional (Costs) and Cost Savings	Total New (Costs) or Cost Savings
Prevention Costs:		
Reengineer the production process	$(750,000)	
Supplier screening and certification	(25,000)	
Preventive maintenance on equipment	(75,000)	
Total additional prevention costs		$ (850,000)
Appraisal Costs:		
Inspect raw materials	$(100,000)	
Total additional appraisal costs		(100,000)
Internal Failure Costs:		
Reduction of rework costs	$ 250,000	
Total internal failure cost savings		250,000
External Failure Costs:		
Reduction of lost profits from lost sales	$ 800,000	
Reduction of sales returns	150,000	
Reduction of warranty costs	225,000	
Total external failure cost savings		1,175,000
Total savings (costs) from quality program		$ 475,000

The analysis shown in Exhibit 4-28 appears very straightforward. However, quality costs can be hard to measure. For example, design engineers may spend only part of their time on quality. Allocating their salaries to various activities is subjective. It is especially hard to measure external failure costs. The largest external failure cost—profits lost because of the company's reputation for poor quality—does not even appear in the accounting records. This cost must be estimated based on the experiences and judgments of the sales department. Because these estimates may be subjective, TQM programs also emphasize nonfinancial measures such as defect rates, number of customer complaints, and number of warranty repairs that can be objectively measured.

Decision Guidelines

Lean Production and the Costs of Quality

Dell, a worldwide leader in PC sales, is famous for its complete commitment to both the lean production and TQM philosophies. The following are several decisions Dell's managers made when adopting these two modern management techniques.

Decision	Guidelines	
How do we change a traditional production system to a lean production system?	**Traditional**	**Lean Production**
	Like machines grouped together	Production cells
	Longer setup times	Shorter setup times
	Larger batches	Smaller batches
	Higher inventories	Lower inventories
	An individual does fewer tasks	An individual does wider range of tasks
	Longer manufacturing cycle times	Shorter manufacturing cycle times
	Emphasis on using sample inspections to limit the number of defective products sold	Emphasis on "building-in" quality to every product
	Many suppliers	Fewer, but well-coordinated, suppliers
What are the four types of quality costs?	1. Prevention costs	
	2. Appraisal costs	
	3. Internal failure costs	
	4. External failure costs	
How do we make trade-offs among the four types of quality costs?	Investment in prevention costs and appraisal costs reduces internal and external failure costs.	

Summary Problem 2

The CEO of IAP is concerned with the quality of its products and the amount of resources currently spent on customer returns. The CEO would like to analyze the costs incurred in conjunction with the quality of the product.

The following information was collected from various departments within the company:

Warranty returns...	$120,000
Training personnel	10,000
Litigation on product liability claims...................................	175,000
Inspecting 10% of final products	5,000
Rework	10,000
Production loss due to machine breakdowns........................	45,000
Inspection of raw materials	5,000

Requirements

1. Prepare a Costs of Quality report. In addition to listing the costs by category, determine the percentage of the total costs of quality incurred in each cost category.

2. Do any additional subjective costs appear to be missing from the report?

3. What can be learned from the report?

Solutions

Requirement 1

	Costs Incurred	Total Costs of Quality	Percentage of Total Costs of Quality (rounded)
Prevention Costs:			
Personnel training	$ 10,000		
Total prevention costs		$ 10,000	3%*
Appraisal Costs:			
Inspecting raw materials	$ 5,000		
Inspecting 10% of final products	5,000		
Total appraisal costs		$ 10,000	3%
Internal Failure Costs:			
Rework	$ 10,000		
Production loss due to machine breakdown	45,000	$ 55,000	15%
Total internal failure costs			
External Failure Costs:			
Litigation costs from product liability claims	$175,000		
Warranty return costs	120,000		
Total external failure costs		$295,000	79%
Total costs of quality		$370,000	100%

*The percentage of total is computed as the total cost of the category divided by the total costs of quality. For example: 3% = $10,000 ÷ $370,000.

Requirement 2

Because the company has warranty returns and product liability litigation, it is very possible that the company suffers from a reputation for poor-quality products. If so, it is losing profits from losing sales. Unsatisfied customers will probably avoid buying from the company in the future. Worse yet, customers may tell their friends and family not to buy from the company. This report does not include an estimate of the lost profits arising from the company's reputation for poor-quality products.

Requirement 3

The Cost of Quality report shows that very little is being spent on prevention and maintenance, which is probably why the internal and external failure costs are so high. The CEO should use this information to develop quality initiatives in the areas of prevention and appraisal. Such initiatives should reduce future internal and external failure costs.

REVIEW

Accounting Vocabulary

Activity-Based Costing (ABC). (p. 179)   Focuses on *activities* as the fundamental cost objects. The costs of those activities become building blocks for compiling the indirect costs of products, services, and customers.

Activity-Based Management (ABM). (p. 185)   Using activity-based cost information to make decisions that increase profits while satisfying customers' needs.

Appraisal Costs. (p. 196)   Costs incurred to *detect* poor-quality goods or services.

Batch-Level Activities. (p. 184)   Activities and costs incurred for every batch, regardless of the number of units in the batch.

Cost Distortion. (p. 173)   Overcosting some products while undercosting other products.

Cost of Quality Report. (p. 195)   A report that lists the costs incurred by the company related to quality. The costs are categorized as prevention costs, appraised costs, internal failure costs, and external failure costs.

Departmental Overhead Rates. (p. 175)   Separate manufacturing overhead rates established for each department.

External Failure Costs. (p. 196)   Costs incurred when the company does not detect poor-quality goods or services until *after* delivery is made to customers.

Facility-Level Activities. (p. 185)   Activities and costs incurred no matter how many units, batches, or products are produced in the plant.

Internal Failure Costs. (p. 196)   Costs incurred when the company detects and corrects poor-quality goods or services *before* making delivery to customers.

Lean Production. (p. 192)   A philosophy and business strategy of manufacturing without waste.

Non-Value-Added Activities. (p. 186)   Activities that neither enhance the customer's image of the product or service nor provide a competitive advantage; also known as waste activities.

Plantwide Overhead Rate. (p. 173)   When overhead is allocated to every product using the same manufacturing overhead rate.

Prevention Costs. (p. 196)   Costs incurred to *avoid* poor-quality goods or services.

Product-Level Activities. (p. 185)   Activities and costs incurred for a particular product, regardless of the number of units or batches of the product produced.

Total Quality Management (TQM). (p. 195)   A management philosophy of delighting customers with superior products and services by continually setting higher goals and improving the performance of every business function.

Unit-Level Activities. (p. 184)   Activities and costs incurred for every unit produced.

Value Engineering. (p. 186)   Eliminating waste in the system by making the company's processes as effective and efficient as possible.

Value-Added Activities. (p. 186)   Activities for which the customer is willing to pay because these activities add value to the final product or service.

Waste Activities. (p. 186)   Activities that neither enhance the customer's image of the product or service nor provide a competitive advantage; also known as non-value-added activities.

Quick Check

1. *(Learning Objective 1)* Which of the following reasons would indicate that a company should consider using departmental overhead rates rather than using a single plantwide overhead rate?

   a. Each product is in each department for a different length of time.

   b. Each department spends different amounts on manufacturing overhead.

   c. Each department incurs different types of manufacturing overhead.

   d. All of the above statements are reasons that a company would choose departmental overhead rates rather than using a single plantwide overhead rate.

2. *(Learning Objective 2)* Which of the following is *not* a step in computing ABC cost allocation rates?

   a. Costs from each activity are allocated to individual jobs that use those activities.

   b. Manufacturing overhead costs associated with each primary production activity are estimated.

   c. The amounts of the allocation base to be used for each primary production activity are estimated.

   d. All of the above statements are steps in calculating ABC cost allocation rates.

3. *(Learning Objective 2)* Manufacturing overhead is allocated to jobs in an ABC system by using the following formula:

   a. Activity cost allocation rate × Estimated amount of activity allocation base used by the job

   b. Activity cost allocation rate ÷ Estimated amount of activity allocation base used by the job

   c. Activity cost allocation rate × Actual amount of activity allocation base used by the job

   d. Activity cost allocation rate ÷ Actual amount of activity allocation base used by the job

4. *(Learning Objective 2)* The legal costs associated with filing a patent for a new model of oven at an appliance manufacturer is an example of which type of activity?

   a. Unit-level

   b. Batch-level

   c. Product-level

   d. Facility-level

5. *(Learning Objective 3)* Which of the following is *false*?

   a. ABC focuses on allocating indirect costs.

   b. Advances in information technology have made it feasible for more companies to adopt ABC.

   c. ABC is only for manufacturing firms.

   d. A system that uses ABC is more refined than one that uses departmental overhead rates.

6. *(Learning Objective 3)* Dell can use ABC information for what decisions?
   a. Pricing
   b. Cost cutting
   c. Evaluating managers' performance
   d. All of the above

7. *(Learning Objective 3)* Which of the following is *not* a good reason for Dell to use ABC?
   a. The computer industry is highly competitive.
   b. Dell produces many more desktops than servers, and servers are more difficult to assemble.
   c. Most costs are direct; indirect costs are a small proportion of total costs.
   d. Dell has advanced information technology, including bar-coded materials and labor.

8. *(Learning Objective 4)* Dell enjoys many benefits from committing to lean production. Which is *not* a benefit of adopting a lean production philosophy?
   a. Lower inventory carrying costs
   b. More space available for production
   c. Ability to respond more quickly to changes in customer demand
   d. Ability to continue production despite disruptions in deliveries of raw materials

9. *(Learning Objective 5)* The cost of lost future sales after a customer finds flaws in a product or service is which of the following quality costs?
   a. External failure cost
   b. Internal failure cost
   c. Appraisal cost
   d. Prevention cost

10. *(Learning Objective 5)* Dell's spending on testing its computers before shipping them to customers helps *reduce* which of the following costs?
    a. Prevention cost
    b. Appraisal cost
    c. External failure cost
    d. None of the above

ASSESS YOUR PROGRESS

Learning Objectives

1 Develop and use departmental overhead rates to allocate indirect costs

2 Develop and use activity-based costing (ABC) to allocate indirect costs

3 Understand the benefits and limitations of ABC/ABM systems

4 Describe a lean production system

5 Describe and use the costs of quality framework

Short Exercises

S4-1 Understand key terms *(Learning Objectives 1, 2, 3, 4, & 5)*

Listed below are several terms. Complete the following statements with one of these terms. You may use a term more than once, and some terms may not be used at all.

Plantwide overhead rate	Unit-level costs	Overcosted	Batch-level costs
Internal failure costs	Non-value added activities	Cost distortion	Value-added activities
Appraisal costs	Product-level costs	External failure costs	Activity-based costing
Undercosted	Lean production	Facility-level costs	Prevention costs

a. _____ are incurred to avoid producing poor-quality goods or services.
b. The philosophy and business strategy of manufacturing without waste is called _____.
c. The more detailed information provided by _____ helps managers control costs.
d. _____ are costs incurred to detect poor-quality goods or services.
e. _____ are incurred for every individual unit.
f. _____ are activities for which the customer is willing to pay.

g. _____ are costs that arise from product defects that are discovered before the product is shipped to the customer.

h. The cost to design a new product is an example of _____.

i. _____ include storage, moving, and inspecting activities.

j. The costs of providing warranty service are _____.

k. _____ are incurred for each batch of products.

l. Total manufacturing overhead is divided by one cost allocation base to calculate a _____.

m. It is likely that _____ will result if a single plantwide overhead rate is used when products vary widely in their usage of various manufacturing overhead activities.

n. _____ are incurred to support the entire organization and cannot be traced to any particular product or batch.

S4-2 Use departmental overhead rates to allocate manufacturing overhead *(Learning Objective 1)*

Quality Furniture uses departmental overhead rates (rather than a plantwide overhead rate) to allocate its manufacturing overhead to jobs. The company's two production departments have the following departmental overhead rates:

Cutting Department:	$10 per machine hour
Finishing Department:	$17 per direct labor hour

Job 392 used the following direct labor hours and machine hours in the two manufacturing departments:

JOB 392	Cutting Department	Finishing Department
Direct labor hours	2	6
Machine hours	8	1

1. How much manufacturing overhead should be allocated to Job 392?

2. Assume that direct labor is paid at a rate of $25 per hour and Job 392 used $2,500 of direct materials. What was the total manufacturing cost of Job 392?

S4-3 Compute departmental overhead rates *(Learning Objective 1)*

Uncle Bruce's Snacks makes potato chips, corn chips, and cheese puffs using three different production lines within the same manufacturing plant. Currently, Uncle Bruce uses a single plantwide overhead rate to allocate its $3,500,000 of annual manufacturing overhead. Of this amount, $1,800,000 is associated with the potato chip line, $1,000,000 is associated with the corn chip line, and $700,000 is associated with the cheese puff line. Uncle Bruce's plant is currently running a total of 17,500 machine hours: 11,250 in the potato chip line, 3,450 in the corn chip line, and 2,800 in the cheese puff line. Uncle Bruce considers machine hours to be the cost driver of manufacturing overhead costs.

1. What is Uncle Bruce's plantwide overhead rate?

2. Calculate the departmental overhead rates for Uncle Bruce's three production lines. Round all answers to the nearest cent.

3. Which products had been overcosted by the plantwide rate? Which products had been undercosted by the plantwide rate?

S4-4 Compute activity cost allocation rates *(Learning Objective 2)*

Uncle Bruce produces different styles of potato chips (ruffled, flat, thick-cut, gourmet) for different corporate customers. Each style of potato chip requires different preparation time, different cooking and draining times (depending on desired fat content), and different packaging (single serving versus bulk). Therefore, Uncle Bruce has decided to try ABC costing to better capture the manufacturing overhead costs incurred by each style of chip.

Uncle Bruce has identified the following activities related to yearly manufacturing overhead costs and cost drivers associated with producing potato chips:

Activity	Manufacturing Overhead	Cost Driver
Preparation..............................	$600,000	Preparation time
Cooking and draining..............	$900,000	Cooking and draining time
Packaging................................	$300,000	Units packaged

Compute the activity cost allocation rates for each activity assuming the following total estimated activity for the year: 12,000 preparation hours, 30,000 cooking and draining hours, and 6 million packages.

S4-5 Continuation of S4-4: Use ABC to allocate overhead *(Learning Objective 2)*

Uncle Bruce just received an order to produce 12,000 single-serving bags of gourmet, fancy-cut, low-fat potato chips. The order will require 16 preparation hours and 32 cooking and draining hours. Use the activity rates you calculated in S4-4 to compute the following:

1. What is the total amount of manufacturing overhead that should be allocated to this order?

2. How much manufacturing overhead should be assigned to each bag?

3. What other costs will Uncle Bruce need to consider to determine the total manufacturing costs of this order?

S4-6 Calculate a job cost using ABC *(Learning Objective 2)*

Berg Industries, a family-run small manufacturer, has adopted an ABC costing system. The following manufacturing activities, indirect manufacturing costs, and usage of cost drivers have been estimated for the year:

Activity	Estimated Total Manufacturing Overhead Costs	Estimated Total Usage of Cost Driver
Machine setup.......................	$ 150,000	3,000 setups
Machining............................	$1,000,000	5,000 machine hours
Quality control......................	$ 337,500	4,500 tests run

During May, Evan and Stephanie Berg machined and assembled Job 624. Evan worked a total of 10 hours on the job, while Stephanie worked 5 hours on the job. Evan is paid a $25 per hour wage rate, while Stephanie is paid $30 per hour because of her additional experience level. Direct materials requisitioned for Job 624 totaled $1,050. The following additional information was collected on Job 624: The job required 1 machine setup, 5 machine hours, and 2 quality control tests.

1. Compute the activity cost allocation rates for the year.

2. Complete the following job cost record for Job 624:

Job Cost Record JOB 624	Manufacturing Costs
Direct materials..	?
Direct labor..	?
Manufacturing overhead..	?
Total job cost...	$?

S4-7 Apply activity cost allocation rates *(Learning Objective 2)*

Narnia Technology uses ABC to allocate all of its manufacturing overhead. Narnia's Cell Phone Department, which assembles and tests digital processors, reports the following data regarding processor G27:

Direct materials cost..	$14.00
Direct labor cost...	$42.00
Manufacturing overhead allocated	?
Manufacturing product cost...	$?

The activities required to build the processors are as follows:

Activity	Allocation Base	Cost Allocated to Each Board			
Start station	Number of processor boards	1	× $ 0.90 =	$0.90
Dip insertion	Number of dip insertions	20	× $ 0.25 =	?
Manual insertion	Number of manual insertions	5	× $? =	2.00
Wave solder	Number of processor boards soldered	1	× $ 4.50 =	4.50
Backload	Number of backload insertions	?	× $ 0.70 =	2.80
Test	Standard time each processor board is in test activity (hr.)	0.15	× $90.00 =	?
Defect analysis	Standard time for defect analysis and repair (hr.)	0.16	× $? =	8.00
Total				$?

1. Fill in the blanks in both the opening schedule and the list of activities.
2. Why might managers favor this ABC system instead of the older system that allocated all manufacturing overhead costs on the basis of direct labor?

S4-8 Classifying costs within the cost hierarchy *(Learning Objective 2)*

Classify each of the following costs as either unit-level, batch-level, product-level, and facility-level.
a. Product line manager salary
b. CEO salary
c. Machine setup costs that are incurred whenever a new production order is started
d. Direct materials
e. Order processing
f. Factory utilities
g. Patent for new product
h. Direct labor
i. Cost to inspect each product as it is finished
j. Depreciation on factory
k. Engineering costs for new product
l. Shipment of an order to a customer

S4-9 Classifying costs within the cost hierarchy *(Learning Objective 2)*

Halliwell Manufacturing produces a variety of plastic containers using an extrusion blow molding process. The following activities are part of Halliwell Manufacturing's operating process:
1. Each container is cut from the mold once the plastic has cooled and hardened.
2. Patents are obtained for each new type of container mold.
3. Plastic resins are used as the main direct material for the containers.
4. A plant manager oversees the entire manufacturing operation.

5. The sales force incurs travel expenses to attend various trade shows throughout the country to market the containers.

6. Each container product line has a product line manager.

7. The extrusion machine is calibrated for each batch of containers made.

8. Each type of container has its own unique molds.

9. Routine maintenance is performed on the extrusion machines.

10. Rent is paid for the building that houses the manufacturing processes.

Classify each activity as either unit-level, batch-level, product-level, and facility-level.

S4-10 Determine the usefulness of refined costing systems in various situations *(Learning Objective 3)*

In each of the following situations, determine whether the company would be (1) more likely or (2) less likely to benefit from refining its costing system.

1. The company has reengineered its production process but has not changed its accounting system.

2. The company produces few products, and the products consume resources in a similar manner.

3. The company operates in a very competitive industry.

4. The company has very few indirect costs.

5. The company produces high volumes of some of its products and low volumes of other products.

6. In bidding for jobs, managers lost bids they expected to win and won bids they expected to lose.

Mission, Inc., Data Set for S4-11 through S4-14:

Mission, Inc., is a technology consulting firm focused on Web site development and integration of Internet business applications. President Susan Nelson's ear is ringing after an unpleasant call from client Jerry Webb. Webb was irate after opening his bill for Mission's redesign of his company's Web site. Webb said that Mission's major competitor, Delta Applications, charged much lower fees to another company for which Webb serves on the board of directors.

Nelson is puzzled for two reasons. First, she is confident that her firm knows Web site design and support as well as any of Mission's competitors. Nelson cannot understand how Delta Applications can undercut Mission's rates and still make a profit. But Delta Applications is reputed to be very profitable. Second, just yesterday Nelson received a call from client Keith Greg. Greg was happy with the excellent service and reasonable fees Nelson charged him for adding a database-driven job-posting feature to his company's Web site. Nelson was surprised by Greg's compliments because this was an unusual job for Mission that required development of complex database management and control applications, and she had felt a little uneasy accepting it.

Like most consulting firms, Mission traces direct labor to individual engagements (jobs). Mission allocates indirect costs to engagements using a budgeted rate based on direct labor hours. Nelson is happy with this system, which she has used since she established Mission in 1995.

Nelson expects to incur $706,000 of indirect costs this year, and she expects her firm to work 5,000 direct labor hours. Nelson and the other systems consultants earn $350 per hour. Clients are billed at 150% of direct labor cost. Last month, Mission's consultants spent 100 hours on Webb's engagement. They also spent 100 hours on Greg's engagement.

S4-11 Compute and use traditional allocation rate *(Learning Objective 1)*

Refer to the Mission Data Set.

1. Compute Mission's indirect cost allocation rate.

2. Compute the total costs assigned to the Webb and Greg engagements.

3. Compute the operating income from the Webb and Greg engagements.

S4-12 Identify clues that old system is broken *(Learning Objective 3)*

Refer to the Mission Data Set. List all of the signals or clues indicating that Mission's cost system may be "broken."

S4-13 Compute activity cost allocation rates *(Learning Objective 2)*

Refer to the Mission Data Set. Nelson suspects that her allocation of indirect costs could be giving misleading results, so she decides to develop an ABC system. She identifies three activities: documentation preparation, information technology support, and training. Nelson figures that documentation costs are driven by the number of pages, information technology support costs are driven by the number of software applications used, and training costs are most closely associated with the number of direct labor hours worked. Estimates of the costs and quantities of the allocation bases follow:

Activity	Estimated Cost	Allocation Base	Estimated Quantity of Cost Driver
Documentation preparation	$100,000	Pages	3,125 pages
Information technology support	156,000	Applications used	780 applications
Training	450,000	Direct labor hours	5,000 hours
Total indirect costs	$706,000		

Compute the cost allocation rate for each activity.

S4-14 Continuation of S4-13: Compute job costs using ABC *(Learning Objective 2)*

Refer to the Mission Data Set and the activity cost allocation rates you computed in S4-13. The Webb and Greg engagements used the following resources last month:

Cost Driver	Webb	Greg
Direct labor hours	100	100
Pages	50	300
Applications used	1	78

1. Compute the cost assigned to the Webb engagement and to the Greg engagement using the ABC system.

2. Compute the operating income from the Webb engagement and from the Greg engagement using the ABC system.

S4-15 Identifying costs as value-added or non-valued-added *(Learning Objective 3)*

Identify which of the following manufacturing overhead costs are value-added and which are non-value added.
a. Cost of moving raw materials into production
b. Product inspection
c. Engineering design costs for a new product
d. Costs arising from backlog in production
e. Costs of warehousing raw materials
f. Wages of the workers assembling products
g. Salary for supervisor on the factory floor
h. Costs of reworking of defective units

S4-16 Identifying activities as value-added or non-valued-added *(Learning Objective 3)*

Identify which of the following manufacturing overhead costs are value-added and which are non-value added.

1. Moving raw materials from the receiving area to the storage area.

2. Storing raw materials until needed in production.

3. Inspecting raw materials when they arrive to make sure that they meet specifications.

4. Assembling parts into a completed product.

5. Partially completed units are stacked while awaiting the next production step.

6. Some of the raw materials are broken while in storage.

7. Product warranty work is performed on units which malfunctioned for customers.

8. Product is delivered to customer.

S4-17 Identify lean production characteristics *(Learning Objective 4)*

Indicate whether each of the following is characteristic of a lean production system or a traditional production system.

a. Management works with suppliers to ensure defect-free raw materials.

b. Products are produced in large batches.

c. Large stocks of finished goods protect against lost sales if customer demand is higher than expected.

d. Suppliers make frequent deliveries of small quantities of raw materials.

e. Setup times are long.

f. Employees do a variety of jobs, including maintenance and setups as well as operation of machines.

g. Machines are grouped into self-contained production cells or production lines.

h. Machines are grouped according to function. For example, all cutting machines are located in one area.

i. Suppliers can access the company's intranet.

j. The final operation in the production sequence "pulls" parts from the preceding operation.

k. Each employee is responsible for inspecting his or her own work.

l. There is an emphasis on building in quality.

m. The manufacturing cycle times are longer.

S4-18 Classifying costs of quality *(Learning Objective 5)*

Classify each of the following quality-related costs as prevention costs, appraisal costs, internal failure costs, or external failure costs.

1. Reworking defective units

2. Litigation costs from product liability claims

3. Inspecting incoming raw materials

4. Training employees

5. Warranty repairs

6. Redesigning the production process

7. Lost productivity due to machine break down

8. Inspecting products that are halfway through the production process

9. Incremental cost of using a higher-grade raw material

10. Cost incurred producing and disposing of defective units

S4-19 Quality initiative decision *(Learning Objective 5)*

Wharfedale manufactures high-quality speakers. Suppose Wharfedale is considering spending the following amounts on a new quality program:

Additional 20 minutes of testing for each speaker	$ 600,000
Negotiating with and training suppliers to obtain higher-quality materials and on-time delivery	300,000
Redesigning the speakers to make them easier to manufacture	1,400,000

Wharfedale expects this quality program to save costs as follows:

Reduced warranty repair costs	$200,000
Avoid inspection of raw materials	400,000
Rework avoided because of fewer defective units	650,000

It also expects this program to avoid lost profits from the following:

Lost sales due to disappointed customers	$850,000
Lost production time due to rework	300,000

1. Classify each of these costs into one of the four categories of quality costs (prevention, appraisal, internal failure, external failure).
2. Should Wharfedale implement the quality program? Give your reasons.

S4-20 Categorize different costs of quality *(Learning Objective 5)*

Millan & Co. makes electronic components. Mike Millan, the president, recently instructed Vice President Steve Bensen to develop a total quality control program: "If we don't at least match the quality improvements our competitors are making," he told Bensen, "we'll soon be out of business." Bensen began by listing various "costs of quality" that Millan incurs. The first six items that came to mind were as follows:

▪ Costs of electronic components returned by customers

▪ Costs incurred by Millan & Co.'s customer representatives traveling to customer sites to repair defective products

▪ Lost profits from lost sales due to reputation for less-than-perfect products

▪ Costs of inspecting components in one of Millan & Co.'s production processes

▪ Salaries of engineers who are designing components to withstand electrical overloads

▪ Costs of reworking defective components after discovery by company inspectors

1. Classify each item as a prevention cost, an appraisal cost, an internal failure cost, or an external failure cost.

Exercises—Group A

E4-21A Compare traditional and departmental cost allocations *(Learning Objective 1)*

Cermak's Fine Furnishings manufactures upscale custom furniture. Cermak Fine Furnishings currently uses a plantwide overhead rate based on direct labor hours to allocate its $1,100,000 of manufacturing overhead to individual jobs. However, Ernie Cermak, owner and CEO, is considering refining the company's costing system by using departmental overhead rates. Currently, the Machining Department incurs $750,000 of manufacturing overhead while the Finishing Department incurs $350,000 of manufacturing overhead. Ernie has identified machine hours (MH) as the primary manufacturing overhead cost driver in the Machining Department and direct labor (DL) hours as the primary cost driver in the Finishing Department.

Cermak Fine Furnishings's plant completed Jobs 450 and 455 on May 15. Both jobs incurred a total of 6 DL hours throughout the entire production process. Job 450 incurred 2 MH in the Machining Department and 5 DL hours in the Finishing Department (the other DL hour occurred in the Machining Department). Job 455 incurred 6 MH in the Machining Department and 4 DL hours in the Finishing Department (the other two DL hours occurred in the Machining Department).

Requirements

1. Compute the plantwide overhead rate assuming that Cermak expects to incur 25,000 total DL hours during the year.
2. Compute departmental overhead rates assuming that Cermak expects to incur 15,000 MH in the Machining Department and 17,500 DL hours in the Finishing Department during the year.
3. If Cermak continues to use the plantwide overhead rate, how much manufacturing overhead would be allocated to Job 450 and Job 455?
4. If Cermak uses departmental overhead rates, how much manufacturing overhead would be allocated to Job 450 and Job 455?
5. Based on your answers to Requirements 3 and 4, does the plantwide overhead rate overcost or undercost either job? Explain. If Cermak sells his furniture at 125% of cost, will his choice of allocation systems affect product pricing? Explain.

E4-22A Compute activity rates and apply to jobs *(Learning Objective 2)*

Northstar uses ABC to account for its chrome wheel manufacturing process. Company managers have identified four manufacturing activities that incur manufacturing overhead costs: materials handling, machine setup, insertion of parts, and finishing. The budgeted activity costs for the upcoming year and their allocation bases are as follows:

Activity	Total Budgeted Manufacturing Overhead Cost	Allocation Base
Materials handling	$ 12,000	Number of parts
Machine setup	3,400	Number of setups
Insertion of parts	48,000	Number of parts
Finishing	80,000	Finishing direct labor hours
Total	$143,400	

Northstar expects to produce 1,000 chrome wheels during the year. The wheels are expected to use 3,000 parts, require 10 setups, and consume 2,000 hours of finishing time.

Job 420 used 150 parts, required 1 setup, and consumed 120 finishing hours.
Job 510 used 425 parts, required 2 setups, and consumed 320 finishing hours.

Requirements

1. Compute the cost allocation rate for each activity.
2. Compute the manufacturing overhead cost that should be assigned to Job 420.
3. Compute the manufacturing overhead cost that should be assigned to Job 510.

E4-23A Apply activity cost allocation rates *(Learning Objective 2)*

The Electronics Manufacturing Department of Imagine uses ABC to allocate all of its manufacturing overhead. The company assembles and tests electronic components used in hand-held video phones. Consider the following data regarding component T24:

Direct materials cost	$51.00
Direct labor cost	$30.00
Manufacturing overhead allocated	?
Manufacturing product cost	$?

The activities required to build the component follow:

Activity	Allocation Base			Cost Allocated to Each Unit
Start station	Number of raw component chassis	2	× $ 1.30 =	$ 2.60
Dip insertion	Number of dip insertions	?	× $ 0.40 =	12.00
Manual insertion	Number of manual insertions	12	× $ 0.80 =	?
Wave solder	Number of components soldered	1	× $ 1.40 =	1.40
Backload	Number of backload insertions	7	× $? =	4.20
Test	Standard time each component is in test activity	0.40	× $80.00 =	?
Defect analysis	Standard time for defect analysis and repair	0.10	× $? =	5.00
Total				$?

Requirements

1. Fill in the blanks in both the opening schedule and the list of activities.

2. Why might managers favor this ABC system instead of the older system, which allocated all manufacturing overhead costs on the basis of direct labor?

E4-24A Using ABC to bill clients at a service firm *(Learning Objective 2)*

Curtis & Company is an architectural firm specializing in home remodeling for private clients and new office buildings for corporate clients.

Curtis & Company charges customers at a billing rate equal to 135% of the client's total job cost. A client's total job cost is a combination of (1) professional time spent on the client ($65 per hour cost of employing each professional) and (2) operating overhead allocated to the client's job. Curtis allocates operating overhead to jobs based on professional hours spent on the job. Curtis estimates its five professionals will incur a total of 10,000 professional hours working on client jobs during the year.

All operating costs other than professional salaries (travel reimbursements, copy costs, secretarial salaries, office lease, and so forth) can be assigned to the three activities. Total activity costs, cost drivers, and total usage of those cost drivers are estimated as follows:

Activity	Total Activity Cost	Cost Driver	Total Usage by Corporate Clients	Total Usage by Private Clients
Transportation to clients........	$ 9,000	Round-trip mileage to clients...........	3,000 miles	12,000 miles
Blueprint copying.................	35,000	Number of copies............	300 copies	700 copies
Office support......................	190,000	Secretarial time................	2,200 secretarial hours	2,800 secretarial hours
Total operating overhead.....	$234,000			

Amy Lee hired Curtis & Company to design her kitchen remodeling. A total of 24 professional hours were incurred on this job. In addition, Amy's remodeling job required one of the professionals to travel back and forth to her house for a total of 125 miles. The blueprints had to be copied four times because Amy changed the plans several times. In addition, 18 hours of secretarial time were used lining up the subcontractors for the job.

Requirements

1. Calculate the current indirect cost allocation rate per professional hour.

2. Calculate the amount that would be billed to Amy Lee given the current costing structure.

3. Calculate the activity cost allocation rates that could be used to allocate operating overhead costs to client jobs.

4. Calculate the amount that would be billed to Amy Lee using ABC costing.

5. Which type of billing system is fairer to clients? Explain.

E4-25A Reassess product costs using ABC *(Learning Objective 2)*

Owens, Inc., manufactures only two products, Medium (42-inch) and Large (63-inch) plasma screen TVs. To generate adequate profit and cover its expenses throughout the value chain, Owens prices its TVs at 300% of manufacturing cost. The company is concerned because the Large model is facing severe pricing competition, whereas the Medium model is the low-price leader in the market. The CEO questions whether the cost numbers generated by the accounting system are correct. He has just learned about ABC and wants to reanalyze this past year's product costs using an ABC system.

Information about the company's products this past year is as follows:

Medium (42-inch) Plasma TVs

Total direct material cost: $660,000

Total direct labor cost: $216,000

Production volume: 3,000 units

Large (63-inch) Plasma TVs:

Total direct material cost: $1,240,000

Total direct labor cost: $384,000

Production volume: 4,000 units

Currently, the company applies manufacturing overhead on the basis of direct labor hours. The company incurred $800,000 of manufacturing overhead this year and 25,000 direct labor hours (9,000 direct labor hours making Medium TVs and 16,000 making Large TVs). The ABC team identified three primary production activities that generate manufacturing overhead costs:

Materials Handling ($150,000); driven by number of material orders handled

Machine Processing ($560,000); driven by machine hours

Packaging ($90,000); driven by packaging hours

The company's only two products required the following activity levels during the year:

	Material Orders Handled	Machine Hours	Packaging Hours
Medium	300	20,000	4,000
Large	200	20,000	6,000

Requirements

1. Use the company's current costing system to find the total cost of producing all Medium (42-inch) TVs and the total cost of producing all Large (63-inch) TVs. What was the average cost of making each unit of each model? Round your answers to the nearest cent.

2. Use ABC to find the total cost of producing all Medium (42-inch) TVs and the total cost of producing all Large (63-inch) TVs. What was the average cost of making each unit of each model? Round your answers to the nearest cent.

3. How much cost distortion was occurring between Owens' two products? Calculate the cost distortion in total and on a per unit basis. Could the cost distortion explain the CEO's confusion about pricing competition? Explain.

E4-26A Use ABC to allocate manufacturing overhead (Learning Objective 2)

Several years after reengineering its production process, Enke, Corp. hired a new controller, Natalie Babin. She developed an ABC system very similar to the one used by Enke's chief rival, Northstar. Part of the reason Babin developed the ABC system was because Enke's profits had been declining even though the company had shifted its product mix toward the product that had appeared most profitable under the old system. Before adopting the new ABC system, Enke had used a plantwide overhead rate based on direct labor hours that was developed years ago.

For the upcoming year, Enke's budgeted ABC manufacturing overhead allocation rates are as follows:

Activity	Allocation Base	Activity Cost Allocation Rate
Materials handling....................	Number of parts	$ 3.75 per part
Machine setup...........................	Number of setups	300.00 per setup
Insertion of parts......................	Number of parts	24.00 per part
Finishing	Finishing direct labor hours	50.00 per hour

The number of parts is now a feasible allocation base because Enke recently purchased bar-coding technology. Enke produces two wheel models: Standard and Deluxe. Budgeted data for the upcoming year are as follows:

	Standard	Deluxe
Parts per wheel...	4.0	6.0
Setups per 1,000 wheels	15.0	15.0
Finishing direct labor hours per wheel.......................	1.0	2.5
Total direct labor hours per wheel	2.0	3.0

The company's managers expect to produce 1,000 units of each model during the year.

Requirements

1. Compute the total budgeted manufacturing overhead cost for the upcoming year.

2. Compute the manufacturing overhead cost per wheel of each model using ABC.

3. Compute Enke's traditional plantwide overhead rate. Use this rate to determine the manufacturing overhead cost per wheel under the traditional system.

E4-27A Continuation of E4-26A: Determine product profitability (Learning Objectives 2 & 3)

Refer to your answers in E4-26A. In addition to the manufacturing overhead costs, the following data are budgeted for the company's Standard and Deluxe models for next year:

	Standard	Deluxe
Sales price per wheel	$300.00	$440.00
Direct materials per wheel...	30.00	46.00
Direct labor per wheel...	45.00	50.00

Requirements

1. Compute the gross profit per wheel if managers rely on the ABC unit cost data computed in E4-26A.

2. Compute the gross profit per wheel if the managers rely on the plantwide allocation cost data.

3. Which product line is more profitable for Enke?

4. Why might controller Natalie Babin have expected ABC to pass the cost-benefit test? Were there any warning signs that Enke's old direct-labor-based allocation system was broken?

E4-28A   Work backward to determine ABC rates (Learning Objective 2)

Channell Fabricators completed two jobs in June. Channell Fabricators recorded the following costs assigned to the jobs by the company's activity-based costing system:

		Allocated Cost	
Activity	Allocation Base	Job 409	Job 622
Materials handling...............	Number of parts	$ 500	$ 1,500
Lathe work..........................	Number of lathe turns	5,000	15,000
Milling................................	Number of machine hours	4,000	28,000
Grinding..............................	Number of parts	300	1,500
Testing................................	Number of output units	126	2,700

Job 622 required 3,000 parts, 60,000 lathe turns, and 1,400 machine hours. All 300 of the job's output units were tested. All units of Job 409 were tested.

Requirements

1. How do you know that at least one of the costs recorded for the two jobs is inaccurate?

2. Disregard materials handling costs. How many parts were used for Job 409? How many lathe turns did Job 409 require? How many machine hours? How many units were produced in Job 409?

3. A nearby company has offered to test all product units for $13 each. On the basis of ABC data, should Channell Fabricators accept or reject the offer? Give your reason.

E4-29A   Differentiate between traditional and lean production (Learning Objective 4)

Briefly describe how lean production systems differ from traditional production systems along each of the following dimensions:

1. Inventory levels

2. Batch sizes

3. Setup times

4. Physical layout of plant

5. Roles of plant employees

6. Manufacturing cycle times

7. Quality

E4-30A   Prepare a Cost of Quality report (Learning Objective 5)

The CEO of Smith Snackfoods is concerned about the amount of resources currently spent on customer warranty claims. Each box of snacks is printed with the following logo: "Satisfaction guaranteed, or your money back." Since the claims are so high, she would like to evaluate what costs are being incurred to ensure the quality of the product. The following information was collected from various departments within the company:

Warranty claims..	$420,000
Cost of defective products found at the inspection point......................	94,000
Training factory personnel	26,000
Recall of Batch #59374...	175,000
Inspecting products when halfway through the production process.......	55,000
Cost of disposing of rejected products...	12,000
Preventive maintenance on factory equipment...................................	7,000
Production loss due to machine breakdowns.....................................	15,000
Inspection of raw materials	5,000

Requirements

1. Prepare a Cost of Quality report. In addition to listing the costs by category, determine the percentage of the total costs of quality incurred in each cost category.

2. Do any additional subjective costs appear to be missing from the report?

3. What can be learned from the report?

E4-31A Classify costs and make a quality-initiative decision *(Learning Objective 5)*

Chihooli manufactures radiation-shielding glass panels. Suppose Chihooli is considering spending the following amounts on a new TQM program:

Strength-testing one item from each batch of panels	$65,000
Training employees in TQM	30,000
Training suppliers in TQM	40,000
Identifying preferred suppliers who commit to on-time delivery of perfect quality materials	60,000

Chihooli expects the new program to save costs through the following:

Avoid lost profits from lost sales due to disappointed customers	$90,000
Avoid rework and spoilage	55,000
Avoid inspection of raw materials	45,000
Avoid warranty costs	15,000

Requirements

1. Classify each item as a prevention cost, an appraisal cost, an internal failure cost, or an external failure cost.

2. Should Chihooli implement the new quality program? Give your reason.

Exercises—Group B

E4-32B Compare traditional and departmental cost allocations *(Learning Objective 1)*

Garvey's Fine Furnishings manufactures upscale custom furniture. Garvey's Fine Furnishings currently uses a plantwide overhead rate, based on direct labor hours, to allocate its $1,200,000 of manufacturing overhead to individual jobs. However, Ernie Garvey, owner and CEO, is considering refining the company's costing system by using departmental overhead rates. Currently, the Machining Department incurs $800,000 of manufacturing overhead while the Finishing Department incurs $400,000 of manufacturing overhead. Ernie has identified machine hours (MH) as the primary manufacturing overhead cost driver in the Machining Department and direct labor (DL) hours as the primary cost driver in the Finishing Department.

Garvey's Fine Furnishings' plant completed Jobs 450 and 455 on May 15. Both jobs incurred a total of 7 DL hours throughout the entire production process. Job 450 incurred 3 MH in the Machining Department and 6 DL hours in the Finishing Department (the other DL hour occurred in the Machining Department). Job 455 incurred 4 MH in the Machining Department and 5 DL hours in the Finishing Department (the other two DL hours occurred in the Machining Department).

Requirements

1. Compute the plantwide overhead rate, assuming Garvey expects to incur 25,000 total DL hours during the year.

2. Compute departmental overhead rates, assuming Garvey expects to incur 15,400 MH in the Machining Department and 17,800 DL hours in the Finishing Department during the year.

3. If Garvey continues to use the plantwide overhead rate, how much manufacturing overhead would be allocated to Job 450 and Job 455?

4. If Garvey uses departmental overhead rates, how much manufacturing overhead would be allocated to Job 450 and Job 455?

5. Based on your answers to Requirements 3 and 4, does the plantwide overhead rate overcost or undercost either of the jobs? Explain. If Garvey sells his furniture at 125% of cost, will his choice of allocation systems affect product pricing?

E4-33B Compute activity rates and apply to jobs (Learning Objective 2)

Central Plain uses ABC to account for its chrome wheel manufacturing process. Company managers have identified four manufacturing activities that incur manufacturing overhead costs: materials handling, machine setup, insertion of parts, and finishing. The budgeted activity costs for the upcoming year and their allocation bases are as follows:

Activity	Total Budgeted Manufacturing Overhead Cost	Allocation Base
Materials handling	$ 5,600	Number of parts
Machine setup	6,400	Number of setups
Insertion of parts	39,200	Number of parts
Finishing	96,800	Finishing direct labor hours
Total	$148,000	

Central Plain expects to produce 1,000 chrome wheels during the year. The wheels are expected to use 2,800 parts, require 20 setups, and consume 2,200 hours of finishing time.
Job 420 used 250 parts, required 3 setups, and consumed 130 finishing hours.
Job 510 used 475 parts, required 6 setups, and consumed 300 finishing hours.

Requirements

1. Compute the cost allocation rate for each activity.

2. Compute the manufacturing overhead cost that should be assigned to Job 420.

3. Compute the manufacturing overhead cost that should be assigned to Job 510.

E4-34B Apply activity cost allocation rates (Learning Objective 2)

The Electronics Manufacturing Department of Best Gadgets uses ABC to allocate all of its manufacturing overhead. The company assembles and tests electronic components used in handheld video phones. Consider the following data regarding component T24:

Direct materials cost	$44.00
Direct labor cost	32.00
Manufacturing overhead allocated	?
Manufacturing product cost	$?

The activities required to build the component follow:

Activity	Allocation Base			Cost Allocated to Each Unit
Start station	Number of raw component chassis	8	× $ 1.80 =	$14.40
Dip insertion	Number of dip insertions	?	× $ 0.40 =	16.00
Manual insertion	Number of manual insertions	18	× $ 1.60 =	?
Wave solder	Number of components soldered	7	× $ 2.20 =	15.40
Backload	Number of backload insertions	15	× $? =	5.10
Test	Standard time each component is in test activity	0.70	× $110.00 =	?
Defect analysis	Standard time for defect analysis and repair	0.50	× $? =	11.00
Total				$?

Requirements

1. Fill in the blanks in both the opening schedule and the list of activities.

2. Why might managers favor this ABC system instead of the older system, which allocated all conversion costs on the basis of direct labor?

E4-35B Using ABC to bill clients at a service firm (Learning Objective 2)

Grenier & Company is an architectural firm, specializing in home remodeling for private clients and new office buildings for corporate clients.

Grenier & Company charges customers at a billing rate equal to 131% of the client's total job cost. A client's total job cost is a combination of (1) professional time spent on the client ($63 per hour cost of employing each professional) and (2) operating overhead allocated to the client's job. Grenier allocates operating overhead to jobs based on professional hours spent on the job. Grenier estimates its five professionals will incur a total of 10,000 professional hours working on client jobs during the year.

All operating costs other than professional salaries (travel reimbursements, copy costs, secretarial salaries, office lease, and so forth) can be assigned to the three activities. Total activity costs, cost drivers, and total usage of those cost drivers are estimated as follows:

Activity	Total Activity Cost	Cost Driver	Total Usage by Corporate Clients	Total Usage by Private Clients
Transportation to clients........	$ 11,000	Round-trip mileage to clients...........	4,000 miles	11,000 miles
Blueprint copying.................	31,000	Number of copies............	500 copies	500 copies
Office support.....................	194,000	Secretarial time................	2,200 secretarial hours	2,800 secretarial hours
Total operating overhead	$236,000			

Amy Lee hired Grenier & Company to design her kitchen remodeling. A total of 21 professional hours were incurred on this job. In addition, Amy's remodeling job required one of the professionals to travel back and forth to her house for a total of 123 miles. The blueprints had to be copied four times because Amy changed the plans several times. In addition, 13 hours of secretarial time were used lining up the subcontractors for the job.

Requirements

1. Calculate the current operating overhead allocation rate per professional hour.

2. Calculate the amount that would be billed to Amy Lee given the current costing structure.

3. Calculate the activity cost allocation rates that could be used to allocate operating overhead costs to client jobs.

4. Calculate the amount that would be billed to Amy Lee using ABC costing.

5. Which type of billing system is fairer to clients? Explain.

E4-36B Reassess product costs using ABC (Learning Objective 2)

Jefferis, Inc., manufactures only two products, Medium (42-inch) and Large (63-inch) plasma screen TVs. To generate adequate profit and cover its expenses throughout the value chain, Jefferis prices its TVs at 300% of manufacturing cost. The company is concerned, because the Large model is facing severe pricing competition, whereas the Medium model is the low-price leader in the market. The CEO questions whether the cost numbers generated by the accounting system are correct. He's just learned about ABC and wants to reanalyze this past year's product costs using an ABC system. Information about the company's products this past year is as follows:

Medium (42-inch) Plasma TVs
Total direct material cost: $661,000
Total direct labor cost: $223,000
Production volume: 3,180 units

Large (63-inch) Plasma TVs:
Total direct material cost: $1,240,000
Total direct labor cost: $386,000
Production volume: 4,120 units

Currently, the company applies manufacturing overhead on the basis of direct labor hours. The company incurred $828,000 of manufacturing overhead this year, and 26,500 direct labor hours (9,600 direct labor hours making Medium TVs and 16,900 making Large TVs). The ABC team identified three primary production activities that generate manufacturing overhead costs:

Materials Handling ($156,000); driven by number of material orders handled
Machine Processing ($570,000); driven by machine hours
Packaging ($102,000); driven by packaging hours

The company's only two products required the following activity levels during the year:

	Material Orders Handled	Machine Hours	Packaging Hours
Medium	340	20,000	4,040
Large	240	23,400	6,040

Requirements

1. Use the company's current costing system to find the total cost of producing all Medium (42-inch) TVs and the total cost of producing all Large (63-inch) TVs. What was the average cost of making each unit of each model? Round your answers to the nearest cent.

2. Use ABC to find the total cost of producing all Medium (42-inch) TVs and the total cost of producing all Large (63-inch) TVs. What was the average cost of making each unit of each model? Round your answers to the nearest cent.

3. How much cost distortion was occurring between Jefferis' two products? Calculate the cost distortion in total, and on a per unit basis. Could the cost distortion explain the CEO's confusion about pricing competition? Explain.

E4-37B Use ABC to allocate manufacturing overhead (Learning Objective 2)

Several years after reengineering its production process, Zeke, Corp. hired a new controller, Georgia Taylor. She developed an ABC system very similar to the one used by Zeke's chief rival, Hotbeach. Part of the reason Taylor developed the ABC system was because Zeke's profits had been declining even though the company had shifted its product mix toward the product that had appeared most profitable under the old system. Before adopting the new ABC system, Zeke had used a plantwide overhead rate, based on direct labor hours that was developed years ago.

For the upcoming year, Zeke's budgeted ABC manufacturing overhead allocation rates are as follows:

Activity	Allocation Base	Activity Cost Allocation Rate
Materials handling	Number of parts	$ 3.85 per part
Machine setup	Number of setups	345.00 per setup
Insertion of parts	Number of parts	27.00 per part
Finishing	Finishing direct labor hours	55.00 per hour

The number of parts is now a feasible allocation base because Zeke recently purchased bar-coding technology. Zeke produces two wheel models: Standard and Deluxe. Budgeted data for the upcoming year are as follows:

	Standard	Deluxe
Parts per wheel	4.0	6.0
Setups per 1,000 wheels	10.0	10.0
Finishing direct labor hours per wheel	1.1	3.5
Total direct labor hours per wheel	2.7	3.8

The company's managers expect to produce 1,000 units of each model during the year.

Requirements

1. Compute the total budgeted manufacturing overhead cost for the upcoming year.
2. Compute the manufacturing overhead cost per wheel of each model using ABC.
3. Compute Zeke's traditional plantwide overhead rate. Use this rate to determine the manufacturing overhead cost per wheel under the traditional system.

E4-38B Continuation of E4-37B: Determine product profitability (Learning Objectives 2 & 3)

Refer to your answers in E4-37B. In addition to the manufacturing overhead costs, the following data are budgeted for the company's Standard and Deluxe models for next year:

	Standard	Deluxe
Sales price per wheel	$470.00	$640.00
Direct materials per wheel	31.00	47.00
Direct labor per wheel	45.50	51.50

Requirements

1. Compute the gross profit per wheel if managers rely on the ABC unit cost data.

2. Compute the gross profit per unit if the managers rely on the plantwide allocation cost data.

3. Which product line is more profitable for Zeke?

4. Why might controller Georgia Taylor have expected ABC to pass the cost-benefit test? Were there any warning signs that Zeke's old direct-labor-based allocation system was broken?

E4-39B Work backward to determine ABC rates *(Learning Objective 2)*

Burke Fabricators completed two jobs in June. Burke Fabricators recorded the following costs assigned to the jobs by the company's activity-based costing system:

Activity	Allocation Base	Allocated Cost Job 409	Allocated Cost Job 622
Materials handling.............	Number of parts	$ 400	$ 1,200
Lathe work........................	Number of lathe turns	4,700	15,500
Milling..............................	Number of machine hours	3,600	26,000
Grinding...........................	Number of parts	336	1,680
Testing.............................	Number of output units	125	2,500

Job 622 required 2,400 parts +, 77,500 lathe turns, and 1,625 machine hours. All 400 of the job's output units were tested. All units of Job 409 were tested.

Requirements

1. How do you know that at least one of the costs recorded for the two jobs is inaccurate?

2. Disregard materials handling costs. How many parts were used for Job 409? How many lathe turns did Job 409 require? How many machine hours did Job 409 require? How many units were produced in Job 409?

3. A nearby company has offered to test all product units for $10 each. On the basis of ABC data, should Burke Fabricators accept or reject the offer? Give your reason.

E4-40B Differentiate between traditional and lean production *(Learning Objective 4)*

Categorize each of the following characteristics as being either more representative of traditional manufacturing or lean production.

1. Quality tends to be "inspect-in" rather than "build-in"

2. Manufacturing plants tend to be organized with self-contained production cells

3. Maintain greater quantities of raw materials, work in process, and finished goods inventories

4. Setup times are longer

5. High quality is stressed in every aspect of production

6. Produce in smaller batches

7. Emphasis is placed on shortening manufacturing cycle times

8. Manufacturing plants tend to group like machinery together in different parts of the plant

9. Setup times are shorter

10. Produce in larger batches

11. Strive to maintain low inventory levels

12. Cycle time tends to be longer

E4-41B Prepare a Cost of Quality report *(Learning Objective 5)*

The CEO of Shaun Snackfoods is concerned with the amounts of resources currently spent on customer warranty claims. Each box of snacks is printed with the following logo: "Satisfaction guaranteed, or your money back." Since the claims are so high, she would like to evaluate what costs are being incurred to ensure the quality of the product. The following information was collected from various departments within the company:

Warranty claims	$436,000
Cost of defective products found at the inspection point	91,000
Training factory personnel	25,000
Recall of Batch #59374	175,000
Inspecting products when halfway through the production process	52,000
Cost of disposing of rejected products	11,000
Preventative maintenance on factory equipment	8,000
Production loss due to machine breakdowns	16,000
Inspection of raw materials	4,000

Requirements

1. Prepare a Cost of Quality report. In addition to listing the costs by category, determine the percentage of the total costs of quality incurred in each cost category.

2. Do any additional subjective costs appear to be missing from the report?

3. What can be learned from the report?

E4-42B   Classify costs and make a quality-initiative decision *(Learning Objective 5)*

Clegg manufactures radiation-shielding glass panels. Suppose Clegg is considering spending the following amounts on a new TQM program:

Strength-testing one item from each batch of panels	$68,000
Training employees in TQM	30,000
Training suppliers in TQM	32,000
Identifying preferred suppliers who commit to on-time delivery of perfect quality materials	60,000

Clegg expects the new program would save costs through the following:

Avoid lost profits from lost sales due to disappointed customers	$95,000
Avoid rework and spoilage	67,000
Avoid inspection of raw materials	57,000
Avoid warranty costs	16,000

Requirements

1. Classify each item as a prevention cost, an appraisal cost, an internal failure cost, or an external failure cost.

2. Should Clegg implement the new quality program? Give your reason.

Problems—Group A

P4-43A   Implementation and analysis of departmental rates *(Learning Objective 1)*

Perreth Products manufactures its products in two separate departments: machining and assembly. Total manufacturing overhead costs for the year are budgeted at $1 million. Of this amount, the Machining Department incurs $600,000 (primarily for machine operation and depreciation) while the Assembly Department incurs $400,000. Perreth Products estimates that it will incur 4,000 machines hours (all in the Machining Department) and 12,500 direct labor hours (2,500 in the Machining Department and 10,000 in the Assembly Department) during the year.

Perreth Products currently uses a plantwide overhead rate based on direct labor hours to allocate overhead. However, the company is considering refining its overhead allocation system by using departmental overhead rates. The Machining Department would allocate its overhead using machine hours (MH), but the Assembly Department would allocate its overhead using direct labor (DL) hours.

The following chart shows the machine hours (MH) and direct labor (DL) hours incurred by Jobs 500 and 501 in each production department:

	Machining Department	Assembly Department
Job 500	3 MH	12 DL hours
	2 DL hours	
Job 501	6 MH	12 DL hours
	2 DL hours	

Both Jobs 500 and 501 used $1,000 of direct materials. Wages and benefits total $25 per direct labor hour. Perreth Products prices its products at 110% of total manufacturing costs.

Requirements

1. Compute Perreth Products' current plantwide overhead rate.

2. Compute refined departmental overhead rates.

3. Which job (Job 500 or Job 501) uses more of the company's resources? Explain.

4. Compute the total amount of overhead allocated to each job if Perreth Products uses its current plantwide overhead rate.

5. Compute the total amount of overhead allocated to each job if Perreth Products uses departmental overhead rates.

6. Do both allocation systems accurately reflect the resources that each job used? Explain.

7. Compute the total manufacturing cost and sales price of each job using Perreth Products' current plantwide overhead rate.

8. Based on the current (plantwide) allocation system, how much profit did Perreth Products *think* it earned on each job? Based on the departmental overhead rates and the sales price determined in Requirement 7, how much profit did it *really* earn on each job?

9. Compare and comment on the results you obtained in Requirements 7 and 8.

P4-44A Use ABC to compute full product costs *(Learning Objective 2)*

Hone's Office Department manufactures computer desks in its Topeka, Kansas, plant. The company uses activity-based costing to allocate all manufacturing conversion costs (direct labor and manufacturing overhead). Its activities and related data follow.

Activity	Budgeted Cost of Activity	Allocation Base	Cost Allocation Rate
Materials handling	$ 300,000	Number of parts	$ 0.60
Assembling	2,500,000	Direct labor hours	15.00
Painting	170,000	Number of painted desks	5.00

Hone produced two styles of desks in March: the Standard desk and Unpainted desk. Data for each follow:

Product	Total Units Produced	Total Direct Materials Costs	Total Number of Parts	Total Assembling Direct Labor Hours
Standard desk...........................	6,000	$96,000	120,000	6,000
Unpainted desk	1,500	21,000	30,000	900

Requirements

1. Compute the per-unit manufacturing product cost of Standard desks and Unpainted desks.

2. Premanufacturing activities, such as product design, were assigned to the Standard desks at $5 each and to the Unpainted desks at $3 each. Similar analyses were conducted of post manufacturing activities, such as distribution, marketing, and customer service. The post-manufacturing costs were $25 per Standard and $22 per Unpainted desk. Compute the full product costs per desk.

3. Which product costs are reported in the external financial statements? Which costs are used for management decision making? Explain the difference.

4. What price should Hone's managers set for Standard desks to earn a $42 profit per desk?

P4-45A   Comprehensive ABC implementation (Learning Objectives 2 & 3)

Xnet develops software for Internet applications. The market is very competitive, and Xnet's competitors continue to introduce new products at low prices. Xnet offers a wide variety of software—from simple programs that enable new users to create personal Web pages to complex commercial search engines. Like most software companies, Xnet's raw material costs are insignificant.

Xnet has just hired Tom Merrell, a recent graduate of State University's accounting program. Merrell asks Software Department Manager Jeff Gire to join him in a pilot activity-based costing study. Merrell and Gire identify the following activities, related costs, and cost-allocation bases:

Activity	Estimated Indirect Activity Costs	Allocation Base	Estimated Quantity of Allocation Base
Applications development	$1,600,000	New applications	4 new applications
Content production..	2,400,000	Lines of code	12 million lines
Testing..	288,000	Testing hours	1,800 testing hours
Total indirect costs...	$4,288,000		

Xnet is planning to develop the following new applications:

- X-Page—software for developing personal Web pages

- X-Secure—commercial security and firewall software

X-Page requires 500,000 lines of code and 100 hours of testing, while X-Secure requires 7.5 million lines of code and 600 hours of testing. Xnet expects to produce and sell 30,000 units of X-Page and 10 units of X-Secure.

Requirements

1. Compute the cost allocation rate for each activity.

2. Use the activity-based cost allocation rates to compute the indirect cost of each unit of X-Page and X-Secure. (*Hint:* Compute the total activity costs allocated to each product line and then compute the cost per unit.)

3. Xnet's original single-allocation-based cost system allocated indirect costs to products at $100 per programmer hour. X-Page requires 10,000 programmer hours, while X-Secure requires 15,000 programmer hours. Compute the total indirect costs allocated to X-Page and X-Secure under the original system. Then, compute the indirect cost per unit for each product.

4. Compare the activity-based costs per unit to the costs from the simpler original system. How have the unit costs changed? Explain why the costs changed as they did.

5. What are the clues that Xnet's ABC system is likely to pass the cost-benefit test?

P4-46A Comprehensive ABC implementation (*Learning Objectives 2 & 3*)

HCI Pharmaceuticals manufactures an over-the-counter allergy medication called Breathe. HCI Pharmaceuticals is trying to win market share from Sudafed and Tylenol. HCI Pharmaceuticals has developed several different Breathe products tailored to specific markets. For example, the company sells large commercial containers of 1,000 capsules to health-care facilities and travel packs of 20 capsules to shops in airports, train stations, and hotels.

HCI Pharmaceuticals' controller, Sandra Dean, has just returned from a conference on ABC. She asks Keith Yeung, supervisor of the Breathe product line, to help her develop an ABC system. Dean and Yeung identify the following activities, related costs, and cost allocation bases:

Activity	Estimated Indirect Activity Costs	Allocation Base	Estimated Quantity of Allocation Base
Materials handling	$190,000	Kilos	19,000 kilos
Packaging	400,000	Machine hours	2,000 hours
Quality assurance	112,500	Samples	1,875 samples
Total indirect costs	$702,500		

The commercial-container Breathe product line had a total weight of 8,000 kilos, used 1,200 machine hours, and required 200 samples. The travel-pack line had a total weight of 6,000 kilos, used 400 machine hours, and required 300 samples. HCI produced 2,500 commercial containers of Breathe and 50,000 travel packs.

Requirements

1. Compute the cost allocation rate for each activity.

2. Use the activity-based cost allocation rates to compute the indirect cost of each unit of the commercial containers and the travel packs. (*Hint:* Compute the total activity costs allocated to each product line and then compute the cost per unit.)

3. HCI Pharmaceuticals' original single-allocation-based cost system allocated indirect costs to products at $300 per machine hour. Compute the total indirect costs allocated to the commercial containers and to the travel packs under the original system. Then, compute the indirect cost per unit for each product.

4. Compare the activity-based costs per unit to the costs from the original system. How have the unit costs changed? Explain why the costs changed as they did.

P4-47A Using ABC in conjunction with quality decisions *(Learning Objectives 2 & 5)*

Real Toys is using a costs-of-quality approach to evaluate design engineering efforts for a new toy robot. The company's senior managers expect the engineering work to reduce appraisal, internal failure, and external failure activities. The predicted reductions in activities over the two-year life of the toy robot follow. Also shown is the cost allocation rate for each activity.

Activity	Predicted Reduction in Activity Units	Activity Cost Allocation Rate per Unit
Inspection of incoming materials............................	300	$20
Inspection of finished goods.................................	300	30
Number of defective units discovered in-house..............	3,200	15
Number of defective units discovered by customers	900	35
Lost sales to dissatisfied customers........................	300	55

Requirements

1. Calculate the predicted quality cost savings from the design engineering work.

2. Real Toys spent $60,000 on design engineering for the new toy robot. What is the net benefit of this "preventive" quality activity?

3. What major difficulty would Real Toys' managers have had in implementing this costs-of-quality approach? What alternative approach could they use to measure quality improvement?

Problems–Group B

P4-48B Implementation and analysis of departmental rates *(Learning Objective 1)*

Quintana Products manufactures its products in two separate departments: machining and assembly. Total manufacturing overhead costs for the year are budgeted at $1.09 million. Of this amount, the Machining Department incurs $670,000 (primarily for machine operation and depreciation) while the Assembly Department incurs $420,000. Quintana Products estimates it will incur 4,000 machines hours (all in the Machining Department) and 14,000 direct labor hours (2,000 in the Machining Department and 12,000 in the Assembly Department) during the year.

Quintana Products currently uses a plantwide overhead rate based on direct labor hours to allocate overhead. However, the company is considering refining its overhead allocation system by using departmental overhead rates. The Machining Department would allocate its overhead using machine hours (MH), but the Assembly Department would allocate its overhead using direct labor (DL) hours.

The following chart shows the machine hours (MH) and direct labor (DL) hours incurred by Jobs 500 and 501 in each production department.

	Machining Department	Assembly Department
Job 500...	8 MH	15 DL hours
	5 DL hours	
Job 501	16 MH	15 DL hours
	5 DL hours	

Both Jobs 500 and 501 used $1,200 of direct materials. Wages and benefits total $30 per direct labor hour. Quintana Products prices its products at 130% of total manufacturing costs.

Requirements

1. Compute Quintana Products' current plantwide overhead rate.

2. Compute refined departmental overhead rates.

3. Which job (Job 500 or Job 501) uses more of the company's resources? Explain.

4. Compute the total amount of overhead allocated to each job if Quintana Products uses its current plantwide overhead rate.

5. Compute the total amount of overhead allocated to each job if Quintana Products uses departmental overhead rates.

6. Do both allocation systems accurately reflect the resources that each job used? Explain.

7. Compute the total manufacturing cost and sales price of each job using Quintana Products' current plantwide overhead rate.

8. Based on the current (plantwide) allocation system, how much profit did Quintana Products *think* it earned on each job? Based on the departmental overhead rates and the sales price determined in Requirement 7, how much profit did it *really* earn on each job?

9. Compare and comment on the results you obtained in Requirements 7 and 8.

P4-49B Use ABC to compute full product costs *(Learning Objective 2)*

Johnston's Office Department manufactures computer desks in its Topeka, Kansas, plant. The company uses activity-based costing to allocate all manufacturing conversion costs (direct labor and manufacturing overhead). Its activities and related data follow:

Activity	Budgeted Cost of Activity	Allocation Base	Cost Allocation Rate
Materials handling.......	$ 330,000	Number of parts	$ 0.60
Assembling..................	2,300,000	Direct labor hours	13.00
Painting......................	140,000	Number of painted desks	5.30

Johnston's produced two styles of desks in March: the Standard desk and Unpainted desk. Data for each follow:

Product	Total Units Produced	Total Direct Materials Costs	Total Number of Parts	Total Assembling Direct Labor Hours
Standard desk..........................	6,500	$98,000	120,500	6,300
Unpainted desk	2,000	18,000	30,500	1,000

Requirements

1. Compute the per-unit manufacturing product cost of Standard desks and Unpainted desks.

2. Premanufacturing activities, such as product design, were assigned to the Standard desks at $4 each and to the Unpainted desks at $3 each. Similar analyses were conducted of post-manufacturing activities such as distribution, marketing, and customer service. The post-manufacturing costs were $22 per Standard and $19 per Unpainted desk. Compute the full product costs per desk.

3. Which product costs are reported in the external financial statements? Which costs are used for management decision making? Explain the difference.

4. What price should Johnston's managers set for Standard desks to earn a $39 profit per desk?

P4-50B Comprehensive ABC implementation (*Learning Objectives 2 & 3*)

Gibson Networking develops software for Internet applications. The market is very competitive, and Gibson Networking's competitors continue to introduce new products at low prices. Gibson Networking offers a wide variety of different software from simple programs that enables new users to create personal Web pages to complex commercial search engines. Like most software companies, Gibson Networking's raw material costs are insignificant.

Gibson Networking's has just hired Tom Merrell, a recent graduate of State University's accounting program. Merrell asks Software Department Manager Jeff Gire to join him in a pilot activity-based costing study. Merrell and Gire identify the following activities, related costs, and cost-allocation bases:

Activity	Estimated Indirect Activity Costs	Allocation Base	Estimated Quantity of Allocation Base
Applications development	$1,500,000	New applications	3 new applications
Content production	2,700,000	Lines of code	9 million lines
Testing	270,000	Testing hours	1,500 testing hours
Total indirect costs	$4,470,000		

Gibson Networking is planning to develop the following new applications:

- X-Page software for developing personal Web pages
- X-Secure commercial security and firewall software

X-Page requires 480,000 lines of code and 70 hours of testing, while X-Secure requires 7.2 million lines of code and 420 hours of testing. Gibson Networking expects to produce and sell 25,000 units of X-Page and 9 units of X-Secure.

Requirements

1. Compute the cost allocation rate for each activity.

2. Use the activity-based cost allocation rates to compute the indirect cost of each unit of X-Page and X-Secure. (*Hint:* Compute the total activity costs allocated to each product line and then compute the cost per unit.)

3. Gibson Networking's original single-allocation-base costing system allocated indirect costs to products at $104 per programmer hour. X-Page requires 14,000 programmer hours, while X-Secure requires 21,000 programmer hours. Compute the total indirect costs allocated to X-Page and X-Secure under the original system. Then, compute the indirect cost per unit for each product.

4. Compare the activity-based costs per unit to the costs from the simpler original system. How have the unit costs changed? Explain why the costs changed as they did.

5. What are the clues that Gibson Networking's ABC system is likely to pass the cost-benefit test?

P4-51B Comprehensive ABC implementation (*Learning Objectives 2 & 3*)

Maloney Pharmaceuticals manufactures an over-the-counter allergy medication called Breathe. Maloney Pharmaceuticals is trying to win market share from Sudafed and Tylenol. Maloney Pharmaceuticals has developed several different Breathe products tailored to specific markets. For example, the company sells large commercial containers of 1,000 capsules to health-care facilities and travel packs of 20 capsules to shops in airports, train stations, and hotels.

Maloney Pharmaceuticals' controller, Sandra Dean, has just returned from a conference on ABC. She asks Keith Yeung, supervisor of the Breathe product line, to help her develop an ABC system. Dean and Yeung identify the following activities, related costs, and cost allocation bases:

Activity	Estimated Indirect Activity Costs	Allocation Base	Estimated Quantity of Allocation Base
Materials handling	$160,000	Kilos	20,000 kilos
Packaging	390,000	Machine hours	2,000 hours
Quality assurance	110,000	Samples	2,200 samples
Total indirect costs	$660,000		

The commercial-container Breathe product line had a total weight of 8,200 kilos, used 1,200 machine hours, and 270 required samples. The travel-pack line had a total weight of 6,500 kilos, used 400 machine hours, and 370 required samples. Maloney produced 2,700 commercial containers of Breathe and 40,000 travel packs.

Requirements

1. Compute the cost allocation rate for each activity.

2. Use the activity-based cost allocation rates to compute the indirect cost of each unit of the commercial containers and the travel packs. (*Hint:* Compute the total activity costs allocated to each product line and then compute the cost per unit.)

3. Maloney Pharmaceuticals' original single-allocation-based cost system allocated indirect costs to products at $350 per machine hour. Compute the total indirect costs allocated to the commercial containers and to the travel packs under the original system. Then, compute the indirect cost per unit for each product.

4. Compare the activity-based costs per unit to the costs from the simpler original system. How have the unit costs changed? Explain why the costs changed as they did.

P4-52B Using ABC in conjunction with quality decisions *(Learning Objectives 2 & 5)*

Teensy Toys is using a costs-of-quality approach to evaluate design engineering efforts for a new toy robot. The company's senior managers expect the engineering work to reduce appraisal, internal failure, and external failure activities. The predicted reductions in activities over the two-year life of the toy robot follow. Also shown are the cost allocation rates for each activity.

Activity	Predicted Reduction in Activity Units	Activity Cost Allocation Rate per Unit
Inspection of incoming materials	310	$16
Inspection of finished goods	310	26
Number of defective units discovered in-house	3,200	15
Number of defective units discovered by customers	850	42
Lost sales to dissatisfied customers	330	61

Requirements

1. Calculate the predicted quality cost savings from the design engineering work.

2. Teensy Toys spent $75,000 on design engineering for the new toy robot. What is the net benefit of this "preventive" quality activity?

3. What major difficulty would Teensy Toys' managers have had in implementing this costs-of-quality approach? What alternative approach could they use to measure quality improvement?

APPLY YOUR KNOWLEDGE

Decision Cases

C4-53   Comprehensive ABC (Learning Objectives 2 & 3)

Axis Systems specializes in servers for work-group, e-commerce, and ERP applications. The company's original job cost system has two direct cost categories: direct materials and direct labor. Overhead is allocated to jobs at the single rate of $22 per direct labor hour.

A task force headed by Axis's CFO recently designed an ABC system with four activities. The ABC system retains the current system's two direct cost categories. Thus, it budgets only overhead costs for each activity. Pertinent data follow:

Activity	Allocation Base	Cost Allocation Rate
Materials handling	Number of parts	$ 0.85
Machine setup	Number of setups	500.00
Assembling	Assembling hours	80.00
Shipping	Number of shipments	1,500.00

Axis Systems has been awarded two new contracts that will be produced as Job A and Job B. Budget data relating to the contracts follow:

	Job A	Job B
Number of parts	15,000	2,000
Number of setups	6	4
Number of assembling hours	1,500	200
Number of shipments	1	1
Total direct labor hours	8,000	600
Number of output units	100	10
Direct materials cost	$210,000	$30,000
Direct labor cost	$160,000	$12,000

Requirements

1. Compute the product cost per unit for each job using the original costing system (with two direct cost categories and a single overhead allocation rate).

2. Suppose Axis Systems adopts the ABC system. Compute the product cost per unit for each job using ABC.

3. Which costing system more accurately assigns to jobs the costs of the resources consumed to produce them? Explain.

4. A dependable company has offered to produce both jobs for Axis for $5,400 per output unit. Axis may outsource (buy from the outside company) Job A only, Job B only, or both jobs. Which course of action will Axis's managers take if they base their decision on (a) the original system? (b) ABC system costs? Which course of action will yield more income? Explain.

C4-54   Continues C4-53: Meeting target costs

To remain competitive, Axis Systems' management believes the company must produce Job B–type servers (from C4-53) at a target cost of $5,400. Axis Systems has just joined a B2B e-market site that management believes will enable the firm to cut direct material costs by 10%. Axis's management also believes that a value-engineering team can reduce assembly time.

Requirement

1. Compute the assembly cost savings per Job B-type server required to meet the $5,400 target cost. (*Hint:* Begin by calculating the direct material, direct labor, and allocated activity cost per server.)

Ethical Issue

I4-55   ABC and ethical dilemma *(Learning Objective 2 & 3)*

Mary Lipe is assistant controller at Stone Packaging, a manufacturer of cardboard boxes and other packaging materials. Lipe has just returned from a packaging industry conference on ABC. She realizes that ABC may help Stone meet its goal of reducing costs by 5% over each of the next three years.

Stone Packaging's Order Department is a likely candidate for ABC. While orders are entered into a computer that updates the accounting records, clerks manually check customers' credit history and hand-deliver orders to shipping. This process occurs whether the sales order is for a dozen specialty boxes worth $80 or 10,000 basic boxes worth $8,000.

Lipe believes that identifying the cost of processing a sales order would justify (1) further computerizing the order process and (2) changing the way the company processes small orders. However, the significant cost savings would arise from elimination of two positions in the Order Department. The company's sales order clerks have been with the company many years. Lipe is uncomfortable with the prospect of proposing a change that will likely result in terminating these employees.

Requirement

1. Use the IMA *Statement of Ethical Professional Practice* (Exhibit 1-6) to consider Lipe's responsibility when cost comes at the expense of employees' jobs.

Discussion & Analysis

Discussion Questions

1. Explain why departmental overhead rates might be used instead of a single plantwide overhead rate.

2. Using activity-based costing, why are indirect costs allocated while direct costs are not allocated? Discuss the difference between "allocate" and "assign."

3. Compare and contrast activity-based costing (ABC) and activity-based management (ABM).

4. How can using a single predetermined manufacturing overhead rate based on a unit-level cost driver cause a high-volume product to be overcosted?

5. Assume a company uses a plantwide predetermined manufacturing overhead rate that is calculated using direct labor hours as the cost driver. The use of this plantwide predetermined manufacturing overhead rate has resulted in cost distortion. The company's high-volume products are overcosted and its low-volume products are undercosted. What effects of this cost distortion will the company most likely be experiencing? Why might the cost distortion be harmful to the company's competitive position in the market?

6. A hospital can use activity-based costing (ABC) for costing its services. In a hospital, what activities might be considered to be value-added activities? What activities at that hospital might be considered to be non-value-added?

Quick Check Answers

1. *d* 2. *d* 3. *c* 4. *c* 5. *c* 6. *d*
7. *c* 8. *d* 9. *a* 10. *c*

For online homework, exercises, and problems that provide you with immediate feedback, please visit www.myaccountinglab.com.

7. A company makes shatterproof, waterproof cases for iPhones. The company makes only one model and has been very successful in marketing its case; no other company in the market has a similar product. The only customization available to the customer is the color of the case. There is no manufacturing cost difference between the different colors of the cases. Since this company has a high-volume product, its controller thinks that the company should adopt activity-based costing. Why might activity-based costing not be as beneficial for this company as for other companies?

8. Compare a traditional production system with a lean production system. Discuss the similarities and the differences.

9. It has been said that external failure costs can be catastrophic and much higher than the other categories. What are some examples of external failure costs? Why is it often difficult to arrive at the cost of external failures?

10. What are the four categories of quality-related costs? Name a cost in each of the four categories for each of the following types of organizations:
    a. Restaurant
    b. Hospital
    c. Law firm
    d. Bank
    e. Tire manufacturer
    f. University

Application & Analysis

4-1 ABC in Real Companies

Choose a company in any of the following categories: airline, florist, bookstore, bank, grocery store, restaurant, college, retail clothing shop, movie theatre, or lawn service. In this activity, you will be making reasonable estimates of the types of costs and activities associated with this company; companies do not typically publish internal cost or process information. Be reasonable in your cost estimates and include your assumptions used in selecting costs.

Basic Discussion Questions

1. Describe the company selected, including its products or services.

2. List eight key activities performed at this company. Choose at least one activity in the areas of production, sales, human resources, and accounting.

3. For each of the key activities, list a potential cost driver for that activity and describe why this cost driver would be appropriate for the associated activity.

Classroom Applications

Web: Post the discussion questions on an electronic discussion board. Have small groups of students choose a product for each of their groups. Each student should watch the clip for the product for his or her group.

Classroom: Form groups of 3–4 students. Your group should choose a company from one of the listed categories. After deciding upon a company, discuss each of the listed questions. Prepare a 5 minute presentation about your group's company that addresses the listed questions.

Independent: Write a paper that addresses each of the listed questions for the company of your choice from one of the given categories. Turn in a 2–3 page typed paper (12 point font, double-spaced with 1" margins).

For additional Application & Analysis projects and implementation tips, see the Instructor Resources in MyAccountingLab.com.

CMA-1 SANSCOM Corporation utilized an activity-based costing system for applying costs to its two products, P and Q. In the assembly department, material handling costs vary directly with the number of parts inserted into the product. Machinery is recalibrated and oiled each weekend regardless of the number of parts inserted during the previous week. Both material handling and machinery maintenance costs are charged to the product on the basis of the number of parts inserted. Due to reengineering of the production process for Product P, the number of insertion parts per finished unit has been reduced. How will the redesign of the production process for Product P affect the activity-based cost of Product Q?

a. Material handling cost per Q unit will remain unchanged, and machinery maintenance cost per Q unit will remain unchanged.

b. Material handling cost per Q unit will increase, and machinery maintenance cost per Q unit will remain unchanged.

c. Material handling cost per Q unit will remain unchanged, and machinery maintenance cost per Q unit will increase.

d. Material handling cost per Q unit will increase, and machinery maintenance cost per Q unit will increase.

(CMA Adapted)

What's your favorite Jelly Belly flavor? Chocolate Pudding?

Very Cherry? Lemon Drop? Peanut Butter? Or maybe Piña Colada? Have you ever wondered how these tasty gems are made?

Each tiny Jelly Belly jelly bean spends seven to ten days going through eight different processes:

1. Cooking the centers
2. Shaping hot liquid centers into jelly beans
3. Drying
4. Sugar shower
5. Shell-building
6. Polishing
7. Stamping (name of the company on each bean)
8. Packaging

The family that owns Jelly Belly needs to know how much it costs to make each batch. That helps the owners set selling prices and measure profits. They also want to know how efficiently each process is operating. That helps them control costs. The owners use accounting information to answer these questions.

Jelly Belly mass-produces its jelly beans in a sequence of processes and accumulates the costs for each *process*. Then, the company spreads these costs over the pounds of jelly beans passing through each process. This *process costing* approach differs from the job costing approach that Life Fitness uses for its exercise equipment. Why the difference? Jelly Belly mass-produces its products, while Life Fitness makes many unique models, often on a custom-ordered basis. It certainly would not be practical to use job cost records to compile the cost of individual jelly beans!

Source: http://jellybelly.com

CHAPTER 5

Process Costing

Learning Objectives

1 Distinguish between the flow of costs in process costing and job costing

2 Compute equivalent units

3 Use process costing in the first production department

4 Prepare journal entries for a process costing system

5 Use process costing in a second or later production department

A s the chapter-opening story explains, managers need to know how much it costs to make their products. Why? So they can control costs, set selling prices, and identify their most profitable products. But finding unit cost at companies that mass manufacture requires a different approach than it does at companies that manufacture small batches of unique products. Simply put, job-costing doesn't "fit" a mass-production environment. Mass manufacturers need an accounting system that is specifically geared to match their production environment. For these types of companies, process costing is the answer. Process costing helps mass-manufacturers find the unit cost of their products, as well as the cost of each manufacturing process involved.

1 Distinguish between the flow of costs in process costing and job costing

Process Costing: An Overview

Let's start by contrasting the two basic types of costing systems: *job costing* and *process costing*.

Two Basic Costing Systems: Job Costing and Process Costing

We saw in Chapter 3 that Life Fitness and Boeing use job costing to determine the cost of producing unique goods in relatively small batches. Service companies such as law firms and hospitals also use job costing to determine the cost of serving individual clients. In contrast, companies such as Jelly Belly and Shell Oil use a series of steps (called *processes*) to make large quantities of identical units. These companies typically use *process costing* systems.

To simplify our discussion, we'll consolidate Jelly Belly's eight separate processes into three processes. We'll combine cooking, shaping, and drying the jelly bean centers into a single process called *Centers*. We'll also combine the sugar shower, shell-building, polishing, and stamping steps into a second process called *Shells*. The third and final process is *Packaging*.

Jelly Belly *accumulates* the costs of each process and then *assigns* these costs to the units (pounds of jelly beans) passing through that process.

Suppose the Centers process incurs $1,350,000 of costs to produce centers for 1,000,000 pounds of jelly beans, the Shells process incurs $800,000, and Packaging incurs $700,000. The total cost to produce a pound of jelly beans is the sum of the cost per pound for each of the three processes.

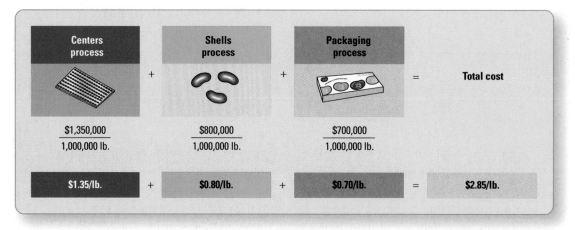

Jelly Belly's owners use the cost per pound of each process to help control costs. For example, they can compare the actual cost of producing centers for a pound of jelly beans (assumed to be $1.35 in our example) to the budget or plan. If the actual cost of the Centers process exceeds the budget, they can look for ways to cut costs in that process. Jelly Belly's owners also consider the total cost of making a pound of jelly beans (assumed to be $2.85 in our example) when setting selling prices. The price should be high enough to cover costs *and* to return a profit. Jelly Belly also uses the total cost of making a pound of jelly beans for financial reporting:

- To value the ending inventory of jelly beans for the balance sheet ($2.85 per pound still in ending inventory)

- To value cost of goods sold for the income statement ($2.85 per pound sold)

The simple computation of the cost to make a pound of jelly beans is correct *only if there are no work in process inventories*, but it takes seven to ten days to complete all of the processes. So, Jelly Belly *does* have inventories of partially complete jelly beans. These inventories make the costing more complicated. In the rest of this chapter, you'll learn how to do process costing when there are work in process inventories.

How Does the Flow of Costs Differ Between Job and Process Costing?

Exhibit 5-1 compares the flow of costs in

- a job costing system for Life Fitness (Panel A), and

- a process costing system for Jelly Belly (Panel B).

EXHIBIT 5-1   Flow of Costs in Job Costing

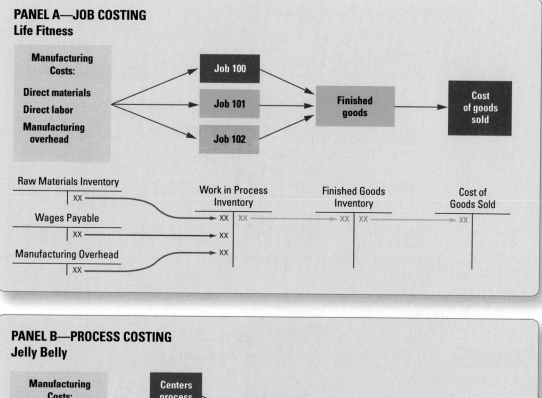

PANEL A—JOB COSTING
Life Fitness

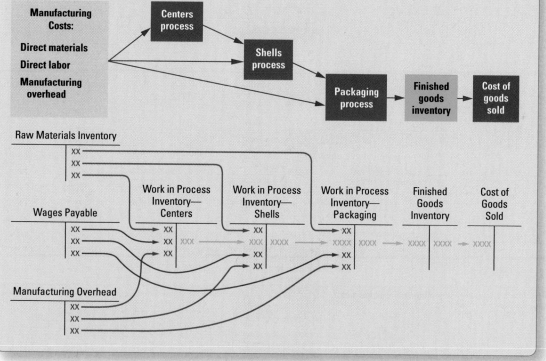

PANEL B—PROCESS COSTING
Jelly Belly

Panel A shows that Life Fitness's job costing system has a single Work in Process Inventory control account supported by individual job cost records for each job that is being worked on. Life Fitness assigns direct materials, direct labor, and manufacturing overhead to individual jobs, as explained in Chapter 3. When a job is finished, its costs flow directly into Finished Goods Inventory. When the job is sold, the cost flows out of Finished Goods Inventory and into Cost of Goods Sold.

In contrast to Life Fitness's individual jobs, Jelly Belly uses a series of three *manufacturing processes* to produce jelly beans. The movement of jelly beans through these three processes is shown in Exhibit 5-2.

EXHIBIT 5-2   Flow of Costs in Production of Jelly Beans

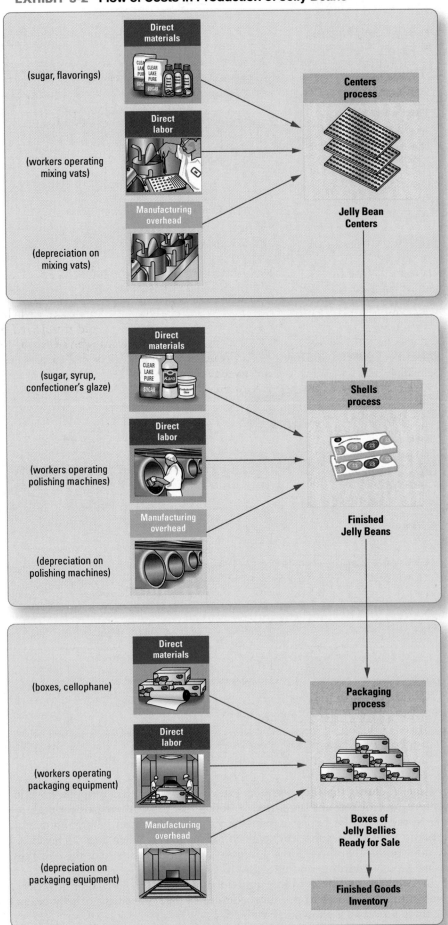

Take a moment to follow along as we describe Exhibit 5-2. In the first process (Centers process) Jelly Belly converts sugar and flavorings (the direct materials) into jelly bean centers using direct labor and manufacturing overhead, such as depreciation on the mixing vats. Once the jelly bean centers are made, they are transferred to the Shells process. In the Shells process, Jelly Belly uses different labor and equipment to coat the jelly bean centers with sugar, syrup, and glaze (the direct materials) to form the crunchy shells. Once that process is complete, the finished jelly beans are transferred to the Packaging process. In the Packaging process, Jelly Belly packages the finished jelly beans into various boxes and bags, using other labor and equipment. The boxed and bagged jelly beans are then transferred to finished goods inventory until they are sold.

Now, let's see how Panel B of Exhibit 5-1 summarizes the flow of costs through this process costing system. Study the exhibit carefully, paying particular attention to the following key points:

1. Each process (Centers, Shells, and Packaging) has its own separate Work in Process Inventory account.

2. Direct materials, direct labor, and manufacturing overhead are assigned to *each* processing department's Work in Process Inventory account based on the manufacturing costs incurred by that process. Exhibit 5-2 shows that each of Jelly Belly's processes uses different direct materials, direct labor, and manufacturing overhead costs.

3. Recall from Exhibit 5-2 that when the Centers process is complete, the jelly bean centers are physically *transferred out* of the Centers process and *transferred in* to the Shells process. Likewise, the *cost* of the centers is also *transferred out* of "Work in Process Inventory—Centers" and *transferred in* to "Work in Process Inventory—Shells." The transfer of costs between accounts is pictured in Panel B of Exhibit 5-1 as a series of green *x*s. As a rule of thumb consider the following:

> In process costing, the manufacturing costs assigned to the product must always follow the physical movement of the product. Therefore, when units are physically transferred out of one process and into the next, the *costs* assigned to those units must *also* be transferred out of the appropriate Work in Process Inventory account and into the next.

To simplify the accounting, the journal entry to record this transfer of costs between accounts is generally made once a month to reflect *all* physical transfers that occurred during the month.

4. When the Shells process is complete, the finished jelly beans are transferred out of the Shells process and into the Packaging process. Likewise, the *cost* assigned to the jelly beans thus far (cost of making the centers and adding the shells) is *transferred out* of "Work in Process Inventory—Shells" and *transferred in* to "Work in Process Inventory—Packaging."

5. When the Packaging process is complete, the finished packages of jelly beans are transferred to finished goods inventory. Likewise, the *cost* assigned to the jelly beans thus far (cost of making and packaging the jelly beans) is transferred out of "Work in Process—Packaging" and into "Finished Goods Inventory." *In process costing, costs are transferred into Finished Goods Inventory only from the Work in Process Inventory of the **last** manufacturing process. The transferred cost includes all costs assigned to the units from every process the units have completed (Centers, Shells, and Packaging).* Finally, when the jelly beans are sold, their cost is transferred out of "Finished Goods Inventory" and into "Cost of Goods Sold."

What are the Building Blocks of Process Costing?

Before we illustrate process costing in more detail, we must first learn about the three building blocks of process costing: conversion costs, equivalent units, and inventory flow assumptions.

Conversion Costs

Chapter 2 introduced three kinds of manufacturing costs: direct materials, direct labor, and manufacturing overhead. Most companies, like Jelly Belly, that mass-produce a product use automated production processes. Therefore, direct labor is only a small part of total manufacturing costs. Companies that use automated production processes often condense the three manufacturing costs into two categories:

1. Direct materials

2. Conversion costs

   Recall from Chapter 2 that conversion costs are direct labor plus manufacturing overhead. Combining these costs in a single category simplifies the process costing procedures. We call this category *conversion costs* because it is the cost to *convert* direct materials into new finished products.

Equivalent Units

2 Compute equivalent units

When a company has work in process inventories of partially completed goods, we use **equivalent units** to express the amount of work done during a period in terms of fully completed units of output.

To illustrate equivalent units, let's look at Callaway Golf, a manufacturer of golf balls and golf clubs. As shown in Exhibit 5-3, let's assume that Callaway's golf ball production plant has 5,000 partially completed balls in ending work in process inventory. Each ball is 80% of the way through the production process. If conversion costs are incurred evenly throughout the process, then getting each of 5,000 balls 80% of the way through the process takes about the same amount of work as getting 4,000 balls (5,000 × 80%) all the way through the process.

EXHIBIT 5-3 Callaway Production Plant Time Line

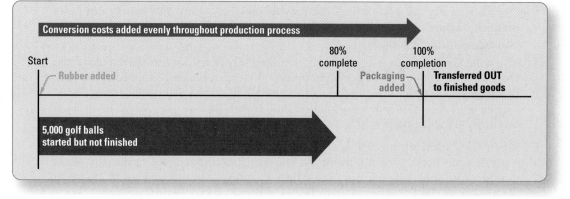

Equivalent units are calculated as follows:

Number of partially complete physical units × Percentage of process completed = Number of equivalent units

So, the number of equivalent units of conversion costs in Callaway's ending work in process inventory is calculated as follows:

$$5,000 \times 80\% = 4,000$$

Conversion costs are usually incurred *evenly* throughout production. However, direct materials are often added at a particular point in the process. For example, Callaway adds rubber at the *beginning* of the production process, but doesn't add packaging materials until the *end*. How many equivalent units of rubber and packaging materials are in the ending inventory of 5,000 balls?

All 5,000 balls are 80% complete, so they all have passed the point at which rubber is added. Each ball has its full share of rubber (100%), so the balls have 5,000 equivalent units of rubber. In contrast, the time line in Exhibit 5-3 shows that *none* of the 5,000 balls has made it to the end of the process, where the packaging materials are added. The ending inventory, therefore, has *zero* equivalent units of packaging materials.

To summarize, the 5,000 balls in ending work in process inventory have the following:

- 5,000 equivalent units of rubber (5,000 units × 100% of rubber)

- 0 equivalent units of packaging materials (5,000 units × 0% of packaging materials)

- 4,000 equivalent units of conversion costs (5,000 units × 80% converted)

Be careful to distinguish the *end of the production process* from the *end of the accounting period*. Goods at the end of the production process are transferred to the next process or to finished goods. For example, Callaway's completed golf balls proceed to the finished goods warehouse. By contrast, at the end of the accounting period, goods that are only partway through the production process are the ending work in process inventory. Callaway's ending work in process inventory includes 5,000 golf balls that have their rubber cores but no packaging.

STOP & THINK

Colleges and universities use the equivalent-unit concept to describe the number of faculty as well as the number of students. The University of Georgia has about 2,000 full-time faculty and 400 part-time faculty. Assume the following:

1. A full-time faculty member teaches six courses per year.
2. 100 part-time faculty teach three courses per year.
3. 300 part-time faculty teach two courses per year.

What is the "full-time equivalent" faculty—the number of equivalent units of faculty?

Answer: Compute the full-time equivalent faculty as follows:

Full-time faculty	$2,000 \times 6/6 = 2,000$
Half-time faculty	$100 \times 3/6 = 50$
One-third-time faculty	$300 \times 2/6 = 100$
Full-time equivalent faculty	$\underline{\underline{2,150}}$

Inventory Flow Assumptions

Firms compute process costing using either the weighted-average or first-in, first-out (FIFO) method. Throughout the rest of the chapter, we will use the **weighted-average method of process costing** rather than the FIFO method because it is simpler and the differences between the two methods' results are usually immaterial. *The two costing methods differ only in how they treat beginning inventory.* The FIFO method requires that any units in beginning inventory be costed *separately* from any units started in the current period. The weighted-average method *combines* any beginning inventory units (and costs) with the current period's units (and costs) to get a weighted-average cost. From a cost-benefit standpoint, many firms prefer to use the weighted-average method because the extra cost of calculating the FIFO method does not justify the additional benefits they gain from using FIFO information. Therefore, throughout the remainder of the text and throughout all assignment material, we will assume that the weighted-average method is used. The FIFO method is discussed in advanced managerial accounting textbooks.

3 Use process costing in the first production department

How Does Process Costing Work in the First Processing Department?

To illustrate process costing, we'll be following SeaView, a manufacturer that mass produces swim masks. We'll see how SeaView uses the weighted-average method of process costing to measure (1) the average cost of producing each swim mask and (2) the cost of the two major processes it uses to make the masks (Shaping and Insertion).

Exhibit 5-4 illustrates SeaView's production process. The Shaping Department begins with plastic and metal fasteners (direct materials) and uses labor and equipment (conversion costs) to transform the materials into shaped masks. The direct materials are added at the *beginning* of the process, but conversion costs are incurred *evenly* throughout the process. After shaping, the masks move to the Insertion Department, where the shaped masks are polished and then the clear faceplates are inserted.

Let's assume that the Shaping Department begins October with no work in progress inventory. During October, the Shaping Department incurs the following costs while working on 50,000 masks:

Beginning work in process inventory		$ 0
Direct materials		140,000
Conversion costs:		
Direct labor	$21,250	
Manufacturing overhead	46,750	
Total conversion costs		68,000
Total costs to account for		$208,000

How did SeaView arrive at these costs? SeaView traces direct materials and direct labor to each processing department using materials requisitions and labor time records (just as we used these documents to trace direct materials and direct labor to individual *jobs* in Chapter 3). SeaView allocates manufacturing overhead to each processing department using a either a plantwide rate, departmental overhead rates, or ABC (just as we allocated manufacturing overhead to individual *jobs* in Chapters 3 and 4).

If, at the end of October, all 50,000 masks have been completely shaped and transferred out of the Shaping Department and into the Insertion Department, the entire $208,000 of manufacturing cost associated with these masks should *likewise* be transferred out of "Work in Process—Shaping" and into "Work in Process—Insertion." In this case, the unit cost for *just* the shaping process is $4.16 per mask ($208,000/50,000 masks).

But what if only 40,000 masks are completely through the shaping process? Let's say that at October 31, the Shaping Department still has 10,000 masks that are only one-quarter of the way through the shaping process. How do we split the $208,000 between the following?

■ 40,000 completely shaped masks transferred to the Insertion Department

■ 10,000 partially shaped masks remaining in the Shaping Department's ending work in process inventory

Why is this important?

"Most food and consumer products are mass produced. Managers need to know 1) the cost of each manufacturing process, to make each one as cost-efficient as possible; and 2) the cost of each unit, to aid in pricing and other business decisions."

EXHIBIT 5-4 **SeaView's Production Process**

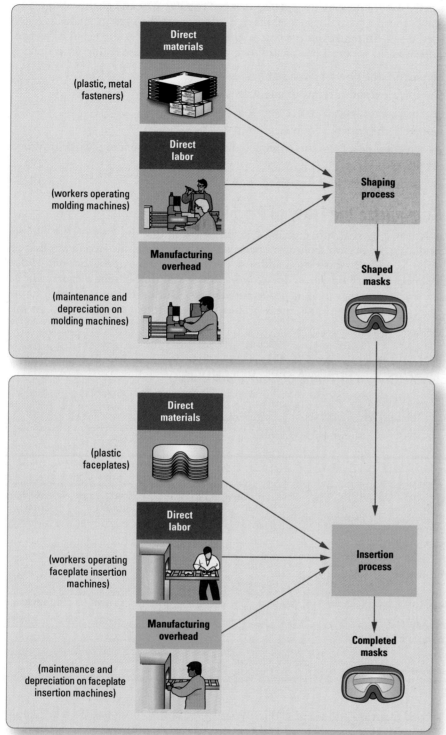

In other words, how do we determine the cost of making the *completely* shaped masks versus the cost of making the *partially* shaped masks? We can't simply assign $4.16 to each mask because a partially shaped mask does *not* cost the same to make as a completely shaped mask. To figure out the cost of making a *completely* shaped mask versus a *partially* shaped mask, we must use the following five-step process costing procedure:

Step 1) Summarize the flow of physical units

Step 2) Compute output in terms of equivalent units

Step 3) Summarize total costs to account for

Step 4) Compute the cost per equivalent unit

Step 5) Assign total costs to units completed and to units in ending Work in Process inventory

We'll walk through each of these steps now.

Step 1: Summarize the Flow of Physical Units

Step 1 tracks the physical movement of swim masks into and out of the Shaping Department during the month. Follow along as we walk through this step in the first column of Exhibit 5-5. The first question addressed is this: *How many physical units did the Shaping Department work on during the month?* Recall that the Shaping Department had no masks in the beginning work in process inventory. During the month, the Shaping Department began work on 50,000 masks. Thus, the department needs to account for a *total* of 50,000 masks.

EXHIBIT 5-5 **Step 1: Summarize the Flow of Physical Units**
Step 2: Compute Output in Terms of Equivalent Units

	Step 1	Step 2 Equivalent Units	
SEAVIEW SHAPING DEPARTMENT Month Ended October 31			
Flow of Production	**Flow of Physical Units**	**Direct Materials**	**Conversion Costs**
Units to account for:			
Beginning work in process, October 1	0		
Started in production during October	50,000		
Total physical units to account for	50,000		
Units accounted for:			
Completed and transferred out during October	40,000	40,000	40,000
Ending work in process, October 31	10,000	10,000	2,500*
Total physical units accounted for	50,000		
Total equivalent units		50,000	42,500

*10,000 units each 25% complete = 2,500 equivalent units

The second question addressed is this: *What happened to those masks?* The Shaping Department reports that it completed and transferred out 40,000 masks to the Insertion Department during October. The remaining 10,000 partially shaped masks are still in the Shaping Department's ending work in process inventory on October 31. Notice that the *Total physical units to account for* (50,000) must equal the *Total physical units accounted for* (50,000). In other words, the Shaping Department must account for the whereabouts of every mask it worked on during the month.

Step 2: Compute Output in Terms of Equivalent Units

Step 2 computes all of the Shaping Department's output for the month in terms of equivalent units. Step 2 is shown in the last two columns of Exhibit 5-5. First, let's consider the 40,000 masks that were *completed and transferred out* to the Insertion Department during October. These units have been fully completed in the Shaping Department; therefore, these 40,000 completed masks have incurred 40,000 equivalent units of direct materials (40,000 masks × 100% of direct materials) and 40,000 equivalent units of conversion costs (40,000 masks × 100% of conversion costs).

Now, let's consider the 10,000 masks still in ending work in process. These masks are only 25% of the way through the shaping process on October 31. The time line in Exhibit 5-6 reminds us that all direct materials are added at the *beginning* of the shaping process. Therefore, the partially shaped masks have made it past the point where direct materials are added. As a result, these masks have incurred 10,000 equivalent units of direct materials (10,000 masks × 100% of direct materials).

EXHIBIT 5-6 SeaView's Shaping Department Time Line

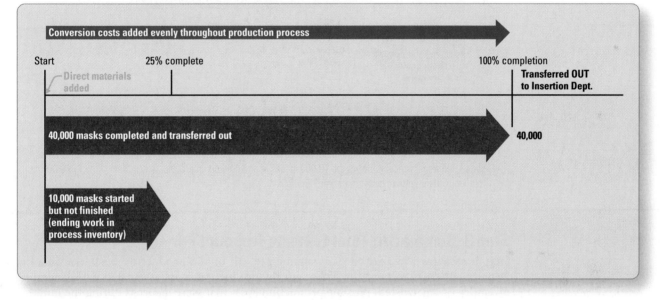

Unlike direct materials, the conversion costs are added *evenly* throughout the shaping process. For these partially shaped masks, the equivalent units of conversion costs are as follows:

$$10,000 \times 25\% = 2,500 \text{ equivalent units of conversion costs}$$

Our last step is to calculate the Shaping Department's output in terms of *total equivalent units* for the month. We must calculate totals separately for direct materials and conversion costs because they will differ in most circumstances. To find the totals, we simply add the equivalent units of all masks worked on during the month. For example, the *total equivalent units of direct materials* (50,000 as shown in Exhibit 5-5) is simply the sum of the 40,000 equivalent units completed and transferred out *plus* the 10,000 equivalent units still in ending work in process. Likewise, the *total equivalent units of conversion costs* (42,500 shown in Exhibit 5-5) is the sum of the 40,000 equivalent units completed and transferred out plus the 2,500 equivalent units still in ending work in process.

STOP & THINK

Suppose the Shaping Department adds direct materials at the end of the shaping process rather than at the beginning.

1. Draw a new time line similar to Exhibit 5-6.

2. Use the time line to determine the number of equivalent units of direct materials.

Answers

1.

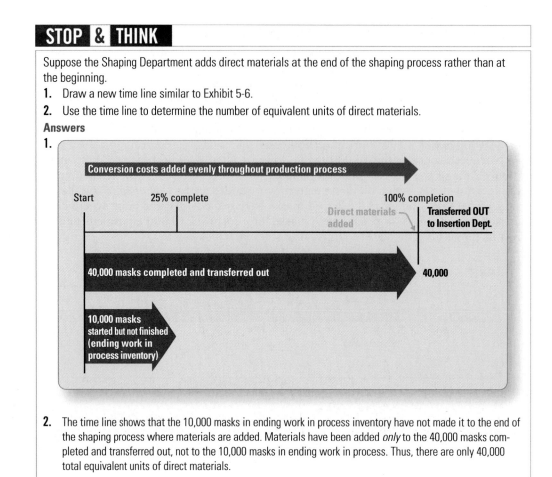

2. The time line shows that the 10,000 masks in ending work in process inventory have not made it to the end of the shaping process where materials are added. Materials have been added *only* to the 40,000 masks completed and transferred out, not to the 10,000 masks in ending work in process. Thus, there are only 40,000 total equivalent units of direct materials.

Step 3: Summarize Total Costs to Account For

Step 3, as shown in Exhibit 5-7, summarizes all of the production costs the Shaping Department must account for. These are the production costs associated with beginning inventory (if any existed) plus the production costs that were incurred during the month.[1]

EXHIBIT 5-7   Step 3: Summarize Total Costs to Account For

			Direct Materials	Conversion Costs	Total
		SEAVIEW SHAPING DEPARTMENT Month Ended October 31			
		Beginning work in process, October 1	$ 0	$ 0	$ 0
		Costs added during October:	140,000	68,000*	208,000
		Total costs to account for	**$140,000**	**$68,000**	**$208,000**

*21,250 of direct labor plus $46,750 of manufacturing overhead = $68,000 of conversion costs

Once again, we must show separate totals for each of the two cost categories: direct materials and conversion costs. Because the Shaping Department did not have any beginning inventory of partially shaped masks, the beginning balance in the "Work in Process Inventory—Shaping" account is zero. During the month, the Shaping Department used $140,000 of direct material and $68,000 of conversion costs ($21,250 of direct labor plus $46,750 of manufacturing overhead).

[1]The Shaping Department did not have a beginning inventory. Summary Problem 1 illustrates a department that does have a beginning inventory. As long as we assume the weighted-average method of process costing, we include the beginning balance to arrive at total costs to account for, as shown in Exhibit 5-7.

We've calculated the Shaping Department's total equivalent units (Step 2) and summarized its total costs to account for (Step 3). Our next step is to calculate the cost per equivalent unit.

Step 4: Compute the Cost per Equivalent Unit

The word *per* means "divided by," so the *cost per equivalent unit* is the *total costs to account for* (from Step 3) divided by the *total equivalent units* (from Step 2). Because the total equivalent units for direct materials (50,000) and conversion costs (42,500) differ, we must compute a separate cost per equivalent unit for each cost category: direct materials and conversion costs. Exhibit 5-8 shows the computations:

EXHIBIT 5-8   Step 4: Compute the Cost per Equivalent Unit

SEAVIEW SHAPING DEPARTMENT
Month Ended October 31

		Direct Materials	Conversion Costs
Total costs to account for (from Exhibit 5-7)		$140,000	$68,000
Divided by total equivalent units (from Exhibit 5-5)		÷ 50,000	÷ 42,500
Cost per equivalent unit		$ 2.80	$ 1.60

What do these figures mean? During October, SeaView's Shaping Department incurred an average of $2.80 of direct materials cost and $1.60 of conversion costs to completely shape the equivalent of one mask. In addition to using the cost per equivalent unit in the five-step process costing procedure, managers also use this information to determine how well they have controlled costs. Managers compare the actual cost per equivalent unit to the budgeted cost per equivalent unit for both direct materials and conversion costs. If the cost per equivalent unit is the same as or lower than budgeted, the manager has successfully controlled costs.

Step 5: Assign Total Costs to Units Completed and to Units in Ending Work in Process Inventory

The goal of Step 5 (Exhibit 5-9) is to determine how much of the Shaping Department's $208,000 total costs should be assigned to (1) the 40,000 completely shaped masks transferred out to the Insertion Department and (2) the 10,000 partially shaped masks remaining in the Shaping Department's ending work in process inventory. Exhibit 5-9 shows how the equivalent units computed in Step 2 (Exhibit 5-5) are costed at the cost per equivalent unit computed in Step 4 (Exhibit 5-8).

EXHIBIT 5-9   Step 5: Assign Costs to Units Completed and to Units in Ending Work in Process Inventory

SEAVIEW SHAPING DEPARTMENT
Month Ended October 31

	Direct Materials	Conversion Costs	Total
Completed and transferred out (40,000)	[40,000 × ($2.80 + $1.60)]		= $176,000
Ending work in process inventory (10,000):			
Direct materials	[10,000 × $2.80]		= $ 28,000
Conversion costs		[2,500 × $1.60]	= 4,000
Total cost of ending work in process inventory			$ 32,000
Total costs accounted for			$208,000

Note: Equivalent units are from Exhibit 5-5; Costs per equivalent are from Exhibit 5-8.

First, consider the 40,000 masks completed and transferred out. Exhibit 5-5 shows 40,000 equivalent units for both direct materials and conversion costs. In Exhibit 5-8 we learned that the company spent $2.80 on direct materials for each equivalent unit, and $1.60 on conversion costs for each equivalent unit. Thus, the total cost of these completed masks is 40,000 × ($2.80 + $1.60) = $176,000, as shown in Exhibit 5-9. We've accomplished our first goal—now we know how much cost ($176,000) should be assigned to the completely shaped masks transferred to the Insertion Department.

Next, consider the 10,000 masks still in ending work in process. These masks have 10,000 equivalent units of direct materials (which cost $2.80 per equivalent unit), so the direct material cost is $28,000 (= 10,000 × $2.80). These masks also have 2,500 equivalent units of conversion costs, which cost $1.60 per equivalent unit, so the conversion costs is $4,000 (= 2,500 × $1.60). Therefore, the total cost of the 10,000 partially completed masks in the Shaping Department's ending work in process inventory is the sum of these direct material and conversion costs: $28,000 + $4,000 = $32,000. Now, we've accomplished our second goal—we know how much cost ($32,000) should be assigned to the partially shaped masks still in ending work in process inventory.

In summary, Exhibit 5-9 has accomplished our goal of splitting the $208,000 *total cost to account for* between the 40,000 masks completed and transferred out to the Insertion Department and the 10,000 partially shaped masks remaining in Work in Process Inventory.

Average Unit Costs

How does this information relate to unit costs? The average cost of making one *completely shaped* unit is $4.40 ($176,000 transferred to Insertion ÷ 40,000 completely shaped masks transferred to Insertion). This average unit cost ($4.40) is the sum of the direct material cost per equivalent unit ($2.80) and the conversion cost per equivalent unit ($1.60). The average cost of one *partially* shaped unit that is 25% of the way through the production process is $3.20 ($32,000 in ending inventory of Shaping ÷ 10,000 partially shaped masks). We needed the five-step process costing procedure to find these average costs per unit. If the Shaping Department manager ignored the five-step process and simply spread the entire production cost over all units worked on during the period, each unit would be assigned a cost of $4.16 ($208,000 ÷ 50,000 masks)—whether completely shaped or not. That would be wrong. The average cost per unit should be (and is) higher for completely shaped units transferred to the Insertion Department than it is for partially shaped units remaining in the Shaping Department's ending work in process inventory.

Recall that once the masks are shaped, they still need to have the faceplates inserted. In the second half of the chapter, we will discuss how the second process—Insertion—uses the same five-step procedure to find the *total* unit cost of making a completed mask, from start to finish.

STOP & THINK

Assume that the Shaping Department manager incorrectly assigned all of October's production costs ($208,000) to the completely shaped masks rather than using the five-step process to divide the costs between the completely shaped and partially shaped masks. What would be the results of this error?
Answer: If the manager incorrectly assigned all production costs to the completely shaped masks, the unit cost of completely shaped masks would be too high ($208,000 ÷ 40,000 = $5.20). In addition, the unit cost of the partially shaped masks would be too low ($0.00). In essence, the manager would be saying that the partially shaped units were "free" to make because he or she assigned all of the production costs to the completely shaped units. To assign production costs properly, managers must use the five-step process.

What Journal Entries are Needed in a Process Costing System?

4 Prepare journal entries for a process costing system

The journal entries used in a process costing system are very similar to those in a job costing system. The basic difference is that the manufacturing costs (direct materials, direct labor, and manufacturing overhead) are assigned to *processing departments*, rather than *jobs*. In addition, at the end of the month a journal entry must be made to transfer cost to the next processing department. Let's now look at the journal entries that would have been made in October for the Shaping Department.

During October, $140,000 of direct materials were requisitioned for use by the Shaping Department. In the following journal entry, notice how these costs are recorded specifically to the Shaping Department's Work in Process Inventory account. In process costing, each processing department maintains a separate Work in Process Inventory account.

	Work in Process Inventory—Shaping	140,000	
	Raw Materials Inventory		140,000
	(To record direct materials used by the Shaping Department in October.)		

Labor time records show that $21,250 of direct labor was used in the Shaping Department during October, resulting in the following journal entry:

	Work in Process Inventory—Shaping	21,250	
	Wages Payable		21,250
	(To record direct labor used in the Shaping Department in October)		

Manufacturing overhead is allocated to the Shaping Department using the company's predetermined overhead rate(s). Just as in a job costing environment, the company may use a single plantwide rate, departmental overhead rates, or ABC to allocate its manufacturing overhead costs. For example, let's say that the Shaping Department's overhead rate is $50 per machine hour and the department used 935 machine hours during the month. That means $46,750 ($50 × 935) of MOH should be allocated to the Shaping Department during October:

	Work in Process Inventory—Shaping	46,750	
	Manufacturing Overhead		46,750
	(To record manufacturing overhead allocated to the Shaping Department in October.)		

After making these journal entries during the month, the "Work in Process Inventory—Shaping" T-account appears as follows:

Work in Process Inventory—Shaping		
Balance, October 1	$ 0	
Direct materials	140,000	
Direct labor $208,000	21,250	
Manufacturing overhead	46,750	

Notice how the sum of the costs currently in the T-account is $208,000. This is the *same total costs to* account for summarized in Exhibit 5-7. By performing the five step process at the end of the month, SeaView was able to determine how much of the $208,000 should be assigned to units still being worked on ($32,000) and how much should be assigned to the units completed and transferred out to the Insertion Department ($176,000). The company uses this information (pictured in Exhibit 5-9) to make the following journal entry:

	Work in Process Inventory—Insertion	176,000	
	Work in Process Inventory—Shaping		176,000
	(To record transfer of cost out of the Shaping Department and into the Insertion Department.)		

After this journal entry is posted, the "Work in Process Inventory—Shaping" account appears as follows. Notice that the new ending balance in the account—$32,000—agrees with the amount assigned to the partially shaped masks in Exhibit 5-9.

Work in Process Inventory—Shaping			
Balance, October 1	0	Transferred to Insertion	176,000
Direct materials	140,000		
Direct labor	21,250		
Manufacturing overhead	46,750		
Balance, October 31	32,000		

In the next half of the chapter, we'll look at the journal entries made by the Insertion Department to record the completion and sale of the swim masks.

Decision Guidelines

Process Costing—First Processing Department

Here are some of the key decisions SeaView made in setting up its process costing system.

Decision	Guidelines
Should SeaView use job or process costing?	SeaView mass-produces large quantities of identical swim masks using two production processes: shaping and insertion. It uses *process costing* to do the following: 1. *Accumulate* the cost of each process 2. *Assign* these costs to the masks passing through that process
How do costs flow from Work in Process Inventory to Finished Goods Inventory in SeaView's process costing system?	In SeaView's process costing system, costs flow from the following: Work in Process Inventory—Shaping ↓ Work in Process Inventory—Insertion ↓ Finished Goods Inventory More generally, costs flow from one Work in Process Inventory account to the next until the last process, after which they flow into Finished Goods Inventory.
How many Work in Process Inventory accounts does SeaView's process costing system have?	SeaView uses a separate Work in Process Inventory account for each of its two major processes: Shaping and Insertion.
How does SeaView account for partially completed products?	SeaView uses equivalent units.
Which costs require separate equivalent-unit computations?	Equivalent units should be calculated separately for each input added at a different point in the production process. SeaView computes equivalent units separately for direct materials and conversion costs because it adds direct materials at a particular point in the production process but incurs conversion costs evenly throughout the process.

Decision	Guidelines
How does SeaView compute equivalent units of conversion costs?	SeaView's *conversion costs* are incurred evenly throughout the production process, so the equivalent units are computed as follows: $$\text{Equivalent units} = \text{Number of partially complete units} \times \text{Percentage of process completed}$$
How does SeaView compute equivalent units of direct materials?	SeaView's *materials* are added at specific points in the production process, so the equivalent units are computed using the following percentages: • If physical units have passed the point at which materials are added, then the units are 100% complete with respect to materials. • If physical units have *not* passed the point at which materials are added, then the units are 0% complete with respect to materials.
How do you compute the cost per equivalent unit?	For each category (direct materials and conversion), divide the total cost to account for by the total equivalent units.
How do you split the costs of the shaping process between the following? • Swim masks completed and transferred out • Partially completed swim masks in ending work in process inventory	Multiply the cost per equivalent unit by the following: • Number of equivalent units completed and transferred out • Number of equivalent units in the ending work in process inventory
How well did the manager of the Shaping Department control the department's costs?	If direct material and conversion cost per equivalent unit is the same or lower than the target unit cost per equivalent unit, the manager has done a good job controlling costs.

Summary Problem 1

Florida Tile produces ceramic tiles using two sequential production departments: Tile-Forming and Tile-Finishing. The following information was found for Florida Tile's first production process, the Tile-Forming Department.

FLORIDA TILE
TILE-FORMING DEPARTMENT
Month Ended May 31

Information about units:

Beginning work in process, May 1	2,000 units
Started in production during May	18,000 units
Completed and transferred to Finishing Department during May	16,000 units
Ending work in process, May 31 (25% complete as to direct materials, 55% complete as to conversion cost)	4,000 units

Information about costs:

Beginning work in process, May 1 (consists of $800 of direct materials cost and $4,000 of conversion costs)	$ 4,800
Direct materials used in May..	$ 6,000
Conversion costs incurred in May	$32,400

continued

Requirement

Use the five steps of process costing to calculate the cost that should be assigned to (1) units completed and transferred out and (2) units still in ending work in process inventory. Then prepare the journal entry needed at month-end to transfer the costs associated with the formed tiles to the next department, Tile Finishing.

Solution

Step 1: Summarize the flow of physical units.

Step 2: Compute output in terms of equivalent units.

FLORIDA TILE
TILE-FORMING DEPARTMENT
Month Ended May 31

Flow of Production	Step 1 Flow of Physical Units	Step 2: Equivalent Units Direct Materials	Step 2: Equivalent Units Conversion Costs
Units to account for:			
Beginning work in process, May 1	2,000		
Started in production during May	18,000		
Total physical units to account for	20,000		
Units accounted for:			
Completed and transferred out in May	16,000	16,000	16,000
Ending work in process, May 31	4,000	1,000*	2,200**
Total physical units accounted for	20,000		
Total equivalent units		17,000	18,200

*Direct materials: 4,000 units each 25% complete = 1,000 equivalent units.
**Conversion costs: 4,000 units each 55% complete = 2,200 equivalent units.

Step 3: Summarize total costs to account for.

FLORIDA TILE
TILE-FORMING DEPARTMENT
Month Ended May 31

	Direct Materials	Conversion Costs	Total
Beginning work in process, May 1	$ 800	$ 4,000	$ 4,800
Costs added during May	6,000	32,400	38,400
Total costs to account for	$6,800	$36,400	$43,200

Note: All cost information is from the summary problem data set.

Step 4: Compute the cost per equivalent unit.

FLORIDA TILE
TILE-FORMING DEPARTMENT
Month Ended May 31

	Direct Materials	Conversion Costs
Total costs to account for (from Step 3)	$ 6,800	$36,400
Divided by total equivalent units (from Step 2)	÷ 17,000	÷ 18,200
Cost per equivalent unit	$ 0.40	$ 2.00

Step 5: Assign total costs to units completed and to units in ending work in process inventory.

FLORIDA TILE
TILE-FORMING DEPARTMENT
Month Ended May 31

	Direct Materials	Conversion Costs	Total
Units completed and transferred out (16,000)	[16,000 × ($0.40 + $2.00)]		= $38,400
Units in ending work in process inventory (4,000):			
Direct materials	[1,000 × $0.40]		= $ 400
Conversion costs		[2,200 × $2.00]	= 4,400
Total cost of ending work in process inventory			$ 4,800
Total costs accounted for			$43,200

The journal entry needed to transfer costs is as follows:

Work in Process Inventory—Finishing		38,400	
Work in Process Inventory—Tile Forming			38,400

The cost of making one completely formed tile in the Forming Department is $2.40. This is the sum of the direct materials cost per equivalent unit ($0.40) and the conversion cost per equivalent unit ($2.00). The completely formed tiles must still be finished in the Finishing Department before we will know the final cost of making one tile from start to finish.

How Does Process Costing Work in a Second or Later Processing Department?

Use process costing in a second or later production department   **5**

Most products require a series of processing steps. Recall that Jelly Belly uses eight processing steps to make its jelly beans. In the last section, we saw how much it costs SeaView to *shape* one mask. In this section, we consider a second department, SeaView's Insertion Department. After units pass through the *final* department (Insertion, in SeaView's case), managers can determine the *entire* cost of making one unit—from start to finish. In the second or later department, we use the same five-step process costing procedure that we used for the Shaping Department, with one major difference: we separately consider the costs *transferred in* to the Insertion Department from the Shaping Department when calculating equivalent units and the cost per equivalent unit. **Transferred-in costs** are incurred in a previous process (the Shaping Department, in the SeaView example) and are carried forward as part of the product's cost when it moves to the next process.

To account for transferred-in costs, we will add one more column to our calculations in Steps 2–5. Let's walk through the Insertion Department's process costing to see how this is done.

Process Costing in SeaView's Insertion Department

The Insertion Department receives the shaped masks and polishes them before inserting the faceplates at the end of the process. Exhibit 5-10 shows that the following:

- Shaped masks are transferred in from the Shaping Department at the beginning of the Insertion Department's process.

- The Insertion Department's conversion costs are added evenly throughout the process.

- The Insertion Department's direct materials (faceplates) are not added until the *end* of the process.

Why is this important?

"Most products are manufactured through a series of production processes. To find the total cost of making one unit—*from start to finish*—managers must perform the five-step process costing procedure in *each* production department."

EXHIBIT 5-10 **SeaView's Insertion Department Time Line**

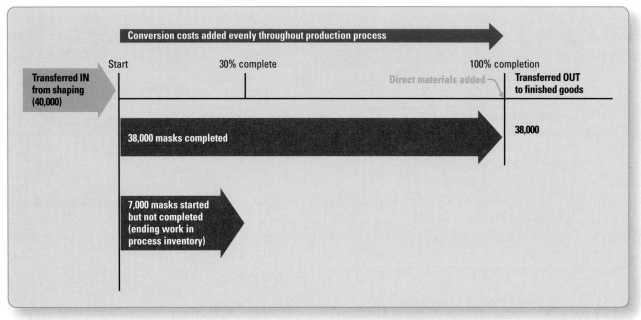

Keep in mind that *direct materials* in the Insertion Department refer *only* to the face-plates and not to the materials (the plastic and metal fasteners) added in the Shaping Department. Likewise, *conversion costs* in the Insertion Department refer to the direct labor and manufacturing overhead costs incurred *only* in the Insertion Department.

Exhibit 5-11 lists SeaView's Insertion Department data for October. The top portion of the exhibit lists the unit information, while the lower portion lists the costs. Let's walk through this information together.

Exhibit 5-11 shows that SeaView's Insertion Department started the October period with 5,000 masks that had made it partway through the insertion process in September. During October, the Insertion Department started work on the 40,000 masks received from the Shaping Department. By the end of the month, the Insertion Department had completed 38,000 masks, while 7,000 remained partially complete.

Exhibit 5-11 also shows that the Insertion Department started October with a beginning balance of $23,100 in its Work in Process Inventory account, which is associated with the 5,000 partially completed masks in its beginning inventory. During the month, $176,000 was transferred in from the Shaping Department (recall the journal entry on page 249) for the 40,000 masks transferred into the department from Shaping. Additionally, the Insertion Department incurred $19,000 in direct material costs (face-plates) and $12,935 in conversion costs during the month.

Just as in the Shaping Department, our goal is to split the total cost in the Insertion Department ($231,035) between the following:

- The 38,000 masks that the Insertion Department completed and transferred out (this time, to Finished Goods Inventory)

- The 7,000 partially complete masks remaining in the Insertion Department's ending work in process inventory at the end of October

After splitting the total cost, we'll be able to determine the cost of making one complete mask—from start to finish. We use the same five-step process costing procedure that we used for the Shaping Department.

Steps 1 and 2: Summarize the Flow of Physical Units and Compute Output in Terms of Equivalent Units

Step 1: Summarize the Flow of Physical Units

This step is the same as in the Shaping Department—we must track the movement of swim masks into and out of the Insertion Department. Exhibit 5-12 (on page 256) shows that the Insertion Department had a beginning work in process inventory of 5,000 masks

EXHIBIT 5-11 SeaView's Insertion Department Data for October

<u>**Information about units:**</u>

Beginning work in process, October 1

    (0% complete as to direct materials, 60% complete

    as to conversion work) .... 5,000 masks*

Transferred in from Shaping Department during

    October (from Exhibit 5-6) .... 40,000 masks

Completed and transferred out to Finished Goods

    Inventory during October.. 38,000 masks

Ending work in process, October 31

    (0% complete as to direct materials, 30% complete

    as to conversion work) .... 7,000 masks

<u>**Information about costs:**</u>

Beginning work in process, October 1

    Transferred-in costs... $ 22,000

    Conversion costs 1,100*

    Beginning balance... $ 23,100

Transferred in from Shaping Department during October

    (from journal entry on page 249)... $176,000

Direct materials added during October in Insertion Department......... $ 19,000

Conversion costs added during October in Insertion Department:

    Direct labor.. $ 3,710

    Manufacturing overhead 9,225

    Conversion costs .... $ 12,935

Total costs to account for $231,035

*This information would have been obtained from Step 5 of the process costing procedure from September. The September 30 balance in work in process becomes the October 1 balance.

that were partway through the insertion process at the start of the period. Recall that during October, the Shaping Department finished 40,000 masks and transferred them *into* the Insertion Department. Thus, Exhibit 5-12 shows that the Insertion Department has 45,000 masks to account for (5,000 + 40,000).

Where did these 45,000 masks go? Exhibits 5-10 and 5-11 show that the Insertion Department completed and transferred 38,000 masks out to Finished Goods Inventory while the remaining 7,000 masks were only partway through the insertion process on October 31. Thus, Exhibit 5-12 shows that the department has accounted for all 45,000 masks (38,000 completed and transferred out + 7,000 in ending work in process inventory).

Step 2: Compute Output in Terms of Equivalent Units

As mentioned earlier, process costing in a second or later department must separately calculate equivalent units for transferred-in costs, much like they separately calculate equivalent units for direct materials and conversion costs. Therefore, Step 2 in Exhibit 5-12 shows *three* columns for the Insertion Department's *three* categories of equivalent units: transferred-in, direct materials, and conversion costs. Let's consider each in turn.

Exhibit 5-10 shows that transferred-in masks are added at the very *beginning* of the insertion process. You might think of the shaped masks transferred in as raw materials added at the very *beginning* of the insertion process. All masks worked on in the Insertion Department—whether completed or not by the end of the month—started in the department as a shaped mask. Therefore, they are *all 100% complete with respect to transferred-in work and costs.* So, the "Transferred-In" column of Exhibit 5-12 shows

EXHIBIT 5-12   Step 1: Summarize the Flow of Physical Units
Step 2: Compute Output in Terms of Equivalent Units

SEAVIEW INSERTION DEPARTMENT
Month Ended October 31

| | Step 1 | Step 2: Equivalent Units | | |
| | Flow of Physical Units | Transferred-in | Direct Materials | Conversion Costs |
Flow of Production				
Units to account for:				
Beginning work in process, October 1	5,000			
Transferred in during October	40,000			
Total physical units to account for	45,000			
Units accounted for:				
Completed and transferred out during October	38,000	38,000	38,000*	38,000*
Ending work in process, October 31	7,000	7,000	0†	2,100†
Total physical units accounted for	45,000			
Total equivalent units		45,000	38,000	40,100

In the Insertion Department:
*Units completed and transferred out
    Direct materials: 38,000 units each 100% completed = 38,000 equivalent units
    Conversion costs: 38,000 units each 100% completed = 38,000 equivalent units
†Ending inventory
    Direct materials: 7,000 units each 0% completed = 0 equivalent units
    Conversion costs: 7,000 units each 30% completed = 2,100 equivalent units

38,000 equivalent units completed and transferred out (38,000 physical units × **100%**) and 7,000 equivalent units still in ending inventory (7,000 physical units × **100%**).

> The following rule holds: *All physical units, whether completed and transferred out or still in ending work in process, are considered 100% complete with respect to transferred-in work and costs.*

The Insertion Department calculates equivalent units of direct material the same way as in the Shaping Department. However, in the Insertion Department, the direct materials (faceplates) are added at the *end* of the process rather than at the beginning of the process. The 38,000 masks completed and transferred out contain faceplates (have 100% of the Insertion Department's direct materials). On the other hand, the 7,000 masks in ending work in process inventory have *not* made it to the end of the process, so they *do not* contain faceplates. As we see in Exhibit 5-12, these unfinished masks have zero equivalent units of the Insertion Department's direct materials (7,000 physical units × 0%).

Now, consider the conversion costs. The 38,000 finished masks are 100% complete with respect to the Insertion Department's conversion costs. However, the 7,000 unfinished masks are only 30% converted (see Exhibits 5-10 and 5-11), so the equivalent units of conversion costs equal 2,100 (7,000 × 30%).

Now, the equivalent units in each column are summed to find the *total* equivalent units for each of the three categories: transferred-in (45,000), direct materials (38,000), and conversion costs (40,100). We'll use these equivalent units in Step 4.

Steps 3 and 4: Summarize Total Costs to Account for and Compute the Cost per Equivalent Unit

Exhibit 5-13 accumulates the Insertion Department's total costs to account for based on the data in Exhibit 5-11.

In addition to direct material and conversion costs, the Insertion Department must account for transferred-in costs. Recall that transferred-in costs are incurred in a previous process (the Shaping Department, in the SeaView example) and are carried forward as part of the product's cost when the physical product is transferred to the next process.

If the Insertion Department had bought these shaped masks from an outside supplier, it would have to account for the costs of purchasing the masks. However, the Insertion

EXHIBIT 5-13 **Step 3: Summarize Total Costs to Account For**
Step 4: Compute the Cost per Equivalent Unit

SEAVIEW INSERTION DEPARTMENT Month Ended October 31				
	Transferred-in	Direct Materials	Conversion Costs	Total
Beginning work in process, October 1 (from Exhibit 5-11)	$ 22,000	$ 0	$ 1,100	$ 23,100
Costs added during October (from Exhibit 5-11)	176,000	19,000	12,935	207,935
Total costs to account for	$198,000	$19,000	$14,035	$231,035
Divide by total equivalent units (from Exhibit 5-12)	÷ 45,000	÷ 38,000	÷ 40,100	
Cost per equivalent unit	$ 4.40	$ 0.50	$ 0.35	

Department receives the masks from an *internal* supplier—the Shaping Department. Thus, the Insertion Department must account for the costs the Shaping Department incurred to provide the shaped masks (the Insertion Department's transferred-in costs) as well as the Insertion Department's own direct materials (faceplates) and conversion costs (labor and overhead to insert the faceplates).

Exhibit 5-13 shows that in Step 3, the Insertion Department's total costs to account for ($231,035) is the sum of the following:

- The cost incurred in September to start the insertion process on the 5,000 masks in the Insertion Department's beginning work in process inventory ($23,100)

- The costs added to "Work in Process Inventory—Insertion" during October ($207,935 = $176,000 transferred in from the Shaping Department + $19,000 direct materials incurred in the Insertion Department + $12,935 conversion costs incurred in the Insertion Department)

Exhibit 5-13 also shows the results of Step 4—the cost per equivalent unit. For each of the three cost categories, SeaView divides the total cost of that category by the total number of equivalent units in that category.

Step 5: Assign Total Costs to Units Completed and to Units in Ending Work in Process Inventory

Exhibit 5-14 shows how SeaView assigns the Insertion Department's total costs to account for ($231,035, from Exhibit 5-13) to (1) units completed and transferred out to finished

EXHIBIT 5-14 **Step 5: Assign Total Costs to Units Completed and to Units in Ending Work in Process Inventory**

SEAVIEW INSERTION DEPARTMENT Month Ended October 31				
	Transferred-in	Direct Materials	Conversion Costs	Total
Units completed and transferred out to Finished Goods Inventory (38,000)	[38,000 × ($4.40 + $0.50 + $0.35)]			$199,500
Ending work in process, October 31 (7,000):				
Transferred-in costs	[7,000 × $4.40]			$ 30,800
Direct materials		[0 × $0.50]		0
Conversion costs			[2,100 × $0.35]	735
Total ending work in process, October 31				31,535
Total costs accounted for				$231,035

goods inventory and (2) units remaining in the Insertion Department's ending work in process inventory. SeaView uses the same approach as it used for the Shaping Department in Exhibit 5-9. SeaView multiplies the number of equivalent units from Step 2 (Exhibit 5-12) by the cost per equivalent unit from Step 4 (Exhibit 5-13).

Exhibit 5-15 illustrates how the costs were assigned in Step 5.

EXHIBIT 5-15 **Assigning Insertion Department's Costs to Units Completed and Transferred Out and to Ending Work in Process Inventory**

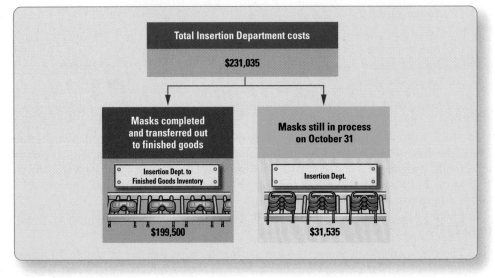

Unit Costs and Gross Profit

SeaView's managers can now compute the cost of manufacturing one swim mask, from start to finish. Step 5 shows that $199,500 should be transferred to the Finished Goods Inventory account for the 38,000 masks completed during the month. Therefore, SeaView's cost of making one completed mask is $5.25 ($199,500 ÷ 38,000 finished masks). Exhibit 5-14 shows that this cost includes the costs from both processing departments:

- $4.40 from the Shaping Department[2]

- $0.85 from the Insertion Department ($0.50 for direct materials and $0.35 for conversion costs)

SeaView's managers use this information to help control costs, set prices, and assess the profitability of the swim masks. Let's assume SeaView is able to charge customers $10 for each mask. If so, the gross profit on the sale of each of these masks will be as follows:

Sales Revenue (per mask)	$10.00
Less: Cost of Goods Sold (per mask)	5.25
Gross Profit (per mask)	$ 4.75

For SeaView to be profitable, the total gross profit (gross profit per mask × number of masks sold) will need to be high enough to cover all of SeaView's operating expenses, such

---

[2]This is the same $4.40 per unit we saw the Shaping Department transfer out to the Insertion Department in the first half of the chapter. Notice how the transferred in cost carries through from one department to the next. The weighted-average method of process costing *combines* the current period's costs ($176,000) with any costs in beginning inventory ($23,100) to yield a weighted-average cost per unit ($4.40). Therefore, the weighted average cost could be different than $4.40 if the beginning inventory had cost more or less than $4.40 per unit to make in September.

as marketing and distribution expenses, incurred in non-manufacturing elements of the value chain. In addition to using the unit cost for valuing Cost of Goods Sold (on the income statement), the unit cost will also be used to value ending Finished Goods Inventory ($5.25 for each mask still in finished goods inventory at the end of October).

Production Cost Reports

Most companies prepare a **production cost report**, which summarizes the entire five-step process on one schedule. Notice how the production cost report for the Insertion Department shown in Exhibit 5-16 on page 261 simply brings together all of the steps that we showed separately in Exhibits 5-12, 5-13, and 5-14. The top half of the schedule focuses on units (Steps 1 and 2), while the bottom half of the schedule focuses on costs (Steps 3, 4, and 5). Each processing department prepares its own production cost report each month. The transferred-in costs, direct materials cost, and conversion costs assigned to the units in *ending* work in process inventory become the *beginning* work in process inventory balances on the next month's cost report.

SeaView's managers monitor production costs by comparing the actual direct materials and conversion costs—particularly the equivalent-unit costs—with expected amounts. If actual costs are higher than expected, managers will try to uncover the reason for the increase, and look for ways to cut costs in the future without sacrificing quality.

Journal Entries in a Second Processing Department

The Insertion Department's journal entries are similar to those of the Shaping Department.

The following summary entry records the manufacturing costs incurred in the Insertion Department during the month of October (data from Exhibit 5-11):

Work in Process Inventory—Insertion	31,935	
Raw Materials Inventory		19,000
Wages Payable		3,710
Manufacturing Overhead		9,225
(*To record manufacturing costs incurred in the Insertion Department during October.*)		

Next, recall the journal entry made to transfer the cost of shaped masks out of the Shaping Department and into the Insertion Department at the end of October (page 249). This journal entry would only be made *once*, but is repeated here simply as a reminder:

Work in Process Inventory—Insertion	176,000	
Work in Process Inventory—Shaping		176,000
(*To record the transfer cost out of the Shaping Department and into the Insertion Department.*)		

After completing the fifth step of the process costing procedure (shown in Exhibit 5-14), the Insertion Department knows that $199,500 should be assigned to the completed masks, while $31,535 should be assigned to the units still being worked on in the Insertion Department. Therefore, the following journal entry is made to transfer cost out of the Insertion Department and into Finished Goods Inventory:

Finished Goods Inventory	199,500	
Work in Process Inventory—Insertion		199,500
(*To record transfer of cost out of the Insertion Department and into Finished Goods Inventory.*)		

After posting, the key accounts appear as follows:

Work in Process Inventory—Shaping

Balance, September 30	0	Transferred to Insertion	176,000
Direct materials	140,000		
Direct labor	21,250		
Manufacturing overhead	46,750		
Balance, October 31	32,000		

Work in Process Inventory—Insertion

Balance, September 30	23,100	Transferred to Finished	
Transferred in from Shaping	176,000	Goods Inventory	199,500
Direct materials	19,000		
Direct labor	3,710		
Manufacturing overhead	9,225		
Balance, October 31	31,535		

Finished Goods Inventory

Balance, September 30	0	
Transferred in from Insertion	199,500	

STOP & THINK

Assume that SeaView sells 36,000 of the masks for $10 each. Assuming that SeaView uses a perpetual inventory system, what journal entries would SeaView make to record the sales transaction?

Answer: The unit cost of making one mask from start to finish is $5.25 ($199,500 transferred to Finished Goods ÷ 38,000 finished masks). SeaView will make one journal entry to record the sales revenue, and a second journal entry to record the cost of goods sold:

	Accounts Receivable (36,000 × $10.00)	360,000	
	Sales Revenue		360,000

	Cost of Goods Sold (36,000 × 5.25)	189,000	
	Finished Goods Inventory		189,000

EXHIBIT 5-16 **Production Cost Report**

SEAVIEW INSERTION DEPARTMENT
Product Cost Report
Month Ended October 31

Flow of Production	Step 1 Flow of Physical Units	Step 2: Equivalent Units Transferred-in	Direct Materials	Conversion Costs	
Units to account for:					
Beginning work in process, Oct. 1	5,000				
Transferred in during October	40,000				
Total physical units to account for	45,000				
Units accounted for:					
Completed and transferred out during October	38,000	38,000	38,000	38,000	
Ending work in process, Oct. 31	7,000	7,000	0	2,100	
Total physical units accounted for	45,000				
Total equivalent units		45,000	38,000	40,100	

Flow of Costs	Steps 3, 4, and 5 Transferred-in	Direct Materials	Conversion Costs	Total
Beginning work in process, October 1	$ 22,000	$ 0	$ 1,100	$ 23,100
Costs added during October	176,000	19,000	12,935	207,935
Total costs to account for	$198,000	$19,000	$14,035	$231,035
÷ Total equivalent units	÷ 45,000	÷ 38,000	÷ 40,100	
Cost per equivalent unit	$ 4.40	$ 0.50	$ 0.35	
Assignment of total costs:				
Units completed during October	[38,000 × ($4.40 + $0.50 + $0.35)]			$199,500
Ending work in process, October 31:				
Transferred-in costs	[7,000 × $4.40]			$ 30,800
Direct materials		[0 × $0.50]		0
Conversion costs			[2,100 × $0.35]	735
Total ending work in process, October 31				31,535
Total costs accounted for				$231,035

Decision Guidelines

Process Costing—Second Process

Let's use SeaView's Insertion Department to review some of the key process costing decisions that arise in a second (or later) process.

Decision	Guidelines
At what point in the insertion process are transferred-in costs (from the shaping process) incurred?	Transferred-in costs are incurred at the *beginning* of the insertion process. The masks must be completely shaped before the insertion process begins.
What percentage of completion is used to calculate equivalent units in the "Transferred-In" column?	All units, whether completed and transferred out or still in ending work in process, are considered 100% complete with respect to transferred-in work and costs.
What checks and balances does the five-step process costing procedure provide?	The five-step procedure provides two important checks: 1. The total units to account for (beginning inventory + units started or transferred in) *must equal* the total units accounted for (units completed and transferred out + units in ending inventory). 2. The total costs to account for (cost of beginning inventory + costs incurred in the current period) *must equal* the total costs accounted for (cost of units completed and transferred out + cost of ending inventory).
What are the two main goals of the Insertion Department's process costing?	The first goal is to split total costs between swim masks completed and transferred out to finished goods inventory and the masks that remain in the Insertion Department's ending work in process inventory. The second goal is to determine the cost of making each swim mask—from start to finish.
What is a production cost report and how do managers use the information found on it?	A production cost report simply summarizes all five steps on one schedule. SeaView's managers use the cost per equivalent unit to determine the cost of producing a swim mask. These costs provide a basis for setting selling prices, performing profitability analysis to decide which products to emphasize, and so forth. These costs are also the basis for valuing inventory on the balance sheet and cost of goods sold on the income statement. Managers also use the cost per equivalent unit to control material and conversion costs and to evaluate the performance of production department managers.

Summary Problem 2

This problem extends the Summary Problem 1 to a second department. During May, Florida Tile Industries reports the following in its Finishing Department:

Finishing Department Data for May	
Information about units:	
Beginning work in process, May 1 (20% complete as to direct materials, 70% complete as to conversion work)	4,000 units
Transferred in from Tile-Forming Department during May	16,000 units
Completed and transferred out to Finished Goods Inventory during May	15,000 units
Ending work in process, May 31 (36% complete as to direct materials, 80% complete as to conversion work)	5,000 units
Information about costs:	
Work in process, May 1 (transferred-in costs, $10,000; direct materials costs, $488; conversion costs, $5,530)	$16,018
Transferred in from Tile-Forming Department during May (page 253)	38,400
Finishing Department direct materials added during May	6,400
Finishing Department conversion costs added during May	24,300

Requirements

1. Assign the Finishing Department's *total costs to account for* to units completed and to units in ending work in process inventory. (*Hint:* Don't confuse the Finishing Department with finished goods inventory. The Finishing Department is Florida Tile's second process. The tiles do not become part of finished goods inventory until they have completed the second process, which happens to be called the Finishing Department.)

2. Make the journal entry to transfer the appropriate amount of cost to Finished Goods Inventory.

3. What is the cost of making one unit of product from start to finish?

continued

Solution

Steps 1 and 2: Summarize the flow of physical units; compute output in terms of equivalent units.

FLORIDA TILE
FINISHING DEPARTMENT
Month Ended May 31

	Step 1	Step 2: Equivalent Units		
Flow of Production	Flow of Physical Units	Transferred-in	Direct Materials	Conversion Costs
Units to account for:				
Beginning work in process, May 1	4,000			
Transferred in from Tile-Forming				
Department during May	16,000			
Total physical units to account for	20,000			
Units accounted for:				
Completed and transferred out during May	15,000	15,000	15,000	15,000
Ending work in process, May 31	5,000	5,000	1,800*	4,000*
Total physical units accounted for	20,000			
Total equivalent units		20,000	16,800	19,000

*Ending inventory:
  Direct materials: 5,000 units each 36% completed = 1,800 equivalent units
  Converted costs: 5,000 units each 80% completed = 4,000 equivalent units

Steps 3 and 4: Summarize total costs to account for; compute the cost per equivalent unit.

FLORIDA TILE
FINISHING DEPARTMENT
Month Ended May 31

	Step 1	Step 2: Equivalent Units		
	Transferred-in	Direct Materials	Conversion Costs	Total
Beginning work in process, May 1	$10,000	$ 488	$ 5,530	$16,018
Costs added during May	38,400	6,400	24,300	69,100
Total costs to account for	$48,400	$ 6,888	$29,830	$85,118
Divide by total equivalent units	÷ 20,000	÷ 16,800	÷ 19,000	
Cost per equivalent unit	$ 2.42	$ 0.41	$ 1.57	

Step 5: Assign total costs to units completed and to units in ending work in process inventory.

FLORIDA TILE
FINISHING DEPARTMENT
Month Ended May 31

Flow of Production	Transferred-in	Direct Materials	Conversion Costs	Total
Units completed and transferred out to				
Finished Goods Inventory	[15,000 × ($2.42 + $0.41 + $1.57)]			$66,000
Ending work in process, May 31:				
Transferred-in costs	[5,000 × $2.42]			12,100
Direct materials		[1,800 × $0.41]		738
Conversion costs			[4,000 × $1.57]	6,280
Total ending work in process, May 31				19,118
Total costs accounted for				$85,118

Requirement 2

Journal entry:

	Finished Goods Inventory	66,000	
	Work in Process Inventory—Finishing Department		66,000
	(*To record the transfer of cost out of the Finishing Department and into Finished Goods Inventory.*)		

Requirement 3

The cost of making one unit from start to finish is $4.40 ($66,000 transferred to Finished Goods Inventory divided by the 15,000 completed tiles). This consists of $2.42[3] of cost incurred in the Tile-Forming Department and $1.98 of cost incurred in the Finishing Department ($0.41 of direct materials and $1.57 of conversion costs).

---

[3]In Summary Problem 1, we saw that the average cost per unit in May was $2.40. The weighted-average method combines the current period's costs (May's costs) with any costs in beginning inventory to yield a weighted-average cost of $2.42 per unit.

REVIEW

Accounting Vocabulary

Equivalent Units. (p. 240)   Express the amount of work done during a period in terms of fully completed units of output.

Production Cost Report. (p. 259)   Summarizes a processing department's operations for a period.

Transferred-In Costs. (p. 253)   Costs incurred in a previous process that are carried forward as part of the product's cost when it moves to the next process.

Weighted-Average Method of Process Costing. (p. 241)   A process costing method that *combines* any beginning inventory units (and costs) with the current period's units (and costs) to get a weighted-average cost.

Quick Check

1. *(Learning Objective 1)* Which of these companies would use process costing?
   a. Saatchi & Saatchi advertising firm
   b. Pace Foods, producer of Pace picante sauce
   c. Accenture management consultants
   d. Amazon.com
2. *(Learning Objective 1)* Which of these companies would use job costing?
   a. An oil refinery
   b. A dairy farm
   c. A paint manufacturer
   d. A hospital
3. *(Learning Objective 1)* All of the following statements are correct *except* for which of the following?
   a. Costs are accumulated by department when using process costing.
   b. Units produced are indistinguishable from each other in a process costing system.
   c. Process costing has the same basic purposes as job costing.
   d. Process costing would be appropriate for a custom cabinet maker.
4. *(Learning Objective 2)* Tucker Manufacturing uses weighted-average process costing. All materials at Tucker are added at the beginning of the production process. The equivalent units for materials at Tucker would be
   a. the units started plus the units in beginning work in process.
   b. the units completed and transferred out plus the units in beginning work in process.
   c. the units started plus the units in ending work in process.
   d. the units started and completed plus the units in ending work in process.
5. *(Learning Objective 2)* An equivalent unit of conversion costs is equal to
   a. an equivalent unit of material costs.
   b. the amount of conversion costs needed to produce one unit.
   c. the amount of conversion costs necessary to start a unit into work in process.
   d. half of the conversion costs necessary to produce one unit.
6. *(Learning Objective 2)* When using the weighted-average method of process costing, the computation of the cost per equivalent unit includes
   a. costs incurred during the current period only.
   b. costs incurred during the current period plus the cost of the beginning work in process inventory.
   c. costs incurred during the current period plus the cost of the ending work in process inventory.
   d. costs incurred during the current period plus all of the costs incurred in the prior period.
7. *(Learning Objective 3)* All of the following statements about process costing are true *except* for which of the following?
   a. Process costing is appropriate for those production processes where similar units are produced in a continuous flow.
   b. Equivalent units for materials and equivalent units for conversion costs are the same.
   c. Units in beginning work in process plus the units started into production should equal units in ending work in process plus units completed.
   d. Each process will have its own separate Work in Process Inventory account.
8. *(Learning Objective 3)* Which of the following statements describes Jelly Belly's process costing system?
   a. Direct materials and direct labor are traced to each specific order.
   b. Costs flow directly from a single Work in Process Inventory account to Finished Goods Inventory.
   c. Costs flow through a sequence of Work in Process Inventory accounts and then into Finished Goods Inventory from the final Work in Process Inventory account.
   d. The subsidiary Work in Process Inventory accounts consist of separate records for each individual order, detailing the materials, labor, and overhead assigned to that order.
9. *(Learning Objective 4)* The journal entry to record the transfer of units from Department A to the next processing department, Department B, includes a debit to
   a. Work in Process Inventory for Dept. B and a credit to Raw Materials Inventory.
   b. Work in Process Inventory for Dept. A and a credit to Work in Process Inventory for Dept. B.
   c. Work in Process Inventory for Dept. B and a credit to Work in Process Inventory for Dept. A.
   d. Finished Goods Inventory and a credit to Work in Process for Dept. A.
10. *(Learning Objective 5)* In general, transferred-in costs include
    a. costs incurred in the previous period.
    b. costs incurred in all prior periods.
    c. costs incurred in only the previous process.
    d. costs incurred in all prior processes.

ASSESS YOUR PROGRESS

Learning Objectives

1 Distinguish between the flow of costs in process costing and job costing

2 Compute equivalent units

3 Use process costing in the first production department

4 Prepare journal entries for a process costing system

5 Use process costing in a second or later production department

Short Exercises

S5-1 Compare flow of costs *(Learning Objective 1)*

Use Exhibit 5-1 to help you describe in your own words the major difference in the flow of costs between a job costing system and a process costing system.

S5-2 Flow of costs through Work in Process Inventory *(Learning Objective 1)*

As shown in Exhibits 5-1 and 5-2, Jelly Belly produces jelly beans in three sequential processing departments: Centers, Shells, and Packaging. Assume that the Shells processing department began September with $18,340 of unfinished jelly bean centers. During September, the Shells process used $42,600 of direct materials, used $12,130 of direct labor, and was allocated $17,260 of manufacturing overhead. In addition, $126,400 was transferred out of the Centers processing department during the month and $196,420 was transferred out of the Shells processing department during the month. These transfers represent the cost of the jelly beans transferred from one process to another.

1. Prepare a T-account for the "Work in Process Inventory—Shells" showing all activity that took place in the account during September.

2. What is the ending balance in the "Work in Process Inventory—Shells" on September 30? What does this figure represent?

S5-3 Recompute SeaView's equivalent units *(Learning Objective 2)*

Look at SeaView's Shaping Department's equivalent-unit computation in Exhibit 5-5. Suppose the ending work in process inventory is 30% of the way through the shaping process rather than 25% of the way through. Compute the total equivalent units of direct materials and conversion costs.

S5-4 Determine the physical flow of units (process costing Step 1) *(Learning Objective 2)*

Kunde Winery's bottling department had 20,000 units in the beginning inventory of Work in Process on June 1. During June, 110,000 units were started into production. On June 30, 30,000 units were left in ending work in process inventory. Summarize the physical flow of units in a schedule similar to Exhibit 5-5 (Step 1 column).

S5-5 Compute equivalent units (process costing Step 2) *(Learning Objective 2)*

Blumhoff's Packaging Department had the following information at March 31. All direct materials are added at the *end* of the conversion process. The units in ending work in process inventory were only 30% of the way through the conversion process.

			Equivalent Units		
		Physical Units	Direct Materials	Conversion Costs	
Units accounted for:					
Completed and transferred out		115,000			
Ending work in process, March 31		15,000			
Total physical units accounted for:		130,000			
Total equivalent units					

1. Complete the schedule by computing the total equivalent units of direct materials and conversion costs for the month.

S5-6 Compute equivalent units (process costing Step 2) *(Learning Objective 2)*

The Frying Department of Rummel's Potato Chips had 100,000 partially completed units in work in process at the end of August. All of the direct materials had been added to these units, but the units were only 60% of the way through the conversion process. In addition, 1,200,000 units had been completed and transferred out of the Frying Department to the Packaging Department during the month.

1. How many equivalent units of direct materials and equivalent units of conversion costs are associated with the 1,200,000 units completed and transferred out?

2. Compute the equivalent units of direct materials and the equivalent units of conversion costs associated with the 100,000 partially completed units still in ending work in process.

3. What are the total equivalent units of direct materials and the total equivalent units of conversion costs for the month?

S5-7 Summarize total costs to account for (process costing Step 3) *(Learning Objective 3)*

McIntyre Industries' Work in Process Inventory account had a $68,000 beginning balance on May 1 ($40,000 of this related to direct materials used during April, while $28,000 related to conversion costs incurred during April). During May, the following costs were incurred in the department:

Direct materials used..	$106,000
Direct labor..	18,000
Manufacturing overhead allocated to the department..........................	154,000

Summarize the department's "Total costs to account for." Prepare a schedule (similar to Exhibit 5-7) that summarizes the department's total costs to account for by direct materials and conversion costs.

S5-8 Compute the cost per equivalent unit (process costing Step 4) *(Learning Objective 3)*

At the end of July, Baker's mixing department had "Total costs to account for" of $752,420. Of this amount, $287,045 related to direct materials costs, while the remainder related to conversion costs. The department had 52,190 total equivalent units of direct materials and 45,625 total equivalent units of conversion costs for the month.

Compute the cost per equivalent unit for direct materials and the cost per equivalent unit for conversion costs.

S5-9 Recompute SeaView's cost per equivalent unit *(Learning Objective 3)*

Return to the original SeaView example in Exhibits 5-5 and 5-7. Suppose direct labor is $34,000 rather than $21,250. Now what is the conversion cost per equivalent unit? (Use Exhibit 5-8 to format your answer.)

S5-10 Assign costs (process costing Step 5) *(Learning Objective 3)*

Tabor Industries produces its product using a *single* production process. For the month of December, Tabor Industries determined its "cost per equivalent unit" to be as follows:

	Direct Materials	Conversion Costs
Cost per equivalent unit:	$4.10	$3.25

During the month, Tabor completed and transferred out 410,000 units to finished goods inventory. At month-end, 80,000 partially complete units remained in ending work in process inventory. These partially completed units were equal to 70,000 equivalent units of direct materials and 50,000 equivalent units of conversion costs.

1. Determine the total cost that should be assigned to the following:

   a. Units completed and transferred out

   b. Units in ending work in process inventory (*Hint:* Use Exhibit 5-9 as a guide.)

2. What was the total costs accounted for?

3. What was Tabor's average cost of making one unit of its product?

S5-11 Flow of costs through Work in Process Inventory *(Learning Objective 4)*

True-Tile produces its product in two processing departments: Forming and Finishing. The following T-account shows the Forming Department's Work in Process Inventory at August 31 prior to completing the five-step process costing procedure:

Work in Process Inventory—Forming Department	
Beginning balance $ 53,250	
Direct materials used 78,360	
Direct labor 14,920	
Manufacturing overhead allocated 126,250	

1. What is the Forming Department's "Total costs to account for" for the month of August?

2. Assume that after using the five-step process costing procedure, the company determines that the "cost to be assigned to units completed and transferred out" is $243,800. What journal entry is needed to record the transfer of costs to the Finishing Department?

3. After the journal entry is made, what will be the new ending balance in the Forming Department's Work in Process Inventory account?

S5-12 Assign total costs in a second processing department *(Learning Objective 5)*

After completing Steps 1–4 of the process costing procedure, Dale Corp. arrived at the following equivalent units and costs per equivalent unit for its *final* production department for the month of February:

	Equivalent Units		
	Transferred-in	Direct Materials	Conversion Costs
Units completed and transferred out	70,000	70,000	70,000
Units in ending work in process,			
February 28...	10,000	8,000	4,000
Total equivalent units	80,000	78,000	74,000
Cost per equivalent unit	$2.64	$0.15	$1.26

1. How much cost should be assigned to the
   a. units completed and transferred out to Finished Goods Inventory during February?
   b. partially complete units still in ending work in process inventory at the end of February?

2. What was the "Total cost accounted for" during February? What other important figure must this match? What does this figure tell you?

3. What is Dale Corporation's average cost of making *each unit* of its product from the first production department all the way through the final production department?

S5-13 Find unit cost and gross profit on a final product *(Learning Objective 5)*

Beach Co. produces Formica countertops in two sequential production departments: Forming and Polishing. The Polishing Department calculated the following costs per equivalent unit (square feet) on its April production cost report:

	Transferred-in	Direct Materials	Conversion Costs
Cost per equivalent unit:	$2.64	$0.10	$1.26

During April, 150,000 square feet were completed and transferred out of the Polishing Department to Finished Goods Inventory. The countertops were subsequently sold for $12 per square foot.

1. What was the cost per square foot of the finished product?

2. Did most of the production cost occur in the Forming Department or in the Polishing Department? Explain how you can tell.

3. What was the gross profit per square foot?

4. What was the total gross profit on the countertops produced in April?

The following data set is used for S5-14 through S5-18:

Polar Springs Data Set: Filtration Department

Polar Springs produces premium bottled water. Polar Springs purchases artesian water, stores the water in large tanks, and then runs the water through two processes:

- Filtration, where workers microfilter and ozonate the water
- Bottling, where workers bottle and package the filtered water

During February, the filtration process incurs the following costs in processing 200,000 liters:

Wages of workers operating the filtration equipment............................	$ 11,100
Wages of workers operating ozonation equipment.................................	12,850
Manufacturing overhead allocated to filtration	24,050
Water...	120,000

Polar Springs has no beginning inventory in the Filtration Department.

S5-14 Compute cost per liter *(Learning Objective 1)*

Refer to the Polar Springs Filtration Department Data Set.

1. Compute the February conversion costs in the Filtration Department.

2. If the Filtration Department completely processed 200,000 liters, what would be the average filtration cost per liter?

3. Now, assume that the total costs of the filtration process listed in the previous chart yield 160,000 liters that are completely filtered and ozonated, while the remaining 40,000 liters are only partway through the process at the end of February. Is the cost per completely filtered and ozonated liter higher, lower, or the same as in Requirement 2? Why?

S5-15 Summarize physical flow and compute equivalent units *(Learning Objective 2)*

Refer to the Polar Springs Filtration Department Data Set. At Polar Spring, water is added at the beginning of the filtration process. Conversion costs are added evenly throughout the process, and in February, 160,000 liters have been completed and transferred out of the Filtration Department to the Bottling Department. The 40,000 liters remaining in the Filtration Department's ending work in process inventory are 80% of the way through the filtration process. Recall that Polar Spring has no beginning inventories.

1. Draw a time line for the filtration process similar to the one in Exhibit 5-6.

2. Complete the first two steps of the process costing procedure for the Filtration Department: summarize the physical flows of units and then compute the equivalent units of direct materials and conversion costs. Your answer should look similar to Exhibit 5-5.

S5-16 Continuation of S5-15: Summarize total costs to account for and compute cost per equivalent unit *(Learning Objective 3)*

Refer to the Polar Springs Filtration Department Data Set and your answer to S5-15. Complete Steps 3 and 4 of the process costing procedure: Summarize total costs to account for and then compute the cost per equivalent unit for both direct materials and conversion costs.

S5-17 Continuation of S5-15 and S5-16: Assign costs *(Learning Objective 3)*

Refer to the Polar Springs Filtration Department Data Set and your answer to S5-15 and S5-16. Complete Step 5 of the process costing procedure: Assign costs to units completed and to units in ending inventory. Prepare a schedule similar to Exhibit 5-9 that answers the following questions.

1. What is the cost of the 160,000 liters completed and transferred out of the Filtration Department?

2. What is the cost of 40,000 liters remaining in the Filtration Department's ending work in process inventory?

S5-18 Continuation of S5-17: Record journal entry and post to T-account *(Learning Objective 4)*

Refer to the Polar Springs Filtration Department Data Set and your answer to S5-17.

1. Record the journal entry to transfer the cost of the 160,000 liters completed and transferred out of the Filtration Department and into the Bottling Department.

2. Record all of the transactions in the "Work in Process Inventory—Filtration" T-account.

The following data set is used for S5-19 through S5-22.

> **Polar Springs Data Set: Bottling Department**
> Polar Spring produces premium bottled water. The preceding Short Exercises considered Polar Spring's first process—filtration. We now consider Polar Spring's second process—bottling. In the Bottling Department, workers bottle the filtered water and pack the bottles into boxes. Conversion costs are incurred evenly throughout the bottling process, but packaging materials are not added until the end of the process.
>
> February data from the Bottling Department follow:
>
> | | |
> |---|---:|
> | Beginning work in process inventory | |
> | (40% of the way through the process) .... | 8,000 liters |
> | Transferred in from Filtration* .... | 160,000 liters |
> | Completed and transferred out to Finished Goods | |
> | Inventory in February .... | 154,000 liters |
> | Ending work in process inventory | |
> | (70% of the way through the bottling process) .... | 14,000 liters |
>
> | Costs in beginning work in process inventory | | Costs added during February | |
> |---|---:|---|---:|
> | Transferred in .... | $1,760 | Transferred in* .... | $136,000 |
> | Direct materials.................. | 0 | Direct materials.............. | 30,800 |
> | Direct labor........................ | 600 | Direct labor................... | 33,726 |
> | Manufacturing overhead.... | 520 | Manufacturing overhead.... | 22,484 |
> | Total beginning work in process inventory as of February 1.......................... | $2,880 | Total costs added during February .... | $223,010 |
>
> *S5-17 showed that Polar Spring's Filtration Department completed and transferred out 160,000 liters at a total cost of $136,000.

S5-19 Compute equivalent units in second department (Learning Objectives 2 & 5)

Refer to the Polar Springs Bottling Department Data Set.

1. Draw a time line similar to the one in Exhibit 5-10.

2. Complete the first two steps of the process costing procedure for the Bottling Department: summarize the physical flow of units and then compute the equivalent units of direct materials and conversion costs. Your answer should look similar to Exhibit 5-12.

S5-20 Continuation of S5-19: Compute cost per equivalent unit in second department
(Learning Objective 5)

Refer to the Polar Springs Bottling Department Data Set and your answer to S5-19. Complete Steps 3 and 4 of the process costing procedure: Summarize total costs to account for and then compute the cost per equivalent unit for both direct materials and conversion costs. Your answer should look similar to Exhibit 5-13.

S5-21 Continuation of S5-19 and S5-20: Assign costs in second department (Learning Objective 5)

Refer to the Polar Springs Bottling Department Data Set and your answers to S5-19 and 5-20. Complete Step 5 of the process costing procedure: Assign costs to units completed and to units in ending inventory. Your answer should look similar to Exhibit 5-14.

S5-22 Continuation of S5-21: Record journal entry and post to T-account (Learning Objective 4)

Refer to the Polar Springs Bottling Department Data Set and your answer to S5-21.

1. Prepare the journal entry to record the cost of units completed and transferred to finished goods.

2. Post all transactions to the "Work in Process Inventory—Bottling" T-account. What is the ending balance?

Exercises—Group A

E5-23A Diagram flow of costs (Learning Objective 1)

Pule produces kitchen cabinets in a three-stage process that includes milling, assembling, and finishing, in that order. Direct materials are added in the Milling and Finishing departments. Direct labor and overhead are incurred in all three departments. The company's general ledger includes the following accounts:

Cost of Goods Sold	Materials Inventory
Manufacturing Wages	Finished Goods Inventory
Work in Process Inventory—Milling	Manufacturing Overhead
Work in Process Inventory—Assembling	
Work in Process Inventory—Finishing	

Outline the flow of costs through the company's accounts, including a brief description of each flow. Include a T-account for each account title given.

E5-24A Analyze flow of costs through inventory T-accounts (Learning Objective 1)

Healthy Start Bakery mass-produces bread using three sequential processing departments: Mixing, Baking, and Packaging. The following transactions occurred during January:

1. Direct materials used in the Packaging Department	$ 30,000
2. Costs assigned to units completed and transferred out of Mixing	225,000
3. Direct labor incurred in the Mixing Department	11,000
4. Beginning balance: Work in Process Inventory—Baking	15,000
5. Manufacturing overhead allocated to the Baking Department	75,000
6. Beginning balance: Finished Goods Inventory	4,000
7. Costs assigned to units completed and transferred out of Baking	301,000
8. Beginning balance: Work in Process Inventory—Mixing	12,000
9. Direct labor incurred in the Packaging Department	8,000
10. Manufacturing overhead allocated to the Mixing Department	60,000
11. Direct materials used in the Mixing Department	152,000
12. Beginning balance: Raw Materials Inventory	23,000
13. Costs assigned to units completed and transferred out of Packaging	381,000
14. Beginning balance: Work in Process Inventory—Packaging	8,000
15. Purchases of Raw Materials	170,000
16. Direct labor incurred in the Baking Department	4,000
17. Manufacturing overhead allocated to the Packaging Department	40,000
18. Cost of goods sold	382,000

Note: No direct materials were used by the Baking Department.

Requirements

1. Post each of these transactions to the company's inventory T-accounts. You should set up separate T-accounts for the following:

▪ Raw Materials Inventory

▪ Work in Process Inventory—Mixing Department

▪ Work in Process Inventory—Baking Department

▪ Work in Process Inventory—Packaging Department

▪ Finished Goods Inventory

2. Determine the balance at month-end in each of the inventory accounts.

3. Assume that 3,175,000 loaves of bread were completed and transferred out of the Packaging Department during the month. What was the cost per unit of making each loaf of bread (from start to finish)?

E5-25A   Summarize physical units and compute equivalent units (process costing Steps 1 and 2)
(Learning Objective 2)

Alice's Apple Pies collected the following production information relating to June's baking operations:

	Physical Units	Direct Materials (% complete)	Conversion Costs (% complete)
Beginning work in process.........	200,000	—	—
Ending work in process.............	150,000	75%	80%
Units started during the month..	1,000,000		

Requirements

Complete the first two steps in the process costing procedure:

1. Summarize the flow of physical units.

2. Compute output in terms of equivalent units. (*Hint:* Your answer should look similar to Exhibit 5-5.)

E5-26A   Compute equivalent units in a second processing department *(Learning Objectives 2 & 5)*

Mogyardy's Mayonnaise uses a process costing system to determine its product's cost. The last of the three processes is packaging. The Packaging Department reported the following information for the month of May:

		Equivalent Units		
	Physical Units	Transferred-in	Direct Materials	Conversion Costs
Units to account for:				
Beginning work in process......	25,000			
Transferred in during May.....	225,000			
Total units to account for.......	(a)			
Units accounted for:				
Completed and transferred out	(b)	(d)	(g)	(j)
Ending work in process..........	30,000	(e)	(h)	(k)
Total units accounted for:	(c)			
Total equivalent units............		(f)	(i)	(l)

The units in ending work in process inventory were 90% complete with respect to direct materials, but only 60% complete with respect to conversion.

Requirement

1. Summarize the flow of physical units and compute output in terms of equivalent units in order to arrive at the missing figures (a) through (l).

E5-27A Complete five-step procedure in first department *(Learning Objective 3)*

Color World prepares and packages paint products. Color World has two departments: (1) blending and (2) packaging. Direct materials are added at the beginning of the blending process (dyes) and at the end of the packaging process (cans). Conversion costs are added evenly throughout each process. Data from the month of May for the Blending Department are as follows:

Gallons:	
Beginning work in process inventory	0
Started production	8,000 gallons
Completed and transferred out to Packaging in May	6,000 gallons
Ending work in process inventory (30% of the way through the blending process)	2,000 gallons
Costs:	
Beginning work in process inventory	$ 0
Costs added during May:	
Direct materials (dyes)	4,800
Direct labor	800
Manufacturing overhead	1,840
Total costs added during May	$7,440

Requirements

1. Draw a time line for the Blending Department similar to Exhibit 5-6.

2. Summarize the physical flow of units and compute total equivalent units for direct materials and for conversion costs.

3. Summarize total costs to account for and find the cost per equivalent unit for direct materials and conversion costs.

4. Assign total costs to units (gallons):
   a. Completed and transferred out to the Packaging Department
   b. In the Blending Department ending work in process inventory

5. What is the average cost per gallon transferred out of the Blending Department to the Packaging Department? Why would Color World's managers want to know this cost?

E5-28A Continuation of E5-27A: Journal entries *(Learning Objective 4)*

Return to the Blending Department for Color World in E5-27A.

Requirements

1. Present the journal entry to record the use of direct materials and direct labor and the allocation of manufacturing overhead to the Blending Department. Also, give the journal entry to record the costs of the gallons completed and transferred out to the Packaging Department.

2. Post the journal entries to the "Work in Process Inventory—Blending" T-account. What is the ending balance?

E5-29A   Record journal entries *(Learning Objective 4)*

Record the following process costing transactions in the general journal:

a. Purchase of raw materials on account, $9,000

b. Requisition of direct materials to
   Assembly Department, $4,000
   Finishing Department, $2,000

c. Incurrence and payment of manufacturing labor, $10,800

d. Incurrence of manufacturing overhead costs:
   Property taxes—plant, $1,900
   Utilities—plant, $4,500
   Insurance—plant, $1,100
   Depreciation—plant, $3,400

e. Assignment of conversion costs to the Assembly Department:
   Direct labor, $4,700
   Manufacturing overhead, $2,900

f. Assignment of conversion costs to the Finishing Department:
   Direct labor, $4,400
   Manufacturing overhead, $6,200

g. Cost of goods completed and transferred out of the Assembly Department to the Finishing Department, $10,250

h. Cost of goods completed and transferred out of the Finishing Department into Finished Goods Inventory, $15,600

E5-30A   Compute equivalent units and assign costs *(Learning Objectives 2, 3, & 4)*

The Assembly Department of ZAP Surge Protectors began September with no work in process inventory. During the month, production that cost $39,860 (direct materials, $9,900, and conversion costs, $29,960) was started on 23,000 units. ZAP completed and transferred to the Testing Department a total of 15,000 units. The ending work in process inventory was 37.5% complete as to direct materials and 80% complete as to conversion work.

Requirements

1. Compute the equivalent units for direct materials and conversion costs.

2. Compute the cost per equivalent unit.

3. Assign the costs to units completed and transferred out and ending work in process inventory.

4. Record the journal entry for the costs transferred out of the Assembly Department to the Testing Department.

5. Post all of the transactions in the "Work in Process Inventory—Assembly" T-account. What is the ending balance?

E5-31A   Complete five-step procedure in first department *(Learning Objective 3)*

Royal Vine Winery in Kingston, New York, has two departments: Fermenting and Packaging. Direct materials are added at the beginning of the fermenting process (grapes) and at the end of the packaging process (bottles). Conversion costs are added evenly throughout each process. Data from the month of March for the Fermenting Department are as follows:

Gallons:	
Beginning work in process inventory	2,000 gallons
Started production	6,000 gallons
Completed and transferred out to Packaging in March	6,550 gallons
Ending work in process inventory (80% of the way through the fermenting process)	1,450 gallons
Costs:	
Beginning work in process inventory($2,800 of direct materials and $2,855 of conversion cost)	$ 5,655
Costs added during March:	
Direct materials	8,800
Direct labor	1,600
Manufacturing overhead	2,484
Total costs added during March	$12,884

Requirements

1. Draw a time line for the Fermenting Department similar to Exhibit 5-6.
2. Summarize the flow of physical units and compute the total equivalent units.
3. Summarize total costs to account for and compute the cost per equivalent unit for direct materials and conversion costs.
4. Assign total costs to units (gallons):
   a. Completed and transferred out to the Packaging Department
   b. In the Fermenting Department ending work in process inventory
5. What is the average cost per gallon transferred out of Fermenting into Packaging? Why would Royal Vine's managers want to know this cost?

E5-32A Continuation of E5-31A: Journal entries (Learning Objective 4)
Return to the Fermenting Department for Royal Vine Winery in E5-31A.

Requirements

1. Present the journal entries to record the use of direct materials and direct labor and the allocation of manufacturing overhead to the Fermenting Department. Also, give the journal entry to record the cost of the gallons completed and transferred out to the Packaging Department.
2. Post the journal entries to the "Work in Process Inventory—Fermenting" T-account. What is the ending balance?

E5-33A Complete five-step procedure and journalize result (Learning Objectives 3 & 4)
The following information was taken from the ledger of Denver Roping:

Work in Process—Forming			
Beginning inventory, October 1	$ 47,820	Transferred to Finishing	$?
Direct materials	193,620		
Conversion costs	168,640		
Ending inventory	?		

The Forming Department had 10,000 partially complete units in beginning work in process inventory. The department started work on 70,000 units during the month and ended the month with 8,000 units still in work in process. These unfinished units were 60% complete as to direct materials but 20% complete as to conversion work. The beginning balance of $47,820 consisted of $21,420 of direct materials and $26,400 of conversion costs.

Requirement

1. Journalize the transfer of costs to the Finishing Department. (*Hint:* Complete the five-step process costing procedure to determine how much cost to transfer.)

E5-34A   Compute equivalent units in two later departments *(Learning Objectives 2 & 5)*

Selected production and cost data of Martha's Fudge follow for May:

| | Flow of Physical Units | |
| | Mixing | Heating |
Flow of Production	Department	Department
Units to account for:		
Beginning work in process, May 1......................	20,000	6,000
Transferred in during May.................................	70,000	80,000
Total physical units to account for.....................	90,000	86,000
Units accounted for:		
Completed and transferred out during May........	80,000	76,000
Ending work in process, May 31	10,000	10,000
Total physical units accounted for..........................	90,000	86,000

On May 31, the Mixing Department's ending work in process inventory was 70% complete as to materials and 20% complete as to conversion costs.

On May 31, the Heating Department's ending work in process inventory was 65% complete as to materials and 55% complete as to conversion costs.

Requirement

1. Compute the equivalent units for transferred-in costs, direct materials, and conversion costs for both the Mixing and the Heating Departments.

E5-35A   Complete five-step procedure in second department *(Learning Objective 5)*

Alpha Semiconductors experienced the following activity in its Photolithography Department during December. Materials are added at the beginning of the photolithography process.

Units:	
Work in process, December 1 (80% of the way	
through the process)	8,000 units
Transferred in from the Polishing and Cutting	
Department during December.................................	27,000 units
Completed during December	? units
Work in process, December 31 (70% of the	
way through the process)...	9,000 units
Costs:	
Work in process, December 1 (transferred-in costs, $20,050;	
direct materials costs, $20,250; and conversion costs, $19,816)	$60,116
Transferred in from the Polishing and Cutting	
Department during December...	97,200
Direct materials added during December	74,250
Conversion costs added during December.....................................	90,650

Requirements

(*Hint:* Use Exhibits 5-12, 5-13, and 5-14 as guides if needed.)

1. Summarize flow of physical units and compute total equivalent units for three cost categories: transferred-in, direct materials, and conversion costs.

2. Summarize total costs to account for and compute the cost per equivalent unit for each cost category.

3. Assign total costs to (a) units completed and transferred to Finished Goods Inventory and (b) units in December 31 Work in Process Inventory.

Exercises—Group B

E5-36B Diagram flow of costs *(Learning Objective 1)*

Wood Again, Inc., produces tables from recycled wood in a three-stage process that includes cutting, assembling, and finishing, in that order. Direct materials are added in the Cutting and Finishing Departments. Direct labor and overhead are incurred in all three departments. The company's general ledger includes the following accounts:

Cost of Goods Sold	Materials Inventory
Manufacturing Wages	Finished Goods Inventory
Work in Process Inventory—Cutting	Manufacturing Overhead
Work in Process Inventory—Assembling	
Work in Process Inventory—Finishing	

Outline the flow of costs through the company's accounts, including a brief description of each flow. Include a T-account for each account title given.

E5-37B Analyze flow of costs through inventory T-accounts *(Learning Objective 1)*

Best Friends Bakery mass-produces bread using three sequential processing departments: Mixing, Baking, and Packaging. The following transactions occurred during May:

1.	Direct materials used in the Packaging Department	$ 35,000
2.	Costs assigned to units completed and transferred out of Mixing	228,000
3.	Direct labor incurred in the Mixing Department	11,600
4.	Beginning balance: Work in Process Inventory—Baking	15,600
5.	Manufactured overhead allocated to the Baking Department	70,000
6.	Beginning balance: Finished Goods Inventory	4,700
7.	Costs assigned to units completed and transferred out of Baking	302,000
8.	Beginning balance: Work in Process Inventory—Mixing	12,700
9.	Direct labor incurred in the Packaging Department	8,400
10.	Manufacturing overhead allocated to the Mixing Department	62,000
11.	Direct materials used in the Mixing Department	153,000
12.	Beginning balance: Raw Materials Inventory	23,500
13.	Costs assigned to units completed and transferred out of Packaging	382,000
14.	Beginning balance: Work in Process Inventory—Packaging	8,000
15.	Purchases of Raw Materials	178,000
16.	Direct labor incurred in the Baking Department	4,000
17.	Manufacturing overhead allocated to the Packaging Department	43,000
18.	Cost of goods sold	383,000

Requirements

1. Post each of these transactions to the company's inventory T-accounts. You should set up separate T-accounts for the following:

- Raw Materials Inventory

- Work in Process Inventory—Mixing Department

- Work in Process Inventory—Baking Department

- Work in Process Inventory—Packaging Department

- Finished Goods Inventory

2. Determine the balance at month-end in each of the inventory accounts.

3. Assume 3,375,000 loaves of bread were completed and transferred out of the Packaging Department during the month. What was the cost per unit of making each loaf of bread (from start to finish)?

E5-38B Summarize physical units and compute equivalent units (process costing Steps 1 and 2)
(Learning Objective 2)

Pauline's Pecan Pies collected the following production information relating to September's baking operations:

	Physical Units	Direct Materials (% complete)	Conversion Costs (% complete)
Beginning work in process.........	206,000	—	—
Ending work in process.............	156,000	65%	90%
Units started during the month..	1,015,000		

Requirements

Complete the first two steps in the process costing procedure:

1. Summarize the flow of physical units.

2. Compute output in terms of equivalent units. (*Hint:* Your answer should look similar to Exhibit 5-5).

E5-39B Compute equivalent units in a second processing department *(Learning Objectives 2 & 5)*

Maxwell's Mayonnaise uses a process costing system to determine its product's cost. The last of the three processes is packaging. The Packaging Department reported the following information for the month of July:

		Equivalent Units		
	Physical Units	Transferred-in	Direct Materials	Conversion Costs
Units to account for:				
Beginning work in process......	23,000			
Transferred in during July......	229,000			
Total units to account for.......	(a)			
Units accounted for:				
Completed and transferred out	(b)	(d)	(g)	(j)
Ending work in process......	28,000	(e)	(h)	(k)
Total units accounted for:	(c)			
Total Equivalent Units		(f)	(i)	(l)

The units in ending work in process inventory were 90% complete with respect to direct materials, but only 60% complete with respect to conversion.

Requirement

1. Summarize the flow of physical units and compute output in terms of equivalent units in order to arrive at the missing figures (a) through (l).

E5-40B Complete five-step procedure in first department (Learning Objective 3)

You Can Paint Too prepares and packages paint products. You Can Paint Too has two departments: (1) Blending and (2) Packaging. Direct materials are added at the beginning of the blending process (dyes) and at the end of the packaging process (cans). Conversion costs are added evenly throughout each process. Data from the month of May for the Blending Department are as follows:

Gallons:	
Beginning work in process inventory	0
Started production	8,500 gallons
Completed and transferred out to Packaging in May	6,400 gallons
Ending work in process inventory (30% of the way through the blending process)	2,100 gallons
Costs:	
Beginning work in process inventory	$ 0
Costs added during May:	
Direct materials (dyes)	4,200
Direct labor	750
Manufacturing overhead	2,500
Total costs added during May	$7,450

Requirements

1. Fill-in the time line for the Blending Department similar to Exhibit 5-6.

2. Summarize the physical flow of units and compute total equivalent units for direct materials and for conversion costs.

3. Summarize total costs to account for and find the cost per equivalent unit for direct materials and for conversion costs.

4. Assign total costs to units (gallons):
   a. Completed and transferred out to the Packaging Department.
   b. In the Blending Department ending work in process inventory.

5. What is the average cost per gallon transferred out of the Blending Department to the Packaging Department? Why would You Can Paint Too's managers want to know this cost?

E5-41B Continuation of E5-40B: Journal entries (Learning Objective 4)

Return to the Blending Department for You Can Paint Too in E5-40B.

Requirements

1. Present the journal entry to record the use of direct materials and direct labor and the allocation of manufacturing overhead to the Blending Department. Also, give the journal entry to record the costs of the gallons completed and transferred out to the Packaging Department.

2. Post the journal entries to the "Work in Process Inventory—Blending" T-account. What is the ending balance?

E5-42B Record journal entries *(Learning Objective 4)*

Record the following process costing transactions in the general journal:

a. Purchase of raw materials on account, $9,900

b. Requisition of direct materials to:

Assembly Department, $4,500

Finishing Department, $2,900

c. Incurrence and payment of manufacturing labor, $10,100

d. Incurrence of manufacturing overhead costs:

Property taxes—plant, $1,600

Utilities—plant, $4,600

Insurance—plant, $1,400

Depreciation—plant, $3,700

e. Assignment of conversion costs to the Assembly Department:

Direct labor, $5,000

Manufacturing overhead, $2,100

f. Assignment of conversion costs to the Finishing Department:

Direct labor, $4,200

Manufacturing overhead, $6,200

g. Cost of goods completed and transferred out of the Assembly Department to the Finishing Department, $10,500

h. Cost of goods completed and transferred out of the Finishing Department into Finished Goods Inventory, $15,500

E5-43B Compute equivalent units and assign costs *(Learning Objectives 2, 3, & 4)*

The Assembly Department of Best Surge Protectors began September with no work in process inventory. During the month, production that cost $41,400 (direct materials, $9,000, and conversion costs, $32,400) was started on 22,000 units. Best completed and transferred to the Testing Department a total of 17,000 units. The ending work in process inventory was 37.5% complete as to direct materials and 80% complete as to conversion work.

Requirements

1. Compute the equivalent units for direct materials and conversion costs.

2. Compute the cost per equivalent unit.

3. Assign the costs to units completed and transferred out and ending work in process inventory.

4. Record the journal entry for the costs transferred out of the Assembly Department to the Testing Department.

5. Post all of the transactions in the "Work in Process Inventory—Assembly" T-account. What is the ending balance?

E5-44B Complete five-step procedure in first department *(Learning Objective 3)*

Paulson Winery in Kingston, New York, has two departments: Fermenting and Packaging. Direct materials are added at the beginning of the fermenting process (grapes) and at the end of the packaging process (bottles). Conversion costs are added evenly throughout each process. Data from the month of March for the Fermenting Department are as follows:

Gallons:	
Beginning work in process inventory	2,000 gallons
Started production	6,000 gallons
Completed and transferred out to Packaging in March	6,500 gallons
Ending work in process inventory (80% of the way through the fermenting process)	1,500 gallons
Costs:	
Beginning work in process inventory ($2,900 of direct materials and $3,000 of conversion cost)	$ 5,900
Costs added during March:	
Direct materials	10,300
Direct labor	2,000
Manufacturing overhead	4,100
Total costs added during March	$16,400

Requirements

1. Draw a time line for the Fermenting Department similar to Exhibit 5-6.
2. Summarize the flow of physical units and compute the total equivalent units.
3. Summarize total costs to account for and compute the cost per equivalent unit for direct materials and conversion costs.
4. Assign total costs to units (gallons):
   a. Completed and transferred out to the Packaging Department.
   b. In the Fermenting Department ending work in process inventory
5. What is the average cost per gallon transferred out of Fermenting into Packaging? Why would Paulson's managers want to know this cost?

E5-45B Continuation of E5-44B: Journal entries *(Learning Objective 4)*

Return to the Fermenting Department for Paulson Winery in E5-44B.

Requirements

1. Present the journal entries to record the use of direct materials and direct labor, and the allocation of manufacturing overhead to the Fermenting Department. Also, give the journal entry to record the cost of the gallons completed and transferred out to the Packaging Department.
2. Post the journal entries to the "Work in Process Inventory—Fermenting" T-account. What is the ending balance?

E5-46B Complete five-step procedure and journalize result *(Learning Objectives 3 & 4)*

The following information was taken from the ledger of Evans Roping:

Work in Process—Forming			
Beginning inventory, October 1	47,200	Transferred to Finishing	?
Direct materials	193,700		
Conversion costs	168,500		
Ending inventory	?		

The Forming Department had 9,000 partially complete units in beginning work in process inventory. The department started work on 69,000 units during the month and ended the month with 7,000 units still in work in process. These unfinished units were 60% complete as to direct materials but 20% complete as to conversion work. The beginning balance of $47,200 consisted of $21,000 of direct materials and $26,200 of conversion costs.

Requirement

1. Journalize the transfer of costs to the Finishing Department. (*Hint*: Complete the five-step process costing procedure to determine how much cost to transfer.)

E5-47B Compute equivalent units in two later departments *(Learning Objectives 2 & 5)*

Selected production and cost data of Anne's Fudge follow for May:

	Flow of Physical Units	
Flow of Production	**Mixing Department**	**Heating Department**
Units to account for:		
Beginning work in process, May 1	24,000	6,000
Transferred in during May................................	79,000	84,000
Total physical units to account for.....................	103,000	90,000
Units accounted for:		
Completed and transferred out during May.......	89,000	78,000
Ending work in process, May 31	14,000	12,000
Total physical units accounted for.........................	103,000	90,000

On May 31, the Mixing Department's ending work in process inventory was 70% complete as to materials and 20% complete as to conversion costs. On May 31, the Heating Department's ending work in process inventory was 75% complete as to materials and 65% complete as to conversion costs.

Requirement

1. Compute the equivalent units for transferred-in costs, direct materials, and conversion costs for both the Mixing and the Heating Departments.

E5-48B   Complete five-step procedure in second department *(Learning Objective 5)*

Brookstein Semiconductors experienced the following activity in its Photolithography Department during December. Materials are added at the beginning of the photolithography process.

Units:	
Work in process, December 1 (80% of the way through the process)	5,500 units
Transferred in from the Polishing and Cutting Department during December.................................	30,000 units
Completed during December	? units
Work in process, December 31 (70% of the way through the process)......................................	9,000 units
Costs:	
Work in process, December 1 (transferred-in costs, $20,200; direct materials costs, $20,400; and conversion costs, $19,100)	$59,700
Transferred in from the Polishing and Cutting Department during December.................................	97,200
Direct materials added during December	73,600
Conversion costs added during December.................................	90,500

Requirements

(Hint: Use Exhibits 5-12, 5-13, and 5-14 as guides if needed.)

1. Summarize flow of physical units and compute total equivalent units for three cost categories: transferred-in, direct materials, and conversion costs.

2. Summarize total costs to account for and compute the cost per equivalent unit for each cost category.

3. Assign total costs to (a) units completed and transferred to Finished Goods Inventory and (b) units in December 31 Work in Process Inventory.

Problems—Group A

P5-49A   Process costing in a single processing department *(Learning Objectives 1, 2, & 3)*

Winter Lips produces a lip balm used for cold-weather sports. The balm is manufactured in a single processing department. No lip balm was in process on May 31, and Winter Lips started production on 20,400 lip balm tubes during June. Direct materials are added at the beginning of the process, but conversion costs are incurred evenly throughout the process. Completed production for June totaled 15,200 units. The June 30 work in process was 40% of the way through the production process. Direct materials costing $4,080 were placed in production during June, and direct labor of $3,315 and manufacturing overhead of $1,005 were assigned to the process.

Requirements

1. Draw a time line for Winter Lips that is similar to Exhibit 5-6.

2. Use the time line to help you compute the total equivalent units and the cost per equivalent unit for June.

3. Assign total costs to (a) units completed and transferred to Finished Goods and (b) units still in process at June 30.

4. Prepare a T-account for Work in Process Inventory to show activity during June, including the June 30 balance.

P5-50A Process costing in a first department *(Learning Objectives 1, 3, & 4)*

The New England Furniture Company produces dining tables in a three-stage process: sawing, assembly, and staining. Costs incurred in the Sawing Department during September are summarized as follows:

Work in Process Inventory—Sawing	
September 1 balance	0
Direct materials	1,860,000
Direct labor	139,100
Manufacturing overhead	153,400

Direct materials (lumber) are added at the beginning of the sawing process, while conversion costs are incurred evenly throughout the process. September activity in the Sawing Department included sawing of 11,000 meters of lumber, which were transferred to the Assembly Department. Also, work began on 1,000 meters of lumber, which on September 30 were 70% of the way through the sawing process.

Requirements

1. Draw a time line for the Sawing Department similar to Exhibit 5-6.

2. Use the time line to help you compute the number of equivalent units and the cost per equivalent unit in the Sawing Department for September.

3. Show that the sum of (a) cost of goods transferred out of the Sawing Department and (b) ending "Work in Process Inventory—Sawing" equals the total cost accumulated in the department during September.

4. Journalize all transactions affecting the company's sawing process during September, including those already posted.

P5-51A Five-step process: Materials added at different points *(Learning Objectives 1, 2, & 3)*

Kun Pow produces canned chicken a la king. The chicken a la king passes through three departments: (1) Mixing, (2) Retort (sterilization), and (3) Packing. In the Mixing Department, chicken and cream are added at the beginning of the process, the mixture is partly cooked, and chopped green peppers and mushrooms are added at the end of the process. Conversion costs are added evenly throughout the mixing process. November data from the Mixing Department are as follows:

Gallons		Costs	
Beginning work in process inventory......	0 gallons	Beginning work in process inventory...	$ 0
Started production	15,000 gallons	Costs added during November:	
Completed and transferred out to		Chicken	12,500
Retort in November..........................	12,900 gallons	Cream..	4,000
Ending work in process inventory		Green peppers and mushrooms.......	11,610
(60% of the way through the		Direct labor	11,108
mixing process).................................	2,100 gallons	Manufacturing overhead.................	3,052
		Total costs..	$42,270

Requirements

1. Draw a time line for the Mixing Department similar to Exhibit 5-6.

2. Use the time line to help you summarize the flow of physical units and compute the equivalent units. *(Hint:* Each direct material added at a different point in the production process requires its own equivalent-unit computation.)

3. Compute the cost per equivalent unit for each cost category.

4. Compute the total costs of the units (gallons):

a. Completed and transferred out to the Retort Department.

b. In the Mixing Department's ending work in process inventory.

P5-52A Prepare a production cost report and journal entries (Learning Objectives 4 & 5)

Off Road manufactures auto roof racks in a two-stage process that includes shaping and plating. Steel alloy is the basic raw material of the shaping process. The steel is molded according to the design specifications of automobile manufacturers (Ford and General Motors). The Plating Department then adds an anodized finish.

At March 31, before recording the transfer of cost from the Plating Department to Finished Goods Inventory, the Off Road general ledger included the following account:

Work in Process Inventory—Plating	
March 1 balance	30,480
Transferred-in from Shaping	36,000
Direct materials	24,200
Direct labor	21,732
Manufacturing overhead	35,388

The direct materials (rubber pads) are added at the end of the plating process. Conversion costs are incurred evenly throughout the process. Work in process of the Plating Department on March 1 consisted of 1,200 racks. The $30,480 beginning balance of "Work in Process—Plating" includes $18,000 of transferred-in cost and $12,480 of conversion cost. During March, 2,400 racks were transferred in from the Shaping Department. The Plating Department transferred 2,200 racks to Finished Goods Inventory in March, and 1,400 were still in process on March 31. This ending inventory was 50% of the way through the plating process.

Requirements

1. Draw a time line for the Plating Department, similar to Exhibit 5-10.

2. Prepare the March production cost report for the Plating Department.

3. Journalize all transactions affecting the Plating Department during March, including the entries that have already been posted.

P5-53A Complete five-step process in a later department (Learning Objectives 1 & 5)

Sidcrome uses four departments to produce plastic handles for screwdrivers: Mixing, Molding, Drying, and Assembly.

Sidcrome's Drying Department requires no direct materials. Conversion costs are incurred evenly throughout the drying process. Other process costing information follows:

Units:	
Beginning work in process	7,000 units
Transferred-in from the Molding Department during the period..	28,000 units
Completed during the period	16,000 units
Ending work in process (20% complete as to conversion work)...	19,000 units
Costs:	
Beginning work in process (transferred-in cost, $140; conversion cost, $231)...	$371
Transferred-in from the Molding Department during the period..	4,760
Conversion costs added during the period	1,947

After the drying process, the screwdrivers are completed by assembling the handles and shanks and packaging for shipment to retail outlets.

Requirements

1. Draw a time line of the Drying Department's process, similar to the one in Exhibit 5-10.

2. Use the time line to compute the number of equivalent units of work performed by the Drying Department during the period, the cost per equivalent unit, and the total costs to account for.

3. Assign total costs to (a) units completed and transferred to the assembly operation and (b) units in the Drying Department's ending work in process inventory.

Problems—Group B

P5-54B Process costing in a single processing department *(Learning Objectives 1, 2, & 3)*

Beautiful Lips produces a lip balm used for cold-weather sports. The balm is manufactured in a single processing department. No lip balm was in process on May 31, and Beautiful Lips started production on 20,100 lip balm tubes during June. Direct materials are added at the beginning of the process, but conversion costs are incurred evenly throughout the process. Completed production for June totaled 15,500 units. The June 30 work in process was 45% of the way through the production process. Direct materials costing $4,060 were placed in production during June, and direct labor of $3,375 and manufacturing overhead of $2,425 were assigned to the process.

Requirements

1. Fill-in the time line for Beautiful Lips.

2. Use the time line to help you compute the total equivalent units and the cost per equivalent unit for June.

3. Assign total costs to (a) units completed and transferred to Finished Goods and (b) units still in process at June 30.

4. Prepare a T-account for Work in Process Inventory to show activity during June, including the June 30 balance.

P5-55B Process costing in a first department *(Learning Objectives 1, 3, & 4)*

The Colorado Table Company produces dining tables in a three-stage process: sawing, assembly, and staining. Costs incurred in the Sawing Department during September are summarized as follows:

Work in Process Inventory—Sawing	
September 1 balance	0
Direct materials	1,863,000
Direct labor	137,100
Manufacturing overhead	157,400

Direct materials (lumber) are added at the beginning of the sawing process, while conversion costs are incurred evenly throughout the process. September activity in the Sawing Department included sawing of 10,000 meters of lumber, which were transferred to the Assembly Department. Also, work began on 3,500 meters of lumber, which on September 30 were 80% of the way through the sawing process.

Requirements

1. Draw a time line for the Sawing Department similar to Exhibit 5-6.

2. Use the time line to help you compute the number of equivalent units and the cost per equivalent unit in the Sawing Department for September.

3. Show that the sum of (a) cost of goods transferred out of the Sawing Department and (b) ending "Work in Process Inventory—Sawing" equals the total cost accumulated in the department during September.

4. Journalize all transactions affecting the company's sawing process during September, including those already posted.

P5-56B Five-step process: Materials added at different points (Learning Objectives 1, 2, & 3)

Happy Giant produces canned chicken a la king. The chicken a la king passes through three departments: (1) Mixing, (2) Retort (sterilization), and (3) Packing. In the Mixing Department, chicken and cream are added at the beginning of the process, the mixture is partly cooked, then chopped green peppers and mushrooms are added at the end of the process. Conversion costs are added evenly throughout the mixing process. November data from the Mixing Department are as follows:

Gallons		Costs	
Beginning work in process inventory......	0 gallons	Beginning work in process inventory...	$ 0
Started production	14,800 gallons	Costs added during November:	
Completed and transferred out to		Chicken	12,500
Retort in November..........................	13,200 gallons	Cream...	4,200
Ending work in process inventory		Green peppers and mushrooms........	11,110
(65% of the way through the		Direct labor	11,808
mixing process)................................	1,600 gallons	Manufacturing overhead.................	3,112
		Total costs..	$42,730

Requirements

1. Draw a time line for the Mixing Department similar to Exhibit 5-6.

2. Use the time line to help you summarize the flow of physical units and compute the equivalent units. (*Hint:* Each direct material added at a different point in the production process requires its own equivalent-unit computation.)

3. Compute the cost per equivalent unit for each cost category.

4. Compute the total costs of the units (gallons):
   a. Completed and transferred out to the Retort Department.
   b. In the Mixing Department's ending work in process inventory.

P5-57B Prepare a production cost report and journal entries (Learning Objectives 4 & 5)

Classic Accessories manufactures auto roof racks in a two-stage process that includes shaping and plating. Steel alloy is the basic raw material of the shaping process. The steel is molded according to the design specifications of automobile manufacturers (Ford and General Motors). The Plating Department then adds an anodized finish.

At March 31, before recording the transfer of cost from the Plating Department to Finished Goods Inventory, the Classic Accessories general ledger included the following account:

Work in Process Inventory—Plating	
March 1 balance	26,370
Transferred-in from Shaping	28,800
Direct materials	28,600
Direct labor	20,867
Manufacturing overhead	36,763

The direct materials (rubber pads) are added at the end of the plating process. Conversion costs are incurred evenly throughout the process. Work in process of the Plating Department on March 1 consisted of 600 racks. The $26,370 beginning balance of "Work in Process—Plating" includes $14,400 of transferred-in cost and $11,970 of conversion cost. During March, 3,000 racks were transferred in from the Shaping Department. The Plating Department transferred 2,200 racks to Finished Goods Inventory in March and 1,400 were still in process on March 31. This ending inventory was 50% of the way through the plating process.

Requirements

1. Draw a time line for the Plating Department, similar to Exhibit 5-10.

2. Prepare the March production cost report for the Plating Department.

3. Journalize all transactions affecting the Plating Department during March, including the entries that have already been posted.

P5-58B Complete the five-step process in a later department *(Learning Objectives 1 & 5)*

Brookman uses four departments to produce plastic handles for screwdrivers: Mixing, Molding, Drying, and Assembly.

Brookman's Drying Department requires no direct materials. Conversion costs are incurred evenly throughout the drying process. Other process costing information follows:

Units:	
Beginning work in process	8,000 units
Transferred-in from the Molding Department	
during the period..	29,000 units
Completed during the period	17,000 units
Ending work in process (20% complete as to	
conversion work)...	20,000 units
Costs:	
Beginning work in process (transferred-in cost, $120;	
conversion cost, $240)..	$ 360
Transferred-in from the Molding Department during the period..	5,800
Conversion costs added during the period	2,700

After the drying process, the screwdrivers are completed by assembling the handles and shanks and packaging them for shipment to retail outlets.

Requirements

1. Draw a time line of the Drying Department's process, similar to the one in Exhibit 5-10.

2. Use the time line to compute the number of equivalent units of work performed by the Drying Department during the period, the cost per equivalent unit, and the total costs to account for.

3. Assign total costs to (a) units completed and transferred to the assembly operation and (b) units in the Drying Department's ending work in process inventory.

APPLY YOUR KNOWLEDGE

Decision Case

C5-59 Cost per unit and gross profit *(Learning Objective 5)*

Jimmy Jones operates Jimmy's Cricket Farm in Eatonton, Georgia. Jimmy's raises about 18 million crickets a month. Most are sold to pet stores at $12.60 for a box of 1,000 crickets. Pet stores sell the crickets for $0.05 to $0.10 each as live feed for reptiles.

Raising crickets requires a two-step process: incubation and brooding. In the first process, incubation employees place cricket eggs on mounds of peat moss to hatch. In the second process, employees move the newly hatched crickets into large boxes filled with cardboard dividers. Depending on the desired size, the crickets spend approximately two weeks in brooding before being shipped to pet stores. In the brooding process, Jimmy's crickets consume about 16 tons of food and produce 12 tons of manure.

Jones has invested $400,000 in the cricket farm, and he had hoped to earn a 24% annual rate of return, which works out to a 2% monthly return on his investment. After looking at the farm's bank balance, Jones fears he is not achieving this return. To get more accurate information on the farm's performance, Jones bought new accounting software that provides weighted-average process cost information. After Jones input the data, the software provided the following reports. However, Jones needs help interpreting these reports.

Jones does know that a unit of production is a box of 1,000 crickets. For example, in June's report, the 7,000 physical units of beginning work in process inventory are 7,000 boxes (each one of the 7,000 boxes contains 1,000 immature crickets). The finished goods inventory is zero because the crickets ship out as soon as they reach the required size. Monthly operating expenses total $2,000 (in addition to the costs that follow).

JIMMY'S CRICKET FARM
Brooding Department
Production Cost Report (part 1 of 2)
Month Ended June 30

			Equivalent Units		
Flow of Production	Flow of Physical Units	Transferred-in	Direct Materials	Conversion Costs
Units to account for:					
Beginning work in process inventory, June 1	7,000				
Transferred in during June	21,000				
Total units to account for	28,000				
Units accounted for:					
Completed and shipped out during June	19,000	19,000	19,000	19,000	
Ending work in process, June 30	9,000	9,000	7,200	3,600	
Total physical units accounted for	28,000				
Total equivalent units		28,000	26,200	22,600	

JIMMY'S CRICKET FARM
Brooding Department
Production Cost Report (part 2 of 2)
Month Ended June 30

	Transferred-in	Direct Materials	Conversion Costs	Total
Unit costs:				
Beginning work in process, June 1	$21,000	$ 39,940	$ 5,020	$ 65,960
Costs added during June	46,200	156,560	51,480	254,240
Total costs to account for	$67,200	$196,500	$56,500	$320,200
Divide by total equivalent units	÷ 28,000	÷ 26,200	÷ 22,600	
Cost per equivalent unit	$ 2.40	$ 7.50	$ 2.50	
Assignment of total cost:				
Units completed and shipped out during June	[19,000 × ($2.40 + $7.50 + $2.50)]			$235,600
Ending work in process, June 30:				
Transferred-in costs	[9,000 × $2.40]			21,600
Direct materials		[7,200 × $7.50]		54,000
Conversion costs			[3,600 × $2.50]	9,000
Total ending work in process, June 30				84,600
Total cost accounted for				$320,200

Requirements

Jimmy Jones has the following questions about the farm's performance during June:

1. What is the cost per box of crickets sold? (*Hint:* This is the cost of the boxes completed and shipped out of brooding.)
2. What is the gross profit per box?
3. How much operating income did Jimmy's Cricket Farm make in June?
4. What is the return on Jones's investment of $400,000 for the month of June? (Compute this as June's operating income divided by Jones's $400,000 investment, expressed as a percentage.)
5. What monthly operating income would provide a 2% monthly rate of return? What price per box would Jimmy's Cricket Farm have had to charge in June to achieve a 2% monthly rate of return?

Ethical Issue

I5-60 Ethical dilemma regarding percentage of completion *(Learning Objectives 2 & 5)*

Rick Penn and Joe Lopus are the plant managers for Pacific Lumber's particle board division. Pacific Lumber has adopted a JIT management philosophy. Each plant combines wood chips with chemical adhesives to produce particle board to order, and all production is sold as soon as it is completed. Laura Green is Pacific Lumber's regional controller. All of Pacific Lumber's plants and divisions send Green their production and cost information. While reviewing the numbers of the two particle board plants, she is surprised that both plants estimate their ending work in process inventories at 80% complete, which is higher than usual. Green calls Lopus, whom she has known for some time. He admits that to ensure that their division met its profit goal and that both he and Penn would make their bonus (which is based on division profit), he and Penn agreed to inflate the percentage completion. Lopus explains, "Determining the percentage completion always requires judgment. Whatever the percentage completion, we'll finish the work in process inventory first thing next year."

Requirements

1. How would inflating the percentage completion of ending work in process inventory help Penn and Lopus get their bonus?
2. The particle board division is the largest of Pacific Lumber's divisions. If Green does not correct the percentage completion of this year's ending work in process inventory, how will the misstatement affect Pacific Lumber's financial statements?
3. Evaluate Lopus's justification, including the effect, if any, on next year's financial statements.
4. In considering what Green should do, answer the following questions:
   a. What is the ethical question?
   b. What are the options?
   c. What are the possible consequences?
   d. What should Green do?

Team Project

T5-61   Calculating costs for a customer order *(Learning Objective 5)*

Hermiston Food Processors in Hermiston, Oregon, processes potatoes into French fries. Production requires two processes: cutting and cooking. The cutting process begins as scalding steam explodes the potatoes' brown skins. Workers using paring knives gouge out black spots before high-pressure water blasts potatoes through a pipe and into blades arranged in a quarter-inch grid. In the cooking process, the raw shoestring fries are cooked in a bleacher, dried, partially fried at 380°F, and immediately flash-frozen at minus 75°F before being dropped into five-pound bags. Direct materials are added at the beginning of the cutting process (potatoes) and at the end of the cooking process (bags). Conversion costs are incurred evenly throughout each process.

Assume that McDonald's offers Hermiston $0.40 per pound to supply restaurants in the Far East. If Hermiston accepts McDonald's offer, the cost (per equivalent unit) that Hermiston will incur to fill the McDonald's order equals the April cost per equivalent unit. J. R. Simlott, manager of the cooking process, must prepare a report explaining whether Hermiston should accept the offer. Simlott gathers the following information from April's cooking operations:

Lola Mendez manages the cutting process. She reports the following data for her department's April operations:

HERMISTON FOOD PROCESSORS	
Cooking Department	
April Activity and Costs	
Beginning work in process inventory, April 1	12,000 pounds
Raw shoestring fries started in April	129,000 pounds
French fries completed and transferred out	130,000 pounds
Ending work in process inventory (30% of way through process), April 30	11,000 pounds
Costs incurred *within* the cooking department in March to start the 12,000 pounds of beginning work in process inventory	$ 576
Costs added during April:	
Direct materials	6,500
Conversion costs	15,420

Split your team into two groups. Each group should meet separately before a meeting of the entire team.

Requirements

1. The first group takes the role of Simlott, manager of the cooking production process. Before meeting with the entire team, determine the maximum transferred-in cost per pound of raw shoestring fries the cooking department can incur from the cutting department if Hermiston is to make a profit on the McDonald's order. (*Hint:* You may find it helpful to prepare a time line and to use Exhibits 5-10–5-13 as a guide for your analysis.)

2. The second group takes the role of Mendez, manager of the cutting process. Before meeting with the entire team, determine the April cost per pound of raw shoestring fries in the cutting process. (*Hint:* You may find it helpful to prepare a time line and to use Exhibits 5-10–5-13 as a guide for your analysis.)

3. After each group meets, the entire team should meet to decide whether Hermiston should accept or reject the McDonald's offer.

Quick Check Answers

1. *b* 2. *d* 3. *d* 4. *a* 5. *b* 6. *b* 7. *b* 8. *c* 9. *c* 10. *d*

For online homework, exercises, and problems that provide you with immediate feedback, please visit www.myaccountinglab.com.

Discussion & Analysis

1. What characteristics of the product or manufacturing process would lead a company to use a process costing system? Give two examples of companies that are likely to be using process costing. What characteristics of the product or manufacturing process would lead a company to use a job costing system? Give two examples of companies that are likely to be using job costing.

2. How are process costing and job costing similar? How are they different?

3. What are conversion costs? In a job costing system, at least some conversion costs are assigned directly to products. Why do all conversion costs need to be assigned to processing departments in a process costing system?

4. Why not assign all costs of production during a period to only the completed units? What happens if a company does this? Why are the costs of production in any period allocated between completed units and units in work in process? Is there any situation where a company can assign all costs of production during a period to the completed units? If so, when?

5. What information generated by a process costing system can be used by management? How can management use this process costing information?

6. Why are the equivalent units for direct materials often different from the equivalent units for conversion costs in the same period?

7. Describe the flow of costs in a process costing system. List each type of journal entry that would be made and describe the purpose of that journal entry.

8. If a company has very little or no inventory, what effect does that lack of inventory have on its process costing system? What other benefits result from having very little to no inventory?

9. How does process costing differ between a first processing department and a second or later processing department?

10. "Process costing is easier to use than job costing." Do you agree or disagree with this statement? Explain your reasoning.

Application & Analysis

5-1 Process Costing in Real Companies

Go to YouTube.com and search for clips from the show *Unwrapped* on Food Network or *How It's Made* on Discovery Channel. Watch a clip for a product that would use process costing. For some of the questions, you may need to make assumptions about the production process (i.e., companies may not publicize their entire production process). If you make any assumptions, be sure to disclose both the assumption and your rationale for that assumption.

Basic Discussion Questions

1. Describe the product selected.

2. Summarize the production process.

3. Justify why you think this production process would dictate the use of a process costing system.

4. List at least two separate processes that are performed in creating this product. What departments would house these processes?

5. Describe at least one department that would have ending work in process. What do the units look like as they are "in process"?

Classroom Applications

Web: Post the discussion questions on an electronic discussion board. Have small groups of students choose a product for their group. Each student should watch the clip for the product for their group.

Classroom: Form groups of 3–4 students. Your group should choose a product and its clip to view. After viewing the clip, prepare a five minute presentation about your group's product and production process that addresses the listed questions.

Independent: Research answers to each of the questions. Turn in a 2–3 page typed paper (12 point font, double-spaced with 1" margins). Include references, including the URL of the clip that you viewed.

For additional Application & Analysis projects and implementation tips, see the Instructor Resources in MyAccountingLab.com.

DEMO DOC CHAPTER 5

Illustrating Process Costing

(Learning Objectives 2 & 3)

Clear Bottled Water produces bottled water. Clear Bottled Water has two production departments: Blending and Packaging. In the Blending Department, materials are added at the beginning of the process. Conversion costs are added evenly throughout the process for blending. Data for the month of April for the Blending Department are as follows:

Units:	
Beginning work in process	0
Started in production during April	116,000 units
Completed and transferred out to Packaging in April	98,000 units
Ending work in process inventory (70% completed)	18,000 units
Costs:	
Beginning work in process	0
Costs added during April:	
Direct materials	$54,520
Conversion costs	32,074
Total costs added during April	$86,594

Requirement

1. Use the five-step process to calculate (1) the cost of the units completed and transferred out to the Packaging Department and (2) the total cost of the units in the Blending Department's ending work in process inventory.

DEMO DOC Solutions

Requirement 1

Use the five-step process costing procedure to calculate (1) the cost of the units completed and transferred out to the Packaging Department and (2) the total cost of the units in the Blending Department's ending work in process inventory.

Step 1: Summarize the flow of physical units.

The first step tracks the physical movement of units into and out of the Blending Department during the month. We first ask ourselves, "How many physical units did the Blending Department work on during the month?" That is the total number of units the Blending Department must account for. Total units to account for (116,000) is the sum of the units in beginning work in process (0) plus the units started in production during the month (116,000).

Next we ask ourselves, "What happened to those units?" The Blending Department accounts for the whereabouts of every unit it worked on during the month by showing that the total units accounted for equals the total units to account for. Total units accounted for (116,000) is the sum of units completed and transferred out of the Blending Department in April (98,000) plus the units in ending work in process at April 30 (18,000).

Flow of Production	Step 1 Flow of Physical Units
Units to account for:	
Beginning work in process, April 1	0
Started in production during April	116,000
Total physical units to account for	116,000
Units accounted for:	
Completed and transferred out during April	98,000
Ending work in process, April 30	18,000
Total physical units accounted for	116,000
Total equivalent units	

Step 2: Compute output in terms of equivalent units.

Now that we have analyzed the flow of physical units, we compute the output in terms of equivalent units. First, the units completed and transferred out during April have 100% of their direct material and conversion costs. Therefore, the equivalent units for direct materials and conversion are the same as their physical units (98,000).

Next, consider the physical units (18,000) still in ending work in process. Materials are added at the beginning of the blending process, so 100% of the direct materials have been added. Therefore, the direct materials equivalent units are also 18,000 (18,000 physical units × 100%).

Conversion costs include both direct labor and manufacturing overhead. Conversion costs are added evenly throughout the blending process, so the conversion equivalent units for the ending work in process are the physical units in ending work in process (18,000) × the percentage complete, (70%), which equals 12,600.

Flow of Production	Step 1 Flow of Physical Units	Step 2 Equivalent Units Direct Materials	Conversion Costs
Units to account for:			
Beginning work in process, April 1	0		
Started in production during April	116,000		
Total physical units to account for	116,000		
Units accounted for:			
Completed and transferred out during April	98,000	98,000	98,000
Ending work in process, April 30	18,000	18,000	12,600
Total physical units accounted for	116,000		
Total equivalent units		116,000	110,600

The total equivalent units for direct materials is 116,000 (98,000 completed units + 18,000 in work in process). The total equivalent units for conversion costs is 110,600 (98,000 completed units + 12,600 in work in process).

Steps 3 and 4: Summarize total costs to account for and compute the cost per equivalent unit.

The next step is to summarize the total costs to account for, which consists of the costs in beginning work in process inventory plus the manufacturing costs incurred during April. The beginning inventory was zero. Direct materials of $54,520 and conversion costs of $32,074 were added during April. The total costs to account for is $86,594:

	Direct Materials	Conversion Costs	Total
Beginning work in process, April 1	$ 0	$ 0	$ 0
Costs added during April	54,520	32,074	86,594
Total costs to account for	$ 54,520	$ 32,074	$ 86,594
Divide by total equivalent units	÷ 116,000	÷ 110,600	
Cost per equivalent unit	$ 0.47	$ 0.29	

The cost per equivalent unit is computed by dividing the total costs to account for by the total equivalent units for each of the cost categories.

To calculate the cost per equivalent unit for direct materials, we divide the total direct materials costs of $54,520 by the equivalent units of direct materials, determined in Step 2 as 116,000 units. The result is $0.47 per equivalent unit for direct materials.

To calculate the cost per equivalent unit for conversion costs, we divide the total conversion cost of $32,074 by the number of equivalent units for conversion (which was determined in Step 2 to be 110,600). Dividing $32,074 by 110,600 gives us $0.29 per equivalent unit for conversion costs.

The cost of completing one unit in the Blending Department is $0.76 ($0.47 for direct materials plus $0.29 for conversion costs).

Step 5: Assign costs to units completed and to units in ending work in process inventory.

Because the units completed and transferred out were finished in the month of April, each unit is assigned the full unit cost of $0.76. Thus, the total cost to be assigned to the units completed and transferred out is $74,480 (98,000 units × $0.76). Shown another way, the total cost to be assigned to the units completed and transferred out is computed by multiplying the number of equivalent units (found in Step 2) by the cost per equivalent unit (found in Step 4):

$$98,000 \times \$0.47 = \$46,060 \text{ (direct materials)}$$
$$98,000 \times \$0.29 = \$28,420 \text{ (conversion costs)}$$
$$\$74,480$$

The total cost to be assigned to the units still in work in process inventory is computed in a similar manner. The number of equivalent units still in ending work in process (from Step 2) is multiplied by the cost per equivalent unit (found in Step 4):

$$18,000 \times \$0.47 = \$ 8,460 \text{ (direct materials)}$$
$$12,600 \times \$0.29 = \$ 3,654 \text{ (conversion costs)}$$
$$\$12,114$$

The total costs to account for ($86,594) is now properly divided between the units completed and transferred out to the Packaging Department ($74,480) and the units still in the Blending Department ending work in process inventory ($12,114).

	Direct Materials	Conversion Costs		Total
Completed and transferred out (98,000)	98,000 × ($0.47 + $0.29)		=	$74,480
Ending work in process inventory:				
Direct materials	18,000 × $0.47		=	$ 8,460
Conversion costs		12,600 × $0.29	=	3,654
Total cost of ending work in process inventory				$12,114
Total costs accounted for				$86,594

High above the rushing waters and mist of Niagara Falls,

hundreds of tourists from around the world return to the 512-room Embassy Suites to enjoy a complimentary afternoon refreshment hour, relax in the hotel's pool and spa, and rest in luxurious suites overlooking the falls. A similar scene occurs across the street at the Sheraton, Marriott, and DoubleTree hotels, as well as at thousands of other travel destinations around the world.

How do hotel managers set prices high enough to cover costs and earn a profit, but low enough to fill most rooms each night? How do they plan for higher occupancy during the busy summer months and lower occupancy during the off-season? They know how their costs behave. Some hotel costs, such as the complimentary morning breakfast and afternoon refreshment hour, vary with the number of guests staying each night. These *variable* costs rise and fall with the number of guests. But most hotel costs, such as depreciation on the building and furniture, stay the same whether 50 or 2,000 guests stay each night. These costs are *fixed*. Most hotel costs are fixed, so the extra costs to serve each additional guest are low. Once these costs are covered, the revenue from extra guests goes toward profits.

CHAPTER 6

Cost Behavior

Learning Objectives

1. Describe key characteristics and graphs of various cost behaviors

2. Use cost equations to express and predict costs

3. Use account analysis and scatter plots to analyze cost behavior

4. Use the high-low method to analyze cost behavior

5. Use regression analysis to analyze cost behavior

6. Prepare contribution margin income statements for service firms and merchandising firms

7. Use variable costing to prepare contribution margin income statements for manufacturers (Appendix)

Up to this point, we have focused our attention on product costing. We have discussed how managers use job costing or process costing to figure out the cost of making a product or providing a service. Product costs are useful for valuing inventory and calculating cost of goods sold. Product costs are also used as a starting place for setting sales prices. However, product costs are not very helpful for planning and some decision making because they contain a mixture of fixed and variable costs. Some of these costs change as volume changes, but other costs do not. To make good decisions and accurate projections, managers must understand **cost behavior**—that is, how costs change as volume changes. In this chapter, we discuss typical cost behaviors and explain methods managers use to determine how their costs behave. The Appendix discusses an alternative product costing system based on cost behavior that manufacturers can use for internal decision making. In the following chapters, we'll show how managers use cost behavior for planning and decision making.

Cost Behavior: How do Changes in Volume Affect Costs?

1 Describe key characteristics and graphs of various cost behaviors

The Embassy Suites at Niagara Falls has 512 guest suites that can accommodate between 512 and 2,048 people (four to a room) per night. This means that if every hotel room is booked (100% occupancy rate), the hotel can accommodate between 3,584 and 14,336 guests per week. How do managers plan for such a wide range of volume? They use historic occupancy patterns to determine the most likely range of volume. The room occupancy rate (percentage of rooms booked) varies depending on the season and day of the week. In addition to understanding occupancy patterns, managers must know how changes in volume (number of guests) affect their costs. We first consider three of the most common cost behaviors:

Why is this important?

"Cost behavior is a key component of most planning and operating decisions. Without a thorough understanding of cost behavior, managers are apt to make less profitable decisions."

1. **Variable costs** are costs that change in total in direct proportion to changes in volume. For Embassy Suites, complimentary morning breakfast, afternoon refreshments, and in-room toiletries (soap, shampoo, and lotion) are variable costs because these costs increase in total with the number of guests.

2. **Fixed costs** are costs that do not change in total despite wide changes in volume. For Embassy Suites, property taxes, insurance, and depreciation on the hotel building and furnishings are fixed costs that will be the same regardless of the number of hotel guests.

3. **Mixed costs** are costs that change in total, but *not* in direct proportion to changes in volume. Mixed costs have both variable and fixed components. For Embassy Suites, utilities (electricity, gas, water) are mixed costs. Some utility costs will be incurred no matter how many guests stay the night. However, utility costs will also rise as the number of guests turning up the heat or air conditioning, taking showers, and using freshly laundered linens rises.

Variable Costs

Every guest at Embassy Suites is entitled to a complimentary morning breakfast and afternoon refreshment hour (drinks and snacks). In addition, guests receive complimentary toiletries, including shampoo, soap, lotion, and mouthwash, that they typically use or take with them. Let's assume that these toiletries cost the hotel $3 per guest and that the breakfast and refreshment hour costs the hotel $10 per guest. Exhibit 6-1 graphs Embassy

EXHIBIT 6-1 **Variable Costs**

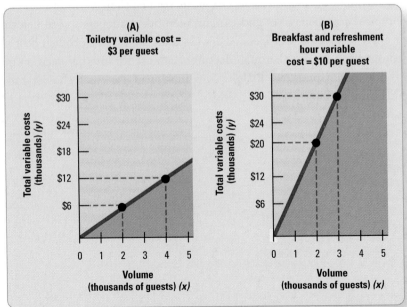

Suites' \$3-per-guest toiletry cost and the \$10-per-guest breakfast and refreshment hour cost. The vertical axis (y-axis) shows total variable costs, while the horizontal axis (x-axis) shows total volume of activity (thousands of guests, in this case).

Look at the total variable toiletry costs in Exhibit 6-1(a). If there are no guests, Embassy Suites doesn't incur any costs for the toiletries, so the total variable cost line begins at the bottom left corner. This point is called the *origin*, and it represents zero volume and zero cost. Total variable cost graphs always begin at the origin. The *slope* of the total variable cost line is the *variable cost per unit of activity*. In Exhibit 6-1(a), the slope of the toiletry variable cost line is \$3 because the hotel spends an additional \$3 on toiletries for each additional guest. If the hotel serves 2,000 guests, it will spend a total of \$6,000 on complimentary toiletries. Doubling the number of guests to 4,000 likewise doubles the total variable cost to \$12,000. This example illustrates several important points about variable costs—total variable costs change in *direct proportion* to changes in volume. If volume of activity doubles, total variable costs double. If volume triples, total variable costs triple.

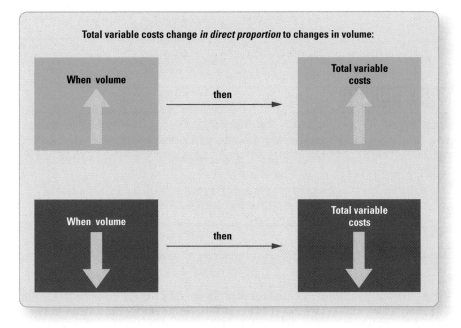

Managers do not need to rely on graphs to predict total variable costs at different volumes of activity. They can use a **cost equation**, a mathematical equation for a straight line, to express how a cost behaves. On cost graphs like the ones pictured in Exhibit 6-1, the vertical (y-axis) always shows total costs, while the horizontal axis (x-axis) shows volume of activity. Therefore, any variable cost line can be mathematically expressed as follows:

Total variable cost (y) = Variable cost per unit of activity (v) × Volume of activity (x)

Or simply:

$$y = vx$$

The hotel's total toiletry cost is as follows:

$$y = \$3x$$

Use cost equations to express and predict costs   **2**

Why is this important?

"Cost equations help managers foresee what their total costs will be at different operating volumes so that they can better plan for the future."

All references to Embassy Suites in this hypothetical example were created by the author solely for academic purposes and are not intended, in any way, to represent the actual business practices of, or costs incurred by, Embassy Suites.

where,

$$y = \text{total toiletry cost}$$
$$\$3 = \text{variable cost per guest}$$
$$x = \text{number of guests}$$

We can confirm the observations made in Exhibit 6-1(a) using the cost equation. If the hotel has no guests ($x = 0$), total toiletry costs are zero, as shown in the graph. If the hotel has 2,000 guests, total toiletry costs will be as follows:

$$y = \$3 \text{ per guest} \times 2,000 \text{ guests}$$
$$= \$6,000$$

If the hotel has 4,000 guests, managers will expect total toiletry costs to be as follows:

$$y = \$3 \text{ per guest} \times 4,000 \text{ guests}$$
$$= \$12,000$$

STOP & THINK

If the hotel serves 3,467 guests next week, how much will the hotel spend on complimentary toiletries?
Answer: You would have a hard time answering this question by simply looking at the graph in Exhibit 6-1(a), but cost equations can be used for any volume. We "plug in" the expected volume to our variable cost equation as follows:

$$y = \$3 \text{ per guest} \times 3,467 \text{ guests}$$
$$= \$10,401$$

Management expects complimentary toiletries next week to cost about $10,401.

Now, look at Exhibit 6-1(b), the total variable costs for the complimentary breakfast and refreshment hour. The slope of the line is $10, representing the cost of providing each guest with the complimentary breakfast and refreshments. We can express the total breakfast and refreshment hour cost as follows:

$$y = \$10x$$

where,

$$y = \text{total breakfast and refreshment hour cost}$$
$$\$10 = \text{variable cost per guest}$$
$$x = \text{number of guests}$$

The total cost of the breakfast and refreshment hour for 2,000 guests is as follows:

$$y = \$10 \text{ per guest} \times 2,000 \text{ guests}$$
$$= \$20,000$$

This is much higher than the $6,000 toiletry cost for 2,000 guests, so the slope of the line is much steeper than it was for the toiletries. *The higher the variable cost per unit of activity (v), the steeper the slope of the total variable cost line.*

Both graphs in Exhibit 6-1 show how *total* variable costs vary with the number of guests. *But note that the variable cost per guest (v) remains constant in each of the graphs.*

That is, Embassy Suites incurs $3 in toiletry costs and $10 in breakfast and refreshment hour costs for each guest no matter how many guests the hotel serves. Some key points to remember about variable costs are shown in Exhibit 6-2.

EXHIBIT 6-2   Key Characteristics of Variable Costs

- *Total* variable costs change in *direct proportion* to changes in volume
- The *variable cost per unit of activity* (*v*) remains constant and is the slope of the variable cost line
- Total variable cost graphs always begin at the origin (if volume is zero, total variable costs are zero)
- Total variable costs can be expressed as follows:

$$y = vx,$$

where,

y = total variable cost

v = variable cost per unit of activity

x = volume of activity

Fixed Costs

In contrast to total variable costs, total fixed costs do *not* change over wide ranges of volume. Many of Embassy Suites' costs are fixed because the hotel continues to operate daily regardless of the number of guests. Some of the hotel's fixed costs include the following:

- Property taxes and insurance
- Depreciation and maintenance on parking ramp, hotel, and room furnishings
- Pool, fitness room, and spa upkeep
- Cable TV and wireless Internet access for all rooms
- Salaries of hotel department managers (housekeeping, food service, special events, etc.)

Most of these costs are **committed fixed costs**, meaning that the hotel is locked in to these costs because of previous management decisions. For example, as soon as the hotel was built, management became locked in to a certain level of property taxes and depreciation, simply because of the location and size of the hotel, and management's choice of furnishings and amenities (pool, fitness room, restaurant, and so forth). Management has little or no control over these committed fixed costs in the short run.

However, the hotel also incurs **discretionary fixed costs**, such as advertising expenses, that are a result of annual management decisions. Companies have more control over discretionary fixed costs because the companies can adjust the costs as necessary in the short run.

Suppose Embassy Suites incurs $100,000 of fixed costs each week. In Exhibit 6-3, the vertical axis (y-axis) shows total fixed costs while the horizontal axis (x-axis) plots volume of activity (thousands of guests). The graph shows total fixed costs as a *flat line* that intersects the y-axis at $100,000 (this is known as the vertical intercept) because the hotel will incur the same $100,000 of fixed costs regardless of the number of guests that stay during the week.

EXHIBIT 6-3   Fixed Costs

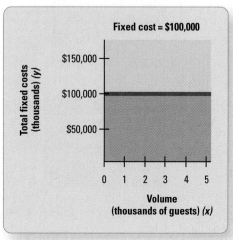

The cost equation for a fixed cost is as follows:

$$\text{Total fixed cost } (y) = \text{Fixed amount over a period of time } (f)$$

Or simply,

$$y = f$$

Embassy Suites' *weekly* fixed cost equation is as follows:

$$y = \$100{,}000$$

where,

$$y = \text{total fixed cost per week}$$

In contrast to the *total fixed costs* shown in Exhibit 6-3, the *fixed cost per guest* depends on the number of guests. If the hotel serves 2,000 guests during the week, the fixed cost per guest is as follows:

$$\$100{,}000 \div 2{,}000 \text{ guests} = \$50/\text{guest}$$

If the number of guests *doubles* to 4,000, the fixed cost per guest is *cut in half*:

$$\$100{,}000 \div 4{,}000 \text{ guests} = \$25/\text{guest}$$

The fixed cost per guest is *inversely proportional* to the number of guests. When volume *increases*, the fixed cost per guest *decreases*. When volume *decreases*, the fixed cost per guest *increases*.

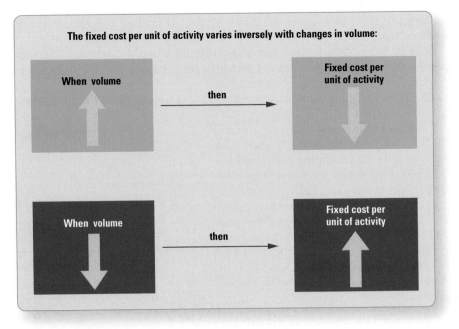

Key points to remember about fixed costs appear in Exhibit 6-4.

EXHIBIT 6-4 **Key Characteristics of Fixed Costs**

- *Total* fixed costs stay *constant* over a wide range of volume
- Fixed costs *per unit of activity* vary *inversely* with changes in volume:
    – Fixed cost per unit of activity *increases* when volume *decreases*
    – Fixed cost per unit of activity *decreases* when volume *increases*
- Total fixed cost graphs are always flat lines with no slope that intersect the *y*-axis at a level equal to total fixed costs
- Total fixed costs can be expressed as $y = f$,
    where
        y = total fixed cost
        f = fixed cost over a given period of time

STOP & THINK

Compute the (a) total fixed cost and (b) fixed cost per guest if the hotel reaches full occupancy of 14,336 guests next week (512 rooms booked with four people per room). Compare the fixed cost per guest at full occupancy to the fixed cost per guest when only 2,000 guests stay during the week. Explain why hotels and other businesses like to operate near 100% capacity.

Answer:

a.   Total fixed costs do not react to wide changes in volume; therefore, total fixed costs will still be $100,000.

b.   Fixed costs per unit decrease as volume increases. At full occupancy, the fixed cost per guest is as follows:

$$\$100,000 \div 14,336 \text{ guests} = \$6.98 \text{ (rounded) per guest}$$

When only 2,000 guests stay, the fixed cost per guest is much higher ($50 = $100,000 ÷ 2,000 guests). Businesses like to operate near full capacity because it lowers their fixed cost per unit. A lower cost per unit gives businesses the flexibility to lower their prices to compete more effectively.

Mixed Costs

Mixed costs contain both variable and fixed cost components. Embassy Suites' utilities are mixed costs because the hotel requires a certain amount of utilities just to operate. However, the more guests at the hotel, the more water, electricity, and gas required. Exhibit 6-5 illustrates mixed costs.

EXHIBIT 6-5 **Mixed Costs**

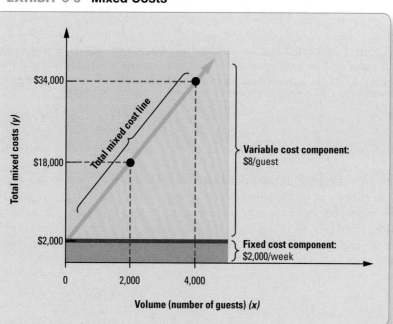

For example, let's assume that utilities for the common areas of the hotel and unoccupied rooms cost $2,000 per week. In addition, these costs increase by $8 per guest as each guest cools or heats his or her room, takes showers, turns on the TV and lights, and uses freshly laundered sheets and towels.

Notice the two components—variable and fixed—of the mixed cost in Exhibit 6-5. Similar to a variable cost, the total mixed cost line increases as the volume of activity increases. However, *the line does **not** begin at the origin.* Rather, it intersects the y-axis at a level equal to the fixed cost component. Even if no guests stay this week, the hotel will still incur $2,000 of utilities cost.

Managers can once again use a cost equation to express the mixed cost line so that they can predict total mixed costs at different volumes. The mixed cost equation simply *combines* the variable cost and fixed cost equations:

$$\text{Total mixed costs} = \text{Variable cost component} + \text{Fixed cost component}$$
$$y = vx + f$$

Embassy Suites' weekly utilities cost equation is as follows:

$$y = \$8x + \$2,000$$

where,

$$y = \text{total utilities cost per week}$$
$$x = \text{number of guests}$$

If the hotel serves 2,000 guests this week, it expects utilities to cost:

$$y = (\$8 \text{ per guest} \times 2,000 \text{ guests}) + \$2,000$$
$$= \$18,000$$

If the hotel serves 4,000 guests this week, it expects utilities to cost:

$$y = (\$8 \text{ per guest} \times 4,000 \text{ guests}) + \$2,000$$
$$= \$34,000$$

Total mixed costs increase as volume increases, *but **not** in direct proportion to changes in volume.* The total mixed cost did *not* double when volume doubled. This is because of the fixed cost component. Additionally, consider the mixed cost *per guest*:

If the hotel serves 2,000 guests: $18,000 total cost ÷ 2,000 guests = $9.00 per guest
If the hotel serves 4,000 guests: $34,000 total cost ÷ 4,000 guests = $8.50 per guest

The mixed cost per guest did *not* decrease by half when the hotel served twice as many guests. This is because of the variable cost component. Mixed costs per unit decrease as volume increases, but ***not** in direct proportion* to changes in volume. Because mixed costs contain both fixed cost and variable cost components, they behave differently than purely variable costs and purely fixed costs. Key points to remember about mixed costs appear in Exhibit 6-6.

EXHIBIT 6-6   Key Characteristics of Mixed Costs

- *Total* mixed costs increase as volume increases because of the variable cost component
- Mixed costs *per unit* decrease as volume increases because of the fixed cost component
- Total mixed cost graphs slope upward but do *not* begin at the origin—they intersect the y-axis at the level of fixed costs
- Total mixed costs can be expressed as a *combination* of the variable and fixed cost equations:

Total mixed costs = variable cost component + fixed cost component

$$y = vx + f$$

where,

y = total mixed cost

v = variable cost per unit of activity (slope)

x = volume of activity

f = fixed cost over a given period of time (vertical intercept)

STOP & THINK

If your cell phone plan charges $10 per month plus $0.15 for each minute you talk, how could you express the monthly cell phone bill as a cost equation? How much will your cell phone bill be if you (a) talk 100 minutes this month or (b) talk 200 minutes this month? If you double your talk time from 100 to 200 minutes, does your total cell phone bill double? Explain.

Answer: The cost equation for the monthly cell phone bill is as follows:

$$y = \$0.15x + \$10$$

where,

y = total cell phone bill for the month

x = number of minutes used

a.   At 100 minutes, the total cost is $25 [= ($0.15 per minute × 100 minutes) + $10].

b.   At 200 minutes, the total cost is $40 [= ($0.15 per minute × 200 minutes) + $10].

The cell phone bill does not double when talk time doubles. The variable portion of the bill doubles from $15 ($0.15 × 100 minutes) to $30 ($0.15 × 200 minutes), but the fixed portion of the bill stays constant ($10).

Relevant Range

Managers always need to keep their **relevant range** in mind when predicting total costs. The relevant range is the band of volume where the following remain constant:

- *Total fixed costs*

- The *variable cost per unit*

A change in cost behavior means a change to a different relevant range.

Let's consider how the concept of relevant range applies to Embassy Suites. As shown in Exhibit 6-3, the hotel's current fixed costs are $100,000 per week. However, since the hotel's popularity continues to grow, room occupancy rates continue to increase. As a result, guests are becoming dissatisfied with the amount of time they have to wait for breakfast tables and elevators. To increase customer satisfaction, management is deciding whether to expand the breakfast facilities and add a 30-passenger elevator to its existing bank of elevators. This expansion, if carried out, will increase the hotel's fixed costs to a new level. Exhibit 6-7 illustrates the hotel's current relevant range and future potential relevant range for fixed costs.

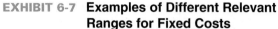

EXHIBIT 6-7   Examples of Different Relevant Ranges for Fixed Costs

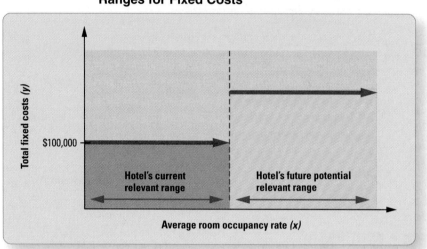

Does the concept of relevant range apply only to fixed costs? No, it also applies to variable costs. As shown in Exhibit 6-1, the hotel's current variable cost for toiletries is $3 per guest. However, as room occupancy rates continue to grow, management hopes to negotiate greater volume discounts on the toiletries from its suppliers. These volume discounts will decrease the variable toiletries cost per guest (for example, down to $2.75 per guest). Exhibit 6-8 illustrates the hotel's current relevant range and future potential relevant range for variable toiletries costs.

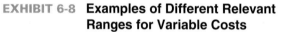

EXHIBIT 6-8   Examples of Different Relevant Ranges for Variable Costs

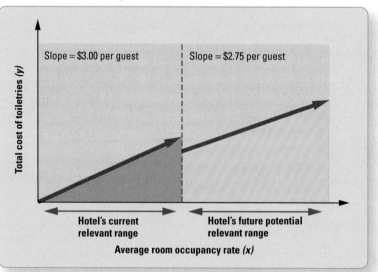

Why is the concept of relevant range important? Managers can predict costs accurately only if they use cost information for the appropriate relevant range. For example, think about your cell phone plan. Many cell phone plans offer a large block of "free" minutes for a set fee each month. If the user exceeds the allotted minutes, the cell phone company charges an additional per-minute fee. Exhibit 6-9 shows a cell phone plan in which the first 1,000 minutes of call time each month cost $50. After the 1,000 minutes are used, the user must pay an additional $0.30 per minute for every minute of call time.

This cell phone plan has two relevant ranges. The first relevant range extends from 0 to 1,000 minutes. In this range, the $50 fee behaves strictly as a fixed cost. You could use 0, 100, or 975 minutes and you would still pay a flat $50 fee that month. The second relevant range starts at 1,001 minutes and extends indefinitely. In this relevant range, the cost is mixed: $50 plus $0.30 per minute. To forecast your cell phone bill each month, you need to know in which relevant range you plan to operate. The same holds true for businesses: To accurately predict costs, they need to know the relevant range in which they plan to operate.

EXHIBIT 6-9 **Example of Relevant Ranges**

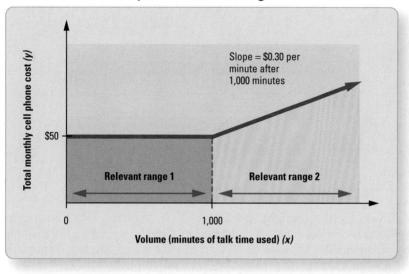

Other Cost Behaviors

While many business costs behave as variable, fixed, or mixed costs, some costs do not neatly fit these patterns. We'll briefly describe other cost behaviors you may encounter.

Step costs resemble stair steps: They are fixed over a small range of activity and then jump up to a new fixed level with moderate changes in volume. Hotels, restaurants, hospitals, and educational institutions typically experience step costs. For example, states usually require day-care centers to limit the caregiver-to-child ratio to 1:7—that is, there must be one caregiver for every seven children. As shown in Exhibit 6-10, a day-care center that takes on an eighth child must incur the cost of employing another caregiver. The new caregiver can watch the eighth through fourteenth child enrolled at the day-care center. If the day-care center takes on a fifteenth child, management will once again need to hire another caregiver, costing another $15,000 in salary. The same step cost patterns occur with hotels (maid-to-room ratio), restaurants (server-to-table ratio), hospitals (nurse-to-bed ratio), and schools (teacher-to-student ratio).

EXHIBIT 6-10 **Step Costs**

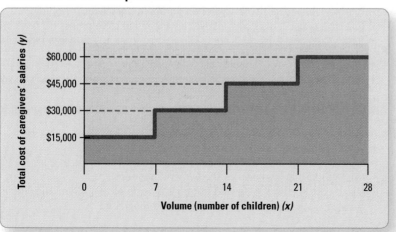

Step costs differ from fixed costs only in that they "step up" to a new relevant range with relatively small changes in volume. Fixed costs hold constant over much larger ranges of volume.

As shown by the red lines in Exhibit 6-11, **curvilinear costs** are not linear (not a straight line) and, therefore, do not fit into any neat pattern.

EXHIBIT 6-11 **Curvilinear Costs and Straight-Line Approximations**

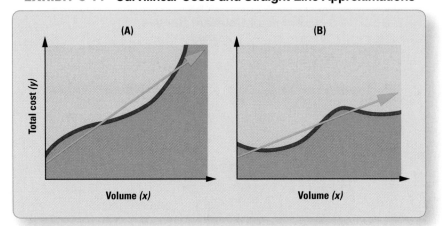

As shown by the straight green arrows in Exhibit 6-11, businesses usually *approximate* these types of costs as mixed costs. Sometimes managers also approximate step costs the same way: They simply draw a straight mixed cost line through the steps. If managers need more accurate predictions, they can simply break these types of costs into smaller relevant ranges and make their predictions based on the particular relevant range. For example, the day-care center may want to predict total caregiver salaries if it enrolls 26 children. The manager knows this enrollment falls into the relevant range of 21 to 28 children, where he or she needs to employ four caregivers. The manager can then predict total caregiver salaries to be $60,000 (four caregivers × $15,000 salary per caregiver).

We have just described the most typical cost behaviors. In the next part of the chapter, we will discuss methods managers use for determining how their costs behave.

Decision Guidelines

Cost Behavior

Suppose you manage a local fitness club. To be an effective manager, you need to know how the club's costs behave. Here are some decisions you will need to make.

Decision	Guidelines
How can you tell if a *total* cost is variable, fixed, or mixed?	• Total variable costs rise in *direct proportion* to increases in volume. • Total fixed costs stay *constant* over a wide range of volumes. • Total mixed costs rise, but *not* in direct proportion to increases in volume.
How can you tell if a *per-unit* cost is variable, fixed, or mixed?	• On a per-unit basis, variable costs stay constant. • On a per-unit basis, fixed costs decrease in proportion to increases in volume (that is to say they are inversely proportional). • On a per-unit basis, mixed costs decrease, but not in direct proportion to increases in volume.
How can you tell by looking at a graph if a cost is variable, fixed, or mixed?	• Variable cost lines slope upward and begin at the origin. • Fixed cost lines are flat (no slope) and intersect the y-axis at a level equal to total fixed costs (this is known as the vertical intercept). • Mixed cost lines slope upward but do *not* begin at the origin. They intersect the y-axis at a level equal to their fixed cost component.

Decision	Guidelines
How can you mathematically express different cost behaviors?	• Cost equations mathematically express cost behavior using the equation for a straight line:

$$y = vx + f$$

where,

> y = total cost
>
> v = variable cost per unit of activity (slope)
>
> x = volume of activity
>
> f = fixed cost (the vertical intercept)

• For a variable cost, f is zero, leaving the following:

$$y = vx$$

• For a fixed cost, v is zero, leaving the following:

$$y = f$$

• Because a mixed cost has both a fixed cost component and a variable cost component, its cost equation is:

$$y = vx + f$$

Summary Problem 1

The previous manager of Fitness-for-Life started the following schedule, but left before completing it. The manager wasn't sure but thought the club's fixed operating costs were $10,000 per month and the variable operating costs were $1 per member. The club's existing facilities could serve up to 750 members per month.

Requirements

1. Complete the following schedule for different levels of monthly membership assuming the previous manager's cost behavior estimates are accurate:

Monthly Operating Costs	100 Members	500 Members	750 Members
Total variable costs....................			
Total fixed costs........................			
Total operating costs.................			
Variable cost per member...........			
Fixed cost per member..............			
Average cost per member			

2. As the manager of the fitness club, why shouldn't you use the average cost per member to predict total costs at different levels of membership?

continued

Solution

Requirement 1

As volume increases, fixed costs stay constant in total but decrease on a per-unit basis. As volume increases, variable costs stay constant on a per-unit basis but increase in total in direct proportion to increases in volume:

	100 Members	500 Members	750 Members
Total variable costs.........................	$ 100	$ 500	$ 750
Total fixed costs.............................	10,000	10,000	10,000
Total operating costs......................	$10,100	$10,500	$10,750
Variable cost per member..............	$ 1.00	$ 1.00	$ 1.00
Fixed cost per member	100.00	20.00	13.33
Average cost per member	$101.00	$ 21.00	$ 14.33

Requirement 2

The average cost per member should not be used to predict total costs at different volumes of membership because it changes as volume changes. The average cost per member decreases as volume increases due to the fixed component of the club's operating costs. Managers should base cost predictions on cost behavior patterns, not on the average cost per member.

How do Managers Determine Cost Behavior?

In real life, managers need to figure out how their costs behave before they can make predictions and good business decisions. In this section, we discuss the most common ways of determining cost behavior.

Account Analysis

3 | Use account analysis and scatter plots to analyze cost behavior

When performing **account analysis**, managers use their judgment to classify each general ledger account as a variable, fixed, or mixed cost. For example, by looking at invoices from his or her supplier, the hotel manager knows that every guest packet of toiletries costs $3. Because guests use or take these toiletries, the total toiletries cost rises in direct proportion to the number of guests. These facts allow the manager to classify the complimentary toiletries expense account as a variable cost.

Likewise, the hotel manager uses account analysis to determine how the depreciation expense accounts behave. Because the hotel uses straight-line depreciation on the parking ramp, building, and furnishings, the manager would classify the depreciation expense accounts as fixed costs. Thus, the manager can use this knowledge of cost behavior and his or her judgment to classify many accounts as variable or fixed.

Scatter Plots

The hotel manager also knows that many of the hotel's costs, such as utilities, are mixed. But how does the manager figure out the portion of the mixed cost that is fixed and the portion that is variable? In other words, how does the manager know from looking at the monthly utility bills that the hotel's utilities cost about $2,000 per week plus $8 more for every guest? One way of figuring this out is by collecting and analyzing historical data about costs and volume.

For example, let's assume that the hotel has collected the information shown in Exhibit 6-12 about last year's guest volume and utility costs.

EXHIBIT 6-12 **Historical Information on Guest Volume and Utility Costs**

Month	Guest Volume (x)	Utility Costs (y)
January	13,250	$114,000
February	15,200	136,000
March	17,600	135,000
April	18,300	157,000
May	22,900	195,400
June	24,600	207,800
July	25,200	209,600
August	24,900	208,300
September	22,600	196,000
October	20,800	176,400
November	18,300	173,600
December	15,420	142,000

As you can see, the hotel's business is seasonal. More people visit in the summer. However, special events such as the annual Festival of Lights, business conferences, and the nearby casino attract people to the hotel throughout the year.

Once the data has been collected, the manager creates a **scatter plot** of the data.

A scatter plot, which graphs the historical cost data on the y-axis and volume data on the x-axis, helps managers visualize the relationship between the cost and the volume of activity (number of guests, in our example). If there is a fairly strong relationship between the cost and volume, the data points will fall in a linear pattern, meaning they will resemble something close to a straight line. However, if there is little or no relationship between the cost and volume, the data points will appear almost random.

Exhibit 6-13 shows a scatter plot of the data in Exhibit 6-12. Scatter plots can be prepared by hand, but they are simpler to create using Microsoft Excel (see the "Technology Makes It Simple" feature). Notice how the data points fall in a pattern that resembles something *close* to a straight line. This shows us that there is a

Why is this important?

"Scatter plots help managers easily visualize the relationship between cost and volume."

EXHIBIT 6-13 **Scatter Plot of Monthly Data**

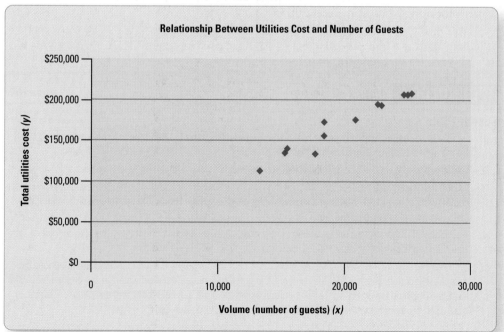

strong relationship between the number of guests and the hotel's utility costs. In other words, the number of guests could be considered a driver of the hotel's utilities costs (recall from our discussion of ABC in Chapter 4 that cost drivers are activities that cause costs to be incurred). On the other hand, if there were a *weaker* relationship between the number of guests and the utility costs, the data points would not fall in such a tight pattern. They would be more loosely scattered, but still in a semilinear pattern. If there were *no* relationship between the number of guests and the utility costs, the data points would appear almost random.

Why is this important? If the data points suggest a fairly weak relationship between the cost and the volume of the chosen activity, any cost equation based on that data will not be very useful for predicting future costs. If this is the case, the manager should consider using a different activity for modeling cost behavior. For example, many hotels use "occupancy rate" (the percentage of rooms rented) rather than number of guests as a basis for explaining and predicting variable and mixed costs.

Scatter plots are also very useful because they allow managers to identify **outliers**, or abnormal data points. Outliers are data points that do not fall in the same general pattern as the other data points. Since all data points in Exhibit 6-13 fall in the same basic pattern, no outliers appear to exist in our data. However, if a manager sees a potential outlier in the data, he or she should first determine whether the data is correct. Perhaps a clerical error was made when gathering or inputting the data. However, if the data is correct, the manager may need to consider whether to delete that data from any further analysis.

Once the scatter plot has been prepared and examined for outliers, the next step is to determine the cost behavior that best describes the historical data points pictured in the scatter plot. Take a moment and pencil in the cost behavior line that you think best represents the data points in Exhibit 6-13. Where does your line intersect the y-axis? At the origin or above it? In other words, does the utilities cost appear to be a purely variable cost or a mixed cost? If it's a mixed cost, what portion of it is fixed?

Instead of guessing, managers can use one of the following methods to estimate the cost equation that describes the data in the scatter plot:

- High-low method

- Regression analysis

The biggest difference between these methods is that the high-low method *uses only two* of the historical data points for this estimate, whereas regression analysis uses *all* of the historical data points. Therefore, regression analysis is theoretically the better of the two methods.

We'll describe both of these methods in the next sections. Before continuing, check out the "Technology Makes It Simple" feature. It shows you just how easy it is to make a scatter plot using Microsoft Excel 2007.

TECHNOLOGY *makes it simple*   Excel 2007

Scatter Plots

1. In an Excel 2007 spreadsheet, type in your data as pictured in Exhibit 6-12. Put the volume data in one column and the associated cost data in the next column.

2. Highlight all of the volume and cost data with your cursor.

3. Click on the "Insert" tab on the menu bar and then choose "Scatter" as the chart type. Next, click the plain scatter plot (without any lines). You'll see the scatter plot on your screen. Make sure the volume data is on the x-axis and the cost data is on the y-axis.

4. To add labels for the scatter plot and titles for each axis, choose "Layout 1" from the "Chart Layout" menu tab. Customize the titles and labels to reflect your data set.

5. If you want to change the way your graph looks, right-click on the graph to check out customizing options. For example, if your data consists of large numbers, the graph may not automatically start at the origin. If you want to see the origin on the graph, right-click on either axis (where the number values are) and choose "Format Axis." Then, fix the minimum value at zero.

High-Low Method

The **high-low method** is an easy way to estimate the variable and fixed cost components of a mixed cost. The high-low method basically fits a mixed cost line through the highest and lowest *volume* data points, as shown in Exhibit 6-14, hence the name *high-low*. The high-low method produces the cost equation describing this mixed cost line.

Use the high-low method to analyze cost behavior   **4**

EXHIBIT 6-14   Mixed Cost Line Using High-Low Method

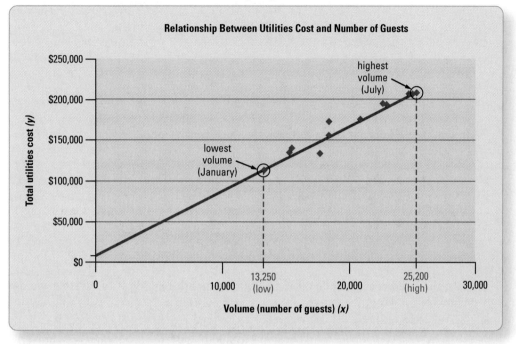

To use the high-low method, we must first identify the months with the highest and lowest volume of activity. Looking at Exhibit 6-12, we see that the hotel served the *most* guests in July and the *fewest* guests in January. *Therefore, we use the data from only these two months in our analysis. We ignore data from all other months.* Even if a month other than July had the highest utility cost, we would still use July. Why? Because we choose the "high" data point based on the month with the highest volume of activity (number of guests)—not the highest cost. We choose the "low" data point in a similar fashion.

Step 1) The first step is to find *the slope of the mixed cost line* that connects the January and July data points. The slope is the variable cost per unit of activity. We can determine the slope of a line as "rise over run." The *rise* is simply the difference in cost between the high and low data points (July and January in our case), while the *run* is the difference in *volume* between the high and low data points:

$$\text{Slope} = \text{Variable cost per unit of activity } (v) = \frac{\text{Rise}}{\text{Run}} = \frac{\text{Change in cost}}{\text{Change in volume}} = \frac{y\,(\text{high}) - y\,(\text{low})}{x\,(\text{high}) - x\,(\text{low})}$$

Using the data from July (as our high) and January (as our low), we calculate the slope as follows:

$$\frac{(\$209{,}600 - \$114{,}000)}{(25{,}200 \text{ guests} - 13{,}250 \text{ guests})} = \$8 \text{ per guest}$$

The slope of the mixed cost line, or variable cost per unit of activity, is $8 per guest.

Step 2) The second step is to find the vertical intercept—the place where the line connecting the January and July data points intersects the y-axis. This is the fixed cost component of the mixed cost. We insert the slope found in Step 1 ($8 per guest) and the volume and cost data from *either* the high or low month into a mixed cost equation:

$$\text{Total mixed costs} = \text{Variable cost component} + \text{Fixed cost component}$$
$$y \quad = \quad vx \quad + \quad f$$

For example, we can insert July's cost and volume data as follows:

$$\$209,600 = (\$8 \text{ per guest} \times 25,200 \text{ guests}) + f$$

And then solve for f:

$$f = \$8,000$$

Or we can use January's data to reach the same conclusion:

$$y \quad = \quad vx \quad + f$$
$$\$114,000 = (\$8 \text{ per guest} \times 13,250 \text{ guests}) + f$$

And then solve for f:

$$f = \$8,000$$

Thus, the fixed cost component is $8,000 per month regardless of whether we use July or January's data.

Step 3) Using the variable cost per unit of activity found in Step 1 ($8 per guest) and the fixed cost component found in Step 2 ($8,000), write the equation representing the costs' behavior. This is the equation for the line connecting the January and July data points on our graph.

$$y = \$8x + \$8,000$$

where,

$$y = \text{total } monthly \text{ utilities cost}$$
$$x = \text{number of guests}$$

Recall that this equation was based on *monthly* utility bills and *monthly* guest volume. In our discussion of the hotel's mixed costs in the first half of the chapter, we said that the mixed utilities cost was $8 per guest plus $2,000 per *week*. The manager had used the high-low method; but because there are about four weeks in a month, the hotel manager approximated the fixed costs to be about $2,000 *per week* ($8,000 per month ÷ approximately four weeks per month).

One major drawback of the high-low method is that it uses only two data points: January and July. Because we ignored every other month, the line might not be representative of those months. In our example, the high-low line is representative of the other data points, but in other situations, it may not be. Despite this drawback, the high-low method is quick and easy to use.

Regression Analysis

 5 Use regression analysis to analyze cost behavior

Regression analysis is a statistical procedure for determining the line and cost equation that best fits the data by using *all of the data points, not just the high-volume and low-volume data points*. In fact, some refer to regression analysis as "the line of best fit." Therefore, it is usually more accurate than the high-low method. A statistic (called the R-square) generated by regression analysis also tells us *how well* the line fits the data points. Regression analysis is tedious to complete by hand but simple to do using Microsoft Excel (see the

"Technology Makes It Simple" feature on page 326). Many graphing calculators also perform regression analysis.

Regression analysis using Microsoft Excel gives us the output shown in Exhibit 6-15.

EXHIBIT 6-15   Output of Microsoft Excel Regression Analysis

Regression Statistics

Multiple R	0.973273
R Square	0.94726
Adjusted R Square	0.941986
Standard Error	8053.744
Observations	12

ANOVA

	df	SS	MS	F	Significance F
Regression	1	11650074512	1.17E + 10	179.6110363	1.02696E-07
Residual	10	648627988.2	64862799		
Total	11	12298702500			

	Coefficients	Standard Error	t Stat	P-value	Lower 95%	Upper 95%	Lower 95.0%	Upper 95.0%
Intercept	14538.05	11898.3624	1.221853	0.249783701	-11973.15763	41049.25	-11973.16	41049.25
X Variable 1	7.849766	0.585720166	13.4019	1.02696E-07	6.5446997	9.154831	6.5447	9.154831

It looks complicated, but for our purposes, we need to consider only three highlighted pieces of information from the output:

1. Intercept coefficient (this refers to the vertical intercept) = 14,538.05

2. X Variable 1 coefficient (this refers to the slope) = 7.85 (rounded)

3. The R-square value (the "goodness-of-fit" statistic) = 0.947 (rounded)

Let's look at each piece of information, starting with the highlighted information at the bottom of the output:

1. The "Intercept coefficient" is the vertical intercept of the mixed cost line. It's the fixed cost component of the mixed cost. Regression analysis tells us that the fixed component of the monthly utility bill is $14,538 (rounded). Why is this different from the $8,000 fixed component we found using the high-low method? It's because regression analysis considers *every* data point, not just the high- and low-volume data points, when forming the best fitting line.

2. The "X Variable 1 coefficient" is the line's slope, or our variable cost per guest. Regression analysis tells us that the hotel spends an extra $7.85 on utilities for every guest it serves. This is slightly lower than the $8 per guest amount we found using the high-low method.

Using the regression output, we can write the utilities *monthly* cost equation as follows:

$$y = \$7.85x + \$14,538$$

where,

y = total *monthly* utilities cost

x = number of guests

> ### Why is this important?
>
> "Regression analysis is fast and easy to perform using Excel 2007. Regression analysis usually gives managers the most representative cost equations, allowing them to make the most accurate cost projections."

3. Now, let's look at the R-square statistic highlighted near the top of Exhibit 6-15. The R-square statistic is often referred to as a "goodness-of-fit" statistic because it tells us how well the regression line fits the data points. The R-square can range in value from zero to one, as shown in Exhibit 6-16. If there were no relationship between the number of guests and the hotel's utility costs, the data points would be scattered randomly (rather than being in a linear pattern) and the R-square would be close to zero. If there were a *perfect* relationship between the number of guests and the hotel's utility cost, a *perfectly* straight line would run through *every* data point and the R-square would be 1.00. In our case, the R-square of 0.947 means that the regression line fits the data quite well (it's very close to 1.00). In other words, the data points *almost* fall in a straight line (as you can see in Exhibit 6-13).

EXHIBIT 6-16 **Range of R-square Values**

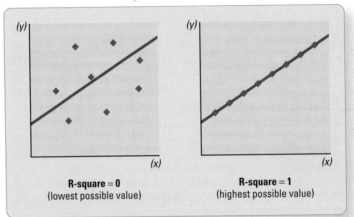

The R-square provides managers with very helpful information. The higher the R-square, the stronger the relationship between cost and volume. The stronger the relationship, the more confidence the manager would have in using the cost equation to predict costs at different volumes within the same relevant range. As a rule of thumb, an R-square over 0.80 generally indicates that the cost equation is very reliable for predicting costs at other volumes within the relevant range. An R-square between 0.50 and 0.80 means that the manager should use the cost equation with caution. However, if the R-square is fairly low (for example, less than 0.50), the manager should try using a different activity base (for example, room occupancy rate) for cost analysis because the current measure of volume is only weakly related to the costs.

Regression analysis can also help managers implement ABC. Recall from Chapter 4 that managers must choose a cost allocation base for every activity cost pool. The cost allocation base should be the primary cost driver of the costs in that pool. Management will use logic to come up with a short list of potential cost drivers for each activity cost pool. Then, management can run a regression analysis for each potential cost driver to see how strongly related it is to the activity costs in the pool. Managers compare the R-squares from each regression to see which one is highest. The regression with the highest R-square identifies the primary cost driver.

TECHNOLOGY *makes it simple*   Excel 2007

Regression Analysis

1. If you created a scatter plot, you have already done this first step. In an Excel spreadsheet, type in your data as pictured in Exhibit 6-12. Put the volume data in one column and the associated cost data in the next column.

2. Click on the "Data" tab on the menu bar.

3. Next, click on "Data Analysis." If you don't see it on your menu bar, follow the directions for add-ins given next before continuing.

4. From the list of data analysis tools, select "Regression," then "OK."

5. Follow the two instructions on the screen:
   i.   Highlight (or type in) the y-axis data range (this is your cost data).
   ii. Highlight (or type in) the x-axis data range (this is your volume data).
   iii. Click "OK."
6. That's all. Excel gives you the output shown in Exhibit 6-15.

DIRECTIONS FOR ADD-INs: It's easy and free to add the "Data Analysis Toolpak" if it's not already on your menu bar. You'll need to add it only once, and then it will always be on your menu bar. Simply follow these instructions:

1. While in Excel, click the Microsoft Office button (the colorful button in the upper-left-hand corner) and then click on the "Excel Options" box shown at the bottom.
2. Click "Add-Ins."
3. In the "Manage" box at the bottom of the screen, select "Excel Add-ins" and click "GO."
4. In the "Add-Ins available" box, select the "Analysis Toolpak" check box and then click "OK."
5. If asked, click "Yes" to install.

Predicting Costs

Managers use the results of the high-low method or regression analysis to plan for costs at different volumes. Managers should make predictions only for volumes falling in the same relevant range. In other words, they shouldn't use the cost equation to predict costs at a volume that is vastly different from the volumes used to generate the cost equation. Of the two methods, the regression analysis equation usually gives better predictions. Why? Because the regression analysis equation uses more historical data. However, remember that both methods just provide *estimates*.

Let's assume that management wants to predict total monthly utility costs if the hotel serves 23,000 guests one month. If management uses the high-low equation, the total utility cost is predicted to be the following:

$$y = (\$8 \text{ per guest} \times 23{,}000 \text{ guests}) + \$8{,}000$$
$$y = \$192{,}000$$

But if management uses the regression equation, the total utility cost is predicted to be the following:

$$y = (\$7.85 \text{ per guest} \times 23{,}000 \text{ guests}) + \$14{,}538$$
$$y = \$195{,}088$$

The predictions are similar in this situation. However, that won't always be the case, especially if the high- and low-volume data points aren't representative of the other data points.

Data Concerns

Cost equations are only as good as the data on which they are based. For example, if the hotel's utility bills are seasonal, management may want to develop separate cost equations for each season. For example, it might develop a winter utility bill cost equation using historical data from only the winter months. Management would do likewise for every other season. Inflation can also affect predictions. If inflation is running rampant, managers should adjust projected costs by the inflation rate. Even if the economy has generally low inflation, certain industries may be experiencing large price changes. For example, the 2005 hurricanes resulted in above-average increases in building supply and fuel costs.

Another cause for concern is outliers, or abnormal data points. Outliers can distort the results of the high-low method and regression analysis. Recall that the high-low method uses only two data points—the data points associated with the highest and lowest volumes of activity. If either of these points is an outlier, the resulting line and cost equation will be skewed. Because regression analysis uses all data points, any outlier in the data will affect the resulting line and cost equation. To find outliers, management should first plot the data like we did in Exhibit 6-13. None of the data points in Exhibit 6-13 appear to be outliers since they all fall in the same general pattern. However, if we saw a data point that was atypical of the others, we would investigate it to see if it was accurate, then possibly exclude it from further analysis—in other words, we would probably not use it in either the high-low method or regression analysis.

What is a Contribution Margin Income Statement?

> **6** Prepare contribution margin income statements for service firms and merchandising firms

Almost all businesses, including Embassy Suites, have some fixed costs, some variable costs, and some mixed costs. Companies use account analysis, the high-low method, or regression analysis (or a combination of these methods) to determine how their costs behave. They may analyze cost behavior on an account-by-account basis, as we did in the previous examples (they prepare separate cost equations for toiletry costs, complimentary breakfast and refreshment costs, utilities costs, and so forth). Or if they do not need so much detail, companies may develop *one* mixed cost equation for *all* operating costs lumped together. Once they have cost behavior information, how do companies communicate it to their managers so that the managers can use it for planning and decision making? Let's look at some potential options.

Traditional Income Statements are Organized by Cost Function

Unfortunately, traditional income statements provide managers with little, if any, cost behavior information. Traditional income statements are organized by *function*, not by cost behavior. Costs related to the production or purchases function of the value chain appear as cost of goods sold, *above* the gross profit line, when the manufactured products or merchandise is sold. All other costs (related to all other value-chain functions) appear as operating expenses, *below* the gross profit line.

Exhibit 6-17 illustrates this *functional* separation of costs for a retailer specializing in fitness equipment. Notice how the traditional format does not provide managers with much information, if any, on cost behavior. The cost of goods sold is a variable cost for a retailer, but contains a mixture of variable and fixed production costs for manufacturers. Recall from Chapter 2 that manufacturers usually classify direct materials and direct labor as variable costs, but treat manufacturing overhead as a mixed cost. In addition,

EXHIBIT 6-17 **Traditional Income Statement of a Retailer**

AAA FITNESS EQUIPMENT
Income Statement
Month Ended July 31

Sales revenue	$ 52,500
Less: Cost of goods sold	(27,300)
Gross profit	25,200
Less: Operating expenses	(14,600)
Operating income	$ 10,600

traditional income statements do not distinguish fixed operating costs from variable operating costs. While external users such as investors and creditors find traditional income statements useful, these statements are not very useful for internal managers who need cost behavior information for planning and decision making.

Contribution Margin Income Statements are Organized by Cost Behavior

To provide managers with cost behavior information, companies often prepare **contribution margin income statements**. Contribution margin income statements can only be used internally. GAAP does not allow companies to use the contribution margin format for external reporting purposes. Contribution margin income statements organize costs by *behavior* rather than by *function*. Therefore, managers find contribution margin income statements more helpful than traditional income statements for planning and decision making. The contribution margin income statement (shown in Exhibit 6-18) presents *all variable costs*—whether relating to the merchandise sold or selling and administrative activities—*above* the contribution margin line. The contribution margin income statement shows *all fixed costs*—whether relating to the merchandise sold or selling and administrative activities—*below* the contribution margin line. The contribution margin, not the gross profit, is the dividing line. The **contribution margin** is equal to sales revenue minus variable expenses.

> ### Why is this important?
> "The contribution margin income statement allows managers to quickly see which costs will change with volume, and which will remain fixed."

EXHIBIT 6-18 **Contribution Margin Income Statement**

AAA FITNESS EQUIPMENT
Contribution Margin Income Statement
Month Ended July 31

Sales revenue	$ 52,500
Less: Variable expenses	(30,900)
Contribution margin	21,600
Less: Fixed expenses	(11,000)
Operating income	$ 10,600

Managers can use contribution margin income statements to predict how changes in volume will affect operating income. Changes in volume will affect total sales revenue and total variable costs (and, therefore, the contribution margin). However, changes in volume will *not* affect fixed costs within the same relevant range. Therefore, the contribution margin income statement distinguishes the financial figures that *will* change from those that *will not* change in response to fluctuations in volume. Traditional income statements do not make this distinction.

In the next chapter, we will discuss many ways managers use the contribution margin to answer business questions, including how changes in volume and costs affect the firm's profits.

The appendix in this chapter is devoted to variable costing. Variable costing is an optional product costing system that *manufacturers* can use for internal purposes. Variable costing results in contribution margin income statements for manufacturers.

Decision Guidelines

Cost Behavior

As the manager of a local fitness club, Fitness-for-Life, you'll want to plan for operating costs at various levels of membership. Before you can make forecasts, you'll need to make some of the following decisions.

Decision	Guidelines
How can I sort out the fixed and the variable components of mixed costs?	• Managers typically use the high-low method or regression analysis. • The high-low method is fast and easy but uses only two historical data points to form the cost equation and, therefore, may not be very indicative of the costs' true behavior. • Regression analysis uses every data point provided to determine the cost equation that best fits the data. It is simple to do with Excel, but tedious to do by hand.
I've used the high-low method to formulate a cost equation. Can I tell how well the cost equation fits the data?	The only way to determine how well the high-low cost equation fits the data is by (1) plotting the data, (2) drawing a line through the data points associated with the highest and lowest volume, and (3) "visually inspecting" the resulting graph to see if the line is representative of the other plotted data points.
I've used regression analysis to formulate a cost equation. Can I tell how well the cost equation fits the data?	The R-square is a "goodness-of-fit" statistic that tells how well the regression analysis cost equation fits the data. The R-square ranges from 0 to 1, with 1 being a perfect fit. When the R-square is high, the cost equation should render fairly accurate predictions.
Do I need to be concerned about anything before using the high-low method or regression analysis?	Cost equations are only as good as the data on which they are based. Managers should plot the historical data to see if a relationship between cost and volume exists. In addition, scatter plots help managers identify outliers. Managers should remove outliers before further analysis. Managers should also adjust cost equations for seasonal data, inflation, and price changes.
Can I present the club's financial statements in a manner that will help with planning and decision making?	Managers often use contribution margin income statements for internal planning and decision making. Contribution margin income statements organize costs by *behavior* (fixed versus variable) rather than by *function* (product versus period).

Summary Problem 2

As the new manager of a local fitness club, Fitness-for-Life, you have been studying the club's financial data. You would like to determine how the club's costs behave in order to make accurate predictions for next year. Here is information from the last six months:

Month	Club Membership (number of members)	Total Operating Costs	Average Operating Costs per Member
July	450	$ 8,900	$19.78
August	480	$ 9,800	$20.42
September	500	$10,100	$20.20
October	550	$10,150	$18.45
November	560	$10,500	$18.75
December	525	$10,200	$19.43

Requirements

1. By looking at the "Total Operating Costs" and the "Operating Costs per Member," can you tell whether the club's operating costs are variable, fixed, or mixed? Explain your answer.

2. Use the high-low method to determine the club's monthly operating cost equation.

3. Using your answer from Requirement 2, predict total monthly operating costs if the club has 600 members.

4. Can you predict total monthly operating costs if the club has 3,000 members? Explain your answer.

5. Prepare the club's traditional income statement and its contribution margin income statement for the month of July. Assume that your cost equation from Requirement 2 accurately describes the club's cost behavior. The club charges members $30 per month for unlimited access to its facilities.

6. *Optional:* Perform regression analysis using Microsoft Excel. What is the monthly operating cost equation? What is the R-square? Why is the cost equation different from that in Requirement 2?

Solution

Requirement 1

By looking at "Total Operating Costs," we can see that the club's operating costs are not purely fixed; otherwise, total costs would remain constant. Operating costs appear to be either variable or mixed because they increase in total as the number of members increases. By looking at the "Operating Costs per Member," we can see that the operating costs aren't purely variable; otherwise, the "per-member" cost would remain constant. Therefore, the club's operating costs are mixed.

Requirement 2

Use the high-low method to determine the club's operating cost equation:

Step 1) The highest volume month is November, and the lowest volume month is July. Therefore, we use *only these two months* to determine the cost equation. The first step is to find the variable cost per unit of activity, which is the slope of the line connecting the November and July data points:

$$\frac{\text{Rise}}{\text{Run}} = \frac{\text{Change in } y}{\text{Change in } x} = \frac{y\,(\text{high}) - y\,(\text{low})}{x\,(\text{high}) - x\,(\text{low})} = \frac{(\$10,500 - \$8,900)}{(560 - 450 \text{ members})} = \$14.55 \text{ per member (rounded)}$$

Step 2) The second step is to find the fixed cost component (vertical intercept) by plugging in the slope and either July or November data to a mixed cost equation:

$$y = vx + f$$

Using November data:

$$\$10,500 = (\$14.55/\text{member} \times 560 \text{ guests}) + f$$

Solving for *f*:

$$f = \$2,352$$

Or we can use July data to reach the same conclusion:

$$\$8,900 = (\$14.55/\text{members} \times 450 \text{ guests}) + f$$

continued

Solving for f:

$$f = \$2,352 \text{ (rounded)}$$

Step 3: Write the monthly operating cost equation:

$$y = \$14.55x + \$2,352$$

where,

$$x = \text{number of members}$$
$$y = \text{total monthly operating costs}$$

Requirement 3

Predict total monthly operating costs when volume reaches 600 members:

$$y = (\$14.55 \times 600) + \$2,352$$
$$y = \$11,082$$

Requirement 4

Our current data and cost equation are based on 450 to 560 members. If membership reaches 3,000, operating costs could behave much differently. That volume falls outside our current relevant range.

Requirement 5

The club had 450 members in July and total operating costs of $8,900. Thus, its traditional income statement is as follows:

FITNESS-FOR-LIFE Income Statement Month Ended July 31	
Club membership revenue (450 × $30)	$13,500
Less: Operating expenses (given)	(8,900)
Operating income	$ 4,600

To prepare the club's contribution margin income statement, we need to know how much of the total $8,900 operating costs is fixed and how much is variable. If the cost equation from Requirement 2 accurately reflects the club's cost behavior, fixed costs will be $2,352 and variable costs will be $6,548 (= $14.55 × 450). The contribution margin income statement would look like this:

FITNESS-FOR-LIFE Contribution Margin Income Statement Month Ended July 31	
Club membership revenue (450 × $30)	$13,500
Less: Variable expenses (450 × $14.55)	(6,548)
Contribution margin	6,952
Less: Fixed expenses	(2,352)
Operating income	$ 4,600

Requirement 6

Regression analysis using Microsoft Excel results in the following cost equation and R-square:

$$y = \$11.80x + \$3,912$$

where,

x = number of members
y = total monthly operating costs

R-square = 0.8007

The regression analysis cost equation uses all of the data points, not just the data from November and July. Therefore, it better represents all of the data. The high R-square means that the regression line fits the data well and predictions based on this cost equation should be quite accurate.

APPENDIX 6A

How Does Variable Costing Differ from Absorption Costing?

> **7** Use variable costing to prepare contribution margin income statements for manufacturers (Appendix)

Once they know how their costs behave, managers of *manufacturing* companies can use **variable costing**, which assigns only *variable* manufacturing costs (direct materials, direct labor, and variable manufacturing overhead) to products. They use variable costing to prepare the contribution margin income statements discussed in the preceding section. Managers can use variable costing and contribution margin income statements only for internal management decisions.

GAAP *requires* managers to use absorption costing, which results in traditional income statements, for *external reporting*. Under **absorption costing**, products "absorb" fixed manufacturing costs as well as variable manufacturing costs. In other words, both fixed and variable manufacturing costs are treated as inventoriable product costs. Supporters of absorption costing argue that companies cannot produce products without fixed manufacturing costs, so these costs are an important part of the inventoriable product costs. In all preceding chapters, we have treated fixed manufacturing costs as an inventoriable product cost; therefore, we have been using absorption costing.

Variable costing assigns only variable manufacturing costs to products. Variable costing treats fixed manufacturing costs as period costs (so they are expensed in the period in which they are incurred). Supporters of variable costing argue that fixed manufacturing costs (such as depreciation on the plant) provide the capacity to produce during a period. Because the company incurs these fixed expenses whether or not it produces any products, they are period costs, not product costs.

All other costs are treated the same way under both absorption and variable costing:

- Variable manufacturing costs are inventoriable products costs.

- All nonmanufacturing costs are period costs.

Exhibit 6-19 summarizes the differences between variable and absorption costing.

EXHIBIT 6-19 **Differences Between Absorption Costing and Variable Costing**

	Absorption Costing	Variable Costing
Product Costs (Capitalized as Inventory until expensed as Cost of Goods Sold)	Direct materials Direct labor Variable manufacturing overhead Fixed manufacturing overhead	Direct materials Direct labor Variable manufacturing overhead
Period Costs (Expensed in periods incurred)	Variable nonmanufacturing costs Fixed nonmanufacturing costs	Fixed manufacturing overhead Variable nonmanufacturing costs Fixed nonmanufacturing costs
Focus	External reporting—required by GAAP	Internal reporting only
Income Statement Format	Conventional income statement, as in Chapters 1–5	Contribution margin statement

Variable Versus Absorption Costing: Sportade

To see how absorption costing and variable costing differ, let's consider the following example. Sportade incurred the following costs for its powdered sports beverage mix in March:

Direct materials cost per case	$ 6.00
Direct labor cost per case	3.00
Variable manufacturing overhead cost per case	2.00
Sales commission per case	2.50
Total fixed manufacturing overhead expenses	50,000
Total fixed marketing and administrative expenses	25,000

Sportade produced 10,000 cases of powdered mix as planned but sold only 8,000 cases at a price of $30 per case. There were no beginning inventories, so Sportade has 2,000 cases of powdered mix in ending finished goods inventory (10,000 cases produced – 8,000 cases sold).

What is Sportade's inventoriable product cost per case under absorption costing and variable costing?

	Absorption Costing	Variable Costing
Direct materials	$ 6.00	$ 6.00
Direct labor	3.00	3.00
Variable manufacturing overhead	2.00	2.00
Fixed manufacturing overhead	5.00*	
Total cost per case	$16.00	$11.00

*$\dfrac{\$50{,}000 \text{ fixed manufacturing overhead}}{10{,}000 \text{ cases}} = \$5 \text{ per case}$

The only difference between absorption and variable costing is that fixed manufacturing overhead is a product cost under absorption costing but a period cost under variable costing. That is why the cost per case is $5 higher under absorption costing (total cost of $16) than under variable costing ($11).

Exhibit 6-20 shows that absorption costing results in a traditional income statement.

EXHIBIT 6-20   Absorption Costing Income Statement

SPORTADE
Income Statement (Absorption Costing)
Month Ended March 31

Sales revenue (8,000 × $30)...		$ 240,000
Deduct: Cost of goods sold:		
Beginning finished goods inventory	$ 0	
Cost of goods manufactured (10,000 × $16)...................	160,000	
Cost of goods available for sale......................................	160,000	
Ending finished goods inventory (2,000 × $16)...............	(32,000)	
Cost of goods sold		(128,000)
Gross profit...		112,000
Deduct: Operating expenses [(8,000 × $2.50) + $25,000].........		(45,000)
Operating income...		$ 67,000

Notice the following:

- The absorption costing income statement in Exhibit 6-20 groups costs by function: manufacturing costs versus nonmanufacturing costs. *We subtract manufacturing costs of goods sold **before** gross profit, whereas we subtract all nonmanufacturing costs (operating expenses) **after** gross profit.*

- Total cost of goods manufactured is the number of cases *produced* multiplied by the $16 total manufacturing cost per case. In contrast, total variable marketing expense (for sales commissions) equals the number of cases *sold* times the sales commission per case.

- Absorption costing holds back as an asset (ending inventory) $32,000 of the manufacturing cost that Sportade incurred this period (2,000 cases × $16 total manufacturing cost per case). This $32,000 is not expensed in the month when Sportade incurred these manufacturing costs. Instead, these manufacturing costs are held back as the asset *Inventory* until the related 2,000 cases are sold.

- The absorption costing income statement does not distinguish between variable and fixed costs. This limits the statement's usefulness for managerial decisions. If the CEO of Sportade wants to predict how a 10% increase in sales will affect operating income, the absorption costing income statement is of little help: It does not separate variable costs (which increase with sales) from fixed costs (which will not change).

The limitations of absorption costing-based income statements lead many manufacturing managers to prefer variable costing and contribution margin income statements *for internal reporting and decision making.* Exhibit 6-21 recasts the Sportade information using variable costing and a contribution margin income statement that groups costs by behavior—variable versus fixed.

Why is this important?

"Variable costing helps manufacturers identify the variable cost of making each unit of a product. This information will be critical to making many of the business decisions, such as whether or not to outsource the product."

EXHIBIT 6-21 **Variable Costing Contribution Margin Income Statement**

SPORTADE Contribution Margin Income Statement (Variable Costing) Month Ended March 31			
Sales revenue (8,000 × $30)..			$ 240,000
Deduct: Variable expenses:			
Variable cost of goods sold:			
Beginning finished goods inventory	$ 0		
Variable cost of goods manufactured (10,000 × $11)	110,000		
Variable cost of goods available for sale	110,000		
Ending finished goods inventory (2,000 × $11)	(22,000)		
Variable cost of goods sold	88,000		
Sales commission expense (8,000 × $2.50).....................	20,000	(108,000)	
Contribution margin...		132,000	
Deduct: Fixed expenses:			
Fixed manufacturing overhead..	50,000		
Fixed marketing and administrative expenses	25,000	(75,000)	
Operating income...		$ 57,000	

Compare the general format of the absorption costing income statement in Exhibit 6-20 with the variable costing contribution margin income statement in Exhibit 6-21. The conventional absorption costing income statement subtracts cost of goods sold (including both variable and fixed manufacturing costs) from sales to obtain *gross profit*. In contrast, the contribution margin income statement subtracts all variable costs (both manufacturing and nonmanufacturing) to obtain *contribution margin*. The following chart highlights the differences between gross profit and contribution margin:

Conventional Income Statement	Contribution Margin Income Statement
Sales revenue	Sales revenue
Deduct Cost of Goods Sold:	Deduct Variable Expenses:
Variable manufacturing cost of goods sold	Variable manufacturing cost of goods sold
Fixed manufacturing cost of goods sold	Variable nonmanufacturing expenses
= Gross profit	= Contribution margin

The two major differences are as follows:

1. Fixed manufacturing cost of goods sold is subtracted from sales to compute gross profit, but not to compute contribution margin.

2. Variable nonmanufacturing expenses are subtracted from sales to calculate contribution margin, but not to compute gross profit.

Now, let's look more closely at the variable costing contribution margin income statement in Exhibit 6-21. First, notice that the details of the (variable) cost of goods sold computation in Exhibit 6-21 parallel those in the absorption costing income statement *except* that we use the $11 variable costing product cost per case rather than the $16 absorption cost per case. Second, variable costing holds back as an asset (ending inventory) only $22,000 (2,000 cases × $11 variable manufacturing cost per case). Third, the variable costing contribution margin income statement subtracts *all* of the variable costs (*both* the $88,000 manufacturing variable cost of goods sold *and* the $20,000 variable sales commission expense) from sales to get contribution margin. Finally, we subtract fixed costs (both the $50,000 fixed manufacturing overhead and the $25,000 fixed marketing and administrative costs) from contribution margin to get operating income. To summarize, the variable costing contribution margin income statement subtracts all variable costs before contribution margin and all fixed costs *after* contribution margin.

By separating variable and fixed costs, the variable costing contribution margin income statement (Exhibit 6-21) allows managers to estimate how changes in sales, costs, or volume will affect profits.

Stop & Think

Suppose Sportade can increase the number of cases sold by 10% using its existing capacity. Compute the likely effect on operating income.

Answer: Because Sportade can accommodate the increased production using existing capacity, fixed costs will be unaffected. Thus, the entire increase in contribution margin flows through to operating income. A 10% increase in sales is an extra 800 cases (10% × 8,000).

Increase in sales revenue (800 cases × $30/case)	$ 24,000
Increase in variable costs (800 cases × $13.50/case*)	(10,800)
Increase in contribution margin..	$ 13,200
Increase in fixed costs..	0
Increase in operating income..	$ 13,200

*Total variable costs per case = $6.00 direct materials + $3.00 direct labor + $2.00 variable manufacturing overhead + $2.50 sales commission. (All variable costs, including the sales commission as well as variable manufacturing costs, must be considered to estimate how the sales increase will affect contribution margin and operating profit.)

Reconciling the Difference in Income

Exhibit 6-20 shows that Sportade's absorption costing operating income is $67,000. Exhibit 6-21 shows that variable costing yields only $57,000 of operating income. Why? To answer this question, we need to understand what happened to the $160,000 ($110,000 variable + $50,000 fixed) total manufacturing costs under each costing method.

Manufacturing costs incurred in March are either

- expensed in March, or

- held back in inventory (an asset).

Exhibit 6-22 shows that of the $160,000 total manufacturing costs incurred during March, absorption costing holds back $32,000 (2,000 × $16) as inventory. This $32,000 assigned to inventory is not expensed until next month, when the units are sold. Thus, only $128,000 ($160,000 – $32,000) of the manufacturing costs are expensed as cost of goods sold during March.

Variable costing holds back in ending inventory only $22,000 (2,000 × $11) of the total manufacturing costs. This is $10,000 ($22,000 – $32,000) *less* than what absorption costing holds back. The difference arises because absorption costing assigns the $5 per case fixed manufacturing overhead costs to the 2,000 cases in ending inventory. In contrast, variable costing does not—it expenses all of the fixed manufacturing overhead in the current month.

Costs that are not held back in inventory are expensed in the current period, so variable costing expenses are $138,000 ($160,000 – $22,000) of manufacturing costs in March. (This $138,000 also equals the $88,000 variable cost of goods sold plus the $50,000 fixed manufacturing overhead.) This is $10,000 more than the $128,000 absorption costing manufacturing expenses during March. *Variable costing has $10,000 more expense in March, so its income is $10,000 lower than absorption costing income.*

EXHIBIT 6-22 Inventory Versus Expenses Under Absorption and Variable Costing

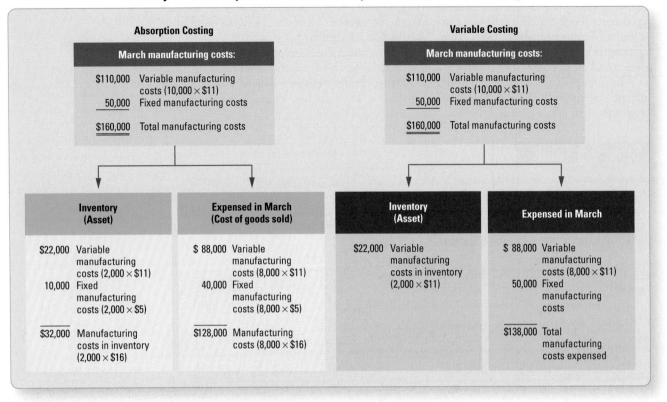

Stop & Think

Suppose Sportade has no inventory at the end of the next month, April. Will absorption costing report higher or lower operating income than variable costing for the month of April?

Answer: Absorption costing will report lower income than variable costing during April. Ending inventory in March becomes the beginning inventory of April. Absorption costing assigns a higher value to beginning inventory in April. When that beginning inventory is sold, the higher beginning inventory costs increase cost of goods sold for April, which, in turn, reduces income.

Absorption Costing and Manager's Incentives

The general rule is this: When inventories increase (more units are produced than sold), absorption costing income is higher than variable costing income. When inventories decline (when fewer units are produced than sold), absorption costing income is lower than variable costing income. Suppose the Sportade manager receives a bonus based on absorption costing income. Will the manager want to increase or decrease production?

The manager knows that absorption costing assigns each case of Sportade $5 of fixed manufacturing overhead.

- For every case produced but not sold, absorption costing "hides" $5 of fixed overhead in ending inventory (an asset).

- The more cases that are added to inventory, the more fixed overhead that is "hidden" in ending inventory at the end of the month.

- The more fixed overhead in ending inventory, the smaller the cost of goods sold and the higher the operating income.

To maximize the bonus under absorption costing, the manager may try to increase production to build up inventory. This incentive conflicts with the JIT philosophy, which emphasizes minimal inventory levels.

Decision Guidelines

Absorption and Variable Costing

As the CEO of Sportade, you are considering whether to use variable costing. Here are some decisions you will have to make.

Decision	Guidelines
When should Sportade use absorption costing? Variable costing?	Sportade must use absorption costing for external reporting. Sportade can use variable costing only for internal reporting.
What is the difference between absorption and variable costing?	Fixed manufacturing costs are treated as follows: • Inventoriable product costs under absorption costing • Period costs under variable costing

How should Sportade compute inventoriable product costs under absorption costing and variable costing?

Absorption Costing	*Variable Costing*
Direct materials	Direct materials
+ Direct labor	+ Direct labor
+ Variable overhead	+ Variable overhead
+ Fixed overhead	
= Product cost	= Product cost

Will absorption costing income be higher than, lower than, or the same as variable costing income?

If units produced > units sold:

    Absorption costing income > Variable costing income

If units produced < units sold:

    Absorption costing income < Variable costing income

If units produced = units sold:

    Absorption costing income = Variable costing income

Decision	Guidelines
Why should Sportade use variable costing for internal reporting?	• Managers can use variable costing contribution margin income statements to estimate how changes in sales or costs will affect profits. • Variable costing does not give Sportade's managers incentives to build up inventory.

Summary Problem 3

Continue the Sportade illustration from pages 334–338. In April, Sportade produces 10,000 cases of the powdered sports beverage and sells 12,000 cases (the 2,000 cases of inventory on March 31, plus the 10,000 cases produced during April). The variable costs per case and the total fixed costs are the same as in March.

Requirements

1. Prepare an income statement for the month ended April 30, using absorption costing.

2. Prepare an income statement for the month ended April 30, using variable costing.

3. Reconcile (explain the difference between) operating income under absorption versus variable costing.

Solution

Requirement 1

SPORTADE
Income Statement (Absorption Costing)
Month Ended April 30

Sales revenue (12,000 × $30)		$360,000
Deduct: Cost of goods sold:		
Beginning finished goods inventory	$ 32,000*	
Cost of goods manufactured (10,000 × $16)	160,000†	
Cost of goods available for sale	192,000	
Ending finished goods inventory	(0)	
Cost of goods sold		192,000
Gross profit		168,000
Deduct: Operating expenses [(12,000 × $2.50) + $25,000]		(55,000)
Operating income		$113,000

*Ending inventory from March 31 (Exhibit 6-20).
†Absorption costing cost per case = $6 + $3 + $2 + $5.

Requirement 2

SPORTADE
Contribution Margin Income Statement (Variable Costing)
Month Ended April 30

Sales revenue (12,000 × $30)		$360,000
Deduct: Variable expenses:		
Variable cost of goods sold:		
Beginning finished goods inventory	$ 22,000*	
Variable cost of goods manufactured (10,000 × $11)	110,000†	
Variable cost of goods available for sale	132,000	
Ending finished goods inventory	(0)	
Variable cost of goods sold	132,000	
Sales commission expense (12,000 × $2.50)	30,000	(162,000)
Contribution margin		198,000
Deduct: Fixed expenses:		
Fixed manufacturing overhead	50,000	
Fixed marketing and administrative expenses	25,000	(75,000)
Operating income		$ 123,000

*Ending inventory from March 31 (Exhibit 6-21).
†Absorption costing cost per case = $6 + $3 + $2.

Requirement 3

April operating income is $10,000 higher under variable costing than under absorption costing. Why? Both methods expense all of April's $160,000 manufacturing costs ($110,000 variable + $50,000 fixed) during April. However, the two methods differ in the amount of March manufacturing cost expensed in April. Absorption costing holds $32,000 of March manufacturing costs in inventory and expenses them in April when the goods are sold. Variable costing holds only $22,000 of March manufacturing costs in inventory and expenses them in April.

Thus, absorption costing operating income is as follows:

- $10,000 higher than variable costing income in March (because absorption costing defers $10,000 more of March costs to April)

- $10,000 lower than variable costing income in April (because absorption costing expenses $10,000 more of March costs in April)

REVIEW

Accounting Vocabulary

Absorption Costing. (p. 325)   The costing method where products "absorb" both fixed and variable manufacturing costs.

Account Analysis. (p. 312)   A method for determining cost behavior that is based on a manager's judgment in classifying each general ledger account as a variable, fixed, or mixed cost.

Committed Fixed Costs. (p. 303)   Fixed costs that are locked in because of previous management decisions; management has little or no control over these costs in the short run.

Contribution Margin. (p. 321)   Sales revenue minus variable expenses.

Contribution Margin Income Statement. (p. 321)   Income statement that organizes costs by *behavior* (variable costs or fixed costs) rather than by *function*.

Cost Behavior. (p. 299)   Describes how costs change as volume changes.

Cost Equation. (p. 301)   A mathematical equation for a straight line that expresses how a cost behaves.

Curvilinear Costs. (p. 310)   A cost behavior that is not linear (not a straight line).

Discretionary Fixed Costs. (p. 303)   Fixed costs that are a result of annual management decisions; fixed costs that are controllable in the short run.

Fixed Costs. (p. 300)   Costs that do not change in total despite wide changes in volume.

High-Low Method. (p. 315)   A method for determining cost behavior that is based on two historical data points: the highest and lowest volume of activity.

Mixed Cost. (p. 300)   Costs that change, but *not* in direct proportion to changes in volume. Mixed costs have both variable cost and fixed cost components.

Regression Analysis. (p. 316)   A statistical procedure for determining the line that best fits the data by using *all of the historical data points, not just the high and low data points*.

Relevant Range. (p. 307)   The band of volume where total fixed costs remain constant at a certain level and where the variable cost *per unit* remains constant at a certain level.

Scatter Plot. (p. 313)   A graph that plots historical cost and volume data.

Step Costs. (p. 309)   A cost behavior that is fixed over a small range of activity and then jumps to a different fixed level with moderate changes in volume.

Outliers. (p. 314)   Abnormal data points; data points that do not fall in the same general pattern as the other data points.

Variable Costs. (p. 300)   Costs that change in total in direct proportion to changes in volume.

Variable Costing. (p. 325)   The costing method that assigns only *variable* manufacturing costs to products.

Quick Check

1. *(Learning Objective 1)* If a *per-unit* cost remains constant over a wide range of volume, the cost is most likely a
   a. variable cost.
   b. fixed cost.
   c. mixed cost.
   d. step cost.

2. *(Learning Objective 1)* The cost per unit decreases as volume increases for which of the following cost behaviors?
   a. Variable costs and fixed costs
   b. Variable costs and mixed costs
   c. Fixed costs and mixed costs
   d. Only fixed costs

3. *(Learning Objective 2)* In the following mixed cost equation, what amount represents the **total variable cost component**: $y = vx + f$?
   a. y
   b. v
   c. f
   d. vx

4. *(Learning Objective 2)* Which of the following would generally be considered a committed fixed cost for a retailing firm?
   a. Cost of a trip to Cancun given to the employee who is "Employee of the Year"
   b. Lease payments made on the store building
   c. Cost of sponsoring the local golf tournament for charity
   d. Cost of annual sales meeting for all employees

5. *(Learning Objective 3)* Which method is used to see if a relationship between the cost driver and total cost exists?
   a. Scatter plot
   b. Variance analysis
   c. Outlier
   d. Account analysis

6. *(Learning Objective 4)* When choosing the high point for the high-low method, how is the high point selected?
   a. The point with the highest total cost is chosen.
   b. The point with the highest volume of activity is chosen.
   c. The point that has the highest cost and highest volume of activity is always chosen.
   d. Both the high point and the low point are selected at random.

7. *(Learning Objective 5)* What is the advantage of using regression analysis to determine the cost equation?
   a. The method is objective.
   b. All data points are used to calculate the equation for the cost equation.
   c. It will generally be more accurate than the high-low method.
   d. All of the above statements are true about regression analysis.

8. *(Learning Objective 6)* The contribution margin income statement
   a. provides owners with cash flow information.
   b. is required for external reporting.
   c. is useful to managers in decision making and planning.
   d. arrives at operating income by subtracting operating expenses from gross profit.

9. *(Learning Objective 7)* The only difference between variable costing and absorption costing lies in the treatment of
   a. fixed manufacturing overhead costs.
   b. variable manufacturing overhead costs.
   c. direct materials and direct labor costs.
   d. variable nonmanufacturing costs.

10. *(Learning Objective 7)* When inventories decline, operating income under variable costing is
    a. lower than operating income under absorption costing.
    b. the same as operating income under absorption costing.
    c. higher than operating income under absorption costing.

ASSESS YOUR PROGRESS

Learning Objectives

1 Describe key characteristics and graphs of various cost behaviors

2 Use cost equations to express and predict costs

3 Use account analysis and scatter plots to analyze cost behavior

4 Use the high-low method to analyze cost behavior

5 Use regression analysis to analyze cost behavior

6 Prepare contribution margin income statements for service firms and merchandising firms

7 Use variable costing to prepare contribution margin income statements for manufacturers (Appendix)

Short Exercises

S6-1 Identify cost behavior *(Learning Objective 1)*

The following chart shows three different costs: Cost A, Cost B, and Cost C. For each cost, the chart shows the total cost and cost per unit at two different volumes within the same relevant range. Based on this information, identify each cost as fixed, variable, or mixed. Explain your answers.

	At 5,000 units		At 6,000 units	
	Total Cost	Cost per Unit	Total Cost	Cost per Unit
Cost A............	$30,000	$6.00	$36,000	$6.00
Cost B............	$30,000	$6.00	$30,000	$5.00
Cost C............	$30,000	$6.00	$33,000	$5.50

S6-2 Sketch cost behavior graphs *(Learning Objective 1)*

Sketch graphs of the following cost behaviors. In each graph, the y-axis should be "total costs" and the x-axis should be "volume of activity."
a. Step
b. Fixed
c. Curvilinear
d. Mixed
e. Variable

S6-3 Computer fixed costs per unit *(Learning Objective 2)*

Sport-time produces high-quality basketballs. If the fixed cost per basketball is $3 when the company produces 12,000 basketballs, what is the fixed cost per basketball when it produces 15,000 basketballs? Assume that both volumes are in the same relevant range.

S6-4 Define various cost equations *(Learning Objective 2)*

Write the cost equation for each of the following cost behaviors. Define the variables in each equation.
a. Fixed
b. Mixed
c. Variable

S6-5 Predict total mixed costs *(Learning Objective 2)*

Ritter Razors produces deluxe razors that compete with Gillette's Mach line of razors. Total manufacturing costs are $100,000 when 20,000 packages are produced. Of this amount, total variable costs are $40,000. What are the total production costs when 25,000 packages of razors are produced? Assume the same relevant range.

S6-6 Predict and graph total mixed costs *(Learning Objectives 1 & 2)*

Suppose World-Link offers an international calling plan that charges $5.00 per month plus $0.35 per minute for calls outside the United States.

1. Under this plan, what is your monthly international long-distance cost if you call Europe for
   a. 20 minutes?
   b. 40 minutes?
   c. 80 minutes?

2. Draw a graph illustrating your total cost under this plan. Label the axes and show your costs at 20, 40, and 80 minutes.

S6-7 Classify cost behavior *(Learning Objective 3)*

Ariel builds innovative loudspeakers for music and home theater. Identify the following costs as variable or fixed:

a. Depreciation on equipment used to cut wood enclosures

b. Wood for speaker enclosures

c. Patents on crossover relays (internal components)

d. Crossover relays

e. Grill cloth

f. Glue

g. Quality inspector's salary

S6-8 Prepare and analyze a scatter plot *(Learning Objective 3)*

Lube-for-Less is a car care center specializing in ten-minute oil changes. Lube-for-Less has two service bays, which limits its capacity to 3,600 oil changes per month. The following information was collected over the past six months:

Month	Number of Oil Changes	Operating Expenses
January	3,400	$36,800
February	2,700	$32,100
March	3,000	$33,300
April	2,900	$32,900
May	3,500	$37,700
June	3,100	$34,100

1. Prepare a scatter plot graphing the volume of oil changes (x-axis) against the company's monthly operating expenses (y-axis). Graph by hand or use Excel.

2. How strong of a relationship does there appear to be between the company's operating expenses and the number of oil changes performed each month? Explain. Do there appear to be any outliers in the data? Explain.

3. Based on the graph, do the company's operating costs appear to be fixed, variable, or mixed? Explain how you can tell.

4. Would you feel comfortable using this information to project operating costs for a volume of 4,000 oil changes per month? Explain.

S6-9 Use the high-low method *(Learning Objective 4)*

Refer to the Lube-for-Less data in S6-8. Use the high-low method to determine the variable and fixed cost components of Lube-for-Less's operating costs. Use this information to project the monthly operating costs for a month in which the company performs 3,600 oil changes.

S6-10 Use the high-low method *(Learning Objective 4)*

Mason Company uses the high-low method to predict its total overhead costs. Past records show that total overhead cost was $25,000 for 800 labor hours worked and $27,500 for 900 for labor hours worked. If Mason Company plans to work 825 labor hours next month, what is the expected total overhead cost?

S6-11 Critique the high-low method *(Learning Objective 4)*

You have been assigned an intern to help you forecast your firm's costs at different volumes. He thinks he will get cost and volume data from the two most recent months, plug them in to the high-low method equations, and turn in the cost equation results to your boss before the hour is over. As his mentor, explain to him why the process isn't quite as simple as he thinks. Point out some of the concerns he is overlooking, including your concerns about his choice of data and method.

S6-12 Analyze a scatter plot *(Learning Objectives 3 & 4)*

The local Holiday Inn collected seven months of data on the number of room-nights rented per month and the monthly utilities cost. The data was graphed, resulting in the following scatter plot:

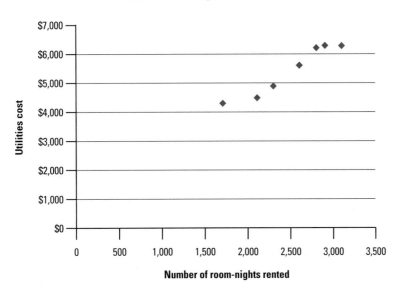

Number of room-nights rented and utilities cost

1. Based on this scatter plot, how strong of a relationship does there appear to be between the number of room-nights rented per month and the monthly utilities cost?

2. Do there appear to be any outliers in the data? Explain.

3. Suppose management performs the high-low method using this data. Do you think the resulting cost equation would be very accurate? Explain.

S6-13 Theoretical comparison of high-low and regression analysis *(Learning Objectives 4 & 5)*

Refer to the Holiday Inn scatter plot in S6-12.

1. Would the high-low method or regression analysis result in a more accurate cost equation for the data pictured in the scatter plot? Explain.

2. A regression analysis of the data revealed an R-squared figure of 0.939. Interpret this figure in light of the lowest and highest possible R-squared values.

3. As a manager, would you be confident predicting utilities costs for other room-night volumes within the same relevant range?

S6-14 Write a cost equation given regression output *(Learning Objective 5)*

A firm wanted to determine the relationship between its monthly operating costs and a potential cost driver, machine hours. The output of a regression analysis performed using Excel 2007 showed the following information:

SUMMARY OUTPUT

Regression Statistics

Multiple R	0.87
R Square	0.86
Adjusted R Square	0.84
Standard Error	398.49
Observations	12

ANOVA

	df	SS	MS	F	Significance F
Regression	1	2365870.5	2365871	14.89886	0.0032
Residual	10	1587954.5	158795		
Total	11	3953825			

	Coefficients	Standard Error	t Stat	P-value	Lower 95%	Upper 95%	Lower 95.0%	Upper 95.0%
Intercept	9942.83	406.44	24.46	2.97	9037.23	10848.43	9037.23	10848.43
X Variable 1	0.89	0.23	3.86	0.00	0.37	1.40	0.37	1.40

a. Given this output, write the firm's monthly cost equation.

b. Should management use this equation to predict monthly operating costs? Explain your answer.

S6-15 Prepare a contribution margin income statement *(Learning Objective 6)*

Pam's Quilt Shoppe sells homemade Amish quilts. Pam buys the quilts from local Amish artisans for $250 each, and her shop sells them for $350 each. Pam also pays a sales commission of 5% of sales revenue to her sales staff. Pam leases her country-style shop for $1,000 per month and pays $1,200 per month in payroll costs in addition to the sales commissions. Pam sold 80 quilts in February. Prepare Pam's traditional income statement and contribution margin income statement for the month.

S6-16 Prepare income statement using variable costing *(Learning Objective 7)*

(Appendix) Consider the Sportade example on pages 334–338. Suppose that during April, the company produces 10,000 cases of powdered drink mix and sells 11,000 cases. Sales price, variable cost per case, and total fixed expenses remain the same as in March. Prepare the April income statement using variable costing.

S6-17 Continuation of S6-16: Absorption costing *(Learning Objective 7)*

(Appendix) Refer to the Sportade example on pages 334–338 and the data and your answer to S6-16.

1. Prepare the April income statement under absorption costing.

2. Is absorption costing income higher or lower than variable costing income? Explain.

Exercises—Group A

E6-18A Graph specific costs *(Learning Objective 1)*

Graph these cost behavior patterns over a relevant range of 0–10,000 units:

a. Variable expenses of $8 per unit

b. Mixed expenses made up of fixed costs of $20,000 and variable costs of $3 per unit

c. Fixed expenses of $15,000

E6-19A   Identify cost behavior graph *(Learning Objective 1)*

Following are a series of cost behavior graphs. The total cost is shown on the vertical (y) axis and the volume (activity) is shown on the horizontal (x) axis.

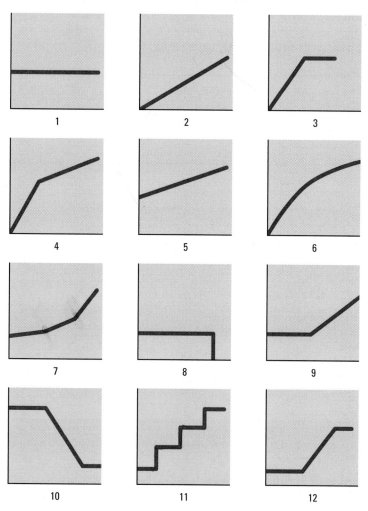

For each of the following situations, identify the graph that most closely represents the cost behavior pattern of the cost in that situation. Some graphs may be used more than once or not at all.

a. Straight-line depreciation of equipment (based on years of life)

b. Monthly electric bill, which consists of a flat monthly service charge plus $0.002 per kilowatt hour used

c. Factory rent of $3,000 per month will be forgiven by the city (which owns the building) if the company employs twelve disadvantaged youth in the month (the activity on the horizontal axis is the number of disadvantaged youths employed)

d. Office rent of $1,500 per month (the activity on the horizontal axis is sales in units)

e. Tuition is $384 per semester credit hour up to 10 credit hours; tuition for 11 credit hours or more is a flat fee of $4,215 per semester

f. Salaries of delivery workers, where a delivery person is needed for every 200 deliveries scheduled in a given month

g. The cost of direct materials for picnic tables when the wood in each table costs $45

h. Cost of water used in plant. To encourage conservation, the water company has the following price schedule per gallon of water in addition to the monthly service fee of $20:

Up to 10,000 gallons...	$0.005 per gallon
10,001–20,000 gallons...	$0.006 per gallon
More than 20,000 gallons.....................................	$0.008 per gallon

i. Cell phone bill, which is $29.99 for 450 anytime minutes in a month plus $0.25 per minute for any minutes used above the included 450 minutes

j. Assembly-line workers are paid $15.00 per hour

E6-20A Identify cost behavior terms *(Learning Objectives 1, 2, 3, 4, & 5)*

Complete the following statements with one of the terms listed here. You may use a term more than once, and some terms may not be used at all.

Account analysis	Step cost(s)	High-low method
Variable cost(s)	Fixed cost(s)	Regression analysis
Curvilinear cost(s)	Total cost(s)	Average cost per unit
R-square	Mixed cost(s)	Committed fixed costs

a. _____ remain constant in total over a wide range of volume.

b. _____ is often referred to as the "goodness-of-fit" statistic.

c. _____ and _____ increase in total as volume increases.

d. Graphs of _____ always begin at the origin.

e. _____ uses the manager's judgment to determine the cost behavior of various accounts.

f. _____ remain constant in total over small ranges of activity.

g. _____ and _____ increase on a per unit basis as volume decreases.

h. _____ uses only two historical data points to determine the cost line and cost equation.

i. _____ remain constant on a per unit basis.

j. When graphing cost equations, _____ are always shown on the y-axis.

k. The _____ should not be used to predict total costs at various volumes unless it is strictly a/an _____.

l. _____ uses all historical data points provided to determine the cost equation.

m. _____ are the result of previous management decisions and are not usually controllable in the short run.

E6-21A Forecast costs at different volumes *(Learning Objectives 1 & 2)*

Perreth Drycleaners has capacity to clean up to 5,000 garments per month.

Requirements

1. Complete the following schedule for the three volumes shown.

	2,000 Garments	3,500 Garments	5,000 Garments
Total variable costs		$2,625	
Total fixed costs			
Total operating costs			
Variable cost per garment			
Fixed cost per garment		$ 2.00	
Average cost per garment			

2. Why does the average cost per garment change?

3. Suppose the owner, Dan Perreth, erroneously uses the average cost per unit *at full capacity* to predict total costs at a volume of 2,000 garments. Would he overestimate or underestimate his total costs? By how much?

E6-22A Prepare income statement in two formats *(Learning Objective 6)*

Refer to the Perreth Drycleaners in E6-21A. Assume that Perreth charges customers $7 per garment for dry cleaning. Prepare Perreth's *projected* income statement if 4,252 garments are cleaned in March. First, prepare the income statement using the traditional format; then, prepare Perreth's contribution margin income statement.

E6-23A Use the high-low method *(Learning Objective 4)*

Jackson Company, which uses the high-low method to analyze cost behavior, has determined that machine hours best predict the company's total utilities cost. The company's cost and machine hour usage data for the first six months of the year follow.

Month	Total Cost	Machine Hours
January	$3,400	1,050
February	$3,700	1,150
March	$3,500	1,000
April	$3,780	1,200
May	$4,000	1,350
June	$4,200	1,400

Requirements

Using the high-low method, answer the following questions:

1. What is the variable utilities cost per machine hour?
2. What is the fixed cost of utilities each month?
3. If Jackson Company uses 1,280 machine hours in a month, what will its total costs be?

E6-24A Use unit cost data to forecast total costs *(Learning Objective 2)*

Mailbox Magic produces decorative mailboxes. The company's average cost per unit is $26.43 when it produces 1,000 mailboxes.

Requirements

1. What is the total cost of producing 1,000 mailboxes?
2. If $18,000 of the total costs is fixed, what is the variable cost of producing each mailbox?
3. Write Mailbox Magic's cost equation.
4. If the plant manager uses the average cost per unit to predict total costs, what would the forecast be for 1,200 mailboxes?
5. If the plant manager uses the cost equation to predict total costs, what would the forecast be for 1,200 mailboxes?
6. What is the dollar difference between your answers to questions 4 and 5? Which approach to forecasting costs is appropriate? Why?

E6-25A Use account analysis to determine cost behavior *(Learning Objective 3)*

Use your judgment (just as a manager would use his or her judgment for account analysis) to determine the cost behavior of each of the following personal costs:

a. Apartment rental, $500 per month
b. Local phone service with unlimited local calls, $19.99 per month
c. Cell phone plan, the first 700 minutes are included for $39.99 per month and every minute thereafter costs $0.30
d. Utilities, $0.475 per kilowatt hour
e. Car payment, $350 per month
f. Car insurance, $250 per month
g. Gas, $2.59 per gallon and your car averages 25 miles per gallon
h. Cable TV, $50 per month for 120 channels plus $4.99 per pay-per-view movie
i. Commuter rail tickets, $2 per ride
j. Student activity pass, $100 plus $5 per event
k. Campus meal plan, $3 per meal

E6-26A Create a scatter plot *(Learning Objective 3)*

Alice Jungemann, owner of Flower Power, operates a local chain of floral shops. Each shop has its own delivery van. Instead of charging a flat delivery fee, Jungemann wants to set the delivery fee based on the distance driven to deliver the flowers. Jungemann wants to separate the fixed and variable portions of her van operating costs so that she has a better idea how delivery distance affects these costs. She has the following data from the past seven months:

Month	Miles Driven	Van Operating Costs
January	15,800	$5,460
February	17,300	5,680
March	14,600	4,940
April	16,000	5,310
May	17,100	5,830
June	15,400	5,420
July	14,100	4,880

February and May are always Flower Power's biggest months because of Valentine's Day and Mother's Day, respectively.

Requirements

1. Prepare a scatter plot of Alice's volume (miles driven) and van operating costs.

2. Does the data appear to contain any outliers? Explain.

3. How strong of a relationship is there between miles driven and van operating costs?

E6-27A High-low method *(Learning Objective 4)*

Refer to Alice's Flower Power data in E6-26A. Use the high-low method to determine Flower Power's cost equation for van operating costs. Use your results to predict van operating costs at a volume of 15,000 miles.

E6-28A Continuation of E6-26A: Regression analysis *(Learning Objective 5)*

Refer to the Flower Power data in E6-26A. Use Microsoft Excel to do the following:

Requirements

1. Run a regression analysis.

2. Determine the firm's cost equation (use the output from the Excel regression).

3. Determine the R-square (use the output from the Excel regression). What does Flower Power's R-square indicate?

4. Predict van operating costs at a volume of 15,000 miles.

E6-29A   Regression analysis using Excel output *(Learning Objective 5)*

Assume that Alice's Flower Power does a regression analysis on the next year's data using Excel 2007. The output generated by Excel is as follows:

SUMMARY OUTPUT

Regression Statistics

Multiple R	0.96
R Square	0.92
Adjusted R Square	0.90
Standard Error	112.91
Observations	7

ANOVA

	df	SS	MS	F	Significance F
Regression	1	689408.19	689408.19	54.08	0.0007
Residual	5	63745.52	12749.10		
Total	6	753153.71			

	Coefficients	Standard Error	t Stat	P-value	Lower 95%	Upper 95%	Lower 95.0%	Upper 95.0%
Intercept	826.04	629.77	1.31	0.25	-792.83	2444.91	-792.83	2444.91
X Variable 1	0.28	0.04	7.35	0.00	0.18	0.37	0.18	0.37

Requirements

1. Determine the firm's cost equation (use the output from the Excel regression).
2. Determine the R-square (use the output from the Excel regression). What does Flower Power's R-square indicate?
3. Predict van operating costs at a volume of 16,000 miles.

E6-30A   Prepare and interpret a scatter plot *(Learning Objective 3)*

Dave's "Golden Brown" Pancake Restaurant features sourdough pancakes made from a strain of sourdough dating back to the Alaskan gold rush. To plan for the future, Dave needs to figure out his cost behavior patterns. He has the following information about his operating costs and the number of pancakes served:

Month	Number of Pancakes	Total Operating Costs
July	3,600	$2,340
August	3,900	$2,390
September	3,200	$2,320
October	3,300	$2,270
November	3,850	$2,560
December	3,620	$2,530

Requirements

1. Prepare a scatter plot of Dave's pancake volume and operating costs. (*Hint*: If you use Excel, be sure to force the vertical axis to zero.)
2. Does the data appear sound, or do there appear to be any outliers? Explain.
3. Based on the scatter plot, do operating costs appear to be variable, fixed, or mixed costs?
4. How strong of a relationship is there between pancake volume and operating costs?

E6-31A High-low method *(Learning Objective 4)*

Refer to Dave's "Golden Brown" Pancake Restaurant in E6-30A.

Requirements

1. Use the high-low method to determine Dave's operating cost equation.

2. Use your answer from Requirement 1 to predict total monthly operating costs if Dave serves 4,000 pancakes one month.

3. Can you predict total monthly operating costs if Dave serves 10,000 pancakes a month? Explain.

E6-32A Regression analysis *(Learning Objective 5)*

Refer to Dave's "Golden Brown" Pancake Restaurant in E6-30A.

Requirements

1. Use Microsoft Excel to perform regression analysis on Dave's monthly data. Based on the output, write Dave's monthly operating cost equation.

2. Based on the R-square shown on the regression output, how well does this cost equation fit the data?

E6-33A Regression analysis using Excel output *(Learning Objective 5)*

Assume that Dave's "Golden Brown" Pancake Restaurant does a regression analysis on the next year's data using Excel 2007. The output generated by Excel is as follows:

SUMMARY OUTPUT

Regression Statistics

Multiple R	0.72
R Square	0.51
Adjusted R Square	0.39
Standard Error	99.45
Observations	6

ANOVA

	df	SS	MS	F	Significance F
Regression	1	41497.60	41497.60	4.20	0.11
Residual	4	39561.23	9890.31		
Total	5	81058.83			

	Coefficients	Standard Error	t Stat	P-value	Lower 95%	Upper 95%	Lower 95.0%	Upper 95.0%
Intercept	1423.60	564.95	2.52	0.07	-144.96	2992.16	-144.96	2992.16
X Variable 1	0.31	0.15	2.05	0.11	-0.11	0.72	-0.11	0.72

Requirements

1. What is the fixed cost per month?

2. What is the variable cost per pancake?

3. If Dave's "Golden Brown" Pancake Restaurant serves 3,700 pancakes in a month, what would the company's total operating costs be?

E6-34A Determine cost behavior and predict operating costs *(Learning Objective 4)*

Bayview Apartments is a 500-unit apartment complex. When the apartments are 90% occupied, monthly operating costs total $200,000. When occupancy dips to 80%, monthly operating costs fall to $197,000. The owner of the apartment complex is worried because many of the apartment residents work at a nearby manufacturing plant that has just announced that it will close in three months. The apartment owner fears that occupancy of her apartments will drop to 60% if residents lose their jobs and move away. Assuming the same relevant range, what can the owner expect her operating costs to be if occupancy falls to 60%?

E6-35A Prepare a contribution margin income statement (Learning Objective 6)

Precious Pets is a small e-tail business specializing in the sale of exotic pet gifts and accessories over the Web. The business is owned by a sole proprietor and operated out of her home. Results for last year are shown next:

PRECIOUS PETS
Income Statement
Year Ended December 31

Sales revenue	$ 987,000
Cost of goods sold	(665,000)
Gross profit	322,000
Operating expenses:	
Selling and marketing expenses	$61,000
Web site maintenance expenses	56,000
Other operating expenses	17,000
Total operating expenses	(134,000)
Operating income	$ 188,000

For internal planning and decision-making purposes, the owner of Precious Pets would like to translate the company's income statement into the contribution margin format. Since Precious Pets is an e-tailer, all of its cost of goods sold is variable. A large portion of the selling and marketing expenses consists of freight-out charges ($19,000), which were also variable. Only 20% of the remaining selling and marketing expenses and 25% of the Web site expenses were variable. Of the other operating expenses, 90% were fixed.

Based on this information, prepare Precious Pets' contribution margin income statement for last year.

E6-36A Prepare a contribution margin income statement (Learning Objective 6)

Charleston Carriage Company offers guided horse-drawn carriage rides through historic Charleston, South Carolina. The carriage business is highly regulated by the city. Charleston Carriage Company has the following operating costs during April:

Monthly depreciation expense on carriages and stable	$2,000
Fee paid to the City of Charleston	15% of ticket revenue
Cost of souvenir set of postcards given to each passenger	$0.50/set of postcards
Brokerage fee paid to independent ticket brokers (60% of tickets are issued through these brokers; 40% are sold directly by the Charleston Carriage Company)	$1.00/ticket sold by broker
Monthly cost of leasing and boarding the horses	$45,000
Carriage drivers (tour guides) are paid on a per passenger basis	$3.00 per passenger
Monthly payroll costs of non–tour guide employees	$7,500
Marketing, Web site, telephone, and other monthly fixed costs	$7,000

During April (a month during peak season) Charleston Carriage Company had 12,960 passengers. Eighty-five percent of passengers were adults ($20 fare) while 15% were children ($12 fare).

Requirements

1. Prepare the company's contribution margin income statement for the month of April. Round all figures to the nearest dollar.

2. Assume that passenger volume increases by 10% in May. Which figures on the income statement would you expect to change, and by what percentage would they change? Which figures would remain the same as in April?

E6-37A Absorption and variable costing income statements *(Learning Objective 7)*

(Appendix) The annual data that follow pertain to Rays, a manufacturer of swimming goggles (Rays had no beginning inventories):

Sales price	$ 35
Variable manufacturing expense per unit	15
Sales commission expense per unit	5
Fixed manufacturing overhead	2,000,000
Fixed operating expenses	250,000
Number of goggles produced	200,000
Number of goggles sold	185,000

Requirements

1. Prepare both conventional (absorption costing) and contribution margin (variable costing) income statements for Rays for the year.

2. Which statement shows the higher operating income? Why?

3. Rays' marketing vice president believes a new sales promotion that costs $150,000 would increase sales to 200,000 goggles. Should the company go ahead with the promotion? Give your reason.

Exercises—Group B

E6-38B Graph specific costs *(Learning Objective 1)*

Graph these cost behavior patterns over a relevant range of 0–10,000 units:
a. Variable expenses of $6 per unit
b. Mixed expenses made up of fixed costs of $30,000 and variable costs of $2 per unit
c. Fixed expenses of $20,000

E6-39B Identify cost behavior graph (*Learning Objective 1*)

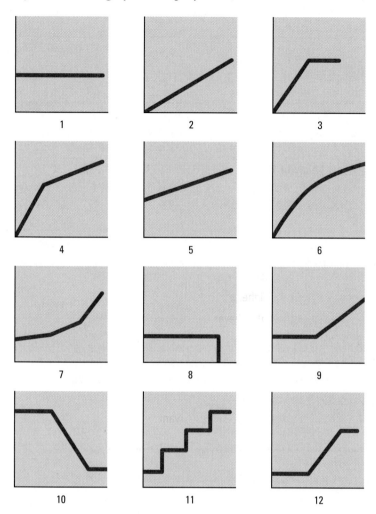

For each of the following situations, identify the graph that most closely represents the cost behavior pattern of the cost in that situation. Some graphs may be used more than once or not at all.

a. Cell phone bill, which is $59.99 for 1,400 anytime minutes in a month plus $0.30 per minute for any minutes used above the included 1,400 minutes

b. Rent on local specialty chocolates store building of $900 per month (the activity on the horizontal axis is sales dollars)

c. Mortgage loan processors are paid $20.00 per hour (the activity on the horizontal axis is number of mortgage loans processed)

d. Tuition is $400 per semester credit hour up to 10 credit hours; tuition for 11 credit hours or more is a flat fee of $4,400 per semester

e. Factory rent of $5,000 per month will be forgiven by the city (which owns the building) if the company employs twenty displaced workers in the month (the activity on the horizontal axis is the number of displaced workers employed)

f. The cost of materials for salsa chips when the ingredients in each pound of chips cost $0.85

g. Salaries of sales team managers, where a manager is needed for every 30 salespeople employed (the activity on the horizontal axis is the number of sales people)

h. Straight-line depreciation of computer network; depreciation is taken over a projected five-year life

i. Cost of electricity used in the plant. To encourage conservation, the electric company has the following price schedule per kilowatt hour in addition to the monthly service fee of $20:

Up to 1,000 kilowatt hours..	$0.050 per kilowatt hour
1,0001–20,000 kilowatt hours.....................................	$0.055 per kilowatt hour
More than 20,000 kilowatt hours	$0.075 per kilowatt hour

j. Monthly natural gas bill, which consists of a flat monthly service charge of $15.50 plus $13.01 per thousand cubic foot (Mcf) of natural gas used

E6-40B Identify cost behavior terms *(Learning Objectives 1, 2, 3, 4, & 5)*

Complete the following statements with one of the terms listed here. You may use a term more than once, and some terms may not be used at all.

R-square	Committed fixed costs	Regression analysis
Average cost per unit	Curvilinear cost(s)	Fixed cost(s)
Variable cost(s)	Total cost(s)	Mixed cost(s)
Step cost(s)	Account analysis	High-low method

a. The manager's judgment is used to determine the cost behavior of various accounts when using the _____ method of cost estimation.

b. _____ are always shown on the y-axis in cost equations graphs.

c. The _____ should not be used to predict total costs at various volumes unless it is strictly a/an _____.

d. As volume increases, _____ and _____ increase in total.

e. _____ are the result of previous management decisions and are not usually controllable in the short run.

f. _____ remain constant in total over a wide range of volume.

g. _____ remain constant in total over small ranges of activity.

h. Graphs of _____ always begin at the origin.

i. One of the disadvantages of the _____ is that it uses only two historical data points to determine the cost line and cost equation.

j. The "goodness-of-fit" statistic is also known as the _____.

k. _____ remain constant on a per unit basis.

l. All historical data points provided are used when performing a _____ to determine the cost equation.

m. As volume decreases, _____ and _____ increase on a per unit basis.

E6-41B Forecast costs at different volumes *(Learning Objectives 1 & 2)*

Pillard Drycleaners has capacity to clean up to 6,000 garments per month.

Requirements

1. Complete the following schedule for the three volumes shown.

	3,000 Garments	4,500 Garments	6,000 Garments
Total variable costs		$3,375	
Total fixed costs			
Total operating costs			
Variable cost per garment			
Fixed cost per garment		$ 2.20	
Average cost per garment			

2. Why does the average cost per garment change?

3. The owner, Dan Pillard, uses the average cost per unit *at full capacity* to predict total costs at a volume of 3,000 garments.

   Would he overestimate or underestimate his total costs? By how much?

E6-42B Prepare income statement in two formats *(Learning Objective 6)*

Refer to the Pillard Drycleaners in E6-41B. Assume that Pillard charges customers $8 per garment for dry cleaning. Prepare Pillard's *projected* income statement if 4,280 garments are cleaned in March. First, prepare the income statement using the traditional format; then, prepare Pillard's contribution margin income statement.

E6-43B Use the high-low method *(Learning Objective 4)*

Smith Company, which uses the high-low method to analyze cost behavior, has determined that machine hours best predict the company's total utilities cost. The company's cost and machine hour usage data for the first six months of the year follow:

Month	Total Cost	Machine Hours
January	$3,420	1,090
February	3,720	1,160
March	3,590	1,040
April	3,760	1,200
May	4,600	1,310
June	4,086	1,440

Requirements

Using the high-low method, answer the following questions:

1. What is the variable utilities cost per machine hour?

2. What is the fixed cost of utilities each month?

3. If Smith Company uses 1,220 machine hours in a month, what will its total costs be?

E6-44B Use unit cost data to forecast total costs *(Learning Objective 2)*

Acme Mailboxes produces decorative mailboxes. The company's average cost per unit is $23.43 when it produces 1,400 mailboxes.

Requirements

1. What is the total cost of producing 1,400 mailboxes?

2. If $15,000 of the total costs are fixed, what is the variable cost of producing each mailbox?

3. Write Acme Mailboxes' cost equation.

4. If the plant manager uses the average cost per unit to predict total costs, what would his forecast be for 1,700 mailboxes?

5. If the plant manager uses the cost equation to predict total costs, what would his forecast be for 1,700 mailboxes?

6. What is the dollar difference between your answers to Questions 4 and 5? Which approach to forecasting costs is appropriate? Why?

E6-45B   Use account analysis to determine cost behavior *(Learning Objective 3)*

Use your judgment (just as a manager would use his or her judgment for account analysis) to determine the cost behavior of each of the following personal costs:

a. Satellite TV, $40 per month for 150 channels plus $2.99 per pay-per-view movie

b. Bus ticket to local mall, $1 per ride

c. Condo rental, $750 per month

d. Local phone service with unlimited local calls, $19.99 per month plus $0.05 per minute for long-distance calls

e. Student activity pass, $50 plus $5 per event

f. Campus meal plan, $3 per meal

g. Pay-as-you-go cell phone plan with no monthly service fee and $0.20 per minute used

h. Utilities, $20 per month plus $0.475 per kilowatt hour

i. Car payment, $400 per month

j. Gas, $2.79 per gallon and your car averages 45 miles per gallon

k. Car insurance, $175 per month

E6-46B   Create a scatter plot *(Learning Objective 3)*

Alice Coughlin, owner of Tulip Time, operates a local chain of floral shops. Each shop has its own delivery van. Instead of charging a flat delivery fee, Coughlin wants to set the delivery fee based on the distance driven to deliver the flowers. Coughlin wants to separate the fixed and variable portions of her van operating costs so that she has a better idea how delivery distance affects these costs. She has the following data from the past seven months:

Month	Miles Driven	Van Operating Costs
January	15,500	$5,400
February	17,500	5,350
March	14,400	4,980
April	16,400	5,280
May	16,900	5,580
June	15,300	5,010
July	13,500	4,590

February and May are always Tulip Time's biggest months because of Valentine's Day and Mother's Day, respectively.

Requirements

1. Prepare a scatter plot of Alice's volume (miles driven) and van operating costs.

2. Does the data appear to contain any outliers? Explain.

3. How strong of a relationship is there between miles driven and van operating expenses?

E6-47B   High-low method *(Learning Objective 4)*

Refer to Alice's Tulip Time data in E6-46B. Use the high-low method to determine Tulip Time's cost equation for van operating costs. Use your results to predict van operating costs at a volume of 14,500 miles.

E6-48B   Continuation of E6-46BA: Regression analysis *(Learning Objective 5)*

Refer to the Tulip Time data in E6-46B. Use Microsoft Excel to run a regression analysis, then do the following calculations.

Requirements

1. Determine the firm's cost equation (use the output from the Excel regression).

2. Determine the R-square (use the output from the Excel regression). What does Tulip Time's R-square indicate?

3. Predict van operating costs at a volume of 14,500 miles.

E6-49B Regression analysis using Excel output *(Learning Objective 5)*

Assume that Alice's Tulip Time does a regression analysis on the next year's data using Excel 2007. The output generated by Excel is as follows:

Regression Statistics

Multiple R	0.85
R Square	0.72
Adjusted R Square	0.66
Standard Error	205.01
Observations	7

ANOVA

	df	SS	MS	F	Significance F
Regression	1	539222.81	539222.81	12.83	0.0158
Residual	5	210148.62	42029.72		
Total	6	749371.43			

	Coefficients	Standard Error	t Stat	P-value	Lower 95%	Upper 95%	Lower 95.0%	Upper 95.0%
Intercept	678.76	1316.00	0.52	0.63	-2704.12	4061.65	-2704.12	4061.65
X Variable 1	0.29	0.08	3.58	0.02	0.08	0.51	0.08	0.51

Requirements

1. Determine the firm's cost equation (use the output from the Excel regression).

2. Determine the R-square (use the output from the Excel regression). What does Tulip Time's R-square indicate?

3. Predict van operating costs at a volume of 15,500 miles.

E6-50B Prepare and interpret a scatter plot *(Learning Objective 3)*

Cliff's "Fresh Stacks" Pancake Restaurant features sourdough pancakes made from a strain of sourdough dating back to the Alaskan gold rush. To plan for the future, Cliff needs to figure out his cost behavior patterns. He has the following information about his operating costs and the number of pancakes served:

Month	Number of Pancakes	Total Operating Costs
July	3,900	$2,340
August	4,200	2,530
September	3,600	2,440
October	3,700	2,290
November	4,000	2,560
December	3,850	2,510

Requirements

1. Prepare a scatter plot of Cliff's pancake volume and operating costs.

2. Does the data appear sound, or do there appear to be any outliers? Explain.

3. Based on the scatter plot, do operating costs appear to be variable, fixed, or mixed costs?

4. How strong of a relationship is there between pancake volume and operating costs?

E6-51B   High-low method *(Learning Objective 4)*

Refer to Cliff's "Fresh Stacks" Pancake Restaurant in E6-50B.

Requirements

1. Use the high-low method to determine Cliff's operating cost equation.

2. Use your answer from Requirement 1 to predict total monthly operating costs if Cliff serves 4,500 pancakes a month.

3. Can you predict total monthly operating costs if Cliff serves 12,000 pancakes a month? Explain.

E6-52B   Regression analysis *(Learning Objective 5)*

Refer to Cliff's "Fresh Stacks" Pancake Restaurant in E6-50B.
Use Microsoft Excel to run a regression analysis, then do the following calculations:

Requirements

1. Determine Cliff's monthly operating cost equation (use the output from the Excel regression).

2. Based on the R-square shown on the regression output, how well does this cost equation fit the data?

E6-53B   Regression analysis using Excel output *(Learning Objective 5)*

Assume that Cliff's "Fresh Stack" Pancake Restaurant does a regression analysis on the next year's data using Excel 2007. The output generated by Excel is as follows:

Regression Statistics

Multiple R	0.56
R Square	0.31
Adjusted R Square	0.14
Standard Error	107.40
Observations	6

ANOVA

	df	SS	MS	F	Significance F
Regression	1	20542.55	20542.55	1.78	0.25
Residual	4	46140.78	11535.19		
Total	5	66683.33			

	Coefficients	Standard Error	t Stat	P-value	Lower 95%	Upper 95%	Lower 95.0%	Upper 95.0%
Intercept	1626.18	632.59	2.57	0.06	-130.18	3382.54	-130.18	3382.54
X Variable 1	0.22	0.16	1.33	0.25	-0.24	0.67	-0.24	0.67

Requirements

1. What is the fixed cost per month?

2. What is the variable cost per pancake?

3. If Cliff's "Fresh Stack" Pancake Restaurant serves 4,200 pancakes in a month, what would its total operating costs be?

E6-54B   Determine cost behavior and predict operating costs *(Learning Objective 4)*

Bayside Apartments is a 750-unit apartment complex. When the apartments are 90% occupied, monthly operating costs total $216,825. When occupancy dips to 80%, monthly operating costs fall to $212,400. The owner of the apartment complex is worried because many of the apartment residents work at a nearby manufacturing plant that has just announced it will close in three months. The apartment owner fears that occupancy of his apartments will drop to 60% if residents lose their jobs and move away. Assuming the same relevant range, what should the owner expect his operating costs to be if occupancy falls to 60%?

E6-55B Prepare a contribution margin income statement *(Learning Objective 6)*

Pretty Pets is a small e-tail business specializing in the sale of exotic pet gifts and accessories over the Web. The business is owned by a sole proprietor and operated out of her home. Results for last year are shown next:

PRETTY PETS
Income Statement
Year Ended December 31

Sales revenue		$1,011,000
Cost of goods sold		(671,000)
Gross profit		340,000
Operating expenses:		
Selling and marketing expenses	$61,000	
Web site maintenance expenses	60,000	
Other operating expenses	17,800	
Total operating expenses		(138,800)
Operating income		$ 201,200

For internal planning and decision making purposes, the owner of Pretty Pets would like to translate the company's income statement into the contribution margin format. Since Pretty Pets is an e-tailer, all of its cost of goods sold is variable. A large portion of the selling and marketing expenses consists of freight-out charges ($20,400), which were also variable. Only 20% of the remaining selling and marketing expenses and 25% of the Web site expenses were variable. Of the other operating expenses, 90% were fixed. Based on this information, prepare Pretty Pets's contribution margin income statement for last year.

E6-56B Prepare a contribution margin income statement *(Learning Objective 6)*

Counton Carriage Company offers guided horse-drawn carriage rides through historic Charleston, South Carolina. The carriage business is highly regulated by the city. Counton Carriage Company has the following operating costs during April:

Monthly depreciation expense on carriages and stable	$2,900
Fee paid to the City of Charleston	15% of ticket revenue
Cost of souvenir set of postcards given to each passenger	$0.75/set of postcards
Brokerage fee paid to independent ticket brokers (60% of tickets are issued through these brokers; 40% are sold directly by the Counton Carriage Company)	$1.20/ticket sold by broker
Monthly cost of leasing and boarding the horses	$48,000
Carriage drivers (tour guides) are paid on a per passenger basis	$3.00 per passenger
Monthly payroll costs of non–tour guide employees	$7,500
Marketing, Web site, telephone, and other monthly fixed costs	$7,250

During April (a month during peak season) Counton Carriage Company had 12,970 passengers. Eighty-five percent of passengers were adults ($26 fare) while 15% were children ($18 fare).

Requirements

1. Prepare the company's contribution margin income statement for the month of April. Round all figures to the nearest dollar.

2. Assume that passenger volume increases by 18% in May. Which figures on the income statement would you expect to change, and by what percentage would they change? Which figures would remain the same as in April?

E6-57B Absorption and variable costing income statements *(Learning Objective 7) (Appendix)*

The annual data that follow pertain to Swim Clearly, a manufacturer of swimming goggles (Swim Clearly has no beginning inventories):

Sale price	$42	Fixed manufacturing overhead	$1,935,000
Variable manufacturing		Fixed operating expense	265,000
expense per unit	20	Number of goggles produced	215,000
Sales commission expense per unit	5	Number of goggles sold	200,000

Requirements

1. Prepare both conventional (absorption costing) and contribution margin (variable costing) income statements for Swim Clearly for the year.

2. Which statement shows the higher operating income? Why?

3. Swim Clearly's marketing vice president believes a new sales promotion that costs $145,000 would increase sales to 215,000 goggles. Should the company go ahead with the promotion? Give your reason.

Problems—Group A

P6-58A Analyze cost behavior *(Learning Objectives 1, 2, 3, & 4)*

Berg Industries is in the process of analyzing its manufacturing overhead costs. Berg Industries is not sure if the number of units produced or number of direct labor (DL) hours is the best cost driver to use for predicting manufacturing overhead (MOH) costs. The following information is available:

Month	Manufacturing Overhead Costs	Direct Labor Hours	Units Produced	MOH Cost per DL Hour	MOH Cost per Unit Produced
July	$460,000	23,000	3,600	$20.00	$127.78
August	515,000	26,400	4,320	19.51	119.21
September	425,000	19,000	4,200	21.36	101.19
October	448,000	21,600	3,400	20.74	131.76
November	527,000	27,000	5,750	19.52	91.65
December	437,000	19,400	3,250	22.53	134.46

Requirements

1. Are manufacturing overhead costs fixed, variable, or mixed? Explain.

2. Graph Berg Industries' manufacturing overhead costs against DL hours. Use Excel or graph by hand.

3. Graph Berg Industries' manufacturing overhead costs against units produced. Use Excel or graph by hand.

4. Do the data appear to be sound, or do you see any potential data problems? Explain.

5. Use the high-low method to determine Berg Industries' manufacturing overhead cost equation using DL hours as the cost driver. Assume that management believes that all data is accurate and wants to include all of it in the analysis.

6. Estimate manufacturing overhead costs if Berg Industries incurs 24,000 DL hours in January.

P6-59A   Continuation of P6-58A: Regression analysis *(Learning Objective 5)*

Refer to Berg Industries in P6-58A.

Requirements

1. Use Excel regression analysis to determine Berg Industries' manufacturing overhead cost equation using DL hours as the cost driver. Comment on the R-square. Estimate manufacturing overhead costs if Berg Industries incurs 24,000 DL hours in January.

2. Use Excel regression analysis to determine Berg's manufacturing overhead cost equation using number of units produced as the cost driver. Use all of the data provided. Project total manufacturing overhead costs if Berg Industries produces 5,000 units. Which cost equation is better—this one or the one from Question 1? Why?

3. Use Excel regression analysis to determine Berg Industries' manufacturing overhead cost equation using number of units produced as the cost driver. This time, remove any potential outliers before performing the regression. How does this affect the R-square? Project total manufacturing overhead costs if 5,000 units are produced.

4. In which cost equation do you have the most confidence? Why?

P6-60A   Prepare traditional and contribution margin income statements *(Learning Objective 6)*

Kelsey's Ice Cream Shoppe sold 9,000 servings of ice cream during June for $3 per serving. Kelsey purchases the ice cream in large tubs from the BlueBell Ice Cream Company. Each tub costs Kelsey $15 and has enough ice cream to fill 30 ice cream cones. Kelsey purchases the ice cream cones for $0.05 each from a local warehouse club. Kelsey's Shoppe is located in a local strip mall, and she pays $1,800 a month to lease the space. Kelsey expenses $250 a month for the depreciation of the Shoppe's furniture and equipment. During June, Kelsey incurred an additional $2,500 of other operating expenses (75% of these were fixed costs).

Requirements

1. Prepare Kelsey's June income statement using a traditional format.

2. Prepare Kelsey's June income statement using a contribution margin format.

P6-61A   Determine financial statement components *(Learning Objective 7) (Appendix)*

Violins-by-Hannah produces student-grade violins for beginning violin students. The company produced 2,000 violins in its first month of operations. At month-end, 600 finished violins remained unsold. There was no inventory in work in process. Violins were sold for $112.50 each. Total costs from the month are as follows:

Direct materials used	$80,000
Direct labor	50,000
Variable manufacturing overhead	30,000
Fixed manufacturing overhead	40,000
Variable selling and administrative expenses	10,000
Fixed selling and administrative expenses	15,000

The company prepares traditional (absorption costing) income statements for its bankers. Hannah would also like to prepare contribution margin income statements for her own management use. Compute the following amounts that would be shown on these income statements:

1. Gross profit

2. Contribution margin

3. Total expenses shown **below** the **gross profit** line

4. Total expenses shown **below** the **contribution margin** line

5. Dollar value of ending inventory under absorption costing

6. Dollar value of ending inventory under variable costing

Which income statement will have a higher operating income? By how much? Explain.

P6-62A Absorption and variable costing income statements *(Learning Objective 7)* *(Appendix)*

Mario's Foods produces frozen meals, which it sells for $7 each. The company uses the FIFO inventory costing method, and it computes a new monthly fixed manufacturing overhead rate based on the actual number of meals produced that month. All costs and production levels are exactly as planned. The following data are from Mario's Foods' first two months in business:

	January	February
Sales...	1,000 meals	1,200 meals
Production	1,400 meals	1,000 meals
Variable manufacturing expense per meal..............	$ 4	$ 4
Sales commission expense per meal........................	$ 1	$ 1
Total fixed manufacturing overhead	$ 700	$ 700
Total fixed marketing and administrative expenses	$ 600	$ 600

Requirements

1. Compute the product cost per meal produced under absorption costing and under variable costing. Do this first for January and then for February.

2. Prepare separate monthly income statements for January and for February, using the following:
   a. Absorption costing
   b. Variable costing

3. Is operating income higher under absorption costing or variable costing in January? In February? Explain the pattern of differences in operating income based on absorption costing versus variable costing.

Problems—Group B

P6-63B Analyze cost behavior *(Learning Objectives 1, 2, 3, & 4)*

Carmichael Industries is in the process of analyzing its manufacturing overhead costs. Carmichael Industries is not sure if the number of units produced or the number of direct labor (DL) hours is the best cost driver to use for predicting manufacturing overhead (MOH) costs. The following information is available:

Month	Manufacturing Overhead Costs	Direct Labor Hours	Units Produced	MOH Cost per DL Hour	MOH Cost per Unit Produced
July	$463,000	23,100	3,620	$20.04	$127.90
August......................	513,000	26,500	4,300	19.36	119.30
September	435,000	20,000	4,230	21.75	102.84
October....................	450,000	21,400	3,380	21.03	133.14
November	562,000	30,000	5,790	18.73	97.06
December.................	438,000	20,500	3,300	21.37	132.73

Requirements

1. Are manufacturing overhead costs fixed, variable, or mixed? Explain.
2. Graph Carmichael Industries' manufacturing overhead costs against DL hours.
3. Graph Carmichael Industries' manufacturing overhead costs against units produced.
4. Do the data appear to be sound or do you see any potential data problems? Explain.

5. Use the high-low method to determine Carmichael Industries' manufacturing overhead cost equation using DL hours as the cost driver. Assume that management believes that all the data is accurate and wants to include all of it in the analysis.

6. Estimate manufacturing overhead costs if Carmichael Industries incurs 25,500 DL hours in January.

P6-64B Continuation of P6-63B: Regression analysis *(Learning Objective 5)*

Refer to Carmichael Industries in P6-63B.

Requirements

1. Use Excel regression analysis to determine Carmichael Industries' manufacturing overhead cost equation using DL hours as the cost driver. Comment on the R-square. Estimate manufacturing overhead costs if Carmichael Industries incurs 25,500 DL hours in January.

2. Use Excel regression analysis to determine Carmichael's manufacturing overhead cost equation using number of units produced as the cost driver. Use all of the data provided. Project total manufacturing overhead costs if Carmichael Industries produces 5,200 units. Which cost equation is better this one or the one from Question 1? Why?

3. Use Excel regression analysis to determine Carmichael Industries' manufacturing overhead cost equation using number of units produced as the cost driver. This time, remove any potential outliers before performing the regression. How does this affect the R-square? Project total manufacturing overhead costs if 5,200 units are produced.

4. In which cost equation do you have the most confidence? Why?

P6-65B Prepare traditional and contribution margin income statements *(Learning Objective 6)*

Mary's Ice Cream Shoppe sold 9,100 servings of ice cream during June for $4 per serving. Mary purchases the ice cream in large tubs from the Organic Ice Cream Company. Each tub costs Mary $14 and has enough ice cream to fill 28 ice cream cones. Mary purchases the ice cream cones for $0.20 each from a local warehouse club. Mary's Shoppe is located in a local strip mall, and she pays $2,050 a month to lease the space. Mary expenses $210 a month for the depreciation of the Shoppe's furniture and equipment. During June, Mary incurred an additional $2,000 of other operating expenses (75% of these were fixed costs).

Requirements

1. Prepare Mary's June income statement using a traditional format.

2. Prepare Mary's June income statement using a contribution margin format.

P6-66B Determine financial statement components *(Learning Objective 7) (Appendix)*

Music World produces student-grade violins for beginning violin students. The company produced 2,100 violins in its first month of operations. At month-end, 550 finished violins remained unsold. There was no inventory in work in process. Violins were sold for $122.50 each. Total costs from the month are as follows:

Direct materials used	$87,200
Direct labor	60,000
Variable manufacturing overhead	25,000
Fixed manufacturing overhead	44,100
Variable selling and administrative expenses	8,000
Fixed selling and administrative expenses	13,900

The company prepares traditional (absorption costing) income statements for its bankers. Hannah would also like to prepare contribution margin income statements for her own management use. Compute the following amounts that would be shown on these income statements:

1. Gross profit

2. Contribution margin

3. Total expenses shown **below** the **gross profit** line

4. Total expenses shown **below** the **contribution margin** line

5. Dollar value of ending inventory under absorption costing

6. Dollar value of ending inventory under variable costing

Which income statement will have a higher operating income? By how much? Explain.

P6-67B Absorption and variable costing income statements *(Learning Objective 7) (Appendix)*

Marty's Entrees produces frozen meals, which it sells for $9 each. The company uses the FIFO inventory costing method, and it computes a new monthly fixed manufacturing overhead rate based on the actual number of meals produced that month. All costs and production levels are exactly as planned. The following data are from Marty's Entrees' first two months in business:

	January	February
Sales	1,400 meals	1,800 meals
Production	2,000 meals	1,400 meals
Variable manufacturing expense per meal	$ 5	$ 5
Sales commission expense per meal	$ 1	$ 1
Total fixed manufacturing overhead	$ 700	$ 700
Total fixed marketing and administrative expenses	$ 500	$ 500

Requirements

1. Compute the product cost per meal produced under absorption costing and under variable costing. Do this first for January and then for February.

2. Prepare separate monthly income statements for January and for February, using (a) absorption costing and (b) variable costing.

3. Is operating income higher under absorption costing or variable costing in January? In February? Explain the pattern of differences in operating income based on absorption costing versus variable costing.

APPLY YOUR KNOWLEDGE

Decision Case

C6-68 Appendix *(Learning Objective 7)*

Suppose you serve on the board of directors of American Faucet, a manufacturer of bathroom fixtures that recently adopted a lean production philosophy. Part of your responsibility is to develop a compensation contract for Toni Moen, the vice president of manufacturing. To give her the incentive to make decisions that will increase the company's profits, the board decides to give Moen a year-end bonus if American Faucet meets a target operating income.

Write a memo to Chairperson of the Board Herbert Kohler explaining whether the bonus contract should be based on absorption costing or variable costing. Use the following format:

Date: _____

To: _____

From: _____

Subject: _____

C6-69 Analyze cost behavior using a variety of methods *(Learning Objectives 1, 2, 3, 4, & 5)*

Braunhaus Microbrewery is in the process of analyzing its manufacturing overhead costs. Braunhaus Microbrewery is not sure if the number of cases or the number of processing hours is the best cost driver of manufacturing overhead (MOH) costs. The following information is available:

Month	Manufacturing Overhead Costs	Processing Hours	Cases	MOH Cost per Processing Hour	MOH Cost per Case
January	$29,500	680	8,000	$43.38	$3.69
February............	27,800	575	6,750	48.35	4.12
March	24,500	500	5,500	49.00	4.45
April.................	29,000	600	7,250	48.33	4.00
May	28,000	650	7,800	43.08	3.59
June.................	29,750	710	5,600	41.90	5.31

Requirements

1. Are manufacturing overhead costs fixed, variable, or mixed? Explain.

2. Graph Braunhaus Microbrewery's manufacturing overhead costs against processing hours. Use Excel or graph by hand.

3. Graph Braunhaus Microbrewery's manufacturing overhead costs against cases produced. Use Excel or graph by hand.

4. Does the data appear to be sound, or do you see any potential data problems? Explain.

5. Use the high-low method to determine Braunhaus Microbrewery's manufacturing overhead cost equation using processing hours as the cost driver. Assume that management believes all of the data to be accurate and wants to include all of it in the analysis.

6. Estimate manufacturing overhead costs if Braunhaus Microbrewery incurs 550 processing hours in July, using the results of the high-low analysis in Requirement 5.

7. Use Excel regression analysis to determine Braunhaus Microbrewery's manufacturing overhead cost equation using processing hours as the cost driver. Comment on the R-square. Estimate manufacturing overhead costs if Braunhaus Microbrewery incurs 550 processing hours in July.

8. Use Excel regression analysis to determine Braunhaus Microbrewery's manufacturing overhead cost equation using number of cases produced as the cost driver. Use all of the data provided. Project total manufacturing overhead costs if Braunhaus Microbrewery produces 6,000 cases. Which cost equation is better—this one or the one from Requirement 7? Why?

9. Use Excel regression analysis to determine Braunhaus Microbrewery's manufacturing overhead cost equation using number of cases produced as the cost driver. This time, remove any potential outliers before performing the regression. How does this affect the R-square? Project total manufacturing overhead costs if Braunhaus Microbrewery produces 6,000 cases.

10. In which cost equation do you have the most confidence? Why?

Quick Check Answers
1. *a* 2. *c* 3. *d* 4. *b* 5. *a* 6. *b* 7. *d* 8. *c* 9. *a* 10. *c*

For online homework, exercises, and problems that provide you with immediate feedback, please visit www.myaccountinglab.com.

Discussion & Analysis

1. Briefly describe an organization with which you are familiar. Describe a situation when a manager in that organization could use cost behavior information and how the manager could use the information.

2. How are fixed costs similar to step fixed costs? How are fixed costs different from step fixed costs? Give an example of a step fixed cost and describe why that cost is not considered to be a fixed cost.

3. Describe a specific situation when a scatter plot could be useful to a manager.

4. What is a mixed cost? Give an example of a mixed cost. Sketch a graph of this example.

5. Compare discretionary fixed costs to committed fixed costs. Think of an organization with which you are familiar. Give two examples of discretionary fixed costs and two examples of committed fixed costs which that organization may have. Explain why the costs you have chosen as examples fit within the definitions of "discretionary fixed costs" and "committed fixed costs."

6. Define the terms "independent variable" and "dependent variable," as used in regression analysis. Illustrate the concepts of independent variables and dependent variables by selecting a cost a company would want to predict and what activity it might use to predict that cost. Describe the independent variable and the dependent variable in that situation.

7. Define the term "relevant range." Why is it important to managers?

8. Describe the term "R-square." If a regression analysis for predicting manufacturing overhead using direct labor hours as the dependent variable has an R-square of 0.40, why might this be a problem? Given the low R-square value, describe the options a manager has for predicting manufacturing overhead costs. Which option do you think is the best option for the manager? Defend your answer.

9. Over the past year, a company's inventory has increased significantly. The company uses absorption costing for financial statements, but internally, the company uses variable costing for financial statements. Which set of financial statements will show the highest operating income? What specifically causes the difference between the two sets of financial statements?

10. A company has adopted a lean production philosophy and, as a result, has cut its inventory levels significantly. Describe the impact on the company's external financial statements as a result of this inventory reduction. Also describe the impact of the inventory reduction on the company's internal financial statements which are prepared using variable costing.

Application & Analysis

6-1 Cost Behavior in Real Companies

Choose a company with which you are familiar that manufactures a product or provides a service. In this activity, you will be making reasonable estimates of the costs and activities associated with this company; companies do not typically publish internal cost or process information.

Basic Discussion Questions

1. Describe the company you selected and the products or services it provides.

2. List ten costs that this company would incur. Include costs from a variety of departments within the company, including human resources, sales, accounting, production (if a manufacturer), service (if a service company), and others. Make sure that you have at least one cost from each of the following categories: fixed, variable, and mixed.

3. Classify each of the costs you listed as either fixed, variable, or mixed. Justify why you classified each cost as you did.

4. Describe a potential cost driver for each of the variable and mixed costs you listed. Explain why each cost driver would be appropriate for its associated cost.

5. Discuss how easy or difficult it was for you to decide whether each cost was fixed, variable, or mixed. Describe techniques a company could use to determine whether a cost is fixed, variable, or mixed.

Classroom Applications

Web: Post the discussion questions on an electronic discussion board. Have small groups of students choose a company for their group.

Classroom: Form groups of 3–4 students. Your group should choose a company that manufactures a product or provides a service. After deciding upon a company, discuss each of the listed questions. Prepare a five-minute presentation about your group's company that addresses the listed questions.

Independent: Write a paper that addresses each of the listed questions for a company of your choice that manufacturers a product or provides a service. Turn in a 2–3 page typed paper (12 point font, double-spaced with 1" margins).

For additional Application & Analysis projects and implementation tips, see Instructor Resources in MyAccountingLab.com.

CMA-1. Ace, Inc., estimates its total materials handling costs at two production levels as follows.

Cost	Gallons
$160,000	80,000
$132,000	60,000

What is the estimated total cost for handling 75,000 gallons?

a. $146,000.

b. $150,000.

c. $153,000.

d. $165,000.

CMA-2. Huntington Corporation pays bonuses to its managers based on operating income, as calculated under variable costing. It is now two months before year-end, and earnings have been depressed for some time. Which one of the following should Wanda Richards, production manager, **definitely** implement if she desires to maximize her bonus for this year?

a. Step up production so that more manufacturing costs are deferred into inventory.

b. Cut $2.3 million of advertising and marketing costs.

c. Postpone $1.8 million of discretionary equipment maintenance until next year.

d. Implement, with the aid of the controller, an activity-based costing and activity-based management system.

(CMA Adapted)

Founded in 1995, Art.com, Inc., has become the world's

largest online retailer of fine art, photography, posters, and other wall décor. The company offers over 500,000 different products to customers ranging from budget-minded college students to professional decorators searching for high-end art. With over one million people visiting the company's Web site each month, Internet Retailer named Art.com one of the "Hot 100 Best Retail Web Sites in 2008." Even though Art.com doesn't face many of the fixed costs of traditional retail outlets, the company still incurs fixed costs related to its Web site, distribution centers, and custom-framing facilities. It also incurs variable costs for each piece of art. The bottom line is e-tail or retail, every business faces fixed and variable costs, and Art.com is no exception. Before they launched the company, how did Art.com managers figure out what sales volume they had to reach to break even? How did they forecast the volume needed to achieve their target profit? And as the company continues to operate, how do managers respond to fluctuating business conditions, changing variable and fixed costs, and pricing pressure from new competitors? Cost-volume-profit (CVP) analysis helps managers answer such questions.

Source: http://corporate.art.com

CHAPTER 7

Cost-Volume-Profit Analysis

Learning Objectives

1. Calculate the unit contribution margin and the contribution margin ratio
2. Use CVP analysis to find breakeven points and target profit volumes
3. Perform sensitivity analysis in response to changing business conditions
4. Find breakeven and target profit volumes for multiproduct companies
5. Determine a firm's margin of safety and operating leverage

In the last chapter, we discussed cost behavior patterns and the methods managers use to determine how the company's costs behave. We showed how managers use the contribution margin income statement to separately display the firm's variable and fixed costs. In this chapter, we show how managers identify the volume of sales necessary to achieve breakeven or a target profit. We also look at how changes in costs, sales price, and volume affect the firm's profit. Finally, we discuss ways to identify the firm's risk level, including ways to gauge how easily a firm's profits could turn to loss if sales volume declines.

How Does Cost-Volume-Profit Analysis Help Managers?

Cost-volume-profit, or CVP, analysis is a powerful tool that helps managers make important business decisions. **Cost-volume-profit analysis** expresses the relationships among costs, volume, and profit or loss. For example, at Art.com, managers need to determine how many pieces of art the company must sell each month just to cover costs or to break even. CVP can provide the answer. CVP also helps Art.com's managers determine how many pieces of art the company must sell to earn a target profit, such as $1,000,000 per month. And if costs or sales prices change, CVP can help managers decide how sales volume would need to change to achieve the same profit level.

However, to use CVP, managers need certain data. They must also make sure the data are consistent with the assumptions underlying CVP analysis. In addition, managers need a solid understanding of the contribution margin concept introduced in the last chapter. In this section, we'll take a look at the data requirements, assumptions, and contribution margin in more detail.

Data Required for Effective CVP Analysis

CVP analysis relies on the interdependency of five components, or pieces of information, shown in Exhibit 7-1.

EXHIBIT 7-1 **Components of CVP Analysis**

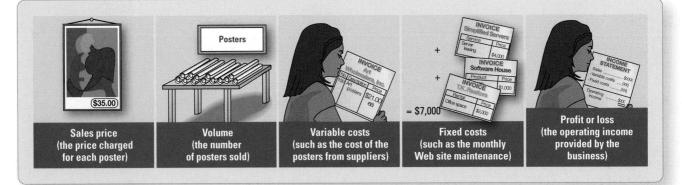

If you know or can estimate four of these five components, you can use CVP analysis to compute the remaining unknown amount. Therefore, CVP helps managers discover how changes in any of these components will affect their business. Because business conditions are always changing, CVP helps managers prepare for and respond to economic changes. Now, let's review the assumptions required for CVP analysis.

CVP Assumptions

CVP analysis assumes the following:

1. A change in volume is the only factor that affects costs.

2. Managers can classify each cost (or the components of mixed costs) as either variable or fixed. These costs are linear throughout the relevant range of volume.

3. Revenues are linear throughout the relevant range of volume.

4. Inventory levels will not change.

5. The sales mix of products will not change. **Sales mix** is the combination of products that make up total sales. For example, Art.com may sell 15% posters, 25% unframed photographs, and 60% framed prints. If profits differ across products, changes in sales mix will affect CVP analysis.

Let's start by looking at a simple firm that has only one product. Later, we'll expand the firm to include a wider selection of products. Kay Martin, an entrepreneur, has just started an e-tail business selling art posters on the Internet. Kay is a "virtual retailer" and carries no inventory. Kay's software tabulates all customer orders each day and then automatically places the order to buy posters from a wholesaler. Kay buys only what she needs to fill the prior day's sales orders. The posters cost $21 each, and Kay sells them for $35 each. Customers pay the shipping costs, so there are no other variable selling costs. Monthly fixed costs for server leasing and maintenance, software, and office rental total $7,000. Kay's relevant range extends from 0 to 2,000 posters a month. Beyond this volume, Kay will need to hire an employee and upgrade her Web site software in order to handle the increased volume.

Let's see if Kay's business meets the CVP assumptions:

1. Sales volume is the only factor that affects Kay's costs.

2. The $21 purchase cost for each poster is a variable cost. Thus, Kay's *total variable cost* increases in direct proportion to the number of posters she sells (an extra $21 in cost for each extra poster she sells). The $7,000 monthly server leasing and maintenance, software, and office rental costs are fixed and do not change no matter how many posters she sells within the relevant range. We could graph each of these costs as a straight line, so they are linear within the relevant range.

3. Kay's revenue is also linear. She sells each poster for $35, so a graph of her revenues is a straight line beginning at the origin (if she doesn't sell any posters, she won't have any revenue) that slopes upward at a rate of $35 per poster.

4. Kay has no inventory. If she did carry inventory, she wouldn't need to worry about this assumption as long as she didn't allow her inventory levels to fluctuate too much.

5. Kay sells just one size poster, so her sales mix is constant at 100% art posters. Later, we'll expand her product line to include two different sized posters—each with a different sales price and variable cost. The resulting CVP modification works for any firm that offers two or more products as long as it assumes that sales mix will remain constant.

Kay's business meets all five assumptions, so her CVP analysis will be accurate. Because most business conditions do not meet these assumptions *perfectly*, managers regard CVP analysis as approximate, not exact.

The Unit Contribution Margin

The last chapter introduced the **contribution margin income statement**, which separates costs by behavior rather than function. Many managers prefer the contribution margin income statement because it gives them the information for CVP analysis in a "ready-to-use" format. On these income statements, the contribution margin is the "dividing line"—all variable expenses go above the line, and all fixed expenses go below the line. The results of Kay's first month of operations is shown in Exhibit 7-2.

> Calculate the unit contribution margin and the contribution margin ratio **1**

EXHIBIT 7-2 Contribution Margin Income Statement

KAY MARTIN POSTERS
Contribution Margin Income Statement
Month Ended August 31

Sales revenue (550 posters)	$ 19,250
Less: Variable expenses	(11,550)
Contribution margin	7,700
Less: Fixed expenses	(7,000)
Operating income	$ 700

Notice that the **contribution margin** is the excess of sales revenue over variable expenses. The contribution margin tells managers how much revenue is left—after paying variable expenses—for *contributing* toward covering fixed costs and then generating a profit, hence the name contribution margin.

Why is this important?

"The unit contribution margin tells managers how much profit they make on each unit before considering fixed costs."

The contribution margin is stated as a *total* amount on the contribution margin income statement. However, managers often state the contribution margin on a *per unit* basis and as a *percentage,* or *ratio.* A product's **contribution margin per unit**—or unit contribution margin—is the excess of the selling price per unit over the variable cost of obtaining *and* selling each unit. Some businesses pay a sales commission on each unit or have other variable costs, such as shipping costs, for each unit sold. However, Kay's variable cost per unit is simply the price she pays for each poster. Therefore, her unit contribution margin is as follows:

Sales price per poster............................	$ 35
Less: Variable cost per poster...............	(21)
Contribution margin per poster............	$ 14

The unit contribution margin indicates how much profit each unit provides *before* fixed costs are considered. Each unit *first* contributes this profit toward covering the firm's fixed costs. Once the company sells enough units to cover its fixed costs, the unit contribution margin contributes *directly* to profit. For example, every poster Kay sells generates $14 of contribution margin that can be used to pay for the monthly $7,000 of fixed costs. After Kay sells enough posters to cover fixed costs, each additional poster she sells will generate $14 of operating income.

Managers can use the unit contribution margin to quickly forecast income at any volume within their relevant range. First, they project the total contribution margin by multiplying the unit contribution margin by the number of units they expect to sell. Then, they subtract fixed costs. For example, let's assume that Kay hopes to sell 650 posters next month. She can project her operating income as follows:

Contribution margin (650 posters × $14 per poster)	$ 9,100
Less: Fixed expenses..	(7,000)
Operating income...	$ 2,100

If Kay sells 650 posters next month, her operating income should be $2,100.

The Contribution Margin Ratio

In addition to computing the unit contribution margin, managers often compute the **contribution margin ratio,** which is the ratio of contribution margin to sales revenue. Kay can compute her contribution margin ratio at the unit level as follows:

$$\text{Contribution margin ratio} = \frac{\text{Unit contribution margin}}{\text{Sales price per unit}} = \frac{\$14}{\$35} = 40\%$$

Kay could also compute the contribution margin ratio using any volume of sales. Let's use her current sales volume, pictured in Exhibit 7-2:

$$\text{Contribution margin ratio} = \frac{\text{Contribution margin}}{\text{Sales revenue}} = \frac{\$7,700}{\$19,250} = 40\%$$

The contribution margin ratio is the percentage of each sales dollar that is available for covering fixed expenses and generating a profit. As shown in Exhibit 7-3, each *$1.00* of sales revenue contributes $0.40 toward fixed expenses and profit while the remaining $0.60 of each sales dollar is used to pay for variable costs.

EXHIBIT 7-3 **Breakdown of $1
of Sales Revenue**

Managers can also use the contribution margin ratio to quickly forecast operating income within their relevant range. When using the contribution margin ratio, managers project income based on sales *dollars* (revenue) rather than sales *units*. For example, if Kay generates $70,000 of sales revenue one month, what operating income should she expect? To find out, Kay simply multiplies her projected sales revenue by the contribution margin ratio to get the total contribution margin. Then she subtracts fixed expenses:

Contribution margin ($70,000 sales × 40%)...........	$28,000
Less: Fixed expenses...	(7,000)
Operating income...	$21,000

Let's verify. If Kay has $70,000 of sales revenue, she has sold 2,000 posters ($70,000 ÷ $35 per poster). Her complete contribution margin income statement would be calculated as follows:

Sales revenue (2,000 posters × $35/poster)..........................	$ 70,000
Less: Variable expenses (2,000 posters × $21/poster)	(42,000)
Contribution margin (2,000 posters × $14/poster)	$ 28,000
Less: Fixed expenses...	(7,000)
Operating income...	$ 21,000

The contribution margin per unit and contribution margin ratio help managers quickly and easily project income at different sales volumes. However, when projecting profits, managers must keep in mind the relevant range. For instance, if Kay wants to project income at a volume of 5,000 posters, she shouldn't use the existing contribution margin and fixed costs. Her current relevant range extends to only 2,000 posters per month. At a higher volume of sales, her variable cost per unit may be lower than $21 (due to volume discounts from her suppliers) and her monthly fixed costs may be higher than $7,000 (due to upgrading her system and hiring an employee to handle the extra sales volume).

Rather than using the individual unit contribution margins on each of their products, large companies that offer hundreds or thousands of products (like Art.com) use their contribution margin *ratio* to predict profits. As long as the sales mix remains constant (one of our CVP assumptions), the contribution margin ratio will remain constant.

We've seen how managers use the contribution margin to project income; but managers use the contribution margin for other purposes too, such as motivating the sales force. Salespeople who know the contribution margin of each product can generate more profit by emphasizing high-margin products. This is why many companies base sales commissions on the contribution margins produced by sales rather than on sales revenue alone.

In the next section, we'll see how managers use the contribution margin in CVP analysis to determine their breakeven point and to determine how many units they need to sell to reach target profits.

How do Managers Find the Breakeven Point?

2 Use CVP analysis to find breakeven points and target profit volumes

A company's **breakeven point** is the sales level at which *operating income is zero*. Sales below the breakeven point result in a loss. Sales above the breakeven point provide a profit. Before Kay started her business, she wanted to figure out how many posters she would have to sell just to break even.

There are three ways to calculate the breakeven point. All of the approaches are based on the income statement, so they all reach the same conclusion. The first two methods find breakeven in terms of sales *units*. The last approach finds breakeven in terms of sales *dollars* (sales *revenue*).

Why is this important?

"Businesses don't want to operate at a loss. CVP analysis helps managers figure how many units they need to sell *just* to break even."

1. The income statement approach
2. The shortcut approach using the *unit* contribution margin
3. The shortcut approach using the contribution margin *ratio*

Let's examine these three approaches in detail.

The Income Statement Approach

The income statement approach starts with the contribution margin income statement, and then breaks it down into smaller components:

SALES REVENUE − VARIABLE EXPENSES − FIXED EXPENSES = OPERATING INCOME

$$\left(\frac{\text{Sales price}}{\text{per unit}} \times \text{Units sold}\right) - \left(\frac{\text{Variable cost}}{\text{per unit}} \times \text{Units sold}\right) - \text{Fixed expenses} = \text{Operating income}$$

Let's use this approach to find Kay's breakeven point. Recall that Kay sells her posters for $35 each and that her variable cost is $21 per poster. Kay's fixed expenses total $7,000. At the breakeven point, operating income is zero. We use this information to solve the income statement equation for the number of posters Kay must sell to break even.

SALES REVENUE − VARIABLE EXPENSES − FIXED EXPENSES = OPERATING INCOME

$$\left(\frac{\text{Sales price}}{\text{per unit}} \times \text{Units sold}\right) - \left(\frac{\text{Variable cost}}{\text{per unit}} \times \text{Units sold}\right) - \text{Fixed expenses} = \text{Operating income}$$

($35 × Units sold) −	($21 × Units sold) −	$7,000 =	$ 0
($35 −	$21) × Units sold −	$7,000 =	$ 0
	$14 × Units sold	=	$7,000
	Units sold	=	$7,000/$14
	Sales in units	=	500 posters

Kay must sell 500 posters to break even. Her breakeven point in sales dollars is $17,500 (500 posters × $35).

You can check your answer by substituting the breakeven number of units into the income statement and checking that this level of sales results in zero profit:

Sales revenue (500 posters × $35)..........................	$ 17,500
Less: Variable expenses (500 posters × $21)..........	(10,500)
Contribution margin......................................	$ 7,000
Less: Fixed expenses......................................	(7,000)
Operating income...	$ 0

Notice that at breakeven, a firm's fixed expenses ($7,000) equal its contribution margin ($7,000). In other words, the firm has generated *just* enough contribution margin to cover its fixed expenses, but *not* enough to generate a profit.

The Shortcut Approach Using the Unit Contribution Margin

To develop the shortcut approach, we start with the contribution margin income statement, and then rearrange some of its terms:

SALES REVENUE – VARIABLE EXPENSES – FIXED EXPENSES = OPERATING INCOME

Contribution margin	– Fixed expenses	= Operating income
Contribution margin		= Fixed expenses + Operating income
(Contribution margin per unit × Units sold)		= Fixed expenses + Operating income

As a final step, we divide both sides of the equation by the contribution margin per unit. Now we have the shortcut formula:

$$\text{Sales in units} = \frac{\text{Fixed expenses + Operating income}}{\text{Contribution margin per unit}}$$

Kay can use this shortcut approach to find her breakeven point in units. Kay's fixed expenses total $7,000, and her unit contribution margin is $14. At the breakeven point, operating income is zero. Thus, Kay's breakeven point in units is as follows:

$$\text{Sales in units} = \frac{\$7,000 + \$0}{\$14}$$

$$= 500 \text{ posters}$$

Why does this shortcut approach work? Recall that each poster provides $14 of contribution margin. To break even, Kay must generate enough contribution margin to cover $7,000 of fixed expenses. At the rate of $14 per poster, Kay must sell 500 posters ($7,000/$14) to cover her $7,000 of fixed expenses. Because the shortcut formula simply rearranges the income statement equation, the breakeven point is the same under both methods (500 posters).

STOP & THINK

What would Kay's operating income be if she sold 501 posters? What would it be if she sold 600 posters?

Answer: Every poster sold provides $14 of contribution margin, which first contributes toward covering fixed costs, then profit. Once Kay reaches her breakeven point (500 posters), she has covered all fixed costs. Therefore, each additional poster sold after the breakeven point contributes $14 *directly to profit.* If Kay sells 501 posters, she has sold one more poster than breakeven. Her operating income is $14. If she sells 600 posters, she has sold 100 more posters than breakeven. Her operating income is $1,400 ($14 per poster × 100 posters). We can verify this as follows:

Contribution margin (600 posters × $14 per poster)	$ 8,400
Less: Fixed expenses...	(7,000)
Operating income..	$ 1,400

Once a company achieves breakeven, each additional unit sold contributes its unique unit contribution margin directly to profit.

The Shortcut Approach Using the Contribution Margin Ratio

It is easy to compute the breakeven point in *units* for a simple business like Kay's that has only one product. But what about companies that have thousands of products such as Art.com, Home Depot, and Amazon.com? It doesn't make sense for these companies to determine the number of each various product they need to sell to break even. Can you imagine a Home Depot manager describing breakeven as 100,000 wood screws, two million nails, 3,000 lawn mowers, 10,000 gallons of paint, and so forth? It simply doesn't make sense. Therefore, multiproduct companies usually compute breakeven in terms of *sales dollars (revenue)*.

This shortcut approach differs from the other shortcut we've just seen in only one way: Fixed expenses plus operating income are divided by the contribution margin *ratio* (not by contribution margin *per unit*) to yield sales in *dollars* (not *units*):

$$\text{Sales in dollars} = \frac{\text{Fixed expenses} + \text{Operating income}}{\text{Contribution margin ratio}}$$

Recall that Kay's contribution margin ratio is 40%. At the breakeven point, operating income is $0, so Kay's breakeven point in sales revenue is as follows:

$$\text{Sales in dollars} = \frac{\$7,000 + \$0}{0.40}$$
$$= \$17,500$$

This is the same breakeven sales revenue we calculated earlier (500 posters × $35 sales price = $17,500).

Why does the contribution margin ratio formula work? Each dollar of Kay's sales contributes $0.40 to fixed expenses and profit. To break even, she must generate enough contribution margin at the rate of $0.40 per sales dollar to cover the $7,000 fixed expenses ($7,000 ÷ 0.40 = $17,500).

> *To recall which shortcut formula gives which result, remember this: Dividing fixed costs by the* **unit** *contribution margin provides breakeven in sales* **units**. *Dividing fixed costs by the contribution margin* **ratio** *provides breakeven in sales* **dollars**.

How do Managers Find the Volume Needed to Earn a Target Profit?

Why is this important?

"Companies want to a make profit. CVP analysis helps managers determine how many units they need to sell to earn a target amount of profit."

For established products and services, managers are more interested in the sales level needed to earn a target profit than in the breakeven point. Managers of new business ventures are also interested in the profits they can expect to earn. For example, Kay doesn't want to just break even—she wants her business to be her sole source of income. She would like the business to earn $4,900 of profit each month. How many posters must Kay sell each month to reach her target profit?

How Much Must We Sell to Earn a Target Profit?

The only difference from our prior analysis is that instead of determining the sales level needed for *zero profit* (breakeven), Kay now wants to know how many posters she must sell to earn a $4,900 profit. We can use the income statement approach or the shortcut approach to find the answer. Because Kay wants to know the number of *units*, we'll use the shortcut formula based on the *unit* contribution margin.

This time, instead of an operating income of zero (breakeven), we'll insert Kay's target operating income of $4,900:

$$\text{Sales in } \textit{units} = \frac{\text{Fixed expenses + Operating income}}{\text{Contribution margin } \textit{per unit}}$$

$$= \frac{\$7,000 + \$4,900}{\$14}$$

$$= \frac{\$11,900}{\$14}$$

$$= 850 \text{ posters}$$

This analysis shows that Kay must sell 850 posters each month to earn profits of $4,900 a month. Notice that this level of sales falls within Kay's current relevant range (0–2,000 posters per month), so the conclusion that she would earn $4,900 of income at this sales volume is valid. If the calculation resulted in a sales volume outside the current relevant range (greater than 2,000 units), we would need to reassess our cost assumptions.

Assume that Kay also wants to know how much sales revenue she needs to earn $4,900 of monthly profit. Because she already knows the number of units needed (850), she can easily translate this volume into sales revenue:

$$850 \text{ posters} \times \$35 \text{ sales price/poster} = \$29,750 \text{ sales revenue}$$

If Kay only wanted to know the sales revenue needed to achieve her target profit rather than the number of units needed, she could have found the answer directly by using the shortcut formula based on the contribution margin *ratio*:

$$\text{Sales in } \textit{dollars} = \frac{\text{Fixed expenses + Operating income}}{\text{Contribution margin } \textit{ratio}}$$

$$= \frac{\$7,000 + \$4,900}{0.40}$$

$$= \frac{\$11,900}{0.40}$$

$$= \$29,750$$

Finally, Kay could have used the income statement approach to find the same answers:

SALES REVENUE	–	VARIABLE EXPENSES	–	FIXED EXPENSES	=	OPERATING INCOME
($35 × Units sold)	–	($21 × Units sold)	–	$7,000	=	$ 4,900
($35	–	$21) × Units sold	–	$7,000	=	$ 4,900
		$14 × Units sold			=	$11,900
				Units sold	=	$11,900/$14
				Units sold	=	850 posters

We can prove that our answers (from any of the three approaches) are correct by preparing Kay's income statement for a sales volume of 850 units:

Sales revenue (850 posters × $35)............................	$ 29,750
Less: Variable expenses (850 posters × $21)	(17,850)
Contribution margin	$ 11,900
Less: Fixed expenses...	(7,000)
Operating income..	$ 4,900

Graphing CVP Relationships

By graphing the CVP relationships for her business, Kay can see at a glance how changes in the levels of sales will affect profits. As in the last chapter, the volume of units (posters) is placed on the horizontal x-axis, while dollars is placed on the vertical y-axis. Then, she follows five steps to graph the CVP relations for her business, as illustrated in Exhibit 7-4.

EXHIBIT 7-4 **Cost-Volume-Profit Graph**

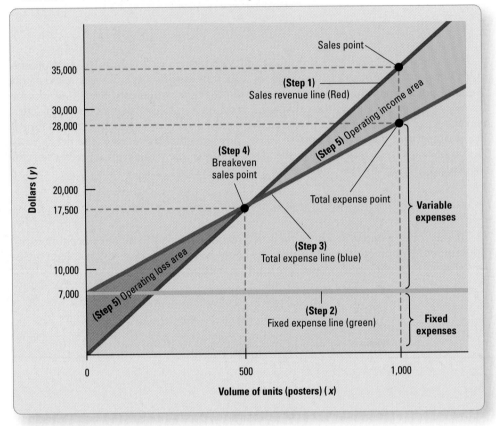

Step 1) Choose a sales volume, such as 1,000 posters. Plot the point for total sales revenue at that volume: 1,000 posters × $35 per poster = sales of $35,000. Draw the *sales revenue line* from the origin (0) through the $35,000 point. Why does the sales revenue line start at the origin? If Kay does not sell any posters, there is no sales revenue.

Step 2) Draw the *fixed expense line*, a horizontal line that intersects the y-axis at $7,000. Recall that the fixed expense line is flat because fixed expenses are the same ($7,000) no matter how many posters Kay sells within her relevant range (up to 2,000 posters per month).

Step 3) Draw the *total expense line*. Total expense is the sum of variable expense plus fixed expense. Thus, total expense is a *mixed* cost. So, the total expense line follows the form of the mixed cost line. Begin by computing variable expense at the chosen sales volume: 1,000 posters × $21 per poster = variable expense of $21,000. Add variable expense to fixed expense: $21,000 + $7,000 = $28,000. Plot the total expense point ($28,000) for 1,000 units. Then, draw a line through this point from the $7,000 fixed expense intercept on the dollars axis. This is the *total expense line*. Why does the total expense line start at the fixed expense line? If Kay sells no posters, she still incurs the $7,000 fixed cost for the server leasing, software, and office rental, but she incurs no variable costs.

Step 4) Identify the *breakeven point*. The breakeven point is the point where the sales revenue line intersects the total expense line. This is the point where sales revenue equals total expenses. Our previous analyses told us that Kay's breakeven point is 500 posters, or $17,500 in sales. The graph shows this information visually.

Step 5) Mark the *operating income* and the *operating loss* areas on the graph. To the left of the breakeven point, the total expense line lies above the sales revenue line. Expenses exceed sales revenue, leading to an operating loss. If Kay sells only 300 posters, she incurs an operating loss. The amount of the loss is the vertical distance between the total expense line and the sales revenue line:

Sales revenue − Variable expenses − Fixed expenses = Operating income (Loss)

$(300 \times \$35)$ − $(300 \times \$21)$ − $7,000   = $(2,800)$

To the right of the breakeven point, the business earns a profit. The vertical distance between the sales revenue line and the total expense line equals income. Exhibit 7-4 shows that if Kay sells 1,000 posters, she earns operating income of $7,000 ($35,000 sales revenue − $28,000 total expenses).

Why bother with a graph? Why not just use the income statement approach or the shortcut approach? Graphs like Exhibit 7-4 help managers visualize profit or loss over a range of volume. The income statement and shortcut approaches estimate income or loss for only a single sales volume.

Decision Guidelines

CVP Analysis

Your friend wants to open her own ice cream parlor after college. She needs help making the following decisions:

Decision	Guidelines
How much will I earn on every ice cream cone I sell?	The unit contribution margin shows managers how much they earn on each unit sold after paying for variable costs *but before considering fixed expenses*. The unit contribution margin is the amount each unit earns that contributes toward covering fixed expenses and generating a profit. It is computed as follows:

Sales price per unit

Less: Variable cost per unit

Contribution margin per unit

The contribution margin ratio shows managers how much contribution margin is earned on every $1 of sales. It is computed as follows:

$$\text{Contribution margin ratio} = \frac{\text{Contribution margin}}{\text{Sales revenue}}$$

continued

Decision	Guidelines
Can I quickly forecast my income without creating a full income statement?	The contribution margin concept allows managers to forecast income quickly at different sales volumes. First, find the total contribution margin (by multiplying the forecasted number of units by the unit contribution margin *or* by multiplying the forecasted sales revenue by the contribution margin ratio) and then subtract all fixed expenses.
How can I compute the *number of ice cream cones* I'll have to sell to break even or earn a target profit?	**Income Statement Approach:** $$\text{SALES REVENUE} - \text{VARIABLE EXPENSES} - \begin{array}{c}\text{FIXED}\\\text{EXPENSE}\end{array} = \begin{array}{c}\text{OPERATING}\\\text{INCOME}\end{array}$$ $$\left(\begin{array}{c}\text{Saleprice per unit}\\ \times \text{Units sold}\end{array}\right) - \left(\begin{array}{c}\text{Variable cost per unit}\\ \times \text{Units sold}\end{array}\right) - \begin{array}{c}\text{Fixed}\\\text{expenses}\end{array} = \begin{array}{c}\text{Operating}\\\text{income}\end{array}$$ **Shortcut Unit Contribution Margin Approach:** $$\text{Sales in } \textit{units} = \frac{\text{Fixed expenses} + \text{Operating income}}{\text{Contribution margin } \textit{per unit}}$$
How can I compute the *amount of sales revenue* (in dollars) I'll have to generate to break even or earn a target profit?	**Shortcut Contribution Margin Ratio Approach:** $$\text{Sales in } \textit{dollars} = \frac{\text{Fixed expenses} + \text{Operating income}}{\text{Contribution margin } \textit{ratio}}$$
What will my profits look like over a range of volumes?	CVP graphs show managers, at a glance, how different sales volumes will affect profits.

Summary Problem 1

Fleet Foot buys hiking socks for $6 a pair and sells them for $10. Management budgets monthly fixed expenses of $10,000 for sales volumes between 0 and 12,000 pairs.

Requirements

1. Use the income statement approach and the shortcut unit contribution margin approach to compute monthly breakeven sales in units.

2. Use the shortcut contribution margin ratio approach to compute the breakeven point in sales revenue (sales dollars).

3. Compute the monthly sales level (in units) required to earn a target operating income of $14,000. Use either the income statement approach or the shortcut contribution margin approach.

4. Prepare a graph of Fleet Foot's CVP relationships, similar to Exhibit 7-4. Draw the sales revenue line, the fixed expense line, and the total expense line. Label the axes, the breakeven point, the operating income area, and the operating loss area.

Solution

Requirement 1

Income Statement Approach:

SALES REVENUE		−	VARIABLE EXPENSES		− FIXED EXPENSES	= OPERATING INCOME
$\left(\begin{array}{c}\text{Sales price}\\\text{per unit}\end{array}\times \text{Units sold}\right)$		−	$\left(\begin{array}{c}\text{Variable cost}\\\text{per unit}\end{array}\times \text{Units sold}\right)$		− Fixed expenses	= Operating income
($10	× Units sold) −		($6	× Units sold) −	$10,000	= $ 0
($10		−	$6)	× Units sold		= $10,000
			$4	× Units sold		= $10,000
				Units sold		= $10,000 ÷ $4
				Breakeven sales in units		= 2,500 units

Shortcut Unit Contribution Margin Approach:

$$\text{Sales in units} = \frac{\text{Fixed expenses} + \text{Operating income}}{\text{Contribution margin per unit}}$$

$$= \frac{\$10,000 + \$0}{(\$10 - \$6)}$$

$$= \frac{\$10,000}{\$4}$$

$$= 2,500 \text{ units}$$

Requirement 2

$$\text{Sales in dollars} = \frac{\text{Fixed expenses} + \text{Operating income}}{\text{Contribution margin ratio}}$$

$$= \frac{\$10,000 + \$0}{0.40^*}$$

$$= \$25,000$$

$$^*\text{Contribution margin ratio} = \frac{\text{Contribution margin per unit}}{\text{Sales price per unit}} = \frac{\$4}{\$10} = 0.40$$

Requirement 3

Income Statement Equation Approach:

SALES REVENUE		−	VARIABLE EXPENSES		− FIXED EXPENSES	= OPERATING INCOME
$\left(\begin{array}{c}\text{Sales price}\\\text{per unit}\end{array}\times \text{Units sold}\right)$		−	$\left(\begin{array}{c}\text{Variable cost}\\\text{per unit}\end{array}\times \text{Units sold}\right)$		− Fixed expenses	= Operating income
($10	× Units sold) −		($6	× Units sold) −	$10,000	= $14,000
($10		−	$6)	× Units sold		= $10,000 + $14,000
			$4	× Units sold		= $24,000
				Units sold		= $24,000 ÷ $4
				Units sold		= 6,000 units

continued

Shortcut Unit Contribution Margin Approach:

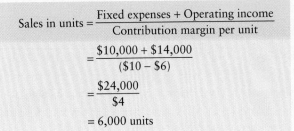

$$\text{Sales in units} = \frac{\text{Fixed expenses} + \text{Operating income}}{\text{Contribution margin per unit}}$$

$$= \frac{\$10,000 + \$14,000}{(\$10 - \$6)}$$

$$= \frac{\$24,000}{\$4}$$

$$= 6,000 \text{ units}$$

Requirement 4

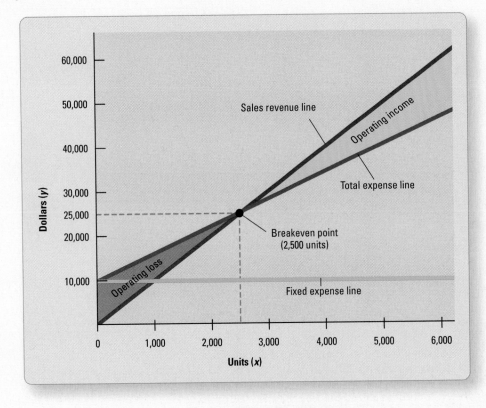

How do Managers Use CVP to Plan for Changing Business Conditions?

3 Perform sensitivity analysis in response to changing business conditions

In today's fast-changing business world, managers need to be prepared for increasing costs, pricing pressure from competitors, and other changing business conditions.

Managers use CVP analysis to conduct **sensitivity analysis.** Sensitivity analysis is a "what-if" technique that asks what results will be if actual prices or costs change or if an underlying assumption such as sales mix changes. For example, increased competition may force Kay to lower her sales price, while at the same time her suppliers increase poster costs. How will these changes affect Kay's breakeven and target profit volumes? What will happen if Kay changes her sales mix by offering posters in two different sizes? We'll tackle these issues next.

Changing the Sales Price

Let's assume that Kay has now been in business for several months. Because of competition, Kay is considering cutting her sales price to $31 per poster. If her variable expenses remain $21 per poster and her fixed expenses stay at $7,000, how many posters will she need to sell to break even? To answer this question, Kay calculates a new unit contribution margin using the new sales price:

New sales price per poster............................	$ 31
Less: Variable cost per poster.......................	(21)
New contribution margin per poster............	$ 10

She then uses the new unit contribution margin to compute breakeven sales in units:

$$\text{Sales in units} = \frac{\text{Fixed expenses} + \text{Operating income}}{\text{Contribution margin per unit}}$$

$$= \frac{\$7,000 + \$0}{\$10}$$

$$= 700 \text{ posters}$$

With the original $35 sale price, Kay's breakeven point was 500 posters. If Kay lowers the sales price to $31 per poster, her breakeven point increases to 700 posters. The lower sales price means that each poster contributes *less* toward fixed expenses ($10 versus $14 before the price change), so Kay must sell 200 *more* posters to break even. Each dollar of sales revenue would contribute $0.32 ($10/$31) rather than $0.40 toward covering fixed expenses and generating a profit.

If Kay reduces her sales price to $31, how many posters must she sell to achieve her $4,900 monthly target profit? Kay again uses the new unit contribution margin to determine how many posters she will need to sell to reach her profit goals:

$$\text{Sales in units} = \frac{\$7,000 + \$4,900}{\$10}$$

$$= 1,190 \text{ posters}$$

> ### Why is this important?
>
> "CVP analysis helps managers prepare for and respond to economic changes, such as increasing costs and pressure to drop sales prices, so companies can remain competitive and profitable."

With the original sales price, Kay needed to sell only 850 posters per month to achieve her target profit level. If Kay cuts her sales price (and, therefore, her contribution margin), she must sell more posters to achieve her financial goals. Kay could have found these same results using the income statement approach. Exhibit 7-5 shows the effect of changes in sales price on breakeven and target profit volumes.

EXHIBIT 7-5   The Effect of Changes in Sales Price on Breakeven and Target Profit Volumes

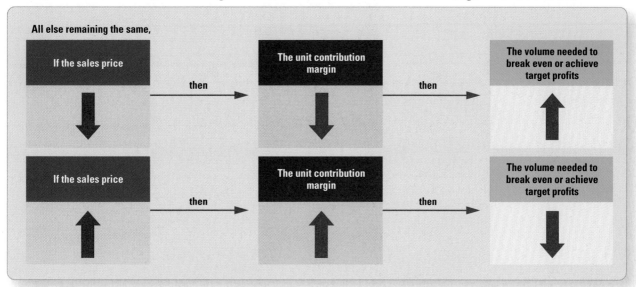

STOP & THINK

Kay believes she could dominate the e-commerce art poster business if she cut the sales price to $20. Is this a good idea?

Answer: No. The variable cost per poster is $21. If Kay sells posters for $20 each, she loses $1 on each poster. Kay will incur a loss if the sales price is less than the variable cost.

Changing Variable Costs

Let's assume that Kay does *not* lower her sales price. However, Kay's supplier raises the price for each poster to $23.80 (instead of the original $21). Kay does not want to pass this increase on to her customers, so she holds her sales price at the original $35 per poster. Her fixed costs remain $7,000. How many posters must she sell to break even after her supplier raises the prices? Kay's new contribution margin per unit drops to $11.20 ($35 sales price per poster − $23.80 variable cost per poster). So, her new breakeven point is as follows:

$$\text{Sales in units} = \frac{\text{Fixed expenses} + \text{Operating income}}{\text{Contribution margin per unit}}$$

$$= \frac{\$7,000 + \$0}{\$11.20}$$

$$= 625 \text{ posters}$$

Higher variable costs per unit have the same effect as lower selling prices per unit—they both reduce the product's unit contribution margin. As a result, Kay will have to sell *more* units to break even and achieve target profits. As shown in Exhibit 7-6, a *decrease* in variable costs would have just the opposite effect. Lower variable costs increase the contribution margin each poster provides and, therefore, lowers the breakeven point.

EXHIBIT 7-6   **The Effect of Changes in Variable Costs on Breakeven and Target Profit Volumes**

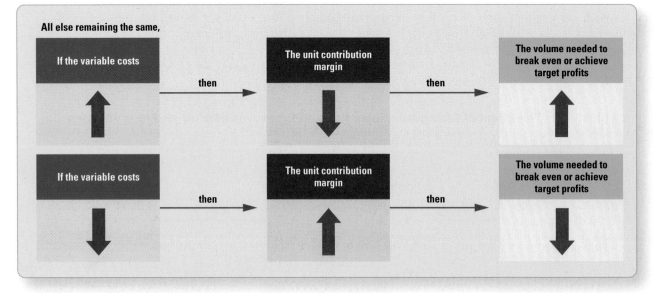

STOP & THINK

Suppose Kay is squeezed from both sides: Her supply costs have increased to $23.80 per poster, yet she must lower her price to $31 in order to compete. Under these conditions, how many posters will Kay need to sell to achieve her monthly target profit of $4,900? If Kay doesn't think she can sell that many posters, how else might she attempt to achieve her profit goals?

Answer: Kay is now in a position faced by many companies—her unit contribution margin is squeezed by both higher supply costs and lower sales prices:

New sales price per poster............................	$ 31.00
Less: New variable cost per poster	(23.80)
New contribution margin per poster............	$ 7.20

Kay's new contribution margin is about half of what it was when she started her business ($14). To achieve her target profit, her volume will have to increase dramatically (yet, it would still fall within her current relevant range for fixed costs—which extends to 2,000 posters per month):

$$\text{Sales in units} = \frac{\text{Fixed expenses + Operating income}}{\text{Contribution margin per unit}}$$

$$= \frac{\$7,000 + \$4,900}{\$7.20}$$

$$= 1,653 \text{ posters (rounded)}$$

Based on her current volume, Kay may not believe she can sell so many posters. To maintain a reasonable profit level, Kay may need to take other measures. For example, she may try to find a different supplier with lower poster costs. She may also attempt to lower her fixed costs. For example, perhaps she could negotiate a cheaper lease on her office space or move her business to a less expensive location. She could also try to increase her volume by spending *more* on fixed costs, such as advertising. Kay could also investigate selling other products, in addition to her regular-size posters, that would have higher unit contribution margins. We'll discuss these measures next.

Changing Fixed Costs

Let's return to Kay's original data ($35 selling price and $21 variable cost). Kay has decided she really doesn't need a storefront office at the retail strip mall because she doesn't have many walk-in customers. She could decrease her monthly fixed costs from $7,000 to $4,200 by moving her office to an industrial park.

How will this decrease in fixed costs affect Kay's breakeven point? *Changes in fixed costs do not affect the contribution margin.* Therefore, Kay's unit contribution margin is still $14 per poster. However, her breakeven point changes because her fixed costs change:

$$\text{Sales in units} = \frac{\text{Fixed expenses + Operating income}}{\text{Contribution margin per unit}}$$

$$= \frac{\$4,200 + \$0}{\$14.00}$$

$$= 300 \text{ posters}$$

Because of the decrease in fixed costs, Kay will need to sell only 300 posters, rather than 500 posters, to break even. The volume needed to achieve her monthly $4,900 target profit will also decline. However, if Kay's fixed costs *increase*, she will have to sell *more* units to break even. Exhibit 7-7 shows the effect of changes in fixed costs on breakeven and target profit volumes.

EXHIBIT 7-7   The Effect of Changes in Fixed Costs on Breakeven and Target Profit Volumes

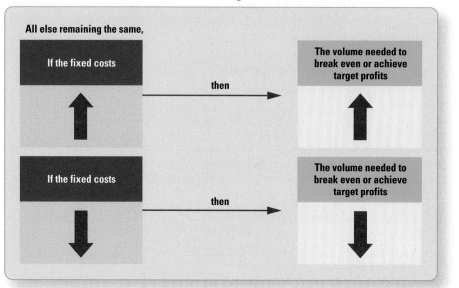

We have seen that changes in sales prices, variable costs, and fixed costs can have dramatic effects on the volume of product that companies must sell to achieve breakeven and target profits. Companies often turn to automation to decrease variable costs (direct labor); but this, in turn, increases their fixed costs (equipment depreciation). Companies often move production overseas to decrease variable and fixed production costs, feeling forced to take these measures to keep their prices as low as their competitors. For example, Charbroil, the maker of gas grills, said that if it didn't move production overseas, profits would decline, or worse yet, the company would go out of business.

STOP & THINK

Kay has been considering advertising as a means to increase her sales volume. Kay could spend an extra $3,500 per month on Web site banner ads. How many *extra* posters would Kay have to sell *just to pay for the advertising?* (Use Kay's original data.)

Answer: Instead of using *all* of Kay's fixed costs, we can isolate *just* the fixed costs relating to advertising. This will allow us to figure out how many *extra* posters Kay would have to sell each month to break even on (or pay for) the advertising cost. Advertising is a fixed cost, so Kay's contribution margin remains $14 per unit.

$$\text{Sales in units} = \frac{\text{Fixed expenses} + \text{Operating income}}{\text{Contribution margin per unit}}$$

$$= \frac{\$3,500 + \$0}{\$14.00}$$

$$= 250 \text{ posters}$$

Kay must sell 250 *extra* posters each month just to pay for the cost of advertising. If she sells fewer than 250 extra posters, she'll increase her volume but lose money on the advertising. If she sells more than 250 extra posters, her plan will have worked—she'll increase her volume *and* her profit. Even though investing in the Web banner ads increases Kay's breakeven point to 750 units (500 plus another 250 to cover the advertising costs), Kay may be willing to pay the extra $3,500 if she expects the ads to stimulate enough extra sales to *more than* cover the additional advertising expense. Companies often face this issue. How many *extra* 12-packs of soda do you think Coca-Cola has to sell to pay for one 30-second advertisement during the Super Bowl?

Another way that companies can offset cost and pricing pressures is to expand their product lines to include products with higher contribution margins. In the next section, we'll see what happens when Kay decides to sell higher-margin, large-size posters in addition to regular-size posters.

Changing the Mix of Products Offered for Sale

So far, we have assumed that Kay sold only one size poster. What would happen if she offered different types of products? Companies that sell more than one product must consider their *sales mix* when performing CVP analysis. All else being equal, a company earns more income by selling high-contribution margin products than by selling an equal number of low-contribution margin products.

> **4** Find breakeven and target profit volumes for multi-product companies

The same CVP formulas that are used to perform CVP analysis for a company with a single product can be used for any company that sells more than one product. However, the formulas use the *weighted-average contribution margin* of all products, rather than the contribution margin of a sole product. Each unit's contribution margin is *weighted* by the relative number of units sold. As before, the company can find the breakeven or the target profit volume in terms of units, or in terms of sales revenue. We'll consider each in turn.

Multiproduct Company: Finding Breakeven in Terms of Sales Units

Suppose Kay plans to sell two types of posters. In addition to her regular-size posters, Kay plans to sell large posters. Let's assume that none of Kay's original costs have changed. Exhibit 7-8 shows that each regular poster will continue to generate $14 of contribution margin, while each large poster will generate $30 of contribution margin. Kay is adding the large-poster line because it carries a higher unit contribution margin.

EXHIBIT 7-8 **Calculating the Weighted-Average Contribution Margin per Unit**

	Regular Posters	Large Posters	Total
Sales price per unit	$ 35	$ 70	
Less: Variable cost per unit	(21)	(40)	
Contribution margin per unit	$ 14	$ 30	
Sales mix	× 5	× 3	8
Contribution margin	$ 70	$ 90	$160
Weighted-average contribution margin per unit ($160/8)			$ 20

For every five regular posters sold, Kay expects to sell three large posters. In other words, she expects 5/8 of the sales to be regular posters and 3/8 to be large posters. This is a 5:3 sales mix. Exhibit 7-8 shows how Kay uses this expected sales mix to find the weighted-average contribution margin per unit.

Notice that none of Kay's products actually generates $20 of contribution margin. However, if the sales mix is 5:3, as expected, it is *as if* the contribution margin is $20 per unit. Once Kay has computed the weighted-average contribution margin per unit, she uses it in the shortcut formula to determine the total number of posters that would need to be sold to break even:

$$\text{Sales in total units} = \frac{\text{Fixed expenses} + \text{Operating income}}{\text{Weighted-average contribution margin per unit}}$$

$$= \frac{\$7,000 + \$0}{\$20}$$

$$= 350 \text{ posters}$$

As a final step, Kay splits the total number of posters into the regular and large sizes using the same sales mix ratios she assumed previously:

Breakeven sales of regular posters ($350 \times 5/8$).............	<u>218.75</u> regular posters
Breakeven sales of large posters ($350 \times 3/8$)	<u>131.25</u> large posters

As is often the case in real situations, these computations don't yield round numbers. Because Kay cannot sell partial posters, she must sell 219 regular posters and 132 large posters to avoid a loss. Using these rounded numbers would lead to a small rounding error in our check figures, however, so the rest of our computations will use the exact results: 218.75 regular posters and 131.25 large posters.

If Kay wants, she can now use the number of units to find her breakeven point in terms of sales revenue (amounts rounded to the nearest dollar):

218.75 regular posters at $35 each............	$ 7,656
131.25 large posters at $70 each..............	<u>9,188</u>
Total revenues	<u>$16,844</u>

We can prove this breakeven point as follows:

	Total
Contribution margin:	
Regular posters ($218.75 \times \$14$)	$ 3,063
Large posters ($131.25 \times \$30$)...............	<u>3,937</u>
Contribution margin	$ 7,000
Less: Fixed expenses.................................	<u>(7,000)</u>
Operating income.....................................	<u>$ 0</u>

We just found Kay's *breakeven* point, but Kay can also use the same steps to calculate the number of units she must sell to achieve a target profit. The only difference, as before, is that she would use *target profit*, rather than *zero*, as the operating income in the shortcut formula.

STOP & THINK

Suppose Kay would still like to earn a monthly profit of $4,900. Recall that she needed to sell 850 posters to achieve this profit level when she was selling only regular posters. If her sales mix is 5:3, as planned, will she need to sell *more than* or *fewer than* 850 posters to achieve her target profit? Why?

Answer: Kay will need to sell *fewer* than 850 posters because she is now selling some large posters that have a higher unit contribution margin. We can verify this as follows:

$$\text{Sales in total units} = \frac{\text{Fixed expenses} + \text{Operating income}}{\text{Weighted-average contribution margin per unit}}$$

$$= \frac{\$7,000 + \$4,900}{\$20}$$

$$= 595 \text{ posters}$$

Kay would have to sell a *total* of 595 posters—372 regular posters ($595 \times 5/8$) and 223 large posters ($595 \times 3/8$)—to achieve her target profit.

Multiproduct Company: Finding Breakeven in Terms of Sales Revenue

Companies that offer hundreds or thousands of products (such as Wal-Mart and Amazon.com) will not want to find the breakeven point in terms of units. Rather, they'll want to know breakeven (or target profit volumes) in terms of sales revenue. To find this sales volume, the company needs to know, or estimate, its weighted-average contribution margin ratio. If a company prepares contribution margin income statements, it easily calculates the contribution margin ratio by dividing the total contribution margin by total sales. The contribution margin ratio is *already* weighted by the company's *actual* sales mix! The following "Stop and Think" illustrates how Amazon.com would use this approach to calculating breakeven.

STOP & THINK

Suppose Amazon.com's total sales revenue is $4.50 billion, its variable expenses total $3.15 billion, and its fixed expenses total $1.1 billion. What is the breakeven point in sales revenue?

Answer: First, Amazon computes its total contribution margin:

Sales revenue............................	$4.50 billion
Less: Variable expenses	3.15 billion
Contribution margin	$1.35 billion

Now Amazon is able to compute its overall contribution margin ratio, which is already weighted by the company's actual sales mix: $1.35 billion ÷ 4.50 billion = 30%.

Finally, Amazon uses the contribution margin ratio in the shortcut formula to predict the breakeven point:

$$\text{Sales in dollars} = \frac{\text{Fixed expenses} + \text{Operating income}}{\text{Contribution margin ratio}}$$

$$= \frac{\$1.1 \text{ billion} + \$0}{0.30}$$

$$= \$3.667 \text{ billion (rounded)}$$

Amazon.com must achieve sales revenue of $3.667 billion just to break even.

Unlike Amazon, Kay's business to this point has been limited to a sole product (regular posters), which had a 40% contribution margin ratio. Once Kay starts selling large posters in addition to the regular posters, her overall weighted-average contribution margin ratio will change. Recall that Kay expects to sell five regular posters for every three large posters. Exhibit 7-9 shows how Kay weights the individual contribution margins and sales revenue, using the anticipated sales mix, to arrive at her anticipated weighted-average contribution margin ratio for this particular sales mix:

EXHIBIT 7-9 **Estimating the Weighted-Average Contribution Margin Ratio**

Expected contribution margin:		
Regular posters (5 × $14)	$ 70	
Large posters (3 × $30)	$ 90	
Expected contribution margin		$160
Divided by expected sales revenue:		
Regular posters (5 × $35)	$175	
Large posters (3 × $70)	$210	
Expected sales revenue		÷ 385
Weighted-average contribution margin ratio		= 41.558%

Notice how Kay's weighted-average contribution margin ratio (41.558%) will be higher than it was when she sold only regular posters (40%). That's because she expects to sell some large posters that have a 42.9% contribution margin ratio ($30/$70) in addition to the regular-sized posters. Because her sales mix is changing, she now has a different contribution margin ratio.

Once Kay knows her weighted-average contribution margin ratio, she can use the shortcut formula to estimate breakeven in terms of sales revenue:

$$\text{Sales in dollars} = \frac{\text{Fixed expenses} + \text{Operating income}}{\text{Contribution margin ratio}}$$

$$= \frac{\$7,000 + \$0}{0.41558}$$

$$= \$16,844 \text{ (rounded)}$$

Notice that this is the same breakeven point in sales revenue we found earlier by first finding breakeven in *units*. Kay could also use the formula to find the total sales revenue she would need to meet her target monthly operating income of $4,900.

If Kay's actual sales mix is not five regular posters to three large posters, her actual operating income will differ from the projected amount. The sales mix greatly influences the breakeven point. When companies offer more than one product, they do not have a unique breakeven point. Every sales mix assumption leads to a different breakeven point.

Stop & Think

Suppose Kay plans to sell 800 total posters in the 5:3 sales mix (five regular posters sold for every three large posters). She actually does sell 800 posters—375 regular and 425 large. The sale prices per poster, variable costs per poster, and fixed expenses are exactly as predicted. Without doing any computations, is Kay's actual operating income greater than, less than, or equal to her expected income?

Answer: Kay's actual sales mix did not turn out to be the 5:3 mix she expected. She actually sold *more* of the higher-margin large posters than the lower-margin regular posters. This favorable change in the sales mix causes her to earn a higher operating income than she expected.

Information Technology and Sensitivity Analysis

We have just seen that Kay's breakeven point and target profit volumes are very sensitive to changes in her business environment, including changes in sales prices, variable costs, fixed costs, and sales mix assumptions. Information technology allows managers to perform a wide array of sensitivity analyses before committing to decisions. Managers of small- to medium-sized companies use Excel spreadsheets to perform sensitivity analyses like those we just did for Kay. Spreadsheets allow managers to estimate how one change (or several simultaneous changes) affects business operations. Managers also use spreadsheet software to create CVP graphs like the one in Exhibit 7-4.

Many large companies use sophisticated enterprise resource planning software such as SAP, Oracle, and PeopleSoft to provide detailed data for CVP analysis. For example, after Sears stores lock their doors at 9 P.M., records for each individual transaction flow into a massive database. From a DieHard battery sold in Texas to a Trader Bay polo shirt sold in New Hampshire, the system compiles an average of 1.5 million transactions a day. With the click of a mouse, managers access sales price, variable cost, and sales volume for individual products to conduct breakeven or profit planning analyses.

What are Some Common Indicators of Risk?

A company's level of risk depends on many factors, including the general health of the economy and the specific industry in which the company operates. In addition, a firm's risk depends on its current volume of sales and the relative amount of fixed and variable costs that make up its total costs. Next, we discuss how a firm can gauge its level of risk, to some extent, by its margin of safety and its operating leverage.

Margin of Safety

5 | Determine a firm's margin of safety and operating leverage

The **margin of safety** is the excess of actual or expected sales over breakeven sales. This is the "cushion," or drop in sales, the company can absorb without incurring a loss. The higher the margin of safety, the greater the cushion against loss and the less risky the business plan. Managers use the margin of safety to evaluate the risk of current operations as well as the risk of new plans.

Let's continue to assume that Kay has been in business for several months and that she generally sells 950 posters a month. Kay's breakeven point in our original data is 500 posters. Kay can express her margin of safety in units, as follows:

Margin of safety in units = Expected sales in units – Breakeven sales in units					
	=	950 posters	–	500 posters	
	=	450 posters			

Kay can also express her margin of safety in sales revenue (sales dollars):

Margin of safety in dollars = Expected sales in dollars – Breakeven sales in dollars				
	=	(950 posters × \$35)	– (500 posters × \$35)	
	=	\$33,250	–	\$17,500
	=	\$15,750		

Sales can drop by 450 posters, or \$15,750 a month, before Kay incurs a loss. This is a fairly comfortable margin.

Managers can also compute the margin of safety as a percentage of sales. Simply divide the margin of safety by sales. We obtain the same percentage whether we use units or dollars.

In units:

$$\text{Margin of safety as a percentage} = \frac{\text{Margin of safety in units}}{\text{Expected sales in units}}$$

$$= \frac{450 \text{ posters}}{950 \text{ posters}}$$

$$= 47.4\% \text{ (rounded)}$$

In dollars:

$$\text{Margin of safety as a percentage} = \frac{\text{Margin of safety in dollars}}{\text{Expected sales in dollars}}$$

$$= \frac{\$15,750}{\$33,250}$$

$$= 47.4\% \text{ (rounded)}$$

The margin of safety percentage tells Kay that sales would have to drop by more than 47.4% before she would incur a loss. If sales fall by less than 47.4%, she would still earn a profit. If sales fall exactly 47.4%, she would break even. This ratio tells Kay that her business plan is not unduly risky.

Operating Leverage

A company's **operating leverage** refers to the relative amount of fixed and variable costs that make up its total costs. Most companies have both fixed and variable costs. However, companies with *high* operating leverage have *relatively more fixed costs* and relatively fewer variable costs. Companies with high operating leverage include golf courses, airlines, and hotels. Because they have fewer variable costs, their contribution margin ratio is relatively high. Recall from the last chapter that Embassy Suites' variable cost of servicing each guest is low, which means that the hotel has a high contribution margin and high operating leverage.

What does high operating leverage have to do with risk? If sales volume decreases, the total contribution margin will drop significantly because each

Why is this important?

"The margin of safety and operating leverage help managers understand their risk if volume decreases due to a recession, competition, or other changes in the marketplace."

sales dollar contains a high percentage of contribution margin. Yet, the high fixed costs of running the company remain. Therefore, the operating income of these companies can easily turn from profit to loss if sales volume declines. For example, airlines were financially devastated after September 11, 2001, because the number of people flying suddenly dropped, creating large reductions in contribution margin. Yet, the airlines had to continue paying their high fixed costs. High operating leverage companies are at *more* risk because their income declines drastically when sales volume declines.

What if the economy is growing and sales volume *increases*? High operating leverage companies will reap high rewards. Remember that after breakeven, each unit sold contributes its unit contribution margin directly to profit. Because high operating leverage companies have high contribution margin ratios, each additional dollar of sales will contribute more to the firm's operating income. Exhibit 7-10 summarizes these characteristics.

EXHIBIT 7-10   Characteristics of High Operating Leverage Firms

- High operating leverage companies have the following:
    —*Higher* levels of fixed costs and *lower* levels of variable costs
    —*Higher* contribution margin ratios
- For high operating leverage companies, changes in volume significantly affect operating income, so they face the following:
    —*Higher* risk
    —*Higher* potential for reward

Examples include golf courses, hotels, rental car agencies, theme parks, airlines, cruise lines, etc.

However, companies with low operating leverage have relatively *fewer* fixed costs and relatively *more* variable costs. For example, retailers incur significant levels of fixed costs, but more of every sales dollar is used to pay for the merchandise (a variable cost), so less ends up as contribution margin. If sales volume declines, these companies have relatively fewer fixed costs to cover, so they are at *less* risk of incurring a loss. If sales volume increases, their relatively small contribution margins ratios add to the bottom line, but in smaller increments. Therefore, they reap less reward than high operating leverage companies experiencing the same volume increases. *In other words, at low operating leverage companies changes in sales volume do not have as much impact on operating income as they do at high operating leverage companies.* Exhibit 7-11 summarizes these characteristics.

EXHIBIT 7-11   Characteristics of Low Operating Leverage Firms

- Low operating leverage companies have the following:
    —*Higher* levels of variable costs and *lower* levels of fixed costs
    —*Lower* contribution margin ratios
- For low operating leverage companies, changes in volume do NOT have as significant an effect on operating income, so they face the following:
    —*Lower* risk
    —*Lower* potential for reward

Examples include merchandising companies and fast-food restaurants.

A company's **operating leverage factor** tells us how responsive a company's operating income is to changes in volume. The greater the operating leverage factors, the greater the impact a change in sales volume has on operating income.

The operating leverage factor, *at a given level of sales*, is calculated as follows:

$$\text{Operating leverage factor} = \frac{\text{Contribution margin}}{\text{Operating income}}$$

Why do we say, "at a given level of sales"? A company's operating leverage factor will depend, to some extent, on the sales level used to calculate the contribution margin and operating income. Most companies compute the operating leverage factor at their current or expected volume of sales, which is what we'll do in our examples.

What does the operating leverage factor tell us?

The operating leverage factor, at a given level of sales, indicates the percentage change in operating income that will occur from a 1% change in volume. In other words, it tells us how responsive a company's operating income is to changes in volume.

The *lowest* possible value for this factor is 1, which occurs only if the company has *no* fixed costs (an *extremely low* operating leverage company). *For a minute, let's assume that Kay has no fixed costs.* Given this scenario, her unit contribution margin ($14 per poster) contributes directly to profit because she has no fixed costs to cover. In addition, she has *no* risk. The worst she can do is break even, and that will occur only if she doesn't sell any posters. Let's continue to assume that she generally sells 950 posters a month, so this will be the level of sales at which we calculate the operating leverage factor:

Sales revenue (950 posters × $35/poster)	$ 33,250
Less: Variable expenses (950 posters × $21/poster)	(19,950)
Contribution margin (950 posters × $14/poster)	$ 13,300
Less: Fixed expenses	(0)
Operating income	$ 13,300

Her operating leverage factor is as follows:

$$\text{Operating leverage factor} = \frac{\$13,300}{\$13,300}$$
$$= 1$$

What does this tell us? If Kay's volume changes by 1%, her operating income will change by 1% (her operating leverage factor of 1 multiplied by a 1% change in volume). What would happen to Kay's operating income if her volume changed by 15% rather than 1%? Her operating income would then change by 15% (her operating leverage factor of 1 multiplied by a 15% change in volume).

Let's now see what happens if we assume, as usual, that Kay's fixed expenses are $7,000. We'll once again calculate the operating leverage factor given Kay's current level of sales (950 posters per month):

Contribution margin (950 posters × $14/poster)	$13,300
Less: Fixed expenses	(7,000)
Operating income	$ 6,300

Now that we have once again assumed that Kay's fixed expenses are $7,000, her operating leverage factor is as follows:

$$\text{Operating leverage factor} = \frac{\$13,300}{\$6,300}$$

$$= 2.11 \text{ (rounded)}$$

Notice that her operating leverage factor is *higher* (2.11 versus 1) when she has *more* fixed costs ($7,000 versus $0). If Kay's sales volume changes by 1%, her operating income will change by 2.11% (her operating leverage factor of 2.11 multiplied by a 1% change in volume). Again, what would happen to Kay's operating income if her volume changed by 15% rather than 1%? Her operating income would then change by 31.65% (her operating leverage factor of 2.11 multiplied by a 15% change in volume).

Managers use the firm's operating leverage factor to determine how vulnerable their operating income is to changes in sales volume—both positive and negative. The larger the operating leverage factor is, the greater the impact a change in sales volume has on operating income. This is true for both increases *and* decreases in volume. Therefore, companies with higher operating leverage factors are particularly vulnerable to changes in volume. In other words, they have *both* higher risk of incurring losses if volume declines *and* higher potential reward if volume increases. Hoping to capitalize on the reward side, many companies have intentionally increased their operating leverage by lowering their variable costs while at the same time increasing their fixed costs. This strategy works well during periods of economic growth but can be detrimental when sales volume declines.

STOP & THINK

Assume Kay's original data ($14 unit contribution margin, $7,000 fixed costs, and 950 posters per month sales volume). Use Kay's operating leverage factor to determine the percentage impact of a 10% *decrease* in sales volume on Kay's operating income. Prove your results.

Answer: If sales volume decreases by 10%, Kay's operating income will decrease by 21.1% (her operating leverage factor of 2.11 multiplied by a 10% decrease in volume).

Proof:		
Current volume of posters..........................		950
Less: Decrease in volume		
(10% × 950) of posters......................		(95)
New volume of posters..............................		855
Multiplied by: Unit contribution margin ...	× $	14
New total contribution margin..................		$11,970
Less: Fixed expenses................................		(7,000)
New operating income		$ 4,970
Versus operating income		
before change in volume....................		$ 6,300 *
Decrease in operating income..................		$ (1,330)
Percentage change ($1,330/$6,300)..........		21.1%(rounded)

*(950 posters × $14/unit contribution margin) – $7,000 fixed expenses

In this chapter, we have discussed how managers use the contribution margin and CVP analysis to predict profits, determine the volume needed to achieve breakeven or a target profit, and assess how changes in the business environment affect their profits. In the next chapter, we look at several types of short-term decisions managers must make. Cost behavior and the contribution margin will continue to play an important role in these decisions.

Decision Guidelines

CVP Analysis

Your friend did decide to open an ice cream parlor. But now she's facing changing business conditions. She needs help making the following decisions:

Decision	Guidelines
The cost of ice cream is rising, yet my competitors have lowered their prices. How will these factors affect the sales volume I'll need to break even or achieve my target profit ?	Increases in variable costs (such as ice cream) and decreases in sales prices both decrease the unit contribution margin and contribution margin ratio. You will have to sell more units in order to achieve breakeven or a target profit. You can use sensitivity analysis to better pinpoint the actual volume you'll need to sell. Simply compute your new unit contribution margin and use it in the shortcut unit contribution margin formula.
Would it help if I could renegotiate my lease with the landlord?	Decreases in fixed costs do not affect the firm's contribution margin. However, a decrease in fixed costs means that the company will have to sell fewer units to achieve breakeven or a target profit. Increases in fixed costs have the opposite effect.
I've been thinking about selling other products in addition to ice cream. Will this affect the sales volume I'll need to earn my target profit?	Your contribution margin ratio will change as a result of changing your sales mix. A company earns more income by selling higher-margin products than by selling an equal number of lower-margin products. If you can shift sales toward higher contribution margin products, you will have to sell fewer units to reach your target profit.
If the economy takes a downturn, how much risk do I face of incurring a loss?	The margin of safety indicates how far sales volume can decline before you would incur a loss:

$$\text{Margin of safety} = \text{Expected sales} - \text{Breakeven sales}$$

The operating leverage factor indicates the percentage change in operating income that will occur from a 1% change in volume. It tells you how sensitive your company's operating income is to changes in volume. At a given level of sales, the operating leverage factor is as follows:

$$\text{Operating leverage factor} = \frac{\text{Contribution margin}}{\text{Operating income}}$$

Summary Problem 2

Recall from Summary Problem 1 that Fleet Foot buys hiking socks for $6 a pair and sells them for $10. Monthly fixed costs are $10,000 (for sales volumes between 0 and 12,000 pairs), resulting in a breakeven point of 2,500 units. Assume that Fleet Foot has been selling 8,000 pairs of socks per month.

Requirements

1. What is Fleet Foot's current margin of safety in units, in sales dollars, and as a percentage? Explain the results.

2. At this level of sales, what is Fleet Foot's operating leverage factor? If volume declines by 25% due to increasing competition, by what percentage will the company's operating income decline?

3. Competition has forced Fleet Foot to lower its sales price to $9 a pair. How will this affect Fleet's breakeven point?

4. To compensate for the lower sales price, Fleet Foot wants to expand its product line to include men's dress socks. Each pair will sell for $7.00 and cost $2.75 from the supplier. Fixed costs will not change. Fleet expects to sell four pairs of dress socks for every one pair of hiking socks (at its new $9 sales price). What is Fleet's weighted-average contribution margin per unit? Given the 4:1 sales mix, how many of each type of sock will it need to sell to break even?

continued

Solution
Requirement 1

Margin of safety in units = Expected sales in units − Breakeven sales in units

= 8,000 − 2,500

= 5,500 units

Margin of safety in dollars = Expected sales in dollars − Breakeven sales in dollars

= (8,000 × $10) − (2,500 × $10)

= $55,000

$$\text{Margin of safety as a percentage} = \frac{\text{Margin of safety in units}}{\text{Expected sales in units}}$$

$$= \frac{5,500 \text{ pairs}}{8,000 \text{ pairs}}$$

= 68.75%

Fleet Foot's margin of safety is quite high. Sales have to fall by more than 5,500 units (or $55,000) before Fleet incurs a loss. Fleet will continue to earn a profit unless sales drop by more than 68.75%.

Requirement 2

At its current level of volume, Fleet's operating income is as follows:

Contribution margin (8,000 pairs × $4/pair)	$ 32,000
Less: Fixed expenses	(10,000)
Operating income	$ 22,000

Fleet's operating leverage factor at this level of sales is computed as follows:

$$\text{Operating leverage factor} = \frac{\text{Contribution margin}}{\text{Operating income}}$$

$$= \frac{\$32,000}{\$22,000}$$

= 1.45 (rounded)

If sales volume declines by 25%, operating income will decline by 36.25% (Fleet's operating leverage factor of 1.45 multiplied by 25%).

Requirement 3

If Fleet drops its sales price to $9 per pair, its contribution margin per pair declines to $3 (sales price of $9 − variable cost of $6). Each sale contributes less toward covering fixed costs. Fleet's new breakeven point *increases* to 3,334 pairs of socks ($10,000 fixed costs ÷ $3 unit contribution margin).

Requirement 4

	Hiking Socks	Dress Socks	Total
Sales price per unit	$ 9.00	$ 7.00	
Deduct: Variable expense per unit	(6.00)	(2.75)	
Contribution margin per unit	$ 3.00	$ 4.25	
Sales mix	× 1	× 4	5
Contribution margin	$ 3.00	$17.00	$20.00
Weighted-average contribution margin per unit ($20/5)			$ 4.00

$$\text{Sales in total units} = \frac{\text{Fixed expenses} + \text{Operating income}}{\text{Weighted-average contribution margin per unit}}$$

$$= \frac{\$10,000 + \$0}{\$4}$$

$$= 2,500 \text{ pairs of socks}$$

Breakeven sales of dress socks (2,500 × 4/5)	2,000 pairs dress socks
Breakeven sales of hiking socks (2,500 × 1/5)	500 pairs hiking socks

By expanding its product line to include higher-margin dress socks, Fleet is able to decrease its breakeven point back to its original level (2,500 pairs). However, to achieve this breakeven point, Fleet must sell the planned ratio of four pairs of dress socks to every one pair of hiking socks.

REVIEW

Accounting Vocabulary

Breakeven Point. (p. 368) The sales level at which operating income is zero: Total revenues equals total expenses.

Contribution Margin. (p. 365) Sales revenue minus variable expenses.

Contribution Margin Per Unit. (p. 366) The excess of the unit sales price over the variable cost per unit; also called unit contribution margin.

Contribution Margin Income Statement. (p. 365) An income statement that groups costs by behavior rather than function; it can be used only by internal management.

Contribution Margin Ratio. (p. 366) Ratio of contribution margin to sales revenue.

Cost-Volume-Profit (CVP) Analysis. (p. 364) Expresses the relationships among costs, volume, and profit or loss.

Margin of Safety. (p. 384) Excess of expected sales over breakeven sales; the drop in sales a company can absorb without incurring an operating loss.

Operating Leverage. (p. 385) The relative amount of fixed and variable costs that make up a firm's total costs.

Operating Leverage Factor. (p. 386) At a given level of sales, the contribution margin divided by operating income; the operating leverage factor indicates the percentage change in operating income that will occur from a 1% change in sales volume.

Sales Mix. (p. 364) The combination of products that make up total sales.

Sensitivity Analysis. (p. 376) A "what-if" technique that asks what results will be if actual prices or costs change or if an underlying assumption changes.

Quick Check

1. *(Learning Objective 1)* When a company is operating at its breakeven point
   a. its selling price will be equal to its variable expense per unit.
   b. its contribution margin will be equal to its variable expenses.
   c. its fixed expenses will be equal to its variable expenses.
   d. its total revenues will be equal to its total expenses.

2. *(Learning Objective 1)* If a company sells one unit above its breakeven sales volume, then its operating income would be equal to
   a. the unit selling price.
   b. the unit contribution margin.
   c. the fixed expenses.
   d. zero.

3. *(Learning Objective 2)* How is the unit sales volume necessary to reach a target profit calculated?
   a. Target profit / unit contribution margin
   b. Target profit / contribution margin ratio
   c. (Fixed expenses + target profit)/unit contribution margin
   d. (Fixed expenses + target profit)/contribution margin ratio

4. *(Learning Objective 2)* The number of units to be sold to reach a certain target profit is calculated as
   a. target profit / unit contribution margin.
   b. target profit / contribution margin ratio.
   c. (fixed expenses + target profit)/unit contribution margin.
   d. (fixed expenses + target profit)/contribution margin ratio.

5. *(Learning Objective 3)* The breakeven point on a CVP graph is
   a. the intersection of the sales revenue line and the total expense line.
   b. the intersection of the fixed expense line and the total expense line.
   c. the intersection of the fixed expense line and the sales revenue.
   d. the intersection of the sales revenue line and the y-axis.

6. *(Learning Objective 3)* If the sales price of a product increases while everything else remains the same, what happens to the breakeven point?
   a. The breakeven point will increase.
   b. The breakeven point will decrease.
   c. The breakeven point will remain the same.
   d. The effect cannot be determined without further information.

7. *(Learning Objective 4)* Target profit analysis is used to calculate the sales volume that is needed to
   a. cover all fixed expenses.
   b. cover all expenses.
   c. to avoid a loss.
   d. earn a specific amount of net operating income.

8. *(Learning Objective 4)* A shift in the sales mix from a product with a high contribution margin ratio toward a product with a low contribution margin ratio will cause the breakeven point to
   a. increase.
   b. decrease.
   c. remain the same.
   d. increase or decrease, but the direction of change cannot be determined from the information given.

9. *(Learning Objective 5)* If the degree of operating leverage is 3, then a 2% change in the number of units sold should result in a 6% change in
   a. sales.
   b. variable expense.
   c. unit contribution margin.
   d. operating income.

10. *(Learning Objective 5)* What is the margin of safety?
    a. The amount of fixed and variable costs that make up a company's total costs
    b. The difference between the sales price per unit and the variable cost per unit
    c. The excess of expected sales over breakeven sales
    d. The sales level at which operating income is zero

ASSESS YOUR PROGRESS

Learning Objectives

 1 Calculate the unit contribution margin and the contribution margin ratio

2 Use CVP analysis to find breakeven points and target profit volumes

3 Perform sensitivity analysis in response to changing business conditions

4 Find breakeven and target profit volumes for multiproduct companies

 **5** Determine a firm's margin of safety and operating leverage

Short Exercises

Bay Cruiseline Data Set used for S7-1 through S7-12:

Bay Cruiseline offers nightly dinner cruises off the coast of Miami, San Francisco, and Seattle. Dinner cruise tickets sell for $50 per passenger. Bay Cruiseline's variable cost of providing the dinner is $20 per passenger, and the fixed cost of operating the vessels (depreciation, salaries, docking fees, and other expenses) is $210,000 per month. The company's relevant range extends to 15,000 monthly passengers.

S7-1 Compute unit contribution margin and contribution margin ratio *(Learning Objective 1)*

Use the information from the Bay Cruiseline Data Set to compute the following:
a. What is the contribution margin per passenger?
b. What is the contribution margin ratio?
c. Use the unit contribution margin to project operating income if monthly sales total 10,000 passengers.
d. Use the contribution margin ratio to project operating income if monthly sales revenue totals $400,000.

S7-2 Project change in income *(Learning Objective 1)*

Use the information from the Bay Cruiseline Data Set. If Bay Cruiseline sells an additional 500 tickets, by what amount will its operating income increase (or operating loss decrease)?

S7-3 Find breakeven *(Learning Objective 2)*

Use the information from the Bay Cruiseline Data Set to compute the number of dinner cruise tickets it must sell to break even.
a. Use the income statement equation approach.
b. Using the shortcut *unit* contribution margin approach, perform a numerical proof to ensure that your answer is correct.
c. Use your answers from a and b to determine the sales revenue needed to break even.
d. Use the shortcut contribution margin *ratio* approach to verify the sales revenue needed to break even.

S7-4 Find target profit volume *(Learning Objective 2)*

Use the information from the Bay Cruiseline Data Set. If Bay Cruiseline has a target operating income of $60,000 per month, how many dinner cruise tickets must the company sell?

S7-5 Prepare a CVP graph *(Learning Objective 2)*

Use the information from the Bay Cruiseline Data Set. Draw a graph of Bay Cruiseline's CVP relationships. Include the sales revenue line, the fixed expense line, and the total expense line. Label the axes, the breakeven point, the income area, and the loss area.

S7-6 Interpret a CVP graph *(Learning Objective 2)*

Describe what each letter stands for in the CVP graph.

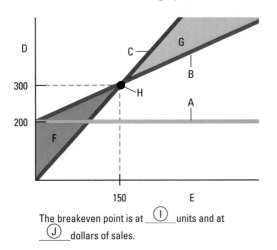

The breakeven point is at ⓘ units and at ⓙ dollars of sales.

S7-7 Changes in sales price and variable costs *(Learning Objective 3)*

Use the information from the Bay Cruiseline Data Set.

1. Suppose Bay Cruiseline cuts its dinner cruise ticket price from $50 to $40 to increase the number of passengers. Compute the new breakeven point in units and in sales dollars. Explain how changes in sales price generally affect the breakeven point.

2. Assume that Bay Cruiseline does *not* cut the price. Bay Cruiseline could reduce its variable costs by no longer serving an appetizer before dinner. Suppose this operating change reduces the variable expense from $20 to $10 per passenger. Compute the new breakeven point in units and in dollars. Explain how changes in variable costs generally affect the breakeven point.

S7-8 Changes in fixed costs *(Learning Objective 3)*

Use the information from the Bay Cruiseline Data Set. Suppose Bay Cruiseline embarks on a cost-reduction drive and slashes fixed expenses from $210,000 per month to $180,000 per month.

1. Compute the new breakeven point in units and in sales dollars.

2. Is the breakeven point higher or lower than in S7-3? Explain how changes in fixed costs generally affect the breakeven point.

S7-9 Compute weighted-average contribution margin *(Learning Objective 4)*

Use the information from the Bay Cruiseline Data Set. Suppose Bay Cruiseline decides to offer two types of dinner cruises: regular cruises and executive cruises. The executive cruise includes complimentary cocktails and a five-course dinner on the upper deck. Assume that fixed expenses remain at $210,000 per month and that the following ticket prices and variable expenses apply:

	Regular Cruise	Executive Cruise
Sales price per ticket....................................	$50	$130
Variable expense per passenger	$20	$ 40

Assuming that Bay Cruiseline expects to sell four regular cruises for every executive cruise, compute the weighted-average contribution margin per unit. Is it higher or lower than a *simple* average contribution margin? Why? Is it higher or lower than the regular cruise contribution margin calculated in S7-1? Why? Will this new sales mix cause Bay Cruiseline's breakeven point to increase or decrease from what it was when it sold only regular cruises?

S7-10 Continuation of S7-9: Breakeven *(Learning Objective 4)*

Refer to your answer to S7-9.

a. Compute the total number of dinner cruises that Bay Cruiseline must sell to breakeven.

b. Compute the number of regular cruises and executive cruises the company must sell to break even.

S7-11 Compute margin of safety *(Learning Objective 5)*

Use the information from the Bay Cruiseline Data Set. If Bay Cruiseline sells 10,000 dinner cruises, compute the margin of safety

a. in units (dinner cruise tickets).

b. in sales dollars.

c. as a percentage of sales.

S7-12 Compute and use operating leverage factor *(Learning Objective 5)*

Use the information from the Bay Cruiseline Data Set.

a. Compute the operating leverage factor when Bay Cruiseline sells 12,000 dinner cruises.

b. If volume increases by 10%, by what percentage will operating income increase?

c. If volume decreases by 5%, by what percentage will operating income decrease?

S7-13 Compute margin of safety *(Learning Objective 5)*

Kay has an e-tail poster business. Suppose Kay expects to sell 1,000 posters. Her average sales price per poster is $30 and her average cost per poster is $24. Her fixed expenses total $3,600. Compute her margin of safety

a. in units (posters).

b. in sales dollars.

c. as a percentage of expected sales.

S7-14 Compute and use operating leverage factor *(Learning Objective 5)*

Suppose Kay sells 1,000 posters. Use the original data from S7-13 to compute her operating leverage factor. If sales volume increases 10%, by what percentage will her operating income change? Prove your answer.

Exercises—Group A

E7-15A   Prepare contribution margin income statements *(Learning Objective 1)*

Aussie Travel uses the contribution margin income statement internally. Aussie's first-quarter results are as follows:

AUSSIE TRAVEL	
Contribution Margin Income Statement	
Three Months Ended March 31	
Sales revenue	$500,000
Less: Variable expenses	100,000
Contribution margin	$400,000
Less: Fixed expenses	150,000
Operating income	$250,000

Aussie's relevant range is between sales of $100,000 and $700,000.

Requirements

1. Prepare contribution margin income statements at sales levels of $150,000 and $600,000. (*Hint*: Use the contribution margin ratio.)

2. Compute breakeven sales in dollars.

E7-16A   Work backward to find missing information *(Learning Objectives 1 & 2)*

Berg Drycleaners has determined the following about its costs: Total variable expenses are $40,000, total fixed expenses are $30,000, and the sales revenue needed to breakeven is $40,000. Use the contribution margin income statement and the shortcut contribution margin approaches to determine Berg Drycleaners' current (1) sales revenue and (2) operating income. (*Hint*: First, find the contribution margin ratio; then, prepare the contribution margin income statement.)

E7-17A   Find breakeven and target profit volume *(Learning Objectives 1 & 2)*

Big Foot produces sports socks. The company has fixed expenses of $85,000 and variable expenses of $1.20 per package. Each package sells for $2.00.

Requirements

1. Compute the contribution margin per package and the contribution margin ratio.

2. Find the breakeven point in units and in dollars using the contribution margin shortcut approaches.

3. Find the number of packages Big Foot needs to sell to earn a $25,000 operating income.

E7-18A   Continuation of E7-17A: Changing costs *(Learning Objective 3)*

Refer to Big Foot in E7-17A. If Big Foot can decrease its variable costs to $1.00 per package by increasing its fixed costs to $100,000, how many packages will it have to sell to generate $25,000 of operating income? Is this more or less than before? Why?

E7-19A   Find breakeven and target profit volume *(Learning Objectives 1 & 2)*

Owner Shan Lo is considering franchising her Happy Wok restaurant concept. She believes people will pay $5 for a large bowl of noodles. Variable costs are $1.50 a bowl. Lo estimates monthly fixed costs for franchisees at $8,400.

Requirements

1. Use the contribution margin ratio shortcut approach to find a franchisee's breakeven sales in dollars.

2. Is franchising a good idea for Lo if franchisees want a minimum monthly operating income of $8,750 and Lo believes that most locations could generate $25,000 in monthly sales?

E7-20A   Continuation of E7-19A: Changing business conditions *(Learning Objective 3)*

Refer to Happy Wok in E7-19A. Lo did franchise her restaurant concept. Because of Happy Wok's success, Noodles-n-More has come on the scene as a competitor. To maintain its market share, Happy Wok will have to lower its sales price to $4.50 per bowl. At the same time, Happy Wok hopes to increase each restaurant's volume to 6,000 bowls per month by embarking on a marketing campaign. Each franchise will have to contribute $500 per month to cover the advertising costs. Prior to these changes, most locations were selling 5,500 bowls per month.

Requirements

1. What was the average restaurant's operating income before these changes?

2. Assuming that the price cut and advertising campaign are successful at increasing volume to the projected level, will the franchisees still earn their target profit of $8,750 per month? Show your calculations.

E7-21A   Compute breakeven and project income *(Learning Objectives 1 & 2)*

Dave's Steel Parts produces parts for the automobile industry. The company has monthly fixed expenses of $600,000 and a contribution margin of 80% of revenues.

Requirements

1. Compute Dave's Steel Parts' monthly breakeven sales in dollars. Use the contribution margin ratio shortcut approach.

2. Use the contribution margin ratio to project operating income (or loss) if revenues are $700,000 and if they are $1,000,000.

3. Do the results in Requirement 2 make sense given the breakeven sales you computed in Requirement 1? Explain.

E7-22A   Continuation of E7-21A: Changing business conditions *(Learning Objective 3)*

Refer to Dave's Steel Parts in E7-21A. Dave feels like he's in a giant squeeze play: The automotive manufacturers are demanding lower prices, and the steel producers have increased raw material costs. Dave's contribution margin has shrunk to 50% of revenues. Dave's monthly operating income, prior to these pressures, was $200,000.

Requirements

1. To maintain this same level of profit, what sales volume (in sales revenue) must Dave now achieve?

2. Dave believes that his monthly sales revenue will go only as high as $1,000,000. He is thinking about moving operations overseas to cut fixed costs. If monthly sales are $1,000,000, by how much will he need to cut fixed costs to maintain his prior profit level of $200,000 per month?

E7-23A   Identify information on a CVP graph *(Learning Objective 2)*

Chad Brown is considering starting a Web-based educational business, e-Prep MBA. He plans to offer a short-course review of accounting for students entering MBA programs. The materials would be available on a password-protected Web site, and students would complete the course through self-study. Brown would have to grade the course assignments, but most of the work is in developing the course materials, setting up the site, and marketing. Unfortunately, Brown's hard drive crashed before he finished his financial analysis. However, he did recover the following partial CVP chart:

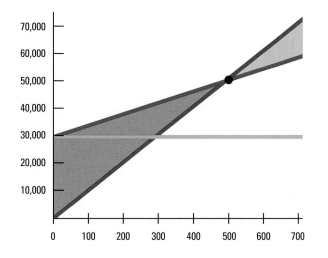

Requirements

1. Label each axis, sales revenue line, total expense line, fixed expense line, operating income area, and operating loss area.
2. If Brown attracts 400 students to take the course, will the venture be profitable?
3. What are the breakeven sales in students and dollars?

E7-24A Prepare a CVP graph (Learning Objective 2)

Suppose that Turner Field, the home of the Atlanta Braves, earns total revenue that averages $24 for every ticket sold. Assume that annual fixed expenses are $24 million and that variable expenses are $4 per ticket.

Requirements

1. Prepare the ballpark's CVP graph under these assumptions. Label the axes, sales revenue line, fixed expense line, total expense line, operating loss area, and operating income area on the graph.
2. Show the breakeven point in dollars and in tickets.

E7-25A Work backward to find new breakeven point (Learning Objectives 2 & 3)

Bevil Industries is planning on purchasing a new piece of equipment that will increase the quality of its production. It hopes the increased quality will generate more sales. The company's contribution margin ratio is 40%, and its current breakeven point is $500,000 in sales revenue. If Bevil Industries' fixed expenses increase by $40,000 due to the equipment, what will its new breakeven point be (in sales revenue)?

E7-26A Find consequence of rising fixed costs (Learning Objectives 1 & 3)

DeAnna Braun sells homemade knit scarves for $16 each at local crafts shows. Her contribution margin ratio is 62.5%. Currently, the crafts show entrance fees cost DeAnna $1,000 per year. The crafts shows are raising their entrance fees by 15% next year. How many *extra* scarves will DeAnna have to sell next year just to pay for rising entrance fee costs?

E7-27A Extension of E7-26A: Multiproduct firm (Learning Objective 4)

Arlan Braun admired his wife's success at selling scarves at local crafts shows (E7-26A), so he decided to make two types of plant stands to sell at the shows. Arlan makes twig stands out of downed wood from his backyard and the yards of his neighbors, so his variable cost is minimal (wood screws, glue, and so forth). However, Arlan has to purchase wood to make his oak plant stands. His unit prices and costs are as follows:

	Twig Stands	Oak Stands
Sales price	$15.00	$35.00
Variable cost	2.50	10.00

The twig stands are more popular, so Arlan sells four twig stands for every one oak stand. DeAnna charges her husband $300 to share her booth at the crafts shows (after all, she has paid the entrance fees). How many of each plant stand does Arlan need to sell to break even? Will this affect the number of scarves DeAnna needs to sell to break even? Explain.

E7-28A Find breakeven for a multiproduct firm (Learning Objective 4)

Racer Scooters plans to sell a motorized standard scooter for $54 and a motorized chrome scooter for $78. Racer Scooters purchases the standard scooter for $36 and the chrome scooter for $50. Racer Scooters expects to sell two chrome scooters for every three standard scooters. Racer Scooters' monthly fixed expenses are $9,680. How many of each type of scooter must Racer Scooters sell monthly to break even? To earn $6,600?

E7-29A Work backward to find missing data (Learning Objective 4)

Kenisha manufactures two styles of watches—the Digital and the Classic. The following data pertain to the Digital:

Variable manufacturing cost	$120
Variable operating cost	30
Sale price	200

Kenisha's monthly fixed expenses total $190,000. When Digitals and Classics are sold in the mix of 7:3, respectively, the sale of 2,000 total watches results in an operating income of $60,000. Compute the contribution margin per watch for the Classic.

E7-30A Breakeven and an advertising decision at a multiproduct company (Learning Objectives 3, 4, & 5)

Grand's Sporting Goods is a retailer of sporting equipment. Last year, Grand's Sporting Goods' sales revenues totaled $6,000,000. Total expenses were $2,100,000. Of this amount, approximately $1,500,000 were variable, while the remainder were fixed. Since Grand's Sporting Goods offers thousands of different products, its managers prefer to calculate the breakeven point in terms of sales dollars rather than units.

Requirements

1. What is Grand's Sporting Goods' current operating income?

2. What is Grand's Sporting Goods' contribution margin ratio?

3. What is Grand's Sporting Goods' breakeven point in sales dollars (*Hint*: The contribution margin ratio calculated in requirement two is already weighted by Grand's Sporting Goods' actual sales mix.)

4. Grand's Sporting Goods' top management is deciding whether to embark on a $200,000 advertisement campaign. The marketing firm has projected annual sales volume to increase by 15% as a result of this campaign. Assuming that the projections are correct, what effect would this advertising campaign have on Grand's Sporting Goods' annual operating income?

E7-31A Compute margin of safety and operating leverage *(Learning Objective 5)*

Use the Aussie Travel data in E7-15A to answer the following questions:

Requirements

1. What is Aussie Travel's current margin of safety (in dollars)?

2. What is Aussie Travel's current operating leverage factor?

3. If sales volume increases 5% next quarter, by what percentage will Aussie's operating income increase? What will the new operating income be?

E7-32A Work backward through margin of safety *(Learning Objective 5)*

Bill's Bait Shop had budgeted bait sales for the season at $10,000, with a $2,000 margin of safety. However, due to unseasonable weather, bait sales reached only $9,200. Actual sales exceeded breakeven sales by what amount?

E7-33A Compute margin of safety and operating leverage *(Learning Objective 5)*

Ronnie's Repair Shop has a monthly target operating income of $32,000. *Variable expenses* are 75% of sales, and monthly fixed expenses are $8,000.

Requirements

1. Compute the monthly margin of safety in dollars if the shop achieves its income goal.

2. Express Ronnie's margin of safety as a percentage of target sales.

3. What is Ronnie's operating leverage factor at the target level of operating income?

4. Assume that Ronnie reaches his target. By what percentage will Ronnie's operating income fall if sales volume declines by 10%?

E7-34A Use operating leverage factor to find fixed costs *(Learning Objective 5)*

Murray Manufacturing had a 1.25 operating leverage factor when sales were $50,000. Murray Manufacturing's contribution margin ratio was 20%. What were Murray Manufacturing's fixed expenses?

E7-35A Comprehensive CVP analysis *(Learning Objectives 1, 2, 3, 4, & 5)*

Gary Finch is evaluating a business opportunity to sell grooming kits at dog shows. Gary can buy the grooming kits at a wholesale cost of $30 per set. He plans to sell the grooming kits for $80 per set. He estimates fixed costs such as travel costs, booth rental cost, and lodging to be $900 per dog show.

Requirements

1. Determine the number of grooming kits Gary must sell per show to break even.

2. Assume Gary wants to earn a profit of $1,100 per show.
   a. Determine the sales volume in units necessary to earn the desired profit.
   b. Determine the sales volume in dollars necessary to earn the desired profit.
   c. Using the contribution margin format, prepare an income statement (condensed version) to confirm your answers to parts 1 and 2.

3. Determine the margin of safety between the sales volume at the break-even point and the sales volume required to earn the desired profit. Determine the margin of safety in both sales dollars, units, and as a percentage.

E7-36A Comprehensive CVP analysis *(Learning Objectives 1, 2, 3, 4, & 5)*

Bowerston Company manufactures and sells a single product. The company's sales and expenses for last year follow:

	Total	Per Unit	%
Sales..	$100,000	$20	?
Variable expenses......................................	60,000	12	?
Contribution margin	?	?	?
Fixed expenses	12,000		
Operating income.......................................	$ 28,000		

Requirements

1. Fill in the missing numbers in the preceding table. Use the table to answer the following questions:
    a. What is the total contribution margin?
    b. What is the per unit contribution margin?
    c. What is the operating income?
    d. How many units were sold?

2. Answer the following questions about breakeven analysis:
    a. What is the quarterly breakeven point in units?
    b. What is the quarterly breakeven point in sales dollars?

3. Answer the following questions about target profit analysis and safety margin:
    a. How many units must the company sell in order to earn a profit of $50,000?
    b. What is the margin of safety in units?
    c. What is the margin of safety in sales dollars?
    d. What is the margin of safety in percentage?

E7-37A   Comprehensive CVP analysis *(Learning Objectives 1, 2, 3, 4, & 5)*

FlashCo. manufactures 1 GB flash drives (jump drives). Price and cost data for a relevant range extending to 200,000 units per month are as follows:

Sales price per unit (current monthly sales volume is 120,000 units)	$ 20.00
Variable costs per unit:	
Direct materials	6.40
Direct labor	5.00
Variable manufacturing overhead	2.20
Variable selling and administrative expenses	1.40
Monthly fixed expenses:	
Fixed manufacturing overhead	$191,400
Fixed selling and administrative expenses	276,600

Requirements

1. What is the company's contribution margin per unit? Contribution margin percentage? Total contribution margin?

2. What would the company's monthly operating income be if the company sold 150,000 units?

3. What would the company's monthly operating income be if the company had sales of $4,000,000?

4. What is the breakeven point in units? In sales dollars?

5. How many units would the company have to sell to earn a target monthly profit of $260,000?

6. Management is currently in contract negotiations with the labor union. If the negotiations fail, direct labor costs will increase by 10% and fixed costs will increase by $22,500 per month. If these costs increase, how many units will the company have to sell each month to break even?

7. Return to the original data for this question and the rest of the questions. What is the company's current operating leverage factor (round to two decimals)?

8. If sales volume increases by 8%, by what percentage will operating income increase?

9. What is the firm's current margin of safety in sales dollars? What is its margin of safety as a percentage of sales?

10. Say FlashCo. adds a second line of flash drives (2 GB rather than 1 GB). A package of the 2 GB flash drives will sell for $45 and have variable cost per unit of $20 per unit. The

expected sales mix is three of the small flash drives (1 GB) for every one large flash drive (2 GB). Given this sales mix, how many of each type of flash drive will FlashCo. need to sell to reach its target monthly profit of $260,000? Is this volume higher or lower than previously needed (in Question 5) to achieve the same target profit? Why?

Exercises–Group B

E7-38B   Prepare contribution margin income statements (Learning Objective 1)

Airborne Travel uses the contribution margin income statement internally. Airborne's first quarter results are as follows:

Airborne Travel
Contribution Margin Income Statement
Three Months Ended March 31

Sales revenue	$ 318,500
Less: Variable expenses	(129,000)
Contribution margin	189,500
Less: Fixed expenses	(179,000)
Operating income	$ 10,500

Airborne's relevant range is between sales of $201,000 and $463,000.

Requirements

1. Prepare contribution margin income statements at sales levels of $251,000 and $363,000. (*Hint:* Use the contribution margin ratio.)

2. Compute breakeven sales in dollars.

E7-39B   Work backward to find missing information (Learning Objectives 1 & 2)

Stancil Drycleaners has determined the following about its costs: Total variable expenses are $38,000, total fixed expenses are $36,000, and the sales revenue needed to break even is $45,000. Use the contribution margin income statement and the shortcut contribution margin approaches to determine Stancil Drycleaners' current (1) sales revenue and (2) operating income. (*Hint:* First, find the contribution margin ratio; then, prepare the contribution margin income statement.)

E7-40B   Find breakeven and target profit volume (Learning Objectives 1 & 2)

Happy Ten produces sports socks. The company has fixed expenses of $80,000 and variable expenses of $0.80 per package. Each package sells for $1.60.

Requirements

1. Compute the contribution margin per package and the contribution margin ratio.

2. Find the breakeven point in units and in dollars, using the contribution margin shortcut approaches.

3. Find the number of packages Happy Ten needs to sell to earn a $22,000 operating income.

E7-41B   Continuation of E7-40B: Changing costs (Learning Objective 3)

Refer to Happy Ten in E7-40B. If Happy Ten can decrease its variable costs to $0.70 per package by increasing its fixed costs to $95,000, how many packages will it have to sell to generate $22,000 of operating income? Is this more or less than before? Why?

E7-42B   Find breakeven and target profit volume (Learning Objectives 1 & 2)

Owner Kay Fay is considering franchising her Oriental Express restaurant concept. She believes people will pay $5.50 for a large bowl of noodles. Variable costs are $2.75 a bowl. Fay estimates monthly fixed costs for franchisees at $8,750.

Requirements

1. Use the contribution margin ratio shortcut approach to find a franchisees' breakeven sales in dollars.

2. Is franchising a good idea for Fay if franchisees want a minimum monthly operating income of $3,500 and Fay believes most locations could generate $24,000 in monthly sales?

E7-43B Continuation of E7-42B: Changing business conditions *(Learning Objective 3)*

Refer to Oriental Express in E7-42B. Since franchising Oriental Express, the restaurant has not been very successful due to Noodles Plus coming on the scene as a competitor. To increase its market share, Oriental Express will have to lower its sales price to $5.00 per bowl. At the same time, Oriental Express hopes to increase each restaurant's volume to 7,000 bowls per month by embarking on a marketing campaign. Each franchise will have to contribute $500 per month to cover the advertising costs. Prior to these changes, most locations were selling 6,500 bowls per month. Fay believed people would pay $5.50 for a large bowl of noodles. Variable costs would be $2.75 a bowl creating a contribution margin of $2.75 per bowl. Kay Fay estimated monthly fixed costs for franchisees at $8,750. Franchisees wanted a minimum monthly operating income of $3,500.

Requirements

1. What was the average restaurant's operating income before these changes?
2. Assuming the price cut and advertising campaign are successful at increasing volume to the projected level, will the franchisees earn their target profit of $3,500 per month?

E7-44B Compute breakeven and project income *(Learning Objectives 1 & 2)*

Gary's Steel Parts produces parts for the automobile industry. The company has monthly fixed expenses of $620,000 and a contribution margin of 90% of revenues.

Requirements

1. Compute Gary's Steel Parts' monthly breakeven sales in dollars. Use the contribution margin ratio shortcut approach.
2. Use the contribution margin ratio to project operating income (or loss) if revenues are $500,000 and if they are $1,030,000.
3. Do the results in Requirement 2 make sense given the breakeven sales you computed in Requirement 1? Explain.

E7-45B Continuation of E7-44B: Changing business conditions *(Learning Objective 3)*

Refer to Dave's Steel Parts in E7-44B. Gary feels like he's in a giant squeeze play: The automotive manufacturers are demanding lower prices, and the steel producers have increased raw material costs. Gary's contribution margin has shrunk to 60% of revenues. Gary's monthly operating income, prior to these pressures, was $307,000.

Requirements

1. To maintain this same level of profit, what sales volume (in sales revenue) must Gary now achieve?
2. Gary believes that his monthly sales revenue will only go as high as $1,030,000. He is thinking about moving operations overseas to cut fixed costs. If monthly sales are $1,030,000, by how much will he need to cut fixed costs to maintain his prior profit level of $307,000 per month?

E7-46B Identify information on a CVP graph *(Learning Objective 2)*

Susannah Chardon is thinking about starting an upscale gift basket service. She would create gift baskets for corporate clients and then arrange for delivery. She is trying to decide if the gift basket service would be profitable. Unfortunately, Chardon's hard drive crashed before she finished her financial analysis. However, she did recover the following partial CVP chart:

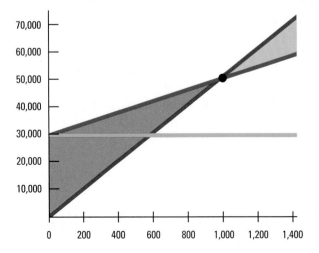

Requirements

1. Label each axis, sales revenue line, total expense line, fixed expense line, operating income area, and operating loss area.
2. If Susannah sells 825 gift baskets in her first year, will the venture be profitable?
3. What are the breakeven sales in baskets and dollars?

E7-47B Prepare a CVP graph *(Learning Objective 2)*

Suppose that Grant Field, the home of the Bay Area Gophers, earns total revenue that averages $28 for every ticket sold. Assume that annual fixed expenses are $22 million, and that variable expenses are $6 per ticket.

Requirements

1. Prepare the ballpark's CVP graph under these assumptions. Label the axes, sales revenue line, fixed expense line, total expense line, operating loss area, and operating income area on the graph.
2. Show the breakeven point in dollars and in tickets.

E7-48B Work backward to find new breakeven point *(Learning Objectives 2 & 3)*

Flow Industries is planning on purchasing a new piece of equipment that will increase the quality of its production. It hopes the increased quality will generate more sales. The company's contribution margin ratio is 20%, and its current breakeven point is $650,000 in sales revenue. If Flow Industries' fixed expenses increase by $50,000 due to the equipment, what will its new breakeven point be (in sales revenue)?

E7-49B Find consequence of rising fixed costs *(Learning Objectives 1 & 3)*

Julie Braun sells homemade knit scarves for $25 each at local craft shows. Her contribution margin ratio is 60%. Currently, the craft show entrance fees cost Julie $1,500 per year. The craft shows are raising their entrance fees by 25% next year. How many *extra* scarves will Julie have to sell next year just to pay for rising entrance fee costs?

E7-50B Extension of E7-49B: Multiproduct firm *(Learning Objective 4)*

Bobby Braun admired his wife's success at selling scarves at local craft shows (E7-49B), so he decided to make two types of plant stands to sell at the shows. Bobby makes twig stands out of downed wood from his backyard and the yards of his neighbors, so his variable cost is minimal (wood screws, glue, and so forth). However, Bobby has to purchase wood to make his oak plant stands. His unit prices and costs are as follows.

	Twig Stands	Oak Stands
Sales price	$13.00	$30.00
Variable cost	2.50	7.00

The twig stands are more popular so Bobby sells four twig stands for every one oak stand. Julie charges her husband $455 to share her booths at the craft shows (after all, she has paid the entrance fees). How many of each plant stand does Bobby need to sell to break even? Will this affect the number of scarves Julie needs to sell to break even? Explain.

E7-51B Find breakeven for a multiproduct firm *(Learning Objective 4)*

Rapid Scooters plans to sell a motorized standard scooter for $65 and a motorized chrome scooter for $75. Rapid Scooters purchases the standard scooter for $50 and the chrome scooter for $55. Rapid Scooters expects to sell two chrome scooters for every three standard scooters. Rapid Scooters' monthly fixed expenses are $15,300. How many of each type of scooter must Rapid Scooters sell monthly to break even? To earn $9,350?

E7-52B Work backward to find missing data *(Learning Objective 4)*

Amanda manufactures two styles of watches the Digital and the Classic. The following data pertain to the Digital:

Variable manufacturing cost	$140
Variable operating cost	20
Sale price	240

Amanda's monthly fixed expenses total $210,000. When Digitals and Classics are sold in the mix of 6:4, respectively, the sale of 2,500 total watches results in an operating income of $80,000. Compute the contribution margin per watch for the Classic.

E7-53B Breakeven and an advertising decision at a multiproduct company *(Learning Objectives 3, 4, & 5)*

Peter's Sporting Goods is a retailer of sporting equipment. Last year, Peter's Sporting Goods sales revenues totaled $6,400,000. Total expenses were $2,800,000. Of this amount, approximately $1,792,000 were variable, while the remainder were fixed. Since Peter's Sporting Goods offers thousands of different products, its managers prefer to calculate the breakeven point in terms of sales dollars, rather than units.

Requirements

1. What is Peter's Sporting Goods' current operating income?

2. What is Peter's Sporting Goods' contribution margin ratio?

3. What is Peter's Sporting Goods' breakeven point in sales dollars? (*Hint:* The contribution margin ratio calculated in Requirement 2 is already weighted by Peter's Sporting Goods' actual sales mix.) What does it mean?

4. Peter's Sporting Goods' top management is deciding whether to embark on a $190,000 advertisement campaign. The marketing firm has projected annual sales volume to increase by 20% as a result of this campaign. Assuming that the projections are correct, what effect would this advertising campaign have on Peter's Sporting Goods' annual operating income?

E7-54B Compute margin of safety and operating leverage *(Learning Objective 5)*

Use the Airborne Travel data in E7-38B to answer the following questions.

Requirements

1. What is Airborne Travel's current margin of safety (in dollars)?

2. What is Airborne Travel's current operating leverage factor?

3. If sales volume increases 4% next quarter, by what percent will Airborne's operating income increase? What will the new operating income be?

E7-55B Work backward through margin of safety *(Learning Objective 5)*

Ben's Bait Shop had budgeted bait sales for the season at $13,000, with a $6,000 margin of safety. However, due to unseasonable weather, bait sales only reached $12,100. Actual sales exceeded breakeven sales by what amount?

E7-56B Compute margin of safety and operating leverage *(Learning Objective 5)*

Foster's Repair Shop has a monthly target operating income of $13,500. *Variable expenses* are 70% of sales, and monthly fixed expenses are $10,000.

Requirements

1. Compute the monthly margin of safety in dollars if the shop achieves its income goal.

2. Express Foster's margin of safety as a percentage of target sales.

3. What is Foster's operating leverage factor at the target level of operating income?

4. Assume that Foster reaches his target. By what percentage will Foster's operating income fall if sales volume declines by 9%?

E7-57B Use operating leverage factor to find fixed costs *(Learning Objective 5)*

Popley Manufacturing had a 1.40 operating leverage factor when sales were $60,000. Popley Manufacturing's contribution margin ratio was 35%. What were Popley Manufacturing's fixed expenses?

E7-58B Comprehensive CVP analysis *(Learning Objectives 1, 2, 3, 4, & 5)*

Larry Stenback is evaluating a business opportunity to sell grooming kits at dog shows. Larry can buy the grooming kits at a wholesale cost of $32 per set. He plans to sell the grooming kits for $62 per set. He estimates fixed costs such as travel costs, booth rental cost, and lodging to be $600 per dog show.

Requirements

1. Determine the number of grooming kits Larry must sell per show to break even.

2. Assume Larry wants to earn a profit of $900 per show.

   a. Determine the sales volume in units necessary to earn the desired profit.

   b. Determine the sales volume in dollars necessary to earn the desired profit.

   c. Using the contribution margin format, prepare an income statement (condensed version) to confirm your answers to parts 1 and 2.

3. Determine the margin of safety between the sales volume at the breakeven point and the sales volume required to earn the desired profit. Determine the margin of safety in both sales dollars, units, and as a percentage.

E7-59B Comprehensive CVP analysis *(Learning Objectives 1, 2, 3, 4, & 5)*

Austen Company manufactures and sells a single product. The company's sales and expenses for last year follow:

	Total	Per Unit	%
Sales...	$81,250	$25	?
Variable expenses..................................	48,750	15	?
Contribution margin	?	?	?
Fixed expenses	13,000		
Operating income.................................	$19,500		

Requirements

1. Fill in the missing numbers in the table. Use the table to answer the following questions:

   a. What is the total contribution margin?

   b. What is the per unit contribution margin?

   c. What is the operating income?

   d. How many units were sold?

2. Answer the following questions about breakeven analysis:

   a. What is the quarterly breakeven point in units?

   b. What is the quarterly breakeven point in sales dollars?

3. Answer the following questions about target profit analysis and safety margin:

   a. How many units must the company sell in order to earn a profit of $53,000?

   b. What is the margin of safety in units?

   c. What is the margin of safety in sales dollars?

   d. What is the margin of safety in percentage?

E7-60B Comprehensive CVP analysis *(Learning Objectives 1, 2, 3, 4, & 5)*

GigaCo. manufactures 1 GB flash drives (jump drives). Price and cost data for a relevant range extending to 200,000 units per month are as follows:

Sales price per unit	
(current monthly sales volume is 130,000 units)	$ 20.00
Variable costs per unit:	
Direct materials	6.20
Direct labor	7.00
Variable manufacturing overhead..	2.00
Variable selling and administrative expenses............................	1.80
Monthly fixed expenses:	
Fixed manufacturing overhead..	$102,300
Fixed selling and administrative expenses	187,800

Requirements

1. What is the company's contribution margin per unit? Contribution margin percentage? Total contribution margin?

2. What would the company's monthly operating income be if it sold 160,000 units?

3. What would the company's monthly operating income be if it had sales of $4,000,000?

4. What is the breakeven point in units? In sales dollars?

5. How many units would the company have to sell to earn a target monthly profit of $260,100?

6. Management is currently in contract negotiations with the labor union. If the negotiations fail, direct labor costs will increase by 10 % and fixed costs will increase by $22,500 per month. If these costs increase, how many units will the company have to sell each month to break even?

7. Return to the original data for this question and the rest of the questions. What is the company's current operating leverage factor (round to two decimal)?

8. If sales volume increases by 7%, by what percentage will operating income increase?

9. What is the firm's current margin of safety in sales dollars? What is its margin of safety as a percentage of sales?

10. Say GigaCo. adds a second line of flash drives (2 GB rather than 1 GB). A package of the 2 GB flash drives will sell for $45 and have variable cost per unit of $28 per unit. The expected sales mix is six of the smaller flash drives (1 GB) for every one larger flash drive (2 GB). Given this sales mix, how many of each type of flash drive will GigaCo. need to sell to reach its target monthly profit of $260,100? Is this volume higher or lower than previously needed (in Question 5) to achieve the same target profit? Why?

Problems—Group A

P7-61A Find missing data in CVP relationships (Learning Objectives 1 & 2)

The budgets of four companies yield the following information:

	Company			
	Q	R	S	T
Target sales..............................	$720,000	$400,000	$190,000	$
Variable expenses......................	216,000			270,000
Fixed expenses		156,000	90,000	
Operating income (loss)	$154,000	$	$	140,000
Units sold.................................		125,000	12,000	15,750
Contribution margin per unit....	$ 6		$ 9.50	$ 40
Contribution margin ratio.........		0.65		

Requirements

1. Fill in the blanks for each company.

2. Compute breakeven, in sales dollars, for each company. Which company has the lowest breakeven point in sales dollars? What causes the low breakeven point?

P7-62A Find breakeven and target profit and prepare income statements (Learning Objectives 1 & 2)

A traveling production of *The Phantom of the Opera* performs each year. The average show sells 800 tickets at $50 a ticket. There are 100 shows each year. The show has a cast of 40, each earning an average of $260 per show. The cast is paid only after each show. The other variable expense is program printing costs of $6 per guest. Annual fixed expenses total $942,400.

Requirements

1. Compute revenue and variable expenses for each show.

2. Use the income statement equation approach to compute the number of shows needed annually to break even.

3. Use the shortcut unit contribution margin approach to compute the number of shows needed annually to earn a profit of $1,438,400. Is this goal realistic? Give your reason.

4. Prepare *The Phantom of the Opera*'s contribution margin income statement for 100 shows each year. Report only two categories of expenses: variable and fixed.

P7-63A Comprehensive CVP problem *(Learning Objectives 1, 2, & 5)*

Team Spirit imprints calendars with college names. The company has fixed expenses of $1,035,000 each month plus variable expenses of $3.60 per carton of calendars. Of the variable expense, 70% is Cost of Goods Sold, while the remaining 30% relates to variable operating expenses. Team Spirit sells each carton of calendars for $10.50.

Requirements

1. Use the income statement equation approach to compute the number of cartons of calendars that Team Spirit must sell each month to break even.

2. Use the contribution margin ratio shortcut formula to compute the dollar amount of monthly sales Team Spirit needs in order to earn $285,000 in operating income (round the contribution margin ratio to two decimal places).

3. Prepare Team Spirit's contribution margin income statement for June for sales of 450,000 cartons of calendars.

4. What is June's margin of safety (in dollars)? What is the operating leverage factor at this level of sales?

5. By what percentage will operating income change if July's sales volume is 13% higher? Prove your answer.

P7-64A Compute breakeven, prepare CVP graph, and respond to change *(Learning Objectives 1, 2, & 3)*

Personal Investors is opening an office in Lexington, Kentucky. Fixed monthly expenses are office rent ($2,500), depreciation on office furniture ($260), utilities ($280), special telephone lines ($600), a connection with an online brokerage service ($640), and the salary of a financial planner ($3,320). Variable expenses include payments to the financial planner (10% of revenue), advertising (5% of revenue), supplies and postage (2% of revenue), and usage fees for the telephone lines and computerized brokerage service (3% of revenue).

Requirements

1. Use the contribution margin ratio CVP formula to compute the investment firm's breakeven revenue in dollars. If the average trade leads to $475 in revenue for Personal Investors, how many trades must it make to break even?

2. Use the income statement equation approach to compute dollar revenues needed to earn monthly operating income of $3,040.

3. Graph Personal Investors' CVP relationships. Assume that an average trade leads to $400 in revenue for Personal Investors. Show the breakeven point, sales revenue line, fixed expense line, total expense line, operating loss area, operating income area, and sales in units (trades) and dollars when monthly operating income of $3,840 is earned. The graph should range from 0 to 40 units (trades).

4. Assume that the average revenue that Personal Investors earns decreases to $375 per trade. How does this affect the breakeven point in number of trades?

P7-65A   CVP analysis at a multiproduct firm (*Learning Objectives 4 & 5*)

The contribution margin income statement of Extreme Coffee for February follows:

EXTREME COFFEE
Contribution Margin Income Statement
For the Month Ended February 29

Sales revenue		$90,000
Variable expenses:		
Cost of goods sold	$32,000	
Marketing expense	10,000	
General and administrative expense	3,000	45,000
Contribution margin		45,000
Fixed expenses:		
Marketing expense	16,500	
General and administrative expense	3,500	20,000
Operating income		$25,000

Extreme Coffee sells three small coffees for every large coffee. A small coffee sells for $2, with a variable expense of $1. A large coffee sells for $4, with a variable expense of $2.

Requirements

1. Determine Extreme Coffee's monthly breakeven point in the numbers of small coffees and large coffees. Prove your answer by preparing a summary contribution margin income statement at the breakeven level of sales. Show only two categories of expenses: variable and fixed.

2. Compute Extreme Coffee's margin of safety in dollars.

3. Use Extreme Coffee's operating leverage factor to determine its new operating income if sales volume increases 15%. Prove your results using the contribution margin income statement format. Assume that sales mix remains unchanged.

Problems–Group B

P7-66B   Find missing data in CVP relationships (*Learning Objectives 1 & 2*)

The budgets of four companies yield the following information:

	Company			
	Q	R	S	T
Target sales	$828,125	$415,625	$181,250	$
Variable expenses	298,125			270,000
Fixed expenses		160,000	98,000	
Operating income (loss)	$230,000	$	$	133,000
Units sold		118,750	11,600	18,000
Contribution margin per unit	$ 6.25		$ 10.00	$ 35.00
Contribution margin ratio		0.64		

Requirements

1. Fill in the blanks for each company.

2. Compute breakeven, in sales dollars, for each company. Which company has the lowest breakeven point in sales dollars? What causes the low breakeven point?

P7-67B   Find breakeven and target profit and prepare income statements *(Learning Objectives 1 & 2)*

A traveling production of *Grease* performs each year. The average show sells 1,000 tickets at $65 per ticket. There are 120 shows a year. The show has a cast of 45, each earning an average of $320 per show. The cast is paid only after each show. The other variable expense is program printing expenses of $6 per guest. Annual fixed expenses total $802,800.

Requirements

1. Compute revenue and variable expenses for each show.

2. Use the income statement equation approach to compute the number of shows needed annually to break even.

3. Use the shortcut unit contribution margin approach to compute the number of shows needed annually to earn a profit of $5,708,800. Is this goal realistic? Give your reason.

4. Prepare *Grease's* contribution margin income statement for 120 shows each year. Report only two categories of expenses: variable and fixed.

P7-68B   Comprehensive CVP problem *(Learning Objectives 1, 2, & 5)*

Vast Spirit imprints calendars with college names. The company has fixed expenses of $1,045,000 each month plus variable expenses of $3.90 per carton of calendars. Of the variable expense, 66% is Cost of Goods Sold, while the remaining 34% relates to variable operating expenses. Vast Spirit sells each carton of calendars for $11.50.

Requirements

1. Use the income statement equation approach to compute the number of cartons of calendars that Vast Spirit must sell each month to break even.

2. Use the contribution margin ratio shortcut formula to compute the dollar amount of monthly sales Vast Spirit needs in order to earn $275,000 in operating income (round the contribution margin ratio to two decimal places).

3. Prepare Vast Spirit's contribution margin income statement for June for sales of 460,000 cartons of calendars.

4. What is June's margin of safety (in dollars)? What is the operating leverage factor at this level of sales?

5. By what percentage will operating income change if July's sales volume is 10% higher? Prove your answer.

P7-69B   Compute breakeven, prepare CVP graph, and respond to change *(Learning Objectives 1, 2, & 3)*

Personal Investors is opening an office in Atlanta, Georgia. Fixed monthly costs are office rent ($2,800), depreciation on office furniture ($310), utilities ($260), special telephone lines ($670), a connection with an online brokerage service ($700), and the salary of a financial planner ($2,760). Variable expenses include payments to the financial planner (10% of revenue), advertising (5% of revenue), supplies and postage (2% of revenue), and usage fees for the telephone lines and computerized brokerage service (23% of revenue).

Requirements

1. Use the contribution margin ratio CVP formula to compute the investment firm's breakeven revenue in dollars. If the average trade leads to $500 in revenue for Personal Investors, how many trades must be made to break even?

2. Use the income statement equation approach to compute dollar revenues needed to earn monthly operating income of $3,900.

3. Graph Personal Investors' CVP relationships. Assume that an average trade leads to $500 in revenue for Personal Investors. Show the breakeven point, sales revenue line, fixed expense line, total expense line, operating loss area, operating income area, and sales in units (trades) and dollars when monthly operating income of $3,900 is earned.

   The graph should range from 0 to 40 units (trades).

4. Assume that the average revenue Personal Investors earns decreases to $400 per trade. How does this affect the breakeven point in number of trades?

P7-70B CVP analysis at a multiproduct firm *(Learning Objectives 4 & 5)*

The contribution margin income statement of Cosmic Coffee for February follows:

Cosmic Coffee
Contribution Margin Income Statement
For the Month Ended February 29

Sales revenue		$88,000
Variable expenses:		
Cost of goods sold	$30,000	
Marketing expense	8,000	
General and administrative expense	2,000	40,000
Contribution margin		48,000
Fixed expenses:		
Marketing expense	34,650	
General and administrative expense	7,350	42,000
Operating income		$ 6,000

Cosmic Coffee sells three small coffees for every large coffee. A small coffee sells for $3.00, with a variable expense of $1.50. A large coffee sells for $5.00, with a variable expense of $2.50.

Requirements

1. Determine Cosmic Coffee's monthly breakeven point in numbers of small coffees and large coffees. Prove your answer by preparing a summary contribution margin income statement at the breakeven level of sales. Show only two categories of expenses: variable and fixed.

2. Compute Cosmic Coffee's margin of safety in dollars.

3. Use Cosmic Coffee's operating leverage factor to determine its new operating income if sales volume increases by 15%. Prove your results using the contribution margin income statement format. Assume the sales mix remains unchanged.

APPLY YOUR KNOWLEDGE

Decision Cases

C7-71 Determine the feasibility of a business plan *(Learning Objective 2)*

Brian and Nui Soon live in Macon, Georgia. Two years ago, they visited Thailand. Nui, a professional chef, was impressed with the cooking methods and the spices used in the Thai food. Macon does not have a Thai restaurant, and the Soons are contemplating opening one. Nui would supervise the cooking, and Brian would leave his current job to be the maitre d'. The restaurant would serve dinner Tuesday through Saturday.

Brian has noticed a restaurant for lease. The restaurant has seven tables, each of which can seat four. Tables can be moved together for a large party. Nui is planning two seatings per evening, and the restaurant will be open 50 weeks per year.

The Soons have drawn up the following estimates:

Average revenue, including beverages and dessert	$	40 per meal
Average cost of the food..	$	12 per meal
Chef's and dishwasher's salaries..	$50,400 per *year*
Rent (premises, equipment)	$	4,000 per month
Cleaning (linen and premises)...	$	800 per month
Replacement of dishes, cutlery, glasses	$	300 per month
Utilities, advertising, telephone..	$	1,900 per month

Requirement

1. Compute *annual* breakeven number of meals and sales revenue for the restaurant. Also, compute the number of meals and the amount of sales revenue needed to earn operating income of $75,600 for the year. How many meals must the Soons serve each night to earn their target income of $75,600? Should the couple open the restaurant? Support your answer.

Ethical Issue

I7-72   Ethical dilemma with CVP analysis error *(Learning Objective 2)*

You have just begun your summer internship at Tmedic. The company supplies sterilized surgical instruments for physicians. To expand sales, Tmedic is considering paying a commission to its sales force. The controller, Jane Hewitt, asks you to compute (1) the new breakeven sales figure and (2) the operating profit if sales increase 15% under the new sales commission plan. She thinks you can handle this task because you learned CVP analysis in your accounting class.

You spend the next day collecting information from the accounting records, performing the analysis, and writing a memo to explain the results. The company president is pleased with your memo. You report that the new sales commission plan will lead to a significant increase in operating income and only a small increase in breakeven sales.

The following week, you realize that you made an error in the CVP analysis. You overlooked the sales personnel's $2,500 monthly salaries, and you did not include this fixed marketing expense in your computations. You are not sure what to do. If you tell Hewitt of your mistake, she will have to tell the president. In this case, you are afraid Tmedic might not offer you permanent employment after your internship.

Requirements

1. How would your error affect breakeven sales and operating income under the proposed sales commission plan? Could this cause the president to reject the sales commission proposal?

2. Consider your ethical responsibilities. Is there a difference between (a) initially making an error and (b) subsequently failing to inform the controller?

3. Suppose you tell Hewitt of the error in your analysis. Why might the consequences not be as bad as you fear? Should Hewitt take any responsibility for your error? What could Hewitt have done differently?

4. After considering all of the factors, should you inform Hewitt or simply keep quiet?

Team Project

P7-73   Advertising campaign and production level decisions *(Learning Objectives 1 & 3)*

EZPAK Manufacturing produces filament packaging tape. In 2010, EZPAK Manufacturing produced and sold 15 million rolls of tape. The company has recently expanded its capacity, so it can now produce up to 30 million rolls per year. EZPAK Manufacturing's accounting records show the following results from 2010:

Sale price per roll	$ 3.00
Variable manufacturing expenses per roll......................................	$ 2.00
Variable marketing and administrative expenses per roll	$ 0.50
Total fixed manufacturing overhead costs.....................................	$8,400,000
Total fixed marketing and administrative expenses	$ 600,000
Sales...	15 million rolls
Production	15 million rolls

There were no beginning or ending inventories in 2010.

In January 2011, EZPAK Manufacturing hired a new president, Kevin McDaniel. McDaniel has a one-year contract specifying that he will be paid 10% of EZPAK Manufacturing's 2011 operating income (based on traditional absorption costing) instead of a salary. In 2011, McDaniel must make two major decisions:

1. Should EZPAK Manufacturing undertake a major advertising campaign? This campaign would raise sales to 25 million rolls. This is the maximum level of sales that EZPAK Manufacturing can expect to make in the near future. The ad campaign would add an additional $3.5 million in marketing and administrative costs. Without the campaign, sales will be 15 million rolls.

2. How many rolls of tape will EZPAK Manufacturing produce?

At the end of the year, EZPAK Manufacturing's board of directors will evaluate McDaniel's performance and decide whether to offer him a contract for the following year.

Requirements

Within your group form two subgroups. The first subgroup assumes the role of Kevin McDaniel, EZPAK Manufacturing's new president. The second subgroup assumes the role of EZPAK Manufacturing's board of directors. McDaniel will meet with the board of directors shortly after the end of 2011 to decide whether he will remain at EZPAK Manufacturing. Most of your effort should be devoted to advance preparation for this meeting. Each subgroup should meet separately to prepare for the meeting between the board and McDaniel. (*Hint:* Keep computations [other than per-unit amounts] in millions.)

Kevin McDaniel should do the following:

1. Compute EZPAK Manufacturing's 2010 operating income.

2. Decide whether to adopt the advertising campaign by calculating the projected increase in operating income from the advertising campaign. Do not include the executive bonus in this calculation. Prepare a memo to the board of directors explaining this decision. Use the following format:

Date:	_____
To:	_____
From:	_____
Subject:	_____

Give this memo to the board of directors as soon as possible (before the joint meeting).

3. Assume that EZPAK Manufacturing adopts the advertising campaign. Decide how many rolls of tape to produce in 2011. Assume that no safety stock is considered necessary to EZPAK's business.

4. Given your response to Question 3, prepare an absorption costing income statement for the year ended December 31, 2011, ending with operating income before bonus. Then, compute your bonus separately. The variable cost per unit and the total fixed expenses (with the exception of the advertising campaign) remain the same as in 2010. Give this income statement and your bonus computation to the board of directors as soon as possible (before your meeting with the board).

5. Decide whether you want to remain at EZPAK Manufacturing for another year. You currently have an offer from another company. The contract with the other company is identical to the one you currently have with EZPAK Manufacturing—you will be paid 10% of absorption costing operating income instead of a salary.

The board of directors should do the following:

1. Compute EZPAK Manufacturing's 2010 operating income.

2. Determine whether EZPAK Manufacturing should adopt the advertising campaign by calculating the projected increase in operating income from the advertising campaign. Do not include the executive bonus in this calculation.

3. Determine how many rolls of tape EZPAK Manufacturing should produce in 2011. Assume that no safety stock is considered necessary to EZPAK's business.

4. Evaluate McDaniel's performance based on his decisions and the information he provided to the board. (*Hint:* You may want to prepare a variable costing income statement.)

5. Evaluate the contract's bonus provision. Are you satisfied with this provision? If so, explain why. If not, recommend how it should be changed.

After McDaniel has given the board his memo and income statement and after the board has had a chance to evaluate McDaniel's performance, McDaniel and the board should meet. The purpose of the meeting is to decide whether it is in everyone's mutual interest for McDaniel to remain with EZPAK Manufacturing and, if so, the terms of the contract EZPAK Manufacturing will offer McDaniel.

Discussion & Analysis

1. Define breakeven point. Why is the breakeven point important to managers?

2. Describe four different ways cost-volume-profit analysis could be useful to management.

3. The purchasing manager for Rockwell Fashion Bags has been able to purchase the material for its signature handbags for $2 less per bag. Keeping everything else the same, what effect would this reduction in material cost have on the breakeven point for Rockwell Fashion Bags? Now assume that the sales manager decides to reduce the selling price of each handbag by $2. What would the net effect of both of these changes be on the breakeven point in units for Rockwell Fashion Bags?

4. Describe three ways that cost-volume-profit concepts could be used by a service organization.

5. "Breakeven analysis isn't very useful to a company because companies need to do more than break even to survive in the long run." Explain why you agree or disagree with this statement.

6. What conditions must be met for cost-volume-profit analysis to be accurate?

7. Why is it necessary to calculate a weighted-average contribution margin ratio for a multi-product company when calculating the breakeven point for that company? Why can't all of the products' contribution margin ratios just be added together and averaged?

8. Is the contribution margin ratio of a grocery store likely to be higher or lower than that of a plastics manufacturer? Explain the difference in cost structure between a grocery store and a plastics manufacturer. How does the cost structure difference impact operating risk?

9. Alston Jewelry had sales revenues last year of $2.4 million, while its breakeven point (in dollars) was $2.2 million. What was Alston Jewelry's margin of safety in dollars? What does the term margin of safety mean? What can you discern about Alston Jewelry from its margin of safety?

10. Rondell Pharmacy is considering switching to the use of robots to fill prescriptions that consist of oral solids or medications in pill form. The robots will assist the human pharmacists and will reduce the number of human pharmacy workers needed. This change is

Quick Check Answers
1. *d* 2. *b* 3. *c* 4. *c* 5. *a* 6. *b* 7. *d* 8. *a* 9. *d* 10. *c*

For online homework, exercises, and problems that provide you with immediate feedback, please visit www.myaccountinglab.com.

expected to reduce the number of prescription filling errors, to reduce the customer's wait time, and to reduce the total overall costs. How does the use of the robots affect Rondell Pharmacy's cost structure? Explain the impact of this switch to robotics on Rondell Pharmacy's operating risk.

Application & Analysis

7-1 CVP for a Product

Select one product that you could make yourself. Examples of possible products could be cookies, birdhouses, jewelry, or custom t-shirts. Assume that you have decided to start a small business producing and selling this product. You will be applying the concepts of cost-volume-profit analysis to this potential venture.

Basic Discussion Questions

1. Describe your product. What market are you targeting this product for? What price will you sell your product for? Make projections of your sales in units over each of the upcoming five years.

2. Make a detailed list of all of the materials needed to make your product. Include quantities needed of each material. Also include the cost of the material on a per-unit basis.

3. Make a list of all of the equipment you will need to make your product. Estimate the cost of each piece of equipment that you will need.

4. Make a list of all other expenses that would be needed to create your product. Examples of other expenses would be rent, utilities, and insurance. Estimate the cost of each of these expenses per year.

5. Now classify all of the expenses you have listed as being either fixed or variable. For mixed expenses, separate the expense into the fixed component and the variable component.

6. Calculate how many units of your product you will need to sell to break even in each of the five years you have projected.

7. Calculate the margin of safety in units for each of the five years in your projection.

8. Now decide how much you would like to make in before-tax operating income (target profit) in each of the upcoming five years. Calculate how many units you would need to sell in each of the upcoming years to meet these target profit levels.

9. How realistic is your potential venture? Do you think you would be able to break even in each of the projected five years? How risky is your venture (use the margin of safety to help answer this question). Do you think your target profits are achievable?

Classroom Applications

Web: Post the discussion questions on an electronic discussion board. Have small groups of students choose a product for their group. Students should collaboratively answer the questions.
Classroom: Form groups of 3–4 students. Your group should choose a product. After estimating costs and making the calculations, prepare a five-minute presentation about your group's product that addresses the listed questions.
Independent: Research answers to each of the questions. Turn in a 2–3 page typed paper (12 point font, double-spaced with 1" margins). Include tables that include the estimated fixed costs and estimated variable costs. Also show all calculations.

For additional Application & Analysis projects and implementation tips, see Instructor Resources in MyAccountingLab.com.

Using CVP for Sensitivity Analysis

(Learning Objectives 1, 2, 3, & 4)

Hacker Golf has developed a unique swing trainer golf club. The company currently pays a production company to produce the golf club at a cost of $32 each. Other variable costs total $6 per golf club, and monthly fixed expenses are $18,000. Hacker Golf currently sells the trainer golf club for $68.

NOTE: Solve each requirement as a separate situation.

Requirements

1. Calculate Hacker Golf's breakeven point in units.
2. Hacker Golf is considering raising the club's selling price to $78. Calculate the new breakeven in units.
3. Hacker Golf has found a new company to produce the golf club at a lower cost of $26. Calculate the new breakeven in units.
4. Because many customers have requested a golf glove to go along with the trainer club. Hacker Golf is considering selling gloves. The company expects to sell only one glove for every four trainer clubs it sells. Hacker Golf can purchase the gloves for $4 each and sell them for $9. Total fixed costs should remain the same at $18,000 per month. Calculate the breakeven point in units for trainer clubs and golf gloves.
5. Use a contribution margin income statement to prove the breakeven point calculated in Requirement 4.

DEMO DOC Solution

Requirement 1

Calculate Hacker's breakeven point in units.

To determine the breakeven point, we first must calculate the contribution margin per unit. The contribution margin is calculated by subtracting variable costs from the sales revenue.

> Contribution margin per unit = Sales price per unit − Variable cost per unit

Hacker Golf's variable cost per club (unit) is the price it pays for each club ($32) plus its additional variable costs per golf club ($6). Therefore, its unit contribution margin is as follows:

Selling price per club	$ 68
Variable cost per club ($32 + $6)	(38)
Contribution margin per club	$ 30

The contribution margin represents the amount from each unit sold that is available to cover fixed expenses. That means Hacker Golf earns $30 per club, which contributes toward fixed expenses until fixed expenses are covered. After fixed expenses are covered, each club sold contributes $30 directly to the company's operating income.

continued

Breakeven is the level of sales at which income is zero. The breakeven point can be calculated as follows:

$$\text{Breakeven in units} = \frac{\text{Fixed expenses} + \text{Operating income}}{\text{Contribution margin per unit}}$$

$$\text{Breakeven in units} = \frac{\$18,000 + 0}{\$30}$$

$$= 600 \text{ trainer clubs}$$

Requirement 2

Hacker Golf is considering raising the club's selling price to $78. Calculate the new breakeven in units.

Even if Hacker Golf raises its sales price per club to $78, its variable costs ($38 per unit) and fixed expenses ($18,000) will stay the same. As a result of increasing the sales price, the company will now have a higher contribution margin per unit:

Selling price per club	$ 78
Variable cost per club ($32 + $6)	(38)
Contribution margin per club........................	$ 40

Once again, you can use the breakeven formula to find the new breakeven point:

$$\text{Breakeven in units} = \frac{\text{Fixed expenses} + \text{Operating income}}{\text{Contribution margin per unit}}$$

$$\text{Breakeven in units} = \frac{\$18,000 + 0}{\$40}$$

$$= 450 \text{ trainer clubs}$$

With the increased selling price, breakeven has been reduced from 600 clubs to 450 clubs. The higher price means that each club contributes more to fixed expenses.

You can prove the answer by preparing an income statement for a sales volume of 450 units:

Sales revenue (450 × $78)...........................	$ 35,100
Less: Variable expenses (450 × $38)	(17,100)
Total contribution margin	18,000
Less: Fixed expenses...................................	(18,000)
Operating income..	0

If the selling price increases, the volume required to break even or achieve target profit goals decreases (provided costs do not change). Conversely, if the selling price decreases, the volume required to break even or achieve target profit goals increases.

Requirement 3

Hacker Golf has found a new company to produce the golf club at a lower cost of $26. Calculate the new breakeven in units.

Let's return to Hacker Golf's original sales price ($68). Assuming that Hacker Golf has found a new company to produce the golf club for $26 each, the company's variable costs per club will decrease. However, fixed expenses remain the same ($18,000). Once again, Hacker Golf's contribution margin per unit will increase as a result of this change in business conditions:

Selling price per club	$ 68
Variable cost per club ($26 + $6)	(32)
Contribution margin per club..................	$ 36

The new breakeven point is found as follows:

$$\text{Breakeven in units} = \frac{\text{Fixed expenses} + \text{Operating income}}{\text{Contribution margin per unit}}$$

$$\text{Breakeven in units} = \frac{\$18,000 + 0}{\$36}$$

$$= 500 \text{ trainer clubs}$$

With the reduced variable cost, Hacker Golf's breakeven in units decreases from 600 clubs to 500 clubs. Using this information, Hacker Golf's management must decide if it is worth the risk to switch to a new producer.

You can also prove this result by preparing an income statement:

Sales revenue (500 × $68).............................	$ 34,000
Less: Variable expenses (500 × $32)	(16,000)
Total contribution margin	18,000
Less: Fixed expenses...................................	(18,000)
Operating income.......................................	0

As variable or fixed expenses increase, so does the volume needed to break even or achieve target profits. Conversely, as these expenses decrease, the volume needed to break even or achieve target profits also decreases.

Requirement 4

Because many customers have requested a golf glove to go along with the trainer club. Hacker Golf is considering selling gloves. The company expects to sell only one glove for every four trainer clubs it sells. Hacker Golf can purchase the gloves for $4 each, and sell them for $9. Total fixed expenses should remain the same at $18,000 per month. Calculate the breakeven point in units for trainer clubs and golf gloves.

Calculating the breakeven point is fairly straightforward when a company is selling only one product. But Hacker Golf is now considering selling two products. Now, breakeven becomes more complicated. Different products will have different effects on the contribution margins because of different costs and selling prices. So, the company needs to consider the sales mix (a combination of products that make up total sales) in determining CVP relationships.

Finding the breakeven point for multiproduct firms involves a simple three-step process. The first step is to calculate a combined weighted-average contribution margin for all of the products that the company sells.

Step 1: Calculate the weighted-average contribution margin.

Hacker Golf believes that it can sell one glove for every four clubs that it sells. This would give the company a 4:1 sales mix. So, Hacker expects that 1/5 (or 20%) of sales will be gloves and 4/5 (or 80%) of sales will be trainer clubs.

Let's return to Hacker's original selling price and variable costs for the trainer club. Recall that Hacker Golf earns a $30 contribution margin on each golf club that it sells. Hacker will also earn a $5 contribution margin on each golf glove that it sells:

	Clubs	Gloves
Sales price per unit	$ 68	$ 9
Less: Variable cost per unit	(38)	(4)
Contribution margin per unit...	$ 30	$ 5

continued

The weighted-average contribution margin is calculated by multiplying the contribution margin per unit by the sales mix expected for each product. Once we have a total contribution margin for the bundle of products ($120 + $5 = $125, in this case), we divide it by the total number of units (5) in the sales mix, as follows:

	Clubs	Gloves	Total
Sales price per unit	$ 68	$ 9	
Less: Variable cost per unit	(38)	(4)	
Contribution margin per unit...........................	$ 30	$ 5	
Sales mix in units	× 4	× 1	5
Contribution margin	$ 120	$ 5	$ 125
Weighted-average contribution margin per unit ($125/5)...............................			$ 25

The $25 represents a weighted-average contribution margin for all of the products that Hacker Golf sells. The golf clubs are weighted more heavily because Hacker Golf expects to sell four times as many clubs as golf gloves.

The next step is to calculate the breakeven in units for the bundle of products.

Step 2: Calculate the breakeven point in units for the total of both products combined.

This is calculated using the breakeven formula modified for the weighted-average contribution margin in the denominator:

$$\text{Sales in total units} = \frac{\text{Fixed expenses} + \text{Operating income}}{\text{Weighted-average contribution margin per unit}}$$

We know from the question that fixed expenses will not be affected, so they should remain at $18,000. The weighted-average contribution margin, as we just calculated, is $25 per unit. So, we compute total sales as follows:

$$\text{Sales in total units} = \frac{\$18,000 + \$0}{\$25}$$
$$= 720$$

Hacker Golf must sell 720 clubs and gloves combined to break even. Management needs to know how many units of *each* product must be sold to break even. Therefore, the next step is to determine how many of the total sales units (720) need to be clubs and how many need to be gloves in order to break even.

Step 3: Calculate the breakeven in units for each product line.

Because Hacker Golf believes that it will sell four trainer clubs for every one glove, the total number of units, 720, is multiplied by each product's sales mix percentage:

$$\text{Breakeven sales of clubs: } [720 \times (4/5)] = 576$$
$$\text{Breakeven sales of gloves: } [720 \times (1/5)] = 144$$

From this analysis, we know that Hacker Golf needs to sell 576 trainer clubs and 144 golf gloves to break even.

Requirement 5

Use a contribution margin income statement to prove the breakeven point calculated in Requirement 4.

To test the calculation of the breakeven point, you would add the revenue generated from all sales, subtract the variable costs associated with all sales, and subtract the total fixed expenses. The result should balance to zero (or close to zero in cases in which rounding occurs).

	Clubs	Gloves	Total
Sales revenue:			
Trainer clubs (576 × $68)	$ 39,168		
Gloves (144 × $9)		$1,296	$ 40,464
Less: Variable expenses:			
Trainer clubs (576 × $38)	(21,888)		
Gloves (144 × $4)		(576)	(22,464)
Contribution margin	$ 17,280	$ 720	$ 18,000
Less: Fixed expenses			(18,000)
Operating income			$ 0

Most major airlines, including Delta, outsource work.

Delta saves approximately $25 million a year by outsourcing its reservation work to call centers in the Philippines and India. Delta estimates is has been able to cut maintenance costs by $240 million over a five-year period by outsourcing much of its airplane maintenance to Miami- and Canadian-based firms. Delta also has a 10-year arrangement to outsource its European finance and accounting functions to Accenture and a 7-year contract to outsource much of its domestic human resource functions to ACS. But why would Delta outsource so much of its work? Primarily to cut costs. Most of the major airlines are experiencing financial difficulties due to rising fuel costs and cut-throat competition, so they need to find ways to cut costs. One way is through outsourcing.

Outsourcing also enables companies to concentrate on their core competencies—the operating activities in which they are experts. When companies focus on just their core competencies, they often outsource the activities that do not give them a competitive advantage. Delta's strategy is to focus on its core competency—flying passengers—and outsource other operating activities, such as reservations, heavy airplane maintenance, finance, and human resource functions to companies that excel at those activities. By doing so, Delta not only saves money, but also integrates the best practices offered by world-class firms into its company operations.

Sources:
www.CNN.com, "Outsourcing Comes to Airlines", Dec. 25, 2004
www.allbusiness.com, "Outsourcing of HR Functions to Regain Momentum in 2008, According to Everest Research Institute", Nov. 2, 2007
www.newratings.com, "Delta AirLines to reduce costs through maintenance outsourcing", March 30, 2005
www.accenture.com, "Helping Delta Air Lines Achieve High Performance Through Financial Outsourcing", 2006

CHAPTER 8

Short-Term Business Decisions

Learning Objectives

1. Describe and identify information relevant to short-term business decisions
2. Make special order decisions
3. Make pricing decisions
4. Make dropping a product, department, or territory decisions
5. Make product mix decisions
6. Make outsourcing (make-or-buy) decisions
7. Make sell as is or process further decisions

In the last chapter, we saw how managers use cost behavior to determine the company's breakeven point and to estimate the sales volume needed to achieve target profits. In this chapter, we'll see how managers use their knowledge of cost behavior to make six special business decisions, such as whether to outsource operating activities. The decisions we'll discuss in this chapter usually pertain to short periods of time, so managers do not need to worry about the time value of money. In other words, they do not need to compute the present value of the revenues and expenses relating to the decision. In Chapter 12, we will discuss longer-term decisions (such as buying equipment and undertaking plant expansions) in which the time value of money becomes important. Before we look at the six business decisions in detail, let's consider a manager's decision-making process and the information managers need to evaluate their options.

How do Managers Make Decisions?

Exhibit 8-1 illustrates how managers decide among alternative courses of action. Management accountants help gather and analyze *relevant information* to compare alternatives. Management accountants also help with the follow-up: comparing the actual results of a decision to those originally anticipated. This feedback helps management as it faces similar types of decisions in the future. It also helps management adjust current operations if actual results of its decision are markedly different from those anticipated.

EXHIBIT 8-1 **How Managers Make Decisions**

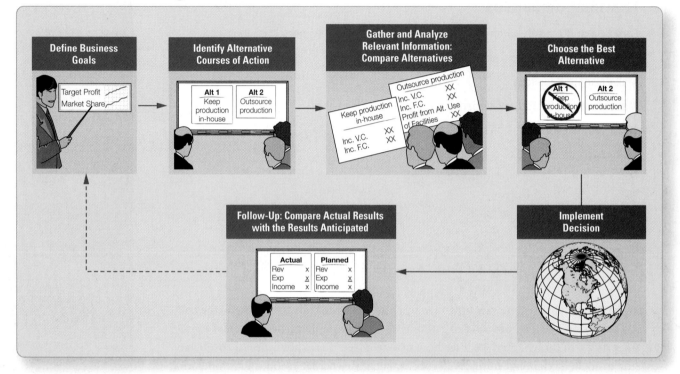

Relevant Information

1 Describe and identify information relevant to short-term business decisions

When managers make decisions, they focus on costs and revenues that are relevant to the decisions. Exhibit 8-2 shows that **relevant information**

1. is expected *future* data.

2. *differs* among alternatives.

Recall our discussion of relevant costs in Chapter 2. In deciding whether to purchase a Toyota Corolla or Nissan Sentra, the cost of the car, the sales tax, and the insurance premium are relevant because these costs

■ are incurred in the *future* (after you decide to buy the car).

■ *differ between alternatives* (each car has a different invoice price, sales tax, and insurance premium).

These costs are *relevant* because they affect your decision of which car to purchase. *Irrelevant* costs are costs that *do not* affect your decision. For example, because the Corolla and Sentra both have similar fuel efficiency and maintenance ratings, we do not expect the car operating costs to differ between alternatives. Because these costs do not differ, they do not affect your decision. In other words, they are *irrelevant* to the decision.

EXHIBIT 8-2 **Relevant Information**

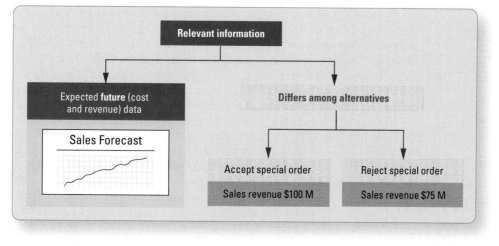

Similarly, the cost of a campus parking sticker is also irrelevant because the sticker costs the same whether you buy the Sentra or the Corolla.

Sunk costs are also irrelevant to your decision. Sunk costs are costs that were incurred in the *past* and cannot be changed regardless of which future action is taken. Perhaps you want to trade in your current truck when you buy your new car. The amount you paid for the truck—which you bought for $15,000 a year ago—is a sunk cost. In fact, it doesn't matter whether you paid $15,000 or $50,000—it's still a sunk cost. No decision made *now* can alter the past. You already bought the truck, so *the price you paid for it is a sunk cost.* All you can do *now* is keep the truck, trade it in, or sell it for the best price you can get, even if that price is substantially less than what you originally paid for the truck.

What *is* relevant is what you can get for your truck in the future. Suppose the Nissan dealership offers you $8,000 for your truck. The Toyota dealership offers you $10,000. Because the amounts differ and the transaction will take place in the future, the trade-in value is relevant to your decision.

The same principle applies to all situations—*only relevant data affect decisions.* Let's consider another application of this general principle.

Suppose Pendleton Woolen Mills is deciding whether to use pure wool or a wool blend in a new line of sweaters. Assume that Pendleton Woolen Mills predicts the following costs under the two alternatives:

	Expected Materials and Labor Cost per Sweater		
	Wool	Wool Blend	Cost Difference
Direct materials..	$10	$6	$4
Direct labor..	2	2	0
Total cost of direct materials and direct labor	$12	$8	$4

The cost of direct materials is relevant because this cost differs between alternatives (the wool costs $4 more than the wool blend). The labor cost is irrelevant because that cost is the same for both kinds of wool.

Why is this important?

"The accounting information used to make business decisions in this chapter considers only one factor: profitability. However in real life, managers should consider many more factors, including the effect of the decision on employees, the local community, and the environment."

Relevant Nonfinancial Information

Nonfinancial, or qualitative factors, also play a role in managers' decisions. For example, closing manufacturing plants or laying off employees can seriously hurt the local community and employee morale. Outsourcing can reduce control over delivery time and product quality. Offering discounted prices to select customers can upset regular customers and tempt them to take their business elsewhere. Managers must think through the likely quantitative *and* qualitative effects of their decisions.

Managers who ignore qualitative factors can make serious mistakes. For example, the City of Nottingham, England, spent $1.6 million on 215 solar-powered parking meters after seeing how well the parking meters worked in countries along the Mediterranean Sea. However, the city did not adequately consider that British skies are typically overcast. The result? The meters didn't always work because of the lack of sunlight. The city *lost* money because people ended up parking for free! Relevant qualitative information has the same characteristics as relevant financial information: The qualitative factor occurs in the *future*, and it *differs* between alternatives. The amount of *future* sunshine required *differed* between alternatives: The mechanical meters didn't require any sunshine, but the solar-powered meters needed a great deal of sunshine.

Likewise, in deciding between the Corolla and Sentra, you will likely consider qualitative factors that differ between the cars (legroom, trunk capacity, dashboard design, and so forth) before making your final decision. Since you must live with these factors in the future, they become relevant to your decision.

Keys to Making Short-Term Special Decisions

Our approach to making short-term special decisions is called the *relevant information approach* or the *incremental analysis approach*. Instead of looking at the company's *entire* income statement under each decision alternative, we'll just look at how operating income would *change or differ* under each alternative. Using this approach, we'll leave out irrelevant information—the costs and revenues that won't differ between alternatives.

We'll consider six kinds of decisions in this chapter:

1. Special sales orders

2. Pricing

3. Dropping products, departments, and territories

4. Product mix

5. Outsourcing (make or buy)

6. Selling as is or processing further

As you study these decisions, keep in mind the two keys in analyzing short-term special business decisions shown in Exhibit 8-3:

1. **Focus on relevant revenues, costs, and profits.** Irrelevant information only clouds the picture and creates information overload. That's why we'll use the incremental analysis approach.

2. **Use a contribution margin approach that separates variable costs from fixed costs.** Because fixed costs and variable costs behave differently, they must be analyzed separately. Traditional (absorption costing) income statements, which blend fixed and variable costs, can mislead managers. Contribution margin income statements, which isolate costs by behavior (variable or fixed), help managers gather the cost-behavior information they need. Keep in mind that unit manufacturing costs are mixed costs, too, so they can also mislead managers. If you use unit manufacturing costs in your analysis, make sure you separate the cost's fixed and variable components first.

We'll use these two keys in each decision.

EXHIBIT 8-3 Two Keys to Making Short-Term Special Decisions

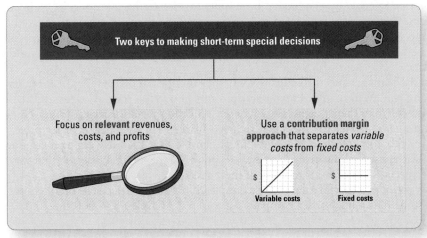

How do Managers Make Special Order and Regular Pricing Decisions?

We'll start our discussion on the six business decisions by looking at special sales order decisions and regular pricing decisions. In the past, managers did not consider pricing to be a short-term decision. However, product life cycles are shrinking in most industries. Companies often sell products for only a few months before replacing them with an updated model. The clothing and technology industries have always had short life cycles. Even auto and housing styles change frequently. Pricing has become a shorter-term decision than it was in the past.

Let's examine a special sales order in detail; then we will discuss regular pricing decisions.

Make special order decisions **2**

Special Sales Order Decisions

A special order occurs when a customer requests a one-time order at a *reduced* sales price. Often, these special orders are for large quantities. Before agreeing to the special deal, management must consider the questions shown in Exhibit 8-4.

EXHIBIT 8-4 Special Order Considerations

- Do we have excess capacity available to fill this order?

- Will the reduced sales price be high enough to cover the *incremental* costs of filling the order (the variable costs and any additional fixed costs)?

- Will the special order affect regular sales in the long run?

First, managers must consider available capacity. If the company is already making as many units as possible and selling them all at its *regular* sales price, it wouldn't make sense to fill a special order at a *reduced* sales price. Therefore, available excess capacity is a necessity for accepting a special order. This is true for service firms (law firms, caterers, and so forth) as well as manufacturers.

Second, managers need to consider whether the special reduced sales price is high enough to cover the incremental costs of filling the order. The special price *must* exceed the variable costs of filling the order, or the company will lose money on the deal. In other words, the special order must provide a positive contribution margin. Next, the company must consider fixed costs. If the company has excess capacity, fixed costs probably won't be affected by producing more units (or delivering more service). However, in some cases, management may need to hire a consultant or incur some other fixed cost to fill the special order. If so, management will need to consider whether the special sales price is high enough to generate a positive contribution margin *and* cover the additional fixed costs.

Finally, managers need to consider whether the special order will affect regular sales in the long run. Will regular customers find out about the special order and demand a lower price or take their business elsewhere? Will the special order customer come back *again and again*, asking for the same reduced price? Will the special order price start a price war with competitors? Managers must gamble that the answers to these questions are "no" or consider how customers will respond. Managers may decide that any profit from the special sales order is not worth these risks.

Let's consider a special sales order example. Suppose ACDelco sells oil filters for $3.20 each. Assume that a mail-order company has offered ACDelco $35,000 for 20,000 oil filters, or $1.75 per filter ($35,000 ÷ 20,000 = $1.75). This sale will

- use manufacturing capacity that would otherwise be idle.

- not change fixed costs.

- not require any variable *nonmanufacturing* expenses (because no extra marketing costs are incurred with this special order).

- not affect regular sales.

We have addressed every consideration except one: Is the special sales price high enough to cover the variable *manufacturing* costs associated with the order? Let's take a look at the *wrong* way and then the *right* way to figure out the answer to that question.

Suppose ACDelco made and sold 250,000 oil filters before considering the special order. Using the traditional (absorption costing) income statement on the left-hand side of Exhibit 8-5, the manufacturing cost per unit is $2 ($500,000 ÷ 250,000). A manager who does not examine these numbers carefully may believe that ACDelco should *not* accept the special order at a sale price of $1.75 because each oil filter costs $2.00 to manufacture. But appearances can be deceiving! Remember that the unit manufacturing cost of a product ($2) is a *mixed* cost containing both fixed and variable cost components. To correctly answer our question, we need to find only the variable portion of the manufacturing unit cost.

EXHIBIT 8-5   Traditional (Absorption Costing) Format and Contribution Margin Format Income Statements

INCOME STATEMENT
(at a production and sales level of 250,000 units)
Year Ended December 31

Traditional (Absorption Costing) Format		Contribution Margin Format		
Sales revenue	$800,000	Sales revenue		$800,000
Less cost of goods sold	(500,000)	Less variable expenses:		
Gross profit	300,000	Manufacturing	$(300,000)	
Less marketing and administrative expenses	(200,000)	Marketing and administrative	(75,000)	(375,000)
		Contribution margin		425,000
		Less fixed expenses:		
		Manufacturing	$(200,000)	
		Marketing and administrative	(125,000)	(325,000)
Operating income	$100,000	Operating income		$100,000

The right-hand side of Exhibit 8-5 shows the contribution margin income statement that separates variable expenses from fixed expenses. The contribution margin income statement shows that the *variable* manufacturing cost per unit is only $1.20 ($300,000 ÷ 250,000). The special sales price of $1.75 is *higher* than the variable manufacturing cost of $1.20. Therefore, the special order will provide a positive contribution margin of $0.55 per unit ($1.75 − $1.20). Since the special order is for 20,000 units, ACDelco's total contribution margin should increase by $11,000 (20,000 units × $0.55 per unit) if it accepts this order. Remember that in this example, ACDelco's variable marketing expenses are irrelevant because the company will not incur the usual variable marketing expenses on this special order. However, this won't always be the case. Many times, companies will also incur variable operating expenses (such as freight-out or sales commissions) on special orders.

Using an incremental analysis approach, ACDelco compares the additional revenues from the special order with the incremental expenses to see if the special order will contribute to profits. Exhibit 8-6 shows that the special sales order will increase revenue by $35,000 (20,000 × $1.75), but it will also increase variable manufacturing cost by $24,000 (20,000 × $1.20). As a result, ACDelco's contribution margin will increase by $11,000, as previously anticipated.

EXHIBIT 8-6   **Incremental Analysis of Special Sales Order**

Expected increase in revenues—sale of 20,000 oil filters × $1.75 each	$ 35,000
Expected increase in expenses—variable manufacturing costs:	
20,000 oil filters × $1.20 each	(24,000)
Expected increase in operating income	$ 11,000

The other costs shown in Exhibit 8-5 are irrelevant. Variable marketing and administrative expenses will be the same whether or not ACDelco accepts the special order because ACDelco made no marketing efforts to get this sale. Fixed manufacturing expenses won't change because ACDelco has enough idle capacity to produce 20,000 extra oil filters without requiring additional facilities. Fixed marketing and administrative expenses won't be affected by this special order either. Because there are no additional fixed costs, the total increase in contribution margin flows directly to operating income. As a result, the special sales order will increase operating income by $11,000.

Notice that the analysis follows the two keys to making short-term special business decisions discussed earlier: (1) focus on relevant data (revenues and costs that *will change* if ACDelco accepts the special order) and (2) use a contribution margin approach that separates variable costs from fixed costs.

To summarize, for special sales orders, the decision rule is as follows:

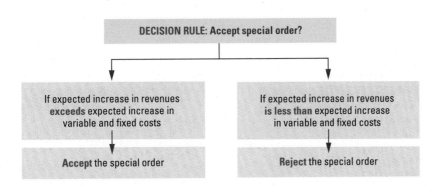

STOP & THINK

The absorption costing income statement on the left-hand side of Exhibit 8-5 shows that the total cost of manufacturing 250,000 filters is $500,000. What is the flaw in reasoning that ACDelco should accept special orders only if the sale price exceeds $2 each?

Answer: The flaw in this analysis arises from treating a mixed cost as though it were variable. Manufacturing one extra oil filter will cost only $1.20—the variable manufacturing cost. Fixed expenses are irrelevant because ACDelco will incur $200,000 of fixed manufacturing overhead expenses whether or not the company accepts the special order. Producing 20,000 more oil filters will not increase *total* fixed expenses, so manufacturing costs increase at the rate of $1.20 per unit, not $2.00 per unit.

Regular Pricing Decisions

3 Make pricing decisions

In the special order decision, ACDelco decided to sell a limited quantity of oil filters for $1.75 each even though the normal price was $3.20 per unit. But how did ACDelco decide to set its regular price at $3.20 per filter? Exhibit 8-7 shows that managers start with three basic questions when setting regular prices for their products or services.

EXHIBIT 8-7 Regular Pricing Considerations

- What is our target profit?
- How much will customers pay?
- Are we a price-taker or a price-setter for this product?

The answers to these questions are often complex and ever-changing. Stockholders expect the company to achieve certain profits. Economic conditions, historical company earnings, industry risk, competition, and new business developments all affect the level of profit that stockholders expect. Stockholders usually tie their profit expectations to the amount of assets invested in the company. For example, stockholders may expect a 10% annual return on their investment. A company's stock price tends to decline if the company does not meet target profits, so managers must keep costs low while generating enough revenue to meet target profits.

This leads to the second question: How much will customers pay? Managers cannot set prices above what customers are willing to pay, or sales will decline. The amount customers will pay depends on the competition, the product's uniqueness, the effectiveness of marketing campaigns, general economic conditions, and so forth.

To address the third pricing question, imagine a continuum with price-takers at one end and price-setters at the other end. A company's products and services fall somewhere along this continuum, shown in Exhibit 8-8. Companies are price-takers when they have little or no control over the prices of their products or services. This occurs when their products and services are *not* unique or when competition is heavy. Examples include food commodities (milk and corn), natural resources (oil and lumber), and generic consumer products and services (paper towels, dry cleaning, and banking).

EXHIBIT 8-8 Price-Takers Versus Price-Setters

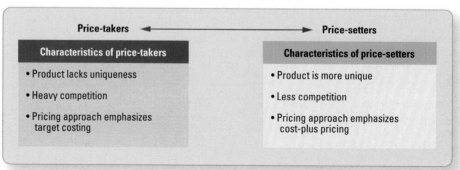

Price-takers ←————————→ Price-setters	
Characteristics of price-takers	**Characteristics of price-setters**
• Product lacks uniqueness	• Product is more unique
• Heavy competition	• Less competition
• Pricing approach emphasizes target costing	• Pricing approach emphasizes cost-plus pricing

Companies are price-setters when they have more control over pricing—in other words, they can "set" prices to some extent. Companies are price-setters when their products are unique, which results in less competition. Unique products such as original art and jewelry, specially manufactured machinery, patented perfume scents, and custom-made furniture can command higher prices.

Obviously, managers would rather be price-setters than price-takers. To gain more control over pricing, companies try to differentiate their products. They want to make their products unique in terms of features, service, or quality—or at least make you *think* their product is unique or somehow better even if it isn't. How do they do this? Primarily through advertising. Consider Nike's tennis shoes, Starbucks' coffee, Hallmark's wrapping paper, Nexus' shampoo, Tylenol's acetaminophen, General Mills' cereal, Capital One's credit cards, Shell's gas, Abercrombie and Fitch's jeans—the list goes on and on. Are these products really better or significantly different from their lower-priced competitors? Possibly. If these companies can make you think so, they've gained more control over their pricing because you are willing to pay *more* for their products or services. The downside? These companies must charge higher prices or sell more just to cover their advertising costs.

A company's approach to pricing depends on whether its product or service is on the price-taking or price-setting side of the spectrum. Price-takers emphasize a target-costing approach. Price-setters emphasize a cost-plus pricing approach. Keep in mind that many products fall somewhere along the continuum. Therefore, managers tend to use both approaches to some extent. We'll now discuss each approach in turn.

Why is this important?

"Both branding and product differentiation give managers more control over pricing. Without such features, a company must often settle for selling its product at the same price as its competitors."

Target Costing

When a company is a price-taker, it emphasizes a target costing approach to pricing. **Target costing** starts with the market price of the product (the price customers are willing to pay) and subtracts the company's desired profit to determine the product's target total cost—the *total* cost to develop, design, produce, market, deliver, and service the product. In other words, the total cost includes *every* cost incurred throughout the value chain relating to the product.

Revenue at market price
Less: Desired profit
Target total cost

In this relationship, the market price is "taken." If the product's current cost is higher than the target cost, the company must find ways to reduce costs, otherwise it will not meet its profit goals. Managers often use ABC along with value engineering (as discussed in Chapter 4) to find ways to cut costs. Let's look at an example of target costing.

Let's assume that oil filters are a commodity and that the current market price is $3.00 per filter (not the $3.20 sales price assumed in the earlier ACDelco example). Because the oil filters are a commodity, ACDelco will emphasize a target-costing approach. Let's assume that ACDelco's stockholders expect a 10% annual return on the company's assets. If the company has $1,000,000 of assets, the desired profit is $100,000 ($1,000,000 × 10%). Exhibit 8-9 calculates the target total cost at the current sales volume (250,000 units). Once we know the target total cost, we can analyze the fixed and variable cost components separately.

Can ACDelco make and sell 250,000 oil filters at a target total cost of $650,000 or less? We know from ACDelco's contribution margin income statement (Exhibit 8-5) that the company's variable costs are $1.50 per unit ($375,000 ÷ 250,000 units). This variable cost per unit includes both manufacturing costs ($1.20 per unit) and marketing and

EXHIBIT 8-9 **Calculating Target Full Cost**

	Calculations	Total
Revenue at market price	250,000 units × $3.00 price =	$ 750,000
Less: Desired profit	10% × $1,000,000 of assets	(100,000)
Target total cost		$ 650,000

administrative costs ($0.30 per unit). We also know that the company incurs $325,000 in fixed costs in its current relevant range. Again, some fixed cost stems from manufacturing and some from marketing and administrative activities. *In setting regular sales prices, companies must cover **all** of their costs—it doesn't matter if these costs are inventoriable product costs or period costs, or whether they are fixed or variable.*

Making and selling 250,000 filters currently costs the company $700,000 [(250,000 units × $1.50 variable cost per unit) + $325,000 of fixed costs], which is more than the target total cost of $650,000 (shown in Exhibit 8-9). So, what are ACDelco's options?

1. Accept a lower profit.

2. Cut fixed costs.

3. Cut variable costs.

4. Use other strategies. For example, ACDelco could attempt to increase sales volume. Recall that the company has excess capacity, so making and selling more units would affect only variable costs. The company could also consider changing or adding to its product mix. Finally, it could attempt to differentiate its oil filters (or strengthen its name brand) to gain more control over sales prices.

Let's look at some of these options. ACDelco may first try to cut fixed costs. As shown in Exhibit 8-10, the company would have to reduce fixed costs to $275,000 to meet its target profit. Since current fixed costs are $325,000 (Exhibit 8-5), that means the company would have to cut fixed costs by $50,000.

EXHIBIT 8-10 **Calculating Target Fixed Cost**

	Calculations	Total
Target total cost		$ 650,000
Less: Current variable costs	250,000 units × $1.50	(375,000)
Target fixed cost		$ 275,000

The company would start by considering whether any discretionary fixed costs could be eliminated without harming the company. Since committed fixed costs are nearly impossible to change in the short run, ACDelco will probably not be able to reduce this type of fixed cost.

If the company can't reduce its fixed costs by $50,000, it would have to lower its variable cost to $1.30 per unit, as shown in Exhibit 8-11.

EXHIBIT 8-11 **Calculating Target Unit Variable Cost**

	Total
Target total cost	$ 650,000
Less: Current fixed costs	(325,000)
Target total variable costs	$ 325,000
Divided by number of units	÷ 250,000
Target variable cost per unit	$ 1.30

Perhaps the company could renegotiate raw materials costs with its suppliers or find a less costly way of packaging or shipping the air filters.

However, if ACDelco can't reduce variable costs to $1.30 per unit, could it meet its target profit through a combination of lowering both fixed costs and variable costs?

STOP & THINK

Suppose ACDelco can reduce its current fixed costs but only by $25,000. If it wants to meet its target profit, by how much will it have to reduce the variable cost of each unit? Assume that sales volume remains at 250,000 units.

Answer: Companies typically try to cut both fixed and variable costs. Because ACDelco can cut its fixed costs only by $25,000, to meet its target profit, it would have to cut its variable costs as well:

Target total cost	$ 650,000
Less: Reduced fixed costs ($325,000 – $25,000)............	(300,000)
Target total variable costs	$ 350,000
Divided by number of units..	÷ 250,000
Target variable cost per unit..	$ 1.40

In addition to cutting its fixed costs by $25,000, the company must reduce its variable costs by $0.10 per unit ($1.50 – $1.40) to meet its target profit at the existing volume of sales.

Another strategy would be to increase sales. ACDelco's managers can use CVP analysis, as you learned in Chapter 7, to figure out how many oil filters the company would have to sell to achieve its target profit. How could the company increase demand for the oil filters? Perhaps it could reach new markets or advertise. How much would advertising cost—and how many extra oil filters would the company have to sell to cover the cost of advertising? These are only some of the questions managers must ask. As you can see, managers don't have an easy task when the current total cost exceeds the target total cost. Sometimes, companies just can't compete given the current market price. If that's the case, they may have no other choice than to exit the market for that product.

Cost-Plus Pricing

When a company is a price-setter, it emphasizes a cost-plus approach to pricing. This pricing approach is essentially the *opposite* of the target-pricing approach. **Cost-plus pricing** starts with the product's total costs (as a given) and *adds* its desired profit to determine a cost-plus price.

Total cost
Plus: Desired profit
Cost-plus price

When the product is unique, the company has more control over pricing. However, the company still needs to make sure that the cost-plus price is not higher than what customers are willing to pay. Let's go back to our original ACDelco example. This time, let's assume that the oil filters benefit from brand recognition, so the company has some control over the price it charges for its filters. Exhibit 8-12 on the following page takes a cost-plus pricing approach assuming the current level of sales.

If the current market price for generic oil filters is $3.00, as we assumed earlier, can ACDelco sell its brand-name filters for $3.20 apiece? The answer depends on how well the company has been able to differentiate its product or brand name. The company may use focus groups or marketing surveys to find out how customers would respond to its cost-plus price. The company may find out that its cost-plus price is too high, or it may find that it could set the price even higher without jeopardizing sales.

EXHIBIT 8-12 Calculating Cost-Plus Price

	Calculations	Total
Current variable costs	250,000 units × $1.50 per unit =	$375,000
Plus: Current fixed costs		+ 325,000
Current total costs		$700,000
Plus: Desired revenue	10% × $1,000,000 of assets	+ 100,000
Target revenue		$800,000
Divided by number of units		÷ 250,000
Cost-plus price per unit		$ 3.20

STOP & THINK

Which costing system (job costing or process costing) do you think price-setters and price-takers typically use?

Answer: Companies tend to be price-setters when their products are unique. Unique products are produced as single items or in small batches. Therefore, these companies use job costing to determine the product's cost. However, companies are price-takers when their products are high-volume commodities. Process costing better suits this type of product.

Notice how pricing decisions used our two keys to decision making: (1) focus on relevant information and (2) use a contribution margin approach that separates variable costs from fixed costs. In pricing decisions, all cost information is relevant because the company must cover *all* costs along the value chain before it can generate a profit. However, we still needed to consider variable costs and fixed costs separately because they behave differently at different volumes.

Our pricing decision rule is as follows:

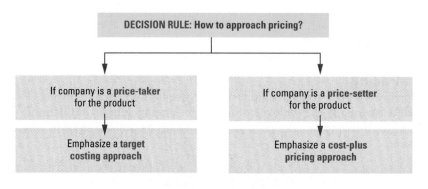

Decision Guidelines

Relevant Information for Business Decisions

Nike makes special order and regular pricing decisions. Even though it sells mass-produced tennis shoes and sports clothing, Nike has differentiated its products with advertising. Nike's managers consider both quantitative and qualitative factors as they make pricing decisions. Here are key guidelines that Nike's managers follow in making their decisions.

Decision	Guidelines
What information is relevant to a short-term special business decision?	Relevant information is as follows: 1. Pertains to the *future* 2. *Differs* between alternatives

Decision	Guidelines
What are two key guidelines in making short-term special business decisions?	**1.** Focus on *relevant* data. **2.** Use a *contribution margin* approach that separates variable costs from fixed costs.
Should Nike accept a lower sales price than the regular price for a large order from a customer in São Paulo, Brazil?	If the revenue from the order exceeds the extra variable and fixed costs incurred to fill the order, then accepting the order will increase operating income.
What should Nike consider in setting its regular product prices?	Nike considers the following: **1.** What profit stockholders expect **2.** What price customers will pay **3.** Whether it is a price-setter or a price-taker
What approach should Nike take to pricing?	Nike has differentiated its products through advertising its brand name. Thus, Nike tends to be a price-setter. Nike's managers can emphasize a cost-plus approach to pricing.
What approach should discount shoe stores such as Payless ShoeSource take to pricing?	Payless ShoeSource sells generic shoes (no-name brands) at low prices. Payless is a price-taker, so managers use a target-costing approach to pricing.

Summary Problem 1

Linger Industries makes tennis balls. Linger's only plant can produce up to 2.5 million cans of balls per year. Current production is two million cans. Annual manufacturing, selling, and administrative fixed costs total $700,000. The variable cost of making and selling each can of balls is $1. Stockholders expect a 12% annual return on the company's $3 million of assets.

Requirements

1. What is Linger Industries' current total cost of making and selling two million cans of tennis balls? What is the current cost per unit of each can of tennis balls?

2. Assume that Linger Industries is a price-taker and the current market price is $1.45 per can of balls (this is the price at which manufacturers sell to retailers). What is the *target* total cost of producing and selling two million cans of balls? Given Linger Industries' current total costs, will the company reach stockholders' profit goals?

3. If Linger Industries cannot reduce its fixed costs, what is the target variable cost per can of balls?

4. Suppose Linger Industries could spend an extra $100,000 on advertising to differentiate its product so that it could be more of a price-setter. Assuming the original volume and costs plus the $100,000 of new advertising costs, what cost-plus price will Linger Industries want to charge for a can of balls?

5. Nike has just asked Linger Industries to supply 400,000 cans of balls at a special order price of $1.20 per can. Nike wants Linger Industries to package the balls under the Nike label (Linger will imprint the Nike logo on each ball and can). As a result, Linger Industries will have to spend $10,000 to change the packaging machinery. Assuming the original volume and costs, should Linger Industries accept this special order? (Unlike the chapter problem, assume that Linger will incur variable selling costs as well as variable manufacturing costs related to this order.)

continued

Solution

Requirement 1

The current total cost, and cost per unit are calculated as follows:

Fixed costs	$ 700,000
Plus: Total variable costs (2 million cans × $1 per unit)	+ 2,000,000
Current total costs	$2,700,000
Divided by number of units	÷ 2,000,000
Current cost per can	$ 1.35

Requirement 2

The target total cost is as follows:

Revenue at market price (2,000,000 cans × $1.45 price)	$2,900,000
Less: Desired profit (12% × $3,000,000 of assets)	(360,000)
Target total cost	$2,540,000

Linger Industries' *current* total costs ($2,700,000 from Requirement 1) are $160,000 higher than the *target* total costs ($2,540,000). If Linger Industries can't cut costs, it won't be able to meet stockholders' profit expectations.

Requirement 3

Assuming that Linger Industries cannot reduce its fixed costs, the target variable cost per can is as follows:

Target total cost (from Requirement 2)	$ 2,540,000
Less: Fixed costs	(700,000)
Target total variable costs	$ 1,840,000
Divided by number of units	÷ 2,000,000
Target variable cost per unit	$ 0.92

Since Linger Industries cannot reduce its fixed costs, it needs to reduce variable costs by $0.08 per can ($1.00 – $0.92) to meet its profit goals. This would require an 8% cost reduction in variable costs, which may not be possible.

Requirement 4

If Linger Industries can differentiate its tennis balls, it will gain more control over pricing. The company's new cost-plus price would be as follows:

Current total costs (from Requirement 1)	$ 2,700,000
Plus: Additional cost of advertising	+ 100,000
Plus: Desired profit (from Requirement 2)	+ 360,000
Target revenue	$ 3,160,000
Divided by number of units	÷ 2,000,000
Cost-plus price per unit	$ 1.58

Linger Industries must study the market to determine whether retailers would pay $1.58 per can of balls.

Requirement 5

First, Linger determines that it has enough extra capacity (500,000 cans) to fill this special order (400,000). Next, Linger compares the revenue from the special order with the extra costs that will be incurred to fill the order. Notice that Linger shouldn't compare the special order price ($1.20) with the current unit cost of each can ($1.35) because the unit cost contains both a fixed and variable component. Since the company has excess capacity, the existing fixed costs won't be affected by the order. The correct analysis is as follows:

Revenue from special order (400,000 × $1.20 per unit)	$ 480,000
Less: Variable cost of special order (400,000 × $1.00)	(400,000)
Contribution margin from special order....................................	$ 80,000
Less: Additional fixed costs of special order............................	(10,000)
Operating income provided by special order...........................	$ 70,000

Linger Industries should accept the special order because it will increase operating income by $70,000. However, Linger Industries also needs to consider whether its regular customers will find out about the special price and demand lower prices, too. If Linger had simply compared the special order price of $1.20 to the current unit cost of each can ($1.35), it would have rejected the special order and missed out on the opportunity to make an additional $70,000 of profit.

How do Managers Make Other Special Business Decisions?

In this part of the chapter we'll consider four more special business decisions:

- When to drop a product, department, or territory
- Which products to emphasize in product mix decisions
- When to outsource
- When to sell as is or process further

Decisions to Drop Products, Departments, or Territories

Managers often must decide whether to drop products, departments, stores, or territories that are not as profitable as desired. Newell Rubbermaid—maker of Sharpie markers, Graco strollers, and Rubbermaid plastics—recently dropped some of its European product lines. Home Depot closed its Expo stores. Kroger food stores replaced some in-store movie rental departments with health food departments. How do managers make these decisions? Exhibit 8-13 shows some questions managers must consider when deciding whether to drop a product line, department, retail store location, or territory.

Make dropping a product, department, or territory decisions   **4**

EXHIBIT 8-13   Considerations for Dropping Products, Departments, or Territories

- Does the product provide a positive contribution margin?
- Will fixed costs continue to exist even if we drop the product?
- Are there any direct fixed costs that can be avoided if we drop the product?
- Will dropping the product affect sales of the company's other products?
- What could we do with the freed capacity?

In the first half of the chapter we assumed that ACDelco offered only one product—oil filters. Now, let's assume that it makes and sells air cleaners, too. Exhibit 8-14 shows the company's contribution margin income statement by product line. Because the air cleaner product line has an operating loss of $19,074, management is considering dropping it.

EXHIBIT 8-14 **Contribution Margin Income Statements by Product Line**

| | | Product Line | |
	Total (270,000 units)	Oil Filters (250,000 units)	Air Cleaners (20,000 units)
Sales revenue.............................	$ 835,000	$ 800,000	$ 35,000
Less: Variable expenses	(405,000)	(375,000)	(30,000)
Contribution margin	430,000	425,000	5,000
Less: Fixed expenses:			
Manufacturing..............................	(200,000)	(185,185)*	(14,815)*
Marketing and administrative..........	(125,000)	(115,741)†	(9,259)†
Total fixed expenses......................	(325,000)	(300,926)	(24,074)
Operating income (loss)	$ 105,000	$ 124,074	$(19,074)

* $200,000 ÷ 270,000 units = $0.74074 per unit; 250,000 units × $0.74074 = $185,185; 20,000 units × $0.74074 = $14,815
† $125,000 ÷ 270,000 units = $0.462963 per unit; 250,000 units × $0.462963 = $115,741; 20,000 units × $0.462963 = $9,259

The first question management should ask is, does the product provide a positive contribution margin? If the product line has a negative contribution margin, the product is not even covering its variable costs. Therefore, the company should drop the product line. However, if the product line has a positive contribution margin, it is *helping* to cover at least some of the company's fixed costs. In ACDelco's case, the air cleaners provide a $5,000 positive contribution margin. ACDelco's managers now need to consider fixed costs.

Suppose ACDelco allocates fixed expenses between product lines in proportion to the number of units sold. Dividing the fixed manufacturing expense of $200,000 by 270,000 total units (oil filters, 250,000; air cleaners, 20,000) yields a fixed manufacturing cost of $0.74074 per unit. Allocating this unit cost to the 250,000 oil filters assigns fixed manufacturing cost of $185,185 to this product, as shown in Exhibit 8-14. The same procedure allocates $14,815 to the 20,000 air cleaners. Fixed marketing and administrative expenses are allocated in the same manner.

It is important to note that this allocation method is arbitrary. ACDelco could allocate fixed costs in many different ways, and each way would have allocated a different amount of fixed costs to each product line. Since the amount of fixed costs allocated to each product line will differ depending on the allocation method used, we need to look at fixed costs in a different light. What matters is this:

1. Will the total fixed costs continue to exist *even if* the product line is dropped?

2. Can any *direct* fixed costs of the air cleaners be avoided if the product line is dropped?

Fixed Costs Continue to Exist (Unavoidable Fixed Costs)

Fixed costs that will continue to exist even after a product is dropped are often called unavoidable fixed costs. Unavoidable fixed costs are irrelevant to the decision because they *will not* differ between alternatives—they will be incurred regardless of whether the product line is dropped. Let's assume that all of ACDelco's fixed costs ($325,000) will continue to exist even if the company drops the air cleaners. Perhaps ACDelco makes the air cleaners in the same manufacturing facilities as the oil filters and uses the same administrative overhead. If that is the case, only the contribution margin the air cleaners provide is relevant. If ACDelco drops the air cleaners, it will lose the $5,000 contribution margin that they provide.

The incremental analysis shown in Exhibit 8-15 verifies the loss. If ACDelco drops the air cleaners, revenue will decrease by $35,000; but variable expenses will decrease by only $30,000, resulting in a net $5,000 decrease in operating income. Because the company's total fixed costs are unaffected, they aren't included in the analysis. This analysis suggests that management should *not* drop the air cleaners.

EXHIBIT 8-15   Incremental Analysis for Dropping a Product When Fixed Costs Continue to Exist

Expected decrease in revenues:	
Sale of air cleaners (20,000 × $1.75)	$35,000
Expected decrease in expenses:	
Variable manufacturing expenses (20,000 × $1.50)	30,000
Expected *decrease* in operating income	$ (5,000)

We could also verify that our analysis is correct by looking at what would *remain* if the air cleaners were dropped:

Contribution margin from oil filters..............................	$ 425,000
Less: Company's fixed expenses (all unavoidable)...........	(325,000)
Remaining operating income...	$ 100,000

The company's operating income after dropping the air cleaners ($100,000) would be $5,000 less than before ($105,000). This verifies our earlier conclusion: ACDelco's income would decrease by $5,000 if it dropped the air cleaners. Keep in mind that most companies have many product lines. Therefore, analyzing the decision to drop a particular product line is accomplished more easily by performing an incremental analysis (as we did in Exhibit 8-15) rather than adding up all of the revenues and expenses that would remain after dropping one product line. We simply show this second analysis as a means of proving our original result.

Direct Fixed Costs that Can be Avoided

Even though ACDelco allocates its fixed costs between product lines, some of the fixed costs might *belong* strictly to the air cleaner product line. These would be direct fixed costs of the air cleaners.[1] For example, suppose ACDelco employs a part-time supervisor to oversee *just* the air cleaner product line. The supervisor's $13,000 salary is a direct fixed cost that ACDelco can *avoid* if it stops producing air cleaners. Avoidable fixed costs, such as the supervisor's salary, *are relevant* to the decision because they differ between alternatives (they will be incurred if the company keeps the product line; they will *not* be incurred if the company drops the product line).

Exhibit 8-16 shows that in this situation, operating income will *increase* by $8,000 if ACDelco drops air cleaners. Why? Because revenues will decline by $35,000 but expenses will decline even more—by $43,000. The result is a net increase to operating income of $8,000. This analysis suggests that management should drop the air cleaners.

---

[1]To aid in decision making, companies should separate direct fixed costs from indirect fixed costs on their contribution margin income statements. Companies should *trace direct fixed costs* to the appropriate product line and *allocate only indirect fixed costs* among product lines. As in the ACDelco example, companies do not always make this distinction on the income statement.

EXHIBIT 8-16 **Incremental Analysis for Dropping a Product When Direct Fixed Costs Can Be Avoided**

Expected decrease in revenues:		
Sale of air cleaners (20,000 × $1.75)		$35,000
Expected decrease in expenses:		
Variable manufacturing expenses (20,000 × $1.50)	$30,000	
Direct fixed expenses—supervisor's salary	13,000	
Expected decrease in total expenses		43,000
Expected *increase* in operating income		$ 8,000

Other Considerations

Management must also consider whether dropping the product line, department, or territory would hurt other sales. In the examples given so far, we assumed that dropping the air cleaners would not affect oil filter sales. However, think about a grocery store. Even if the Produce Department is not profitable, would managers drop it? Probably not, because if they did, they would lose customers who want one-stop shopping. In such situations, managers must also include the loss of contribution margin from *other* departments affected by the change when performing the financial analysis shown previously.

Management should also consider what it could do with freed capacity. In the ACDelco example, we assumed that the company produces oil filters and air cleaners using the same manufacturing facilities. If ACDelco drops the air cleaners, could it make and sell another product using the freed capacity? Managers should consider whether using the facilities to produce a different product would be more profitable than using the facilities to produce air cleaners.

STOP & THINK

Assume that all of ACDelco's fixed costs are unavoidable. If the company drops air cleaners, they could make spark plugs with the freed capacity. The company expects spark plugs would provide $50,000 of sales, incur $30,000 of variable costs, and incur $10,000 of new direct fixed costs. Should ACDelco drop the air cleaners and use the freed capacity to make spark plugs?

Answer: If all fixed costs are unavoidable, ACDelco would lose $5,000 of contribution margin if it dropped air cleaners. ACDelco should compare this loss with the expected gain from producing and selling spark plugs with the freed capacity:

Sales of spark plugs	$ 50,000
Less: Variable cost of spark plugs	(30,000)
Less: Direct fixed costs of spark plugs	(10,000)
Operating income gained from spark plugs	$ 10,000

The gain from producing spark plugs ($10,000) outweighs the loss from dropping air cleaners ($5,000). This suggests that management should replace air cleaner production with spark plug production.

Business decisions should take into account all costs affected by the choice of action. Managers must ask what total costs—variable and fixed—will change. As Exhibits 8-15 and 8-16 show, the key to deciding whether to drop products, departments, or territories is to compare the lost revenue against the costs that can be saved and to consider what would be done with the freed capacity. The decision rule is as follows:

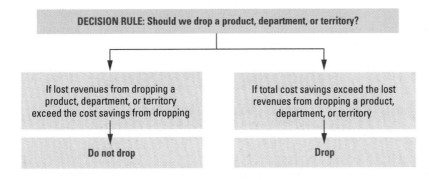

Product Mix Decisions

Companies do not have unlimited resources. **Constraints** that restrict production or sale of a product vary from company to company. For a manufacturer, the production constraint is often the number of available machine hours. For a merchandiser such as Wal-Mart, the primary constraint is cubic feet of display space. In order to determine which products to emphasize displaying or producing, companies facing constraints consider the questions shown in Exhibit 8-17.

Make product mix decisions   **5**

EXHIBIT 8-17   Product Mix Considerations

- What constraint(s) stops us from making (or displaying) all of the units we can sell?
- Which products offer the highest contribution margin per unit of the constraint?
- Would emphasizing one product over another affect fixed costs?

Consider Union Bay, a manufacturer of shirts and jeans. Let's say the company can sell all of the shirts and jeans it produces, but it has only 2,000 machine hours of capacity. The company uses the same machines to produce both jeans and shirts. In this case, machine hours is the constraint. Note that this is a short-term decision, because in the long run, Union Bay could expand its production facilities to meet sales demand if it made financial sense to do so. The following data suggest that shirts are more profitable than jeans:

	Per Unit	
	Shirts	**Jeans**
Sale price...	$30	$60
Less: Variable expenses	(12)	(48)
Contribution margin	$18	$12
Contribution margin ratio:.................................		
Shirts—$18 ÷ $30	60 %	
Jeans—$12 ÷ $60...		20 %

However, an important piece of information is missing—the time it takes to make each product. Let's assume that Union Bay can produce either 20 pairs of jeans *or* 10 shirts per machine hour. *The company will incur the same fixed costs either way, so fixed costs are irrelevant.* Which product should it emphasize?

To maximize profits when fixed costs are irrelevant, follow this decision rule:

> **DECISION RULE: Which product to emphasize?**
>
> ↓
>
> Emphasize the product with the **highest contribution margin per unit of the constraint.**

Because *machine hours* is the constraint, Union Bay needs to figure out which product has the *highest contribution margin per machine hour*. Exhibit 8-18 shows the contribution margin per machine hour for each product.

EXHIBIT 8-18   **Product Mix—Which Product to Emphasize**

	Shirts	Jeans
(1) Units that can be produced each machine hour	10	20
(2) Contribution margin per unit	× $18	× $12
Contribution margin per machine hour (1) × (2)	$180	$240
Available capacity—number of machine hours	× 2,000	× 2,000
Total contribution margin at full capacity	$360,000	$480,000

Jeans have a higher contribution margin per machine hour ($240) than shirts ($180). Therefore, Union Bay will earn more profit by producing jeans. Why? Because even though jeans have a lower contribution margin *per unit*, Union Bay can make twice as many jeans as shirts in the available machine hours. Exhibit 8-18 also proves that Union Bay earns more total profit by making jeans. Multiplying the contribution margin per machine hour by the available number of machine hours shows that Union Bay can earn $480,000 of contribution margin by producing jeans but only $360,000 by producing shirts.

To maximize profit, Union Bay should make 40,000 jeans (2,000 machine hours × 20 jeans per hour) and zero shirts. Why zero shirts? Because for every machine hour spent making shirts, Union Bay would *give up* $60 of contribution margin ($240 per hour for jeans versus $180 per hour for shirts).

Changing Assumptions: Product Mix When Demand is Limited

We made two assumptions about Union Bay: (1) Union Bay's sales of other products, if any, won't be hurt by this decision and (2) Union Bay can sell as many jeans and shirts as it can produce. Let's challenge these assumptions. First, how could making only jeans (and not shirts) hurt sales of the company's other products? Using other production equipment, Union Bay also makes ties and jackets that coordinate with their shirts. Tie and jacket sales might fall if Union Bay no longer offers coordinating shirts.

Let's challenge our second assumption. A new competitor has decreased the demand for Union Bay's jeans. Now, the company can sell only 30,000 pairs of jeans. Union Bay should make only as many jeans as it can sell and use the remaining machine hours to produce shirts. Let's see how this constraint in sales demand changes profitability.

Recall from Exhibit 8-18 that Union Bay will earn $480,000 of contribution margin from using all 2,000 machine hours to produce jeans. However, if Union Bay makes only 30,000 jeans, it will use only 1,500 machine hours (30,000 jeans ÷ 20 jeans per machine hour). That leaves 500 machine hours available for making shirts. Union Bay's new contribution margin will be as follows:

	Shirts	Jeans	Total
Contribution margin per machine hour (from Exhibit 8-18)...........	$ 180	$ 240	
Machine hours devoted to product.................................	× 500	× 1,500	2,000
Total contribution margin at full capacity.......................	$90,000	$360,000	$450,000

Because of the change in product mix, Union Bay's total contribution margin will fall from $480,000 to $450,000, a $30,000 decline. Union Bay had to give up $60 of contribution margin per machine hour ($240 – $180) on the 500 hours it spent producing shirts rather than jeans. However, Union Bay had no choice—the company would have incurred an *actual loss* from producing jeans that it could not sell. If Union Bay had produced 40,000 jeans but sold only 30,000, the company would have spent $480,000 to make the unsold jeans (10,000 jeans × $48 variable cost per pair of jeans) yet would have received no sales revenue from them.

What about fixed costs? In most cases, changing the product mix emphasis in the short run will not affect fixed costs, so fixed costs are irrelevant. However, fixed costs could differ when a different product mix is emphasized. What if Union Bay had a month-to-month lease on a zipper machine used only for making jeans? If Union Bay made only shirts, it could *avoid* the lease cost. However, if Union Bay makes any jeans, it needs the machine. In this case, the fixed costs become relevant because they differ between alternative product mixes (shirts only *versus* jeans only or jeans and shirts).

STOP & THINK

Would Union Bay's product mix decision change if it had a $20,000 cancelable lease on a zipper machine needed only for jean production? Assume that Union Bay can sell as many units as it makes.
Answer: We would compare the profitability as follows:

	Shirts	Jeans
Total contribution margin at full capacity (from Exhibit 8-18)......................................	$360,000	$480,000
Less: Avoidable fixed costs.................................	-0-	(20,000)
Net benefit...	$360,000	$460,000

Even considering the zipper machine lease, producing jeans is more profitable than producing shirts. Union Bay would prefer producing jeans over shirts unless demand for jeans drops so low that the net benefit from jeans is less than $360,000 (the benefit gained from solely producing shirts).

Notice that the analysis again follows the two guidelines for special business decisions: (1) focus on relevant data (only those revenues and costs that differ) and (2) use a contribution margin approach, which separates variable from fixed costs.

Outsourcing Decisions (Make-or-Buy)

Recall from the chapter's opening story that Delta outsources much of its reservation work and airplane maintenance. **Outsourcing** decisions are sometimes called **make-or-buy** decisions because managers must decide whether to buy a product or service or produce it in-house. The heart of these decisions is *how best to use available resources.*

Make outsourcing (make-or-buy) decisions **6**

Let's see how managers make outsourcing decisions. DefTone, a manufacturer of music CDs, is deciding whether to make paper liners for CD jewel boxes (the plastic cases in which CDs are sold) in-house or whether to outsource them to Mūz-Art, a company that specializes in producing paper liners. DefTone's cost to produce 250,000 liners is as follows:

	Total Cost (250,000 liners)
Direct materials	$ 40,000
Direct labor	20,000
Variable manufacturing overhead	15,000
Fixed manufacturing overhead	50,000
Total manufacturing cost	$125,000
Number of liners	÷ 250,000
Cost per liner	$ 0.50

Mūz-Art offers to sell DefTone the liners for $0.37 each. Should DefTone make the liners or buy them from Mūz-Art? DefTone's $0.50 cost per unit to make the liner is $0.13 higher than the cost of buying it from Mūz-Art. It first appears that DefTone should outsource the liners. But the correct answer is not so simple. Why? Because manufacturing unit costs contain both fixed and variable components. In deciding whether to outsource, managers must consider fixed and variable costs separately. Exhibit 8-19 shows some of the questions management must consider when deciding whether to outsource.

EXHIBIT 8-19 Outsourcing Considerations

- How do our variable costs compare to the outsourcing cost?
- Are any fixed costs avoidable if we outsource?
- What could we do with the freed capacity?

Why is this important?

"Almost any business activity can be outsourced (for example, manufacturing, marketing, payroll). Companies often choose to retain only their core competencies—things they are *really* good at doing—and outsource just about everything else to companies that can do it *better* for them."

Let's see how these considerations apply to DefTone. By purchasing the liners, DefTone can avoid all variable manufacturing costs—$40,000 of direct materials, $20,000 of direct labor, and $15,000 of variable manufacturing overhead. In total, the company will save $75,000 in variable manufacturing costs, or $0.30 per liner ($75,000 ÷ 250,000 liners). However, DefTone will have to pay the variable outsourcing cost of $0.37 per unit, or $92,500 for the 250,000 liners. Based only on variable costs, the lower cost alternative is to manufacture the liners in-house. However, managers must still consider fixed costs.

Assume that DefTone cannot avoid any of the fixed costs by outsourcing. In this case, the company's fixed costs are irrelevant to the decision because DefTone would continue to incur $50,000 of fixed costs regardless of whether the company outsources the liners. The fixed costs are irrelevant because they do not differ between alternatives. DefTone should continue to make its own liners because the variable cost of outsourcing the liners ($92,500) exceeds the variable cost of making the liners ($75,000).

However, what if DefTone can avoid some fixed costs by outsourcing the liners? Let's assume that management can reduce fixed overhead cost by $10,000 by outsourcing the liners. DefTone will still incur $40,000 of fixed overhead ($50,000 – $10,000) even if they outsource the liners. In this case, fixed costs become relevant to the decision because they differ between alternatives. Exhibit 8-20 shows the differences in costs between the make and buy alternatives under this scenario.

EXHIBIT 8-20 Incremental Analysis for Outsourcing Decision

Liner Costs	Make Liners	Buy Liners	Difference
Variable costs:			
Direct materials	$ 40,000	—	$40,000
Direct labor	20,000	—	20,000
Variable overhead	15,000	—	15,000
Purchase cost from Mūz-Art			
(250,000 × $0.37)	—	$ 92,500	(92,500)
Fixed overhead	50,000	40,000	10,000
Total cost of liners	$125,000	$132,500	$ (7,500)

Exhibit 8-20 shows that it would still cost DefTone less to make the liners than to buy them from Mūz-Art, even with the $10,000 reduction in fixed costs. The net savings from making 250,000 liners is $7,500. Exhibit 8-20 also shows that outsourcing decisions follow our two key guidelines for special business decisions: (1) focus on relevant data (differences in costs in this case) and (2) use a contribution margin approach that separates variable costs from fixed costs.

Note how the unit cost—which does not separate costs according to behavior—can be deceiving. If DefTone's managers made their decision by comparing the total manufacturing cost per liner ($0.50) to the outsourcing unit cost per liner ($0.37), they would have incorrectly decided to outsource. Recall that the manufacturing unit cost ($0.50) contains both fixed and variable components whereas the outsourcing cost ($0.37) is strictly variable. To make the correct decision, DefTone had to separate the two cost components and analyze them separately.

Our decision rule for outsourcing is as follows:

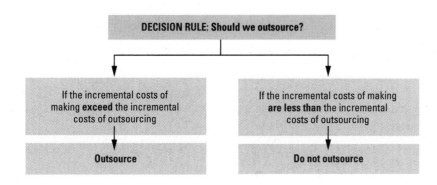

STOP & THINK

Assuming that DefTone could save $10,000 in fixed costs by outsourcing, what is the most the company would be willing to pay per liner to outsource production of 250,000 liners?

Answer: To answer that question, we must find the outsourcing price at which DefTone would be *indifferent* making the liners or outsourcing the liners. DefTone would be indifferent if the total costs were the *same* either way:

$$\text{Costs if making liners} = \text{Costs if outsourcing liners}$$

$$\text{Variable manufacturing costs} + \text{Fixed costs} = \text{Variable outsourcing costs} + \text{Fixed costs}$$

$$(250,000 \text{ units} \times \$0.30 \text{ per unit}) + \$50,000 = (250,000 \times \text{outsourcing cost per unit}) + \$40,000$$

$$\$75,000 + \$50,000 - \$40,000 = (250,000 \times \text{outsourcing cost per unit})$$

$$\$85,000 = (250,000 \times \text{outsourcing cost per unit})$$

$$\$85,000 \div 250,000 = \text{outsourcing cost per unit}$$

$$\$0.34 = \text{outsourcing cost per unit}$$

DefTone would be indifferent about making or outsourcing the liners if the outsourcing cost price was $0.34 per unit. At that price, DefTone would incur the same cost to manufacture or outsource the liners. DefTone would save money only if the outsourcing price was less than $0.34 per unit. Therefore, the most DefTone would pay to outsource is $0.33 per liner.

We haven't considered what DefTone could do with the freed capacity it would have if it decided to outsource the liners. The analysis in Exhibit 8-20 assumes no other use for the production facilities if DefTone buys the liners from Mūz-Art. But suppose DefTone has an opportunity to use its freed capacity to make more CDs for an additional profit of $18,000. Now, DefTone must consider its **opportunity cost**—the benefit forgone by not choosing an alternative course of action. In this case, DefTone's opportunity cost of making the liners is the $18,000 profit it forgoes if it does not free its production facilities to make the additional CDs.

Let's see how DefTone's managers decide among three alternatives:

1. Use the facilities to make the liners.

2. Buy the liners and leave facilities idle (continue to assume $10,000 of avoidable fixed costs from outsourcing liners).

3. Buy the liners and use facilities to make more CDs (continue to assume $10,000 of avoidable fixed costs from outsourcing liners).

The alternative with the lowest *net* cost is the best use of DefTone's facilities. Exhibit 8-21 compares the three alternatives.

EXHIBIT 8-21 Best Use of Facilities Given Opportunity Costs

	Make Liners	Buy Liners Facilities Idle	Buy Liners Make Additional CDs
Expected cost of 250,000 liners (from Exhibit 8-20)	$125,000	$132,500	$132,500
Expected *profit* from additional CDs	—	—	(18,000)
Expected net cost of obtaining 250,000 liners	$125,000	$132,500	$114,500

DefTone should buy the liners from Mūz-Art and use the vacated facilities to make more CDs. If DefTone makes the liners or buys the liners from Mūz-Art but leaves its production facilities idle, it will forgo the opportunity to earn $18,000.

STOP & THINK

How will the $18,000 opportunity cost change the *maximum* amount DefTone is willing to pay to outsource each liner?

Answer: DefTone will now be willing to pay *more* to outsource its liners. In essence, the company is willing to pay for the opportunity to make more CDs.

DefTone's managers should consider qualitative factors as well as revenue and cost differences in making their final decision. For example, DefTone managers may believe they can better control quality or delivery schedules by making the liners themselves. This argues for making the liners, even if the cost is slightly higher.

Sell As Is or Process Further Decisions

At what point in processing should a company sell its product? Many companies, especially in the food processing and natural resource industries, face this business decision. Companies in these industries process a raw material (milk, corn, livestock, crude oil, lumber, and so forth) to a point before it is saleable. For example, Kraft pasteurizes raw milk before it is saleable. Kraft must then decide whether it should sell the pasteurized milk as is or process it further into other dairy products (reduced-fat milk, butter, sour cream, cottage cheese, yogurt, blocks of cheese, shredded cheese, and so forth). Managers consider the questions shown in Exhibit 8-22 when deciding whether to sell as is or process further.

Make sell as is or process further decisions **7**

EXHIBIT 8-22   Sell As Is or Process Further Considerations

- How much revenue will we receive if we sell the product as is?
- How much revenue will we receive if we sell the product *after* processing it further?
- How much will it cost to process the product further?

Let's consider Bertolli, the manufacturer of Italian food products. Suppose Bertolli spends $100,000 to process raw olives into 50,000 quarts of plain virgin olive oil. Should Bertolli sell the olive oil as is or should it spend more to process the olive oil into gourmet dipping oils, such as a Basil and Garlic Infused Dipping Oil? In making the decision, Bertolli's managers consider the following relevant information[2]:

- Bertolli could sell the plain olive oil for $5 per quart, for a total of $250,000 (50,000 × $5).

- Bertolli could sell the gourmet dipping oil for $7 per quart, for a total of $350,000 (50,000 × $7).

- Bertolli would have to spend $0.75 per quart, or $37,500 (50,000 gallons × $0.75), to further process the plain olive oil into the gourmet dipping oil. This cost would include the extra direct materials required (such as basil, garlic, and the incremental cost of premium glass containers) as well as the extra conversion costs incurred (the cost of any *additional* machinery and labor that the company would need to purchase in order to complete the extra processing).

By examining the incremental analysis shown in Exhibit 8-23, Bertolli's managers can see that they can increase operating income by $62,500 by

Why is this important?

"Some companies are able to sell their products at different points of completion. For example, some furniture manufacturers sell flat-packed bookshelves, TV stands, and home office furniture that the consumer must finish assembling. A cost-benefit analysis helps managers choose the most profitable point at which to sell the company's products."

---

[2]All references to Bertolli in this hypothetical example were created by the author solely for academic purposes and are not intended, in any way, to represent the actual business practices of, or costs incurred by Bertolli.

further processing the plain olive oil into the gourmet dipping oil. The extra $100,000 of revenue greatly exceeds the incremental $37,500 of cost incurred to further process the olive oil.

EXHIBIT 8-23   Incremental Analysis for Sell As Is or Process Further Decision

	Sell As Is	Process Further	Difference
Expected revenue from selling 50,000 quarts of plain olive oil at $5.00 per quart	$250,000		
Expected revenue from selling 50,000 quarts of gourmet dipping oil at $7.00 per quart		$350,000	$100,000
Additional costs of $0.75 per quart to convert 50,000 quarts of plain olive oil into gourmet dipping oil		(37,500)	(37,500)
Total net benefit	$250,000	$312,500	$ 62,500

Notice that Bertolli's managers do *not* consider the $100,000 originally spent on processing the olives into olive oil. Why? It is a sunk cost. Recall from our previous discussion that a sunk cost is a past cost that cannot be changed regardless of which future action the company takes. Bertolli has incurred $100,000 regardless of whether it sells the olive oil as is or processes it further into gourmet dipping oils. Therefore, the cost is *not* relevant to the decision.

Thus, the decision rule is as follows:

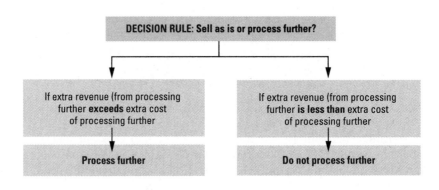

Decision Guidelines

Short-Term Special Business Decisions

Amazon.com has confronted most of the special business decisions we've covered. Here are the key guidelines Amazon.com's managers follow in making their decisions.

Decision	Guidelines
Should Amazon.com drop its electronics product line?	If the cost savings exceed the lost revenues from dropping the electronics product line, then dropping will increase operating income.
Given limited warehouse space, which products should Amazon.com focus on selling?	Amazon.com should focus on selling the products with the highest contribution margin per unit of the constraint, which is cubic feet of warehouse space
Should Amazon.com outsource its warehousing operations?	If the incremental costs of operating its own warehouses exceed the costs of outsourcing, then outsourcing will increase operating income.
How should a company decide whether to sell a product as is or process further?	Process further only if the extra sales revenue (from processing further) exceeds the extra costs of additional processing.

Summary Problem 2

Requirements

1. Aziz produces Standard and Deluxe sunglasses:

	Per Pair	
	Standard	**Deluxe**
Sale price..	$20	$30
Variable expenses..	16	21

The company has 15,000 machine hours available. In one machine hour, Aziz can produce 70 pairs of the Standard model or 30 pairs of the Deluxe model. Assuming machine hours is a constraint, which model should Aziz emphasize?

2. Just Do It! incurs the following costs for 20,000 pairs of its high-tech hiking socks:

Direct materials..	$ 20,000
Direct labor..	80,000
Variable manufacturing overhead	40,000
Fixed manufacturing overhead..	80,000
Total manufacturing cost	$220,000
Cost per pair ($220,000 ÷ 20,000)...	$ 11

Another manufacturer has offered to sell Just Do It! similar socks for $10 a pair, a total purchase cost of $200,000. If Just Do It! outsources *and* leaves its plant idle, it can save $50,000 of fixed overhead cost. Or the company can use the released facilities to make other products that will contribute $70,000 to profits. In this case, the company will not be able to avoid any fixed costs. Identify and analyze the alternatives. What is the best course of action?

Solution

Requirement 1

	Style of Sunglasses	
	Standard	**Deluxe**
Sale price per pair..	$ 20	$ 30
Variable expense per pair	(16)	(21)
Contribution margin per pair	$ 4	$ 9
Units produced each machine hour	× 70	× 30
Contribution margin per machine hour....................	$ 280	$ 270
Capacity—number of machine hours	× 15,000	× 15,000
Total contribution margin at full capacity............	$4,200,000	$4,050,000

Decision: Emphasize the Standard model because it has the higher contribution margin per unit of the constraint—machine hours—resulting in a higher contribution margin for the company.

continued

Requirement 2

| | Buy Socks | | |
	Make Socks	Facilities Idle	Make Other Products
Relevant costs:			
Direct materials	$ 20,000	—	—
Direct labor	80,000	—	—
Variable overhead	40,000	—	—
Fixed overhead	80,000	$ 30,000	$ 80,000
Purchase cost from outsider (20,000 × $10)	—	200,000	200,000
Total cost of obtaining socks	220,000	230,000	280,000
Profit from other products	—	—	(70,000)
Net cost of obtaining 20,000 pairs of socks	$220,000	$230,000	$210,000

Decision: Just Do It! should buy the socks from the outside supplier and use the released facilities to make other products.

REVIEW

Accounting Vocabulary

Constraint. (p. 439) A factor that restricts production or sale of a product.

Cost-Plus Pricing. (p. 431) An approach to pricing used by price-setters; Cost-plus pricing begins with the product's total costs and adds the company's desired profit to determine a cost-plus price.

Opportunity Cost. (p. 444) The benefit forgone by not choosing an alternative course of action.

Outsourcing. (p. 441) A make-or-buy decision: Managers decide whether to buy a product or service or produce it in-house.

Relevant Information. (p. 422) Expected *future* data that *differs* among alternatives.

Sunk Cost. (p. 423) A past cost that cannot be changed regardless of which future action is taken.

Target Costing (p. 429) An approach to pricing used by price-takers; Target Costing begins with the revenue at market price and subtracts the company's desired profit to arrive at the target total cost.

Quick Check

1. *(Learning Objective 1)* In making short-term special decisions, you should
   a. focus on total costs.
   b. separate variable from fixed costs.
   c. use a traditional absorption costing approach.
   d. focus only on quantitative factors.
2. *(Learning Objective 1)* When making decisions, managers should
   a. consider sunk costs.
   b. consider costs that do not differ between alternatives.
   c. consider only variable costs.
   d. consider revenues that differ between alternatives.

3. *(Learning Objective 1)* Which of the following costs are irrelevant to business decisions?
   a. Sunk costs
   b. Costs that differ between alternatives
   c. Variable costs
   d. Avoidable costs
4. *(Learning Objective 2)* Which of the following is relevant to Amazon.com's decision to accept a special order at a lower sale price from a large customer in China?
   a. The cost of Amazon.com's warehouses in the United States
   b. Amazon.com's investment in its Web site
   c. The cost of shipping the order to the customer
   d. Founder Jeff Bezos's salary

5. *(Learning Objective 3)* When companies are price-setters, their products and services
   a. are priced by managers using a target-pricing emphasis.
   b. tend to be unique.
   c. tend to have a great many competitors.
   d. tend to be commodities.

6. *(Learning Objective 3)* When pricing a product or service, managers must consider which of the following?
   a. Only variable costs
   b. Only period costs
   c. Only manufacturing costs
   d. All costs

7. *(Learning Objective 4)* In deciding whether to drop its electronics product line, Amazon.com would consider
   a. the costs it could save by dropping the product line.
   b. the revenues it would lose from dropping the product line.
   c. how dropping the electronics product line would affect sales of its other products, such as CDs.
   d. all of the above.

8. *(Learning Objective 5)* In deciding which product lines to emphasize, Amazon.com should focus on the product line that has the highest
   a. contribution margin per unit of the constraining factor.
   b. contribution margin per unit of product.
   c. contribution margin ratio.
   d. profit per unit of product.

9. *(Learning Objective 6)* When making outsourcing decisions
   a. the manufacturing full unit cost of making the product in-house is relevant.
   b. the variable cost of producing the product in-house is relevant.
   c. avoidable fixed costs are irrelevant.
   d. expected use of the freed capacity is irrelevant.

10. *(Learning Objective 7)* When deciding whether to sell as is or process a product further, managers should ignore which of the following?
    a. The revenue if the product is processed further
    b. The cost of processing further
    c. The costs of processing the product thus far
    d. The revenue if the product is sold as is

ASSESS YOUR PROGRESS

Learning Objectives

1 Describe and identify information relevant to short-term business decisions

2 Make special order decisions

3 Make pricing decisions

4 Make dropping a product, department, or territory decisions

5 Make product mix decisions

6 Make outsourcing (make-or-buy) decisions

7 Make sell as is or process further decisions

Short Exercises

S8-1 Determine relevance of information *(Learning Objective 1)*

You are trying to decide whether to trade in your ink-jet printer for a more recent model. Your usage pattern will remain unchanged, but the old and new printers use different ink cartridges. Are the following items relevant or irrelevant to your decision?
a. The price of the new printer
b. The price you paid for the old printer
c. The trade-in value of the old printer
d. Paper costs
e. The difference between the cost of ink cartridges

S8-2 Special order decision given revised data *(Learning Objective 2)*

Consider the ACDelco special sales order example on pages 426–427. Suppose ACDelco's variable manufacturing cost is $1.35 per oil filter (instead of $1.20). In addition, ACDelco would have to buy a special stamping machine that costs $9,000 to mark the customer's logo on the special-order oil filters. The machine would be scrapped when the special order is complete.

Would you recommend that ACDelco accept the special order under these conditions? Show your analysis.

S8-3 Determine pricing approach and target price *(Learning Objective 3)*

SnowDreams operates a Rocky Mountain ski resort. The company is planning its lift ticket pricing for the coming ski season. Investors would like to earn a 15% return on the company's $100 million of assets. The company incurs primarily fixed costs to groom the runs and operate the lifts. SnowDreams projects fixed costs to be $33,750,000 for the ski season. The resort serves about 750,000 skiers and snowboarders each season. Variable costs are about $10 per guest. Currently, the resort has such a favorable reputation among skiers and snowboarders that it has some control over the lift ticket prices.

1. Would SnowDreams emphasize target costing or cost-plus pricing. Why?

2. If other resorts in the area charge $70 per day, what price should SnowDreams charge?

S8-4 Use target costing to analyze data *(Learning Objective 3)*

Consider SnowDreams from S8-3. Assume that SnowDreams' reputation has diminished and other resorts in the vicinity are charging only $65 per lift ticket. SnowDreams has become a price-taker and won't be able to charge more than its competitors. At the market price, SnowDreams' managers believe they will still serve 750,000 skiers and snowboarders each season.

1. If SnowDreams can't reduce its costs, what profit will it earn? State your answer in dollars and as a percent of assets. Will investors be happy with the profit level? Show your analysis.

2. Assume that SnowDreams has found ways to cut its fixed costs to $30 million. What is its new target variable cost per skier/snowboarder? Compare this to the current variable cost per skier/snowboarder. Comment on your results.

S8-5 Decide whether to drop a department *(Learning Objective 4)*

Knight Fashion in New York operates three departments: Men's, Women's, and Accessories. Knight Fashion allocates all fixed expenses (unavoidable building depreciation and utilities) based on each department's square footage. Departmental operating income data for the third quarter of the current year are as follows:

	Department			
	Men's	Women's	Accessories	Total
Sales revenue	$105,000	$54,000	$100,000	$259,000
Variable expenses	60,000	30,000	80,000	170,000
Fixed expenses	25,000	20,000	25,000	70,000
Total expenses	85,000	50,000	105,000	240,000
Operating income (loss)	$20,000	$4,000	$(5,000)	$19,000

The store will remain in the same building regardless of whether any of the departments are dropped. Should Knight Fashion drop any of the departments? Give your reason.

S8-6 Drop a department: Revised information *(Learning Objective 4)*

Consider Knight Fashion from S8-5. Assume that the fixed expenses assigned to each department include only direct fixed costs of the department (rather than unavoidable fixed costs as given in S8-5):

▪ Salary of the department's manager

▪ Cost of advertising directly related to that department

If Knight Fashion drops a department, it will not incur these fixed expenses. Under these circumstances, should Knight Fashion drop any of the departments? Give your reason.

S8-7 Replace a department *(Learning Objective 4)*

Consider Knight Fashion from S8-5. Assume once again that all fixed costs are unavoidable. If Knight Fashion drops one of the current departments, it plans to replace the dropped department with a Shoe Department. The company expects the Shoe Department to produce $80,000 in sales and have $50,000 of variable costs. Because the shoe business would be new to Knight Fashion, the company would have to incur an additional $7,000 of fixed costs (advertising, new shoe display racks, and so forth) per quarter related to the department. What should Knight Fashion do now?

S8-8 Product mix decision: Unlimited demand *(Learning Objective 5)*

StoreAll produces plastic storage bins for household storage needs. The company makes two sizes of bins: Large (50 gallon) and Regular (35 gallon). Demand for the product is so high that StoreAll can sell as many of each size as it can produce. The company uses the same machinery to produce both sizes. The machinery can be run for only 3,000 hours per period. StoreAll can produce 10 Large bins every hour compared to 15 regular bins in the same amount of time. Fixed expenses amount to $100,000 per period. Sales prices and variable costs are as follows:

	Regular	Large
Sales price per unit	$8.00	$10.00
Variable cost per unit	$3.00	$4.00

1. Which product should StoreAll emphasize? Why?
2. To maximize profits, how many of each size bin should StoreAll produce?
3. Given this product mix, what will the company's operating income be?

S8-9 Product mix decision: Limited demand *(Learning Objective 5)*

Consider StoreAll in S8-8. Assume that demand for Regular bins is limited to 30,000 units and demand for Large bins is limited to 25,000 units.

1. How many of each size bin should StoreAll make now?
2. Given this product mix, what will be the company's operating income?
3. Explain why the operating income is less than it was when StoreAll was producing its optimal product mix.

S8-10 Outsourcing production decision *(Learning Objectives 1 & 6)*

Suppose an Olive Garden restaurant is considering whether to (1) bake bread for its restaurant in-house or (2) buy the bread from a local bakery. The chef estimates that variable costs of making each loaf include $0.50 of ingredients, $0.25 of variable overhead (electricity to run the oven), and $0.75 of direct labor for kneading and forming the loaves. Allocating fixed overhead (depreciation on the kitchen equipment and building) based on direct labor assigns $1.00 of fixed overhead per loaf. None of the fixed costs are avoidable. The local bakery would charge Olive Garden $1.75 per loaf.

1. What is the unit cost of making the bread in-house (use absorption costing)?
2. Should Olive Garden bake the bread in-house or buy from the local bakery? Why?
3. In addition to the financial analysis, what else should Olive Garden consider when making this decision?

S8-11 Relevant information for outsourcing delivery function *(Learning Objectives 1 & 6)*

U.S. Food in Lexington, Kentucky, manufactures and markets snack foods. Betsy Gonzalez manages the company's fleet of 200 delivery trucks. Gonzalez has been charged with "reengineering" the fleet-management function. She has an important decision to make.

▨ Should she continue to manage the fleet in-house with the five employees reporting to her? To do so, she will have to acquire new fleet-management software to streamline U.S. Food's fleet-management process.

▨ Should she outsource the fleet-management function to Fleet Management Services, a company that specializes in managing fleets of trucks for other companies? Fleet Management Services would take over the maintenance, repair, and scheduling of U.S. Food's fleet (but U.S. Food would retain ownership). This alternative would require Gonzalez to lay off her five employees. However, her own job would be secure, as she would be U.S. Food's liaison with Fleet Management Services.

Assume that Gonzalez's records show the following data concerning U.S. Food's fleet:

Book value of U.S. Food's trucks, with an estimated five-year life	$3,500,000
Annual leasing fee for new fleet-management software	8,000
Annual maintenance of trucks	145,500
Fleet Supervisor Gonzalez's annual salary	60,000
Total annual salaries of U.S. Food's five other fleet-management employees	150,000

Suppose that Fleet Management Services offers to manage U.S. Food's fleet for an annual fee of $290,000.

Which alternative will maximize U.S. Food's short-term operating income?

S8-12 Outsourcing qualitative considerations *(Learning Objectives 1 & 6)*

Refer to U.S. Food in S8-11. What qualitative factors should Gonzalez consider before making a final decision?

S8-13 Scrap or process further decision *(Learning Objective 7)*

Auto Components has an inventory of 500 obsolete remote entry keys that are carried in inventory at a manufacturing cost of $80,000. Production Supervisor Terri Smith must decide to do one of the following:

▪ Process the inventory further at a cost of $20,000, with the expectation of selling it for $28,000

▪ Scrap the inventory for a sale price of $6,000

What should Smith do? Present figures to support your decision.

S8-14 Determine most profitable final product *(Learning Objective 7)*

Chocolite processes cocoa beans into cocoa powder at a processing cost of $10,000 per batch. Chocolite can sell the cocoa powder as is, or it can process the cocoa powder further into chocolate syrup or boxed assorted chocolates. Once processed, each batch of cocoa beans would result in the following sales revenue:

Cocoa powder	$ 15,000
Chocolate syrup	$100,000
Boxed assorted chocolates	$200,000

The cost of transforming the cocoa powder into chocolate syrup would be $70,000. Likewise, the company would incur $180,000 to transform the cocoa powder into boxed assorted chocolates. The company president has decided to make boxed assorted chocolates owing to its high sales value and to the fact that the $10,000 cost of processing cocoa beans "eats up" most of the cocoa powder profits. Has the president made the right or wrong decision? Explain your answer. Be sure to include the correct financial analysis in your response.

Exercises—Group A

E8-15A   Determine relevant and irrelevant information *(Learning Objective 1)*

The Plastic Lumber Company is considering whether it should replace an extrusion machine. The new machine will produce 40% more finished lumber than the old machine. The increase in production will cause fixed selling costs to increase, but variable selling costs will not increase. The new machine will require installation by an engineering firm; the old machine had required a similar installation. If the new machine is purchased, the old machine can be sold as scrap. The old machine requires frequent repairs and maintenance to keep it running. The new machine will require maintenance once a year. The new machine will be paid for by signing a notes payable with the bank that will cover the cost of the new machine. The Plastic Lumber Company will pay interest on the notes payable. The notes payable that was used to pay for the old machine was fully paid off last year.

In the following chart, indicate whether each of the costs described would be relevant or not to The Plastic Lumber Company's decision about whether to purchase the new extrusion machine or to keep using the old extrusion machine.

	Item	Relevant	Not Relevant
a.	Cost of new machine...		
b.	Cost of old machine...		
c.	Added profits from increase in production from new machine...		
d.	Fixed selling costs...		
e.	Variable selling costs...		
f.	Scrap value of old machine...		
g.	Interest expense on new machine...		
h.	Interest expense on old machine...		
i.	Book value of old machine...		
j.	Maintenance cost of new machine...		
k.	Repairs and maintenance costs of old machine...		
l.	Installation costs of new machine...		
m.	Installation costs of old machine...		
n.	Salary of company's CEO...		
o.	Accumulated depreciation on old machine........		

E8-16A Special order decisions given two scenarios *(Learning Objective 2)*

Suppose the Baseball Hall of Fame in Cooperstown, New York, has approached Sports-Cardz with a special order. The Hall of Fame wants to purchase 50,000 baseball card packs for a special promotional campaign and offers $0.40 per pack, a total of $20,000. Sports-Cardz's total production cost is $0.60 per pack, as follows:

Variable costs:	
Direct materials	$0.14
Direct labor	0.08
Variable overhead..	0.13
Fixed overhead..	0.25
Total cost..	$0.60

Sports-Cardz has enough excess capacity to handle the special order.

Requirements

1. Prepare an incremental analysis to determine whether Sports-Cardz should accept the special sales order assuming fixed costs would not be affected by the special order.

2. Now assume that the Hall of Fame wants special hologram baseball cards. Sports-Cardz must spend $5,000 to develop this hologram, which will be useless after the special order is completed. Should Sports-Cardz accept the special order under these circumstances? Show your analysis.

E8-17A Special order decision and considerations (*Learning Objective 2*)

Maui Jane Sunglasses sell for about $150 per pair. Suppose the company incurs the following average costs per pair:

Direct materials	$40
Direct labor	12
Variable manufacturing overhead	8
Variable marketing expenses	4
Fixed manufacturing overhead	20*
Total costs	$84

$$* \frac{\$2,000,000 \text{ total fixed manufacturing overhead}}{100,000 \text{ pairs of sunglasses}}$$

Maui Jane has enough idle capacity to accept a one-time-only special order from LensCrafters for 20,000 pairs of sunglasses at $76 per pair. Maui Jane will not incur any variable marketing expenses for the order.

Requirements

1. How would accepting the order affect Maui Jane's operating income? In addition to the special order's effect on profits, what other (longer-term qualitative) factors should Maui Jane's managers consider in deciding whether to accept the order?

2. Maui Jane's marketing manager, Jim Revo, argues against accepting the special order because the offer price of $76 is less than Maui Jane's $84 cost to make the sunglasses. Revo asks you, as one of Maui Jane's staff accountants, to write a memo explaining whether his analysis is correct.

E8-18A Pricing decisions given two scenarios (*Learning Objective 3*)

Bennett Builders builds 1,500-square-foot starter tract homes in the fast-growing suburbs of Atlanta. Land and labor are cheap, and competition among developers is fierce. The homes are "cookie-cutter," with any upgrades added by the buyer after the sale. Bennett Builders' costs per developed sublot are as follows:

Land	$ 50,000
Construction	$125,000
Landscaping	$ 5,000
Variable marketing costs	$ 2,000

Bennett Builders would like to earn a profit of 15% of the variable cost of each home sale. Similar homes offered by competing builders sell for $200,000 each.

Requirements

1. Which approach to pricing should Bennett Builders emphasize? Why?

2. Will Bennett Builders be able to achieve its target profit levels? Show your computations.

3. Bathrooms and kitchens are typically the most important selling features of a home. Bennett Builders could differentiate the homes by upgrading bathrooms and kitchens. The upgrades would cost $20,000 per home but would enable Bennett Builders to increase the selling prices by $35,000 per home (in general, kitchen and bathroom upgrades typically add at least 150% of their cost to the value of any home). If Bennett Builders upgrades, what will the new cost-plus price per home be? Should the company differentiate its product in this manner? Show your analysis.

E8-19A   Decide whether to drop a product line *(Learning Objective 4)*

Top managers of Video Avenue are alarmed by their operating losses. They are considering dropping the DVD product line. Company accountants have prepared the following analysis to help make this decision:

	Total	Blu-ray Discs	DVDs
Sales revenue	$420,000	$300,000	$120,000
Variable expenses	230,000	150,000	80,000
Contribution margin	190,000	150,000	40,000
Fixed expenses:			
Manufacturing	125,000	70,000	55,000
Marketing and administrative	70,000	55,000	15,000
Total fixed expenses	195,000	125,000	70,000
Operating income (loss)	$ (5,000)	$ 25,000	$(30,000)

Total fixed costs will not change if the company stops selling DVDs.

Requirements

1. Prepare an incremental analysis to show whether Video Avenue should drop the DVD product line. Will dropping DVDs add $30,000 to operating income? Explain.

2. Assume that Video Avenue can avoid $30,000 of fixed expenses by dropping the DVD product line (these costs are direct fixed costs of the DVD product line). Prepare an incremental analysis to show whether Video Avenue should stop selling DVDs.

3. Now, assume that all $70,000 of fixed costs assigned to DVDs are direct fixed costs and can be avoided if the company stops selling DVDs. However, marketing has concluded that Blu-ray disc sales would be adversely affected by discontinuing the DVD line (retailers want to buy both from the same supplier). Blu-ray disc production and sales would decline 10%. What should the company do?

E8-20A   Dropping a product line *(Learning Objective 4)*

Suppose Kellogg's is considering dropping its Special-K product line. Assume that during the past year, Special-K's product line income statement showed the following:

Sales	$7,600,000
Cost of goods sold	6,400,000
Gross profit	1,200,000
Operating expenses	1,400,000
Operating loss	$ (200,000)

Fixed manufacturing overhead costs account for 40% of the cost of goods, while only 30% of the operating expenses are fixed. Since the Special-K line is only one of Kellogg's breakfast cereals, only $750,000 of direct fixed costs (the majority of which is advertising) will be eliminated if the product line is discontinued. The remainder of the fixed costs will still be incurred by Kellogg's. If the company decides to drop the product line, what will happen to the company's operating income? Should Kellogg's drop the product line?

E8-21A Identify constraint, then determine product mix *(Learning Objective 5)*

Lifemaster produces two types of exercise treadmills: Regular and Deluxe. The exercise craze is such that Lifemaster could use all of its available machine hours producing either model. The two models are processed through the same Production Department.

	Per Unit	
	Deluxe	**Regular**
Sale price...	$1,000	$ 550
Costs:		
Direct materials	$ 290	$ 100
Direct labor	80	180
Variable manufacturing overhead...........................	240	80
Fixed manufacturing overhead*..............................	120	40
Variable operating expenses...................................	115	65
Total cost	845	465
Operating income..	$ 155	$ 85

*Allocated on the basis of machine hours.

What product mix will maximize operating income? (*Hint:* Use the allocation of fixed manufacturing overhead to determine the proportion of machine hours used by each product.)

E8-22A Determine product mix for retailer *(Learning Objective 5)*

Vivace sells both designer and moderately priced fashion accessories. Top management is deciding which product line to emphasize. Accountants have provided the following data:

	Per Item	
	Designer	**Moderately Priced**
Average sale price...	$200	$84
Average variable expenses.................................	85	24
Average fixed expenses (allocated)	20	10
Average operating income..................................	$ 95	$50

The Vivace store in Reno, Nevada, has 10,000 square feet of floor space. If Vivace emphasizes moderately priced goods, it can display 650 items in the store. If Vivace emphasizes designer wear, it can display only 300 designer items to create more of a boutique-like atmosphere. These numbers are also the average monthly sales in units.

Prepare an analysis to show which product to emphasize.

E8-23A Determine product mix for retailer—two stocking scenarios *(Learning Objective 5)*

Each morning, Max Imery stocks the drink case at Max's Beach Hut in Myrtle Beach, South Carolina. Max's Beach Hut has 100 linear feet of refrigerated display space for cold drinks. Each linear foot can hold either six 12-ounce cans or four 20-ounce plastic or glass bottles. Max's Beach Hut sells three types of cold drinks:

1. Coca-Cola in 12-oz. cans for $1.50 per can

2. A&W Root Beer in 20-oz. plastic bottles for $1.75 per bottle

3. Mountain Dew in 20-oz. glass bottles for $2.20 per bottle

Max's Beach Hut pays its suppliers the following:

1. $0.25 per 12-oz. can of Coca-Cola

2. $0.40 per 20-oz. bottle of A&W Root Beer

3. $0.75 per 20-oz. bottle of Mountain Dew

Max's Beach Hut's monthly fixed expenses include the following:

Hut rental	$ 375
Refrigerator rental	75
Max's salary	1,550
Total fixed expenses	$2,000

Max's Beach Hut can sell all drinks stocked in the display case each morning.

Requirements

1. What is Max's Beach Hut's constraining factor? What should Max stock to maximize profits? What is the maximum contribution margin he could generate from refrigerated drinks each day?

2. To provide variety to customers, suppose Max refuses to devote more than 60 linear feet and no less than 10 linear feet to any individual product. Under this condition, how many linear feet of each drink should Max stock? How many units of each product will be available for sale each day?

3. Assuming the product mix calculated in Requirement 2, what contribution margin will Max generate from refrigerated drinks each day?

E8-24A Make-or-buy product component *(Learning Objective 6)*

Fiber Systems manufactures an optical switch that it uses in its final product. Fiber Systems incurred the following manufacturing costs when it produced 70,000 units last year:

Direct materials	$ 630,000
Direct labor	105,000
Variable overhead	140,000
Fixed overhead	455,000
Total manufacturing cost for 70,000 units	$1,330,000

Fiber Systems does not yet know how many switches it will need this year; however, another company has offered to sell Fiber Systems the switch for $14 per unit. If Fiber Systems buys the switch from the outside supplier, the manufacturing facilities that will be idle cannot be used for any other purpose, yet none of the fixed costs are avoidable.

Requirements

1. Given the same cost structure, should Fiber Systems make or buy the switch? Show your analysis.

2. Now, assume that Fiber Systems can avoid $100,000 of fixed costs a year by outsourcing production. In addition, because sales are increasing, Fiber Systems needs 75,000 switches a year rather than 70,000. What should Fiber Systems do now?

3. Given the last scenario, what is the most Fiber Systems would be willing to pay to outsource the switches?

E8-25A Make-or-buy with alternative use of facilities *(Learning Objective 6)*

Refer to E8-24A. Fiber Systems needs 80,000 optical switches next year (assume same relevant range). By outsourcing them, Fiber Systems can use its idle facilities to manufacture another product that will contribute $220,000 to operating income, but none of the fixed costs will be avoidable. Should Fiber Systems make or buy the switches? Show your analysis.

E8-26A Determine maximum outsourcing price *(Learning Objective 6)*

DefTone's sales have increased; as a result, the company needs 400,000 jewel-case liners rather than 250,000. DefTone has enough existing capacity to make all of the liners it needs. In addition, due to volume discounts, its variable costs of making each liner will decline to $0.28 per liner. Assume that by outsourcing, DefTone can reduce its current fixed costs ($50,000) by $10,000. There is no alternative use for the factory space freed through outsourcing, so it will just remain idle. What is the maximum DefTone will pay to outsource production of its CD liners?

E8-27A Sell as is or process further (Learning Objective 7)

Dairymaid processes organic milk into plain yogurt. Dairymaid sells plain yogurt to hospitals, nursing homes, and restaurants in bulk, one-gallon containers. Each batch, processed at a cost of $800, yields 500 gallons of plain yogurt. Dairymaid sells the one-gallon tubs for $6.00 each and spends $0.10 for each plastic tub. Dairymaid has recently begun to reconsider its strategy. Dairymaid wonders if it would be more profitable to sell individual-sized portions of fruited organic yogurt at local food stores. Dairymaid could further process each batch of plain yogurt into 10,667 individual portions (3/4 cup each) of fruited yogurt. A recent market analysis indicates that demand for the product exists. Dairymaid would sell each individual portion for $0.50. Packaging would cost $0.08 per portion, and fruit would cost $0.10 per portion. Fixed costs would not change. Should Dairymaid continue to sell only the gallon-sized plain yogurt (sell as is) or convert the plain yogurt into individual-sized portions of fruited yogurt (process further)? Why?

Exercises—Group B

E8-28B Determine relevant and irrelevant information (Learning Objective 1)

Joe Roberts, production manager for Fabricut, invested in computer-controlled production machinery last year. He purchased the machinery from Advanced Design at a cost of $2 million. A representative from Advanced Design recently contacted Joe because the company has designed an even more efficient piece of machinery. The new design would double the production output of the year-old machinery but cost Fabricut another $3 million. The old machinery was installed by an engineering firm; the same firm will be required to install the new machinery. Fixed selling costs would not increase if the new machinery were to be purchased, but variable selling costs would increase. Fabricut paid off the notes payable it used to pay for the machinery last year. If Fabricut purchases the new machinery, it will sign a new notes payable. Maintenance costs for the new machinery would be the same as for the current machinery. If Fabricut purchases the new machinery, it can trade in the old machinery; Advanced Design will credit Fabricut's account for the trade-in value.

In the following chart, indicate whether each of the costs described would be relevant or not to Fabricut's decision about whether to purchase the new machinery or to keep using the older machinery.

	Item	Relevant	Not Relevant
a.	Cost of new machinery		
b.	Cost of old machinery		
c.	Book value of old machinery		
d.	Maintenance cost of new machinery		
e.	Maintenance cost of old machinery		
f.	Trade-in value of old machinery		
g.	Interest expense on new machinery		
h.	Interest expense on old machinery		
i.	Added profits from increase in production from new machinery		
j.	Fixed selling costs		
k.	Variable selling costs		
l.	Accumulated depreciation on old machinery		
m.	Installation costs of new machinery		
n.	Installation costs of old machinery		
o.	Salary of company's CEO		

E8-29B Special order decisions given two scenarios *(Learning Objective 2)*

Suppose the Baseball Hall of Fame in Cooperstown, New York, has approached Star-Cardz with a special order. The Hall of Fame wishes to purchase 54,000 baseball card packs for a special promotional campaign and offers $0.38 per pack, a total of $20,520. Star-Cardz's total production cost is $0.58 per pack, as follows:

Variable costs:	
Direct materials	$0.11
Direct labor	0.07
Variable overhead	0.10
Fixed overhead	0.30
Total cost	$0.58

Star-Cardz has enough excess capacity to handle the special order.

Requirements

1. Prepare an incremental analysis to determine whether Star-Cardz should accept the special sales order assuming fixed costs would not be affected by the special order.

2. Now assume that the Hall of Fame wants special hologram baseball cards. Star-Cardz will spend $5,300 to develop this hologram, which will be useless after the special order is completed. Should Star-Cardz accept the special order under these circumstances? Show your analysis.

E8-30B Special order decision and considerations *(Learning Objective 2)*

Maui Juda Sunglasses sell for about $154 per pair. Suppose the company incurs the following average costs per pair:

Direct materials	$38
Direct labor	10
Variable manufacturing overhead	8
Variable marketing expenses	2
Fixed manufacturing overhead	16*
Total costs	$74

*$2,200,000 total fixed manufacturing overhead / 137,500 pairs of sunglasses

Maui Juda has enough idle capacity to accept a one-time-only special order from LA Glasses for 19,000 pairs of sunglasses at $49 per pair. Maui Juda will not incur any variable marketing expenses for the order.

Requirements

1. How would accepting the order affect Maui Juda's operating income? In addition to the special order's effect on profits, what other (longer-term, qualitative) factors should Maui Juda's managers consider in deciding whether to accept the order?

2. Maui Juda's marketing manager, Jim Revo, argues against accepting the special order because the offer price of $49 is less than Maui Juda's $74 cost to make the sunglasses. Revo asks you, as one of Maui Juda's staff accountants, to explain whether his analysis is correct.

E8-31B Pricing decisions given two scenarios *(Learning Objective 3)*

Rouse Builders builds 1,500-square-foot starter tract homes in the fast-growing suburbs of Hartford. Land and labor are cheap, and competition among developers is fierce. The homes are "cookie-cutter," with any upgrades added by the buyer after the sale. Rouse Builders' costs per developed sublot are as follows:

Land	$ 51,000
Construction	$123,000
Landscaping	$ 6,000
Variable marketing costs	$ 1,000

Rouse Builders would like to earn a profit of 16% of the variable cost of each home sale. Similar homes offered by competing builders sell for $201,000 each.

Requirements

1. Which approach to pricing should Rouse Builders emphasize? Why?

2. Will Rouse Builders be able to achieve its target profit levels? Show your computations.

3. Bathrooms and kitchens are typically the most important selling features of a home. Rouse Builders could differentiate the homes by upgrading bathrooms and kitchens. The upgrades would cost $16,000 per home but would enable Rouse Builders to increase the selling prices by $28,000 per home (in general, kitchen and bathroom upgrades typically add at least 150% of their cost to the value of any home.) If Rouse Builders upgrades, what will the new cost-plus price per home be? Should the company differentiate its product in this manner? Show your analysis.

E8-32B Decide whether to drop a product line *(Learning Objective 4)*

Top managers of NY Video are alarmed by their operating losses. They are considering dropping the DVD product line. Company accountants have prepared the following analysis to help make this decision:

	Total	Blu-ray Discs	DVDs
Sales revenue	$428,000	$308,000	$120,000
Variable expenses	238,000	150,000	88,000
Contribution margin	190,000	158,000	32,000
Fixed expenses:			
Manufacturing	133,000	76,000	57,000
Marketing and administrative	65,000	54,000	11,000
Total fixed expenses	198,000	130,000	68,000
Operating income (loss)	$ (8,000)	$ 28,000	$ (36,000)

Total fixed costs will not change if the company stops selling DVDs.

Requirements

1. Prepare an incremental analysis to show whether NY Video should drop the DVD product line. Will dropping the DVDs add $36,000 to operating income? Explain.

2. Assume that NY Video can avoid $36,000 of fixed expenses by dropping the DVD product line (these costs are direct fixed costs of the DVD product line). Prepare an incremental analysis to show whether NY Video should stop selling DVDs.

3. Now, assume that all $68,000 of fixed costs assigned to DVDs are direct fixed costs and can be avoided if the company stops selling DVDs. However, marketing has concluded that Blu-ray disc sales would be adversely affected by discontinuing the DVD line (retailers want to buy both from the same supplier). Blu-ray disc production and sales would decline 10%. What should the company do?

E8-33B Dropping a product line (Learning Objective 4)

Suppose Crispy Pop's is considering dropping its Special Oats product line. Assume that during the past year, Special Oats' product line income statement showed the following:

Sales	$7,400,000
Cost of goods sold	6,150,000
Gross profit	1,250,000
Operating expenses	1,350,000
Operating loss	$ (100,000)

Fixed manufacturing overhead costs account for 40% of the cost of goods, while only 30% of the operating expenses are fixed. Since the Special Oats line is only one of Crispy Pop's breakfast cereals, only $730,000 of direct fixed costs (the majority of which is advertising) will be eliminated if the product line is discontinued. The remainder of the fixed costs will still be incurred by Crispy Pop's. If the company decides to drop the product line, what will happen to the company's operating income? Should Crispy Pop's drop the product line?

E8-34B Identify constraint, then determine product mix (Learning Objective 5)

FitTime produces two types of exercise treadmills: Regular and Deluxe. The exercise craze is such that FitTime could use all of its available machine hours producing either model. The two models are processed through the same Production Department.

	Per Unit	
	Deluxe	Regular
Sale price	$ 990	$ 560
Costs:		
Direct materials	$ 290	$ 100
Direct labor	86	188
Variable manufacturing overhead	172	86
Fixed manufacturing overhead*	80	40
Variable operating expenses	115	61
Total cost	743	475
Operating income	$ 247	$ 85

*Allocated on the basis of machine hours.

What product mix will maximize operating income? (*Hint:* Use the allocation of fixed manufacturing overhead to determine the proportion of machine hours used by each product.)

E8-35B Determine product mix for retailer (Learning Objective 5)

Juda sells both designer and moderately priced fashion accessories. Top management is deciding which product line to emphasize. Accountants have provided the following data:

	Per Item	
	Designer	Moderately Priced
Average sale price	$205	$78
Average variable expenses	80	27
Average fixed expenses (allocated)	15	5
Average operating income	$110	$46

The Juda store in Orlando, Florida, has 14,000 square feet of floor space. If Juda emphasizes moderately priced goods, it can display 840 items in the store. If Juda emphasizes designer wear, it can display only 560 designer items to create more of a boutique-like atmosphere. These numbers also are the average monthly sales in units. Prepare an analysis to show which product to emphasize.

E8-36B Determine product mix for retailer—two stocking scenarios (*Learning Objective 5*)

Each morning, Murry Cole stocks the drink case at Murry's Beach Hut in Charlotte, North Carolina. Murry's Beach Hut has 105 linear feet of refrigerated display space for cold drinks. Each linear foot can hold either five 12-ounce cans or four 20-ounce plastic or glass bottles. Murry's Beach Hut sells three types of cold drinks:

1. Grand-Cola in 12-oz. cans, for $1.50 per can

2. Fizzle Pop in 20-oz. plastic bottles, for $1.75 per bottle

3. Value-Soda in 20-oz. glass bottles, for $2.30 per bottle

Murry's Beach Hut pays its suppliers the following:

1. $0.25 per 12-oz. can of Grand-Cola

2. $0.40 per 20-oz. bottle of Fizzle Pop

3. $0.80 per 20-oz. bottle of Value-Soda

Murry's Beach Hut's monthly fixed expenses include the following:

Hut rental	$ 365
Refrigerator rental	65
Murry's salary	1,750
Total fixed expenses	$2,180

Murry's Beach Hut can sell all the drinks stocked in the display case each morning.

Requirements

1. What is Murry's Beach Hut's constraining factor? What should Murry stock to maximize profits? What is the maximum contribution margin he could generate from refrigerated drinks each day?

2. To provide variety to customers, suppose Murry refuses to devote more than 60 linear feet and no less than 5 linear feet to any individual product. Under this condition, how many linear feet of each drink should Murry stock? How many units of each product will be available for sale each day?

3. Assuming the product mix calculated in Requirement 2, what contribution margin will Murry generate from refrigerated drinks each day?

E8-37B Make-or-buy product component (*Learning Objective 6*)

Tech Systems manufactures an optical switch that it uses in its final product. Tech Systems incurred the following manufacturing costs when it produced 68,000 units last year:

Direct materials	$ 680,000
Direct labor	136,000
Variable overhead	68,000
Fixed overhead	374,000
Manufacturing cost for 68,000 units	$1,258,000

Tech Systems does not yet know how many switches it will need this year; however, another company has offered to sell Tech Systems the switch for $11.00 per unit. If Tech Systems buys the switch from the outside supplier, the manufacturing facilities that will be idle cannot be used for any other purpose, yet none of the fixed costs are avoidable.

Requirements

1. Given the same cost structure, should Tech Systems make or buy the switch? Show your analysis.

2. Now, assume that Tech Systems can avoid $100,000 of fixed costs a year by outsourcing production. In addition, because sales are increasing, Tech Systems needs 73,000 switches a year rather than 68,000. What should Tech Systems do now?

3. Given the last scenario, what is the most Tech Systems would be willing to pay to outsource the switches?

E8-38B Make-or-buy with alternative use of facilities *(Learning Objective 6)*

Refer to E8-37B. Tech Systems needs 80,000 optical switches next year (assume same relevant range). By outsourcing them, Tech Systems can use its idle facilities to manufacture another product that will contribute $130,000 to operating income, but none of the fixed costs will be avoidable. Should Tech Systems make or buy the switches? Show your analysis.

			Cost to Make Minus
	Make Unit	Buy Unit	Cost to Buy
Variable cost per unit:			
Direct materials	$10.00	$ —	$ 10.00
Direct labor	2.00	—	2.00
Variable overhead........................	1.00	—	1.00
Purchase price from outsider.......	—	11.00	(11.00)
Variable cost per unit...................	$13.00	$11.00	$ 2.00

Tech Systems
Incremental Analysis for Outsourcing Decision

E8-39B Determine maximum outsourcing price *(Learning Objective 6)*

CoolTone's sales have increased; as a result, the company needs 430,000 jewel-case liners rather than 280,000. CoolTone has enough existing capacity to make all of the liners it needs. In addition, due to volume discounts, its variable costs of making each liner will decline to $0.26 per liner. Assume that by outsourcing, CoolTone can reduce its current fixed costs ($58,800) by $8,600. There is no alternative use for the factory space freed through outsourcing, so it will just remain idle. What is the maximum CoolTone will pay to outsource production of its CD liners?

E8-40B Sell as is or process further *(Learning Objective 7)*

Organicplus processes organic milk into plain yogurt. Organicplus sells plain yogurt to hospitals, nursing homes, and restaurants in bulk, one-gallon containers. Each batch, processed at a cost of $810, yields 550 gallons of plain yogurt. Organicplus sells the one-gallon tubs for $8.00 each, and spends $0.12 for each plastic tub. Organicplus has recently begun to reconsider its strategy. Organicplus wonders if it would be more profitable to sell individual-sized portions of fruited organic yogurt at local food stores. Organicplus could further process each batch of plain yogurt into 11,733 individual portions (3/4 cup each) of fruited yogurt. A recent market analysis indicates that demand for the product exists. Organicplus would sell each individual portion for $0.50. Packaging would cost $0.05 per portion, and fruit would cost $0.10 per portion. Fixed costs would not change. Should Organicplus continue to sell only the gallon-sized plain yogurt (sell as is) or convert the plain yogurt into individual-sized portions of fruited yogurt (process further)? Why?

Problems—Group A

P8-41A Special order decision and considerations *(Learning Objective 2)*

Buoy manufactures flotation vests in Tampa, Florida. Buoy's contribution margin income statement for the most recent month contains the following data:

Sales in units	31,000
Sales revenue	$434,000
Variable expenses:	
Manufacturing	$ 93,000
Marketing and administrative	107,000
Total variable expenses	200,000
Contribution margin	234,000
Fixed expenses:	
Manufacturing	126,000
Marketing and administrative	90,000
Total fixed expenses	216,000
Operating income	$ 18,000

Suppose Overton's wants to buy 5,000 vests from Buoy. Acceptance of the order will not increase Buoy's variable marketing and administrative expenses or any of its fixed expenses. The Buoy plant has enough unused capacity to manufacture the additional vests. Overton's has offered $10 per vest, which is below the normal sale price of $14.

Requirements

1. Prepare an incremental analysis to determine whether Buoy should accept this special sales order.

2. Identify long-term factors Buoy should consider in deciding whether to accept the special sales order.

P8-42A Pricing of nursery plants *(Learning Objective 3)*

GreenThumb operates a commercial plant nursery where it propagates plants for garden centers throughout the region. GreenThumb has $5 million in assets. Its yearly fixed costs are $600,000, and the variable costs for the potting soil, container, label, seedling, and labor for each gallon-sized plant total $1.25. GreenThumb's volume is currently 500,000 units. Competitors offer the same quality plants to garden centers for $3.50 each. Garden centers then mark them up to sell to the public for $8 to $10, depending on the type of plant.

Requirements

1. GreenThumb's owners want to earn a 12% return on the company's assets. What is GreenThumb's target full cost?

2. Given GreenThumb's current costs, will its owners be able to achieve their target profit? Show your analysis.

3. Assume that GreenThumb has identified ways to cut its variable costs to $1.10 per unit. What is its new target fixed cost? Will this decrease in variable costs allow the company to achieve its target profit? Show your analysis.

4. GreenThumb started an aggressive advertising campaign strategy to differentiate its plants from those grown by other nurseries. Monrovia Plants made this strategy work, so GreenThumb has decided to try it, too. GreenThumb doesn't expect volume to be affected, but it hopes to gain more control over pricing. If GreenThumb has to spend $100,000 this year to advertise and its variable costs continue to be $1.10 per unit, what will its cost-plus price be? Do you think GreenThumb will be able to sell its plants to garden centers at the cost-plus price? Why or why not?

P8-43A Prepare and use contribution margin statements for dropping a line decision (Learning Objective 4)

Members of the board of directors of Security Systems have received the following operating income data for the year just ended:

	Industrial Systems	Household Systems	Total
	Product Line		
Sales revenue	$300,000	$310,000	$610,000
Cost of goods sold:			
Variable	$ 38,000	$ 42,000	$ 80,000
Fixed	210,000	69,000	279,000
Total cost of goods sold	248,000	111,000	359,000
Gross profit	52,000	199,000	251,000
Marketing and administrative expenses:			
Variable	66,000	71,000	137,000
Fixed	40,000	22,000	62,000
Total marketing and administrative expenses	106,000	93,000	199,000
Operating income (loss)	$ (54,000)	$106,000	$ 52,000

Members of the board are surprised that the industrial systems product line is losing money. They commission a study to determine whether the company should drop the line. Company accountants estimate that dropping industrial systems will decrease fixed cost of goods sold by $80,000 and decrease fixed marketing and administrative expenses by $12,000.

Requirements

1. Prepare an incremental analysis to show whether Security Systems should drop the industrial systems product line.

2. Prepare contribution margin income statements to show Security Systems' total operating income under the two alternatives: (a) with the industrial systems line and (b) without the line. Compare the *difference* between the two alternatives' income numbers to your answer to Requirement 1. What have you learned from this comparison?

P8-44A Product mix decision under constraint (Learning Objective 5)

Brun, located in St. Cloud, Minnesota, produces two lines of electric toothbrushes: Deluxe and Standard. Because Brun can sell all of the toothbrushes it produces, the owners are expanding the plant. They are deciding which product line to emphasize. To make this decision, they assemble the following data:

	Deluxe Toothbrush	Standard Toothbrush
	Per Unit	
Sale price	$80	$48
Variable expenses	20	18
Contribution margin	$60	$30
Contribution margin ratio	75%	62.5%

After expansion, the factory will have a production capacity of 4,500 machine hours per month. The plant can manufacture either 60 Standard electric toothbrushes or 24 Deluxe electric toothbrushes per machine hour.

Requirements

1. Identify the constraining factor for Brun.

2. Prepare an analysis to show which product line to emphasize.

P8-45A Outsourcing decision given alternative use of capacity *(Learning Objective 6)*

X-Perience manufactures snowboards. Its cost of making 1,800 bindings is as follows:

Direct materials	$17,520
Direct labor	3,100
Variable manufacturing overhead	2,080
Fixed manufacturing overhead	6,800
Total manufacturing costs	$29,500
Cost per pair ($29,500 ÷ 1,800)	$ 16.39 (rounded)

Suppose O'Brien will sell bindings to X-Perience for $14 each. X-Perience will pay $1.00 per unit to transport the bindings to its manufacturing plant, where it will add its own logo at a cost of $0.20 per binding.

Requirements

1. X-Perience's accountants predict that purchasing the bindings from O'Brien will enable the company to avoid $2,200 of fixed overhead. Prepare an analysis to show whether X-Perience should make or buy the bindings.

2. The facilities freed by purchasing bindings from O'Brien can be used to manufacture another product that will contribute $3,100 to profit. Total fixed costs will be the same as if X-Perience had produced the bindings. Show which alternative makes the best use of X-Perience's facilities: (a) make bindings, (b) buy bindings and leave facilities idle, or (c) buy bindings and make another product.

P8-46A Sell or process further decisions *(Learning Objective 7)*

Vision Chemical has spent $240,000 to refine 72,000 gallons of acetone, which can be sold for $2.16 a gallon. Alternatively, Vision Chemical can process the acetone further. This processing will yield a total of 60,000 gallons of lacquer thinner that can be sold for $3.20 a gallon. The additional processing will cost $0.62 per gallon of lacquer thinner. To sell the lacquer thinner, Vision Chemical must pay shipping of $0.22 a gallon and administrative expenses of $0.10 a gallon on the thinner.

Requirements

1. Diagram Vision's decision, using Exhibit 8-23 as a guide.

2. Identify the sunk cost. Is the sunk cost relevant to Vision's decision? Why or why not?

3. Should Vision sell the acetone or process it into lacquer thinner? Show the expected net revenue difference between the two alternatives.

Problems–Group B

P8-47B Special order decision and considerations *(Learning Objective 2)*

Deep Blue manufactures flotation vests in Charleston, South Carolina. Deep Blue's contribution margin income statement for the most recent month contains the following data:

Sales in units	31,000
Sales revenue	$434,000
Variable expenses:	
Manufacturing	$186,000
Marketing and administrative	110,000
Total variable expenses	296,000
Contribution margin	138,000
Fixed expenses:	
Manufacturing	130,000
Marketing and administrative	92,000
Total fixed expenses	222,000
Operating income (loss)	$ (84,000)

Suppose Boats-n-More wishes to buy 4,600 vests from Deep Blue. Acceptance of the order will not increase Deep Blue's variable marketing and administrative expenses. The Deep Blue plant has enough unused capacity to manufacture the additional vests. Boats-n-More has offered $5 per vest, which is below the normal sale price of $14.

Requirements

1. Prepare an incremental analysis to determine whether Deep Blue should accept this special sales order.

2. Identify long-term factors Deep Blue should consider in deciding whether to accept the special sales order.

P8-48B Pricing of nursery plants *(Learning Objective 3)*

Plant City operates a commercial plant nursery where it propagates plants for garden centers throughout the region. Plant City has $5.25 million in assets. Its yearly fixed costs are $668,500, and the variable costs for the potting soil, container, label, seedling, and labor for each gallon-sized plant total $1.20. Plant City's volume is currently 490,000 units. Competitors offer the same quality plants to garden centers for $3.70 each. Garden centers then mark them up to sell to the public for $8 to $9, depending on the type of plant.

Requirements

1. Plant City's owners want to earn a 12% return on the company's assets. What is Plant City's target full cost?

2. Given Plant City's current costs, will its owners be able to achieve their target profit? Show your analysis.

3. Assume that Plant City has identified ways to cut its variable costs to $1.05 per unit. What is its new target fixed cost? Will this decrease in variable costs allow the company to achieve its target profit? Show your analysis.

4. Plant City started an aggressive advertising campaign strategy to differentiate its plants from those grown by other nurseries. Monrovia Plants made this strategy work so Plant City has decided to try it, too. Plant City doesn't expect volume to be affected, but it hopes to gain more control over pricing. If Plant City has to spend $53,900 this year to advertise and its variable costs continue to be $1.05 per unit, what will its cost-plus price be? Do you think Plant City will be able to sell its plants to garden centers at the cost-plus price? Why or why not?

P8-49B Prepare and use contribution margin statements for dropping a line decision (*Learning Objective 4*)

Members of the board of directors of Security Force have received the following operating income data for the year just ended:

	Product Line		
	Industrial Systems	Household Systems	Total
Sales revenue...	$360,000	$370,000	$730,000
Cost of goods sold:			
Variable..	$ 35,000	$ 42,000	$ 77,000
Fixed	260,000	66,000	326,000
Total cost of goods sold.......................	295,000	108,000	403,000
Gross profit...	65,000	262,000	327,000
Marketing and administrative expenses:			
Variable	66,000	71,000	137,000
Fixed..	42,000	22,000	64,000
Total marketing and administrative expenses................	108,000	93,000	201,000
Operating income (loss)	$ (43,000)	$169,000	$126,000

Members of the board are surprised that the industrial systems product line is losing money. They commission a study to determine whether the company should drop the line. Company accountants estimate that dropping industrial systems will decrease fixed cost of goods sold by $82,000 and decrease fixed marketing and administrative expenses by $15,000.

Requirements

1. Prepare an incremental analysis to show whether Security Force should drop the industrial systems product line.

2. Prepare contribution margin income statements to show Security Force's total operating income under the two alternatives: (a) with the industrial systems line and (b) without the line. Compare the *difference* between the two alternatives' income numbers to your answer to Requirement 1. What have you learned from this comparison?

P8-50B Product mix decision under constraint (*Learning Objective 5*)

Brinn located in Ann Arbor, Michigan, produces two lines of electric toothbrushes: Deluxe and Standard. Because Brinn can sell all the toothbrushes it can produce, the owners are expanding the plant. They are deciding which product line to emphasize. To make this decision, they assemble the following data:

	Per Unit	
	Deluxe Toothbrush	Regular Toothbrush
Sale price...	$98	$50
Variable expenses...	19	16
Contribution margin	79	34
Contribution margin ratio......................................	80.6%	68%

After expansion, the factory will have a production capacity of 4,200 machine hours per month. The plant can manufacture either 55 Standard electric toothbrushes or 25 Deluxe electric toothbrushes per machine hour.

Requirements

1. Identify the constraining factor for Brinn.

2. Prepare an analysis to show which product line to emphasize.

P8-51B Outsourcing decision given alternative use of capacity *(Learning Objective 6)*

Winter Sports manufactures snowboards. Its cost of making 23,600 bindings is as follows:

Direct materials..	$ 24,000
Direct labor..	82,000
Variable manufacturing overhead	48,000
Fixed manufacturing overhead...	82,000
Total manufacturing costs..	$236,000
Cost per pair ($236,000 / 23,600)...	$ 10.00

Suppose Monroe will sell bindings to Winter Sports for $11 each. Winter Sports would pay $2.00 per unit to transport the bindings to its manufacturing plant, where it would add its own logo at a cost $0.50 of per binding.

Requirements

1. Winter Sports' accountants predict that purchasing the bindings from Monroe will enable the company to avoid $10,000 of fixed overhead. Prepare an analysis to show whether Winter Sports should make or buy the bindings.

2. The facilities freed by purchasing bindings from Monroe can be used to manufacture another product that will contribute $25,000 to profit. Total fixed costs will be the same as if Winter Sports had produced the bindings. Show which alternative makes the best use of Winter Sports' facilities: (a) make bindings, (b) buy bindings and leave facilities idle, or (c) buy bindings and make another product.

P8-52B Sell or process further decisions *(Learning Objective 7)*

Preston Chemical has spent $243,000 to refine 73,000 gallons of acetone, which can be sold for $2.00 a gallon. Alternatively, Preston Chemical can process the acetone further. This processing will yield a total of 58,000 gallons of lacquer thinner that can be sold for $3.30 a gallon. The additional processing will cost $0.40 per gallon of lacquer thinner. To sell the lacquer thinner, Preston Chemical must pay shipping of $0.24 a gallon and administrative expenses of $0.14 a gallon on the thinner.

Requirements

1. Fill in the diagram for Preston's decision.

2. Identify the sunk cost. Is the sunk cost relevant to Preston's decision? Why or why not?

3. Should Preston sell the acetone or process it into lacquer thinner? Show the expected net revenue difference between the two alternatives.

APPLY YOUR KNOWLEDGE

Decision Case

C8-53 Outsourcing e-mail *(Learning Objective 6)*

BKFin.com provides banks access to sophisticated financial information and analysis systems via the Web. The company combines these tools with benchmarking data access, including e-mail and wireless communications, so that banks can instantly evaluate individual loan applications and entire loan portfolios.

BKFin.com's CEO, Jon Wise, is happy with the company's growth. To better focus on client service, Wise is considering outsourcing some functions. CFO Jenny Lee suggests that the company's e-mail may be the place to start. She recently attended a conference and learned that companies such as Continental Airlines, DellNet, GTE, and NBC were outsourcing their e-mail function. Wise asks Lee to identify costs related to BKFin.com's in-house Microsoft Exchange e-mail application, which has 2,300 mailboxes. This information follows:

Variable costs:	
E-mail license...	$7 per mailbox per month
Virus protection license...	$1 per mailbox per month
Other variable costs...	$8 per mailbox per month
Fixed costs:	
Computer hardware costs.......................................	$94,300 per month
$8,050 monthly salary for two information technology staff members who work only on e-mail..	$16,100 per month

Requirements

1. Compute the *total cost* per mailbox per month of BKFin.com's current e-mail function.

2. Suppose Mail.com, a leading provider of Internet messaging outsourcing services, offers to host BKFin.com's e-mail function for $9 per mailbox per month. If BKFin.com outsources its e-mail to Mail.com, BKFin.com will still need the virus protection software; its computer hardware; and one information technology staff member who would be responsible for maintaining virus protection, quarantining suspicious e-mail, and managing content (e.g., screening e-mail for objectionable content). Should CEO Wise accept Mail.com's offer? Why or why not?

3. Suppose for an additional $5 per mailbox per month, Mail.com will also provide virus protection, quarantine, and content-management services. Outsourcing these additional functions would mean that BKFin.com would not need an e-mail information technology staff member or the separate virus protection license. Should CEO Wise outsource these extra services to Mail.com? Why or why not?

Ethical Issue

I8-54   **Outsourcing and ethics** *(Learning Objective 6)*

Mary Tan is the controller for Duck Associates, a property management company in Portland, Oregon. Each year, Tan and payroll clerk Toby Stock meet with the external auditors about payroll accounting. This year, the auditors suggest that Tan consider outsourcing Duck Associates' payroll accounting to a company specializing in payroll processing services. This would allow Tan and her staff to focus on their primary responsibility: accounting for the properties under management. At present, payroll requires 1.5 employee positions—payroll clerk Toby Stock and a bookkeeper who spends half her time entering payroll data in the system.

Tan considers this suggestion, and she lists the following items relating to outsourcing payroll accounting:

a. The current payroll software that was purchased for $4,000 three years ago would not be needed if payroll processing were outsourced.

b. Duck Associates' bookkeeper would spend half her time preparing the weekly payroll input form that is given to the payroll processing service. She is paid $450 a week.

c. Duck Associates would no longer need payroll clerk Toby Stock, whose annual salary is $42,000.

d. The payroll processing service would charge $2,000 a month.

Requirements

1. Would outsourcing the payroll function increase or decrease Duck Associates' operating income?

2. Tan believes that outsourcing payroll would simplify her job, but she does not like the prospect of having to lay off Stock, who has become a close personal friend. She does not believe there is another position available for Stock at his current salary. Can you think of other factors that might support keeping Stock rather than outsourcing payroll processing? How should each of the factors affect Tan's decision if she wants to do what is best for Duck Associates and act ethically?

Team Project

T8-55   Relevant information to outsourcing decision (*Learning Objective 6*)

John Menard is the founder and sole owner of Menards. Analysts have estimated that his chain of home improvement stores scattered around nine midwestern states generate about $3 billion in annual sales. But how can Menards compete with giant Home Depot?

Suppose Menard is trying to decide whether to invest $45 million in a state-of-the-art manufacturing plant in Eau Claire, Wisconsin. Menard expects the plant would operate for 15 years, after which it would have no residual value. The plant would produce Menards's own line of Formica countertops, cabinets, and picnic tables.

Suppose Menards would incur the following unit costs in producing its own product lines:

	Per Unit		
	Countertops	Cabinets	Picnic Tables
Direct materials..	$15	$10	$25
Direct labor..	10	5	15
Variable manufacturing overhead	5	2	6

Rather than Menard making these products, assume that he can buy them from outside suppliers. Suppliers would charge Menards $40 per countertop, $25 per cabinet, and $65 per picnic table.

Whether Menard makes or buys these products, assume that he expects the following annual sales:

- Countertops—487,200 at $130 each
- Picnic tables—100,000 at $225 each
- Cabinets—150,000 at $75 each

If "making" is sufficiently more profitable than outsourcing, Menard will build the new plant. John Menard has asked your consulting group for a recommendation. Menard uses the straight-line depreciation method.

Requirements

1. Are the following items relevant or irrelevant in Menard's decision to build a new plant that will manufacture his own products?
    a. The unit sale prices of the countertops, cabinets, and picnic tables (the sale prices that Menards charges its customers)
    b. The prices that outside suppliers would charge Menards for the three products if Menards decides to outsource the products rather than make them
    c. The $45 million to build the new plant
    d. The direct materials, direct labor, and variable overhead that Menards would incur to manufacture the three product lines
    e. Menard's salary

2. Determine whether Menards should make or outsource the countertops, cabinets, and picnic tables *assuming that the company has already built the plant and, therefore, has the manufacturing capacity to produce these products*. In other words, what is the annual difference in cash flows if Menards decides to make rather than outsource each of these three products?

3. Write a memo giving your recommendation to Menard. The memo should clearly state your recommendation and briefly summarize the reasons for your recommendation.

Discussion & Analysis

1. A beverage company is considering whether to drop its line of grape soda. What factors will affect the company's decision? What is a qualitative factor? Which of the factors you listed are qualitative?

2. What factors would be relevant to a restaurant that is considering whether to make its own dinner rolls or to purchase dinner rolls from a local bakery?

3. How would outsourcing change a company's cost structure? How might this change in cost structure help or harm a company's competitive position?

4. What is an opportunity cost? List possible opportunity costs associated with a make-or-buy decision.

5. What undesirable result can arise from allocating common fixed costs to product lines?

6. Why could a manager be justified in ignoring fixed costs when making a decision about a special order? When would fixed costs be relevant when making a decision about a special order?

7. What is the difference between segment margin and contribution margin? When would each be used?

8. Do joint costs affect a sell or process further decision? Why or why not?

9. How can "make-or-buy" concepts be applied to decisions at a service organization? What types of "make-or-buy" decisions might a service organization face?

10. Oscar Company builds outdoor furniture using a variety of woods and plastics. What is a constraint? List at least four possible constraints at Oscar Company.

Quick Check Answers

1. *b* 2. *d* 3. *a* 4. *c* 5. *b* 6. *d* 7. *d* 8. *a* 9. *b* 10. *c*

For online homework, exercises, and problems that provide you with immediate feedback, please visit www.myaccountinglab.com.

Application & Analysis

8-1 Outsourcing Decision at a Real Company

Go to the New York Times Web site (http://www.nytimes.com/) or to USA Today (http://www.usatoday.com/) and search for the term "outsource." Find an article about a company making a decision to outsource a part of its business operations.

Basic Discussion Questions

1. Describe the company that is making the decision to outsource. What area of the business is the company either looking to outsource or did it already outsource?

2. Why did the company decide to outsource (or is considering outsourcing)?

3. List the revenues and costs that might be impacted by this outsourcing decision. The article will not list many, if any, of these revenues and costs; you should make reasonable guesses about what revenues and/or costs would be associated with the business operation being outsourced.

4. List the qualitative factors that could influence the company's decision whether to outsource this business operation or not. Again, you need to make reasonable guesses about the qualitative factors that might influence the company's decision to outsource or not.

Classroom Applications

Web: Post the discussion questions on an electronic discussion board. Have small groups of students choose a news article for their groups. Each student should read the article for the product for his or her group.

Classroom: Form groups of 3–4 students. Your group should choose a news article as described. After reading the article, prepare a five-minute presentation about your group's company and its outsourcing decision which addresses the listed questions.

Independent: Research answers to each of the questions. Turn in a 2–3 page typed paper (12 point font, double-spaced with 1" margins). Include references, including the URL for the article that you referenced.

For additional Application & Analysis projects and implementation tips, see the Instructor Resources in MyAccountingLab.com.

CMA-1. Breegle Company produces three products (B-40, J-60, and H-102) from a single process. Breegle uses the physical volume method to allocate joint costs of $22,500 per batch to the products. Based on the following information, which product(s) should Breegle continue to process after the splitoff point in order to maximize profit?

	B-40	J-60	H-102
Physical units produced per batch	1,500	2,000	3,200
Sales value per unit a splitoff	$10.00	$4.00	$7.25
Cost per unit of further processing after splitoff	3.05	1.00	2.50
Sales value per unit after further processing	12.25	5.70	9.75

a. B-40 only.
b. J-60 only.
c. H-102 only.
d. B-40 and H-102 only.

(CMA Adapted)

Campbell Soup Company's goal is "to win in both the

marketplace and the workplace with integrity as the world's most extraordinary food company." How will the company attain this goal? First, it identifies key strategies. Some of Campbell's key strategies include expanding its icon brands (such as Campbell's Soup, V8 Juice, and Pepperidge Farms Snacks), increasing margins through improving productivity, and advancing its commitment to organizational excellence and social responsibility. These strategies require detailed plans be put into place. The company's managers express these plans, in financial terms, through budgets. The company's budgets reflect and support each of these key strategies. For example, management has budgeted millions of dollars toward researching new products in order to expand its icon brands. Management has also budgeted millions of dollars towards new, more productive manufacturing equipment and an ERP information system that should improve profit margins and increase organizational excellence. Is the company on track for reaching its goal of winning in both the marketplace and the workplace? For the past three years, Campbell's return to shareowners has exceeded the Standard & Poor's 500 Stock Index. And for the last two years, Gallup has recognized Campbell as one of the "Best Places to Work" in America. The company's budget is a vital tool in making it all happen.

Source: Campbell Soup Company, 2008 Annual Report

CHAPTER 9

The Master Budget and Responsibility Accounting

Learning Objectives

1 Describe how and why managers use budgets

2 Prepare the operating budgets

3 Prepare the financial budgets

4 Describe the four types of responsibility centers and prepare performance reports

5 Prepare a merchandiser's Cost of Goods Sold, Inventory, and Purchases Budget (Appendix)

Budgeting is perhaps the most widely used management accounting tool employed by companies, organizations, and governments throughout the world. Even individuals, such as you and I, can benefit from creating a personal budget that shows how we plan to use our resources and to make sure our spending does not get out of control. For example, if your goal is to buy a house five years after graduating from college, then you need to plan for that goal. Your budget for each of the next five years would include saving enough money each year to accumulate the down payment you'll need for the house. By carefully planning how you'll spend and save your resources, you'll have a better chance of reaching your goals.

How and Why do Managers Use Budgets?

As you'll see throughout this chapter, management uses budgeting to express its plans and to assess how well it's reaching its goals. In this section, we'll take a closer look at how budgets are used and developed, the benefits of budgeting, and the particular budgets that are prepared as part of the company's master budget.

How are Budgets Used?

All companies and organizations use budgets for the same reasons you would in your personal life—to plan for the future and control the revenues and expenses related to those plans. Exhibit 9-1 shows how managers use budgets in fulfilling their major responsibilities of planning, directing, and controlling operations. Budgeting is an on-going cycle: Company strategies lead to detailed plans, which in turn lead to actions. Results are then compared to the budget to provide managers feedback. This feedback allows managers to take corrective actions and if necessary, revise strategies, which starts the cycle over.

EXHIBIT 9-1 **Managers Use Budgets to Plan and Control Business Activities**

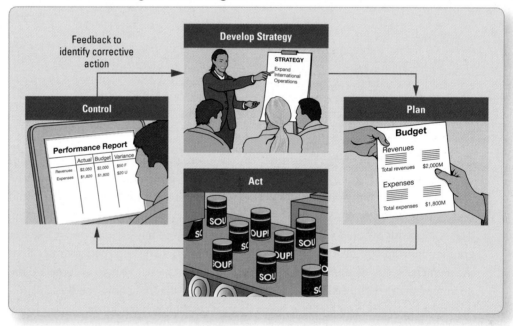

How are Budgets Developed?

A few years ago Campbell was not performing up to expectations. The first step toward getting the company back on track was management's decision to create long-term strategic goals. **Strategic planning** involves setting long-term goals that may extend 5–10 years into the future. Long-term, loosely-detailed budgets are often created to reflect expectations for these long-term goals.

Once the goals are set, management designs key strategies for attaining the goals. These strategies, such as Campbell's expansion of its icon brands and improvements to production efficiency, are then put into place through the use of shorter-term budgets for an entire fiscal year. However, even a yearly budget is not detailed enough to guide many management decisions. For example, Campbell's soup production managers must know what month of the year they expect to receive and start using new production machinery. They must also decide how much of each raw material (vegetables, chicken, and so forth) to purchase each month to meet production requirements for both existing and new products. In turn, this will affect monthly cash needs. Therefore, companies usually prepare a budget for every month of the fiscal year.

Many companies set aside time during the last two quarters of the fiscal year to create their budget for the upcoming fiscal year. Other companies prepare rolling, or continuous budgets. A **rolling budget** is a budget that is continuously updated so that the next 12 months of operations are always budgeted. For example, as soon as January is over, the next January is added to the budget. The benefit of a rolling budget is that managers always have a budget for the next 12 months.

Who is Involved in the Budgeting Process?

Rather than using a "top-down" approach in which top management determines the budget, most companies use some degree of participative budgeting. As the term implies, **participative budgeting** involves the participation of many levels of management. Participative budgeting is beneficial because

- lower level managers are closer to the action, and should have a more detailed knowledge for creating realistic budgets.

- managers are more likely to accept, and be motivated by budgets they helped to create.

However, participative budgeting also has disadvantages:

- The budget process can become much more complex and time consuming as more people participate in the process.

- Managers may intentionally build **slack** into the budget for their area of operation by overbudgeting expenses or underbudgeting revenue. Why would they do this? They would do so for three possible reasons: 1) because of uncertainty about the future, 2) to make their performance look better when actual results are compared against budgeted amounts at the end of the period, and 3) to have the resources they need in the event of budget cuts.

Even with participative budgeting, someone must still have the "final say" on the budget. Often, companies use a **budget committee** to review the submitted budgets, remove unwarranted slack, and revise and approve the final budget. The budget committee often includes upper management, such as the CEO and CFO, as well as managers from every area of the value chain (such as Research and Development, Marketing, Distribution, and so forth). By using a cross-functional budget committee, the final budget is more likely to reflect a comprehensive view of the organization and be accepted by managers than if the budget were prepared by one person or department for the entire organization. The budget committee is often supported by full-time staff personnel devoted to updating and analyzing the budgets.

What is the Starting Point for Developing the Budgets?

Many companies use the prior year's budgeted figures, or actual results, as the *starting point* for creating the budget for the coming year. Of course, those figures will then be modified to reflect

- new products, customers, or geographical areas;

- changes in the marketplace caused by competitors;

- changes in labor contracts, raw material, and fuel costs;

- general inflation;

- and any new strategies.

However, this approach to budgeting may cause year-after-year increases that after time, grow out of control. To prevent perpetual increases in budgeted expenses, many companies intermittently use zero-based budgeting. When a company implements **zero-based budgeting**, all managers begin with a budget of zero and must justify *every dollar* they put in the budget. This budgeting approach is very time-consuming and labor intensive. Therefore, companies only use it from time to time in order to keep their expenses in check.

What are the Benefits of Budgeting?

Exhibit 9-2 summarizes three key benefits of budgeting. Budgeting forces managers to plan, promotes coordination and communication, and provides a benchmark for motivating employees and evaluating actual performance.

EXHIBIT 9-2 Benefits of Budgeting

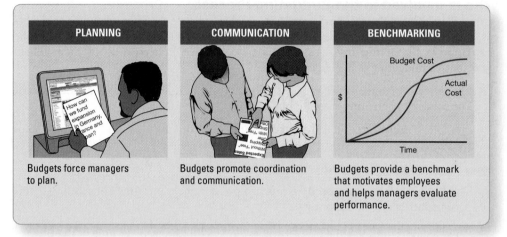

Planning

Business managers are extremely busy directing the day-to-day operations of the company. The budgeting process forces managers to spend time planning for the future, rather than only concerning themselves with daily operations. The sooner companies develop a plan and have time to act on the plan, the more likely they will achieve their goals.

Coordination and Communication

The budget coordinates a company's activities. It forces managers to consider relations among operations across the entire value chain. For example, Campbell's decision to expand its icon brands will first affect the research and development function. However, once new products are developed, the design and production teams will need to focus on how and where the products will be mass produced. The marketing team will need to develop attractive labeling and create a successful advertising campaign. The distribution team may need to alter its current distribution system to accommodate the new products. And customer service will need to be ready to handle any complaints or warranty issues. All areas of the value chain are ultimately affected by management's plans. The budget process helps to communicate and coordinate the effects of the plan.

Benchmarking

Budgets provide a benchmark that motivates employees and helps managers evaluate performance. The budget provides a target that most managers will try to achieve, especially if they participated in the budgeting process and the budget has been set at a realistic level. Budgets should be achievable with effort. Budgets that are too "tight" (too hard to achieve) or too "loose" (too easy to achieve) do not provide managers with much motivation.

Think about exams for a moment. Some professors have a reputation for giving "impossible" exams while others may be known for giving "easy" exams. In either of these cases, students are rarely motivated to put much effort into learning the material because they feel they won't be rewarded for their additional efforts. However, if students feel that a professor's exam can be achieved with effort, they will be more likely to devote themselves to learning the material. In other words, the perceived "fairness" of the exam affects how well the exam motivates students to study. Likewise, if a budget is perceived to be "fair," employees are likely to be motivated by it.

Budgets also provide a benchmark for evaluating performance. At the end of the period, companies use performance reports, such as the one pictured in Exhibit 9-3, to compare "actual" revenues and expenses against "budgeted" revenues and expenses. The

variance, or difference between actual and budgeted figures, is used to evaluate how well the manager controlled operations and to determine whether the plan needs to be revised. The second half of this chapter delves more deeply into this aspect of budgeting.

EXHIBIT 9-3 **Summary Performance Report**

	Actual	Budget	Variance (Actual – Budget)
Sales revenue	$550	$600	$(50)
Less: Total expenses	90	68	(22)
Net income	$460	$532	$(72)

What is the Master Budget?

The **master budget** is the comprehensive planning document for the entire organization. It consists of all of the supporting budgets needed to create the company's budgeted financial statements. Exhibit 9-4 shows all of the components of the master budget for a manufacturer, and the order in which they are usually prepared. The master budgets of service and merchandising firms are less complex, and are described in Appendix 9A.

EXHIBIT 9-4 **Master Budget for a Manufacturing Company**

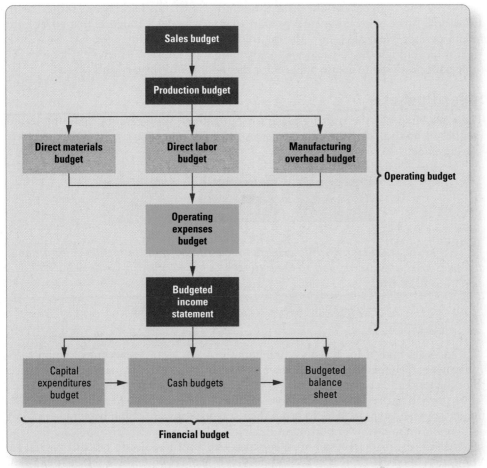

The **operating budgets** are the budgets needed to run the daily operations of the company. The operating budgets culminate in a budgeted income statement. As Exhibit 9-4 shows, the starting point of the operating budgets is the sales budget because it affects most other components of the master budget. After estimating sales, manufacturers prepare the production budget, which determines how many units need to be produced. Once production volume is established, managers prepare the budgets determining the amounts of direct materials, direct labor, and manufacturing overhead that will be needed to meet production. Next, managers prepare the operating expenses budget. After all of these budgets are prepared, management will be able to prepare the budgeted income statement.

As you'll see throughout the chapter, cost behavior will be important in forming most of the operating budgets. Total fixed costs will not change as volume changes within the relevant range. However, total variable costs will fluctuate as volume fluctuates.

The **financial budgets** project the collection and payment of cash, as well as forecast the company's budgeted balance sheet. The capital expenditure budget shows the company's plan for purchasing property, plant, and equipment. The cash budget projects the cash that will be available to run the company's operations and determines whether the company will have extra funds to invest or whether the company will need to borrow cash. Finally, the budgeted balance sheet forecasts the company's position at the end of the budget period.

How are the Operating Budgets Prepared?

| 2 | Prepare the operating budgets |

We will be following the budget process for Tucson Tortilla, a fairly small, independently owned manufacturer of tortilla chips. The company sells its product, by the case, to restaurants, grocery stores, and convenience stores. To keep our example simple, we will just show the budgets for the first three months of the fiscal year, rather than all 12 months. Since many companies prepare quarterly budgets (budgets that cover a three-month period), we'll also show the quarterly figures on each budget. For every budget, we'll walk through the calculations for the month of January. Then we'll show how the same pattern is used to create budgets for the months of February and March.

Sales Budget

The sales budget is the starting place for budgeting. Managers multiply the expected number of unit sales by the expected sales price per unit to arrive at the expected total sales revenue.

For example, Tucson Tortilla expects to sell 30,000 cases of tortilla chips in January, at a sales price of $20 per case, so the estimated sales revenue for January is as follows:

$$30,000 \text{ cases} \times \$20 \text{ per case} = \$600,000$$

The sales budget for the first three months of the year is shown in Exhibit 9-5. As you can see, the monthly sales volume is expected to fluctuate. January sales are expected to be higher than February sales due to the extraordinary number of chips purchased for Super Bowl™ parties. Also, since more tortillas chips are sold when the weather warms up, the company expects sales to begin their seasonal upward climb beginning in March.

As shown in the lower portion of Exhibit 9-5, managers may also indicate the type of sale that will be made. Tucson Tortilla expects 20% of its sales to be cash (COD) sales. Companies often use **COD** ("collect on delivery"[1]) collection terms if the customer is new, has a poor credit rating, or has not paid on time in the past. Tucson Tortilla will still sell to these customers, but will demand payment immediately when the inventory is delivered.

---

[1]In the past, COD meant "cash on delivery." However, as other forms of payment (such as checks, credit cards, and debit cards) have become more common, the word "cash" has been replaced with the word "collect" to incorporate these additional types of payments.

EXHIBIT 9-5 Sales Budget

Tucson Tortilla Sales Budget For the Quarter Ended March 31				
	Month			
	January	**February**	**March**	**1st Quarter**
Unit sales (cases)	30,000	20,000	25,000	75,000
Unit selling price	× $ 20	× $ 20	× $ 20	× $ 20
Total sales revenue	$600,000	$400,000	$500,000	$1,500,000
Type of Sale:				
Cash sales (20%)	$120,000	$ 80,000	$100,000	$ 300,000
Credit sales (80%)	480,000	320,000	400,000	1,200,000
Total sales revenue	$600,000	$400,000	$500,000	$1,500,000

The remaining 80% of sales will be made on credit. Tucson Tortilla's credit terms are "net 30," meaning the customer has up to 30 days to pay for its purchases. Having this information available on the sales budget will help managers prepare the cash collections budget later.

Production Budget

Once managers have estimated how many units they expect to sell, they can figure out how many units they need to produce. Most manufacturers maintain some ending finished goods inventory, or **safety stock**, which is inventory kept on hand in case demand is higher than predicted, or the problems in the factory slow production (such as machine breakdown, employees out sick, and so forth). As a result, managers need to factor in the desired level of ending inventory when deciding how much inventory to produce. They do so as follows:

> ### Why is this important?
> "The sales budget is the basis for every other budget. If sales are not projected as accurately as possible, all other budgets will be off target."

Let's walk through this calculation step-by-step:

- First, managers figure out how many total units they need. To do this, they add the number of units they plan to sell to the number of units they want on hand at the end of the month. *Let's assume Tucson Tortilla wants to maintain an ending inventory equal to 10% of the next month's expected sales (20,000 cases in February). Thus, the total number of cases needed in January is as follows:*

> 30,000 cases for January sales + (10% × 20,000) = 32,000 total cases needed

- Next, managers calculate the amount of inventory they expect to have on hand at the beginning of the month. *Since Tucson Tortilla desires ending inventory to be 10% of the next month's sales, managers expect to have 10% of January's sales on hand on December 31, which becomes the beginning balance on January 1st:*

> 10% × 30,000 cases = 3,000 cases in beginning inventory on January 1

▧ Finally, by subtracting what the company already has in stock at the beginning of the month from the total units needed, the company is able to calculate how many units to produce:

> 32,000 cases needed – 3,000 cases in beginning inventory = 29,000 cases to produce

Exhibit 9-6 shows Tucson Tortilla's Production Budget for the first three months of the year. As the red arrows show, the ending inventory from one month (January 31) always becomes the beginning inventory for the next month (February 1).

EXHIBIT 9-6 **Production Budget**

Tucson Tortilla
Production Budget
For the Quarter Ended March 31

	Month			
	January	February	March	1st Quarter
Unit sales (from Sales Budget)	30,000 ×10% 20,000 ×10% 25,000			75,000
Plus: Desired end inventory	2,000	2,500	3,200* →	3,200**
Total needed	32,000	22,500	28,200	78,200
Less: Beginning inventory	(3,000)	(2,000)	(2,500)	(3,000)**
Units to produce	29,000	20,500	25,700	75,200

* April sales are projected to be 32,000 units.
** Since the quarter begins January 1 and ends March 31, the beginning inventory for the quarter is the balance on January 1 and the ending inventory for the quarter is the balance on March 31.

Now that the company knows how many units it plans to produce every month, it can figure out the amount of direct materials, direct labor, and manufacturing overhead that will be needed. As shown in the following sections, the company will create separate budgets for each of these three manufacturing costs. Each budget will be driven by the number of units to be produced each month.

Direct Materials Budget

The format of the direct materials budget is quite similar to the production budget:

Let's walk through the process using January as an example:

▧ First, the company figures out the quantity of direct materials (DM) needed for production. *Let's assume Tucson Tortilla's only direct material is masa harina, the special corn flour used to make tortilla chips. Each case of tortilla chips requires 5 pounds of this corn flour. Therefore, the quantity of direct materials needed for January production is as follows:*

> 29,000 cases to be produced × 5 pounds per case = 145,000 pounds

■ Next, the company adds in the desired ending inventory of direct materials. Some amount of direct materials safety stock is usually needed in case suppliers do not deliver all of the direct materials needed on time. *Let's assume that Tucson Tortilla wants to maintain an ending inventory of direct materials equal to 10% of the materials needed for next month's production (102,500 required in February, as shown in Exhibit 9-7):*

$$145,000 \text{ pounds} + (10\% \times 102,500) = 155,250 \text{ total pounds needed}$$

■ Next, managers determine the direct material inventory they expect to have on hand at the beginning of the month. *Tucson Tortilla expects to have 10% of the materials needed for January's production in stock on December 31, which becomes the opening balance on January 1:*

$$10\% \times 145,000 \text{ pounds} = 14,500 \text{ pounds in beginning inventory}$$

Finally, by subtracting what the company already has in stock at the beginning of the month from the total quantity needed, the company is able to calculate the quantity of direct materials they need to purchase:

$$155,250 \text{ pounds needed} - 14,500 \text{ pounds in beginning inventory} = 140,750 \text{ pounds to buy}$$

■ Finally, the company calculates the expected cost of purchasing those direct materials. *Let's say Tucson Tortilla can buy the Masa Harina corn flour in bulk for $1.50 per pound.*

$$140,750 \text{ pounds} \times \$1.50 = \$211,125$$

Exhibit 9-7 shows Tucson Tortilla's direct materials budget for the first three months of the year.

EXHIBIT 9-7 **Direct Materials Budget**

Tucson Tortilla
Direct Materials Budget for Masa Harina Corn Flour
For the Quarter Ended March 31

	Month			
	January	February	March	1st Quarter
Unit to be produced (from Production Budget)	29,000	20,500	25,700	75,200
× Quantity (pounds) of DM needed per unit	× 5 lbs	× 5 lbs	× 5 lbs	× 5 lbs
Quantity (pounds) needed for production	145,000	102,500	128,500	376,000
Plus: Desired end inventory of DM	10,250	12,850	16,150*	16,150**
Total quantity (pounds) needed	155,250	115,350	144,650	392,150
Less: Beginning inventory of DM	(14,500)	(10,250)	(12,850)	(14,500)**
Quantity (pounds) to purchase	140,750	105,100	131,800	377,650
× Cost per pound	× $1.50	× $1.50	× $1.50	× $1.50
Total cost of DM purchases	$211,125	$157,650	$197,700	$566,475

* 161,500 pounds are needed for production in April.
** Since the quarter begins January 1 and ends March 31, the beginning inventory for the quarter is the balance on January 1 and the ending inventory for the quarter is the balance on March 31.

Direct Labor Budget

The direct labor (DL) budget is determined as follows:

Tucson Tortilla's factory is fairly automated, so very little direct labor is required. *Let's assume that each case requires only 0.05 of an hour. Direct laborers are paid $22 per hour. Thus, the direct labor cost for January is projected to be as follows:*

> 29,000 cases × 0.05 hours per case = 1,450 hours required × $22 per hour = $31,900

The Direct Labor budget for the first three months of the year is shown in Exhibit 9-8:

EXHIBIT 9-8   Direct Labor Budget

Tucson Tortilla
Direct Labor Budget
For the Quarter Ended March 31

	Month			
	January	February	March	1st Quarter
Units to be produced (from Production Budget)	29,000	20,500	25,700	75,200
× Direct labor hours per unit	× 0.05	× 0.05	× 0.05	× 0.05
Total hours required	1,450	1,025	1,285	3,760
× Direct labor cost per hour	× $ 22	× $ 22	× $ 22	× $ 22
Total Direct labor cost	$31,900	$22,550	$28,270	$82,720

Manufacturing Overhead Budget

The manufacturing overhead budget is highly dependent on cost behavior. Some overhead costs, such as indirect materials, are variable. For example, Tucson Tortilla considers the oil used for frying the tortilla chips to be an indirect material. Since a portion of the oil is absorbed into the chips, the amount of oil required increases as production volume increases. Thus, the cost is variable. The company also considers salt and cellophane packaging to be variable indirect materials. *Tucson Tortilla expects to spend $1.25 on indirect materials for each case of tortilla chips produced, so January's budget for indirect materials is as follows:*

> 29,000 cases × $1.25 = $36,250 of indirect materials

Costs such as utilities and indirect labor are mixed costs. Mixed costs are usually separated into their variable and fixed components using one of the cost behavior estimation methods already discussed in Chapter 6. *Based on engineering and cost studies, Tucson Tortilla has determined that each case of chips requires $0.75 of variable indirect labor, and $0.50 of variable utility costs as a result of running the production machinery. These variable costs are budgeted as follows for January:*

> 29,000 cases × $0.75 = $21,750 of variable indirect labor
> 29,000 cases × $0.50 = $14,500 of variable factory utilities

Finally, many manufacturing overhead costs are fixed. *Tucson Tortilla's fixed costs include depreciation, insurance, and property taxes on the factory. The company also incurs some fixed indirect labor (salaried production engineers that oversee the daily manufacturing operation) and a fixed amount of utilities just to keep the lights, heat, or air conditioning on in the plant regardless of the production volume.*

Exhibit 9-9 shows that the manufacturing overhead budget usually has separate sections for variable and fixed overhead costs so that managers can easily see which costs will change as production volume changes.

EXHIBIT 9-9 **Manufacturing Overhead Budget**

	Month			
	January	February	March	1st Quarter
Units to be Produced (from Production Budget)	29,000	20,500	25,700	75,200
Variable Costs:				
Indirect materials ($1.25 per case)	$ 36,250	$25,625	$32,125	$ 94,000
Indirect labor—variable portion ($0.75 per case)	21,750	15,375	19,275	56,400
Utilities—variable portion ($0.50 per case)	14,500	10,250	12,850	37,600
Total variable MOH	$ 72,500	$51,250	$64,250	$188,000
Fixed MOH Costs:				
Depreciation on factory and production equipment	$ 10,000	$10,000	$10,000	$ 30,000
Insurance and property taxes on the factory	3,000	3,000	3,000	9,000
Indirect labor—fixed portion	15,000	15,000	15,000	45,000
Utilities—fixed portion	2,000	2,000	2,000	6,000
Total fixed MOH	$ 30,000	$30,000	$30,000	$ 90,000
Total manufacturing overhead	$102,500	$81,250	$94,250	$278,000

Table title: Tucson Tortilla — Manufacturing Overhead Budget — For the Quarter Ended March 31

Now that we have completed budgets for each of the three manufacturing costs (direct materials, direct labor, and manufacturing overhead), we turn our attention to operating expenses.

Operating Expenses Budget

Recall that all costs incurred in every area of the value chain, except production, must be expensed as operating expenses in the period incurred. Thus all research and development, design, marketing, distribution, and customer service costs will be shown on the operating expenses budget.

Some operating expenses are variable, based on how many units will be *sold* (not produced). *For example, to motivate its sales force to generate sales, Tucson Tortilla pays its sales representatives a $1.50 sales commission for every case they sell.*

30,000 sales units × $1.50 = $45,000 sales commission expense in January

The company also incurs $2.00 of shipping costs on every case sold.

30,000 sales units × $2.00 = $60,000 shipping expense in January

Finally, the company knows that not all of the sales made on credit will eventually be collected. Based on experience, Tucson Tortilla expects monthly bad debt expense to be

1% of its credit sales. Since January credit sales are expected to be $480,000 (from Sales Budget, Exhibit 9-5), the company's bad debt expense for January is as follows:

$480,000 of credit sales in January × 1% = $4,800 bad debt expense for January

Other operating expenses are fixed: They will stay the same each month even though sales volume fluctuates. *For example, Tucson Tortilla's fixed expenses include salaries, office rent, depreciation on office equipment and the company's vehicles, advertising, telephone, and internet service.*

As shown in Exhibit 9-10, operating expenses are usually shown according to their cost behavior.

EXHIBIT 9-10 Operating Expenses Budget

Tucson Tortilla
Operating Expenses Budget
For the Quarter Ended March 31

	Month			1st Quarter
	January	February	March	
Sales units (from Sales Budget)	30,000	20,000	25,000	75,000
Variable Operating Expenses:				
Sales commissions expense ($1.50 per case sold)	$ 45,000	$ 30,000	$ 37,500	$112,500
Shipping expense ($2.00 per case sold)	60,000	40,000	50,000	150,000
Bad debt expense (1% of credit sales)	4,800	3,200	4,000	12,000
Variable operating expenses	$109,800	$ 73,200	$ 91,500	$274,500
Fixed Operating Expenses:				
Salaries	$ 20,000	$ 20,000	$ 20,000	$ 60,000
Office rent	4,000	4,000	4,000	12,000
Depreciation	6,000	6,000	6,000	18,000
Advertising	2,000	2,000	2,000	6,000
Telephone and Internet	1,000	1,000	1,000	3,000
Fixed operating expenses	$ 33,000	$ 33,000	$ 33,000	$ 99,000
Total operating expenses	$142,800	$106,200	$124,500	$373,500

Budgeted Income Statement

A budgeted income statement looks just like a regular income statement, except for the fact that it uses budgeted data. Recall the general format for an income statement:

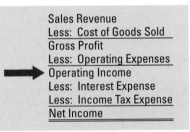

Sales Revenue
Less: Cost of Goods Sold
Gross Profit
Less: Operating Expenses
→ Operating Income
Less: Interest Expense
Less: Income Tax Expense
Net Income

This textbook has focused on a company's operating income, rather than net income. However, a complete income statement would include any interest expense (and/or interest income) as well as a provision for income taxes. These additional costs are subtracted from operating income to arrive at net income.

We have already computed the budgeted sales revenue and operating expenses on separate budgets. But we still need to calculate the Cost of Goods Sold before we can prepare the income statement.

Tucson Tortilla computes its Cost of Goods Sold as follows:

This will be relatively simple for Tucson Tortilla since the company produces only one product.

The cost of manufacturing each case of tortilla chips is shown in Exhibit 9-11. Almost all of the information presented has already been presented and used to prepare the budgets for direct materials, direct labor, and manufacturing overhead. The only new piece of information is the total production volume for the year, budgeted to be 400,000 cases.

Why is this important?

"The budgeted income statement helps managers know in advance whether their plans will result in an acceptable level of income. If not, management will need to consider how it can cut expenses or increase sales revenues."

EXHIBIT 9-11   Budgeted Manufacturing Cost per Unit

Tucson Tortilla
Budgeted Manufacturing Cost per Unit

Direct materials (5 pounds of corn flour per case × $1.50 per pound)	$ 7.50
Direct labor (0.05 hours per case × $22 per hour)	1.10
Manufacturing overhead:	
Variable—indirect materials ($1.25 per case), variable indirect labor	
($0.75 per case), and variable utilities ($0.50 per case)	2.50
Fixed—$30,000 per month × 12 months = $360,000 for the year	
So, the fixed cost per unit is $360,000 ÷ 400,000* cases	.90
Cost of manufacturing each case	$12.00

*Recall that companies base their predetermined MOH rate on the total estimated cost and volume for the *entire year*, rather than on monthly costs and volumes that will fluctuate.

Exhibit 9-12 shows the company's budgeted income statement for January. Interest expense is budgeted to be zero since the company has no outstanding debt. The income tax expense is budgeted to be 35% of income before taxes. The company will prepare budgeted income statements for each month and quarter, as well as for the entire year.

EXHIBIT 9-12   Budgeted Income Statement

Tucson Tortilla
Budgeted Income Statement
For the month ended January 31

Sales (30,000 cases × $20 per case, from Exhibit 9-5)	$ 600,000
Less: Cost of goods sold (30,000 cases × $12.00 per case, from Exhibit 9-11)	(360,000)
Gross profit	240,000
Less: Operating expenses (from Exhibit 9-10)	(142,800)
Operating income	$ 97,200
Less: Interest expense (or add interest income)	0
Less: Income tax expense*	(34,020)
Net income	$ 63,180

*The corporate income tax rate for most companies is currently 35% of income before tax ($97,200 × 35% = $34,020).

We have now completed the operating budgets for Tucson Tortilla. In the second half of the chapter we'll prepare Tucson Tortilla's financial budgets.

Decision Guidelines

The Master Budget

Let's consider some of the decisions Campbell Soup Company made as it set up its budgeting process.

Decision	Guidelines
What should be the driving force behind the budgeting process?	The company's long-term goals and strategies drive the budgeting of the company's resources.
What are budgets used for?	Managers use budgets to help them fulfill their primary responsibilities: planning, directing, and controlling operations. Managers use feedback from the budgeting process to take corrective actions and, if necessary, revise strategies.
Who should be involved in the budgeting process?	Budgets tend to be more realistic and more motivational if lower level managers, as well as upper level managers, are allowed to participate in the budgeting process. The budgeting process tends to encompass a more comprehensive view when managers from all areas of the value chain participate in the process and serve on the budget committee.
What period of time should the budgets cover?	Long-term, strategic planning often results in forecasts of revenues and expenses 5–10 years into the future. Monthly and yearly budgets provide much more detailed information to aid management's shorter-term decisions.
How tough should the budget be to achieve?	Budgets are more useful for motivating employees and evaluating performance if they can be achieved with effort. Budgets that are too tight (too hard to achieve) or too loose (too easy to achieve) are not as beneficial.
What benefits should a company expect to obtain from developing a budget?	Benefits include the following: • Planning • Coordination and Communication • Benchmarking (used for both motivation and performance evaluation)
What budgets should be included in the master budget?	The *operating budgets* includes all budgets necessary to create a budgeted income statement. For a manufacturer, this includes the following: • Sales Budget • Production Budget • Direct Materials Budget • Direct Labor Budget • Manufacturing Overhead Budget • Operating Expenses Budget • Budgeted Income Statement The operating budgets for merchandising and service companies are less complex (see Appendix 9A). The *financial budgets* include the capital expenditures budget, the cash budgets, and the budgeted balance sheet.

Summary Problem   1

Pillows Unlimited makes decorative throw pillows for home use. The company sells the pillows to home décor retailers for $14 per pillow. Each pillow requires 1.25 yards of fabric, which the company obtains at a cost of $6 per yard. The company would like to maintain an ending stock of fabric equal to 10% of the next month's production requirements. The company would also like to maintain an ending stock of finished pillows equal to 20% of the next month's sales. Sales (in units) are projected to be as follows for the first three months of the year:

January	100,000
February	110,000
March	115,000

Requirements

Prepare the following budgets for the first three months of the year, as well as a summary budget for the quarter

1. Prepare the sales budget, including a separate section that details the type of sales made. For this section, assume that 10% of the company's pillows are cash sales, while the remaining 90% are sold on credit terms.

2. Prepare the production budget. Assume that the company anticipates selling 120,000 units in April.

3. Prepare the direct materials purchases budget. Assume the company needs 150,000 yards of fabric for production in April.

Solutions

Requirement 1

Pillows Unlimited
Sales Budget
For the Quarter ended March 31

	Month			
	January	February	March	1st Quarter
Unit sales	100,000	110,000	115,000	325,000
Unit selling price	× $ 14	× $ 14	× $ 14	× $ 14
Total sales revenue	$1,400,000	$1,540,000	$1,610,000	$4,550,000
Type of Sale:				
Cash sales (10%)	$ 140,000	$ 154,000	$ 161,000	$ 455,000
Credit sales (90%)	1,260,000	1,386,000	1,449,000	4,095,000
Total sales revenue	$1,400,000	$1,540,000	$1,610,000	$4,550,000

Requirement 2

Pillows Unlimited
Production Budget
For the Quarter ended March 31

	Month			
	January	February	March	1st Quarter
Unit sales	100,000	110,000	115,000	325,000
Plus: Desired end inventory (20% of next month's unit sales)	22,000	23,000	24,000	24,000
Total needed	122,000	133,000	139,000	349,000
Less: Beginning inventory	(20,000)*	(22,000)	(23,000)	(20,000)
Units to produce	102,000	111,000	116,000	329,000

*January 1 balance (equal to December 31 balance) is 20% of the projected unit sales in January (100,000).

continued

Requirement 3

		Pillows Unlimited Direct Materials Budget For the Quarter ended March 31		
	Month			
	January	**February**	**March**	**1st Quarter**
Units to be produced (from Production Budget)	102,000	111,000	116,000	329,000
× Quantity (yards) of DM needed per unit	× 1.25	× 1.25	× 1.25	× 1.25
Quantity (yards) needed for production	127,500	138,750	145,000	411,250
Plus: Desired end inventory of DM (10% of the amount needed for next month's production)	13,875	14,500	15,000	15,000
Total quantity (yards) needed	141,375	153,250	160,000	426,250
Less: Beginning inventory of DM	(12,750)*	(13,875)	(14,500)	(12,750)
Quantity (yards) to purchase	128,625	139,375	145,500	413,500
× Cost per pound	× $ 6.00	× $ 6.00	× $ 6.00	× $ 6.00
Total cost of DM purchases	$771,750	$836,250	$873,000	$2,481,000

*January 1 balance (equal to December 31 balance) is 10% of the quantity needed for January's production (127,500).

How are the Financial Budgets Prepared?

3 Prepare the financial budgets

In the first half of the chapter, we prepared Tucson Tortilla's operating budgets, culminating with the company's budgeted income statement. In this part of the chapter we turn our attention to Tucson Tortilla's financial budgets. Managers typically prepare a capital expenditures budget as well as three separate cash budgets:

1. Cash collections (or receipts) budget

2. Cash payments (or disbursements) budget

3. Combined cash budget, complete with financing arrangements

Finally, managers prepare the budgeted balance sheet. Each of these budgets is illustrated next.

Capital Expenditure Budget

The capital expenditure budget shows the company's intentions to invest in new property, plant, or equipment (capital investments).When planned capital investments are significant, this budget must be developed early in the process because the additional investments may affect depreciation expense, interest expense (if funds are borrowed to pay for the investments), or dividend payments (if stock is issued to pay for the investments). Chapter 12 contains a detailed discussion of the capital budgeting process, including the techniques managers use in deciding whether to make additional investments.

Exhibit 9-13 shows Tucson Tortilla's capital expenditure budget for the first three months of the year. *Tucson Tortilla expects to purchase a new piece of production equipment in January. The equipment will cost $125,000. No other capital investments are planned in the first quarter of the year.*

EXHIBIT 9-13   Capital Expenditure Budget

<table>
<tr><th colspan="5">Tucson Tortilla
Capital Expenditure Budget
For the Quarter Ended March 31</th></tr>
<tr><th></th><th colspan="3">Month</th><th></th></tr>
<tr><th></th><th>January</th><th>February</th><th>March</th><th>1st Quarter</th></tr>
<tr><td>New investments in property, plant and equipment</td><td>$125,000</td><td>0</td><td>0</td><td>$125,000</td></tr>
</table>

Cash Collections Budget

The cash collections budget is all about timing: *When* does Tucson Tortilla expect to receive cash from its sales? Of course, Tucson Tortilla will receive cash immediately on its cash (COD) sales. From the Sales Budget (Exhibit 9-5) we see that the company expects the following cash sales in January:

> Cash (COD) sales = $120,000

However, most of the company's sales are made on credit. Recall that Tucson Tortilla's credit terms are "net 30 days," meaning customers have 30 days to pay. Therefore, most customers will wait nearly 30 days (a full month) before paying. However, some companies may be experiencing cash flow difficulties and may not be able to pay Tucson Tortilla on time. Because of this, Tucson Tortilla doesn't expect to receive payment on all of its credit sales the month after the sale.

Based on collection history, Tucson Tortilla expects 85% of its credit sales to be collected in the month after sale, and 14% to be collected two months after the sale. Tucson Tortilla expects that 1% of credit sales will never be collected, and therefore, has recognized a 1% bad debt expense in its operating expenses budget. Furthermore, assume that December credit sales were $500,000 and November credit sales were $480,000.

> Anticipated January Collections of Credit Sales:
> 85% × $500,000 (December credit sales) = $425,000
> 14% × $480,000 (November credit sales) = $ 67,200

Exhibit 9-14 shows Tucson Tortilla's expected cash collections for the first three months of the year:

EXHIBIT 9-14   Cash Collections Budget

<table>
<tr><th colspan="5">Tucson Tortilla
Cash Collections Budget
For the Quarter Ended March 31</th></tr>
<tr><th></th><th colspan="3">Month</th><th></th></tr>
<tr><th></th><th>January</th><th>February</th><th>March</th><th>1st Quarter</th></tr>
<tr><td>Cash sales (from Sales Budget)</td><td>$120,000</td><td>$ 80,000</td><td>$100,000</td><td>$ 300,000</td></tr>
<tr><td>Collections on Credit Sales:</td><td></td><td></td><td></td><td></td></tr>
<tr><td>85% of credit sales made last month</td><td>425,000</td><td>408,000[b]</td><td>272,000[d]</td><td>1,105,000</td></tr>
<tr><td>14% of credit sales made two months ago</td><td>67,200</td><td>70,000[c]</td><td>67,200[e]</td><td>204,400</td></tr>
<tr><td>Total cash collections</td><td>$612,200</td><td>$558,000</td><td>$439,200</td><td>$1,609,400</td></tr>
</table>

[b] 85% × $480,000 (January credit sales, Exhibit 9-5) = $408,000
[c] 14% × $500,000 (December credit sales, Exhibit 9-5) = $70,000
[d] 85% × $320,000 (February credit sales, Exhibit 9-5) = $272,000
[e] 14% × $480,000 (January credit sales, Exhibit 9-5) = $67,200

Cash Payments Budget

The cash payments budget is also about timing: *When* will Tucson Tortilla pay for its direct materials purchases, direct labor costs, manufacturing overhead costs, operating expenses, capital expenditures, and income taxes? Let's tackle each cost, one at a time.

DIRECT MATERIALS PURCHASES   *Tucson Tortilla has been given "net 30 days" payment terms from its suppliers of the corn flour used to make the tortilla chips. Therefore, Tucson Tortilla waits a month before it pays for the direct material purchases shown in the Direct Materials Budget (Exhibit 9-7). So, the company will pay for its December purchases (projected to be $231,845) in January, its January purchases of $211,125 (Exhibit 9-7) in February, its February purchases of $157,650 (Exhibit 9-7) in March, and so forth:*

	January	February	March	1st Quarter
Cash payments for DM purchases	$231,845	$211,125	$157,650	$600,620

DIRECT LABOR   *Tucson Tortilla's factory employees are paid twice a month for the work they perform during the month. Therefore, January's direct labor cost of $31,900 (Exhibit 9-8) will be paid in January, and likewise, for each month.*

	January	February	March	1st Quarter
Cash payments for direct labor	$31,900	$22,550	$28,270	$82,720

MANUFACTURING OVERHEAD   Tucson Tortilla must consider when it pays for its manufacturing overhead costs. *Let's assume that the company pays for all manufacturing overhead costs (other than depreciation), insurance, and property taxes **in the month in which they are incurred.** Depreciation is a non-cash expense, so it never appears on the cash disbursements budget. Insurance and property taxes are typically paid on a semiannual basis. While Tucson Tortilla budgets a cost of $3,000 per month for factory insurance and property tax, it doesn't actually pay these costs on a monthly basis. Rather, Tucson Tortilla prepays its insurance and property tax twice a year, in January and July. The amount of these semiannual payments is calculated as shown:*

$$3,000 \text{ monthly cost} \times 12 \text{ months} = \$36,000 \div 2 = \$18,000 \text{ payments in January and July}$$

So, the cash payments for manufacturing overhead costs are expected to be as follows:

	January	February	March	1st Quarter
Total manufacturing overhead (from Exhibit 9-9)	$102,500	$ 81,250	$ 94,250	$278,000
Less: Depreciation (not a cash expense)	(10,000)	(10,000)	(10,000)	(30,000)
Less: Property tax and insurance (paid twice a year, not monthly)	(3,000)	(3,000)	(3,000)	(9,000)
Plus: Semiannual payments for property taxes and insurance	18,000	0	0	18,000
Cash payments for MOH costs	$107,500	$ 68,250	$ 81,250	$257,000

OPERATING EXPENSES   *Let's assume that the company pays for all operating expenses, except depreciation and bad debt expense, **in the month in which they are incurred.** Both depreciation and bad debt expense are non-cash expenses, so they never appear on the cash payments budget. Bad debt expense simply recognizes the sales revenue that will never be* *collected. Therefore, these non-cash expenses need to be deducted from the total operating expenses to arrive at **cash** payments for operating expenses:*

	January	February	March	1st Quarter
Total operating expenses (from Exhibit 9-10)	$142,800	$106,200	$124,500	$373,500
Less: Depreciation expense	(6,000)	(6,000)	(6,000)	(18,000)
Less: Bad debt expense	(4,800)	(3,200)	(4,000)	(12,000)
Cash payments for operating expenses	$132,000	$ 97,000	$114,500	$343,500

CAPITAL EXPENDITURES The timing of these cash payments have already been scheduled on the Capital Expenditures Budget in Exhibit 9-13.

INCOME TAXES Corporations must make quarterly income tax payments for their estimated income tax liability. For corporations like Tucson Tortilla that have a December 31 fiscal year end, the first income tax payment is not due until April 15. The remaining payments are due June 15, September 15, and December 15. *As a result, Tucson Tortilla will not show any income tax payments in the first quarter of the year.*

DIVIDENDS Like many corporations, Tucson Tortilla pays dividends to its shareholders on a quarterly basis. Tucson Tortilla plans to pay $25,000 in cash dividends in January for the company's earnings in the fourth quarter of the previous year.

Finally, we pull all of these cash payments together onto a single budget, as shown in Exhibit 9-15.

EXHIBIT 9-15 Cash Payments Budget

Tucson Tortilla
Cash Payments Budget
For the Quarter Ended March 31

	Month			
	January	February	March	1st Quarter
Cash payments for direct materials purchases	$231,845	$211,125	$157,650	$ 600,620
Cash payments for direct labor	31,900	22,550	28,270	82,720
Cash payments for manufacturing overhead	107,500	68,250	81,250	257,000
Cash payments for operating expenses	132,000	97,000	114,500	343,500
Cash payments for capital investments	125,000	0	0	125,000
Cash payments for income taxes	0	0	0	0
Cash dividends	25,000	0	0	25,000
Total cash payments	$653,245	$398,925	$381,670	$1,433,840

Combined Cash Budget

The combined cash budget simply merges the budgeted cash collections and cash payments to project the company's ending cash position. Exhibit 9-16 shows the following:

- Budgeted cash collections for the month are added to the beginning cash balance to determine the total cash available.

- Budgeted cash payments are then subtracted to determine the ending cash balance before financing.

- Based on the ending cash balance before financing, the company knows whether it needs to borrow money or whether it has excess funds with which to repay debt or invest.

By looking at Exhibit 9-16, we see that Tucson Tortilla expects to begin the month with $36,100 of cash. However, by the end of the month, it will be short of cash. Therefore, the company's managers must plan for how they will handle this shortage. One strategy would be to delay the purchase of equipment planned for January. Another strategy would be to borrow money. Let's say Tucson Tortilla has prearranged a line of credit that carries an interest rate of prime plus 1%. A **line of credit** is a lending arrangement from a bank in which a company is allowed to borrow money as needed, up to a specified maximum amount, yet only pay interest on the portion that is actually borrowed until it is repaid.

EXHIBIT 9-16   Combined Cash Budget

Tucson Tortilla
Combined Cash Budget
For the Quarter Ended March 31

	Month			1st Quarter
	January	February	March	
Beginning balance of cash	$ 36,100	$ 15,055	$ 153,980	$ 36,100
Cash collections (Exhibit 9-14)	612,200	558,000	439,200	1,609,400
Total cash available	648,300	573,055	593,180	1,645,500
Less: Cash payments (Exhibit 9-15)	(653,245)	(398,925)	(381,670)	(1,433,840)
Ending cash balance before financing	(4,945)	174,130	211,510	211,660
Financing:				
Borrowings	20,000	0	0	20,000
Repayments	0	(20,000)	0	(20,000)
Interest payments	0	(150)	0	(150)
End cash balance	$ 15,055	$ 153,980	$ 211,510	$ 211,510

The line of credit will enable Tucson Tortilla to borrow funds to meet its short-term cash deficiencies. Let's say that Tucson Tortilla wants to maintain an ending cash balance of at least $15,000. By borrowing $20,000 on its line of credit at the end of January, the company will have slightly more ($15,055) than its minimum desired balance.

The cash budget also shows that Tucson Tortilla will be able to repay this borrowing, along with the accrued interest, in February. Assuming Tucson Tortilla borrows the $20,000 for a full month at an interest rate of 9%, February's interest payment would be calculated as follows:

$20,000 loan × 1/12 of the year × 9% interest rate = $150

Why is this important?

"The combined cash budget lets managers know in advance when they will be short on cash and need to borrow money, or when they may have extra funds to invest."

Exhibit 9-16 also shows that Tucson Tortilla expects to have a fairly substantial cash balance at the end of both February and March. The company's managers use the cash budgets to determine when this cash will be needed and to decide how to invest it accordingly. Since the first quarterly income tax payment is due April 15, management will want to invest most of this excess cash in a safe, short term investment, such as a money market fund or short-term certificate of deposit. The company will also need cash in April to pay shareholders a quarterly dividend. Any cash not needed in the short run can be invested in longer-term investments. Managers exercising good cash management should have a plan in place for both cash deficiencies and cash excesses.

Budgeted Balance Sheet

Exhibit 9-17, shows Tucson Tortilla's budgeted balance sheet as of January 31. The company will prepare a budgeted balance sheet for each month of the year.

EXHIBIT 9-17 **Budgeted Balance Sheet**

Tucson Tortilla
Budgeted Balance Sheet
January 31

Assets

Cash (from Cash Budget, Exhibit 9-16)..	$ 15,055	
Accounts receivable, net of allowance[A]..	549,450	
Raw materials inventory (from Direct Materials Budget: 10,250 lbs end inventory × $1.50)	15,375	
Finished goods inventory (from Production Budget: 2,000 cases × $12.00 unit cost)	24,000	
Prepaid property taxes and insurance[B]	15,000	
Total current assets		$ 618,880
Property, plant, and equipment[C]	6,350,000	
Less: Accumulated depreciation[D]..	(1,920,000)	
Property, plant, and equipment, net		4,430,000
Total assets..		$5,048,880

Liabilities and Stockholders' Equity

Accounts payable[E]..	$ 211,125	
Income tax liability (from income statement, Exhibit 9-12).............................	34,020	
Other current liabilities (line of credit) (from Cash Budget, Exhibit 9-16)	20,000	
Total liabilities		$ 265,145
Stockholders' equity[F]...		4,783,735
Total liabilities and owner's equity..		$5,048,880

[A] Accounts Receivable, Net of Allowance

January credit sales (from Sales Budget, Exhibit 9-5)	$480,000
15% of December's credit sales ($500,000) yet to be collected	75,000
Accounts receivable, January 31...	$555,000
Less: Allowance for uncollectible accounts (Assume $750 balance	
prior to additional $4,800 bad debt expense, Exhibit 9-10)...........	(5,550)
Accounts receivable, net of allowance for uncollectible accounts	$549,450

[B] Prepaid Property Tax and Insurance

Semiannual payment made in January (cash payments for	
MOH, p. 492)	$18,000
Less: January cost (MOH Budget, Exhibit 9-9)	3,000
Prepaid property tax and insurance, January 31..................................	$15,000

^{C} **Property, Plant, and Equipment**	
December 31 balance (assumed)..	$6,225,000
Plus: January's investment in new equipment (Capital Expenditure Budget, Exhibit 9-13).........	125,000
Property, plant, and equipment, January 31..	$6,350,000

^{D} **Accumulated Depreciation**	
December 31 balance (assumed)..	$1,904,000
Plus: January's depreciation from Manufacturing Overhead Budget, Exhibit 9-9........................	10,000
Plus: January's depreciation from Operating Expenses Budget, Exhibit 9-10	6,000
Accumulated depreciation, January 31	$1,920,000

^{E} **Accounts Payable**	
January's DM purchases to be paid in February (p. 492 and Exhibit 9-15).................................	211,125
Accounts payable, January 31	$211,125

^{F} **Stockholders' Equity**	
December 31 balance of common stock and retained earnings (assumed)	$4,720,555
Plus: January's net income (Budgeted Income Statement, Exhibit 9-12)	63,180
Stockholders' equity, January 31	$4,783,735

Sensitivity Analysis

The master budget models the company's *planned* activities. Managers try to use the best estimates possible when creating budgets. However, managers do not have a crystal ball for making predictions. Some of the key assumptions (such sales volume) used to create the budgets may turn out to be different than originally predicted. How do managers prepare themselves for potentially different scenarios? They use sensitivity analysis.

As shown in Exhibit 9-18, **sensitivity analysis** is a *what if* technique that asks *what* a result will be *if* a predicted amount is not achieved or *if* an underlying assumption changes. *What if* demand for tortilla chips is less than expected? *What if* shipping costs increase due to increases in gasoline prices? *What if* the cost of the corn flour increases or union workers negotiate a wage increase? *What if* sales are 15% cash and 85% credit, rather than 20% cash and 80% credit? How will any or all of these changes in key assumptions affect Tucson Tortilla's budgeted income and budgeted cash position? Will Tucson Tortilla have to borrow more cash? On the other hand, *what if* sales are greater

EXHIBIT 9-18 **Sensitivity Analysis**

than expected? Management must be prepared to meet the additional demand for its product, or its customers may turn to competing suppliers.

Technology makes it cost effective to perform comprehensive sensitivity analyses. Most companies use computer spreadsheet programs or special budget software to prepare the master budget and all of its components. Managers perform sensitivity analysis by simply changing one or several of the underlying assumptions in the budgets, such as sales quantity, direct material cost, and collection terms. The budget software automatically computes a complete set of revised budgets based on the changes.

Armed with a better understanding of how changes in key assumption will affect the company's bottom line and cash position, today's managers can be prepared to lead the company when business conditions change.

What is Responsibility Accounting?

You've seen how managers set strategic goals and develop plans and budgets that help reach those goals. Let's return to Campbell Soup Company and look more closely at how managers *use* budgets to control operations.

Each manager is responsible for planning and controlling some part of the firm's activities. A **responsibility center** is a part or subunit of an organization whose manager is accountable for specific activities. Lower-level managers are often responsible for budgeting and controlling costs of a single value chain function. For example, one manager is responsible for planning and controlling the *production* of Campbell's soup at the plant, while another is responsible for planning and controlling the *distribution* of the product to customers. Lower-level managers report to higher-level managers, who have broader responsibilities. Managers in charge of production and distribution report to senior managers responsible for profits earned by an entire product line.

Four Types of Responsibility Centers

Responsibility accounting is a system for evaluating the performance of each responsibility center and its manager. Responsibility accounting performance reports compare plans (budgets) with actions (actual results) for each center. Superiors then evaluate how well each manager controlled the operations for which he or she was responsible.

Exhibit 9-19 illustrates four types of responsibility centers. We'll briefly describe each type of responsibility center.

> Describe the four types of responsibility centers and prepare performance reports **4**

> **Why is this important?**
>
> "Responsibility accounting allows upper management to 'divide and conquer.' The company's operations are divided into various responsibility centers and a manager is held responsible for making sure the center is run as effectively and efficiently as possible."

EXHIBIT 9-19 Four Types of Responsibility Centers

Cost Center	Revenue Center	Profit Center	Investment Center
In a **cost center**, such as a manufacturing plant, managers are responsible for costs.	In a **revenue center**, such as the Midwest sales region, managers are responsible for generating sales revenue.	In a **profit center**, such as a line of products, managers are responsible for generating income.	In an **investment center**, such as Campbell's Soup, Sauces and Beverages division, managers are responsible for income and invested capital.

Cost Center

In a **cost center**, managers are accountable for costs only. Manufacturing operations, such as the Campbell's Chicken Noodle Soup manufacturing plant, are cost centers. The plant manager controls costs by ensuring that the entire production process runs efficiently. The plant manager is *not* responsible for generating revenues because he or she is not involved in selling the product. The plant manager is evaluated on his or her ability to control *costs* by comparing actual costs to budgeted costs. All else being equal (for example, holding quality and volume constant), the plant manager is likely to receive a more favorable evaluation when actual costs are less than budgeted costs.

Revenue Center

In a **revenue center**, managers are accountable primarily for revenues. Many times, revenue centers are sales territories, such as Campbell's Soups Midwest and Southeast sales regions. Managers of revenue centers may also be responsible for the costs of their own sales operations. Revenue center performance reports compare actual with budgeted revenues. All else being equal, the manager is likely to receive a more favorable evaluation when actual revenues exceed the budget.

Profit Center

In a **profit center**, managers are accountable for both revenues and costs and, therefore, profits. For example, at the Campbell Soup Company, a (higher-level) manager is responsible for the entire Campbell's soup line of products. This manager is accountable for increasing sales revenue *and* controlling costs to achieve the profit goals for the entire line of soups. Profit center reports include both revenues and expenses to show the profit center's income. Superiors evaluate the manager's performance by comparing actual revenues, expenses, and profits to the budget. All else being equal, the manager is likely to receive a more favorable evaluation when actual profits exceed the budget.

Investment Center

In an **investment center**, managers are accountable for investments, revenues, and costs. Investment centers are generally large divisions of a corporation. For example, the Campbell Soup Company has four different divisions. The "U.S. Soup, Sauces and Beverages" division includes all of Campbell's different soups, Pace Mexican sauces, Prego pasta sauces and V8 Juices. Campbell's "Baking and Snacking" division includes such products as Pepperidge Farms bread and Goldfish snacks. Managers of investment centers are responsible for (1) generating sales, (2) controlling costs, and (3) efficiently managing the division's assets (the company's investment in the division). Investment centers are treated almost as if they were stand-alone companies. Managers have decision-making authority over how the division's assets are used. As a result, managers are held responsible for generating as much income as they can with those assets.

In addition to using performance reports, top management often evaluates investment center managers based on performance measures such as return on investment (ROI), residual income, and Economic Value Added (EVA). Chapter 11 explains how these measures are calculated and used. All else being equal, the manager will receive a more favorable evaluation if the division's actual ROI, residual income, or EVA exceeds the amount budgeted.

Responsibility Accounting Performance Reports

Exhibit 9-20 shows how an organization such as the Campbell Soup Company assigns responsibility.

At the top level, the CEO oversees each of the four divisions. Division managers generally have broad responsibility, including deciding how to use assets to maximize ROI. Most companies consider divisions as *investment centers*.

Each division manager supervises all of the product lines in that division. Exhibit 9-20 shows that the VP of U.S. Soup, Sauces and Beverages oversees the Prego pasta sauces, Pace Mexican sauces, V8 juice and juice drinks, and Campbell's condensed and ready-to-serve soups. Each of these product lines is considered to be a *profit center*. The manager of the Pace Mexican sauces product line is responsible for evaluating lower-level managers of *cost centers* (such as plants that make Pace products) and *revenue centers* (such as managers responsible for selling Pace products).

EXHIBIT 9-20 **Partial Organization Chart**

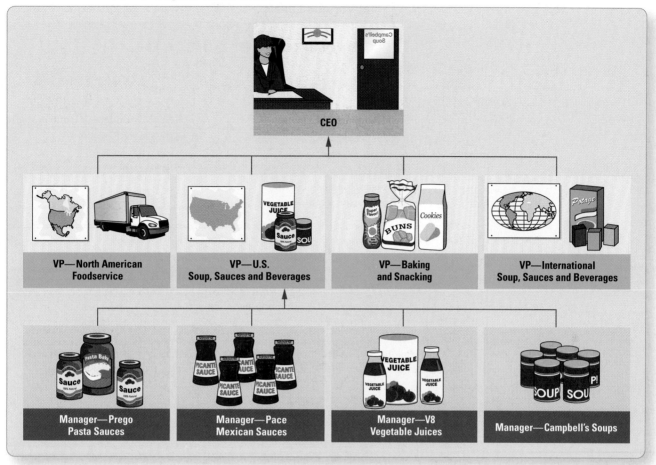

Exhibit 9-21 illustrates responsibility accounting performance reports for each level of management shown in Exhibit 9-20, using hypothetical figures.

Start with the lowest level and move to the top. Follow the $25 million budgeted operating income from the Pace Mexican sauces product line report to the report of the VP—U.S. Soup, Sauces and Beverages. The VP's report summarizes the budgeted and actual operating incomes for each of the product lines he or she supervises.

Now, trace the $70 million budgeted operating income from the VP's report to the CEO's report. The CEO's report includes a summary of each division's actual and budgeted profits, as well as the costs incurred by corporate headquarters, which are not assigned to any of the divisions.

Management by Exception

Managers use a technique called **management by exception** when they analyze performance reports. Management by exception means that managers will only investigate budget variances that are material in amount, meaning they are a relatively large deviation from what was expected (in terms of a percentage or dollar amount). Look at the CEO's report. The International Soup, Sauces and Beverages Division's actual operating income of $34 million is very close to the budgeted $35 million. Unless there are other signs of trouble, the CEO will not waste time investigating such a relatively small variance.

In contrast, the U.S. Soup, Sauces and Beverages Division earned a great deal more profit than budgeted. The CEO will want to know why. Suppose the VP of the division believes that a national sales promotion was especially effective. That promotion may be repeated or adapted by other divisions. One reason managers investigate large, favorable variances (not just large, unfavorable ones) is to identify the reason for exceptional results so that other parts of the organization may benefit. Another is to ensure that employees are not skimping on ingredients, marketing, or R&D, which could hurt the

EXHIBIT 9-21 **Responsibility Accounting Performance Reports at Various Levels**

CEO'S QUARTERLY RESPONSIBILITY REPORT
(in millions of dollars*)

Operating Income of Divisions and Corporate Headquarters Expense	Actual	Budget	Variance Favorable/ (Unfavorable)
North American Foodservice	$209	$218	$ (9)
U.S. Soups, Sauces and Beverages	84	70	14
Baking and Snacking	87	79	8
International Soups, Sauces and Beverages	34	35	(1)
Corporate Headquarters Expense	(29)	(33)	4
Operating Income	$385	$369	$16

VP—U.S. SOUPS, SAUCES AND BEVERAGES QUARTERLY RESPONSIBILITY REPORT
(in millions of dollars)

Operating Income of Product Lines	Actual	Budget	Variance Favorable/ (Unfavorable)
Prego Pasta Sauces	$18	$20	$ (2)
Pace Mexican Sauces	38	25	13
V8 Vegetable Juices	15	10	5
Campbell's Soups	13	15	(2)
Operating Income	$84	$70	$14

MANAGER—PACE MEXICAN SAUCES QUARTERLY RESPONSIBILITY REPORT
(in millions of dollars)

Revenue and Expenses	Actual	Budget	Variance Favorable/ (Unfavorable)
Sales revenue	$ 84	$ 80	$ 4
Cost of goods sold	(30)	(36)	6
Gross profit	54	44	10
Marketing expenses	(9)	(12)	3
Research and development expenses	(3)	(2)	(1)
Other expenses	(4)	(5)	1
Operating income	$ 38	$ 25	$13

* All figures are hypothetical.

company's long-term success. Also, it's possible that large variances are the result of unrealistic budgets.

The CEO would likely focus on improving the North American Foodservice Division because its actual income fell $9 million below budget. The CEO would want to see which product lines caused the shortfall so that he or she and the VP of the division could work together to correct any problems.

Exhibit 9-21 also shows how summarized data can hide problems. Although as a whole, the U.S. Soup, Sauces and Beverages Division performed well, the pasta sauces and soup lines did not. If the CEO received only the condensed report at the top of the exhibit, he or she would rely on division managers to spot and correct problems in individual product lines.

Not a Question of Blame

Responsibility accounting assigns managers responsibility for their unit's actions and provides a way to evaluate both the managers and their unit's performance. But superiors should not misuse responsibility accounting to find fault or place blame. The question is not who is to blame for an unfavorable variance. Instead, the question is who can best explain why a specific variance occurred. Consider the North American Foodservice in Exhibit 9-21. Suppose a hurricane devastated a distribution facility. The remaining facilities may have operated very efficiently, and this efficiency kept the income variance down to $9 million. If so, the North American Foodservice Division and its VP actually did a good job.

Flexible Budgets

The performance report pictured in Exhibit 9-21 compares actual costs to the amounts that were originally budgeted. One potential problem with this type of performance report is that the actual volume may differ from that which was originally budgeted. For example, say the budgeted cost was for 100 million units, yet 120 million units were actually produced. Is it "fair" to compare the actual cost (which is probably higher) to the budgeted cost in such a situation? In the next chapter, we discuss a different type of performance report that adjusts the budgeted amounts to reflect the actual volume produced and sold (these are called flexible budgets). Some companies prefer these types of performance reports since they provide more of an "apples to apples" comparison.

Other Performance Measures

Top management uses responsibility accounting performance reports to assess each responsibility center's *financial* performance. Top management also often assesses each responsibility center's nonfinancial *operating* performance. Typical nonfinancial performance measures include customer satisfaction ratings, delivery time, product quality, and employee expertise. Chapter 11 discusses the broader view of performance evaluation, known as the "balanced scorecard." In that chapter, we will look at how managers use both financial and nonfinancial performance measures to form a "balanced view" of each responsibility center's performance.

Decision Guidelines

The Master Budget and Responsibility Accounting

Let's consider some additional decisions with respect to budgeting.

Decision	Guidelines
What is the key to preparing the cash collections and cash payments budgets?	The key to preparing the cash budgets is *timing*. *When* will cash be received, and *when* will cash be paid? The timing of cash collections and cash payments often differs from the period in which the related revenues and expenses are recognized on the income statement.
What can be done to prepare for possible changes in key, underlying budget assumptions?	Management uses sensitivity analysis to understand how changes in key, underlying assumptions might affect the company's financial results. This awareness helps managers cope with changing business conditions when they occur.
What should managers be held responsible for?	**Cost center:** Manager is responsible for costs. **Revenue center:** Manager is responsible for revenues. **Profit center:** Manager is responsible for both revenues and costs and, therefore, profits. **Investment center:** Manager is responsible for revenues, costs, and the efficient use of the assets invested in the division.
How should upper management evaluate the performance of the responsibility centers and their managers?	Actual performance should be compared with the budget. Using management by exception, any large variances should be investigated, with an emphasis on uncovering information, rather than placing blame.

Summary Problem 2

The following information was taken from Pillows Unlimited Sales Budget, found in Summary Problem 1 on page 489:

Pillows Unlimited
Sales Budget—Type of Sale
For the Quarter Ended March 31

Type of Sale:	Month			
	January	February	March	1st Quarter
Cash sales (10%)	$ 140,000	$ 154,000	$ 161,000	$ 455,000
Credit sales (90%)	1,260,000	1,386,000	1,449,000	4,095,000
Total sales revenue	$1,400,000	$1,540,000	$1,610,000	$4,550,000

The company's collection history indicates that 75% of credit sales are collected in the month after the sale, 15% are collected two months after the sale, 8% are collected three months after the sale, and the remaining 2% are never collected.

Assume the following additional information was gathered about the types of sales made in the fourth quarter (October through December) of the previous year:

Pillows Unlimited
Sales Budget—Type of Sale
For the Quarter Ended December 31

Type of Sale:	Month			
	October	November	December	4th Quarter
Cash sales (10%)	$ 142,800	$ 151,200	$ 137,200	$ 431,200
Credit sales (90%)	1,285,200	1,360,800	1,234,800	3,880,800
Total sales revenue	$1,428,000	$1,512,000	$1,372,000	$4,312,000

The following information was taken from Pillows Unlimited Direct Materials Budget, found in Summary Problem 1 on page 490:

	January	February	March	1st Quarter
Total cost of DM purchases	$771,750	$836,250	$873,000	$2,481,000

Assume that the total cost of direct materials purchases in December was $725,000. The company pays 40% of its direct materials purchases in the month of purchase, and pays the remaining 60% in the month after purchase.

Requirements

1. Prepare the Cash Collections Budget for January, February, and March, as well as a summary for the first quarter.
2. Prepare the Cash Disbursements Budget for Direct Materials purchases for the months of January, February, and March, as well as a summary for the quarter.

Solution

Requirement 1

Pillows Unlimited
Cash Collections Budget
For the Quarter Ended March 31

	Month			
	January	February	March	1st Quarter
Cash sales	$ 140,000	$ 154,000	$ 161,000	$ 455,000
Collections on credit sales:				
75% of credit sales made last month	926,100[A]	945,000[D]	1,039,500[G]	2,910,600
15% of credit sales made two months ago	204,120[B]	185,220[E]	189,000[H]	578,340
8% of credit sales made two months ago	102,816[C]	108,864[F]	98,784[I]	310,464
Total cash collections	$1,373,036	$1,393,084	$1,488,284	$4,254,404

[A]December credit sales ($1,234,800) × 75% = $ 926,100
[B]November credit sales ($1,360,800) × 15% = $ 204,120
[C]October credit sales   ($1,285,200) × 8% = $ 102,816

[D]January credit sales   ($1,260,000) × 75% = $ 945,000
[E]December credit sales ($1,234,800) × 15% = $ 185,220
[F]November credit sales ($1,360,800) × 8% = $ 108,864

[G]February credit sales   ($1,386,000) × 75% = $1,039,500
[H]January credit sales   ($1,260,000) × 15% = $ 189,000
[I]December credit sales ($1,234,800) × 8% = $ 98,784

Requirement 2

Pillows Unlimited
Cash Payments Budget—Direct Materials
For the Quarter Ended March 31

	Month			
	January	February	March	1st Quarter
40% of current month DM purchases	$308,700[A]	$334,500[C]	$349,200[E]	$ 992,400
60% of last month's DM purchases	435,000[B]	463,050[D]	501,750[F]	1,399,800
Total cash payments for DM	$743,700	$797,550	$850,950	$2,392,200

[A]January DM purchases   ($771,750) × 40% = $308,700
[B]December DM purchases ($725,000) × 60% = $435,000

[C]February DM purchases   ($836,250) × 40% = $334,500
[D]January DM purchases   ($771,750) × 60% = $463,050

[E]March DM purchases   ($873,000) × 40% = $349,200
[F]February DM purchases   ($836,250) × 60% = $501,750

APPENDIX 9A

5 Prepare a merchandiser's Cost of Goods Sold, Inventory, and Purchases Budget

The Master Budget for Service and Merchandising Companies

In this chapter, we presented the master budget for a manufacturing company. The components of the master budget were summarized in Exhibit 9-4. The master budgets for service companies and merchandising companies are somewhat less complex.

- *Service companies:* Since service companies have no merchandise inventory, their operating budgets only include the Sales Budget, the Operating Expenses Budget, and the Budgeted Income Statement. The financial budgets are the same as those shown in Exhibit 9-4: the Capital Expenditures Budget, Cash Budgets, and Budgeted Balance Sheet.

- *Merchandising companies:* Since merchandising companies purchase ready-made products, they do not need to prepare the Production, Direct Materials, Direct Labor, or Manufacturing Overhead Budgets. Replacing these budgets is a combined **Cost of Goods Sold, Inventory, and Purchases Budget**. This budget follows the same general format as the manufacturer's production budget except that it is calculated at cost (in dollars) rather than in units:[2]

Cost of Goods Sold	(the inventory we plan to sell during the month, at cost)
Plus: Desired Ending Inventory	(the amount of inventory we want on hand at month's end)
= Total Inventory Needed	(the total amount of inventory needed)
Less: Beginning Inventory	(the amount of inventory we have on hand)
Purchases of Inventory	(the amount of inventory we need to purchase)

Let's try an example:

Let's say one Circle J convenience store expects sales of $500,000 in January, $520,000 in February, $530,000 in March, and $550,000 in April. Let's also assume that management sets its prices to achieve a 40% gross profit. As a result, Cost of Goods Sold is 60% of the sales revenue (100% − 40%). Finally, management wishes to have ending inventory equal to 10% of the next month's Cost of Goods Sold. Exhibit 9-22 shows the Cost of Goods Sold, Inventory, and Purchases budget for January and February. Keep in mind that all figures (other than Sales Revenue) are shown at cost.

EXHIBIT 9-22 Merchandiser's Cost of Goods Sold, Inventory, and Purchases Budget

Circle J Convenience Store Cost of Goods Sold, Inventory, and Purchases Budget For the months of January and February	Month		
	January	February	March
Sales revenue (from Sales Budget)	$500,000	$520,000	$530,000
Cost of goods sold (60% of sales revenue)	$300,000	$312,000	$318,000
Plus: Desired ending inventory 10% of next month's cost of goods sold)	31,200	31,800	33,000[b]
Total inventory required	331,200	343,800	351,000
Less: Beginning inventory	(30,000)[a]	(31,200)	(31,800)
Purchases of inventory	$301,200	$312,600	$319,200

[a] December 31 balance (equal to January 1 balance) is 10% of January's Cost of Goods Sold.
[b] April sales of $550,000 × 60% = $330,000; April Cost of Goods Sold × 10% = $33,000

[2] A merchandiser could first prepare this budget in units, and then convert it to dollars. However, merchandisers usually have hundreds or thousands of products for sale, so it is often simpler to directly state it in dollars.

Figures from this budget are then used as follows:

- *Cost of Goods Sold* is used in preparing the budgeted income statement.
- *Ending Inventory* is used in preparing the budgeted balance sheet.
- *Purchases of Inventory* is used in preparing the cash payments budget.

In summary, a merchandising company's *operating* budgets include the following:

- Sales Budget
- Cost of Goods Sold, Inventory, and Purchases Budget
- Operating Expenses Budget
- Budgeted Income Statement

The *financial* budgets are the same as those shown in Exhibit 9-4: the Capital Expenditures Budget, Cash Budgets, and Budgeted Balance Sheet.

REVIEW

Accounting Vocabulary

Budget Committee. (p. 477) A committee comprised of upper management, as well as cross-functional managers, who review, revise, and approve the final budget.

COD. (p. 480) Collect on Delivery, or Cash on Delivery. A sales term indicating that the inventory must be paid for at the time of delivery.

Cost Center. (p. 498) A responsibility center for which the manager is responsible for costs only.

Cost of Goods Sold, Inventory, and Purchases Budget. (p. 504) A merchandiser's budget that computes the Cost of Goods Sold, the amount of desired ending inventory, and amount of merchandise to be purchased.

Financial Budgets. (p. 480) The budgets that project the collection and payment of cash, as well as forecast the company's budgeted balance sheet.

Investment Center. (p. 498) A responsibility center for which the manager is accountable for revenues, costs, and the efficient use of the assets.

Line of Credit. (p. 494) A lending arrangement from a bank in which a company is allowed to borrow money as needed, up to a specified maximum amount, yet only pay interest on the portion that is actually borrowed until it is repaid.

Management by Exception. (p. 499) Directs management's attention to important differences between actual and budgeted amounts.

Master Budget. (p. 479) The comprehensive planning document for the entire organization. The master budget includes the operating budgets and the financial budgets.

Operating Budgets. (p. 479) The budgets needed to run the daily operations of the company. The operation budgets culminate in a budgeted income statement.

Participative Budgeting. (p. 477) Budgeting that involves the participation of many levels of management.

Profit Center. (p. 498) A responsibility center for which the manager is responsible for both costs and revenues, and therefore profit.

Responsibility Accounting. (p. 497) A system for evaluating the performance of each responsibility center and its manager.

Responsibility Center. (p. 497) A part or subunit of an organization whose manager is accountable for specific activities.

Revenue Center. (p. 498) A responsibility center for which the manager is accountable for revenues only.

Rolling Budget. (p. 477) A budget that is continuously updated so that the next 12 months of operations are always budgeted; also known as a continuous budget.

Safety Stock. (p. 481) Extra inventory kept on hand in case demand is higher than expected or problems in the factory slow production.

Sensitivity Analysis. (p. 496) A *what if* technique that asks what a result will be if a predicted amount is not achieved or if an underlying assumption changes.

Slack. (p. 477) Intentionally overstating budgeted expenses or understating budgeted revenues in order to cope with uncertainty, make performance appear better, or make room for potential budget cuts.

Strategic Planning. (p. 476) Setting long-term goals that may extend 5–10 years into the future.

Variance. (p. 479) The difference between actual and budgeted figures (revenues and expenses).

Zero-Based Budgeting. (p. 477) A budgeting approach in which managers begin with a budget of zero and must justify every dollar put into the budget.

Quick Check

1. *(Learning Objective 1)* Amazon.com expects to receive which of the following benefits when it uses its budgeting process?
   a. The planning required to develop the budget helps managers foresee and avoid potential problems before they occur.
   b. The budget helps motivate employees to achieve Amazon.com's sales growth and cost reduction goals.
   c. The budget provides Amazon.com's managers with a benchmark against which to compare actual results for performance evaluation.
   d. All of the above.

2. *(Learning Objective 1)* Budgets are
   a. required by Generally Accepted Accounting Principles (GAAP).
   b. future oriented.
   c. only used by large corporations.
   d. prepared by the controller for the entire company.

3. *(Learning Objective 1)* Technology has made it easier for managers to perform all of the following tasks *except*
   a. sensitivity analyses.
   b. combining individual units' budgets to create the companywide budget.
   c. removing slack from the budget.
   d. preparing responsibility center performance reports that identify variances between actual and budgeted revenues and costs.

4. *(Learning Objective 2)* Which of the following is the starting point for the master budget?
   a. The sales budget
   b. The direct materials budget
   c. The production budget
   d. The operating expenses budget

5. *(Learning Objective 2)* The income statement is part of which element of a company's master budget?
   a. The operating budgets
   b. The capital expenditures budget
   c. The financial budgets
   d. The cash budgets

6. *(Learning Objective 2)* The usual starting point for a direct labor budget for a manufacturer is the
   a. direct materials budget.
   b. sales budget.
   c. cash budget.
   d. production budget.

7. *(Learning Objective 3)* The following budgets are all financial budgets *except* for the
   a. combined cash budget.
   b. budgeted balance sheet.
   c. budgeted income statement.
   d. capital expenditures budget.

8. *(Learning Objective 3)* Which of the following expenses would *not* appear in a cash budget?
   a. Depreciation expense
   b. Wages expense
   c. Interest expense
   d. Marketing expense

9. *(Learning Objective 4)* Which of the following responsibility centers is a profit center?
   a. The Accounting Department for a local bank
   b. The sales office for a charter airline service
   c. The headquarters for an international tire manufacturer
   d. The local branch office for a national bank

10. *(Learning Objective 4)* Which of the following managers is at the highest level of the organization?
    a. Cost center manager
    b. Revenue center manager
    c. Profit center manager
    d. Investment center manager

ASSESS YOUR PROGRESS

Learning Objectives

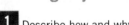 Describe how and why managers use budgets

 Prepare the operating budgets

 Prepare the financial budgets

 Describe the four types of responsibility centers and prepare performance reports

5 Prepare a merchandiser's Cost of Goods Sold, Inventory, and Purchases Budget (Appendix)

Short Exercises

S9-1 Order of preparation and components of master budget *(Learning Objective 1)*

Identify the order in which a manufacturer would prepare the following budgets. Also note whether each budget is an operating budget or a financial budget.

a.   Budgeted income statement

b.   Combined cash budget

c.   Sales budget

d.   Budgeted balance sheet

e.   Cash payments budget

f.   Direct materials budget

g.   Production budget

S9-2 Understand key terms and definitions *(Learning Objectives 1 & 2)*

Listed next are several terms. Complete the following statements with one of these terms. You may use a term more than once, and some terms may not be used at all.

Operating budgets	Production budget	Master budget	Participative budgeting
Financial budgets	Slack	Zero-based budgeting	Strategic planning
Safety stock	Variance	Budget committee	Rolling budget

a.   _____ is a budget that is continuously updated by adding months to the end of the budgeting period.

b.   _____ is the comprehensive planning document for the entire organization.

c.   These budgets, _____, project both the collection and payment of cash and forecast the company's budgeted balance sheet.

d.   The _____ is used to forecast how many units should be made to meet the sales projects.

e.   When an organization builds its budgets from the ground up, it is using _____.

f.   _____ is the process of setting long-term goals that may extend several years into the future.

g.   Managers will sometimes build _____ into their budgets to protect themselves against unanticipated expenses or lower revenues.

h.   The _____ is the difference between actual and budgeted figures and is used to evaluate how well the manager controlled operations during the period.

i.   _____ are often used by companies to review submitted budgets, make revisions as needed, and approve the final budgets.

j.   _____ is extra inventory of finished goods that is kept on hand in case demand is higher than predicted or problems in the factory slow production.

k.   The sales budget and production budget are examples of _____.

l.   _____ is a budgeting process that begins with departmental managers and flows up through middle management to top management.

S9-3 Sales budget *(Learning Objective 2)*

Gibbs Company manufactures two sizes of cargo containers. The small model sells for $100, while the large containers sell for $700. In the second quarter of the upcoming year, Gibbs Company expects to sell 1,000 small containers and 450 large containers in April, 1,300 small containers and 500 large containers in May, and 1,500 small containers and 670 large containers in June. Prepare the sales budget for the second quarter, with a column for each month and for the quarter in total.

S9-4 Production budget *(Learning Objective 2)*

Thomas Cycles manufactures chainless bicycles. On March 31, Thomas Cycles had 200 bikes in inventory. The company has a policy that the ending inventory in any month must be 20% of the following month's expected sales. Thomas Cycles expects to sell the following number of bikes in each of next four months:

April	1,000 bikes
May	1,100 bikes
June	1,300 bikes
July	1,200 bikes

Prepare a production budget for the second quarter, with a column for each month and for the quarter.

S9-5 Direct materials budget *(Learning Objective 2)*

The Bakery by the Bay produces organic bread that is sold by the loaf. Each loaf requires 1/2 of a pound of flour. The company pays $3.00 per pound of the organic flour used in its loaves. The Bakery by the Bay expects to produce the following number of loaves in each of the upcoming four months:

July	1,500 loaves
August	1,800 loaves
September	1,600 loaves
October	1,500 loaves

The company has a policy that it will have 10% of the following month's flour needs on hand at the end of each month. At the end of June, there were 75 pounds of flour on hand. Prepare the direct materials budget for the third quarter, with a column for each month and for the quarter.

S9-6 Direct labor budget *(Learning Objective 2)*

The Production Department of Connor Manufacturing has prepared the following schedule of units to be produced over the first quarter of the upcoming year:

	January	February	March
Units to be produced	500	600	800

Each unit requires 2.0 hours of direct labor. Direct labor workers are paid an average of $15 per hour. How many hours will be required in January? In February? In March?

S9-7 Manufacturing overhead budget *(Learning Objective 2)*

Probe Corporation is preparing its manufacturing overhead budget. The direct labor budget for the upcoming quarter is as follows:

	April	May	June
Budgeted direct labor hours	400	700	600

The company's variable manufacturing overhead rate is $1.50 per direct labor hour and the company's fixed manufacturing overhead is $3,500 per month. How much manufacturing overhead will be budgeted for April? For May? For June?

S9-8 Operating expenses budget (Learning Objective 2)

Davenport Corporation is preparing its operating expenses budget. The budgeted unit sales for the upcoming quarter is as follows:

	July	August	September
Budgeted unit sales...	1,200	1,400	1,700

The company's variable operating expenses are $4.00 per unit. Fixed monthly operating expenses include $5,000 for salaries, $3,000 for office rent, and depreciation of $2,500. How much operating expenses will be budgeted for July? For August? For September?

S9-9 Budgeted income statement (Learning Objective 2)

Bell & Smythe manufactures hearing aid devices. For January, Bell & Smythe expects to sell 600 hearing aid devices at an average price of $2,300 per unit. Bell & Smythe's average manufacturing cost of each unit sold is $1,400. Variable operating expenses for Bell & Smythe will be $1.50 per unit sold and fixed operating expenses are expected to be $7,500 for the month. Monthly interest expense is $3,700. Bell & Smythe has a tax rate of 30% of income before taxes. Prepare Bell & Smythe's budgeted income statement for January.

S9-10 Cash collections budget (Learning Objective 3)

Diamond Service anticipates the following sales revenue over a five-month period:

	November	December	January	February	March
Sales revenue................	$16,000	$10,000	$15,000	$12,000	$14,000

Diamond Service's sales are 25% cash and 75% credit. Diamond Service's collection history indicates that credit sales are collected as follows:

30% in the month of the sale
60% in the month after the sale
6% two months after the sale
4% are never collected

How much cash will be collected in January? In February? In March?

S9-11 Cash payments budget (Learning Objective 3)

Sentinel Corporation is preparing its cash payments budget for next month. The following information pertains to the cash payments:

a. Sentinel Corporation pays for 50% of its direct materials purchases in the month of purchase and the remainder the following month. Last month's direct material purchases were $70,000, while Sentinel Corporation anticipates $80,000 of direct material purchases next month.

b. Direct labor for the upcoming month is budgeted to be $32,000 and will be paid at the end of the upcoming month.

c. Manufacturing overhead is estimated to be 150% of direct labor cost each month and is paid in the month in which it is incurred. This monthly estimate includes $11,000 of depreciation on the plant and equipment.

d. Monthly operating expenses for next month are expected to be $43,000, which includes $2,000 of depreciation on office equipment and $1,000 of bad debt expense. These monthly operating expenses are paid during the month in which they are incurred.

e. Sentinel Corporation will be making an estimated tax payment of $7,000 next month. How much cash will be paid out next month?

S9-12 Cash budget (Learning Objective 3)

Grippers Manufacturing has $8,300 cash on hand on January 1. The company requires a minimum cash balance of $7,500. January cash collections are $548,330. Total cash payments for January are $583,200. Prepare a cash budget for January. How much cash, if any, will Grippers need to borrow by the end of January?

S9-13 Budgeted balance sheet *(Learning Objective 3)*

Ireland Company's budgeted data for the upcoming year showed total projected assets of $1,275,500 and total projected liabilities of $812,000. The balance of common stock for the year is projected to remain stable at $250,000. The stockholders' equity section of the balance sheet is made up of common stock and retained earnings. No cash dividends will be paid during the year. Ireland Company is budgeting net income for the year of $158,500. Prepare a budgeted balance sheet for end of the year. What was the balance of retained earnings at the beginning of the year?

S9-14 Identify responsibility centers *(Learning Objective 4)*

Fill in the blanks with the phrase that best completes the sentence.

A cost center	A responsibility center	Lower
An investment center	A revenue center	Higher
A profit center		

    a. The Maintenance Department at the San Diego Zoo is _____.

    b. The concession stand at the San Diego Zoo is _____.

    c. The Menswear Department at Bloomingdale's, which is responsible for buying and selling merchandise, is _____.

    d. A production line at a PalmPilot plant is _____.

    e. _____ is any segment of the business whose manager is accountable for specific activities.

    f. Quaker, a division of PepsiCo, is _____.

    g. The sales manager in charge of Nike's Northwest sales territory oversees _____.

    h. Managers of cost and revenue centers are at _____ levels of the organization than are managers of profit and investment centers.

S9-15 Identify types of responsibility centers *(Learning Objective 4)*

Identify each responsibility center as a cost center, a revenue center, a profit center, or an investment center.

    a. The Bakery Department of a Publix supermarket reports income for the current year.

    b. Pace Foods is a subsidiary of Campbell Soup Company.

    c. The Personnel Department of State Farm Insurance Companies prepares its budget and subsequent performance report on the basis of its expected expenses for the year.

    d. The Shopping Section Burpee.com reports both revenues and expenses.

    e. Burpee.com's investor relations Web site provides operating and financial information to investors and other interested parties.

    f. The manager of a BP service station is evaluated based on the station's revenues and expenses.

    g. A charter airline records revenues and expenses for each airplane each month. Each airplane's performance report shows its ratio of operating income to average book value.

    h. The manager of the Southwest sales territory is evaluated based on a comparison of current period sales against budgeted sales.

S9-16 Inventory, purchases, and cost of goods sold *(Learning Objective 5)*

Grippers sells its rock-climbing shoes worldwide. Grippers expects to sell 4,000 pairs of shoes for $185 each in January and 3,500 pairs of shoes for $220 each in February. All sales are cash only. Grippers expects cost of goods sold to average 65% of sales revenue and the company expects to sell 4,300 pairs of shoes in March for $240 each. Grippers' target ending inventory is $10,000 plus 50% of the next month's cost of goods sold.

    1. Prepare the sales budget for January and February.

    2. Prepare Grippers' inventory, purchases, and cost of goods sold budget for January and February.

Exercises—Group A

E9-17A Prepare summary performance report *(Learning Objective 1)*

Hanna White owns a chain of travel goods stores. Management anticipated selling 10,000 suitcases at an average sales price of $150. Variable expenses were budgeted to be 80% of sales revenue, and the total fixed expense was budgeted to be $100,000. The actual results for the year showed that 8,000 suitcases were sold at an average price of $200. The actual variable expense percentage was 80% of sales revenue and the total fixed expenses were as budgeted.

Requirement

1. Prepare a performance report for this year, similar to Exhibit 9-3. How would you improve White's performance evaluation system to better analyze this year's results?

E9-18A Prepare a sales budget for a retail organization *(Learning Objective 2)*

Middlestate College Bookstore is the bookstore on campus for students and faculty. Middlestate College Bookstore shows the following sales projections in units by quarter for the upcoming year:

Quarter	Books	School Supplies	Apparel	Miscellaneous
1st	1,500	200	500	660
2nd	800	150	350	520
3rd	1,700	240	800	840
4th	600	140	550	490

The average price of an item in each of the departments is as follows:

	Average sales per unit
Books	$80
School supplies	$10
Apparel	$25
Miscellaneous	$ 5

Requirement

1. Prepare a sales budget for the upcoming year by quarter for the Middlestate College Bookstore, with sales categorized by the four product groupings (books, school supplies, apparel, and miscellaneous).

E9-19A Prepare a sales budget for a not-for-profit organization *(Learning Objective 2)*

Bright Star Preschool operates a not-for-profit morning preschool. Each family pays a nonrefundable registration fee of $120 per child per school year. Monthly tuition for the nine-month school year varies depending on the number of days per week that the child attends preschool. The monthly tuition is $115 for the two-day program, $130 for the three-day program, $145 for the four-day program, and $160 for the five-day program. The following enrollment has been projected for the coming year:

Two-day program:	56 children
Three-day program:	32 children
Four-day program:	48 children
Five-day program:	16 children

In addition to the morning preschool, Bright Star Preschool offers a Lunch Bunch program where kids have the option of staying an extra hour for lunch and playtime. Bright Star Preschool charges an additional $3 per child for every Lunch Bunch attended. Historically, half the children stay for Lunch Bunch an average of 10 times a month.

Requirement

1. Calculate Bright Star Preschool's budgeted revenue for the school year.

E9-20A   Production budget *(Learning Objective 2)*

Ringer Foods produces specialty soup sold in jars. The projected sales in dollars and jars for each quarter of the upcoming year are as follows:

	Total sales revenue	Number of jars sold
1st quarter	$180,000	150,000
2nd quarter	$216,000	180,000
3rd quarter	$252,000	210,000
4th quarter	$192,000	160,000

Ringer anticipates selling 220,000 jars with total sales revenue of $264,000 in the first quarter of the year *following* the year given in the preceding table. Ringer has a policy that the ending inventory of jars must be 25% of the following quarter's sales. Prepare a production budget for the year that shows the number of jars to be produced each quarter and for the year in total.

E9-21A   Direct materials budget *(Learning Objective 2)*

Beckett Industries manufactures a popular interactive stuffed animal for children that requires three computer chips inside each toy. Beckett Industries pays $2 for each computer chip. To help to guard against stockouts of the computer chip, Beckett Industries has a policy that states that the ending inventory of computer chips should be at least 20% of the following month's production needs. The production schedule for the first four months of the year is as follows:

	Stuffed animals to be produced
January	5,000
February	4,400
March	4,800
April	4,200

Requirement

1. Prepare a direct materials budget for the first quarter that shows both the number of computer chips needed and the dollar amount of the purchases in the budget.

E9-22A   Production and direct materials budgets *(Learning Objective 2)*

Mason Manufacturing produces self-watering planters for use in upscale retail establishments. Sales projections for the first five months of the upcoming year shows the estimated unit sales of the planters each month to be as follows:

	Number of planters to be sold
January	3,500
February	3,400
March	3,600
April	4,000
May	4,200

Inventory at the start of the year was 350 planters. The desired inventory of planters at the end of each month should be equal to 10% of the following month's budgeted sales. Each planter requires two pounds of polypropylene (a type of plastic). The company wants to have 20% of the polypropylene required for next month's production on hand at the end of each month. The polypropylene costs $0.25 per pound.

Requirements

1. Prepare a production budget for each month in the first quarter of the year, including production in units for each month and for the quarter.

2. Prepare a direct materials budget for the polypropylene for each month in the first quarter of the year, including the pounds of polypropylene required, and the total cost of the polypropylene to be purchased.

E9-23A   Direct labor budget *(Learning Objective 2)*

Madden Industries manufactures three models of a product in a single plant with two departments: Cutting and Assembly. The company has estimated costs for each of the three product models: the Zip, the Flash, and the Royal models. The company is currently analyzing direct labor hour requirements for the upcoming year.

	Cutting	Assembly
Estimated hours per unit:		
Zips	1.0	2.0
Flashes	1.5	2.4
Royals	1.2	2.3
Direct labor hour rate	$10	$12

Budgeted unit production for each of the products is as follows:

	Number of units to be produced
Product model:	
Zips	500
Flashes	700
Royals	800

Requirement

1. Prepare a direct labor budget for the upcoming year that shows the budgeted direct labor costs for each department and for the company as a whole.

E9-24A   Manufacturing overhead budget *(Learning Objective 2)*

The Carlyle Company is in the process of preparing its manufacturing overhead budget for the upcoming year. Sales are projected to be 40,000 units. Information about the various manufacturing overhead costs follows:

	Variable rate per unit	Total fixed costs
Indirect materials	$1.00	
Supplies	$0.80	
Indirect labor	$0.50	$60,000
Plant utilities	$0.10	$30,000
Repairs and maintenance	$0.40	$12,000
Depreciation on plant and equipment		$48,000
Insurance on plant and equipment		$20,000
Plant supervision		$65,000

Requirement

1. Prepare the manufacturing overhead budget for the Carlyle Company for the upcoming year.

E9-25A Prepare an operating expenses budget and an income statement *(Learning Objective 2)*

Great Start Preschool operates a not-for-profit morning preschool that operates nine months of the year. Great Start has 152 kids enrolled in its various programs. Great Start's primary expense is payroll. Teachers are paid a flat salary each of the nine months as follows:

Teachers of two-day program:	$ 432 per month
Teachers of three-day program:	$ 648 per month
Teachers of four-day program:	$ 864 per month
Teachers of five-day program:	$1,080 per month
Preschool director's salary:	$1,500 per month

Great Start has 7 two-day program teachers, 4 three-day program teachers, 6 four-day program teachers, and 2 five-day program teachers. Great Start also has a director who is paid a monthly salary of $1,500.

In addition to the salary expense, Great Start must pay federal payroll taxes (FICA taxes) in the amount of 7.65% of salary expense. Great Start leases its facilities from a local church, paying $4,012 every month it operates. Fixed operating expenses (telephone, Internet access, bookkeeping services, and so forth) amount to $850 per month over the nine-month school year. Variable monthly expenses (over the nine-month school year) for art supplies and other miscellaneous supplies are $12 per child. Revenue for the entire nine-month school year from tuition, registration fees, and the lunch program is projected to be $219,840.

Requirements

1. Prepare Great Start Preschool's monthly operating budget. Round all amounts to the nearest dollar.

2. Using your answer from Requirement 1, create Great Start Preschool's budgeted income statement for the entire nine-month school year. Assume that the operating revenue is $219,840. You may group all operating expenses together.

3. Great Start is a not-for-profit preschool. What might Great Start do with its projected income for the year?

E9-26A Budgeted income statement *(Learning Objective 2)*

Samson Foods produces a specialty chocolate chip cookie that is sold to hotel chains by the case for $50 per case. For the upcoming quarter, Samson Foods is projecting the following sales:

	January	February	March
Cases of cookies	5,000	4,500	5,700

The budgeted cost of manufacturing each case is $23. Operating expenses are projected to be $58,000 in January, $53,000 in February, and $61,000 in March. Samson Foods is subject to a corporate tax rate of 30%.

Requirement

1. Prepare a budgeted income statement for the first quarter, with a column for each month and for the quarter.

E9-27A Prepare budgeted income statement *(Learning Objective 2)*

Wheels is an exotic car dealership. Sales in the fourth quarter of last year were $4,000,000. Suppose its Miami office projects that its current year's quarterly sales will increase by 3% in quarter 1, by another 4% in quarter 2, by another 6% in quarter 3, and by another 5% in quarter 4. Management expects cost of goods sold to be 50% of revenues every quarter, while operating expenses should be 30% of revenues during each of the first two quarters, 25% of revenues during the third quarter, and 35% during the fourth quarter.

Requirement

1. Prepare a budgeted income statement for each of the four quarters and for the entire year.

E9-28A   Cash collections budget *(Learning Objective 3)*

Brandon Wholesalers has found that 80% of its sales in any given month are credit sales, while the remainder are cash sales. Of the credit sales, Brandon Wholesalers has experienced the following collection pattern:

> 25% paid in the month of the sale
>
> 50% paid in the month after the sale
>
> 20% paid two months after the sale
>
> 5% of the sales are never collected

November sales for last year were $100,000, while December sales were $120,000. Projected sales for the next three months are as follows:

January sales	$160,000
February sales	$125,000
March sales..	$180,000

Requirement

1. Prepare a cash collections budget for the first quarter, with a column for each month and for the quarter.

E9-29A   Cash payments budget *(Learning Objective 3)*

Dwight Corporation is preparing its cash payments budget. The following items relate to cash payments Dwight Corporation anticipates making during the second quarter of the upcoming year.

a. Dwight Corporation pays for 50% of its direct materials purchases in the month of purchase and the remainder the following month. Dwight Corporation's direct material purchases for March through June are anticipated to be as follows:

March	April	May	June
$112,000	$135,000	$128,000	$145,000

b. Direct labor is paid in the month in which it is incurred. Direct labor for each month of the second quarter is budgeted as follows:

April	May	June
$50,000	$60,000	$75,000

c. Manufacturing overhead is estimated to be 150% of direct labor cost each month. This monthly estimate includes $35,000 of depreciation on the plant and equipment. All manufacturing overhead (excluding depreciation) is paid in the month in which it is incurred.

d. Monthly operating expenses for March through June are projected to be as follows:

March	April	May	June
$72,000	$87,000	$84,000	$93,000

Monthly operating expenses are paid in the month after they are incurred. Monthly operating expenses include $12,000 for monthly depreciation on administrative offices and equipment, and $3,000 for bad debt expense.

e. Dwight Corporation plans to pay $5,000 (cash) for a new server in May.

f. Dwight Corporation must make an estimated tax payment of $12,500 on June 15.

Requirement

1. Prepare a cash payments budget for April, May, and June and for the quarter.

E9-30A Combined cash budget *(Learning Objective 3)*

Woodlawn Manufacturing produces a variety of industrial valves. The company is preparing its cash budget for the upcoming third quarter. The following transactions are expected to occur:

a. Cash collections from sales in July, August, and September are projected to be $90,000, $152,000, and $121,000 respectively.

b. Cash payments for the upcoming third quarter are projected to be $140,000 in July, $100,000 in August, and $135,000 in September.

c. The cash balance as of the first day of the third quarter is projected to be $30,000.

d. Woodlawn Manufacturing has a policy that it must maintain a minimum cash balance of $25,000.

The company has a line of credit with the local bank that allows it to borrow funds in months that it would not otherwise have a minimum balance of $25,000. If the company has more than $25,000 at the end of any given month, it uses the excess funds to pay off any outstanding line of credit balance. Each month, Woodlawn Manufacturing pays interest on the prior month's line of credit ending balance. The actual interest rate that Woodlawn Manufacturing will pay floats since it is tied to the prime rate. However, the interest rate paid during the budget period is expected to be 1% of the prior month's line of credit ending balance (if the company did not have an outstanding balance at the end of the prior month, then Woodlawn Manufacturing does not have to pay any interest). All line of credit borrowings are taken or paid off on the first day of the month. As of the first day of the third quarter, Woodlawn Manufacturing did not have a balance on its line of credit.

Requirement

1. Prepare a combined cash budget for Woodlawn Manufacturing for the third quarter, with a column for each month and for the quarter total.

E9-31A Compute cash receipts and payments *(Learning Objective 3)*

Aqua Pure is a distributor of bottled water. For each of the items a through f, compute the amount of cash receipts or payments Aqua Pure will budget for September. The solution to one item may depend on the answer to an earlier item.

a. The company expenses $5,000 per month for insurance on its fleet of delivery vehicles. The insurance premium is paid semiannually in September and March.

b. Management expects to sell 7,500 cases of water in August and 9,200 in September. Each case sells for $12. Cash sales average 30% of total sales, and credit sales make up the rest. On average, three-fourths of credit sales are collected in the month of sale, with the balance collected the following month.

c. The company pays commissions and other expenses of $4,200 per month.

d. Depreciation expense of $4,500 is recognized each month.

e. Aqua Pure declares $100,000 in dividends to stockholders of record as of September 14.

f. The payment date for the dividends declared in Part e is September 30.

E9-32A Prepare sales and cash collections budgets *(Learning Objectives 2 & 3)*

Rovniak Reeds, a manufacturer of saxophone, oboe, and clarinet reeds, has projected sales to be $890,000 in October, $950,000 in November, $1,025,000 in December, and $920,000 in January. Rovniak's sales are 25% cash and 75% credit. Rovniak's collection history indicates that credit sales are collected as follows:

25% in the month of the sale
65% in the month after the sale
8% two months after the sale
2% are never collected

Requirements

1. Prepare a sales budget for all four months, showing the breakdown between cash and credit sales.

2. Prepare a cash collections budget for December and January. Round all answers up to the nearest dollar.

E9-33A Prepare budgeted balance sheet (*Learning Objective 3*)

Use the following information to prepare a budgeted balance sheet for Marine.com at March 31. Show computations for the cash and owners' equity amounts.

a. March 31 inventory balance, $15,000.

b. March payments for inventory, $4,600.

c. March payments of accounts payable and accrued liabilities, $8,200.

d. March 31 accounts payable balance, $4,300.

e. February 28 furniture and fixtures balance, $34,800; accumulated depreciation balance, $29,870.

f. February 28 owners' equity, $26,700.

g. March depreciation expense, $600.

h. Cost of goods sold, 60% of sales.

i. Other March expenses, including income tax, total $5,000; paid in cash.

j. February 28 cash balance, $11,400.

k. March budgeted sales, $12,200.

l. March 31 accounts receivable balance, one-fourth of March sales.

m. March cash receipts, $14,300.

E9-34A Prepare cash budget, then revise (*Learning Objective 3*)

Battery Power, a family-owned battery store, began October with $10,500 cash. Management forecasts that collections from credit customers will be $11,000 in October and $15,000 in November. The store is scheduled to receive $6,000 cash on a business note receivable in October. Projected cash payments include inventory purchases ($13,000 in October and $13,900 in November) and operating expenses ($3,000 each month).

Battery Power's bank requires a $10,000 minimum balance in the store's checking account. At the end of any month when the account balance dips below $10,000, the bank automatically extends credit to the store in multiples of $1,000. Battery Power borrows as little as possible and pays back loans in quarterly installments of $2,000 plus 4% interest on the entire unpaid principal. The first payment occurs three months after the loan.

Requirement

1. Prepare Battery Power's cash budget for October and November.

E9-35A Finish an incomplete cash budget (*Learning Objective 3*)

You recently began a job as an accounting intern at Outdoor Adventures. Your first task was to help prepare the cash budget for February and March. Unfortunately, the computer with the budget file crashed, and you did not have a backup or even a hard copy. You ran a program to salvage bits of data from the budget file. After entering the following data in the budget, you may have just enough information to reconstruct the budget.

Outdoor Adventures eliminates any cash deficiency by borrowing the exact amount needed from State Street Bank, where the current interest rate is 8%. Outdoor Adventures pays interest on its outstanding debt at the end of each month. The company also repays all borrowed amounts at the end of the month as cash becomes available.

Requirement

1. Complete the following cash budget:

OUTDOOR ADVENTURES LTD.
Cash Budget
February and March

	February	March
Beginning cash balance	$ 16,900	$?
Cash collections	?	79,600
Cash from sale of plant assets	0	1,800
Cash available	106,900	?
Cash payments:		
Purchase of inventory	$?	$41,000
Operating expenses	47,200	?
Total payments	98,000	?
(1) Ending cash balance before financing	?	25,100
Minimum cash balance desired	20,000	20,000
Cash excess (deficiency)	$?	$?
Financing of cash deficiency:		
Borrowing (at end of month)	$?	$?
Principal repayments (at end of month)	?	?
Interest expense	?	?
(2) Total effects of financing	?	?
Ending cash balance (1) + (2)	$?	$?

E9-36A Prepare performance reports at different organizational levels (Learning Objective 4)

InTouch is a Seattle company that sells cell phones and PDAs on the Web. InTouch has assistant managers for its digital and video cell phone operations. These assistant managers report to the manager of the total cell phone product line, who, with the manager of PDAs, reports to the manager for all sales of handheld devices, Beth Beverly. Beverly received the following data for November operations:

	Cell Phones		PDAs
	Digital	Video	
Revenues, budget	$204,000	$800,000	$300,000
Expenses, budget	140,000	390,000	225,000
Revenues, actual	214,000	840,000	290,000
Expenses, actual	135,000	400,000	230,000

Requirement

1. Arrange the data in a performance report similar to Exhibit 9-21. Show November results, in thousands of dollars, for digital cell phones, for the total cell phone product line, and for all devices. Should Beverly investigate the performance of digital cell phone operations? Why or why not?

E9-37A Prepare inventory, purchases, and cost of goods sold budget *(Learning Objective 5)*

Leno sells tire rims. Its sales budget for the nine months ended September 30 follows:

	Mar 31	Jun 30	Sep 30	Nine-Month Total
	Quarter Ended			
Cash sales, 30%	$ 30,000	$ 45,000	$ 37,500	$112,500
Credit sales, 70%	70,000	105,000	87,500	262,500
Total sales, 100%	$100,000	$150,000	$125,000	$375,000

In the past, cost of goods sold has been 60% of total sales. The director of marketing and the financial vice president agree that each quarter's ending inventory should not be below $20,000 plus 10% of cost of goods sold for the following quarter. The marketing director expects sales of $220,000 during the fourth quarter. The January 1 inventory was $19,000.

Requirement

1. Prepare an inventory, purchases, and cost of goods sold budget for each of the first three quarters of the year. Compute cost of goods sold for the entire nine-month period (use Exhibit 9-22 as a model).

Exercises—Group B

E9-38B Prepare summary performance report *(Learning Objective 1)*

Daniel Kyler owns a chain of travel goods stores. Management anticipated selling 10,500 suitcases at an average sale price of $180. Variable expenses were budgeted to be 65% of sales revenue, and the total fixed expenses was budgeted to be $115,000. The actual results for the year showed that 9,000 suitcases were sold at an average price of $280. The actual variable expense percentage was 65% of sales revenue and the total fixed expenses were as budgeted. Prepare a performance report for this year. How would you improve Kyler's performance evaluation system to better analyze this year's results?

E9-39B Prepare a sales budget for a retail organization *(Learning Objective 2)*

Seattle College Bookstore is the bookstore on campus for students and faculty. Seattle College Bookstore shows the following sales projections in units by quarter for the upcoming year:

Quarter	Books	School Supplies	Apparel	Miscellaneous
1st	1,580	260	520	620
2nd	890	110	380	510
3rd	1,790	280	870	800
4th	610	160	560	450

The average price of an item in each of the departments is as follows:

	Average sales per unit
Books	$84
School supplies	$19
Apparel	$23
Miscellaneous	$ 8

Requirement

1. Prepare a sales budget for the upcoming year by quarter for the Seattle College Bookstore, with sales categorized by the four product groupings (books, school supplies, apparel, and miscellaneous).

E9-40B Prepare a sales budget for a not-for-profit organization *(Learning Objective 2)*

Wonderland Preschool operates a not-for-profit morning preschool. Each family pays a non-refundable registration fee of $100 per child per school year. Monthly tuition for the eight-month school year varies depending on the number of days per week that the child attends preschool. The monthly tuition is $130 for the two-day program, $150 for the three-day program, $175 for the four-day program, and $190 for the five-day program. The following enrollment has been projected for the coming year:

Two-day program: 80 children	Four-day program: 54 children
Three-day program: 42 children	Five-day program: 12 children

In addition to the morning preschool, Wonderland Preschool offers a Lunch Bunch program where kids have the option of staying an extra hour for lunch and playtime. Wonderland Preschool charges an additional $3 per child for every Lunch Bunch attended. Historically, half the children stay for Lunch Bunch an average of fifteen times a month.

Requirement

1. Calculate Wonderland Preschool's budgeted revenue for the school year.

E9-41B Production budget *(Learning Objective 2)*

Smith Foods produces specialty soup sold in jars. The projected sales in dollars and jars for each quarter of the upcoming year are as follows:

	Total sales revenue	Number of jars sold
1st quarter	$182,000	150,000
2nd quarter	$210,000	180,500
3rd quarter	$251,000	213,500
4th quarter	$195,000	164,500

Smith anticipates selling 223,000 jars with total sales revenue of $265,000 in the first quarter of the year following the year given in the preceding table. Smith has a policy that the ending inventory of jars must be 30% of the following quarter's sales. Prepare a production budget for the year that shows the number of jars to be produced each quarter and for the year in total.

E9-42B Direct materials budget *(Learning Objective 2)*

Gable Industries manufactures a popular interactive stuffed animal for children that requires two computer chips inside each toy. Gable Industries pays $3 for each computer chip. To help to guard against stockouts of the computer chip, Gable Industries has a policy that states that the ending inventory of computer chips should be at least 30% of the following month's production needs. The production schedule for the first four months of the year is as follows:

	Stuffed animals to be produced
January	5,700
February	4,600
March	4,300
April	4,900

Requirement

1. Prepare a direct materials budget for the first quarter that shows both the number of computer chips needed and the dollar amount of the purchases in the budget.

E9-43B Production and direct materials budgets *(Learning Objective 2)*

Preston Manufacturing produces self-watering planters for use in upscale retail establishments. Sales projections for the first five months of the upcoming year shows the estimated unit sales of the planters each month to be as follows:

	Number of planters to be sold
January	3,300
February	3,100
March	3,500
April	4,800
May	4,600

Inventory at the start of the year was 330 planters. The desired inventory of planters at the end of each month should be equal to 10% of the following month's budgeted sales. Each planter requires four pounds of polypropylene (a type of plastic). The company wants to have 30% of the polypropylene required for next month's production on hand at the end of each month. The polypropylene costs $0.30 per pound.

Requirements

1. Prepare a production budget for each month in the first quarter of the year, including production in units for each month and for the quarter.

2. Prepare a direct materials budget for the polypropylene for each month in the first quarter of the year, including the pounds of polypropylene required, and the total cost of the polypropylene to be purchased.

E9-44B Direct labor budget *(Learning Objective 2)*

Austen Industries manufactures three models of a product in a single plant with two departments: Cutting and Assembly. The company has estimated costs for each of the three product models, which are the Imperial, the Zip, and the Zoom models.

The company is currently analyzing direct labor hour requirements for the upcoming year.

	Cutting	Assembly
Estimated hours per unit:		
Imperials	1.6	2.1
Zips	1.1	2.4
Zooms	1.7	2.9
Direct labor hour rate	$9	$11

Budgeted unit production for each of the products is as follows:

	Number of units to be produced
Product model:	
Imperials	540
Zips	770
Zooms	830

Requirement

1. Prepare a direct labor budget for the upcoming year that shows the budgeted direct labor costs for each department and for the company as a whole.

E9-45B Manufacturing overhead budget *(Learning Objective 2)*

The Anderson Company is in the process of preparing its manufacturing overhead budget for the upcoming year. Sales are projected to be 44,000 units. Information about the various manufacturing overhead costs follows:

	Variable rate per unit	Total fixed costs
Indirect materials	$0.80	
Supplies	$0.90	
Indirect labor	$0.60	$68,000
Plant utilities	$0.20	$30,000
Repairs and maintenance	$0.30	$14,000
Depreciation on plant and equipment		$45,000
Insurance on plant and equipment		$20,000
Plant supervision		$66,000

Requirement

1. Prepare the manufacturing overhead budget for the Anderson Company for the upcoming year.

E9-46B Prepare an operating expenses budget and an income statement *(Learning Objective 2)*

Nice Place Preschool operates a not-for-profit morning preschool that operates nine months of the year. Nice Place has 161 kids enrolled in its various programs. Nice Place's primary expense is payroll. Teachers are paid a flat salary each of the nine months as follows:

Salary data	
Teachers of two-day program:	$ 438 per month
Teachers of three-day program:	$ 651 per month
Teachers of four-day program:	$ 872 per month
Teachers of five-day program:	$1,040 per month
Preschool director's salary:	$1,250 per month

Nice Place has 8 two-day program teachers, 5 three-day program teachers, 7 four-day program teachers, and 3 five-day program teachers. Nice Place also has a director who is paid a monthly salary of $1,250.

In addition to the salary expense, Nice Place must pay federal payroll taxes (FICA taxes) in the amount of 7.65% of salary expense. Nice Place leases its facilities from a local church, paying $2,200 per month plus 10.75% of monthly tuition revenue. Fixed operating expenses (telephone, Internet access, bookkeeping services, and so forth) amount to $890 per month over the nine-month school year. Variable monthly expenses (over the nine-month school year) for art supplies and other miscellaneous supplies are $10 per child. Revenue for the entire nine-month school year from tuition, registration fees, and the lunch program is projected to be $291,865.

Requirements

1. Prepare Nice Place Preschool's monthly operating budget. Round all amounts to the nearest dollar.

2. Using your answer from Requirement 1, create Nice Place Preschool's budgeted income statement for the entire nine-month school year. Assume that the operating revenue is $291,865. You may group all operating expenses together.

3. Nice Place is a not-for-profit preschool. What might Nice Place do with its projected income for the year?

E9-47B   Budgeted income statement (*Learning Objective 2*)

Fielding Foods produces a specialty brownie that is sold to hotel chains by the case for $55 per case. For the upcoming quarter, Fielding Foods is projecting the following sales:

	January	February	March
Cases of brownies	5,700	4,900	5,500

The budgeted cost of manufacturing each case is $27. Operating expenses are projected to be $61,000 in January, $57,000 in February, and $64,000 in March. Fielding Foods is subject to a corporate tax rate of 30%.

Requirement

1. Prepare a budgeted income statement for the first quarter, with a column for each month and for the quarter in total.

E9-48B   Prepare budgeted income statement (*Learning Objective 2*)

Monette is an exotic car dealership. Sales in the fourth quarter of last year were $4,400,000. Suppose its Boston office projects that its current year's quarterly sales will increase by 2% in quarter 1, by another 6% in quarter 2, by another 4% in quarter 3, and by another 3% in quarter 4. Management expects cost of goods sold to be 45% of revenues every quarter, while operating expenses should be 35% of revenues during each of the first two quarters, 20% of revenues during the third quarter, and 25% during the fourth quarter.

Requirement

1. Prepare a budgeted income statement for each of the four quarters and for the entire year.

E9-49B   Cash collections budget (*Learning Objective 3*)

Bentfield Wholesalers has found that 60% of its sales in any given month are credit sales, while the remainder are cash sales. Of the credit sales, Bentfield Wholesalers has experienced the following collection pattern:

25% paid in the month of the sale

50% paid in the month after the sale

15% paid two months after the sale

10% of the sales are never collected

November sales for last year were $90,000, while December sales were $125,000. Projected sales for the next three months are as follows:

January sales	$180,000
February sales	$135,000
March sales	$190,000

Requirement

1. Prepare a cash collections budget for the first quarter, with a column for each month and for the quarter.

E9-50B Cash payments budget *(Learning Objective 3)*

Monachino Corporation is preparing its cash payments budget. The following items relate to cash payments Monachino Corporation anticipates making during the second quarter of the upcoming year.

a. Monachino Corporation pays for 55% of its direct materials purchases in the month of purchase and the remainder the following month. Monachino Corporation's direct material purchases for March through June are anticipated to be as follows:

March	April	May	June
$117,000	$134,000	$129,000	$148,000

b. Direct labor is paid in the month in which it is incurred. Direct labor for each month of the second quarter is budgeted as follows:

April	May	June
$54,000	$64,000	$79,000

c. Manufacturing overhead is estimated to be 130% of direct labor cost each month. This monthly estimate includes $34,000 of depreciation on the plant and equipment. All manufacturing overhead (excluding depreciation) is paid in the month in which it is incurred.

d. Monthly operating expenses for March through June are projected to be as follows:

March	April	May	June
$77,000	$84,000	$86,000	$97,000

Monthly operating expenses are paid in the month after they are incurred. Monthly operating expenses include $13,000 for monthly depreciation on administrative offices and equipment, and $3,500 for bad debt expense.

e. Monachino Corporation plans to pay $6,000 (cash) for a new server in May.

f. Monachino Corporation must make an estimated tax payment of $12,500 on June 15.

Requirement

1. Prepare a cash payments budget for April, May, and June and for the quarter.

E9-51B Combined cash budget *(Learning Objective 3)*

Berkner Manufacturing produces a variety of industrial valves. The company is preparing its cash budget for the upcoming third quarter. The following transactions are expected to occur:

a. Cash collections from sales in July, August, and September are projected to be $93,000, $158,000, and $120,000 respectively.

b. Cash payments for the upcoming third quarter are projected to be $143,000 in July, $108,000 in August, and $132,000 in September.

c. The cash balance as of the first day of the third quarter is projected to be $34,000.

Berkner Manufacturing has a policy that it must maintain a minimum cash balance of $27,000. The company has a line of credit with the local bank that allows it to borrow funds in months that it would not otherwise have a minimum balance of $27,000. If the company has more than $27,000 at the end of any given month, it uses the excess funds to pay off any outstanding line of credit balance. Each month, Berkner Manufacturing pays interest on the prior month's line of credit ending balance. The actual interest rate that Berkner Manufacturing will pay floats since it is tied to the prime rate. However, the interest rate paid during the budget period is expected to be 1% of the prior month's line of credit ending balance (if it did not have an outstanding balance at the end of the prior month, then Berkner Manufacturing does not have to pay any interest). All line of credit borrowings are taken or paid off on the first day of the month. As of the first day of the third quarter, Berkner Manufacturing did not have a balance on its line of credit.

Requirement

1. Prepare a combined cash budget for Berkner Manufacturing for the third quarter, with a column for each month and for the quarter total.

E9-52B Compute cash receipts and payments *(Learning Objective 3)*

Aqua Cool is a distributor of bottled water. For each of items a through f, compute the amount of cash receipts or payments Aqua Cool will budget for September. The solution to one item may depend on the answer to an earlier item.

a. The company expenses $5,200 per month for insurance on its fleet of delivery vehicles. The insurance premium is paid semiannually, in September and March.

b. Management expects to sell 7,900 cases of water in August and 9,600 in September. Each case sells for $13. Cash sales average 30% of total sales, and credit sales make up the rest. Three-fourths of credit sales are collected in the month of sale, with the balance collected the following month.

c. The company pays commissions and other expenses of $4,100 per month.

d. Depreciation expense of $3,500 is recognized each month.

e. Aqua Cool declares $106,000 in dividends to stockholders of record as of September 14.

f. The payment date for the dividends declared in Part e is September 30.

E9-53B Prepare sales and cash collections budgets *(Learning Objectives 2 & 3)*

Yung Reeds, a manufacturer of saxophone, oboe, and clarinet reeds, has projected sales to be $900,000 in October, $954,000 in November, $1,040,000 in December, and $924,000 in January. Yung's sales are 20% cash and 80% on credit. Yung's collection history indicates that credit sales are collected as follows:

> 25% in the month of the sale
> 60% in the month after the sale
> 14% two months after the sale
> 1% are never collected

Requirements

1. Prepare a sales budget for all four months, showing the breakdown between cash and credit sales.

2. Prepare a cash collection budget for December and January. Round all answers up to the nearest dollar.

E9-54B Prepare budgeted balance sheet *(Learning Objective 3)*

Use the following information to prepare a budgeted balance sheet for Rescue.com at March 31. Show computations for the cash and owners' equity amounts.

a. March 31 inventory balance, $17,535.

b. March payments for inventory, $4,400.

c. March payments of accounts payable and accrued liabilities, $8,300.

d. March 31 accounts payable balance, $2,200.

e. February 28 furniture and fixtures balance, $34,600; accumulated depreciation balance, $29,880.

f. February 28 owners' equity, $28,510.

g. March depreciation expense, $800.

h. Cost of goods sold, 40% of sales.

i. Other March expenses, including income tax, total $6,000; paid in cash.

j. February 28 cash balance, $11,400.

k. March budgeted sales, $12,700.

l. March 31 accounts receivable balance, one-fourth of March sales.

m. March cash receipts, $14,200.

E9-55B Prepare cash budget, then revise *(Learning Objective 3)*

Energy Power, a family-owned battery store, began October with $10,000 cash. Management forecasts that collections from credit customers will be $11,400 in October and $14,800 in November. The store is scheduled to receive $4,500 cash on a business note receivable in October. Projected cash payments include inventory purchases ($9,700 in October and $13,200 in November) and operating expenses ($4,200 each month).

Energy Power's bank requires a $11,000 minimum balance in the store's checking account. At the end of any month when the account balance dips below $11,000, the bank automatically extends credit to the store in multiples of $2,000. Energy Power borrows as little as possible and pays back loans in quarterly installments of $4,000, plus 6% interest on the entire unpaid principal. The first payment occurs three months after the loan.

Requirement

1. Prepare Energy Power's cash budget for October and November.

E9-56B Finish an incomplete cash budget *(Learning Objective 3)*

You recently began a job as an accounting intern at Backyard Adventures. Your first task was to help prepare the cash budget for February and March. Unfortunately, the computer with the budget file crashed, and you did not have a backup or even a hard copy. You ran a program to salvage bits of data from the budget file. After entering the following data in the budget, you may have just enough information to reconstruct the budget.

Backyard Adventures eliminates any cash deficiency by borrowing the exact amount needed from State Street Bank, where the current interest rate is 6%. Backyard Adventures pays interest on its outstanding debt at the end of each month. The company also repays all borrowed amounts at the end of the month, as cash becomes available.

Requirement

1. Complete the following cash budget:

Backyard Adventures, LTD.
Cash Budget
February and March

	February	March
Beginning cash balance	$ 16,500	$?
Cash collections	?	80,000
Cash from sale of plant assets	0	1,900
Cash available	106,500	?
Cash payments:		
Purchase of inventory	$?	$ 41,100
Operating expenses	47,400	?
Total payments	98,300	?
(1) Ending cash balance before financing	?	23,700
Minimum cash balance desired	(21,000)	(21,000)
Cash excess (deficiency)	$?	$?
Financing of cash deficiency:		
Borrowing (at end of month)	$?	$?
Principal repayments (at end of month)	?	?
Interest expense	?	?
(2) Total effects of financing	?	?
Ending cash balance (1) + (2)	$?	$?

E9-57B Prepare performance reports at different organizational levels *(Learning Objective 4)*

Web True is a Tulsa company that sells cell phones and PDAs on the Web. Web True has assistant managers for its digital and video cell phone operations. These assistant managers report to the manager of the total cell phone product line, who, with the manager of PDAs reports to the manager for sales of all handheld devices, Mary Burton. Burton received the following data for November operations:

	Cell Phones		
	Digital	Video	PDAs
Revenues, budget.............................	$205,000	$805,000	$300,000
Expenses, budget.............................	144,000	430,000	228,000
Revenues, actual..............................	217,000	865,000	280,000
Expenses, actual..............................	134,000	400,000	240,000

Requirement

1. Arrange the data in the performance reports. Show November results, in thousands of dollars, for digital cell phones, for the total cell phone product line, and for all handheld devices. Should Burton investigate the performance of digital cell phone operations? Why or why not?

E9-58B Prepare inventory, purchases, and cost of goods sold budget (Learning Objective 5)

Sullivan sells tire rims. Its sales budget for the nine months ended September 30 follows:

	Quarter Ended			Nine-Month
	Mar 31	Jun 30	Sep 30	Total
Cash sales, 40%....................	$ 40,000	$ 60,000	$ 50,000	$150,000
Credit sales, 60%...................	60,000	90,000	75,000	225,000
Total sales, 100%	$100,000	$150,000	$125,000	$375,000

In the past, cost of goods sold has been 65% of total sales. The director of marketing and the financial vice president agree that each quarter's ending inventory should not be below $10,000 plus 15% of cost of goods sold for the following quarter. The marketing director expects sales of $200,000 during the fourth quarter. The January 1 inventory was $17,000.

Requirement

1. Prepare an inventory, purchases, and cost of goods sold budget for each of the first three quarters of the year. Compute cost of goods sold for the entire nine-month period (use Exhibit 9-22 as a model).

Problems—Group A

P9-59A Comprehensive budgeting problem (Learning Objectives 2 & 3)

Silverman Manufacturing is preparing its master budget for the first quarter of the upcoming year. The following data pertain to Silverman Manufacturing's operations:

Current Assets as of December 31 (prior year):	
Cash	$ 4,500
Accounts receivable, net..	$ 49,000
Inventory..	$ 15,320
Property, plant, and equipment, net	$121,500
Accounts payable	$ 42,400
Capital stock..	$125,000
Retained earnings..	$ 22,920

a. Actual sales in December were $70,000. Selling price per unit is projected to remain stable at $10 per unit throughout the budget period. Sales for the first five months of the upcoming year are budgeted to be as follows:

January	$80,000
February	$92,000
March	$99,000
April	$97,000
May	$85,000

b. Sales are 30% cash and 70% credit. All credit sales are collected in the month following the sale.

c. Silverman Manufacturing has a policy that states that each month's ending inventory of finished goods should be 25% of the following month's sales (in units).

d. Of each month's direct material purchases, 20% are paid for in the month of purchase, while the remainder is paid for in the month following purchase. Two pounds of direct material is needed per unit at $2 per pound. Ending inventory of direct materials should be 10% of next month's production needs.

e. Monthly manufacturing conversion costs are $5,000 for factory rent, $3,000 for other fixed manufacturing expenses, and $1.20 per unit for variable manufacturing overhead. No depreciation is included in these figures. All expenses are paid in the month in which they are incurred.

f. Computer equipment for the administrative offices will be purchased in the upcoming quarter. In January, Silverman Manufacturing will purchase equipment for $5,000 (cash), while February's cash expenditure will be $12,000 and March's cash expenditure will be $16,000.

g. Operating expenses are budgeted to be $1 per unit sold plus fixed operating expenses of $1,000 per month. All operating expenses are paid in the month in which they are incurred.

h. Depreciation on the building and equipment for the general and administrative offices is budgeted to be $4,800 for the entire quarter, which includes depreciation on new acquisitions.

i. Silverman Manufacturing has a policy that the ending cash balance in each month must be at least $4,000. It has a line of credit with a local bank. The company can borrow in increments of $1,000 at the beginning of each month, up to a total outstanding loan balance of $100,000. The interest rate on these loans is 1% per month simple interest (not compounded). Silverman Manufacturing would pay down on the line of credit balance if it has excess funds at the end of the quarter. The company would also pay the accumulated interest at the end of the quarter on the funds borrowed during the quarter.

j. The company's income tax rate is projected to be 30% of operating income less interest expense. The company pays $10,000 cash at the end of February in estimated taxes.

Requirements

1. Prepare a schedule of cash collections for January, February, and March, and for the quarter in total. Use the following format:

Cash Collections Budget

	January	February	March	Quarter
Cash sales				
Credit sales				
Total cash collections				

2. Prepare a production budget, using the following format:

Production Budget

	January	February	March	Quarter
Unit sales*				
Plus: Desired ending inventory				
Total needed				
Less: Beginning inventory				
Units to produce				

*Hint: Unit sales = Sales in dollars ÷ Selling price per unit

3. Prepare a direct materials budget, using the following format:

Direct Materials Budget

	January	February	March	Quarter
Units to be produced				
× Pounds of DM needed per unit				
Quantity (pounds) needed for production				
Plus: Desired ending inventory of DM				
Total quantity (pounds) needed				
Less: Beginning inventory of DM				
Quantity (pounds) to purchase				
× Cost per pound				
Total cost of DM purchases				

4. Prepare a cash payments budget for the direct material purchases from Requirement 3, using the following format:

Cash Payments for Direct Material Purchases Budget

	January	February	March	Quarter
December purchases (from Accounts Payable)				
January purchases				
February purchases				
March purchases				
Total cash payments for direct material purchases				

5. Prepare a cash payments budget for conversion costs, using the following format:

Cash Payments for Conversion Costs Budget

	January	February	March	Quarter
Variable conversion costs				
Rent (fixed)				
Other fixed MOH				
Total payments for conversion costs				

6. Prepare a cash payments budget for operating expenses, using the following format:

Cash Payments for Operating Expenses Budget

	January	February	March	Quarter
Variable operating expenses				
Fixed operating expenses				
Total payments for operating expenses				

7. Prepare a combined cash budget, using the following format:

Combined Cash Budget

	January	February	March	Quarter
Cash balance, beginning				
Add cash collections				
Total cash available				
Less cash payments:				
Direct material purchases				
Conversion costs				
Operating expenses				
Equipment purchases				
Tax payment				
Total cash payments				
Ending cash balance before financing				
Financing:				
Borrowings				
Repayments				
Interest payments				
Ending cash balance				

8. Calculate the budgeted manufacturing cost per unit, using the following format (assume that fixed manufacturing overhead is budgeted to be $0.80 per unit for the year):

Budgeted Manufacturing Cost per Unit	
Direct materials cost per unit	
Conversion costs per unit	
Fixed manufacturing overhead per unit	
Budgeted cost of manufacturing each unit	

9. Prepare a budgeted income statement for the quarter ending March 31, using the following format:

Budgeted Income Statement
For the Quarter Ending March 31

Sales...
Cost of goods sold*...
Gross profit...
Operating expenses ....
Depreciation...
Operating income...
Less interest expense ....
Less provision for income taxes....................................
Net income..

*Cost of goods sold = Budgeted cost of manufacturing each unit × Number of units sold

P9-60A   Prepare budgeted income statement *(Learning Objective 2)*

The budget committee of Vinning Office Supply has assembled the following data. As the business manager, you must prepare the budgeted income statements for May and June.

a. Sales in April were $50,000. You forecast that monthly sales will increase 10% in May and 3% in June.

b. Vinning Office Supply maintains inventory of $9,000 plus 30% of sales revenues budgeted for the following month. Monthly purchases average 50% of sales revenues in that same month. Actual inventory on April 30 is $14,000. Sales budgeted for July are $55,000.

c. Monthly salaries amount to $4,000. Sales commissions equal 10% of sales for that month. Combine salaries and commissions into a single figure.

d. Other monthly expenses are as follows:

Rent expense..	$3,000, paid as incurred
Depreciation expense	$ 600
Insurance expense......................................	$ 200, expiration of prepaid amount
Income tax	20% of operating income

Requirement

1. Prepare Vinning Office Supply's budgeted income statements for May and June. Show cost of goods sold computations.

P9-61A Cash budgets *(Learning Objective 3)*

Daniel's Manufacturing is preparing its cash budgets for the first two months of the upcoming year. Here is the information about the company's upcoming cash receipts and cash disbursements:

a. Sales are 70% cash and 30% credit. Credit sales are collected 20% in the month of sale and the remainder in the month after sale. Actual sales in December were $55,000. Schedules of budgeted sales for the two months of the upcoming year are as follows:

	Budgeted Sales Revenue
January	$60,000
February	$68,000

b. Actual purchases of direct materials in December were $24,000. Daniel's purchases of direct materials in January are budgeted to be $22,000 and $26,000 in February. All purchases are paid 50% in the month of purchase and 50% the following month.

c. Salaries and sales commissions are also paid half in the month earned and half the next month. Actual salaries were $8,000 in December. Budgeted salaries in January are $9,000 and February budgeted salaries are $10,500. Sales commissions each month are 10% of that month's sales.

d. Rent expense is $3,000 per month.

e. Depreciation is $2,500 per month.

f. Estimated income tax payments are made at the end of January. The estimated tax payment is projected to be $12,500.

g. The cash balance at the end of the prior year was $21,000.

Requirements

1. Prepare schedules of (a) budgeted cash collections, (b) budgeted cash payments for purchases, and (c) budgeted cash payments for operating expenses. Show amounts for each month and totals for January and February.

2. Prepare a combined cash budget similar to Exhibit 9-16. If no financing activity took place, what is the budgeted cash balance on February 28?

P9-62A Prepare a combined cash budget and a budgeted balance sheet *(Learning Objective 3)*

Alliance Printing of Baltimore has applied for a loan. Bank of America has requested a budgeted balance sheet as of April 30, and a combined cash budget for April. As Alliance Printing's controller, you have assembled the following information:

a. March 31 equipment balance, $52,400; accumulated depreciation, $41,300.

b. April capital expenditures of $42,800 budgeted for cash purchase of equipment.

c. April depreciation expense, $900.

d. Cost of goods sold, 60% of sales.

e. Other April operating expenses, including income tax, total $13,200, 25% of which will be paid in cash and the remainder accrued at April 30.

f. March 31 owners' equity, $93,700.

g. March 31 cash balance, $40,600.

h. April budgeted sales, $90,000, 70% of which is for cash. Of the remaining 30%, half will be collected in April and half in May.

i. April cash collections on March sales, $29,700.

j. April cash payments of March 31 liabilities incurred for March purchases of inventory, $17,300.

k. March 31 inventory balance, $29,600.

l. April purchases of inventory, $10,000 for cash and $36,800 on credit. Half of the credit purchases will be paid in April and half in May.

Requirements

1. Prepare the budgeted balance sheet for Alliance Printing at April 30. Show separate computations for cash, inventory, and owners' equity balances.

2. Prepare the combined cash budget for April.

3. Suppose Alliance Printing has become aware of more efficient (and more expensive) equipment than it budgeted for purchase in April. What is the total amount of cash available for equipment purchases in April, before financing, if the minimum desired ending cash balance is $21,000? (For this requirement, disregard the $42,800 initially budgeted for equipment purchases.)

4. Before granting a loan to Alliance Printing, Bank of America asks for a sensitivity analysis assuming that April sales are only $60,000 rather than the $90,000 originally budgeted. (While the cost of goods sold will change, assume that purchases, depreciation, and the other operating expenses will remain the same as in the earlier requirements.)

   a. Prepare a revised budgeted balance sheet for Alliance Printing, showing separate computations for cash, inventory, and owners' equity balances.

   b. Suppose Alliance Printing has a minimum desired cash balance of $23,000. Will the company need to borrow cash in April?

   c. In this sensitivity analysis, sales declined by 33 1/3% ($30,000 ÷ $90,000). Is the decline in expenses and income more or less than 33 1/3%? Explain.

P9-63A Prepare performance reports for various organizational levels (*Learning Objective 4*)

Winnie's World operates a chain of pet stores in the Midwest. The manager of each store reports to the region manager, who, in turn, reports to the headquarters in Milwaukee, Wisconsin. The *actual* income statements for the Dayton store, the Ohio region (including the Dayton store), and the company as a whole (including the Ohio region) for July are as follows:

	Dayton	Ohio	Companywide
Revenue	$148,900	$1,647,000	$4,200,000
Expenses:			
Region manager/			
headquarters office	$ —	$ 60,000	$ 116,000
Cost of materials	81,100	871,900	1,807,000
Salary expense	38,300	415,100	1,119,000
Depreciation expense..............	7,200	91,000	435,000
Utilities expense.....................	4,000	46,200	260,000
Rent expense	2,400	34,700	178,000
Total expenses.........................	133,000	1,518,900	3,915,000
Operating income......................	$ 15,900	$ 128,100	$ 285,000

Budgeted amounts for July were as follows:

	Dayton	Ohio	Companywide
Revenue	$162,400	$1,769,700	$4,450,000
Expenses:			
Region manager/			
headquarters office	$ —	$ 65,600	$ 118,000
Cost of materials	86,400	963,400	1,972,000
Salary expense	38,800	442,000	1,095,000
Depreciation expense..............	7,200	87,800	449,000
Utilities expense.....................	4,400	54,400	271,000
Rent expense	3,600	32,300	174,000
Total expenses.........................	140,400	1,645,500	4,079,000
Operating income......................	$ 22,000	$ 124,200	$ 371,000

Requirements

1. Prepare a report for July that shows the performance of the Dayton store, the Ohio region, and the company as a whole. Follow the format of Exhibit 9-21.

2. As the Ohio region manager, would you investigate the Dayton store on the basis of this report? Why or why not?

3. Briefly discuss the benefits of budgeting. Base your discussion on Winnie's World's performance report.

P9-64A Prepare an inventory, purchases, and cost of goods sold budget *(Learning Objective 5)*

University Logos buys logo-imprinted merchandise and then sells it to university bookstores. Sales are expected to be $2,000,000 in September, $2,160,000 in October, $2,376,000 in November, and $2,500,000 in December. University Logos sets its prices to earn an average 30% gross profit on sales revenue. The company does not want inventory to fall below $400,000 plus 15% of the next month's cost of goods sold.

Requirement

1. Prepare an inventory, purchases, and cost of goods sold budget for the months of October and November.

Problems—Group B

P9-65B Comprehensive budgeting problem *(Learning Objectives 2 & 3)*

Osborne Manufacturing is preparing its master budget for the first quarter of the upcoming year. The following data pertain to Osborne Manufacturing's operations:

Current assets as of December 31 (prior year):	
Cash	$ 4,640
Accounts receivable, net	$ 51,000
Inventory	$ 15,600
Property, plant, and equipment, net	$121,500
Accounts payable	$ 42,800
Capital stock	$124,500
Retained earnings	$ 22,800

a. Actual sales in December were $72,000. Selling price per unit is projected to remain stable at $12 per unit throughout the budget period. Sales for the first five months of the upcoming year are budgeted to be as follows:

January	$104,400
February	$108,000
March	$112,800
April	$109,200
May	$105,600

b. Sales are 20% cash and 80% credit. All credit sales are collected in the month following the sale.

c. Osborne Manufacturing has a policy that states that each month's ending inventory of finished goods should be 10% of the following month's sales (in units).

d. Of each month's direct material purchases, 20% are paid for in the month of purchase, while the remainder is paid for in the month following purchase. Three pounds of direct material is needed per unit at $2.00 per pound. Ending inventory of direct materials should be 30% of next month's production needs.

e. Monthly manufacturing conversion costs are $4,500 for factory rent, $2,800 for other fixed manufacturing expenses, and $1.10 per unit for variable manufacturing overhead. No depreciation is included in these figures. All expenses are paid in the month in which they are incurred.

f. Computer equipment for the administrative offices will be purchased in the upcoming quarter. In January, Osborne Manufacturing will purchase equipment for $6,000 (cash), while February's cash expenditure will be $12,800 and March's cash expenditure will be $15,600.

g. Operating expenses are budgeted to be $1.30 per unit sold plus fixed operating expenses of $1,800 per month. All operating expenses are paid in the month in which they are incurred.

h. Depreciation on the building and equipment for the general and administrative offices is budgeted to be $4,600 for the entire quarter, which includes depreciation on new acquisitions.

i. Osborne Manufacturing has a policy that the ending cash balance in each month must be at least $4,200. The company has a line of credit with a local bank. It can borrow in increments of $1,000 at the beginning of each month, up to a total outstanding loan balance of $130,000. The interest rate on these loans is 2% per month simple interest (not compounded). Osborne Manufacturing would pay down on the line of credit balance if it has excess funds at the end of the quarter. The company would also pay the accumulated interest at the end of the quarter on the funds borrowed during the quarter.

j. The company's income tax rate is projected to be 30% of operating income less interest expense. The company pays $10,800 cash at the end of February in estimated taxes.

Requirements

1. Prepare a schedule of cash collections for January, February, and March, and for the quarter in total.

Cash Collections Budget

	January	February	March	Quarter
Cash sales				
Credit sales				
Total cash collections				

2. Prepare a production budget. (Hint: Unit sales = Sales in dollars / Selling price per unit.)

Production Budget

	January	February	March	Quarter
Unit sales				
Plus: Desired ending inventory				
Total needed				
Less: Beginning inventory				
Units to produce				

3. Prepare a direct materials budget.

Direct Materials Budget

	January	February	March	Quarter
Units to be produced				
× Pounds of DM needed per unit				
Quantity (pounds) needed for production				
Plus: Desired ending inventory of DM				
Total quantity (pounds) needed				
Less: Beginning inventory of DM				
Quantity (pounds) to purchase				
× Cost per pound				
Total cost of DM purchases				

4. Prepare a cash payments budget for the direct material purchases from Requirement 3.

Cash Payments for Direct Material Purchases Budget

	January	February	March	Quarter
December purchases (from Accounts Payable)				
January purchases				
February purchases				
March purchases				
Total cash payments for DM purchases				

5. Prepare a cash payments budget for conversion costs.

Cash Payments for Conversion Costs Budget

	January	February	March	Quarter
Variable conversion costs				
Rent (fixed)				
Other fixed MOH				
Total payments for conversion costs				

6. Prepare a cash payments budget for operating expenses.

Cash Payments for Operating Expenses Budget

	January	February	March	Quarter
Variable operating expenses				
Fixed operating expenses				
Total payments for operating expenses				

7. Prepare a combined cash budget.

Combined Cash Budget

	January	February	March	Quarter
Cash balance, beginning				
Add cash collections				
Total cash available				
Less cash payments:				
Direct material purchases				
Conversion costs				
Operating expenses				
Equipment purchases				
Tax payment				
Total disbursements				
Ending cash balance before financing				
Financing:				
Borrowings				
Repayments				
Interest payments				
Total financing				
Cash balance, ending				

8. Calculate the budgeted manufacturing cost per unit (assume that fixed manufacturing overhead is budgeted to be $0.80 per unit for the year).

Budgeted Manufacturing Cost per Unit

Direct materials cost per unit	
Conversion costs per unit	
Fixed manufacturing overhead per unit	
Budgeted cost of manufacturing each unit	

9. Prepare a budgeted income statement for the quarter ending March 31. (Hint: Cost of goods sold = Budgeted cost of manufacturing each unit × Number of units sold)

Budgeted Income Statement
For the Quarter Ended March 31

Sales..

Cost of goods sold...

Gross profit...

Operating expenses ....

Depreciation expense ....

Operating income..

Less interest expense ....

Less provision for income taxes.......................................

Net income...

P9-66B Prepare budgeted income statement (*Learning Objective 2*)

The budget committee of Omaha Office Supply has assembled the following data. As the business manager, you must prepare the budgeted income statements for May and June.

a. Sales in April were $42,000. You forecast that monthly sales will increase 12% in May and 3% in June.

b. Omaha Office Supply maintains inventory of $8,000 plus 30% of the sales revenue budgeted for the following month. Monthly purchases average 50% of sales revenue in that same month. Actual inventory on April 30 is $15,000. Sales budgeted for July are $45,000.

c. Monthly salaries amount to $6,000. Sales commissions equal 12% of sales for that month. Combine salaries and commissions into a single figure.

d. Other monthly expenses are as follows:

Rent expense	$2,200, paid as incurred
Depreciation expense	$ 300
Insurance expense	$ 100, expiration of prepaid amount
Income tax	20% of operating income

Requirement

1. Prepare Omaha's budgeted income statements for May and June. Show cost of goods sold computations.

P9-67B Cash budgets (*Learning Objective 3*)

Roan's Manufacturing is preparing its cash budgets for the first two months of the upcoming year. Here is the information about the company's upcoming cash receipts and cash disbursements:

a. Sales are 65% cash and 35% credit. Credit sales are collected 30% in the month of sale and the remainder in the month after sale. Actual sales in December were $51,000. Schedules of budgeted sales for the two months of the upcoming year are as follows:

	Budgeted sales revenue
January	$60,000
February	$69,000

b. Actual purchases of direct materials in December were $25,500. Daniel's purchases of direct materials in January are budgeted to be $23,500 and $28,000 in February. All purchases are paid 30% in the month of purchase and 70% the following month.

c. Salaries and sales commissions are also paid half in the month earned and half the next month. Actual salaries were $8,000 in December. Budgeted salaries in January are $9,000 and February budgeted salaries are $10,500. Sales commissions each month are 8% of that month's sales.

d. Rent expense is $3,300 per month.

e. Depreciation is $2,800 per month.

f. Estimated income tax payments are made at the end of January. The estimated tax payment is projected to be $12,000.

g. The cash balance at the end of the prior year was $18,000.

Requirements

1. Prepare schedules of (a) budgeted cash collections, (b) budgeted cash payments for purchases, and (c) budgeted cash payments for operating expenses. Show amounts for each month and totals for January and February.

2. Prepare a combined cash budget. If no financing activity took place, what is the budgeted cash balance on February 28?

P9-68B **Prepare a combined cash budget and a budgeted balance sheet** *(Learning Objective 3)*

Sheet Printing of Atlanta has applied for a loan. Bank of America has requested a budgeted balance sheet at April 30 and a combined cash budget for April. As Sheet Printing's controller, you have assembled the following information:

a. March 31 equipment balance, $52,600; accumulated depreciation, $41,700.

b. April capital expenditures of $42,000 budgeted for cash purchase of equipment.

c. April depreciation expense, $900.

d. Cost of goods sold, 65% of sales.

e. Other April operating expenses, including income tax, total $14,000, 20% of which will be paid in cash and the remainder accrued at April 30.

f. March 31 owners' equity, $91,700.

g. March 31 cash balance, $40,100.

h. April budgeted sales, $84,000, 60% of which is for cash; of the remaining 40%, half will be collected in April and half in May.

i. April cash collections on March sales, $29,200.

j. April cash payments of March 31 liabilities incurred for March purchases of inventory, $17,600.

k. March 31 inventory balance, $29,100.

l. April purchases of inventory, $10,300 for cash and $36,300 on credit. Half of the credit purchases will be paid in April and half in May.

Requirements

1. Prepare the budgeted balance sheet for Sheet Printing at April 30. Show separate computations for cash, inventory, and owners' equity balances.

2. Prepare the combined cash budget for April.

3. Suppose Sheet Printing has become aware of more efficient (and more expensive) equipment than it budgeted for purchase in April. What is the total amount of cash available for equipment purchases in April, before financing, if the minimum desired ending cash balance is $14,000? (For this requirement, disregard the $42,000 initially budgeted for equipment purchases.)

4. Before granting a loan to Sheet Printing, Bank of America asks for a sensitivity analysis assuming that April sales are only $56,000 rather than the $84,000 originally budgeted. (While the cost of goods sold will change, assume that purchases, depreciation, and the other operating expenses will remain the same as in the earlier requirements.)

   a. Prepare a revised budgeted balance sheet for Sheet Printing, showing separate computations for cash, inventory, and owners' equity balances.

   b. Suppose Sheet Printing has a minimum desired cash balance of $16,000. Will the company need to borrow cash in April?

   c. In this sensitivity analysis, sales declined by 33 1/3% ($28,000/$84,000). Is the decline in expenses and income more or less than 33 1/3%? Explain.

P9-69B **Prepare performance reports for various organizational levels** *(Learning Objective 4)*

Animal World operates a chain of pet stores in the Midwest. The manager of each store reports to the region manager, who, in turn, reports to headquarters in Naperville, Illinois. The actual and budgeted income statements for the Chesterfield store, the Missouri region (including the Chesterfield store), and the company as a whole (including the Missouri region) for July are as follows:

	Chesterfield	Missouri	Companywide
Revenue	$148,400	$1,645,000	$4,300,000
Expenses:			
Region manager/ headquarters office	$ —	$ 55,000	$ 118,000
Cost of materials	81,800	871,800	1,808,000
Salary expense	38,800	415,700	1,121,000
Depreciation expense	7,700	93,000	439,000
Utilities expense	4,600	46,500	265,000
Rent expense	2,500	34,400	178,000
Total expenses	135,400	1,516,400	3,929,000
Operating income	$ 13,000	$ 128,600	$ 371,000

Budgeted amounts for July were as follows:

	Chesterfield	Missouri	Companywide
Revenue	$162,400	$1,768,000	$4,550,000
Expenses:			
Region manager/ headquarters office	$ —	$ 60,600	$ 120,000
Cost of materials	86,700	963,600	1,974,000
Salary expense	38,900	440,000	1,092,000
Depreciation expense	7,700	87,400	447,000
Utilities expense	4,700	54,400	274,000
Rent expense	4,000	32,700	172,000
Total expenses	142,000	1,613,700	4,079,000
Operating income	$ 20,400	$ 154,300	$ 471,000

Requirements

1. Prepare a report for July that shows the performance of the Chesterfield store, the Missouri region, and the company as a whole.
2. As the Missouri region manager, would you investigate the Chesterfield store on the basis of this report? Why or why not?
3. Briefly discuss the benefits of budgeting. Base your discussion on Animal World's performance report.

P9-70B Prepare an inventory, purchases, and cost of goods sold budget *(Learning Objective 5)*

Cool Logos buys logo-imprinted merchandise and then sells it to university bookstores. Sales are expected to be $2,006,000 in September, $2,240,000 in October, $2,381,000 in November, and $2,570,000 in December. Cool Logos sets its prices to earn an average 40% gross profit on sales revenue. The company does not want inventory to fall below $420,000 plus 15% of the next month's cost of goods sold.

Requirement

1. Prepare an inventory, purchases, and cost of goods sold budget for the months of October and November.

APPLY YOUR KNOWLEDGE

Decision Cases

C9-71   Suggest performance improvements *(Learning Objective 1)*

Donna Tse recently joined Cycle World, a bicycle store in St. Louis, as an assistant manager. She recently finished her accounting courses. Cycle World's manager and owner, Jeff Towry, asks Tse to prepare a budgeted income statement for the upcoming year based on the information he has collected. Tse's budget follows:

CYCLE WORLD
Budgeted Income Statement
For the Year Ending July 31

Sales revenue		$244,000
Cost of goods sold		177,000
Gross profit		67,000
Operating expenses:		
Salary and commission expense	$46,000	
Rent expense	8,000	
Depreciation expense	2,000	
Insurance expense	800	
Miscellaneous expenses	12,000	68,800
Operating loss		(1,800)
Interest expense		225
Net loss		$ (2,025)

Requirement

1. Tse does not want to give Towry this budget without making constructive suggestions for steps Towry could take to improve expected performance. Write a memo to Towry outlining your suggestions. Your memo should take the following form:

> **Date:** _____
>
> **To:** Mr. Jeff Towry, Manager
>   Cycle World
>
> **From:** Donna Tse
>
> **Subject:** Cycle World's budgeted income statement

C9-72   Prepare cash budgets under two alternatives *(Learning Objectives 2 & 3)*

Each autumn, as a hobby, Suzanne De Angelo weaves cotton place mats to sell at a local crafts shop. The mats sell for $20 per set of four. The shop charges a 10% commission and remits the net proceeds to De Angelo at the end of December. De Angelo has woven and sold 25 sets each of the last two years. She has enough cotton in inventory to make another 25 sets. She paid $7 per set for the cotton. De Angelo uses a four-harness loom that she purchased for cash exactly two years ago. It is depreciated at the rate of $10 per month. The accounts payable relate to the cotton inventory and are payable by September 30.

De Angelo is considering buying an eight-harness loom so that she can weave more intricate patterns in linen. The new loom costs $1,000; it would be depreciated at $20 per month. Her bank has agreed to lend her $1,000 at 18% interest, with $200 principal plus accrued interest payable each December 31. De Angelo believes she can weave 15 linen place mat sets in time for the Christmas rush if she does not weave any cotton mats. She predicts that each linen set will sell for $50. Linen costs $18 per set. De Angelo's supplier will sell her linen on credit, payable December 31.

De Angelo plans to keep her old loom whether or not she buys the new loom. The balance sheet for her weaving business at August 31 is as follows:

SUZANNE DE ANGELO, WEAVER
Balance Sheet
August 31

Current assets:			Current liabilities:		
Cash		$ 25	Accounts payable		$ 74
Inventory of cotton		175			
		200			
Fixed assets:					
Loom		500	Owner's equity		386
Accumulated depreciation		(240)			
		260			
Total assets		$ 460	Total liabilities and owner's equity		$460

Requirements

1. Prepare a combined cash budget for the four months ending December 31, for two alternatives: weaving the place mats in cotton using the existing loom and weaving the place mats in linen using the new loom. For each alternative, prepare a budgeted income statement for the four months ending December 31, and a budgeted balance sheet at December 31.
2. On the basis of financial considerations only, what should De Angelo do? Give your reason.
3. What nonfinancial factors might De Angelo consider in her decision?

Ethical Issue

I9-73   Ethical considerations for padded budgets (Learning Objectives 1 & 5)

Residence Suites operates a regional hotel chain. Each hotel is operated by a manager and an assistant manager/controller. Many of the staff who run the front desk, clean the rooms, and prepare the breakfast buffet work part-time or have a second job, so turnover is high.

Assistant manager/controller Terry Dunn asked the new bookkeeper to help prepare the hotel's master budget. The master budget is prepared once a year and submitted to company headquarters for approval. Once approved, the master budget is used to evaluate the hotel's performance. These performance evaluations affect hotel managers' bonuses; they also affect company decisions about which hotels deserve extra funds for capital improvements.

When the budget was almost complete, Dunn asked the bookkeeper to increase amounts budgeted for labor and supplies by 15%. When asked why, Dunn responded that hotel manager Clay Murry told her to do this when she began working at the hotel. Murry explained that this budgetary cushion gave him flexibility in running the hotel. For example, because company headquarters tightly controls capital improvement funds, Murry can use the extra money budgeted for labor and supplies to replace broken televisions or to pay "bonuses" to keep valued employees. Dunn initially accepted this explanation because she had observed similar behavior at her previous place of employment.

Put yourself in Dunn's position. In deciding how to deal with the situation, answer the following questions:

1. What is the ethical issue?
2. What are my options?
3. What are the possible consequences?
4. What should I do?

Team Project

T9-74   Analyzing and discussing budget concerns *(Learning Objectives 1, 2, & 3)*

Xellnet provides e-commerce software for the pharmaceuticals industry. Xellnet is organized into several divisions. A companywide planning committee sets general strategy and goals for the company and its divisions, but each division develops its own budget.

Rick Watson is the new division manager of wireless communications software. His division has two departments: Development and Sales. Carrie Pronai manages the 20 or so programmers and systems specialists typically employed in the Development Department to create and update the division's software applications. Liz Smith manages the Sales Department.

Xellnet considers the divisions to be investment centers. To earn his bonus next year, Watson must achieve a 30% return on the $3 million invested in his division. This amounts to $900,000 of income (30% × $3 million). Within the wireless division, development is a cost center, while sales is a revenue center.

Budgeting is in progress. Pronai met with her staff and is now struggling with two sets of numbers. Alternative A is her best estimate of next year's costs. However, unexpected problems can arise in the writing of software, and finding competent programmers is an ongoing challenge. She knows that Watson was a programmer before he earned an MBA, so he should be sensitive to this uncertainty. Consequently, she is thinking of increasing her budgeted costs (Alternative B). Her department's bonuses largely depend on whether the department meets its budgeted costs.

<table>
<tr><td colspan="3" align="center">**XELLNET**
Wireless Division
Development Budget</td></tr>
<tr><td></td><td>**Alternative A**</td><td>**Alternative B**</td></tr>
<tr><td>Salaries expense (including overtime and part-time)</td><td>$2,400,000</td><td>$2,640,000</td></tr>
<tr><td>Software expense</td><td>120,000</td><td>132,000</td></tr>
<tr><td>Travel expense</td><td>65,000</td><td>71,500</td></tr>
<tr><td>Depreciation expense</td><td>255,000</td><td>255,000</td></tr>
<tr><td>Miscellaneous expense</td><td>100,000</td><td>110,000</td></tr>
<tr><td>Total expense</td><td>$2,940,000</td><td>$3,208,500</td></tr>
</table>

Liz Smith is also struggling with her sales budget. Companies have made their initial investments in communications software, so it is harder to win new customers. If things go well, she believes her sales team can maintain the level of growth achieved over the last few years. This is Alternative A in the sales budget. However, if Smith is too optimistic, sales may fall short of the budget. If this happens, her team will not receive bonuses. Therefore, Smith is considering reducing the sales numbers and submitting Alternative B.

<table>
<tr><td colspan="3" align="center">**XELLNET**
Wireless Division
Sales Budget</td></tr>
<tr><td></td><td>**Alternative A**</td><td>**Alternative B**</td></tr>
<tr><td>Sales revenue</td><td>$5,000,000</td><td>$4,500,000</td></tr>
<tr><td>Salaries expense</td><td>360,000</td><td>360,000</td></tr>
<tr><td>Travel expense</td><td>240,000</td><td>210,500</td></tr>
</table>

Split your team into three groups. Each group should meet separately before the entire team meets.

Requirements

1. The first group plays the role of Development Manager Carrie Pronai. Before meeting with the entire team, determine which set of budget numbers you are going to present to Rick Watson. Write a memo supporting your decision. Give this memo to the third group before the team meeting.

2. The second group plays the role of Sales Manager Liz Smith. Before meeting with the entire team, determine which set of budget numbers you are going to present to Rick Watson. Write a memo supporting your decision. Give this memo to the third group before the team meeting.

3. The third group plays the role of Division Manager Rick Watson. Before meeting with the entire team, use the memos that Pronai and Smith provided to prepare a division budget based on the sales and development budgets. Your divisional overhead costs (additional costs beyond those incurred by the Development and Sales Departments) are approximately $390,000. Determine whether the wireless division can meet its targeted 30% return on assets given the budgeted alternatives submitted by your department managers.

During the meeting of the entire team, the group playing Watson presents the division budget and considers its implications. Each group should take turns discussing its concerns with the proposed budget. The team as a whole should consider whether the division budget must be revised. The team should prepare a report that includes the division budget and a summary of the issues covered in the team meeting.

Discussion & Analysis

1. "The sales budget is the most important budget." Do you agree or disagree? Explain your answer.

2. List at least four reasons why a company would use budgeting.

3. Describe the difference between an operating budget and a capital budget.

4. Describe the process for developing a budget.

5. Compare and contrast "participative budgeting" with "top-down" budgeting.

6. What is a budget committee? What is the budget committee's role in the budgeting process?

7. What are operating budgets? List at least four operating budgets.

8. What are financial budgets? List at least three financial budgets.

9. What is a responsibility center? List the four types of responsibility centers. Describe an example of each of the four types of responsibility centers.

10. How does the master budget for a service company differ from a master budget for a manufacturing company? Which (if any) operating budgets differ and how specifically do they differ? Which (if any) financial budgets differ and how specifically do they differ?

Application & Analysis

9-1 Budgeting for a Single Product

In this activity, you will be creating budgets for a single product for each of the months in an upcoming quarter. Select a product that you could purchase in large quantities (at a Sam's Club or other warehouse retail chain) and repackage into smaller quantities to offer for sale at a sidewalk café, a sporting event, a flea market, or other similar venue. Investigate the price and quantity at which this product is available at the warehouse. Choose a selling price for the smaller (repackaged) package. Make reasonable assumptions about how many of the smaller units you can sell in each of the next four months (you will need the fourth month's sales in units for the operating budgets).

Basic Discussion Questions

1. Describe your product. What is your cost of this product? What size (quantity) will you purchase? At what price will you sell your repackaged product? Make projections of your sales in units in each of the upcoming three months.

2. Estimate how many hours you will spend in each of the upcoming three months doing the purchasing, repackaging, and selling. Select a reasonable wage rate for yourself. What will your total labor costs be in each of the upcoming three months?

3. Prepare a sales budget for each of the upcoming three months.

4. Prepare the direct material budgets for the upcoming three months, assuming that you need to keep 10% of the direct materials needed for next month's sales on hand at the end of each month (this requirement is why you needed to estimate unit sales for four months).

6. Prepare a direct labor budget (for your labor) for each of the upcoming three months.

7. Think about any other expenses you are likely to have (i.e., booth rental at a flea market or a vendor license). Prepare the operating expenses budget for each of the upcoming three months.

8. Prepare a budgeted income statement that reflects the budgets you prepared, including the sales budget, direct materials budget, direct labor budget, and the operating expenses budget. This budgeted income statement should include one column for each of the three months in the quarter and it should also include a total column that represents the totals of the three months. What is your projected profit by month and for the quarter?

Classroom Applications

Web: Post the activity description and discussion questions on an electronic discussion board. Have small groups of students choose a product for their groups. The group should collaborate on estimating selling price, sales volume, and costs and on preparing the budgets. The group should discuss the results of the budget and the budgeting process.

Classroom: Form groups of 3–4 students. Your group should choose a product. Your group should collaborate on estimating selling price, sales volume, and costs and on preparing the budgets. Discuss the results of the budget and the budgeting process itself. Prepare a five-minute presentation about your group's product and its budgets.

Independent: Select a product as described in the introduction for this activity. Prepare the budgets as listed. Be sure to include your assumptions about estimated selling price, estimated sales volume, and your estimates of all of your costs. Turn in a 3–4 page typed paper (12 point font, double-spaced with 1" margins). The paper should include your budgets for each of the three months and for the quarter in total. These budgets can be tables within your Word document.

For additional Application & Analysis projects and implementation tips, see the Instructor Resources in MyAccountingLab.com.

CMA-1. Crisper, Inc. plans to sell 80,000 bags of potato chips in June, and each of these bags requires five potatoes. Pertinent data includes:

	Bags of potato chips	Potatoes
Actual June inventory	15,000 bags	27,000 potatoes
Desired June 30 inventory	18,000 bags	23,000 potatoes

What number of units of raw material should Crisper plan to purchase?

    a. 381,000

    b. 389,000

    c. 411,000

    d. 419,000

CMA-2. Holland Company is in the process of projecting its cash position at the end of the second quarter. Shown below is pertinent information from Holland's records.

Cash balance at end of 1st quarter	$ 36,000
Cash collections from customers for 2nd quarter	1,300,000
Accounts payable at end of 1st quarter	100,000
Accounts payable at end of 2nd quarter	75,000
All 2nd quarter costs and expenses (accrual basis)	1,200,000
Depreciation (accrued expense included above)	60,000
Purchases of equipment (for cash)	50,000
Gain on sale of asset (for cash)	5,000
Net book value of asset sold	35,000
Repayment of notes payable	66,000

From the data above, determine Holland's projected cash balance at the end of the second quarter.

    a. Zero
    b. $25,000
    c. $60,000
    d. $95,000

(CMA Adapted)

Quick Check Answers

1. *d* 2. *b* 3. *c* 4. *a* 5. *a* 6. *d*
7. *c* 8. *a* 9. *d* 10. *d*

For online homework, exercises, and problems that provide you with immediate feedback, please visit www.myaccountinglab.com.

Production and Direct Materials Budgets

(Learning Objective 2)

Collegiate Basket Company makes high-quality picnic baskets marketed to the enthusiastic tailgater. The baskets are hand-painted in school colors with the college mascot on the top. The company's sales budget for the third quarter of the fiscal year is as follows:

Collegiate Basket Company
Sales Budget
For the Quarter ended September 30

	Month			
	July	August	September	3rd Quarter
Unit Sales (baskets)	1,225	1,300	1,350	3,875
Unit Selling Price	× $70	× $70	× $70	× $70
Total Sales Revenue	$85,750	$91,000	$94,500	$271,250

Additionally, the company has estimated October sales to be 1,400 units.

Collegiate doesn't want its inventory to fall below 10% of the next month's unit sales, but it started July with only 100 completed baskets in stock.

Collegiate buys the wood it uses to make the baskets from a local lumber company at a price of $3 per foot. Each basket requires 4 feet of lumber. Collegiate wants to maintain an ending inventory of direct materials equal to 20% of the materials needed for next month's production. On July 1, the company had 1,000 feet of lumber on hand.

Requirement

1. Prepare the following budgets for July, August, and September, as well as a budget for the third quarter:

    a. Production budget

    b. Direct material budget

DEMO DOC Solutions

Requirement 1

a. Production budget

To prepare the production budget, we start with the unit sales (baskets) from the sales budget and add the amount of inventory that Collegiate wants to have on hand at the end of the month. We know that Collegiate doesn't want its inventory to fall below 10% of the next month's unit sales.

So, we can calculate the company's desired ending inventory each month as follows:

$$\text{July: } 1,300 \quad \text{(August unit sales)} \times 10\% = 130 \text{ units}$$
$$\text{August: } 1,350 \text{ (September unit sales)} \times 10\% = 135 \text{ units}$$
$$\text{September: } 1,400 \quad \text{(October unit sales)} \times 10\% = 140 \text{ units}$$

We begin to build our production budget with this data:

Collegiate Basket Company
Production Budget
For the Quarter ended September 30

	Month			3rd Quarter
	July	August	September	
Unit Sales (baskets)	1,225	1,300	1,350	3,875
Plus: Desired Ending Inventory	130	135	140 ⟶	140
Total Needed	1,355	1,435	1,490	4,015

Notice that we don't add up the desired ending inventory for each month and put that amount in the quarter column. The third quarter begins on July 1 and ends on September 30, so the ending inventory for the quarter is the balance at September 30, as shown by the blue arrow in the budget.

Now we know the total number of units needed each month. To complete the production budget, we need to subtract what the company already has in stock at the beginning of the month. After doing so, we'll know how many units the company will need to produce each month.

We were told that the company had 100 completed baskets on July 1. To determine the beginning inventory for August and September, we simply take the ending inventory from the previous month (the ending inventory one month, becomes the beginning inventory the next month). This is shown by the red arrows in the budget below.

Collegiate Basket Company
Production Budget
For the Quarter ended September 30

	Month			3rd Quarter
	July	August	September	
Unit Sales (baskets)	1,225	1,300	1,350	3,875
Plus: Desired Ending Inventory	130	135	140 ⟶	140
Total Needed	1,355	1,435	1,490	4,015
Less: Beginning Inventory	(100)	(130)	(135)	(100)
Units to produce	1,255	1,305	1,355	3,915

Finally, we subtract the beginning inventory from the total units need to determine the number of units to produce each month.

Notice from the orange arrow that the beginning inventory for the third quarter is the July 1 balance of 100 units. That's because the third quarter of the fiscal year begins on July 1. Don't make the mistake of adding up all of the beginning inventory units and placing that in the third quarter column.

b. Direct materials budget

Now that we know how many baskets Collegiate needs to produce, we are ready to prepare the direct materials budget. Each basket requires 4 feet of lumbers, so we figure out the quantity of direct materials (DM) needed for production each month as follows:

Collegiate Basket Company
Direct Materials Budget
For the Quarter ended September 30

	Month			
	July	August	September	3rd Quarter
Units to be produced (from Production Budget)	1,255	1,305	1,355	3,915
× Quantity (feet) of DM needed per unit	× 4	× 4	× 4	× 4
Quantity (feet) needed for production	5,020	5,220	5,420	15,660

Let's also assume that the Fourth quarter production budget indicates that 1,408 units will be produced in October, resulting in 5,632 feet of lumber needed for production in October (1,408 × 4 feet = 5,632 feet).

Next, we need to calculate the amount of lumber that Collegiate wants to have on hand at the end of each month. We know that Collegiate wants to maintain an ending stock of lumber equal to 20% of the materials needed for next month's production. So, the desired ending inventory of lumber for each month can be calculated as follows:

July: 5,220 feet (August quantity needed) × 20% = 1,044 feet

August: 5,420 feet (September quantity needed) × 20% = 1,084 feet

September: 5,632 feet (October quantity needed) × 20% = 1,126 feet

continued on the next page

By adding the desired ending inventory to the amount of lumber needed for production, we are able to figure out the total amount of lumber needed each month:

Collegiate Basket Company
Direct Materials Budget
For the Quarter ended September 30

	Month			3rd Quarter
	July	August	September	
Units to be produced (from Production Budget)	1,255	1,305	1,355	3,915
× Quantity (feet) of DM needed per unit	× 4	× 4	× 4	× 4
Quantity (feet) needed for production	5,020	5,220	5,420	15,660
Plus: Desired End Inventory of DM	1,044	1,084	1,126 ⟶	1,126
Total Quantity (feet) Needed	6,064	6,304	6,546	16,786

Notice again from the blue arrow that the ending inventory for the quarter is the ending inventory on September 30.

Will Collegiate need to buy all of this inventory? No, because it begins each month with some lumber on hand. So the next step is to subtract the beginning inventory of lumber from the total needed in order to arrive at the amount of lumber to purchase.

We were told that the company had 1,000 yards of lumber in stock on July 1. To determine the beginning inventory for August and September, we just take the ending inventory from the previous month. This is shown by the red arrows in the budget below.

Collegiate Basket Company
Direct Materials Budget
For the Quarter ended September 30

	Month			3rd Quarter
	July	August	September	
Units to be produced (from Production Budget)	1,255	1,305	1,355	3,915
× Quantity (feet) of DM needed per unit	× 4	× 4	× 4	× 4
Quantity (feet) needed for production	5,020	5,220	5,420	15,660
Plus: Desired End Inventory of DM	1,044	1,084	1,126 ⟶	1,126
Total Quantity (feet) Needed	6,064	6,304	6,546	16,786
Less: Beginning Inventory of DM	1,000	1,044	1,084	1,000
Quantity (feet) to purchase	5,064	5,260	5,462	15,786

Notice again from the orange arrow that the beginning inventory for the quarter is the July 1 inventory balance.

Now we know the total amount of lumber that Collegiate needs to purchase each month. The final step is to figure out how much these purchases will cost. To do so, we simply multiply the total feet of lumber to purchase by the $3 cost per foot:

Collegiate Basket Company
Direct Materials Budget
For the Quarter ended September 30

	Month			
	July	August	September	3rd Quarter
Units to be produced (from Production Budget)	1,255	1,305	1,355	3,915
× Quantity (feet) of DM needed per unit	× 4	× 4	× 4	× 4
Quantity (feet) needed for production	5,020	5,220	5,420	15,660
Plus: Desired End Inventory of DM	1,044	1,084	1,126	1,126
Total Quantity (feet) Needed	6,064	6,304	6,546	16,786
Less: Beginning Inventory of DM	1,000	1,044	1,084	1,000
Quantity (feet) to purchase	5,064	5,260	5,462	15,786
× Cost per foot	× $ 3	× $ 3	× $ 3	× $ 3
Total Cost of DM purchases	$15,192	$15,780	$16,386	$47,358

How does McDonald's make sure that its 30,000

restaurants deliver quality, service, cleanliness, and value to over 46 million customers worldwide each day? It does so by using budgets, standards, and variances. Managers budget sales for each hour and schedule just enough workers to handle the budgeted level of sales. During the day, the manager computes variances for sales (for example, actual sales minus budgeted sales) and for direct labor. If actual sales fall short of the budget, the manager can send employees home early. This helps control direct labor cost.

McDonald's also sets budgets and standards for direct materials. From Beijing to Miami, the standards for a regular McDonald's hamburger are the same: 1 bun, 1 hamburger patty, 1 pickle slice, 1/8 teaspoon of onion, 1/4 teaspoon of mustard, and 1/2 ounce of ketchup. To control direct materials costs, for example, the manager compares the number of hamburger patties actually used with the number of patties that should have been used, given the store's actual sales.

McDonald's uses budgets, standards, and variances to control costs so prices remain low enough that customers believe McDonald's provides good *value*. McDonald's also uses standards and variances to motivate employees to focus on the following:

- Quality—sandwiches unsold within 10 minutes are thrown away.
- Service—customers should receive food within 90 seconds of ordering.
- Cleanliness—mystery shoppers score restaurants' cleanliness.

Source: www.mcdonalds.com (2009)

CHAPTER 10

Flexible Budgets and Standard Costs

Learning Objectives

1 Prepare a flexible budget for planning purposes

2 Use the sales volume variance and flexible budget variance to explain why actual results differ from the master budget

3 Identify the benefits of standard costs and learn how to set standards

4 Compute standard cost variances for direct materials and direct labor

5 Compute manufacturing overhead variances

6 (Appendix) Record transactions at standard cost and prepare a standard cost income statement

In the last chapter, we saw how managers use budgets for planning and performance evaluation. We saw that managers compare actual results to budgeted figures, and investigate any variances they deem to be significant. This chapter builds on your knowledge of budgeting to show how managers can use more in-depth variance analysis techniques to learn *why* actual results differ from budgets. Why is this important? Because you must know *why* actual costs differ from the budget to identify problems and to decide what, if any, action to take.

In this chapter, you'll learn how managers of companies can use flexible budgets, standard costs, and variance analysis to better pinpoint *why* actual results differ from the budget. This is the first step in determining how to correct problems.

How do Managers Use Flexible Budgets?

In this chapter we'll see how Kool-Time Pools, an installer of in-ground swimming pools, uses flexible budgets and standard costs to help control its operations. Kool-Time uses direct materials, direct labor, and manufacturing overhead (such as the monthly lease on the earth moving equipment) to manufacture the swimming pools directly on the customer's site. In addition to manufacturing costs, the company incurs selling and administrative expenses in conjunction with its marketing and sales efforts. As with most companies, some of these costs are variable, while others are fixed.

What Is a Static Budget?

At the beginning of the year, Kool-Time's managers prepared a master budget like the one in Chapter 9. The master budget is a **static budget**, which means that it is prepared for *one* level of sales volume. Once the master budget is developed, it does not change.

Exhibit 10-1 compares June's actual results with the static (master) budget for June. The difference between actual results and the budget is called a **variance**. In this case, because we are comparing actual results against the static budget, this particular variance is called the static budget variance. Variances are considered favorable (F) when a higher actual amount increases operating income and unfavorable (U) when a higher actual amount decreases operating income. Favorable variances should not necessarily be interpreted as "good." Likewise, unfavorable variances should not be interpreted as "bad." Rather, they simply indicate the variance's effect on operating income. Exhibit 10-1 shows that Kool-Time's revenues were $25,000 higher than expected and its expenses were $21,000 higher than expected. Together, these variances resulted in a $4,000 favorable static budget variance for operating income.

EXHIBIT 10-1 Actual Results Versus Static Budget

KOOL-TIME POOLS Comparison of Actual Results with Static Budget Month Ended June 30			
	Actual Results	**Static (Master) Budget**	**Static Budget Variance**
Output units (pools installed)	10	8	2 F
Sales revenue	$ 121,000	$ 96,000	$ 25,000 F
Expenses	(105,000)	(84,000)	(21,000) U
Operating income	$ 16,000	$ 12,000	$ 4,000 F

What Is a Flexible Budget?

The static budget variance in Exhibit 10-1 is hard to analyze because the static budget is based on 8 pools, but actual results are for 10 pools. Trying to compare actual results against a budget prepared for a different volume is like comparing apples to oranges. Why did the $21,000 unfavorable expense variance occur? Were materials wasted? Did the cost of materials suddenly increase? How much of the additional expense and revenues arose because Kool-Time installed 10 pools rather than 8? The simple comparison presented in Exhibit 10-1 does not give managers enough information to answer these questions.

However, flexible budgets can help managers answer such questions. Exhibit 10-2 shows that in contrast to the static budget developed for a single level of sales volume, **flexible budgets** are summarized budgets prepared for different levels of volume. Flexible budgets can be used to help managers plan for future periods *and* to evaluate performance after the period has ended. We'll consider both uses and then get back to the question of why the $21,000 unfavorable expense variance occurred.

Using Flexible Budgets for Planning

1 Prepare a flexible budget for planning purposes

Managers can use flexible budgets for planning revenues and expenses at different sales volumes. Even though Kool-Time's managers believe the company will install eight pools in June, they also know that they might not be correct about this estimate. Pool sales

EXHIBIT 10-2 **Static Versus Flexible Budgets**

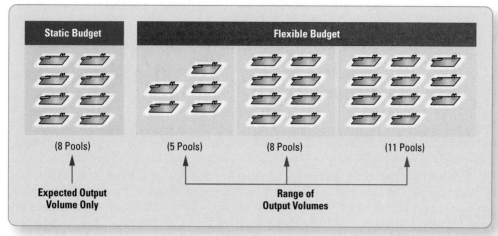

could be higher or lower during the month, and managers need to be prepared for both possibilities. Flexible budgets show how Kool-Time's revenues and expenses *should* vary as the number of pools installed varies.

Let's prepare flexible budgets for Kool-Time, assuming pool sales for the month could be as low as 5 or as high as 11. We'll start with revenues: The budgeted sales price per pool is $12,000, so each additional pool sale should yield another $12,000 of revenue. Exhibit 10-3 shows projected revenues at three possible volumes: 5 pools, 8 pools, and 11 pools.

EXHIBIT 10-3 **Flexible Budget**

KOOL-TIME POOLS
Flexible Budget
Month Ended June 30

		Output Units (Pools Installed)		
	Flexible Budget per Output Unit	5	8	11
Sales revenue	$12,000	$60,000	$96,000	$132,000
Variable expenses	8,000	40,000	64,000	88,000
Fixed expenses		20,000	20,000	20,000
Total expenses		60,000	84,000	108,000
Operating income		$ 0	$12,000	$ 24,000

To project expenses at different volumes, managers must know how the company's costs behave. Total fixed costs will be the same regardless of volume as long as the volume is within the same relevant range. However, total variable costs will change as volume changes. Managers use a mixed cost equation, such as the one we discussed in Chapter 6, to budget expenses at different volumes. This is sometimes referred to as a flexible budget formula:

Flexible budget total cost = (Number of output units × Variable cost per output unit) + Total fixed cost

Kool-Time's variable costs are $8,000 per pool. Of this amount, $7,000 is for variable manufacturing costs (direct materials, direct labor, and variable manufacturing overhead such as gasoline to operate the earthmoving equipment), while $1,000 is for variable selling and administrative expenses (such as the commission paid to sales staff on every pool sold). It is these variable expenses that put the "flex" in the flexible budget because budgeted total monthly fixed costs remain constant. Kool-Time's monthly fixed costs are $20,000. This includes $12,000 of fixed monthly manufacturing overhead (such as the the monthly lease of earth-moving equipment), while $8,000 relates to fixed selling and administrative expenses (sales and administrative salaries, lease of sales office, telephone and Internet service, and so forth).

Using this information on cost behavior, managers can predict costs at different volumes, just as we did in Chapter 6. For example, the total budgeted cost for five pools is as follows:

$$\$60,000 = (5 \text{ pools} \times \$8,000 \text{ variable cost per pool}) + \$20,000 \text{ fixed cost}$$

Likewise, the total budgeted cost for 11 pools is as follows:

$$\$108,000 = (11 \text{ pools} \times \$8,000 \text{ variable cost per pool}) + \$20,000 \text{ fixed cost}$$

Exhibit 10-3 shows the revenues and expenses anticipated if Kool-Time sells 5, 8, or 11 pools during the month. Kool-Time's best estimate is 8 pools, but by acknowledging that sales could be as low as 5 or as high as 11, Kool-Time's managers will be better prepared for any differences in volume that may arise.

Managers develop flexible budgets like Exhibit 10-3 for any number of volumes using a simple Excel spreadsheet or more sophisticated Web-based budget management software. However, managers must be careful: *They must consider the company's relevant range.* Why? They do so because total monthly fixed costs and the variable cost per pool change outside this range. Kool-Time's relevant range is 0 to 11 pools. If the company installs 12 pools, it will have to lease additional equipment, so fixed monthly costs will exceed $20,000. Kool-Time also will have to pay workers an overtime premium, so the variable cost per pool will be more than $8,000.

GRAPHING FLEXIBLE BUDGET COSTS Sometimes, it's helpful for managers to see a graph of the flexible budget costs. Exhibit 10-4 shows budgeted total costs for the entire relevant range of 0 to 11 pools. Because Kool-Time has both fixed and variable costs, its total costs are mixed. Kool-Time's flexible budget graph has the same characteristics as the mixed cost graphs we discussed in Chapter 6. The total cost line intersects the vertical axis at the level of total fixed cost ($20,000) that Kool-Time will incur whether it installs 0 pools or 11 pools. The total cost line also slopes upward at the rate of $8,000 per pool, which is Kool-Time's variable cost per pool. Each additional pool, up to 11 pools, should cost Kool-Time an extra $8,000.

EXHIBIT 10-4 Kool-Time Pools' Monthly Flexible Budget Graph

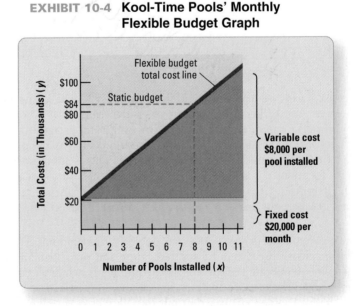

As shown by the dotted line in Exhibit 10-4, Kool-Time expects to install 8 pools in June (at a total cost of $84,000). But managers also can use this graph to *plan* costs for anywhere from 0 to 11 pools.

Using Flexible Budgets for Evaluating Performance

We just saw how managers can use flexible budgets for planning purposes. But managers can also use flexible budgets *at the end of the period* to evaluate the company's financial performance and help control costs. Rather than comparing actual revenues and expenses against the static budget (as shown in Exhibit 10-1), managers can compare the actual results against the flexible budget *for the actual volume of output* that occurred during the period.

Consider June, when Kool-Time *actually* installed 10 pools. The flexible budget graph in Exhibit 10-5 show that *flexible budgeted* total costs for 10 pools are as follows:

Variable costs (10 × $8,000)	$ 80,000
Fixed costs	20,000
Total costs	$100,000

June's *actual* costs were $105,000 (Exhibit 10-1). Consequently, June's actual costs for 10 pools ($105,000) slightly exceed the budget for 10 pools ($100,000). Managers can use graphs such as Exhibit 10-5 to see at a glance whether actual costs are either of the following:

■ Higher than budgeted for the actual volume of output (as in April, June, and August)

■ Lower than budgeted for the actual volume of output (as in May and July).

EXHIBIT 10-5 Kool-Time Pools' Graph of Actual and Budgeted Monthly Costs

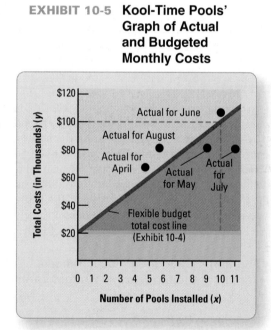

Why is this important?

"Flexible budgets allow managers to compare actual results with the results they would have expected for the particular volume achieved."

We used a simple graph to illustrate how Kool-Time's managers can compare actual costs against flexible budgeted costs. Unlike the apples-to-oranges comparison in Exhibit 10-1, comparing actual costs against flexible budgeted costs allows managers to make an apples-to-apples comparison. Why? Because both the actual costs and the flexible budgeted costs are based on the *same actual volume of activity (10 pools)*. In other words, if management would have had a crystal ball before the month began, it would have budgeted for 10 pools rather than eight. By comparing the actual costs with the flexible budgeted costs for 10 pools, Kool-Time's managers see that their expenses were only $5,000 higher than anticipated *for this volume*. This explains a portion of the $21,000 unfavorable expense variance shown in Exhibit 10-1. In the next section, we'll see how managers can perform a more in-depth analysis to find out more about why the $21,000 unfavorable expense variance shown in Exhibit 10-1 occurred.

STOP & THINK

Use the graph in Exhibit 10-5 and Kool-Time's flexible budget mixed cost equation to answer the following questions:

1. How many pools did Kool-Time install in July?
2. What were Kool-Time's actual costs in July?
3. Using Kool-Time's flexible budget mixed cost equation, what is the flexible budget total cost for the month of July?
4. Is Kool-Time's variance for total costs favorable or unfavorable in July?

Answer:

1. Exhibit 10-5 shows that Kool-Time installed 11 pools in July.
2. Exhibit 10-5 shows that Kool-Time's actual costs in July were about $80,000.
3. Using Kool-Time's flexible budget mixed cost equation the flexible budget total cost for the month of July is as follows:

Variable costs (11 × $8,000)	$ 88,000
Fixed costs	20,000
Total costs...	$108,000

4. Kool-Time's July variance for total costs is $28,000 ($108,000 − $80,000) favorable because actual costs are less than the budget.

2 Use the sales volume variance and flexible budget variance to explain why actual results differ from the master budget

How do Managers Compute the Sales Volume Variance and Flexible Budget Variance?

Managers must know *why* a variance occurred to pinpoint problems and to identify corrective action. Recall that Kool-Time's managers had a hard time understanding why the static budget variances in Exhibit 10-1 occurred because comparing the figures in that exhibit was like comparing apples to oranges: The actual results were based on the 10 pools installed, yet the budget was for 8 pools. To get more answers as to why the static budget variance occurred, managers often separate the static budget variance into two different parts: (1) the sales volume variance and (2) the flexible budget variance. Exhibit 10-6 shows how the static budget variance can be separated into these two variances. To obtain these variances managers first need to prepare a flexible budget for the actual level of output for the period (10 pools).

EXHIBIT 10-6 **The Static Budget Variance, the Sales Volume Variance, and the Flexible Budget Variance**

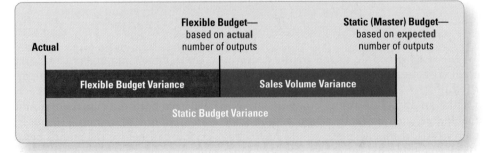

Exhibit 10-6 shows the following:

- The **sales volume variance** is the difference between the *static* (master) budget and the *flexible* budget (for the actual number of outputs). As the name suggests, this variance arises *only* because the number of units actually sold differs from the volume originally planned for in the static master budget.

The **flexible budget variance** is the difference between the *flexible* budget and the *actual* results. This variance arises because the company actually earned more or less revenue or incurred more or less expense than expected *for the actual level of output (10 pools)*. In other words, this variance is due to factors *other than* volume.

Let's see how Kool-Time's managers calculate and interpret these two different variances. Exhibit 10-7 shows Kool-Time's performance report for June. Column 1 shows Kool-Time's actual results for the period. This information is gathered from the general ledger. Now, consider the static master budget amounts presented in column 5. Recall that at the *beginning* of the period, Kool-Time *expected* to sell eight pools. For these eight pools, Kool-Time's

- budgeted sales revenue is $96,000 (8 × $12,000).

- budgeted variable expenses are $64,000 (8 × $8,000).

- budgeted fixed expenses are $20,000.

Notice that the amounts shown in columns 1 and 5 are the same as those shown in Exhibit 10-1. The only difference is that here we show a little more detail: Variable and fixed costs are shown separately; they are not lumped together.

EXHIBIT 10-7 Income Statement Performance Report

KOOL-TIME POOLS
Income Statement Performance Report
Month Ended June 30

	(1) Actual Results at Actual Prices	(2) (1)–(3) Flexible Budget Variance	(3) Flexible Budget for Actual Number of Output Units*	(4) (3)–(5) Sales Volume Variance	(5) Static (Master) Budget*
Output units (pools installed)	10	–0–	10	2 F	8
Sales revenue	$121,000	$ 1,000 F	$120,000	$ 24,000 F	$ 96,000
Variable expenses	83,000	3,000 U	80,000	16,000 U	64,000
Fixed expenses	22,000	2,000 U	20,000	–0–	20,000
Total expenses	105,000	5,000 U	100,000	16,000 U	84,000
Operating income	$ 16,000	$ 4,000 U	$ 20,000	$ 8,000 F	$ 12,000

Flexible budget variance, $4,000 U   Sales volume variance, $8,000 F

Static budget variance, $4,000 F

*Budgeted sales price is $12,000 per pool, budgeted variable expense is $8,000 per pool, and budgeted total monthly fixed expenses are $20,000.

Finally, consider column 3. In contrast to the static budget, which is developed *before* the period, the flexible budget used in the performance report is not developed until the *end* of the period. Why? Because *flexible budgets used in performance reports are based on the actual number of outputs, which is not known until the end of the period.* For Kool-Time, this flexible budget is based on the *10 pools actually installed*:

- Budgeted sales revenue is $120,000 (10 × $12,000).

- Budgeted variable expenses are $80,000 (10 × $8,000).

- Budgeted fixed expenses are $20,000.

Now that you know how this performance report was developed, let's take a look at the variances in more detail.

Why is this important?

"This type of performance report allows managers to see, at a glance, how much of the overall variance is due to a difference in sales volume, and how much is due to other factors, such as unexpected increases in the cost of materials or labor."

Sales Volume Variance

The sales volume variance (shown in column 4 of Exhibit 10-7) is the difference between the static master budget (column 5) and the flexible budget (column 3). The *only difference* between the static and flexible budgets in the performance report is the *number of outputs on which the budget is based* (8 pools versus 10 pools). Both budgets use the same

- budgeted sales price per unit ($12,000 per pool).
- budgeted variable cost per unit ($8,000 per pool).
- budgeted total fixed costs ($20,000 per month).

Holding selling price per unit, variable cost per unit, and total fixed costs constant highlights the effects of differences in sales volume—the variance shown in column 4. Exhibit 10-7 shows that by installing two more pools than initially expected, Kool-Time's

- sales revenue *should* increase from $96,000 (8 × $12,000) to $120,000 (10 × $12,000)—a $24,000 favorable sales volume variance.
- variable costs *should* increase from $64,000 (8 × $8,000) to $80,000 (10 × $8,000)—a $16,000 unfavorable sales volume variance.

Budgeted total fixed expenses are unaffected because 8 pools and 10 pools are within the relevant range where fixed expenses total $20,000. Consequently, installing two more pools should increase operating income by $8,000 ($24,000 F – $16,000 U). So, Kool-Time's June sales volume variance is $8,000 F.

Since the sales volume variance arises *only* because the number of units actually sold differs from the volume originally planned for in the master budget, this variance is typically marketing's responsibility.

Answer: Marketing

STOP & THINK

When is there a sales volume variance for fixed expenses?

Answer: The only time managers would see a sales volume variance for fixed expenses is when the number of units actually sold falls within a *different* relevant range than the static budget sales volume. When actual and expected number of units sold fall in the same relevant range, there is no sales volume variance for fixed expenses.

Flexible Budget Variance

As the name suggests, the flexible budget variance (shown in column 2 of Exhibit 10-7) is the difference between the *flexible* budget (column 3) and the *actual* results (column 1). Recall that the flexible budget is based on the actual level of output (10 pools), so it shows the revenues and expenses that Kool-Time's managers expect for a volume of 10 pools. Therefore, the flexible budget *variance* highlights *unexpected* revenues and expenses.

Exhibit 10-7 shows a $1,000 favorable flexible budget variance for sales revenue. Kool-Time actually received $121,000 for installing 10 pools rather than the $120,000 expected for 10 pools (10 pools × $12,000). This variance means that the average sales price was $12,100 per pool ($121,000 ÷ 10 pools), which is $100 higher than the budgeted sales price of $12,000 per pool. This variance is typically marketing's responsibility.

Exhibit 10-7 also shows a $3,000 unfavorable flexible budget variance for variable expenses. Kool-Time actually incurred $83,000 of variable expenses rather than the $80,000 expected for 10 pools (10 pools × $8,000 per pool). The company also spent $2,000 more on fixed expenses than was budgeted ($22,000 − $20,000). Consequently, the flexible budget variance for total expenses is $5,000 unfavorable ($3,000 U + $2,000 U). In other words, Kool-Time spent $5,000 more than it would expect to spend for installing 10 pools. This is the same $5,000 flexible budget expense variance we saw graphed in Exhibit 10-5. This variance is typically the responsibility of the purchasing, production, and human resources managers.

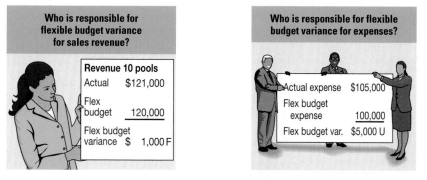

Who is responsible for flexible budget variance for sales revenue?

Revenue 10 pools	
Actual	$121,000
Flex budget	120,000
Flex budget variance	$ 1,000 F

Answer: Marketing

Who is responsible for flexible budget variance for expenses?

Actual expense	$105,000
Flex budget expense	100,000
Flex budget var.	$5,000 U

Answer: Purchasing, Production, HR

Interpreting the Variances

How would Kool-Time's managers use these variances? The favorable sales volume variance reveals that strong sales should have increased Kool-Time's income by $8,000. In addition, the sales staff increased sales without discounting prices: The favorable $1,000 flexible budget variance for sales revenue shows that the sales price was, on average, *higher* than budgeted. These favorable variances due to the quantity of pools sold (the $8,000 favorable sales volume variance) and the sales price per pool (the $1,000 favorable sales revenue price variance) suggest that Kool-Time's marketing staff did a better-than-expected job in selling pools and maintaining sales prices. Perhaps the high sales commissions paid on each pool sale is doing a good job of motivating the sales staff.

However, higher-than-expected expenses offset much of the favorable sales volume variance. Exhibit 10-7 shows a $5,000 unfavorable flexible budget variance for expenses. Management will want to find out why. The reason might be an uncontrollable increase in the cost of materials. Or higher costs might have resulted from more-controllable factors, such as employees wasting materials or working inefficiently. If so, managers can take action to reduce waste or inefficiency. Although Kool-Time does not have any favorable expense variances, in general, managers can benefit from examining favorable as well as unfavorable expense variances. Favorable variances may be the result of some type of efficiency that could be used in other areas of the company, too.

Let's get back to Kool-Time's original question from Exhibit 10-1: Why did the company have an unfavorable static budget variance of $21,000 for expenses? The *sales volume variance* shows that $16,000 of this amount is due to the fact that Kool-Time installed two more pools than it originally planned to install. The *flexible budget variance* shows that the remaining $5,000 (of the $21,000 variance) is due to cost overruns caused by other factors. In the second part of this chapter, we will see how managers drill down deeper to find the root cause(s) for this $5,000 flexible budget expense variance. Once managers identify the reason for the cost overruns, they can decide what action to take to avoid similar overruns in the future.

Decision Guidelines

Flexible Budgets

You and your roommate have started a business printing T-shirts for special customer requests (for example, including school or student organization logos). How can you use flexible budgets to plan and control your costs?

Decision	Guidelines
How should we estimate sales revenues, costs, and profits over the range of likely sales (output) levels?	Prepare a set of flexible budgets for different sales levels.
How should we prepare a flexible budget for total costs?	Use a mixed cost equation to predict costs at different volumes within the relevant range: $$\text{Flexible budget total cost} = \left(\text{Number of T-shirts} \times \text{Variable cost per T-shirts} \right) + \text{Fixed cost}$$
How should we use budgets to help evaluate performance?	• Graph actual costs versus flexible budget costs, as in Exhibit 10-5. • Prepare an income statement performance report, as in Exhibit 10-7.
On which output level is the budget based?	Static (master) budget—*expected* number of T-shirts, estimated before the period. Flexible budget—*actual* number of T-shirts, not known until the end of the period.
How can we better understand why actual results differed from the master budget?	Prepare an income statement performance report comparing actual results, flexible budget for actual number of T-shirts sold, and static (master) budget, as in Exhibit 10-7.
How do we interpret favorable and unfavorable variances?	• Favorable variances increase operating income. • Unfavorable variances decrease operating income.
How much of the static budget variance is because the actual number of T-shirts sold does not equal budgeted sales?	Compute the sales volume variance (SVV) by comparing the flexible budget with the static budget. • Favorable SVV— Actual number of T-shirts sold > Expected. • Unfavorable SVV— Actual number of T-shirts sold < Expected.
How much of the static budget variance occurs because actual revenues and costs are not what they should have been for the actual number of T-shirts sold?	Compute the flexible budget variance (FBV) by comparing actual results with the flexible budget. • Favorable FBV— Actual sales revenue > Flexible budget sales revenue OR Actual expenses < Flexible budget expenses • Unfavorable FBV— Actual sales revenue < Flexible budget sales revenue OR Actual expenses > Flexible budget expenses
What actions can we take to avoid an unfavorable sales volume variance?	• Design more-attractive T-shirts to increase demand. • Provide marketing incentives to increase the number of T-shirts sold.

Summary Problem 1

Exhibit 10-7 indicates that Kool-Time installed 10 swimming pools during June. Now, assume that Kool-Time installed 7 pools (instead of 10) and that the actual sales price averaged $12,500 per pool. Actual variable expenses were $57,400, and actual fixed expenses were $19,000.

Requirements

1. Prepare a revised income statement performance report using Exhibit 10-7 as a guide.

2. Show that the sum of the flexible budget variance and the sales volume variance for operating income equals the static budget variance for operating income.

3. What should be done with the information provided by the performance report?

Solution

Requirements 1 and 2

KOOL-TIME POOLS
Income Statement Performance Report—Revised
Month Ended June 30

	(1) Actual Results at Actual Prices	(2) (1)–(3) Flexible Budget Variance	(3) Flexible Budget for Actual Number of Output Units	(4) (3)–(5) Sales Volume Variance	(5) Static (Master) Budget
Output units	7	–0–	7	1 U	8
Sales revenue	$ 87,500	$ 3,500 F	$ 84,000	$ 12,000 U	$ 96,000
Variable expenses	57,400	1,400 U	56,000	8,000 F	64,000
Fixed expenses	19,000	1,000 F	20,000	—	20,000
Total expenses	76,400	400 U	76,000	8,000 F	84,000
Operating income	$ 11,100	$ 3,100 F	$ 8,000	$ 4,000 U	$ 12,000

Flexible budget variance,
$3,100 F

Sales volume variance,
$4,000 U

Static budget variance,
$900 U

Requirement 3

The performance report helps managers determine the amount of the static budget variance that is due to sales volume and the amount of the variance that is due to other factors (the flexible budget variance). The manager will want to investigate the cause of any significant variances and determine whether they were due to controllable factors. For example, the largest variance was the unfavorable sales volume variance. This variance could be due to insufficient advertising (a controllable factor), or a general recession in the economy (an uncontrollable factor). The manager uses this feedback to adjust operations as necessary.

3 Identify the benefits of standard costs and learn how to set standards

What are Standard Costs?

Think of a **standard cost** as a budget for a single unit. In Kool-Time's case, a single unit would be one swimming pool. Most companies use standard costs to develop their flexible budgets. Recall that Kool-Time developed its flexible budget using a *standard variable cost per pool* of $8,000 (see Exhibit 10-3). Of the total standard variable cost per pool, $7,000 relates to the cost of variable manufacturing inputs: the direct materials, direct labor, and variable manufacturing overhead costs necessary to install one pool. The other $1,000 relates to selling and administrative costs associated with *selling* each pool (sales commission, for example). For the rest of this chapter, we are going to concentrate on *standard manufacturing costs*, although the same concepts apply to selling, general, and administrative costs.

In a standard cost system, each manufacturing input (such as direct materials) has a quantity standard and a price standard. For example, McDonald's has a standard for the amount of beef used per hamburger and a standard for the price paid per pound of beef. Likewise, Kool-Time has a standard for the amount of gunite (a concrete-like material) used per pool and a standard for the price it pays per cubic foot of gunite. Let's see how managers set these quantity and price standards.

Why is this important?

"Standard costs give managers a benchmark, or goal, for how much each unit should cost."

Quantity Standards

Engineers and production managers set direct material and direct labor quantity standards, usually allowing for unavoidable waste and spoilage. For example, each pool that Kool-Time installs requires 975 cubic feet of gunite. As part of the normal installation process, an additional 25 cubic feet of gunite is typically wasted due to unavoidable spoilage from hardened, unusable gunite. Kool-Time calculates the standard quantity of gunite per pool as follows:

Gunite required......................................	975 cubic feet per pool
Unavoidable waste and spoilage............	25 cubic feet per pool
Standard quantity of gunite..................	1,000 cubic feet per pool

Kool-Time also develops quantity standards for direct labor based on time records from past pool installations and current installation requirements. In setting labor standards, managers usually allow for unavoidable work interruptions and normal downtime for which the employee would still be paid. Considering these factors, Kool-Time has set its direct labor quantity standard at 400 direct labor hours per pool.

Price Standards

Now, let's turn our attention to price standards. Accountants help managers set direct material price standards after considering the base purchase price of materials, early-payment discounts, receiving costs, and freight-in. For example, the manager in charge of purchasing gunite for Kool-Time indicates that the purchase price, net of discounts, is $1.90 per cubic foot and that freight-in costs $0.10 per cubic foot. Kool-Time calculates its price standard for gunite as follows:

Purchase price, net of discounts............	$1.90 per cubic foot
Freight-in	0.10 per cubic foot
Standard cost of gunite.........................	$2.00 per cubic foot

For direct labor, accountants work with personnel or human resources managers to determine standard labor rates, taking into account payroll taxes and fringe benefits as well as the hourly wage rate. Kool-Time's Human Resources Department indicates that the hourly wage rate for production workers is $8.00 and that payroll taxes and fringe benefits total $2.50 per direct labor hour. Kool-Time's direct labor price (or rate) standard is as follows:

Hourly wage rate	$ 8.00 per direct labor hour
Payroll taxes and fringe benefits............	2.50 per direct labor hour
Standard direct labor rate.....................	$10.50 per direct labor hour

Standard Manufacturing Overhead Rates

In addition to direct materials and direct labor price and quantity standards, companies also set standard manufacturing overhead rates. The standard predetermined manufacturing overhead rates are calculated as you learned in Chapter 3 except that *two* rates are calculated: one for fixed overhead and one for variable overhead. Why? Because isolating the variable overhead component helps managers create flexible budgets for different volumes. For setting standard overhead rates, accountants work with production managers to estimate variable and fixed manufacturing overhead expenses. Managers then identify an appropriate allocation base for computing the standard manufacturing overhead rates.

For example, recall that Kool-Time's fixed manufacturing overhead costs are expected to be $12,000 per month (the other $8,000 of fixed costs related to selling and administrative expenses). Production managers also estimate variable manufacturing overhead costs to be $800 per pool, or a total of $6,400 for the 8 pools they plan to produce during the month ($800 × 8 = $6,400). Kool-Time has decided to use direct labor hours as its overhead allocation base, so managers estimate the total number of direct labor hours they expect to incur during the month:

8 pools × 400 standard direct labor hours per pool = 3,200 direct labor hours

Kool-Time computes the standard variable overhead rate as follows:

$$\text{Standard } variable \text{ overhead rate} = \frac{\text{Estimated total } variable \text{ overhead cost}}{\text{Estimated total quality of allocation base}}$$

$$= \frac{\$6,400}{3,200 \text{ direct labor hours}}$$

$$= \underline{\$2.00} \text{ per direct labor hour}$$

Kool-Time computes the standard fixed overhead rate in a similar way:

$$\text{Standard } fixed \text{ overhead rate} = \frac{\text{Estimated total } fixed \text{ overhead cost}}{\text{Estimated total quality of allocation base}}$$

$$= \frac{\$12,000}{3,200 \text{ direct labor hours}}$$

$$= \underline{\$3.75} \text{ per direct labor hour}$$

The standard total overhead rate is the *sum* of the standard *variable* overhead and the standard *fixed* overhead rates:

| Variable overhead rate | + | Fixed overhead rate | = | Standard overhead rate |

$2.00 per direct labor hour + $3.75 per direct labor hour = $5.75 per direct labor hour

Notice that the standard manufacturing overhead rate ($5.75 per direct labor hour) is the rate we would have computed in Chapter 3 based on all anticipated manufacturing overhead costs, regardless of cost behavior ($5.75 = $18,400 total estimated manufacturing overhead costs ÷ 3,200 total estimated direct labor hours).

Standard Cost of Inputs

Once managers have developed quantity and price standards, they calculate the standard cost of *each input* (such as direct materials, direct labor, and manufacturing overhead) by multiplying the quantity standard by the price standard:

Quantity standard × Price standard = Standard cost of input

For example, Kool-Time's standard direct materials cost per pool is as follows:

1,000 cubic feet of gunite × $2.00 per cubic foot = $2,000 of direct materials per pool

Likewise, Kool-Time's standard direct labor cost per pool is as follows:

400 direct labor hours × $10.50 per direct labor hour = $4,200 of direct labor per pool

Exhibit 10-8 shows Kool-Time's standard costs for variable and fixed overhead. The exhibit also shows that by adding the standard cost of all of the inputs Kool-Time can find the standard cost of *manufacturing* one pool ($8,500). However, this cost can be misleading to managers because it contains a fixed overhead component. It's really only valid when Kool-Time installs exactly eight pools in a month.

EXHIBIT 10-8 **Kool-Time's Standard Manufacturing Costs per Pool**

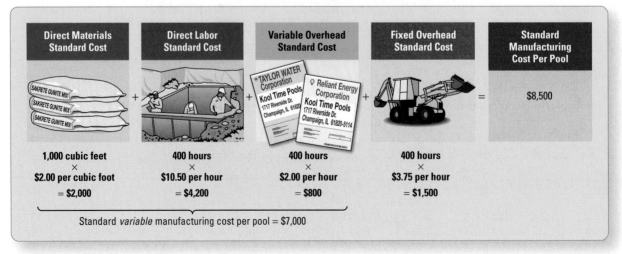

Rather than run the risk of misleading managers, it is often more helpful to highlight just the standard *variable* manufacturing cost per pool. Exhibit 10-8 shows that Kool-Time's standard costs for direct materials ($2,000), direct labor ($4,200), and variable overhead ($800) amount to $7,000 variable manufacturing cost per pool. How does this correspond with variable cost per pool used for flexible budgeting? In addition to variable *manufacturing* costs, recall that Kool-Time expects to incur $1,000 of variable *selling and administrative* expenses per pool (for sales commissions, for example). Added together, these two costs total the $8,000 variable cost per pool that Kool-Time used for flexible budgeting in Exhibit 10-3.

Kool-Time is not alone in its use of standards. U.S. surveys have shown that more than 80% of responding companies use standard costs. International surveys show that over half of responding companies in the United Kingdom, Ireland, Sweden, and Japan use standard costs. Why? Most companies believe that the benefits from using standard costs outweigh the costs of developing the standards and periodically revising them as business conditions change.

For example, companies should reassess their price standards when input prices such as the price of raw materials or labor rates change due to nontemporary market conditions. They should also reassess quantity standards when the product or production process is modified and, as a result, different quantities of materials or labor are required.

Exhibit 10-9 shows five benefits that companies, such as McDonald's, obtain from using standard costs.

EXHIBIT 10-9   **The Benefits of Standard Costs**

Now, let's take a look at how Kool-Time uses its standard costs to analyze flexible budget variances.

How do Managers Use Standard Costs to Analyze Direct Material and Direct Labor Variances?

Let's return to our Kool-Time example. Exhibit 10-7 showed that the main cause for concern at Kool-Time is the $5,000 unfavorable flexible budget variance for expenses. The first step in identifying the causes of this variance is to take a more detailed look at what is included in the *expenses*. Panel A of Exhibit 10-10 does just this. Note that Panel A of Exhibit 10-10 is different from Exhibit 10-7 in three ways: (1) It shows *only* expenses (it leaves out all revenue data), (2) it contains only actual and flexible budget data (it leaves out the static master budget and sales volume variance), and (3) it shows the *components* of Kool-Time's variable and fixed expenses (detailed production costs are shown separately from marketing and administrative expenses). Take a moment to see that the total variable expenses ($83,000 actual versus $80,000 budgeted), total fixed expenses

EXHIBIT 10-10 Data for Standard Costing Example

KOOL-TIME POOLS
Data for Standard Costing Example
Month Ended June 30

PANEL A—Comparison of Actual Results with Flexible Budget for 10 Swimming Pools

	(1) Actual Results at Actual Prices	(2) Flexible Budget for 10 Pools	(1) – (2) Flexible Budget Variance
Variable expenses:			
Direct materials	$ 23,100*	$ 20,000†	$3,100 U
Direct labor	41,800*	42,000†	200 F
Variable overhead	9,000	8,000†	1,000 U
Marketing and administrative expenses	9,100	10,000	900 F
Total variable expenses	83,000	80,000	3,000 U
Fixed expenses:			
Fixed overhead	12,300	12,000‡	300 U
Marketing and administrative expenses	9,700	8,000	1,700 U
Total fixed expenses	22,000	20,000	2,000 U
Total expenses	$105,000	$100,000	$5,000 U

PANEL B—Computation of Flexible Budget for Direct Materials, Direct Labor, and Variable Overhead for 10 Swimming Pools

	(1) Standard Quantity of Inputs Allowed for 10 Pools	(2) Standard Price per Unit of Input	(1) × (2) Flexible Budget for 10 Pools
Direct materials	1,000 cubic feet per pool × 10 pools = 10,000 cubic feet	× $ 2.00	= $20,000
Direct labor	400 hours per pool × 10 pools = 4,000 hours	× 10.50	= 42,000
Variable overhead	400 hours per pool × 10 pools = 4,000 hours	× 2.00	= 8,000

PANEL C—Computation of Actual Costs for Direct Materials and Direct Labor for 10 Swimming Pools

	(1) Actual Quantity of Inputs Used for 10 Pools	(2) Actual Price per Unit of Input	(1) × (2) Actual Cost for 10 Pools
Direct materials	11,969 cubic feet actually used ×	$1.93 actual cost/cubic foot	= $23,100
Direct labor	3,800 hours actually used ×	$11.00 actual cost/hour	= 41,800

*See Panel C.
†See Panel B.
‡Fixed overhead was budgeted at $12,000 per month.

($22,000 actual versus $20,000 budgeted), and total expenses ($105,000 actual versus $100,000 budgeted) agree with Exhibit 10-7. The total $5,000 unfavorable flexible budget variance for expenses also agrees with Exhibit 10-7.

Study Exhibit 10-10 carefully because we will continue to refer to it throughout the rest of the chapter. Panel B shows how we used Kool-Time's price and quantity standards to compute the flexible budget amounts shown in Panel A. Panel C shows how we computed the actual direct materials and direct labor costs shown in Panel A.

Direct Material Variances

The largest single component of the flexible budget variance in Panel A of Exhibit 10-10 is the $3,100 unfavorable variance in direct materials. Recall that the flexible budget variance is the difference between the actual cost incurred and the flexible budget (as shown in Exhibits 10-6 and 10-7). Exhibit 10-11 shows that Kool-Time computes the direct materials flexible budget variance as the difference between (1) the actual amount paid for gunite and (2) the flexible budget amount (*not the static budget amount*) that Kool-Time should have spent on gunite for the 10 pools that it actually installed.

EXHIBIT 10-11 **Kool-Time Pools' Direct Materials Flexible Budget Variance**

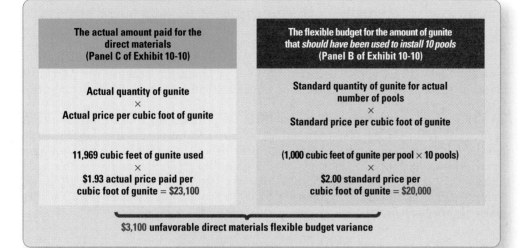

Now that Kool-Time knows that it spent $3,100 more than it should have on gunite, the next question is why. Did the $3,100 unfavorable variance arise because Kool-Time

- did not meet the price standard because it paid too much for each cubic foot of gunite?

- did not meet the quantity standard because workers used more gunite than they should have used to install 10 pools?

To answer those questions, Kool-Time's managers separate the flexible budget variance for direct materials into price and efficiency components, as shown in Exhibit 10-12.

EXHIBIT 10-12 **The Relations Among Price, Efficiency, Flexible Budget, Sales Volume, and Static Budget Variances**

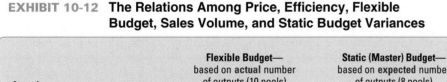
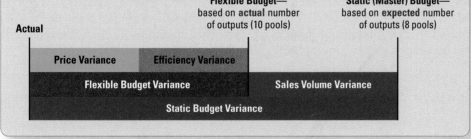

Exhibit 10-12 emphasizes two points. First, added together, the price and efficiency variances equal the flexible budget variance. Second, *static budgets (like column 5 of Exhibit 10-7) play no role in computing the flexible budget variance or in determining how it is split into price and efficiency variances.* The static budget is used *only* in computing the sales volume variance—never in computing the flexible budget variance or its component price and efficiency variances.

DIRECT MATERIALS PRICE VARIANCE A **price variance** measures how well the business keeps unit prices of material and labor inputs within standards. As the name suggests, the price variance is the *difference in prices* (actual price per unit – standard price per unit) of an input, multiplied by the *actual quantity* of the input:

Price variance = (Actual price per input unit – Standard price per input unit) × (Actual quantity of input)

For Kool-Time, the direct materials price variance for gunite is:

$$\text{Direct materials price variance} = (\$1.93 \text{ per cubic foot} - \$2.00 \text{ per cubic foot}) \times 11{,}969 \text{ cubic feet}$$
$$= (\$0.07 \text{ per cubic foot}) \times 11{,}969 \text{ cubic feet}$$
$$= \$838 \text{ F (rounded)}$$

The $838 direct materials price variance is *favorable* because the purchasing manager spent $0.07 *less* per cubic foot of gunite than budgeted ($1.93 actual price – $2.00 standard price).

The purchasing manager is responsible for the price variance on the *actual quantity* of materials he or she buys, so we multiply the $0.07 favorable price variance per cubic foot by the 11,969 cubic feet of gunite he or she *actually purchased*. Thus, Kool-Time's June operating income is $838 higher [($1.93 – $2.00) × 11,969] than the flexible budget because the purchasing manager paid less than the standard price for gunite. (If the purchasing manager had paid *more* than the $2.00 per cubic foot standard price, the direct materials price variance would have been *unfavorable*.)

Answer: Purchasing

DIRECT MATERIALS EFFICIENCY VARIANCE An **efficiency variance** measures whether the firm meets its quantity standards. In other words, it measures whether the quantity of materials actually used to make the *actual number of outputs* is within the standard allowed for that number of outputs. The efficiency variance is the *difference in quantities* (actual quantity of input used – standard quantity of input allowed for the actual number of outputs) multiplied by the *standard price per unit* of the input.

$$\text{Efficiency variance} = \left(\text{Actual quantity of input} - \begin{array}{c} \text{Standard quantity of input allowed} \\ \text{for the actual number of outputs} \end{array} \right) \times (\text{Standard price per input unit})$$

The standard quantity of inputs is the *quantity that should have been used*, or the standard quantity of inputs *allowed*, for the actual output. For Kool-Time, the *standard quantity of inputs (gunite) that workers should have used for the actual number of outputs* (10 pools) is as follows:

1,000 cubic feet of gunite per pool × 10 pools installed = 10,000 cubic feet of gunite

Thus, the direct materials efficiency variance is as follows:

$$\text{Direct materials efficiency variance} = (11,969 \text{ cubic feet} - 10,000 \text{ cubic feet}) \times \$2 \text{ per cubic foot}$$
$$= (1,969 \text{ cubic feet}) \times \$2 \text{ per cubic foot}$$
$$= \$3,938 \text{ U}$$

The $3,938 direct materials efficiency variance is *unfavorable* because workers actually used 1,969 *more* cubic feet of gunite than they should have used to install 10 pools (11,969 actual cubic feet – 10,000 standard cubic feet).

The manager in charge of installing the pools is responsible for the variance in the quantity of the materials (gunite) used—in this case, the extra 1,969 cubic feet of gunite. However, this manager generally is *not* the person who purchases the gunite. The manager who installs the pools often has no control over the actual price paid for the gunite. Thus, we multiply the extra 1,969 cubic feet of gunite his or her workers used by the *standard price* of $2 per cubic foot to obtain the direct materials efficiency variance. Kool-Time's operating income is $3,938 lower [(11,969 – 10,000) × $2] than the flexible budget because workers used more gunite than they should have to install the 10 pools in June. (If workers had used *less* than the standard 10,000 cubic feet to install the 10 pools, the direct materials efficiency variance would have been *favorable*.)

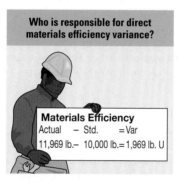

Answer: Pool Installation Manager

SUMMARY OF DIRECT MATERIAL VARIANCES Exhibit 10-13 summarizes how Kool-Time splits the $3,100 unfavorable direct materials flexible budget variance first identified in Panel A of Exhibit 10-10 into price and efficiency variances.

Kool-Time actually spent $3,100 more than it should have for gunite because a good price for the gunite increased profits by $838, but inefficient use of the gunite reduced profits by $3,938.

Why is this important?

"By separating the flexible budget variance into its price and efficiency components, managers can better pinpoint why the variance occurred. This information helps managers to better control costs in the future."

EXHIBIT 10-13 **Kool-Time Pools' Direct Materials Variances**

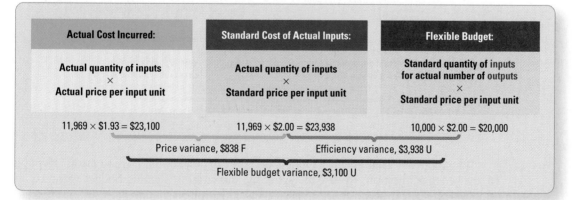

Let's review who is responsible for each of these variances and consider why each variance may have occurred.

1. *Purchasing managers typically are responsible for direct materials price variances* because they should know why the actual price differs from the standard price. Kool-Time's purchasing manager may have negotiated a good price for gunite, or perhaps the supplier did not increase the price of gunite as much as expected when Kool-Time developed its standard cost. In either case, the purchasing manager is in the best position to explain the favorable price variance.

2. *Production managers typically are responsible for direct materials efficiency variances* because they are responsible for ensuring that workers use materials efficiently and effectively. The manager in charge of installing pools should be able to explain why workers used more gunite than they should have to install the 10 pools. Was the gunite of lower quality? Did workers waste materials? Did their equipment malfunction? Kool-Time's top management needs answers to those questions in order to decide what corrective action to take. Should management require purchasing to buy higher-quality gunite, train and supervise workers more closely to reduce waste, or improve maintenance of equipment?

Smart managers know that these variances raise questions that can help pinpoint problems. But be careful! A favorable variance does not necessarily mean that a manager did a good job, nor does an unfavorable variance mean that a manager did a bad job. Perhaps Kool-Time's purchasing manager obtained a lower price by purchasing inferior-quality gunite, which, in turn, led to waste and spoilage. If so, the purchasing manager's decision hurt the company because the $838 favorable price variance is more than offset by the $3,938 unfavorable efficiency variance. This illustrates why good managers (1) use variances as a guide for investigation rather than as a simple tool to assign blame and (2) investigate favorable as well as unfavorable variances.

Direct Labor Variances

Kool-Time uses a similar approach to analyze the direct labor flexible budget variance. Using the information from Panels B and C of Exhibit 10-10, Exhibit 10-14 shows how Kool-Time computes this variance as the difference between the actual amount paid for direct labor and the flexible budget amount that Kool-Time should have spent on direct labor for 10 pools.

EXHIBIT 10-14 **Kool-Time Pools' Direct Labor Flexible Budget Variance**

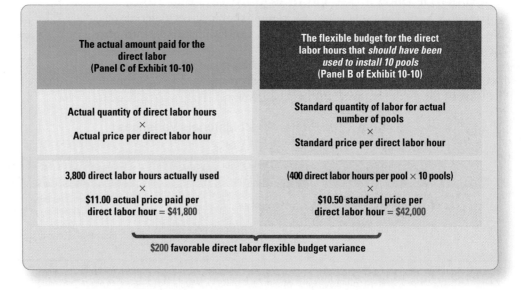

Why did Kool-Time spend $200 less on labor than it should have to install 10 pools? To answer that question, Kool-Time splits the direct labor flexible budget variance into price and efficiency variances the same way it did for direct materials.

DIRECT LABOR PRICE VARIANCE The direct labor price variance is computed the same way as the direct materials price variance, so we use the same formula for price variance shown earlier:

Price variance = (Actual price per input unit − Standard price per input unit) × (Actual quantity of input)

$$\text{Direct labor price variance} = (\$11.00 \text{ per hour} - \$10.50 \text{ per hour}) \times 3,800 \text{ hours}$$
$$= (\$0.50 \text{ per hour}) \times 3,800 \text{ hours}$$
$$= \$1,900 \text{ U}$$

The $1,900 direct labor price variance is *unfavorable* because the Human Resources (or Personnel) Department hired workers at $0.50 *more* per direct labor hour than budgeted ($11.00 actual price − $10.50 standard price).

The human resources manager is responsible for the price variance on the *actual quantity* of labor he or she hires, so we multiply the $0.50 unfavorable price variance per direct labor hour by the 3,800 hours of labor he or she *actually purchased*.

Answer: HR Department

DIRECT LABOR EFFICIENCY VARIANCE The direct labor efficiency variance is computed the same way as the direct materials efficiency variance, so once again, we use the same formula for efficiency variance shown earlier:

$$\text{Efficiency variance} = \left(\text{Actual quantity of input} - \begin{array}{c} \text{Standard quantity of input allowed} \\ \text{for the actual number of outputs} \end{array} \right) \times \text{Standard price per input unit}$$

For Kool-Time, the *standard quantity of direct labor hours that workers should have used for the actual number of outputs* (10 pools) is as follows:

400 direct labor hours per pool × 10 pools installed × 4,000 direct labor hours

Thus, the direct labor efficiency variance is as follows:

$$\text{Direct labor efficiency variance} = (3,800 \text{ hours} - 4,000 \text{ hours}) \times \$10.50 \text{ per hour}$$
$$= (200 \text{ hours}) \times \$10.50 \text{ per hour}$$
$$= \$2,100 \text{ F}$$

The $2,100 direct labor efficiency variance is *favorable* because installers actually worked 200 *fewer* hours than they should have to install 10 pools (3,800 actual hours – 4,000 standard hours).

The manager in charge of installing the pools is responsible for the variance in the quantity of direct labor hours used—in this case, the 200 fewer hours used. Assuming that this manager is not also responsible for setting employees' pay rates (which is usually the responsibility of the Human Resources or Personnel Department), the manager in charge of installing the pools has little control over the actual price paid per labor hour. Thus, we multiply the 200 fewer direct labor hours by the *standard price* of $10.50 per direct labor hour to obtain the direct labor efficiency variance.

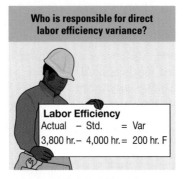

Answer: Pool Installation Manager

SUMMARY OF DIRECT LABOR VARIANCES Exhibit 10-15 summarizes how Kool-Time splits the $200 favorable direct labor flexible budget variance into price and efficiency variances. Had they looked only at the $200 favorable direct labor flexible budget variance, Kool-Time's managers might have thought direct labor costs were close to expectations. But this illustrates the danger in ending the analysis after computing only the flexible budget variance. "Peeling the onion" to examine the price and efficiency variances yields more insight:

- The unfavorable direct labor price variance means that Kool-Time's operating income is $1,900 lower than expected because the company paid its employees an average of $11.00 per hour in June instead of the standard rate of $10.50. But this unfavorable variance was more than offset by the favorable direct labor efficiency variance.

- The favorable direct labor efficiency variance means that Kool-Time's operating income is $2,100 higher than expected because workers installed 10 pools in 3,800 hours instead of the budgeted 4,000 hours.

EXHIBIT 10-15 **Kool-Time Pools' Direct Labor Variances**

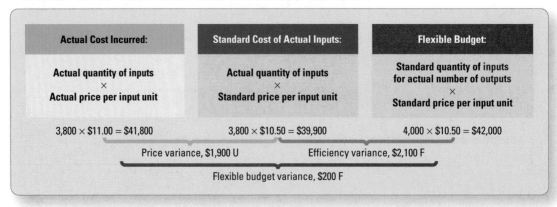

Kool-Time's top management will ask the Human Resources Department to explain the unfavorable labor price variance, and it will ask the manager in charge of installing the pools to explain the favorable labor efficiency variance. Once again, there might have been a trade-off. Kool-Time might have hired more-experienced (and thus more highly paid) workers and traded off an unfavorable price variance for a favorable efficiency variance. If so, the strategy was successful—the overall effect on profits was favorable. This possibility reminds us that managers should be careful in using variances to evaluate performance.

You have now seen how Kool-Time analyzes flexible budget variances for direct materials and direct labor. Variances for variable marketing and administrative expenses could be calculated the same way, but for simplicity, we limit our detailed analysis to the variances in the production element of the value chain. Before leaving this topic, we need to examine three common pitfalls in computing price and efficiency variances.

Price and Efficiency Variances: Three Common Pitfalls

Here are three common pitfalls to avoid in computing price and efficiency variances for direct materials and direct labor:

1. *Static budgets like column 5 of Exhibit 10-7 play no role in computing the flexible budget variance or in determining how it is split into the price and efficiency variances.* Exhibit 10-12 shows that the static budget is used *only* in computing the sales volume variance—never in computing the flexible budget variance or its component price and efficiency variances.

2. In the efficiency variance, the standard quantity is the *standard quantity of inputs allowed for the actual number of outputs*—the basis for the flexible budget. To compute the standard quantity of inputs allowed, determine the actual number of outputs. For Kool-Time, the actual number of outputs is 10 pools. Next, compute how many inputs should have been used to produce the actual number of outputs (10 pools). For example, each pool should use 400 direct labor hours, so the standard quantity of direct labor hours allowed for 10 pools is 10 × 400 hours = 4,000 hours.

3. In the direct materials price variance, the difference in prices is multiplied by the *actual quantity* of materials. In the direct materials efficiency variance, the difference in quantities is multiplied by the *standard price* of the materials. The following explanation can help you remember this difference:

   ▪ The materials price variance is usually the responsibility of purchasing personnel; they purchase the actual quantity used, not just the amount of materials that should have been used (the standard quantity). So, the price variance is the difference in prices multiplied by the *actual quantity* of materials purchased.

   ▪ The materials efficiency variance is usually the responsibility of production personnel; they have no influence over the actual price paid. So, the efficiency variance is computed as the difference in quantities multiplied by the *standard* price (the price that should have been paid).

   Similar logic applies to the direct labor price and efficiency variances.

Using Variances

Let's look at some practical tips for using variances.

HOW OFTEN ARE VARIANCES COMPUTED? Many firms monitor sales volume, direct materials efficiency, and direct labor efficiency variances day to day, or even hour to hour. McDonald's restaurants compute variances for sales and direct labor each hour. Material efficiencies are computed for each shift. The Brass Products Division of Parker Hannifin computes efficiency variances for each job the day after workers finish the job. This allows managers to ask questions about any large variances while the job is still fresh in workers' minds.

Technology such as the bar coding of materials and even labor and computerized data entry allows McDonald's and Parker Hannifin to compute efficiency variances quickly. In contrast to efficiency variances, monthly computations of material and labor price variances may be sufficient if long-term contracts with suppliers or labor unions make large price variances unlikely.

USING VARIANCES TO EVALUATE EMPLOYEES' PERFORMANCE Good managers use variances as a way to raise questions, not as simple indicators of whether employees performed well or poorly. Why should you take care in using variances to evaluate performance?

- Some variances are caused by factors that managers cannot control. For example, perhaps Kool-Time used more gunite than budgeted because workers had to repair cracked foundations resulting from an earthquake.

- Sometimes, variances are the result of inaccurate or outdated standards. Management must take care to review and update standards on a regular basis. If the production process changes or if supply prices change, the standards will need to be updated to reflect current operating conditions.

- Managers often make trade-offs among variances. Chrysler intentionally accepted a large order for customized Dodge vans because it expected the favorable sales volume variance to more than offset the unfavorable direct labor price variance from the overtime premium and the unfavorable sales revenue price variance from extra rebates offered to the customer. Similarly, managers often trade off price variances against efficiency variances. Purchasing personnel may decide to buy higher-quality (but more expensive) direct materials to reduce waste and spoilage. The unfavorable price variance may be more than offset by a favorable efficiency variance.

- Evaluations based primarily on one variance can encourage managers to take actions that make the variance look good but hurt the company in the long run. For example, Kool-Time's managers could do the following:

  - Purchase low-quality gunite or hire less-experienced labor to get favorable price variances.

  - Use less gunite or less labor (resulting in lower-quality installed pools) to get favorable efficiency variances.

How can upper management discourage such actions? One approach is to base performance evaluation on *nonfinancial* measures as well, such as quality indicators (for example, variances in the grade of gunite or labor used) or customer satisfaction measures. For instance, McDonald's discourages skimping on labor by evaluating nonfinancial measures, such as the difference between actual and standard time to serve drive-through customers. If the McDonald's shift manager does not have enough workers, drive-through customers may have to wait to get their french fries. They may take their business to Wendy's or Burger King. In Chapter 11, we'll discuss nonfinancial performance evaluation in more detail.

STOP & THINK

Why might an auto assembly plant experience a favorable direct labor efficiency variance? Should managers investigate favorable as well as unfavorable efficiency variances? Why or why not?

Answer:

1. The plant may have redesigned the manufacturing process to avoid wasted motion. For example, a Dodge van plant in Canada significantly reduced direct labor by reorganizing production so employees reach for raw materials as needed rather than carry armloads of materials across the plant floor.

2. Employees may have worked harder or more intensely than budgeted.

3. Employees may have rushed through the work and skimped on quality.   There are two reasons why managers should investigate favorable efficiency variances. First, managers want to maximize improvements that increase profits. For example, can managers capitalize on 1 and 2 to further improve labor efficiency at this or other plants? Second, managers want to prevent employees from achieving favorable variances at the expense of long-run profits through strategies like 3.

How do Managers Use Standard Costs to Analyze Manufacturing Overhead Variances?

In the last section, we looked at how managers analyze direct materials and direct labor variances. In this section, we look at manufacturing overhead variances. A company's total manufacturing overhead variance *is the difference between the actual overhead incurred and the standard overhead allocated to production.* In other words, this is the amount by which manufacturing overhead has been overallocated or underallocated to production. The total manufacturing overhead variance can be broken into two components: (1) overhead flexible budget variance and (2) production volume variance.

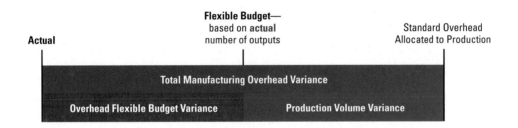

Overhead Flexible Budget Variance

The **overhead flexible budget variance** shows how well management has controlled overhead costs. Therefore, this variance is often referred to as the overhead controllable variance. It is computed *the same way* as the flexible budget variances for direct materials and direct labor. It is the *difference between actual overhead costs and the flexible budget overhead for the actual number of outputs (10 pools).*

The following information about Kool-Time's overhead is taken directly from Exhibit 10-10.

	(1) Actual Results	(2) Flexible Budget for 10 Pools	(1) – (2) Flexible Budget Variance
Variable overhead ($800 per pool)	$ 9,000	$ 8,000	$1,000 U
Fixed overhead	12,300	12,000	300 U
Total overhead	$21,300	$20,000	$1,300 U

Before continuing, let's quickly review how we arrived at the flexible budget numbers shown previously.

The amount of *variable* overhead budgeted for the actual output is calculated as follows:

(400 direct labor hours allowed per pool × $2.00 per direct labor hour variable overhead rate) × 10 pools = $8,000

Since 10 pools falls within the relevant range of 0 to 11, *fixed* production overhead for the month is budgeted at $12,000. Therefore, the total flexible budget for overhead is $20,000. Actual overhead for the month is $21,300. Therefore, Kool-Time's calculates the overhead flexible budget variance as follows:

Overhead flexible budget variance = Actual overhead – Flexible budget overhead for actual output

$$= \$21,300 - \$20,000$$
$$= \$1,300 \text{ U}$$

Why did Kool-Time spend $1,300 more on overhead items than it should have to install the 10 pools in June? You can see that $1,000 ($9,000 – $8,000) of the variance is due to higher-than-expected spending on variable overhead items and that the remaining $300 ($12,300 – $12,000) is due to higher spending on fixed overhead items. Kool-Time will investigate the reason for each of these variances.

Most companies compile actual and budget cost information for the individual component items that make up overhead, such as indirect materials, indirect labor, utilities, and depreciation on plant and equipment. Managers "drill down" by comparing actual costs to budgeted costs for each of these items. For example, Kool-Time's drill-down analysis might reveal that variable overhead costs were higher than expected because the price of gasoline for the earthmoving equipment increased. Perhaps spending on fixed overhead increased because Kool-Time's monthly lease on its earthmoving equipment expired and it had to negotiate a new lease. Advanced books on cost accounting explain this drill-down variance analysis in more detail.

Production Volume Variance

The second component of the total manufacturing overhead variance is the **production volume variance**. *The production volume variance is the difference between the flexible budget overhead and the standard overhead allocated to production.* As the name suggests, this variance arises when actual production volume differs from expected production volume. The production volume variance arises because companies treat fixed overhead as if it were variable in order to allocate it.

Recall from our discussion on standard costs that Kool-Time allocates overhead at a rate of $5.75 per direct labor hour. The total standard overhead rate consists of $2.00 per direct labor hour for variable overhead and $3.75 per direct labor hour for fixed overhead. Kool-Time computed these standard overhead rates based on the assumption that it would sell eight pools. Because Kool-Time actually installed 10 pools, the amount of standard overhead *allocated* to production was as follows:

Standard overhead rate per direct labor hour...	$ 5.75
Standard direct labor hours (400 DL hours per pool × 10 pools)	× 4,000
Standard overhead allocated to production...	$23,000

Notice that when companies use standard costing, they allocate manufacturing overhead to the units produced using the standard overhead rate multiplied by the *standard quantity of the allocation base allowed* (400 DL hours per pool × 10 pools), *not by the actual quantity* of the allocation base used (3,800 hours for the 10 pools), as you did in Chapter 3.

The production volume variance is calculated as follows:

Production volume variance = Flexible budget overhead for actual output – Standard overhead allocated to production

$$= \$20,000 - \$23,000$$
$$= \$3,000 \text{ F}$$

The production volume variance is favorable whenever actual output (10 pools for Kool-Time) exceeds expected output (8 pools). By installing 10 pools instead of 8, Kool-Time used its production capacity more fully than originally planned. In other words, it used its capacity more efficiently, resulting in a favorable variance. If Kool-Time had installed seven or fewer pools, the production volume variance would have been unfavorable because the company would have used less production capacity than expected.

The production volume variance is due only to *fixed* overhead. Why? Because the amount of *variable* overhead in the flexible budget ($8,000) is the *same* as the variable overhead allocated to production ($8,000 = 10 pools × 400 DL hours/pool × $2/DL hour). *In essence, the production volume variance arises because companies treat fixed overhead ($12,000) as if it were variable ($3.75 per DL hour) to allocate it.* The $3,000 favorable production volume variance arises because Kool-Time budgeted fixed overhead of $12,000 (Exhibit 10-10) but allocated $15,000 of fixed overhead to the 10 pools it installed (10 pools × 400 DL hours/pool × $3.75 *fixed* overhead per DL hour).

Another way to see this is by examining the hours used to determine the overhead allocation rate versus the hours used to actually allocate overhead. Since the variance is due *strictly* to the fixed overhead, we multiply the difference in hours by the fixed overhead rate:

Total hours used to determine allocation rate (*8 pools* × 400 direct labor hours)	= 3,200
Total hours used to allocate overhead (*10 pools* × 400 direct labor hours)	= 4,000
Difference in hours (additional hours of overhead allocated)	800
Fixed overhead rate per hour	× $ 3.75
Production volume variance	$3,000

As you can see, the production volume variance is due to the fact that Kool-Time allocated more fixed overhead than it had budgeted.

Overview of Kool-Time's Manufacturing Overhead Variances

Kool-Time's overhead variances are summarized as follows:

Total overhead variance:	
Actual overhead cost	
($9,000 variable + $12,300 fixed)	$21,300
Standard overhead allocated to production	
(10 pools × 400 standard direct labor hours per pool × $5.75)	23,000
Total overhead variance	$ 1,700 F
Overhead flexible budget variance:	
Actual overhead cost (from above)	$21,300
Flexible budget overhead for actual outputs	
($8,000 variable + $12,000 fixed)	20,000
Overhead flexible budget variance	$ 1,300 U
Production volume variance:	
Flexible budget overhead for actual outputs (from above)	$20,000
Standard overhead allocated to production (from above)	23,000
Production volume variance	$ 3,000 F

As we have just seen, many companies use standard costs independent of the general ledger accounting system to develop flexible budgets and evaluate performance through variance analysis. Once managers know the causes of the variances, they can use that information to improve operations.

Other companies integrate standards directly into their general ledger accounting. This method of accounting, called standard costing, is discussed in the Appendix to this chapter.

Decision Guidelines

Standard Costs and Variance Analysis

You've seen how managers use standard costs and variances in actual and budgeted costs to identify potential problems. Variances help managers see *why* actual costs differ from the budget. This is the first step in determining how to correct problems.

Let's review how Kool-Time made some of the key decisions in setting up and using its standard cost system.

Decision	Guidelines
How does Kool-Time set standards?	Historical performance data
	Engineering analysis/time-and-motion studies
How does Kool-Time compute a price variance for materials or labor?	$$\text{Price variance} = \left(\begin{array}{c}\text{Actual price} \\ \text{per input unit}\end{array} - \begin{array}{c}\text{Standard price} \\ \text{per input unit}\end{array}\right) \times \begin{array}{c}\text{Actual} \\ \text{quantity of} \\ \text{input}\end{array}$$
How does Kool-Time compute an efficiency variance for materials or labor?	$$\text{Efficiency variance} = \left(\begin{array}{c}\text{Actual} \\ \text{quantity of} \\ \text{input}\end{array} - \begin{array}{c}\text{Standard quantity} \\ \text{of input allowed for the} \\ \text{actual number of outputs}\end{array}\right) \times \begin{array}{c}\text{Standard} \\ \text{price per} \\ \text{input unit}\end{array}$$
Who is most likely responsible for the:	
Sales volume variance?	Marketing Department
Sales revenue flexible budget variance?	Marketing Department
Direct materials price variance?	Purchasing Department
Direct materials efficiency variance?	Production Department
Direct labor price variance?	Human Resources or Personnel Department
Direct labor efficiency variance?	Production Department
How does Kool-Time allocate manufacturing overhead in a standard costing system?	$$\begin{array}{c}\text{Manufacturing} \\ \text{overhead} \\ \text{allocated}\end{array} = \left(\begin{array}{c}\text{Standard} \\ \text{predetermined} \\ \text{manufacturing} \\ \text{overhead rate}\end{array}\right) \times \left(\begin{array}{c}\text{Standard quantity} \\ \text{of allocation base} \\ \text{allowed for} \\ \text{actual outputs}\end{array}\right)$$
How does Kool-Time analyze overallocated or underallocated manufacturing overhead? Split overallocated or underallocated overhead as follows:	$$\text{Flexible budget variance} = \begin{array}{c}\text{Actual} \\ \text{overhead}\end{array} - \begin{array}{c}\text{Flexible budget} \\ \text{overhead for} \\ \text{actual outputs}\end{array}$$
	$$\begin{array}{c}\text{Production volume} \\ \text{variance}\end{array} = \begin{array}{c}\text{Flexible budget} \\ \text{overhead for} \\ \text{actual outputs}\end{array} - \begin{array}{c}\text{Standard overhead} \\ \text{allocated to} \\ \text{actual outputs}\end{array}$$

Summary Problem 2

Suppose Kool-Time had installed seven pools in June and that actual expenses were as follows:

Direct materials (gunite).............................	7,400 cubic feet @ $2 per cubic foot
Direct labor..	2,740 hours @ $10 per hour
Variable overhead	$ 5,400
Fixed overhead..	$11,900

Recall from Exhibit 10-8 that Kool-Time has the following quantity and price standards:

Direct materials (gunite)..........	1000 cubic feet per pool; $2.00 per cubic feet
Direct labor.............................	400 hours per pool; $10.50 per hour
Variable overhead rate	$2.00 per hour ⎫
Fixed overhead rate.................	$3.75 per hour ⎬ $5.75 per hour overhead rate

Requirements

1. Compute price variances for direct materials and direct labor.
2. Compute efficiency variances for direct materials and direct labor.
3. Compute the total overhead variance, the overhead flexible budget variance, and the production volume variance. Prepare a summary similar to the one on page 579.

Solution

Requirement 1

$$\text{Price variance} = (\text{Actual price per input unit} - \text{Standard price per input unit}) \times \text{Actual quantity of input}$$

Direct materials:

$$\text{Price variance} = (\$2.00 - \$2.00) \times 7,400 \text{ cubic feet} = \$0$$

Direct labor:

$$\text{Price variance} = (\$10.00 - \$10.50) \times 2,740 \text{ hours} = \$1,370 \text{ F}$$

Requirement 2

$$\text{Efficiency variance} = \left(\text{Actual quantity of input} - \frac{\text{Standard quantity of input allowed}}{\text{for the actual number of outputs}} \right) \times (\text{Standard price per input unit})$$

continued

Direct materials:

Since 7 pools were installed the standard quantity of material allowed for the actual output is 7,000 cubic feet (1,000 cubic feet per pool × 7 pools). Thus the efficiency variance is as follows:

Efficiency variance = (7,400 cubic feet − 7,000 cubic feet) × $2.00 per cubic foot = $800 U

Direct labor:

Since 7 pools were installed the standard quantity of labor allowed for the actual output is 2,800 hours (400 direct labor hours per pool × 7 pools). Thus the efficiency variance is as follows:

Efficiency variance = (2,740 hours − 2,800 hours) × $10.50 per hour = $630 F

Requirement 3

Total overhead variance:	
Actual overhead cost ($5,400 variable + $11,900 fixed)	$17,300
Standard overhead allocated to production	
(2,800 standard direct labor hours × $5.75)	16,100
Total overhead variance...	$ 1,200 U
Overhead flexible budget variance:	
Actual overhead cost ($5,400 + $11,900)...............................	$17,300
Flexible budget overhead for actual	
outputs ($5,600* + $12,000)..	17,600
Overhead flexible budget variance	$ 300 F
Production volume variance:	
Flexible budget overhead for actual	
outputs ($5,600* variable + $12,000 fixed).............................	$17,600
Standard overhead allocated to (actual) production	
(2,800 standard direct labor hours × $5.75)	16,100
Production volume variance...	$ 1,500 U

* 2,800 standard DL hours × $2.00 variable overhead rate = $5,600

APPENDIX 10A

Standard Cost Accounting Systems

Many companies integrate standards directly into their general ledger accounting by recording inventory-related costs at standard cost rather than actual cost. This method of accounting is called standard costing or standard cost accounting. Standard costing not only saves on bookkeeping costs but it also isolates price and efficiency variances as soon as they occur. Before we go through the journal entries, keep the following key points in mind:

1. Each type of variance discussed has its own general ledger account. A debit balance means that the variance is unfavorable since it decreases income (just like an expense). A credit balance means that the variance is favorable since it increases income (just like a revenue).

2. Just as in job costing, the manufacturing costs flow through the inventory accounts in the following order: raw materials → work in process → finished goods → cost of goods sold. The difference is that *standard costs* rather than actual costs are used to record the manufacturing costs put into the inventory accounts.

3. At the end of the period, the variance accounts are closed to cost of goods sold to "correct" for the fact that the standard costs recorded in the accounts were different from actual costs. Assuming that most inventory worked on during the period has been sold, any "error" from using standard costs rather than actual costs is contained in cost of goods sold. Closing the variances to cost of goods sold corrects the account balance.

Why is this important?

"By incorporating standard costing into the company's general ledger, managers have immediate information about the variances as they are occurring."

Journal Entries

We use Kool-Time's June transactions to demonstrate standard costing in a job-costing context.

1. **Recording Raw Materials Purchases**—Kool-Time debits Raw Materials Inventory for the *actual quantity* purchased (11,969 cubic feet) costed at the *standard price* ($2 per cubic foot). It credits Accounts Payable for the *actual quantity* of gunite purchased (11,969 cubic feet) costed at the *actual price* ($1.93 per cubic foot) because this is the amount owed to Kool-Time's suppliers. The difference is the direct material *price* variance. When Kool-Time purchases raw materials, it is immediately able to tell whether it paid more or less than the standard price for the materials; therefore, the direct materials *price* variance "pops out" when the purchase is recorded:

(1)	Raw materials inventory (11,969 × $2.00)	23,938	
	Direct materials price variance		838
	Accounts payable (11,969 × $1.93)		23,100
	(*to record purchases of direct materials*)		

Recall that Kool-Time's direct materials price variance was $838 favorable (page 570). So, the variance has a credit balance and increases Kool-Time's June profits.

2. **Recording Use of Direct Materials**—When Kool-Time uses direct materials, it debits Work in Process Inventory for the *standard price × standard quantity* of direct materials that should have been used for the actual output of 10 pools. *This maintains Work in Process Inventory at a purely standard cost.* Raw Materials Inventory is credited for the *actual quantity* of materials put into production (11,969 cubic feet) costed at the *standard price* at which journal entry 1 entered them into the Raw Materials Inventory account ($2). The difference is the direct materials *efficiency* variance. The direct materials efficiency variance "pops out" when Kool-Time records the *use* of direct materials:

(2)	Work in process inventory (10,000 × $2)	20,000	
	Direct materials efficiency variance	3,938	
	Raw materials inventory (11,969 × $2)		23,938
	(*to record use of direct materials*)		

Kool-Time's direct materials efficiency variance was $3,938 unfavorable (page 571), which decreases June profits. See how a debit to the variance account corresponds with an unfavorable variance.

3. **Recording Direct Labor Costs**—Since Work in Process Inventory is maintained at standard cost, Kool-Time debits Work in Process Inventory for the *standard price* of direct labor × *standard quantity* of direct labor that should have been used for the actual output of 10 pools (just like it did for direct materials in journal entry 2). Kool-Time credits Wages Payable for the *actual* hours worked at the *actual* wage rate since this is the amount owed to employees. At the same time, Kool-Time records the direct labor price and efficiency variances calculated on page 573. The *unfavorable* price variance is recorded as a *debit*, while the *favorable* efficiency variance is recorded as a credit.

(3)	Work in process inventory (4,000 × $10.50)	42,000	
	Direct labor price variance	1,900	
	Direct labor efficiency variance		2,100
	Wages payable (3,800 × $11.00)		41,800
	(*to record direct labor costs incurred*)		

4. **Recording Manufacturing Overhead Costs Incurred**—Kool-Time Pools records manufacturing overhead costs as usual, debiting the manufacturing overhead account and crediting various accounts:

(4)	Manufacturing overhead	21,300	
	Accounts payable, accumulated depreciation, and so forth		
	[to record actual overhead costs incurred (from Exhibit 10-10)]		21,300

5. **Allocating Overhead**—In standard costing, the overhead allocated to Work in Process Inventory is computed as the standard overhead rate ($5.75 per DL hour) × standard quantity of the allocation base allowed for the actual output (10 pools × 400 DL hours per pool). As usual, the manufacturing overhead account is credited when assigning overhead:

(5)	Work in process inventory (4,000 × $5.75)	23,000	
	Manufacturing overhead		23,000
	(to allocate overhead)		

This journal entry corresponds with our calculation, on page 578, of the standard overhead allocated to production.

6. **Recording the Completion of Pools**—So far, Work in Process has been debited with $85,000 of manufacturing cost ($20,000 of direct materials + $42,000 of direct labor + $23,000 of manufacturing overhead). Does this make sense? According to Exhibit 10-8, the standard manufacturing cost of 1 pool is $8,500 ($2,000 direct material + $4,200 direct labor + $2,300 overhead). The sum of 10 pools, costed at *standard* rather than actual cost, is $85,000. As the pools are completed, the standard cost of each is transferred out of Work in Process and into Finished Goods:

(6)	Finished goods inventory	85,000	
	Work in process inventory		85,000
	(to record completion of 10 pools)		

7. **Recording the Sale and Release of Inventory**—When the pools are sold, *sales revenue* is recorded at the standard sales price, but accounts receivable is recorded at the actual sales price. The difference between the standard sales price and actual sales price received is the flexible budget sales revenue variance shown in Exhibit 10-7. It is favorable (a credit) because the company sold the pools for a higher price than it anticipated.

(7a)	Cash or accounts receivable (at actual price)	121,000	
	Flexible budget sales revenue variance		1,000
	Sales revenue (at standard)		120,000
	(to record the sale of 10 pools)		

Kool-Time must also release inventory for the pools it has sold. Since these pools were recorded at standard cost ($8,500 each), they must be removed from finished goods inventory and go into cost of goods sold at the same (standard) cost:

(7b)	Cost of goods sold	85,000	
	Finished goods inventory		85,000
	(to record the cost of sales of 10 pools)		

8. **Closing Manufacturing Overhead**—Kool-Time Pools closes Manufacturing Overhead to the two overhead variance accounts using the calculations performed on pages 577 and 578 ($1,300 unfavorable Overhead Flexible Budget Variance and $3,000 favorable Production Volume Variance).

(8)	Manufacturing overhead	1,700	
	Overhead flexible budget variance	1,300	
	Production volume variance		3,000
	(to record overhead variances and close the Manufacturing Overhead account)		

Exhibit 10-16 shows selected Kool-Time accounts after posting these entries.

EXHIBIT 10-16   Kool-Time Pools' Flow of Costs in Standard Costing System

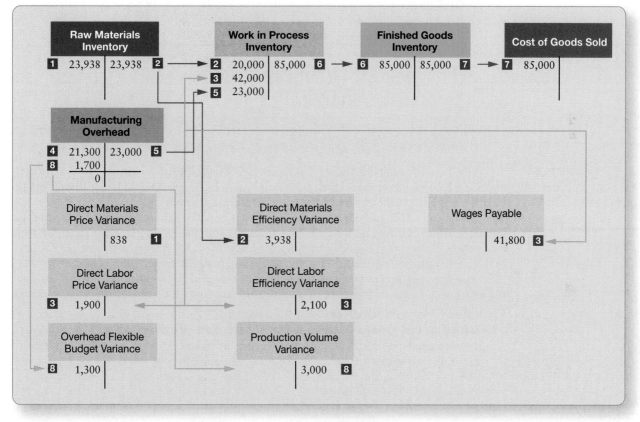

Standard Cost Income Statement for Management

Exhibit 10-17 shows a standard cost income statement that highlights the variances for Kool-Time's management. The statement shows sales revenue at standard and then adds the favorable flexible budget sales revenue variance to yield actual sales revenue. Next, the statement shows the cost of goods sold at standard cost. Then, the statement separately lists each manufacturing cost variance followed by the cost of goods sold at actual cost. (Recall that since Kool-Time had no raw materials, work in process, or finished goods inventories, all of the variances relate to June's sales.)

EXHIBIT 10-17 Standard Cost Income Statement

KOOL-TIME POOLS
Standard Cost Income Statement
Month Ended June 30

Sales revenue at standard (10 × $12,000)		$120,000
Flexible budget sales revenue variance		1,000
Sales revenue at actual		121,000
Cost of goods sold at standard cost		85,000
Manufacturing cost variances:		
Direct materials price variance	$ (838)	
Direct materials efficiency variance	3,938	
Direct labor price variance	1,900	
Direct labor efficiency variance	(2,100)	
Manufacturing overhead flexible		
budget variance	1,300	
Production volume variance	(3,000)	
Total manufacturing variances		1,200
Cost of goods sold at actual cost		86,200
Gross profit		34,800
Marketing and administrative expenses*		(18,800)
Operating income		$ 16,000

*$9,100 + $9,700 from Exhibit 10-10.

The income statement shows that the net effect of all of the manufacturing cost variances is $1,200 unfavorable. Thus, June's operating income is $1,200 lower than it would have been if all actual costs had been equal to standard amounts.

At the end of the period, all of the cost variance accounts are closed to zero-out their balances. Why? For two reasons: (1) The financial statements prepared for *external* users never show variances (variances are only for internal management's use) and (2) the general ledger must be "corrected" for the fact that standard rather than actual costs were used to record manufacturing costs. Since all of the pools were sold, the "error" in costing currently exists in the cost of goods sold account. Therefore, the cost variance accounts are closed to cost of goods sold:

9. **Closing the Cost Variance Accounts to Cost of Goods Sold**—To close, or zero-out, the variance accounts, all unfavorable variances (debit balances) must be credited, while all favorable variances (credit balances) must be debited:

(9a)	Cost of goods sold	1,200	
	Direct materials price variance	838	
	Direct labor efficiency variance	2,100	
	Production volume variance	3,000	
	Direct labor price variance		1,900
	Direct materials efficiency variance		3,938
	Overhead flexible budget variance		1,300
	(*to close cost variance accounts to cost of goods sold*)		

Likewise, the favorable flexible budget sales revenue variance (1,000) is closed to sales revenue (to zero-out the variance account and correct the revenue account).

(9b)	Flexible budget sales revenue variance	1,000	
	Sales revenue		1,000
	(*to close the revenue variance account*)		

Accounting Vocabulary

Efficiency Variance. (p. 570)   Measures whether the quantity of materials or labor used to make the actual number of outputs is within the standard allowed for that number of outputs.

Flexible Budget. (p. 554)   A summarized budget prepared for different levels of volume.

Flexible Budget Variance. (p. 559)   The difference arising because the company actually earned more or less revenue or incurred more or less cost than expected for the actual level of output.

Overhead Flexible Budget Variance. (p. 577)   The difference between the actual overhead cost and the flexible budget overhead for the actual number of outputs.

Price Variance. (p. 570)   The difference in prices (actual price per unit minus standard price per unit) of an input multiplied by the actual quantity of the input.

Production Volume Variance. (p. 578)   The difference between the manufacturing overhead cost in the flexible budget for actual outputs and the standard overhead allocated to production.

Sales Volume Variance. (p. 558)   The difference between a static budget amount and a flexible budget amount arising only because the number of units actually sold differs from the static budget units.

Standard Cost. (p. 564)   A budget for a single unit.

Static Budget. (p. 554)   The budget prepared for only one level of sales volume; also called the master budget.

Variance. (p. 554)   The difference between an actual amount and the budget.

Quick Check

1. *(Learning Objective 1)* A budget that is based on the actual activity level of a period is a
   a. static budget.
   b. rolling budget.
   c. master budget.
   d. flexible budget.

2. *(Learning Objective 1)* A flexible budget
   a. contains a plan for a range of activity levels so that the plan can be adjusted to reflect changes in activity levels.
   b. is the plan for one level of activity and cannot be adjusted for changes in the level of activity.
   c. can be used to evaluate performance after the period has ended but is not used for planning.
   d. contains only variable costs but does not include fixed costs since fixed costs do not change.

3. *(Learning Objective 2)* Assuming that all activity is within the relevant range, an increase in the activity level in a flexible budget will
   a. increase total fixed costs.
   b. increase the variable cost per unit.
   c. increase total costs.
   d. decrease the variable cost per unit.

4. *(Learning Objective 3)* Advantages of using standard costs include all of the following *except* that
   a. standard costing allows companies to create flexible budgets.
   b. managers can evaluate the efficiency of production workers.
   c. differences between the static budget and the flexible budget can be broken down into price and quantity components.
   d. the price sensitivity of consumers can be analyzed.

5. *(Learning Objective 3)* A sales volume variance will occur when
   a. the actual selling price of a unit is lower than the selling price originally planned for in the master budget.
   b. the number of units actually sold differs from the volume originally planned for in the master budget.
   c. the actual cost of the inputs differ from the costs originally planned for in the master budget.
   d. the actual selling price of a unit is higher than the selling price originally planned for in the master budget.

6. *(Learning Objective 4)* A favorable material quantity variance indicates that
   a. the standard material price is less than the actual material price.
   b. the actual material price is less than the standard material price.
   c. the actual quantity of material used is less than the standard material allowed for the actual quantity of output.
   d. the standard material allowed for the actual quantity of output is less than the actual quantity of material used.

7. *(Learning Objective 4)* The formula for calculating a direct materials quantity variance is
   a. (Actual price per input unit – Standard price per input unit) × Actual quantity of input.
   b. (Actual quantity of input – Standard quantity of input allowed for the actual number of outputs) × Standard price per input unit.
   c. (Actual price per input unit – Actual quantity of input) × Standard price per input unit.
   d. (Actual quantity of input – Standard price per input unit) × Standard quantity of input allowed for the actual number of outputs.

8. *(Learning Objective 5)* The production volume variance is favorable whenever
   a. actual output exceeds expected output.
   b. expected output exceeds actual output.
   c. the actual variable overhead rate exceeds the standard variable overhead rate.
   d. the standard variable overhead rate exceeds the actual variable overhead rate.

9. *(Learning Objective 5)* The total manufacturing overhead variance is composed of
   a. price variance and efficiency variance.
   b. price variance and production volume variance.
   c. efficiency variance and production volume variance.
   d. flexible budget variance and production volume variance.

10. *(Learning Objective 6: Appendix)* When a company *uses* direct materials, the amount of the debit to Work in Process Inventory is based on the
    a. actual quantity of the materials used × actual price per unit of the materials.
    b. standard quantity of the materials allowed for the actual production of 75 connectors × actual price per unit of the materials.
    c. standard quantity of the materials allowed for the actual production of 75 connectors × standard price per unit of the materials.
    d. actual quantity of the materials used × standard price per unit of the materials.

ASSESS YOUR PROGRESS

Learning Objectives

1 Prepare a flexible budget for planning purposes

2 Use the sales volume variance and flexible budget variance to explain why actual results differ from the master budget

3 Identify the benefits of standard costs and learn how to set standards

4 Compute standard cost variances for direct materials and direct labor

5 Compute manufacturing overhead variances

6 (Appendix) Record transactions at standard cost and prepare a standard cost income statement

Short Exercises

S10-1 Prepare a flexible budget *(Learning Objective 1)*

Turn to Kool-Time's flexible budget in Exhibit 10-3.

1. Using the data from Exhibit 10-3, develop flexible budgets for four- and nine-pool levels of output.

2. Would Kool-Time's managers use the flexible budgets you developed in Requirement 1 for planning or for controlling? What specific insights can Kool-Time's managers gain from the flexible budgets you prepared in Requirement 1?

S10-2 Interpret a flexible budget graph *(Learning Objective 1)*

Look at Kool-Time's graph of actual and budgeted monthly costs in Exhibit 10-5.

1. How many pools did Kool-Time install in May?

2. How much were Kool-Time's actual expenses in May?

3. Using Kool-Time's flexible budget formula, what is the flexible budget total cost for May?

4. What is Kool-Time's flexible budget variance for total costs? Is the variance favorable or unfavorable in May?

S10-3 Interpret a performance report *(Learning Objective 2)*

The following is a partially completed performance report for Surf-Side Pools, one of Kool-Time's competitors:

	Actual Results at Actual Prices	Flexible Budget Variance	Flexible Budget for Actual Number of Output Units	Sales Volume Variance	Static (Master) Budget
SURF-SIDE POOLS Income Statement Performance Report Year Ended April 30					
Output units (pools installed)	6	?	?	?	5
Sales revenue	$102,000	?	$108,000	?	$90,000
Variable expenses	57,000	?	60,000	?	50,000
Fixed expenses	21,000	?	25,000	?	25,000
Total expenses	78,000	?	85,000	?	75,000
Operating income	$24,000	?	$23,000	?	$15,000

1. How many pools did Surf-Side originally think it would install in April?
2. How many pools did Surf-Side actually install in April?
3. How many pools is the flexible budget based on? Why?
4. What was the budgeted sales price per pool?
5. What was the budgeted variable cost per pool?
6. Define the sales volume variance. What causes it?
7. Define the flexible budget variance. What causes it?

S10-4 Complete a performance report *(Learning Objective 2)*

Complete the performance report shown in S10-3 by filling in all missing values. Be sure to label each variance as favorable (F) or unfavorable (U). Then, answer the following questions:

1. What was the *total* static budget variance?
2. What was the *total* sales volume variance?
3. What was the *total* flexible budget variance?
4. Show that the total sales volume variance and total flexible budget variance sum to the total static budget variance.
5. Interpret the variances and then give one plausible explanation for the variances shown in this performance report.

S10-5 Interpret the sales volume variance *(Learning Objective 2)*

Recall that Kool-Time's relevant range is 0 to 11 pools per month.
Explain whether Kool-Time would have a sales volume variance for fixed expenses in Exhibit 10-7 if
a. Kool-Time installs 14 pools per month.
b. Kool-Time installs 7 pools per month.

S10-6 Understand key terms *(Learning Objectives 1 & 2)*

Fill in the blank with the phrase that best completes the sentence.

Actual number of outputs	Beginning of the period	Static budget variance
Expected number of outputs	End of the period	
Sales volume variance	Flexible budget variance	

a. The static budget is developed at the _____.
b. The flexible budget used in an income statement performance report is based on the _____.

c. The master budget is based on the _____.

d. The flexible budget used in an income statement performance report is developed at the _____.

e. The difference between actual costs and the costs that should have been incurred for the actual number of outputs is the _____.

S10-7 Calculate a standard price *(Learning Objective 3)*

The Bolognese Corporation is in the process of setting price standards for its direct materials. Polymer clay is used in one product. The polymer clay is purchased for $14 per pound. The Bolognese Corporation always pays its suppliers within 10 days, so it is able to take advantage of a 5% early-payment discount offered by the polymer clay vendor. Freight-in for the polymer clay is $0.25 per pound of clay, while receiving costs are $0.05 per pound. What is the standard price per pound of polymer clay?

McDonald's Data Set used for S10-8 through S10-12:

As explained in the chapter opening story, the standard direct materials for a regular McDonald's hamburger are as follows:

1 bun	1 pickle slice	1/4 teaspoon of mustard
1 hamburger patty	1/8 teaspoon of onion	1/2 ounce of ketchup

Assume that the company has set the following standard materials prices:

Buns.............................	$0.10 each	Onion..............	$0.08 per teaspoon
Hamburger patties	$0.20 each	Mustard	$0.04 per teaspoon
Pickle slices	$0.03 per slice	Ketchup...........	$0.10 per ounce

In addition to the direct materials standards, the company sets standards for direct labor. The standard labor wage rate is $6 per hour. Since the griddles are so large, the restaurants cook the hamburgers in batches of 20. The standard time allotted to cook, apply condiments, and wrap each batch of 20 hamburgers is 4 minutes.

Assume that a San Diego, California, McDonald's sold 5,000 hamburgers yesterday and actually used the following materials:

5,150 buns	4,800 pickle slices	1,400 teaspoons of mustard
5,100 hamburger patties	800 teaspoons of onion	2,750 ounces of ketchup

S10-8 Compute standard cost of direct materials *(Learning Objective 3)*

Refer to the McDonald's Data Set on this page. Compute the standard direct materials cost per hamburger.

S10-9 Compute standard cost of direct labor *(Learning Objective 3)*

Refer to the McDonald's Data Set on this page. Compute the standard direct labor cost per hamburger. (*Hint:* Find the quantity and price standards in minutes.)

S10-10 Compute direct materials efficiency variances *(Learning Objective 4)*

Refer to the McDonald's Data Set on this page.

1. Compute the direct materials efficiency variance for buns, hamburger patties, and pickle slices.

2. As a manager, what would you learn from the variances and supporting data?

S10-11 Compute more direct materials efficiency variances *(Learning Objective 4)*

Refer to the McDonald's Data Set on this page.

1. Compute the direct materials efficiency variance for an onion, mustard, and ketchup.

2. As a manager, what would you learn from the variances and supporting data?

S10-12 Compute direct materials price variances *(Learning Objective 4)*

Refer to the McDonald's Data Set on page 602.

Actual prices paid for ingredients purchased during the week were as follows:

Buns.............................	$0.12 each	Onion..............	$0.07 per teaspoon
Hamburger patties	$0.25 each	Mustard	$0.01 per teaspoon
Pickle slices	$0.02 per slice	Ketchup............	$0.12 per ounce

1. Compute the direct materials price variance for each ingredient.

2. As a manager, what would you learn from the variances and supporting data?

S10-13 Compute standard overhead allocation rates *(Learning Objective 3)*

McDonald's supplies its restaurants with many premanufactured ingredients (such as bags of frozen french fries), while other ingredients (such as lettuce and tomatoes) are obtained from local suppliers. Assume that the manufacturing plant processing the fries anticipated incurring a total of $3,080,000 of manufacturing overhead during the year. Of this amount, $1,320,000 is fixed. Manufacturing overhead is allocated based on machine hours. The plant anticipates running the machines 220,000 hours next year.

1. Compute the standard *variable* overhead rate.

2. Compute the *fixed* overhead rate.

3. Compute the standard *total* overhead rate.

S10-14 Compute manufacturing overhead variances *(Learning Objective 5)*

Assume that the McDonald's french fries manufacturing facility actually incurred $2,975,000 of manufacturing overhead for the year. Based on the actual output of french fries, the flexible budget indicated that total manufacturing overhead should have been $3,000,000. Using a standard costing system, the company allocated $2,940,000 of manufacturing overhead to production.

1. Calculate the total manufacturing overhead variance. What does this tell managers?

2. Determine the overhead flexible budget variance. What does this tell managers?

3. Determine the production volume variance. What does this tell managers?

4. Double-check: Do the two variances (computed in Requirements 2 and 3) sum to the total overhead variance computed in Requirement 1?

S10-15 Compute manufacturing overhead variances *(Learning Objective 5)*

Rovnovsky Industries produces high-end flutes for professional musicians across the globe. Actual manufacturing overhead for the year was $1,240,000. The flexible budget indicated that fixed overhead should have been $800,000 and variable overhead should have been $400,000 for the number of flutes actually produced. Using a standard costing system, the company allocated $1,300,000 of overhead to production.

1. Calculate the total overhead variance. What does this tell managers?

2. Determine the overhead flexible budget variance. What does this tell managers?

3. Determine the production volume variance. What does this tell managers?

S10-16 (Appendix) Record direct materials purchase and use *(Learning Objective 6)*

During the week, McDonald's french fry manufacturing facility purchased 10,000 pounds of potatoes at a price of $1.10 per pound. The standard price per pound is $1.05. During the week, 9,760 pounds of potatoes were used. The standard quantity of potatoes that should have been used for the actual volume of output was 9,700 pounds. Record the following transactions using a standard cost accounting system:

1. The purchase of potatoes

2. The use of potatoes

Are the variances favorable or unfavorable? Explain.

S10-17 (Appendix) Record direct labor purchase and use *(Learning Objective 6)*

During the week, McDonald's french fry manufacturing facility incurred 2,000 hours of direct labor. Direct laborers were paid $12.25 per hour. The standard hourly labor rate is $12. Standards indicate that for the volume of output actually achieved, the factory should have used 2,100 hours. Record the following transactions using a standard cost accounting system:

1. The accumulation of labor costs

2. The assignment of direct labor to production

Are the variances favorable, or unfavorable? Explain.

Exercises—Group A

E10-18A Prepare flexible budgets for planning *(Learning Objective 1)*

Logiclik sells its main product, ergonomic mouse pads, for $11 each. Its variable cost is $5 per pad. Fixed expenses are $200,000 per month for volumes up to 60,000 pads. Above 60,000 pads, monthly fixed expenses are $250,000.

Requirement

1. Prepare a monthly flexible budget for the product, showing sales, variable expenses, fixed expenses, and operating income or loss for volume levels of 40,000, 50,000, and 70,000 pads.

E10-19A Graph flexible budget costs *(Learning Objective 1)*

Graph the flexible budget total cost line for Logiclik in Exercise 10-18A. Show total costs for volume levels of 40,000, 50,000, and 70,000 pads.

E10-20A Complete and interpret a performance report *(Learning Objective 2)*

Joe Boxer Company's managers received the following incomplete performance report:

JOE BOXER COMPANY
Income Statement Performance Report
Year Ended July 31

	Actual Results at Actual Prices	Flexible Budget Variance	Flexible Budget for Actual Number of Output Units	Sales Volume Variance	Static (Master) Budget
Output units	36,000	?	36,000	4,000 F	?
Sales revenue	$216,000	?	$216,000	$24,000 F	?
Variable expenses	84,000	?	81,000	9,000 U	?
Fixed expenses	106,000	?	100,000	–0–	?
Total expenses	190,000	?	181,000	9,000 U	?
Operating income	$ 26,000	?	$ 35,000	$15,000 F	?

Complete the performance report. Identify the employee group that may deserve praise and the group that may be subject to criticism. Give your reasons.

E10-21A Prepare an income statement performance report *(Learning Objective 2)*

Kool-Times installed nine pools during May. Prepare an income statement performance report for Kool-Time for May, using Exhibit 10-7 as a guide. Assume that the actual sales price per pool is $12,000, actual variable expenses total $61,000, and actual fixed expenses are $19,000 in May. The master budget was prepared with the following assumptions: variable cost of $8,000 per pool, fixed expenses of $20,000 per month, and anticipated sales volume of eight pools at $12,000 per pool.

Requirement

1. Compute the sales volume variance and flexible budget variance. Use these variances to explain to Kool-Time's management why May's operating income differs from operating income shown in the static budget.

E10-22A Compute sales volume and flexible budget variances *(Learning Objective 2)*

Top managers of Manion Industries predicted the following year's sales of 145,000 units of its product at a unit price of $8. Actual sales for the year were 140,000 units at $9.50 each. Variable expenses were budgeted at $2.20 per unit and actual variable expenses were $2.30 per unit. Actual fixed expenses of $420,000 exceeded budgeted fixed expenses by $20,000. Prepare Manion Industries' income statement performance report in a format similar to E10-20. What variance contributed most to the year's favorable results? What caused this variance?

E10-23A Work backward to find missing values *(Learning Objective 2)*

Hanco has a relevant range extending to 30,000 units each month. The following performance report provides information about Hanco's budget and actual performance for April.

HANCO
Income Statement Performance Report
Month Ended April 30

	Actual Results at Actual Prices	(A)	Flexible Budget for Actual Number of Output Units	(B)	Static (Master) Budget
Output units	25,000		(C)		30,000
Sales revenue	$240,000	$ 5,000 (F)	(D)		
Variable cost			(E)		$187,500
Fixed cost	$ 15,000	(F)			$ 20,000
Operating income					(G)

Requirement

1. Find the missing data for letters A–G. Be sure to label any variances as favorable or unfavorable. (*Hint:* A and B are titles.)

E10-24A Calculate standard costs *(Learning Objective 3)*

Rachel's Bakery makes desserts for local restaurants. Each pan of gourmet brownies requires 2 cups flour, 1/2 cup chopped pecans, 1/4 cup cocoa, 1 cup sugar, 1/2 cup chocolate chips, 2 eggs, and 1/3 cup oil. Each pan requires 10 minutes of direct labor for mixing, cutting, and packaging. Each pan must bake for 30 minutes. Restaurants purchase the gourmet brownies by the pan, not by the individual serving. Each pan is currently sold for $12. Standard costs are $1.92 per bag of flour (16 cups in a bag), $6.00 per bag of pecans (3 cups per bag), $2.40 per tin of cocoa (2 cups per tin), $2.40 per 5-pound bag of sugar (16 cups in a bag), $1.80 per bag of chocolate chips (2 cups per bag), $1.08 per dozen eggs, $1.26 per bottle of oil (6 cups per bottle), and $0.50 for packaging materials. The standard wage rate is $12 per hour. Rachel allocates bakery overhead at $7.00 per oven hour.

Requirements

1. What is the standard cost per pan of gourmet brownies?

2. What is the standard gross profit per pan of gourmet brownies?

3. How often should Rachel reassess her standard quantities and standard prices for inputs?

E10-25A Calculate materials and labor variances *(Learning Objective 4)*

McDonald's manufactures the bags of frozen french fries used at its franchised restaurants. Last week, McDonald's purchased and used 100,000 pounds of potatoes at a price of $0.75 per pound. During the week, 2,000 direct labor hours were incurred in the plant at a rate of $12.25 per hour. The standard price per pound of potatoes is $0.85, and the standard direct labor rate is $12.00 per hour. Standards indicate that for the number of bags of frozen fries produced, the factory should have used 97,000 pounds of potatoes and 1,900 hours of direct labor.

Requirements

1. Determine the direct materials price and efficiency variances. Be sure to label each variance as favorable or unfavorable.

2. Think of a plausible explanation for the variances found in Requirement 1.

3. Determine the direct labor price and efficiency variances. Be sure to label each variance as favorable or unfavorable.

4. Could the explanation for the labor variances be tied to the material variances? Explain.

E10-26A Compute direct materials variance *(Learning Objective 4)*

The following direct materials variance computations are incomplete:

$$\text{Price variance} = (\$? - \$10) \times 9{,}600 \text{ pounds} = \$4{,}800 \text{ U}$$

$$\text{Efficiency variance} = (? - 10{,}400 \text{ pounds}) \times \$10 = ? \text{ F}$$

$$\text{Flexible budget variance} = \$?$$

Requirement

1. Fill in the missing values and identify the flexible budget variance as favorable or unfavorable.

E10-27A Calculate materials and labor variances *(Learning Objective 4)*

Dock Guard, which uses a standard cost accounting system, manufactured 200,000 boat fenders during the year, using 1,450,000 feet of extruded vinyl purchased at $1.05 per foot. Production required 4,500 direct labor hours that cost $14 per hour. The materials standard was 7 feet of vinyl per fender at a standard cost of $1.10 per foot. The labor standard was 0.025 direct labor hour per fender at a standard cost of $13 per hour. Compute the price and efficiency variances for direct materials and direct labor. Does the pattern of variances suggest that Dock Guard's managers have been making trade-offs? Explain.

E10-28A Compute standard manufacturing overhead rates *(Learning Objective 3)*

Fresh-Cut processes bags of organic frozen vegetables sold at specialty grocery stores. Fresh-Cut allocates manufacturing overhead based on direct labor hours. Fresh-Cut has projected total overhead for the year to be $800,000. Of this amount, $600,000 relates to fixed overhead expenses. Fresh-Cut expects to process 160,000 cases of frozen organic vegetables this year. The direct labor standard for each case is 1/4 of an hour.

Requirements

1. Compute the standard *variable* overhead rate.

2. Compute the *fixed* overhead rate.

3. Compute the standard *total* overhead rate.

E10-29A Continuation of E10-28A: Compute overhead variances *(Learning Objective 5)*

Fresh-Cut actually processed 180,000 cases of frozen organic vegetables during the year and incurred $840,000 of manufacturing overhead. Of this amount, $610,000 was fixed.

Requirements

1. What is the flexible budget (for the actual output) for variable overhead? for fixed overhead? for total overhead?

2. How much overhead would have been allocated to production?

3. Use your answer from Requirement 1 to determine the overhead flexible budget variance. What does this tell managers?

4. Use your answer from Requirements 1 and 2 to determine the production volume variance. What does this tell managers?

5. What is the total overhead variance?

E10-30A Compute manufacturing overhead variances *(Learning Objective 5)*

Deelux manufactures paint. The company charges the following standard unit costs to production on the basis of static budget volume of 30,000 gallons of paint per month:

Direct materials	$2.50
Direct labor	2.00
Manufacturing overhead	1.50
Standard unit cost	$6.00

Deelux allocates overhead based on standard machine hours, and it uses the following monthly flexible budget for overhead:

	Number of Outputs (gallons)		
	27,000	30,000	33,000
Standard machine hours....................................	2,700	3,000	3,300
Budgeted manufacturing overhead cost:			
Variable..	$13,500	$15,000	$16,500
Fixed...	30,000	30,000	30,000

Deelux actually produced 33,000 gallons of paint using 3,100 machine hours. Actual variable overhead was $16,200, and fixed overhead was $32,500. Compute the total overhead variance, the overhead flexible budget variance, and the production volume variance.

Watermate Data Set used for E10-31A through E10-36A:

Watermate is a manufacturer of ceramic bottles. The company has these standards:

Direct materials (clay)	1 pound per bottle, at a cost of $0.40 per pound
Direct labor..	1/5 hour per bottle, at a cost of $14 per hour
Static budget variable overhead...	$70,000
Static budget fixed overhead	$30,000
Static budget direct labor hours...	10,000 hours
Static budget number of bottles...	50,000

Watermate allocates manufacturing overhead to production based on standard direct labor hours. Last month, Watermate reported the following actual results for the production of 70,000 bottles:

Direct materials..	1.1 pound per bottle, at a cost of $0.50 per pound
Direct labor..	1/4 hour per bottle, at a cost of $13 per hour
Actual variable overhead..	$104,000
Actual fixed overhead	$ 28,000

E10-31A Compute the standard cost of one unit *(Learning Objective 3)*

Refer to the Watermate Data Set on this page.

Requirements

1. Compute the standard predetermined variable manufacturing overhead rate, the standard predetermined fixed manufacturing overhead rate, and the total standard predetermined overhead rate.

2. Compute the standard cost of each of the following inputs: direct materials, direct labor, variable manufacturing overhead, and fixed manufacturing overhead.

3. Determine the standard cost of one ceramic bottle.

E10-32A Compute and interpret direct materials variances *(Learning Objective 4)*

Refer to the Watermate Data Set on this page.

Requirements

1. Compute the direct materials price variance and the direct materials efficiency variance.

2. What is the total flexible budget variance for direct materials?

3. Who is generally responsible for each variance?

4. Interpret the variances.

E10-33A Compute and interpret direct labor variances *(Learning Objective 4)*

Refer to the Watermate Data Set on page 607.

Requirements

1. Compute the direct labor price variance and the direct labor efficiency variance.
2. What is the total flexible budget variance for direct labor?
3. Who is generally responsible for each variance?
4. Interpret the variances.

E10-34A Compute and interpret manufacturing overhead variances *(Learning Objective 5)*

Refer to the Watermate Data Set on page 607.

Requirements

1. Compute the total manufacturing overhead variance. What does this tell management?
2. Compute the overhead flexible budget variance. What does this tell management?
3. Compute the production volume variance. What does this tell management?

E10-35A Record journal entries in a standard costing system *(Learning Objective 6)*

Refer to the Watermate Data Set on page 607. Use a standard cost accounting system to do the following:

Requirements

1. Record Watermate's direct materials and direct labor journal entries.
2. Record Watermate's journal entries for manufacturing overhead, including the entry that records the overhead variances and closes the Manufacturing Overhead account.
3. Record the journal entries for the completion and sale of the 70,000 bottles, assuming Watermate sold (on account) all of the 70,000 bottles at a sales price of $8 each (there were no beginning or ending inventories).

E10-36A Prepare a standard cost income statement *(Learning Objective 6)*

Refer to the Watermate Data Set on page 607. Prepare a standard cost income statement for Watermate's management, using Exhibit 10-17 as a guide. Assume that sales were $560,000 and actual marketing and administrative expenses were $76,500.

E10-37A (Appendix) Record materials and labor transactions *(Learning Objective 6)*

Make the journal entries to record the purchase and use of direct materials and direct labor made by Dock Guard in E10-27A.

E10-38A (Appendix) Interpret a standard cost income statement *(Learning Objective 6)*

The managers of Viewx, a contract manufacturer of DVD drives, are seeking explanations for the variances in the following report. Explain the meaning of each of Viewx's materials, labor, and overhead variances.

VIEWX CO.
Standard Cost Income Statement
Year Ended December 31

Sales revenue		$1,200,000
Cost of goods sold at standard cost		700,000
Manufacturing cost variances:		
Direct materials price variance	$ 8,000 F	
Direct materials efficiency variance	32,000 U	
Direct labor price variance	24,000 F	
Direct labor efficiency variance	10,000 U	
Manufacturing overhead flexible budget variance	28,000 U	
Production volume variance	8,000 F	
Total manufacturing variances		30,000
Cost of goods sold at actual cost		730,000
Gross profit		470,000
Marketing and administrative expenses		418,000
Operating income		$ 52,000

E10-39A (Appendix) Prepare a standard cost income statement *(Learning Objective 6)*

Western Outfitters' revenue and expense information for April follows:

Sales revenue	$560,000
Cost of good sold (standard)	342,000
Direct materials price variance	2,000 F
Direct materials efficiency variance	6,000 F
Direct labor price variance	4,000 U
Direct labor efficiency variance	2,000 F
Overhead flexible budget variance	3,500 U
Production volume variance	8,000 F

Requirement

1. Prepare a standard cost income statement for management through gross profit. Report all standard cost variances for management's use. Has management done a good or poor job of controlling costs? Explain.

Exercises—Group B

E10-40B Prepare flexible budgets for planning *(Learning Objective 1)*

Office Plus sells its main product, ergonomic mouse pads, for $8 each. Its variable cost is $2 per pad. Fixed costs are $200,000 per month for volumes up to 80,000 pads. Above 80,000 pads, monthly fixed costs are $265,000.

Requirement

1. Prepare a monthly flexible budget for the product, showing sales revenue, variable costs, fixed costs, and operating income for volume levels of 60,000, 70,000, and 90,000 pads.

E10-41B Graph flexible budget costs *(Learning Objective 1)*

Graph the flexible budget total cost line for Office Plus in Exercise 10-40B. Show total cost for volume levels of 60,000, 70,000, and 90,000 pads.

E10-42B Complete and interpret a performance report *(Learning Objective 2)*

McKnight Company's managers received the following incomplete performance report:

McKnight Company				
Income Statement Performance Report				
Year Ended July 31				

	Actual Results at Actual Prices	Flexible Budget Variance	Flexible Budget for Actual Number of Output Units	Sales Volume Variance	Static (Master) Budget
Output units	38,000	—	38,000	2,000 F	—
Sales revenue	$219,000	—	$219,000	$24,000 F	—
Variable costs	81,000	—	80,000	10,000 U	—
Fixed costs	107,000	—	100,000	0	—
Total costs	188,000	—	180,000	10,000 U	—
Operating income	$ 31,000	—	$ 39,000	$14,000 F	—

Requirement

1. Complete the performance report. Identify the employee group that may deserve praise and the group that may be subject to criticism. Give your reasons.

E10-43B Prepare an income statement performance report (Learning Objective 2)

Time 2 Kool installed 10 pools during March. Prepare an income statement report for Time 2 Kool for March, using the following table as a guide.

	(1) Actual Results at Actual Prices	(2) = [(1)–(3)] Flexible Budget Variance	(3) Flexible Budget for Actual Number of Output Units*	(4) = [(3)–(5)] Sales Volume Variance	(5) Static (Master) Budget
Time 2 Kool Pools **Income Statement Performance Report** **Month Ended June 30**					
Output units (pools installed)	10	–0–	10	2 F	8
Sales revenue	$121,000	$1,000 F	$120,000	$24,000 F	$96,000
Variable expenses	83,000	3,000 U	80,000	16,000 F	64,000
Fixed expenses	22,000	2,000 U	20,000	–0–	20,000
Total expenses	105,000	5,000 U	100,000	16,000 U	84,000
Operating income	$ 16,000	$4,000 U	$ 20,000	$ 8,000 F	$12,000

Flexible budget variance, $4,000 U   Sales volume variance, $8,000 F

Static budget variance, $4,000 F

*Budgeted sales price is $12,000 per pool, budgeted variable expense is $8,000 per pool, and budgeted total monthly fixed expenses are $20,000.

Assume that the actual sale price per pool is $12,400, actual variable expenses total $65,500, and actual fixed expenses are $19,100 in March. The master budget was prepared with the following assumptions: variable cost of $8,900 per pool, fixed expenses of $20,700 per month, and anticipated sales volume of nine pools at $12,400 per pool.

Requirement

1. Compute the sales volume variance and flexible budget variances. Use these variances to explain to Time 2 Kool's management why March's operating income differs from the operating income shown in the static budget.

E10-44B Compute sales volume and flexible budget variances (Learning Objective 2)

Top managers of Lortan Industries predicted the following year's sales of 147,000 units of its product at a unit price of $9.20. Actual sales for the year were 144,000 units at $11.60 each. Variable expenses were budgeted at $2.35 per unit, and actual variable expenses were $2.80 per unit. Actual fixed expenses of $430,000 exceeded budgeted fixed expenses by $27,500. Prepare Lortan Industries' income statement performance report. What variance contributed most to the year's favorable results? What caused this variance?

E10-45B Work backward to find missing values (Learning Objective 2)

Manco has a relevant range extending to 31,000 units each month. The following performance report provides information about Manco's budget and actual performance for November.

Manco
Income Statement Performance Report
Month Ended November 30

	Actual Results at Actual Prices	(A)	Flexible Budget for Actual Number of Output Units	(B)	Static (Master) Budget
Output units	26,000		(C)		31,000
Sales revenue	$251,000	$ 5,300 (F)	(D)		
Variable expenses			(E)		$190,650
Fixed expenses	$ 15,000	(F)			$ 23,000
Operating income					(G)

Requirement

1. Find the missing data for letters A through G. Be sure to label any variances as favorable or unfavorable. (*Hint*: A and B are titles.)

E10-46B Calculate standard costs *(Learning Objective 3)*

Lilian's Bakery makes desserts for local restaurants. Each pan of gourmet bars requires 3 cups of flour, 1/2 cup chopped pecans, 1/4 cup cocoa, 1 cup sugar, 1/2 cup chocolate chips, 3 eggs, and 1/3 cup oil. Each pan requires 15 minutes of direct labor for mixing, cutting, and packaging. Each pan must bake for 30 minutes. Restaurants purchase the gourmet bars by the pan, not by the individual serving. Each pan is currently sold for $12. Standard costs are as follows: $1.60 per bag of flour (16 cups in a bag), $3.00 per bag of pecans (3 cups per bag), $4.20 per tin of cocoa (3 cups per tin), $2.20 per 5 pound bag of sugar (11 cups in a bag), $1.80 per bag of chocolate chips (2 cups per bag), $0.84 per dozen eggs, $1.68 per bottle of oil (8 cups per bottle), and $0.60 for packaging materials. The standard wage rate is $15 per hour. Lilian allocates bakery overhead at $5.00 per oven hour.

Requirements

1. What is the standard cost per pan of gourmet bars?
2. What is the standard gross profit per pan of gourmet bars?
3. How often should Lilian reassess her standard quantities and standard prices for inputs?

E10-47B Calculate materials and labor variances *(Learning Objective 4)*

Curly's manufactures the bags of frozen french fries used at its franchised restaurants. Last week, Curly's purchased and used 99,000 pounds of potatoes at a price of $0.70 per pound. During the week, 2,300 direct labor hours were incurred in the plant at a rate of $12.30 per hour. The standard price per pound of potatoes is $0.90 and the standard direct labor rate is $12.05 per hour. Standards indicate that for the number of bags of frozen fries produced, the factory should have used 97,000 pounds of potatoes and 22,000 hours of direct labor.

Requirements

1. Determine the direct materials price and efficiency variances. Be sure to label each variance as favorable or unfavorable.
2. Think of a plausible explanation for the variances found in Requirement 1.
3. Determine the direct labor price and efficiency variances. Be sure to label each variance as favorable or unfavorable.
4. Could the explanation for the labor variances be tied to the material variances? Explain.

E10-48B Compute direct materials variance *(Learning Objective 4)*

The following direct materials variance computations are incomplete:

$$\text{Price variance} = (\$? - \$7) \times 10,800 \text{ pounds} = \$5,400 \text{ U}$$
$$\text{Efficiency variance} = (? - 10,400 \text{ pounds}) \times \$7 = ? \text{ U}$$
$$\text{Flexible budget variance} = \$?$$

Requirement

1. Fill in the missing values and identify the flexible budget variance as favorable or unfavorable.

E10-49B Calculate materials and labor variances *(Learning Objective 4)*

Great Guard, which uses a standard cost accounting system, manufactured 210,000 boat fenders during the year, using 1,730,000 feet of extruded vinyl purchased at $1.45 per foot. Production required 4,500 direct labor hours that cost $14.50 per hour. The materials standard was 8 feet of vinyl per fender at a standard cost of $1.60 per foot. The labor standard was 0.023 direct labor hour per fender, at a standard cost of $13.00 per hour. Compute the price and efficiency variances for direct materials and direct labor. Does the pattern of variances suggest that Great Guard's managers have been making trade-offs? Explain.

E10-50B Compute standard manufacturing overhead rates *(Learning Objective 3)*

Great-Cut processes bags of organic frozen vegetables sold at specialty grocery stores. Great-Cut allocates manufacturing overhead based on direct labor hours. Great-Cut has projected total overhead for the year to be $765,000. Of this amount, $595,000 relates to fixed overhead expenses. Great-Cut expects to process 170,000 cases of frozen organic vegetables this year. The direct labor standard for each case is 1/4 hour.

Requirements

1. Compute the standard *variable* overhead rate.

2. Compute the *fixed* overhead rate.

3. Compute the standard *total* overhead rate.

E10-51B Continuation of E10-50B: Compute overhead variances *(Learning Objective 5)*

Great-Cut actually processed 195,000 cases of frozen organic vegetables during the year and incurred $795,000 of manufacturing overhead. Of this amount, $605,000 was fixed.

Requirements

1. What is the flexible budget (for the actual output) for variable overhead? For fixed overhead? For total overhead?

2. How much overhead would have been allocated to production?

3. Use your answer from Requirement 1 to determine the overhead flexible budget variance. What does this tell managers?

4. Use your answer from Requirements 1 and 2 to determine the production volume variance. What does this tell managers?

5. What is the total overhead variance?

E10-52B Compute manufacturing overhead variances *(Learning Objective 5)*

Canvas manufactures paint. The company charges the following standard unit costs to production on the basis of static budget volume of 35,000 gallons of paint per month:

Direct materials	$2.60
Direct labor	2.30
Manufacturing overhead	1.60
Standard unit cost	$6.50

Canvas allocates overhead based on standard machine hours, and it uses the following monthly flexible budget for overhead:

	Number of Outputs (gallons)		
	32,000	35,000	40,000
Standard machine hours.....................................	3,200	3,500	4,000
Budgeted manufacturing overhead cost:			
Variable..	$22,400	$24,500	$28,000
Fixed..	35,000	35,000	35,000

Canvas actually produced 40,000 gallons of paint, using 3,180 machine hours. Actual variable overhead was $16,400, and fixed overhead was $33,000. Compute the total overhead variance, the overhead flexible budget variance, and the production volume variance.

E10-53B Compute the standard cost of one unit (Learning Objective 3)

Groovy Bottles is a manufacturer of ceramic bottles. The company has the following standards:

Direct materials (clay)	1.3 pound per bottle, at a cost of $0.40 per pound
Direct labor...	1/5 hour per bottle, at a cost of $14.80 per hour
Static budget variable overhead.......................................	$70,500
Static budget fixed overhead	$30,500
Static budget direct labor hours.......................................	10,000 hours
Static budget number of bottles.......................................	52,000

Groovy Bottles allocates manufacturing overhead to production based on standard direct labor hours. Last month the company reported the following actual results for the production of 69,000 bottles:

Direct materials...	1.5 pound per bottle, at a cost of $0.70 per pound
Direct labor...	1/4 hour per bottle, at a cost of $12.90 per hour
Actual variable overhead...	$104,600
Actual fixed overhead	$ 28,700

Requirements

1. Compute the standard predetermined variable manufacturing overhead rate, the standard predetermined fixed manufacturing overhead rate, and the total standard predetermined overhead rate.

2. Compute the standard cost of each of the following inputs: direct materials, direct labor, variable manufacturing overhead, and fixed manufacturing overhead.

3. Determine the standard cost of one ceramic bottle.

E10-54B Compute and interpret direct materials variances (Learning Objective 4)

Refer to the Groovy Bottles Data Set in E10-53B.

Requirements

1. Compute the direct materials price variance and the direct materials efficiency variance.

2. What is the total flexible budget variance for direct materials?

3. Who is generally responsible for each variance?

4. Interpret the variances.

E10-55B Compute and interpret direct labor variances *(Learning Objective 4)*

Refer to the Groovy Bottles Data Set in E10-53B.

Requirements

1. Compute the direct labor price variance and the direct labor efficiency variance.

2. What is the total flexible budget variance for direct labor?

3. Who is generally responsible for each variance?

4. Interpret the variances.

E10-56B Compute and interpret manufacturing overhead variances *(Learning Objective 5)*

Refer to the Groovy Bottles Data Set in E10-53B.

Requirements

1. Compute the total manufacturing overhead variance. What does this tell management?

2. Compute the overhead flexible budget variance. What does this tell management?

3. Compute the production volume variance. What does this tell management?

E10-57B Record journal entries in a standard costing system *(Learning Objective 6)*

Refer to the Groovy Bottles Data Set in E10-53B. The standard predetermined variable manufacturing overhead rate is $7.05 and the standard predetermined fixed manufacturing overhead rate is $3.05.
Use a standard cost accounting system to do the following:

Requirements

1. Record Groovy Bottles' direct materials and direct labor journal entries.

2. Record Groovy Bottles' journal entries for manufacturing overhead, including the entry that records the overhead variances and closes the Manufacturing Overhead account.

3. Record the journal entries for the completion and sale of the 69,000 bottles, assuming Groovy Bottle sold (on account) all of the 69,000 bottles at a sale price of $8.70 each (there were no beginning or ending inventories).

E10-58B Prepare a standard cost income statement *(Learning Objective 6)*

Refer to the Groovy Bottles Data Set in E10-53B. The cost of goods sold at standard cost totaled $377,844. Prepare a standard cost income statement for Groovy Bottles' management, using Exhibit 10-17 as a guide. Assume that sales were $600,300 and actual marketing and administrative expenses were $80,500.

E10-59B (Appendix) Record materials and labor transactions *(Learning Objective 6)*

Make the journal entries to record the purchase and use of direct materials and direct labor made by Great Guard in E10-49B.

E10-60B (Appendix) Interpret a standard cost income statement *(Learning Objective 6)*

The managers of Monachino, a contract manufacturer of DVD drives, are seeking explanations for the variances in the following report. Explain the meaning of each of Monachino's materials, labor, and overhead variances.

Monachino Company
Standard Cost Income Statement
Year Ended December 31

Sales revenue		$1,180,000
Cost of goods sold at standard cost		700,000
Manufacturing cost variances:		
Direct materials price variance	$32,000 U	
Direct materials efficiency variance	8,000 F	
Direct labor price variance	10,000 U	
Direct labor efficiency variance	24,000 F	
Manufacturing overhead flexible budget variance	9,000 F	
Production volume variance	30,000 U	
Total manufacturing variances		31,000
Cost of goods sold at actual cost		731,000
Gross profit		449,000
Marketing and administrative expenses		426,000
Operating income		$ 23,000

E10-61B (Appendix) Prepare a standard cost income statement *(Learning Objective 6)*

Special Outfitters' revenue and expense information for April follows:

Sales revenue	$561,000
Cost of good sold (standard)	344,000
Direct materials price variance	2,950 F
Direct materials efficiency variance	6,400 F
Direct labor price variance	4,300 U
Direct labor efficiency variance	2,200 F
Overhead flexible budget variance	3,650 U
Production volume variance	8,450 F

Requirement

1. Prepare a standard cost income statement for management through gross profit. Report all standard cost variances for management's use. Has management done a good or poor job of controlling costs? Explain.

Problems—Group A

P10-62A Prepare a flexible budget for planning *(Learning Objective 1)*

Lasting Bubbles, Inc., produces multicolored bubble solution used for weddings and other events. The company's static budget income statement for August follows. It is based on expected sales volume of 55,000 bubble kits.

LASTING BUBBLES, INC.
Static Budget Income Statement
Month Ended August 31

Sales revenue	$165,000
Variable expenses:	
Cost of goods sold	63,250
Sales commissions	13,750
Utilities expense	11,000
Fixed expenses:	
Salary expense	32,000
Depreciation expense	20,000
Rent expense	11,000
Utilities expense	5,000
Total expenses	156,000
Operating income	$ 9,000

Lasting Bubbles' plant capacity is 62,500 kits. If actual volume exceeds 62,500 kits, the company must expand the plant. In that case, salaries will increase by 10%, depreciation by 15%, and rent by $5,800. Fixed utilities will be unchanged by any volume increase.

Requirements

1. Prepare flexible budget income statements for the company, showing output levels of 55,000, 60,000, and 65,000 kits.

2. Graph the behavior of the company's total costs.

3. Why might Lasting Bubbles' managers want to see the graph you prepared in Requirement 2 as well as the columnar format analysis in Requirement 1? What is the disadvantage of the graphic approach?

P10-63A Prepare and interpret a performance report *(Learning Objective 2)*

Refer to the Lasting Bubbles data in P10-62A. The company sold 60,000 bubble kits during August, and its actual operating income was as follows:

LASTING BUBBLES, INC.
Income Statement
Month Ended August 31

Sales revenue	$185,000
Variable expenses:	
Cost of goods sold	$ 69,500
Sales commissions	18,000
Utilities expense	12,000
Fixed expenses:	
Salary expense	34,000
Depreciation expense	20,000
Rent expense	10,000
Utilities expense	5,000
Total expenses	168,500
Operating income	$ 16,500

Requirements

1. Prepare an income statement performance report for August in a format similar to Exhibit 10-7.

2. What accounts for most of the difference between actual operating income and static budget operating income?

3. What is Lasting Bubbles' static budget variance? Explain why the income statement performance report provides Lasting Bubbles' managers with more useful information than the simple static budget variance. What insights can Lasting Bubbles' managers draw from this performance report?

P10-64A Comprehensive flexible budget, standards, and variances problem (Learning Objectives 2, 3, 4, & 5)

One System assembles PCs and uses flexible budgeting and a standard cost system. One System allocates overhead based on the number of direct materials parts. The company's performance report includes the following selected data:

	Static Budget (20,000 PCs)	Actual Results (22,000 PCs)
Sales (20,000 PCs × $400)	$8,000,000	
(22,000 PCs × $420)		$9,240,000
Variable manufacturing expenses:		
Direct materials (200,000 parts × $10.00)	2,000,000	
(214,200 parts × $9.80)		2,099,160
Direct labor (40,000 hr × $14.00)	560,000	
(42,500 hr × $14.60)		620,500
Variable overhead (200,000 parts × $4.00)	800,000	
(214,200 parts × $4.10)		878,220
Fixed manufacturing expenses:		
Fixed overhead	900,000	930,000
Total cost of goods sold	4,260,000	4,527,880
Gross profit	$3,740,000	$4,712,120

Requirements

1. Determine the company's standard cost for one unit.

2. Prepare a flexible budget based on the actual number of PCs sold.

3. Compute the price variance for direct materials and for direct labor.

4. Compute the efficiency variances for direct materials and direct labor.

5. For manufacturing overhead, compute the total variance, the flexible budget variance, and the production volume variance.

6. What is the total flexible budget variance for One System's manufacturing costs? Show how the total flexible budget variance is divided into materials, labor, and overhead variances.

7. Have One System's managers done a good job or a poor job controlling material and labor costs? Why?

8. Describe how One System's managers can benefit from the standard costing system.

P10-65A Work backward through labor variances *(Learning Objective 4)*

Amanda's Music manufactures harmonicas. Amanda uses standard costs to judge performance. Recently, a clerk mistakenly threw away some of the records, and Amanda has only partial data for October. She knows that the direct labor flexible budget variance for the month was $330 F and that the standard labor price was $10 per hour. A recent pay cut caused a favorable labor price variance of $0.50 per hour. The standard direct labor hours for actual October output were 5,600.

Requirements

1. Find the actual number of direct labor hours worked during October. First, find the actual direct labor price per hour. Then, determine the actual number of direct labor hours worked by setting up the computation of the direct labor flexible budget variance of $330 F.

2. Compute the direct labor price and efficiency variances. Do these variances suggest that the manager may have made trade-offs? Explain.

P10-66A Determine all variances *(Learning Objectives 4 & 5)*

Avanti manufactures embroidered jackets. The company prepares flexible budgets and uses a standard cost system to control manufacturing costs. The following standard unit cost of a jacket is based on the static budget volume of 14,000 jackets per month:

Direct materials (3.0 sq. ft × $4.00 per sq. ft)............................		$ 12.00
Direct labor (2 hours × $9.40 per hour)		18.80
Manufacturing overhead:		
Variable (2 hours × $0.65 per hour).....................................	$1.30	
Fixed (2 hours × $2.20 per hour)	4.40	5.70
Total cost per jacket..		$36.50

Data for November of the current year include the following:
a. Actual production was 13,600 jackets.
b. Actual direct materials usage was 2.70 square feet per jacket at an actual cost of $4.15 per square foot.
c. Actual direct labor usage of 24,480 hours cost $235,008.
d. Total actual overhead cost was $79,000.

Requirements

1. Compute the price and efficiency variances for direct materials and direct labor.

2. For manufacturing overhead, compute the total variance, the flexible budget variance, and the production volume variance.

3. Avanti's management intentionally purchased superior materials for November production. How did this decision affect the other cost variances? Overall, was the decision wise? Explain.

P10-67A (Appendix) Journalize standard cost transactions (Learning Objective 6)

Refer to the data in P10-66A. Journalize the usage of direct materials and the assignment of direct labor, including the related variances.

P10-68A Compute variances and prepare standard cost income statement (Learning Objectives 4, 5, & 6)

Happ and Sons makes ground covers to prevent weed growth. During May, the company produced and sold 44,000 rolls and recorded the following cost data:

	Standard Unit Cost	Actual Total Cost
Direct materials:		
Standard (3 lb × $1.10 per pound)...............	$3.30	
Actual (136,600 lb × $1.05 per pound).........		$143,430
Direct labor:		
Standard (0.1 hr × $9.00 per hr)..................	0.90	
Actual (4,600 hrs × $8.80 per hr).................		40,480
Manufacturing overhead:		
Standard:		
Variable (0.2 machine hr × $9.00 per hr)......... $1.80		
Fixed ($96,000 for static budget		
volume of 40,000 units and		
8,000 machine hours) 2.40		
Actual..	4.20	168,800
Total manufacturing costs................................	$8.40	$352,710

Requirements

1. Compute the price and efficiency variances for direct materials and direct labor.

2. For manufacturing overhead, compute the total variance, the flexible budget variance, and the production volume variance.

3. Prepare a standard cost income statement through gross profit to report all variances to management. Sales price was $10.60 per roll.

4. Happ and Sons intentionally purchased cheaper materials during May. Was the decision wise? Discuss the trade-off between the two materials variances.

Problems—Group B

P10-69B Prepare a flexible budget for planning *(Learning Objective 1)*

Creative Bubbles produces multicolored bubble solution used for weddings and other events. Creative Bubbles' plant capacity is 72,500 kits. If actual volume exceeds 72,500 kits, the company must expand the plant. In that case, salaries will increase by 10%, depreciation by 15%, and rent by $6,000. Fixed utilities will be unchanged by any volume increase.

The company's static budget income statement for December follows. It is based on expected sales volume of 65,000 bubble kits.

Creative Bubbles, Inc.
Static Budget Income Statement
Month Ended December 31

Sales revenue	$201,500
Variable expenses:	
Cost of goods sold	81,250
Sales commissions	13,000
Utilities expense	9,750
Fixed expenses:	
Salary expense	33,000
Depreciation expense	18,000
Rent expense	9,000
Utilities expense	3,000
Total expenses	167,000
Operating income	$ 34,500

Requirements

1. Prepare flexible budget income statements for the company, showing output levels of 65,000, 70,000, and 75,000 kits.

2. Graph the behavior of the company's total costs.

3. Why might Creative Bubbles' managers want to see the graph you prepared in Requirement 2 as well as the columnar format analysis in Requirement 1? What is the disadvantage of the graphic approach?

P10-70B Prepare and interpret a performance report *(Learning Objective 2)*

Refer to the Creative Bubbles data in P10-69B. The company sold 70,000 bubble kits during December, and its actual operating income was as follows:

Creative Bubbles, Inc.
Income Statement
Month Ended December 31

Sales revenue	$226,000
Variable expenses:	
Cost of goods sold	$ 87,800
Sales commissions	16,500
Utilities expense	10,500
Fixed costs:	
Salary expense	35,100
Depreciation expense	18,000
Rent expense	8,250
Utilities expense	3,000
Total expenses	179,150
Operating income	$ 46,850

Requirements

1. Prepare an income statement performance report for December.

2. What accounts for most of the difference between actual operating income and static budget operating income?

3. What is Creative Bubbles' static budget variance? Explain why the income statement performance report provides Creative Bubbles' managers with more useful information than the simple static budget variance. What insights can Creative Bubbles' managers draw from this performance report?

P10-71B Comprehensive flexible budget, standards, and variances problem *(Learning Objectives 2, 3, 4, & 5)*

Gray System assembles PCs and uses flexible budgeting and a standard cost system. Gray System allocates overhead based on the number of direct materials parts. The company's performance report includes the following selected data:

	Static Budget (20,500 PCs)	Actual Results (22,500 PCs)
Sales (20,500 PCs × $415)..................................	$8,507,500	
(22,500 PCs × $435).................................		$9,787,500
Variable manufacturing expenses:		
Direct materials (205,000 parts × $9.50)...........	1,947,500	
(218,500 parts × $9.30).........		2,032,050
Direct labor (41,000 hrs × $14.00)	574,000	
(43,500 hrs × $14.60)		635,100
Variable overhead (205,000 parts × $3.90)	799,500	
(218,500 parts × $4.00)		874,000
Fixed manufacturing costs:		
Fixed overhead	902,000	932,000
Total cost of goods sold	4,223,000	4,473,150
Gross profit	$4,284,500	$5,314,350

Requirements

1. Determine the company's standard cost for one unit.

2. Prepare a flexible budget based on the actual number of PCs sold.

3. Compute the price variance for direct materials and for direct labor.

4. Compute the efficiency variances for direct materials and direct labor.

5. For manufacturing overhead, compute the total variance, the flexible budget variance, and the production volume variance.

6. What is the total flexible budget variance for Gray System's manufacturing costs? Show how the total flexible variance is divided into materials, labor, and overhead variances.

7. Have Gray System's managers done a good job or a poor job controlling material and labor costs? Why?

8. Describe how Gray System's managers can benefit from the standard costing system.

P10-72B Work backward through labor variances *(Learning Objective 4)*

Laura's Music manufactures harmonicas. Laura uses standard costs to judge performance. Recently, a clerk mistakenly threw away some of the records, and Laura has only partial data for May. She knows that the direct labor flexible budget variance for the month was $360 F and that the standard labor price was $9 per hour. A recent pay cut caused a favorable labor price variance of $0.70 per hour. The standard direct labor hours for actual May output were 5,850.

Requirements

1. Find the actual number of direct labor hours worked during May. First, find the actual direct labor price per hour. Then, determine the actual number of direct labor hours worked by setting up the computation of the direct labor flexible budget variance of $360 F.

2. Compute the direct labor price and efficiency variances. Do these variances suggest that the manager may have made trade-offs? Explain.

P10-73B Determine all variances *(Learning Objectives 4 & 5)*

Preston manufactures embroidered jackets. The company prepares flexible budgets and uses a standard cost system to control manufacturing costs. The following standard unit cost of a jacket is based on the static budget volume of 13,800 jackets per month:

Direct materials (3.0 sq. ft × $3.90 per sq. ft).........................		$ 11.70
Direct labor (2 hours × $9.00 per hour)		18.00
Manufacturing overhead:		
Variable (2 hours × $0.67 per hour)..................................	$1.34	
Fixed (2 hours × $2.40 per hour)	4.80	6.14
Total cost per jacket..		$35.84

Data for November of the current year include the following:

a. Actual production was 13,400 jackets.

b. Actual direct materials usage was 2.80 square feet per jacket at an actual price of $4.00 per square foot.

c. Actual direct labor usage of 24,600 hours cost $223,860.

d. Total actual overhead cost was $83,000.

Requirements

1. Compute the price and efficiency variances for direct materials and direct labor.

2. For manufacturing overhead, compute the total variance, the flexible budget variance, and the production volume variance.

3. Preston's management intentionally purchased superior materials for November production. How did this decision affect the other cost variances?

   Overall, was the decision wise?

P10-74B (Appendix) Journalize standard cost transactions *(Learning Objective 6)*

Refer to the data in P10-73B. Journalize the usage of direct materials and the assignment of direct labor, including the related variances.

P10-75B Compute variances and prepare standard cost income statement *(Learning Objectives 4, 5, & 6)*

Greg and Sons makes ground covers to prevent weed growth. During May, the company sold 44,300 rolls and recorded the following cost data:

	Standard Unit Cost	Actual Total Cost
Direct materials:		
Standard (3 lb × $1.25 per pound)...............	$3.75	
Actual (136,800 lb × $1.20 per pound).........		$164,160
Direct labor:		
Standard (0.1 hr × $7.00 per hr)..................	0.70	
Actual (4,630 hrs × $6.80 per hr).................		31,484
Manufacturing overhead:		
Standard:		
Variable (0.2 machine hr × $8.00 per hr).........	$1.60	
Fixed ($99,000 for static budget volume of 40,300 units and 8,060 machine hours)...............................	2.50	
Actual...	4.10	168,400
Total manufacturing costs................................	$8.55	$364,044

Requirements

1. Compute the price and efficiency variances for direct materials and direct labor.

2. For manufacturing overhead, compute the total variance, the flexible budget variance, and the production volume variance.

3. Prepare a standard cost income statement through gross profit to report all variances to management. Sales price was $10.60 per roll.

4. Greg and Sons intentionally purchased cheaper materials during May. Was the decision wise? Discuss the trade-off between the two materials variances.

APPLY YOUR KNOWLEDGE

Decision Cases

C10-76 Compute flexible budget and sales volume variances *(Learning Objective 2)*

ReelTime distributes DVDs to movie retailers, including dot-coms. ReelTime's top management meets monthly to evaluate the company's performance. Controller Terri Lon prepared the following performance report for the meeting.

Lon also revealed that the actual sales price of $20 per movie was equal to the budgeted sales price and that there were no changes in inventories for the month.

Management is disappointed by the operating income results. CEO Lyle Nesbitt exclaims, "How can actual operating income be roughly 13% of the static budget amount when there are so many favorable variances?"

REELTIME, INC.
Income Statement Performance Report
Month Ended July 31

	Actual Results	Static Budget	Variance	
Sales revenue	$1,640,000	$1,960,000	$320,000	U
Variable expenses:				
Cost of goods sold	773,750	980,000	206,250	F
Sales commissions	77,375	107,800	30,425	F
Shipping expense	42,850	53,900	11,050	F
Fixed expenses:				
Salary expense	311,450	300,500	10,950	U
Depreciation expense	208,750	214,000	5,250	F
Rent expense	128,250	108,250	20,000	U
Advertising expense	81,100	68,500	12,600	U
Total expenses	1,623,525	1,832,950	209,425	F
Operating income	$ 16,475	$ 127,050	$110,575	U

Requirements

1. Prepare a more informative performance report. Be sure to include a flexible budget for the actual number of DVDs bought and sold.
2. As a member of ReelTime's management team, which variances would you want investigated? Why?
3. Nesbitt believes that many consumers are postponing purchases of new movies until after the introduction of a new format for recordable DVD players. In light of this information, how would you rate the company's performance?

C10-77 Calculate efficiency variances (Learning Objective 4)

Assume that you manage your local Marble Slab Creamery ice cream parlor. In addition to selling ice cream cones, you make large batches of a few flavors of milk shakes to sell throughout the day. Your parlor is chosen to test the company's "Made-for-You" system. The system allows patrons to customize their milk shakes by choosing different flavors.

Customers like the new system, and your staff appears to be adapting, but you wonder whether this new made-to-order system is as efficient as the old system where you made just a few large batches. Efficiency is a special concern because your performance is evaluated in part on the restaurant's efficient use of materials and labor. Assume that your superiors consider efficiency variances greater than 5% unacceptable.

You decide to look at your sales for a typical day. You find that the parlor used 390 pounds of ice cream and 72 hours of direct labor to produce and sell 2,000 shakes. Assume that the standard quantity allowed for a shake is 0.2 pound of ice cream and 0.03 hours (1.8 minutes) of direct labor. Further, assume that standard costs are $1.50 per pound for ice cream and $8.00 an hour for labor.

Requirements

1. Compute the efficiency variances for direct labor and direct materials.
2. Provide likely explanations for the variances. Do you have reason to be concerned about your performance evaluation? Explain.

3. Write a memo to Marble Slab Creamery's national office explaining your concern and suggesting a remedy. Use the following format for your memo:

Date: _____

    To: Marble Slab Creamery's National Office

From: _____

Subject: "Made-for-You" System

Ethical Issues

C10-78 Ethical dilemmas relating to standards *(Learning Objective 3)*

Austin Landers is the accountant for Sun Coast, a manufacturer of outdoor furniture that is sold through specialty stores and Internet companies. Annually, Landers is responsible for reviewing the standard costs for the following year. While reviewing the standard costs for the coming year, two ethical issues arise. Use the IMA's *Statement of Ethical Professional Practice* (in Chapter 1) to identify the ethical dilemma in each situation. Identify the relevant factors in each situation and suggest what Landers should recommend to the controller.

Issue 1: Landers has been approached by Kara Willis, a former colleague who worked with Landers when they were both employed by a public accounting firm. Willis recently started her own firm, Willis Benchmarking Associates, which collects and sells data on industry benchmarks. She offers to provide Landers with benchmarks for the outdoor furniture industry free of charge if he will provide her with the last three years of Sun Coast's standard and actual costs. Willis explains that this is how she obtains most of her firm's benchmarking data. Landers always has a difficult time with the standard-setting process and believes that the benchmark data would be very useful.

Issue 2: Sun Coast's management is starting a continuous improvement policy that requires a 10% reduction in standard costs each year for the next three years. Dan Jones, manufacturing supervisor of the Teak furniture line, asks Landers to set loose standard costs this year before the continuous improvement policy is implemented. Jones argues that there is no other way to meet the tightening standards while maintaining the high quality of the Teak line.

Team Project

T10-79 Evaluate standard setting approaches *(Learning Objective 3)*

Pella is the world's second-largest manufacturer of wood windows and doors. In 1992, Pella entered the national retail market with its ProLine windows and doors, manufactured in Carroll, Iowa. Since then, Pella has introduced many new product lines with manufacturing facilities in several states.

Suppose Pella has been using a standard cost system that bases price and quantity standards on Pella's historical long-run average performance. Assume Pella's controller has engaged your team of management consultants to recommend whether Pella should use some basis other than historical performance for setting standards.

Requirements

1. List the types of variances you recommend that Pella compute (for example, direct materials price variance for glass). For each variance, what specific standards would Pella need to develop? In addition to cost standards, do you recommend that Pella develop any nonfinancial standards? Explain.

2. There are many approaches to setting standards other than simply using long-run average historical prices and quantities.

   a. List three alternative approaches that Pella could use to set standards and explain how Pella could implement each alternative.

   b. Evaluate each alternative method of setting standards, including the pros and cons of each method.

   c. Write a memo to Pella's controller detailing your recommendations. First, should Pella retain its historical data-based standard cost approach? If not, which alternative approach should it adopt? Use the following format for your memo:

Date: _____

To: Controller, Pella Corporation

From: _____ , Management Consultants

Subject: Standard Costs

Quick Check Answers

1. *d* 2. *a* 3. *c* 4. *d* 5. *b* 6. *c*
7. *b* 8. *a* 9. *d* 10. *c*

For online homework, exercises, and problems that provide you with immediate feedback, please visit www.myaccountinglab.com.

Discussion & Analysis

1. Compare and contrast a static budget and a flexible budget.

2. Describe two ways managers can use flexible budgets.

3. How is the sales volume variance calculated? What does it measure? Who within the organization is typically held responsible for the sales volume variance?

4. How is the flexible budget variance calculated? What does it measure? Who within the organization is typically held responsible for the flexible budget variance?

5. What does the direct materials price variance measure? Who is generally responsible for the direct materials price variance? Describe two situations that could result in a favorable materials price variance. Describe two situations that could result in an unfavorable materials price variance.

6. What does the direct materials efficiency variance measure? Who is generally responsible for the direct materials efficiency variance? Describe two situations that could result in a favorable direct materials efficiency variance. Describe two situations that could result in an unfavorable direct materials efficiency variance.

7. What does the direct labor price variance measure? Who is generally responsible for the direct labor price variance? Describe two situations that could result in a favorable direct labor price variance. Describe two situations that could result in an unfavorable direct labor price variance.

8. What does the direct labor efficiency variance measure? Who is generally responsible for the direct labor efficiency variance? Describe two situations that could result in a favorable labor efficiency variance. Describe two situations that could result in an unfavorable labor efficiency variance.

9. Describe at least four ways a company could use standard costing and variance analysis.

10. What are the two manufacturing overhead variances? What does each measure? Who within the organization would be responsible for each of these variances?

Application & Analysis

10-1   Analyzing Variances and Potential Causes

Go to YouTube.com and search for clips from the show "Unwrapped" on Food Network or "How It's Made" on Discovery Channel. Watch a clip for a product you find interesting. Companies are not likely to disclose everything about their production process and other trade secrets. When you answer the following questions, you may have to make reasonable assumptions or guesses about the manufacturing process, materials, and labor.

Basic Discussion Questions

1. Describe the product that is being produced. Briefly outline the production process.

2. What direct materials are used to make this product? In general, what has happened to the cost of these materials over the past year? To find information about the price of materials, you might try one of these sources (or a combination of these sources):

   a. Go to the New York Times website (http://www.nytimes.com/) or to USA Today (http://www.usatoday.com/) and search for each of the materials.

   b. Find the company's annual report on its Web site and read its discussion about its costs of production.

3. Given what you have discovered about the cost of materials for this product, were the price variances for each material likely to be favorable or unfavorable (answer separately for each individual material)?

4. In general, what has probably occurred to the cost of direct labor for this company? Again, to find clues about its labor costs, you might try one of the options listed in Question 2. If you cannot find anything specific about this company, then discuss what has happened to the cost of labor in general over the past year.

5. Given what you have discovered about the cost of labor, was the labor price variance likely to be favorable or unfavorable?

6. It is unlikely that the company has released information about its efficiency variances. In general, though, what could cause this company's material efficiency variances to be favorable? What could cause these material efficiency variances to be unfavorable?

7. In general, what could cause this company's labor efficiency variances to be favorable? What could cause these labor efficiency variances to be unfavorable?

Classroom Applications

Web: Post the discussion questions on an electronic discussion board. Have small groups of students choose a product for their groups. Each student should watch the clip for the product for his or her group. The students should then collaborate to form answers for all of the discussion questions for their product/company.

Classroom: Form groups of 3–4 students. Your group should choose a product and its clip to view. After viewing the clip, prepare a five-minute presentation about your group's product that addresses the listed questions.

Independent: Research answers to each of the questions. Turn in a 2–3 page typed paper (12 point font, double-spaced with 1" margins). Include references, including the URL for the clip that you viewed.

For additional Application & Analysis projects and implementation tips, see the Instructor Resources in MyAccountingLab.com.

United Parcel Service (UPS) delivers over 5.4 billion

packages a year in over 200 countries. To achieve such astonishing volume, UPS employs over 425,000 people and flies more than 1,900 flight segments each day into 800 airports around the world. How does management successfully guide the actions of all of these employees? First, it divides—or decentralizes—the company into three segments: domestic packaging, international packaging, and nonpackaging services (such as supply chain and logistics). It further breaks each packaging segment into geographic regions and each region into districts. Management gives each district manager authority to make decisions for his or her district. Because top management wants *every* employee to know how his or her day-to-day job contributes to the company's goals, it implemented a system, called the balanced scorecard, for communicating strategy to all district managers and employees. Management can also use the balanced scorecard to measure whether each district is meeting its goals and to assess where changes should be made. According to one UPS executive, "The balanced scorecard provided a road map—the shared vision of our future goals—with action elements that let *everyone* contribute to our success."

Has the balanced scorecard helped UPS become an industry leader? In 2008, *Fortune* rated UPS as the "World's Most Admired Company in its Industry" for the tenth consecutive year. Year after year, UPS continues to win awards in the areas of E-commerce, technology, business excellence, and corporate citizenship.

Sources: Robert Kaplan and David Norton, *The Strategy-Focused Organization: How Balanced Scorecard Companies Thrive in the New Business Environment*, Harvard Business School Press, Boston, 2001, pp. 21–22, 239–241; www.ups.com (2009).

CHAPTER 11

Performance Evaluation and the Balanced Scorecard

Learning Objectives

1. Explain why and how companies decentralize

2. Explain why companies use performance evaluation systems

3. Describe the balanced scorecard and identify key performance indicators for each perspective

4. Use performance reports to evaluate cost, revenue, and profit centers

5. Use ROI, RI, and EVA to evaluate investment centers

Many companies, such as UPS, decentralize their operations into subunits. Decentralization provides large companies with many advantages. But once a company decentralizes its operations, top management is no longer directly involved in running the day-to-day operations of each subunit. Therefore, upper management needs a system—such as the balanced scorecard—for communicating the company's strategy to subunit managers and for measuring how well the subunits are achieving their goals.

As you'll see in this chapter, the balanced scorecard helps management view the performance of company subunits from several different perspectives. Each perspective gives management unique insight into the factors that will drive the success of the company, as a whole.

Why do Companies Decentralize Operations?

1 Explain why and how companies decentralize

In a small company, the owner or top manager often makes all planning and operating decisions. Small companies can use **centralized** decision making because of the smaller scope of their operations. However, when a company grows, it is impossible for a single person to manage the entire organization's daily operations. Therefore, most companies **decentralize** as they grow.

Companies that decentralize split their operations into different divisions or operating units. Top management delegates decision-making responsibility to the unit managers. Top management determines the type of decentralization that best suits the company's strategy. For example, decentralization may be based on geographic area, product line, customer base, business function, or some other business characteristic. Citizens Bank segments its operations by state (different geographic areas). Sherwin-Williams segments by customer base (commercial and consumer paint divisions). PepsiCo segments by type of product (Pepsi brand beverages; Frito-Lay snack foods; and Quaker brand food products). And UPS segmented first by function (domestic packaging, international packaging, and nonpackaging services), then by geographic area.

Advantages of Decentralization

What advantages does decentralization offer large companies? Let's take a look.

FREES TOP MANAGEMENT'S TIME By delegating responsibility for daily operations to unit managers, top management can concentrate on long-term strategic planning and higher-level decisions that affect the entire company.

SUPPORTS USE OF EXPERT KNOWLEDGE Decentralization allows top management to hire the expertise each business unit needs to excel in its specific operations. For example, decentralizing by state allows Citizens Bank to hire managers with specialized knowledge of the banking laws in each state. Such specialized knowledge can help unit managers make better decisions than the company's top managers could make about product and business improvements within the business unit.

IMPROVES CUSTOMER RELATIONS Unit managers focus on just one segment of the company; therefore, they can maintain close contact with important customers. Thus, decentralization often leads to improved customer relations and quicker customer response time.

PROVIDES TRAINING Decentralization also provides unit managers with training and experience necessary to become effective top managers. Companies often choose CEOs based on their past performance as division managers.

IMPROVES MOTIVATION AND RETENTION Empowering unit managers to make decisions increases managers' motivation and retention and improves job performance and satisfaction.

Disadvantages of Decentralization

As Exhibit 11-1 illustrates, the many advantages of decentralization usually outweigh the disadvantages.

Despite its advantages, decentralization can also cause potential problems, including those outlined in this section.

DUPLICATION OF COSTS Decentralization may cause the company to duplicate certain costs or assets. For example, each business unit may hire its own Payroll Department and purchase its own payroll software. Companies can often avoid such duplications by providing

EXHIBIT 11-1 **Advantages Outweigh Disadvantages**

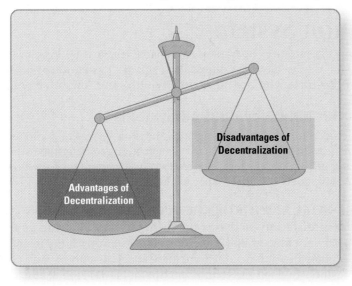

centralized services. For example, Doubletree Hotels segments its business by property, yet each property shares one centralized reservations office and one centralized Web site.

PROBLEMS ACHIEVING GOAL CONGRUENCE **Goal Congruence** occurs when unit managers' goals align with top management's goals. Decentralized companies often struggle to achieve goal congruence. Unit managers may not fully understand the big picture of the company. They may make decisions that are good for their division but may harm another division or the rest of the company. For example, the Purchasing Department may buy cheaper components to decrease product cost. However, cheaper components may hurt the product line's quality, and the company's brand, *as a whole*, may suffer. Later in this chapter, we'll see how management accountants can design performance evaluation systems that foster goal congruence.

Responsibility Centers

Decentralized companies delegate responsibility for specific decisions to each subunit, creating responsibility centers. Recall from Chapter 9 that a **responsibility center** is a part or subunit of an organization whose manager is accountable for specific activities. Exhibit 11-2 reviews the four most common types of responsibility centers.

EXHIBIT 11-2 **The Four Most Common Types of Responsibility Centers**

Responsibility Center	Manager is responsible for...	Examples
Cost center	Controlling costs	Production line at Dell Computer; Legal Department and Accounting Department at Nike
Revenue center	Generating sales revenue	Midwest sales region at Pace Foods; central reservation office at Delta
Profit center	Producing profit through generating sales and controlling costs	Product line at Colgate-Palmolive; individual Home Depot stores
Investment center	Producing profit and managing the division's invested capital	Company divisions such as Walt Disney World Resorts and Toon Disney

What are Performance Evaluation Systems?

2 Explain why companies use performance evaluation systems

Once a company decentralizes operations, top management is no longer involved in running the subunits' day-to-day operations. Performance evaluation systems provide top management with a framework for maintaining control over the entire organization.

Goals of Performance Evaluation Systems

When companies decentralize, top management needs a system to communicate its goals to subunit managers. In addition, top management needs to determine whether the decisions being made at the subunit level are effectively meeting company goals. We'll now consider the primary goals of performance evaluation systems.

PROMOTING GOAL CONGRUENCE AND COORDINATION As previously mentioned, decentralization increases the difficulty of achieving goal congruence. Unit managers may not always make decisions consistent with the overall goals of the organization. A company will be able to achieve its goals only if each unit moves in a synchronized fashion toward the overall company goals. Like a flock of birds or a school of fish, each individual subunit must move in harmony with the other subunits. The performance measurement system should provide incentives for coordinating the subunits' activities and direct them toward achieving the overall company goals.

COMMUNICATING EXPECTATIONS To make decisions that are consistent with the company's goals, unit managers must know the goals and the specific part that their units play in attaining those goals. The performance measurement system should spell out the unit's most critical objectives. Without a clear picture of what management expects, unit managers have little to guide their daily operating decisions.

MOTIVATING UNIT MANAGERS Unit managers are usually motivated to make decisions that will help to achieve top management's expectations. For additional motivation, upper management may offer bonuses to unit managers who meet or exceed performance targets. Top management must exercise extreme care in setting performance targets. For example, a manager measured solely by his or her ability to control costs may take whatever actions are necessary to achieve that goal, including sacrificing quality or customer service. But such actions would *not* be in the best interests of the company as a whole. Therefore, upper management must consider the ramifications of the performance targets it sets for unit managers.

PROVIDING FEEDBACK In decentralized companies, top management is no longer involved in the day-to-day operations of each subunit. Performance evaluation systems provide upper management with the feedback it needs to maintain control over the entire organization, even though it has delegated responsibility and decision-making authority to unit managers. If targets are not met at the unit level, upper management will take corrective actions, ranging from modifying unit goals (if the targets are unrealistic) to replacing the unit manager (if the targets are achievable but the manager fails to reach them).

BENCHMARKING Performance evaluation results are often used for **benchmarking**, which is the practice of comparing the unit's achievements against other company subunits, other companies in the same industry, the best practices in the industry, or the subunit's past performance. By comparing current results against past performance, managers can assess whether their decisions are improving, having no effect, or adversely affecting subunit performance. However, comparing current results against industry benchmarks is often more revealing than comparing results against budgets or past performance. To survive, a company must keep up with its competitors.

Why is this important?

"Performance evaluation systems help managers identify operations that fall short of company goals, focusing their attention on what needs to be improved."

Limitations of Financial Performance Measurement

In the past, performance evaluation systems revolved almost entirely around *financial* performance. Until 1995, 95% of UPS's performance measures were financial. On the one hand, this focus makes sense because the ultimate goal of a company is to generate profit. On the other hand, *current* financial performance tends to reveal the results of *past* actions rather than indicate *future* performance. For this reason, financial measures tend to be **lag indicators** rather than **lead indicators**. Management needs to know the results of past decisions, but it also needs to know how current decisions may affect the future. To adequately assess the performance of subunits, managers need lead indicators in addition to lag indicators.

Another limitation of financial performance measures is that they tend to focus on the company's short-term achievements rather than on long-term performance. Why is this the case? Because financial statements are prepared on a monthly, quarterly, or annual basis. To remain competitive, top management needs clear signals that assess and predict the company's performance over longer periods of time.

The Balanced Scorecard

In the early 1990s, Robert Kaplan and David Norton introduced the **balanced scorecard**.[1] The balanced scorecard recognizes that management must consider *both* financial performance measures (which tend to measure the results of actions already taken) and operational performance measures (which tend to drive future performance) when judging the performance of a company and its subunits. These measures should be linked with the company's goals and its strategy for achieving those goals. The balanced scorecard represents a major shift in corporate performance measurement: Financial indicators are no longer the sole measure of performance; they are now only one measure among a broader set of performance measures. Keeping score of operating measures *and* traditional financial measures gives management a "balanced," comprehensive view of the organization.

Kaplan and Norton use the analogy of an airplane pilot to illustrate the necessity for a balanced scorecard approach to performance evaluation. The pilot of an airplane cannot rely on only one factor, such as wind speed, to fly a plane. Rather, the pilot must consider other critical factors, such as altitude, direction, and fuel level. Likewise, management cannot rely on only financial measures to guide the company. Management needs to consider other critical factors, such as customer satisfaction, operational efficiency, and employee excellence. Similar to the way a pilot uses cockpit instruments to measure critical factors, management uses *key performance indicators*—such as customer satisfaction ratings and market share—to measure critical factors that affect the success of the company. As shown in Exhibit 11-3, **key performance indicators (KPIs)** are summary performance measures that help managers assess whether the company is achieving its goals.

> **3** Describe the balanced scorecard and identify key performance indicators for each perspective

EXHIBIT 11-3 Linking Company Goals to Key Performance Indicators

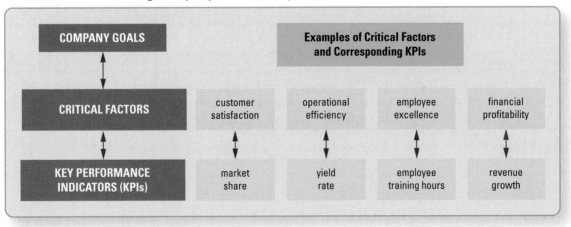

[1]Robert Kaplan and David Norton, "The Balanced Scorecard—Measures That Drive Performance," *Harvard Business Review on Measuring Corporate Performance*, Boston, 1991, pp. 123–145; Robert Kaplan and David Norton, *Translating Strategy into Action: The Balanced Scorecard*, Boston, Harvard Business School Press, 1996.

Why is this important?

"Rather than focusing strictly on financial performance, the balanced scorecard includes operational performance measures that give managers a holistic view of the company's performance."

The Four Perspectives of the Balanced Scorecard

The balanced scorecard views the company from four different perspectives, each of which evaluates a specific aspect of organizational performance:

1. Financial perspective
2. Customer perspective
3. Internal business perspective
4. Learning and growth perspective

Exhibit 11-4 illustrates how the company's strategy affects, and, in turn, is affected by all four perspectives. In addition, it shows the cause-and-effect relationship linking the four perspectives.

EXHIBIT 11-4 **The Four Perspectives of the Balanced Scorecard**

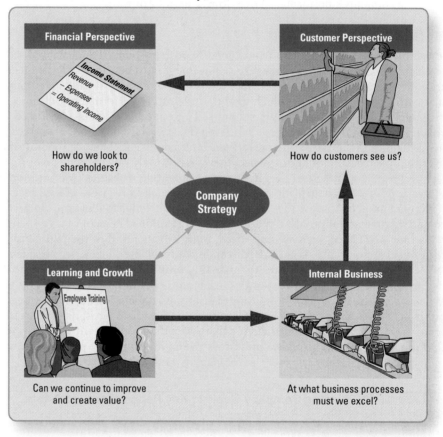

Companies that adopt the balanced scorecard usually have specific objectives they want to achieve within each of the four perspectives. Once management clearly identifies the objectives, it develops KPIs that will assess how well the objectives are being achieved. To focus attention on the most critical elements and prevent information overload, management should use only a few KPIs for each perspective. Let's now look at each of the perspectives and discuss the links between them.

Financial Perspective

The financial perspective helps managers answer the question, how do we look to shareholders? The ultimate goal of a company is to generate income for its owners. Therefore, company strategy revolves around increasing the company's profits through increasing revenue, controlling costs, and increasing productivity. Companies grow revenue through introducing new products, gaining new customers, and increasing sales to existing customers. At the same time, companies must carefully monitor their costs. Companies increase productivity by using the company's assets more efficiently. For example, CVS, the drugstore chain, simply changed the direction of its store aisles and lowered its shelves to create a more user-friendly store layout. As a result, profits increased. Managers may implement seemingly sensible strategies and initiatives, but the test of their judgment is whether these decisions increase company profits.

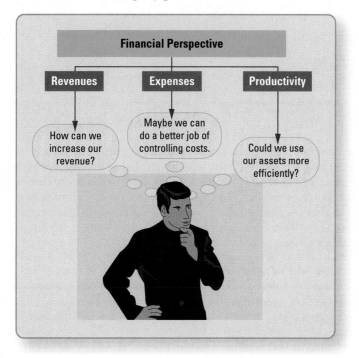

The financial perspective focuses management's attention on KPIs that assess financial objectives such as revenue growth and cost cutting. Some commonly used KPIs include *sales revenue growth*, *gross margin growth*, and *return on investment*. Later in the chapter, the most commonly used financial perspective KPIs will be discussed in detail.

Customer Perspective

The customer perspective helps managers evaluate the question, how do customers see us? Customer satisfaction is a top priority for long-term company success. If customers aren't happy, they won't come back. Therefore, customer satisfaction is critical for the company to achieve its financial goals. Notice in Exhibit 11-4 how the customer perspective influences the finan-cial perspective.

Customers are typically concerned with four specific product or service attributes: (1) the product's price, (2) the product's quality, (3) the sales service quality, and (4) the product's delivery time (the shorter the better). Since each of these attributes is critical to making the customer happy, most companies have specific targets for each of them.

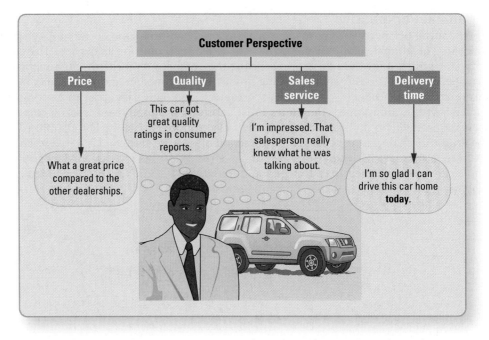

Businesses commonly use *customer satisfaction ratings* to assess how they are performing on these attributes. No doubt, you have filled out a customer satisfaction survey. Because customer satisfaction is crucial, customer satisfaction ratings determine the extent to which bonuses are granted to Bahama Breeze restaurant managers. In addition to customer satisfaction ratings, the customer perspective is often measured using KPIs such as *percentage of market share*, *increase in the number of customers*, *number of repeat customers*, and *rate of on-time deliveries*.

Internal Business Perspective

The internal business perspective helps managers address the question, "At what business processes must we excel to satisfy customer and financial objectives?" The answer to that question incorporates three factors: (1) innovation, (2) operations, and (3) post-sales service. All three factors critically affect customer satisfaction, which will affect the company's financial success, as shown in Exhibit 11-4.

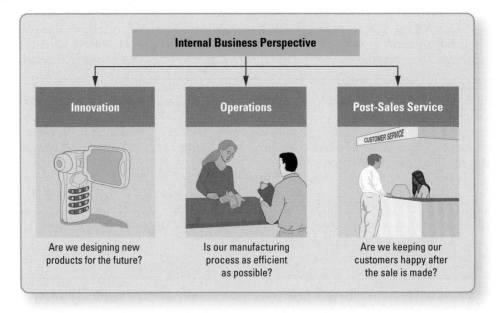

Satisfying customers once does not guarantee future success, which is why the first important factor of the internal business perspective is innovation. Customers' needs and wants change as the world around them changes. Not all that long ago, digital cameras, flat-panel computer monitors, plasma screen televisions, and digital video recorders (DVRs) did not exist. Companies must continually improve existing products (such as the addition of cameras to cell phones) and develop new products (such as the iPhone and the Wii) to succeed in the future. Companies commonly assess innovation using KPIs such as the *number of new products developed* or *new-product development time.*

The second important factor of the internal business perspective is operations. Efficient and effective internal operations allow the company to meet customers' needs and expectations. For example, the time it takes to manufacture a product *(manufacturing cycle time)* affects the company's ability to deliver quickly to meet a customer's demand. Production efficiency *(number of units produced per hour)* and product quality *(defect rate)* also affect the price charged to the customer. To remain competitive, companies must be as good as the industry leader at those internal operations that are essential to their businesses.

The third factor of the internal business perspective is post-sales service. How well does the company service customers after the sale? Claims of excellent post-sales service help to generate more sales. Management assesses post-sales service through the following typical KPIs: *number of warranty claims received, average repair time,* and *average wait time on the phone for a customer service representative.*

Learning and Growth Perspective

The learning and growth perspective helps managers assess the question, can we continue to improve and create value? The learning and growth perspective focuses on three factors: (1) employee capabilities, (2) information system capabilities, and (3) the company's "climate for action." As shown in Exhibit 11-4, the learning and growth perspective lays the foundation needed to improve internal business operations, sustain customer satisfaction, and generate financial success. Without skilled employees, updated technology, and a positive corporate culture, the company will not be able to meet the objectives of the other perspectives.

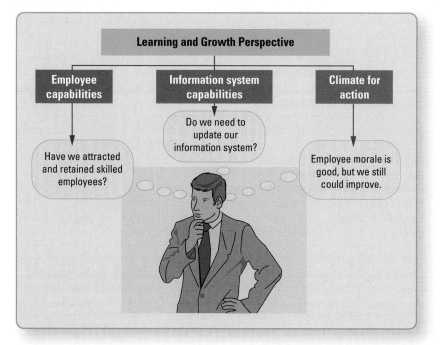

Let's consider each of these factors. First, because most routine work is automated, employees are free to be critical and creative thinkers who help achieve the company's goals. The learning and growth perspective measures employees' skills, knowledge, motivation, and empowerment. KPIs typically include *hours of employee training, employee satisfaction, employee turnover,* and *number of employee suggestions implemented.* Second, employees need timely and accurate information on customers, internal processes, and finances; therefore, other KPIs measure the maintenance and improvement of the company's information system. For example, KPIs might include the *percentage of employees having online access to information about customers* and the *percentage of processes with real-time feedback on quality, cycle time, and cost.* Finally, management must create a corporate culture that supports communication, change, and growth. For example, UPS used the balanced scorecard to communicate strategy to all employees and to show them how their daily work contributed to company success.

In summary, the balanced scorecard focuses performance measurement on progress toward the company's goals in each of the four perspectives. In designing the scorecard, managers start with the company's goals and its strategy for achieving those goals and then identify the *most* important measures of performance that will predict long-term success. Some of these measures are operational lead indicators, while others are financial lag indicators. Managers must consider the linkages between strategy and operations and the way those operations will affect finances now and in the future.

So far, we have looked at why companies decentralize, why they need to measure subunit performance, and how the balanced scorecard can help. In the second half of the chapter, we'll focus on how companies measure the financial perspective of the balanced scorecard.

Decision Guidelines

Performance Evaluation and the Balanced Scorecard

UPS had to make the following types of decisions when it decentralized and developed its balanced scorecard for performance evaluation.

Decision	Guidelines
How should we decentralize?	The manner of decentralization should fit the company's strategy. Many companies decentralize based on geographic region, product line, business function, or customer type.
Will decentralization have a negative impact on the company?	Decentralization usually provides many benefits; however, decentralization also has potential drawbacks: • Subunits may duplicate costs or assets. • Subunit managers may not make decisions that are favorable to the entire company or consistent with top managers' goals.
How can responsibility accounting be incorporated at decentralized companies?	Subunit managers are given responsibility for specific activities and are held accountable only for the results of those activities. Subunits generally fall into one of the following four categories according to their responsibilities: 1. **Cost centers**—responsible for controlling costs 2. **Revenue centers**—responsible for generating revenue 3. **Profit centers**—responsible for controlling costs and generating revenue 4. **Investment centers**—responsible for controlling costs, generating revenue, and efficiently managing the division's invested capital (assets)
Is a performance evaluation system necessary?	While not mandatory, most companies will reap many benefits from implementing a well-designed performance evaluation system. Such systems will promote goal congruence, communicate expectations, motivate managers, provide feedback, and enable benchmarking.
Should the performance evaluation system include lag or lead measures?	Better performance evaluation systems include *both* lag and lead measures. Lag measures reveal the results of past actions, while lead measures project future performance.
What are the four balanced scorecard perspectives?	1. Financial perspective 2. Customer perspective 3. Internal business perspective 4. Learning and growth perspective.
Must all four perspectives be included in the company's balanced scorecard?	Every company's balanced scorecard will be unique to its business and strategy. Because each of the four perspectives is causally linked, most companies benefit from developing performance measures for each of the four perspectives.

Summary Problem 1

Requirements

1. Each of the following describes a key performance indicator. Determine which of the balanced scorecard perspectives is being addressed (financial, customer, internal business, or learning and growth).

   a. Employee turnover

   b. Earnings per share

   c. Percentage of on-time deliveries

   d. Revenue growth rate

   e. Percentage of defects discovered during manufacturing

   f. Number of warranties claimed

   g. New product development time

   h. Number of repeat customers

   i. Number of employee suggestions implemented

2. Read the following company initiatives and determine which of the balanced scorecard perspectives is being addressed (financial, customer, internal business, or learning and growth).

   a. Purchasing efficient production equipment

   b. Providing employee training

   c. Updating retail store lighting

   d. Paying quarterly dividends

   e. Updating the company's information system

Solution

Requirement 1

a. Learning and growth

b. Financial

c. Customer

d. Financial

e. Internal business

f. Internal business

g. Internal business

h. Customer

i. Learning and growth

Requirement 2

a. Internal business

b. Learning and growth

c. Customer

d. Financial

e. Learning and growth

How do Managers Evaluate the Financial Performance of Cost, Revenue, and Profit Centers?

4 Use performance reports to evaluate cost, revenue, and profit centers

In this half of the chapter, we'll take a more detailed look at how companies measure the financial perspective of the balanced scorecard for different subunits of the company. We'll focus on the financial performance measurement of each type of responsibility center. Because each type of responsibility center is unique, each will use different performance measures.

Responsibility accounting performance reports capture the financial performance of cost, revenue, and profit centers. Recall from Chapter 9 that responsibility accounting performance reports compare *actual* results with *budgeted* amounts and display a variance, or difference, between the two amounts. Because **cost centers** are responsible only for controlling costs, the only information their performance reports include is the actual versus budgeted *costs*. Likewise, performance reports for **revenue centers** contain only the actual versus budgeted *revenue*. However, **profit centers** are responsible for controlling costs and generating revenue. Therefore, performance reports contain actual and budgeted information on both *revenues and costs*. In addition to the performance report, a cost center may be evaluated on KPIs such as *cost per unit of output*.

Why is this important?

"Performance reports should only hold managers responsible for the operations that are directly under their control."

Cost Center Performance Reports

Cost center performance reports typically focus on the *flexible budget variance*—the difference between actual results and the flexible budget (as described in Chapter 10). Exhibit 11-5 shows an example of a cost center performance report for a regional Payroll Processing Department of House and Garden Depot, a home improvement warehouse chain. Because the Payroll Processing Department only incurs expenses and does not generate revenue, it is classified as a cost center.

EXHIBIT 11-5 **Example of Cost Center Performance Report**

HOUSE AND GARDEN DEPOT—NORTH FLORIDA REGION
Payroll Processing Department Performance Report
July 2008

	Actual	Flexible Budget	Flexible Budget Variance (U or F)	% Variance* (U or F)
Salary and wages	$18,500	$18,000	$ 500 U	2.8% U
Payroll benefits	6,100	5,000	1,100 U	22.0% U
Equipment depreciation	3,000	3,000	0	0%
Supplies	1,850	2,000	150 F	7.5% F
Other	1,900	2,000	100 F	5.0% F
Total Expenses	$31,350	$30,000	$1,350 U	4.5% U

*Flexible budget variance ÷ flexible budget.

Managers use **management by exception** to determine which variances in the performance report are worth investigating. For example, management may investigate only those variances that exceed a certain dollar amount (for example, over $1,000) or a certain percentage of the budgeted figure (for example, over 10%). Smaller variances signal that operations are close to target and do not require management's immediate attention. For example, in the cost center performance report illustrated in Exhibit 11-5, management might investigate "payroll benefits" because the variance exceeds $1,000 and 10%. As discussed in Chapter 10, management should investigate favorable as well as unfavorable variances that meet its investigation criteria. Companies that use standard costs can compute price and efficiency variances, as described in Chapter 10, to better understand why significant flexible budget variances occurred.

Revenue Center Performance Reports

Revenue center performance reports often highlight both the flexible budget variance and the sales volume variance. The Paint Department at House and Garden Depot's Tallahassee store might look similar to Exhibit 11-6, with detailed sales volume and revenue shown for each brand and type of paint sold (for simplicity, the exhibit shows volume and revenue for only one item). The cash register bar-coding system provides managment with the sales volume and sales revenue generated by individual products.

EXHIBIT 11-6 Example of a Revenue Center Performance Report

HOUSE AND GARDEN DEPOT—Tallahassee Store Paint Department Performance Report July 2008					
Sales Revenue	**Actual Sales**	**Flexible Budget Variance**	**Flexible Budget**	**Sales Volume Variance**	**Static (Master) Budget**
Glidden—Flat:					
Volume (gallons)	2,480	–0–	2,480	155 F	2,325
Revenue	$40,920	$3,720 U	$44,640	$2,790 F	$41,850
Glidden—Semigloss:					
Volume (gallons)					
Revenue					
Glidden—Glossy:					
Volume (gallons)					
Revenue					

Recall from Chapter 10 that the sales volume variance is due strictly to volume differences—selling more or fewer units (gallons of paint) than originally planned. The flexible budget variance, however, is due strictly to differences in the sales price—selling units for a higher or lower price than originally planned. Both the sales volume variance and the flexible budget variance help revenue center managers understand why they have exceeded or fallen short of budgeted revenue. In addition to the performance report, revenue centers may be evaluated on KPIs such as *revenue growth percentage* for different product lines.

Profit Center Performance Reports

Managers of profit centers are responsible for generating revenue and controlling costs so their performance reports include both revenues and expenses. Exhibit 11-7 shows an example of a profit center performance report for the Tallahassee House and Garden Depot store.

EXHIBIT 11-7 Example of a Profit Center Performance Report

HOUSE AND GARDEN DEPOT Tallahassee Store—Performance Report July 2008				
	Actual	**Flexible Budget**	**Flexible Budget Variance**	**% Variance**
Sales revenue	$5,243,600	$5,000,000	$243,600 F	4.9% F
Operating expenses	4,183,500	4,000,000	183,500 U	4.6% U
Income from operations before service				
department charges	1,060,100	1,000,000	60,100 F	6.0% F
Service department charges (allocated)	84,300	75,000	9,300 U	12.4% U
Income from operations	$ 975,800	$ 925,000	$ 50,800 F	5.5% F

Notice how this profit center performance report contains the line "Service department charges." Recall that one drawback of decentralization is that subunits may duplicate costs or assets. Many companies avoid this problem by providing centralized service departments where several subunits, such as profit centers, share assets or costs. For example, the payroll processing cost center shown in Exhibit 11-5 serves all of the House and Garden Depot stores in the northern Florida region. In addition to centralized payroll departments, companies often provide centralized human resource departments, legal departments, and information systems.

When subunits share centralized services, should those services be "free" to the subunits? If they are free, the subunits' performance reports will *not* include any charge for using those services. However, if they are not free, the performance reports will show a charge, as you see in Exhibit 11-7. Most companies charge subunits for their use of centralized services because the subunit would otherwise have to buy those services on its own. For example, if House and Garden Depot didn't operate a Centralized Payroll Department, the Tallahassee House and Garden Depot store would have to hire its own payroll department personnel and purchase any computers, payroll software, and supplies necessary to process the store's payroll. As an alternative, it could outsource payroll to a company such as Paychex or ADP. In either event, the store would incur a cost for processing payroll. It only seems fair that the store is charged for using the Centralized Payroll Processing Department. In addition, subunits tend to use centralized services more judiciously when they are charged for using the services. The appendix to this chapter describes how companies allocate service department costs between subunits. Because the charges are the result of allocation rather than a direct cost of the profit center, they are usually shown on a separate line rather than "buried" in the subunit's other operating expenses.

Exhibit 11-8 shows the basic decisions management must make regarding centralized service departments.

EXHIBIT 11-8 **Centralized Services Decision Tree**

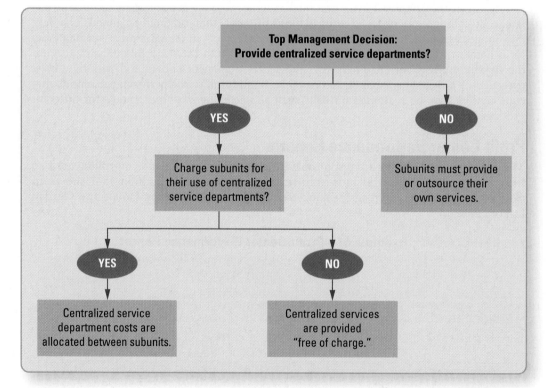

Regardless of the type of responsibility center, performance reports should focus on information, not blame. Analyzing budget variances helps managers understand the underlying reasons for the unit's performance. Once management understands these reasons, it may be able to take corrective actions. But some variances are uncontrollable. For example, the 2005 hurricanes along the Gulf Coast increased the price of gasoline (due to damaged oil refineries) and building materials (as people repaired hurricane-damaged homes). These price increases resulted in unfavorable cost variances for many companies. Managers should not be responsible for conditions they cannot control. Responsibility accounting can help management identify the causes of variances, thus allowing them to determine what was controllable and what was not.

We have just looked at the *detailed* financial information presented in responsibility accounting performance reports. In addition to these detailed reports, upper management often uses *summary* measures—financial KPIs—to assess the financial performance of cost, revenue, and profit centers. Examples include the *cost per unit of output* (for cost centers), *revenue growth* (for revenue centers), and *gross margin growth* (for profit centers). KPIs such as these are used to address the financial perspective of the balanced scorecard for cost, revenue, and profit centers. In the next section, we'll look at the most commonly used KPIs for investment centers.

STOP & THINK

We have just seen that companies like House and Garden Depot use responsibility accounting performance reports to evaluate the financial performance of cost, revenue, and profit centers. Are these types of performance reports sufficient for evaluating the financial performance of investment centers? Why or why not?

Answer: Investment centers are responsible not only for generating revenue and controlling costs but also for efficiently managing the subunit's invested capital. The performance reports we have just seen address how well the subunits control costs and generate revenue, but they do not address how well the subunits manage their assets. Therefore, these performance reports will be helpful but not sufficient for evaluating investment center performance.

How do Managers Evaluate the Financial Performance of Investment Centers?

Investment centers are typically large divisions of a company, such as the Frito-Lay division of PepsiCo. The duties of an investment center manager are similar to those of a CEO. The CEO is responsible for maximizing income in relation to the company's invested capital by using company assets efficiently. Likewise, investment center managers are responsible not only for generating profit but also for making the best use of the investment center's assets.

How does an investment center manager influence the use of the division's assets? An investment center manager has the authority to open new stores or close old stores. The manager may also decide how much inventory to hold, what types of investments to make, how aggressively to collect accounts receivable, and whether to invest in new equipment. In other words, the manager has decision-making responsibility over all of the division's assets.

Companies cannot evaluate investment centers the way they evaluate profit centers based only on operating income. Why? Because income does not indicate how *efficiently* the division is using its assets. The financial evaluation of investment centers must measure two factors: (1) how much income the division is generating and (2) how efficiently the division is using its assets.

Consider House and Garden Depot. In addition to its home improvement warehouse stores, House and Garden Depot operates a Landscaping Division and a Design Division. Operating income, total assets, and sales for the two divisions follow (in thousands of dollars):

House and Garden Depot	Landscaping Division	Design Division
Operating income	$ 450,000	$ 600,000
Total assets	2,500,000	4,000,000
Sales	7,500,000	10,000,000

Use ROI, RI, and EVA to evaluate investment centers

5

Why is this important?

"Return on investment (ROI), residual income (RI), and Economic Value Added (EVA) measure how well large company divisions are using their assets to generate profit."

Based on operating income alone, the Design Division (with operating income of $600,000) appears to be more profitable than the Landscaping Division (with operating income of $450,000). However, this comparison is misleading because it does not consider the assets invested in each division. The Design Division has more assets to use for generating income than does the Landscaping Division.

To adequately evaluate an investment center's financial performance, companies need summary performance measures—or KPIs—that include *both* the division's operating income *and* its assets. In the next sections, we discuss three commonly used performance measures: return on investment (ROI), residual income (RI), and Economic Value Added (EVA). As shown in Exhibit 11-9, all three measures incorporate both the division's assets and its operating income. For simplicity, we will leave the word *divisional* out of the equations. However, keep in mind that all of the equations use divisional data when evaluating a division's performance.

EXHIBIT 11-9   Summary Performance Measures (KPIs) for Investment Centers

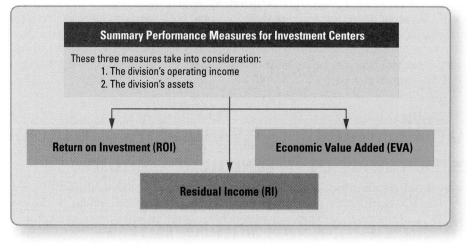

Return on Investment (ROI)

Return on Investment (ROI) is one of the most commonly used KPIs for evaluating an investment center's financial performance. Companies typically define ROI as follows:

$$\text{ROI} = \frac{\text{Operating income}}{\text{Total assets}}$$

ROI measures the amount of income an investment center earns relative to the size of its assets. Let's calculate each division's ROI:

$$\text{Landscaping Division ROI} = \left(\frac{\$450,000}{\$2,500,000}\right) = 18\%$$

$$\text{Design Division ROI} = \left(\frac{\$600,000}{\$4,000,000}\right) = 15\%$$

Although the Design Division has a higher operating income than the Landscaping Division, the Design Division is actually *less* profitable than the Landscaping Division when we consider that the Design Division has more assets from which to generate its profit.

If you had $1,000 to invest, would you rather invest it in the Design Division or Landscaping Division? The Design Division earns a profit of $0.15 on every $1.00 of assets, but the Landscaping Division earns $0.18 on every $1.00 of assets. When top management decides how to invest excess funds, they often consider each division's ROI. A division with a higher ROI is more likely to receive extra funds because it has a track record of providing a higher return.

In addition to comparing ROI across divisions, management also compares a division's ROI across time to determine whether the division is becoming more or less profitable in relation to its assets. In addition, management often benchmarks divisional ROI with other companies in the same industry to determine how each division is performing compared to its competitors.

To determine what is driving a division's ROI, management often restates the ROI equation in its expanded form:

$$\text{ROI} = \frac{\text{Operating income}}{\text{Sales}} \times \frac{\text{Sales}}{\text{Total assets}} = \frac{\text{Operating income}}{\text{Total assets}}$$

Notice that Sales is incorporated in the denominator of the first term and in the numerator of the second term. When the two terms are multiplied together, Sales cancels out, leaving the original ROI formula.

Why do managers rewrite the ROI formula this way? Because it helps them better understand how they can improve their ROI. The first term in the expanded equation is called the **sales margin**:

$$\text{Sales margin} = \frac{\text{Operating income}}{\text{Sales}}$$

The sales margin shows how much operating income the division earns on every $1 of sales, so this term focuses on profitability. Let's calculate each division's sales margin:

$$\text{Landscaping Division's sales margin} = \left(\frac{\$450,000}{\$7,500,000}\right) = 6\%$$

$$\text{Design Division's sales margin} = \left(\frac{\$600,000}{\$10,000,000}\right) = 6\%$$

Both the Landscaping Division and the Design Division have a sales margin of 6%, meaning that both divisions earn a profit of $0.06 on every $1.00 of sales.

If both divisions have identical sales margins, why do their ROIs differ (18% for Landscaping versus 15% for Design)? The answer is found in the second term of the expanded ROI equation, **capital turnover**:

$$\text{Capital turnover} = \frac{\text{Sales}}{\text{Total assets}}$$

Capital turnover shows how efficiently a division uses its assets to generate sales. Rather than focusing on profitability, capital turnover focuses on efficiency. Let's calculate each division's capital turnover:

$$\text{Landscaping Division's capital turnover} = \left(\frac{\$7,500,000}{\$2,500,000}\right) = 3$$

$$\text{Design Division's capital turnover} = \left(\frac{\$10,000,000}{\$4,000,000}\right) = 2.5$$

The Landscaping Division has a capital turnover of 3. This means that the Landscaping Division generates $3 of sales with every $1 of assets. The Design Division's capital turnover is only 2.5. The Design Division generates only $2.50 of sales with every $1.00 of assets. The Landscaping Division uses its assets more efficiently in generating sales than does the Design Division.

Let's put the two terms back together in the expanded ROI equation:

	Sales margin	×	Capital turnover	= ROI
Landscaping Division:	6%	×	3	= 18%
Design Division:	6%	×	2.5	= 15%

As you can see, the expanded ROI equation gives management more insight into the division's ROI. Management can now see that both divisions are equally profitable on their sales (6%), but the Landscaping Division is doing a better job of generating sales with its assets than is the Design Division. Consequently, the Landscaping Division has a higher ROI.

If a manager is not satisfied with the division's capital turnover rate, how can the manager improve it? He or she might try to eliminate nonproductive assets—for example, by being more aggressive in collecting accounts receivables or decreasing inventory levels, as JoAnn Fabrics decided to do. The manager might decide to change the layout of retail stores to generate sales. Recall that CVS successfully increased sales just by lowering shelves and changing the direction of the aisles.

What if management is not satisfied with the current sales margin? To increase the sales margin, management must increase the operating income earned on every dollar of sales. Management may cut product costs or selling and administrative costs, but it needs to be careful when trimming costs. Cutting costs in the short term can hurt long-term ROI. For example, sacrificing quality or cutting back on research and development could decrease costs in the short run but may hurt long-term sales. The balanced scorecard helps management carefully consider the consequences of cost-cutting measures before acting on them.

ROI has one major drawback. Evaluating division managers based solely on ROI gives them an incentive to adopt *only* projects that maintain or increase their current ROI. Assume that top management has set a companywide target ROI of 16%. Both divisions are considering investing in in-store video display equipment that shows customers how to use featured products. This equipment will increase sales because customers are more likely to buy the products after they see these infomercials. The equipment would cost each division $100,000 and is expected to provide each division with $17,000 of annual income. The *equipment's* ROI is as follows:

$$\text{Equipment ROI} = \frac{\$17,000}{\$100,000} = 17\%$$

Upper management would want the divisions to invest in this equipment since the equipment will provide a 17% ROI, which is higher than the 16% target rate. But what will the managers of the divisions do? Because the Design Division currently has an ROI of 15%, the new equipment (with its 17% ROI) will *increase* the division's *overall* ROI. Therefore, the Design Division manager will buy the equipment. However, the Landscaping Division currently has an ROI of 18%. If the Landscaping Division invests in the equipment, its *overall* ROI will *decrease*. Therefore, the manager of the Landscaping Division will probably turn down the investment. In this case, goal congruence is *not* achieved—only one division will invest in equipment. Yet, top management wants both divisions to invest in the equipment because the equipment return exceeds the 16% target ROI. Next, we discuss a performance measure that overcomes this weakness of ROI.

Residual Income (RI)

Residual income (RI) is another commonly used KPI for evaluating an investment center's financial performance. Essentially, RI looks at whether the division has created any excess (or residual) income above and beyond management's expectations. Similar to ROI, RI incorporates the division's operating income and its total assets, thereby measuring the division's profitability and the efficiency with which it uses its assets. RI also incorporates another piece of information: top management's target rate of return (such as the 16% target return in the previous example). The target rate of return is the minimum acceptable rate of return that top management expects a division to earn with its assets. Management's target rate of return is based on many factors. Some of these factors include the risk level of the division's business, interest rates, investor's expectations, return being earned by other divisions, and general economic conditions. Since these factors change over time, management's target rate of return may also change over time.

RI compares the division's operating income with the minimum operating income that top management expects *given the size of the division's assets*. A positive RI means that the division's operating income exceeds top management's target rate of return. A negative RI means the division is not meeting the target rate of return. Let's look at the RI equation and calculate the RI for both divisions using the 16% target rate of return from the previous example.

$$RI = \text{Operating income} - \text{Minimum acceptable income}$$

In this equation, the minimum acceptable income is defined as top management's target rate of return multiplied by the division's total assets. Thus,

$$RI = \text{Operating income} - (\text{Target rate of return} \times \text{Total assets})$$

Let's calculate the residual income for the Landscaping Division:

$$\text{Landscaping Division RI} = \$450,000 - (16\% \times \$2,500,000)$$
$$= \$450,000 - \$400,000$$
$$= \$50,000$$

The positive RI indicates that the Landscaping Division exceeded top management's 16% target return expectations. The RI calculation also confirms what we learned about the Landscaping Division's ROI. Recall that the Landscaping Division's ROI was 18%, which is higher than the targeted 16%.

Let's also calculate the RI for the Design Division:

$$\text{Design Division RI} = \$600,000 - (16\% \times \$4,000,000)$$
$$= \$600,000 - \$640,000$$
$$= (\$40,000)$$

The Design Division's RI is negative. This means that the Design Division did not use its assets as effectively as top management expected. Recall that the Design Division's ROI of 15% fell short of the target rate of 16%.

Why would a company prefer to use RI over ROI for performance evaluation? The answer is that RI is more likely to lead to goal congruence than is ROI. Let's once again consider the video display equipment that both divisions could buy. In both divisions, the equipment is expected to generate a 17% return. If the divisions are evaluated based on ROI, the Design Division will buy the equipment because doing so will increase the division's ROI. The Landscaping Division will probably not buy the equipment because doing so will lower the division's ROI.

However, if management evaluates divisions based on RI rather than ROI, what will the divisions do? The answer depends on whether the project yields a positive or negative RI. Recall that the equipment would cost each division $100,000 but would provide $17,000 of operating income each year. The RI provided by *just* the equipment would be as follows:

$$\text{Equipment RI} = \$17,000 - (\$100,000 \times 16\%)$$
$$= \$17,000 - \$16,000$$
$$= \$1,000$$

If purchased, this equipment will *improve* each division's current RI by $1,000. As a result, both divisions will be motivated to invest in the equipment. Goal congruence is achieved because both divisions take the action that top management desires. That is, both divisions invest in the equipment.

Another benefit of RI is that management may set different target returns for different divisions. For example, management might require a higher target rate of return from a division operating in a riskier business environment. If the design industry were riskier than the landscape industry, top management might decide to set a higher target return—perhaps 17%—for the Design Division.

Economic Value Added (EVA)

Economic Value Added (EVA) is a special type of RI calculation. Unlike the RI calculation we've just discussed, EVA looks at a division's RI through the eyes of the company's primary stakeholders: its investors and long-term creditors (such as bondholders). Since these stakeholders provide the company's capital, management often wants to evaluate how efficiently a division is using its assets from these two stakeholders' viewpoints. EVA calculates RI for these stakeholders by specifically considering the following:

1. The income available to these stakeholders

2. The assets used to generate income for these stakeholders

3. The minimum rate of return required by these stakeholders (referred to as the **weighted average cost of capital**, or WACC)

Let's compare the EVA equation with the RI equation and then look at the differences in more detail:

RI = Operating income   − (Total assets   × Target rate of return)

EVA = After-tax operating income − [(Total assets − Current liabilities) × WACC%]

Both equations calculate whether the division created any income above and beyond expectations. They do this by comparing actual income with the minimum acceptable income. But note the differences in the EVA calculation:

1. The EVA calculation uses *after-tax operating income*, which is the income left over after income taxes are subtracted. Why? Because the portion of income paid to the government is not available to investors and long-term creditors.

2. *Total assets is reduced by current liabilities.* Why? Because funds owed to short-term creditors, such as suppliers (accounts payable) and employees (wages payable), will be paid in the immediate future and will not be available for generating income in the long run. The division is not expected to earn a return for investors and long-term creditors on those funds that will soon be paid out to short-term creditors.

3. The *WACC* replaces management's target rate of return. Since EVA focuses on investors and creditors, it's *their* expected rate of return that should be used, not management's expected rate of return. The WACC, which represents the minimum rate of return that *investors and long-term creditors* expect, is based on the company's cost of raising capital from both groups of stakeholders. The riskier the business, the higher the expected return. Detailed WACC computations are discussed in advanced accounting and finance courses.

In summary, EVA incorporates all of the elements of RI from the perspective of investors and long-term creditors. Now that we've walked through the equation's components, let's calculate EVA for the Landscape and Design Divisions discussed earlier. We'll need the following additional information:

Effective income tax rate	30%
WACC	13%
Landscaping Division's current liabilities	$150,000
Design Division's current liabilities	$250,000

The 30% effective income tax rate means that the government takes 30% of the company's income, leaving only 70% to the company's stakeholders. Therefore, we calculate *after-tax operating income* by multiplying the division's operating income by 70%, or (100%—effective tax rate of 30%).

EVA = After-tax operating income − [(Total assets − Current liabilities) × WACC%]

Landscaping Division EVA = ($450,000 × 70%) − [($2,500,000 − $150,000) × 13%]

$\qquad$ =$315,000 $\qquad$ −($2,350,000) × 13%)

$\qquad$ =$315,000 $\qquad$ −$305,500

$\qquad$ =$9,500

Design Division EVA = ($600,000 × 70%) − [($4,000,000 − $250,000) × 13%]

$\qquad$ =$420,000 $\qquad$ −($3,750,000) × 13%)

$\qquad$ =$420,000 $\qquad$ −$487,500

$\qquad$ =($67,500)

These EVA calculations show that the Landscaping Division has generated income in excess of expectations for its investors and long-term debtholders whereas the Design Division has not.

Many firms, such as Coca-Cola and JCPenney, measure the financial performance of their investment centers using EVA. EVA promotes goal congruence, just as RI does. In addition, EVA looks at the income generated by the division in excess of expectations solely from the perspective of investors and long-term creditors. Therefore, EVA specifically addresses the financial perspective of the balanced scorecard that asks this question: "How do we look to shareholders?"

Exhibit 11-10 (shown on the next page) summarizes the three performance measures and some of their advantages.

Limitations of Financial Performance Measures

We have just finished looking at three KPIs (ROI, RI, and EVA) commonly used to evaluate the financial performance of investment centers. As discussed in the following sections, all of these measures have drawbacks that management should keep in mind when evaluating the financial performance of investment centers.

MEASUREMENT ISSUES The ROI, RI, and EVA calculations appear to be very straightforward; however, management must make some decisions before these calculations can be made. For example, all three equations use the term *total assets*. Recall that total assets is a balance sheet figure, which means that it is a snapshot at any given point in time. Because the total assets figure will be *different* at the beginning of the period than at the end of the

EXHIBIT 11-10 **Three Investment Center Performance Measures: A Summary**

	ROI:		
Equation	$\text{ROI} = \dfrac{\text{Operating income}}{\text{Sales}} \times \dfrac{\text{Sales}}{\text{Total assets}} = \dfrac{\text{Operating income}}{\text{Total assets}}$		
Advantages	• The expanded equation provides management with additional information on profitability and efficiency • Management can compare ROI across divisions and with other companies • ROI is useful for resource allocation		

	RI:		
Equation	**RI = Operating income − (Total assets × Target rate of return)**		
Advantages	• Promotes goal congruence better than ROI • Incorporates management's minimum required rate of return • Management can use different target rates of return for divisions with different levels of risk		

	EVA:		
Equation	**EVA = (After-tax operating income) − [(Total assets − Current liabilities) × WACC%]**		
Advantages	• Considers income generated for investors and long-term creditors in excess of their expectations • Promotes goal congruence		

period, many companies choose to use a simple average of the two figures in their ROI, RI, and EVA calculations.

Management must also decide if it really wants to include *all* assets in the total asset figure. Many firms, such as Kohls and ALDI, are continually buying land on which to build future retail outlets. Until those stores are built and opened, the land (including any construction in progress) is a nonproductive asset, which is not adding to the company's operating income. Including nonproductive assets in the total asset figure will drive down the ROI, RI, and EVA figures. Therefore, some firms do not include nonproductive assets in these calculations.

Another asset measurement issue is whether to use the gross book value of assets (the historical cost of the assets) or the net book value of assets (historical cost less accumulated depreciation). Many firms use the net book value of assets because the figure is consistent with and easily pulled from the balance sheet. Because depreciation expense factors into the firm's operating income, the net book value concept is consistent with the measurement of operating income. However, using the net book value of assets has a definite drawback. Over time, the net book value of assets decreases because accumulated depreciation continues to grow until the assets are fully depreciated. Therefore, ROI, RI, and EVA get *larger over time simply because of depreciation* rather than from actual improvements in operations. In addition, the rate of this depreciation effect will depend on the depreciation method used.

In general, calculating ROI based on the net book value of assets gives managers incentive to continue using old, outdated equipment because its low net book value results in a higher ROI. However, top management may want the division to invest in new technology to create operational efficiency (internal business perspective of the balanced scorecard) or to enhance its information systems (learning and growth perspective). The long-term effects of using outdated equipment may be devastating as competitors use new technology to produce cheaper products and sell at lower prices. Thus, to create goal congruence, some firms prefer calculating ROI based on the gross book value of assets or even based on their current replacement cost. The same general rule holds true for RI and EVA calculations: All else being equal, using the net book value will increase RI and EVA over time.

SHORT-TERM FOCUS One serious drawback of financial performance measures is their short-term focus. Companies usually prepare performance reports and calculate ROI, RI, and EVA figures using a time frame of one year or less. If upper management uses a short time frame, division managers have an incentive to take actions that will lead to an immediate increase in these measures, even if such actions may not be in the company's long-term interest (such as cutting back on R&D or advertising). On the other hand, for some potentially positive actions that subunit managers consider, it may take longer than one year to generate income at the targeted level. Many **product life cycles** start slow, even incurring losses in the early stages, before generating profit. If managers are measured on short-term financial performance only, they may not introduce new products because they are not willing to wait several years for the positive effect to show up in their financial performance measures.

As a potential remedy, management can measure financial performance using a longer time horizon, such as three to five years. Extending the time frame gives subunit managers the incentive to think long term rather than short term and make decisions that will positively impact the company over the next several years.

The limitations of financial performance measures confirm the importance of the balanced scorecard. The deficiencies of financial measures can be overcome by taking a broader view of performance—including KPIs from all four balanced scorecard perspectives—rather than concentrating on only the financial measures.

Decision Guidelines

Performance Evaluation and the Balanced Scorecard

When managers at UPS developed the financial perspective of their balanced scorecard, they had to make decisions such as these.

Decision	Guidelines
How should the financial section of the balanced scorecard be measured for cost, revenue, and profit centers?	Responsibility accounting performance reports measure the financial performance of cost, revenue, and profit centers. These reports typically highlight the variances between budgeted and actual performance.
How should the financial section of the balanced scorecard be measured for investment centers?	Investment centers require measures that take into account the division's operating income *and* the division's assets. Typical measures include the following: • Return on investment (ROI) • Residual income (RI) • Economic Value Added (EVA)
How is ROI computed and interpreted?	$$\text{ROI} = \text{Operating income} \div \text{Total assets}$$ ROI measures the amount of income earned by a division relative to the size of its assets—the higher, the better.
Can managers learn more by writing the ROI formula in its expanded form?	In its expanded form, ROI is written as follows: $$\text{ROI} = \text{Sales margin} \times \text{Capital turnover}$$ where, $$\text{Sales margin} = \text{Operating income} \div \text{Sales}$$ $$\text{Capital turnover} = \text{Sales} \div \text{Total assets}$$ Sales margin focuses on profitability (the amount of income earned on every dollar of sales), while capital turnover focuses on efficiency (the amount of sales generated with every dollar of assets).

Decision	Guidelines
How is RI computed and interpreted?	$$RI = \text{Operating income} - (\text{Target rate of return} \times \text{Total assets})$$
	If RI is positive, the division is earning income at a rate that exceeds management's minimum expectations.
How is EVA computed? How does it differ from RI?	$$EVA = \text{After-tax operating income} - [(\text{Total assets} - \text{Current liabilities}) \times \text{WACC\%}]$$
	EVA is a special type of RI calculation that focuses on the income (in excess of expectations) the division created for two specific stakeholders: investors and long-term creditors.
When calculating ROI, RI, or EVA, what, if any, measurement issues are of concern?	1. What date should be used to measure the assets? Many firms use the average balance of total assets rather than the beginning or ending balance of assets.
	2. Should the net book value or gross book value of the assets be used? If the net book value of assets is used to measure total assets, ROI, RI, and EVA will "artificially" rise over time due to the depreciation of the assets. Using gross book value to measure total assets eliminates this measurement issue.

Summary Problem 2

Assume that House and Garden Depot expects each division to earn a 16% target rate of return. House and Garden Depot's weighted average cost of capital (WACC) is 13%, and its effective tax rate is 30%. Assume that the company's original Retail Division had the following results last year (in millions of dollars):

Operating income..	$ 1,450
Total assets	16,100
Current liabilities	3,600
Sales..	26,500

Requirements

1. Compute the Retail Division's sales margin, capital turnover, and ROI. Round your results to three decimal places. Interpret the results in relation to the Landscaping and Design Divisions discussed in the chapter.

2. Compute and interpret the Retail Division's RI.

3. Compute the Retail Division's EVA. What does this tell you?

4. What can you conclude based on all three financial performance KPIs?

Solution

Requirement 1

$$
\begin{aligned}
ROI = \quad & \text{Sales margin} \quad \times \quad \text{Capital turnover} \\
= \ & (\text{Operating income} \div \text{Sales}) \times (\text{Sales} \div \text{Total assets}) \\
= \ & (\$1,450 \div \$26,500) \qquad \times (\$26,500 \div \$16,100) \\
= \ & .055 \qquad\qquad\qquad\quad \times 1.646 \\
= \ & .091
\end{aligned}
$$

The original Retail Division is far from meeting top management's expectations. Its ROI is only 9.1%. The sales margin (5.5%) is slightly lower than the Landscaping and Design Divisions (6% each), but the capital turnover (1.646) is much lower than the other divisions (3.0 and 2.5). This means that the original Retail Division is not generating sales from its assets as efficiently as the Landscaping and Design Divisions. Division management needs to consider ways to increase the efficiency of their use of divisional assets.

Requirement 2

$$RI = \text{Operating income} - (\text{Target rate of return} \times \text{Total assets})$$

$$= \$1,450 \qquad - (16\% \times \$16,100)$$

$$= \$1,450 \qquad - \$2,576$$

$$= (\$1,126)$$

The negative RI confirms the ROI results: The division is not meeting management's target rate of return.

Requirement 3

$$EVA = \text{After-tax operating income} - [(\text{Total assets} - \text{Current liabilities}) \times WACC\%]$$

$$= (\$1,450 \times 70\%) \qquad - [(\$16,100 - \$3,600) \times 13\%]$$

$$= \$1,015 \qquad - (\$12,500 \times 13\%)$$

$$= \$1,015 \qquad - \$1,625$$

$$= (\$610)$$

The negative EVA means that the division is not generating income for investors and long-term creditors at the rate that these stakeholders desire.

Requirement 4

All three investment center performance measures (ROI, RI, and EVA) point to the same conclusion: The original Retail Division is not meeting financial expectations. Either top management and stakeholders' expectations are unrealistic or the division is not *currently* performing up to par. Recall, however, that financial performance measures tend to be lag indicators—measuring the results of decisions made in the past. The division's managers may currently be implementing new initiatives to improve the division's future profitability. Lead indicators should be used to project whether such initiatives are pointing the company in the right direction.

APPENDIX 11A

Allocating Service Department Costs

How do companies charge subunits for their use of service departments? For example, suppose House and Garden Depot incurs $30,000 per month to operate the North Florida Region's centralized payroll department. To simplify the illustration, let's assume that the region has only three stores: Tallahassee, Gainesville, and Jacksonville. How should the company split, or allocate, the $30,000 cost among the three stores? Splitting the cost equally—charging each store $10,000—may not be fair, especially if the three units don't use the services equally.

Ideally, the company should allocate the $30,000 based on each subunit's use of centralized payroll services. The company should use the primary activity that drives the cost of central payroll services as the allocation base. As you may recall from Chapter 5, companies identify cost drivers when they implement ABC. Thus, a company that has already implemented ABC should know what cost drivers would be suitable for allocating service department charges. For example, payroll processing cost may be driven by the number of employee payroll checks or direct deposits processed. The cost driver chosen for allocating the $30,000 might be the number of employees employed by each store, as shown in the following table.

Subunits Sharing Central Payroll Services	Number of Employees (allocation base)	Percentage of Total Employees	Service Department Charge ($30,000 × %)
Tallahassee	100	25%	$ 7,500
Gainesville	140	35%	10,500
Jacksonville	160	40%	12,000
Total	400	100%	$30,000

Most companies use some type of usage-related cost driver to allocate service department costs. The following table lists additional centralized services and common allocation bases.

Centralized Service Departments	Typical Allocation Base
Human resources	Number of employees
Legal	Number of hours spent on legal matters
Travel	Number of business trips booked

However, when usage data are not available or are too costly to collect, companies resort to allocating service department costs based on each subunit's ability to bear the cost. In such cases, companies allocate the service department cost based on the relative amount of revenue or operating income each subunit generates. The following table illustrates this type of allocation.

Subunits Sharing Centralized Payroll Services	Unit Operating Income Before Service Department Charges	Percentage of Total Operating Income	Service Department Charge ($30,000 × %)
Tallahassee	$ 320,000	20%	$ 6,000
Gainesville	480,000	30%	9,000
Jacksonville	800,000	50%	15,000
Total	$1,600,000	100%	$30,000

This type of allocation is like a tax: The higher the subunit's income, the higher the charge.

Even usage-related allocation systems have limitations. What if the cost of running the service department is fixed rather than variable? Then, much of the cost cannot be attributed to a specific cost driver. In our payroll example, suppose $20,000 of the total $30,000 is straight-line depreciation on the equipment and software. Should the company still use the number of employees to allocate the entire $30,000 of cost? As another example, suppose the Tallahassee store downsizes and its relative percentage of employees drops from 25% to 10% while the number of employees in each of the other two stores stays constant. If that happens, the Gainesville and Jacksonville stores will be charged higher costs even though they did nothing to cause an increase. These are just two examples of how the best allocation systems are still subject to inherent flaws. More complex service department allocation systems, such as the step-down and reciprocal methods, are discussed in more advanced accounting texts.

Accounting Vocabulary

Balanced Scorecard. (p. 621)   Measures that recognize that management must consider financial performance measures and operational performance measures when judging the performance of a company and its subunits.

Benchmarking. (p. 620)   Comparing actual performance to similar companies in the same industry, to other divisions, or to world-class standards.

Capital Turnover. (p. 633)   The amount of sales revenue generated for every dollar of invested assets; a component of the ROI calculation computed as sales divided by total assets.

Centralized. (p. 618)   Refers to companies in which all major planning and operating decisions are made by top management.

Cost Center. (p. 628)   A subunit responsible only for controlling costs.

Decentralized. (p. 618)   Refers to companies that are segmented into smaller operating units; unit managers make planning and operating decisions for their units.

Economic Value Added (EVA). (p. 636)   A residual income measure calculating the amount of income generated by the company or its divisions in excess of stockholders' and long-term creditors' expectations.

Goal Congruence. (p. 619)   Aligning the goals of subunit managers with the goals of top management.

Investment Center. (p. 631)   A subunit responsible for generating profits and efficiently managing the division's invested capital (assets).

Key Performance Indicator (KPI). (p. 621)   Summary performance measures that help managers assess whether the company is achieving its long-term and short-term goals.

Lag Indicators. (p. 621)   Performance measures that indicate past performance.

Lead Indicators. (p. 621)   Performance measures that forecast future performance.

Management by Exception (p. 628)   Directs management's attention to important differences between actual and budgeted amounts.

Product Life Cycle. (p. 639)   The length of time between a product's initial development and its discontinuance in the market.

Profit Center. (p. 628)   A subunit responsible for generating revenue and controlling costs.

Residual Income (RI). (p. 634)   A measure of profitability and efficiency computed as the excess of actual income over a specified minimum acceptable income.

Responsibility Center. (p. 619)   A part or subunit of an organization whose manager is accountable for specific activities.

Return on Investment (ROI). (p. 632)   A measure of profitability and efficiency computed as operating income divided by total assets.

Revenue Center. (p. 628)   A subunit responsible only for generating revenue.

Sales Margin. (p. 633)   The amount of income earned on every dollar of sales; a component of the ROI calculation computed as operating income divided by sales.

Weighted Average Cost of Capital (WACC). (p. 636)   The company's cost of capital; the target rate of return used in EVA calculations to represent the return that investors and long-term creditors expect.

Quick Check

1. *(Learning Objective 1)* Which is *not* one of the potential advantages of decentralization?
   a. Improves customer relations
   b. Increases goal congruence
   c. Improves motivation and retention
   d. Supports use of expert knowledge
2. *(Learning Objective 1)* The Quaker Foods division of PepsiCo is most likely treated as a
   a. cost center.
   b. revenue center.
   c. profit center.
   d. investment center.
3. *(Learning Objective 1)* Decentralization is often based on all the following *except*
   a. geographic region.
   b. product line.
   c. revenue size.
   d. business function.
4. *(Learning Objective 2)* Which of the following is *not* a reason for a company to use a performance evaluation system?
   a. Controlling assets
   b. Communicating expectations
   c. Motivating managers
   d. Providing feedback
5. *(Learning Objective 3)* Manufacturing yield rate (number of units produced per unit of time) would be a typical measure for which of the following balanced scorecard perspectives?
   a. Financial
   b. Customer
   c. Internal business
   d. Learning and growth
6. *(Learning Objective 3)* Which of the following balanced scorecard perspectives essentially asks the question "Can we continue to improve and create value?"
   a. Financial
   b. Customer
   c. Internal business
   d. Learning and growth

7. *(Learning Objective 4)* The performance evaluation of a cost center is typically based on its
   a. sales volume variance.
   b. ROI.
   c. flexible budget variance.
   d. static budget variance.

8. *(Learning Objective 5)* Which of the following is a disadvantage of financial performance measures such as return on investment (ROI), residual income, and Economic Value Added (EVA)?
   a. Not readily understood by managers
   b. Focus on short-term performance
   c. Cannot be used in a balanced scorecard
   d. Cannot be used to evaluate division performance

9. *(Learning Objective 5)* Which performance measurement tool is most likely to cause goal incongruence between division managers and the corporate headquarters?
   a. Return on investment (ROI)
   b. Residual income
   c. Economic Value Added (EVA)
   d. Balanced scorecard

10. (Learning Objective 5) For which type of responsibility center would it be appropriate to measure performance using return on investment (ROI)?
   a. Cost center
   b. Revenue center
   c. Profit center
   d. Investment center

ASSESS YOUR PROGRESS

Learning Objectives

 1 Explain why and how companies decentralize

2 Explain why companies use performance evaluation systems

3 Describe the balanced scorecard and identify key performance indicators for each perspective

4 Use performance reports to evaluate cost, revenue, and profit centers

5 Use ROI, RI, and EVA to evaluate investment centers

Short Exercises

S11-1 Explain how and why companies decentralize *(Learning Objective 1)*

Explain why companies decentralize. Describe some typical methods of decentralization.

S11-2 Give advice about decentralization *(Learning Objective 1)*

Grandma Jones's Cookie Company sells homemade cookies made with organic ingredients. Her sales are strictly Web-based. The business is exceeding Grandma Jones's expectations, with orders coming in from consumers and corporate event planners across the country. Even by employing a full-time baker and a Web designer, Grandma Jones can no longer handle the business on her own. She wants your advice on whether she should decentralize and, if so, how she should do it. Explain some of the advantages and disadvantages of decentralization and offer her three ways she might decentralize her company.

S11-3 Describe each type of responsibility center *(Learning Objective 1)*

Most decentralized subunits can be described as one of four types of responsibility centers. List the four most common types of responsibility centers and describe their responsibilities.

S11-4 Classify types of subunits *(Learning Objective 1)*

Each of the following managers has been given certain decision-making authority. Classify each manager according to the type of responsibility center he or she manages.

1. Manager of Holiday Inn's central reservation office
2. Managers of various corporate-owned Holiday Inn locations
3. Manager of the Holiday Inn corporate division
4. Manager of the Housekeeping Department at a Holiday Inn
5. Manager of the Holiday Inn Express corporate division
6. Manager of the complimentary breakfast buffet at a Holiday Inn Express

S11-5 Goals of performance evaluation systems *(Learning Objective 2)*

Well-designed performance evaluation systems accomplish many goals. State which goal is being achieved by the following actions:

a. Comparing targets to actual results
b. Providing subunit managers with performance targets
c. Comparing actual results with industry standards
d. Providing bonuses to subunit managers who achieve performance targets
e. Aligning subunit performance targets with company strategy
f. Comparing actual results to the results of competitors
g. Using the adage "you get what you measure" when designing the performance evaluation system

S11-6 Classify KPIs by balanced scorecard perspective *(Learning Objective 3)*

Classify each of the following key performance indicators according to the balanced scorecard perspective it addresses. Choose from financial perspective, customer perspective, internal business perspective, or learning and growth perspective.

a. Number of employee suggestions implemented
b. Revenue growth
c. Number of on-time deliveries
d. Percentage of sales force with access to real-time inventory levels
e. Customer satisfaction ratings
f. Number of defects found during manufacturing
g. Number of warranty claims
h. ROI

S11-7 Classify KPIs by balanced scorecard perspective *(Learning Objective 3)*

Classify each of the following key performance indicators according to the balanced scorecard perspective it addresses. Choose from financial perspective, customer perspective, internal business perspective, or learning and growth perspective.

a. Variable cost per unit
b. Percentage of market share
c. Number of hours of employee training
d. Number of new products developed
e. Yield rate (number of units produced per hour)
f. Average repair time
g. Employee satisfaction
h. Number of repeat customers

S11-8 Describe management by exception *(Learning Objective 4)*

Describe management by exception and how it is used in the evaluation of cost, revenue, and profit centers.

S11-9 Assess profitability *(Learning Objective 5)*

Which of the following corporate divisions is more profitable? Explain.

	Domestic	International
Operating income	$ 6 million	$10 million
Total assets	$20 million	$35 million

Racer Sports Data Set used for S11-10 through S11-14:

Racer Sports Company makes snowboards, downhill skis, cross-country skis, skateboards, surfboards, and in-line skates. The company has found it beneficial to split operations into two divisions based on the climate required for the sport: Snow Sports and Non-Snow Sports. The following divisional information is available for the past year:

	Sales	Operating Income	Total Assets	Current Liabilities
Snow Sports......................	$5,000,000	$ 800,000	$4,000,000	$350,000
Non-Snow Sports..............	9,000,000	1,440,000	6,000,000	600,000

Racer's management has specified a target 15% rate of return. The company's weighted average cost of capital (WACC) is 12%, and its effective tax rate is 35%.

S11-10   Calculate ROI *(Learning Objective 5)*

Refer to the Racer Sports Data Set.

1. Calculate each division's ROI.

2. Top management has extra funds to invest. Which division will most likely receive those funds? Why?

3. Can you explain why one division's ROI is higher? How could management gain more insight?

S11-11   Compute sales margin *(Learning Objective 5)*

Refer to the Racer Sports Data Set. Compute each division's sales margin. Interpret your results.

S11-12   Continuation of S11-10 and S11-11: Capital turnover *(Learning Objective 5)*

Refer to the Racer Sports Data Set.

1. Compute each division's capital turnover (round to two decimal places). Interpret your results.

2. Use your answers to Question 1 along with your answers to S11-11 to recalculate ROI using the expanded formula. Do your answers agree with your ROI calculations in S11-10?

S11-13   Compute RI *(Learning Objective 5)*

Refer to the Racer Sports Data Set. Compute each division's RI. Interpret your results. Are your results consistent with each division's ROI?

S11-14   Compute EVA *(Learning Objective 5)*

Refer to the Racer Sports Data Set. Compute each division's EVA. Interpret your results.

Exercises—Group A

E11-15A Identify centralized and decentralized organizations *(Learning Objective 1)*

The following table lists a series of descriptions of decentralized organizations or centralized organizations. For each description, indicate whether that scenario is more typical of a decentralized organization or a centralized organization.

Characteristic	Decentralized (D) or Centralized (C)
a. Lawrence Company has a policy that they promote from within the company whenever possible. They have formal training programs for lower-level managers.	
b. Walker Corporation is divided into several operating units.	
c. Two Turtles is a small independent pet shop in Akron, Ohio. The owner is also the manager of the store.	
d. The managers at Veeson Company have the authority to make decisions about product offerings and pricing becauseVeeson Company wants its managers to be able to respond quickly to changes in local market demand.	
e. Bobbins Crafts, Inc., wants to empower its managers to make decisions so that the managers' motivation is increased and retention of managers increases.	
f. The duplication of services caused the Rondell Company to "flatten" its organization structure. The Rondell Company now has a single payroll department, a single human resource department, and a single administrative headquarters.	
g. The Plastic Lumber Company, Inc., is managed by its owner, who oversees production, sales, engineering, and the other admininistrative functions.	

E11-16A Identify type of responsibility center *(Learning Objective 2)*

Each of the following situations describes an organizational unit. Identify which type of responsibility center each underlined item is (cost, revenue, profit, or investment center).

Organization	Type of Responsibility Center (Cost, Revenue, Profit, or Investment)
a. <u>Sherwin-Williams Store #1933</u> is located in Copley, Ohio. The store sells paints, wallpapers, and supplies to do-it-yourself customers and to professional wall covering installers.	
b. The <u>Accounting Research and Compliance Department</u> at FirstEnergy is responsible for researching how new accounting pronouncements and rules will impact FirstEnergy's financial statements.	
c. The <u>Southwestern Sales Region</u> of McDermott Foods is responsible for selling the various product lines of McDermott.	
d. The <u>Taxation Department</u> at Verizon Communications, Inc., is responsible for preparing the federal, state, and local income and franchise tax returns for the corporation.	
e. The <u>Roseville Chipotle restaurant</u> in Minnesota, is owned by its parent Chipotle Mexican Grill, Inc. The Roseville Chipotle, like other Chipotle restaurants, serves burritos, fajitas, and tacos and competes in the "fast-casual" dining category.	
f. <u>Trek Bicycle Corporation</u> manufactures and distributes bicycles and cycling products under the Trek, Gary Fisher, Bontrager, and Klein brand names.	
g. <u>The Hershey Company</u> is one of the oldest chocolate companies in the United States. Its product lines include the Mauna Loa Macadamia Nuts, Dagoba Organic Chocolates, and Joseph Schmidt Confections.	
h. The <u>Human Resources Department</u> is responsible for recruiting and training for Kohl's Corporation.	
i. The <u>reservation office</u> for BlueSky Airlines, Inc., is responsible for both Web sales and counter sales.	
j. The <u>Disney Store</u> at Spring Hill Mall in West Dundee, Illinois, is owned by The Walt Disney Company.	
k. H & R Block Tax Services, H & R Block Bank, and RSM McGladrey are all divisions of their parent corporation, <u>H & R Block.</u>	

E11-17A Differentiate between lag and lead indicators *(Learning Objective 2)*

Explain the difference between lag and lead indicators. Are financial performance measures typically referred to as lag or lead indicators? Explain, using L.L.Bean (a catalog clothing merchandiser) as an example. Are operational measures (such as customer satisfaction ratings, defect rate, and number of on-time deliveries) typically referred to as lag or lead indicators? Explain using L.L.Bean as an example.

E11-18A Construct balanced scorecard (*Learning Objective 3*)

Sarvan Corporation is preparing its balanced scorecard for the past quarter. The balanced scorecard contains four perspectives: financial, customer, internal business process, and learning and growth. Through its strategic management planning process, Sarvan Corporation has selected two specific objectives for each of the four perspectives; these specific objectives are listed in the following table.

Specific Objective
Improve post-sales service
Increase market share
Increase profitability of core product line
Improve employee job satisfaction
Increase sales of core product line
Develop new core products
Improve employee product knowledge
Increase customer satisfaction

Sarvan Corporation has collected key performance indicators (KPIs) to measure progress towards achieving its specific objectives. The following table contains the KPIs and corresponding data that Sarvan Corporation has collected for the past quarter.

KPI	Goal	Actual
Core product line profit as a percentage of core product line sales...	15 %	12 %
Market share percentage	17 %	18 %
Number of new core products	15	21
Customer satisfaction rating (1–5, with 1 being most satisfied)	1.3	1.2
Hours of employee training provided	2,200	2,350
Average repair time (number of days)	1.0	1.4
Sales revenue growth—Core product line	$ 2,000,000	$ 2,200,000
Employee turnover rate (number of employees leaving company/number of total employees)	5 %	7 %

Requirement

1. Prepare a balanced scorecard report for Sarvan Corporation, using the following format.

Sarvan Corporation
Balanced Scorecard Report
For Quarter Ended December 31

Perspective	Objective	KPI	Goal	Actual	Goal Achieved? (√ if met)
Financial					
Customer					
Internal Business Process..............					
Learning and Growth..................					

For each of the specific objectives listed, place that objective under the appropriate perspective heading in the report. Select a KPI from the list of KPIs that would be appropriate to measure progress towards each objective. (There are two specific objectives for each perspective and one KPI for each of the specific objectives.) In the last column in the Balanced Scorecard Report, place a checkmark if the associated KPI goal has been achieved.

E11-19A Classify KPIs by balanced scorecard perspective *(Learning Objective 3)*

Classify each of the following key performance indicators according to the balanced score-card perspective it addresses. Choose from financial perspective, customer perspective, internal business perspective, or learning and growth perspective.

a. Number of customer complaints
b. Number of information system upgrades completed
c. Economic Value Added (EVA)
d. New product development time
e. Employee turnover rate
f. Percentage of products with online help manuals
g. Customer retention
h. Percentage of compensation based on performance
i. Percentage of orders filled each week
j. Gross margin growth
k. Number of new patents
l. Employee satisfaction ratings

E11-20A Complete and analyze a performance report *(Learning Objective 4)*

One subunit of Racer Sports Company had the following financial results last month:

Racer—Subunit X	Actual	Flexible Budget	Flexible Budget Variance (U or F)	% Variance* (U or F)
Direct materials....................	$ 21,500	$ 20,000		
Direct labor.........................	14,250	15,000		
Indirect labor	29,250	25,000		
Utilities	10,950	10,000		
Depreciation.......................	25,000	25,000		
Repairs and maintenance	4,200	5,000		
Total.................................	$105,150	$100,000		

*Flexible budget variance ÷ Flexible budget

Requirements

1. Complete the performance evaluation report for this subunit (round to four decimals).
2. Based on the data presented, what type of responsibility center is this subunit?
3. Which items should be investigated if part of management's decision criteria is to investigate all variances exceeding $3,000 or 10%?
4. Should only unfavorable variances be investigated? Explain.

E11-21A Complete and analyze a performance report (Learning Objective 4)

The accountant for a subunit of Racer Sports Company went on vacation before completing the subunit's monthly performance report. This is as far she got:

Racer—Subunit X Revenue by Product	Actual	Flexible Budget Variance	Flexible Budget	Sales Volume Variance	Static (Master) Budget
Downhill					
Model RI..	$ 326,000			$20,000 (F)	$ 300,000
Downhill					
Model RII.......................................	155,000		$165,000		150,000
Cross-Country					
Model EXI......................................	283,000	$2,000 (U)	285,000		300,000
Cross-Country					
Model EXII	252,000		245,000	17,500 (U)	262,500
Snowboard					
Model LXI.......................................	425,000	5,000 (F)			400,000
Total	$1,441,000				$1,412,500

Requirements

1. Complete the performance evaluation report for this subunit.
2. Based on the data presented, what type of responsibility center is this subunit?
3. Which items should be investigated if part of management's decision criteria is to investigate all variances exceeding $15,000? Interpret your results. (What could cause these variances? What impact might these variances have on company inventory levels and operations?)

E11-22A Compute and interpret the expanded ROI equation (Learning Objective 5)

Toro, a national manufacturer of lawn-mowing and snowblowing equipment, segments its business according to customer type: Professional and Residential. The following divisional information was available for the past year (in thousands of dollars):

	Sales	Operating Income	Total Assets	Current Liabilities
Residential	$ 635,500	$ 63,500	$205,000	$ 70,000
Professional.............	$1,031,250	$165,000	$375,000	$150,000

Assume that management has a 25% target rate of return for each division. Also, assume that Toro's weighted average cost of capital is 15% and its effective tax rate is 30%.

Requirements

Round all of your answers to four decimal places.
1. Calculate each division's ROI.
2. Calculate each division's sales margin. Interpret your results.
3. Calculate each division's capital turnover. Interpret your results.
4. Use the expanded ROI formula to confirm your results from Requirement 1. What can you conclude?

E11-23A Compute RI and EVA *(Learning Objective 5)*

Refer to the data about Toro in E11-22A.

Requirements

1. Calculate each division's RI. Interpret your results.
2. Calculate each division's EVA. Interpret your results.
3. Describe the conceptual and computational similarities and differences between RI and EVA.

E11-24A Relationship between ROI and residual income *(Learning Objective 5)*

Data on three unrelated companies are given in the following table.

	Alston Company	Baxter Industries	Calloway, Inc.
Sales	$100,000	?	$500,000
Operating income	$ 40,000	$120,000	?
Total assets	$ 80,000	?	?
Sales margin	?	15 %	10%
Capital turnover	?	5.00	?
Return on investment (ROI)	?	?	25%
Target rate of return	10%	20 %	?
Residual income	?	?	$ 12,000

Requirement

1. Fill in the missing information in the preceding table.

E11-25A Compute ROI, residual income, and EVA *(Learning Objective 5)*

Results from First Corporation's most recent year of operations is presented in the following table.

Operating income	$ 9,000
Total assets	$15,000
Current liabilities	$ 4,000
Sales	$36,000
Target rate of return	15%
Weighted average cost of capital	12%
Tax rate	30%

Requirements

1. Calculate the sales margin, capital turnover, and return on investment (ROI).
2. Calculate the residual income.
3. Calculate the Economic Value Added (EVA).

E11-26A Comparison of ROI and residual income (*Learning Objective 5*)

Hawkins Ceramics, a division of Piper Corporation, has an operating income of $64,000 and total assets of $400,000. The required rate of return for the company is 12%. The company is evaluating whether it should use return on investment (ROI) or residual income (RI) as a measurement of performance for its division managers.

The manager of Hawkins Ceramics has the opportunity to undertake a new project that will require an investment of $100,000. This investment would earn $14,000 for Hawkins Ceramics.

Requirements

1. What is the original return on investment (ROI) for Hawkins Ceramics (before making any additional investment)?

2. What would the ROI be for Hawkins Ceramics if this investment opportunity were undertaken? Would the manager of the Hawkins Ceramics division want to make this investment if she were evaluated based on ROI? Why or why not?

3. What is the ROI of the investment opportunity? Would the investment be desirable from the standpoint of Piper Corporation? Why or why not?

4. What would the residual income (RI) be for Hawkins Ceramics if this investment opportunity were to be undertaken? Would the manager of the Hawkins Ceramics division want to make this investment she were evaluated based on RI? Why or why not?

5. What is the RI of the investment opportunity? Would the investment be desirable from the standpoint of Piper Corporation? Why or why not?

6. Which performance measurement method, ROI or RI, promotes goal congruence? Why?

Exercises—Group B

E11-27B Identify centralized and decentralized organizations

The following table lists a series of descriptions of decentralized organizations or centralized organizations. For each description, indicate whether that scenario is more typical of a decentralized organization or a centralized organization.

Characteristic	Decentralized or Centralized
a. Fulton Holdings wants its managers to be able to respond quickly to changes in local market demand so the managers have the authority to make decisions about product offerings and pricing.	
b. Craft Supplies & More is a small independent craft shop and is managed by its owner.	
c. Mayflower Corporation now has a single payroll department, a single human resource department, and a single administrative headquarters since Mayflower Corporation "flattened" its organization structure.	
d. Smythe Resorts and Hotels, Inc., wants to empower its managers to make decisions so that the managers' motivation is increased and retention of managers increases.	
e. Phillips Corporation has formal training programs for lower-level managers and has a policy that they promote from within the company whenever possible.	
f. The Plastic Lumber Company, Inc., is managed by its owner, who oversees production, sales, engineering, and the other admininistrative functions.	
g. Daniels Furniture, Inc., is divided into several operating units.	

E11-28B Identify type of responsibility center

Each of the following situations describes an organizational unit. Identify which type of responsibility center each underlined item is (cost, revenue, profit, or investment center).

Organization	Type of Responsibility Center (Cost, Revenue, Profit, or Investment)
a. The <u>Goodyear Tire & Rubber Company</u> is one of the oldest tire companies in the world. Its geographic regions include North America, Europe, Africa, South America, Asia, and Australia.	
b. The <u>Dairy Group Account team</u> of the Dean Foods Company is responsible for sales and servicing for the SUPERVALU, Target, and Costco accounts.	
c. The Fairmont Chicago, The Fairmont Royal York in Toronto, and The Fairmont Orchid in Hawaii are all hotels owned by their parent corporation, <u>Fairmont Hotels & Resorts.</u>	
d. The <u>J.M. Smucker Company Store and Café</u> is located in Wooster, Ohio. The store sells a variety of company products, while the café offers items made with ingredients from the Smucker's brands.	
e. The <u>3M Company</u> manufactures and distributes products under the Post-it, Scotch, Nexcare, and Thinsulate brand names.	
f. The <u>Barnes & Noble bookstore</u> in Asheville, North Carolina, is owned by its parent, Barnes & Noble, Inc. The Asheville bookstore, like other Barnes & Noble bookstores, sells books, magazines, music CDs, coffee, and a variety of other items.	
g. The <u>Human Resources Department</u> at American Greetings is responsible for hiring and training new associates.	
h. The <u>JCPenney store</u> in the Oakpark Shopping Center in Kansas City is owned by the JCPenney Company, Inc.	
i. The <u>Information Systems Department</u> is responsible for designing, installing, and servicing the information systems throughout Kohl's Corporation.	
j. The <u>reservation office</u> for CharterNow Airlines, Inc., is responsible for both Web sales and counter sales.	
k. In addition to other accounting duties, the <u>Financial Reporting and Control & Analysis Department</u> at Progressive Insurance is responsible for performing a monthly analysis of general ledger accounts and fluctuations as a control mechanism.	

E11-29B Differentiate between lag and lead indicators *(Learning Objective 2)*

Explain the difference between lag and lead indicators. Are financial performance measures typically referred to as lag or lead indicators? Explain, using Research in Motion (a manufacturer of mobile communication devices such as BlackBerry smartphones) as an example. Are operational measures (such as customer satisfaction ratings, defect rate, and number of on-time deliveries) typically referred to as lag or lead indicators? Explain, again using Research in Motion as an example.

E11-30B Construct balanced scorecard *(Learning Objective 3)*

Byrne Corporation is preparing its balanced scorecard for the past quarter. The balanced scorecard contains four perspectives: financial, customer, internal business process, and learning and growth. Through its strategic management planning process, Byrne Corporation has selected two specific objectives for each of the four perspectives; these specific objectives are listed in the following table.

Specific Objective
1. Improve post-sales service
2. Increase number of customers
3. Increase gross margin
4. Improve employee morale
5. Increase profitability of core product line
6. Increase plant safety
7. Improve employee job satisfaction
8. Increase customer retention

Byrne Corporation has collected key performance indicators (KPIs) to measure progress towards achieving its specific objectives. The following table contains the KPIs and corresponding data that Byrne Corporation has collected for the past quarter.

KPI	Goal		Actual	
Gross margin growth percentage	24	%	23	%
Number of customers	130,000		135,000	
Number of plant accidents	1		3	
Number of repeat customers	105,000		98,000	
Employee turnover rate (number of employees leaving/number of total employees)	6	%	9	%
Average repair time (number of days)	1.2		1.1	
Core product line profit as a percentage of core product line sales	18	%	12	%
Employee satisfaction survey (1–5, with 1 as most satisfied)	1.7		1.9	

Requirement

1. Prepare a balanced scorecard report for Byrne Corporation, using the following format:

Bryne Corporation Balanced Scorecard Report For Quarter Ended December 31					
Perspective	Objective	KPI	Goal	Actual	Goal Achieved? (√ if met)
Financial					
Customer					
Internal Business Process					
Learning and Growth					

For each of the specific objectives listed, place that objective under the appropriate perspective heading in the report. Select a KPI from the list of KPIs that would be appropriate to measure progress towards each objective. (There are two specific objectives for each perspective and one KPI for each of the specific objectives.) In the last column in the Balanced Scorecard Report, place a checkmark if the associated KPI goal has been achieved.

E11-31B Classify KPIs by balanced scorecard perspective *(Learning Objective 3)*

Classify each of the following key performance indicators according to the balanced scorecard perspective it addresses. Choose from financial perspective, customer perspective, internal business perspective, or learning and growth perspective.

a. Manufacturing cycle time (average length of production process)
b. Earnings growth
c. Average machine setup time
d. Number of new customers
e. Employee promotion rate
f. Cash flow from operations
g. Customer satisfaction ratings
h. Machine downtime
i. Finished products per day per employee
j. Percentage of employees with access to upgraded system
k. Wait time per order prior to start of production
l. Capital turnover

E11-32B Complete and analyze a performance report *(Learning Objective 4)*

One subunit of Speed Sports Company had the following financial results last month:

Speed—Subunit X	Actual	Flexible Budget	Flexible Budget Variance (U or F)	% Variance (U or F)
Direct materials....................	$ 12,930	$12,000		
Direct labor.........................	13,265	14,000		
Indirect labor	23,380	20,000		
Utilities	16,455	15,000		
Depreciation.......................	30,250	30,250		
Repairs and maintenance	4,205	5,000		
Total..................................	$100,485	$96,250		

Requirements

1. Complete the performance evaluation report for this subunit (round to four decimals).
2. Based on the data presented, what type of responsibility center is this subunit?
3. Which items should be investigated if part of management's decision criteria is to investigate all variances exceeding or $2,900 or 11%?
4. Should only unfavorable variances be investigated? Explain.

E11-33B Complete and analyze a performance report (Learning Objective 4)

The accountant for a subunit of Speed Sports Company went on vacation before completing the subunit's monthly performance report. This is as far as she got:

Speed—Subunit X Revenue by Product	Actual	Flexible Budget Variance	Flexible Budget	Sales Volume Variance	Static (Master) Budget
Downhill Model RI...	$ 324,000			$19,000 (F)	$ 301,000
Downhill Model RII..	152,000		$162,000		145,000
Cross-Country Model EXI..	289,000	$3,000 (U)	292,000		308,000
Cross-Country Model EXII	255,000		248,000	20,500 (U)	268,500
Snowboard Model LXI..	423,000	4,000 (F)			401,000
Total	$1,443,000				$1,423,500

Requirements

1. Complete the performance evaluation report for this subunit.

2. Based on the data presented, what type of responsibility center is this subunit?

3. Which items should be investigated if part of management's decision criteria is to investigate all variances exceeding $16,000? Interpret your results. (What could cause these variances? What impact might these variances have on company inventory levels and operations?)

E11-34B Compute and interpret the expanded ROI equation (Learning Objective 5)

Zuds, a national manufacturer of lawn-mowing and snow-blowing equipment, segments its business according to customer type: Professional and Residential. The following divisional information was available for the past year (in thousands of dollars):

	Sales	Operating Income	Total Assets	Current Liabilities
Residential	$ 925,000	$ 64,750	$185,000	$ 76,000
Professional............	$1,794,000	$179,400	$390,000	$165,000

Management has a 26% target rate of return for each division. Zuds' weighted average cost of capital is 17% and its effective tax rate is 32%.

Requirements

1. Calculate each division's ROI. Round all of your answers to four decimal places.

2. Calculate each division's sales margin. Interpret your results.

3. Calculate each division's capital turnover. Interpret your results.

4. Use the expanded ROI formula to confirm your results from Requirement 1. What can you conclude?

E11-35B Compute RI and EVA *(Learning Objective 5)*

Refer to the data about Zuds in E11-34B.

Requirements

1. Calculate each division's RI. Interpret your results.

2. Calculate each division's EVA. Interpret your results.

3. Describe the conceptual and computational similarities and differences between RI and EVA.

E11-36B Relationship between ROI and residual income *(Learning Objective 5)*

Data on three unrelated companies are given in the following table.

	Juda Company	Gammaro Industries	Sesnie, Inc.
Sales	$108,000	?	$522,000
Operating income	$ 43,200	$117,900	?
Total assets	$ 72,000	?	?
Sales margin	?	15 %	10%
Capital turnover	?	4.80	?
Return on investment (ROI)	?	?	29%
Target rate of return	9%	20 %	?
Residual income	?	?	$ 21,600

Requirement

1. Fill in the missing information.

E11-37B Compute ROI, residual income, and EVA *(Learning Objective 5)*

Results from Extreme Corporation's most recent year of operations is presented in the following table:

Operating income	$ 9,100
Total assets	$14,000
Current liabilities	$ 3,600
Sales	$35,000
Target rate of return	14%
Weighted average cost of capital	12%
Tax rate	30%

Requirements

1. Calculate the sales margin, capital turnover, and return on investment (ROI).

2. Calculate the residual income.

3. Calculate the Economic Value Added (EVA).

E11-38B Comparison of ROI and residual income *(Learning Objective 5)*

Johnson Ceramics, a division of Sesnie Corporation, has an operating income of $63,000 and total assets of $360,000. The required rate of return for the company is 13%. The company is evaluating whether it should use return on investment (ROI) or residual income (RI) as a measurement of performance for its division managers.

The manager of Johnson Ceramics has the opportunity to undertake a new project that will require an investment of $90,000. This investment would earn $9,000 for Johnson Ceramics.

Requirements

1. What is the original return on investment (ROI) for Johnson Ceramics (before making any additional investment)?

2. What would the ROI be for Johnson Ceramics if this investment opportunity were undertaken? Would the manager of the Johnson Ceramics division want to make this investment if she were evaluated based on ROI? Why or why not?

3. What is the ROI of the investment opportunity? Would the investment be desirable from the standpoint of Sesnie Corporation? Why or why not?

4. What would the residual income (RI) be for Johnson Ceramics if this investment opportunity were to be undertaken? Would the manager of the Johnson Ceramics division want to make this investment if she were evaluated based on RI? Why or why not?

5. What is the RI of the investment opportunity? Would the investment be desirable from the standpoint of Sesnie Corporation? Why or why not?

6. Which performance measurement method, ROI or RI, promotes goal congruence? Why?

Problems—Group A

P11-39A Evaluate subunit performance (Learning Objectives 3 & 4)

One subunit of Racer Sports Company had the following financial results last month:

Racer—Subunit X	Actual	Flexible Budget	Flexible Budget Variance (U or F)	Percentage Variance* (U or F)
Sales	$486,000	$450,000		
Cost of goods sold	260,000	250,000		
Gross margin	$226,000	$200,000		
Operating expenses	52,000	50,000		
Operating income before service department charges	$174,000	$150,000		
Service department charges (allocated)	35,000	25,000		
Operating income	$139,000	$125,000		

*Flexible budget variance ÷ Flexible budget

Requirements

1. Complete the performance evaluation report for this subunit (round to three decimal places).

2. Based on the data presented, what type of responsibility center is this subunit?

3. Which items should be investigated if part of management's decision criteria is to investigate all variances equal to or exceeding $10,000 *and* exceeding 10% (both criteria must be met)?

4. Should only unfavorable variances be investigated? Explain.

5. Is it possible that the variances are due to a higher-than-expected sales volume? Explain.

6. Do you think management will place equal weight on each of the $10,000 variances? Explain.

7. Which balanced scorecard perspective is being addressed through this performance report? In your opinion, is this performance report a lead or lag indicator? Explain.

8. Give one key performance indicator for the other three balanced scorecard perspectives. Indicate which perspective is being addressed by the indicators you list. Are they lead or lag indicators? Explain.

P11-40A Evaluate divisional performance *(Learning Objective 5)*

Sherwin-Williams is a national paint manufacturer and retailer. The company is segmented into five divisions: Paint Stores (branded retail locations), Consumer (paint sold through stores such as Sears, Home Depot, and Lowe's), Automotive (sales to auto manufacturers), International, and Administration. The following is selected divisional information for the company's two largest divisions: Paint Stores and Consumer (in thousands of dollars).

	Sales	Operating Income	Total Assets	Current Liabilities
Paint stores.............	$3,920,000	$490,000	$1,400,000	$350,000
Consumer................	$1,200,000	$180,000	$1,600,000	$600,000

Assume that management has specified a 20% target rate of return. Further assume that the company's weighted average cost of capital is 15% and its effective tax rate is 32%.

Requirements

Round all calculations to two decimal places.

1. Calculate each division's ROI.

2. Calculate each division's sales margin. Interpret your results.

3. Calculate each division's capital turnover. Interpret your results.

4. Use the expanded ROI formula to confirm your results from Requirement 1. Interpret your results.

5. Calculate each division's RI. Interpret your results and offer recommendations for any division with negative RI.

6. Calculate each division's EVA. Interpret your results.

7. Describe the conceptual and computational similarities and differences between RI and EVA.

8. Total asset data were provided in this problem. If you were to gather this information from an annual report, how would you measure total assets? Describe your measurement choices and some of the pros and cons of those choices.

9. Describe some of the factors that management considers when setting its minimum target rate of return.

10. Explain why some firms prefer to use RI rather than ROI for performance measurement.

11. Explain why budget versus actual performance reports are insufficient for evaluating the performance of investment centers.

P11-41A Collect and analyze division data from an annual report (Learning Objective 5)

HardyCo segments its company into four distinct divisions. The net revenues, operating profit, and total assets for these divisions are disclosed in the footnotes to HardyCo's consolidated financial statements and presented here.

Notes to Consolidated Financial Statements
Note 1—Basis of Presentation and Our Divisions:

We manufacture, market, and sell a variety of products through our divisions, including furniture and fixtures for the home, office, stores, and health-care facilities. The accounting policies are the same for each division, as indicated in Note 2. There is, however, one exception. HardyCo centrally manages commodity derivatives and does not allocate any gains and losses incurred by these contracts to individual divisions. These derivatives are used to hedge the underlying price risk to the commodities used in production. The resulting gains and losses from these contracts are recorded under corporate expenses rather than allocated to specific divisions.

	Net Revenue			Operating Profit		
	2010	2009	2008	2010	2009	2008
Home furnishings	$10,500	$ 9,400	$ 9,000	$2,625	$2,350	$1,800
Office furniture	9,000	8,100	7,800	1,800	1,620	1,560
Store displays	12,200	11,000	10,500	1,464	1,320	1,260
Health-care furnishings	1,750	1,600	1,500	525	500	480
Total division	33,450	30,100	28,800	6,414	5,790	5,100
Corporate	—	—	—	(300)	(260)	(215)
Total	$33,450	$30,100	$28,800	$6,114	$5,530	$4,885

Corporate includes the costs of our corporate headquarters, centrally-managed initiatives, and certain gains and losses that cannot be accurately allocated to specific divisions, such as derivative gains and losses.

	Amortization of Intangible Assets			Depreciation & Other Amortization		
	2010	2009	2008	2010	2009	2008
Home furnishings	$ 10	$ 5	$ 5	$ 430	$ 420	$ 425
Office furniture	80	75	75	280	260	255
Store displays	75	70	68	475	420	380
Health-care furnishings	—	—	5	30	35	32
Total division	165	150	153	1,215	1,135	1,092
Corporate	—	—	—	20	25	24
Total	$165	$150	$153	$1,235	$1,160	$1,116

	Total Assets			Capital Spending		
	2010	2009	2008	2010	2009	2008
Home furnishings	$ 6,250	$ 5,000	$ 4,500	$ 500	$ 510	$ 470
Office furniture	6,000	5,400	5,200	490	320	265
Store displays	10,000	8,800	8,400	835	665	530
Health-care furnishings	1,000	800	750	30	30	35
Total division	23,250	20,000	18,850	1,855	1,525	1,300
Corporate	1,740	5,300	3,500	200	205	90
Total	$24,990	$25,300	$22,350	$2,055	$1,730	$1,390

Corporate Assets consist of cash, short-term investments, and property, plant, and equipment. The corporate property, plant, and equipment includes the headquarters building, equipment within, and the surrounding property.

Requirements

1. What are HardyCo's four business divisions? Make a table listing each division, its net revenues, operating profit, and total assets.

2. Use the data you collected in Requirement 1 to calculate each division's sales margin. Interpret your results.

3. Use the data you collected in Requirement 1 to calculate each division's capital turnover. Interpret your results.

4. Use the data you collected in Requirement 1 to calculate each division's ROI. Interpret your results.

5. Can you calculate RI and/or EVA using the data presented? Why or why not?

Problems—Group B

P11-42B Evaluate subunit performance *(Learning Objectives 3 & 4)*

One subunit of Speed Sports Company had the following financial results last month:

Speed—Subunit X	Actual	Flexible Budget	Flexible Budget Variance (U or F)	Percentage Variance* (U or F)
Sales	$486,900	$450,000		
Cost of goods sold	259,500	250,000	_____	
Gross margin	$227,400	$200,000		
Operating expenses	51,750	50,000	_____	
Operating income before service department charges	$175,650	$150,000		
Service department charges (allocated)	40,750	31,250	_____	
Operating income	$134,900	$118,750	_____	

*Flexible budget variance ÷ Flexible budget

Requirements

1. Complete the performance evaluation report for the subunit (round to three decimal places).

2. Based on the data presented, what type of responsibility center is this subunit?

3. Which items should be investigated if part of management's decision criteria is to investigate all variances equal to or exceeding $9,500 *and* exceeding 16% (both criteria must be met)?

4. Should only unfavorable variances be investigated? Explain.

5. Is it possible that the variances are due to a higher-than-expected sales volume? Explain.

6. Do you think management will place equal weight on each of the $9,500 variances? Explain.

7. Which balanced scorecard perspective is being addressed through this performance report? In your opinion, is this performance report a lead or lag indicator? Explain.

8. List one key performance indicator for the other three balanced scorecard perspectives. Indicate which perspective is being addressed by the indicators you list. Are they lead or lag indicators? Explain.

P11-43B Evaluate divisional performance *(Learning Objective 5)*

NYC Paints is a national paint manufacturer and retailer. The company is segmented into five divisions: Paint Stores (branded retail locations), Consumer (paint sold through stores like Sears, Home Depot, and Lowe's), Automotive (sales to auto manufacturers), International, and Administration. The following is selected divisional information for its two largest divisions: Paint Stores and Consumer (in thousands of dollars).

	Sales	Operating Income	Total Assets	Current Liabilities
Paint stores..............	$3,950,000	$553,000	$1,975,000	$350,000
Consumer.................	$1,300,000	$221,000	$2,600,000	$590,000

Assume that management has specified a 23% target rate of return. Further assume that the company's weighted average cost of capital is 14% and its effective tax rate is 32%.

Requirements

Round all calculations to four decimal places.

1. Calculate each division's ROI.

2. Calculate each division's sales margin. Interpret your results.

3. Calculated each division's capital turnover. Interpret your results.

4. Use the expanded ROI formula to confirm your results from Requirement 1. Interpret your results.

5. Calculate each division's RI. Interpret your results and offer recommendations for any division with negative RI.

6. Calculate each division's EVA. Interpret your results.

7. Describe the conceptual and computational similarities and differences between RI and EVA.

8. Total asset data was provided in this problem. If you were to gather this information from an annual report, how would you measure total assets? Describe your measurement choices and some of the pros and cons of those choices.

9. Describe some of the factors that management considers when setting its minimum target rate of return.

10. Explain why some firms prefer to use RI rather than ROI for performance measurement.

11. Explain why budget versus actual performance reports are insufficient for evaluating the performance of investment centers.

P11-44B Collect and analyze division data from an annual report *(Learning Objective 5)*

GlennCo segments its company into four distinct divisions. The net revenues, operating profit, and total assets for these divisions are disclosed in the footnotes to GlennCo's consolidated financial statements and presented here.

Net Revenue and Operating Profit

	Net Revenue			Operating Profit		
	2010	2009	2008	2010	2009	2008
Home furnishings............................	$11,250	$10,150	$ 9,750	$3,150	$2,875	$2,325
Office furniture	9,500	8,600	8,300	1,995	1,815	1,755
Store displays	12,750	11,550	11,050	1,785	1,645	1,585
Health-care furnishings	1,500	1,350	1,250	480	455	435
Total division..................................	35,000	31,650	30,350	7,410	6,790	6,100
Corporate...	-	-	-	(330)	(290)	(245)
Total	$35,000	$31,650	$30,350	$7,080	$6,500	$5,855

Total Assets and Other Information

	Amortization of Intangible Assets			Depreciation & Other Amortization		
	2010	2009	2008	2010	2009	2008
Home furnishings.......................	$ 16	$ 11	$ 11	$ 425	$ 415	$ 420
Office furniture	82	77	77	280	260	255
Store displays	72	67	65	465	410	370
Health-care furnishings	-	-	5	45	50	47
Total division..............................	170	155	158	1,215	1,135	1,092
Corporate......................................	-	-	-	15	20	19
Total	$170	$155	$158	$1,230	$1,155	$1,111

	Total Assets			Capital Spending		
	2010	2009	2008	2010	2009	2008
Home furnishings............................	$ 7,500	$ 6,250	$ 5,750	$ 495	$ 505	$ 465
Office furniture	7,600	7,000	6,800	500	330	275
Store displays	10,625	9,425	9,025	865	695	560
Health-care furnishings	750	550	500	20	20	25
Total division..................................	26,475	23,225	22,075	1,880	1,550	1,325
Corporate...	1,710	5,270	3,470	210	215	100
Total	$28,185	$28,495	$25,545	$2,090	$1,765	$1,425

Notes to Consolidated Financial Statements

Note 1—Basis of Presentation and Our Divisions:

We manufacture, market, and sell a variety of products through our divisions, including furniture and fixtures for the home, office, stores, and health-care facilities. The accounting policies are the same for each division. as indicated in Note 2. There is, however, one exception. GlennCo centrally manages commodity derivatives and does not allocate any gains and losses incurred by these contracts to individual divisions. These derivatives are used to hedge the underlying price risk to the commodities used in production. The resulting gains and losses from these contracts are recorded under corporate expenses rather than allocated to specific divisions.

Corporate includes the costs of our corporate headquarters, centrally-managed initiatives, and certain gains and losses that cannot be accurately allocated to specific divisions, such as derivative gains and losses.

Corporate Assets consist of cash, short-term investments, and property, plant, and equipment. The corporate property, plant, and equipment includes the headquarters building, equipment within, and the surrounding property.

Requirements

1. What are GlennCo's four business divisions? Make a table listing each division, its net revenues, operating profit, and total assets.

2. Use the data you collected in Requirement 1 to calculate each division's sales margin. Interpret your results.

3. Use the data you collected in Requirement 1 to calculate each division's capital turnover. Interpret your results.

4. Use the data you collected in Requirement 1 to calculate each division's ROI. Interpret your results.

5. Can you calculate RI and/or EVA using the data presented? Why or why not?

APPLY YOUR KNOWLEDGE

Decision Case

C11-45 Collect and analyze division data *(Learning Objective 5)*

Colgate-Palmolive operates two product segments. Using the company's Web site, locate segment information for 2008 in the company's 2008 annual report. (*Hint:* Look under investor relations.) Then, look in the financial statement footnotes.

Quick Check Answers
1. *b* 2. *d* 3. *c* 4. *a* 5. *c* 6. *d*
7. *c* 8. *b* 9. *a* 10. *d*

For online homework, exercises, and problems that provide you with immediate feedback, please visit www.myaccountinglab.com.

Requirements

1. What are the two segments (ignore geographical subsets of the one product segment)? Gather data about each segment's net sales, operating income, and identifiable assets.

2. Calculate ROI for each segment.

3. Which segment has the highest ROI? Explain why.

4. If you were on the top management team and could allocate extra funds to only one division, which division would you choose? Why?

Discussion & Analysis

1. Describe at least four advantages of decentralization. Also describe at least two disadvantages to decentralization.

2. Describe at least four reasons a company would use a performance evaluation system.

3. Explain why using financial statements as the sole performance evaluation tool for a company is probably not a good idea. What issues can arise from using only financial measures for performance evaluation?

4. Define key performance indicator (KPI). What is the relationship between KPIs and a company's objectives? Select a company of any size with which you are familiar. List at least four examples of specific objectives that company might have and one potential KPI for each of those specific objectives.

5. List and describe the four perspectives found on a balanced scorecard. For each perspective, list at least two examples of KPIs that might be used to measure performance on that perspective.

6. Compare and contrast a cost center, a revenue center, a profit center, and an investment center. List a specific example of each type of responsibility center. How is the performance of managers evaluated in each type of responsibility center?

7. Contrast lag indicator with lead indicator. Provide an example of each type of indicator.

8. Explain the potential problem that could arise from using ROI as the incentive measure for managers. What are some specific actions a company might take to resolve this potential problem?

9. Describe at least two specific actions that a company could take to improve its ROI.

10. Define residual income. How is it calculated? Describe the major weakness of residual income.

Application & Analysis

11-1 Segmented Financial Information

Select a company you are interested in and obtain its annual reports by going the company's Web site. Download the annual report for the most recent year. (On many company's Web sites, you will need to visit the Investor Relations section to obtain the company's financial statements.) You may also collect the information from the company's Form 10-K, which can be found at http://www.sec.gov/idea/searchidea/companysearch_idea.html.

Basic Discussion Questions

1. Locate the company's annual report as outlined previously. Find the company's segment information; it should be in the "Notes to Consolidated Financial Statements" or other similarly named section. Look for the word "Segment" in a heading—that is usually the section you need.

2. List the segments as reported in the annual report. Make a table listing each operating segment, its revenues, income, and assets.

3. Use the data you collected in Requirement 2 to calculate each segment's sales margin. Interpret your results.

4. Use the data you collected in Question 2 to calculate each segment's capital turnover. Interpret your results.

5. Use the data you collected in Requirement 2 to calculate each segment's ROI. Interpret your results.

6. Can you calculate RI and/or EVA using the data presented? Why or why not?

7. The rules for how segments should be presented in the annual report are governed by external financial accounting rules. The information you gathered for the previous requirements would be used by investors and other external stakeholders in their analysis of the company and its stock. Internally, the company most likely has many segments. Based on what you know about the company and its products or services, list at least five potential segments that the company might use for internal reporting. Explain why this way of segmenting the company for internal reporting could be useful to managers.

Classroom Applications

Web: Post the discussion questions on an electronic discussion board. Have small groups of students choose a company for their groups. The students should answer the listed questions in their discussion.

Classroom: Form groups of 3–4 students. Your group should choose a company. Prepare a five-minute presentation about your group's company that addresses the listed questions.

Independent: Research answers to each of the questions. Turn in a 2–3 page typed paper (12 point font, double-spaced with 1" margins). Include references, including the URL for annual report you used for this activity.

For additional Application & Analysis projects and implementation tips, see the Instructor Resources in MyAccountingLab.com.

Cedar Fair Entertainment Company is the leading

operator of amusement parks in the United States and Canada, entertaining over 22 million guests each year. The company's flagship park, Cedar Point, in Sandusky, Ohio, is known as the "Roller Coaster Capital of the World." The park has a world-record breaking collection of 17 roller coasters, as well as an abundance of non-coaster rides and activities. These roller coasters include some of the *fastest* and *tallest* roller coasters in North America. The newest roller coaster, "Maverick," cost over $21 million to build. The company doesn't mind paying that kind of money for a new ride, as long as it is expected to generate handsome returns in years to come. According to Cedar Fair's chief executive officer, "the key to the company's future is to continue to invest in our product and create an even better experience for our guests." One way of doing that is to bring customers back by offering thrilling new rides. As a result, Cedar Point has been voted the "Best Amusement Park in the World" for 11 consecutive years by *Amusement Today's* international survey.

Sources: Cedarpoint.com;
Cedar Fair Entertainment Company, 2007 summary annual report and 2008 10-K filing.

CHAPTER 12

Capital Investment Decisions and the Time Value of Money

Learning Objectives

1. Describe the importance of capital investments and the capital budgeting process

2. Use the payback and accounting rate of return methods to make capital investment decisions

3. Use the time value of money to compute the present and future values of single lump sums and annuities

4. Use discounted cash flow models to make capital investment decisions

5. Compare and contrast the four capital budgeting methods

As the chapter opening story shows, companies must continually evaluate whether they need to invest in new property, buildings, equipment, or projects in order to remain competitive or increase their revenue stream. Many companies also initiate capital improvements in order to save on existing costs, such as the cost of manual labor. Management must carefully consider whether the additional revenues or cost savings will be worth the high price of these new capital investments. In this chapter, we'll see how companies such as Cedar Point use net present value, payback period, and other capital investment analysis techniques to decide which long-term capital investments to make.

1 Describe the importance of capital investments and the capital budgeting process

What is Capital Budgeting?

The process of making capital investment decisions is often referred to as **capital budgeting**. Companies make capital investments when they acquire *capital assets*—assets used for a long period of time. Capital investments include buying new equipment, building new plants, automating production, and developing major commercial Web sites. In addition to affecting operations for many years, capital investments usually require large sums of money. Cedar Point's decision to spend $21 million on the Maverick roller coaster will tie up resources for years to come—as will Marriott's decision to spend $187 million to renovate its Marco Island Marriott Beach Resort, Golf Club, and Spa.

Capital investment decisions affect all types of businesses as they try to become more efficient by automating production and implementing new technologies. Grocers and retailers such as Wal-Mart have invested in expensive self-scan check-out machines, while airlines such as Delta and Continental have invested in self-check-in kiosks. These new technologies cost money. How do managers decide whether these expansions in plant and equipment will be good investments? They use capital budgeting analysis. Some companies, such as Georgia Pacific, employ staff dedicated solely to capital budgeting analysis. They spend thousands of hours a year determining which capital investments to pursue.

Why is this important?

"Each of these four methods help managers decide whether it would be wise to invest large sums of money in new projects, buildings, or equipment."

Four Popular Methods of Capital Budgeting Analysis

In this chapter, we discuss four popular methods of analyzing potential capital investments:

1. Payback period

2. Accounting rate of return (ARR)

3. Net present value (NPV)

4. Internal rate of return (IRR)

The first two methods, payback period and accounting rate of return, are fairly quick and easy to calculate and work well for capital investments that have a relatively short life span, such as computer equipment and software that may have a useful life of only two to three years. Management often uses the payback period and accounting rate of return to screen potential investments from those that are less desirable. The payback period provides management with valuable information on how fast the cash invested will be recouped. The accounting rate of return shows the effect of the investment on the company's accrual-based income. However, these two methods are inadequate if the capital investments have a longer life span. Why? Because these methods do not consider the time value of money. The last two methods, net present value and internal rate of return, factor in the time value of money, so they are more appropriate for longer-term capital investments such as Cedar Point's new roller coasters and rides. Management often uses a combination of methods to make final capital investment decisions.

Capital budgeting is not an exact science. Although the calculations these methods require may appear precise, remember that they are based on predictions about an uncertain future. These predictions must consider many unknown factors, such as changing consumer preferences, competition, and government regulations. The further into the future the decision extends, the more likely actual results will differ from predictions. Long-term decisions are riskier than short-term decisions.

Focus on Cash Flows

Generally Accepted Accounting Principles (GAAP) are based on accrual accounting, but capital budgeting focuses on cash flows. The desirability of a capital asset depends on its ability to generate *net cash inflows*—that is, inflows in excess of outflows—over the asset's useful life. Recall that operating income based on accrual accounting contains noncash expenses such as depreciation expense and bad-debt expense. The capital investment's *net cash inflows*, therefore, will differ from its operating income. Of the four capital budgeting methods covered in this chapter, only the accounting rate of return method uses accrual-based accounting income. The other three methods use the investment's projected *net cash inflows*.

What do the projected net cash inflows include? Cash *inflows* include future cash revenue generated from the investment, any future savings in ongoing cash operating costs resulting from the investment, and any future residual value of the asset. To determine the investment's *net* cash inflows, the inflows are *netted* against the investment's future cash *outflows*, such as the investment's ongoing cash operating costs and refurbishment, repairs, and maintenance costs. The initial investment itself is also a significant cash outflow. However, in our calculations, *we refer to the amount of the investment separately from all other cash flows related to the investment*. The projected net cash inflows are "given" in our examples and in the assignment material. In reality, much of capital investment analysis revolves around projecting these figures as accurately as possible using input from employees throughout the organization (production, marketing, and so forth, depending on the type of capital investment).

Capital Budgeting Process

As shown in Exhibit 12-1, the first step in the capital budgeting process is to identify potential investments—for example, new technology and equipment that may make the company more efficient, competitive, and profitable. Employees, consultants, and outside sales vendors often offer capital investment proposals to management. After identifying potential capital investments, managers next project the investments' net cash inflows. As discussed previously, this step can be very time-consuming and difficult. However, managers make the best projections possible given the information they have. The third step is to analyze the investments using one or more of the four methods listed previously. Sometimes the analysis involves a two-stage process. In the first stage, managers screen the investments using one or both of the methods that do *not* incorporate the time value of money: payback period or accounting rate of return. These simple methods quickly weed out undesirable investments. Potential investments that "pass the initial test" go on to a second stage of analysis. In the second stage, managers further analyze the potential investments using the net present value or internal rate of return method. Because these methods consider the time value of money, they provide more accurate information about the potential investment's profitability. Since each method evaluates the potential investment from a different angle, some companies use all four methods to get the most "complete picture" they can about the investment.

EXHIBIT 12-1   Capital Budgeting Process

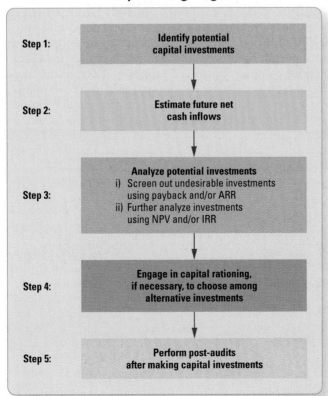

Some companies can pursue all of the potential investments that meet or exceed their decision criteria. However, because of limited resources, other companies must engage in **capital rationing** and choose among alternative capital investments. This is the fourth step pictured in Exhibit 12-1. Based on the availability of funds, managers determine if and when to make specific capital investments. For example, management may decide to wait three years to buy a certain piece of equipment because it considers other investments to be more important. In the intervening three years, the company will reassess whether it should still invest in the equipment. Perhaps technology has changed and even better equipment is available. Perhaps consumer tastes have changed, so the company no longer needs the equipment. Because of changing factors, long-term capital budgets are rarely "set in stone."

As a final step, most companies perform **post-audits** of their capital investments. After investing in the assets, they compare the actual net cash inflows generated from the investment to the projected net cash inflows. Post-audits help companies determine whether the investments are going as planned and deserve continued support or whether they should abandon the project and sell the assets (if possible). Managers also use feedback from post-audits to better estimate net cash inflow projections for future projects. If managers expect routine post-audits, they will more likely submit realistic net cash inflow estimates with their capital investment proposals.

How do Managers Calculate the Payback Period and Accounting Rate of Return?

Payback Period

> **2** Use the payback and accounting rate of return methods to make capital investment decisions

Payback is the length of time it takes to recover, in net cash inflows, the cost of the capital outlay. The payback model measures how quickly managers expect to recover their investment dollars. The shorter the payback period, the more attractive the asset, *all else being equal*. Why? The quicker an investment pays itself back, the less inherent risk that the investment will become unprofitable. Computing the payback period depends on whether net cash inflows are equal each year or whether they differ over time. We consider each in turn.

Why is this important?

"Companies want to recover their cash as quickly as possible. The payback period tells managers how long it will take before the investment is recouped."

Payback with Equal Annual Net Cash Inflows

Tierra Firma makes camping gear. The company is considering investing $240,000 in hardware and software to develop a business-to-business (B2B) portal. Employees throughout the company will use the B2B portal to access company-approved suppliers. Tierra Firma expects the portal to save $60,000 each year for the six years of its useful life. The savings will arise from a reduction in the number of purchasing personnel the company employs and from lower prices on the goods and services purchased. Net cash inflows arise from an increase in revenues, a decrease in expenses, or both. In Tierra Firma's case, the net cash inflows result from lower expenses.

When net cash inflows are equal each year, managers compute the payback period as follows:

$$\text{Payback period} = \frac{\text{Amount invested}}{\text{Expected annual net cash inflow}}$$

Tierra Firma computes the investment's payback as follows:

$$\text{Payback period for B2B portal} = \frac{\$240,000}{\$60,000} = 4 \text{ years}$$

Exhibit 12-2 verifies that Tierra Firma expects to recoup the $240,000 investment in the B2B portal by the end of Year 4, when the accumulated net cash inflows total $240,000.

EXHIBIT 12-2 Payback—Equal Annual Net Cash Inflows

| | | Net Cash Inflows | | | |
| | | B2B Portal | | Web Site Development | |
Year	Amount Invested	Annual	Accumulated	Annual	Accumulated
0	$240,000	—	—	—	—
1	—	$60,000	$ 60,000	$80,000	$ 80,000
2	—	60,000	120,000	80,000	160,000
3	—	60,000	180,000	80,000	240,000
4	—	60,000	240,000		
5	—	60,000	300,000		
6	—	60,000	360,000		

Tierra Firma is also considering investing $240,000 to develop a Web site. The company expects the Web site to generate $80,000 in net cash inflows each year of its three-year life. The payback period is computed as follows:

$$\text{Payback period for Web site development} = \frac{\$240,000}{\$80,000} = 3 \text{ years}$$

Exhibit 12-2 verifies that Tierra Firma will recoup the $240,000 investment for Web site development by the end of Year 3, when the accumulated net cash inflows total $240,000.

Payback with Unequal Net Cash Inflows

The payback equation works only when net cash inflows are the same each period. When periodic cash flows are unequal, you must accumulate net cash inflows until the amount invested is recovered. Assume that Tierra Firma is considering an alternate investment, the Z80 portal. The Z80 portal differs from the B2B portal and Web site in two respects: (1) it has *unequal* net cash inflows during its life, and (2) it has a $30,000 residual value at the end of its life. The Z80 portal will generate net cash inflows of $100,000 in Year 1, $80,000 in Year 2, $50,000 each year in Years 3–5, $30,000 in Year 6, and $30,000 when it is sold at the end of its life. Exhibit 12-3 shows the payback schedule for these unequal annual net cash inflows.

EXHIBIT 12-3 Payback—Unequal Annual Net Cash Inflows

| | | Net Cash Inflows Z80 Portal | |
Year	Amount Invested	Annual	Accumulated
0	$240,000	—	—
1	—	100,000	$100,000
2	—	80,000	180,000
3	—	50,000	230,000
4	—	50,000	280,000
5	—	50,000	330,000
6	—	30,000	360,000
Residual Value		30,000	390,000

By the end of Year 3, the company has recovered $230,000 of the $240,000 initially invested and is only $10,000 short of payback. Because the expected net cash inflow in Year 4 is $50,000, by the end of Year 4, the company will have recovered *more* than the initial investment. Therefore, the payback period is somewhere between three and four years. Assuming that the cash flow occurs evenly throughout the fourth year, the payback period is calculated as follows:

$$\text{Payback} = 3 \text{ years} + \frac{\$10,000 \text{ (amount needed to complete recovery in Year 4)}}{\$50,000 \text{ (projected net cash inflow in Year 4)}}$$

$$= 3.2 \text{ years}$$

Criticism of the Payback Period Method

A major criticism of the payback method is that it focuses only on time, not on profitability. The payback period considers only those cash flows that occur *during* the payback period. This method ignores any cash flows that occur *after* that period, including any residual value. For example, Exhibit 12-2 shows that the B2B portal will continue to generate net cash inflows for two years after its payback period. These additional net cash inflows amount to $120,000 ($60,000 × 2 years), yet the payback method ignores this extra cash. A similar situation occurs with the Z80 portal. As shown in Exhibit 12-3, the Z80 portal will provide an additional $150,000 of net cash inflows, including residual value, after its payback period of 3.2 years. In contrast, the Web site's useful life, as shown in Exhibit 12-2, is the *same* as its payback period (three years). Since no additional cash flows occur after the payback period, the Web site will merely cover its cost and provide no profit. Because this is the case, the company has little or no reason to invest in the Web site even though its payback period is the shortest of all three investments.

Exhibit 12-4 compares the payback period of the three investments. As the exhibit illustrates, the payback method does not consider the asset's profitability. *The method only tells management how quickly it will recover its cash.* Even though the Web site has the shortest payback period, both the B2B portal and the Z80 portal are better investments because they provide profit. The key point is that the investment with the shortest payback period is best *only when all other factors are the same.* Therefore, managers usually use the payback method as a screening device to "weed out" investments that will take too long to recoup. They rarely use payback period as the sole method for deciding whether to invest in the asset.

EXHIBIT 12-4 **Comparing Payback Periods Between Investments**

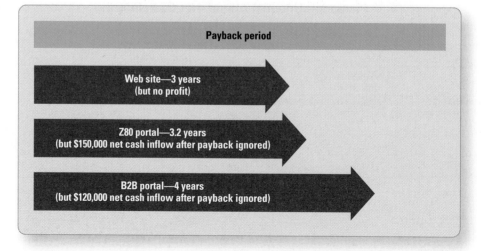

When using the payback period method, managers are guided by the following decision rule:

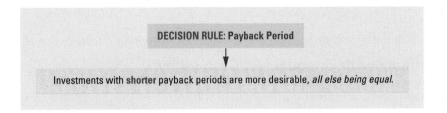

DECISION RULE: Payback Period

↓

Investments with **shorter** payback periods are more desirable, *all else being equal.*

Accounting Rate of Return (ARR)

Companies are in business to earn profits. One measure of profitability is the **accounting rate of return (ARR)** on an asset:[1]

$$\text{Accounting rate of return} = \frac{\text{Average annual operating income from asset}}{\text{Initial investment}^1}$$

The ARR focuses on the *operating income, not the net cash inflow*, that an asset generates. The ARR measures the average annual rate of return over the asset's life. Recall that operating income is based on *accrual accounting*. Therefore, any noncash expenses such as depreciation expense must be subtracted from the asset's net cash inflows to arrive at its operating income. Assuming that depreciation expense is the only noncash expense relating to the investment, we can rewrite the ARR formula as follows:

$$\text{ARR} = \frac{\text{Average annual net cash flow} - \text{Annual depreciation expense}}{\text{Initial investment}}$$

Exhibit 12-5 reviews how to calculate annual depreciation expense using the straight-line method.

EXHIBIT 12-5   **Review of Straight-Line Depreciation Expense Calculation**

$$\text{Annual depreciation expense} = \frac{\text{Initial cost of asset} - \text{Residual value}}{\text{Useful life of asset (in years)}}$$

Investments with Equal Annual Net Cash Inflows

Recall that the B2B portal, which costs $240,000, has equal annual net cash inflows of $60,000, a six-year useful life, and no residual value.

First, we must find the B2B portal's annual depreciation expense:

$$\text{Annual depreciation expense} = \frac{\$240,000 - 0}{6 \text{ years}} = \$40,000$$

---

[1]Some managers prefer to use the average investment, rather than the initial investment, as the denominator. For simplicity, we will use the initial investment.

Now, we can complete the ARR formula:

$$\text{ARR} = \frac{\$60,000 - \$40,000}{\$240,000} = \frac{\$20,000}{\$240,000} = 8.33\% \text{ (rounded)}$$

The B2B portal will provide an average annual accounting rate of return of 8.33%.

Investments with Unequal Net Cash Inflows

Now, consider the Z80 portal. Recall that the Z80 portal would also cost $240,000 but it had unequal net cash inflows during its life (as pictured in Exhibit 12-3) and a $30,000 residual value at the end of its life. Since the yearly cash inflows vary in size, we need to first calculate the Z80's *average* annual net cash inflows:[2]

Total net cash inflows *during* operating life of asset (does not include the residual value at the end of life)[2] (Year 1 + Year 2, and so forth) from Exhibit 12-3...........	$360,000
Divide by: Asset's operating life (in years).............................	÷ 6 years
Average annual net cash inflow from asset...........................	$ 60,000

Now, let's calculate the asset's annual depreciation expense:

$$\text{Annual depreciation expense} = \frac{\$240,000 - \$30,000}{6 \text{ years}} = \$35,000$$

Finally, we can complete the ARR calculation:

$$\text{ARR} = \frac{\$60,000 - \$35,000}{\$240,000} = \frac{\$25,000}{\$240,000} = 10.42\% \text{ (rounded)}$$

Notice that the Z80 portal's average annual operating income ($25,000) is higher than the B2B portal's average operating income ($20,000). Since the Z80 asset has a residual value at the end of its life, less depreciation is expensed each year, leading to a higher average annual operating income and a higher ARR.

Companies that use the ARR model set a minimum required accounting rate of return. If Tierra Firma required an ARR of at least 10%, its managers would not approve an investment in the B2B portal but would approve an investment in the Z80 portal.

The decision rule is as follows:

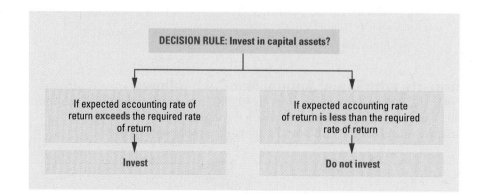

Decision rule: Invest in capital assets?

If expected accounting rate of return **exceeds** the required rate of return → Invest

If expected accounting rate of return **is less** than the required rate of return → Do not invest

---

[2]The residual value is not included in the net cash inflows *during* the asset's operating life because we are trying to find the asset's average *annual operating* income. We assume that the asset will be sold for its expected residual value ($30,000) at the *end* of its life, resulting in no additional accounting gain or loss.

In summary, the payback period focuses on the time it takes for the company to recoup its cash investment but ignores all cash flows occurring after the payback period. Because it ignores any additional cash flows (including any residual value), the method does not consider the profitability of the project.

The ARR, however, measures the profitability of the asset over its entire life using accrual accounting figures. It is the only method that uses accrual accounting rather than net cash inflows in its computations. As discussed in Chapter 11, company divisions are often evaluated based on accounting income. Therefore, the investment's ARR helps managers see how the investment will impact their division's profitability. The payback period and ARR methods are simple and quick to compute, so managers often use them to screen out undesirable investments and to gain a more complete picture of the investment's desirability. However, both methods ignore the time value of money.

Decision Guidelines

Capital Budgeting

Amazon.com started as a virtual retailer. It held no inventory. Instead, it bought books and CDs only as needed to fill customer orders. As the company grew, its managers decided to invest in their own warehouse facilities. Why? Owning warehouse facilities allows Amazon.com to save money by buying in bulk. Also, shipping all items in the customer's order in one package from one location saves shipping costs. Here are some of the guidelines Amazon.com's managers used as they made the major capital budgeting decision to invest in building warehouses.

Decision	Guidelines
Why is this decision important?	Capital budgeting decisions typically require large investments and affect operations for years to come.
What method shows us how soon we will recoup our cash investment?	The payback method shows how quickly managers will recoup their investment. The method highlights investments that are too risky due to long payback periods. However, it doesn't reveal any information about the investment's profitability.
Does any method consider the impact of the investment on accrual-based accounting income?	The accounting rate of return is the only capital budgeting method that shows how the investment will affect accrual-based accounting income, which is important to financial statement users. All other methods of capital investment analysis focus on the investment's net cash inflows.
How do we compute the payback period if cash flows are *equal*?	$$\text{Payback period} = \frac{\text{Amount invested}}{\text{Expected annual net cash inflow}}$$
How do we compute the payback period if cash flows are *unequal*?	Accumulate net cash inflows until the amount invested is recovered.
How do we compute the ARR?	$$\text{Accounting rate of return} = \frac{\text{Average annual operating income from asset}}{\text{Initial investment}}$$ We can also write this formula as follows: $$\text{ARR} = \frac{\text{Average annual net cash flow} - \text{Annual depreciation expense}}{\text{Initial investment}}$$

Summary Problem 1

Zetamax is considering buying a new bar-coding machine for its Austin, Texas plant. The company screens its potential capital investments using the payback period and accounting rate of return methods. If a potential investment has a payback period of less than four years and a minimum 7% accounting rate of return, it will be considered further. The data for the machine follow:

Cost of machine	$48,000
Estimated residual value	$ 0
Estimated annual net cash inflow (each year for five years)	$13,000
Estimated useful life	5 years

Requirements

1. Compute the bar-coding machine's payback period.
2. Compute the bar-coding machine's ARR.
3. Should Zetamax turn down this investment proposal or consider it further?

Solution

Requirement 1

$$\text{Payback period} = \frac{\text{Amount invested}}{\text{Expected annual net cash inflow}} = \frac{\$48,000}{\$13,000} = 3.7 \text{ years (rounded)}$$

Requirement 2

$$\text{Accounting rate of return} = \frac{\text{Average annual net cash inflow} - \text{Annual depreciation expense}}{\text{Initial investment}}$$

$$= \frac{\$13,000 - \$9,600^*}{\$48,000}$$

$$= \frac{\$3,400}{\$48,000}$$

$$= 7.08\%$$

*Depreciation expense = $48,000 ÷ 5 years = $9,600

Requirement 3

The bar-coding machine proposal passes both initial screening tests. The payback period is slightly less than four years, and the accounting rate of return is slightly higher than 7%. Zetamax should further analyze the proposal using a method that incorporates the time value of money.

How do Managers Compute the Time Value of Money?

A dollar received today is worth more than a dollar to be received in the future. Why? Because you can invest today's dollar and earn extra income. The fact that invested money earns income over time is called the **time value of money,** and this explains why we would prefer to receive cash sooner rather than later. The time value of money means that the timing of capital investments' net cash inflows is important. Two methods of capital investment analysis incorporate the time value of money: the NPV and IRR. This section reviews time value of money concepts to make sure you have a firm foundation for discussing these two methods.

> **3** Use the time value of money to compute the present and future values of single lump sums and annuities

Factors Affecting the Time Value of Money

The time value of money depends on several key factors:

1. The principal amount (p)

2. The number of periods (n)

3. The interest rate (i)

The principal (p) refers to the amount of the investment or borrowing. Because this chapter deals with capital investments, we'll primarily discuss the principal in terms of investments. However, the same concepts apply to borrowings (which you probably discussed in your financial accounting course when you studied bonds payable). We state the principal as either a single lump sum or an annuity. For example, if you want to save money for a new car after college, you may decide to invest a single lump sum of $10,000 in a certificate of deposit (CD). However, you may not currently have $10,000 to invest. Instead, you may invest funds as an annuity, depositing $2,000 at the end of each year in a bank savings account. An **annuity** is a stream of *equal installments* made at *equal time intervals*.[3] An *ordinary annuity* is an annuity in which the installments occur at the *end* of each period.

The number of periods (n) is the length of time from the beginning of the investment until termination. All else being equal, the shorter the investment period, the lower the total amount of interest earned. If you withdraw your savings after four years rather than five years, you will earn less interest. If you begin to save for retirement at age 22 rather than age 45, you will earn more interest before you retire (you let time do the work). In this chapter, the number of periods is stated in years.[4]

The interest rate (i) is the annual percentage earned on the investment. **Simple interest** means that interest is calculated *only* on the principal amount. **Compound interest** means that interest is calculated on the principal *and* on all interest earned to date. *Compound interest assumes that all interest earned will remain invested at the same interest rate, not withdrawn and spent.* Exhibit 12-6 compares simple interest (6%) on a five-year, $10,000 CD with interest compounded yearly (rounded to the nearest dollar). As you can see, the amount of compound interest earned yearly grows as the base on which it is calculated (principal plus cumulative interest to date) grows. Over the life of this particular investment, the total amount of compound interest is about 13% more than the total amount of simple interest. Most investments yield compound interest, so we assume compound interest rather than simple interest for the rest of this chapter.

> ### Why is this important?
>
> "The time value of money is a critical factor in many management decisions. In addition to its use in capital investment analysis, it's also used for personal financial planning (such as retirement planning), business valuation (for purchasing businesses), and financing decisions (borrowing and lending)."

---

[3]An *ordinary annuity* is an annuity in which the installments occur at the *end* of each period. An *annuity due* is an annuity in which the installments occur at the *beginning* of each period. Throughout this chapter we use ordinary annuities since they are better suited to capital budgeting cash flow assumptions.

[4]The number of periods can also be stated in days, months, or quarters. If so, the interest rate needs to be adjusted to reflect the number of time periods in the year.

EXHIBIT 12-6 Simple Versus Compound Interest for a Principal Amount of $10,000 at 6% over Five Years

Year	Simple Interest Calculation	Simple Interest	Compound Interest Calculation	Compound Interest
1	$ 10,000 × 6% =	$ 600	$10,000 × 6% =	$ 600
2	$ 10,000 × 6% =	600	($10,000 + 600) × 6% =	636
3	$ 10,000 × 6% =	600	($10,000 + 600 + 636) × 6% =	674
4	$ 10,000 × 6% =	600	($10,000 + 600 + 636 + 674) × 6% =	715
5	$ 10,000 × 6% =	600	($10,000 + 600 + 636 + 674 + 715) × 6% =	758
	Total interest	$3,000	Total interest	$3,383

Fortunately, time value calculations involving compound interest do not have to be as tedious as shown in Exhibit 12-6. Formulas and tables (or proper use of business calculators programmed with these formulas) simplify the calculations. In the next sections, we will discuss how to use these tools to perform time value calculations.

Future Values and Present Values: Points Along the Time Continuum

Consider the time line in Exhibit 12-7. The future value or present value of an investment simply refers to the value of an investment at different points in time.

EXHIBIT 12-7 Present Value and Future Value Along the Time Continuum

We can calculate the future value or the present value of any investment by knowing (or assuming) information about the three factors listed earlier: (1) the principal amount, (2) the period of time, and (3) the interest rate. For example, in Exhibit 12-6, we calculated the interest that would be earned on (1) a $10,000 principal (2) invested for five years (3) at 6% interest. The future value of the investment is its worth at the end of the five-year time frame—the original principal *plus* the interest earned. In our example, the future value of the investment is as follows:

$$\text{Future value} = \text{Principal} + \text{Interest earned}$$
$$= \$10,000 + \$3,383$$
$$= \$13,383$$

If we invest $10,000 *today*, its *present value* is simply the $10,000 principal amount. So, another way of stating the future value is as follows:

$$\text{Future value} = \text{Present value} + \text{Interest earned}$$

We can rearrange the equation as follows:

$$\text{Present value} = \text{Future value} - \text{Interest earned}$$
$$\$10,000 \quad = \quad \$13,383 \quad - \quad \$3,383$$

The only difference between present value and future value is the amount of interest that is earned in the intervening time span.

Future Value and Present Value Factors

Calculating each period's compound interest, as we did in Exhibit 12-6, and then adding it to the present value to figure the future value (or subtracting it from the future value to figure the present value) is tedious. Fortunately, mathematical formulas simplify future value and present value calculations. Mathematical formulas have been developed that specify future values and present values for unlimited combinations of interest rates (i) and time periods (n). Separate formulas exist for single lump-sum investments and annuities.

The formulas have been calculated using various interest rates and time periods. The results are displayed in tables. The formulas and resulting tables are shown in Appendix 12A at the end of this chapter:

1. Present Value of $1 (Table A, p. 696)—*used for lump-sum amounts*

2. Present Value of Annuity of $1 (Table B, p. 697)—*used for annuities*

3. Future Value of $1 (Table C, p. 698)—*used for lump-sum amounts*

4. Future Value of Annuity of $1 (Table D, p. 699)—*used for annuities*

Take a moment to look at these tables because we are going to use them throughout the rest of the chapter. Note that the columns are interest rates (i) and the rows are periods (n).

The data in each table, known as future value factors (FV factors) and present value factors (PV factors), are for an investment (or loan) of $1. To find the future value of an amount other than $1, you simply multiply the FV factor found in the table by the principal amount. To find the present value of an amount other than $1, you multiply the PV factor found in the table by the principal amount.

Rather than using these tables, you may want to use a business calculator or scientific calculator that has been programmed with time value of money functions. Programmed calculators such as Texas Instruments' TI-83 (Plus) and TI-84 (Plus) make time value of money computations much easier because you do not need to find the correct PV and FV factors in the tables. Rather, you simply enter the principal amount, interest rate, and number of time periods in the calculator and instruct the calculator to solve for the unknown value.

Appendix 12B, at the end of this chapter, shows step-by-step directions for using the TI-83(Plus) and TI-84 (Plus) to perform basic time value of money computations as well as NPV and IRR computations. Instructions for operating other programmed calculators can usually be found on the manufacturer's Web site. In addition, Web sites such as atomiclearning.com offer free online video tutorials for some calculators.

Appendix 12B also shows step-by-step use of these calculators for every problem illustrated throughout the rest of the chapter. As you will see in Appendix 12B, using a programmed calculator results in slightly different answers than those presented in the text when using the tables. The differences are due to the fact that the PV and FV factors found in the tables have been rounded to three digits. Finally, all end-of-chapter material has been solved using both the tables and programmed calculators so that you will have the exact solution for the method you choose to use.

Calculating Future Values of Single Sums and Annuities Using FV Factors

Let's go back to our $10,000 lump-sum investment. If we want to know the future value of the investment five years from now at an interest rate of 6%, we determine the FV factor from the table labeled Future Value of $1 (Appendix 12A, Table C). We use this table for lump-sum amounts. We look down the 6% column and across the 5 periods row and find that the future value factor is 1.338. We finish our calculations as follows:

Future value = Principal amount × (FV factor for i = 6%, n = 5)

= $10,000 × (1.338)

= $13,380

This figure agrees with our earlier calculation of the investment's future value ($13,383) in Exhibit 12-6. (The difference of $3 is due to two facts: (1) the tables round the FV and PV factors to three decimal places, and (2) we rounded our earlier yearly interest calculations in Exhibit 12-6 to the nearest dollar.)

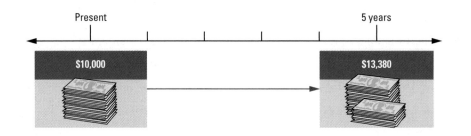

Let's also consider our alternative investment strategy: investing $2,000 at the end of each year for five years. The procedure for calculating the future value of an annuity is similar to calculating the future value of a lump-sum amount. This time, we use the Future Value of Annuity of $1 table (Appendix 12A, Table D). Assuming 6% interest, we once again look down the 6% column. Because we will be making five annual installments, we look across the row marked 5 periods. The Annuity FV factor is 5.637. We finish the calculation as follows:

Future value = Amount of each cash installment × (Annuity FV factor for i = 6%, n = 5)

= $2,000 × (5.637)

= $11,274

This is considerably less than the future value ($13,380) of the lump sum of $10,000 even though we invested $10,000 out of pocket either way.

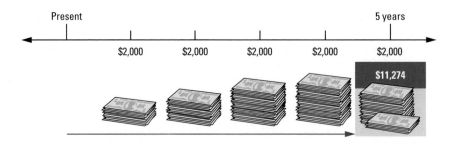

STOP & THINK

Explain why the future value of the annuity ($11,274) is less than the future value of the lump sum ($13,380). Prove that the $11,274 future value is correct by calculating interest using the "longhand" method shown earlier.

 Answer: Even though you invested $10,000 out of pocket under both investments, the timing of the investment significantly affects the amount of interest earned. The $10,000 lump sum invested immediately earns interest for the full five years. However, the annuity doesn't begin earning interest until Year 2 (because the first installment isn't made until the *end* of Year 1). In addition, the amount invested begins at $2,000 and doesn't reach a full $10,000 until the end of Year 5. Therefore, the base on which the interest is earned is smaller than the lump-sum investment for the entire five-year period. As shown here, the $11,274 future value of a $2,000 annuity for five years is correct.

Year	Interest Earned During Year (6%) (rounded)	Investment Installment (end of year)	Cumulative Balance at End of Year (investments plus interest earned to date)*
1	$ 0	$2,000	$ 2,000
2	120	2,000	4,120
3	247	2,000	6,367
4	382	2,000	8,749
5	525	2,000	11,274

*This is the base on which the interest is earned the next year.

Calculating Present Values of Single Sums and Annuities Using PV Factors

The process for calculating present values—often called discounting cash flows—is similar to the process for calculating future values. The difference is the point in time at which you are assessing the investment's worth. Rather than determining its value at a future date, you are determining its value at an earlier point in time (today). For our example, let's assume that you've just won the lottery after purchasing one $5 lottery ticket. The state offers you three payout options for your after-tax prize money:

Option #1: $1,000,000 now

Option #2: $150,000 at the end of each year for the next 10 years

Option #3: $2,000,000 10 years from now

Which alternative should you take? You might be tempted to wait 10 years to "double" your winnings. You may be tempted to take the money now and spend it. However, let's assume that you plan to prudently invest all money received—no matter when you receive it—so that you have financial flexibility in the future (for example, for buying a house, retiring early, and taking vacations). How can you choose among the three payment alternatives when the *total amount* of each option varies ($1,000,000 versus $1,500,000 versus $2,000,000) and the *timing* of the cash flows varies (now versus some each year versus later)? Comparing these three options is like comparing apples to oranges—we just can't do it—unless we find some common basis for comparison. Our common basis for comparison will be the prize money's worth at a certain point in time—namely, today. In other words, if we convert each payment option to its *present value*, we can compare apples to apples.

We already know the principal amount and timing of each payment option, so the only assumption we'll have to make is the interest rate. The interest rate will vary depending on the amount of risk you are willing to take with your investment. Riskier investments (such as stock investments) command higher interest rates; safer investments (such as FDIC-insured bank deposits) yield lower interest rates. Let's assume that after investigating possible investment alternatives, you choose an investment contract with an 8% annual return.

We already know that the present value of Option #1 is $1,000,000. Let's convert the other two payment options to their present values so that we can compare them. We'll need to use the Present Value of Annuity of $1 table (Appendix 12A, Table B) to convert payment Option #2 (since it's an annuity) and the Present Value of $1 table (Appendix 12A, Table A) to convert payment Option #3 (since it's a single lump sum). To obtain the PV factors, we look down the 8% column and across the 10 period row. Then, we finish the calculations as follows:

Option #1

Present value = $1,000,000

Option #2

Present value = Amount of each cash installment × (Annuity PV factor for $i = 8\%$, $n = 10$)
Present value = $150,000 × (6.710)
Present value = $1,006,500

Option #3

Present value = Principal amount × (PV factor for $i = 8\%$, $n = 10$)
Present value = $2,000,000 × (0.463)
Present value = $926,000

Exhibit 12-8 shows that we have converted each payout option to a common basis—its worth today—so we can make a valid comparison of the options. Based on this comparison, we should choose Option #2 because its worth, in today's dollars, is the highest of the three options.

EXHIBIT 12-8 **Comparing Present Values of Lottery Payout Options at *i* = 8%**

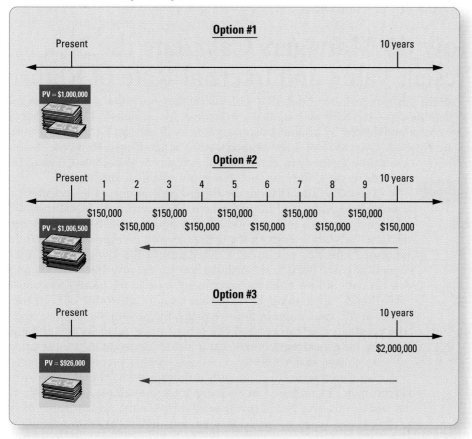

STOP & THINK

Suppose you decide to invest your lottery winnings very conservatively. You decide to invest in a risk-free investment that earns only 3%. Would you still choose payout Option #2? Explain your decision.

Answer: Using a 3% interest rate, the present values of the payout options are as follows:

Payment Options	Present Value of Lottery Payout (Present value calculation, *i* = 3%, *n* = 10)
Option #1...	$1,000,000 (already stated at its present value)
Option #2...	$1,279,500 (= $150,000 × 8.530)
Option #3...	$1,488,000 (= $2,000,000 × .744)

When the lottery payout is invested at 3% rather than 8%, the present values change. Option #3 is now the best alternative because its present value is the highest. Present values and future values are extremely sensitive to changes in interest rate assumptions, especially when the investment period is relatively long.

Now that we have studied time value of money concepts, we will discuss the two capital budgeting methods that incorporate the time value of money: net present value (NPV) and internal rate of return (IRR).

How do Managers Calculate the Net Present Value and Internal Rate of Return?

4 Use discounted cash flow models to make capital investment decisions

Neither the payback period nor the ARR incorporate the time value of money. *Discounted cash flow models*—the NPV and the IRR—overcome this weakness. These models incorporate compound interest by assuming that companies will reinvest future cash flows when they are received. Over 85% of large industrial firms in the United States use discounted cash flow methods to make capital investment decisions. Companies that provide services, such as Cedar Point, also use these models.

The NPV and IRR methods rely on present value calculations to *compare* the amount of the investment (the investment's initial cost) with its expected net cash inflows. Recall that an investment's *net cash inflows* includes all *future* cash flows related to the investment, such as future increased sales and cost savings netted against the investment's future cash operating costs. Because the cash outflow for the investment occurs *now* but the net cash inflows from the investment occur in the *future*, companies can make valid "apple-to-apple" comparisons only when they convert the cash flows to the *same point in time*—namely, the present value. Companies use the present value rather than the future value to make the comparison because the investment's initial cost is already stated at its present value.[5]

Why is this important?

"The NPV method lets managers make an 'apples-to-apples' comparison between the cash flows they will receive in the future from the investment and the price they must currently pay to 'purchase' those future cash flows (the cost of the investment)."

As shown in Exhibit 12-9, in a favorable investment, the present value of the investment's net cash inflows exceeds the initial cost of the investment. In terms of our earlier lottery example, the lottery ticket turned out to be a "good investment" because the present value of its net cash inflows (the present value of the lottery payout under *any* of the three payout options) exceeded the cost of the investment (the $5 lottery ticket). Let's begin our discussion by taking a closer look at the NPV method.

EXHIBIT 12-9 **Comparing the Present Value of an Investment's Net Cash Inflows Against the Investment's Initial Cost**

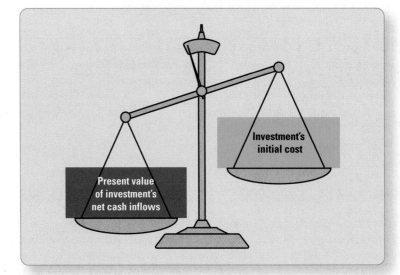

---

[5]If the investment is to be purchased through lease payments, rather than a current cash outlay, we would still use the current cash price of the investment as its initial cost. If no current cash price is available, we would discount the future lease payments back to their present value to estimate the investment's current cash price.

Net Present Value (NPV)

Allegra is considering producing CD players and digital video recorders (DVRs). The products require different specialized machines, each costing $1 million. Each machine has a five-year life and zero residual value. The two products have different patterns of predicted net cash inflows:

	Annual Net Cash Inflows	
Year	CD Players	DVRs
1	$ 305,450	$ 500,000
2	305,450	350,000
3	305,450	300,000
4	305,450	250,000
5	305,450	40,000
Total............................	$1,527,250	$1,440,000

The CD-player project generates more net cash inflows, but the DVR project brings in cash sooner. To decide how attractive each investment is, we find its **net present value** (**NPV**). The NPV is the *difference* between the present value of the investment's net cash inflows and the investment's cost. We *discount* the net cash inflows to their present value—just as we did in the lottery example—using Allegra's minimum desired rate of return. This rate is called the **discount rate** because it is the interest rate used for the present value calculations. It's also called the **required rate of return** or **hurdle rate** because the investment must meet or exceed this rate to be acceptable. The discount rate depends on the riskiness of investments. The higher the risk, the higher the discount rate. Allegra's discount rate for these investments is 14%.

We compare the present value of the net cash inflows to the investment's initial cost to decide which projects meet or exceed management's minimum desired rate of return. In other words, management is deciding whether the $1 million is worth more (because the company would have to give it up now to invest in the project) or whether the project's future net cash inflows are worth more. Managers can make a valid comparison between the two sums of money only by comparing them at the *same* point in time—namely at their present value.

NPV with Equal Annual Net Cash Inflows (Annuity)

Allegra expects the CD-player project to generate $305,450 of net cash inflows each year for five years. Because these cash flows are equal in amount and occur every year, they are an annuity. Therefore, we use the Present Value of Annuity of $1 table (Appendix 12A, Table B) to find the appropriate Annuity PV factor for $i = 14\%$, $n = 5$.

The present value of the net cash inflows from Allegra's CD-player project is as follows:

Present value = Amount of each cash inflow × (Annuity PV factor for $i = 14\%$, $n = 5$)

$$= \$305,450 \times (3.433)$$
$$= \$1,048,610$$

Next, we subtract the investment's initial cost ($1 million) from the present value of the net cash inflows ($1,048,610). The difference of $48,610 is the net present value (NPV), as shown in Exhibit 12-10 (on the next page).

EXHIBIT 12-10 **NPV of Equal Net Cash Inflows—CD-Player Project**

	Annuity PV Factor ($i = 14\%$, $n = 5$)	Net Cash Inflow	Present Value
Present value of annuity of equal annual net cash inflows for 5 years at 14%	3.433* ×	$305,450 =	$ 1,048,610
Investment			(1,000,000)
Net present value of the CD-player project			$ 48,610

*Annuity PV factor is found in Appendix 12A, Table B.

A *positive* NPV means that the project earns *more* than the required rate of return. A *negative* NPV means that the project fails to earn the required rate of return. This leads to the following decision rule:

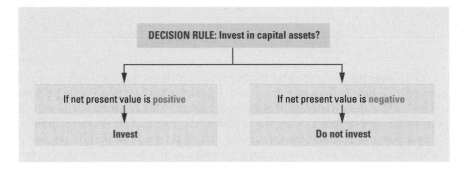

In Allegra's case, the CD-player project is an attractive investment. The $48,610 positive NPV means that the CD-player project earns *more than* Allegra's 14% target rate of return. In other words, management would prefer to give up $1 million today to receive the CD-player project's future net cash inflows. Why? Because those future net cash inflows are worth more than $1 million in today's dollars (they are worth $1,048,610).

Another way managers can use present value analysis is to start the capital budgeting process by computing the total present value of the net cash inflows from the project to determine the *maximum* the company can invest in the project and still earn the target rate of return. For Allegra, the present value of the net cash inflows is $1,048,610. This means that Allegra can invest a maximum of $1,048,610 and still earn the 14% target rate of return. Because Allegra's managers believe they can undertake the project for $1 million, the project is an attractive investment.

NPV with Unequal Annual Net Cash Inflows

In contrast to the CD-player project, the net cash inflows of the DVR project are unequal—$500,000 in Year 1, $350,000 in Year 2, and so forth. Because these amounts vary by year, Allegra's managers *cannot* use the annuity table to compute the present value of the DVR project. They must compute the present value of each individual year's net cash inflows *separately (as separate lump sums received in different years)* using the Present Value of $1 table (Appendix 12A, Table A).

Exhibit 12-11 shows that the $500,000 net cash inflow received in Year 1 is discounted using a PV factor of $i = 14\%$, $n = 1$, while the $350,000 net cash inflow received in Year 2 is discounted using a PV factor of $i = 14\%$, $n = 2$, and so forth. After separately discounting each of the five year's net cash inflows, we find that the *total* present value of the DVR project's net cash inflows is $1,078,910. Finally, we subtract the investment's cost ($1 million) to arrive at the DVR project's NPV: $78,910.

EXHIBIT 12-11   NPV with Unequal Net Cash Inflows—DVR Project

	PV Factor ($i = 14\%$)		Net Cash Inflow		Present Value
Present value of each year's net cash inflows discounted at 14%:					
Year 1 ($n = 1$)	0.877*	×	$500,000	=	$ 438,500
Year 2 ($n = 2$)	0.769	×	350,000	=	269,150
Year 3 ($n = 3$)	0.675	×	300,000	=	202,500
Year 4 ($n = 4$)	0.592	×	250,000	=	148,000
Year 5 ($n = 5$)	0.519	×	40,000	=	20,760
Total present value of net cash inflows					1,078,910
Investment					(1,000,000)
Net present value of the DVR project					$ 78,910

*PV factors are found in Appendix 12A, Table A.

Because the NPV is positive, Allegra expects the DVR project to earn more than the 14% target rate of return, making this an attractive investment.

Capital Rationing and the Profitability Index

Exhibits 12-10 and 12-11 show that both the CD-player and DVR projects have positive NPVs. Therefore, both are attractive investments. Because resources are limited, companies are not always able to invest in all capital assets that meet their investment criteria. For example, Allegra may not have the funds to invest in both the DVR and CD-player projects at this time. In this case, Allegra should choose the DVR project because it yields a higher NPV. The DVR project should earn an additional $78,910 beyond the 14% required rate of return, while the CD-player project returns an additional $48,610.

> **Why is this important?**
>
> "The profitability index allows managers to compare potential investments of different sizes so that they can choose the most profitable investment."

This example illustrates an important point. The CD-player project promises more *total* net cash inflows. But the *timing* of the DVR cash flows—loaded near the beginning of the project—gives the DVR investment a higher NPV. The DVR project is more attractive because of the time value of money. Its dollars, which are received sooner, are worth more now than the more distant dollars of the CD-player project.

If Allegra had to choose between the CD and DVR project, it would choose the DVR project because that project yields a higher NPV ($78,910). However, comparing the NPV of the two projects is valid *only* because both projects require the same initial cost—$1 million. In contrast, Exhibit 12-12 summarizes three capital investment options that Raycor, a sporting goods manufacturer, faces. Each capital project requires a different initial investment. All three projects are attractive because each yields a positive NPV. Assuming that Raycor can invest in only one project at this time, which one should it choose? Project B yields the highest NPV, but it also requires a larger initial investment than the alternatives.

EXHIBIT 12-12   Raycor's Capital Investment Options

	Project A	Project B	Project C
Present value of net cash inflows	$150,000	$238,000	$182,000
Investment	(125,000)	(200,000)	(150,000)
Net present value (NPV)	$ 25,000	$ 38,000	$ 32,000

To choose among the projects, Raycor computes the **profitability index** (also known as the **present value index**). The profitability index is computed as follows:

> Profitability index = Present value of net cash inflows ÷ Investment

The profitability index computes the number of dollars returned for every dollar invested, *with all calculations performed in present value dollars*. It allows us to compare alternative investments in present value terms (like the NPV method) but also considers differences in the investments' initial cost. Let's compute the profitability index for all three alternatives.

Present value of net cash inflows	÷ Investment	= Profitability index
Project A: $150,000	÷ $125,000 =	1.20
Project B: $238,000	÷ $200,000 =	1.19
Project C: $182,000	÷ $150,000 =	1.21

The profitability index shows that Project C is the best of the three alternatives because it returns $1.21 (in present value dollars) for every $1.00 invested. Projects A and B return slightly less.

Let's also compute the profitability index for Allegra's CD-player and DVR projects:

Present value of net cash inflows	÷ Investment	= Profitability index
CD: $1,048,610	÷ $1,000,000 =	1.049
DVR: $1,078,910	÷ $1,000,000 =	1.079

The profitability index confirms our prior conclusion that the DVR project is more profitable than the CD-player project. The DVR project returns $1.079 (in present value dollars) for every $1.00 invested. This return is beyond the 14% return already used to discount the cash flows. We did not need the profitability index to determine that the DVR project was preferable because both projects required the same investment ($1 million).

NPV of a Project with Residual Value

Many assets yield cash inflows at the end of their useful lives because they have residual value. Companies discount an investment's residual value to its present value when determining the *total* present value of the project's net cash inflows. The residual value is discounted as a single lump sum—not an annuity—because it will be received only once, when the asset is sold.

Suppose Allegra expects the CD project equipment to be worth $100,000 at the end of its five-year life. This represents an additional future cash inflow from the CD-player project. To determine the CD-player project's NPV, we discount the residual value ($100,000) using the Present Value of $1 table ($i = 14\%$, $n = 5$) (see Appendix 12A, Table A). We then *add* its present value ($51,900) to the present value of the CD project's other net cash inflows ($1,048,610) as shown in Exhibit 12-13:

EXHIBIT 12-13   NPV of a Project with Residual Value

	PV Factor ($i = 14\%$, $n = 5$)	Net Cash Inflow	Present Value
Present value of annuity	3.433	× $305,450 =	$ 1,048,610
Present value of residual value (single lump sum)	0.519	× 100,000 =	51,900
Total present value of net cash inflows			$ 1,100,510
Investment			$(1,000,000)
Net present value (NPV)			$ 100,510

Because of the expected residual value, the CD-player project is now more attractive than the DVR project. If Allegra could pursue only the CD or DVR project, it would now choose the CD project because its NPV ($100,510) is higher than the DVR project ($78,910) and both projects require the same investment ($1 million).

Sensitivity Analysis

Capital budgeting decisions affect cash flows far into the future. Allegra's managers might want to know whether their decision would be affected by any of their major assumptions. For example consider the following:

- Changing the discount rate from 14% to 12% or to 16%

- Changing the net cash flows by 10%

- Changing an expected residual value

Managers can use spreadsheet software or programmed calculators to quickly perform sensitivity analysis.

Internal Rate of Return (IRR)

The NPV method only tells management whether the investment exceeds the hurdle rate. Since both the CD-player and DVR projects yield positive NPVs, we know they provide *more* than a 14% rate of return. But what exact rate of return would these investments provide? The IRR method answers that question.

The **internal rate of return (IRR)** is the rate of return, based on discounted cash flows, that a company can expect to earn by investing in the project. *It is the interest rate that makes the NPV of the investment equal to zero:*

$$NPV = 0$$

Let's look at this concept in another light by inserting the definition of NPV:

Present value of the investment's net cash inflows − Investment's cost = 0

Or if we rearrange the equation:

Investment's cost = Present value of the investment's net cash inflows

In other words, the IRR is the *interest rate* that makes the cost of the investment equal to the present value of the investment's net cash inflows. The higher the IRR, the more desirable the project. Like the profitability index, the IRR can be used in the capital rationing process.

IRR computations are very easy to perform on programmed calculators (see Appendix 12B). However, IRR computations are much more cumbersome to perform using the tables.

IRR with Equal Annual Net Cash Inflows (Annuity)

When the investment is an annuity, we can develop a formula that will tell us the Annuity PV factor associated with the investment's IRR. We start with the equation given previously and then substitute in as follows:

Investment's cost = Present value of the investment's net cash inflows

Investment's cost = Amount of each equal net cash inflow × Annuity PV factor (*i* = ?, *n* = given)

Finally, we rearrange the equation to obtain the following formula:

$$\frac{\text{Investment's cost}}{\text{Amount of each equal net cash inflow}} = \text{Annuity PV factor } (i = ?, n = \text{given})$$

Let's use this formula to find the Annuity PV factor associated with Allegra's CD-player project. Recall that the project would cost $1 million and result in five equal yearly cash inflows of $305,450:

$$\frac{\$1,000,000}{\$305,450} = \text{Annuity PV factor } (i = ?, n = 5)$$

$$3.274 = \text{Annuity PV factor } (i = ?, n = 5)$$

Next, we find the interest rate that corresponds to this Annuity PV factor. Turn to the Present Value of Annuity of $1 table (Appendix 12A, Table B). Scan the row corresponding to the project's expected life—five years, in our example. Choose the column(s) with the number closest to the Annuity PV factor you calculated using the formula. The 3.274 annuity factor is in the 16% column.

Therefore, the IRR of the CD-play project is 16%.

Allegra expects the project to earn an internal rate of return of 16% over its life. Exhibit 12-14 confirms this result: Using a 16% discount rate, the project's NPV is zero. In other words, 16% is the discount rate that makes the investment cost equal to the present value of the investment's net cash inflows.

EXHIBIT 12-14   IRR–CD-Player Project

	Annuity PV Factor $(i = 16\%, n = 5)$		Net Cash Inflow		Total Present Value
Present value of annuity of equal annual net cash inflows for 5 years at 16%	3.274	×	$305,450	=	$ 1,000,000†
Investment					(1,000,000)
Net present value of the CD-player project					$ 0‡

†Slight rounding error.
‡The zero difference proves that the IRR is 16%.

To decide whether the project is acceptable, compare the IRR with the minimum desired rate of return. The decision rule is as follows:

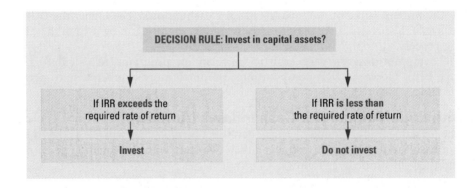

Recall that Allegra's hurdle rate is 14%. Because the CD project's IRR (16%) is higher than the hurdle rate (14%), Allegra would invest in the project.

In the CD-player project, the exact Annuity PV factor (3.274) appears in the Present Value of an Annuity of $1 table (Appendix 12A, Table B). Many times, the exact factor will not appear in the table. For example, let's find the IRR of Tierra Firma's B2B Portal. Recall that the B2B portal had a six-year life with annual net cash inflows of $60,000. The investment cost $240,000. We find its Annuity PV factor using the formula given previously:

$$\frac{\text{Investment's cost}}{\text{Amount of each equal net cash inflow}} = \text{Annuity PV factor } (i = ?, n = \text{given})$$

$$\frac{\$240,000}{\$60,000} = \text{Annuity PV factor } (i = ?, n = 6)$$

$$4.00 = \text{Annuity PV factor } (i = ?, n = 6)$$

Now, look in the Present Value of Annuity of $1 table in the row marked 6 periods (Appendix 12A, Table B). You will not see 4.00 under any column. The closest two factors are 3.889 (at 14%) and 4.111 (at 12%).

Thus, the B2B portal's IRR is somewhere between 12% and 14%.

If we used a calculator programmed with the IRR function, we would find the exact IRR is 12.98%. If Tierra Firma had a 14% hurdle rate, it would *not* invest in the B2B portal because the portal's IRR is less than 14%.

IRR with Unequal Annual Net Cash Inflows

Because the DVR project has unequal cash inflows, Allegra cannot use the Present Value of Annuity of $1 table to find the asset's IRR. Rather, Allegra must use a trial-and-error procedure to determine the discount rate that makes the project's NPV equal to zero. Recall from Exhibit 12-11 that the DVR's NPV using a 14% discount rate is $78,910. Since the NPV is *positive*, the IRR must be *higher* than 14%. Allegra performs the trial-and-error process using *higher* discount rates until it finds the rate that brings the net present value of the DVR project to *zero*. Exhibit 12-15 shows that at 16%, the DVR has an NPV of $40,390; therefore, the IRR must be higher than 16%. At 18%, the NPV is $3,980, which is very close to zero. Thus, the IRR must be slightly higher than 18%. If we use a calculator programmed with the IRR function rather than the trial-and-error procedure, we would find that the IRR is 18.23%.

EXHIBIT 12-15   Finding the DVR's IRR Through Trial and Error

	Net Cash Inflow	PV Factor (for $i = 16\%$)		Present Value at 16%	Net Cash Inflow	PV Factor (for $i = 18\%$)		Present Value at 18%
Year 1 ($n = 1$)	$500,000	×	0.862* =	$ 431,000	$500,000	×	0.847* =	$ 423,500
Year 2 ($n = 2$)	350,000	×	0.743 =	260,050	350,000	×	0.718 =	251,300
Year 3 ($n = 3$)	300,000	×	0.641 =	192,300	300,000	×	0.609 =	182,700
Year 4 ($n = 4$)	250,000	×	0.552 =	138,000	250,000	×	0.516 =	129,000
Year 5 ($n = 5$)	40,000	×	0.476 =	19,040	40,000	×	0.437 =	17,480
Total present value of net cash inflows				$ 1,040,390				$ 1,003,980
Investment				(1,000,000)				(1,000,000)
Net present value (NPV)				$ 40,390				$ 3,980

*PV factors are found in Appendix 12A, Table A.

The DVR's internal rate of return is higher than Allegra's 14% hurdle rate, so the DVR project is attractive.

How do the Capital Budgeting Methods Compare?

We have discussed four capital budgeting methods commonly used by companies to make capital investment decisions—two that ignore the time value of money (payback period and ARR) and two that incorporate the time value of money (NPV and IRR). Exhibit 12-16 summarizes the similarities and differences between the two methods that ignore the time value of money.

EXHIBIT 12-16 Capital Budgeting Methods That *Ignore* the Time Value of Money

Payback Period	ARR
• Simple to compute	• The only method that uses accrual accounting figures
• Focuses on the time it takes to recover the company's cash investment	• Shows how the investment will affect operating income, which is important to financial statement users
• Ignores any cash flows occurring after the payback period, including any residual value	• Measures the average profitability of the asset over its entire life
• Highlights risks of investments with longer cash recovery periods	• Ignores the time value of money
• Ignores the time value of money	

Exhibit 12-17 considers the similarities and differences between the two methods that incorporate the time value of money.

EXHIBIT 12-17 Capital Budgeting Methods That *Incorporate* the Time Value of Money

NPV	IRR
• Incorporates the time value of money and the asset's net cash flows over its entire life	• Incorporates the time value of money and the asset's net cash flows over its entire life
• Indicates whether the asset will earn the company's minimum required rate of return	• Computes the project's unique rate of return
• Shows the excess or deficiency of the asset's present value of net cash inflows over its initial investment cost	• No additional steps needed for capital rationing decisions
• The profitability index should be computed for capital rationing decisions when the assets require different initial investments	

Keep in mind that managers often use more than one method to gain different perspectives on the risks and returns of potential capital investments.

STOP & THINK

A pharmaceutical company is considering two research projects that require the same initial investment. Project A has an NPV of $232,000 and a 3-year payback period. Project B has an NPV of $237,000 and a payback period of 4.5 years. Which project would you choose?

Answer: Many managers would choose Project A even though it has a slightly lower NPV. Why? The NPV is only $5,000 lower, yet the payback period is significantly shorter. The uncertainty of receiving operating cash flows increases with each passing year. Managers often forgo small differences in expected cash inflows to decrease the risk of investments.

Decision Guidelines

Capital Budgeting

Here are more of the guidelines Amazon.com's managers used as they made the major capital budgeting decision to invest in building warehouses.

Decision	Guidelines
Which capital budgeting methods are best?	No one method is best. Each method provides a different perspective on the investment decision.
Why do the NPV and IRR models calculate the present value of an investment's net cash flows?	Because an investment's cash inflows occur in the future, yet the cash outlay for the investment occurs now, all of the cash flows must be converted to a common point in time. These methods use the *present* value as the common point in time.
How do we know if investing in warehouse facilities will be worthwhile?	Investment in warehouse facilities may be worthwhile if the NPV is positive or the IRR exceeds the required rate of return.
How do we compute the net present value (NPV) if the investment has equal annual cash inflows?	Compute the present value of the investment's net cash inflows using the Present Value of an Annuity of $1 table and then subtract the investment's cost.
How do we compute the net present value (NPV) if the investment has unequal annual cash inflows?	Compute the present value of each year's net cash inflows using the Present Value of $1 (lump sum) table, sum the present value of the inflows, and then subtract the investment's cost.
How do we compute the internal rate of return (IRR) if the investment has equal annual cash inflows?	Find the interest rate that yields the following Annuity PV factor: $$\text{Annuity PV factor} = \frac{\text{Investment's cost}}{\text{Amount of each equal net cash inflow}}$$
How do we compute the internal rate of return (IRR) if the investment has unequal annual cash inflows?	Use trial and error, a business calculator, or spreadsheet software to find the IRR.

Summary Problem 2

Recall from Summary Problem 1 that Zetamax is considering buying a new bar-coding machine. The investment proposal passed the initial screening tests (payback period and accounting rate of return), so the company now wants to analyze the proposal using the discounted cash flow methods. Recall that the bar-coding machine costs $48,000, has a five-year life, and has no residual value. The estimated net cash inflows are $13,000 per year over its life. The company's hurdle rate is 16%.

Requirements

1. Compute the bar-coding machine's NPV.
2. Find the bar-coding machine's IRR (exact percentage not required).
3. Should Zetamax buy the bar-coding machine? Why or why not?

Solution

Requirement 1

Present value of annuity of equal annual net cash inflows at 16% ($13,000 × 3.274*)	$ 42,562
Investment	(48,000)
Net present value	$ (5,438)

*Annuity PV factor ($i = 16\%$, $n = 5$).

continued

Requirement 2

$$\frac{\text{Investment's cost}}{\text{Amount of each equal net cash inflow}} = \text{Annuity PV factor } (i = ?, n = \text{given})$$

$$\frac{\$48{,}000}{\$13{,}000} = \text{Annuity PV factor } (i = ?, n = 5)$$

$$3.692 = \text{Annuity PV factor } (i = ?, n = 5)$$

Because the cash inflows occur for five years, we look for the PV factor 3.692 in the row marked $n = 5$ on the Present Value of Annuity of $1 table (Appendix 12A, Table B). The PV factor is 3.605 at 12% and 3.791 at 10%. Therefore, the bar-coding machine has an IRR that falls between 10% and 12%. (*Optional:* Using a programmed calculator, we find an 11.038% internal rate of return.)

Requirement 3

Decision: Do not buy the bar-coding machine. It has a negative NPV and its IRR falls below the company's required rate of return. Both methods show that this investment does not meet management's minimum requirements for investments of this nature.

APPENDIX 12A

Present Value Tables and Future Value Tables
Table A Present Value of $1

Present Value of $1

Periods	1%	2%	3%	4%	5%	6%	8%	10%	12%	14%	16%	18%	20%
1	0.990	0.980	0.971	0.962	0.952	0.943	0.926	0.909	0.893	0.877	0.862	0.847	0.833
2	0.980	0.961	0.943	0.925	0.907	0.890	0.857	0.826	0.797	0.769	0.743	0.718	0.694
3	0.971	0.942	0.915	0.889	0.864	0.840	0.794	0.751	0.712	0.675	0.641	0.609	0.579
4	0.961	0.924	0.888	0.855	0.823	0.792	0.735	0.683	0.636	0.592	0.552	0.516	0.482
5	0.951	0.906	0.863	0.822	0.784	0.747	0.681	0.621	0.567	0.519	0.476	0.437	0.402
6	0.942	0.888	0.837	0.790	0.746	0.705	0.630	0.564	0.507	0.456	0.410	0.370	0.335
7	0.933	0.871	0.813	0.760	0.711	0.665	0.583	0.513	0.452	0.400	0.354	0.314	0.279
8	0.923	0.853	0.789	0.731	0.677	0.627	0.540	0.467	0.404	0.351	0.305	0.266	0.233
9	0.914	0.837	0.766	0.703	0.645	0.592	0.500	0.424	0.361	0.308	0.263	0.225	0.194
10	0.905	0.820	0.744	0.676	0.614	0.558	0.463	0.386	0.322	0.270	0.227	0.191	0.162
11	0.896	0.804	0.722	0.650	0.585	0.527	0.429	0.350	0.287	0.237	0.195	0.162	0.135
12	0.887	0.788	0.701	0.625	0.557	0.497	0.397	0.319	0.257	0.208	0.168	0.137	0.112
13	0.879	0.773	0.681	0.601	0.530	0.469	0.368	0.290	0.229	0.182	0.145	0.116	0.093
14	0.870	0.758	0.661	0.577	0.505	0.442	0.340	0.263	0.205	0.160	0.125	0.099	0.078
15	0.861	0.743	0.642	0.555	0.481	0.417	0.315	0.239	0.183	0.140	0.108	0.084	0.065
20	0.820	0.673	0.554	0.456	0.377	0.312	0.215	0.149	0.104	0.073	0.051	0.037	0.026
25	0.780	0.610	0.478	0.375	0.295	0.233	0.146	0.092	0.059	0.038	0.024	0.016	0.010
30	0.742	0.552	0.412	0.308	0.231	0.174	0.099	0.057	0.033	0.020	0.012	0.007	0.004
40	0.672	0.453	0.307	0.208	0.142	0.097	0.046	0.022	0.011	0.005	0.003	0.001	0.001

The factors in the table were generated using the following formula:

$$\text{Present Value of } \$1 = \frac{1}{(1+i)^n}$$

where:
i = annual interest rate
n = number of periods

Table B Present Value of Annuity of $1

Present Value of Annuity of $1

Periods	1%	2%	3%	4%	5%	6%	8%	10%	12%	14%	16%	18%	20%
1	0.990	0.980	0.971	0.962	0.952	0.943	0.926	0.909	0.893	0.877	0.862	0.847	0.833
2	1.970	1.942	1.913	1.886	1.859	1.833	1.783	1.736	1.690	1.647	1.605	1.566	1.528
3	2.941	2.884	2.829	2.775	2.723	2.673	2.577	2.487	2.402	2.322	2.246	2.174	2.106
4	3.902	3.808	3.717	3.630	3.546	3.465	3.312	3.170	3.037	2.914	2.798	2.690	2.589
5	4.853	4.713	4.580	4.452	4.329	4.212	3.993	3.791	3.605	3.433	3.274	3.127	2.991
6	5.795	5.601	5.417	5.242	5.076	4.917	4.623	4.355	4.111	3.889	3.685	3.498	3.326
7	6.728	6.472	6.230	6.002	5.786	5.582	5.206	4.868	4.564	4.288	4.039	3.812	3.605
8	7.652	7.325	7.020	6.733	6.463	6.210	5.747	5.335	4.968	4.639	4.344	4.078	3.837
9	8.566	8.162	7.786	7.435	7.108	6.802	6.247	5.759	5.328	4.946	4.607	4.303	4.031
10	9.471	8.983	8.530	8.111	7.722	7.360	6.710	6.145	5.650	5.216	4.833	4.494	4.192
11	10.368	9.787	9.253	8.760	8.306	7.887	7.139	6.495	5.938	5.553	5.029	4.656	4.327
12	11.255	10.575	9.954	9.385	8.863	8.384	7.536	6.814	6.194	5.660	5.197	4.793	4.439
13	12.134	11.348	10.635	9.986	9.394	8.853	7.904	7.103	6.424	5.842	5.342	4.910	4.533
14	13.004	12.106	11.296	10.563	9.899	9.295	8.244	7.367	6.628	6.002	5.468	5.008	4.611
15	13.865	12.849	11.938	11.118	10.380	9.712	8.559	7.606	6.811	6.142	5.575	5.092	4.675
20	18.046	16.351	14.878	13.590	12.462	11.470	9.818	8.514	7.469	6.623	5.929	5.353	4.870
25	22.023	19.523	17.413	15.622	14.094	12.783	10.675	9.077	7.843	6.873	6.097	5.467	4.948
30	25.808	22.396	19.600	17.292	15.373	13.765	11.258	9.427	8.055	7.003	6.177	5.517	4.979
40	32.835	27.355	23.115	19.793	17.159	15.046	11.925	9.779	8.244	7.105	6.234	5.548	4.997

The factors in the table were generated using the following formula:

$$\text{Present value of annuity of } \$1 = \frac{1}{i}\left[1 - \frac{1}{(1+i)^n}\right]$$

where:

i = annual interest rate
n = number of periods

Table C Future Value of $1

						Future Value of $1							
Periods	1%	2%	3%	4%	5%	6%	8%	10%	12%	14%	16%	18%	20%
1	1.010	1.020	1.030	1.040	1.050	1.060	1.080	1.100	1.120	1.140	1.160	1.180	1.200
2	1.020	1.040	1.061	1.082	1.103	1.124	1.166	1.210	1.254	1.300	1.346	1.392	1.440
3	1.030	1.061	1.093	1.125	1.158	1.191	1.260	1.331	1.405	1.482	1.561	1.643	1.728
4	1.041	1.082	1.126	1.170	1.216	1.262	1.360	1.464	1.574	1.689	1.811	1.939	2.074
5	1.051	1.104	1.159	1.217	1.276	1.338	1.469	1.611	1.762	1.925	2.100	2.288	2.488
6	1.062	1.126	1.194	1.265	1.340	1.419	1.587	1.772	1.974	2.195	2.436	2.700	2.986
7	1.072	1.149	1.230	1.316	1.407	1.504	1.714	1.949	2.211	2.502	2.826	3.185	3.583
8	1.083	1.172	1.267	1.369	1.477	1.594	1.851	2.144	2.476	2.853	3.278	3.759	4.300
9	1.094	1.195	1.305	1.423	1.551	1.689	1.999	2.358	2.773	3.252	3.803	4.435	5.160
10	1.105	1.219	1.344	1.480	1.629	1.791	2.159	2.594	3.106	3.707	4.411	5.234	6.192
11	1.116	1.243	1.384	1.539	1.710	1.898	2.332	2.853	3.479	4.226	5.117	6.176	7.430
12	1.127	1.268	1.426	1.601	1.796	2.012	2.518	3.138	3.896	4.818	5.936	7.288	8.916
13	1.138	1.294	1.469	1.665	1.886	2.133	2.720	3.452	4.363	5.492	6.886	8.599	10.669
14	1.149	1.319	1.513	1.732	1.980	2.261	2.937	3.798	4.887	6.261	7.988	10.147	12.839
15	1.161	1.346	1.558	1.801	2.079	2.397	3.172	4.177	5.474	7.138	9.266	11.974	15.407
20	1.220	1.486	1.806	2.191	2.653	3.207	4.661	6.728	9.646	13.743	19.461	27.393	38.338
25	1.282	1.641	2.094	2.666	3.386	4.292	6.848	10.835	17.000	26.462	40.874	62.669	95.396
30	1.348	1.811	2.427	3.243	4.322	5.743	10.063	17.449	29.960	50.950	85.850	143.371	237.376
40	1.489	2.208	3.262	4.801	7.040	10.286	21.725	45.259	93.051	188.884	378.721	750.378	1,469.772

The factors in the table were generated using the following formula:

Future Value of $1 = (1 + i)^n$

where:
i = annual interest rate
n = number of periods

Table D Future Value of Annuity of $1

						Future Value of Annuity of $1							
Periods	1%	2%	3%	4%	5%	6%	8%	10%	12%	14%	16%	18%	20%
1	1.000	1.000	1.000	1.000	1.000	1.000	1.000	1.000	1.000	1.000	1.000	1.000	1.000
2	2.010	2.020	2.030	2.040	2.050	2.060	2.080	2.100	2.120	2.140	2.160	2.180	2.200
3	3.030	3.060	3.091	3.122	3.153	3.184	3.246	3.310	3.374	3.440	3.506	3.572	3.640
4	4.060	4.122	4.184	4.246	4.310	4.375	4.506	4.641	4.779	4.921	5.066	5.215	5.368
5	5.101	5.204	5.309	5.416	5.526	5.637	5.867	6.105	6.353	6.610	6.877	7.154	7.442
6	6.152	6.308	6.468	6.633	6.802	6.975	7.336	7.716	8.115	8.536	8.977	9.442	9.930
7	7.214	7.434	7.662	7.898	8.142	8.394	8.923	9.487	10.089	10.730	11.414	12.142	12.916
8	8.286	8.583	8.892	9.214	9.549	9.897	10.637	11.436	12.300	13.233	14.240	15.327	16.499
9	9.369	9.755	10.159	10.583	11.027	11.491	12.488	13.579	14.776	16.085	17.519	19.086	20.799
10	10.462	10.950	11.464	12.006	12.578	13.181	14.487	15.937	17.549	19.337	21.321	23.521	25.959
11	11.567	12.169	12.808	13.486	14.207	14.972	16.645	18.531	20.655	23.045	25.733	28.755	32.150
12	12.683	13.412	14.192	15.026	15.917	16.870	18.977	21.384	24.133	27.271	30.850	34.931	39.581
13	13.809	14.680	15.618	16.627	17.713	18.882	21.495	24.523	28.029	32.089	36.786	42.219	48.497
14	14.947	15.974	17.086	18.292	19.599	21.015	24.215	27.975	32.393	37.581	43.672	50.818	59.196
15	16.097	17.293	18.599	20.024	21.579	23.276	27.152	31.772	37.280	43.842	51.660	60.965	72.035
20	22.019	24.297	26.870	29.778	33.066	36.786	45.762	57.275	72.052	91.025	115.380	146.630	186.690
25	28.243	32.030	36.459	41.646	47.727	54.865	73.106	98.347	133.330	181.870	249.210	342.600	471.980
30	34.785	40.568	47.575	56.085	66.439	79.058	113.280	164.490	241.330	356.790	530.310	790.950	1,181.900
40	48.886	60.402	75.401	95.026	120.800	154.760	259.060	442.590	767.090	1,342.000	2,360.800	4,163.200	7,343.900

The factors in the table were generated using the following formula:

$$\text{Future Value of Annuity of } \$1 = \frac{(1+i)^n - 1}{i}$$

where:
  i = annual interest rate
  n = number of periods

APPENDIX 12B

Using a TI-83, TI-83 Plus, TI-84, or TI-84 Plus Calculator to Perform Time Value of Money Calculations

TECHNOLOGY *makes it simple*

Time Value of Money Calculations
Using a TI-83, TI-83 Plus, TI-84, or TI-84 Plus Calculator to Perform Time Value of Money Calculations:
Steps to perform basic present value and future value calculations:

1. On the TI-83 Plus or TI-84 Plus: Press [APPS] *to show the applications menu.*
   On the TI-83 or TI-84: Press [2nd] [X⁻¹] [ENTER] *to show the applications menu.*
2. Choose **Finance** to see the finance applications menu.
3. Choose **TVM solver** to obtain the list of time value of money (TVM) variables:
   N = *number of periods (years)*
   I% = *interest rate per year* **(do not convert percentage to a decimal)**
   PV = *present value*
   PMT = *amount of each annuity installment*
   FV = *future value*
   P/Y = *number of compounding periods per year* **(leave setting at 1)**
   C/Y = *number of coupons per year* **(leave setting at 1)**
   PMT: **End** or Begin *(leave setting on **End** to denote an ordinary annuity)*
4. **Enter the known variables** and **set all unknown variables to zero** (except P/Y and C/Y, which need to be left set at 1).
5. To compute the unknown variable, scroll to the line for the variable you want to solve and then press [ALPHA] [ENTER].
6. The answer will now appear on the calculator.
7. Press [2nd] [QUIT] *to exit the TVM solver when you are finished.* **If you would like to do more TVM calculations, you do not need to exit. Simply repeat Steps 4 and 5 using the new data.**

Comments:
   i. The order in which you input the variables does not matter.
   ii. The answer will be shown as a negative number unless you input the original cash flow data as a negative number. **Use the [(-)] key to enter a negative number, not the minus key; otherwise you will get an error message.** The calculator follows a cash flow sign convention that assumes that all positive figures are cash inflows and all negative figures are cash outflows.
   iii. The answers you get will vary slightly from those found using the PV and FV tables in Appendix A. Why? Because the PV and FV factors in the tables have been rounded to three digits.

Example 1: Future Value of a Lump Sum
Let's use our lump-sum investment example from the text. Assume that you invest $10,000 for five years at an interest rate of 6%. Use the following procedures to find its future value five years from now:

1. On the TI-83 Plus or TI-84 Plus: Press [APPS] *to show the applications menu.*
   On the TI-83 or TI-84: Press [2nd] [X⁻¹] [ENTER] *to show the applications menu.*
2. Choose **Finance** to see the finance applications menu.
3. Choose **TVM solver** *to obtain the list of time value of money (TVM) variables.*
4. Fill in the variables as follows:
   N = **5**
   I% = **6**
   PV = **–10000** *(Be sure to use the negative number (-) key, not the minus sign.)*
   PMT = **0**
   FV = **0**
   P/Y = 1
   C/Y = 1
   PMT: **End** or Begin

5. To compute the unknown future value, scroll down to **FV** and press [ALPHA] [ENTER].

6. The answer will now appear as **FV** = **13,382.26** (rounded).

If you forgot to enter the $10,000 principal as a negative number (in Step 4), the FV will be displayed as a negative.

Example 2: Future Value of an Annuity

Let's use the annuity investment example from the text. Assume that you invest $2,000 at the end of each year for five years. The investment earns 6% interest. Use the following procedures to finds the investment's future value five years from now:

1. On the TI-83 Plus or TI-84 Plus: Press [APPS] *to show the applications menu.*

   On the TI-83 or TI-84: Press [2nd] [X⁻¹] [ENTER] *to show the applications menu.*

2. Choose **Finance** *to see the finance applications menu.*

3. Choose **TVM solver** *to obtain the list of time value of money (TVM) variables.*

4. Fill in the variables as follows:

   N = **5**

   I%= **6**

   PV = **0**

   PMT = **–2000** *(Be sure to use the negative number (-) key, not the minus sign.)*

   FV = **0**

   P/Y = 1

   C/Y = 1

   PMT: **End** or Begin

5. To compute the unknown future value, scroll down to **FV** and press [ALPHA] [ENTER].

6. The answer will now appear as **FV = 11,274.19 (rounded)**.

If you forgot to enter the $2,000 annuity as a negative number (in Step 4), the FV will be displayed as a negative.

Example 3: Present Value of an Annuity—Lottery Option #2

Let's use the lottery payout Option #2 from the text for our example. Option #2 was to receive $150,000 at the end of each year for the next 10 years. The interest rate was assumed to be 8%. Use the following procedure to find the present value of this payout option:

1. On the TI-83 Plus or TI-84 Plus: Press [APPS] *to show the applications menu.*

   On the TI-83 or TI-84: Press [2nd] [X⁻¹] [ENTER] *to show the applications menu.*

2. Choose **Finance** *to see the finance applications menu.*

3. Choose **TVM solver** *to obtain the list of time value of money (TVM) variables.*

4. Fill in the variables as follows:

   N = **10**

   I%= **8**

   PV = **0**

   PMT = **–150000** *(Be sure to use the negative number (-) key, not the minus sign.)*

   FV = **0**

   P/Y = 1

   C/Y = 1

   PMT: **End** or Begin

5. To compute the unknown future value, scroll down to **PV** and press [ALPHA] [ENTER].

6. The answer will now appear as **PV = 1,006,512.21** (rounded).

Had we not entered the annuity as a negative figure, the present value would have been shown as a negative.

Example 4: Present Value of a Lump Sum—Lottery Option #3

Let's use the lottery payout Option #3 from the text as our example. Option #3 was to receive $2 million 10 years from now. The interest rate was assumed to be 8%. Use the following procedure to find the present value of this payout option:

1. On the TI-83 Plus or TI-84 Plus: Press [APPS] *to show the applications menu.*

   On the TI-83 or TI-84: Press [2nd] [X⁻¹] [ENTER] *to show the applications menu.*

2. Choose **Finance** *to see the finance applications menu.*

3. Choose **TVM solver** *to obtain the list of time value of money (TVM) variables.*

4. Fill in the variables as follows:

   N = **10**

   I%= **8**

PV = **0**

PMT = **0**

FV = **–2000000** *(Be sure to use the negative number (-) key, not the minus sign.)*

P/Y = 1

C/Y = 1

5. PMT: **End** or Begin

6. To compute the unknown future value, scroll down to **PV** and press [ALPHA] [ENTER].

7. The answer will now appear as **PV = 926,386.98** (rounded).

Had we not entered the $2 million future cash flow as a negative, the present value would have been shown as a negative.

TECHNOLOGY *makes it simple*

NPV Calculations

Using a TI-83, TI-83 Plus, TI-84, or TI-84 Plus calculator to perform NPV calculations
Steps to performing NPV calculations:
If you are currently in the TVM solver mode, exit by pressing [2nd] [Quit].

1. On the TI-83 Plus or TI-84 Plus: Press [APPS] *to show the applications menu.*

   On the TI-83 or TI-84: Press [2nd] [X⁻¹] [ENTER] *to show the applications menu.*

2. Choose **Finance** *to see the finance applications menu.*

3. Choose **npv** *to obtain the NPV prompt:* **npv(**.

4. Fill in the following information, paying close attention to using the correct symbols:

   npv (hurdle rate, initial investment*, {cash flow in Year 1, cash flow in Year 2, etc.})

5. To compute the NPV, press [ENTER].

6. The answer will now appear on the calculator.

7. To exit the worksheet, press [CLEAR]. Alternatively, if you would like to change any of the assumptions for sensitivity analysis, you may press [2nd] [ENTER] to recall the formula, edit any of the values, and then recompute the new NPV by pressing [ENTER].

Note: If you would like to find just the present value (not the NPV) of a stream of unequal cash flows, use a zero (0) for the initial investment.

Example 1: NPV of Allegra's CD-Player Project—An Annuity

Recall that the CD-player project required an investment of $1 million and was expected to generate equal net cash inflows of $305,450 each year for five years. The company's discount, or hurdle rate, was 14%.

1. On the TI-83 Plus or TI-84 Plus: Press [APPS] *to show the applications menu.*

   On the TI-83 or TI-84: Press [2nd] [X⁻¹] [ENTER] *to show the applications menu.*

2. Choose **Finance** *to see the finance applications menu.*

3. Choose **npv** *to obtain the NPV prompt:* **npv(**.

4. Fill in the following information, paying close attention to using the correct symbols:

   npv (14, –1000000, {305450, 305450, 305450, 305450, 305450}) *(Be sure to use the negative number (-) key, not the minus sign.)*

5. To compute the NPV, press [ENTER].

6. The answer will now appear on the calculator: **48,634.58** (rounded).

7. [CLEAR] the worksheet or recall it [2nd] [ENTER] for sensitivity analysis.

Example 2: NPV of Allegra's DVR Project—Unequal Cash Flows

Recall that the DVR project required an investment of $1 million and was expected to generate the unequal periodic cash inflows shown in Exhibit 12-11.

1. On the TI-83 Plus or TI-84 Plus: Press [APPS] *to show the applications menu.*

   On the TI-83 or TI-84: Press [2nd] [X⁻¹] [ENTER] *to show the applications menu.*

2. Choose **Finance** *to see the finance applications menu.*

3. Choose **npv** *to obtain the NPV prompt:* **npv(**.

---

*The initial investment must be entered as a negative number.

4. Fill in the following information, paying close attention to using the correct symbols:

   npv (14, –1000000, {500000, 350000, 300000, 250000, 40000}) *(Be sure to use the negative number (-) key, not the minus sign.)*

5. To compute the NPV, press [ENTER].

6. The answer will now appear on the calculator: **79,196.40** (rounded).

7. [CLEAR] the worksheet or recall it [2nd] [ENTER] for sensitivity analysis.

Example 3: Investment with a Residual Value

If an investment has a residual value, simply add the residual value as an additional cash inflow in the year in which it is to be received. For example, assume as we did in Exhibit 12-13 that the CD project equipment will be worth $100,000 at the end of its five-year life. This represents an additional expected cash inflow to the company in Year 5, so we'll show the cash inflow in Year 5 to be $405,450 (= $305,450 + $100,000).

1. On the TI-83 Plus or TI-84 Plus: Press [APPS] *to show the applications menu.*

   On the TI-83 or TI-84: Press [2nd] [X⁻¹] [ENTER] *to show the applications menu.*

2. Choose **Finance** *to see the finance applications menu.*

3. Choose **npv** *to obtain the NPV prompt:* **npv(**.

4. Fill in the following information, paying close attention to using the correct symbols:

   npv (14, –1000000, {305450, 305450, 305450, 305450, 405450}) *(Be sure to use the negative number (-) key, not the minus sign.)*

5. To compute the NPV, press [ENTER].

6. The answer will now appear on the calculator: **100,571.45** (rounded).

7. [CLEAR] the worksheet or recall it [2nd] [ENTER] for sensitivity analysis.

TECHNOLOGY *makes it simple*

IRR Calculations

Using a TI-83, TI-83 Plus, TI-84, or TI-84 Plus calculator to perform IRR calculations

The procedure for finding the IRR is virtually identical to the procedure used to find the NPV. The only differences are that we choose IRR rather than NPV from the Finance menu and we don't insert a given hurdle rate.

Steps to performing IRR calculations:

If you are currently in the TVM solver mode, exit by pressing [2nd] [Quit].

1. On the TI-83 Plus or TI-84 Plus: Press [APPS] *to show the applications menu.*

   On the TI-83 or TI-84: Press [2nd] [X⁻¹] [ENTER] *to show the applications menu.*

2. Choose **Finance** *to see the finance applications menu.*

3. Choose **irr** *to obtain the IRR prompt:* **irr(**.

4. Fill in the following information, paying close attention to using the correct symbols:

   irr (initial investment*, {cash flow in Year 1, cash flow in Year 2, etc.})

5. To compute the IRR press [ENTER].

6. The answer will now appear on the calculator.

7. To exit the worksheet, press [CLEAR]. Alternatively, if you would like to change any of the assumptions for sensitivity analysis, you may press [2nd] [ENTER] to recall the formula, edit any of the values, and then recompute the new IRR by pressing [ENTER].

Example 1: IRR of Allegra's CD-Player Project—An Annuity

Recall that the CD-player project required an investment of $1 million and was expected to generate equal net cash inflows of $305,450 each year for five years. Use the following procedures to find the investment's IRR:

1. On the TI-83 Plus or TI-84 Plus: Press [APPS] *to show the applications menu.*

   On the TI-83 or TI-84: Press [2nd] [X⁻¹] [ENTER] *to show the applications menu.*

2. Choose **Finance** *to see the finance applications menu.*

3. Choose **irr** *to obtain the IRR prompt:* **irr(**.

4. Fill in the following information, paying close attention to using the correct symbols:

   irr (–1000000, {305450, 305450, 305450, 305450, 305450}) *(Be sure to use the negative number (-) key, not the minus sign.)*

---

*The initial investment must be entered as a negative number.

5. To compute the IRR, press [ENTER].

6. The answer will now appear on the calculator: **16.01** (rounded).

7. [CLEAR] the worksheet or recall it [2nd] [ENTER] for sensitivity analysis.

Example 2: IRR of Allegra's DVR Project—Unequal Cash Flows

Recall that the DVR project required an investment of $1 million and was expected to generate the unequal periodic cash inflows shown in Exhibit 12-11. Use the following procedures to find the investment's IRR:

1. On the TI-83 Plus or TI-84 Plus: Press [APPS] *to show the applications menu.*

On the TI-83 or TI-84: Press [2nd] [X⁻¹] [ENTER] *to show the applications menu.*

2. Choose **Finance** *to see the finance applications menu.*

3. Choose **irr** *to obtain the IRR prompt: **irr(**.*

4. Fill in the following information, paying close attention to using the correct symbols:

irr (–1000000, {500000, 350000, 300000, 250000, 40000}) *(Be sure to use the negative number (-) key, not the minus sign.)*

5. To compute the IRR, press [ENTER].

6. The answer will now appear on the calculator: **18.23** (rounded).

7. [CLEAR] the worksheet or recall it [2nd] [ENTER] for sensitivity analysis.

Example 3: Investment with a Residual Value

If an investment has a residual value, simply add the residual value as an additional cash inflow in the year in which it is to be received. For example, assume as we did in Exhibit 12-13 that the CD project equipment will be worth $100,000 at the end of its five-year life. This represents an additional expected cash inflow to the company in Year 5, so we'll show the cash inflow in Year 5 to be $405,450 (= $305,450 + $100,000).

1. On the TI-83 Plus or TI-84 Plus: Press [APPS] *to show the applications menu.*

On the TI-83 or TI-84: Press [2nd] [X⁻¹] [ENTER] *to show the applications menu.*

2. Choose **Finance** *to see the finance applications menu.*

3. Choose **irr** *to obtain the IRR prompt: **irr(**.*

4. Fill in the following information, paying close attention to using the correct symbols:

irr (–1000000, {305450, 305450, 305450, 305450, 405450}) *(Be sure to use the negative number (-) key, not the minus sign.)*

5. To compute the IRR, press [ENTER].

6. The answer will now appear on the calculator: **17.95** (rounded).

7. [CLEAR] the worksheet or recall it [2nd] [ENTER] for sensitivity analysis.

REVIEW

Accounting Vocabulary

Accounting Rate of Return. (p. 675) A measure of profitability computed by dividing the average annual operating income from an asset by the initial investment in the asset.

Annuity. (p. 679) A stream of equal installments made at equal time intervals.

Capital Budgeting. (p. 670) The process of making capital investment decisions. Companies make capital investments when they acquire *capital assets*—assets used for a long period of time.

Capital Rationing. (p. 672) Choosing among alternative capital investments due to limited funds.

Compound Interest. (p. 679) Interest computed on the principal *and* all interest earned to date.

Discount Rate. (p. 687) Management's minimum desired rate of return on an investment; also called the hurdle rate and required rate of return.

Hurdle Rate. (p. 687) Management's minimum desired rate of return on an investment; also called the discount rate and required rate of return.

Internal Rate of Return (IRR). (p. 691) The rate of return (based on discounted cash flows) that a company can expect to earn by investing in a capital asset. The interest rate that makes the NPV of the investment equal to zero.

Net Present Value (NPV). (p. 687) The *difference* between the present value of the investment's net cash inflows and the investment's cost.

Payback. (p. 672) The length of time it takes to recover, in net cash inflows, the cost of a capital outlay.

Post-Audits. (p. 672) Comparing a capital investment's actual net cash inflows to its projected net cash inflows.

Present Value Index. (p. 690) An index that computes the number of dollars returned for every dollar invested, *with all calculations performed in present value dollars*. It is computed as present value of net cash inflows divided by investment; also called profitability index.

Profitability Index. (p. 690) An index that computes the number of dollars returned for every dollar invested, *with all calculations performed in present value dollars*. Computed as present value of net cash inflows divided by investment; also called present value index.

Required Rate of Return. (p. 687) Management's minimum desired rate of return on an investment; also called the discount rate and hurdle rate.

Simple Interest. (p. 679) Interest computed *only* on the principal amount.

Time Value of Money. (p. 679) The fact that money can be invested to earn income over time.

Quick Check

1. Examples of capital budgeting investments could include all of the following *except*
   a. building a new store.
   b. installing a new computer system.
   c. paying bonuses to the sales force.
   d. developing a new Web site.

2. Suppose Amazon.com is considering investing in warehouse-management software that costs $500,000, has $50,000 residual value, and should lead to cost savings of $120,000 per year for its five-year life. In calculating the ARR, which of the following figures should be used as the equation's denominator?
   a. $225,000
   b. $500,000
   c. $250,000
   d. $275,000

3. Using the information from Question 2, which of the following figures should be used in the equation's numerator (average annual operating income)?
   a. $120,000
   b. $20,000
   c. $30,000
   d. $10,000

4. Which of the following affects the present value of an investment?
   a. The interest rate
   b. The number of time periods (length of the investment)
   c. The type of investment (annuity versus single lump sum)
   d. All of the above

5. When making capital rationing decisions, the size of the initial investment required may differ between alternative investments. The profitability index can be used in conjunction with which of the following methods to help managers choose between alternatives?
   a. IRR
   b. ARR
   c. Payback Period
   d. NPV

6. The IRR is
   a. the same as the ARR.
   b. the firm's hurdle rate.
   c. the interest rate at which the NPV of the investment is zero.
   d. none of the above.

7. Which of the following methods uses accrual accounting rather than net cash flows as a basis for calculations?
   a. Payback
   b. ARR
   c. NPV
   d. IRR

8. Which of the following methods does not consider the investment's profitability?
   a. Payback
   b. ARR
   c. NPV
   d. IRR

9. Which of the following is *true* regarding capital rationing decisions?
   a. Companies should always choose the investment with the shortest payback period.
   b. Companies should always choose the investment with the highest NPV.
   c. Companies should always choose the investment with the highest ARR.
   d. None of the above

10. Which of the following is the most reliable method for making capital budgeting decisions?
    a. NPV method
    b. ARR method
    c. Payback method
    d. Post-audit method

ASSESS YOUR PROGRESS

Learning Objectives

 1 Describe the importance of capital investments and the capital budgeting process

2 Use the payback and accounting rate of return methods to make capital investment decisions

3 Use the time value of money to compute the present and future values of single lump sums and annuities

4 Use discounted cash flow models to make capital investment decisions

5 Compare and contrast the four capital budgeting methods

Short Exercises

S12-1 Order the capital budgeting process *(Learning Objective 1)*

Place the following activities in sequence to illustrate the capital budgeting process:
a. Budget capital investments
b. Project investments' cash flows
c. Perform post-audits
d. Make investments
e. Use feedback to reassess investments already made
f. Identify potential capital investments
g. Screen/analyze investments using one or more of the methods discussed

Allegra Data Set used for S12-2 through S12-5:

Allegra is considering producing CD players and digital video recorders (DVRs). The products require different specialized machines, each costing $1 million. Each machine has a five-year life and zero residual value. The two products have different patterns of predicted net cash inflows:

	Annual Net Cash Inflows	
Year	CD Players	DVRs
1	$ 312,500	$ 500,000
2	312,500	350,000
3	312,500	300,000
4	312,500	250,000
5	312,500	40,000
Total	$1,562,500	$1,440,000

Allegra will consider making capital investments only if the payback period of the project is less than 3.5 years and the ARR exceeds 8%.

S12-2 Compute payback period—equal cash inflows *(Learning Objective 2)*

Refer to the Allegra Data Set. Calculate the CD-player project's payback period. If the CD project had a residual value of $100,000, would the payback period change? Explain and recalculate if necessary. Does this investment pass Allegra's payback period screening rule?

S12-3 Compute payback period—unequal cash inflows *(Learning Objective 2)*

Refer to the Allegra Data Set. Calculate the DVR project's payback period. If the DVR project had a residual value of $100,000, would the payback period change? Explain and recalculate if necessary. Does this investment pass Allegra's payback period screening rule?

S12-4 Compute ARR—equal cash inflows *(Learning Objective 2)*

Refer to the Allegra Data Set. Calculate the CD-player project's ARR. If the CD project had a residual value of $100,000, would the ARR change? Explain and recalculate if necessary. Does this investment pass Allegra's ARR screening rule?

S12-5 Compute ARR—unequal cash inflows *(Learning Objective 2)*

Refer to the Allegra Data Set. Calculate the DVR project's ARR. If the DVR project had a residual value of $100,000, would the ARR change? Explain and recalculate if necessary. Does this investment pass Allegra's ARR screening rule?

S12-6 Compute annual cash savings *(Learning Objective 2)*

Suppose Allegra is deciding whether to invest in a DVD-HD project. The payback period for the $5 million investment is four years, and the project's expected life is seven years. What equal annual net cash inflows are expected from this project?

S12-7 Find the present values of future cash flows *(Learning Objective 3)*

Your grandfather would like to share some of his fortune with you. He offers to give you money under one of the following scenarios (you get to choose):

1. $8,000 a year at the end of each of the next eight years

2. $50,000 (lump sum) now

3. $100,000 (lump sum) eight years from now

Calculate the present value of each scenario using a 6% interest rate. Which scenario yields the highest present value? Would your preference change if you used a 12% interest rate?

S12-8 Show how timing affects future values *(Learning Objective 3)*

Assume that you make the following investments:
a. You invest a lump sum of $5,000 for four years at 12% interest. What is the investment's value at the end of four years?
b. In a different account earning 12% interest, you invest $1,250 at the end of each year for four years. What is the investment's value at the end of four years?
c. What general rule of thumb explains the difference in the investments' future values?

S12-9 Compare payout options at their future values *(Learning Objective 3)*

Refer to the lottery payout options on page 685. Rather than compare the payout options at their present values (as is done in the chapter), compare the payout options at their future value 10 years from now.
a. Using an 8% interest rate, what is the future value of each payout option?
b. Rank your preference of payout options.
c. Does computing the future value rather than the present value of the options change your preference of payout options? Explain.

S12-10 Relationship between the PV tables *(Learning Objective 3)*

Use the Present Value of $1 table (Appendix 12A, Table A) to determine the present value of $1 received one year from now. Assume a 14% interest rate. Use the same table to find the present value of $1 received two years from now. Continue this process for a total of five years.
a. What is the *total* present value of the cash flows received over the five-year period?
b. Could you characterize this stream of cash flows as an annuity? Why or why not?
c. Use the Present Value of Annuity of $1 table (Appendix 12A, Table B) to determine the present value of the same stream of cash flows. Compare your results to your answer in Part a.
d. Explain your findings.

S12-11 Compute NPV—equal net cash inflows *(Learning Objective 4)*

Skyline Music is considering investing $750,000 in private lesson studios that will have no residual value. The studios are expected to result in annual net cash inflows of $100,000 per year for the next 10 years. Assuming that Skyline Music uses an 8% hurdle rate, what is net present value (NPV) of the studio investment? Is this a favorable investment?

S12-12 Compute IRR—equal net cash inflows *(Learning Objective 4)*

Refer to Skyline Music in S12-11. What is the approximate internal rate of return (IRR) of the studio investment?

S12-13 Compute NPV—unequal net cash inflows *(Learning Objective 4)*

The local Giant Eagle supermarket is considering investing in self-check-out kiosks for its customers. The self-check-out kiosks will cost $45,000 and have no residual value. Management expects the equipment to result in net cash savings over three years as customers grow accustomed to using the new technology: $14,000 the first year; $19,000 the second year; $24,000 the third year. Assuming a 10% discount rate, what is the NPV of the kiosk investment? Is this a favorable investment? Why or why not?

S12-14 Compute IRR—unequal net cash inflows *(Learning Objective 4)*

Refer to Giant Eagle in S12-13. What is the approximate internal rate of return (IRR) of the kiosk investment?

S12-15 Compare the capital budgeting methods *(Learning Objective 5)*

Fill in each statement with the appropriate capital budgeting method: payback period, ARR, NPV, or IRR.

a. _____ and _____ incorporate the time value of money.

b. _____ focuses on time, not profitability.

c. _____ uses accrual accounting income.

d. _____ finds the discount rate that brings the investment's NPV to zero.

e. In capital rationing decisions, the profitability index must be computed to compare investments requiring different initial investments when the _____ method is used.

f. _____ ignores salvage value.

g. _____ uses discounted cash flows to determine the asset's unique rate of return.

h. _____ highlights risky investments.

i. _____ measures profitability but ignores the time value of money.

Exercises—Group A

E12-16A Identify capital investments *(Learning Objective 1)*

Which of the following purchases would be considered to be capital investments?

Purchase Item	Capital Investment?
a. Land for the new administrative offices will cost $250,000.	
b. Salary costs for the upcoming year are projected to be $2,000,000.	
c. The cost of electricity and other utilities for the manufacturing facility is approximately $575,000 per year.	
d. The construction and installation of special-use machinery to produce a new model of washer is projected to cost $450,000.	
e. The new advertising campaign for the first quarter of the upcoming year will cost $175,000.	
f. Twelve new cars are purchased for a total of $300,000 to expand the fleet of cars used by the salespeople.	
g. New self-scan registers are purchased for all store locations at a total cost of $700,000.	
h. A new network system throughout corporate headquarters will be installed for a cost of $200,000.	
i. The cost of paper and toner for the company printers is projected to be $150,000 for the upcoming year.	
j. The purchase cost plus installation for a second extrusion machine in a plastics recycling firm will be $500,000.	

E12-17A Compute payback period—equal cash inflows *(Learning Objective 2)*

Quiksilver is considering acquiring a manufacturing plant. The purchase price is $1,236,100. The owners believe the plant will generate net cash inflows of $309,025 annually. It will have to be replaced in eight years. To be profitable, the investment payback must occur before the investment's replacement date. Use the payback method to determine whether Quiksilver should purchase this plant.

E12-18A Compute payback period—unequal cash inflows *(Learning Objective 2)*

Sikes Hardware is adding a new product line that will require an investment of $1,500,000. Managers estimate that this investment will have a 10-year life and generate net cash inflows of $315,000 the first year, $285,000 the second year, and $240,000 each year thereafter for eight years. The investment has no residual value. Compute the payback period.

E12-19A ARR with unequal cash inflows *(Learning Objective 2)*

Refer to the Sikes Hardware information in E12-18. Compute the ARR for the investment.

E12-20A Compute and compare ARR *(Learning Objective 2)*

Engineered Products is shopping for new equipment. Managers are considering two investments. Equipment manufactured by Atlas costs $1,000,000 and will last five years and have no residual value. The Atlas equipment will generate annual operating income of $160,000. Equipment manufactured by Veras costs $1,200,000 and will remain useful for six years. It promises annual operating income of $238,800, and its expected residual value is $100,000.

Which equipment offers the higher ARR?

E12-21A Compare retirement savings plans *(Learning Objective 3)*

Assume that you want to retire early at age 52. You plan to save using one of the following two strategies: (1) save $3,000 a year in an IRA beginning when you are 22 and ending when you are 52 (30 years) or (2) wait until you are 40 to start saving and then save $7,500 per year for the next 12 years. Assume that you will earn the historic stock market average of 10% per year.

Requirements

1. How much out-of-pocket cash will you invest under the two options?
2. How much savings will you have accumulated at age 52 under the two options?
3. Explain the results.
4. If you let the savings continue to grow for 10 more years (with no further out-of-pocket investments), under each scenario, what will the investment be worth when you are age 62?

E12-22A Show the effect of interest rate on future values *(Learning Objective 3)*

Your best friend just received a gift of $5,000 from his favorite aunt. He wants to save the money to use as starter money after college. He can (1) invest it risk-free at 3%, (2) take on moderate risk at 8%, or (3) take on high risk at 16%. Help your friend project the investment's worth at the end of four years under each investment strategy and explain the results to him.

E12-23A Fund future cash flows *(Learning Objective 3)*

Janet wants to take the next five years off work to travel around the world. She estimates her annual cash needs at $30,000 (if she needs more, she'll work odd jobs). Janet believes she can invest her savings at 8% until she depletes her funds.

Requirements

1. How much money does Janet need now to fund her travels?
2. After speaking with a number of banks, Janet learns she'll be able to invest her funds only at 6%. How much does she need now to fund her travels?

E12-24A Choosing a lottery payout option *(Learning Objective 3)*

Congratulations! You've won a state lotto. The state lottery offers you the following (after-tax) payout options:

Option #1: $12,000,000 five years from now

Option #2: $2,250,000 at the end of each year for the next five years

Option #3: $10,000,000 three years from now

Requirement

1. Assuming that you can earn 8% on your funds, which option would you prefer?

E12-25A Solve various time value of money scenarios *(Learning Objective 3)*

1. Suppose you invest a sum of $2,500 in an account bearing interest at the rate of 14% per year. What will the investment be worth six years from now?

2. How much would you need to invest now to be able to withdraw $5,000 at the end of every year for the next 20 years? Assume a 12% interest rate.

3. Assume that you want to have $150,000 saved seven years from now. If you can invest your funds at a 6% interest rate, how much do you currently need to invest?

4. Your aunt Betty plans to give you $1,000 at the end of every year for the next 10 years. If you invest each of her yearly gifts at a 12% interest rate, how much will they be worth at the end of the 10-year period?

5. Suppose you want to buy a small cabin in the mountains four years from now. You estimate that the property will cost $52,500 at that time. How much money do you need to invest each year in an account bearing interest at the rate of 6% per year to accumulate the $52,500 purchase price?

E12-26A Calculate NPV—equal annual cash inflows *(Learning Objective 4)*

Use the NPV method to determine whether Salon Products should invest in the following projects:

■ *Project A* costs $272,000 and offers eight annual net cash inflows of $60,000. Salon Products requires an annual return of 14% on projects like A.

■ *Project B* costs $380,000 and offers nine annual net cash inflows of $70,000. Salon Products demands an annual return of 12% on investments of this nature.

Requirement

1. What is the NPV of each project? What is the maximum acceptable price to pay for each project?

E12-27A Calculate IRR—equal cash inflows *(Learning Objective 4)*

Refer to Salon Products in E12-26A. Compute the IRR of each project and use this information to identify the better investment.

E12-28A Calculate NPV—unequal cash flows *(Learning Objective 4)*

Bevil Industries is deciding whether to automate one phase of its production process. The manufacturing equipment has a six-year life and will cost $900,000. Projected net cash inflows are as follows:

Year 1	$260,000
Year 2	$250,000
Year 3	$225,000
Year 4	$210,000
Year 5	$200,000
Year 6	$175,000

Requirements

1. Compute this project's NPV using Bevil Industries' 14% hurdle rate. Should Bevil Industries invest in the equipment? Why or why not?

2. Bevil Industries could refurbish the equipment at the end of six years for $100,000. The refurbished equipment could be used one more year, providing $75,000 of net cash inflows in Year 7. In addition, the refurbished equipment would have a $50,000 residual value at the end of Year 7. Should Bevil Industries invest in the equipment and refurbish it after six years? Why or why not? (*Hint*: In addition to your answer to Requirement 1, discount the additional cash outflow and inflows back to the present value.)

E12-29A Compute IRR—unequal cash flows *(Learning Objective 4)*

Ritter Razors is considering an equipment investment that will cost $950,000. Projected net cash inflows over the equipment's three-year life are as follows: Year 1: $500,000; Year 2: $400,000; and Year 3: $300,000. Ritter wants to know the equipment's IRR.

Requirement

1. Use trial and error to find the IRR within a 2% range. (*Hint*: Use Ritter's hurdle rate of 10% to begin the trial-and-error process.)

   Optional: Use a business calculator to compute the exact IRR.

E12-30A Capital rationing decision *(Learning Objective 4)*

Sheffield Manufacturing is considering three capital investment proposals. At this time, Sheffield Manufacturing has funds available to pursue only one of the three investments.

	Equipment A	Equipment B	Equipment C
Present value of			
net cash inflows...............	$1,695,000	$1,960,000	$2,200,000
Investment.............................	($1,500,000)	($1,750,000)	($2,000,000)
NPV...	$ 195,000	$ 210,000	$ 200,000

Requirement

1. Which investment should Sheffield Manufacturing pursue at this time? Why?

Flint Valley Expansion Data Set used for E12-31A through E12-34A:

Assume that Flint Valley's managers developed the following estimates concerning the expansion (all numbers assumed):	
Number of additional skiers per day	125
Average number of days per year that weather conditions allow skiing at Flint Valley	160
Useful life of expansion (in years)..	8
Average cash spent by each skier per day	$ 240
Average variable cost of serving each skier per day	$ 140
Cost of expansion	$8,000,000
Discount rate..	12%

Assume that Flint Valley uses the straight-line depreciation method and expects the lodge expansion to have a residual value of $960,000 at the end of its eight-year life.

E12-31A Compute payback and ARR with residual value *(Learning Objective 2)*

Consider how Flint Valley, a popular ski resort could use capital budgeting to decide whether the $8 million Snow Park Lodge expansion would be a good investment.

Requirements

1. Compute the average annual net cash inflow from the expansion.

2. Compute the average annual operating income from the expansion.

3. Compute the payback period.

4. Compute the ARR.

E12-32A Continuation of E12-31A: Compute payback and ARR with no residual value *(Learning Objective 2)*

Refer to the Flint Valley Expansion Data Set. *Assume that the expansion has zero residual value.*

Requirements

1. Will the payback period change? Explain and recalculate if necessary.

2. Will the project's ARR change? Explain and recalculate if necessary.

3. Assume that Flint Valley screens its potential capital investments using the following decision criteria:

Will Flint Valley consider this project further or reject it?

Maximum payback period	five years
Minimum accounting rate of return	10%

E12-33A Calculate NPV with and without residual value *(Learning Objective 4)*

Refer to the Flint Valley Expansion Data Set.

Requirements

1. What is the project's NPV? Is the investment attractive? Why or why not?

2. *Assume that the expansion has no residual value.* What is the project's NPV? Is the investment still attractive? Why or why not?

E12-34A Calculate IRR with no residual value *(Learning Objective 4)*

Refer to the Flint Valley Expansion Data Set. *Assume that the expansion has no residual value.* What is the project's IRR? Is the investment attractive? Why or why not?

E12-35A Comparing capital budgeting methods *(Learning Objective 5)*

The following table contains information about four projects in which Hughes Corporation has the opportunity to invest. This information is based on estimates that different managers have prepared about their potential project.

Project	Investment Required	Net Present Value	Life of Project	Internal Rate of Return	Profitability Index	Payback Period in Years	Accounting Rate of Return
A.....	$ 200,000	$ 52,350	5	22%	1.26	2.86	18%
B.....	$ 400,000	$ 72,230	6	25%	1.18	2.96	15%
C.....	$1,000,000	$224,075	3	20%	1.22	2.11	11%
D.....	$1,500,000	$ 85,000	4	13%	1.06	3.00	22%

Requirements

1. Rank the four projects in order of preference by using the
   a. net present value.
   b. project profitability index.
   c. internal rate of return.
   d. payback period.
   e. accounting rate of return.

2. Which method(s) do you think is best for evaluating capital investment projects in general? Why?

Exercises—Group B

E12-36B Identify capital investments *(Learning Objective 1)*

Which of the following purchases would be considered capital investments?

Purchase Item	Capital Investment?
a. The plant manager wants to purchase twelve new forklifts for use in materials management for a total of $660,000.	
b. The company purchases $368,000 of a raw material to be used in the construction of its most popular product.	
c. A company purchased a parcel of land for $550,000; the company's new manufacturing facility will be built on this land next year.	
d. The company has $125,000 in a money market account.	
e. The payroll for the administrative and sales staff is projected to be $580,000 for the upcoming year.	
f. Salespersons for the company are provided with new cars for business use; the cost of these new vehicles is $512,000.	
g. New clothing racks and display shelves are installed in four of the company's retail locations; the total cost of these new displays and their installation is $325,000.	
h. A clothing retailer purchases clothing merchandise for $8,200,000 to be resold in its 20 retail locations.	
i. The company's utility costs for the year are projected to be $800,000.	
j. A merchandiser adds 80,000 square feet of floor space to its flagship store for a total cost of $3,300,000.	

E12-37B Compute payback period—equal cash inflows *(Learning Objective 2)*

McKnight is considering acquiring a manufacturing plant. The purchase price is $2,480,000. The owners believe the plant will generate net cash inflows of $310,000 annually. It will have to be replaced in five years. To be profitable, the investment payback must occur before the investment's replacement date. Use the payback method to determine whether McKnight should purchase this plant.

E12-38B Compute payback period—unequal cash inflows *(Learning Objective 2)*

Walken Hardware is adding a new product line that will require an investment of $1,418,000. Managers estimate that this investment will have a 10-year life and generate net cash inflows of $300,000 the first year, $280,000 the second year, and $250,000 each year thereafter for eight years. The investment has no residual value. Compute the payback period.

E12-39B ARR with unequal cash inflows *(Learning Objective 2)*

Refer to the Walken Hardware information in E12-38B. Compute the ARR for the investment.

E12-40B Compute and compare ARR *(Learning Objective 2)*

Zoom Products is shopping for new equipment. Managers are considering two investments. Equipment manufactured by Preston costs $800,000 and will last for four years with no residual value. The Preston equipment will generate annual operating income of $156,000. Equipment manufactured by Root costs $1,100,000 and will remain useful for five years. It promises annual operating income of $236,500, and its expected residual value is $105,000. Which equipment offers the higher ARR?

E12-41B Compare retirement savings plans *(Learning Objective 3)*

Assume you want to retire early at age 54. You plan to save using one of the following two strategies: (1) save $3,300 a year in an IRA beginning when you are 24 and ending when you are 54 (30 years) or (2) wait until you are 42 to start saving and then save $8,250 per year for the next 12 years. Assume you will earn the historic stock market average of 14% per year.

Requirements

1. How much out-of-pocket cash will you invest under the two options?

2. How much savings will you have accumulated at age 54 under the two options?

3. Explain the results.

4. If you were to let the savings continue to grow for eight more years (with no further out-of-pocket investments), under each scenario, what will the investments be worth when you are age 62?

E12-42B Show the effect of interest rate on future values *(Learning Objective 3)*

Your best friend just received a gift of $5,000 from his favorite aunt. He wants to save the money to use as starter money after college. He can (1) invest it risk-free at 3%, (2) take on moderate risk at 10%, or (3) take on high risk at 14%. Help your friend project the investment's worth at the end of three years under each investment strategy and explain the results to him.

E12-43B Fund future cash flows *(Learning Objective 3)*

Samantha wants to take the next six years off work to travel around the world. She estimates her annual cash needs at $35,000 (if she needs more, she'll work odd jobs). Samantha believes she can invest her savings at 8% until she depletes her funds.

Requirements

1. How much money does Samantha need now to fund her travels?

2. After speaking with a number of banks, Samantha learns she'll be able to invest her funds at 10%. How much does she need now to fund her travels?

E12-44B Choosing a lottery payout option *(Learning Objective 3)*

Congratulations! You've won a state lotto. The state lottery offers you the following (after-tax) payout options:

Option #1: $13,500,000 four years from now

Option #2: $2,050,000 at the end of each year for the next six years

Option #3: $12,500,000 three years from now

Requirement

1. Assuming that you can earn 10% on your funds, which option would you prefer?

E12-45B Solve various time value of money scenarios *(Learning Objective 3)*

Solve these various time value of money scenarios.

1. Suppose you invest a sum of $5,000 in an account bearing interest at the rate of 10% per year. What will the investment be worth six years from now?

2. How much would you need to invest now to be able to withdraw $9,000 at the end of every year for the next 20 years? Assume a 12% interest rate.

3. Assume that you want to have $145,000 saved seven years from now. If you can invest your funds at an 8% interest rate, how much do you currently need to invest?

4. Your aunt Betty plans to give you $3,000 at the end of every year for the next 10 years. If you invest each of her yearly gifts at a 12% interest rate, how much will they be worth at the end of the 10-year period?

5. Suppose you would like to buy a small cabin in the mountains four years from now. You estimate that the property will cost $51,500 at that time. How much money would you need to invest each year in an account bearing interest at the rate of 6% per year in order to accumulate the $51,500 purchase price?

E12-46B Calculate NPV—equal annual cash inflows *(Learning Objective 4)*

Use the NPV method to determine whether Vargas Products should invest in the following projects:

- *Project A* costs $285,000 and offers eight annual net cash inflows of $64,000. Vargas Products requires an annual return of 12% on projects like A.

■ *Project B* costs $390,000 and offers 10 annual net cash inflows of $74,000. Vargas Products demands an annual return of 10% on investments of this nature.

Requirement

1. What is the NPV of each project? What is the maximum acceptable price to pay for each project?

E12-47B Calculate IRR—equal cash inflows *(Learning Objective 4)*

Refer to Vargas Products in E12-46B. Compute the IRR of each project and use this information to identify the better investment.

E12-48B Calculate NPV—unequal cash flows *(Learning Objective 4)*

Fielding Industries is deciding whether to automate one phase of its production process. The manufacturing equipment has a six-year life and will cost $910,000.

Projected net cash inflows are as follows:	
Year 1	$264,000
Year 2	$254,000
Year 3	$222,000
Year 4	$210,000
Year 5	$204,000
Year 6	$178,000

Requirements

1. Compute this project's NPV using Fielding Industries' 16% hurdle rate. Should Fielding Industries invest in the equipment? Why or why not?

2. Fielding Industries could refurbish the equipment at the end of six years for $105,000. The refurbished equipment could be used for one more year, providing $77,000 of net cash inflows in Year 7. Additionally, the refurbished equipment would have a $55,000 residual value at the end of Year 7. Should Fielding Industries invest in the equipment and refurbish it after six years? Why or why not? (*Hint:* In addition to your answer to Requirement 1, discount the additional cash outflows and inflows back to the present value.)

E12-49B Compute IRR—unequal cash flows *(Learning Objective 4)*

Tracey Tables is considering an equipment investment that will cost $965,000. Projected net cash inflows over the equipment's three-year life are as follows: Year 1: $494,000; Year 2: $382,000; and Year 3: $282,000. Tracey wants to know the equipment's IRR.

Requirement

1. Use trial and error to find the IRR within a 2% range. (*Hint:* Use Tracey's hurdle rate of 8% to begin the trial-and-error process.)

E12-50B Capital rationing decision *(Learning Objective 4)*

Bradfield Manufacturing is considering three capital investment proposals. At this time, Bradfield Manufacturing only has funds available to pursue one of the three investments.

	Equipment A	Equipment B	Equipment C
Present value of net cash inflows	$1,690,000	$1,955,000	$2,190,000
Investment	($1,625,000)	($1,700,000)	($1,825,000)
NPV	$ 65,000	$ 255,000	$ 365,000

Requirement

1. Which investment should Bradfield Manufacturing pursue at this time? Why?

Cherry Valley Data Set used for E12-51B–E12-54B.

Assume that Cherry Valley's managers developed the following estimates concerning the expansion (all numbers assumed):	
Number of additional skiers per day	122
Average number of days per year that weather conditions allow skiing at Cherry Valley	162
Useful life of expansion (in years)..	9
Average cash spent by each skier per day .... $	245
Average variable cost of serving each skier per day .... $	135
Cost of expansion	$10,000,000
Discount rate..	10%

E12-51B Compute payback and ARR with residual value *(Learning Objective 2)*

Consider how Cherry Valley, a popular ski resort, could use capital budgeting to decide whether the $10 million Brook Park Lodge expansion would be a good investment.

Requirements

1. Compute the average annual net cash inflow from the expansion.
2. Compute the average annual operating income from the expansion.
3. Compute the payback period.
4. Compute the ARR.

E12-52B Continuation of E12-51B: Compute payback and ARR with no residual value *(Learning Objective 2)*

Refer to the Cherry Valley data in E12-51B. Now assume the expansion has zero residual value.

Requirements

1. Will the payback period change? Explain and recalculate if necessary.
2. Will the project's ARR change? Explain and recalculate if necessary.
3. Assume Cherry Valley screens its potential capital investments using the following decision criteria: maximum payback period of six years, minimum accounting rate of return of 8%. Will Cherry Valley consider this project further or reject it?

E12-53B Calculate NPV with and without residual value *(Learning Objective 4)*

Refer to the Cherry Valley data in E12-51B. Assume that Cherry Valley uses the straight-line depreciation method and expects the lodge expansion to have a residual value of $950,000 at the end of its nine-year life. It has already calculated the average annual net cash inflow per year to be $2,174,040.

Requirements

1. What is the project's NPV? Is the investment attractive? Why or why not?
2. *Assume the expansion has no residual value.* What is the project's NPV? Is the investment still attractive? Why or why not?

E12-54B Calculate IRR with no residual value *(Learning Objective 4)*

Refer to the Cherry Valley data in E12-51B. Assume that Cherry uses the straight-line depreciation method and expects the lodge expansion to have no residual value at the end of its nine-year life. The company has already calculated the average annual net cash inflow per year to be $2,174,040 and the NPV of the expansion to be $2,923,096. What is the project's IRR? Is the investment attractive? Why?

E12-55B Comparing capital budgeting methods *(Learning Objective 5)*

The following table contains information about four projects in which Andrews Corporation has the opportunity to invest. This information is based on estimates that different managers have prepared about the company's potential project.

Project	Investment Required	Net Present Value	Life of Project	Internal Rate of Return	Profitability Index	Payback Period in Years	Accounting Rate of Return
A.....	$ 215,000	$ 42,475	5	22%	1.20	2.87	20%
B	$ 410,000	$ 72,724	6	25%	1.18	2.97	15%
C.....	$1,020,000	$163,812	3	19%	1.16	2.14	13%
D.....	$1,515,000	$ 85,850	4	13%	1.06	3.00	21%

Requirements

1. Rank the four projects in order of preference by using the
   a. net present value.
   b. project profitability index.
   c. internal rate of return.
   d. payback period.
   e. accounting rate of return.

2. Which method(s) do you think is best for evaluating capital investment projects in general? Why?

Problems—Group A

P12-56A Solve various time value of money scenarios *(Learning Objectives 3 & 4)*

1. Jeff just hit the jackpot in Las Vegas and won $25,000! If he invests it now at a 12% interest rate, how much will it be worth in 20 years?

2. Evan would like to have $2,000,000 saved by the time he retires in 40 years. How much does he need to invest now at a 10% interest rate to fund his retirement goal?

3. Assume that Stephanie accumulates savings of $1 million by the time she retires. If she invests this savings at 8%, how much money will she be able to withdraw at the end of each year for 20 years?

4. Katelyn plans to invest $2,000 at the end of each year for the next seven years. Assuming a 14% interest rate, what will her investment be worth seven years from now?

5. Assuming a 6% interest rate, how much would Danielle have to invest now to be able to withdraw $10,000 at the end of each year for the next nine years?

6. Jim is considering a capital investment that costs $485,000 and will provide the following net cash inflows:

Year	Net Cash Inflow
1	$300,000
2	200,000
3	100,000

Using a hurdle rate of 12%, find the NPV of the investment.

7. What is the IRR of the capital investment described in Question 6?

P12-57A Retirement planning in two stages *(Learning Objective 3)*

You are planning for a very early retirement. You would like to retire at age 40 and have enough money saved to be able to draw $225,000 per year for the next 40 years (based on family history, you think you'll live to age 80). You plan to save for retirement by making 15 equal annual installments (from age 25 to age 40) into a fairly risky investment fund that you expect will earn 12% per year. You will leave the money in this fund until it is completely depleted when you are 80 years old. To make your plan work answer the following:

1. How much money must you accumulate by retirement? (*Hint:* Find the present value of the $225,000 withdrawals. You may want to draw a time line showing the savings period and the retirement period.)

2. How does this amount compare to the total amount you will draw out of the investment during retirement? How can these numbers be so different?

3. How much must you pay into the investment each year for the first 15 years? (*Hint:* Your answer from Requirement 1 becomes the future value of this annuity.)

4. How does the total out-of-pocket savings compare to the investment's value at the end of the 15-year savings period and the withdrawals you will make during retirement?

P12-58A Evaluate an investment using all four methods (*Learning Objectives 2 & 4*)

Water World is considering purchasing a water park in San Antonio, Texas for $1,850,000. The new facility will generate annual net cash inflows of $520,000 for eight years. Engineers estimate that the facility will remain useful for eight years and have no residual value. The company uses straight-line depreciation. Its owners want payback in less than five years and an ARR of 10% or more. Management uses a 12% hurdle rate on investments of this nature.

Requirements

1. Compute the payback period, the ARR, the NPV, and the approximate IRR of this investment. (If you use the tables to compute the IRR, answer with the closest interest rate shown in the tables.)

2. Recommend whether the company should invest in this project.

P12-59A Compare investments with different cash flows and residual values (*Learning Objectives 2 & 4*)

Locos operates a chain of sandwich shops. The company is considering two possible expansion plans. Plan A would open eight smaller shops at a cost of $8,450,000. Expected annual net cash inflows are $1,690,000 with zero residual value at the end of 10 years. Under Plan B, Locos would open three larger shops at a cost of $8,400,000. This plan is expected to generate net cash inflows of $1,120,000 per year for 10 years, the estimated life of the properties. Estimated residual value is $980,000. Locos uses straight-line depreciation and requires an annual return of 8%.

Requirements

1. Compute the payback period, the ARR, and the NPV of these two plans. What are the strengths and weaknesses of these capital budgeting models?

2. Which expansion plan should Locos choose? Why?

3. Estimate Plan A's IRR. How does the IRR compare with the company's required rate of return?

Problems—Group B

P12-60B Solve various time value of money scenarios (*Learning Objectives 3 & 4*)

1. Ben just hit the jackpot in Las Vegas and won $45,000! If he invests it now, at a 14% interest rate, how much will it be worth 20 years from now?

2. Jack would like to have $2,500,000 saved by the time he retires 40 years from now. How much does he need to invest now at a 14% interest rate to fund his retirement goal?

3. Assume that Maria accumulates savings of $1.5 million by the time she retires. If she invests this savings at 12%, how much money will she be able to withdraw at the end of each year for 15 years?

4. Hannah plans to invest $2,500 at the end of each year for the next eight years. Assuming a 14% interest rate, what will her investment be worth eight years from now?

5. Assuming a 12% interest rate, how much would Marisa have to invest now to be able to withdraw $13,000 at the end of every year for the next nine years?

6. Nick is considering a capital investment that costs $505,000 and will provide the following net cash inflows:

Year	Net Cash Inflow
1	$298,000
2	205,000
3	96,000

Using a hurdle rate of 10%, find the NPV of the investment.

7. What is the IRR of the capital investment described in Question 6?

P12-61B Retirement planning in two stages *(Learning Objective 3)*

You are planning for an early retirement. You would like to retire at age 40 and have enough money saved to be able to draw $205,000 per year for the next 35 years (based on family history, you think you'll live to age 75). You plan to save by making 10 equal annual install-ments (from age 30 to age 40) into a fairly risky investment fund that you expect will earn 14% per year. You will leave the money in this fund until it is completely depleted when you are 75 years old.

To make your plan work, answer the following:

1. How much money must you accumulate by retirement? *(Hint:* Find the present value of the $205,000 withdrawals. You may want to draw a time line showing the savings period and the retirement period.)

2. How does this amount compare the total amount you will draw out of the investment during retirement? How can these numbers be so different?

3. How much must you pay into the investment each year for the first 10 years? *(Hint:* Your answer from Requirement 1 becomes the future value of this annuity.)

4. How does the total out-of-pocket savings compare to the investment's value at the end of the 10-year savings period and the withdrawals you will make during retirement?

P12-62B Evaluate an investment using all four methods *(Learning Objectives 2 & 4)*

River Wild is considering purchasing a water park in Oakland, California for $2,000,000. The new facility will generate annual net cash inflows of $510,000 for nine years. Engineers estimate that the facility will remain useful for nine years and have no residual value. The company uses straight-line depreciation. Its owners want payback in less than five years and an ARR of 12% or more. Management uses a 10% hurdle rate on invest-ments of this nature.

Requirements

1. Compute the payback period, the ARR, the NPV, and the approximate IRR of this investment.

2. Recommend whether the company should invest in this project.

P12-63B Compare investments with different cash flows and residual values *(Learning Objectives 2 & 4)*

Franks operates a chain of sub shops. The company is considering two possible expansion plans. Plan A would open eight smaller shops at a cost of $8,840,000. Expected annual net cash inflows are $1,600,000, with zero residual value at the end of nine years. Under Plan B, Franks would open three larger shops at a cost of $8,240,000. This plan is expected to generate net cash inflows of $1,250,000 per year for nine years, the estimated life of the properties. Estimated residual value for Plan B is $1,125,000. Franks uses straight-line depreciation and requires an annual return of 8%.

Requirements

1. Compute the payback period, the ARR, and the NPV of these two plans. What are the strengths and weaknesses of these capital budgeting models?

2. Which expansion plan should Franks choose? Why?

3. Estimate Plan A's IRR. How does the IRR compare with the company's required rate of return?

APPLY YOUR KNOWLEDGE

Decision Case

C12-64 Apply time value of money to a personal decision *(Learning Objective 3)*

Ted Christensen, a second-year business student at the University of Utah, will graduate in two years with an accounting major and a Spanish minor. Christensen is trying to decide where to work this summer. He has two choices: work full-time for a bottling plant or work part-time in the accounting department of a meat-packing plant. He probably will work at the same place next summer as well. He is able to work 12 weeks during the summer.

The bottling plant would pay Christensen $380 per week this year and 7% more next summer. At the meat-packing plant, he would work 20 hours per week at $8.75 per hour. By working only part-time, he would take two accounting courses this summer. Tuition is $225 per hour for each of the four-hour courses. Christensen believes that the experience he gains this summer will qualify him for a full-time accounting position with the meat-packing plant next summer. That position will pay $550 per week.

Christensen sees two additional benefits of working part-time this summer. First, he could reduce his studying workload during the fall and spring semesters by one course each term. Second, he would have the time to work as a grader in the university's accounting department during the 15-week fall term. Grading pays $50 per week.

Requirements

1. Suppose that Christensen ignores the time value of money in decisions that cover this short of a time period. Suppose also that his sole goal is to make as much money as possible between now and the end of next summer. What should he do? What nonquantitative factors might Ted consider? What would *you* do if you were faced with these alternatives?

2. Now, suppose that Christensen considers the time value of money for all cash flows that he expects to receive one year or more in the future. Which alternative does this consideration favor? Why?

Discussion & Analysis

1. Describe the capital budgeting process in your own words.

2. Define capital investment. List at least three examples of capital investments other than the examples provided in the chapter.

3. "As the required rate of return increases, the net present value of a project also increases." Explain why you agree or disagree with this statement.

4. Summarize the net present value method for evaluating a capital investment opportunity. Describe the circumstances that create a positive net present value. Describe the circumstances that may cause the net present value of a project to be negative. Describe the advantages and disadvantages of the net present value method.

5. Net cash inflows and net cash outflows are used in the net present value method and in the internal rate of return method. Explain why accounting net income is not used instead of cash flows.

6. Suppose you are a manager and you have three potential capital investment projects from which to choose. Funds are limited, so you can only choose one of the three projects. Describe at least three methods you can use to select the one project in which to invest.

7. The net present value method assumes that future cash inflows are immediately reinvested at the required rate of return, while the internal rate of return method assumes that future cash inflows are immediately invested at the internal rate of return rate. Which assumption is better? Explain your answer.

8. The decision rule for NPV analysis states that the project with the highest NPV should be selected. Describe at least two situations when the project with the highest NPV may not necessarily be the best project to select.

9. List and describe the advantages and disadvantages of the internal rate of return method.

10. List and describe the advantages and disadvantages of the payback method.

Application & Analysis

12-1 Evaluating the Purchase of an Asset with Various Capital Budgeting Methods

In this activity, you will be evaluating whether you should purchase a hybrid car or its gasoline-engine counterpart. Select two car models that are similar, with one being a hybrid model and one being the non-hybrid model. (For example, the Honda Civic is available as a hybrid or a gasoline-engine model.) Assume that you plan on keeping your car for 10 years and that at the end of the 10 years, the resale value of both models will be negligible.

Quick Check Answers

1. *c* 2. *b* 3. *c* 4. *d* 5. *d* 6. *c*
7. *b* 8. *a* 9. *d* 10. *a*

For online homework, exercises, and problems that provide you with immediate feedback, please visit www.myaccountinglab.com.

Basic Discussion Questions

1. Research the cost of each model (include taxes and title costs). Also, obtain an estimate of the miles per gallon fuel efficiency of each model.

2. Estimate the number of miles you drive each year. Also estimate the cost of a gallon of fuel.

3. Given your previous estimates from 1 and 2, estimate the total cost of driving the hybrid model for one year. Also estimate the total cost of driving the non-hybrid model for one year. Calculate the savings offered by the hybrid model over the non-hybrid model.

4. Calculate the NPV of the hybrid model, using the annual fuel savings as the annual cash inflow for the 10 years you would own the car.

5. Compare the NPV of the hybrid model with the cost of the gasoline-engine model. Which model has the lowest cost (the lowest NPV)? From a purely financial standpoint, does the hybrid model make sense?

6. Now look at the payback period of the hybrid model. Use the difference between the cost of the hybrid model and the gasoline-engine model as the investment. Use the annual fuel savings as the expected annual net cash inflow. Ignoring the time value of money, how long does it take for the additional cost of the hybrid model to pay for itself through fuel savings?

7. What qualitative factors might affect your decision about which model to purchase?

Classroom Applications

Web: Post the discussion questions on an electronic discussion board. Have small groups of students choose a hybrid model of car and its gasoline-engine counterpart for the groups to analyze. Students should collaborate to perform the analysis as outlined in the discussion questions.

Classroom: Form groups of 3–4 students. Your group should choose a hybrid model of car and its gasoline-engine counterpart for your group to analyze. Collaborate to perform the analysis as outlined in the discussion questions. Prepare a five-minute presentation that covers your group's responses to the discussion questions.

Independent: Research answers to each of the questions. Turn in a 2–3 page typed paper (12 point font, double-spaced with 1" margins). Include references, including the URLs for sites containing the cost information used in your analysis.

For additional Application & Analysis projects and implementation tips, see the Instructor Resources in MyAccountingLab.com.

In the past 20 years the United States has seen the

proliferation of credit card debt. From 1985 to 2008, total consumer debt grew from $355 billion to $2.6 trillion. As of 2008, the average American household carried nearly $8,700 of credit card debt. Why do people use credit cards? Some people use credit cards simply as a matter of convenience, so they don't have to carry cash or personal checks. But many people use credit cards because they do not have enough funds to pay for the things they need or want. In other words, the cash they generate from their salary or wages is not high enough to cover their expenses (such as food, clothing, housing, and entertainment) and make necessary debt payments (such as monthly car and student loan payments). In the end, credit card debt is incurred because cash inflows are not high enough to cover cash outflows.

Just as cash flows are important to personal finances, they are equally important to a company's finances. To better understand the financial health of a company, we must understand how the company generates cash, and how the cash is being used. That's exactly the kind of information that is presented in the statement of cash flows.

Source: www.money-zine.com/Financial-Planning/Debt-Consolidation/Credit-Card-Debt-statistics/

CHAPTER 13

Statement of Cash Flows

Learning Objectives

1. Classify cash flows as operating, investing, or financing activities
2. Prepare the statement of cash flows using the indirect method
3. Prepare the statement of cash flows using the direct method

As the opening story shows, good cash management is critical to individuals and companies, alike. Managers use cash budgets, as discussed in Chapter 9, to plan for their cash needs. But investors and creditors, who want to understand how the company is generating and using cash, do not have access to internal cash budgets. Rather, they must rely on the company's financial statements to provide them with information on whether the company's cash increased or decreased over the course of the year, and the reasons for the change. In this chapter, we'll discuss how the statement of cash flows presents investors, creditors, and managers with important information on how a company generated and used cash over a given period of time.

What is the Statement of Cash Flows?

Companies prepare four basic financial statements:

1. Income statement

2. Balance sheet

3. Statement of stockholders' equity

4. Statement of cash flows

You are already familiar with the first three statements from your financial accounting course. These statements do not present much information about the company's cash. For example, the balance sheet gives a "snapshot" of the company's ending cash balance, but it does not report *whether* cash increased or decreased during the period or *why*. The **statement of cash flows** is an important and necessary statement because it shows the overall increase or decrease in cash during the period, as well as *how* the company *generated* and *used* cash during the period. Exhibit 13-1 shows the basic format of a statement of cash flows.

EXHIBIT 13-1 **Basic Format of the Statement of Cash Flows**

SportsTime, Inc.
Statement of Cash Flows
For the Year Ending December 31, 2010

Cash provided (or used) by operating activities (itemized list)	$XXX
Cash provided (or used) by investing activities (itemized list)	XX
Cash provided (or used) by financing activities (itemized list)	XX
Net increase (or decrease) in cash	XXX
Cash, beginning of the period	XX
Cash, end of the period	$XXX

Why is cash so important? It is important because anyone involved with the company has certain expectations regarding the company's cash:

- Employees expect payment of their salaries and wages.

- Suppliers expect payment for their products and services.

- Creditors expect to be repaid loans and interest payments.

- Investors expect dividends.

- Governmental taxing authorities expect payment of income and property taxes.

Why is this important?

"The SCF shows "at a glance," how the company generated and used cash during the year, enabling managers, investors, and creditors to predict whether the company can meet its cash obligations in the future."

The statement of cash flows helps all of these stakeholders evaluate how the company has generated and used cash in the past, which in turn helps them predict whether the company will be able meet its cash obligations in the future. It also helps managers understand if the company is generating sufficient cash from its day-to-day operating activities to enable investments in new equipment, new stores, or new businesses. If insufficient cash is being generated from the day-to-day operations of the company to fund these investments, then the company may need to cut back on expenses or planned investments, or consider raising more capital through selling stocks or taking out loans.

Finally, how is "cash" defined on the statement of cash flows? Typically, the statement of cash flows includes all cash and cash equivalents. Cash generally includes petty cash, checking, and savings accounts. **Cash equivalents** include very safe, highly liquid assets that are readily convertible into cash, such as money market funds, certificates of deposit that mature in less than three months, and U.S. treasury bills. Throughout this chapter, any references to cash will include cash and cash equivalents.

Three Types of Activities That Generate and Use Cash

As Exhibit 13-1 shows, the statement of cash flows classifies all business transactions into three different types of activities. These activities are presented on the statement of cash flows in the following order:

Classify cash flows as operating, investing, or financing activities

1. Operating activities

2. Investing activities

3. Financing activities

Let's take a look at the kind of transactions that would fall under each category.

Operating Activities

Operating activities primarily consist of the day-to-day profit-making activities of the company. These activities include such transactions as making or buying inventory, selling inventory, selling services, paying employees, advertising, and so forth. These activities typically affect current asset accounts such as inventory and accounts receivable, as well as current liability accounts such as salaries payable and accounts payable. Operating activities also include *any other activity that affects net income* (not just operating income). Therefore, this category also includes receiving interest income and paying interest expense; recording gains or losses on the sale of property, plant, and equipment; receiving dividend income; and paying for income tax expense. Keep the following rule of thumb in mind when deciding if an activity should be classified as an operating activity:[1]

> **Why is this important?**
>
> "Financial statement readers want to know how much of the company's cash was generated from day-to-day company operations versus how much was raised by selling investments or company stock, or by borrowing money. A company that doesn't raise sufficient cash from operations won't be able to survive in the long-run."

> *Transactions that affect net income, current assets, and current liabilities are classified as operating activities on the statement of cash flows.*

Investing Activities

Investing activities include transactions that involve buying or selling long-term assets. These activities include buying or selling property, plant, or equipment; buying or selling stock in other companies (if the stock is meant to be held for the long term); or loaning money to other companies with the goal of earning interest income from the loan. Keep the following rule of thumb in mind when deciding if an activity should be classified as an investing activity:

> *Transactions that affect long-term assets are classified as investing activities on the statement of cash flows.*

Financing Activities

Financing activities include transactions that either generate capital for the company or pay it back. These activities include selling company stock, issuing long-term debt (such as notes or bonds), buying back company stock (also known as treasury stock), paying dividends to stockholders, and repaying the principal amount on loans. Keep the following rule of thumb in mind when deciding whether an activity should be classified as a financing activity:

> *Transactions that affect long-term liabilities and owner's equity are classified as financing activities on the statement of cash flows.*

---

[1]Since the entire statement of cash flows, including cash flows from operating, investing, and financing activities is needed to explain the change in the company's cash account during the year, the change in the cash account is the only current asset account excluded from this rule of thumb.

Exhibit 13-2 presents a list of common sources and uses of cash and shows how they are classified on the statement of cash flows. We have italicized those items that you may have difficulty remembering because they are not completely intuitive.

For example, consider the following:

- Even though interest income and dividend income is earned from investments, they are both classified as cash flows from operating activities because they *affect (increase) net income.*

- Interest expense occurs because the company has borrowed money, so you might think this is a financing activity. However, it is classified as an operating activity because it *affects (decreases) net income.*

- The cash received or paid for property, plant, or equipment is classified as an investing activity, yet any *gain* or *loss* on the sale is classified as an operating activity because it *affects net income.*

- The *payment* of dividends is a distribution of the company's equity (not an expense on the income statement); therefore, it is classified as a financing activity.

EXHIBIT 13-2 Classification of Activities on the Statement of Cash Flows

Operating Activities
(Cash flows related to the primary, day-to-day profit making activities of the company; these activities affect net income, current assets, and current liabilities)

- Cash received from sale of services or merchandise
- *Cash received from interest income*
- *Cash received from dividend income*
- Cash paid to purchase inventory
- Cash paid for selling, general, and administrative expenses
- *Cash paid for interest expense*
- Cash paid for income taxes
- *Gain or Loss on sale of property, plant, or equipment*

Investing Activities
(Cash flows related to buying and selling investments; these activities affect long-term assets)

- Cash received from sale of property, plant, or equipment
- Cash received from collection of long-term loans
- Cash received from sale of long-term equity (stock) investments
- Cash paid to purchase property, plant, or equipment
- Cash paid for purchasing long-term equity (stock) investments

Financing Activities
(Cash flows related to generating and repaying capital; these activities affect long-term liabilities and owner's equity accounts)

- Cash received from issuing long-term debt (such as notes and bonds)
- Cash received from issuing stock
- Cash received from using a line of credit
- Cash used to pay back long-term debt
- *Cash used to pay dividends*
- Cash used to buy back company stock (treasury stock)

Noncash Investing and Financing Activities

Sometimes companies have significant investing or financing activities that do not involve cash. For example, a company may purchase property, plant, or equipment by issuing common stock to the seller, rather than paying cash. Liabilities, such as bonds or notes payable, may be extinguished by converting them to common stock.

Any significant noncash investing or financing activity must be disclosed in a supplementary schedule to the statement of cash flows or in a footnote to the financial statements. Why? Because these activities will affect *future* cash flows, such as the future payment of dividends and interest. Since financial statement readers use the statement of cash flows to make predictions about future cash flows, they need to be made aware of any noncash investing or financing transactions that took place during the year.

Two Methods of Presenting Operating Activities

The operating activities section of the statement of cash flows may be presented using either the direct or indirect method. These different methods only affect the *format* of the presentation. Both methods result in the *same* dollar figure for the total cash provided by operating activities. Keep in mind that these methods only affect the operating activities section and have no bearing on the investing or financing sections of the statement.

Direct Method

The **direct method** lists the receipt and payment of cash for specific operating activities. For example, the operating activities would list such line items as the following:

- Cash receipts from customers
- Cash payments (to suppliers) for inventory
- Cash payments (to employees) for salaries and wages
- Cash payments for insurance

In essence, the direct method lists many of the same items shown on the income statement, but calculates them on a cash basis, rather than accrual basis. Recall that the **accrual basis of accounting** requires that revenues are recorded when they are earned (when the sale takes place), rather than when cash is received on the sale. Likewise, expenses are recorded when they are incurred, rather than when they are paid. These timing differences give rise to current assets such as accounts receivable and current liabilities such as wages payable. Thus, accrual-based net income almost always differs from the cash basis.

Indirect Method

The **indirect method** begins with the company's net income, which is prepared on an accrual basis, and then reconciles it back to the cash basis through a series of adjustments. This method reconciles net income to the cash basis by adjusting for 1) noncash revenues (such as gains on sale) or expenses (such as depreciation), and 2) changes in the current asset and current liability accounts. For example, an increase in accounts receivable indicates that more sales were made than were collected. Therefore, an adjustment would be made to net income to reflect this increase in accounts receivable.

Which Method is Most Commonly Used?

Recent surveys show that over 98% of companies currently use the indirect method.[2] Why? Because it is easier and, therefore, less costly to prepare. Furthermore, if a company chooses to use the direct method, it must also provide a supplementary schedule reconciling net income to the cash basis. In essence, a company that chooses to use the direct method must also perform the indirect method for a supplementary disclosure.

Currently, the Financial Accounting Standards Board (FASB) and International Accounting Standards Board (IASB) *encourage* companies to use the direct method. However, the boards have jointly proposed that companies be *required* to use the direct method in the future.[3] The outcome of this proposal is uncertain at this time. The second half of the chapter will illustrate both the indirect and direct methods.

[2]American Institute of Certified Public Accountants, *Accounting Trends and Techniques: 2004*, Jersey City, NJ, 2004.

[3]Financial Accounting Standards Board, *Financial Accounting Series Discussion Paper Number 1630-100: Preliminary Views on Financial Statement Presentation*, Norwalk, CT, October 16, 2008, Paragraph 3.70–3.83.

Before you go on, use the decision guidelines and summary problem to review what you have learned so far.

Decision Guidelines

Statement of Cash Flows

The following guidelines present some decisions that need to be made before preparing the statement of cash flows.

Decision	Guidelines
What financial statements should my company prepare?	A set of financial statements includes the 1) income statement, 2) balance sheet, 3) statement of stockholders' equity, and 4) statement of cash flows.
How should my company define "cash" for the statement of cash flows.	The statement of cash flows usually explains changes in both cash and cash equivalents. Cash and cash equivalents include petty cash, checking and savings account deposits, money markets, short–term certificates of deposit, and U.S. treasury bills.
What types of cash flows should be presented on the statement of cash flows?	All cash flows must be classified into one of the following three categories: 1. Cash flows from operating activities 2. Cash flows from investing activities 3. Cash flows from financing activities
How can I tell if a cash transaction should be classified as an operating activity?	Cash flows from operating activities include the day-to-day profit-making activities of the firm. These activities include any transactions that affect net income (including interest income and expense, dividend income, and gains/losses on sale of property, plant, and equipment), current assets, or current liabilities.
How can I tell if a cash transaction should be classified as an investing activity?	Cash flows from investing activities include all transactions that affect long-term assets.
How can I tell if a cash transaction should be classified as a financing activity?	Cash flows from financing activities include transactions that generate capital for the company or pay it back. These transactions affect long-term liabilities and stockholders' equity.
My company purchased a piece of land in exchange for company stock. Since the transaction didn't affect cash, do we include it on the statement of cash flows?	Even though the transaction didn't affect cash this year, it needs to be disclosed because it will affect *future* cash flows. All significant noncash investing or financing transactions need to be disclosed in either a supplementary schedule to the statement of cash flows or in a footnote to the financial statements.
Should my company use the direct or indirect method for presenting the cash flows from operating activities?	Either method is *currently* acceptable. However, if you use the direct method, you must also present a supplementary schedule that is much like the information presented using the indirect method.

Summary Problem 1

Classify each of the following transactions as an operating, investing, or financing activity.

1. Payment of salaries
2. Purchase of land
3. Issuance of stock
4. Repayment of long-term notes
5. Payment of rent
6. Collection of sales revenue
7. Conversions of bonds payable to common stock

8. Loss on the sale of equipment

9. Purchase of another company's stock (to be held for more than one year)

10. Purchase of merchandise inventory

11. Proceeds from the sale of a building

12. Payment of dividends

13. Collection of interest income

14. Purchase of treasury stock (company buys back its own stock)

15. Payment of interest on long-term debt

Solution

Transaction	Type of Activity
1. Payment of salaries	Operating
2. Purchase of land	Investing
3. Issuance of stock	Financing
4. Repayment of long-term notes	Financing
5. Payment of rent	Operating
6. Collection of sales revenue	Operating
7. Conversion of bonds payable to common stock	Noncash Financing and Investing; must be disclosed even though it doesn't use cash
8. Loss on the sale of equipment	Operating
9. Purchase of another company's stock (to be held for more than one year)	Investing
10. Purchase of merchandise inventory	Operating
11. Proceeds from the sale of a building	Investing
12. Payment of dividends	Financing
13. Collection of interest income	Operating
14. Purchase of treasury stock (company buys back its own stock)	Financing
15. Payment of interest on long-term debt	Operating

How is the Statement of Cash Flows Prepared Using the Indirect Method?

In this section, we'll use the indirect method to prepare the statement of cash flows for SportsTime, Inc., a regional retailer of sporting goods equipment.

> Prepare the statement of cash flows using the indirect method **2**

Information Needed to Prepare the Statement of Cash Flows

In order to prepare the statement of cash flows, the following company information is needed:

1. Income statement for the current year

2. **Comparative balance sheets** (balance sheets for the end of the current year and prior year)

3. Miscellaneous additional information relating to investing and financing transactions

Exhibit 13-3 presents SportsTime's income statement while Exhibit 13-4 presents the company's comparative balance sheets. Additional information about the company's investing and financing transactions will be presented as needed throughout the remainder of the chapter.

EXHIBIT 13-3   Income Statement

SportsTime, Inc.
Income Statement
For the Year Ended December 31, 2010

Sales revenue		$9,500,000
Cost of goods sold		7,125,000
Gross profit		2,375,000
Operating expenses:		
Salaries and wages expense	$580,000	
Insurance expense	25,000	
Depreciation expense	142,000	
Other operating expenses	230,000	977,000
Operating income		1,398,000
Other income and expenses:		
Interest expense	60,000	
Gain on sale of PP&E	1,000	59,000
Income before taxes		1,339,000
Income tax expense		401,700
Net income		$ 937,300

Why is this important?

"Most companies currently use the indirect method, so understanding how it is prepared and interpreted is crucial. This method highlights the differences between accrual based net income and the cash basis."

Preparing the Cash Flows from Operating Activities

The indirect method requires that we begin the operating activities section with the company's accrual based net income, which is found on the income statement. Then, we make all adjustments needed to convert, or reconcile net income back to a cash basis. These adjustments will include the following:

- Noncash expenses and revenues (found on the income statement)
- Changes in the current asset accounts (found on the comparative balance sheets)
- Changes in the current liability accounts (found on the comparative balance sheets)

Noncash Expenses

Depreciation expense is perhaps the most common noncash expense found on the income statement. Depreciation is simply the systematic write-off of the cost of plant and equipment over time. No cash actually trades hands when depreciation expense is recorded. Since depreciation expense reduced net income by $142,000 (Exhibit 13-3), but didn't use cash, we must *add it back* to net income in order to convert net income back to the cash basis. Therefore, we begin our statement of cash flows by adding back depreciation expense, as shown (in blue) in Exhibit 13-5.

We would also add back any amortization (of intangible assets) or depletion (of natural resources) expense for the same reason. SportsTime's income statement does not show any amortization or depletion expense, so these adjustments are not needed.

EXHIBIT 13-4 **Comparative Balance Sheets**

SportsTime, Inc.
Balance Sheets
December 31, 2010 and 2009

	2010	2009	Change Increase/ (Decrease)
Assets			
Current assets:			
Cash	$ 203,500	$ 125,000	$ 78,500
Accounts receivable....................................	365,000	330,000	35,000
Inventory...	632,000	657,000	(25,000)
Prepaid insurance	20,000	15,000	5,000
Total current assets	1,220,500	1,127,000	
Property, plant, and equipment	3,415,000	2,900,000	515,000
Less accumulated depreciation	(499,000)	(380,000)	119,000
Investments	285,000	185,000	100,000
Total assets...	$4,421,500	$3,832,000	
Liabilities			
Current liabilities:			
Accounts payable	$ 245,000	$ 285,000	(40,000)
Wages payable..	57,000	48,500	8,500
Interest payable	3,000	8,000	(5,000)
Income taxes payable	146,700	120,000	26,700
Other accrued expenses payable.................	15,500	28,500	(13,000)
Total current liabilities	467,200	490,000	
Long-term liabilities....................................	550,000	750,000	(200,000)
Total liabilities	1,017,200	1,240,000	
Stockholders' equity			
Common stock..	1,100,000	1,100,000	0
Retained earnings..	2,304,300	1,492,000	812,300
Total Stockholders' equity..........................	3,404,300	2,592,000	
Total liabilities and equity..........................	$4,421,500	$3,832,000	

EXHIBIT 13-5 **Adjusting Net Income for Depreciation Expense**

SportsTime, Inc.
Statement of Cash Flows—Indirect Method
For the Year Ended December 31, 2010

Operating Activities		
Net income...		$937,300
Adjustments to reconcile net income to cash basis:		
Depreciation expense	142,000	

Noncash Revenues

The income statement in Exhibit 13-3 shows a $1,000 gain on the sale of property, plant, and equipment (PP&E). A gain on the sale arises when the equipment is sold for *more* than its net book value. The **net book value** is the original cost of the equipment less its accumulated depreciation. Let's assume that SportsTime sold some old display shelves and dressing room chairs for $3,000. Company records indicate that this equipment originally cost $25,000 and that at the time of sale, accumulated depreciation on this equipment totaled $23,000. The gain on sale would have been calculated as follows:

Sale price of equipment		$3,000
Original cost of the equipment	$25,000	
Less: Accumulated depreciation	23,000	
Net book value of equipment		2,000
Gain on sale		$1,000

The actual cash received on the sale ($3,000) will be reported as a source of cash in the investing section of the statement of cash flows. But the $1,000 gain, which increased accrual based net income, does not actually represent cash received. Therefore, the $1,000 gain must be deducted from net income to convert it back to the cash basis. Exhibit 13-6 incorporates this gain (in blue) on our developing statement of cash flows.

EXHIBIT 13-6 **Adjusting Net Income for Gain on Sale**

SportsTime, Inc. Statement of Cash Flows—Indirect Method For the Year Ended December 31, 2010		
Operating Activities:		
Net income		$937,300
Adjustments to reconcile net income to cash basis:		
Depreciation expense	142,000	
Gain on sale of equipment	(1,000)	

Conversely, a loss on the sale of equipment would have occurred if the equipment was sold for *less* than the equipment's net book value. Since a loss doesn't represent a payout of cash (in fact, cash is received for the sale) we would *add back the loss* to net income to convert it back to the cash basis.

Changes in Current Asset Accounts

The next step in preparing the statement of cash flows is to adjust net income for any changes in current asset accounts. The comparative balance sheets in Exhibit 13-4 shows that the balance in all current asset accounts changed over the year. Remember, the entire statement of cash flows is attempting to explain the change in the cash account. So, we will need to analyze the changes to all current asset accounts *except* for cash.

Let's first look at those accounts that had *increases* over the course of the year: accounts receivable and prepaid insurance.

ACCOUNTS RECEIVABLE   Exhibit 13-4 shows a $35,000 increase in accounts receivable. An *increase* in accounts receivable indicates that *more* sales were made than were collected. To reconcile net income back to the cash basis, we need to subtract any sales that were not yet collected in cash. To do so, we *subtract* the $35,000 *increase* in accounts receivable from net income.

PREPAID INSURANCE   Exhibit 13-4 shows a $5,000 increase in prepaid insurance. An *increase* in prepaid insurance indicates that the company *paid more* for insurance than was recorded as insurance expense. To reconcile net income to the cash basis, we need to subtract more than was expensed. To do so, we *subtract* the $5,000 *increase* in prepaid insurance from net income.

Exhibit 13-7 illustrates the general rule for reconciling net income to cash for *increases* in any current asset accounts.

EXHIBIT 13-7 **General Rule for Increases in Current Asset Accounts**

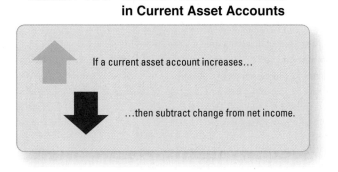

Now let's look at an example of a current asset account that decreased over the course of the year.

INVENTORY   Exhibit 13-4 shows a $25,000 *decrease* in inventory. The *decrease* in inventory indicates that the company sold more merchandise inventory than it purchased. Its inventory level shrunk. So the Cost of Goods Sold expensed on the income statement is greater than the cash paid to purchase the merchandise from the company's suppliers. To reconcile net income back to the cash basis, we need to subtract less than the amount expensed. To do so, we *add back* the $25,000 *decrease* in inventory to net income.

Exhibit 13-8 illustrates the general rule for reconciling net income to cash for *decreases* in any current asset accounts.

EXHIBIT 13-8 **General Rule for Decreases in Current Asset Accounts**

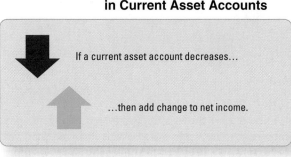

The general rule of thumb for current asset accounts is as follows:

- *If a current asset account **increases**, then **subtract** the change from net income.*
- *If a current asset account **decreases**, then **add** the change to net income.*

Notice that for changes in current assets, we reconcile net income back to the cash basis by adjusting in the *opposite* direction.

Exhibit 13-9 illustrates our developing statement of cash flows after incorporating changes in the current asset accounts (in blue).

EXHIBIT 13-9 **Adjusting Net Income for Changes in Current Asset Accounts**

SportsTime, Inc.
Statement of Cash Flows—Indirect Method
For the Year Ended December 31, 2010

Operating Activities:		
Net income...		$937,300
Adjustments to reconcile net income to cash basis:		
Depreciation expense	142,000	
Gain on sale of equipment	(1,000)	
Increase in accounts receivable..	(35,000)	
Decrease in inventory...	25,000	
Increase in prepaid insurance	(5,000)	

Changes in Current Liability Accounts

Now let's take a look at one current liability account that decreased over the course of the year (interest payable), and another than increased (wages payable).

INTEREST PAYABLE   Exhibit 13-4 shows a $5,000 *decrease* in interest payable. An *decrease* in interest payable indicates that the company paid out more than it expensed for interest expense during the year. Therefore, to reconcile net income to the cash basis, we need to subtract *more* than was expensed. To do so, we subtract the $5,000 decrease in interest payable from net income.

The general rule of thumb for *decreases* in current liabilities is pictured in Exhibit 13-10.

EXHIBIT 13-10 **General Rule for Decreases in Current Liability Accounts**

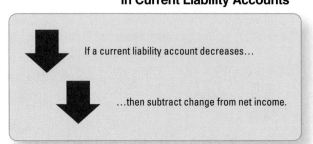

If a current liability account decreases...

...then subtract change from net income.

WAGES PAYABLE   Exhibit 13-4 shows a $8,500 *increase* in wages payable. An *increase* in wages payable indicates that more wage expense was incurred than was paid. To reconcile net income to the cash basis, we need to subtract *less* than was expensed. Therefore, we need to add back the $8,500 increase in wages payable to net income.

The general rule of thumb for *increases* in current liabilities is pictured in Exhibit 13-11.

EXHIBIT 13-11 **General Rule for Increases in Current Liability Accounts**

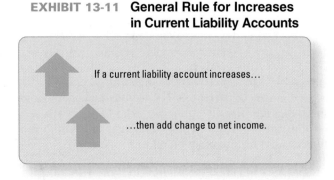

If a current liability account increases...

...then add change to net income.

The general rule of thumb for current liability accounts is as follows:

> • If a current liability account **increases**, then **add** the change to net income.
> • If a current liability account **decreases**, then **subtract** the change from net income.

Notice that for changes in current liabilities, we reconcile net income back to the cash basis by adjusting in the *same* direction. The adjustments for changes in current liability accounts are pictured in blue in Exhibit 13-12.

Interpreting Cash Flows from Operating Activities

Exhibit 13-12 shows the completed operating activities section of the statement of cash flows. As you can see, the day-to-day profit making activities of the company have generated over $1 million in cash during the year. That's a positive sign—a company that is not providing cash from operating activities can't survive in the long-run. It also shows that cash was drained by allowing accounts receivable to increase and by paying down many of the company's current liabilities (such as accounts payable, interest payable, and other accrued expenses). Finally, this reconciliation shows that cash provided by operations was $103,200 higher than net income, once again showing that accrual based net income differs from the cash basis.

EXHIBIT 13-12   Cash Flows from Operating Activities (Indirect Method)

SportsTime, Inc.		
Statement of Cash Flows—Operating Activities (Indirect Method)		
For the Year Ended December 31, 2010		
Operating Activities:		
Net income		$937,300
Adjustments to reconcile net income to cash basis:		
Depreciation expense	142,000	
Gain on sale of equipment	(1,000)	
Increase in accounts receivable	(35,000)	
Decrease in inventory	25,000	
Increase in prepaid insurance	(5,000)	
Decrease in accounts payable	(40,000)	
Increase in wages payable	8,500	
Decrease in interest payable	(5,000)	
Increase in income taxes payable	26,700	
Decrease in other accrued expenses payable	(13,000)	103,200
Net cash provided by operating activities		1,040,500

Now that we have prepared the operating section (using the indirect method), let's take a look at how we prepare the investing and financing sections.

Preparing the Cash Flows from Investing Activities

Recall that transactions affecting long-term asset accounts are classified as investing activities. So the first step in preparing the investing section is to determine whether any changes occurred in the long-term assets accounts during the year. The comparative balance sheets presented in Exhibit 13-4 show changes in three long-term asset accounts:

1. Property, Plant, and Equipment—increase of $515,000

2. Accumulated Depreciation (a contra asset to Property, Plant, and Equipment)—increase of $119,000

3. Investments—increase of $100,000

After noting these changes, we would need to delve into the company's records (such as the general journal) to find more information about these investing activities. The following additional information was found:

a. Equipment originally costing $25,000 was sold for $3,000. The equipment had accumulated depreciation of $23,000, resulting in a gain of $1,000.

b. The company purchased $100,000 of stock in XYZ company. No stock investments were sold during the year.

Now let's see how we use this information to sort out investment activities that took place during the year.

Property, Plant, and Equipment

By analyzing the change in this account, we can figure out how much cash the company paid for new property, plant, and equipment (PP&E) during the year:

Beginning balance, PP&E (from Exhibit 13-4)	$2,900,000
Plus: Purchases of PP&E	?
Less: Original cost of equipment sold (from the additional	
information given)..	(25,000)
Ending balance, PP&E (from Exhibit 13-4)....................................	$3,415,000

We can illustrate this relationship in the form of an equation, and then solve for the unknown amount:

$$\text{Beginning PP\&E} + \text{Purchases of PP\&E} - \text{PPE sold} = \text{Ending PP\&E}$$
$$\$2,900,000 \quad + \quad ??? \quad - \$25,000 = \$3,415,000$$

We can rearrange the equation as follows:

$$\text{Purchases of PP\&E} = \$3,415,000 + \$25,000 - \$2,900,000$$

Solving the equation yields the following:

$$\text{Purchases of PP\&E} = \$540,000$$

On the statement of cash flows, we will show that $540,000 was used to purchase new property, plant, and equipment. Additionally, the sale of the old equipment for $3,000 will be shown as a *receipt* of cash. Notice that the statement of cash flows doesn't just show the net change in the Property, Plant, and Equipment account. Rather, the company needs to show separate line items for new investments purchased and old investments sold.

Accumulated Depreciation

This account is reconciled as follows:

Beginning balance, Accumulated depreciation (Exhibit 13-4)..............	$380,000
Plus: Depreciation expense (Exhibit 13-3)...	142,000
Less: Accumulated depreciation on sold equipment (from the additional	
information given)...	(23,000)
Ending balance, Accumulated depreciation (Exhibit 13-4)..................	$499,000

We already accounted for the depreciation expense as an adjustment to net income in the operating activities section of the statement of cash flows. Likewise, the accumulated depreciation on the sold equipment was taken into account in calculating the gain on sale. This too, became an adjustment to net income in the operating activities section. Since we have completely reconciled the change in this account and have already made the necessary adjustments, no other adjustments are needed.

Investments

Changes in long term investments are analyzed as follows:

Beginning balance, Investments (Exhibit 13-4)	$185,000
Plus: Purchases of stock investments (from the additional information given)	?
Less: Sale of stock investments	?
Ending balance, Investments (Exhibit 13-4)	$285,000

According to the additional information given, SportsTime purchased $100,000 of new stock investments during the year, and did not sell any. Therefore, the investment account is completely reconciled as follows:

Beginning investments + Purchases of investments − Investments sold = Ending investments

| $185,000 | + | $100,000 | − | $0 | = | $285,000 |

Any purchase or sale of long-term investments needs to be listed *separately* on the statement of cash flows. Keep in mind that if the company had sold some investments for an amount that differed from the original purchase price, a gain or loss would have resulted. This gain or loss would be shown as an adjustment to net income in the operating section of the statement, much like a gain or loss on the sale of property, plant, or equipment.

Now that we have analyzed the changes in each long-term asset account, we can prepare the investing section of the statement of cash flows. Exhibit 13-13 shows that the company used much of the cash it generated from operations ($1,040,500, from Exhibit 13-12) to pay for new investments in property, plant, and equipment ($540,000) and new stock investments ($100,000).

EXHIBIT 13-13 Investing Activities Section of the Statement of Cash Flows

SportsTime, Inc.
Statement of Cash Flows—Investing Activities Section
For the Year Ended December 31, 2010

Investing Activities:		
Cash used to purchase property, plant, and equipment	(540,000)	
Proceeds from the sale of equipment	3,000	
Cash used to purchase investments in stock	(100,000)	
Net cash used by investing activities		(637,000)

Preparing the Cash Flows from Financing Activities

Financing activities include transactions that either generate capital for the company or pay it back. Financing activities affect long-term liabilities and owner's equity accounts. The comparative balance sheets shown in Exhibit 13-4 show changes in the company's long-term liabilities, common stock, and retained earnings accounts. We'll have to analyze the changes in each of these accounts to determine the cash provided and used by financing activities. We'll also need the following information obtained from company records.

---

a. $100,000 of new bonds were issued during the year.

b. $300,000 of bonds were repaid during the year.

c. The board of directors declared cash dividends of $125,000 during the year.

Long-Term Liabilities

Any change in long-term liabilities can be explained either by new borrowings (issuance of notes or bonds payable) or the repayment of principal on existing debt:

Beginning balance, Long-term liabilities (Exhibit 13-4)	$750,000
Plus: Cash proceeds from new bond issuance	?
Less: Repayment of principal on existing debt	?
End balance, Long-term liabilities (Exhibit 13-4)	$550,000

The additional information provided reconciles this account as follows:

Beginning long-term liabilities	+	Bond issuance	−	Repayments of principal	=	Ending long-term liabilities
$750,000	+	$100,000	−	$300,000	=	$550,000

We'll need to show the issuance and repayments separately on the statement of cash flows.

Common Stock

There was no change in the common stock account on the balance sheet (Exhibit 13-4); therefore, we can conclude that no transactions involving common stock took place during the year.

Retained Earnings

Retained earnings represents the cumulative earnings of a company, less distributions to the company's owners. We analyze the retained earnings account as follows:

Beginning balance, Retained earnings (Exhibit 13-4)	$1,492,000
Plus: Net income (Exhibit 13-3)	937,300
Less: Dividends declared during the year (from the additional information given)	(125,000)
Ending balance, Retained earnings (Exhibit 13-4)	$2,304,300

Since there was no dividends payable shown on the balance sheet, we can conclude that all dividends declared during the year ($125,000) were also paid out to stockholders. Remember, dividends are a distribution of capital back to the owners; not an expense on the income statement. Therefore, the dividends paid will be shown as a use of cash in the financing section of the statement of cash flows.

Exhibit 13-14 shows the completed statement of cash flows for SportsTime, prepared using the indirect method. The information provided in the financing section shows that that company used $300,000 for paying down long-term debt, but obtained

$100,000 of new debt (perhaps at a lower interest rate). The company used an additional $125,000 to pay dividends to its owners.

EXHIBIT 13-14   Statement of Cash Flows (Indirect Method)

SportsTime, Inc.
Statement of Cash Flows—Indirect Method
For the Year Ended December 31, 2010

Operating Activities:

Net income		$ 937,300
Adjustments to reconcile net income to cash basis:		
Depreciation expense	142,000	
Gain on sale of equipment	(1,000)	
Increase in accounts receivable	(35,000)	
Decrease in inventory	25,000	
Increase in prepaid insurance	(5,000)	
Decrease in accounts payable	(40,000)	
Increase in wages payable	8,500	
Decrease in interest payable	(5,000)	
Increase in income taxes payable	26,700	
Decrease in other accrued expenses payable	(13,000)	103,200
Net cash provided by operating activities		1,040,500
Investing Activities:		
Cash used to purchase property, plant, and equipment	(540,000)	
Proceeds from the sale of equipment	3,000	
Cash used to purchase investments in stock	(100,000)	
Net cash used by investing activities		(637,000)
Financing Activities:		
Proceeds from bond issuance	100,000	
Repayment of long-term debt	(300,000)	
Cash payments for dividends	(125,000)	
Net cash used by investing activities		(325,000)
Net increase in cash		78,500
Cash at the beginning of the year		125,000
Cash at the end of the year		$ 203,500

Interpreting the Statement of Cash Flows

The statement of cash flows shown in Exhibit 13-14 presents a detailed explanation of how SportsTime generated and used cash during the year. In summary, we see that a little over $1 million in cash was generated by the company's day-to-day operating activities. Roughly 61% of this cash was used to purchase new, long-term investments, while 31% was used to decrease company debt and pay dividends. The remaining 8% was added to the company's cash balance, leaving cash $78,500 higher than it was at the beginning of the year.

Free Cash Flow

Many potential investors calculate the company's **free cash flow** using the information provided on the statement of cash flows. Free cash flow represents the amount of excess cash a business generates after taking into consideration the capital expenditures necessary to maintain its business. This cash can then be used for expansion, to pay dividends, pay down debt, or for any other business purpose (which is why it is called "free"). Essentially, it is the cash generated from the company's core business that is "left over" after paying bills and making capital expenditures. Free cash flow is calculated as follows:

Free cash flow = Cash flow from operating activities – capital expenditures

Using the information provided in Exhibit 13-14, we can calculate SportsTime's free cash flow as follows:

$$= \$1,040,500 - \$540,000$$
$$= \$500,500$$

The presence of free cash flow means that SportsTime has the ability to expand, produce new products, pay dividends, buy back treasury stock, or reduce its debt. Potential investors place high value on a company's ability to generate free cash flow and often use it as a means of valuing stock.

Recap: Steps to Preparing the Statement of Cash Flows Using the Indirect Method

Exhibit 13-15 summarizes the steps used to create a statement of cash flows using the indirect method.

EXHIBIT 13-15   Steps for Using the Indirect Method

Step 1. Begin the operating section with the company's net income and add back any noncash expenses (such as depreciation or losses on the sale of property, plant, and equipment) and subtract any noncash revenues (such gains on the sale of property, plant, or equipment). This information is found on the company's income statement.

Step 2. Adjust net income for all changes in current asset and current liability accounts (other than the cash account):
- **Add back** decreases in current asset accounts and increases in current liability accounts.
- **Subtract** increases in current asset accounts and decreases in current liability accounts.

Step 3. Prepare the investing section by analyzing the changes in all long-term asset accounts found on the company's comparative balance sheet. Separately list all cash transactions that took place during the year affecting these accounts (such as buying and selling property). Any gains or losses on sales, depreciation, or amortization of these assets has already been accounted for in the operating section.

Step 4. Prepare the financing section by analyzing the changes in all long-term liability and equity accounts found on the company's comparative balance sheet. Separately list all cash transactions that took place during the year affecting these accounts (such as issuing new debt or paying down existing debt, selling stock, buying treasury stock, or paying dividends).

Step 5. Present a subtotal of the amount of cash provided or used by each of the three types of activities (operating, investing, financing). Use the subtotals to find the overall increase or decrease in cash during the year. Then add the increase to (or subtract the decrease from) the company's beginning cash balance to arrive at the ending cash balance shown on the company's balance sheet.

How is the Statement of Cash Flows Prepared Using the Direct Method?

3 Prepare the statement of cash flows using the direct method

In this section, we'll prepare the statement of cash flows using the direct method. Keep in mind that the choice of method (indirect versus direct) only affects the operating activities section of the statement of cash flows. The investing and financing sections are the same regardless of the method used.

Why is this important?

"In the future, the FASB and IASB may require companies to use the direct method. This method shows, in a straight-forward manner, what the company received and paid cash for during the year."

Overview

The direct method lists the receipt and payment of cash for specific operating activities. For example, the operating activities would list such line items as follows:

- Cash receipts from customers
- Cash payments (to suppliers) for purchase of inventory
- Cash payments (to employees) for salaries and wages

In essence, the direct method lists many of the same items shown on the income statement, but calculates them on a cash, rather than accrual basis.

Exhibit 13-16 shows SportsTime's statement of cash flow using the direct method. Notice the reference number (1-7) provided on the right-hand side of the schedule. These reference numbers are only provided for the sake of instruction, and are never included on an actual statement of cash flows. In the following section, we'll show the supporting calculations for each referenced line item on the statement.

EXHIBIT 13-16 **Statement of Cash Flows (Direct Method)**

SportsTime, Inc.
Statement of Cash Flows—Direct Method
For the Year Ended December 31, 2010

		*Ref.
Operating Activities:		
Cash receipts from customers..	$ 9,465,000	(1)
Cash payments for inventory	(7,140,000)	(2)
Cash payments for insurance	(30,000)	(3)
Cash payments for salaries and wages................................	(571,500)	(4)
Cash payments for interest expense.....................................	(65,000)	(5)
Cash payments for income taxes	(375,000)	(6)
Cash payments for other operating expenses.......................	(243,000)	(7)
Net cash provided by operating activities.....................................	$1,040,500	
Investing Activities:		
Cash used to purchase property, plant, and equipment	(540,000)	
Proceeds from the sale of equipment	3,000	
Cash used to purchase investments in stock	(100,000)	
Net cash used by investing activities..	(637,000)	
Financing Activities:		
Proceeds from bond issuance	100,000	
Repayment of long-term debt..	(300,000)	
Cash payments for dividends	(125,000)	
Net cash used by investing activities..	(325,000)	
Net increase in cash and cash equivalents....................................	78,500	
Cash and cash equivalents at the beginning of the year................	125,000	
Cash and cash equivalents at the end of the year.........................	$ 203,500	

*Reference numbers are provided for the sake of instruction only, and are never actually shown on the statement of cash flows.

Notice that the cash provided by operating activities ($1,040,500) is the *same* as we found using the indirect method (shown in Exhibit 13-14).

Determining Cash Payments and Receipts

The best way to make sure you've captured all cash transactions from operating activities is to analyze *every* current asset and current liability account shown on the balance sheet (Exhibit 13-4), and incorporate related information from the income statement (Exhibit 13-3) as necessary. Let's start with current assets.

(1) Cash Receipts from Customers

To determine the amount of cash received from customers we must analyze accounts receivable. Accounts receivable increases when sales are made and decreases when cash is collected:

Beginning balance, Accounts receivable (Exhibit 13-4)........................	$ 330,000
Plus: Sales revenue (from income statement)	9,500,000
Less: Cash collections of accounts receivable	?
Ending balance, Accounts receivable (Exhibit 13-4)............................	$ 365,000

Solving for the unknown, we determine that cash collections of sales must be $9,465,000.

(2) Cash Payments for Inventory

The next current asset account on the balance sheet is inventory. We'll use this account, along with accounts payable (current liability), to figure out how much cash was used to purchase inventory. First let's think about what affects the inventory account: The account increases for the purchase of inventory, and decreases for the cost of goods sold. Therefore, we can establish the following relationship:

Beginning balance, Inventory (Exhibit 13-4)	$ 657,000
Plus: Purchases of inventory	?
Less: Cost of goods sold (Exhibit 13-3)	(7,125,000)
Ending balance, Inventory (Exhibit 13-4)	$ 632,000

Solving for the unknown, we determine that purchases of inventory must have been $7,100,000.

However, did the company pay for all of these purchases during the year? We'll only know by investigating the changes in accounts payable (we assume SportsTime uses accounts payable only for inventory purchases):

Beginning balance, Accounts payable (Exhibit 13-4)	$ 285,000
Plus: Purchases of inventory	7,100,000
Less: Cash payments for inventory	(?)
Ending balance, Accounts payable (Exhibit 13-4)	$ 245,000

Solving for the unknown, we determine that payments for inventory must have been $7,140,000.

(3) Cash Payments for Insurance

The next current asset on the balance sheet is prepaid insurance. This account will increase for purchases of insurance, and decrease as a result of recording insurance expense:

Beginning balance, Prepaid insurance (Exhibit 13-4)	$ 15,000
Plus: Payments for insurance	?
Less: Insurance expense (Exhibit 13-3)	(25,000)
Ending balance, Prepaid insurance (Exhibit 13-4)	$ 20,000

Solving for the unknown, we determine that payments for insurance must have been $30,000.

We've analyzed all of the current asset accounts found on the company's balance sheet, so now we turn our attention to the current liability accounts shown in Exhibit 13-4. The first current liability shown is accounts payable. We've already analyzed that account when calculating the amount of inventory purchased. The remaining current liability accounts include wages payable, interest payable, income taxes payable, and other accrued expenses payable. We'll examine each of these next.

(4) Cash Payments for Salaries and Wages

Wages payable increases when we record salaries and wages expense, and decreases when the company pays its employees:

Beginning balance, Wages payable (Exhibit 13-4)	$ 48,500
Plus: Salaries and wages expense (Exhibit 13-3)	580,000
Less: Payments for salaries and wages	(?)
Ending balance, Wages payable (Exhibit 13-4)...................................	$ 57,000

Solving for the unknown, we determine that payments for salaries and wages must have been $571,500.

(5) Cash Payments for Interest Expense

Interest payable increases when we record interest expense, and decreases when the company pays interest:

Beginning balance, Interest payable (Exhibit 13-4)...............................	$ 8,000
Plus: Interest expense (Exhibit 13-3)	60,000
Less: Payments for interest	(?)
Ending balance, Interest payable (Exhibit 13-4)	$ 3,000

Solving for the unknown, we determine that payments for interest expense must have been $65,000.

(6) Cash Payments for Income Taxes

Income taxes payable increases when we record income tax expense, and decreases when the company pays income taxes:

Beginning balance, Income taxes payable (Exhibit 13-4).....................	$120,000
Plus: Income tax expense (Exhibit 13-3)..	401,700
Less: Payments for income taxes	(?)
Ending balance, Income taxes payable (Exhibit 13-4)	$146,700

Solving for the unknown, we determine that payments for income taxes must have been $375,000.

(7) Cash Payments for Other Operating Expenses

SportsTime's income statement lists many of operating expenses separately: salaries and wages expense, insurance expense, and depreciation expense. It then lumps together its remaining operating expenses, as shown in Exhibit 13-3. "Other operating expenses" would include such expenses as rent, utilities, telephone and internet, supplies, and so forth. SportsTime records liabilities for these expenses as "other accrued expenses payable":

Beginning balance, Other accrued expenses payable (Exhibit 13-4)........	$ 28,500
Plus: Other operating expenses (Exhibit 13-3).....................................	230,000
Less: Payments for other operating expenses.......................................	(?)
Ending balance, Other accrued expenses payable (Exhibit 13-4)........	$ 15,500

Solving for the unknown, we determine that payments for other operating expenses must have been $243,000.

Cash Flows from Operating Activities

By analyzing each current asset and current liability account, we have figured out the actual cash receipts and cash payments made for each operating activity during the year. After listing each transaction separately (Exhibit 13-16), we see that the cash flows from operating activities totals $1,040,500, just as it did using the indirect method.

Comparing the Direct and Indirect Methods

As you can see, the direct method requires much more analysis than the indirect method. As a result, most companies currently use the indirect method. However, the FASB and IASB have jointly recommended that companies use the direct method because it shows cash receipts and cash payments in a much more straightforward manner. Nonetheless, both methods result in the same *total* amount of cash provided by operating activities (for SportsTime, $1,040,500).

Decision Guidelines

Statement of Cash Flows

Companies have a choice of using the indirect method or direct method. The following decision guidelines provide general guidance for preparing the statement of cash flows using either method.

Decision	Guidelines
What kind of information is needed in order to prepare the statement of cash flows?	The following information is needed: 1. Income statement for the year 2. Balance sheets for the current and prior year (comparative balance sheets) 3. Additional information about investing and financing activities that occurred during the year
If my company uses the indirect method, what adjustments should be shown when reconciling net income to the cash basis?	1. All noncash expenses are **added back** to net income. 2. All noncash revenues are **deducted** from net income. 3. All changes in current asset and current liability accounts will either be added, or deducted from net income (as indicated below).
To reconcile net income to the cash basis, do we add or subtract changes in current asset accounts? (indirect method)	• *If a current asset account **increases**, then **subtract** the change from net income.* • *If a current asset account **decreases**, then **add** the change to net income.*
To reconcile net income to the cash basis, do we add or subtract changes in current liability accounts? (indirect method)	• *If a current liability account **increases**, then **add** the change to net income.* • *If a current liability account **decreases**, then **subtract** the change from net income.*
What process should be used to prepare the investing section of the statement of cash flows?	You will need to analyze the change in every long-term asset account found on the balance sheet. Purchases and sales of investments need to be disclosed separately on the statement of cash flows. (You can't just show the net change in each account.)
What process should be used to prepare the financing section of the statement of cash flows?	You will need to analyze the change in every long-term liability and owner's equity account found on the balance sheet to determine the financing transactions that took place during the year.
My company has decided to use the direct method. What process should be used to prepare the operating section of the statement of cash flows?	Each current asset and current liability account will need to be analyzed to determine the cash transactions underlying the change in the account. These transactions typically include the following: • Receipts from customers • Payments for inventory • Payments for salaries and wages • Payments for other operating expenses (listed separately, or grouped together, depending on the presentation of expenses in the income statement)

Summary Problem 2

Today's Fashion is a local retailer of trend-setting clothing. The company's income statement and comparative balance sheets are presented below. In addition, the following information was gathered from the company's records:

> a. No new debt was issued during the year.
>
> b. Dividends of $200,000 were declared by the board of directors.
>
> c. Equipment with an original cost of $20,000 was sold for $9,000.
> The equipment had accumulated depreciation of $15,000 at the time of sale.

Requirement

Prepare the company's statement of cash flows using the indirect method.

Today's Fashion
Income Statement
For the Year Ended December 31, 2010

Sales revenue		$4,750,000
Cost of goods sold		3,562,500
Gross profit		1,187,500
Operating expenses:		
Salaries and wages expense	$340,000	
Insurance expense	10,000	
Depreciation expense	75,000	
Other operating expenses	125,000	550,000
Operating income		637,500
Other income and expenses:		
Interest expense	8,000	
Gain on sale of PP&E	4,000	4,000
Income before taxes		633,500
Income tax expense		190,050
Net income		$ 443,450

Today's Fashion
Balance Sheets
December 31, 2010 and 2009

	2010	2009	Change Increase/ (Decrease)
Assets			
Current assets:			
Cash and cash equivalents	$ 187,000	$ 85,000	$102,000
Accounts receivable	37,000	57,000	(20,000)
Inventory	337,500	350,000	(12,500)
Prepaid insurance	5,000	3,000	2,000
Total current assets	566,500	495,000	
Property, plant, and equipment	1,860,000	1,660,000	200,000
Less accumulated depreciation	(310,000)	(250,000)	60,000
Investments	50,000	50,000	0
Total assets	$2,166,500	1,955,000	
Liabilities			
Current liabilities:			
Accounts payable	$ 65,000	$ 85,000	(20,000)
Wages payable	29,000	25,000	4,000
Interest payable	2,000	8,000	(6,000)
Income taxes payable	100,050	85,000	15,050
Other accrued expenses payable	13,000	18,000	(5,000)
Total current liabilities	209,050	221,000	
Long-term liabilities	80,000	100,000	(20,000)
Total liabilities	289,050	321,000	
Stockholders' equity			
Common stock	850,000	850,000	0
Retained earnings	1,027,450	784,000	243,450
Total Stockholders' equity	1,877,450	1,634,000	
Total liabilities and equity	$2,166,500	$1,955,000	

Solution

The following steps are taken to prepare the statement of cash flows using the indirect method:

1. We begin the operating section with the company's net income, and add back any noncash expenses (depreciation) and then subtract any noncash revenues (gains on the sale of property, plant, or equipment).

2. We then adjust net income for all changes in current asset and current liability accounts (other than the cash account):

   ▪ We *add* decreases in current asset accounts and increases in current liability accounts.

   ▪ We *subtract* increases in current asset accounts and decreases in current liability accounts.

3. To prepare the investing section, we analyze the changes in all long-term asset accounts. We separately list all cash transactions that took place during the year (for example, buying and selling property, plant, and equipment or long-term investments). Any gains, losses, depreciation, or amortization of these assets has already been accounted for in the operating section.

4. To prepare the financing section, we analyze the changes in all long-term liability and equity accounts. We separately list all cash transactions that took place during the year (for example issuing new debt or paying down existing debt, selling stock, buying treasury stock, or paying dividends).

Today's Fashion
Statement of Cash Flows—Indirect Method
For the Year Ended December 31, 2010

Operating Activities:

Net income..		$ 443,450
Adjustments to reconcile net income to cash basis:		
Depreciation expense	75,000	
Gain on sale of equipment	(4,000)	
Decrease in accounts receivable............................	20,000	
Decrease in inventory..	12,500	
Increase in prepaid insurance	(2,000)	
Decrease in accounts payable	(20,000)	
Increase in wages payable	4,000	
Decrease in interest payable	(6,000)	
Increase in income taxes payable...........................	15,050	
Decrease in other accrued expenses payable.........	(5,000)	89,550
Net cash provided by operating activities.......................		533,000
Investing Activities:		
Cash used to purchase property, plant, and equipment	(220,000)	
Proceeds from the sale of equipment.....................	9,000	
Net cash used by investing activities..............................		(211,000)
Financing Activities:		
Repayment of long-term debt................................	(20,000)	
Cash payments for dividends	(200,000)	
Net cash used by investing activities..............................		(220,000)
Net increase in cash		102,000
Cash, beginning of the year..		85,000
Cash, end of the year..		$ 187,000

Analysis of Investing and Financing Activities:

Property, Plant, and Equipment:

Beginning balance, PP&E..	$1,660,000
Plus: Purchases of PP&E	?
Less: Original cost of equipment sold (given)	(20,000)
Ending balance, PP&E	$1,860,000

Solving for the unknown, the company must have purchases of $220,000 of property, plant, and equipment. This will be shown as an investing activity.

Accumulated Depreciation:

Beginning balance, Accumulated depreciation.....................................	$250,000
Plus: Depreciation expense...	75,000
Less: Accumulated depreciation on sold equipment (given).................	(15,000)
Ending balance, Accumulated depreciation	$310,000

The depreciation expense will be shown as an operating activity.

Gain on Sale of Equipment

Sale price of equipment (given)...		$9,000
Original cost of the equipment...	$20,000	
Less: Accumulated depreciation	15,000	
Net book value of equipment		5,000
Gain on sale		$4,000

The $4,000 gain on sale will be shown as an adjustment to net income in the operating section while the $9,000 cash received will be shown as an investing activity.

Long-Term Liabilities:

Beginning balance, Long-term liabilities...............................	$100,000
Plus: Cash proceeds from new bond issuance (given)	0
Less: Repayment of principal on existing debt....................................	?
End balance, Long-term liabilities	$ 80,000

Solving for the unknown, the company must have repaid $20,000 of principal on the existing long-term debt. This will be shown as an investing activity.

Retained Earnings:

Beginning balance, Retained earnings....................................	$ 784,000
Plus: Net income	443,450
Less: Dividends declared during the year (given)	(200,000)
Ending balance, Retained earnings....................................	$1,027,450

The payment of dividends will be shown as a financing activity.

REVIEW

Accounting Vocabulary

Accrual Basis of Accounting. (p. 727)   Revenues are recorded when they are earned (when the sale takes place), rather than when cash is received on the sale. Likewise, expenses are recorded when they are incurred, rather than when they are paid.

Cash Equivalents. (p. 724)   Very safe, highly liquid assets that are readily convertible into cash, such as money market funds, certificates of deposit that mature in less than three months, and U.S. treasury bills.

Comparative Balance Sheets. (p. 729)   A comparison of the balance sheets from the end of two fiscal periods; usually highlighting the changes in each account.

Direct Method. (p. 727)   A method of presenting cash flows from operating activities that separately lists the receipt and payment of cash for specific operating activities.

Free Cash Flow. (p. 739)   The amount of excess cash a business generates after taking into consideration the capital expenditures necessary to maintain its business. It is calculated as cash flows from operating activities minus capital expenditures.

Indirect Method. (p. 727) A method of presenting the cash flows from operating activities that begins with the company's net income, which is prepared on an accrual basis, and then reconciles it back to the cash basis through a series of adjustments.

Investing Activities. (p. 725) Activities that involve buying or selling long-term assets, such as buying or selling property, plant, or equipment; buying or selling stock in other companies (if the stock is meant to be held for the long term); or loaning money to other companies with the goal of earning interest income from the loan.

Financing Activities. (p. 725) Activities that either generate capital for the company or pay it back, such as issuing stock or long-term debt, paying dividends, and repaying principal

amounts on loans; this includes all activities that affect long-term liabilities and owner's equity.

Net Book Value. (p. 731) The original cost of plant or equipment less its accumulated depreciation.

Operating Activities. (p. 725) The day-to-day profit-making activities of the company, such as making or buying inventory, selling inventory, selling services, paying employees, advertising, and so forth; This also includes *any other activity that affects net income* (not just operating income), current assets, or current liabilities.

Statement of Cash Flows. (p. 724) One of the four basic financial statements; the statement shows the overall increase or decrease in cash during the period as well as how the company generated and used cash during the period.

Quick Check

1. *(Learning Objective 1)* Dividends paid to a company's stockholders would appear on the statement of cash flows as a(n)
   a. increase in the investing section.
   b. decrease in the investing section.
   c. increase in the financing section.
   d. decrease in the financing section.

2. *(Learning Objective 1)* Which of the following would be classified as a decrease in the financing section of the statement of cash flows?
   a. Purchase of new equipment
   b. Issuance of common stock
   c. Retirement of long-term bonds payable
   d. Sale of a building

3. *(Learning Objective 1)* The cash proceeds from a sale of a plant asset would appear on the statement of cash flows as a(n)
   a. increase in the investing section.
   b. decrease in the investing section.
   c. increase in the financing section.
   d. decrease in the financing section.

4. *(Learning Objective 2)* Poppins Corporation prepares its statement of cash flow using the indirect method. Which of the following items would be deducted from net income when calculating the net cash from operations?
   a. A loss on sale of land
   b. A gain on sale of property, plant, and equipment
   c. An increase in salaries payable
   d. A decrease in accounts receivable

5. *(Learning Objective 2)* When preparing the cash provided by operations section of the statement of cash flows using the indirect method, which of the following would provide cash?
   a. A decrease in salaries payable
   b. An increase in accounts receivable
   c. A decrease in long-term investments
   d. An increase in accounts payable

6. *(Learning Objective 2)* When preparing the cash provided by operations section of the statement of cash

flows using the indirect method, which of the following would be shown as a use of cash?
   a. A decrease in prepaid insurance
   b. An increase in accounts receivable
   c. An increase in salaries payable
   d. A decrease in property, plant, and equipment

7. *(Learning Objective 2)* An increase in the Taxes Payable account from the beginning of the year to the end of year would be what type of adjustment to "net cash provided by operations" if the company uses the indirect method when preparing its statement of cash flows?
   a. Would not affect "net cash provided by operations"
   b. A decrease to "net cash provided by operations"
   c. An increase to "net cash provided by operations"
   d. Unable to determine without the amount of the cash paid for taxes

8. *(Learning Objective 3)* Allyson Corporation uses the indirect method to prepare its statement of cash flows. If the "net cash provided by operations" on its statement was $37,500, what would the net cash provided by operations using the direct method be?
   a. Less than $37,500
   b. $37,500
   c. More than $37,500
   d. Cannot be determined from the information provided

9. *(Learning Objective 3)* Sacco Pretzel Company uses the direct method to prepare its statement of cash flows. When calculating the net cash provided (used) by operations, which of the following items would be deducted from net income?
   a. Cash paid for income taxes
   b. Gain on sale of land
   c. Depreciation expense
   d. Cash paid for dividends

10. *(Learning Objective 3)* Which of the following sections will be prepared differently if the direct method is used to prepare the statement of cash flows instead of the indirect method?
    a. Operating activities
    b. Investing activities
    c. Financing activities
    d. All of the sections will be different

ASSESS YOUR PROGRESS

Learning Objectives

1 Classify cash flows as operating, investing, or financing activities

2 Prepare the statement of cash flows using the indirect method

3 Prepare the statement of cash flows using the direct method

Short Exercises

S13-1 Classifying cash flows *(Learning Objective 1)*

Sable Gym Corporation is preparing its statement of cash flows (indirect method) for the past year. Listed below are items used in preparing the company's statement of cash flows. Specify how each item would be treated on Sable Gym Corporation's statement of cash flows by using the following abbreviations:

1. Operating activity—addition to net income (O+)
2. Operating activity—subtraction from net income (O–)
3. Financing activity (F)
4. Investing activity (I)
5. Activity that is not on the statement of cash flows (NA)

Items to Classify in Operating Section of Statement of Cash Flows (Indirect Method)			
a.	Decrease in inventory	—	h.	Depreciation expense	—
b.	Decrease in accounts payable	—	i.	Retained earnings	—
c.	Collection of cash from customers	—	j.	Increase in prepaid expense	—
d.	Gain on sale of land	—	k.	Loss on sale of building	—
e.	Issuance of common stock	—	l.	Payment of dividends	—
f.	Purchase of equipment	—	m.	Increase in accounts receivable	—
g.	Increase in accrued liabilities	—	n.	Net income	—

S13-2 Identifying activities for the statement of cash flows—indirect method *(Learning Objectives 1 & 2)*

Identify each of Palmer Industries' transactions listed below as operating (O), investing (I), financing (F), noncash investing and financing (NIF), or a transaction that is not reported on the statement of cash flows (NA). Also indicate whether the transaction increases (+) or decreases (–) cash. The indirect method is used for operating activities.

a.	Depreciation of equipment	—	i.	Decrease in accrued liabilities	—
b.	Acquisition of building by cash payment	—	j.	Loss on sale of equipment	—
c.	Net income	—	k.	Payment of long-term debt	—
d.	Decrease in raw materials inventory	—	l.	Issuance of common stock for cash	—
e.	Payment of cash dividend	—	m.	Purchase of long-term investment	—
f.	Increase in prepaid expenses	—	n.	Acquisition of equipment by issuance of note payable	—
g.	Purchase of treasury stock	—	o.	Sale of long-term investment	—
h.	Cash sale of land	—	p.	Accrual of salary expense	—

S13-3 Preparing the operation cash flows section (indirect method) *(Learning Objective 2)*

Maxter Corporation began the year with accounts receivable, inventory, and prepaid expenses totaling $50,000. At the end of the year, Maxter had a total of $65,000 for these current assets. At the beginning of the year, it owed current liabilities of $37,000, and at year end, current liabilities totaled $35,000.

Net income for the year was $71,000. Included in net income were a $5,000 gain on the sale of land and depreciation expense of $9,000.

Show how Maxter should report cash flows from operating activities for the year. Maxter uses the indirect method.

S13-4 Classify cash flows as operating, investing, or financing *(Learning Objectives 1 & 2)*

For each of the following situations, identify whether the activity is an operating, investing, or financing activity and compute the cash provided or used by the activity.

Activity	Operating (O) Investing (I) Financing (F)	Amount of Cash Flow	Increase (+) Decrease (−)
a. A building with a cost of $180,000 and accumulated depreciation of $40,000 was sold for a $15,000 gain.			
b. Net income for last year was $112,000. The accumulated depreciation balance increased by $25,000. There were no changes in noncash current assets or liabilities. There were also no sales of plant assets.			
c. Net income was $25,000 for the year. Accounts receivable increased by $5,000 and accounts payable increased by $7,000. There were no other changes in the noncash current assets and current liabilities. There was no depreciation for the year.			
d. Bonds payable with a face value of $50,000 were retired with a cash payment for their face value. New bonds were issued later in the year for $30,000.			
e. Bonds payable were retired for their face value of $60,000 (cash paid). Cash dividends of $18,000 were also paid. A new notes payable was signed for cash proceeds of $28,000.			
f. A plant asset with a cost of $60,000 and accumulated depreciation of $17,000 was sold for a $12,000 loss.			
g. Current assets (not including cash) increased by $5,000 and current liabilities decreased by $9,000. There was no depreciation. Net income was $57,000 for the year.			
h. Common stock was issued for $200,000 cash. Dividends of $24,000 were paid in cash.			
i. Noncash current assets decreased by $7,000 and current liabilities decreased by $11,000. Depreciation was $13,000 for the year, while net income was $57,000.			

S13-5 Calculate investing cash flows *(Learning Objectives 2 & 3)*

Sullivan Company reported the following financial statements for 2009 and 2010:

Sullivan Company
Income Statement
For Year Ended December 31, 2010

Sales revenue		$4,750,000
Cost of goods sold		2,850,000
Gross profit		1,900,000
Operating expenses:		
Salaries and wage expense	340,000	
Insurance expense	10,000	
Depreciation expense	75,000	
Other operating expenses	125,000	550,000
Operating income		1,350,000
Other income and expenses:		
Interest expense		6,400
Income before taxes		1,343,600
Income tax expense		403,080
Net income		$ 940,520

Sullivan Company
Balance Sheets
As of December 31, 2010 and 2009

	2010	2009
Assets		
Current assets:		
Cash and cash equivalents	$ 584,000	$ 464,000
Accounts receivable	72,000	12,000
Inventory	900,000	200,000
Prepaid insurance	4,000	4,000
Total current assets	1,560,500	680,000
Property, plant, and equipment	1,280,000	1,100,000
Less: Accumulated depreciation	(275,000)	(200,000)
Investments	40,000	65,000
Total assets	$2,605,000	$1,645,000
Liabilities		
Current liabilities:		
Accounts payable (inventory purchases)	$ 22,000	$ 42,000
Salaries payable	17,000	18,000
Interest payable	2,400	5,000
Taxes payable	275,080	32,000
Other accrued operating expenses	26,000	11,000
Total current liabilities	342,480	108,000
Bonds payable	65,000	80,000
Total liabilities	407,480	188,000
Stockholders' equity		
Common stock	725,000	775,000
Retained earnings	1,472,520	682,000
Total stockholders' equity	2,197,520	1,457,000
Total liabilities and equity	$2,605,000	$1,645,000

Compute the following investing cash flows:

a. Purchases of plant assets (all were for cash). There were no sales of plant assets.

b. Proceeds from the sale of investments. There were no purchases of investments.

S13-6 Calculate financing cash flows *(Learning Objectives 2 & 3)*

Use the data given in S13-5 for the Sullivan Company to compute the following financing cash flows:

a. New borrowing or payment of long-term notes payable. Sullivan Company had only one long-term note payable transaction during the day.

b. Issuance of common stock or retirement of common stock. The company had only one common stock transaction during the year.

c. Payment of cash dividends (same as dividends declared).

S13-7 Classify cash flows as operating, investing, or financing *(Learning Objectives 1, 2, & 3)*

The items in the following table may or may not appear in a statement of cash flows.

	Operating (O) Investing (I) Financing (F)	Direct (D) Indirect (I) Both (B)	Increase (+) Decrease (−)
1. Decrease in accounts receivable			
2. Increase in wages payable			
3. Cash paid to suppliers			
4. Cash received from customers			
5. Purchase of treasury stock			
6. Increase in taxes payable			
7. Principle payments on long-term note payable			
8. Purchase of plant assets			
9. Depreciation expense			
10. Cash paid for taxes			
11. Dividends paid			
12. Issuance of stock			

For each of the items in the table, indicate the following:

1. Would the item appear on the statement of cash flows under operating activities (O), investing activities (I), or financing activities (F)?

2. Would the item appear on the statement of cash flows using the direct method (D), indirect method (I), or both (B)?

3. Would the item result in an increase (+) or a decrease (−) when computing cash flow?

S13-8 Prepare statement of cash flows (indirect method) *(Learning Objective 2)*

Christabel Corporation uses the indirect method to prepare its statement of cash flows. Data related cash activities for last year appears next.

Net income..	$ 92,500
Dividends paid (cash)..	50,000
Depreciation expense	17,000
Net decrease in current assets...	21,900
Issued new notes payable for cash	31,500
Paid cash for building..	279,000
Net decrease in current liabilities..	5,300
Sold investment for cash...	$100,000

Answer the following questions:

1. What was the net cash flow from operating activities for the year?
2. What was the cash flow from (or used for) investing activities for the year?
3. What was the cash flow from (or used for) financing activities for the year?
4. What was the net change in cash for the year?
5. If the beginning balance of cash for the year was $158,000, what was the balance of cash at the end of the year?

S13-9 Calculate increase or decrease in current assets and liabilities *(Learning Objective 3)*

A recent statement of cash flows for Lamar Company reported the following information:

Net income..	$ 451,100
Depreciation..	67,000
Cash effect of changes in:	
Accounts receivable	24,000
Inventory...	(17,800)
Other current assets...	8,300
Accounts payable..	12,000
Other current liabilities..	(199,000)
Net cash provided by operations...	$ 345,600

Based on the information presented in the statement of cash flows for Lamar Company, determine whether the following accounts increased or decreased during the period: Accounts Receivable, Inventory, Other Current Assets, Accounts Payable, and Other Current Liabilities.

S13-10 Prepare statement of cash flows (direct method) *(Learning Objective 3)*

Ansel Corporation uses the direct method to prepare its statement of cash flows. Data related to cash activities for last year appears next.

Paid for interest..	$ 4,000	Paid for equipment...........................	$12,000
Paid for utilities...	18,000	Paid to suppliers................................	37,000
Paid dividends..	3,000	Paid for insurance	9,000
Received from customers...................................	52,000	Depreciation expense	3,700
Paid for taxes	5,500	Paid for advertising..........................	7,200
Received from issuing long-term note payable	23,000	Received from sale of land	13,000
Paid to employees..	15,000	Received from sale of plant assets ...	6,800

Answer the following questions:

1. What was the net cash flow from operating activities for the year?

2. What was the net cash flow from investing activities for the year?

3. What was the net cash flow from financing activities for the year?

4. What was the net change in cash for the year?

5. If the beginning balance of cash for the year was $342,000, what was the balance of cash at the end of the year?

Exercises—Group A

E13-11A Prepare operating cash flows section (indirect method) *(Learning Objective 2)*

The comparative balance sheet for Desmond Isle Travel Services, Inc., for December 31, 2010 and 2009, is as follows:

Desmond Isle Travel Services, Inc.
Balance Sheets
As of December 31, 2010 and 2009

	2010	2009
Assets		
Cash	$ 45,000	$ 12,000
Accounts receivable (net)......................................	78,000	81,000
Inventories	59,000	19,000
Prepaid insurance...	11,000	13,000
Land	101,000	117,000
Equipment..	76,000	56,000
Accumulated depreciation—equipment	(17,000)	(11,000)
Total	$353,000	$287,000
Liabilities and Stockholders' equity		
Accounts payable	$ 27,000	$ 30,000
Wages payable..	32,000	21,000
Interest payable..	12,000	11,000
Income taxes payable	7,000	5,000
Note payable (long-term)	98,000	88,000
Total liabilities	$176,000	$155,000
Common stock..	125,000	115,000
Retained earnings...	52,000	17,000
Total stockholders' equity..............................	$177,000	$132,000
Total liabilities and stockholders' equity	$353,000	$287,000

The following information is taken from the records of Desmond Isle Travel Services, Inc.:

a. Land was sold for $13,000.

b. Equipment was purchased for cash.

c. There were no disposals of equipment during the year.

d. The common stock was issued for cash.

e. Net income for 2010 was $40,000.

f. Cash dividends paid during the year were $5,000.

Desmond Isle Travel Services, Inc., uses the indirect method for preparing the statement of cash flows. Prepare the operating section of the statement of cash flows for 2010.

E13-12A Prepare statement of cash flow preparation (indirect method) *(Learning Objective 2)*

Using the data given in E13-11A, prepare the statement of cash flows (indirect method) for Desmond Isle Travel Services, Inc., for 2010.

E13-13A Calculate cash flows from operating, investing, and financing activities (direct method) *(Learning Objectives 2 & 3)*

Compute the following cash flows for Express Service Company for the past year:

1. The beginning balance of Retained Earnings was $135,000, while the end of the year balance of Retained Earnings was $177,000. Net income for the year was $65,000. No dividends payable were on the balance sheet. How much was paid in cash dividends during the year?

2. The beginning and ending balances of the Common Stock account were $215,000 and $273,000, respectively. Where would the increase in Common Stock appear on the statement of cash flows?

3. The beginning and ending balances of the Treasury Stock account were $53,000 and $78,000, respectively. Where would the increase in Treasury Stock appear on the statement of cash flows?

4. The Property, Plant, & Equipment (net) increased by $12,000 during the year to have a balance of $152,000 at the end of the year. Depreciation for the year was $19,000. Acquisitions of new plant assets during the year totaled $39,000. Plant assets were sold at a loss of $3,000.

   a. What were the cash proceeds from the sale of plant assets?

   b. What amount would be reported on the investing section of the statement of cash flows? Would it be a source of cash or a use of cash?

   c. What amount, if any, would be reported on the operating section of the statement of cash flows?

E13-14A Calculate operating cash flows (indirect method) *(Learning Objective 2)*

Century Corporation has the following activities for the past year:

Net income..	$?	Cost of goods sold..	$47,000
Payment of dividends.......................	$ 5,000	Other operating expenses............................	$12,000
Proceeds from issuance of stock........	$ 75,000	Depreciation expense	$17,000
Purchase of treasury stock................	$ 12,000	Purchase of equipment	$23,000
Sales revenue.....................................	$120,000	Proceeds from sale of land..........................	$21,000
Payment of note payable	$ 13,000	Increase in current assets other than cash.....	$ 7,000
Decrease in current liabilities.............	$ 10,000		

Requirement

1. Prepare the operating activities section of Century Corporation's statement of cash flows for the year ended, using the indirect method for operating cash flows.

E13-15A Prepare statement of cash flows (indirect method) *(Learning Objective 2)*

Using the data given in E13-14A, prepare statement of cash flows for Century Corporation for the year. Century Corporation uses the indirect method for operating activities.

E13-16A Prepare statement of cash flows (indirect method) *(Learning Objective 3)*

Dragon Corporation is preparing its statement of cash flows for the past year. Minna Yu has gathered the following information about the past year.

Decrease in accounts receivable..................	$ 8,000	Retire bond payable (long-term)............	$15,000
Increase in salaries payable........................	7,500	Paid dividends in cash...........................	31,000
Depreciation expense	11,000	Decrease in inventory............................	7,000
Increase in prepaid insurance	100	Decrease in accounts payable	6,000
Decrease in other short-term liabilities.......	1,500	Sold land (investment)...........................	25,000
Increase in taxes payable...........................	1,000	Increase in interest payable....................	700
Purchase of new computer system.............	14,000	Cash balance, beginning of year............	92,400
Net income..	87,080		

Requirement

1. Prepare a statement of cash flows for the past year using the indirect method.

E13-17A Compute operating cash flows using direct method *(Learning Objective 3)*

Applebrook Spas provides the following data for the year just ended.

Payments to employees.................	$ 63,800	Payment of note payable	$ 5,000
Proceeds from sale of land............	41,500	Depreciation expense	4,300
Payment of dividends	12,000	Purchase of equipment..........................	7,700
Payments to suppliers....................	63,000	Purchase of treasury stock.....................	11,000
Increase in salaries payable...........	11,300	Gain on sale of land..............................	1,200
Payment of income tax..................	9,500	Cost of goods sold................................	114,000
Collections from customers..........	150,000	Proceeds from issuance of common stock............	15,000
Sales revenue..............................	168,000	Beginning balance, cash........................	14,000

Requirement

1. Prepare the operating activities section of Applebrook Spas' statement of cash flows for the year ended, using the direct method for operating cash flows.

E13-18A Prepare statement of cash flows (direct method) *(Learning Objective 3)*

Using the data from E13-17A, prepare the statement of cash flows using the direct method.

E13-19A Prepare statement of cash flows (direct method) *(Learning Objective 3)*

Martin Interiors began the year with cash of $50,000. During the year, Martin Interiors earned service revenue of $400,000. Cash collections for the year were $385,000. Expenses for the year were $375,000, with $360,000 of that total paid in cash. Martin Interiors also used cash to purchase equipment for $80,000 and to pay a cash dividend to stockholders of $35,000. During the year, Martin Interiors also borrowed $50,000 cash by issuing a note payable.

Requirement

1. Prepare the company's statement of cash flows using the direct method.

Exercises—Group B

E13-20B Prepare operating cash flows section (indirect method) *(Learning Objective 2)*

The comparative balance sheet for Eastern Travel Services, Inc., for December 31, 2010 and 2009, is as follows:

Eastern Travel Services, Inc.
Balance Sheet
As of December 31, 2010 and 2009

	2010	2009
Assets		
Cash	$ 42,000	$ 22,000
Accounts receivable (net)	80,000	81,000
Inventories	60,000	23,000
Prepaid insurance	8,000	10,000
Land	107,000	119,000
Equipment, net	79,000	54,000
Accumulated depreciation—equipment	(21,000)	(15,000)
Total	$355,000	$294,000
Liabilities and Stockholders' equity		
Accounts payable	$ 23,000	$ 37,000
Wages payable	36,000	20,000
Interest payable	14,000	12,000
Income tax payable	9,000	6,000
Notes payable, long-term	98,000	92,000
Total liabilities	$180,000	$167,000
Common stock	131,000	116,000
Retained earnings	44,000	11,000
Total stockholders' equity	$175,000	$127,000
Total liabilities and stockholders' equity	$355,000	$294,000

The following information is taken from the records of Eastern Travel Services, Inc.:
a. Land was sold for $8,100.
b. Equipment was purchased for cash.
c. There were no disposals of equipment during the year.
d. The common stock was issued for cash.
e. Net income for 2010 was $38,000.
f. Cash dividends paid during the year were $5,000.

Eastern Travel Services, Inc., uses the indirect method for preparing the statement of cash flows. Prepare the operating section of the statement of cash flows for 2010.

E13-21B Prepare statement of cash flow preparation (indirect method) *(Learning Objective 2)*

Using the data given in E13-20B, prepare the statement of cash flows (indirect method) for Eastern Travel Services, Inc., for 2010.

E13-22B Calculate cash flows from operating, investing, and financing activities (direct method) *(Learning Objectives 2 & 3)*

Compute the following cash flows for Swift Repair Company for the past year:

1. The beginning balance of Retained Earning was $137,000, while the end of the year balance of Retained Earnings was $175,000. Net income for the year was $63,000. No dividends payable were on the balance sheet. How much was paid in cash dividends during the year?

2. The beginning and ending balances of the Common Stock account were $216,000 and $276,000, respectively. Where would the increase in Common Stock appear on the statement of cash flows?

3. The beginning and ending balances of the Treasury Stock account were $51,000 and $76,000, respectively. Where would the increase in Treasury Stock appear on the statement of cash flows?

4. The Property, Plant, & Equipment (net) increased by $15,000 during the year to have a balance of $159,000 at the end of the year. Depreciation for the year was $15,000. Acquisitions of new plant assets during the year totaled $37,000. Plant assets were sold at a loss of $2,000.

   a. What were the cash proceeds from the sale of plant assets?

   b. What amount would be reported on the investing section of the statement of cash flows? Would it be a source of cash or a use of cash?

   c. What amount would be reported on the operating section of the statement of cash flows? How would it be presented?

E13-23B Calculate operating cash flows (indirect method) *(Learning Objective 2)*

Ericson Corporation has the following activities for the past year:

Net income	$?	Cost of goods sold	$52,000
Payment of dividends	5,000	Other operating expenses	10,000
Proceeds from issuance of stock	73,000	Depreciation expense	16,000
Purchase of treasury stock	13,000	Purchase of equipment	20,000
Sales revenue	120,000	Proceeds from sale of land	18,000
Payment of note payable	10,000	Increase in current assets other than cash	8,000
Decrease in current liabilities	6,000		

Requirement

1. Prepare the operating activities section of Ericson Corporation's statement of cash flows for the year ended, using the indirect method for operating cash flows.

E13-24B Prepare statement of cash flows (indirect method) *(Learning Objective 2)*

Using the data given in E13-23B, prepare the statement of cash flows for Ericson Corporation for the year. Ericson Corporation uses the indirect method for operating activities.

E13-25B Prepare statement of cash flows (indirect method) *(Learning Oobjective 3)*

Lantern Corporation is preparing its statement of cash flows for the past year. Manell Yu has gathered the following information about the past year.

Decrease in accounts receivable	$ 7,000	Retire bond payable (long-term)	$11,000
Increase in salaries payable	9,000	Paid dividends in cash	29,000
Depreciation expense	10,000	Decrease in inventory	6,000
Increase in prepaid insurance	500	Decrease in accounts payable	11,000
Decrease in other short-term liabilities	3,000	Sold land (investment)	21,000
Increase in taxes payable	1,000	Increase in interest payable	400
Purchase of new computer system	11,000	Cash balance, beginning of year	90,000
Net income	91,000		

Requirement

1. Prepare a statement of cash flows for the past year using the indirect method.

E13-26B Compute operating cash flows using direct method *(Learning Objective 3)*

Medford Spas provides the following data for the year just ended.

Payments to employees................	$ 64,500	Payment of note payable	$ 6,000
Proceeds from sale of land............	40,500	Depreciation expense	4,300
Payment of dividends	14,000	Purchase of equipment	9,500
Payments to suppliers..................	69,000	Purchase of treasury stock....................................	12,500
Increase in salaries payable...........	13,500	Gain on sale of land	1,100
Payment of income tax.................	11,000	Cost of goods sold...	110,000
Collections from customers..........	153,000	Proceeds from issuance of common stock.............	15,000
Sales revenue..............................	171,000	Beginning balance, cash..	13,500

Requirement

1. Prepare the operating activities section of Medford Spas' statement of cash flows for the year ended using the direct method for operating cash flows.

E13-27B Prepare statement of cash flows (direct method) *(Learning Objective 3)*

Using the data for E13-26B, prepare the statement of cash flows using the direct method.

E13-28B Prepare statement of cash flows (direct method) *(Learning Objective 3)*

Matthew Interiors began the year with cash of $56,000. During the year, Matthew Interiors earned service revenue of $416,000. Cash collections for the year were $390,000. Expenses for the year were $365,000, with $350,000 of that total paid in cash. Matthew Interiors also used cash to purchase equipment for $70,000 and to pay a cash dividend to stockholders of $40,000. During the year, Matthew Interiors borrowed $56,000 cash by issuing a note payable.

Requirement

1. Prepare the company's statement of cash flows using the direct method.

Problems—Group A

P13-29A Prepare statement of cash flows (indirect method) *(Learning Objective 2)*

Prepare statement of cash flows using the indirect method. The income statement for 2010 and the balance sheets for 2010 and 2009 are presented for Harper Industries.

Harper Industries, Inc.
Income Statement
For Year Ended December 31, 2010

Sales revenue		$951,000
Cost of goods sold		380,400
Gross profit		570,600
Operating expenses:		
Salaries and wage expense	189,000	
Insurance expense	12,000	
Depreciation expense	51,000	
Other operating expenses	83,000	335,000
Operating income		235,600
Other income and expenses:		
Gain on sale of equipment	3,000	
Interest expense	5,300	$ 2,300
Income before taxes		233,300
Income tax expense		69,990
Net income		$163,310

Harper Industries, Inc.
Balance Sheets
As of December 31, 2010 and 2009

	2010	2009
Assets		
Current assets:		
Cash and cash equivalents	$ 475,900	$ 289,100
Accounts receivable	75,000	125,000
Inventory	329,700	211,000
Prepaid insurance	7,600	5,500
Total current assets	888,200	630,600
Property, plant, and equipment	607,000	575,000
Less: Accumulated depreciation	(152,100)	(110,000)
Investments	89,000	75,000
Total assets	$1,432,100	$1,170,600
Liabilities		
Current liabilities:		
Accounts payable (inventory purchases)	$ 55,100	$ 37,000
Salaries payable	16,300	17,000
Interest payable	1,600	500
Taxes payable	60,990	11,000
Other accrued operating expenses	6,000	3,300
Total current liabilities	139,990	68,800
Bonds payable	60,000	25,000
Total liabilities	199,990	93,800
Stockholders' equity		
Common stock	600,000	600,000
Retained earnings	632,110	476,800
Total stockholders' equity	1,232,110	1,076,800
Total liabilities and equity	$1,432,100	$1,170,600

Additional information follows:

a. Sold plant asset for $4,100. Original cost of this plant asset was $10,000 and it had $8,900 of accumulated depreciation associated with it.

b. Paid $5,000 on the bonds payable; issued $40,000 of new bonds payable.

c. Declared and paid cash dividends of $8,000.

d. Purchased new investment for $14,000.

e. Purchased new equipment for $42,000.

Requirement

1. Prepare a statement of cash flows for Harper Industries, Inc., for the year ended December 31, 2010, using the indirect method.

P13-30A Prepare statement of cash flows (indirect method) *(Learning Objectives 1 & 2)*

The 2010 and 2009 balance sheets of Waterside Corporation follow. The 2010 income statement is also provided. Waterside had no noncash investing and financing transactions during 2010. During the year, Waterside sold equipment for $15,200, which had originally cost $13,000 and had a book value of $11,000. Waterside did not issue any notes payable during the year but did issue common stock for $28,000.

Requirements

1. Prepare the statement of cash flows for Waterside Corporation for 2010 using the indirect method.

2. Evaluate Waterside's cash flows for the year. Discuss each of the categories of cash flows in your response.

Waterside Corporation
Income Statement
As of December 31, 2010 and 2009

Sales revenue		$341,000
Cost of goods sold		72,000
Gross profit		269,000
Operating expenses:		
Salaries and wage expense	25,100	
Depreciation expense	5,000	
Other operating expenses	13,000	43,100
Operating income		225,900
Other income and expenses:		
Gain on sale of equipment	4,200	
Interest expense	9,500	
Income before taxes		220,600
Income tax expense		36,800
Net income		$183,800

Waterside Corporation
Balance Sheets
For Years Ended December 31, 2010 and 2009

	2010	2009
Assets		
Current assets:		
Cash and cash equivalents	$ 49,800	$ 20,700
Accounts receivable	32,100	29,300
Inventory	86,000	93,100
Prepaid insurance	3,200	2,500
Total current assets	171,100	145,600
Property, plant, and equipment	156,500	135,800
Less: Accumulated depreciation	(30,000)	(27,000)
Investments	110,000	0
Total assets	$407,600	$254,400
Liabilities		
Current liabilities:		
Accounts payable (inventory purchases)	$ 33,600	$ 36,700
Salaries payable	2,800	7,200
Interest payable	1,900	0
Taxes payable	5,400	0
Other accrued operating expenses	18,600	22,000
Total current liabilities	62,300	65,900
Bonds payable	78,000	110,000
Total liabilities	140,300	175,900
Stockholders' equity		
Common stock	103,000	75,000
Retained earnings	164,300	3,500
Total stockholders' equity	267,300	78,500
Total liabilities and equity	$407,600	$254,400

P13-31A Prepare a statement of cash flows (direct method) *(Learning Objectives 1 & 3)*

Superb Digital Services, Inc., has provided the following data from the company's records for the year just ended:

a.	Collection of interest	$ 5,700
b.	Cash sales	$252,000
c.	Credit sales	$675,500
d.	Proceeds from sale of investment	$ 12,300
e.	Gain on sale of investment	$ 2,500
f.	Payments to suppliers	$572,900
g.	Cash payments to purchase plant assets	$ 52,100
h.	Depreciation expense	$ 63,800
i.	Salaries expense	$ 77,500
j.	Payment of short-term note payable by issuing common stock	$ 72,100
k.	Cost of goods sold	$567,600
l.	Proceeds from issuance of note payable	$ 24,300
m.	Income tax expense and payment	$ 38,600
n.	Proceeds from issuance of common stock	$ 22,000
o.	Cash receipt of dividend revenue	$ 6,700
p.	Interest revenue	$ 6,000
q.	Payment of cash dividends	$ 28,900
r.	Collections of accounts receivable	$574,300
s.	Amortization expense	$ 3,400
t.	Payments on long-term notes payable	$ 45,300
u.	Interest expense and payments	$ 12,100
v.	Purchase of equipment by issuing common stock to seller	$ 17,500
w.	Payment of salaries	$ 74,500
x.	Proceeds from sale of plant assets	$ 24,700
y.	Loss on sale of plant assets	$ 3,500
z.	Cash and cash equivalents balance, beginning of year	$ 25,700

Requirements

1. Prepare the statement of cash flows for Superb Digital Services, Inc., using the direct method for cash flows from operations. Note that you will need to calculate the ending balance of cash and cash equivalents. Include a schedule of noncash investing and financing activities.

2. Evaluate Superb's cash flows for the year. Discuss each of the categories of cash flows in your response.

P13-32A Prepare statements of cash flows (indirect and direct method) (Learning objectives 1, 2, & 3)

Marshall Sign Company, Inc., has the following comparative balance sheet as of March 31, 2010.

Marshall Sign Company, Inc.
Balance Sheet
As of March 31, 2010 and 2009

	2010	2009	Increase (Decrease)
Current assets:			
Cash..	55,900	14,300	41,600
Accounts receivable.............................	51,400	53,200	(1,800)
Inventories	65,300	59,800	5,500
Prepaid expenses..................................	4,100	5,200	(1,100)
Long-term investment	9,400	6,800	2,600
Equipment, net......................................	71,300	70,000	1,300
Land	35,100	96,000	(60,900)
Total assets..	292,500	305,300	(12,800)
Current liabilities:			
Note payable, short-term	43,400	48,100	(4,700)
Accounts payable	4,700	3,200	1,500
Income tax payable	14,100	15,400	(1,300)
Salary payable.......................................	9,700	12,400	(2,700)
Interest payable.....................................	8,300	7,300	1,000
Accrued liabilities.................................	1,500	3,500	(2,000)
Long-term note payable	48,100	93,200	(45,100)
Common stock..	69,800	61,200	8,600
Retained earnings..................................	92,900	61,000	31,900
Total liabilities and equity....................	292,500	305,300	(12,800)

Selected transaction data for the year ended March 31, 2010, include the following:

a.	Net income...	76,900
b.	Paid long-term note payable with cash...............................	59,700
c.	Cash payments to employees..	41,700
d.	Loss on sale of land..	9,500
e.	Acquired equipment by issuing long-term note payable....	14,600
f.	Cash payments to suppliers..	147,500
g.	Cash paid for interest...	4,300
h.	Depreciation expense on equipment....................................	13,300
i.	Paid short-term note payable by issuing common stock	4,700
j.	Paid cash dividends	45,000
k.	Received cash for issuance of common stock......................	3,900
l.	Cash received from customers..	297,400
m.	Cash paid for income taxes	11,800
n.	Sold land for cash..	51,400
o.	Interest received (in cash)	1,500
p.	Purchased long-term investment for cash	2,600

Requirements

1. Prepare the statement of cash flows for Marshall Sign Company, Inc., for the year ended March 31, 2010, using the indirect method for operating cash flows. Include a schedule of noncash investing and financing activities. All of the current accounts, except short-term notes payable, result from operating transactions.

2. Also prepare a supplementary schedule of cash flows from operations using the direct method.

Problems—Group B

P13-33B Prepare statement of cash flows (indirect method) *(Learning Objective 2)*

Prepare statement of cash flows using the indirect method. The income statement for 2010 and the balance sheets for 2010 and 2009 are presented for Hall Industries.

Hall Industries, Inc.
Income Statement
For Year Ended December 31, 2010

Sales revenue		$952,000
Cost of goods sold		383,000
Gross profit		569,000
Operating expenses:		
Salary and wage expense	189,000	
Insurance expense	14,500	
Depreciation expense	51,600	
Other operating expense	84,000	339,100
Operating income		229,900
Other income and expense:		
Gain on sale of equipment	3,000	
Interest expense	5,100	2,100
Income before taxes		227,800
Income tax expense		68,340
Net income		$159,460

Hall Industries, Inc.
Comparative Balance Sheet
As of December 31, 2010 and 2009

	2010	2009
Assets		
Current assets:		
Cash and cash equivalents	$ 472,000	$ 292,000
Accounts receivable	78,000	125,000
Inventory	327,000	213,000
Prepaid expenses	9,500	6,500
Total current assets	886,500	636,500
Property, plant, and equipment	620,000	580,000
Less: Accumulated depreciation	(149,000)	(107,000)
Investments	86,000	73,000
Total assets	$1,443,500	$1,182,500
Liabilities		
Current liabilities:		
Accounts payable (inventory purchases)	$ 54,000	$ 36,000
Salaries payable	16,400	17,800
Interest payable	1,900	800
Taxes payable	59,340	12,000
Other accrued operating expenses	6,500	3,200
Total current liabilities	138,140	69,800
Bonds payable	66,000	27,000
Total liabilities	204,140	96,800
Stockholders' equity		
Common stock	602,000	602,000
Retained earnings	637,360	483,700
Total stockholders' equity	1,239,360	1,085,700
Total liabilities and stockholders' equity	$1,443,500	$1,182,500

Additional information follows:

a. Sold plant asset for $4,200. Original cost of this plant asset was $10,800 and it had $9,600 of accumulated depreciation associated with it.

b. Paid $5,500 on the bonds payable; issued $44,500 of new bonds payable.

c. Declared and paid cash dividends of $5,800.

d. Purchased new investment for $13,000.

e. Purchased new equipment for $50,800.

Requirement

1. Prepare a statement of cash flows for Hall Industries, Inc., for the year ended December 31, 2010, using the indirect method.

P13-34B Prepare statement of cash flows (indirect method) *(Learning Objectives 1 & 2)*

The 2010 and 2009 balance sheets of Walker Corporation follow. The 2010 income statement is also provided. Walker had no noncash investing and financing transactions during 2010. During the year, Walker sold equipment for $15,700, which had originally cost $13,200 and had a book value of $11,200. Walker did not issue any notes payable during the year but did issue common stock for $23,000.

Requirements

1. Prepare the statement of cash flows for Walker Corporation for 2010 using the indirect method.

2. Evaluate Walker's cash flows for the year. Discuss each of the categories of cash flows in your response.

Walker Corporation
Income Statement
For Year Ended December 31, 2010

Sales revenue		$346,000
Cost of goods sold		76,000
Gross profit		270,000
Operating expenses:		
Salary and wage expense	$25,500	
Insurance expense	—	
Depreciation expense	5,200	
Other operating expense	14,500	45,200
Operating income		224,800
Other income and expense:		
Gain on sale of equipment	4,500	
Interest expense	9,400	4,900
Income before taxes		219,900
Income tax expense		36,600
Net income		$183,300

Walker Corporation
Comparative Balance Sheet
As of December 31, 2010 and 2009

	2010	2009
Assets		
Current assets:		
Cash and cash equivalents	$ 48,000	$ 21,000
Accounts receivable	31,700	29,900
Inventory	86,100	94,600
Prepaid expenses	3,300	2,700
Total current assets	169,100	148,200
Property, plant, and equipment	157,000	137,000
Less: Accumulated depreciation	(30,800)	(27,600)
Investments	116,000	0
Total assets	$411,300	$257,600
Liabilities		
Current liabilities:		
Accounts payable (inventory purchases)	$ 33,300	$ 36,500
Salaries payable	2,600	7,600
Interest payable	2,600	0
Taxes payable	6,200	0
Other accrued operating expenses	18,900	22,500
Total current liabilities	63,600	66,600
Bonds payable	71,000	113,000
Total liabilities	134,600	179,600
Stockholders' equity		
Common stock	99,000	76,000
Retained earnings	177,700	2,000
Total stockholders' equity	276,700	78,000
Total liabilities and equity	$411,300	$257,600

P13-35B Prepare a statement of cash flows (direct method) *(Learning Objectives 1 & 3)*

Inspired Digital Services, Inc., has provided the following data from the company's records for the year just ended:

a.	Collection of interest	$ 5,200
b.	Cash sales	$254,000
c.	Credit sales	$673,000
d.	Proceeds from sale of investment	$ 12,700
e.	Gain on sale of investment	$ 2,400
f.	Payments to suppliers	$572,500
g.	Cash payments to purchase plant assets	$ 52,900
h.	Depreciation expense	$ 63,500
i.	Salaries expense	$ 77,600
j.	Payment of short-term note payable by issuing common stock	$ 71,800
k.	Cost of goods sold	$567,500
l.	Proceeds from issuance of note payable	$ 24,000
m.	Income tax expense and payment	$ 38,100
n.	Proceeds from issuance of common stock	$ 21,000
o.	Cash receipt of dividend revenue	$ 6,500
p.	Interest revenue	$ 5,600
q.	Payment of cash dividends	$ 28,600
r.	Collections of accounts receivable	$572,500
s.	Amortization expense	$ 3,200
t.	Payments on long-term notes payable	$ 44,500
u.	Interest expense and payments	$ 12,700
v.	Purchase of equipment by issuing common stock to seller	$ 17,600
w.	Payment of salaries	$ 74,600
x.	Proceeds from sale of plant assets	$ 24,800
y.	Loss on sale of plant assets	$ 3,000
z.	Cash and cash equivalents balance, beginning of year	$ 25,800

Requirements

1. Prepare the statement of cash flows for Inspired Digital Services, Inc., using the direct method for cash flows from operations. Note that you will need to calculate the ending balance of cash and cash equivalents. Include a schedule of noncash investing and financing activities.

2. Evaluate Inspired's cash flows for the year. Discuss each of the categories of cash flows in your response.

P13-36B Prepare statements of cash flows (indirect and direct method) *(Learning Objectives 1, 2, & 3)*

Barton Publication Company, Inc., has the following comparative balance sheet as of March 31, 2010.

Barton Publication Company, Inc.
Balance Sheet
As of March 31, 2010 and 2009

	2010	2009	Increase (Decrease)
Current assets:			
Cash...	$ 55,600	$ 14,700	$ 40,900
Accounts receivable.................................	51,400	53,300	(1,900)
Inventories	65,400	59,700	5,700
Prepaid expenses	3,700	5,100	(1,400)
Long-term investment	10,000	6,800	3,200
Equipment, net...	71,700	70,200	1,500
Land	35,500	97,000	(61,500)
Total assets...	293,300	$306,800	$(13,500)
Current liabilities:			
Note payable, short-term	$ 43,200	$ 48,900	$ (5,700)
Accounts payable.....................................	4,300	3,500	800
Income tax payable	13,700	15,500	(1,800)
Salary payable...	9,200	12,400	(3,200)
Interest payable.......................................	8,200	7,400	800
Accrued liabilities....................................	2,900	3,400	(500)
Long-term note payable	48,900	93,100	(44,200)
Common stock..	69,600	61,700	7,900
Retained earnings....................................	93,300	60,900	32,400
Total liabilities and equity........................	$293,300	$306,800	$(13,500)

Selected transaction data for the year ended March 31, 2010, include the following:
a. Net income, $77,000
b. Paid long-term note payable with cash, $59,600
c. Cash payments to employees, $43,000
d. Loss on sale of land, $9,600
e. Acquired equipment by issuing long-term note payable, $15,400
f. Cash payments to suppliers, $147,100
g. Cash paid for interest, $4,100
h. Depreciation expense on equipment, $13,900
i. Paid short-term note payable by issuing common stock, $5,700
j. Paid cash dividends, $44,600
k. Received cash for issuance of common stock, $2,200
l. Cash received from customers, $299,400
m. Cash paid for income taxes, $12,000
n. Sold land for cash, $51,900
o. Interest received (in cash), $1,000
p. Purchased long-term investment for cash, $3,200

Requirements

1. Prepare the statement of cash flows for Barton Publication Company, Inc., for the year ended March 31, 2010, using the indirect method for operating cash flows. Include a schedule of noncash investing and financing activities. All of the current accounts except short-term notes payable result from operating transactions.

2. Also prepare a supplementary schedule of cash flows from operations using the direct method.

APPLY YOUR KNOWLEDGE

Decision Cases

C13-37 Use cash flow data to evaluate potential investments (Learning Objectives 1 & 2)

Your company has some excess cash and would like to invest it in the stock of another company. You investigate several different stocks and are trying to decide which stock would be the best investment for your company. One factor you investigate is each company's cash flow. The summaries of the cash flow statements for your three top stock choices follow:

(000s omitted)	Baxter, Corp.	Meredith Enterprises	Rollyson, Inc.
Net cash provided by (used for)			
operating activities..	(20,000)	28,100	16,000
Cash provided by (used for)			
investing activities:			
Cash used to purchase plant or equipment ...		(12,100)	(25,000)
Proceeds from the sale of equipment............	8,000		
Cash used to purchase investments in stock..		(5,000)	
Net cash provided by (used for)			
investing activities...	8,000	(17,100)	(25,000)
Cash provided by (used for)			
financing activities:			
Proceeds from bond issuance	23,500	4,000	5,000
Repayment of long-term debt......................	(1,000)	(2,000)	
Cash proceeds from issuance of stock			12,000
Cash payments for dividends	(2,500)	(5,000)	
Net cash provided by (used for)			
financing activities...	20,000	(3,000)	17,000
Net increase in cash	8,000	8,000	8,000

Although you will look at many other criteria in your stock purchase recommendation, what can you tell about each of the three companies listed? Based solely on cash flow, which stock appears to be better?

Discussion & Analysis

1. How do managers use the statement of cash flows by managers?

2. Describe at least four needs for cash within a business.

3. Define an "operating activity." List two examples of an operating activity on the statement of cash flows that would *increase* cash. List two examples of an operating activity that would *decrease* cash.

4. Define an "investing activity." List two examples of an investing activity on the statement of cash flows that would *increase* cash. List two examples of an investing activity that would *decrease* cash.

5. Define a "financing activity." List two examples of a financing activity on the statement of cash flows that would *increase* cash. List two examples of a financing activity that would *decrease* cash.

Quick Check Answers

1. *d* 2. *c* 3. *a* 4. *b* 5. *d* 6. *b* 7. *c*
8. *b* 9. *a* 10. *a*

For online homework, exercises, and problems that provide you with immediate feedback, please visit www.myaccountinglab.com.

6. Define a "noncash investing or financing" activity. Describe an activity that would need to be disclosed as a noncash investing or financing activity.

7. Describe the difference between the direct and the indirect methods of preparing the operating section of the statement of cash flows.

8. Describe the process for reconciling net income to the cash basis. What items are added to net income? What items are subtracted from net income?

9. When preparing a statement of cash flows using the indirect method, what information is needed? What documents or statements would be used?

10. Summarize the process for preparing the operations section of the statement of cash flows when using the direct method.

Application & Analysis

13-1　Comparing Cash Flow Statements from Companies in the Same Industry

Select an industry in which you are interested and select two companies within that industry. Obtain their annual reports by going to each company's Web site and downloading the report for the most recent year. (On many company Web sites, you will need to visit the Investor Relations section or other similarly named link to obtain the company's financial statements.)

Basic Discussion Questions

For each of the companies you selected, answer the following:

1. Which method is used to calculate the cash provided or used by operations?

2. What items increased cash provided by operations?

3. What items decreased cash provided by operations?

4. Overall, was cash increased or decreased by operating activities?

5. Did investing activities in total increase cash or decrease cash during the year? What were the major uses or sources of cash related to investing?

6. Did financing activities in total increase cash or decrease cash during the year? What were the major uses or sources of cash related to financing?

7. What items (if any) are disclosed as significant noncash financing or investing activities?

Now that you have looked at each company's cash flow statements individually, compare the two companies. What can you tell about each company from its statement of cash flows? Can you tell if one company is stronger than the other from their statements of cash flows? What clues do you have?

Classroom Applications

Web: Post the discussion questions on an electronic discussion board. Have small groups of students choose an industry and two companies within that industry for their group. Students should discuss their responses to the listed questions.

Classroom: Form groups of 3–4 students. Your group should choose an industry and two companies within that industry. After answering the listed questions, prepare a five-minute presentation about your group's two companies that compares the companies based on the interpretation of their statement of cash flows.

Independent: Select two companies within the same industry. Turn in a 2–3 page typed paper (12 point font, double-spaced with 1" margins) that contains answers to the listed questions. Include the URLs for the annual reports you retrieved.

For additional Application & Analysis projects and implementation tips, see the Instructor Resources in MyAccountingLab.com

With over $63 billion in annual sales, Target Corporation

is currently the fifth largest retailer in the United States. Its trademark symbol, the bull's-eye, is recognized by 96% of people surveyed. This brand recognition even beats out familiar trademarks like Nike's swoosh. Target has a reputation for being one of the largest supporters of corporate social responsibility, donating over $14 million to schools nationwide in 2008 alone. As a result of these corporate practices, *Fortune* magazine has ranked Target Corporation as one of "America's Most Admired Companies."

All of these accolades might lead one to believe that Target must be highly profitable. Indeed, Target *has* earned a profit in each of the past 10 years. But, net income alone does not tell the whole story. Has revenue grown steadily, or have there been large fluctuations—ups and downs—over the course recent years? How big was each year's profit in relation to sales? For every dollar sold, how much of it ended up as gross profit, and how much of it went to pay for operating expenses? What kind of return has the company been providing to shareholders? And how quickly has Target been able to sell its highly seasonable and fashion-trended merchandise?

Financial statement analysis can help us answer these questions.

Sources: www.target.com,
www.stores.org/pdf/09Top100chart.pdf

CHAPTER 14

Financial Statement Analysis

Learning Objectives

1   Perform a horizontal analysis of financial statements

2   Perform a vertical analysis of financial statements

3   Prepare and use common-size financial statements

4   Compute the standard financial ratios

nvestors and creditors can't evaluate a company very well by examining the financial statements from only one year. Performance is better judged by comparing financial statement data:

- From year to year
- With a competitor, such as Wal-Mart
- With industry averages

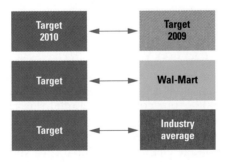

In this chapter, we'll examine several analytical tools that are frequently used to judge the financial performance of a company as a whole. To illustrate, we'll apply these tools to Supermart, a regional retailer of general merchandise that is similar to, but smaller than Target. Then we will apply these analytical tools directly to Target Corporation's financial statements in the mid-chapter and end-of-chapter summary problems.

What are the Most Common Methods of Analysis?

Why is this important?

"Evaluating the performance of a company is difficult without some type of benchmark for comparison. Therefore, managers typically benchmark financial performance over time, against other companies, or against industry averages."

There are three ways to analyze financial statements:

- **Horizontal analysis** provides a year-to-year comparison of a company's performance in different periods.

- **Vertical analysis** provides a means of evaluating the relative size of each line item in the financial statements. It also allows us to compare companies of different size.

- **Ratio analysis** provides a means of evaluating the relationships between key components of the financial statements.

We'll explain the first two methods in this half of the chapter, and then devote the entire second half of the chapter to ratio analysis.

To use these tools, we must begin with the company's financial statements. Exhibit 14-1 presents Supermart's income statement for the last two years, while Exhibit 14-2 presents the company's balance sheet for the last two years.

EXHIBIT 14-1 Supermart Income Statement

Supermart
Income Statement
For the Years Ended December 31, 2010 and 2009

(amounts in thousands)	2010	2009
Sales revenue	$858,000	$803,000
Cost of goods sold	513,000	509,000
Gross profit	345,000	294,000
Operating expenses	244,000	237,000
Operating income	101,000	57,000
Interest expense	20,000	14,000
Income before income taxes	81,000	43,000
Income tax expense	33,000	17,000
Net income	$ 48,000	$ 26,000

Horizontal Analysis

Perform a horizontal analysis of financial statements

Many decisions hinge on whether sales, expenses, and net income are increasing or decreasing. Have sales and other revenues risen from last year? By how much? Sales may have increased by $20,000, but considered alone, this fact is not very helpful. The *percentage change* in sales over time is more helpful. It is better to know that sales increased by 20% than to know that sales increased by $20,000.

The study of percentage changes in comparative statements is called **horizontal analysis**. Computing a percentage change in comparative statements requires two steps:

1. Compute the dollar amount of the change from the earlier period to the later period.

2. Divide the dollar amount of change by the earlier period amount. We call the earlier period the base period.

EXHIBIT 14-2   Supermart Balance Sheet

Supermart
Balance Sheet
December 31, 2010 and 2009

(amounts in thousands)	2010	2009
Assets		
Current assets:		
Cash..	$ 29,000	$ 32,000
Accounts receivables, net....................................	114,000	85,000
Inventory...	113,000	111,000
Other current assets	6,000	8,000
Total current assets	262,000	236,000
Property, plant, and equipment, net	507,000	399,000
Other noncurrent assets	18,000	9,000
Total assets...	$787,000	$644,000
Liabilities		
Current liabilities:		
Accounts payable	$ 73,000	$ 68,000
Notes payable	42,000	27,000
Accrued liabilities..	27,000	31,000
Total current liabilities	142,000	126,000
Long-term liabilities	289,000	198,000
Total liabilities	431,000	324,000
Stockholders' Equity		
Common stock, no par...	186,000	186,000
Retained earnings...	170,000	134,000
Total stockholders' equity	356,000	320,000
Total liabilities and equity..................................	$787,000	$644,000

Let's illustrate with Supermart's sales revenue, shown in Exhibit 14-1:

Step 1) Compute the dollar amount of change in sales revenue from 2009 to 2010:

2010	2009	Increase
$858,000 −	$803,000 =	$55,000

Step 2) Divide the dollar amount of change by the base-period amount. This computes
the percentage change for the period:

$$\text{Percentage change} = \frac{\text{Dollar amount of change}}{\text{Base-year amount}}$$

$$= \frac{\$55,000}{\$803,000} = 0.068 \text{ (rounded)} = 6.8\%$$

We now see that Supermart's sales revenue increased by $55,000, or 6.8%, over the
previous year.

Horizontal Analysis of the Income Statement

Exhibit 14-3 shows a complete horizontal analysis of Supermart's income statement.

EXHIBIT 14-3 **Supermart Comparative Income Statement—Horizontal Analysis**

Supermart
Comparative Income Statements
For the Years Ended December 31, 2010 and 2009

(amounts in thousands)	2010	2009	Increase (Decrease) Change	Increase (Decrease) Percentage*
Sales revenue	$858,000	$803,000	$55,000	6.8%
Cost of goods sold	513,000	509,000	4,000	0.8%
Gross profit	345,000	294,000	51,000	17.3%
Operating expenses	244,000	237,000	7,000	3.0%
Operating income	101,000	57,000	44,000	77.2%
Interest expense	20,000	14,000	6,000	42.9%
Income before income taxes	81,000	43,000	38,000	88.4%
Income tax expense	33,000	17,000	16,000	94.1%
Net income	$ 48,000	$ 26,000	$22,000	84.6%

*rounded

The horizontal analysis shows that sales increased by almost 7%, yet the cost of goods sold increased by less than 1%. Supermart was either able to raise its prices, find cheaper suppliers, or sell products with higher margins. As a result, gross profit was about 17% higher than the previous year. Supermart was also able to hold its operating expenses to a 3% increase. These factors all contributed to increasing operating income by 77% over the previous year! Interest expense increased 42%, either as a result of a higher interest rate, more debt, or a combination of the two. Finally, as a result of the increased income, income taxes also increased substantially. The end result was an 84% increase in net income over the previous year.

Horizontal Analysis of the Balance Sheet

Exhibit 14-4 shows a complete horizontal analysis of Supermart's balance sheet.

The horizontal analysis shows that Supermart's accounts receivable grew substantially over the year (34%), while its cash decreased about 9%. The company may have relaxed its credit terms to generate more sales. The company also has taken on more short- and long-term debt, which may have been used to finance the significant additions to property, plant, and equipment and the increase in noncurrent assets that occurred during the year.

Trend Percentages

Trend percentages are a form of horizontal analysis. Trends indicate the direction a business is taking over a longer period of time, such as three, five, or ten years. For example, in Exhibit 14-3, we saw that Supermart's net income increased a whopping 84% over the previous year. Has income always been increasing at such a significant rate? Or was that an isolated growth spurt limited to a one-year period? Investors typically like to see smooth growth trends over time, rather than large, sporadic fluctuations in sales and net income.

Trend percentages are computed by selecting a base year. The base-year amounts are set equal to 100%. The amounts for each following year are expressed as a percentage of the base amount. To compute trend percentages, divide each item in the following years by the base-year amount.

$$\text{Trend \%} = \frac{\text{Any year \$}}{\text{Base year \$}}$$

EXHIBIT 14-4 Comparative Balance Sheet—Horizontal Analysis

Supermart
Comparative Balance Sheet
December 31, 2010 and 2009

(amounts in thousands)	2010	2009	Increase (Decrease) Change	Percentage*
Assets				
Current assets:				
Cash	$ 29,000	$ 32,000	$ (3,000)	(9.4%)
Accounts receivables, net..................	114,000	85,000	29,000	34.1%
Inventory...	113,000	111,000	2,000	1.8%
Other current assets	6,000	8,000	(2,000)	(25.0%)
Total current assets	262,000	236,000	26,000	11.0%
Property, plant, and equipment, net.......	507,000	399,000	108,000	27.1%
Other noncurrent assets	18,000	9,000	9,000	100.0%
Total assets...............................	$787,000	$644,000	$143,000	22.2%
Liabilities				
Current liabilities:				
Accounts payable	$ 73,000	$ 68,000	$ 5,000	7.4%
Notes payable	42,000	27,000	15,000	55.6%
Accrued liabilities..............................	27,000	31,000	(4,000)	(12.9%)
Total current liabilities	142,000	126,000	16,000	12.7%
Long-term liabilities	289,000	198,000	91,000	46.0%
Total liabilities	431,000	324,000	107,000	33.0%
Stockholders' Equity				
Common stock, no par.......................	186,000	186,000	0	0.0%
Retained earnings..............................	170,000	134,000	36,000	26.9%
Total stockholders' equity	356,000	320,000	36,000	11.3%
Total liabilities and equity.................	$787,000	$644,000	$143,000	22.2%

*rounded

Supermart's sales revenue, and trend percentages from 2005 to 2010, are pictured in Exhibit 14-5. We selected 2005 as the base, so that year's percentage is set equal to 100.

EXHIBIT 14-5 Supermart's Sales Trend

	2010	2009	2008	2007	2006	Base Year 2005
Sales revenue	$858,000	$780,000	$690,000	$648,000	$618,000	$600,000
Trend percentage	143%	130%	115%	108%	103%	100%

From the percentages, we see that sales increased at a fairly slow, even rate in the earlier years (2005–2008). However, the rate of increase picked up in the later years (2009 and 2010). Supermart is obviously experiencing growth, either in existing store sales, or by adding new retail locations. Trend data is often pictured using line graphs. In fact, publically traded companies show the trend of their stock returns in the 10-K filings required by the Securities and Exchange Commission (SEC). Exhibit 14-6 shows Supermart's sales trends. As you can see, sales have increased every year, but the rate of increase has been larger in recent years (as shown by the steeper incline of the line from 2009–2010).

You can perform a trend analysis on any item you consider important. Trend analysis is widely used to predict the future.

EXHIBIT 14-6   Line Graph of Sales Trend

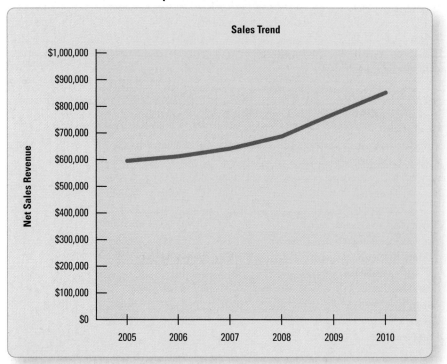

Vertical Analysis

2 Perform a vertical analysis of financial statements

As we have seen, horizontal analysis and trend percentages highlight changes in an item over time. But no single technique gives a complete picture of a business, so we also need vertical analysis.

Vertical analysis of a financial statement shows the relationship of each item to a base amount, which is the 100% figure. Every other item on the statement is then reported as a percentage of that base. When performing vertical analysis of an income statement, sales revenue is usually considered the base (100%).

$$\text{Vertical analysis \% for income statement} = \frac{\text{Each income statement item}}{\text{Revenue (net sales)}}$$

Exhibit 14-7 shows the vertical analysis of Supermart's 2010 income statement.

EXHIBIT 14-7   Income Statement—Vertical Analysis

Supermart
Income Statement
For the Year Ended December 31, 2010

(amounts in thousands)	Amount	Percentage*
Sales revenue	$858,000	100.0%
Cost of goods sold	513,000	59.8%
Gross profit	345,000	40.2%
Operating expenses	244,000	28.4%
Operating income	101,000	11.8%
Interest expense	20,000	2.4%
Income before income taxes	81,000	9.4%
Income tax expense	33,000	3.8%
Net income	$ 48,000	5.6%

*rounded

The vertical analysis shows that the Supermart's gross profit is 40% of sales revenue. Operating expenses use up 28% of each dollar sold, while income taxes and interest use up another 6%. As a result of all of these expenses, only 5.6% of every sales dollar ends up as net income (for every $1.00 of sales revenue, a little less than $0.06 ends up as net income).

When performing vertical analysis of a balance sheet, total assets is usually considered the base (100%).

$$\text{Vertical analysis \% for balance sheet} = \frac{\text{Each balance sheet line item}}{\text{Total assets}}$$

Exhibit 14-8 shows the vertical analysis of Supermart's 2010 balance sheet. The base amount (100%) is total assets.

EXHIBIT 14-8   Balance Sheet—Vertical Analysis

<table>
<tr><td colspan="3" align="center">**Supermart**
Balance Sheet
December 31, 2010</td></tr>
<tr><td>*(amounts in thousands)*</td><td>Amount</td><td>Percentage*</td></tr>
<tr><td colspan="3" align="center">Assets</td></tr>
<tr><td>Current assets:</td><td></td><td></td></tr>
<tr><td>Cash...</td><td>$ 29,000</td><td>3.7%</td></tr>
<tr><td>Accounts receivables, net.................................</td><td>114,000</td><td>14.5%</td></tr>
<tr><td>Inventory..</td><td>113,000</td><td>14.4%</td></tr>
<tr><td>Other current assets ....</td><td>6,000</td><td>0.8%</td></tr>
<tr><td>Total current assets ....</td><td>262,000</td><td>33.3%</td></tr>
<tr><td>Property, plant, and equipment, net ....</td><td>507,000</td><td>64.4%</td></tr>
<tr><td>Other noncurrent assets ....</td><td>18,000</td><td>2.3%</td></tr>
<tr><td>Total assets..</td><td>$787,000</td><td>100.0%</td></tr>
<tr><td colspan="3" align="center">Liabilities</td></tr>
<tr><td>Current liabilities:</td><td></td><td></td></tr>
<tr><td>Accounts payable ....</td><td>$ 73,000</td><td>9.3%</td></tr>
<tr><td>Notes payable ....</td><td>42,000</td><td>5.3%</td></tr>
<tr><td>Accrued liabilities...</td><td>27,000</td><td>3.4%</td></tr>
<tr><td>Total current liabilities ....</td><td>142,000</td><td>18.0%</td></tr>
<tr><td>Long-term liabilities...</td><td>289,000</td><td>36.7%</td></tr>
<tr><td>Total liabilities ....</td><td>431,000</td><td>54.8%</td></tr>
<tr><td colspan="3" align="center">Stockholders' Equity</td></tr>
<tr><td>Common stock, no par.....................................</td><td>186,000</td><td>23.6%</td></tr>
<tr><td>Retained earnings...</td><td>170,000</td><td>21.6%</td></tr>
<tr><td>Total stockholders' equity.................................</td><td>356,000</td><td>45.2%</td></tr>
<tr><td>Total liabilities and equity................................</td><td>$787,000</td><td>100.0%</td></tr>
</table>

*rounded

The vertical analysis of Supermart's balance sheet reveals that most of the company's assets (64%) consist of property, plant, and equipment. Inventory and receivables together make up about 29% of the company's assets. While the company is in the business of selling merchandise and, therefore, needs a fair amount of inventory, the receivables balance may be higher than desirable. Current liabilities is only 18% of total assets, but long-term debt is double that amount. Finally, stockholders' equity makes up a significant portion of assets 45%.

How do we Compare One Company with Another?

Horizontal analysis and vertical analysis provide a great deal of useful data about a company. But the Supermart data apply to only one business. Many times we want to **benchmark**, or compare, a company against either 1) its competitor, or 2) industry averages.

Prepare and use common-size financial statements

3

To compare Supermart to another company, we can use a common-size statement. A **common-size statement** reports only percentages—the same percentages that appear in a vertical analysis. By using only the percentages, rather than gross dollar amounts, we are able to compare companies that vary in terms of size. For example, in Exhibit 14-9 we use common-size income statements to compare Supermart, a smaller regional retailer, to Target, a large national retailer.

EXHIBIT 14-9 **Common-Size Income Statement**

Supermart
Common-Size Income Statement
Supermart Versus Target

	Supermart	Target*
Sales revenue	100.0%	100.0%
Cost of goods sold	59.8%	69.7%
Gross profit	40.2%	30.3%
Operating expenses	28.4%	23.4%
Operating income	11.8%	6.9%
Interest expense	2.4%	1.4%
Income before income taxes	9.4%	5.5%
Income tax expense	3.8%	2.0%
Net income	5.6%	3.5%

*Adapted from Target's 2008 income statement

Exhibit 14-9 shows that Supermart is actually more profitable, on each dollar of sales revenue (5.6%), than Target (3.5%). Supermart's gross margin (40.2%) is about 10 percentage points higher than Target's (30.3%), but its operating expenses use up more of each sales dollar (28.4%) than do Target's operating expenses (24.4%). Likewise, Supermart's income taxes and interest expense also use up a slightly larger percentage of sales revenue. Despite these small differences, none of the line item percentages are drastically different than Target's.

We could also compare Supermart against industry averages, using the same type of anlaysis. However, since Target is the fifth largest retailer in the country, it accounts for a large portion of the industry average. Therefore, we wouldn't expect the results to be much different.

Before going on, be sure to review the decision guidelines. Then practice what you have learned in Summary Problem 1 by performing vertical and horizontal analysis on Target Corporation's financial statements.

Decision Guidelines

Horizontal and Vertical Analysis

In order to make well-informed financial decisions, investors, creditors, and managers need to determine how well the company is performing. The following guidelines help these decision makers judge the financial performance of a company.

Decision	Guidelines
What methods are generally used to evaluate a company's performance?	• Horizontal analysis • Vertical analysis • Ratio analysis
How does trend analysis differ from horizontal analysis?	Horizontal analysis performed over a longer period of time (3–10 years) is usually called trend analysis. When performing trend analysis, a base year is chosen, and set to 100%. All years after the base year are calculated as a percentage of the base year.
What line item on the income statement is used as the base amount (100%) for vertical analysis?	Net sales revenue is generally used as the base (100%) for vertical analysis of the income statement.
What line item on the balance sheet is used as the base amount (100%) for vertical analysis?	Total assets are generally used as the base (100%) for vertical analysis of the balance sheet.
How can I compare two companies that differ in size?	Common-size income statements and balance sheets are generally used to compare companies that differ in size. Common-size financial statements present the vertical analysis percentages of different companies, side-by-side.

Summary Problem 1

Target Corporation's annual sales and net income data for the years 2000–2008 are presented next. Also shown are Target Corporation's 2008 and 2007 comparative income statements (adapted).[1] Keep in mind that the latest recession began in the United States in December 2007. This recession had a far-reaching impact on most sectors of the economy, including retailers.

(in millions)	2008	2007	2006	2005	2004	2003	2002	2001	2000
Sales**	$63,339	$62,530	$58,783	$51,844	$46,102	$41,303	$43,152	$39,363	$36,561
Net income	$ 2,214	$ 2,849	$ 2,787	$ 2,408	$ 3,198	$ 1,809	$ 1,654	$ 1,368	$ 1,264

** Includes the company's credit card operations, including credit card revenue, net of credit card expense.

---

[1]Target Corporation 10-K, March 13, 2009.

**Target Corporation
Income Statement (Adapted)
For the Fiscal Year 2008 and 2007***

(Dollars in millions)	2008	2007
Sales revenue**	$63,339	$62,530
Cost of goods sold	44,157	42,929
Gross profit	19,182	19,601
Operating expenses:		
Selling, general, and administrative	12,954	12,670
Depreciation	1,826	1,659
Operating income	4,402	5,272
Interest expense, net	866	647
Income tax expense	1,322	1,776
Net income	$ 2,214	$ 2,849

*Because of the busy holiday season, retailers rarely end their fiscal year at December 31. Target's 2008 fiscal year ended January 31, 2009, and its 2007 fiscal year ended February 2, 2008.
**Includes the company's credit card operations including credit card revenue, net of credit card expenses.

Requirements

1. Perform a trend analysis for the years 2000–2008, using 2000 as the base year. Comment on the results.

2. Perform a horizontal analysis for the years 2007–2008 and comment on the results.

3. Perform a vertical analysis for the years 2007–2008 and comment on the results.

Solutions

Requirement 1

(in millions)	2008	2007	2006	2005	2004	2003	2002	2001	2000
Sales revenue	$63,339	$62,530	$58,783	$51,844	$46,102	$41,303	$43,152	$39,363	$36,561
Trend percentage*	173%	171%	161%	142%	126%	113%	118%	108%	100%
Net income	$ 2,214	$ 2,849	$ 2,787	$ 2,408	$ 3,198	$ 1,809	$ 1,654	$ 1,368	$ 1,264
Trend percentage*	175%	225%	220%	191%	253%	143%	131%	108%	100%

*rounded

Sales revenue has gradually increased over time. Current sales revenue is 173% of what it had been in the base year, 2000. Likewise, current net income is 175% of what it had been in the base year. However, the increase in net income was not as gradual as the increase in sales. In fact, net income has had significant yearly variations that do not correspond directly with the increase in sales. Operations, other than sales, must have significantly influenced net income in certain years.

Requirement 2

Target Corporation
Horizontal Analysis of Comparative Income Statements
For the Fiscal Years 2008 and 2007

			Increase (Decrease)	
(Dollars in millions)	2008	2007	Amount	Percentage*
Sales revenue...	$63,339	$62,530	$ 809	1.3%
Cost of goods sold.....................................	44,157	42,929	1,228	2.9%
Gross profit..	19,182	19,601	(419)	(2.1%)
Operating expenses:				
Selling, general, and administrative	12,954	12,670	284	2.2%
Depreciation......................................	1,826	1,659	167	10.1%
Operating income.....................................	4,402	5,272	(870)	(16.5%)
Interest expense, net.................................	866	647	219	33.8%
Income tax expense...................................	1,322	1,776	(454)	(25.5%)
Net income..	$ 2,214	$ 2,849	$ (635)	(22.3%)

*rounded

Cost of Goods Sold increased at a greater rate (2.9%) than sales revenue (1.3%), leading to a decline of 2.1% in gross profit. Selling, general, and administrative expenses increased at a similar rate (2.2%) as cost of goods sold. However, depreciation increased significantly (10.1%), perhaps as a result of new retail stores. These increases in operating expenses led to a 16.5% decline in operating income. Interest expense increased dramatically (33.8%). This increase could be a result of the company holding more debt and/or an increase in the interest rate on the debt. Finally, income tax expense decreased at about the same rate (25.5%) as net income (22.3%).

Requirement 3

Target Corporation
Vertical Analysis of Comparative Income Statements
For the Fiscal Years 2008 and 2007

	2008		2007	
	Amount	Percent*	Amount	Percent*
Sales revenue...	$63,339	100.0%	$62,530	100.0%
Cost of goods sold.....................................	44,157	69.7%	42,929	68.7%
Gross profit..	19,182	30.3%	19,601	31.3%
Operating expenses:				
Selling, general, and administrative	12,954	20.5%	12,670	20.3%
Depreciation......................................	1,826	2.9%	1,659	2.7%
Operating income.....................................	4,402	6.9%	5,272	8.4%
Interest expense, net.................................	866	1.4%	647	1.0%
Income tax expense...................................	1,322	2.0%	1,776	2.8%
Net income..	$ 2,214	3.5%	$ 2,849	4.6%

*rounded

The vertical analysis shows that Target's gross profit is roughly 30% of sales revenue, although this amount shrunk by one percent from 2007. Selling, general, and administrative expenses use up about 20% of the company's sales revenue, while depreciation accounts for almost 3% of sales revenue. Interest and income taxes, combined, use up another 3.5% of sales revenue. As a result, net income is only 3.5% of sales revenue, which is down one percent from 2007. That means, for every dollar of sales revenue generated by the company, only three and one half cents ends up as net income.

What are Some of the Most Common Financial Ratios?

4 Compute the standard financial ratios

In this half of the chapter, we'll discuss many different financial ratios that managers, investors, and creditors use when analyzing a company's financial statements. Most of the information needed for these ratios can be found in the company's financial statements (refer to Supermart's income statement and balance sheet in Exhibits 14-1 and 14-2). A few of the ratios require the knowledge of the company's closing market price, which can be found in the *Wall Street Journal*. Other ratios require knowledge of the number of shares outstanding. This information can be obtained in the company's 10-K filing.

The ratios we'll discuss in this chapter may be classified as follows:

1. Measuring ability to pay current liabilities
2. Measuring ability to sell inventory and collect receivables
3. Measuring ability to pay long-term debt
4. Measuring profitability
5. Analyzing stock investments

Why is this important?

"Managers use different financial ratios to evaluate a company's performance, depending on the underlying need. For example, if a manager wants to know how quickly inventory is selling, he or she will calculate inventory turnover. If a manager wants to know how easily the company will be able to meet its current obligations, he or she will calculate the current ratio or quick ratio."

Measuring Ability to Pay Current Liabilities

Working capital is defined as follows:

Working capital = Current assets − Current liabilities

Working capital measures the ability to meet short-term obligations with current assets. Supermart's 2010 working capital is calculated as follows:

$262,000 − $142,000 = $120,000

This shows that Supermart has ample current assets to meet its current obligations. Rather than measuring working capital alone, manager's often measure the company's ability to meet current obligations by calculating two common ratios: the *current ratio* and the *acid-test*, or *quick ratio*.

Current Ratio

The most widely used ratio is the **current ratio**, which is current assets divided by current liabilities. The current ratio measures the ability to pay current liabilities with current assets.

Supermart's current ratio at December 31, 2010 and 2009 is calculated as follows:[2]

		Supermart's Current Ratio	
Formula		2010	2009
Current ratio = $\frac{\text{Current assets}}{\text{Current liabilities}}$		$\frac{\$262,000}{\$142,000}=1.85$	$\frac{\$236,000}{\$126,000}=1.87$

What is an acceptable current ratio? The answer depends on the industry, however, a current ratio of 2.0 is generally considered fairly strong. Compare Supermart's

[2]The solutions to all ratio calculations in this chapter have been rounded.

current ratio of 1.85 with the current ratios of some well-known companies in the same industry:[3]

Company	Current Ratio
Wal-Mart...	0.88
JCPenney...	2.23
Kohl's...	2.04

Acid-Test Ratio

The **acid-test ratio**, or **quick ratio**, tells us whether the entity could pay all of its current liabilities if they came due *immediately*. That is, could the company pass this *acid test*?

To compute the acid-test ratio, we add cash, short-term investments, and net current receivables (accounts and notes receivable, net of allowances) and divide this sum by current liabilities. Inventory and prepaid expenses are *not* included in the acid test because they are the least liquid current assets. Supermart's acid-test ratios for 2010 and 2009 follow:

	Supermart's Acid-Test Ratio	
Formula	2010	2009
$\text{Acid-test ratio} = \dfrac{\text{Cash} + \text{Short-term investments} + \text{Net current receivables}}{\text{Current liabilities}}$	$\dfrac{\$29,000 + \$0 + \$114,000}{\$142,000} = 1.01$	$\dfrac{\$32,000 + \$0 + \$85,000}{\$126,000} = 0.93$

An acid-test ratio of 0.90 to 1.00 is acceptable in most industries. We do not present comparative statistics for Wal-Mart and JC Penney, since their balance sheets do not identify short-term investments separately. However, Kohl's quick ratio is currently 0.37.

Measuring Ability to Sell Inventory and Collect Receivables

The ability to sell inventory and collect receivables is fundamental to business. In this section, we discuss three ratios that measure the company's ability to sell inventory and collect receivables.

Inventory Turnover

Inventory turnover measures the number of times a company sells its average level of inventory during a year. A high rate of turnover indicates ease in selling inventory; a low rate indicates difficulty. A value of "6" means that the company sold its average level of inventory six times—every two months—during the year.

To compute inventory turnover, we divide cost of goods sold by the average inventory for the period. We use the cost of goods sold—not sales—because both cost of goods sold and inventory are stated *at cost*. Sales at *retail prices* are not comparable with inventory at *cost*.

Supermart's inventory turnover for 2010 is as follows:

Formula	Supermart's 2010 Inventory Turnover
$\text{Inventory turnover} = \dfrac{\text{Cost of goods sold}}{\text{Average inventory}}$	$\dfrac{\$513,000}{(\$111,000 + \$113,000)/2} = 4.6$

---

[3]All information given for Wal-Mart Stores, Inc., JCPenney, and Kohl's Corporation, were calculated using the companies' financial statements reported for fiscal year 2008 (fiscal year ended January 31, 2009), as found in each company's SEC 10-K filing.

Notice that average inventory is calculated adding the beginning inventory ($111,000) and ending inventory ($113,000) for the period, and then dividing by two.

Inventory turnover varies widely with the nature of the business. Because of product innovation, some industries (for example, high-technology industries), must turn their inventory very quickly to avoid inventory obsolescence. However, in other industries, the risk of obsolescence is not so great.

Compare Supermart's inventory turnover with that of some well-known companies in the same industry:

Company	Inventory Turnover
Wal-Mart..	8.79
JCPenney..	3.35
Kohl's..	3.65

Accounts Receivable Turnover

Accounts receivable turnover measures the ability to collect cash from credit customers. This means that the higher the ratio, the faster the cash collections. But a receivable turnover that's too high may indicate that credit is too tight, causing the loss of sales to good customers.

For illustrative purposes we'll assume that all of Supermart's sales were made on account. The accounts receivable turnover is computed by dividing net credit sales by average net accounts receivable. Supermart's accounts receivable turnover ratio for 2010 is computed as follows:

Formula	Supermart's 2010 Accounts Receivable Turnover
Accounts receivable turnover $= \dfrac{\text{Net credit sales}}{\text{Average net accounts receivable}}$	$\dfrac{\$858,000}{(\$85,000 + \$114,000)/2} = 8.6$

We don't show comparative statistics for Wal-Mart, JCPenney, or Kohl's since their balance sheets do not show any receivables (most customers pay with cash, debit, or credit cards).

Days' Sales in Receivables

The **days' sales in receivables** ratio also measures the ability to collect receivables. Days' sales in receivables tell us how many days' sales remain in Accounts Receivable. To compute the ratio, we can follow a logical two-step process:

1. Divide net sales by 365 days to figure average sales for one day.

2. Divide this average day's sales amount into average net accounts receivable.

This two-step process is illustrated using Supermart's 2010 data as follows:

Formula	Supermart's 2010 Days' Sales in Accounts Receivable
Days' sales in *average* Accounts receivable:	
1. One day's sales $= \dfrac{\text{Net sales}}{365 \text{ days}}$	$\dfrac{\$858,000}{365 \text{ days}} = \$2,351$
2. $\dfrac{\text{Day's sales in average}}{\text{accounts receivable}} = \dfrac{\text{Average net accounts receivable}}{\text{One day's sales}}$	$\dfrac{(\$85,000 + \$114,000)/2}{\$2,351} = 42 \text{ days}$

Supermart's ratio tells us that 42 average days' sales remain in accounts receivable and need to be collected. Let's assume that like many companies, Supermart gives its customers 30 days to pay. Supermart's ratio shows that on average, customers are taking longer—about 45 days—to pay. This could be a result of general economic conditions (such as a recession), or Supermart's particular customer base. In either event, Supermart may need to increase its efforts to collect receivables more quickly if it expects to be paid within 30 days of sale.

Measuring Ability to Pay Long-Term Debt

The ratios discussed so far yield insight into current assets and current liabilities. They help us measure ability to sell inventory, collect receivables, and pay current liabilities. Most businesses also have long-term debt. Two key indicators of a business's ability to pay long-term liabilities are the *debt ratio* and the *times-interest-earned ratio*.

Debt Ratio

A loan officer at Metro Bank is evaluating loan applications from two companies. Both companies have asked to borrow $500,000 and have agreed to repay the loan over a five-year period. The first firm already owes $600,000 to another bank. The second owes only $100,000. Other things equal, you are more likely to lend money to Company 2 because that company owes less than Company 1.

The relationship between total liabilities and total assets—called the **debt ratio**—shows the proportion of assets financed with debt. When the debt ratio is 1, all of the assets are financed with debt. A debt ratio of 0.50 means that debt finances half the assets; the owners of the business have financed the other half. The higher the debt ratio, the higher the company's financial risk. The debt ratios for Supermart at the ends of 2010 and 2009 follow:

		Supermart's Debt Ratio	
	Formula	2010	2009
Debt ratio =	$\dfrac{\text{Total liabilities}}{\text{Total assets}}$	$\dfrac{\$431,000}{\$787,000} = 0.55$	$\dfrac{\$324,000}{\$644,000} = 0.50$

Supermart's debt ratio increased slightly in 2010. Let's look at the debt ratios of some well-known companies in the same industry:

Company	Debt Ratio
Wal-Mart	0.60
JCPenney	0.65
Kohl's	0.41

Times-Interest-Earned Ratio

The debt ratio says nothing about ability to pay interest expense. Analysts use the **times-interest-earned ratio** to relate income to interest expense. This ratio is also called the **interest-coverage ratio**. It measures the number of times operating income can cover interest expense. A high interest-coverage ratio indicates ease in paying interest expense; a low ratio suggests difficulty.

To compute this ratio, we divide operating income by interest expense. Calculation of Supermart's times-interest-earned ratio follows:

		Supermart's Times-Interest-Earned Ratio	
	Formula	2010	2009
Times-interest-earned ratio =	$\dfrac{\text{Income from operations}}{\text{Interest expense}}$	$\dfrac{\$101,000}{\$20,000} = 5.05$	$\dfrac{\$57,000}{\$14,000} = 4.07$

The company's times-interest-earned ratio shows that in 2010, the company could pay its interest about five times over with the amount of operating income it earned. Therefore,

Supermart should have little trouble paying the interest expense it owes to creditors. Compare Supermart's times-interest-earned ratio with other companies in the same industry:

Company	Times-Interest-Earned Ratio
Wal-Mart...	10.44
JCPenney...	5.04
Kohl's...	11.64

Measuring Profitability

The fundamental goal of business is to earn a profit. Ratios that measure profitability are often reported in the business press. We examine four profitability measures.

Rate of Return on Net Sales

In business, the term *return* is used broadly as a measure of profitability. Consider a ratio called the **rate of return on net sales**, or simply **return on sales**. This ratio shows the percentage of each sales dollar earned as net income. Supermart's rate of return on sales follows:

		Supermart's Rate of Return on Sales	
Formula		2010	2009
Rate of return on sales $= \dfrac{\text{Net income}}{\text{Net sales}}$		$\dfrac{\$48,000}{\$858,000} = 5.6\%$	$\dfrac{\$26,000}{\$803,000} = 3.2\%$

Companies strive for a high rate of return on sales. The higher the rate of return, the more sales dollars end up as profit. Supermart experienced a significant increase in its return on sales in the last year. Return on sales varies greatly depending on the industry. General merchandise retailers typically have a very low return on sales. Compare Supermart's rate of return on sales to the rates of return for some leading companies in the same industry:

Company	Rate of Return on Sales
Wal-Mart...	3.34%
JCPenney...	3.09%
Kohl's...	5.40%

Rate of Return on Total Assets

The **rate of return on total assets**, or simply **return on assets**, measures success in using assets to earn a profit. Two groups finance a company's assets:

1. Creditors have loaned money to the company, and they earn interest.

2. Shareholders have invested in stock, and their return is net income.

The sum of interest expense and net income is the return to the two groups that have financed the company's assets. Computation of the return-on-assets ratio for Supermart follows:

Formula	Supermart's 2010 Rate of Return on Total Assets
Rate of return on assets $= \dfrac{\text{Net income} + \text{Interest expense}}{\text{Average total assets}}$	$\dfrac{\$48,000 + \$20,000}{(\$644,000 + \$787,000)/2} = 9.5\%$

Compare Supermart's rate of return on assets with the rates of some other companies:

Company	Rate of Return on Assets
Wal-Mart	9.53%
JCPenney	6.06%
Kohl's	9.29%

Rate of Return on Common Stockholders' Equity

A popular measure of profitability is **rate of return on common stockholders' equity**, often shortened to **return on equity**. This ratio shows the relationship between net income and common stockholders' equity—how much income is earned for each $1 invested by the common shareholders.

To compute this ratio, we subtract preferred dividends from net income to get net income available to the common stockholders. Then, we divide net income available to common stockholders by average common equity during the year. Common equity is total stockholders' equity minus preferred equity. The 2010 rate of return on common stockholders' equity for Supermart follows:

Formula	Supermart's 2010 Rate of Return on Common Stockholders' Equity
$\dfrac{\text{Rate of return on common}}{\text{stockholders' equity}} = \dfrac{\text{Net income} - \text{Preferred dividends}}{\text{Average common stockholders' equity}}$	$\dfrac{\$48{,}000 - \$0}{(\$320{,}000 + \$356{,}000)/2} = 14.2\%$

Supermart's return on equity (14.2%) is higher than its return on assets (9.5%). This difference results from borrowing at one rate—for example, 8%—and investing the money to earn a higher rate, such as the firm's 14.2% return on equity.

This practice is called **trading on the equity**, or using **leverage**. It is directly related to the debt ratio. The higher the debt ratio reaches, the higher the leverage. Companies that finance operations with debt are said to *leverage* their positions.

During good times, leverage increases profitability. But leverage can have a negative impact on profitability. Therefore, leverage is a double-edged sword, increasing profits during good times but compounding losses during bad times. Compare Supermart's return on equity with the rates of some leading companies in the same industry.

Company	Rate of Return on Common Stockholders' Equity
Wal-Mart	20.63%
JCPenney	12.08%
Kohl's	13.78%

Earnings per Share of Common Stock

Earnings per share of common stock, or simply **earnings per share** (EPS), is perhaps the most widely quoted of all financial statistics. EPS is the only ratio that must appear on the face of the income statement. EPS is the amount of net income earned for each share of the company's outstanding *common* stock. Recall the following:

Outstanding stock = Issued stock − Treasury stock

Earnings per share is computed by dividing net income available to common stockholders by the number of common shares outstanding during the year. Preferred dividends are subtracted from net income because the preferred stockholders have a prior claim to dividends.

Let's assume Supermart has no preferred stock outstanding and no preferred dividends. Let's also assume that Supermart had 10,000 shares of common stock outstanding throughout 2009 and 2010. Given this information, we calculate the company's EPS as follows:

		Supermart's Earnings per Share	
Formula		**2010**	**2009**
Earnings per share of common stock =	$\dfrac{\text{Net income} - \text{Preferred dividends}}{\text{Number of shares of common stock outstanding}}$	$\dfrac{\$48,000 - \$0}{10,000} = \$4.80$	$\dfrac{\$26,000 - \$0}{10,000} = \$2.60$

Supermart's EPS increased significantly. Most companies strive to increase EPS each year, but general economic conditions, such as a recession, can prevent companies from doing so. Other leading companies in the same industry reported the following earnings per share on their income statements:

Company	Earnings Per Share
Wal-Mart	$3.40
JCPenney	$2.58
Kohl's	$2.89

Analyzing Stock Investments

Investors purchase stock to earn a return on their investment. This return consists of two parts: (1) gains (or losses) from selling the stock at a price above (or below) the purchase price and (2) dividends. The ratios we examine in this section help analysts evaluate stock investments.

Price/Earnings Ratio

The **price/earnings ratio** is the ratio of the market price of a share of common stock to the company's earnings per share. It shows the market price of $1 of earnings. This ratio, abbreviated P/E, appears in the stock listings of the *Wall Street Journal*. The daily closing price of all publicly traded stocks can also be found in the *Wall Street Journal*.

Let's say the market price of Supermart's common stock was $60 at the end of 2010 and $35 at the end of 2009. Supermart's P/E ratio is calculated as follows:

		Supermart's 2010 Price/Earnings Ratio	
Formula		**2010**	**2009**
P/E ratio =	$\dfrac{\text{Market price per share of common stock}}{\text{Earnings per share}}$	$\dfrac{\$60.00}{\$4.80} = 12.5$	$\dfrac{\$35.00}{\$2.60} = 13.5$

Supermart's P/E ratio of 12.5 means that the company's stock is selling at 12.5 times earnings. The P/E ratio of other firms in the same industry follows:

Company	Price/Earnings Ratio
Wal-Mart	13.86
JCPenney	6.49
Kohl's	12.70

Dividend Yield

Dividend yield is the ratio of dividends per share to the stock's market price per share. This ratio measures the percentage of a stock's market value that is returned annually as dividends. *Preferred* stockholders, who invest primarily to receive dividends, pay special attention to dividend yield.

Supermart paid annual cash dividends of $1.20 per share of common stock in 2010 and $1.00 in 2009, and market prices of the company's common stock were $60 in 2010 and $35 in 2009. The firm's dividend yield on common stock follow:

		Dividend Yield on Supermart's Common Stock	
Formula		2010	2009
Dividend yield on common stock* = $\dfrac{\text{Dividend per share of common stock}}{\text{Market price per share of common stock}}$		$\dfrac{\$1.20}{\$60.00} = 2.0\%$	$\dfrac{\$1.00}{\$35.00} = 2.9\%$

*Dividend yields may also be calculated for preferred stock.

An investor who buys Supermart common stock for $60 can expect to receive 2% of the investment annually in the form of cash dividends.

The dividends paid by companies varies substantially. Notice that Kohl's Corporation doesn't pay dividends:

Company	Dividend Yield
Wal-Mart..	2.02%
JCPenney..	4.78%
Kohl's..	0%

Book Value per Share of Common Stock

Book value per share of common stock is common equity divided by the number of common shares outstanding. Common equity equals total stockholders' equity less preferred equity. Supermart has no preferred stock outstanding. Its book-value-per-share-of-common-stock ratios follow (10,000 shares of common stock were outstanding).

		Book Value per Share of Supermart's Common Stock	
Formula		2010	2009
Book value per share of common stock $=$ $\dfrac{\text{Total stockholders' equity} - \text{Preferred equity}}{\text{Number of shares of common stock outstanding}}$		$\dfrac{\$356,000 - \$0}{10,000} = \$35.60$	$\dfrac{\$320,000 - \$0}{10,000} = \$32.00$

Many experts argue that book value is not useful for investment analysis. It bears no relationship to market value and provides little information beyond stockholders' equity reported on the balance sheet. But some investors base their investment decisions on book value. For example, some investors rank stocks on the basis of the ratio of market price to book value. To these investors, the lower the ratio, the more attractive the stock, as this implies that the stock might be undervalued.

Red Flags in Financial Statement Analysis

Analysts look for *red flags* that may signal financial trouble. Recent accounting scandals highlight the importance of these red flags. The following conditions may reveal that the company is too risky.

■ **Movement of Sales, Inventory, and Receivables.** Sales, receivables, and inventory generally move together. Increased sales lead to higher receivables and require more inventory to meet demand. Strange movements among sales, inventory, and receivables make the financial statements look suspect.

■ **Earnings Problems.** Has net income decreased significantly for several years in a row? Has income turned into a loss? Most companies cannot survive years of consecutive loss.

■ **Decreased Cash Flow.** Cash flow validates net income. Is cash flow from operations consistently lower than net income? If so, the company is in trouble. Are the sales of plant assets a major source of cash? If so, the company may face a cash shortage.

■ **Too Much Debt.** How does the company's debt ratio compare to that of major competitors? If the debt ratio is too high, the company may be unable to pay its debts.

■ **Inability to Collect Receivables.** Are days' sales in receivables growing faster than those of competitors? A cash shortage may be looming.

■ **Buildup of Inventories.** Is inventory turnover too slow? If so, the company may be unable to sell goods or it may be overstating inventory.

Decision Guidelines

Using Ratios in Financial Statement Analysis

How can investors, creditors, and managers measure a company's ability to pay bills, sell inventory, collect receivables, pay long-term debt and so forth? How can they evaluate stock investments? The decision guidelines summarize the ratios that help to answer these questions.

Ratio	Computation	Information Provided
Measuring ability to pay current liabilities:		
1. Current ratio	$\dfrac{\text{Current assets}}{\text{Current liabilities}}$	Measures ability to pay current liabilities with current assets
2. Acid-test (quick) ratio	$\dfrac{\text{Cash} + \dfrac{\text{Short-term}}{\text{investments}} + \dfrac{\text{Net current}}{\text{receivables}}}{\text{Current liabilities}}$	Shows ability to pay all current liabilities if they come due immediately
Measuring ability to sell inventory and collect receivables:		
3. Inventory turnover	$\dfrac{\text{Cost of goods sold}}{\text{Average inventory}}$	Indicates salability of inventory—the number of times a company sells its average inventory during a year
4. Accounts receivable turnover	$\dfrac{\text{Net credit sales}}{\text{Average net accounts receivable}}$	Measures ability to collect cash from customers
5. Days' sales in receivables	$\dfrac{\text{Average net accounts receivable}}{\text{One day's sales}}$	Shows how many days' sales remain in Accounts Receivable—how many days it takes to collect the average level of receivables

Ratio	Computation	Information Provided
Measuring ability to pay long-term debt:		
6. Debt ratio	$$\frac{\text{Total liabilities}}{\text{Total assets}}$$	Indicates percentage of assets financed with debt
7. Times-interest-earned ratio	$$\frac{\text{Income from operations}}{\text{Interest expense}}$$	Measures the number of times operating income can cover interest expense
Measuring profitability:		
8. Rate of return on net sales	$$\frac{\text{Net income}}{\text{Net sales}}$$	Shows the percentage of each sales dollar earned as net income
9. Rate of return on total assets	$$\frac{\text{Net income} + \text{Interest expense}}{\text{Average total assets}}$$	Measures how profitably a company uses its assets
10. Rate of return on common stockholders' equity	$$\frac{\text{Net income} - \text{Preferred dividends}}{\text{Average common stockholders' equity}}$$	Gauges how much income is earned for each dollar invested by common shareholders
11. Earnings per share of common stock	$$\frac{\text{Net income} - \text{Preferred dividends}}{\substack{\text{Number of shares of} \\ \text{common stock outstanding}}}$$	Gives the amount of net income earned for each share of the company's common stock
Analyzing stock as an investment:		
12. Price/earnings ratio	$$\frac{\text{Market price per share of common stock}}{\text{Earnings per share}}$$	Indicates the market price of $1 of earnings
13. Dividend yield	$$\frac{\substack{\text{Annual dividend per share of} \\ \text{common (or preferred) stock}}}{\substack{\text{Market price per share of} \\ \text{common (or preferred) stock}}}$$	Shows the percentage of a stock's market value returned as dividends to stockholders each year
14. Book value per share of common stock	$$\frac{\text{Total stockholders equity} - \text{Preferred equity}}{\substack{\text{Number of shares of} \\ \text{common stock outstanding}}}$$	Indicates the recorded accounting amount for each share of common stock outstanding

Summary Problem 2

Target Corporation's income statement was presented in Summary Problem 1 on page 784. The company's balance sheet (adapted), at the end of fiscal year 2008 and 2007 is presented below.[4]

Target Corporation
Balance Sheet (Adapted)
End of Fiscal Year*

(Dollars in millions)	2008	2007
Assets		
Current assets:		
Cash and cash equivalents	$ 864	$ 2,450
Credit card receivables, net of allowance	8,084	8,054
Inventory	6,705	6,780
Other current assets	1,835	1,622
Total current assets	17,488	18,906
Property, plant, and equipment, net	25,756	24,095
Other noncurrent assets	862	1,559
Total assets	$44,106	$44,560
Liabilities		
Current liabilities:		
Accounts payable	$ 6,337	$ 6,721
Other current liabilities	4,175	5,061
Total current liabilities	10,512	11,782
Long-term liabilities	19,882	17,471
Total liabilities	30,394	29,253
Stockholders' Equity		
Common stock and Additional paid-in capital	2,825	2,724
Retained earnings*	10,887	12,583
Total stockholders' equity	13,712	15,307
Total liabilities and equity	$44,106	$44,560

*January 31, 2009 (fiscal year 2008) and February 2, 2008 (fiscal year 2007)

Other company information follows:
- Target has no preferred stock issued or outstanding.
- There were 752,712,464 common shares issued and outstanding at the end of fiscal year 2008.
- Cash dividends of $0.62 per share were declared during fiscal year 2008.
- The closing market price per share was $31.20 on Friday, January 30, 2009 (the end of fiscal year 2008) and $57.05 on Friday, February 1, 2008 (the end of fiscal year 2007).[5]

Requirement 1

Calculate the following ratios for fiscal year 2008:
1. Current ratio
2. Acid-test ratio
3. Inventory turnover
4. Days' sales in receivables
5. Debt ratio
6. Times-interest-earned ratio

---

[4]Target Corporation 10-K, March 13, 2009.
[5]http://bigcharts.marketwatch.com.

7. Rate of return on net sales

8. Rate of return on total assets

9. Rate of return on common stockholders' equity

10. Earnings per share of common stock

11. Price/earnings ratio

12. Dividend yield

13. Book value per share of common stock

Requirement 2

Compare Target's ratios to the ratios presented in the chapter for Wal-Mart, JCPenney, and Kohl's. Do any of Target's ratios differ dramatically?

Solution

Requirement 1

$$1)\ \text{Current ratio} = \frac{Current\ assets}{Current\ liabilities}$$

$$= \frac{\$17,488}{\$10,512} = 1.66$$

$$2)\ \text{Acid-test ratio} = \frac{Cash + ST\ investments + Net\ current\ receivables}{Current\ liabilities}$$

$$= \frac{864 + 0^* + 8,084}{10,512} = 0.85$$

*No short-term investments are listed separately on the balance sheet. However, they may be a part of "other current assets." We also assume that all net receivables are current.

$$3)\ \text{Inventory turnover} = \frac{Cost\ of\ goods\ sold}{Average\ inventory}$$

$$= \frac{\$44,157}{(\$6,705 + \$6,780)/2} = 6.54$$

$$4)\ \text{Days' sales in receivables} = \frac{Average\ net\ accounts\ receivable}{One\ day's\ sales}$$

$$= \frac{(\$8,084 + \$8,054)/2}{(\$63,339)/365} = 46.5\ \text{days}$$

$$5)\ \text{Debt ratio} = \frac{Total\ liabilities}{Total\ assets}$$

$$= \frac{\$30,394}{\$44,106} = 0.69$$

$$6)\ \text{Times-interest-earned ratio} = \frac{Income\ from\ operations}{Interest\ expense}$$

$$= \frac{\$4,402}{\$866} = 5.08$$

$$7)\ \text{Rate of return on net sales} = \frac{Net\ income}{Sales\ revenue}$$

$$= \frac{\$2,214}{\$63,339} = 3.5\%$$

8) Rate of return on total assets $= \dfrac{Net\ income + Interest\ expense}{Average\ total\ assets}$

$$= \dfrac{\$2{,}214 + \$866}{(\$44{,}106 + \$44{,}560)/2} = 6.9\%$$

9) Rate of return on common stockholders' equity $= \dfrac{Net\ income - Preferred\ dividends}{Average\ common\ stockholder's\ equity}$

$$= \dfrac{\$2{,}214 - \$0}{(\$13{,}712 + 15{,}307)/2} = 15.3\%$$

10) Earnings per share of common stock $= \dfrac{Net\ income - Preferred\ dividends}{Number\ of\ shares\ of\ common\ stock\ outstanding}$

$$= \dfrac{\$2{,}214\ million}{752{,}712{,}464} = \$2.94$$

11) Price/earnings ratio $= \dfrac{Market\ price\ per\ share\ of\ common\ stock}{Earnings\ per\ share}$

$$= \dfrac{\$31.20}{\$2.94} = 10.61$$

12) Dividend yield $= \dfrac{Dividend\ per\ share\ of\ common\ stock}{Market\ price\ per\ share\ of\ common\ stock}$

$$= \dfrac{\$0.62}{\$31.20} = 2.0\%$$

13) Book value per share of common stock $= \dfrac{Total\ stockholders'\ equity - Preferred\ equity}{Number\ of\ shares\ of\ common\ stock\ outstanding}$

$$= \dfrac{\$13{,}712\ million - 0}{752{,}712{,}464} = \$18.21$$

Requirement 2

All of Target Corporation's ratios are in the same general range as those presented for Wal-Mart, JCPenney, and Kohl's. For example, let's look at one ratio from each of the five categories of ratios discussed earlier:

1. Measuring ability to pay current liabilities

   Current Ratio—Target's current ratio (1.66) is better than Wal-Mart's (0.88), but not as high as JCPenney's (2.23) or Kohl's (2.04). This means Target should have be able to meet its current obligations, using current assets, much easier than Wal-Mart has the ability to do.

2. Measuring ability to sell inventory and collect receivables

   Inventory Turnover—Target's inventory turnover (6.54) is much better than JCPenney's (3.35) and Kohl's (3.65) but not as high as Wal-Mart's (8.79). This means that Target is able to sell its inventory much more quickly JCPenney and Kohl's can.

3. Measuring ability to pay long-term debt

   Debt ratio—Target's debt ratio (0.69) is only slightly higher than Wal-Mart's (0.60) and JCPenney's (0.65) but much higher than Kohl's (0.41). This means that more of Target's assets were funded through debt, than Kohl's.

4. Measuring profitability

Return on equity—Target's return on equity (15.3%) is better than JC Penney's (12.08%) and Kohl's (13.78%), but worse than Wal-Mart's (20.63%). This means that Target is providing a return to its common stockholders of 15 cents on every dollar of stock invested in the company.

5. Analyzing Stock Investments

Dividend yield—Target's dividend yield (2.0%) is much better than Kohl's (0%), about the same as Wal-Mart's (2.02%), but lower than JCPenney's (4.78%). This means that Target is paying shareholders dividends at a rate of 2% of what one share of common stock would have cost investors if they had bought the stock at closing balance sheet date.

REVIEW

Accounting Vocabulary

Accounts Receivable Turnover. (p. 788) Measures a company's ability to collect cash from credit customers. To compute accounts receivable turnover, divide net credit sales by average net accounts receivable.

Acid-Test Ratio. (p. 787) Ratio of the sum of cash plus short-term investments plus net current receivables to total current liabilities. It tells whether the entity can pay all of its current liabilities if they come due immediately; also called the *quick ratio*.

Benchmarking. (p. 781) The practice of comparing a company with other companies or industry averages.

Book Value per Share of Common Stock. (p. 793) Common stockholders' equity divided by the number of shares of common stock outstanding. It is the recorded amount for each share of common stock outstanding.

Common-Size Statement. (p. 782) A financial statement that reports only percentages (no dollar amounts).

Current Ratio. (p. 786) Current assets divided by current liabilities. It measures the ability to pay current liabilities with current assets.

Days' Sales in Receivables. (p. 788) Ratio of average net accounts receivable to one day's sale. It indicates how many days' sales remain in Accounts Receivable awaiting collection.

Debt Ratio. (p. 789) Ratio of total liabilities to total assets. It shows the proportion of a company's assets that is financed with debt.

Dividend Yield. (p. 793) Ratio of dividends per share of stock to the stock's market price per share. It tells the percentage of a stock's market value that the company returns to stockholders annually as dividends.

Earnings per Share (EPS). (p. 791) Amount of a company's net income for each share of its outstanding common stock.

Horizontal Analysis. (p. 776) Study of percentage changes in comparative financial statements.

Interest-Coverage Ratio. (p. 789) Ratio of income from operations to interest expense. It measures the number of times that operating income can cover interest expense; also called the *times-interest earned ratio*.

Inventory Turnover. (p. 787) Ratio of cost of goods sold to average inventory. It indicates how rapidly inventory is sold.

Leverage. (p. 791) Earning more income on borrowed money than the related interest expense, thereby increasing the earnings for the owners of the business; also called *trading on equity*.

Price/Earnings (P/E) Ratio. (p. 792) Ratio of the market price of a share of common stock to the company's earnings per share. It measures the value that the stock market places on $1 of a company's earnings.

Quick Ratio. (p. 787) Ratio of the sum of cash plus short-term investments plus net current receivables to total current liabilities. It tells whether the entity can pay all its current liabilities if they come due immediately; also called the *acid-test ratio*.

Rate of Return on Common Stockholders' Equity. (p. 791) Net income minus preferred dividends divided by average common stockholders' equity. It is a measure of profitability; also called *return on equity*.

Rate of Return on Net Sales. (p. 790) Ratio of net income to net sales. It is a measure of profitability; also called *return on sales*.

Rate of Return on Total Assets. (p. 790) Net income plus interest expense divided by average total assets. This ratio measures a company's success in using its assets to earn income for the people who finance the business; also called *return on assets*.

Ratio Analysis. (p. 776) Evaluating the relationships between two or more key components of the financial statements.

Return on Assets. (p. 790) Net income plus interest expense, divided by average total assets. This ratio measures a company's success in using its assets to earn income for the people who finance the business; also called *rate of return on total assets*.

Return on Equity. (p. 791) Net income minus preferred dividends, divided by average common stockholders' equity. It is a measure of profitability; also called *rate of return on common stockholders' equity*.

Return on Sales. (p. 790) Ratio of net income to net sales. It is a measure of profitability; also called *rate of return on net sales*.

Times-Interest-Earned Ratio. (p. 789) Ratio of income from operations to interest expense. It measures the number of times operating income can cover interest expense; also called the *interest-coverage ratio*.

Trading on Equity. (p. 791) Earning more income on borrowed money than the related interest expense, thereby increasing the earnings for the owners of the business; also called *leverage*.

Trend Percentages. (p. 778) A form of horizontal analysis in which percentages are computed by selecting a base year as 100% and expressing amounts for following years as a percentage of the base amount.

Vertical Analysis. (p. 780) Analysis of a financial statement that reveals the relationship of each statement item to a specified base, which is the 100% figure.

Working Capital. (p. 786) Current assets minus current liabilities; measures a business's ability to meet its short-term obligations with its current assets.

Quick Check

1. *(Learning Objective 1)* Analyzing the percentage changes in comparative financial statements from year to year is known as
   a. horizontal analysis.
   b. benchmarking.
   c. trend analysis.
   d. vertical analysis.

2. *(Learning Objective 1)* What technique would you use to help predict future revenues and expenses of a company?
   a. Capital analysis
   b. Benchmarking
   c. Trend analysis
   d. Vertical analysis

3. *(Learning Objective 2)* Showing each item on the income statement as a percentage of sales is an example of
   a. horizontal analysis.
   b. benchmarking.
   c. trend analysis.
   d. vertical analysis.

4. *(Learning Objective 2)* Which of the following amounts is usually used as the base amount when performing a vertical analysis of a balance sheet?
   a. Current assets
   b. Current liabilities
   c. Total liabilities
   d. Total liabilities and stockholders' equity

5. *(Learning Objective 3)* Analysts can use common-size financial statements to
   a. compare the relative proportion of assets, liabilities, equity, revenues, and expenses within a company over time or between companies of different sizes.
   b. evaluate the financial statements of companies in different industries of the same size.
   c. determine whether a company is in stable financial condition.
   d. determine which company's stock should be purchased.

6. *(Learning Objective 4)* Which of the following ratios is a measure of a company's ability to pay long-term debt?
   a. Times-interest-earned ratio
   b. Rate of return on total assets
   c. Current ratio
   d. Accounts receivable turnover

7. *(Learning Objective 4)* Which of the following ratios is a measure of a company's ability to sell inventory and collect receivables?
   a. Acid-test ratio
   b. Debt ratio
   c. Days' sales in receivables
   d. Times-interest-earned ratio

8. *(Learning Objective 4)* Of the following ratios, which would not be effective in judging a company's ability to pay its current bills?
   a. Quick ratio
   b. Price-earnings ratio
   c. Acid-test ratio
   d. Current ratio

9. *(Learning Objective 4)* (Cash + short-term investments + net current receivables) divided by current liabilities is the formula for
   a. return on assets.
   b. current ratio.
   c. working capital ratio.
   d. acid-test ratio.

10. *(Learning Objective 4)* If Sarhan Corporation has a current ratio of 2.0, which transaction will normally increase Sarhan's current ratio?
    a. Making a sale to a customer on account
    b. Paying a long-term note payable off with cash
    c. Receiving cash from customers on accounts receivables
    d. Purchasing new equipment by issuing a long-term notes payable

ASSESS YOUR PROGRESS

Learning Objectives

1 Perform a horizontal analysis of financial statements

2 Perform a vertical analysis of financial statements

3 Prepare and use common-size financial statements

4 Compute the standard financial ratios

Short Exercises

S14-1 Horizontal analysis of revenue and cost of sales *(Learning Objective 1)*

Micatin reported the following on its comparative income statement:

(in millions)	2009	2008	2007
Revenue	$9,993	$9,489	$8,995
Cost of sales..............................	5,905	5,785	5,404

Perform a horizontal analysis of revenues and gross profit—both in dollar amounts and in percentages—for 2009 and 2008.

S14-2 Find trend percentages *(Learning Objective 2)*

Micatin reported the following revenues and net income amounts:

(in millions)	2009	2008	2007	2006
Revenue	$10,278	$9,774	$9,207	$9,000
Net income...................................	630	594	576	450

a. Show Micatin's trend percentages for revenues and net income. Use 2006 as the base year and round to the nearest percent.

b. Which measure increased faster during 2007–2009?

S14-3 Vertical analysis of assets *(Learning Objective 2)*

TriState Optical Company reported the following amounts on its balance sheet at December 31:

Cash and receivables	$ 50,100
Inventory..	$ 38,800
Property, plant, and equipment, net	$111,100
Total assets	$200,000

Perform a vertical analysis of TriState Optical Company's assets at year end.

S14-4 Prepare common-size income statements (Learning Objective 3)

Compare Sanchez and Alioto by converting their income statements to common size.

	Sanchez	Alioto
Net sales...	$9,500	$19,500
Cost of goods sold...............................	$5,795	$14,040
Other expense......................................	$3,116	$ 4,524
Net income...	$ 589	$ 936

Which company earns more net income? Which company's net income is a higher percentage of its net sales?

Henderson's Data Set used for S14-5 through S14-9:
Henderson's, a home-improvement store chain, reported these summarized figures (in billions):

Henderson's
Income Statement
For the Year Ended December 31, 2009

Net sales	$31,025,000
Cost of goods sold..	21,750,000
Interest expense...	217,210
All other expenses	7,072,190
Net income...	$ 1,985,600

Henderson's
Balance Sheet
December 31,

	2009	2008		2009	2008
Cash...............................	$ 1,200,000	$ 800,000	Total current liabilities	$ 4,400,000	$ 3,600,000
Short-term investments......	200,000	260,000	Long-term liabilities	4,294,000	4,200,000
Accounts receivable...........	100,000	197,500	Total liabilities	8,694,000	7,800,000
Inventory.........................	4,600,000	4,100,000			
Other current assets	500,000	402,500	Common stock.......................	2,506,000	3,000,000
Total current assets	6,600,000	5,760,000	Retained earnings...................	7,700,000	6,650,000
All other assets.................	12,300,000	11,690,000	Total equity............................	10,206,000	9,650,000
Total assets......................	$18,900,000	$17,450,000	Total liabilities and equity......	$18,900,000	$17,450,000

S14-5 Find current ratio (Learning Objective 4)

Refer to the Henderson's Data Set.
a. Compute Henderson's current ratio at December 31, 2009 and 2008.
b. Did Henderson's current ratio improve, deteriorate, or hold steady during 2009?

S14-6 Analyze inventory and receivables (Learning Objective 4)

Use the Henderson's Data Set to compute the following:
a. The rate of inventory turnover for 2009.
b. Days' sales in average receivables during 2009.

S14-7 Compute and interpret debt ratio (Learning Objective 4)

Refer to the Henderson's Data Set.
a. Compute the debt ratio at December 31, 2009.
b. Is Lowe's ability to pay its liabilities strong or weak? Explain your reasoning.

S14-8 Compute profitability ratios *(Learning Objective 4)*

Use the Henderson's Data Set to compute these profitability measures for 2009:

a. Rate of return on net sales

b. Rate of return on total assets (interest expense for 2009 was $217,210)

c. Rate of return on common stockholders' equity

Are these rates of return strong or weak?

S14-9 Determine earnings per share *(Learning Objective 4)*

Use the Henderson's Data Set when making the following calculations:

a. Compute earnings per share (EPS) for Henderson's. The number of shares outstanding was 730,000.

b. Compute Henderson's price/earnings ratio. The price of a share of Henderson's is $74.80.

S14-10 Find missing values on income statement *(Learning Objective 4)*

A skeleton of Heirloom Mills' income statement appears as follows (amounts in thousands):

HEIRLOOM MILLS
Income Statement
Year Ended December 31

Net sales...	$7,200
Cost of goods sold...	(a)
Selling and administrative expenses...	1,710
Interest expense..	(b)
Other expenses...	150
Income before taxes	1,000
Income tax expense...	(c)
Net income..	$ (d)

Use the following ratio data to complete Heirloom Mills' income statement:

a. Inventory turnover was 5.5 (beginning inventory was $790; ending inventory was $750).

b. Rate of return on sales is 0.095.

S14-11 Find missing values on balance sheet *(Learning Objective 4)*

A skeleton of Heirloom Mills' balance sheet appears as follows (amounts in thousands):

HEIRLOOM MILLS
Balance Sheet
December 31

Cash...	$ 50	Total current liabilities	$2,100
Receivables...............................	(a)	Long-term note payable	(e)
Inventories	750	Other long-term liabilities	820
Prepaid expenses	(b)		
Total current assets	(c)		
Plant assets, net........................	(d)		
Other assets.............................	2,150	Stockholders' equity..................	2,400
Total assets..............................	$6,800	Total liabilities and equity.........	$ (f)

Use the following ratio data to complete Heirloom Mills' balance sheet:

a. The current ratio is 0.70.

b. The acid-test ratio is 0.30.

Exercises—Group A

E14-12A Trend analysis of working capital *(Learning Objective 1)*

Compute the dollar amount of change and the percentage of change in Media Enterprises working capital each year during 2008 and 2009. Is this trend favorable or unfavorable?

	2009	2008	2007
Total current assets	$372,250	$340,000	$300,000
Total current liabilities.........	$190,000	$178,000	$150,000

E14-13A Horizontal analysis *(Learning Objective 1)*

Prepare a horizontal analysis of the following comparative income statement of Enchanted Designs.

Enchanted Designs
Comparative Income Statements
Years Ended December 31, 2009 and 2008

	2009	2008
Net sales revenue..	$460,000	$400,000
Expenses:		
Cost of goods sold...	$216,200	$200,000
Selling and general expenses..	$105,800	$100,000
Other expense	$ 27,600	$ 20,000
Total expenses...	$349,600	$320,000
Net income..	$110,400	$ 80,000

Why did net income increase by a higher percentage than net sales revenue during 2009?

E14-14A Compute trend percentages *(Learning Objective 1)*

Compute trend percentages for Thousand Oaks Realty's net revenue and net income for the following five-year period using 2005 as the base year.

(in thousands)	2009	2008	2007	2006	2005
Net revenue..................................	$1,323	$1,197	$1,113	$1,008	$1,050
Net income...................................	$ 174	$ 162	$ 114	$ 102	$ 120

Which grew faster during the period, net revenue or net income?

E14-15A Perform vertical analysis (Learning Objective 2)

Alpha Graphics has requested that you perform a vertical analysis of its balance sheet.

Alpha Graphics, Inc.
Balance Sheet
As of December 31

Assets	
Total current assets	$ 44,250
Property, plant, and equipment, net	216,000
Other assets	39,750
Total assets	$300,000
Liabilities	
Total current liabilities	$ 55,500
Long-term debt	115,500
Total liabilities	171,000
Stockholders' equity	
Total stockholders' equity	129,000
Total liabilities and stockholders' equity	$300,000

E14-16A Prepare common-size income statement (Learning Objective 3)

Prepare a comparative common-size income statement for Enchanted Designs using the 2009 and 2008 data of Exercise 14-13A. To an investor, how does 2009 compare with 2008? Explain your reasoning.

E14-17A Calculate ratios (Learning Objective 4)

Balance sheet:	Current year	Preceding year
Cash	$ 15,000	$ 22,000
Short-term investments	$ 10,000	$ 26,000
Net receivables	$ 53,000	$ 67,000
Inventory	$ 77,000	$ 71,000
Prepaid expenses	$ 19,000	$ 8,000
Total current assets	$174,000	$194,000
Total current liabilities	$120,000	$ 90,000
Income statement:		
Net credit sales	$438,000	
Cost of goods sold	$314,500	

Requirement

1. Compute the following ratios for the current year:
   a. Current ratio
   b. Acid-test ratio
   c. Inventory turnover
   d. Days' sales in average receivables

E14-18A More ratio analysis (*Learning Objective 4*)

Big Bend Picture Frames has asked you to determine whether the company's ability to pay current liabilities and total liabilities improved or deteriorated during 2009. To answer that question, compute these ratios for 2009 and 2008, using the following data:

	2009	2008
Cash...	$ 60,000	$ 47,500
Short-term receivables...............................	27,000	—
Net receivables...	122,000	115,000
Inventory..	239,250	276,250
Total assets	560,000	490,000
Total current liabilities...............................	275,000	203,125
Long-term note payable	38,600	51,675
Income from operations	165,120	156,780
Interest expense..	48,000	39,000

a. Current ratio
b. Acid-test ratio
c. Debt ratio
d. Times-interest-earned ratio

E14-19A Compute profitability ratios (*Learning Objective 4*)

Compute four ratios that measure Bonaparte's ability to earn profits. The company's comparative income statement follows. The data for 2007 are given as needed.

Bonaparte
Comparative Income Statement
Years Ended December 31, 2009, 2008, and 2007

(Dollars in thousands)	2009	2008	2007
Net sales...	$180,000	$160,000	
Cost of goods sold......................................	95,000	86,000	
Selling and administrative expenses................	47,000	40,000	
Interest expense..	9,000	10,000	
Income tax expense....................................	11,000	10,000	
Net income..	$ 18,000	$ 14,000	
Additional data:			
Total assets...	$206,000	$194,000	$181,000
Common stockholders' equity........................	$ 98,000	$ 89,500	$ 70,500
Preferred dividends.....................................	$ 3,000	$ 3,000	$ —
Common shares outstanding during the year.........	20,000	20,000	18,000

Did the company's operating performance improve or deteriorate during 2009?

E14-20A Compute stock ratios *(Learning Objective 4)*

Evaluate the common stock of Shamrock State Bank as an investment. Specifically, use the three stock ratios to determine whether the common stock has increased or decreased in attractiveness during the past year.

	Current year	Last year
Net income..	$ 60,000	$ 52,000
Dividends—common...	$ 19,800	$ 19,800
Dividends—preferred	$ 12,000	$ 12,000
Total stockholders' equity at year end		
(includes 80,000 shares of common stock)	$ 780,000	$600,000
Preferred stock, 6%..	$ 200,000	$200,000
Market price per share of common	$ 16.50	$ 12.50

E14-21A Find missing values *(Learning Objective 4)*

The following data (dollar amounts in millions) are adapted from the financial statements of Super Saver Stores, Inc.

Total current assets	$10,500
Accumulated depreciation...	$ 2,000
Total liabilities...	$15,000
Preferred stock	$ 0
Debt ratio...	60 %
Current ratio..	1.50

Requirement

1. Complete Super Saver's condensed balance sheet.

Current assets..	$?
Property, plant, and equipment...	$?
Less: Accumulated depreciation..	(?)
Total assets	$?
Current liabilities	$?
Long-term liabilities...	?
Stockholders' equity..	?
Total liabilities and stockholders' equity	$?

E14-22A Calculate ratios *(Learning Objective 4)*

Liberty Corporation reported these figures:

Balance sheet	2009	2008	Income statement	2009
Cash and equivalents	$ 3,000	$ 2,300	Sales	$14,600
Receivables	$ 2,400	$ 2,200	Cost of sales	$ 5,400
Inventory	$ 2,100	$ 1,500	Operating expenses	$ 4,500
Prepaid expenses	$ 1,500	$ 2,250	Operating income	$ 4,700
Total current assets	$ 9,000	$ 8,250	Interest expense	$ 200
Other assets	$21,000	$16,750	Other expense	$ 2,200
Total assets	$30,000	$25,000	Net income	$ 2,300
Total current liabilities	$10,000	$ 9,000		
Long-term liabilities	$ 7,000	$ 6,000		
Common equity	$13,000	$10,000		
Total liabilities and equity	$30,000	$25,000		

Liberty has 2,500 shares of common stock outstanding. Its stock has traded recently at $34.50 per share. You would like to gain a better understanding of Liberty's financial position. Calculate the following ratios for 2009 and interpret the results:

a. Inventory turnover

b. Days' sales in receivables

c. Acid-test ratio

d. Times-interest-earned

e. Return on stockholders' equity

f. Earnings per share

g. Price/earnings ratio

Exercises—Group B

E14-23B Trend analysis of working capital *(Learning Objective 1)*

Compute the dollar amount of change and the percentage of change in Memoir Enterprises working capital each year during 2008 and 2009. Is this trend favorable or unfavorable?

	2009	2008	2007
Total current assets	$288,880	$268,000	$233,000
Total current liabilities	184,000	176,000	153,000

E14-24B Horizontal analysis *(Learning Objective 1)*

Prepare a horizontal analysis of the following comparative income statement of Charmed Designs.

Charmed Designs
Comparative Income Statement
Years Ended December 31, 2009 and 2008

	2009	2008
Net sales revenue	$482,580	$420,000
Expenses:		
Cost of goods sold	$227,220	$210,000
Selling and general expenses	95,130	90,000
Other expense	20,685	15,000
Total expenses	343,035	315,000
Net income	$139,545	$105,000

Why did net income increase by a higher percentage than net sales revenue during 2009?

E14-25B Compute trend percentages *(Learning Objective 1)*

Compute trend percentages for Horizons Realty's net revenue and net income for the following five-year period using 2005 as the base year.

(in thousands)	2009	2008	2007	2006	2005
Net revenue	$1,254	$1,026	$988	$893	$950
Net income	204	186	138	126	150

Which grew faster during the period, net revenue or net income?

E14-26B Perform vertical analysis *(Learning Objective 2)*

Dawson Graphics has requested that you perform a vertical analysis of its balance sheet.

Dawson Graphics, Inc.
Balance Sheet
As of December 31

Assets	
Total current assets	$ 49,600
Property, plant, and equipment, net	229,120
Other assets	41,280
Total assets	$320,000
Liabilities	
Total current liabilities	$ 60,160
Long-term debt	124,160
Total liabilities	184,320
Stockholders' equity	
Total stockholders' equity	135,680
Total liabilities and stockholders' equity	$320,000

E14-27B Prepare common-size income statement *(Learning Objective 3)*

Prepare a comparative common-size income statement for Charmed Designs using the 2009 and 2008 data of Exercise 14-24B. To an investor, how does 2009 compare with 2008? Explain your reasoning.

E14-28B Calculate ratios *(Learning Objective 4)*

The financial statements of Jim's Health Foods include the following items:

Balance sheet:	Current year	Preceding year
Cash	$ 16,500	$ 22,000
Short-term investments	10,750	25,500
Net receivables	49,000	77,360
Inventory	81,000	78,500
Prepaid expenses	21,500	9,200
Total current assets	$178,750	$212,560
Total current liabilities	$125,000	$ 89,000
Income statement:		
Net credit sales	$427,050	
Cost of goods sold	319,000	

Requirement

1. Compute the following ratios for the current year:
   a. Current ratio
   b. Acid-test ratio
   c. Inventory turnover
   d. Days' sales in average receivables

E14-29B More ratio analysis *(Learning Objective 4)*

Autumn Picture Frames has asked you to determine whether the company's ability to pay current liabilities and total liabilities improved or deteriorated during 2009. To answer this question, compute these ratios for 2009 and 2008, using the following data:

	2009	2008
Cash	$ 62,000	$ 49,500
Short-term investments	28,000	—
Net receivables	116,460	127,300
Inventory	242,730	284,960
Total assets	556,000	486,000
Total current liabilities	279,000	208,000
Long-term note payable	37,920	30,140
Income from operations	154,350	169,260
Interest expense	45,000	42,000

a. Current ratio
b. Acid-test ratio
c. Debt ratio
d. Times-interest-earned ratio

E14-30B Compute profitability ratios (Learning Objective 4)

Compute four ratios that measure Variline's ability to earn profits. The company's comparative income statement follows. The data for 2007 are given as needed.

Variline
Comparative Income Statement
Years Ended December 31, 2009, 2008, and 2007

(dollars in thousands)	2009	2008	2007
Net sales..	$211,400	$182,910	
Cost of goods sold.................................	105,000	96,000	
Selling and administrative expenses.......................	53,000	46,000	
Interest expense...................................	5,385	6,459	
Income tax expense	22,647	16,160	
Net income..	$ 25,368	$ 18,291	
Additional data:			
Total assets...	$207,000	$195,000	$180,000
Common stockholders' equity........................	$101,000	$ 92,000	$ 61,110
Preferred dividends................................	$ 2,980	$ 2,980	$ 0
Common shares outstanding during the year.........	27,985	27,985	26,000

Did the company's operating performance improve or deteriorate during 2009?

E14-31B Compute stock ratios (Learning Objective 4)

Evaluate the common stock of Warwick State Bank as an investment. Specifically, use the three stock ratios to determine whether the common stock has increased or decreased in attractiveness during the past year.

	Current year	Last year
Net income...	$ 57,280	$ 52,360
Dividends—common..	$ 22,140	$ 22,140
Dividends—preferred	$ 13,000	$ 13,000
Total stockholders' equity at year-end		
(includes 82,000 shares of common stock) ..	$ 796,300	$628,200
Preferred stock, (6%)	$ 210,000	$210,000
Market price per share of common stock	$ 13.50	$ 10.80

E14-32B Find missing values (Learning Objective 4)

The following data (dollar amounts in millions) are adapted from the financial statements of Gammaro Supply Stores, Inc.

Total current assets	$11,200
Accumulated depreciation...	$ 1,600
Total liabilities...	$18,500
Preferred stock	$ 0
Debt ratio..	50 %
Current ratio...	1.40

Requirement

1. Complete Gammaro Supply's condensed balance sheet.

Current assets..	$?
Property, plant, and equipment..	$?
Less: Accumulated depreciation..	(?)
Total assets	$?
Current liabilities	$?
Long-term liabilities	?
Stockholders' equity	?
Total liabilities and stockholders' equity	$?

E14-33B Calculate ratios *(Learning Objective 4)*

Justice Corporation reported these figures:

Balance sheet	2009	2008	Income statement	2009
Cash and equivalents	$ 2,950	$ 2,500	Sales	$15,695
Receivables	3,300	2,720	Cost of sales	5,940
Inventory	2,200	1,400	Operating expenses	7,255
Prepaid expenses	3,050	1,480	Operating income	2,500
Total current assets	11,500	8,100	Interest expense	100
Other assets	20,500	16,000	Other expense	200
Total assets	32,000	24,100	Net income	$ 2,200
Total current liabilities	12,500	11,000		
Long-term liabilities	11,500	3,500		
Common equity	8,000	9,600		
Total liabilities and equity	$32,000	$24,100		

Justice has 2,000 shares of common stock outstanding. Its stock has traded recently at $41.80 per share. You would like to gain a better understanding of Justice's financial position. Calculate the following ratios for 2009 and interpret the results:

a. Inventory turnover

b. Days' sales in receivables

c. Acid-test ratio

d. Times-interest-earned

e. Return on stockholders' equity

f. Earnings per share

g. Price/earnings ratio

Problems—Group A

P14-34A Prepare trend analysis *(Learning Objectives 1 & 4)*

Net sales revenue, net income, and common stockholders' equity for Shawnee Mission Corporation, a manufacturer of contact lenses, follow for a four-year period.

(in thousands)	2009	2008	2007	2006
Net sales revenue.............................	$7,633	$7,191	$6,562	$6,800
Net income...	630	420	360	500
Ending common stockholders' equity.........	3,775	3,725	3,275	3,125

Requirements

1. Compute trend percentages for each item for 2006 through 2009. Use 2006 as the base year.

2. Compute the rate of return on common stockholders' equity for 2007 through 2009.

P14-35A Comprehensive analysis *(Learning Objectives 2, 3, & 4)*

Todd Department Stores' chief executive officer (CEO) has asked you to compare the company's profit performance and financial position with the average for the industry. The CEO has given you the company's income statement and balance sheet, as well as the industry average data for retailers.

Todd Department Stores, Inc.
Income Statement Compared with Industry Average
For Year Ended December 31

	Todd	Industry Average
Net sales..	$780,000	100.0%
Cost of goods sold...	528,060	65.8%
Gross profit..	251,940	34.2%
Operating expenses	163,020	19.7%
Operating income..	88,920	14.5%
Other expenses..	5,070	0.4%
Net income..	$ 83,850	14.1%

Todd Department Stores, Inc.
Balance Sheet Compared with Industry Average
As of December 31

	Todd	Industry Average
Current assets...	$305,010	70.9%
Fixed assets, net	119,340	23.6%
Intangible assets, net	4,050	0.8%
Other assets...	21,600	4.7%
Total assets..	$450,000	100.0%
Current liabilities	$207,000	48.1%
Long-term liabilities	101,025	16.6%
Stockholders' equity..	141,975	35.3%
Total liabilities and stockholders' equity	$450,000	100.0%

Requirements

1. Prepare a common-size income statement and balance sheet for Todd Department Stores. The first column of each statement should present Todd Department Stores' common-size statement, while the second column should present the industry averages.

2. For the profitability analysis, compute Todd Department Stores' (a) ratio of gross profit to net sales, (b) ratio of operating income to net sales, and (c) ratio of net income to net sales. Compare these figures with the industry averages. Is Todd Department Stores' profit performance better or worse than the industry average?

3. For the analysis of financial position, compute Todd Department Stores' (a) ratio of current assets to total assets and (b) ratio of stockholders' equity to total assets. Compare these ratios with the industry averages. Is Todd Department Stores' financial position better or worse than the industry averages?

P14-36A Effect of transactions on ratios *(Learning Objective 4)*

Financial statement data of *Southern Traveler* magazine include the following items (dollars in thousands):

Cash	$ 22,000
Accounts receivable, net	$ 82,000
Inventories	$162,000
Total assets	$637,000
Short-term notes payable	$ 49,000
Accounts payable	$103,000
Accrued liabilities	$ 38,000
Long-term liabilities	$192,200
Net income	$ 72,000
Common shares outstanding	50,000

Requirements

1. Compute *Southern Traveler*'s current ratio, debt ratio, and earnings per share. Round all ratios to two decimal places and use the following format for your answer:

Current Ratio	Debt Ratio	Earnings per Share

2. Compute the three ratios after evaluating the effect of each transaction that follows. Consider each transaction *separately*.

   a. Purchased inventory on account, $50,000
   b. Borrowed $112,500 on a long-term note payable
   c. Issued 6,250 shares of common stock, receiving cash of $98,000
   d. Received cash on account, $19,000

   Format your answer as follows:

Transaction	Current Ratio	Debt Ratio	Earnings per Share
a.			

P14-37A Ratio analysis over two years *(Learning Objective 4)*

Comparative financial statement data of Weinstein, Inc., follow:

Weinstein, Inc.
Comparative Income Statement
Years Ended December 31, 2009 and 2008

	2009	2008
Net sales..	$460,500	$427,000
Cost of goods sold...	$240,000	$218,000
Gross profit...	$220,500	$209,000
Operating expenses	$138,000	$134,000
Income from operations	$ 82,500	$ 75,000
Interest expense..	$ 11,000	$ 12,000
Income before income tax	$ 71,500	$ 63,000
Income tax expense...	$ 25,500	$ 27,000
Net income..	$ 46,000	$ 36,000

Weinstein, Inc.
Comparative Balance Sheet
December 31, 2009 and 2008

	2009	2008	2007*
Current assets:			
Cash..	$ 96,000	$ 97,000	
Current receivables, net............................	$112,000	$115,000	$103,000
Inventories	$138,000	$162,000	$186,800
Prepaid expenses	$ 11,000	$ 6,000	
Total current assets	$357,000	$380,000	
Property, plant, and equipment, net	$204,500	$174,500	
Total assets...	$561,500	$554,500	
Total current liabilities	$212,500	$237,500	
Long-term liabilities	$119,000	$ 97,000	
Total liabilities	$331,500	$334,500	
Preferred stock, 6%.......................................	$100,000	$100,000	
Common stockholders' equity, no par..................	$130,000	$120,000	$ 80,000
Total liabilities and stockholders' equity	$561,500	$554,500	

*Selected 2007 amounts

1. Market price of Weinstein's common stock: $45.36 at December 31, 2009, and $29.25 at December 31, 2008

2. Common shares outstanding: 10,000 during 2009 and 10,000 during 2008

3. All sales are credit sales

Requirements

1. Compute the following ratios for 2009 and 2008:
   a. Current ratio
   b. Times-interest-earned ratio
   c. Inventory turnover
   d. Return on common stockholders' equity
   e. Earnings per share of common stock
   f. Price/earnings ratio

2. Decide (a) whether Weinstein's ability to pay debts and to sell inventory improved or deteriorated during 2009 and (b) whether the investment attractiveness of its common stock appears to have increased or decreased.

P14-38A Make an investment decision *(Learning Objective 4)*

Assume that you are purchasing an investment and have decided to invest in a company in the digital phone business. You have narrowed the choice to Singular or Very Zone and have assembled the following data.

Selected income statement data for the current year follows:

	Singular	Very Zone
Net sales (all on credit)	$456,250	$525,600
Cost of goods sold	$210,000	$258,500
Interest expense	—	$ 19,000
Net income	$ 50,000	$ 72,000

Selected balance sheet data at the *beginning* of the current year follows:

	Singular	Very Zone
Current receivables, net	$ 42,000	$ 47,000
Inventories	$ 83,000	$ 88,000
Total assets	$259,000	$270,000
Common stock:		
$1 par, (10,000 shares)	$ 10,000	
$1 par, (15,000 shares)		$ 15,000

Selected balance sheet and market-price data at the *end* of the current year follows:

	Singular	Very Zone
Current assets:		
Cash	$ 29,200	$ 20,000
Short-term investments	$ 42,000	$ 18,000
Current receivables, net	$ 38,000	$ 43,000
Inventories	$ 67,000	$100,000
Prepaid expenses	$ 2,000	$ 3,000
Total current assets	$178,200	$184,000
Total assets	$300,000	$328,000
Total current liabilities	$105,000	$100,000
Total liabilities	$105,000	$131,200
Common stock:		
$1 par, (10,000 shares)	$ 10,000	
$1 par, (15,000 shares)		$ 15,000
Total stockholders' equity	$195,000	$196,800
Market price per share of common stock	$ 80.00	$ 86.40

Your strategy is to invest in companies that have low price/earnings ratios but appear to be in good shape financially. Assume that you have analyzed all other factors and that your decision depends on the results of ratio analysis.

Requirement

1. Compute the following ratios for both companies for the current year and decide which company's stock better fits your investment strategy.

   a. Acid-test ratio

   b. Inventory turnover

   c. Days' sales in average receivables

   d. Debt ratio

   e. Earnings per share of common stock

   f. Price/earnings ratio

Problems—Group B

P14-39B Prepare trend analysis *(Learning Objectives 1 & 4)*

Net sales revenue, net income, and common stockholders' equity for Moshe Mission Corporation, a manufacturer of contact lenses, follow for a four-year period.

(in thousands)	2009	2008	2007	2006
Net sales revenue..	$7,008	$6,752	$6,032	$6,400
Net income...	702	432	378	540
Ending common stockholders' equity.........	5,340	3,300	4,200	3,000

Requirements

1. Compute trend percentages for each item for 2006 through 2009. Use 2006 as the base year.

2. Compute the rate of return on common stockholders' equity for 2007 through 2009.

P14-40B Comprehensive analysis *(Learning Objectives 2, 3, & 4)*

Timothy Department Stores' chief executive officer (CEO) has asked you to compare the company's profit performance and financial position with the average for the industry. The CEO has given you the company's income statement and balance sheet, as well as the industry average data for retailers.

Timothy Department Stores, Inc.
Income Statement Compared with Industry Average
For Year Ended December 31

	Timothy	Industry Average
Net sales...	$786,000	100.0%
Cost of goods sold...	532,122	65.9%
Gross profit...	253,878	34.1%
Operating expenses	164,274	19.6%
Operating income..	89,604	14.5%
Other expenses..	4,716	0.4%
Net income..	$ 84,888	14.1%

Timothy Department Stores, Inc.
Balance Sheet Compared with Industry Average
As of December 31

	Timothy	Industry Average
Current assets...	$290,680	70.7%
Fixed assets, net	109,220	23.8%
Intangible assets, net	7,310	0.8%
Other assets..	22,790	4.7%
Total assets...	$430,000	100.0%
Current liabilities	$197,800	47.9%
Long-term liabilities...	97,180	16.5%
Stockholders' equity...	135,020	35.6%
Total liabilities and stockholders' equity	$430,000	100.0%

Requirements

1. Prepare a common-size income statement and balance sheet for Timothy Department Stores. The first column of each statement should present Timothy Department Stores' common-size statement, while the second column should present the industry averages.

2. For the profitability analysis, compute Timothy Department Stores' (a) ratio of gross profit to net sales, (b) ratio of operating income to net sales, and (c) ratio of net income to net sales. Compare these figures with the industry averages. Is Timothy Department Stores' profit performance better or worse than the average for the industry?

3. For the analysis of financial position, compute Timothy Department Stores' (a) ratios of current assets to total assets and (b) ratio of stockholders' equity to total assets. Compare these ratios with the industry averages. Is Timothy Department Stores' financial position better or worse than the industry averages?

P14-41B Effect of transactions on ratios (Learning Objective 4)

Financial statement data of *Modern Traveler* magazine include the following information (dollars in thousands):

Cash	$ 21,500
Accounts receivable, net	85,000
Inventories	155,700
Total assets	598,500
Short-term notes payable	48,000
Accounts payable	104,000
Accrued liabilities	38,000
Long-term liabilities	169,100
Net income	65,520
Common shares outstanding	52,000

Requirements

1. Compute *Modern Traveler*'s current ratio, debt ratio, and earnings per share. Round all ratios to two decimal places and use the following format for your answer:

Current Ratio	Debt Ratio	Earnings per Share

2. Compute the three ratios after evaluating the effect of each transaction that follows. Consider each transaction *separately*.

   a. Purchased inventory on account, $98,800
   b. Borrowed $199,500 on a long-term note payable
   c. Issued 6,500 shares of common stock, receiving cash of $119,700
   d. Received cash on account, $21,000

   Format your answer as follows:

Transaction	Current Ratio	Debt Ratio	Earnings per Share
a.			

P14-42B Ratio analysis over two years *(Learning Objective 4)*

Comparative financial statement data of Panfield, Inc., follow:

Panfield, Inc.
Comparative Income Statement
Years Ended December 31, 2009 and 2008

	2009	2008
Net sales...	$449,990	$441,010
Cost of goods sold...	234,000	226,000
Gross profit...	215,990	215,010
Operating expenses	140,000	135,000
Income from operations	75,990	80,010
Interest expense...	10,200	12,600
Income before income tax	65,790	67,410
Income tax expense..	6,690	20,310
Net income..	$ 59,100	$ 47,100

Panfield, Inc.
Comparative Balance Sheet
December 31, 2009 and 2008

	2009	2008	2007*
Current assets:			
Cash...	$ 97,000	$ 98,000	
Current receivables, net.................................	123,500	158,500	$120,000
Inventories	133,000	127,000	155,500
Prepaid expenses...	10,500	7,500	
Total current assets.................................	364,000	391,000	
Property, plant, and equipment, net	206,000	177,000	
Total assets..	$570,000	$568,000	
Total current liabilities	$208,000	$230,000	
Long-term liabilities	138,000	118,000	
Total liabilities	346,000	348,000	
Preferred stock, 7%..	90,000	90,000	
Common stockholders' equity, no par...................	134,000	130,000	110,000
Total liabilities and stockholders' equity	$570,000	$568,000	

*Selected 2007 amounts

1. Market price of Panfield's common stock: $50.60 at December 31, 2009, and $33.49 at December 31, 2008

2. Common shares outstanding: 12,000 during 2009 and 12,000 during 2008

3. All sales are credit sales

Requirements

1. Compute the following ratios for 2009 and 2008:
   a. Current ratio
   b. Times-interest-earned ratio
   c. Inventory turnover
   d. Return on common stockholders' equity
   e. Earnings per share of common stock
   f. Price/earnings ratio

2. Decide (a) whether Panfield's ability to pay debts and to sell inventory improved or deteriorated during 2009 and (b) whether the investment attractiveness of its common stock appears to have increased or decreased.

P14-43B Make an investment decision (*Learning Objective 4*)

Assume that you are purchasing an investment and have decided to invest in a company in the digital phone business. You have narrowed the choice to Digitized or Very Network and have assembled the following data.

Selected income statement data for the current year follows:

	Digitized	Very Network
Net sales (all on credit)	$419,750	$565,750
Cost of goods sold	225,000	247,000
Interest expense	—	20,500
Net income	67,600	67,200

Selected balance sheet data at the *beginning* of the current year follows:

	Digitized	Very Network
Current receivables, net	$ 38,750	$ 55,150
Inventories	88,250	83,000
Total assets	258,000	272,000
Common stock:		
$1 par (13,000 shares)	13,000	
$1 par (16,000 shares)		16,000

Selected balance sheet and market-price data at the *end* of the current year follows:

	Digitized	Very Network
Current assets:		
Cash	$ 30,000	$ 23,000
Short-term investments	49,560	20,830
Current receivables, net	36,000	42,500
Inventories	68,000	107,000
Prepaid expenses	1,440	5,670
Total current assets	$185,000	$199,000
Total assets	$300,000	$250,000
Total current liabilities	108,000	97,000
Total liabilities	108,000	130,000
Common stock:		
$1 par (13,000 shares)	13,000	
$1 par (16,000 shares)		16,000
Total stockholders' equity	192,000	120,000
Market price per share of common stock	$ 88.40	$ 77.70

Your strategy is to invest in companies that have low price/earnings ratios but appear to be in good shape financially. Assume that you have analyzed all other factors and that your decision depends on the results of ratio analysis.

Requirement

1. Compute the following ratios for both companies for the current year and decide which company's stock better fits your investment strategy.

   a. Acid-test ratio

   b. Inventory turnover

   c. Days' sales in average receivables

   d. Debt ratio

   e. Earnings per share of common stock

   f. Price/earnings ratio

APPLY YOUR KNOWLEDGE

Decision Cases

C14-44 Investment recommendation *(Learning Objective 4)*

Take the role of an investment analyst at Prudential Bache. It is your job to recommend investments for your clients. The only information you have are some ratio values for two companies in the pharmaceuticals industry.

Ratio	Healthtime	Mocek
Return on equity	21.5%	32.3%
Return on assets	16.4%	17.1%
Days' sales in receivables	42	36
Inventory turnover	8	6
Gross profit percentage	51 %	53 %
Net income as a percentage of sales	8.3%	7.2%
Times interest earned	9	16

Write a report to Prudential Bache's investment committee. Recommend one company's stock over the other. State the reasons for your recommendation.

C14-45 Effect of transactions on ratios *(Learning Objective 4)*

General Allied Conglomerates (GAC) and First Star Corporation (FSC) both had a bad year in 2009; the companies' auto parts units suffered net losses. The loss pushed some return measures into the negative column, and the companies' ratios deteriorated. Assume that top management of GAC and FSC are pondering ways to improve their ratios. In particular, management is considering the following transactions:

1. Borrow $100 million on long-term debt

2. Purchase treasury stock for $500 million cash

3. Expense one-fourth of the goodwill carried on the books

4. Create a new auto design division at a cash cost of $300 million

5. Purchase patents from another manufacturer, paying $20 million cash

Requirement

1. Top management wants to know the effects of these transactions (increase, decrease, or no effect) on the following ratios:

   a. Current ratio

   b. Debt ratio

   c. Return on equity

C14-46 Identify affected ratios *(Learning Objective 4)*

Lance Berkman is the controller of Saturn, a dance club whose year-end is December 31. Berkman prepares checks for suppliers in December and posts them to the appropriate accounts in that month. However, he holds on to the checks and mails them to the suppliers in January. What financial ratio(s) are most affected by the action? What is Berkman's purpose in undertaking this activity?

Ethical Issue

I14-47 Effect of decisions on ratios *(Learning Objective 4)*

Betsy Ross Flag Company's long-term debt agreements make certain demands on the business. For example, Ross may not purchase treasury stock in excess of the balance of retained earnings. Also, long-term debt may not exceed stockholders' equity, and the current ratio may not fall below 1.50. If Ross fails to meet any of those requirements, the company's lenders have the authority to take over management of the company.

Changes in consumer demand have made it hard for Ross to attract customers. Current liabilities have mounted faster than current assets, causing the current ratio to fall to 1.47. Before releasing financial statements, Ross's management is scrambling to improve the current ratio. The controller points out that an investment can be classified as either long-term or short-term, depending on management's intention. By deciding to convert an investment to cash within one year, Ross can classify the investment as short-term—a current asset. On the controller's recommendation, Ross's board of directors votes to reclassify long-term investments as short-term.

Requirements

1. What effect will reclassifying the investments have on the current ratio? Is Ross's true financial position stronger as a result of reclassifying the investments?

2. Shortly after the financial statements are released, sales improve and so, too, does the current ratio. As a result, Ross's management decides not to sell the investments it had reclassified as short-term. Accordingly, the company reclassifies the investments as long-term. Has management behaved unethically? Give the reasoning underlying your answer.

Team Project

T14-48 Comparison of common-size financials *(Learning Objective 3)*

Select a company and obtain its financial statements. Convert the income statement and the balance sheet to common size and compare the company you selected to the industry average. The Risk Management Association's *Annual Statement Studies*, Dun & Bradstreet's *Industry Norms & Key Business Ratios*, and Prentice Hall's *Almanac of Business and Industrial Financial Ratios* by Leo Troy publish common-size statements for most industries.

Quick Check Answers

1. *a* 2. *c* 3. *d* 4. *d* 5. *a* 6. *a*
7. *c* 8. *b* 9. *d* 10. *a*

For online homework, exercises, and problems that provide you with immediate feedback, please visit www.myaccountinglab.com.

Discussion & Analysis

1. Describe horizontal analysis. Describe vertical analysis. What is each technique used for? How are the two methods similar? How are they different?

2. How is the current ratio calculated? What is it used to measure? How is it interpreted?

3. Assume a company has a current ratio of 2.0. List two examples of transactions that could cause the current ratio to increase. Also list two examples of transactions that could cause the current ratio to decrease.

4. What does the accounts receivable turnover measure? What does a relatively high accounts receivable turnover indicate about a company?

5. Describe the set of circumstances that could result in net income increasing while ROI decreases.

6. Suppose a company has a relatively high inventory turnover. What does the high inventory turnover indicate about the company's short-term liquidity?

7. Describe at least four financial conditions that may signal financial trouble.

8. Describe at least two reasons that a company's ratios might not be comparable over time.

9. Compare and contrast the current ratio and the quick ratio.

10. Describe why book value per share of common stock may not be useful for investment analysis.

Application & Analysis

14-1 Calculating Ratios for Companies Within the Same Industry

Select an industry you are interested in and select three companies within that industry. Obtain their annual reports by going to each company's Web site and downloading the report for the most recent year. (On many companies' Web sites, you will need to visit the Investor Relations section to obtain the company's financial statements.) You may also collect the information from the company's Form 10-K, which can be found at http://www.sec.gov/idea/searchidea/company-search_idea.html.

Basic Discussion Questions

For each of the three companies you selected, answer the following:

1. Calculate two ratios that measure the ability to pay current liabilities.

2. Calculate at least two ratios that measure the ability to sell inventory and collect receivables.

3. Calculate at least two ratios that measure the ability to pay long-term debt.

4. Calculate at least two ratios that measure profitability.

5. Calculate at least two ratios that help to analyze the stock as an investment.

Now that you have crunched the numbers, interpret the ratios. What can you tell about each company and its financial position? Is one company clearly better than the others in terms of its financial position, or are all three companies similar to each other.

Classroom Applications

Web: Post the discussion questions on an electronic discussion board. Have small groups of students choose an industry and three companies within that industry for their groups. Students should calculate the ratios and then collaborate on the interpretation of those ratios.

Classroom: Form groups of 3–4 students. Your group should choose an industry and three companies within that industry. After calculating the ratios, prepare a five-minute presentation about your group's three companies that compares the companies to each other based on the interpretation of their ratios.

Independent: Calculate answers to each of the questions; include these calculations and ratios in a table. Turn in a 3–4 page typed paper (12 point font, double-spaced with 1" margins) that includes the ratio calculation table and focuses the remainder of the paper on the interpretations of the ratios and the comparison between the companies. Include references, including the URLs for the annual reports you retrieved.

For additional Application & Analysis projects and implementation tips, see the Instructor Resources in MyAccountingLab.com.

PHOTO CREDITS

Chapter 1, Page 2, Spencer Grant\PhotoEdit Inc.;

Chapter 2, Page 42, Newscom;

Chapter 3, Page 96, Julian Rovagnati\istockphoto.com;

Chapter 4, Page 170, Shutterstock;

Chapter 5, Page 234, David Young-Wolff\PhotoEdit Inc.;

Chapter 6, Page 298, Karen Braun;

Chapter 7, Page 362, istockphoto.com;

Chapter 8, Page 420, Delta Air Lines;

Chapter 9, Page 474, Michael Newman\PhotoEdit Inc.;

Chapter 10, Page 552, McDonalds Corp.;

Chapter 11, Page 616, Landov Media;

Chapter 12, Page 668, istockphoto.com;

Chapter 13, Page 722, Getty Images - Digital Vision;

Chapter 14, Page 774, Pat Sullivan\AP Wide World Photos

COMPANY INDEX

GLINDEX

A Combined Glossary/Subject Index.

A

ABC. *See* Activity-based costing (ABC)

ABM. *See* Activity-based management (ABM)

Absorption costing. The costing method where products "absorb" both fixed and variable manufacturing costs, 325–330

Absorption costing income statement, 327, 426

Account analysis. A method for determining cost behavior that is based on a manager's judgment in classifying each general ledger account as a variable, fixed, or mixed cost, 312

Accounting rate of return (ARR). A measure of profitability computed by dividing the average annual operating income from an asset by the initial investment in the asset, 670, 675–677

Accounts receivable, 732

Accounts receivable turnover. Measures a company's ability to collect cash from credit customers. To compute accounts receivable turnover, divide net credit sales by average net accounts receivable, 788

Accrual basis of accounting. Revenues are recorded when they are earned (when the sale takes place), rather than when cash is received on the sale. Likewise, expenses are recorded when they are incurred, rather than when they are paid, 727

Accumulated depreciation, 736–737

Acid-test ratio. Ratio of the sum of cash plus short-term investments plus net current receivables to total current liabilities. It tells whether the entity can pay all of its current liabilities if they come due immediately; also called the *quick ratio*, 787

Activity allocation bases, 181

Activity-based costing (ABC). Focuses on *activities* as the fundamental cost objects. The costs of those activities become building blocks for compiling the indirect costs of products, services, and customers, 179, 183–184

   allocating indirect costs with, 179–183

   circumstances favoring, 188

   outside of manufacturing, 187

   results of, 186

Activity-based management (ABM). Using activity-based cost information to make decisions that increase profits while satisfying customers' needs, 185–189

Activity cost pools, 180–181, 184–185

Allocate. To assign an *indirect* cost to a cost object, 49

American Institute of Certified Public Accountants, 21

Annuity. A stream of equal installments made at equal time intervals, 679

   future value of, 682–683, 699

   net present value with, 687–688

   present value of, 683–685, 697

Appraisal costs. Costs incurred to detect poor quality goods or services, 196, 197

Assets

   return on, 790–791

   total, 637–638

Assign. To attach a cost to a cost object, 49

Audit committee. A subcommittee of the board of directors that is responsible for overseeing both the internal audit function and the annual financial statement audit by independent CPAs, 7–8

Average cost. The total cost divided by the number of units, 64–65

Average unit costs, 248

B

Balanced scorecard. Measures that recognize that management must consider financial performance measures and operational performance measures when judging the performance of a company and its subunits, 617, 621–626

Balance sheets

   budgeted, 495–496

   comparative, 729, 731, 779

   comparing, 61

   horizontal analysis of, 778

   vertical analysis of, 781

Batch-level activities. Activities and costs incurred for every batch, regardless of the number of units in the batch, 184

Benchmarking. Comparing actual performance to similar companies in the same industry, to other divisions, or to world-class standards, 620, 781–782

   budgets and, 478–479

Billing rate. The labor rate charged to the customer, which includes both cost and profit components, 131

Bill of materials. A list of all of the raw materials needed to manufacture a job, 102

Blame, 501

Board of Directors. The body elected by shareholders to oversee the company, 7

Book value per share of common stock. Common stockholders' equity divided by the number of shares of common stock outstanding. It is the recorded amount for each share of common stock outstanding, 793

Breakeven point. The sales level at which operating income is zero: Total revenues equals total expenses, 368

   changing fixed costs and, 380

   changing sales prices and, 377

   changing variable costs and, 378

   finding, using CVP analysis, 368–370

   in terms of sales revenue, 382–384

   in terms of sales units, 381–382

Budget. Quantitative expression of a plan that helps managers coordinate and implement the plan, 4, 475. *See also* Capital budgeting; Flexible budgets

   benefits of, 478–479

   capital expenditure, 490–491

   cash collections, 491

   cash payments, 492–493

   combined cash, 493–494

   development of, 476–477

   direct labor, 484

   direct materials, 482–483

   financial, 480, 490–497

   flexible, 501

   manufacturing overhead, 484–485

   master, 479–480, 504–505

   operating, 479–487

   persons involved in, 477

   production, 481–482

   rolling, 477

   sales, 480–481

   sensitivity analysis and, 496–497

   static, 554

   use of, 476–480

Budget committee. A committee comprised of upper management, as well as cross-functional managers, who review, revise, and approve the final budget, 477

Budgeted balance sheet, 495–496

How to Use MyAccountingLab

If you have not yet had a chance to explore the benefits of the MyAccountingLab Web site, I would encourage you to log in now and see what a valuable tool it can be. MyAccountingLab is a terrific tool for helping you grasp the accounting concepts that you are learning. So what exactly is MyAccountingLab? MyAccountingLab is a homework management tool that allows you to complete homework online. ▼

What is so great about completing the homework online, you might wonder?

Well, how about the ability to ask for and receive help *immediately* while you are working the problems? MyAccountingLab allows you to click on a **Help Me Solve This** button at anytime while you are working the problem, and a pop-up window appears with tips to help you solve the specific part of the problem that you are working on. It is similar to having someone standing over your shoulder to help you—right in the middle of the problem—so that you can get through it and understand how to solve it.

MyAccountingLab also has a button that you can click on that will open an **online version of the textbook**—it even takes you right to the section of the textbook that explains the topic related to the problem that you are working on.

Another great feature of MyAccountingLab is the **Ask My Instructor...** button. If your instructor allows you to e-mail questions, you are able to send an e-mail to your instructor in which you can explain what you are having difficulties with. When your instructor receives the e-mail, there will be a link that will take the instructor right to the problem you were working on in MyAccountingLab.

You will also find two different types of problems in MyAccountingLab, **bookmatch** and **algorithmic** problems. The bookmatch problems are the exact problems right out of your textbook (your instructor must make these available in MyAccountingLab). The algorithmic problems are identical to the ones in the textbook, except they have several variables that change in the problem every time it is selected. The algorithmic problems allow you to have an unlimited number of problems you can work in order to master the material. This means that you can see how to do a problem similar to the one in the book.